$3000 Shakespere   PS 389

2003ois

Brths Vocab.

3 examples of death imagery

833 - 837

read + Review 835

Summary on 836

major Type

279 - 90

291 - 99

Read

63

+Essay + 48

Milton Ann Hobart-Vaugh

LE
P

250 - 252

2 comments

254

GINN
Literature Series

Edward J. Gordon
SENIOR AUTHOR

Introduction to Literature
The Study of Literature
Understanding Literature
Types of Literature
American Literature
English Literature

ENGLISH LITERATURE

NEW EDITION

G. ARMOUR CRAIG • FRANK M. RICE
EDWARD J. GORDON

Author Consultant, HARRY L. WALEN

GINN AND COMPANY

Acknowledgments

Grateful acknowledgment is due to the following publishers, authors, and other holders of copyright material for permission to use selections from their publications.

GEORGE ALLEN & UNWIN LTD.: "Calculated Spontaneity," from *This and That,* by John Hilton.

APPLETON-CENTURY-CROFTS: From a translation of *Il Cortegiano,* by Thomas Hoby, from *The Castle of Knowledge* by Robert Recorde, in *Prose of the English Renaissance,* edited by J. William Hebel, Hoyt H. Hudson, Francis R. Johnson, and A. Wigfall Green. Copyright, 1952 by Appleton-Century-Crofts, Inc.; "Description of Spring...," by Henry Howard, Earl of Surrey, "Spring, the Sweet Spring," by Thomas Nashe, first sonnet from *Astrophel and Stella,* by Sir Philip Sidney, in *Poetry of the English Renaissance,* edited by J. William Hebel and Hoyt H. Hudson. Copyright, 1929, by F. S. Crofts and Co., Inc. Reprinted by permission of Appleton-Century-Crofts.

EDWARD ARNOLD (PUBLISHERS) LTD.: From "Notes on the English Character," in *Abinger Harvest,* by Edward Morgan Forster.

MRS. LILIAN BALCH: "Holiday at the Seaside," by Lilian Balch, from *The Oxford Book of English Talk.*

MRS. GEORGE BAMBRIDGE: "Recessional," from *The Five Nations,* by Rudyard Kipling.

CURTIS BROWN LTD.: "On the Dole," from *The Pageant of the Years,* by Dylan Gibbs.

CAMBRIDGE UNIVERSITY PRESS: "The Devout Poor," from *Life and Death of Mr. Badman,* by John Bunyan, edited by John Brown; from "Lecture V, Interlude on Jargon," in *On the Art of Writing,* by Sir Arthur Quiller-Couch.

JONATHAN CAPE LIMITED: "Departure in the Dark," "Watching Post," from *Collected Poems 1954,* by C. Day Lewis, published by Hogarth Press. Reprinted by permission of the Executors of the Estate of C. Day Lewis and Jonathan Cape Limited; "Naming of Parts," from *A Map of Verona,* by Henry Reed. Reprinted by permission of Jonathan Cape Limited.

CHATTO & WINDUS LTD.: "Strange Meeting," from the preface, in *The Poems of Wilfred Owen.*

THE CLARENDON PRESS: "Nightingales," No. 12 in *Poetical Works of Robert Bridges,* from *Lives of the English Poets,* by Samuel Johnson; from *Raleigh's Discovery of Guiana in Voyages of the Elizabethan Seaman in America,* edited by Edward John Payne; from *Centuries, Poems, and Thanksgiving.* Vol. 1, by Thomas Traherne, edited by H. M. Margoliouth.

DODD, MEAD & COMPANY, INC.: "The Soldier," by Rupert Brooke. Reprinted by permission of Dodd, Mead & Company from *The Collected Poems of Rupert Brooke.* Copyright 1915 by Dodd, Mead & Company, Inc. Copyright 1943 by Edward Marsh.

J. M. DENT & SONS LTD.: From the Preface of *The Nigger of the Narcissus,* by Joseph Conrad: "Fern Hill," from *Collected Poems 1934 — 1952,* by Dylan Thomas.

DOUBLEDAY & COMPANY, INC.: "Recessional," by Rudyard Kipling, from *Rudyard Kipling Verse: Definitive Edition.* Reprinted by permission of Mrs. George Bambridge and Doubleday & Company, Inc. "April Rise," from *The Sun My Monument* by Laurie Lee. Copyright, 1944 by Laurie Lee. Reprinted by permission of Doubleday & Company, Inc.

DOVER PUBLICATIONS, INC.: From *The Life of Isaac Newton,* by Louis Trenchard More, Dover Publications, Inc., New York.

FABER AND FABER LIMITED: "Musée des Beaux Arts," "The Unknown Citizen," reprinted by permission of Faber and Faber Ltd from *Collected Poems* by W. H. Auden; "Journey of the Magi," "Preludes," from "The Waste Land," from "The Hollow Men," reprinted by permission of Faber and Faber Ltd from *Collected Poems 1909 — 1962* by T. S. Eliot; "The Truisms," reprinted by permission of Faber and Faber Ltd from *The Collected Poems of Louis MacNeice;* "The Express," "What I Expected," from No. 24 of "Preludes," from No. 35 of "Preludes," reprinted by permission of Faber and Faber Ltd from *Collected Poems 1928 — 1953* by Stephen Spender, from "Tradition and the Individual Talent," by T. S. Eliot. Reprinted by permission of Faber and Faber Ltd from *Selected Essays* by T. S. Eliot.

JOHN FARQUARSON LTD.: From the General Prologue, from "The Nun's Priest's Tale," from the Pardoner's Prologue, in *The Canterbury Tales,* by Geoffrey Chaucer, translated by Nevill Coghill (The Folio Society, 1956).

HARVARD UNIVERSITY PRESS: From "Musophilus," reprinted by permission of the publishers from *Poems and a Defence of Ryme,* by Samuel Daniel, edited by Arthur Colby Sprague. Copyright, 1930 by The President and Fellows of Harvard College; 1958 by Arthur Colby Sprague.

HOLT, RINEHART AND WINSTON: "Loveliest of trees, the cherry now," "On Wenlock Edge," "To an Athlete Dying Young," from "A Shropshire Lad" — Authorized Edition — from *The*

tion," by Richard B. Sheridan, in *Prose of the Romantic Period 1780 — 1830,* edited by Raymond Wright.

A. D. PETERS: From *The Autobiography of Charles Darwin, 1809 — 1882,* edited by Nora Barlow; "The Living," from *Winter's Tales 5,* by Mary Lavin.

PRINCETON UNIVERSITY PRESS: From *Beowulf in Old English Poetry,* translated by J. Duncan Spaeth.

G. P. PUTNAM'S SONS: From *Blood, Sweat and Tears,* by Winston S. Churchill. © 1941 by Winston S. Churchill. Reprinted by permission of G. P. Putnam's Sons; from "Lecture V, Interlude on Jargon," in *On the Art of Writing,* by Sir Arthur Quiller-Couch.

RANDOM HOUSE, INC.: "Elegy for J. F. K.," Copyright © 1965 by W. H. Auden. Reprinted from *Collected Poems,* by W. H. Auden, edited by Edward Mendelson, by permission of Random House, Inc.; "Musée des Beaux Arts," "The Unknown Citizen," Copyright 1940 and renewed 1968 by W. H. Auden. Reprinted from *Collected Poems,* by W. H. Auden, edited by Edward Mendelson by permission of Random House, Inc.; "What I expected, was," "The Express," excerpts from "I think continually of those," and from "Not palaces, an era's crown," Copyright 1934 and renewed 1962 by Stephen Spender. Reprinted from *Collected Poems 1928 — 1953,* by Stephen Spender, by permission of Random House, Inc.; "Riders to the Sea," by J. M. Synge. Reprinted from *The Complete Plays of John M. Synge;* "On the Knocking at the Gate in Macbeth," by Thomas DeQuincey. Reprinted from *The Selected Writing of Thomas DeQuincey.*

THE RONALD PRESS COMPANY: "On his Blindness," "To The Lord General Cromwell," from *Paradise Lost,* in *The Poems of John Milton,* Second Edition, edited by James Holly Hanford. Copyright 1953 The Ronald Press Company.

RUTLEDGE AND KEGAN PAUL LTD.: From a notebook entry by Thomas Hardy, in *Novelists on the Novel,* by Miriam Allott; "The Queen," by Sir John Hayward, in *Portraits in Prose,* edited by Hugh Macdonald.

CHARLES SCRIBNER'S SONS: "Journey to Freedom," reprinted with the permission of Charles Scribner's Sons from *My Early Life: A Roving Commission* by Winston Churchill. Copyright 1930 Charles Scribner's Sons; renewal copyright © 1958 Winston Churchill. "Lucifer in Starlight," from *The Poetical Works of George Meredith.*

THE SOCIETY OF AUTHORS: "The Burning of Leaves," from *The Poems of Our Time 1900 — 1960,* by Laurence Binyon, reprinted by permission of The Society of Authors as the literary representative of the Estate of the late Laurence Binyon; "Loveliest of Trees," "On Wenlock Edge," "To an Athlete Dying Young," from "A Shropshire Lad" in *The Collected Poems of A. E. Housman,* reprinted by permission of The Society of Authors as the literary representative of the Estate of the late A. E. Housman and Messrs. Jonathan Cape Ltd., publishers of A. E. Housman's *Collected Poems;* "The Apple Tree," from *The Scrapbook of Katherine Mansfield,* reprinted by permission of The Society of Authors as the literary representatives of the Estate of the late Katherine Mansfield.

TUDOR PUBLISHING COMPANY: From *The Anatomy of Melancholy,* by Robert Burton, edited by Floyd Dell and Paul Jordan-Smith.

THE VIKING PRESS: "The Rocking-Horse Winner," from *The Complete Short Stories of D. H. Lawrence,* volume 3, Copyright 1933 by the Estate of D. H. Lawrence, renewed © 1961 by Angelo Ravagli and C. Montague Weekly, Executors of the Estate of Frieda Lawrence Ravagli. Reprinted by permission of The Viking Press.

A P. WATT & SON: "Recessional," from *The Five Nations,* by Rudyard Kipling; from "Among School Children," from "The Fisherman," "Sailing to Byzantium," "The Lake Isle of Innisfree," reprinted with permission of the publisher from *Collected Poems,* by W. B. Yeats; from *Essays and Introductions,* by W. B. Yeats.

MRS. W. B. YEATS: From "Among School Children," from "The Fisherman," "Sailing to Byzantium," "The Lake Isle of Innisfree," reprinted with permission of the publisher from *Collected Poems,* by William Butler Yeats; from *Essays and Introductions,* by William Butler Yeats.

The photographs on the pages listed below are from the following sources:

ii: Stephen Maka
ix: Howard Wilson; Harison Forman
x: Ansel Adams in *This Is The American Earth* © 1960 by the Sierra Club; Mal in The Christian Science Monitor © TCSPS.
xi: Ken Heyman; AP
xii: "Yvette Guilbert" by Toulouse-Lautrec, The Rhode Island School of Design; Earnest Baxter from Black Star
xiii: Wide World; Richard McKinnon; Andreas Feininger, LIFE Magazine © Time Inc.; Monkmeyer; Wide World; William Wasserman
xv: Henri Cartier-Bresson from Magnum; NASA
xvi: Weston Kemp; English brass rubbing; Ansel Adams in *This Is The American Earth* © 1960 by the Sierra Club
xvii: Karsh, Ottawa from Rapho Guillumette
xxv: University of London
xxvi: Lon McKee
xxvii: Derby Art Gallery Collection
xxviii: Henry E. Huntington Library, San Marino, California
xxix: "The Mad Tea Party" from *Alice in Wonderland* illustrated by Tenniel
xxx: Bibliotheque Nationale, Paris
xxxi: The Massey Collection of English Art, The National Gallery of Canada, Ottawa

Preface

The basic organization of this anthology of English literature is chronological. The overlapping of the dates assigned to the Middle Ages and the Renaissance is deliberate, for the Middle Ages and the Renaissance did in fact interpenetrate. And although it may seem at first eccentric to begin the Twentieth Century chapter at 1914, yet in many important ways the twentieth century did not begin until World War I. The chapter on the English novel is, of course, an exception to the general chronological arrangement. This discussion of the largest and most varied literary form in English stands between the Victorian and Twentieth Century chapters. There it serves as a recapitulation of the elements that from the 17th century on have formed themselves into the novel as we know it, and it introduces certain elements of 20th-century literature.

The selections within each chapter are arranged both historically and thematically. Earlier writers of the period usually appear early in the chapter. But history is more than a matter of chronology, and the thematic groupings of writers and their works reveal the similarities and differences of the selections; they illuminate one another.

The introduction to each chapter (with the exception of the first) is in two sections: "The Writer's Language" and "The People and Their Times." The first part describes the state of the language and the development it was to undergo during that period; it also describes with relevant quotations what the writers themselves thought they were doing. "The Writer's Language," then, is both linguistic history and the history of criticism. The second part of each introduction offers from contemporary, mainly nonliterary, sources examples of how the people of the time talked and what they thought about. "The People and Their Times" attempts to present a sense of an age.

For those teachers who will want students to view the selections in this anthology thematically, the next several pages (pp. ix–xvii) present an introduction to three basic themes which pervade English literature: The People and Nature, The People and Their Society, The People and Their Beliefs. Students who read works grouped about these concerns will be led to think about the place that humankind occupies in the scheme of things and how we function within that scheme. Photographs, quotations, and probing questions point to human beings as they are, perhaps will be, revealed through their writings. The "People and Their Times" sections at the beginning of each chapter provide more detailed information to supplement and support these introductory theme pages. Footnoted references are made to each pertinent chapter section.

Pages xviii–xxii will assist students of literature in understanding the responsibility and the position of the writers who created the works in this anthology. These pages present the writer as a person skilled at welding ideas in the words of the time; the implication is that the student reader may well also respond to literature as a writer, using the words of *his/her* time. These pages set the stage for the more detailed "The Writer's Language" sections at the beginning of each chapter in the book.

At the end of each selection comes a short passage called "Comment." Its function is to focus students' attention on the center of the work they have just read and to lead into a series of questions that radiate from this center. These detailed questions require that students read and reread the selection. They move from simple levels of comprehension through an analytical examination of the work, up to a final question that requires students to express their sense of what the work has achieved. Very often this last question asks students to write an essay. Even if it does not specifically say so, this last question can almost always be used as a writing assignment. A list of all composition assignments may be found on pages xxiii–xxiv.

The texts of the selections have been chosen with the aim of using what are considered by scholars to be good sources of the works. When a work is less than complete as presented, the word *from* is used before the title; long omissions are marked by three asterisks, and shorter omissions by ellipsis marks.

The spelling of all selections (except those for which the copyright holders stipulated otherwise) has been made to conform to American usage.

The glossary at the end of the book provides a small dictionary for looking up difficult words. The footnotes define unusual words or allusions that students might not be expected to know.

The illustrations will help students understand the themes of the literature, will give them a sense of the period in which the literature was written, and will in some cases supplement what they learn from the selections and editorial material about intellectual, social, and political history of each period. Time charts at the end of each chapter relate literary events to one another and to important people and happenings of the time in England and the world.

The teacher must have, in addition, a large repertory of other material and new approaches which will turn the classroom into a workshop in which students explore not only the literature but their responses to it.

The People and Nature

Listen! you hear the grating roar
Of pebbles which the waves draw back,
   and fling
At their return, up the high strand,
Begin, and cease, and then again begin,
With tremulous cadence slow, and bring
The eternal note of sadness in.
         —from "Dover Beach"
         MATTHEW ARNOLD

      . . . Therefore am I still
A lover of the meadows and the woods,
And mountains; and of all that we behold
From this green earth; of all the mighty world
Of eye, and ear;—both what they half create,
And what perceive; well pleased to recognize
In nature and the language of the sense
The anchor of my purest thoughts, the nurse,
The guide, the guardian of my heart, and soul
Of all my moral being.
      —from "Lines, Composed a Few Miles
        above Tintern Abbey"
      WILLIAM WORDSWORTH

How do humankind fit into the natural order of things? Is humankind always, to some degree, in conflict with nature? Are we the rightful rulers, the "paragon of animals"? Do we acknowledge or deny our natural heritage? If we destroy nature, do we at the same time destroy ourselves?

Selections Illustrating the Theme of *The People and Nature*

The People and Their Society

In love—

Do all humans need to love? . . . and be loved? Does a mechanized society alter our capacity for love?

Do you need anybody?
I just need someone to love.
Could it be anybody?
I want somebody to love.
—*from* "A Little Help from My Friends"
THE BEATLES

But love me for love's sake, that evermore
Thou may'st love on through love's eternity.
—*from* "Sonnet 14"
ELIZABETH BARRETT BROWNING

In conflict—

W. H. Auden called this century The Age of Anxiety; others have called it the Age of Science and the Age of Violence. Does a complex society by its nature breed anxiety and conflict?

I am the enemy you killed, my friend,
I knew you in this dark;. . .
—*from* "Strange Meeting"
WILFRED OWEN

Imperfect—

A wad some Power the giftie gie us
To see oursels as ithers see us!
It wad frae monie a blunder free us,
   An' foolish notion
What airs in dress an' gait wad lea'e us,
   An' ev'n devotion!
       —from "To a Louse"
       ROBERT BURNS

The proper study of mankind is man.
       —from "Essay on Man"
       ALEXANDER POPE

Alone—

Many 20th-century writers have been concerned with our mechanized, industrial society and the pressures that are brought to bear on the individual. Do the conditions of life in this century prevent us from being fully human? *Are* we becoming more and more isolated from nature and from each other?

       . . . , then on the shore
Of the wide world I stand alone, and think
Till love and fame to nothingness do sink.
       —from "When I Have Fears"
       JOHN KEATS

Who leads us—

Selections Illustrating the Theme of *The People and Their Society*

The People and Their Beliefs

The Druids believed in magic and human sacrifice.

To what extent does state of knowledge free or restrict human actions or beliefs?

Can people hold beliefs that concern what is outside of human knowledge?

          . . . Life piled on life
Were all too little, and of one to me
Little remains: but every hour is saved
From that eternal silence, something more,
A bringer of new things; and vile it were
For some three suns to store and hoard myself,
And this gray spirit yearning in desire
To follow knowledge like a sinking star,
Beyond the utmost bound of human thought.
          —from "Ulysses"
          ALFRED, LORD TENNYSON

The earth hath no motion of itself,
no more than a stone, but resteth
quietly; and so the other elements
do except they be forcibly moved.
   —from *The Castle of Knowledge*
   1556

Can a person's beliefs bring him or her into conflict with others?
In conflict, must a person believe that his/her cause is just?

And we are here as on a darkling plain
Swept with confused alarms of struggle and slight,
Where ignorant armies clash by night.
—*from* "Dover Beach"
MATTHEW ARNOLD

. . . we shall defend our Island, whatever the cost may be,
we shall fight on the beaches, we shall fight on the landing grounds,
we shall fight in the fields and in the streets, we shall fight in the
hills; we shall never surrender.

—WINSTON CHURCHILL
June, 1940

What forces shape our personal, individual convictions?

And what I am beheld again
  What is, and no man understands;
  And out of darkness came the hands
That reach thro' nature, molding men.
  —*from* "In Memoriam A. H. H."
  ALFRED LORD TENNYSON

Do we all seek immortality?

Only a sweet and virtuous soul,
  Like seasoned timber, never gives;
But though the whole world would turn to cool,
  Then chiefly lives.

                    —*from* "Virtue"
                    GEORGE HERBERT

Selections Illustrating the Theme of *The People and Their Beliefs*

The Writer and Literature

JULIET: 'Tis but thy name that is my enemy.
Thou art thyself, though not a Montague.
What's Montague? It is nor hand, nor foot,
Nor arm, nor face, nor any other part
Belonging to a man. O, be some other name!
What's in a name? That which we call a rose
By any other name would smell as sweet.
So Romeo would, were he not Romeo call'd,
Retain that dear perfection which he owes
Without that title. Romeo, doff thy name;
And for that name, which is no part of thee,
Take all myself.
    ROMEO: I take thee at thy word.
Call me but love, and I'll be new baptiz'd;
Henceforth I never will be Romeo.
    JULIET: What man art thou that, thus
              bescreen'd in night,
So stumblest on my counsel?
    ROMEO: By a name
I know not how to tell thee who I am.
My name, dear saint, is hateful to myself,
Because I am an enemy to thee.
Had I it written, I would tear the word.
    —from *Romeo and Juliet*
    WILLIAM SHAKESPEARE (1564–1616)

Why does one of the greatest love stories in our language revolve around "What's in a name?" Why does Shakespeare have Romeo and Juliet spend precious time trying to define—or disown—a "name," a "word?" Juliet pleads with Romeo to "be some other name," to "doff" the "hateful" name of Montague. Romeo feels that by denying a "word," his name, he can gain the world of Juliet's love: he sees his name as a barrier to that world and vows to "tear the word" Montague to shreds. "Montague" represents a feud for which he is not responsible and in which he tries, unsuccessfully, not to take part. When Romeo and Juliet try to set up their own private name system, they are closing their eyes to a public reality. Romeo is indeed "love," but he is also part of the tragic feud between the Montagues and the Capulets. When Juliet says, "Thou art thyself, though not a Montague," we know she is deceiving herself. "Montague" does belong to Romeo, as much as his hand, his foot, his arm, or his face. The "word" stands for many things outside his control. Shakespeare was keenly aware of such word power, and his greatness stems from the ways in which he made us more aware of our "other names." He knew that we, like Romeo, are all inheritors, and that what we inherit has a great part in the shaping of our lives.

The inheritance we share, regardless of our varied pasts, is a common language. This book records not only the growth and changes in that language, but the experiences which shaped and were shaped by it. Each time you read, write about, or discuss a work of literature, you add to, and perhaps change, that record. The better you understand the terms of your inheritance, the "codes" of your language, the more you will be able to shape it to your benefit. But how do you achieve this understanding, and thereby the control, of your inheritance?

First, we must recognize that we inherit not only patterns and units of language, sentences and words, but also an unconscious understanding of when these patterns and units are appropriate. We do not have to hear all of an everyday conversation to know what is happening or even to predict what will be said. Second, we must realize that we cannot arbitrarily change parts of this pattern and expect to be understood. Too great or sudden a switch from a "public" to a "private" code throws up barriers to general understanding. Third, we must be willing to put ourselves in others' places, to recognize our "other names," especially when we are readers and cannot demand on-the-spot clarification from the writer.

Because human experience changes, the meanings of our words change. A pattern or unit which makes sense in one place or time may not be clearly understood in another. Although our ancestors would have recognized each part of "countdown" or "blast-off," they simply could not have summoned up the awesome image of a spaceship launching to give the words our meaning. But because we are the living and not the dead, the real comprehension problems are ours, not our ancestors'. If we are to claim our inheritance we must understand its terms: we must be aware of the development and changes in parts of our legacy. The more we understand its "terms"— the accumulated meanings of the words we hear, speak, and write—the more we can benefit from our inheritance. But how do we bridge the comprehension gap we inevitably encounter in surveying over 1,000 years of "accumulated meanings"?

Stepping backward in time may not be as unfamiliar an experience as you might suppose. In fact, in a way you're already quite adept at doing so. Every time you read or view science fiction, you build a bridge to another type of experience, an experience which demands that you either modify your codes or accept new ones. In science fiction an author creates, or has the characters create, a world which is the imagined result of the present. The author creates a modified code to deal with the "new" world. This code must be both public and private. Within the world of the book it is public; outside that world, in the limited world of those who read the book, it is private. If the code has words which shed new light on old, familiar experiences, these words are incorporated. You probably have several words in your vocabulary which come from your "future" inheritance. Because of the painful relevance *1984* has to your present-day world, many of you cannot hear or see "Big Brother" without thinking of the special meaning George Orwell ascribed to it. Whereas some words, then, change or accumulate meanings, others become only superficially recognizable. In another time, parts of a word may seem familiar, but the whole makes no sense unless you know the writer's code. What do you make of *doublething* and *joycamp*, of *oldthink*, *goodthink*, and *crimethink?* To crack science fiction codes, you use the same techniques that you need for reading the writings of your ancestors.

As you step backward in time, you find yourself in both the position of the ancestor who could not grasp the concept of "blast-off" and in the position of your contemporary who hears "Big Brother" but has not read *1984*. The parts of the word or phrase are familiar, but the whole makes little sense, especially if isolated from context. The more you increase the time gap, the more unfamiliar you may expect all units to become. How many units of the 8th-century poem, "The Dream of the Rood" ("The Dream of the Cross") seem familiar or even vaguely familiar?

> Hwæt, iċ swefna cyst   secgan wille,
> hwæt mē ġemætte   to midre nihte,
> siþþan reord-berend   reste wunodon.
> —Anonymous

Some isolated words may be familiar; however, they refuse to add up to a recognizable whole. A full or even free translation is needed if the whole is to make sense.

> I am minded to tell a marvelous dream,
> I will say what I dreamt in the deep of the night,
> When the sons of men lay asleep and at rest.
> —Translated by Kemp Malone

The comprehension gap is bridged with translation, but have you lost something in gaining "understanding"? If you'll place the translation alongside the original, you'll see that the patterns differ. Spacings in the middle of each line of the original have been deleted; lines have been lengthened and words gained in the translation. Rhythm, then, must have changed. Certainly the "sound" of the poem has changed with the change in beat.

As you move from Anglo-Saxon times toward the present, you see evolving a language which looks and sounds increasingly familiar yet retains many of its Anglo-Saxon qualities. The poems of William Langland and Geoffrey Chaucer both are concerned with someone's dreams or imaginings. You won't have too difficult a time breaking the codes: more than half the words will be immediately clear, and the units which need "translation" will be considerably smaller.

In a somer seson • whan soft was the sonne,

     ❁   ❁   ❁

I was werey forwandred • and went me to reste
Vnder a brode banke • by a bornes side,
And as I lay and lened • and loked up þe wateres,
I slombred in a slepyng • it sweyued so merye.
          —from *Piers the Plowman*
             WILLIAM LANGLAND (1332?–1400?)

      Of Decembre the tenthe day,
      Whan hit was night, to slepe I lay
      Right ther as I was wont to done,
      And fil on slepe wonder sone,

             ❁   ❁   ❁

      But as I sleep, me mette I was
      Within a temple y-mad of glas;
      —from *The Hous of Fame*
        GEOFFREY CHAUCER (1340?–1400)

Unfamiliar words still crop up, although they do not greatly impede the flow of the sentences. A few words which seem familiar may carry different meanings than *you* would ascribe to them. These words, nonetheless, do convey the feeling the poet intended. You sense that when Langland says the sun is "soft," it is a mild, lovely summer day, and that the brook which "sweyued so merye" has helped lull the weary traveler into a pleasant slumber. You don't need literal translation; familiar sounds help fill in meaning. You are even more at home with Langland's contemporary. Although Chaucer has slipped back to the "old" ways with one word, he has jumped ahead of Langland into a looser, more modern rhythm and he has relinquished Anglo-Saxon spelling.

As you get closer and closer to today, more language barriers fall: spelling, words, phrases, and sentence patterns offer increasingly less trouble, sometimes none. Do you encounter any real comprehension gaps in the dream-vision below, barely 300 years old?

      As I walked through the wilderness of this world, I lighted
    on a certain place where was a Den, and I laid me down in
    that place to sleep: and as I slept I dreamed a dream.
               —from *The Pilgrim's Progress*
              JOHN BUNYAN (1628–1688)

In comparison with the other three selections, *The Pilgrim's Progress* is easily decoded. Familiar words with "old-fashioned" meanings fall into place readily because of an overwhelmingly familiar pattern. Bunyan appears to be translatable. Or is he?

Have we really cracked *all* the codes? Are we familiar enough with the Bunyan selection so that we could fill in words or meanings had they been left out, or even add to the selection without injuring it?

Are there perhaps not codes larger than the units of words or phrases which might help us carry on a conversation with the writer? There might be. We have left unexamined one element common to, although not exactly the same within, all four selections: all the authors chose to speak to us within the pattern of a dream. What meaning does this larger pattern add? Does it accumulate meanings as it details change through the centuries? Is it not possible, then, that we have inherited codes for writing? Is it not also possible that since writing can be a very private thing, each writer has both accepted and altered the codes he or she has inherited? In directing the past which gives meaning to words, hasn't the writer used the language of literature to assert his or her uniqueness?

If you were to sit down to write your dream, what————?

Composition Assignments

To the Teacher

Additional writing assignments may be found in the *Teachers' Handbook and Key*, pages 33, 43, 49, 51, 136, 161, 184, 185, 254, 314, 334. The "Summing Up" sections of the book include comprehensive questions which are suitable for discussion or composition. Only those which specifically direct the student to write have been included on this list.

This list will help you select the composition assignments most suitable for your students. Because the assignments are stated in the most concise terms, you may want to discuss each topic as you assign it.

To the Student

As you read this book, you may often want to disagree with an idea, take it one step further, or go off in a different direction altogether. This impulse to differ with the printed page is your unique contribution to the meeting of minds between writer and reader. It is an impulse natural to all good readers. But these thoughts are often vague and may be frequently forgotten unless you put them into some kind of permanent form. To make your thoughts concrete and to preserve them for later use, it is a good idea to develop the writing habit.

For this purpose, composition questions have been included after many of the selections in this book. Some of the questions ask you to tell *what* the author is saying; others ask you to comment on the *way* he or she has said it; still others ask you to compare one writer with another, or one group of writers with another group. Gradually, you will become familiar with the characteristics of different writers, the different periods during which they wrote, and the different forms which they used. But even more important, you will become accustomed to converting your thoughts into writing—at dressing *your* ideas in words, phrases, and sentences that will make them attractive and interesting enough to appear in public.

Assignment	Location	Page
1. Describe a poet's powers and limitations as implied by "Thomas Rymer."	C4[1]	55
2. Analyze Macbeth's character in terms of Renaissance "imagination."	PW1[2]	246
3. Evaluate Shakespeare's ability to create character, as illustrated by Lady Macbeth.	PW2	246
4. Compare attitude towards kings in *Macbeth* and *Morte Darthur*.	PW3	246

[1]The abbreviation *C* refers to the "Comments" sections of the text.
[2]The abbreviation *PW* refers to the "Play as a Whole" sections of the text.

³The abbreviation *SU* refers to the "Summing Up" sections of the text.

Contents

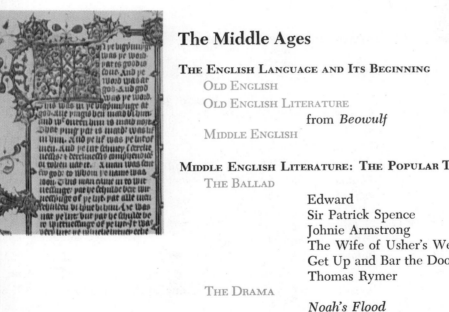

The Renaissance 119

The Enlightenment

The Literature of the Enlightenment

The Romantic Period 427

The Literature of the Romantic Period

The English Novel

The Twentieth Century

The Twentieth Century 707

The Literature of the Twentieth Century

xxxi

Hereford Cathedral Library is the best remaining example in England of the medieval chained library, in which the precious books and manuscripts were chained to the shelves.

The Study
of
Literature

The Student of Literature

One who studies the atom and its nucleus is called a physicist, one who studies the paths of the stars is called an astronomer, and one who studies societies of the past is called a historian. But there is, strangely, no single name for the person who studies literature.

There are scholars who investigate the origins and history of language: they are linguists or philologists, and without their work we could not know how to read the great books of the past. Other scholars edit manuscripts and texts; they put before us in print the words that writers of the past actually wrote. But the student of literature is not only an investigator of words and their changes of form, or only an investigator of manuscripts and printed sources. Sometimes such a person is a historian, for no one can read a book without becoming aware of the conditions of life that surrounded its author. The student of literature is sometimes a philosopher, constantly meeting ideas and constantly discovering how great minds have gone about the very difficult business of thinking—thinking about love, about nature, about youth and age, even about thought itself. And sometimes the student of literature is concerned with religion, with the deepest and strongest beliefs that human beings have held. But there is no simple name for this student of literature, and that is as it should be.

The World of Literature

We open a book, and there before us on the page is an arrangement of words. We see only printed words—not live people, not solid buildings or towering mountains or the endlessly moving sea—only silent, immovable print. And yet as we read this silent print we can sometimes be so moved that no one, not the historian, not the philosopher or the psychologist, not even the theologian, can explain all that we feel

The minstrel with his harp sang the earliest stories of English literature. This illustration is from the Caedmonian Genesis manuscript (ca. 1000).

Mss. Junius 11, Bodleian Library, Oxford

happening to us. We read, and we enter a mysterious world that is both near to us and remote from us. It is a world in which we sometimes find our own concerns—our own hopes and fears, loves and hatreds. It is a world sometimes so remote from our concerns that we forget about them, and return to them to find that they look different. The world of literature is both mysteriously near and mysteriously remote, and no one word can sum up what happens to us when we enter it.

What is so inexhaustibly wonderful about literature is its power to awaken in us awarenesses of life that we did not know we had. We read a poem or a story or a play and discover that we knew more than we suspected we knew, about love and loyalty between men and women, about courage in the face of difficulties, about the desperation of men and women frightened by great events, about what it feels like to meditate upon a great idea, about the way in which comedy dissolves our anxieties and refreshes our presence of mind. When we understand a work of literature we discover powers of judgment and insight in ourselves that we had not known we possessed. We become aware of ranges of experience that we share with every imaginative writer who speaks to us in our language.

The Language of Literature

The writer speaks to us in our language, but of course we know that writers sometimes transform that language so thoroughly that we have real trouble in understanding what they have to say. The writer expresses a vision of life in words—in phrases, clauses, sentences. But

2

sometimes we cannot grasp the sentences because certain words (and they are often words we use ourselves) seem to make no sense to us. We can make sense of them only if we give them meanings we had not thought of before, meanings that we resist giving to them. The words of our language, we feel, ought to mean what they *do* mean, and nothing is more painful or irritating than to have to change the meanings we have lived with, and lived on, all our lives. The words of our language *mean* the values by which we live, and we must resist 'anything that threatens them.

But we cannot resist what deepens our sense of these values, any more than we can resist the deepening and widening of meaning that comes to the words we know best as we grow in wisdom and experience. This deepening and widening of meaning comes as we hear familiar words used around us. It comes perhaps most often when we hear someone use familiar words in a distinctive and individual way: in the sound of an individual voice we may hear fresh meanings that revive and strengthen the values we live by.

Individual Style

And so it is in the world of literature. We open a book, and there is the arrangement of words on the page. And in this arrangement, we find, the words both do and do not have the meanings we expect. We read further and discover something more, more important even than the way the words fit into the sense of values we have brought with us. We begin to hear an original voice. It is a voice, to be sure, that

THE STUDY OF LITERATURE

3

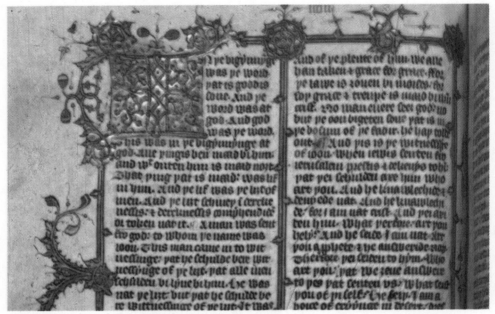

The brilliant colors of illuminated manuscripts, such as this page from the Wyclif Bible, a 14th-century translation, emphasized initial letters and decorated page borders.

reaches us only through words on a page. And it is a voice that reaches us somewhat uncertainly, as if it were muffled in layers of time. But it is a voice, and as clearly the voice of a particular person as is the voice of a close friend in the next room.

It is, of course, not a voice that says things we can predict, as we predict that our friend in the next room is starting to tell a favorite story. We know that story. We know too—or can guess from our friend's tone—just what kind of audience is listening to it this time. After all, we know our friend's style. About the voice from the page we can only know that it comes from a particular time and place. We know that this voice raised itself above the murmur and babble of hundreds and thousands of voices in the background. We may not know at once the location of that background, but we do know in a rough way whether it is "modern" or "old." We may like or dislike what the voice seems to be saying (as we may like or dislike our friend's story), but like it or not we take pleasure in recognizing that it *is* a voice, and this pleasure keeps us listening for more. We feel that someone is expressing a view of experience that is individual and fresh. We know that it comes from an author who wrote for himself or herself and for anyone who will listen. The author wrote to be heard. We read because we cannot resist the pleasure of hearing an individual voice.

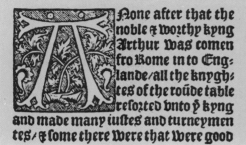

Here foloweth the fyrth boke of the noble and worthy prynce kyng Arthur.

How syr Launcelot and syr Lyonell departed fro the courte for to seke auentures / & how syr Lyonell lefte syr Launcelot sleppynge & was taken. Capital.j.

Anone after that the noble & worthy kyng Arthur was comen fro Rome in to Englande / all the knyghtes of the rounde table resorted vnto ye kyng and made many iustes and turneymentes / & some there were that were good knyghtes / whiche encreased so in armes and worshyp that they passed all theyr felowes in prowesse & noble dedes & that was well proued on many. But in especyall it was proued on syr Launcelot du lake. For in all turneymentes and iustes and dedes of armes / bothe for lyfe and deth he passed all knyghtes & at no tyme he was neuer ouercomen but yf it were by treason or enchauntement. Syr Launcelot encreased so mer uaylously in worshyp & honour / wherfore he is the first knyght ye the frensshe booke maketh mencyon of / after that kynge Arthur came from Rome / wherfore quene Gueneuer had hym in grete fauour aboue all other knyghtes / and certaynly he loued the quene agayne aboue all other ladyes and damoyselles all the dayes of his lyfe / and for her he

A 1529 edition of Malory's Morte Darthur *printed by Wynkyn de Worde, Caxton's assistant and successor, shows how the first printed books modeled the design of their type faces on the black letter writing of manuscripts.*

Worlds Near and Remote

The student of literature, then, is anyone who can hear an imagination expressing itself in its own words. But of course no one can "own" the words he or she uses. The language we use, like the very air we breathe, surrounds us all from the beginning of our lives. It can be no one person's private property. Words belong to each of us; they also belong to all of us. That is why the student of literature again and again encounters experiences that he or she mysteriously knows, even though they are experiences that never have been undergone. That is why the world we enter when we read a play, a poem, or a story, is a world both near to us and remote from us. And it is why the student of literature cannot have a simple name. The subject studied is personal. It is also as general as the experience of all other persons.

Using words from the language in which we conduct our daily lives, a great writer moves us into a world that we have never entered before. Yet when we are there, we find it after all strangely familiar. And it must be so, for it is a world made of the language in which we speak to others and to ourselves. However arranged, the writer's words are our words too. He or she arranges them, of course, in ways that must be studied: the phrases and clauses are more than grammatical arrangements. The great writer's voice is controlled by many re-

TO
THE MOST HIGH,
MIGHTIE
And
MAGNIFICENT
EMPRESSE RENOVV-
MED FOR PIETIE, VER-
TVE, AND ALL GRATIOVS
GOVERNMENT ELIZABETH BY
THE GRACE OF GOD QVEENE
OF ENGLAND FRAVNCE AND
IRELAND AND OF VIRGI-
NIA, DEFENDOVR OF THE
FAITH, &c. HER MOST
HVMBLE SERVAVNT
EDMVND SPENSER
DOTH IN ALL HV-
MILITIE DEDI-
CATE, PRE-
SENT
AND CONSECRATE THESE
HIS LABOVRS TO LIVE
VVITH THE ETERNI-
TIE OF HER
FAME.

*The dedication page of
Edmund Spenser's*
The Faerie Queene, 1590.
*The letters in this page
of Renaissance typography
were modeled on Roman
examples; they provide
the basis for all modern
type faces.*

sources—by irony, by image and metaphor, by meter and rhythm, to name only a few. Some voices are finely modulated by the sonnet, some are amplified by the epic; some carry us through a great novel, some through a short story. But these are the arrangements of words through which we discover meanings that are new to us. They give us meanings that we never quite shake loose from the words in which we find them. For they give us meanings that enrich both our awareness of ourselves and our sense of a background of values without which we could not be "selves" at all.

Two Descriptions of Springtime

Let us consider an example. One experience that everyone shares is the coming of spring. Each of us is aware of the cycle of the seasons and all of us know, perhaps as an inconvenience, perhaps as a blessing, the warm spring rain that dissolves the frosts of winter. Even the city-dweller senses the change of light and air when April comes and life is renewed once more. Certainly no subject appears more often in literature, and no subject has been treated more variously. Here, for example, is one of the oldest and most famous passages in English literature:

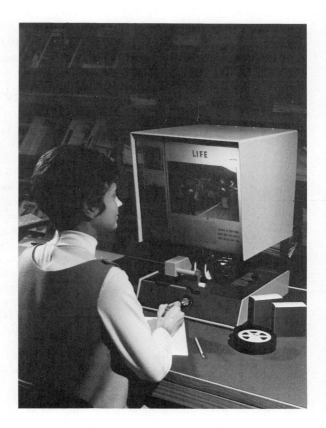

A student using a microfilm machine in a library. The machine projects films of printed material. Its use has made widely available rare manuscripts, books, and other documents; the size of the film permits libraries to store in a small space great quantities of writing.

Whan that Aprill with his shoures soote
The droghte of March hath perced to the roote,
And bathed every veyne in swich licour
Of which vertue engendred is the flour;
Whan Zephirus eek with his sweete breeth   5
Inspired hath in every holt and heeth
The tendre croppes, and the yonge sonne
Hath in the Ram his halve cours yronne,
And smale foweles maken melodye,
That slepen al the nyght with open ye   10
(So priketh hem nature in hir corages);
Thanne longen folk to goon on pilgrimages
And palmeres for to seken straunge strondes,
To ferne halwes, kowthe in sondry londes;
And specially from every shires ende   15
Of Engelond to Caunterbury they wende,
The hooly blisful martir for to seke,
That hem hath holpen whan that they were seeke.

This is the opening sentence from Chaucer's *Canterbury Tales,* written late in the 14th century, though not printed (for there was no printing then) until nearly a hundred years later. The spelling no doubt seems strange, and the sound of the lines when they are correctly pronounced will be even stranger. This six-hundred-year-old passage is printed here, clearly and accurately, the result of many generations of painstaking work in searching and comparing ancient manuscripts.

The following recent translation puts the passage into the language in which we now speak and write:

> When in April the sweet showers fall
> And pierce the drought of March to the root, and all
> The veins are bathed in liquor of such power
> As will bring on the engendering of the flower,
> When also Zephyrus with his sweet breath   5
> Exhales an air in every grove and heath
> Upon the tender shoots, and the young sun
> His half-course in the sign of the Ram has run,
> And the small fowl are making melody,
> That sleep away the night with open eye   10
> (So nature pricks them and their heart engages),
> Then people long to go on pilgrimages,
> And palmers long to seek the stranger strands
> Of far-off saints, hallowed in sundry lands,
> And specially, from every shire's end   15
> In England, down to Canterbury they wend
> To seek the holy blissful martyr, quick
> In giving help to them when they were sick.

Making such a translation requires an accurate and extensive knowledge of the meanings of many ancient words and grammatical forms. It requires too a knowledge of the way in which Chaucer's words sounded and rhymed. Still more knowledge is essential for an understanding of the translation. We have to know that "Zephyrus" is a name for the warm west wind, that the "sign of the Ram" is one of the signs of the zodiac and means that the sun has passed its position of March 21. We have to know that "palmers" are religious pilgrims, that the "holy blissful martyr" is Saint Thomas à Becket, who was murdered in Canterbury Cathedral in 1170 by ambitious agents of the king.

Consider now the opening of another famous English poem, *The Waste Land,* by T. S. Eliot, published in 1922:*

> April is the cruellest month, breeding
> Lilacs out of the dead land, mixing
> Memory and desire, stirring
> Dull roots with spring rain.
> Winter kept us warm, covering   5
> Earth in forgetful snow, feeding
> A little life with dried tubers.

* From "The Waste Land" in *Collected Poems 1909–1962* by T. S. Eliot, copyright, 1936, by Harcourt Brace Jovanovich, Inc.; Copyright © 1963, 1964 by T. S. Eliot. Reprinted by permission of the publisher.

Summer surprised us, coming over the Starnbergersee
With a shower of rain; we stopped in the colonnade,
And went on in sunlight, into the Hofgarten,   10
And drank coffee, and talked for an hour.

Here, certainly, is a very different springtime.

The opening lines of both passages speak of the rain that stirs and awakens the earth in April. For Chaucer the coming of spring is an occasion for joy and gratitude that human life is part of the cycle of nature. The gentle air and rain make flowers spring up and birds sing, and they stir many to make religious pilgrimages in grateful thanks to the saints who have helped them through the sickness and hardship of the long cold winter. And especially in England multitudes of pilgrims set out for the shrine of Saint Thomas à Becket at Canterbury, the most important cathedral in the kingdom. But in the modern poem the coming of spring is painful. The "dead land" does not spring into joyful life; it seems to resist the "breeding," "mixing," "stirring" forced upon it by the spring rain. The passage from Chaucer is one sweeping sentence: *when* all nature awakens, *then* people set out on pilgrimages. Their journey is purposeful, and the onrushing sentence ties the purpose to the rest of creation. But instead of a joyous pilgrimage in England, the person speaking in the modern poem tells us of a casual stroll in a foreign city—in Munich, where there is a famous cafe, the Hofgarten, and a lake, the Starnbergersee, nearby. The "mixing" of "memory and desire" here does not lead to a purposeful religious journey, but only to an unexcited awareness that winter is over, an awareness of pain and boredom. For Chaucer, April is the time of "sweet showers"; for Eliot, April is "the cruellest month."

This small portion of T. S. Eliot's poetry may seem in its way as strange as did the first version of the passage from Chaucer, and at first sight we may like it or we may not. But we cannot help hearing in it, for all its deliberately flat, unexcited, joyless quality, a hauntingly original voice. And the qualities of this voice help us to hear the more clearly the buoyant joyfulness of Chaucer. By themselves Chaucer's lines seem simple and straightforward—as indeed they are. Yet when we read them alongside the passage from *The Waste Land*, their simple joyfulness becomes an expression that is beautifully balanced, beautifully *made*, and made by one of the most original voices in all English literature. To some readers the poet of six hundred years ago may seem nearer, may make more sense, than the poet of the 20th century. And yet all of us will share the latter's vision too, for we recognize his language at once. We may well say that spring is the time for gladness and pilgrimages, if only to the baseball park. Still, as we hear the passage from *The Waste Land* we have a sense of something in us that resists the pull of the seasons, that slows our responses to nature, that will not quickly and joyfully come to life. Chaucer's April is very different from Eliot's, and the difference between them makes us aware of our own April, our own place in history.

Literature and History

For we live in history ourselves, and we come to understand and to express who we are and where we are by using many of the same words that both these poets have used. Chaucer lived a long time ago. The population of London was under 100,000 even a century after he died, and in his lifetime the mysterious and deadly plague, the Black Death, killed at least a third of his fellow citizens. Chaucer scarcely knew about gunpowder, he never saw a printed book, and the whole vast land in which we live did not exist for him. Eliot, who was born twelve years before the 20th century began, has lived through two World Wars, he has seen new nations come into being all over the world, he has seen the airplane, radio, and the television reduce the distances between nations, and he has even seen the beginnings of exploration into outer space. Certainly his place in history must be different from Chaucer's, and certainly his conception of spring—and of much else—must be different from Chaucer's.

The history with which the student of literature is concerned, however, is not just a reflection of what has happened in the worlds of politics, warfare, transportation, communication, technology. It is the history of what has happened in the world of literature, the world in which men and women discover and express their knowledge of themselves. Such a world cannot of course be separated from the way people govern themselves, from the way they earn their livings, fight their wars, establish peace. But the relation between literature and politics or economics or technology is never simple and is sometimes difficult to see.

If we had a magic time-machine that could transport us back to the London of Chaucer's day, we would see much that would confound and amaze us. Indeed, we would perhaps not long survive the ordinary conditions of life—the lack of sanitation, the gross and unvaried diet (for the rich—the poor were often hungry), the vast differences between the squalor of the artisans and the splendor of the nobles, and in winter the bone-chilling damp and cold. (We would indeed welcome April if we survived such a winter.) And the babble of voices around us in the muddy, pestilential streets would assail our ears as a wild and unintelligible noise. And yet—if we survived—after a while we would begin to hear our own language amid that noise. We would begin to pick out the words that we use ourselves in the daily conduct of our lives, such words as *sweet, soft, melody, folk, long, lands, holy, help, sick*. We would find, too, that we understood the ways in which such words were put together—joyously or sadly, defiantly or maliciously. We would find that great as it is, the historical gulf between Chaucer's England and 20th century America is yet bridged by our common language.

Thanks to the work of scholars, printers, and publishers, we need no such machine to go back to Chaucer's time or even to 1922, the year of

Eliot's famous poem. We need only books, books written in our language and using our words. Not using them to say the same things over and over, nor using them to say similar things in better and better ways. Spring did not mean the same thing to Eliot that it did to Chaucer; indeed, one reason Eliot gave to spring the meaning that he did is that he knew what Chaucer's was—Chaucer's and that of many another writer in the long years between them. Eliot made *his* meaning to express himself, who he was and where in all the long history of our language he thought he was. He did not find himself in a joyous world of purpose and worship, and he said so as imaginatively and arrestingly as he could. And as we read these poets, we find ourselves in a position that differs yet again, that differs from the positions of both Chaucer and Eliot. It will be our own position in the long and vast history of the language that we share, and we come to know it only by performing the many, many acts of comparison that a wide, various, and abundant experience of literature can supply.

Literature and the Expression of Oneself

As students of literature, we are not merely readers of other persons' words. We read Eliot's poetry, but we do not read it in isolation; we read it with Chaucer's poetry in mind—and that of as many other writers as we can master. As soon as we see Chaucer and Eliot together—and they are, for all their differences, together in our language—we find ourselves struggling to express many things. We want to understand the differences before us, we want to justify our preferences, we want to know why—and we want to know how—there can be two such different springtimes. And to distinguish, to reconcile, to understand two such writers is a task that calls upon our best efforts as users of the language we share with them.

For as students of literature, we are truly users of language ourselves. We are speakers and writers who, in our own way, express *ourselves* and our place in history. After all, language is the means by which all of us express ourselves—our dreams, our choices, our beliefs, our deepest sense of life. Music is perhaps the most immediate kind of self-expression, but relatively few of us are composers. Painting or sculpture is perhaps the most permanent kind of self-expression, but again relatively few of us can speak our minds in lines and colors or shapes. All of us must learn many special languages in the course of our lives—the language of mathematics, the symbols of the blueprint, the equations of the engineer's formulas, the chemist's table of elements. We *cannot* keep our society going without such special languages as these. But we *do* not keep our lives going without that language in which the symbols are the great words of human experience—*love, fear, humanity, God, family, law*. We do not live without the words that for all their constantly changing meanings are the main words in the language that we share with Shakespeare and Thomas

Hardy as well as with Emerson and Robert Frost. And that is why the literature gathered into this book is English literature.

National Individuality in Literature

Because it is the literature of England, of course, it tells us about a civilization that differs in many respects from our own. Britain, after all, is a constitutional monarchy, and although Queen Elizabeth does not exercise over her subjects the same power as did the Queen Elizabeth of Shakespeare's day, still British society is organized differently from ours. From England we draw our deepest beliefs in the equality of individuals before the law, in the legal traditions of the trial by jury and the common law, and in many other guarantees of political freedom that are written into our Declaration of Independence and our Constitution—and written there by men who thought of themselves as Englishmen, though not English subjects. And yet, until fairly recent times, no one could hold public office or even graduate from either of the two oldest universities, Oxford or Cambridge, without belonging to the Church of England. There originated in Britain some of the greatest achievements and institutions of modern industry, and they originated and developed under a system of private ownership. Yet today in Britain the government owns the railroads and the radio (and some of the television networks as well), it provides general medical and health services for all its citizens, and it administers a vast educational program of scholarships and examinations from grammar school through graduate work in the universities. We all know of commoner differences. The British drive on the left; their currency system is different from ours. Within the British Isles, small as their geographic area is, are other surprises. As one journeys from the Scottish north, south through Wales and the Midlands to Cornwall, one will hear varieties of accent more numerous than in a similar journey from Maine to Texas or from Washington to Florida. And in moving from town to town the traveler will find that the inhabitants of this little island have strong local ties. The English, the Scottish, the Welsh, or the Irish, when you ask them where they live is likely to say, "I belong to . . .": "I belong to Paisley," or "I belong to Exeter," or "I belong to Hull." Do Americans "belong to" Fort Worth or Baltimore or Cleveland Heights?

The literature of England, like that of France or Germany or any other nation, certainly reflects national traits, national uniquenesses, national history. Certainly the student of literature will become aware of these differences, and certainly our own country's institutions will become clearer as he or she encounters variations from them in another nation. One will hear differences of idiom that sometimes go deep into national life: for example, the Englishman stands for Parliament, but the American runs for Congress; the American refers abruptly to "TV," but the Englishman speaks familiarly of "the telly."

English Literature Is Ours

But the American student of literature reads English literature primarily because he or she *is* a student of literature and not only a historian or sociologist. For the literature of England, from Chaucer to T. S. Eliot, has shaped the expectations of American readers and writers ever since there has been an America. It is the literature that has taught us most about the values of original speech and the power of the imagination. It is the literature that has taught us most about how to know ourselves and to appreciate the culture of others. It is the literature that has kept our language fresh, alive, and growing for more than six hundred years.

The frontispiece of Troilus and Criseyde *by Geoffrey Chaucer from an illuminated manuscript of 1400 represents the poet reading to a noble audience.*

to 1500

The Middle Ages

"... *tel forth, and I wol heere.*"

GEOFFREY CHAUCER

The English Language and Its Beginning

ENGLISH LITERATURE to us means books. It means books that we read to ourselves, silently. Often, of course, we see and hear a play; sometimes we listen to the recording of an author reading from his or her works. Yet most of our experience of literature is one in which we "hear" what we read only in our "inner ear." We read to ourselves, silently, alone. Our silent, rapid reading of a page is the result of our long exposure to fixed, uniform print. Our very notions of what literature is and how it works upon us have been fixed by all our experience of the *printed* word, the unchanging, uniform arrangement of words upon the page.

But English literature is older than books. There was literature in England for hundreds of years before the first printed book. It was an oral literature, a literature sung, chanted, recited; and those who listened to it were never alone. They heard it in groups sometimes as small as a family, sometimes as large as a band of warriors sitting in a hall with a chieftain at their head. The earliest English literature was social, communal—and noisy. It was close to the experience of daily life, not something one studied by oneself, but something one understood in experiencing it with others. There was no reading public, as we now say. There was, rather, a live, expectant, sometimes vigorously participating audience.

A Roman parade helmet found at Ribchester in the northwest of England. On the crown is a combat scene between cavalry and foot soldiers.

The first English literature that we know much about was composed by professional poets called scops who sang to warrior bands of the deeds of their forefathers and kinsmen. The scop sometimes was assisted by a gleeman, a subordinate who memorized the scop's compositions and recited them, not letter-perfect, but "sound-perfect." Both must have had prodigious memories, as did the troubadours, the professional poets of France, for they could apparently recite for hours, even days, without stopping or forgetting. Unlike us they could not depend on a book to get their stories right, for the story or poem had nothing to do with writing. They spoke their poetry as they learned it or invented it, by heart, not by eye.

Some of this earliest literature was eventually written down by scribes, but much of it was never set down at all and has been irretrievably lost. And some of it, the ballads and folk songs especially, was not written down until centuries after it came into being. Even those who could read and write in the Middle Ages rarely could do either silently. Every monastery had its room where religious manuscripts were copied and read and studied. The quiet of these rooms was broken not only by the shuffling of pages and the scratching of quill pens; each was filled with the mumble and whisper of men who said aloud to themselves the sentences they read or copied. Even the most learned men were not "eye-readers"; they were "ear-readers." In the beginnings of English literature, men thought of poems and stories as something to be heard: they listened to literature together and shared its impact as they shared the experiences of fighting, of farming, or of worshiping.

MIDDLE AGES

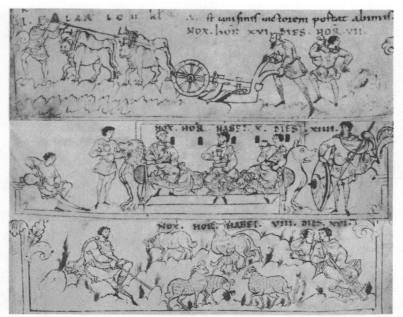

These line drawings from a calendar of about 900 represent scenes of life in Anglo-Saxon England. Each month of the calendar had a different scene; here—plowing the fields, banqueting, and sheepherding.

In each later chapter of this book you will read about two matters: "The Writer's Language" and "The People and Their Times." In this chapter the two topics are not separated. For, as you consider the literature of the Middle Ages, you will see how the history of the peoples who populated England in this era is not separable from the way they spoke and wrote. Their history has indeed affected the very form of the language as it was spoken and written then and now.

The Language: Old English

The "English" of our earliest literature was a language that we find almost unrecognizable now. This language is called Old English— or Anglo-Saxon. Here, for example, are the opening lines of *Beowulf,* the most famous Old English poem, first in Old English, then in a modern English translation:

> Hwæt, we Gar-Dena   in geardagum,
> þeodcyninga   þrym gefrunon,
> hu ða æþelingas   ellen fremedon!

> Lo! we, of the Spear-Danes'   in days of yore,
> of the warrior-kings'   glory have heard,
> how those princes   heroic deeds wrought.

[The signs þ and ð eventually were replaced by our *th.*]

Bamburgh Castle on the northeast coast of England dates from Norman times. The first fortress was built here in the 6th century and was the capital of the Old English kingdom of Bernicia. It is referred to in Arthurian legend as "Joyous Garde."

Such was the English language in the 10th century, though it was then about to change, as it had changed before. And each change was the result of an invasion of the British Isles by warriors from the Continent.

The first such invasion is so remote that we do not know what inhabitants it pushed back or destroyed. The invaders were Celts, and one of the invading tribes called themselves Brythons. They were Druids, practicing a primitive religion of magic and human sacrifice, and were slowly emerging from Bronze Age civilization. Certainly they seemed primitive barbarians to the next invaders. These were the Romans, who crossed the English Channel in 55 B.C. under orders from Julius Caesar. Although the Romans did not fully occupy the land for almost another hundred years, by the end of the 1st century A.D. they had established a province that extended as far north as the Scottish Highlands. The ancient Celtic-speaking Britons, some of whom the Romans called Picts (from the Latin *pictus*, "painted") because they painted themselves blue, were driven into the hills of the west and the north. There, in isolation, they kept their language unmodified by the Latin of the Romans. As the vast Roman Empire began to feel the pressures of the barbarians from the north and east of Europe, the

MIDDLE AGES

The west front of Wells Cathedral, which is a good example of English Gothic architecture, the building being low and rambling, the west front highly decorated with statues and carving. It was built during the period 1207–1242.

remote garrisons were drawn in, and by the year 410 when Rome itself was sacked by barbarians, Britain could no longer be called Roman. The tribes that next invaded England gave the land what was to become the English language we speak today.

These invading tribes came from the shores of the North Sea, and they brought with them a Germanic language. Both Latin and this Germanic Old English (also called Anglo-Saxon) are Indo-European languages. They are dialects within the vast family of Indo-European (sometimes called Aryan) languages that spread from the Mediterranean to Scandinavia, from the Atlantic to India and Persia. Many branches of this huge system of languages have become extinct; many others now seem so different from each other that we find it hard to believe they have a common ancestry.

Old English, like Latin, was an inflected language: its words changed their forms (*inflect* is from the Latin *flecto*, meaning "bend") according to their grammatical function in a sentence. Of course we still retain traces of this inflecting, especially in our use of pronouns. We do not say "I hit he"; we change *he* to the form it must have as a direct object: "I hit him." In such a sentence as "The king gave the warrior a gift,"

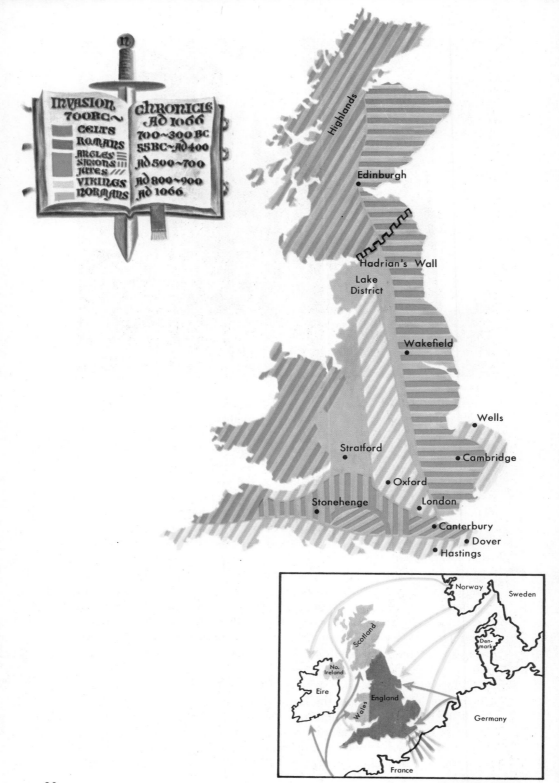

INVASION CHRONICLE
700 BC ~ AD 1066

CELTS	700 ~ 300 BC
ROMANS	55 BC ~ AD 400
ANGLES SAXONS JUTES	AD 500 ~ 700
VIKINGS	AD 800 ~ 900
NORMANS	AD 1066

Highlands

Edinburgh

Hadrian's Wall

Lake District

Wakefield

Wells

Stratford

Cambridge

Oxford

London

Stonehenge

Canterbury

Dover

Hastings

Norway

Sweden

Scotland

Denmark

No. Ireland

Eire

England

Wales

Germany

France

20

the words *king, warrior,* and *gift* all have the same form, though one is
the subject, one the indirect object, and one the object of the action.
The order of the words in the sentence tells us which is which, but in
the Old English we would see differences of form among the three
nouns like the difference between *he* and *him.*

Another characteristic of Old English is its "fixed stress" system, a
habit of stressing the root of a word. This system not only helps make it
a strong language but also is related to a characteristic of earliest
English poetry. All Germanic languages have a "fixed stress" system.
Modern English words which are derived from the Germanic core
of our language have a fixed stress. For instance, compounds of the
word *love,* a Germanic word, keep the stress on the root: *lóver, lóving,
lóvingly, lóvely, lóveliness.* Compounds of the word *kin,* also a Germanic word, similarly keep the stress on the root: *kíndred* and *kínship.*
Most compounds made by adding prefixes to Germanic words keep the
stress on the syllable that contains the root-element of the word: *belóved,
akín.* On the other hand, words borrowed from non-Germanic Indo-
European languages, such as Latin or Greek, frequently show a shift
of stress from the root of the word. For example, in compounds of the
word *family* (borrowed from the Latin word *familia*) the stress shifts:
fámily, famíliar, familiárity. And in compounds of the word *photograph*
(borrowed from Greek words) the stress shifts: *photógrapher, photo-
gráphic.* Of all Indo-European languages, then, only Germanic languages have a fixed stress system. And this habitual stress upon the
most important element of the word, no matter how many prefixes and
suffixes may be fastened to it, is one of the greatest strengths of the
language from which our English has derived. It has enabled the
English language to develop as civilization has developed, without losing its basic strength.

The Germanic stress system also has something to do with art. The
earliest English poetry is alliterative: that is, important syllables in the
line of poetry are bound together by the fact that they begin with
the same sound, and this alliteration is reinforced by the habitual
stress. The pause in the middle of each line is bridged by the alliteration that binds the key words together.

> I will síng of mysélf   a sóng that is trúe
> Téll of my trável,   of tróublous jóurneys.

(These two lines come from an Old English—Anglo-Saxon—poem called
"The Seafarer." The translation approximates the sounds you would hear
in the original.) Of course we still do much the same thing in common
speech: "busy as a bee," "cool as a cucumber," "rack and ruin." We
would rather say "friend or foe" than "friend or enemy"; we would
never say "sticks and pebbles" when we could say "sticks and stones."

The dangers of the sea, well known to the Anglo-Saxons, are shown in a 12th-century manuscript illustration. The sailors have mistaken a whale's back for an island.

This vigorous language, then, was brought into Roman Britain by Germanic tribes called Angles, Saxons, and Jutes in about the 6th century. From the Angles, or Engles, has come the very name for our language, though they were not the most powerful and influential of the Germanic tribes. From the West Saxons of the old kingdom of Wessex has come most of our knowledge of Old English literature, for almost all Old English literature is recorded in the West Saxon dialect.

It was also the West Saxons under King Alfred who dealt most decisively with yet another series of invasions, this time by the Vikings, or Danes. The Danes began in the 8th century a series of invasions of England, and by the 9th century had control of northern England. The Danish and Old English languages resembled each other much more closely than either one resembled Latin, since both came originally from a single parent Germanic language. But many of the Danish words were different enough to seem foreign to speakers of Old English, and as a result of the Danish invasions and settlements, English was enriched by a large number of Scandinavian borrowings. Some of them, such as *cast, sky, take,* and *window,* are among our most common words today.

Old English Literature

But what of the ancient literature of the Anglo-Saxons? What was it about? What was it like? First, it reflected the hard conditions of the seafaring life the Angles, Saxons, and Jutes left behind them when they came to the comparatively fertile and gentle land of Britain. The Germanic peoples believed in Wyrd ("weird"), or Fate, that pitilessly rules humankind. Their other gods and goddesses were violent beings, whose names have given us our words for the days of the week. Tuesday, for example, is the day of *Tiw*, the god of war, and this name renders into English the Latin name of the same day, *Martis Dies*, or the day of Mars, the Roman war-god; the French call this day *mardi*. Any dictionary will show you the derivation of the other six names. The literature of this people had in it a steady note of loneliness, of the terror of the "rime-cold" (frosty) sea, of sadness for departed comrades. Here, for example, is a small fragment, in modern English, of a poem called "The Wanderer":

So the wanderer spake,   his woes remembering,
His misfortunes in fighting   and the fall of his kinsmen:
   "Often alone   at early dawn
I make my moan!   Not a man now lives
To whom I can speak forth   my heart and soul
And tell of its trials.   In truth I know well
That there belongs to a lord   an illustrious trait,
To fetter his feelings   fast in his breast,
To keep his own counsel   though cares oppress him.
The weary in heart   against Wyrd has no help
Nor may the troubled in thought   attempt to get aid."

The melancholy is intense: against Wyrd we are powerless; we must suffer in silence.

To this lonely melancholy came the outlook and the doctrines of Christianity. During their occupation of Britain, the Romans had taught Christianity to some of the Celts. Indeed, one of these, after the Germanic invaders came, made his way back to Ireland bringing Christianity: he was Saint Patrick. The Anglo-Saxons in the 6th century were converted to Christianity by a special mission from Rome. Afterwards, the marauding Vikings destroyed the churches and altars they found during their raids. But they too were eventually converted, and the invading Normans in 1066 were fighting fellow Christians.

There is a passage in the *Ecclesiastical History of the English People*, a long record of history made by the Venerable Bede, a churchman, which suggests how and why the Anglo-Saxons adopted the Christian religion. A missionary has been urging an early king (King Edwin—the time is 627 A.D.) to adopt his religion, and the King turns to his advisers. His high priest says that the new teachings should be accepted if they are better and more effectual than beliefs in the old gods. Another of the King's chief men agrees, and he goes on to say:

> "Your Majesty, when we compare the present life of man with that time of which we have no knowledge, it seems to me like the swift flight of a lone sparrow through the banqueting-hall where you sit in the winter months to dine with your thanes and counselors. Inside there is a comforting fire to warm the room; outside, the wintry storms of snow and rain are raging. This sparrow flies swiftly in through one door of the hall, and out through another. While he is inside, he is safe from the winter storms; but after a few moments of comfort, he vanishes from sight into the darkness whence he came. Similarly, man appears on earth for a little while, but we know nothing of what went before this life, and what follows. Therefore if this new teaching can reveal any more certain knowledge, it seems only right that we should follow it."

If, in other words, the "new teaching" of Christianity could penetrate the darkness of the fate that surrounds man's life, then it would be well indeed to accept it.

Beowulf

Beowulf, the greatest work of Old English literature, probably written about a century after this memorable passage (although our only written copy of it, from which you have seen a brief quotation, dates from the late 10th century), contains elements of the Christian teachings accepted by this King and his council. But it contains many more elements from the beliefs and the folklore of the early Scandinavian peoples. It is an epic—a long narrative poem which sums up the traditions of a whole people in the adventures of a hero. Beowulf, its warrior-hero, belongs to the Jutes, a tribe which lived in what is now Sweden, and all his adventures occur in that land and in southern Denmark, not in England at all. Beowulf battles with threatening monsters and a dragon; he rules benevolently and generously. But his adventures too are played out under the grim, brooding presence of Wyrd, or Fate. The sense of this presence has never completely vanished from English literature: it lies behind the mutterings of the Witches—or Weird Sisters—in *Macbeth;* it dominates the novels of Thomas Hardy, who wrote, much later, of a country he called Wessex after the old Anglo-Saxon kingdom of that name.

The lid of a Northumbrian casket, carved about 700, shows warriors dressed in chain mail. The box is made of whalebone plaques fitted with silver.

Beowulf

Translated by J. Duncan Spaeth

[*The poem begins with a brief account of* Scyld (shYld), *a famous King of the Spear-Danes. It then traces the lineage of* Hrothgar (hrōth' gär), *the present King of the* Spear-Danes, *and tells of the building of Heorot (hā'ə rŏt), Hrothgar's magnificent mead-hall, the place where the warriors slept, ate, and drank mead.[1] Heorot is being plagued by a monster, Grendel, a demon-sprite, who in nightly raids attacks and kills numerous men of Hrothgar's court.*]

> In the darkness dwelt a demon-sprite,
> Whose heart was filled with fury and hate,
> When he heard each night the noise of revel
> Loud in the hall, laughter and song.
> To the sound of the harp the singer chanted   5
> Lays[2] he had learned, of long ago;
> How the Almighty had made the earth,
> Wonder-bright lands, washed by the ocean;
> How he set triumphant, sun and moon
> To lighten all men that live on the earth.   10

1 mead: a fermented honey drink.
2 Lays: songs.

He brightened the land with leaves and branches;
Life he created for every being,
Each in its kind, that moves upon earth.
So, happy in hall, the heroes lived,
Wanting nought, till one began   15
To work them woe, a wicked fiend.
The demon grim was Grendel called,
Marsh stalker[3] huge, the moors he roamed.
The joyless creature had kept long time
The lonely fen,[4] the lairs of monsters,   20
Cast out from men, an exile accurst.
The killing of Abel, on offspring of Cain
Was justly avenged by the Judge Eternal.[5]
Nought gained by the feud the faithless murderer;
He was banished unblest from abode of men. . . .   25

THE RAVAGING OF HEOROT HALL BY THE MONSTER GRENDEL

demon-sprite

When night had fallen, the fiend crept near
To the lofty hall, to learn how the Danes
In Heorot fared, when the feasting was done.
The aethelings[6] all within he saw
Asleep after revel, not recking[7] of danger,   30
And free from care. The fiend accurst,
Grim and greedy, his grip made ready;
Snatched in their sleep, with savage fury,
Thirty warriors; away he sprang
Proud of his prey, to repair to his home,   35
His blood-dripping booty to bring to his lair.
At early dawn, when day-break came,
The vengeance of Grendel was revealed to all;
Their wails after wassail[8] were widely heard,
Their morning-woe. The mighty ruler,   40
The aetheling brave, sat bowed with grief.
The fate of his followers filled him with sorrow,
When they traced the tracks of the treacherous foe,
Fiend accurst. Too fierce was that onset,
Too loathsome and long, nor left them respite.   45
The very next night, anew he began
To maim and to murder, nor was minded to slacken
His fury of hate, too hardened in crime.
'Twas easy to find then earls who preferred
A room elsewhere, for rest at night,   50

---

3 **Marsh stalker:** stalker of the marshes, or wastes.
4 **fen:** low, swampy land.
5 **The killing . . . Eternal:** See Genesis 4:1-16.
6 **aethelings** (ăth'əl ĭngz): noble warriors.
7 **recking:** thinking of.
8 **wassail** (wŏs'əl): the drinking bout of the night before.

"The mighty ruler, / The aetheling brave sat bowed with grief." These figures and others illustrating this poem are chess pieces dating from 900 to 1100.

A bed in the bowers, when they brought this news
Of the hall-foe's hate; and henceforth all
Who escaped the demon, kept distance safe.

So Grendel wrongfully ruled the hall,
One against all till empty stood   55
That lordly mansion, and long remained so.
For the space of twelve winters the Scyldings' Friend[9]
Bore in his breast the brunt of this sorrow,
Measureless woe.   In mournful lays
The tale became known; 'twas told abroad   60
In gleemen's songs, how Grendel had warred
Long against Hrothgar, and wreaked[10] his hate
With murderous fury through many a year,
Refusing to end the feud perpetual,
Or decently deal with the Danes in parley,   65
Take their tribute for treaty of peace;
Nor could their leaders look to receive
Pay from his hands for the harm that he wrought.
The fell destroyer kept feeding his rage
On young and old.   So all night long   70
He prowled o'er the fen and surprised his victims,
Death-shadow dark.   (The dusky realms
Where the hell-runes haunt[11] are hidden from men.)
So the exiled roamer his raids continued;
Wrong upon wrong in his wrath he heaped.   75

9 Scyldings' (shYld′ĭngz) **Friend:** Hrothgar.
10 wreaked (rēkt): gave free play to.

11 hell-runes haunt: mysterious creatures of hell wander.

[The wise men of the Spear-Danes meet often to take counsel and to
pray before their heathen altars for deliverance from the monster.]

Many the wise men that met to discover
Ways of escape from the scourge of affliction.
Often they came for counsel together;
Often at heathen altars they made
Sacrifice-offerings, beseeching their idols   80
To send them deliverance from assault of the foe.
Such was their practice, they prayed to the Devil;
The hope of the heathen on hell was fixed,
The mood of their mind. Their Maker they knew not,
The righteous Judge and Ruler on high.   85
The Wielder of Glory they worshipped not,
The Warden of Heaven. Woe be to him
Whose soul is doomed through spite and envy,
In utter despair and agony hopeless
Forever to burn. But blessed is he   90
Who, after this life, the Lord shall seek,
Eager for peace in the arms of the Father.

[Grendel continues to attack and kill Hrothgar's men. Beowulf, a
brave young warrior in the service of Hygelac (hY̆g' ə läk), *King of the*
Jutes, hears of Hrothgar's trouble. He chooses from the Jutes fourteen
of the bravest men and embarks for the land of the Spear-Danes.
When he and his warriors arrive, they are met by Hrothgar's coast
guard, who, after being told their purpose, directs them to Heorot.
There follows an evening of feasting, mead-drinking, and exchanging
of stories.]

THE FEASTING IN HEOROT AND THE CUSTOMS OF THE HALL

Hrothgar spoke, the Scyldings' defender:
"Thou hast come, dear Beowulf, to bring us help,
For the sake of friendship to fight our battles.   95
[Hrothgar recounts the exploits of Beowulf's father.]
Sad is my spirit and sore it grieves me
To tell to any the trouble and shame
That Grendel hath brought me with bitter hate,
The havoc he wrought in my ranks in the hall.
My war-band dwindles, driven by Wyrd   100
Into Grendel's grasp; but God may easily
End this monster's mad career.
Full often they boasted, my beer-bold warriors,
Brave o'er their ale-cups, the best of my fighters,
They'd meet in the mead-hall the mighty Grendel,   105
End his orgies with edge of the sword.

But always the mead-hall, the morning after,
The splendid building, was blood-bespattered;
Daylight dawned on the drippings of swords,
Soiled with slaughter were sills and benches.   110
My liege-men[12] perished, and left me poor.
Sit down to the board; unbend thy thoughts;
Speak to my men as thy mood shall prompt."
For the band of the Jutes a bench was cleared;
Room in the mead-hall was made for them all.   115
Then strode to their seats the strong-hearted heroes.
The warriors' wants a waiting-thane[13] served;
Held in his hand the highly-wrought ale-cup,
Poured sparkling mead, while the minstrel sang
Gaily in Heorot. There was gladness of heroes,   120
A joyous company of Jutes and of Danes.

[*Hrothgar and his warriors retire, and Beowulf, who has insisted that
he meet Grendel alone and unarmed, begins his watch for Grendel.*]

BEOWULF'S FIGHT WITH GRENDEL

Now Grendel came, from his crags of mist
Across the moor; he was curst of God.
The murderous prowler meant to surprise
In the high-built hall his human prey.   125
He stalked 'neath the clouds, till steep before him
The house of revelry rose in his path,
The gold-hall of heroes, the gaily adorned.
Hrothgar's home he had hunted full often,
But never before had he found to receive him   130
So hardy a hero, such hall-guards there.
Close to the building crept the slayer,
Doomed to misery. The door gave way,
Though fastened with bolts, when his fist fell on it.
Maddened he broke through the breach he had made;   135
Swoln with anger and eager to slay,
The ravening fiend o'er the bright-paved floor
Furious ran, while flashed from his eyes
An ugly glare like embers aglow.
He saw in the hall, all huddled together,   140
The heroes asleep. Then laughed in his heart
The hideous fiend; he hoped ere dawn
To sunder body from soul of each;
He looked to appease his lust of blood,
Glut his maw[14] with the men he would slay.   145

12 **liege**(lēj)-**men:** devoted followers.   14 **glut his maw:** fill his stomach to excess.
13 **thane:** free man in the service of a lord.

But Wyrd had otherwise willed his doom;
Never again should he get a victim
After that night. Narrowly watched
Hygelac's thane how the horrible slayer
Forward should charge in fierce attack. 150
Nor was the monster minded to wait:
Sudden he sprang on a sleeping thane,
Ere he could stir, he slit him open;
Bit through the bone-joints, gulped the blood,
Greedily bolted the body piecemeal. 155
Soon he had swallowed the slain man wholly,
Hands and feet. Then forward he hastened,
Sprang at the hero, and seized him at rest;
Fiercely clutched him with fiendish claw.
But quickly Beowulf caught his forearm, 160
And threw himself on it with all his weight.
Straight discovered that crafty plotter,
That never in all midearth had he met
In any man a mightier grip.
Gone was his courage, and craven fear 165
Sat in his heart, yet helped him no sooner.
Fain[15] would he hide in his hole in the fenland,
His devil's den. A different welcome
From former days he found that night!
Now Hygelac's thane, the hardy, remembered 170
His evening's boast, and bounding up,
Grendel he clenched, and cracked his fingers;
The monster tried flight, but the man pursued;
The ravager hoped to wrench himself free,
And gain the fen, for he felt his fingers 175
Helpless and limp in the hold of his foe.
'Twas a sorry visit the man-devourer
Made to the Hall of the Hart[16] that night.
Dread was the din, the Danes were frighted
By the uproar wild of the ale-spilling fray. 180
The hardiest blenched as the hall-foes wrestled
In terrible rage. The rafters groaned;
'Twas wonder great that the wine-hall stood,
Firm 'gainst the fighters' furious onslaught,
Nor fell to the ground, that glorious building. 185
With bands of iron 'twas braced and stiffened
Within and without. But off from the sill
Many a mead-bench mounted with gold
Was wrung where they wrestled in wrath together.

15 Fain: gladly.

16 Hall of the Hart: literal name for Heorot, so called because it was decorated with the antlers of the hart, or stag.

The Scylding nobles never imagined 190
That open attack, or treacherous cunning,
Could wreck or ruin their royal hall,
The lofty and antlered, unless the flames
Should some day swallow it up in smoke.
The din was renewed, the noise redoubled; 195
Each man of the Danes was mute with dread,
That heard from the wall the horrible wail,
The gruesome song of the godless foe,
His howl of defeat, as the fiend of hell
Bemoaned his hurt. The man held fast; 200
Greatest he was in grip of strength,
Of all that dwelt upon earth that day.

The Defeat of Grendel

Loath in his heart was the hero-deliverer
To let escape his slaughterous guest.
Of little use that life he deemed 205
To human kind. The comrades of Beowulf
Unsheathed their weapons to ward[17] their leader,
Eagerly brandished their ancient blades,
The life of their peerless lord to defend.
Little they deemed, those dauntless warriors, 210
As they leaped to the fray, those lusty fighters,
Laying on boldly to left and to right,
Eager to slay, that no sword upon earth
No keenest weapon could wound that monster:
Point would not pierce, he was proof against iron; 215
'Gainst victory-blades the devourer was charmed.
But a woeful end awaited the wretch,
That very day he was doomed to depart,
And fare afar to the fiends' domain.

Now Grendel found, who in former days 220
So many a warrior had wantonly slain,
In brutish lust, abandoned of God,
That the frame of his body was breaking at last.
Keen of courage, the kinsman of Hygelac
Held him grimly gripped in his hands. 225
Loath was each to the other alive.
The grisly monster got his death-wound:
A huge split opened under his shoulder;
Crunched the socket, cracked the sinews.
Glory great was given to Beowulf. 230
But Grendel escaped with his gaping wound,

17 **ward:** guard.

"When morning arrived, so runs the report,
Around the gift-hall gathered the warriors;"

O'er the dreary moor his dark den sought,
Crawled to his lair. 'Twas clear to him then,
The count of his hours to end had come,
Done were his days. The Danes were glad,   235
The hard fight was over, they had their desire.
Cleared was the hall, 'twas cleansed by the hero
With keen heart and courage, who came from afar.
The lord of the Jutes rejoiced in his work,
The deed of renown he had done that night.   240
His boast to the Danes he bravely fulfilled;
From lingering woe delivered them all;
From heavy sorrow they suffered in heart;
From dire distress they endured so long;
From toil and from trouble. This token they saw: 245
The hero had laid the hand of Grendel
Both arm and claws, the whole forequarter
With clutches huge, 'neath the high-peaked roof.

THE CELEBRATION OF THE VICTORY AND THE SONG OF THE GLEEMAN

When morning arrived, so runs the report,
Around the gift-hall gathered the warriors;   250
The folk-leaders fared from far and near,
The wide ways o'er, the wonder to view,
The wild beast's foot-prints. Not one of them felt
Regret that the creature had come to grief,
When they traced his retreat by the tracks on the moor;   255
Marked where he wearily made his way,
Harried and beaten, to the haunt of the nicors,[18]
Slunk to the water, to save his life.

18 **nicors** (nĭk′ərz): water sprites or water goblins.

MIDDLE AGES

"The folk-leaders fared from far and near,
The wide ways o'er, the wonder to view. . . ."

There they beheld the heaving surges,
Billows abrim with bloody froth,   260
Dyed with gore, where the gruesome fiend,
Stricken and doomed, in the struggle of death
Gave up his ghost in the gloom of the mere,[19]
His heathen soul for hell to receive it.
Then from the mere the thanes turned back,   265
Men and youths from the merry hunt,
Home they rode on their horses gray,
Proudly sitting their prancing steeds.
Beowulf's prowess was praised by all.
They all agreed that go where you will,   270
'Twixt sea and sea, at the south or the north,
None better than he, no braver hero,
None worthier honor could ever be found.

[*But Beowulf's victory over Grendel does not free Heorot from danger.
Grendel's mother, seeking revenge for the death of her monster-son, attacks Heorot and kills Hrothgar's dearest friend. Beowulf follows
Grendel's mother to her lair and there slays her. Thus the young Beowulf triumphs over the forces of evil.*

The second part of Beowulf *tells of an exploit of the mature Beowulf.
After the death of King Hygelac, Beowulf becomes King of the Jutes
and rules wisely for fifty years. In his old age he is once again called
to battle—this time with a dragon which is threatening his kingdom.
Beowulf slays the dragon, thus winning for his people the dragon's
treasure-hoard. But Beowulf is himself mortally wounded in the fight.
After his death, his people prepare a funeral pyre for him; they lament
the loss and praise the valor of their great King.*]

19 mere: pond.

Then built for Beowulf the band of the Jutes
A funeral pyre; 'twas firmly based.   275
They hung it with helmets as he had bidden,
With shining byrnies[20] and battleshields.
In the midst they laid, with loud lament,
Their lord beloved, their leader brave.
On the brow of the cliff they kindled the blaze,   280
Black o'er the flames the smoke shot up;
Cries of woe, in the windless air,
Rose and blent with the roar of the blast,
Till the frame of the body burst with the heat
Of the seething heart. In sorrowing mood   285
They mourned aloud their leader dead.
Joined in the wail a woman old,
With hair upbound for Beowulf grieved,
Chanted a dreary dirge of woe,
Dark forebodings of days to come,   290
Thick with slaughter and throes of battle,
Bondage and shame. The black smoke rose.
High on the headland they heaped a barrow,[21]
Lofty and broad 'twas built by the Weders,[22]
Far to be seen by sea-faring men.   295
Ten days long they toiled to raise it,
The battle-king's beacon. They built a wall
To fence the brands[23] of the funeral burning,
The choicest and best their chiefs could devise.
In the barrow they buried the bracelets and rings,   300
All those pieces of precious treasure
That bold-hearted men had brought from the cave,[24]
Returned to earth the heirloom of heroes,
The gold to the ground, again to become
As useless to men as of yore it had been.   305

Around the barrow the battle-brave rode,
Twelve in the troop, all true-born aethelings,
To make their lament and mourn for the King;
To chant a lay their lord to honor.
They praised his daring; his deeds of prowess   310
They mentioned in song. For meet[25] it is
That men should publish their master's praise,
Honor their chieftain, and cherish him dearly
When he leaves this life, released from the body.

---

20 byrnies: (bûr'nĭz): armor for the body.
21 barrow: large mound of earth over a grave.
22 Weders: another name for the Jutes.

23 brands: burning sticks.
24 the cave: where the dragon's treasure-hoard was found.
25 meet: fitting.

Thus joined the men of the Jutes in mourning
Their hero's end. His hearth-companions
Called him the best among kings of the earth,
Mildest of men, and most beloved,
Kindest to kinsmen, and keenest for fame.

Comment

The unknown author of *Beowulf* wrote about the Jutes and the Spear-Danes, Germanic peoples who lived in pre-Christian times on the continent. Yet he has also left us in the poem a record of his own culture, the culture of the early Anglo-Saxons. Throughout the poem, in fact, the poet fuses elements from the old Germanic life with elements of the life of his own island people.

1. Find in the selection descriptions of the social customs of the warrior. Find evidence of the personal traits of the warrior that the Anglo-Saxons most admired. In the characterization and the actions of Beowulf himself, for example, what traits are presented as most admirable?

2. Although the time of the events narrated in *Beowulf* is pre-Christian, the poem was composed after the Anglo-Saxons had been introduced to Christianity, and it therefore contains certain Christian attitudes and allusions. Find references to the Old or New Testament in the selection.

3. Again, the poem speaks of both Wyrd and God—of both the Germanic Fate that directs men's lives to inevitable destruction, and the Christian God who cares for the lives of his children. Sometimes both Wyrd and God may be referred to in a short passage:

> My war-band dwindles, driven by Wyrd
> Into Grendel's grasp; but God may easily
> End this monster's mad career.

Which seems to you stronger in the poem: the Christian elements; or the note of sadness and loss, a belief that all good things will come to an end, the major note, indeed, of Anglo-Saxon poetry? In the account of Beowulf's funeral (ll. 274-319), especially, what outlook on life seems to you to be expressed?

The illustrations above and facing are from an early 14th-century English prayer book organized according to the months of the year. For September: the Anglo-Saxon laborers feed the swine by knocking fruit from the trees.

The Language: Middle English

The next—and last—invasion brought to England the French, and it changed the English language profoundly. In 1066 William the Conqueror and his Norman soldiers—men whose name indicates their descent from "Northmen," or Vikings, but whose forebears had completely adopted the language and culture they found in France—these Norman invaders overcame Harold the Saxon, and the last great mutation of the English language began.

After their conquest of the English, the Normans brought a new civilization to Britain. The process was a slow one—indeed all the processes and developments of the long period from the invasion of England by Germanic tribes to the late Middle Ages must be reckoned in hundreds of years. The new rulers conducted the affairs of the kingdom in Latin and in French. The Old English language that under Alfred and the Wessex Kingdom had become dominant developed in fragments, spoken in regions isolated from each other. The northernmost regions of the island, of course, as well as Wales, had never been under the influence of the West Saxons, and their special dialects continued undisturbed.

These Norman French imposed their language almost entirely upon the country. In Sir Walter Scott's *Ivanhoe* there is a scene in which a native Saxon complains that the names of the beasts of the field—*ox, cow, calf, sheep, swine*—are English; these are the names by which they are known to the native population who care for them on the farms. But when these animals are changed into meat and served in the hall,

MIDDLE AGES

For January: another view of life in the Middle Ages shows the Norman rich feasting while being entertained by a minstrel.

complains the Saxon, their names become French: *beef, veal, mutton, pork, bacon.* The difference tells us that the French were the masters and the Anglo-Saxons the servants; it also suggests how thoroughly the masters' language was imposed. For virtually all our words for cookery come from the French—*boil, fry, roast, toast*—whereas the Old English words for preparing foods have virtually disappeared.

The words they introduced are a record of how completely the French transformed our civilization. Most of the terms from the realm of government, including *government* itself, come from the French: *people, nation, realm, parliament.* The French introduced a whole new vocabulary for the military world: *officer, lieutenant, sergeant, soldier, company.* They gave us our important legal words: *suit, sue, plaintiff, defendant, crime.* They brought words for the Church: *religion, service, saint, clergy, preach, pray.* They brought words for the world of art and architecture: *beauty, design, color, ornament, arch, column.* There is no branch of civilized life which they did not transform.

And yet the Germanic base of the language survived. It did so partly by reason of the development of what we might call two styles, the high and the low. A vocabulary rich in French and Latin elements is to this very day more formal, learned, and technical than one that is chiefly Anglo-Saxon in origin. Even behind this development we can glimpse the persistent expressive power of the Germanic words. For when we are under pressure or excited we revert to the old language. We cry "Help!" not "Aid!" or "Assistance!" If we are in a hurry, we "begin" rather than "commence." To those we like we are "friendly" rather than "amicable," we prefer a "hearty" to a "cordial" handshake, and we hope, finally, to achieve not "felicity" but "happiness." The simple, emphatic speech of our remote Germanic ancestors has proved its lasting value in our emotions and everyday lives.

A new consolidation of the languages of all the invaders slowly emerged. In the Hundred Years' War with France, a series of raids and battles which lasted from about 1340 to about 1450, the English soldiers, fighting side by side against the French, were men whose ancestors had been Celts, Danes, Saxons, and Normans. These soldiers, especially English archers armed with the deadly accurate longbow, won many a battle against French knights in heavy armor on horseback. By the middle of the 15th century, however, England ruled only the port of Calais on the French side of the Channel. There were wars in England itself, wars between rivals for the throne that William the Conqueror had so firmly established in 1066. All this fighting and turbulence accompanied the slowly growing sense of England as a *nation*.

Commerce and industry flourished, and many native merchants and craftsmen rose to prominence and power. They organized themselves into associations called *guilds*—organizations of men who worked in the same craft or trade, such as carpenters, weavers, or merchants. The merchants' guilds often came to be the most important bodies of a town. And more and more of the administration of the kingdom centered in London. The language in use there, the language of the army, of business, of politics, slowly became the most powerful common language of the kingdom. During the latter half of the 14th century it even became the language of the grammar schools.

This language, the dialect of the Southeast Midlands, is that in which Chaucer, one of the greatest of English poets, spoke and wrote. Indeed, his achievements as a writer were themselves an important influence in establishing London English as the most authoritative dialect. The vocabulary of this language, as we have seen, owes much to the French. But the sinews of the vocabulary—the pronouns, prepositions, and conjunctions that bound it together—were English, and so were its words for the most fundamental concepts.

Middle English, Chaucer's language, had become liberated from some of the rules of Old English. Only two instances will be mentioned here. Old English, you remember, was an inflected language; modern English retains very little of this inflecting, that is, of words changing their forms according to grammatical function. We do not in modern English change the form of the nouns in such a sentence as "The king gave the warrior a gift" as they would have been changed in Old English to show their grammatical function. The fact that so few traces of inflection remain is the result of what happened in the long troubled period between the Conquest and Chaucer. The meaning of a sentence in Chaucer's language, as in modern English, depends upon its word order, not upon the grammatical forms of words.

Or there is the troublesome business of gender that so confuses you if you learn a language such as French. For you must memorize a grammatical gender system that has nothing to do with the difference between male and female. The French say *le crayon* ("pencil," masculine gender) but *la plume* ("pen," feminine gender). And if you study Old English, gender is similarly confusing, for it too is grammatical. There, for example, the word for woman is a noun of neuter gender, as it is in German (*þæt wif, das Weib*). But Chaucer's language, like ours, has dropped these apparently arbitrary distinctions. His nouns no longer have gender; and he uses the pronouns in a natural way, calling male and female beings *he* and *she* and objects *it*. In Old English, the pronouns reflected the gender of the noun they stood for. Thus a "plant," or *wyrt*, being of feminine gender, must be called "she," whereas a "weed," or *coccel*, being of masculine gender, is called "he."

Now such changes as these (and there are many more too complex to describe here) come about when the sounds of a language change in some consistent way. And such changes did occur in the sounds of English, in the spoken language. For example, the Old English word for *name* was *nama* (nä'mä). The final *-a* of this word is pronounced like *a* of the root-syllable, but with much weaker stress. It is also highly significant grammatically. It shows that the word belongs to a certain class, or declension, of nouns, that it is of masculine gender within that class, and that its case is nominative and its number singular. By Chaucer's time this final *-a* had become even less emphatic. It was pronounced (ə), like the *-a* of *tuba*, and was spelled *-e*. This same *-e* was also used when the word was the object of a verb, whereas in Old English the objective case had a different ending, *-an*. Such wearing away of the grammatical and class-endings of words eventually destroys the whole rigid inflectional system. We forget about gender except in the most obvious way, and the order of words in a sentence tells us what is the subject and what is the predicate.

Finally, a word about the sound of Chaucer's Southeast Midland dialect. Generally the vowels were pronounced as they are in French, Spanish, Italian, or Latin: we say *name* and *dame* with what we call a long *a*; in Chaucer's time the vowel of these words was similar in sound to that of modern *father*. It thus had the "continental value" still used in European languages other than English. The consonants were pronounced much as they are now, except that there was a *gh* sound in such words as *night* pronounced like a very strong *ch* (the sound is heard in such Scottish words as *loch*). All final syllables were pronounced, though a final *-e* would disappear into the opening sound of a following word if that word began with a vowel. Here again, in Middle English, is the very beginning of *The Canterbury Tales:*

> Whan that Aprill with his shoures soote
> The droghte of March hath perced to the roote. . . .

The language of these lines would sound strange to you, but it is nearer to our speech than it is to the language of *Beowulf*.

Some musical instruments for popular entertainment in the Middle Ages were (l. to r.) the portative organ, nakers (kettledrums), the symphony (hurdy-gurdy), and bagpipes, as shown in the Luttrell Psalter (psalm book) of 1340.

Middle English Literature
The Popular Tradition

The Ballad

IN ALL ITS various dialects Middle English literature is rich as a literature of the people. They listened to sermons. They heard miracle plays (based on stories from the Bible) and morality plays (designed to teach morality through the speeches and actions of allegorical characters such as Good Deeds and Death). But the popular and native traditions of medieval literature flourished most vigorously in the narrative songs called ballads.

Some of the stories they tell can be found in the folklore of peoples all over the world. Some are about episodes or persons known to history; some about legendary characters and events. The authors of the ballads are unknown. Almost all are told in the ballad stanza, a group of four lines of which the second and fourth are shorter. These lines have one fewer strong beat and are connected by rhyme.

> There lived a wife at Usher's Well,　　　*a*
> 　And a wealthy wife was she;　　　*b*
> She had three stout and stalwart sons,　　　*c*
> 　And sent them oer the sea.　　　*b*

However the ballad stanza came into being, and whether or not the stories told by the ballads we know were composed by one person or a whole community, the four-line stanza with its strong, clear beat has easily and fluently adapted itself to the telling of all kinds of tales. They are tales, moreover, that we value and remember not for their plots, but for the feelings we find beneath the surface of their simple plots.

Most ballads have come to us in versions that were current in the 15th century or later, though some of them, we know, go back much further than that. And most of them have come to us in northern and Scottish dialects, for most of them were collected by scholars (Sir Walter Scott was one) who found them in Scotland and in the Border country, the region between England and Scotland. To put them into modern English not only destroys their charm and vigor, it also falsifies them. For they were first written down as they were sung; and they therefore preserve for us a glimpse of the way their words were first written, at a time when spelling was not standardized. The old spelling also often gives us an idea of the sound of the language in which they were sung.

"Edward"

One of the finest of the popular ballads is this one, which tells of a mysterious and tragic crime. It proceeds entirely by dialogue: the mother questions; the son answers. Moreover, the main part of each question and answer is repeated, and thus only gradually is the situation revealed to us. Such repetition, called incremental repetition, appears often in the ballad as an addition to the traditional four-line rhyming stanza. Each stanza makes an addition, or increment, to our knowledge, and the repetition keeps us in suspense. When the final revelation comes, it comes, as here, with a powerful shock. We may imagine the hush that must have followed upon the singing of such a dark tale as this.

Edward

"Why dois your brand sae drap wi bluid,
        Edward, Edward,
Why dois your brand sae drap wi bluid,
  And why sae sad gang yee O?"
"Oh I hae killed my hauke sae guid,   5
        Mither, mither,
O I hae killed my hauke sae guid,
  And I had nae mair bot hee O."

"Your haukis bluid was nevir sae reid,
        Edward, Edward,   10
Your haukis bluid was nevir sae reid,
  My deir son I tell thee O."
"O I hae killed my reid-roan steid,
        Mither, mither,
O I hae killed my reid-roan steid,   15
  That erst was sae fair and frie O."

"Your steid was auld, and ye hae gat mair,
        Edward, Edward,
Your steid was auld, and ye hae gat mair,
  Sum other dule ye drie O."   20
"O I hae killed my fadir deir,
        Mither, mither,
O I hae killed my fadir deir,
  Alas, and wae is mee O!"

"And whatten penance wul ye drie for that,   25
        Edward, Edward?
And whatten penance will ye drie for that?
  My deir son, now tell me O."
"Ile set my feit in yonder boat,
        Mither, mither,   30
Ile set my feit in yonder boat,
  And Ile fare ovir the sea O."

"And what wul ye doe wi your towirs and your ha,
  Edward, Edward?
And what wul ye doe wi your towirs and your ha,   35
  That were sae fair to see O?"
"Ile let thame stand tul they doun fa,
  Mither, mither,
Ile let thame stand tul they doun fa,
  For here nevir mair maun I bee O."   40

"And what wul ye leive to your bairns and your wife,
  Edward, Edward?
And what wul ye leive to your bairns and your wife,
  Whan ye gang ovir the sea O?"
"The warldis room, late them beg thrae life,   45
  Mither, mither,
The warldis room, late them beg thrae life,
  For thame nevir mair wul I see O."

"And what wul ye leive to your ain mither deir,
  Edward, Edward?   50
And what wul ye leive to your ain mither deir?
  My deir son, now tell me O."
"The curse of hell frae me sall ye beir,
  Mither, mither,
The curse of hell frae me sall ye beir,   55
  Sic counseils ye gave to me O."

Comment

The Scottish dialect of this and other ballads is not difficult to master, particularly if we say them aloud to ourselves. Here, leaving out all but the simple questions and answers, is a translation of "Edward." The translation below also shows the traditional four-line ballad stanza to which the repetitions in the original are attached.

1 "Why does your sword so drip with blood,/And why do you go so sadly?"
 "I have killed my hawk so good,/And I had no other but him."
2 "Your hawk's blood was never so red,/My dear son, I tell you."
 "I have killed my red-gray horse,/That once was so fair and noble."
3 "Your horse was old, and you have more,/Some other grief you are suffering."
 "I have killed my father dear,/Alas and woe is me."
4 "And what penance will you suffer for that?/My dear son, now tell me".
 "I'll set my feet in yonder boat,/And I'll journey over the sea."
5 "And what will you do with your towers and your hall,/That were so fair to see?"

"I'll let them stand till they fall down,/For here never more will I
be."

6 "And what will you leave to your children and your wife,/When you
go over the sea?"
"The space of the world [to wander in], let them beg through life,/
For them never more will I see."

7 "And what will you leave to your own mother dear,/My dear son,
now tell me."
"The curse of hell from me shall you bear,/Such advice you gave to
me."

The ballad "Edward" implies rather than tells its story. How much
responsibility for Edward's crime is his mother's we cannot fully tell,
for at the beginning she seems not to know what he has done. Yet his
dependence upon her and his closeness to her are implied by the fact
that he has returned to her rather than to his own wife and "bairns."
Was his crime the result of her "counseils" to him? Do her questions
imply that she knows what she has done but that she fears to face it?

1. What does the ballad tell you of Edward's rank, his condition in
   society?
2. What do Edward's answers tell you about his condition of mind?
   When he comes to the questions about his wife and children, how
   do you understand his answer—"Let them beg"?
3. What do the mother's questions tell us about her condition of
   mind? Is she in terror for what he has done? Is she sure of the
   "counseils" she has given him?
4. Which interpretation makes this ballad more tragic, that the mother
   knows what her son has done because she urged him to do it, or that
   she is filled with horror because he has done something far beyond
   any "counseils" she ever gave? Why?

"Sir Patrick Spence"

This ballad may well have some connection with history, for late
in the 13th century there were some diplomatic missions that took
Scottish lords to confer with the Danes. And it is indeed historical in
its reflection of a society in which obedience must be absolute and
courage unwavering.

Sir
Patrick
Spence

The king sits in Dumferling[1]
    toune,
  Drinking the blude-reid wine:
"O whar will I get guid sailor,
  To sail this schip of mine?"

Up and spak an eldern knicht,   5
  Sat at the kings richt kne:
"Sir Patrick Spence is the best
    sailor
  That sails upon the se."

The king has written a braid[2] letter
  And signd it wi his hand,   10
And sent it to Sir Patrick Spence,
  Was walking on the sand.

The first line that Sir Patrick red,
  A loud lauch lauched he;[3]
The next line that Sir Patrick red,   15
  The teir blinded his ee.

"O wha is this has don this deid,
  This ill deid don to me,
To send me out this time o' the
    yeir,
  To sail upon the se!   20

"Mak hast, mak haste, my mirry
    men all,
  Our guid schip sails the morne:"
"O say na sae, my master deir,
  For I feir a deadlie storme.

"Late late yestreen I saw the new
    moone,   25
  Wi the auld moone in hir arme,
And I feir, I feir, my deir master,
  That we will cum to harme."

O our Scots nobles wer richt laith
  To weet their cork-heild
    schoone;[4]   30
Bot lang owre a' the play wer
    playd,
  Thair hats they swam aboone.[5]

O lang, lang may their ladies sit,
  Wi thair fans into their hand,
Or eir[6] they se Sir Patrick Spence   35
  Cum sailing to the land.

O lang, lang may the ladies stand,
  Wi thair gold kems[7] in their
    hair,
Waiting for thair ain deir lords,
  For they'll se thame na mair.   40

Haf owre,[8] haf owre to Aberdour,[9]
  It's fiftie fadom deip,
And thair lies guid Sir Patrick
    Spence,
  Wi the Scots lords at his feit.

---

1 **Dumferling:** Dunfermline (dŭn fûrm′lĭn), near
Edinburgh.
2 **braid:** plain; clear.
3 **A loud . . . he:** A loud laugh laughed he.
4 **To weet . . . schoone:** to wet their cork-heeled
shoes (the fancy shoes of courtiers; they did not
wear sailors' boots).
5 **Thair hats . . . aboone:** Their hats floated above
them (after they had drowned).
6 **Or eir:** before.
7 **kems:** combs.
8 **Haf owre:** half over; halfway back.
9 **Aberdour:** port not far from Edinburgh.

Comment

Here again both the story and its main character are revealed indirectly. How good a sailor was Sir Patrick Spence? Why should his loss be so important—more important, apparently, than the loss of the noblemen? The details of the action, rather than direct statements, provoke—and answer—such questions as these.

1. We first meet the hero as he walks by the sea. What do his responses to the letter of the King tell you about him?
2. Sir Patrick is speaking to his men in lines 21-22. The rest of this stanza and all of the next is a speech from another voice. What does the difference between these two speeches tell you about Sir Patrick? Why does he not say "I feir" to his men?
3. Beginning with line 29 we make a long leap, and we resume the story from a different point of view; for Sir Patrick Spence is not again directly described. And yet this ballad does celebrate him, not the well-dressed lords who have drowned or their ladies waiting with golden combs in their hair. How do these four last stanzas continue to make us feel that Sir Patrick Spence was a brave hero?

"Johnie Armstrong"

Among the many ballads about outlaws the most famous are the many loosely connected stories of Robin Hood. None of these, however, is quite so coherent as the following story of Johnie Armstrong, perhaps because, unlike Robin Hood, this outlaw was a real person. He was certainly no Robin Hood, for he and his band early in the 16th century pillaged and preyed on both the English and the Scottish in the Border country, and his interest in plunder was personal and selfish. In this version Johnie is treacherously captured in Edinburgh by the Scottish king; he was probably in fact taken in some such way as this by James V of Scotland in one of the King's efforts to establish law and order. The incident was commemorated in a dramatic story.

Johnie Armstrong

There dwelt a man in faire Westmerland,[1]
   Johnie Armstrong men did him call,
He had nither lands nor rents coming in,
   Yet he kept eight score[2] men in his hall.

He had horse and harness for them all,   5
   Goodly steeds were all milke-white;
O the golden bands an about their necks,[3]
   And their weapons, they were all alike.[4]

Newes then was brought unto the king
   That there was sicke a won[5] as hee,   10
That livèd lyke a bold out-law
   And robbèd all the north country.

The king he writt an a letter then,
   A letter which was large and long;
He signèd it with his owne hand,   15
   And he promised to doe him no wrong.

When this letter came Johnie untill,
   His heart it was as blythe as birds on the tree:
"Never was I sent for before any king,
   My father, my grandfather, nor none but mee.   20

"And if wee goe the king before,
   I would we went most orderly;
Every man of you shall have his scarlet cloak,
   Laced with silver laces three.

"Every won of you shall have his velvett coat,   25
   Laced with sillver lace so white;
O the golden bands an about your necks,
   Black hatts, white feathers, all alyke."

---

1 **Westmerland:** Westmorland, in northwest England.
2 **eight score:** A score is a group of twenty.
3 **an about their necks:** around their necks.

4 **And their weapons . . . alike:** a sign of a well-organized and well-supplied army.
5 **sicke a won:** such a one.

By the morrow morninge at ten of the clock,
  Towards Edenburough gon was hee,
And with him all his eight score men;
  Good lord, it was a goodly sight for to see!   30

When Johnie came befower the king,
  He fell downe on his knee;
"O pardon, my soveraine leige," he said,   35
  "O pardon my eight score men and mee!"

"Thou shalt have no pardon, thou traytor strong,
  For thy eight score men nor thee;
For to-morrow morning by ten of the clock,
  Both thou and them shall hang on the gallow-tree." 40

But Johnie looke'd over his left shoulder,
  Good Lord, what a grevious look looked hee!
Saying, "Asking grace[6] of a graceles face—
  Why there is none for you nor me."

But Johnie had a bright sword by his side,   45
  And it was made of the mettle so free,[7]
That had not the king stept his foot aside,
  He had smitten his head from his faire bodde.

Saying, "Fight on, my merry men all,
  And see that none of you be taine;   50
For rather then men shall say we were hange'd,
  Let them report how we were slaine."

Then, God wott,[8] faire Eddenburrough rose,
  And so besett poore Johnie rounde,
That fowerscore and tenn of Johnies best men   55
  Lay gasping all upon the ground.

Then like a mad man Johnie laide about,
  And like a mad man then fought hee,
Untill a falce Scot came Johnie behinde,
  And runn him through the faire bodde.   60

Saying, "Fight on, my merry men all,
  And see that none of you be taine;
For I will stand by and bleed but awhile,
  And then will I come and fight againe."

---

6 **grace:** good will.
7 **mettle so free:** such noble metal.
8 **God wott:** God knows.

Newes then was brought to young Johnie[9] Armstrong,   65
        As he stood by his nurses knee,
Who vowed if ere he live'd for to be a man,
        O the treacherous Scots revengd hee'd be.

9 **young Johnie:** the outlaw's son; presumably the feud will go on.

Comment

An outlaw presumably lives outside the world of law and order. But where and how does this outlaw find disorder?

1. How does Johnie Armstrong run his band of men? And how does he want them (and himself) to behave before the King?
2. In lines 41-44 Johnie turns to look at his men. His look is "grevious" and he speaks to them in a broken exclamation. What contrast do you see here between Johnie's present plight and the way he has run himself and his men up to this moment? What kind of deed has been done to him here?
3. What kind of society, then, for all his outlawry, does Johnie live in? And does his son, "young Johnie Armstrong," live in, believe in, such a society?

"The Wife of Usher's Well"

The ghost story, especially the story of returning spirits who haunt and terrify the living, is as old as the art of the story itself, and it is the subject of many a ballad. You will soon be reading, too, of a man haunted by ghosts, in Shakespeare's *Macbeth*. But the returning spirit need not reveal to us only the terror and guilt of the living; it may also reveal poignantly the strength of the ties that death has severed. The following ballad, which has been found in many versions here in America as well as in England, moves with apparently sudden breaks in the narrative, and yet the individual scenes clearly follow each other.

The Wife of Usher's Well

There lived a wife at Usher's Well,
    And a wealthy wife was she;
She had three stout and stalwart
      sons,
    And sent them oer the sea.

They hadna been a week from her,   5
    A week but barely ane,[1]
Whan word came to the carline
      wife[2]
    That her three sons were gane.

They hadna been a week from her,
    A week but barely three,   10
When word came to the carlin
      wife
    That her sons she'd never see.

"I wish the wind may never cease,
    Nor fashes in the flood,[3]
Till my three sons come hame to
      me,   15
    In earthly flesh and blood."

It fell about the Martinmass,[4]
    When nights are lang and mirk[5]
The carlin wife's three sons came
      hame,
    And their hats were o the birk.[6]   20

It neither grew in syke[7] nor ditch,
    Nor yet in ony sheugh;[8]
But at the gates o Paradise,
    That birk grew fair eneugh.

"Blow up the fire, my maidens,   25
    Bring water from the well;
For a' my house shall feast this
      night,
    Since my three sons are well."

And she has made to them[9] a bed,
    She's made it large and wide,   30
And she's taen her mantle her
      about,
    Sat down at the bed-side.

Up then crew the red, red cock,
    And up and crew the gray;
The eldest to the youngest said,   35
    " 'Tis time[10] we were away."

The cock he hadna crawd but
      once,
    And clappd his wings at a',[11]
When the youngest to the eldest
      said,
    "Brother, we must awa.   40

---

1 **ane:** one
2 **carline wife:** old woman.
3 **fashes in the flood:** troubles; storms at sea.
4 **Martinmass:** November 11.
5 **mirk:** murky.
6 **hats . . . o the birk:** On their heads they wore birch leaves taken from a tree which grew beside the gates of Paradise.

7 **syke:** trench.
8 **sheugh:** furrow.
9 **to them:** for them.
10 **'Tis time . . . away:** At the first crowing of the cock, signifying the end of night, the dead must return to their graves.
11 **at a':** The cock has crowed, but he has not yet clapped his wings "at all." (When he does, it may be too late; day may be here.)

"The cock doth craw, the day doth
    daw,[12]
  The channerin[13] worm doth
    chide;
Gin we be mist out o our place,
  A sair pain we maun bide.[14]

"Fare ye weel, my mother dear!   45
  Fareweel to barn and byre![15]
And fare ye weel, the bonny lass
  That kindles my mother's fire!"

12 daw: dawn.
13 channerin: fretting. The worms of the grave are chiding and warning the sons to return.
14 Gin . . . bide: If we are missed because we are out of our proper place (our graves), we must suffer a sore penalty.

15 byre: shed for cattle.

Comment

The mother wishes for the return of her sons, and return they do, though obviously (to us) as spirits. The mother prepares a "feast" for her sons; she watches over them as they sleep in the bed she has made for them. But after she says, "my house shall feast this night,/Since my three sons are well," she says nothing. The only other words spoken are said by her sons.

1. The youngest son speaks in the last two stanzas, first to his brothers, then to his mother, and finally to one of the maids of the house. What contrast of imagery do you find between these last two stanzas?
2. The ballad ends with these contrasting stanzas. What does the absence of further words from the mother tell us? What does it suggest about her ties to her sons?

"Get Up and Bar the Door"

One of the favorite themes of medieval literature has been revived in modern literature as the battle of the sexes. The situation of this short ballad could be the subject of one of Chaucer's tales or of a story by James Thurber. It tells us something not only about stubbornness but also about the conditions of life in which stubbornness was exerted some five hundred years ago. There are some American versions of this ballad, but not all of them are quite so printable as this late medieval one.

THE WIFE OF USHER'S WELL

Get Up and Bar
the Door

It fell about the Martinmas¹ time,
  And a gay time it was then,
When our goodwife got puddings²
    to make,
  And she's boild them in the pan.

The wind sae cauld blew south
    and north,   5
  And blew into the floor;
Quoth our goodman to our good-
    wife,³
  "Gae out and bar the door."

"My hand is in my hussyfskap,⁴
  Goodman, as ye may see;   10
And it should nae be barrd this
    hundred year,
  It's no be barrd for me."⁵

They made a paction⁶ tween them
    twa,
  They made it firm and sure,
That the first word whaeer⁷ shoud
    speak,   15
  Shoud rise and bar the door.

Then by there came two gentle-
    men,
  At twelve o clock at night,

And they could neither see house
    nor hall,
  Nor coal nor candle-light.   20

"Now whether is this a rich man's
    house,
  Or whether is it a poor?"
But neer a word wad ane o them
    speak,
  For barring of the door.⁸

And first they ate the white pud-
    dings,   25
  And then they ate the black;⁹
Tho muckle¹⁰ thought the good-
    wife to hersel,
  Yet neer a word she spake.

Then said the one unto the other,
  "Here, man, tak ye my knife;   30
Do ye tak aff the auld man's beard,
  And I'll kiss the goodwife."

"But there's nae water in the house,
  And what shall we do than?"¹¹
"What ails ye at the pudding-
    broo,¹²   35
  That boils into the pan?"

---

1 **Martinmas:** November 11.
2 **puddings:** sausages.
3 **goodman; goodwife:** husband; wife.
4 **hussyfskap:** household chores; housewifery.
5 **It's no . . . me:** I won't shut it!
6 **paction:** agreement.
7 **whaeer:** whoever.

8 **But neer . . . door:** But never a word would one of them speak lest he or she should have to shut the door.
9 **the white puddings . . . the black:** The goodwife had made both dark and light sausage.
10 **muckle:** much.
11 **What shall we do than?:** How shall we shave him without water?
12 **What . . . pudding-broo:** Why not use the water the sausages were boiled in?

O up then started our goodman,
    An angry man was he:
"Will ye kiss my wife before my
      een,
    And scad me wi pudding-
      bree?"[13]   40

Then up and started our goodwife,
    Gied three skips on the floor:
"Goodman, you've spoken the fore-
      most word,
    Get up and bar the door."

13 scad . . . bree: scald me with the pudding water.

Comment

This little ballad is much like the *fabliau*, the rough story of simple life, that Chaucer told more than once. Its structure is simple enough, and there is but one question to ask about it: Who won?

"Thomas Rymer"

In the 13th century lived a certain Thomas of Erceldoune, who after his death was widely remembered as a poet and prophet. The following ballad is one of many popular versions of how he came by his strange powers, and it tells us something about what were believed to be the powers of the poet in the medieval period.

Thomas Rymer

True Thomas lay oer yond grassy bank,
    And he beheld a ladie gay,
A ladie that was brisk and bold,
    Come riding oer the fernie brae.[1]

Her skirt was of the grass-green silk,   5
    Her mantel of the velvet fine,
At ilka tet[2] of her horse's mane
    Hung fifty silver bells and nine.

True Thomas he took off his hat,
    And bowed him low down till his knee: 10
"All hail, thou mighty Queen of Heaven!
    For your peer on earth I never did see."

1 fernie brae: fern-covered hillside.
2 at ilka tet : from every lock.

"O no, O no, True Thomas," she says,
    "That name does not belong to me;
I am but the queen of fair Elfland,   15
    And I'm come here for to visit thee.

"But ye maun[3] go wi me now, Thomas,
    True Thomas, ye maun go wi me,
For ye maun serve me seven years,
    Thro weel or wae[4] as may chance to be."   20

She turned about her milk-white steed,
    And took True Thomas up behind,
And aye wheneer her bridle rang,
    The steed flew swifter than the wind.

For forty days and forty nights   25
    He wade thro red blude to the knee,
And he saw neither sun nor moon,
    But heard the roaring of the sea.

O they rade on, and further on,
    Until they came to a garden green: 30
"Light down, light down, ye ladie free,
    Some of that fruit let me pull to thee."

"O no, O no, True Thomas," she says,
    "That fruit maun not be touched by thee,
For a' the plagues that are in hell   35
    Light on the fruit of this countrie.

"But I have a loaf here in my lap,
    Likewise a bottle of claret wine,[5]
And now ere we go farther on,
    We'll rest a while, and ye may dine."   40

When he had eaten and drunk his fill,
    "Lay down your head upon my knee,"
The lady sayd, "ere we climb yon hill,
    And I will show you fairlies[6] three.

"O see not ye yon narrow road,   45
    So thick beset wi thorns and briers?
That is the path of righteousness,
    Tho after it but few enquires.

---

3 maun: must.
4 weel or wae: well or woe.

5 claret wine: red wine.
6 fairlies: wonders.

"And see not ye that braid[7] braid road,
    That lies across yon lillie leven?[8]   50
That is the path of wickedness,
    Tho some call it the road to heaven.

"And see not ye that bonny road,
    Which winds about the fernie brae?
That is the road to fair Elfland,   55
    Where you and I this night maun gae.

"But Thomas, ye maun hold your tongue,
    Whatever you may hear or see,
For gin[9] ae word you should chance to speak,
    You will neer get back to your ain countrie."   60

He has gotten a coat of the even cloth,
    And a pair of shoes of velvet green.
And till seven years were past and gone
    True Thomas on earth was never seen.

7 **braid:** broad.
8 **lillie leven:** glade carpeted with flowers.
9 **gin:** if.

Comment

The adventures of Thomas on the way to "fair Elfland" are strange. But perhaps taken in turn they may constitute something like a theory of poetry.

1. Thomas first mistakes the lady for the Queen of Heaven. What does her denial of that title tell you about the powers of the poet?
2. Next he rides with her through hard country to a green garden. But Thomas is not permitted to eat of the fruit of the garden. Why not? Is this a "real" garden?
3. And next comes the queen's presentation of the three roads. Why should her country be reached by neither the path of righteousness nor that of wickedness? And why, finally, must Thomas keep silent while he is in Elfland?
4. By speculating upon these questions, write a brief account of the idea of the poet implied by this ballad. What are his powers? What are his limitations?

A wagon which served as the stage for the cycles of medieval religious plays. The wagons moved from place to place, allowing the audience to remain in their own neighborhood and see several plays in a day. This illustration is from a 15th-century manuscript.

The Drama

In many towns in England during the Middle Ages it was possible to see acted out once a year a series of religious pageants called miracle plays. From the early 14th century the occasion for these miracle plays (sometimes called mystery plays) was the festival of Corpus Christi, one of the great festivals of the medieval Church. Corpus Christi occurred approximately two months after Easter.

The miracle play is a dramatization of an episode from the Bible. It was presented as one in a series, or cycle, of such episodes, sometimes as one in a cycle of forty or more. Although few of these cycles have survived (only four in part), it is clear that each began with a dramatization of the Creation, continued with episodes from the Old Testament that were believed most strongly to foreshadow the coming of Christ, and then, after presenting the Nativity, with its manger, shepherds, and wisemen, moved on through the chief events of the life of Jesus to the Crucifixion and finally to the Last Judgment.

Each play was devoted to a "miracle" that prepared the world for Christ's coming or to one from the life of Jesus. The plays were indeed

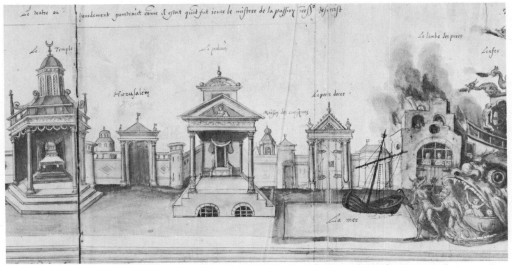

This 16th-century stage setting was used for religious plays that told stories of the Bible from the Creation through the life of Jesus to the Last Judgment. The action moved on the stage from Paradise through a series of mansions (small houses) representing different places and times, to Hell. Each episode was performed on succeeding days for twenty-three days. The part of the stage shown here has on the left the temple and on the far right the mouth of Hell. The illustration is from a script of the play.

extensions of dramatic presentations that began within the church itself of the doctrines and events of Christianity. Such dramatic parts of the service were gradually enlarged and elaborated until they moved outside the service proper and became pageants produced by the people themselves outside the church building.

Noah's Flood

Certainly the people themselves must have watched and participated in the miracle play called *Noah's Flood*. It is called the Chester pageant of the water-leaders and drawers in Dee. This means that it was performed by a group of citizens of the ancient town of Chester near the north border of Wales where the River Dee flows into the Irish Sea. The group who performed it were in fact the guild of water carriers ("water-leaders") and those who drew water for the town from the river. It is, of course, altogether appropriate that those in the business of supplying water should be in charge of the pageant of the Flood. In other towns the first part of the story was presented by the carpenters and shipbuilders (again appropriately, as you will see). Each guild or special trade of the medieval town was responsible for presenting an episode in the cycle. In many towns each guild presented its play

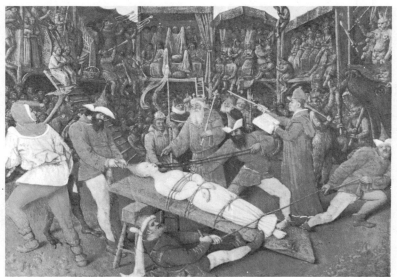

Another kind of stage for medieval religious plays has the mansions, the settings for the various episodes, ranged around half of a circular stage. The production manager is in the right foreground with his baton and prompt-copy of the script; he led the production, giving cues as needed.

from a large wagon that was moved from place to place during the day, from early morning until night, so that every inhabitant might see the whole cycle of plays without moving far from his own neighborhood.

The miracle play, moreover, belonged to the people in yet another sense: it is full of the rough humor and crude make-believe that brings even so far-off and miraculous an event as the building of the Ark and the inundation of the Flood within the understanding of the most unlearned member of the audience. Few who watched the annual cycle of miracle plays could read. They were simple people whose lives moved in patterns shaped by their religion, by the succession of the seasons, and by the human cycle of birth, life, and death. The miracle play brought close to them a wondrous story from the book that shaped their religion, and brought it close not only because it was sponsored and presented by their fellow citizens but also because it incorporated much of the daily experience shared by everyone in the town.

We do not know who wrote the miracle plays. It is likely that they were revised from time to time by the unknown amateurs who produced them. One cycle, performed in the Yorkshire town of Wakefield, does bear the mark of a single writer—he is referred to as "the Wakefield master." But every cycle was the work of many townspeople co-operating in everything from costumes to casting. As in the modernized version presented here, the plays were often, especially in the longer speeches, in eight-line rhyming stanzas.

Noah's Flood

Chester Pageant of the Water-Leaders and Drawers in Dee

(And first in some high place, or in the clouds if it may be, **God** *speaketh unto* **Noah** *standing without the Ark with all his family.)*

     God. I, God, that all the world have wrought,
     Heaven and earth, and all of nought,[1]
     I see my people, in deed and thought,
     Are set foully in sin.
5   My spirit shall abide in man,
     That through fleshly liking[2] is my foe,
     Only till six score years be gone,
     To look if he cease from sin.

     Man that I made I will destroy,
10   Beast, worm, and fowl to fly;[3]
     For on the earth they do me annoy,
     The folk that are thereon.
     It harms me so heartfully,
     The malice now that can multiply,
15   That sore it grieveth me inwardly
     That ever I made man.

     Therefore, Noah, my servant free,[4]
     That righteous man art, as I see,
     A ship soon thou shalt make thee
20   Of trees dry and light.
     Little chambers therein thou make;
     And binding-slitch[5] also thou take:
     Within and out do thou not slake[6]
     To anoint it through all thy might.

25   Three hundred cubits it shall be long,
     And fifty of breadth, to make it strong;
     Of height fifty. Do thou with thong[7]
     Thus measure it about.
     One window work[8] through thy wit,
30   One cubit of length and breadth make it;
     Upon the side a door shall sit,
     For to come in and out.

1 of nought : from nothing.

2 that through . . . liking : who because of bodily appetites.

3 to fly : that flies.

4 free : noble; honorable.

5 binding-slitch : pitch to seal the seams between the timbers.
6 slake : slacken your efforts.

7 thong : tape.

8 work : make.

Eating-places thou make also,
Three roofed chambers on a row;[9]
35 For with water I shall overflow
Man that I did make.
Destroyed all the world shall be,
Save thou; thy wife, thy sons three,
And all their wives also with thee
40 Shall saved be for thy sake.

NOAH. Ah, Lord, I thank thee loud and still,[10]
That to me art in such will,[11]
And sparest me and my house to spill,[12]
As now I soothly[13] find.
45 Thy bidding, Lord, I shall fulfill,
And never more thee grieve nor grill,[14]
That such grace has sent me till[15]
Among all mankind.

(*To his family:*)

Have done, you men and women all!
50 Help, for aught that may befall,
To work this ship, chamber and hall,
As God hath bidden us do.

SHEM. Father, I am all ready bound:[16]
An ax I have, by my crown,[17]
55 As sharp as any in all this town,
For to go thereto.

HAM. I have a hatchet wondrous keen
To bite well, as may be seen;
A better ground one, as I ween,[18]
60 Is not in all this town.

JAPHETH. And I can well make a pin,[19]
And with this hammer knock it in;
Go and work without more din,
And I am ready bound.

65 NOAH'S WIFE. And we shall bring timber to,
For we may nothing else do;
Women be weak to undergo
Any great travail.

SHEM'S WIFE. Here is a good hackstock;[20]
70 On this you may hew and knock;

9 on a row : one above the other.

10 still : all the time.
11 That . . . will : that are so disposed toward me.
12 spill : destroy.
13 soothly : truly.

14 grill : offend.
15 me till : to me.

16 ready bound : prepared; "all set."
17 by my crown : an exclamation.

18 ween : suppose.

19 pin : wooden peg.

20 hackstock : chopping block.

Shall none be idle in this flock,
Nor now may no man fall.[21]

    HAM's WIFE. And I will go to gather slitch,
The ship for to caulk and pitch;
75 Anointed it must be every stitch,[22]
Board, tree[23] and pin.

    JAPHETH's WIFE. And I will gather chips here.
To make a fire for you all here,
And for to make your dinner,
80 Against you come in.[24]

(Then they make signs as if they were working with different tools.)

    NOAH. Now, in the name of God, I will begin
To make the ship that we shall in,
That we be ready for to swim[25]
At the coming of the flood.
85 These boards I join here together,
To keep us safe from the weather,
That we may row both hither and thither,
And safe be from this flood.
Of this tree will I make the mast,
90 Tied with cables that will last,
With a sail yard for each blast,
And each thing in their kind;[26]
With topcastle[27] and bowsprit,
With cords and ropes, I have all meet,[28]
95 To sail forth at the next wet;[29]
This ship is at an end.[30]

Wife, in this castle[31] we shall be kept;
My children and thou, I would, in leapt.[32]

    NOAH's WIFE. In faith, Noah, I had as lief[33] thou slept.
100 For all thy frankish fare,[34]
I will not do after thy rede.[35]

    NOAH. Good wife, do now as I thee bid.

    NOAH's WIFE. By Christ, not ere I see more need,
Though thou stand all the day and stare.

105   NOAH. Lord, that women be crabbed ay,[36]
And never are meek, that dare I say.
This is well seen by me today,

21 fall : fail to do his part.

22 stitch : fastening.
23 tree : beam.

24 Against . . . in : in preparation for your coming in.

25 swim : float.

26 And . . . kind : and every kind of thing we need.
27 topcastle : platform at the head of a ship's masts.
28 meet : ready.
29 wet : rain.
30 at an end : finished.

31 castle : high structure on a ship's deck.
32 My children . . . leapt : I want you and my children to jump in.
33 had as lief : would prefer.
34 frankish fare : frantic behavior.
35 rede : advice.

36 crabbed ay : always cross; always hard to understand.

As witness you[37] each one.
Good wife, let be all this clamor
110 That thou makes in this place here;
For all they ween[38] thou art master—
And so thou art, by Saint John!

God. Noah, take thou thy family,
And in the ship look that thou hie;[39]
115 For none so righteous man to me
Is now on earth living.
Of clean beasts[40] with thee thou take
Seven and seven,[41] ere thou slake;[42]
He and she, mate to mate,
120 Quickly do thou bring.

Of beasts unclean two and two,
Male and female, and no more;
Of clean fowls seven also,
The he and she together;
125 Of fowls unclean two and no more,
As I of beasts said before
These shall be saved through my love,
Against[43] I send the weather.
Of all meats[44] that must be eaten
130 Into the ship look there be gotten,
For that no way may be forgotten;
And do all this right soon,
To sustain man and beast therein
Ay till[45] the water cease falling.
135 This world is filled full of sin,
And that is now well seen.

Seven days be yet coming:
You shall have time them in to bring;
After that it is my liking
140 Mankind for to annoy.
Forty days and forty nights
Rain shall fall for their unrights;
And that I have made through my mights
Now think I to destroy.

145 **Noah.** Lord, at your bidding I am bain;[46]
Since no other grace will gain,
It will I fulfill fain,[47]
For gracious I thee find.
A hundred winters and twenty

37 you : i.e., the audience.

38 ween : suppose.

39 look . . . hie : See that you hurry.

40 clean beasts : animals fit for food.
41 seven and seven : by sevens.
42 slake : stop.

43 Against : before.
44 meats : food.

45 Ay till : until.

46 bain : ready.

47 Since . . . fain : Since nothing else will win grace for me, I will fulfill your bidding gladly.

150 This ship-making tarried have I,
    If[48] through amendment any mercy
    Would fall unto mankind.

48 If : to see if.

    (*To his family:*)

Have done, you men and women all!
Hie you lest this water fall,
155 That each beast were in his stall,
    And into the ship brought.
    Of clean beasts seven shall be,
    Of unclean two; this God bade me.
    This flood is nigh, well may we see;
160 Therefore tarry you nought.

(*Then* NOAH *shall go into the Ark with all his family, his wife except, and the Ark must be boarded round about, and on the boards all the beasts and fowls hereafter rehearsed must be painted, that these words may agree with the pictures.*)

    SHEM. Sir, here are lions, leopards in,
Horses, mares, oxen, and swine;
Goats, calves, sheep, and kine
Here sitten thou may see.

165   HAM. Camels, asses men may find,
    Buck, doe, hart, and hind;
    And beasts of all manner kind
    Here be, as thinketh me.

    JAPHETH. Take here cats and dogs too,
170 Otter, fox, skunk also;
    Hares hopping gaily can go
    Have cabbage here to eat.

    NOAH'S WIFE. And here are bears, wolves set,
Apes, owls, marmoset,
175 Weasels, squirrels, and ferret;
    Here they eat their meat.

    SHEM'S WIFE. Yet more beasts are in this house:
Here cats make it full carouse;
Here a rat and here a mouse,
180 They stand nigh together.

    HAM'S WIFE. And here are fowls, less and more:
Herons, cranes, and bittor,[49]
Swans, peacocks; and them before
Meat for this weather.[50]

49 bittor : bitterns.

50 Meat . . . weather : food to eat during the storm.

NOAH'S FLOOD

185 JAPHETH'S WIFE. Here are cocks, kites, crows,
     Rooks, ravens, many rows,
     Ducks, curlews, whoever knows
     Each one in his kind;[51]
     And here are doves, ducks, drakes,
190 Redshanks running through the lakes;
     And each fowl that singing makes
     In this ship men may find.

     NOAH. Wife, come in! Why stands thou there?
     Thou art ever froward,[52] that dare I swear.
195 Come in, for God's sake! Time it were,
     For fear lest that we drown.

     NOAH'S WIFE. Yea, sir, set up your sail,
     And row forth with evil hail,[53]
     For, without any fail,[54]
200 I will not out of this town
     If I have not my gossips[55] every one,
     One foot further I will not gone;
     They shall not drown, by Saint John,
     If I may save their life.
205 They loved me full well, by Christ,
     Unless thou let them in thy chest,[56]
     Else row forth, Noah, whither thou list,[57]
     And get thee a new wife.

     NOAH. Shem, son, lo! thy mother is wrow:[58]
210 Forsooth, such another I do not know.

     SHEM. Father, I shall fetch her in, I trow,[59]
     Without any fail.

              (*He goes to his mother.*)

     Mother, my father after thee sent,
     And bids thee into yonder ship wend.
215 Look up and see the wind,
     For we be ready to sail.

     NOAH'S WIFE. Son, go again to him, and say
     I will not come therein today.

     NOAH. Come in, wife, in twenty devils' way,[60]
220 Or else stand there without.

     HAM. Shall we all fetch her in?

51 whoever . . . kind : for anyone who knows each species.

52 froward : contrary.

53 hail : health; i.e., "bad luck to you!"
54 fail : doubt.

55 gossips : friends.

56 chest : ark.

57 else . . . list : Then row away, Noah, where you wish.

58 wrow : angry.

59 trow : think.

60 in . . . way : oath.

NOAH. Yea, sons, in Christ's blessing and mine;
I would you hied you betime,[61]
For of this flood I am in doubt.[62]

225   Gossip (to WIFE). The flood comes fleeting[63] in full fast,
On every side it spreads full far;
For fear of drowning I am aghast;
Good gossip, let us draw near.

And let us drink ere we depart,
230 For ofttimes we have done so;
For at a draught thou drink'st a quart
And so will I do ere I go.

NOAH'S WIFE. Here is a pottle of Malmsey,[64] good and
   strong;
It will rejoice both heart and tongue;
235 Though Noah thinks us never so long,
Yet we will drink alike.[65]

JAPHETH. Mother, we pray you altogether—
For we are here your own childer[66]—
Come into the ship for fear of the weather,
240 For his love that you bought![67]

NOAH'S WIFE. That will I not, for all your call,
But[68] I have my gossips all.

SHEM. In faith, mother, yet you shall,
Whether you will or nought.

(Then she shall go.)

245   NOAH. Welcome, wife, into this boat.

NOAH'S WIFE. And have thou that for thy note![69]

(She boxes him on the ear.)

NOAH. Aha! marry, this is hot!
It is good to be still.[70]
Ah, children, methinks my boat removes;[71]
250 Our tarrying here hugely me grieves.
Over the land the water spreads;
God do as he will!
Ah, great God that art so good,
He that works not thy will is wood.[72]

61 betime : without waste of time.
62 in doubt : afraid.
63 fleeting : flowing.
64 pottle of Malmsey (mäm′zĭ) : two-quart jug of a strong sweet wine.
65 alike : a quart apiece.
66 childer : children.
67 For . . . bought : for the love of Christ who redeemed you.
68 But : unless.
69 And . . . note : And take that for your trouble!
70 still : peaceful.
71 removes : is moving.
72 wood : mad.

255 Now all this world is on a flood,
    As I well see in sight.
    This window will I shut anon,[73]
    And into my chamber will I be gone,
    Till this water, so great an one,
260 Be slaked[74] though thy might. . . .

[The old stage directions at this point indicate that NOAH closes the window of the Ark, *"and for a little space within board he shall stand silent"*—to indicate the passage of forty days. Then comes the stage business that we may be sure delighted the audience: NOAH opens the window and sends out a dove to fly in search of dry land. The stage directions read: *"There shall be in the ship another dove bearing an olive-branch in her mouth, which* NOAH *shall let down from the mast by a cord in his hand."* The branch of olive which the dove brings back is a sign that land indeed has been found, and NOAH exclaims:]

    Ah, Lord, honored must thou be!
    All earth dries now, I see;
    But yet, till thou command me,
    Hence will I not hie.
265 All this water is away;
    Therefore, as soon as I may,
    Sacrifice I shall do, in fay,[75]
    To thee devoutly.

      GOD. Noah, take thy wife anon,
270 And thy children every one;
    Out of the ship thou shalt be gone,
    And they all with thee.
    Beasts and all that can fly
    Out anon they shall hie,
275 On earth to grow and multiply;
    I will that it so be.

      NOAH. Lord, I thank thee through[76] thy might;
    Thy bidding shall be done in hight,[77]
    And as fast as I may dight[78]
280 I will do thee honor,
    And to thee offer sacrifice;
    Therefore come, in all wise,[79]
    For of these beasts that be his,
    Offer I will this store.[80]

73 anon : at once.

74 slaked : diminished.

75 fay : faith.

76 through : for.
77 hight : haste.
78 dight : get ready.

79 in all wise : by all means (said to his family).

80 store : large number.

(Then going out of the Ark with all his family he shall take his animals and birds and offer them in sacrifice.)

285　Lord God in majesty,
　　　That such grace has granted me,
　　　Where all was lorn,[81] safe to be,
　　　Therefore now am I bound,
　　　My wife, my children, and family,
290　With sacrifice to honor thee;
　　　Of beasts, fowls, as thou mayst see,
　　　I offer here right soon.

　　　God. Noah, to me thou art full able,[82]
　　　And thy sacrifice acceptable;
295　For I have found thee true and stable,
　　　On thee now must I mind:
　　　I will curse the earth no more
　　　For man's sin that grieves me sore;
　　　For from his youth man full yore
300　Has been inclined to sin.[83]

　　　A covenant, Noah, with thee I make,
　　　And all thy seed[84] for thy sake,
　　　Of such vengeance for to slake,[85]
　　　For now I have my will.
305　Here I give my promise fast
　　　That man, woman, fowl nor beast,
　　　With water, while the world shall last,
　　　I will no more spill.[86]

　　　My bow[87] between you and me
310　In the firmament shall be,
　　　By very token[88] that you may see
　　　That such vengeance shall cease,
　　　That man nor woman never more
　　　Be wasted by[89] water, as is before;[90]
315　But for sin that grieveth me sore,
　　　Therefore this vegeance was.

　　　When clouds are in the heavenly sphere
　　　That same bow shall then appear
　　　In token that my fierce anger
320　Shall no more vengeance take
　　　The string is turned toward you,
　　　And toward me is bent the bow,
　　　That such weather shall never show;
　　　And this promise I make.

81 lorn : lost.

82 full able : obedient.

83 For . . . sin : For from his youth man has long been inclined to sin.

84 seed : descendants.

85 Of . . . slake : to lessen such vengeance (as the flood).

86 spill : destroy.

87 bow : rainbow.

88 by very token : as a true sign.

89 be wasted : be laid waste.
90 as is before : as just happened.

NOAH'S FLOOD

325 My blessing now I give thee here,
   To thee, Noah, my servant dear,
   For vengeance shall no more appear;
   And now farewell, my darling dear.

Comment

It is clear that the original actors of this pageant-like play were
close to their audience. When Noah first tries to get his wife aboard
the Ark, he says that her behavior makes "them," the watching audience, realize that women are contrary—and we can imagine the hoots
of laughter that greeted this old, old joke. The original actors and
producers were close to their audience in another way too, for although the action of their play was supposed to be in far-off, Old
Testament times long before the birth of Jesus, yet Japheth asks his
mother to get aboard the Ark "For his love that you bought"—that is, for
the love of Christ, who by His death redeemed mankind. Again, the
details of tools and construction—hatchets, hackstocks, beams, planks,
and pitch—are drawn from 14th-century life, not from the culture of
the far-off land of Noah. And no one was worried by the long
stretches of time that are a part of the familiar story—120 years seem
to pass between the first and the second stanzas, and the Ark floats on
the Flood for forty days and nights. All these things—the joke, the
anachronisms (that is, the introduction into past times of events that
happened in the future), the easy familiarity of the story and the time
it covered—such things tell us that *Noah's Flood* provided an experience
for its audience that they recognized and entered into with awareness
and enthusiasm.

But we must not forget that the episode presented in this little play
was a religious one—indeed, a miraculous one—for the audience. What,
then, can we, some five hundred years later, make of the religious
attitudes of those who produced and those who watched the presentation in Chester in, say, 1450? The robust humor of Mrs. Noah's reluctance to leave her "gossips" is a feature of the play that must have
amused the spectators of ancient Chester. It is not likely that many
wives of ordinary citizens of a medieval town could afford the time
or money to drink Malmsey with their "gossips," though it is not unlikely that many of them must have wanted to and that some of their
husbands did. Noah's quarrel with his stubborn wife is a farce—a
joke, a "gag" strictly for laughs—that reminds us of the ballad "Get Up
and Bar the Door." And yet in many examples of Christian art and
in many commentaries on the Bible, Noah's wife is described as a
meek, gentle person who foreshadows Mary, the mother of Jesus.
Was *Noah's Flood*, then, an irreverent play? Did it bring religion so
close to its audience that all mystery went out of it? Did it simply
make some irresponsible jokes about serious and sacred matters?

1. Review the speeches of God to Noah. Why, in his first speech, does God say that he is disappointed in man? In his last speech, what sign does he describe to Noah by which all men can tell whether God is really angry with them or not? Do the two appearances of God in the play seem to you presented reverentially?
2. But between the appearances of God, what happens? How do you account for the fact that after Noah's wife goes aboard the Ark (under protest!) she is not heard from again? What does it mean that the last exchange in the play is between God and Noah?
3. It is clear that *Noah's Flood* is a combination of reverence and gaiety—or even more than gaiety, of farce. What does this combination tell you about medieval man's attitude toward his religion?

Sir Geoffrey Luttrell in the elaborate dress and armor of the medieval knight. His wife hands up his helmet; his daughter-in-law holds his shield. The ladies' dresses are ornamented with the Luttrell blazon, the martlet. The illustration is from the Luttrell Psalter of 1340.

Middle English Literature
The Courtly Tradition

THE FAVORITE literature of the lords and ladies of medieval England came from France, and most of it can be described under the term *romance*. A romance is a tale of marvelous adventure involving legendary heroes who were usually associated with the ancient Greeks and Trojans, with the court of the great French King Charlemagne, or with the legendary Celtic hero, King Arthur. The name *romance* comes from the fact that the earliest versions of these stories were in a language derived from Roman Latin—they were in a "romanish" language. They celebrated the honor, courage, and loyalty of the knight who fulfilled his obligations to his king and who also dedicated himself to the protection and fervent admiration of womanhood.

The courtly lover, as he was called, lived by a special code. He was bound to his lady as her servant, he fought in her honor in tourna-

MIDDLE AGES

ments, and he addressed himself to her through an elaborate system of manners called "courtesy." The code of courtly love was developed in the 11th century in southeastern France by poets called troubadours. It had little to do with the realistically arranged marriages of the time, for "love" and marriage were then, and for centuries to come, thought of quite separately. But the code introduced into Western Europe an attitude toward love that spread rapidly and greatly modified civilized manners.

Le Morte Darthur

The traditions of chivalry—of the mounted knight who battles for his lady and his lord—were summed up in the late Middle Ages by one of the first books to be printed in England. This is *Le Morte Darthur* by Thomas Malory. It gathers together a vast number of romances concerning King Arthur and his Round Table, the adventures of his knights in their quest for the Holy Grail, their battles and sufferings and victories. Malory's title is French for "The Death of Arthur," and it is a rewriting of the great mass of French romances on the subject. The title has another relevance, for Malory wrote at a time when the practices of chivalry were dying. Soldiers were fighting now with gunpowder; the new merchants and tradesmen of the middle class were beginning to be heard from, and the end of the Middle Ages was at hand. The aristocratic ideal was about to enter into a new world.

Little is known of Malory's life. He probably came of an ancient landed family, he fought in the latter stages of the Hundred Years' War, and he was at one time a member of Parliament. He himself was the follower of a knight famous for his courtesy, the Earl of Warwick. The last part of Malory's life was as dark as the end of the Round Table itself, for he spent his last twenty years in prison. He seems to have been a violent, turbulent man, and the fighting and dying of the selection which follows must have been well known to him. He died in 1471 shortly after finishing his great work.

The selection, which is here modernized as to spelling and punctuation, begins with Arthur's last battle. Sir Mordred has rebelled against him and in his efforts to seize the kingdom has already fought one battle against the knights still loyal to King Arthur. One more tragic engagement must occur, and what follows describes that battle and its strange aftermath. The selection opens as King Arthur sleeps, the night before he is to meet Mordred in battle near Salisbury. As you will see, the battle expected for the morrow does not occur, but a worse one does.

Le Morte Darthur

Sir Thomas Malory

So UPON TRINITY Sunday[1] at night, King Arthur dreamed a wonderful dream, and that was this: that him seemed he sat upon a chaflet[2] in a chair, and the chair was fast to a wheel, and thereupon sat King Arthur in the richest cloth of gold that might be made; and the King thought there was under him, far from him, an hideous deep black water, and therein were all manner of serpents, and worms, and wild beasts, foul and horrible; and suddenly the King thought the wheel turned up-so-down, and he fell among the serpents, and every beast took him by a limb; and then the King cried as he lay in his bed and slept: "Help." And then knights, squires and yeomen, awaked the King; and then he was so amazed that he wist[3] not where he was; and then he fell a-slumbering again, not sleeping nor thoroughly waking. So the King seemed verily that there came Sir Gawaine[4] unto him with a number of fair ladies with him. And when

King Arthur saw him, then he said: "Welcome, my sister's son; I weened thou hadst been dead, and now I see thee alive, much am I beholding unto Almighty Jesu. O fair nephew and my sister's son, what be these ladies that hither be come with you?" "Sir," said Sir Gawaine, "all these be ladies for whom I have foughten when I was man living, and all these are those that I did battle for in righteous quarrel; and God hath given them that grace[5] at their great prayer, because I did battle for them, that they should bring me hither unto you: thus much hath God given me leave, for to warn you of your death; for an[6] ye fight as to-morn with Sir Mordred, as ye both have assigned, doubt ye not ye must be slain, and the most part of your people on both parties. And for the great grace and goodness that Almighty Jesu hath unto you, and for pity of you, and many more other good men there shall be slain, God hath sent me to you of his special grace, to give you warning that in no wise ye do battle as to-morn, but that ye take a treaty for a month day[7]; and proffer you largely, so as to-morn to be put in a delay.[8] For within a month shall come Sir Lancelot with all his noble knights, and rescue you worshipfully, and slay Sir Mordred, and all that ever will hold with him." Then Sir Gawaine and all the ladies vanished.

And anon the King called upon his knights, squires, and yeomen, and charged them wightly[9] to fetch his noble lords and wise bishops unto him. And when they were come, the King

---

MIDDLE AGES

A woodcut from a 1529 edition of Malory's Morte Darthur *printed by Wynkyn de Worde shows a style of illustration used in many early printed books.*

told them his avision,[10] what Sir Gawaine had told him, and warned him that if he fought on the morn he should be slain. Then the King commanded Sir Lucan the Butler,[11] and his brother Sir Bedivere, with two bishops with them, and charged them in any wise, an they might, "Take a treaty[12] for a month day with Sir Mordred, and spare not, proffer him lands and goods as much as ye think best." So then they departed, and came to Sir Mordred, where he had a grim host of an hundred thousand men. And there they entreated Sir Mordred long time; and at the last Sir Mordred was agreed for to have Cornwall and Kent, by Arthur's days:[13] after, all England, after the days of King Arthur.

[*The next section starts a new chapter: "How by misadventure of an adder the battle began, where Mordred was slain, and Arthur hurt to the death."*]

THEN WERE THEY condescended[14] that King Arthur and Sir Mordred should meet betwixt both their hosts, and everych[15] of them should bring fourteen persons; and they came with this word unto Arthur. Then said he: "I am glad that this is done": and so he went into the field. And when Arthur should depart, he warned all his host that an they

10 **avision:** vision; dream.
11 **Butler:** the head of Arthur's household; not a servant but an officer.
12 **take a treaty:** They made a formal treaty or truce. Lucan and Bedivere represent the King in asking for a truce and in drawing up the general terms of a treaty. The tentative agreements they make must be ratified by a meeting between Arthur and Mordred themselves.

13 **by Arthur's days:** as long as Arthur lived.
14 **condescended:** agreed.
15 **everych:** each.

SIR THOMAS MALORY

see any sword drawn: "Look ye come on fiercely, and slay that traitor, Sir Mordred, for I in no wise trust him." In like wise Sir Mordred warned his host that: "An ye see any sword drawn, look that ye come on fiercely, and so slay all that ever before you standeth; for in no wise I will not trust for this treaty, for I know well my father will be avenged on me." And so they met as their appointment was, and so they were agreed and accorded thoroughly; and wine was fetched, and they drank. Right soon came an adder out of a little heath bush, and it stung a knight on the foot. And when the knight felt him stung, he looked down and saw the adder, and then he drew his sword to slay the adder, and thought of none other harm. And when the host on both parties saw that sword drawn, then they blew beams,[16] trumpets, and horns, and shouted grimly. And so both hosts dressed them together. And King Arthur took his horse, and said: "Alas this unhappy day!" and so rode to his party. And Sir Mordred in like wise. And never was there seen a more dolefuller battle in no Christian land; for there was but rushing and riding, foining[17] and striking, and many a grim word was there spoken either to other, and many a deadly stroke. But ever King Arthur rode throughout the battle[18] of Sir Mordred many times, and did full nobly as a noble king should, and at all times he fainted never; and Sir Mordred that day put him in devoir,[19] and in great peril. And thus they fought all the long day, and never stinted[20] till the noble knights were laid to the cold earth; and ever they fought still till it

was near night, and by that time was there an hundred thousand laid dead upon the down. Then was Arthur wood wroth[21] out of measure, when he saw his people so slain from him.

Then the King looked about him, and then was he ware,[22] of all his host and of all his good knights, were left no more alive but two knights; that one was Sir Lucan the Butler, and his brother Sir Bedivere, and they were full sore wounded. "Jesu mercy," said the King, "where are all my noble knights become? Alas that ever I should see this doleful day, for now," said Arthur, "I am come to mine end. But would to God that I wist where were that traitor Sir Mordred, that hath caused all this mischief." Then was King Arthur ware where Sir Mordred leaned upon his sword among a great heap of dead men. "Now give me my spear," said Arthur unto Sir Lucan, "for yonder I have espied the traitor that all this woe hath wrought." "Sir, let him be," said Sir Lucan, "for he is unhappy;[23] and if ye pass this unhappy day ye shall be right well revenged upon him. Good lord, remember ye of your night's dream, and what the spirit of Sir Gawaine told you this night, yet God of his great goodness hath preserved you hitherto. Therefore, for God's sake, my lord, leave off by this, for blessed be God ye have won the field, for here we be three alive, and with Sir Mordred is none alive; and if ye leave off now this wicked day of destiny is past." "Tide me death, betide me life,"[24] saith the King, "now I see him yonder alone he shall never escape mine hands, for at a better avail shall I never have him." "God speed you well," said Sir Bedivere.

16 **beams:** another name for trumpets.
17 **foining:** thrusting.
18 **battle:** battle line.
19 **put . . . devoir:** drove him to his utmost endeavor.
20 **stinted:** stopped.

21 **wood wroth:** mad with anger.
22 **ware:** aware.
23 **unhappy:** likely to cause misfortune.
24 **Tide . . . life:** whether I live or die.

Then the King gat his spear in both his hands, and ran toward Sir Mordred, crying: "Traitor, now is thy death-day come." And when Sir Mordred heard Sir Arthur, he ran until[25] him with his sword drawn in his hand. And there King Arthur smote Sir Mordred under the shield, with a foin of his spear, throughout the body, more than a fathom.[26] And when Sir Mordred felt that he had his death wound he thrust himself with the might that he had up to the bur[27] of King Arthur's spear. And right so he smote his father Arthur, with his sword holden in both his hands, on the side of the head, that the sword pierced the helmet and the brainpan, and therewithal Sir Mordred fell stark dead to the earth; and the noble Arthur fell in a swoon to the earth, and there he swooned ofttimes. And Sir Lucan the Butler and Sir Bedivere ofttimes heaved him up. And so weakly they led him betwixt them both, to a little chapel not far from the seaside. And when the King was there he thought him well eased.

[*The King, hearing cries on the nearby battlefield, sends Sir Lucan to discover what is happening. Sir Lucan finds thieves pillaging the dead on the battlefield and returns to advise the king to move to a safer place. But as Sir Lucan and Sir Bedivere try to help their wounded king move, Sir Lucan, also badly wounded, falls dead. Arthur grieves "to see this noble duke so die for my sake, for he would have holpen [helped] me, that had more need of help than I."*]

THEN SIR BEDIVERE wept for the death of his brother. "Leave this mourning and weeping," said the King, "for all this will not avail me, for wit[28] thou well an I might live myself, the death of Sir Lucan would grieve me evermore; but my time hieth[29] fast," said the king. "Therefore," said Arthur unto Sir Bedivere, "take thou Excalibur, my good sword, and go with it to yonder water side, and when thou comest there I charge thee throw my sword in that water, and come again and tell me what thou there seest." "My lord," said Bedivere, "your commandment shall be done, and lightly[30] bring you word again."

So Sir Bedivere departed, and by the way he beheld that noble sword, that the pommel and the haft[31] was all of precious stones; and then he said to himself: "If I throw this rich sword in the water, thereof shall never come good, but harm and loss." And then Sir Bedivere hid Excalibur under a tree. And so, as soon as he might, he came again unto the King, and said he had been at the water, and had thrown the sword in the water. "What saw thou there?" said the King. "Sir," he said, "I saw nothing but waves and winds." "That is untruly said of thee," said the King, "therefore go thou lightly again, and do my commandment; as thou art to me lief[32] and dear, spare not, but throw it in." Then Sir Bedivere returned again, and took the sword in his hand; and then him thought sin and shame to throw away that noble sword, and so eft[33] he hid the sword, and returned again, and told to the King that he had been at the water, and done his commandment. "What saw thou there?" said the King. "Sir," he said, "I saw

25 **until:** toward; up to.
26 **fathom:** the length of two outstretched arms, about 6 feet.
27 **bur:** rounded nob between the handle and the blade.

28 **wit:** know.
29 **hieth:** goes quickly.
30 **lightly:** quickly.
31 **pommel and the haft:** round nob of the hilt, and the handle.
32 **lief:** beloved.
33 **eft:** again.

SIR THOMAS MALORY

nothing but the waters wap and waves wan."[34] "Ah, traitor untrue," said King Arthur, "now hast thou betrayed me twice. Who would have weened that, thou that hast been to me so lief and dear? and thou art named a noble knight, and would betray me for the richness of the sword. But now go again lightly, for thy long tarrying putteth me in great jeopardy of my life, for I have taken cold. And but if thou do now as I bid thee, if ever I may see thee, I shall slay thee with mine own hands; for thou wouldst for my rich sword see me dead."

Then Sir Bedivere departed, and went to the sword, and lightly took it up, and went to the water side; and there he bound the girdle[35] about the hilts, and then he threw the sword as far into the water as he might; and there came an arm and an hand above the water and met it, and caught it, and so shook it thrice and brandished,[36] and then vanished away the hand with the sword in the water. So Sir Bedivere came again to the King, and told him what he saw. "Alas," said the King, "help me hence, for I dread me I have tarried over long." Then Sir Bedivere took the King upon his back, and so went with him to that water side. And when they were at the water side, even fast by the bank hoved a little barge with many fair ladies in it, and among them all was a queen, and all they had black hoods, and all they wept and shrieked when they saw King Arthur. "Now put me into the barge," said the King. And so he did softly; and there received him three queens with great mourning; and so they set them down, and in one of their laps King Arthur laid his head. And then that queen said: "Ah, dear brother, why have ye tarried so long from me? alas, this wound on your head hath caught over-much cold." And so then they rowed from the land, and Sir Bedivere beheld all those ladies go from him. Then Sir Bedivere cried: "Ah my lord Arthur, what shall become of me, now ye go from me and leave me here alone among mine enemies?" "Comfort thyself," said the King, "and do as well as thou mayst, for in me is no trust for to trust in; for I will into the vale of Avilion[37] to heal me of my grievous wound: and if thou hear never more of me, pray for my soul." But ever the queens and ladies wept and shrieked, that it was pity to hear. And as soon as Sir Bedivere had lost the sight of the barge, he wept and wailed, and so took the forest; and so he went all that night, and in the morning he was ware betwixt two holts hoar,[38] of a chapel and an hermitage.

[*Sir Bedivere finds a tomb. The hermit tells him that on the night before ladies had brought him a body for burial. Sir Bedivere cries, "Alas! that was my lord King Arthur"; more details of his death and burial have never been told.*]

YET SOME MEN say in many parts of England that King Arthur is not dead, but had by the will of our Lord Jesu into another place; and men say that he shall come again, and he shall win the holy cross. I will not say it shall be so, but rather I will say: here in this world he changed his life. But many men say that there is written upon his tomb this verse: *Hic jacet Arthurus, Rex quondam, Rexque futurus.*[39]

---

34 **waters . . . wan:** tossing waters and dark waves.
35 **girdle:** belt.
36 **brandished:** waved the sword as if preparing to use it.

37 **Avilion:** in medieval romance, an island near the earthly paradise.
38 **holts hoar:** gray woods.
39 **Hic . . . futurus:** "Here lies Arthur, formerly King, and King to be"; or, "the once and future King."

Comment

Soon after the death of King Arthur, Sir Lancelot, one of the great champions of the Round Table, also dies, and he is lamented by his brother, Sir Hector, in this speech:

> "Ah Lancelot," he said, "thou were head of all Christian knights, and now . . . there thou liest, that . . . were never matched of earthly knight's hand. And thou were the courteoustest knight that ever bare shield. And thou were the truest friend to thy lover that ever bestrad horse. . . . And thou were the kindest man that ever struck with sword. And thou were the goodliest [handsomest] person that ever came among press [crowd] of knights. And thou was the meekest man and the gentlest that ever ate in hall among ladies. And thou were the sternest knight to thy mortal foe that ever put spear in the breast." Then there was weeping and dolor out of measure.

This farewell speech is a summary of the virtues of knighthood.

1. What are the highest qualities of the knight in peace? What are his highest qualities in war?
2. How do the qualities of the perfect knight appear in the selection that tells the story of Arthur's death? Which of them figure most largely in King Arthur?

The busy London waterfront as it looked in Chaucer's day. The Tower of London with its Traitors' Gate is in the middle ground and Old London Bridge is in the background.

Middle English Literature
The Writer Emerges

ALTHOUGH MALORY's authorship of *Le Morte Darthur* is known, he was reworking stories whose authors are for the most part unknown to us. The medieval author was largely anonymous because it was not his own story that he told. His function was to *tell*—to gather his audience into a common experience that was familiar enough, but the pleasure of which was the sharing of it with others. With Geoffrey Chaucer, however, we come to our first great author. The tales he told had

MIDDLE AGES

been told by others before him. The audience he wrote for was perhaps no larger than the group of those who, like himself, delighted in the narrator's art. But his voice, his style, is his own. There is nothing anonymous about *The Canterbury Tales;* its authorship strikes us in every line.

Geoffrey Chaucer (1340?–1400)

Geoffrey Chaucer was born in or about 1340 into a prosperous family of vintners, or wine-merchants. His father imported wine from Spain, and from the beginning of his life the continent was in many respects nearer to Chaucer than were the northern regions of the island of Britain itself. He was made a page, or confidential servant, to a daughter-in-law of the reigning King, Edward III, and in this post he continued his education by learning the courtesies, the manners, and the interests of the court. He also began an association with the reigning family that he never relinquished.

But Chaucer's life was not sheltered. In 1359 he fought with English forces in France in one of the many expeditions of the Hundred Years' War, and he was taken prisoner near Rheims (he was ransomed by King Edward). Nor was life in England always easy and civilized, for violence and death were often near. As a child of eight Chaucer lived through the Black Death, a sudden invasion of bubonic plague that killed thousands and that was to return three times in his lifetime. In his early forties he saw the violence of the Peasants' Revolt, a rebellion of farm workers, who, their numbers depleted by the plagues, fought against the conditions that tied them mercilessly to their hard lot. The rebels for a time were so successful that they captured the Tower of London, and they were so enraged that they beheaded many officials of the government and the Church, including an archbishop. Through all this turbulence feudalism was decaying, and the man of business, such as Chaucer was for much of his career, hastened its end.

For Chaucer was very much a man of affairs. He perhaps studied law briefly after his return from the fighting in France. Soon after his marriage in 1366 or 1367 to a woman whose sister was to become the wife of his chief patron, John of Gaunt, son of King Edward III, Chaucer became an Esquire of the Royal Household. In this confidential position he began a series of diplomatic journeys to the continent. He went on an important mission to Genoa, and in Italy he saw the beginnings of the Renaissance. The colors of the great paintings were fresh when he saw them; the great palaces and buildings were new. Although Dante had been dead for fifty years, and although the great poet Petrarch was near the end of his career, Chaucer must have met some of their followers; certainly he brought back with him manuscripts of their works. He saw too the splendor of such Italian noblemen as Bernabo, Lord of Milan, whose scale of life may be sug-

The mass burial of the dead during the time of the Black Death, from a 14th-century town history.

gested by the fact that he was rumored to have kept five thousand hunting dogs!

After his missions abroad, Chaucer entered into important duties in London. In 1374 he was put in charge of all traffic in wool, hides, and sheepskins for the port of London, which is to say that he was the customs officer in control of the most important exports of the kingdom. In about 1385 he went to live for a time in something like retirement outside the city, in Kent. Yet even here he was busy, for he became justice of the peace and a member of Parliament. And in 1389 he returned to royal service: he was made Clerk of the King's Works, or put in charge of the maintenance and repair of the Tower of London, Westminster Palace, and many other royal residences and offices. Toward the end of his life he managed one of the most important royal forests. Chaucer lived an active life. He was so constantly engaged in the highest business and political affairs of the kingdom that it may well seem incredible to us that he should have been a great writer as well.

He was perhaps the greatest amateur that English literature has known. He wrote not for a living but for his own pleasure and interest. And he wrote not for a public, but for an audience who would share his pleasure in "inditing"—in shaping observations and experience in verse.

Wayfarers on the roads in Chaucer's time are the pilgrim with a shell sewn on his hat (an emblem from the shrine of St. James Compostela in Spain), a wandering tinker, a beggar and her child, and an itinerant showman.

The Canterbury Tales

The Canterbury Tales is the great work of Chaucer's maturity, the product of his final interest in literature. His first works were dominated by his interest in French poetry. From these he passed into his "Italian period," when he was much influenced by the narrative poems of such writers as Boccaccio. But his last and greatest period, following upon his mastery of the art of narrative, was what can only be called his English period. For in *The Canterbury Tales* English poetry found its own full voice.

The Prologue gives the frame of the work. The poet introduces a group of people gathered together from all walks of life by their common desire to make a pilgrimage (as you have seen in the introduction to this book). When Chaucer has introduced each of them, he brings on the Host, the genial landlord of the inn where they have met. The Host proposes that he will go with them on their pilgrimage provided each promises to tell two stories on the journey to Canterbury and two on the way back. And he in turn promises that whoever tells the best story ". . . shall be given a supper, paid by all,/Here in this tavern, in this very hall,/When we come back again from Canterbury." And so the frame is provided, and the tales begin.

What is before us, then, is not "literature" as we usually think of it now, but some tellers of tales who are competing for a pleasant prize of good-fellowship. And we not only imagine each tale as *told;* we also think of how the telling of it revealed something of the character of its teller. In other words, Chaucer not only put together a great variety of stories that came to him in a rich lifetime of interest and observation; he also described a great variety of tellers of tales. He did not complete his project; *The Canterbury Tales* would have been a huge work if he had. But, as a later poet and admirer of Chaucer said, what we have is "God's plenty."

The following selection from the Prologue comes from a modern translation, and it includes most but not all of Chaucer's portraits of the pilgrims. You may be interested in reading in Middle English the first eighteen lines of the Prologue (p. 7) and comparing them with the translation that follows.

Prologue

to

The Canterbury Tales

Geoffrey Chaucer

Translated by Nevill Coghill

When in April the sweet showers fall
And pierce the drought of March to the root, and all
The veins are bathed in liquor of such power
As will bring on the engendering of the flower,
When also Zephyrus[1] with his sweet breath   5
Exhales an air in every grove and heath
Upon the tender shoots, and the young sun
His half-course in the sign of the Ram has run,[2]
And the small fowl are making melody,
That sleep away the night with open eye   10
(So nature pricks them and their heart engages),
Then people long to go on pilgrimages,
And palmers[3] long to seek the stranger strands
Of far-off saints, hallowed in sundry lands,
And specially, from every shire's end   15

---

1 **Zephyrus** (zĕf′ə rəs): the warm west wind.
2 **young sun . . . run:** The sign of the Ram is one of the signs of the Zodiac; the sun has passed
half through this period, past March 21.
3 **palmers** (pä′mərz): pilgrims.

MIDDLE AGES

In England, down to Canterbury⁴ they wend
To seek the holy blissful martyr,⁵ quick
In giving help to them when they were sick.
    It happened in that season that one day
In Southwark,⁶ at the Tabard,⁷ as I lay   20
Ready to go on pilgrimage and start
For Canterbury, most devout at heart,
At night there came into that hostelry
Some nine and twenty in a company
Of sundry folk happening then to fall   25
In fellowship, and they were pilgrims all
That towards Canterbury meant to ride.
The rooms and stables of the inn were wide;
They made us easy, all was of the best.
And shortly, when the sun had gone to rest,   30
By speaking to them all upon the trip
I soon was one of them in fellowship,
And promised to rise early and take the way
To Canterbury, as you heard me say.
    But none the less, while I have time and space,   35
Before my story takes a further pace,
It seems a reasonable thing to say
What their condition was, the full array
Of each of them, as it appeared to me,
According to profession and degree,   40
And what apparel they were riding in;
And at a Knight I therefore will begin.

There was a KNIGHT, a most distinguished man,
Who from the day on which he first began
To ride abroad had followed chivalry,   45
Truth, honor, generousness and courtesy.
He had done nobly in his sovereign's war
And ridden into battle, no man more,
As well in Christian as in heathen places,
And ever honored for his noble graces. . . .⁸   50
And though so much distinguished, he was wise
And in his bearing modest as a maid.
He never yet a boorish thing had said
In all his life to any, come what might;
He was a true, a perfect gentle-knight.   55

---

4 **Canterbury:** town about fifty-five miles southeast of London, site of Canterbury Cathedral.
5 **holy, blissful martyr** (mär′tər): Saint Thomas à
Becket, the archbishop who in 1170 was murdered
in Canterbury Cathedral by ambitious agents of
the king. The place where he was murdered became England's most popular shrine.

6 **Southwark** (sŭth′ərk): a town outside London,
where the Canterbury road began.
7 **Tabard** (tăb′ərd): a short, sleeveless coat; here,
the "sign" and the name of the inn.
8 **He had . . . graces:** The Knight has also fought
in three major Crusades, which Chaucer goes on
to specify in detail in the lines omitted here.

Speaking of his equipment, he possessed
Fine horses, but he was not gaily dressed.
He wore a fustian tunic stained and dark
With smudges where his armor had left mark;
Just home from service, he had joined our ranks   60
To do his pilgrimage and render thanks.

He had his son with him, a fine young SQUIRE,
A lover and cadet,[9] a lad of fire
With locks as curly as if they had been pressed.
He was some twenty years of age, I guessed.   65
In stature he was of a moderate length,
With wonderful agility and strength.
He'd seen some service with the cavalry
In Flanders and Artois and Picardy[10]
And had done valiantly in little space   70
Of time, in hope to win his lady's grace.
He was embroidered like a meadow bright
And full of freshest flowers, red and white.
Singing he was, or fluting all the day;
He was as fresh as is the month of May.   75
Short was his gown, the sleeves were long and wide;
He knew the way to sit a horse and ride.
He could make songs and poems and recite,
Knew how to joust and dance, to draw and write.
He loved so hotly that till dawn grew pale   80
He slept as little as a nightingale.
Courteous he was, lowly and serviceable,
And carved to serve his father at the table.[11]

There was a YEOMAN[12] with him at his side,
No other servant; so he chose to ride.   85
This Yeoman wore a coat and hood of green,
And peacock-feathered arrows, bright and keen
And neatly sheathed, hung at his belt the while
—For he could dress his gear in yeoman style,
His arrows never dropped their feathers low—   90
And in his hand he bore a mighty bow.
His head was like a nut, his face was brown.
He knew the whole of woodcraft up and down.
A saucy brace was on his arm to ward

---

9 A lover and cadet: The Squire, following the
code of courtly love and chivalry, is not yet a
knight, but he is already in the service of a lady.
10 In Flanders . . . Picardy (pĭk′ər dy): Like Chaucer himself, he has fought in battles of the Hundred Years' War.

11 And carved . . . table: one of the duties of the
personal squire or attendant.
12 Yeoman (yō′mən): an attendant not so high in
rank as a squire, but a little higher than a page.

MIDDLE AGES

It from the bowstring, and a shield and sword
Hung at one side, and at the other slipped
A jaunty dirk, spear-sharp and well-equipped.
A medal of Saint Christopher[13] he wore
Of shining silver on his breast, and bore
A hunting horn, well slung and burnished clean,

That dangled from a baldrick[14] of bright green.
He was a proper forester I guess.

There also was a N<u>un</u>, a Prioress,[15]
Her way of smiling very simple and coy;
Her greatest oath was only "By Saint Loy!"[16]

And she was known as Madam Eglantyne.
And well she sang a service, with a fine
Intoning through her nose, as was most seemly,
And she spoke daintily in French, extremely,

After the school of Stratford-atte-Bowe;[17]
French in the Paris style she did not know.
At meat her manners were well taught withal;
No morsel from her lips did she let fall,
Nor dipped her fingers in the sauce too deep;

But she could carry a morsel up and keep
The smallest drop from falling on her breast.
For courtliness she had a special zest.
And she would wipe her upper lip so clean
That not a trace of grease was to be seen

Upon the cup when she had drunk; to eat,
She reached a hand sedately for the meat.
She certainly was very entertaining,
Pleasant and friendly in her ways, and straining
To counterfeit a courtly kind of grace,

A stately bearing fitting to her place,
And to seem dignified in all her dealings.
As for her sympathies and tender feelings,
She was so charitably solicitous
She used to weep if she but saw a mouse

Caught in a trap, if it were dead or bleeding.
And she had little dogs she would be feeding
With roasted flesh, or milk, or fine white bread.
Sorely she wept if one of them were dead

---

13 Saint Christopher: patron of foresters and travelers.
14 baldrick: carrying-belt.
15 Prioress: superior officer of a religious order.
16 Saint Loy: Saint Eligious, who was remembered for his courtesy and craftsmanship—he had been a bishop and a goldsmith. The "oath" is a mild one.

17 Stratford-atte-Bow: There was a Benedictine nunnery of Saint Leonard in this village near London; and, if the Prioress did not come from there, she had been educated there. The French taught in the schools of England was by this time much less polished than that of Paris.

GEOFFREY CHAUCER

Or someone took a stick and made it smart; 135
She was all sentiment and tender heart.
Her veil was gathered in a seemly way,
Her nose was elegant, her eyes glass-gray;
Her mouth was very small, but soft and red,
Her forehead, certainly, was fair of spread, 140
Almost a span across the brows, I own;
She was indeed by no means undergrown.
Her cloak, I noticed, had a graceful charm.
She wore a coral trinket on her arm,
A set of beads, the gaudies tricked in green,
Whence hung a golden brooch of brightest sheen 145
On which there first was graven a crowned A,
And lower, *Amor vincit omnia.*[18]

  Another Nun, the chaplain at her cell,
Was riding with her, and three Priests as well.
  A Monk[19] there was, one of the finest sort 150
Who rode the country; hunting was his sport.
A manly man, to be an Abbot able;
Many a dainty horse he had in stable.
His bridle, when he rode, a man might hear
Jingling in a whistling wind as clear, 155
Aye, and as loud as does the chapel bell
Where my lord Monk was Prior of the cell.
The Rule of good Saint Benet or Maur[20]
As old and strict he tended to ignore;
He let go by the things of yesterday 160
And took the modern world's more spacious way.
He did not rate that text at a plucked hen
Which says that hunters are not holy men
And that a monk uncloistered is a mere
Fish out of water, flapping on the pier, 165
That is to say a monk out of his cloister.
That was a text he held not worth an oyster;
And I agreed and said his views were sound;
Was he to study till his head went round
Poring over books in cloisters? Must he toil 170
As Austin[21] bade and till the very soil?
Was he to leave the world upon the shelf?
Let Austin have his labor to himself.
  This Monk was therefore a good man to horse;

---

18 Amor . . . omnia: Latin for "love conquers all."
19 Monk: The monk belongs to the "regular" clergy, those bound to a monastic life by *regulae*, or strict rules of discipline.
20 Saint Benet or Saint Maur: Saint Benedict or

his disciple, Saint Maur. Saint Benedict was the founder of monasticism in western Europe.
21 Austin: Saint Augustine, one of the greatest of the Church Fathers, wrote much upon the subject of self-discipline.

Greyhounds he had, as swift as birds, to course.   175
Hunting a hare or riding at a fence
Was all his fun, he spared for no expense.
I saw his sleeves were garnished at the hand
With fine gray fur, the finest in the land,
And on his hood, to fasten it at his chin   180
He had a wrought-gold cunningly fashioned pin;
Into a lover's knot it seemed to pass.
His head was bald and shone like looking glass;
So did his face, as if it had been greased.
He was a fat and personable priest;   185
His prominent eyeballs never seemed to settle
And glittered like the flame beneath a kettle;
Supple his boots, his horse in fine condition.
He was a prelate[22] fit for exhibition,
He was not pale like a tormented soul.   190
He liked a fat swan best, and roasted whole.
His palfrey was as brown as is a berry. . . .

    There was a MERCHANT with a forking beard
And motley[23] dress; high on his horse he sat,
Upon his head a Flemish beaver hat   195
And on his feet daintily buckled boots.
In solemn tones he spoke of his pursuits,
Harping upon his gains—he never lost.
The sea should be kept free at any cost
(He thought) upon the Harwich-Holland range.[24]   200
He was expert at currency-exchange.
This estimable Merchant so had set
His wits to work, none knew he was in debt,
He was so stately in negotiation,
Loan, bargain and commercial obligation.   205
He was an excellent fellow all the same;
To tell the truth I do not know his name.

    An OXFORD CLERIC,[25] still a student though,
One who had taken logic long ago,
Was there; his horse was thinner than a rake,   210
And he was not too fat, I undertake,
But had a hollow look, a sober stare;
The thread upon his overcoat was bare.
He had found no preferment[26] in the church

---

22 prelate (prĕl′ĭt): one who ranks high in the Church.
23 motley (mŏt′lĭ): cloth of mixed colors.
24 The sea . . . range: The merchant wants the sea between England and Holland kept free of pirates.

25 Oxford Cleric: The Cleric (clerk, or student) is perhaps a Master of Arts, but he is still in training for entrance into the priesthood, or holy orders.
26 preferment: He had no "living" or appointment to any parish.

And he was too unworldly to make search   215
For secular employment. By his bed
He preferred having twenty books in red
And black, of Aristotle's philosophy,
To having fine clothes, fiddle or psaltery.
Though a philosopher, as I have told,   220
He had not found the stone for making gold.[27]
What ever money from his friends he took
He spent on learning or another book
And prayed for them most earnestly, returning
Thanks to them thus for paying for his learning.   225
His only care was study, and indeed
He never spoke a word more than was need,
Formal at that, respectful in the extreme,
Short, to the point, and lofty in his theme.
The thought of moral virtue filled his speech   230
And he would gladly learn, and gladly teach. . . .

There was a FRANKLIN[28] with him, it appeared;
White as a daisy-petal was his beard.
A sanguine man, high-colored and benign,
He loved a morning sop of cake in wine.   235
He lived for pleasure and had always done,
For he was Epicurus'[29] very son,
In whose opinion sensual delight
Was the one true felicity in sight.
As noted as Saint Julian[30] was for bounty   240
He made his household free to all the County.
His bread, his ale were finest of the fine
And no one had a better stock of wine.
His house was never short of bake-meat pies,
Of fish and flesh, and these in such supplies   245
It positively snowed with meat and drink
And all the dainties that a man could think.
According to the seasons of the year
Changes of dish were ordered to appear.
He kept fat partridges in coops, beyond,   250
Many a bream and pike were in his pond.
Woe to the cook whose sauces had no sting
Or who was unprepared in anything!
And in his hall a table stood arrayed
And ready all day long, with places laid.   255

---

27 stone . . . gold: "philosopher's stone," an imaginary stone believed to have the power of trans-
muting base metals into gold.

28 Franklin: a landed proprietor or gentleman
farmer.
29 Epicurus (ĕp'ə kyōŏr'əs): a Greek philosopher.
30 Saint Julian: patron saint of hospitality.

As Justice at the Sessions none stood higher;[31]
He often had been Member for the Shire.[32]
A dagger and a little purse of silk
Hung at his girdle, white as morning milk.
As Sheriff he checked audit,[33] every entry.   260
He was a model among landed gentry. . . .

There was a Skipper hailing from far west;
He came from Dartmouth,[34] so I understood.
He rode a farmer's horse as best he could,
And wore a woolen gown that reached his knee.   265
A dagger on a lanyard falling free
Hung from his neck under his arm and down.
The summer heat had tanned his color brown,
And certainly he was an excellent fellow.
Many a draught of vintage, red and yellow,   270
He'd drawn at Bordeaux, while the trader snored;
The nicer rules of conscience he ignored.
If, when he fought, the enemy vessel sank,
He sent his prisoners home; they walked the plank.
As for his skill in reckoning his tides,   275
Currents and many another risk besides,
Moons, harbors, pilots, he had such dispatch
That none from Hull[35] to Carthage[36] was his match. . . .

A worthy Woman from beside Bath city
Was with us, somewhat deaf, which was a pity.   280
In making cloth she showed so great a bent
She bettered those of Ypres and of Ghent.[37]
In all the parish not a dame dared stir
Towards the altar steps in front of her,
And if indeed they did, so wrath was she   285
As to be quite put out of charity.[38]
Her kerchiefs were of finely woven ground;
I dared have sworn they weighed a good ten pound,
The ones she wore on Sunday, on her head.
Her hose were of the finest scarlet red   290
And gartered tight; her shoes were soft and new.
Bold was her face, handsome, and red in hue.

A worthy woman all her life, what's more
She'd had five husbands, all at the church door,[39]
Apart from other company in youth;   295
No need just now to speak of that, forsooth.
And she had thrice been to Jerusalem,
Seen many strange rivers and passed over them;
She'd been to Rome and also to Boulogne,
St. James of Compostella and Cologne,[40]   300
And she was skilled in wandering by the way.
She had gap-teeth, set widely, truth to say.
Easily on an ambling horse she sat
Well wimpled up, and on her head a hat
As broad as is a buckler or a shield;   305
She had a flowing mantle that concealed
Large hips, her heels spurred sharply under that.
In company she like to laugh and chat
And knew the remedies for love's mischances,
An art in which she knew the oldest dances.   310

    A holy-minded man of good renown
There was, and poor, the PARSON[41] to a town,
Yet he was rich in holy thought and work.
He also was a learned man, a clerk,
Who truly knew Christ's gospel and would preach it   315
Devoutly to parishioners, and teach it.
Benign and wonderfully diligent,
And patient when adversity was sent
(For so he proved in great adversity)
He much disliked extorting tithe[42] or fee,   320
Nay rather he preferred beyond a doubt
Giving to poor parishioners round about
From his own goods and Easter offerings.
He found sufficiency in little things.
Wide was his parish, with houses far asunder,   325
Yet he neglected not in rain or thunder,
In sickness, or in trouble, to pay call
On the remotest whether great or small
Upon his feet, and in his hand a stave.
A noble example to his sheep he gave,   330
A doer of the word before he taught it,
And it was from the gospel he had caught it.
This little proverb he would add thereto
That if gold rust, what then will iron do?

---

39 at the church door: Marriage ceremonies in the
Middle Ages took place at the church door.
40 And she . . . Cologne (kə lōn′)**:** She had made
pilgrimages to most of the important European
religious shrines.

41 Parson: The Parson belongs to the "secular"
clergy, or those who are out in the world and not
bound by monastic rules.
42 tithe: portion of one's income (literally, one-
tenth) contributed by members to support of a
church.

For if a priest be foul in whom we trust 335
No wonder that a common man should rust;
And shame it is to see—let priests take stock—
A dunged-up shepherd and a snowy flock.
The true example that a priest should give
Is one of cleanness, how the sheep should live. 340
He did not set his benefice to hire[43]
And leave his sheep encumbered in the mire
Or run to London to earn easy bread
By singing masses for the wealthy dead,
Or find some Brotherhood and get enrolled.[44] 345
He stayed at home and watched over his fold
So that no wolf should make the sheep miscarry.
He was a shepherd and no mercenary.
Holy and virtuous he was, but then
Never contemptuous of sinful men, 350
Never disdainful, never too proud or fine,
But was discreet in teaching and benign.
His business was to show a fair behavior
And draw men thus to Heaven and their Saviour,
Unless indeed a man were obstinate; 355
And such, whether of high or low estate,
He put to sharp rebuke to say the least.
I think there never was a better priest.
He sought no pomp or glory in his dealings,
No scrupulosity had spiced his feelings. 360
Christ and His Twelve Apostles and their lore
He taught, but followed it himself before.

There was a PLOWMAN with him there, his brother.
Many a load of dung one time or other
He must have carted through the morning dew. 365
He was an honest worker, good and true,
Living in peace and perfect charity.
And, as the gospel bade him, so did he;
God he loved best, with all his heart and mind,
And then his neighbor as himself, repined 370
At no misfortune, slacked for no content,
For steadily about his work he went
To thrash his corn, to dig or to manure
Or make a ditch; and he would help the poor
For love of Christ and never take a penny 375
If he could help it, and, as prompt as any,

---

43 **He did . . . hire:** He did not hire someone to
perform his duties.

44 **Or run . . . enrolled:** The offerings would be
rich in London; the private chaplain to a guild or
association of tradesmen would live well.

He paid his tithes in full when they were due,
On what he owned, and on his earnings too.
He wore a tabard smock and rode a mare. . . .

The MILLER was a chap of sixteen stone,[45]   380
A great stout fellow big in brawn and bone.
He did well out of them, for he could go
And win the ram at any wrestling show.[46]
Broad, knotty and short-shouldered, he would boast
He could heave any door off hinge and post,   385
Or take a run and break it with his head.
His beard, like any sow or fox, was red
And broad as well, as though it were a spade;
And, at its very tip, his nose displayed
A wart on which there stood a tuft of hair   390
Red as the bristles in an old sow's ear.
His nostrils were as black as they were wide,
He had a sword and buckler at his side,
His mighty mouth was like a furnace door.
A wrangler and buffoon, he had a store   395
Of tavern stories, filthy in the main.
His was a master-hand at stealing grain.
He felt it with his thumb and thus he knew
Its quality and took three times his due—
A thumb of gold,[47] by God, to gauge an oat!   400
He wore a hood of blue and a white coat.
He liked to play his bagpipes up and down
And that was how he took us out of town. . . .

The REEVE[48] was old and choleric and thin;
His beard was shaven closely to the skin,   405
His shorn hair came abruptly to a stop
Above his ears, and he was docked on top
Just like a priest; his legs were long and lean,
They were like sticks, no calf was to be seen.
He kept his bins and garners[49] very trim;   410
No auditor could gain a point on him.[50]
And he could judge by watching drought and rain
The yield he might expect from seed and grain.
His master's sheep, his animals and hens,
Pigs, horses, dairies, stores and cattle pens   415

---

45 stone: unit of weight; now fourteen pounds.
46 And win . . . show: Livestock were often the prizes for winning wrestling matches at country fairs.
47 thumb of gold: A proverbial expression: "An honest miller has a golden thumb." But is a golden thumb possible?

48 Reeve: The Reeve is an estate manager.
49 garners: granaries.
50 No auditor . . . him: He knew how to balance (or juggle?) his accounts.

Were wholly trusted to his government.
And he was under contract to present
The accounts, right from his master's earliest years.
No one had ever caught him in arrears.
No bailiff,[51] serf or herdsman dared to kick,   420
He knew their dodges, knew their every trick;
Feared like the plague he was, by those beneath.
He had a charming house upon a heath,
Shadowed in green by trees above the sward.[52]
A better hand at bargains than his lord,   425
He had grown rich and had a store of treasure
Well tucked away, yet out it came to pleasure
His lord with subtle loans or gifts of goods
To earn his thanks, and even coats and hoods.
When young he'd learnt a useful trade and still   430
He was a carpenter of first-rate skill.
The stallion-cob[53] he rode at a slow trot
Was dapple-gray and bore the name of Scot.
He wore an overcoat of bluish shade
And rather long; he had a rusty blade   435
Slung at his side. He came, as I heard tell,
From Norfolk, near a place called Baldeswell.
His coat was tucked under his belt and splayed.
He rode the hindmost of our cavalcade. . . .

He[54] and a gentle PARDONER[55] rode together,   440
A bird from Charing Cross of the same feather,
Just back from visiting the Court of Rome.
He loudly sang, "Come hither, love, come home!"
The Summoner sang deep seconds to this song,
No trumpet ever sounded half so strong.   445
This Pardoner had hair as yellow as wax
Hanging down smoothly like a hank of flax.
In driblets fell these locks behind his head
Down to his shoulders which they overspread;
Thinly they fell, like rattails, one by one.   450
He wore no hood upon his head, for fun;
The hood inside his wallet[56] had been stowed,
He aimed at riding in the latest mode;

---

51 **bailiff:** estate officer.
52 **sward:** grassy land.
53 **stallion-cob:** good solid stallion.
54 **He:** the Summoner, whose description is here omitted. A summoner was one who summoned people to an ecclesiastical court to answer for certain crimes that were not tried in civil court.
55 **Pardoner:** The Pardoner was one (often lower than the priest in the orders of the Church) who had been licensed to grant, in return for offerings to the Church, indulgences, documents that granted remission of punishment in Purgatory for sins already confessed. The office of pardoner was grossly abused in the Middle Ages and was finally abolished by the Church. This Pardoner comes from the Hospital of the Blessed Mary of Rouncivalle, a religious institution near Charing Cross in Chaucer's London.
56 **wallet:** traveling bag.

But for a little cap his head was bare
And he had bulging eyeballs, like a hare.   455
He'd sewed a holy relic on his cap;
His wallet lay before him on his lap,
Brimful of pardons come from Rome all hot.
He had the same small voice a goat has got.
His chin no beard had harbored, nor would harbor,   460
Smoother than ever chin was left by barber. . . .
There was no pardoner of equal grace,
For in his trunk he had a pillowcase
Which he asserted was Our Lady's veil.
He said he had a gobbet of the sail   465
Saint Peter had the time when he made bold
To walk the waves, till Jesu Christ took hold.[57]
He had a cross of metal set with stones
And, in a glass, a rubble of pigs' bones.
And with these relics, any time he found   470
Some poor up-country parson to astound,
On one short day, in money down, he drew
More than the parson in a month or two,
And by his flatteries and prevarication
Made monkeys of the priest and congregation.   475
But still to do him justice first and last
In church he was a noble ecclesiast.
How well he read a lesson or told a story!
But best of all he sang an Offertory,[58]
For well he knew that when that song was sung   480
He'd have to preach and tune his honey-tongue
And (well he could) win silver from the crowd.
That's why he sang so merrily and loud.

    Now I have told you shortly, in a clause,
The rank, the array, the number and the cause   485
Of our assembly in this company
In Southwark, at that high-class hostelry
Known as the Tabard, close beside the Bell.[59]

All the illustrations of the pilgrims are from the Ellesmere manuscript, which is in the Huntington Library, San Marino, California. Made soon after Chaucer's death, it is the most authoritative copy of The Canterbury Tales.

57 the sail . . . took hold: See Matthew 14:24-31.
58 Offertory (ôf′ər tôr′ĭ): anthem sung in the Mass following the Creed while the offerings of the congregation are made.
59 the Bell: another inn.

Comment

The variety of this series of portraits is rich indeed. First there is the variety of "rank" represented. Besides those given here, the full Prologue also describes a Friar, a Lawyer, five Guildsmen, or members of special trades (a Weaver, a Dyer, a Carpenter, a Tapestry-maker, and a Haberdasher), together with their Cook, a Physician, a Manciple, or business manager of a college for lawyers, and the Summoner, who accompanied the Pardoner. Then there is the variety of human nature represented. Some of the pilgrims are quiet, some noisy; some are strong, some weak; some are faithful, some are not. Perhaps the greatest variety is to be found in Chaucer's perceptions of individual traits and characteristics. Sometimes he gives us details of dress, sometimes of facial expression; sometimes he concentrates on the background—the habitual life of the individual pilgrim at home—sometimes he does not. Yet all this variety is held together for us by Chaucer's style, by the attitude he expresses whether he notes a detail or sketches a background.

1. Briefly list the laymen (those not connected with the Church) in what you take to be the order of their rank in society. Who is at the top? Who comes last? Make a similar list of the ecclesiastical pilgrims.
2. Which pilgrims seem to you most worthy in Chaucer's eyes? What trait does he seem most to value and approve? Which seem to you least worthy in his eyes? And what does Chaucer seem to disapprove in them? But about which pilgrims is Chaucer's judgment hard to determine? Are there more or fewer of these than of the other two kinds of character?
3. What seem to you some revealing details of Chaucer's observation? For example, why does the Reeve ride last? What does this fact tell us about him? Again, the Nun feeds her dogs "fine white bread," and this tells us that she was all "sentiment and tender heart." But in keeping pets at all she was breaking a rule of her order, and "fine white bread" was something that the Plowman, for example, would rarely have seen. The Nun is kind, but what else is she? What similarly telling details can you find in the portraits of the Monk, the Skipper, the Woman, or Wife, of Bath?
4. Considering both the large and the fine features of Chaucer's portraits, how do you characterize his attitude toward the band of pilgrims? Running through all the variety, what consistency, what uniformity, do you find in the man who makes all these observations?

"The Pardoner's Tale"

The Pardoner begins his tale by telling the pilgrims this:

"My lords," he said, "in churches where I preach
I cultivate a haughty kind of speech
And ring it out as roundly as a bell;
I've got it all by heart, the tale I tell.
I have a text, it always is the same
And always has been, since I learnt the game,
Old as the hills and fresher than the grass,
Radix malorum est cupiditas."
[The root of evil is greed.]

Greed is, as we know, something the Pardoner knows much of. But this is his "text," the point or moral of the sermon he gives over and over. The tale he tells is an illustration of his text; it is called the *exemplum,* or that part of the sermon which provides a concrete, dramatic example of the sin his sermon attacks. The tale is an ancient one from the Orient; and, wherever Chaucer heard it, we can see why he never forgot it. It is a story of three young rowdies ("riotoures") who will do anything for money. The selection does not include the Pardoner's opening remarks, in which he learnedly sets forth the theme of his sermon, that greed is the root of all evil.

In the introduction to this book (p. 7) and in the discussion of the Middle English language at the beginning of this chapter (p. 39), you saw examples of Chaucer's language and read some explanation of how he would have pronounced it. Now here again are the lines with which the Pardoner introduces his tale, this time not in a modern English translation but in Middle English, the language in which Chaucer spoke and wrote:

"Lordynges,"[1] quod[2] he, "in chirches whan I preche,
I peyne me[3] to han[4] an hauteyn[5] speche,
And rynge it out as round as gooth a belle,
For I kan[6] al by rote that I telle.
My theme is alwey oon,[7] and evere was—
Radix malorum est Cupiditas.[8]

1 lordynges : my lords.
2 quod : quoth; said.
3 peyne me : take pains.
4 han : have.
5 hauteyn : haughty; lofty.
6 kan : know.
7 alwey oon : always one; i.e., the same.
8 Radix . . . Cupiditas : Latin for "The root of evil is greed."

You see—and hear—that this language is not really very different from our own English. By saying words aloud, by considering the sense of the story, and by using the sidenotes in modern English provided here, it is possible to understand and enjoy the story, besides having the opportunity of reading the tale just as it was written by Chaucer. The text of "The Pardoner's Tale" which follows is printed in Middle English.

The Pardoner's Tale

Geoffrey Chaucer

Thise riotoures thre of whiche I telle,
Longe erst er prime rong[1] of any belle,
Were set hem[2] in a taverne for to drynke,
And as they sat, they herde a belle clynke
5 Biforn[3] a cors,[4] was caried to his grave.
That oon of hem gan callen to his knave:[5]
"Go bet,"[6] quod he, "and axe[7] redily
What cors is this that passeth heer forby;
And looke that thou reporte his name weel."
10 "Sire," quod this boy, "it nedeth never-a-deel;[8]
It was me toold er ye cam heer two houres.[9]
He was, pardee,[10] an old felawe[11] of youres;
And sodeynly he was yslayn to-nyght,[12]
Fordronke,[13] as he sat on his bench upright.
15 Ther cam a privee[14] theef men clepeth[15] Deeth,
That in this contree al the peple sleeth,[16]
And with his spere he smoot his herte atwo,[17]
And wente his wey withouten wordes mo.[18]
He hath a thousand slayn this pestilence.[19]
20 And, maister, er ye come in his presence,
Me thynketh that it were necessarie
For to be war[20] of swich[21] an adversarie.
Beth[22] redy for to meete hym everemoore;[23]
Thus taughte me my dame;[24] I sy namoore,"[25]
25 "By seinte Marie!" seyde this taverner,[26]
"The child seith sooth,[27] for he hath slayn this yeer,
Henne over a mile,[28] withinne a greet village,
Bothe man and womman, child, and hyne,[29] and page;
I trowe[30] his habitacioun be there.
30 To been avysed[31] greet wysdom it were,

Er that[1] he dide a man a dishonour."

"Ye, Goddes armes!"[2] quod this riotour,
"Is it swich peril with hym for to meete?
I shal hym seke by wey and eek by strete,[3]
35 I make avow to Goddes digne[4] bones!
Herkneth, felawes, we thre been al ones;[5]
Lat ech of us holde up his hand til[6] oother,
And ech of us bicomen otheres brother,
And we wol sleen this false traytour Deeth.
40 He shal be slayn, he that so manye sleeth,
By Goddes dignitee, er it be nyght!"
Togidres[7] han thise thre hir trouthes plight[8]
To lyve and dyen ech of hem for oother,
As though he were his owene ybore[9] brother.
45 And up they stirte,[10] al dronken in this rage,
And forth they goon[11] towardes that village
Of which the taverner hadde spoke biforn.
And many a grisly ooth[12] thanne han[13] they sworn,
And Cristes blessed body al torente[14]—
50 Deeth shal be deed, if that they may hym hente![15]
Whan they han goon nat fully half a mile,
Right as they wolde han troden over a stile,[16]
An oold man and a povre[17] with hem mette.
This olde man ful[18] mekely hem grette,[19]
55 And seyde thus, "Now, lordes, God yow see!"[20]
The proudeste of thise riotoures three
Answerde agayn, "What, carl, with sory grace![21]
Why artow[22] al forwrapped[23] save thy face?
Why lyvestow[24] so longe in so greet age?"
60 This olde man gan looke[25] in his visage,[26]
And seyde thus: "For I ne kan nat fynde[27]
A man, though that I walked into Ynde,[28]
Neither in citee ne in no village,
That wolde chaunge his youthe for myn age;
65 And therfore moot[29] I han myn age stille,
As longe tyme as it is Goddes wille.
Ne Deeth, allas! ne wol[30] not han my lyf
Thus walke I, lyk a restelees kaityf,[31]
And on the ground, which is my moodres[32] gate,
70 I knokke with my staf, bothe erly and late,
And seye 'Leeve[33] mooder, leet me in!
Lo[34] how I vanysshe, flessh, and blood, and skyn!
Allas! whan shul my bones been at reste?
Mooder, with yow wolde I chaunge my cheste[35]
75 That in my chambre longe tyme hath be,
Ye, for an heyre clowt[36] to wrappe in me!'
But yet to me she wol nat do that grace,

1 Er that : before.
2 Ye, Goddes armes : Yes, by the arms of God.
3 seke . . . strete : seek him in highways and also (eke) in streets.
4 digne : worthy.
5 we . . . ones : We three are as one.
6 til : to.
7 Togidres : together.
8 hir . . . plight : plighted their troth (swore allegiance).
9 ybore : born.
10 stirte : jumped.
11 goon : went.
12 ooth : oath.
13 han : have.
14 torente : tore apart.
15 hente : catch.
16 Right . . . stile : just as they were about to climb over a stile.
17 povre : poor (a poor old man).
18 ful : very.
19 grette : greeted.
20 God yow see : God protect (see) you.
21 carl . . . grace! : peasant, curse you.
22 artow : are you.
23 forwrapped : wrapped up.
24 lyvestow : do you live.
25 gan looke : began to look.
26 visage : face.
27 I ne . . . nat fynde : Note the double negative ("I no can not find . . .") in reputable use in Chaucer's time.
28 Ynde : India.
29 moot : must.
30 wol : will.
31 kaityf : captive.
32 moodres : mother's.
33 Leeve : dear.
34 Lo : see.
35 chaunge my cheste : exchange my clothes chest.
36 heyre clowt : haircloth shirt (a shroud).

For which ful pale and welked[1] is my face.
    But, sires, to yow it is no curteisye
80 To speken to an old man vileynye,[2]
But[3] he trespasse in word, or elles in dede.
In Hooly Writ ye may yourself wel rede:
'Agayns[4] an oold man, hoor[5] upon his heed,
Ye sholde arise;' wherfore I yeve yow reed,[6]
85 Ne dooth unto an oold man noon[7] harm now,
Namoore than that ye wolde men did to yow
In age, if that ye so longe abyde.
And God be with yow, where ye go or ryde![8]
I moot go thider[9] as I have to go."
90   "Nay, olde cherl, by God, thou shalt nat so,"
Seyde this oother hasardour[10] anon;[11]
"Thou partest nat so lightly, by Seint John!
Thou spak right now of thilke[12] traytour Deeth,
That in this contree alle oure freendes sleeth.
95 Have heer my trouthe, as thou art his espye,[13]
Telle where he is, or thou shalt it abye,[14]
By God, and by the hooly sacrement!
For soothly thou art oon of his assent[15]
To sleen us yonge folk, thou false theef!"
100   "Now, sires," quod he, "if that yow be so leef[16]
To fynde Deeth, turne up this croked wey,
For in that grove I lafte hym, by my fey,[17]
Under a tree, and there he wole abyde;
Noght for youre boost[18] he wole him[19] no thyng hyde.
105 Se ye that ook? Right there ye shal hym fynde.
God save yow, that boghte agayn mankynde,[20]
And yow amende!"[21] Thus seyde this olde man;
And everich[22] of thise riotoures ran
Til he cam to that tree, and ther they founde
110 Of floryns[23] fyne of gold ycoyned rounde[24]
Wel ny an eighte busshels, as hem[25] thoughte.
No lenger thanne after Deeth they soughte,
But ech of hem so glad was of that sighte,
For that the floryns been so faire and brighte,
115 That doun they sette hem[26] by this precious hoord.
The worste of hem, he spak the firste word.
    "Bretheren," quod he, "taak kep[27] what that I seye,
My wit[28] is greet, though that I bourde[29] and pleye.
This tresor hath Fortune unto us yiven,[30]
120 In myrthe and jolitee oure lyf to lyven,
And lightly as it comth, so wol we spende.
Ey! Goddes precious dignitee! who wende[31]
To-day that we sholde han so fair a grace?
But myghte this gold be caried fro this place

1 welked : withered.

2 vileynye : rudely.
3 But : unless.
4 Agayns : Before (in the presence of).
5 hoor : hoar (white-headed).
6 Yeve yow reed : give you advice.
7 noon : no.
8 where . . . ryde! : whether you walk or ride.
9 thider : thither.
10 hasardour : gambler.
11 anon : immediately.

12 thilke : that same.

13 espye : spy.
14 it abye : suffer for it.

15 oon . . . assent : one of his opinion (in agreement with him).
16 leef : eager.

17 fey : faith (on my word).

18 boost : boast.
19 him : himself.

20 that boghte agayn : Who redeemed.
21 yow amende : improve you.
22 everich : each.
23 floryns : florins (coins).
24 ycoyned rounde : literally, coined round.
25 hem : they.

26 hem : themselves.

27 taak kep : take heed.
28 wit : wisdom.
29 bourde : jest.
30 yiven : given.

31 wende : would have thought.

125 Hoom to myn hous, or elles unto youres—
For wel ye woot[1] that al this gold is oures—
Thanne were we in heigh felicitee.
But trewely, by daye it may nat bee.
Men wolde seyn that we were theves stronge,
130 And for oure owene tresor doon us honge.[2]
This tresor moste ycaried be by nyghte
As wisely and as slyly as it myghte.
Wherfore I rede[3] that cut[4] among us alle
Be drawe, and lat se[5] wher the cut wol falle;
135 And he that hath the cut with herte blithe
Shal renne to the town, and that ful swithe,[6]
And brynge us breed and wyn ful prively.[7]
And two of us shul kepen subtilly[8]
This tresor wel; and if he wol nat tarie,
140 Whan it is nyght, we wol this tresor carie,
By oon assent, where as us thynketh best."
That oon of hem the cut broghte in his fest,[9]
And bad hem drawe, and looke where it wol falle;
And it fil on the yongeste of hem alle,
145 And forth toward the toun he wente anon.
And also soone as that he was gon,
That oon of hem spak thus unto that oother:
"Thow knowest wel thou art my sworen brother;
Thy profit wol I telle thee anon.
150 Thou woost wel that oure felawe is agon.
And heere is gold, and that ful greet plentee,
That shal departed[10] been among us thre.
But nathelees,[11] if I kan shape it so
That it departed were among us two,
155 Hadde I nat doon a freendes torn[12] to thee?"
    That oother answerde, "I noot[13] hou that may be.
He woot wel that the gold is with us tweye;[14]
What shal we doon? What shal we to hym seye?"
    "Shal it be conseil?"[15] seyde the firste shrewe,[16]
160 "And I shal tellen in a wordes fewe
What we shal doon, and brynge it wel aboute."
    "I graunte," quod that oother, "out of doute,[17]
That, by my trouthe, I wol thee nat biwreye."[18]
    "Now," quod the firste, "thou woost wel we be tweye,
165 And two of us shul strenger be than oon.
Looke whan that he is set, that right anoon[19]
Arys[20] as though thou woldest with hym pleye,
And I shal ryve[21] hym thurgh the sydes tweye
Whil that thou strogelest with hym as in game,
170 And with thy daggere looke thou[22] do the same;
And thanne shal al this gold departed be,

1 woot : know.

2 doon us honge : cause
us to be hanged.

3 rede : advise.
4 cut : lots.
5 lat se : let (us) see.

6 swithe : quickly.
7 prively : secretly.
8 subtilly : craftily.

9 fest : fist.

10 departed : divided.
11 nathelees : nevertheless.

12 torn : turn; deed.
13 noot : know not.
14 tweye : two.

15 counseil : secret.
16 shrewe : scoundrel.

17 "I . . . doute" : "I agree
without a doubt."
18 biwreye : betray.

19 right anoon : right
away; instantly.
20 Arys : arise.
21 ryve : stab.

22 looke thou : you be sure
to.

My deere freend, bitwixen me and thee.
Thanne may we bothe oure lustes all fulfille,
And pleye at dees[1] right at oure owene wille."

175 And thus acorded[2] been thise shrewes tweye
To sleen the thridde, as ye han herd me seye.

This yongeste, which that wente to the toun,
Ful ofte in herte[3] he rolleth up and doun
The beautee of thise floryns newe and brighte.
180 "O Lord!" quod he, "if so were that I myghte
Have al this tresor to myself allone,
Ther is no man that lyveth under the trone[4]
Of God that sholde lyve so murye as I!"
And atte laste the feend,[5] oure enemy,
185 Putte in his thought that he sholde poyson beye,[6]
With which he myghte sleen his felawes tweye;
For-why the feend foond hym in swich lyvynge[7]
That he hadde leve[8] him to sorwe brynge.[9]
For this was outrely[10] his fulle entente,
190 To sleen hem bothe, and nevere to repente.
And forth he gooth, no lenger wolde he tarie,
Into the toun, unto a pothecarie,[11]
And preyde[12] hym that he hym wolde selle
Som poyson, that he myghte his rattes quelle;[13]
195 And eek ther was a polcat in his hawe,[14]
That, as he seyde, his capouns hadde yslawe,[15]
And fayn he wolde wreke hym,[16] if he myghte,
On vermyn that destroyed[17] hym by nyghte.

The pothecarie answerde, "And thou shalt have
200 A thyng that, also God my soule save,
In al this world ther is no creature,
That eten or dronken hath of this confiture[18]
Noght but the montance[19] of a corn[20] of whete,
That he ne shal his lif anon forlete;[21]
205 Ye, sterve[22] he shal, and that in lasse[23] while
Than thou wolt goon a paas[24] nat but a mile,
This poysoun is so strong and violent."

This cursed man hath in his hond yhent[25]
This poysoun in a box, and sith[26] he ran
210 Into the nexte strete unto a man,
And borwed of hym large botelles thre;
And in the two his poyson poured he;
The thridde he kepte clene for his drynke.
For al the nyght he shoop hym for to swynke[27]
215 In cariynge of the gold out of that place.
And whan this riotour, with sory grace,
Hadde filled with wyn his grete botels thre,
To his felawes agayn repaireth he.

1 dees : dice.
2 acorded : agreed.

3 Ful ofte in herte : very often in his imagination.

4 trone : throne.

5 feend : Devil.
6 beye : buy.

7 For-why . . . lyvynge : because the Devil found him living such a life.
8 leve : leave; permission (from God).
9 him to sorwe brynge : to bring him to sorrow.
10 outrely : entirely.
11 pothecarie : apothecary (druggist).
12 preyde : beseeched.
13 quelle : kill.
14 hawe : yard.
15 capouns hadde yslawe : had slain his chickens.
16 fayn . . . hym : He would like to avenge himself.
17 destroyed : annoyed.
18 confiture : preparation.
19 montance : amount.
20 corn : grain.
21 forlete : give up; lose.
22 sterve : die.
23 lasse : less.
24 goon a paas : walk at a footpace.
25 yhent : taken.
26 sith : then.

27 shoop . . . swynke : planned to work.

What nedeth it to sermone of it moore?
220 For right as they hadde cast[1] his deeth bifoore,
Right so they han hym slayn, and that anon.
And whan that this was doon, thus spak that oon:
"Now lat us sitte and drynke, and make us merie,
And afterward we wol his body berie."
225 And with that word it happed hym, par cas,[2]
To take the botel ther the poyson was,
And drank, and yaf[3] his felawe drynke also,
For which anon they storven[4] bothe two.
   But certes,[5] I suppose that Avycen[6]
230 Wroot nevere in no canon, ne in no fen,[7]
Mo wonder signes[8] of empoisonyng
Than hadde thise wrecches two, er hir[9] endyng.
Thus ended been thise homycides two,
And eek the false empoysonere also.
235   O cursed synne of alle cursednesse!
O traytours homycide, O wikkednesse!
O glotonye, luxurie,[10] and hasardrye!
Thou blasphemour of Crist with vileynye
And othes[11] grete, of usage and of pride!
240 Allas! mankynde, how may it bitide[12]
That to thy creatour, which that the wroghte,[13]
And with his precious herte-blood thee boghte,
Thou art so fals and so unkynde,[14] allas?
   Now, goode men, God foryeve yow youre trespas,
245 And ware[15] yow fro the synne of avarice!
Myn hooly pardoun may yow alle warice,[16]
So that ye offre nobles or sterlynges,[17]
Or elles silver broches, spoones, rynges.
Boweth youre heed under this hooly bulle![18]
250 Cometh up, ye wyves, offreth of youre wolle![19]
Youre names I entre heer in my rolle anon;
Into the blisse of hevene shul ye gon.
I yow assoille,[20] by myn heigh power,
Yow that wol offre, as clene and eek as cleer
255 As ye were born.—And lo, sires, thus I preche.
And Jhesu Crist, that is oure soules leche,[21]
So graunte yow his pardoun to receyve,
For that is best; I wol yow nat deceyve.

1 cast : planned.

2 par cas : by chance.

3 yaf : gave.
4 storven : died.
5 certes : certainly.
6 Avycen : Avicenna, an
Arabian authority on medicine.
7 Wroot . . . fen : never
wrote in any rule or section
(of his book).
8 Mo . . . signes : more
wonderful symptoms.
9 hir : their.
10 luxurie : lust (lechery).

11 othes : oaths.
12 bitide : betide (happen).
13 which . . . wroghte :
who made you.

14 unkynde : unnatural.

15 ware : guard; keep.
16 warice : cure.
17 nobles or sterlynges :
valuable coins.

18 hooly bulle : holy edict.
19 wolle : wool.

20 assoille : absolve; pardon.

21 leche : physician.

Comment

Each of the pilgrims tells a tale, and each pilgrim's tale—its subject,
the way in which it is told, its effect on the rest of the group—reveals in
turn something about the one who tells it. And nothing in all *The*

Canterbury Tales is so astonishing as the relation between this story and the man who tells it. As we know from his portrait in the Prologue, the Pardoner himself deals in fraudulent religious relics for the sake of gain; and still his sermon is one against avarice. Does he know himself? Or is he unknowingly as bad as the damned souls of his tale?

The mystery of the Pardoner's character even extends into the tale itself: Who is the strange old man whom the roisterers meet when they set out to "sleen this false traytour Deeth" and who directs them to the bushels of gold that prove their undoing? Is *he* a symbol of death? Does he knowingly direct them to their own deaths?

1. A person dominated by greed will try to outmaneuver others to get what he or she wants. How does the behavior of the three roisterers exemplify the text of the Pardoner's sermon?

2. Suppose the old man of the story is just that—an old man who is weary of life and who does not know about the gold under the tree: do the actions of the three young men still exemplify the text?

3. But suppose the old man is a symbol of death. What do *his* actions mean? What does it mean that he wants to die but cannot? What does it mean that he directs the young men to the gold?

4. Which interpretation of the old man seems to you more in keeping with what Chaucer would have intended: that the old man is no one in particular, or that he is a symbolic figure?

5. And finally, what does this tale suggest to you about the person who tells it? What does it add to the characterization of the Pardoner that Chaucer gives us in the Prologue?

"The Nun's Priest's Tale"

Although Chaucer does not describe the Nun's Priest in the Prologue, he must have been a charming and amusing companion. His tale of the Cock and the Fox is one of the most popular of beast fables; that is, a story in which the adventures of animals provide us with simple moral instruction. Like "The Pardoner's Tale," then, it is an *exemplum*, or illustration of a moral truth.

In the sequence of the pilgrims' tales it follows that of the Monk. The Monk's contribution has been so thoroughly gloomy (he recites a series of tragedies in which princes and kings fall to ruin) that he has been interrupted: the pilgrims are not amused and they will hear no more. The Host then calls on the Nun's Priest to "tell a tale to make our troubles pack." And so he does. He tells a moral tale, but he does so with a gaiety—a lightness of touch—that has made many readers call this the "most Chaucerian" of all the *Tales*; and the translation given here captures much of the tone of the original.

The Nun's Priest's Tale

Geoffrey Chaucer

Translated by Nevill Coghill

Once, long ago, there dwelt a poor old widow
In a small cottage by a little meadow
Beside a grove and standing in a dale.
This widow-woman, of whom I tell my tale,
Since the sad day when last she was a wife,   5
Had let a very patient, simple life.
Little she had in capital or rent,
But still by making do with what God sent
She kept herself and her two daughters going.
Three hefty sows—no more—were all her showing,   10
Three cows as well; there was a sheep called Molly.
    Sooty her hall,[1] her kitchen melancholy,
And there she ate full many a slender meal;
There was no *sauce piquante*[2] to spice her veal,
No dainty morsel ever passed her throat,   15
According to her cloth she cut her coat.
Repletion never left her in disquiet
And all her physic was a temperate diet,
Hard work for exercise and heart's content.
And rich man's gout[3] did nothing to prevent   20
Her dancing, apoplexy[4] struck her not;
She drank no wine, nor white nor red had got.
Her board was mostly served with white and black,
Milk and brown bread, in which she found no lack;
Broiled bacon or an egg or two were common,   25
She was in fact a sort of dairywoman.
    She had a yard that was enclosed about
By a stockade and a dry ditch without,
In which she kept a cock called Chanticleer.
In all the land for crowing he'd no peer;   30
His voice was jollier than the organ blowing

---

1 **hall:** A "hall" would be a combined living and dining room. This is an exaggerated word for a small cottage.
2 **sauce piquante:** French for pungent or sharp sauce.

3 **gout:** a painful disease of the joints, commonly thought to be caused by rich food and drink.
4 **apoplexy** (ăp'ə plĕk'sĭ): stroke; also thought to be caused by overindulgence.

"And every time a seed of corn was found / He gave a chuck, and up his wives ran all." The drawing of an everyday 14th-century scene is from the Luttrell Psalter.

In church on Sundays, he was great at crowing.
Far, far more regular than any clock
Or abbey bell the crowing of this cock.
The equinoctial wheel and its position[5]   35
At each ascent he knew by intuition;
At every hour—fifteen degrees of movement—
He crowed so well there could be no improvement.[6]
His comb was redder than fine coral, tall
And battlemented like a castle wall,   40
His bill was black and shone as bright as jet,
Like azure were his legs and they were set
On azure toes with nails of lily white,
Like burnished gold his feathers, flaming bright.
 This gentlecock was master in some measure   45
Of seven hens, all there to do his pleasure.
They were his sisters and his paramours,
Colored like him in all particulars;
She with the loveliest dyes upon her throat
Was known as gracious Lady Pertelote.   50
Courteous[7] she was, discreet and debonair,
Companionable too, and took such care
In her deportment, since she was seven days old
She held the heart of Chanticleer controlled,
Locked up securely in her every limb;   55
O such a happiness his love to him!

5 **equinoctial** (ē'kwə nŏk'shəl) . . . **position:** position of sun and stars.
6 **At every . . . improvement:** The sun moved through 15 degrees in an hour, by this calculation; Chanticleer was such a good timepiece that he crowed on the hour.

7 **Courteous:** To Chaucer this word meant much more than "polite"; it was applied to both knights and ladies who lived by the code of courtly love.

GEOFFREY CHAUCER

And such a joy it was to hear them sing,
As when the glorious sun began to spring,
In sweet accord "My Love is far from land"[8]
—For in those far-off days I understand   60
All birds and animals could speak and sing.
   Now it befell, as dawn began to spring,
When Chanticleer and Pertelote and all
His wives were perched in this poor widow's hall
(Fair Pertelote was next him on the perch),   65
This Chanticleer began to groan and lurch
Like someone sorely troubled by a dream,
And Pertelote who heard him roar and scream
Was quite aghast and said, "O dearest heart,
What's ailing you? Why do you groan and start?   70
Fie, what a sleeper! What a noise to make!"
"Madam," he said, "I beg you not to take
Offense, but by the Lord I had a dream
So terrible just now I had to scream;
I still can feel my heart racing from fear.   75
God turn my dream to good and guard all here,
And keep my body out of durance[9] vile!
I dreamt that roaming up and down a while
Within our yard I saw a kind of beast,
A sort of hound that tried, or seemed at least   80
To try and seize me—would have killed me dead!
His color was a blend of yellow and red,
His ears and tail were tipped with sable fur
Unlike the rest; he was a russet cur.
Small was his snout, his eyes were glowing bright.   85
It was enough to make one die of fright.
That was no doubt what made me groan and swoon."
   "For shame," she said, "you timorous poltroon!
Alas, what cowardice! By God above,
You've forfeited my heart and lost my love.   90
I cannot love a coward, come what may.
For certainly, whatever we may say,
All women long—and O that it might be!—
For husbands tough, dependable and free,
Secret, discreet, no niggard, not a fool   95
That boasts and then will find his courage cool
At every trifling thing. By God above,
How dare you say for shame, and to your love,
That anything at all was to be feared?
Have you no manly heart to match your beard?   100
And can a dream reduce you to such terror?

---

8 My . . . land: the first line of a popular song.   **9 durance** (dyŏŏr′əns): duress.

Dreams are a vanity, God knows, pure error.
Dreams are engendered in the too-replete
From vapors in the belly, which compete
With others, too abundant, swollen tight.   105
    "No doubt the redness in your dream tonight
Comes from the superfluity and force
Of the red choler in your blood. Of course.
That is what puts a dreamer in the dread
Of crimsoned arrows, fires flaming red,   110
Of great red monsters making as to fight him,
And big red whelps and little ones to bite him. . . ."

*[Pertelote continues learnedly to tell Chanticleer that his dream is just
"something he ate." Her main medical authority is an ancient author
named Dionysius Cato, who presumably argued that dreams arise
simply by fumes from a full stomach. But Chanticleer comes right
back at her. He knows about Cato too, but he knows many other authors on his side as well.]*

    "Madam," he said, "I thank you for your lore,
But with regard to Cato all the same,
His wisdom has, no doubt, a certain fame,   115
But though he said that we should take no heed
Of dreams, by God in ancient books I read
Of many a man of more authority
Than ever Cato was, believe you me,
Who say the very opposite is true   120
And prove their theories by experience too.
Dreams have quite often been significations
As well of triumphs as of tribulations
That people undergo in this our life. . . ."

*[Chanticleer now embarks on his learned argument to prove that
dreams do foretell real events that will happen. And he all but overwhelms Pertelote with a variety of authorities, from the Old Testament
to the* Iliad.]

    And with that word he flew down from the beams,   125
For it was day, and down his hens flew all,
And with a chuck he gave the troupe a call
For he had found a seed upon the floor.
Royal he was, he was afraid no more. . . .
Grim as a lion's was his manly frown   130
As on his toes he sauntered up and down;
He scarcely deigned to set his foot to ground
And every time a seed of corn was found
He gave a chuck, and up his wives ran all.

Thus royal as a prince who strides his hall   135
Leave we this Chanticleer engaged on feeding
And pass to the adventure that was breeding.
    Now when the month in which the world began,
March, the first month, when God created man,[10]
Was over, and the thirty-second day   140
Thereafter ended, on the third of May
It happened that Chanticleer in all his pride,
His seven wives attendant at his side,
Cast his eyes upward to the blazing sun,
Which in the sign of Taurus[11] then had run   145
His twenty-one degrees and somewhat more,
And knew by nature and no other lore
That it was nine o'clock. With blissful voice
He crew triumphantly and said, "Rejoice,
Behold the sun! The sun is up, my seven.   150
Look, it has climbed forty degrees in heaven,
Forty degrees and one in fact, by this,
Dear Madam Pertelote, my earthly bliss,
Hark to those blissful birds and how they sing!
Look at those pretty flowers, how they spring!   155
Solace and revel fill my heart!" He laughed.
    But in that moment Fate let fly her shaft;
Ever the latter end of joy is woe,
God knows that worldly joy is swift to go.
A rhetorician with a flair for style   160
Could chronicle this maxim in his file
Of Notable Remarks with safe conviction.
Then let the wise give ear; this is no fiction.
My story is as true, I undertake,
As that of good Sir Lancelot du Lake[12]   165
Who held all women in such high esteem.
Let me return full circle to my theme.
    A coal-tipped fox of sly iniquity
That had been lurking round the grove for three
Long years, that very night burst through and passed   170
Stockade and hedge, as Providence forecast,
Into the yard where Chanticleer the Fair
Was wont, with all his ladies, to repair.
Still, in a bed of cabbages, he lay
Until about the middle of the day,
Watching the cock and waiting for his cue,   175
As all these homicides[13] so gladly do

---

10 March . . . man: The creation of the world was believed to have occurred at the time of the vernal equinox, March 21.
11 sign of Taurus (tôr′əs): Taurus is the second sign of the zodiac (the Ram is first); the date by this calculation in "signs" and "degrees" would be May 3.
12 Sir Lancelot du Lake: from the Arthurian romances. (See pp. 70-77.)
13 homicides: murderers.

That lie about in wait to murder men.
A false assassin, lurking in thy den!
O new Iscariot, new Ganelon!
And O Greek Sinon,[14] thou whose treachery won   180
Troy town and brought it utterly to sorrow!
O Chanticleer, accursed be that morrow
That brought thee to the yard from thy high beams!
Thou hadst been warned, and truly, by thy dreams
That this would be a perilous day for thee.   185
    But that which God's foreknowledge can foresee
Must needs occur, as certain men of learning
Have said. Ask any scholar of discerning;
He'll say the Schools are filled with altercation
On this vexed matter of predestination[15]   190
Long bandied by a hundred thousand men.
How can I sift it to the bottom then? . . .

[Here the Nun's Priest, with a little sly satire on certain kinds of philo-sophical discussion, describes various learned attempts to understand predestination, "God's foreknowledge." And he even makes fun of the subject, or of pretenses to understand such a subject, by connecting it with the "foreknowledge" of Chanticleer's dream.]

    But I decline discussion of the matter;
My tale is of a cock and of the clatter
That came of following his wife's advice   195
To walk about his yard, on the precise
Morning after the dream of which I told.
    O women's counsel is so often cold!
A woman's counsel brought us first to woe,
Made Adam out of Paradise to go,   200
Where he had been so merry, so well at ease.
But, for I know not whom it may displease
If I suggest that women are to blame,
Pass over that; I only speak in game.
Read the authorities to know about   205
What has been said of women; you'll find out.
These are the cock's words, and not mine, I'm giving;
I think no harm of any woman living.
    Merrily in her dust-bath in the sand
Lay Pertelote. Her sisters were at hand   210
Basking in sunlight. Chanticleer sang free,

---

14 Iscariot (Ĭs kăr′Ĭ ət) . . . **Ganelon** . . . **Sinon:**
Judas Iscariot betrayed Jesus; Ganelon betrayed
Roland to the Saracens (in the *Song of Roland*);
and Sinon persuaded the Trojans to let the wooden
horse of the Greeks inside the walls of Troy.

15. predestination: theory that God has foreor-dained all events.

An English miniature from an early 14th-century papal epistle that gave instructions to the clergy. The illustrations done in the margins use animal figures to enforce the serious message of the text.

More merrily than a mermaid in the sea
(For *Physiologus*[16] reports the thing
And says how well and merrily they sing).
And so it happened as he cast his eye   215
Towards the cabbage at a butterfly,
It fell upon the fox there, lying low.
Gone was all inclination then to crow.
"Cok cok," he cried, giving a sudden start,
As one who feels a terror at his heart,   220
For natural instinct teaches beasts to flee
The moment they perceive an enemy,
Though they had never met with it before.
    This Chanticleer was shaken to the core
And would have fled. The fox was quick to say   225
However, "Sir! Whither so fast away?
Are you afraid of me that am your friend?
A fiend, or worse, I should be, to intend
Your harm, or practice villainy upon you.
Dear sir, I was not even spying on you!   230
Truly I came to do no other thing
Than just to lie and listen to you sing.
You have as merry a voice as God has given
To any angel in the courts of Heaven;
To that you add a musical sense as strong   235
As had Boethius,[17] who was skilled in song.
My Lord your Father (God receive his soul!),
Your mother too—how courtly, what control!—

---

16 *Physiologus:* The **Physiologus,** or Latin "Bestiary," was an encyclopedia about animals, real and imaginary; what it "reports" about the singing of mermaids is an example of its lore.

17 **Boethius** (bō ē′thĭ əs): Among the many works of Boethius, a great medieval philosopher, was a treatise on music.

Have honored my poor house, to my great ease;
And you, sir, too, I should be glad to please.   240
For, when it comes to singing, I'll say this
(Else may these eyes of mine be barred from bliss),
There never was a singer I would rather
Have heard at dawn than your respected father.
All that he sang came welling from his soul,   245
And how he put his voice under control!
The pains he took to keep his eyes tight shut
In concentration—then the tiptoe strut,
The slender neck stretched out, the delicate beak!
No singer could approach him in technique   250
Or rival him in song, still less surpass. . . .
Can you not emulate your sire and sing?"
    This Chanticleer began to beat a wing
As one incapable of smelling treason,
So wholly had this flattery ravished reason.   255
Alas, my lords! there's many a sycophant
And flatterer that fill your courts with cant
And give more pleasure with their zeal forsooth
Than he who speaks in soberness and truth.
Read what Ecclesiasticus[18] records   260
Of flatterers. 'Ware treachery, my lords!
    This Chanticleer stood high upon his toes,
He stretched his neck, his eyes began to close,
His beak to open; with his eyes shut tight
He then began to sing with all his might.   265
    Sir Russel[19] Fox then leapt to the attack,
Grabbing his gorge he flung him o'er his back
And off he bore him to the woods, the brute,
And for the moment there was no pursuit.
    O Destiny that may not be evaded!   270
Alas that Chanticleer had so paraded!
Alas that he had flown down from the beams!
O that his wife took no account of dreams!
And on a Friday,[20] too, to risk their necks!
O Venus, goddess of the joys of sex,   275
Since Chanticleer thy mysteries professed,
And in thy service always did his best,
And more for pleasure than to multiply
His kind, on thine own day is he to die?

---

18 Ecclesiasticus: a book of proverbs; now found
in the Protestant Apocrypha and the Douay Version of the Bible. Not a reference to Ecclesiastes
in the Old Testament.
19 Russel: Reynard is the usual name for the fox,
but this name suggests his color, from the Latin
word *russus*, "red."

20 Friday: the day of the Roman goddess Venus
(the French name for the day is *vendredi*); in
Germanic languages this is the day of the goddess Frigg, or Freya. Venus is the goddess of love,
and, like a courtly lover, Chanticleer is her servant.

GEOFFREY CHAUCER

"Sir Russel Fox then leapt to the attack. . . ." The fox and the cock were familiar decorations in medieval manuscripts.

O Geoffrey,[21] thou my dear and sovereign master   280
Who, when they brought King Richard to disaster
And shot him dead, lamented so his death,
Would that I had thy skill, thy gracious breath,
To chide a Friday half so well as you!   285
(For he was killed upon a Friday too.)
Then I could fashion you a rhapsody
For Chanticleer in dread and agony.
    Sure never such a cry or lamentation
Was made by ladies of high Trojan station,   290
When Ilium fell and Pyrrhus with his sword
Grabbed Priam by the beard, their king, and lord,
And slew him there, as the *Aeneid* tells,[22]
As what was uttered by those hens. Their yells
Surpassed them all in palpitating fear   295
When they beheld the rape of Chanticleer.
Dame Pertelote emitted sovereign shrieks
That echoed up in anguish to the peaks
Louder than those extorted from the wife
Of Hasdrubal[23] when he had lost his life   300
And Carthage all in flame and ashes lay.
She was so full of torment and dismay
That in the very flames she chose her part
And burnt to ashes with a steadfast heart.

21 **Geoffrey:** Geoffrey of Vinsauf, a 12th-century poet and writer on the art of rhetoric, wrote an elegy on the death of Richard the Lion-Hearted, who was killed on a Friday. Chaucer is not really serious in his praise of Geoffrey's "skill and gracious breath," for much of the exaggerated style of this tale is a parody of such rhetoric

22 **Sure . . . *Aeneid* tells:** The Roman poet Virgil, in his *Aeneid*, tells of the fall of Troy (or "Ilium") and of the death of the Trojan King Priam at the hands of Achilles's son Pyrrhus.

23 **Hasdrubal** (häz′drŏŏ bəl)**:** Carthaginian general and ruler, who was killed when Carthage was destroyed by the Romans in 146 B.C.

O woeful hens, louder your shrieks and higher
Than those of Roman matrons when the fire.   305
Consumed their husbands, senators of Rome,
When Nero burnt their city and their home,[24]
Beyond a doubt that Nero was their bale![25]
    Now let me turn again to tell my tale;
This blessed widow and her daughters two   310
Heard all these hens in clamor and halloo
And, rushing to the door at all this shrieking,
They saw the fox towards the covert streaking
And, on his shoulder, Chanticleer stretched flat.
"Look, look!" they cried. "O mercy, look at that!   315
Ha! Ha! the fox!" and after him they ran,
And stick in hand ran many a serving man,
Ran Coll our dog, ran Talbot, Bran and Shaggy,
And with a distaff in her hand ran Maggie,
Ran cow and calf and ran the very hogs   320
In terror at the barking of the dogs;
The men and women shouted, ran and cursed,
They ran so hard they thought their hearts would burst,
They yelled like fiends in Hell, ducks left the water
Quacking and flapping as on point of slaughter,   325
Up flew the geese in terror over the trees,
Out of the hive came forth the swarm of bees;
So hideous was the noise—God bless us all,
Jack Straw[26] and all his followers in their brawl
Were never half so shrill, for all their noise,   330
When they were murdering those Flemish[27] boys,
As that day's hue and cry upon the fox.
They grabbed up trumpets made of brass and box,
Of horn and bone, on which they blew and pooped,
And therewithal they shouted and they whooped   335
So that it seemed the very heavens would fall.
    And now, good people, pay attention all.
See how Dame Fortune quickly changes side
And robs her enemy of hope and pride!
This cock that lay upon the fox's back,   340
In all his dread contrived to give a quack
And said, "Sir Fox, if I were you, as God's
My witness, I would round upon these clods
And shout, 'Turn back, you saucy bumpkins all!
A very pestilence upon you fall!   345

---

24 **those of Roman . . . home:** Nero, a Roman emperor, according to legend, set fire to Rome and had many senators put to death.
25 **their bale:** the cause of their sorrow.
26 **Jack Straw:** one of the leaders of the Peasants' Revolt in 1381.

27 **Flemish:** The Flemish were the enemies of the peasants because they competed against native workers in the woolen industry and because the industry itself encouraged landowners to turn their fields into pasturage for sheep, thus impoverishing general farm workers.

GEOFFREY CHAUCER

Now that I have in safety reached the wood
Do what you like, the cock is mine for good;
I'll eat him there in spite of everyone.' "
    The fox replying, "Faith, it shall be done!"
Opened his mouth and spoke. The nimble bird,   350
Breaking away upon the uttered word,
Flew high into the treetops on the spot.
And when the fox perceived where he had got,
"Alas," he cried, "alas, my Chanticleer,
I've done you grievous wrong, indeed I fear   355
I must have frightened you; I grabbed too hard
When I caught hold and took you from the yard.
But, sir, I meant no harm, don't be offended,
Come down and I'll explain what I intended;
So help me God, I'll tell the truth—on oath!"   360
"No," said the cock, "and curses on us both,
And first on me if I were such a dunce
As let you fool me oftener than once.
Never again, for all your flattering lies,
You'll coax a song to make me blink my eyes;   365
And as for those who blink when they should look,
God blot them from his everlasting Book!"
"Nay, rather," said the fox, "his plagues be flung
On all who chatter that should hold their tongue."
    Lo, such it is not to be on your guard   370
Against the flatterers of the world, or yard,
And if you think my story is absurd
A foolish trifle of a beast and bird,
A fable of a fox, a cock, a hen,
Take hold upon the moral, gentlemen.   375
    Saint Paul himself, a saint of great discerning,
Says that all things are written for our learning;
So take the grain and let the chaff be still.
And, gracious Father, if it be thy will
As saith my Saviour, make us all good men,   380
And bring us to his heavenly bliss. Amen.

Comment

The humor of this tale begins almost at once, with the contrast between the modest circumstances of the widow and the elaborate, courtly airs (not to mention the enormous learning) of her rooster and his favorite hen. It continues in the learned and courtly description of Chanticleer strolling in the May morning with his troupe. Even the Fox is compared to the worst traitors in all literature. In other words, the tale is in a mock-heroic style: it mocks or makes fun of the pretentiousness of Chanticleer's thoughts and behavior, which, after all, occur in a most inelegant and modest barnyard, by describing them in language that reminds us of great characters in ancient and chivalric literature. The tale gently mocks self-importance by exaggerating it, and so reminds us of pretentiousness and self-importance in general.

1. What contrast, like that between the widow's modest cottage and Chanticleer's courtly finery, do you find in the extended description of what happens after Chanticleer is caught by the Fox? (For example, the narrator says that the noise of "lamentation" was like that at the fall of "Ilium." But what really happened?) Point out particular contrasting details.
2. How has Chanticleer been caught? What "treachery" has fooled him?
3. But how does Chanticleer escape? What kind of speech, what kind of gesture to the pursuing crowd, does he persuade the Fox to make?
4. At the end, the narrator—the Nun's Priest—asks us to "take the grain and let the chaff be still." What seems to you the real "grain" of this tale? And what seems to you its "chaff"?
5. But if you leave the "chaff" alone, if you ignore it, what happens to the fun and entertainment of this tale? *Can* you let the "chaff" go?

The Middle Ages
Summing Up

As you look back from this tale to some of the medieval writings you have read, can you see how Chaucer's art sums up and pulls together some of the characteristics of the literature that preceded and surrounded him?

1. Does "The Nun's Priest's Tale" reflect any of the elements of the ballad, of the traditions of popular literature? Be as specific as you can.
2. Does it reflect any of the elements of the courtly tradition—of the romance as retold by Malory? Again, be specific.
3. What has Chaucer added to these two traditions of early literature? If "The Nun's Priest's Tale" is really Chaucerian, then what are Chaucer's most important characteristics?

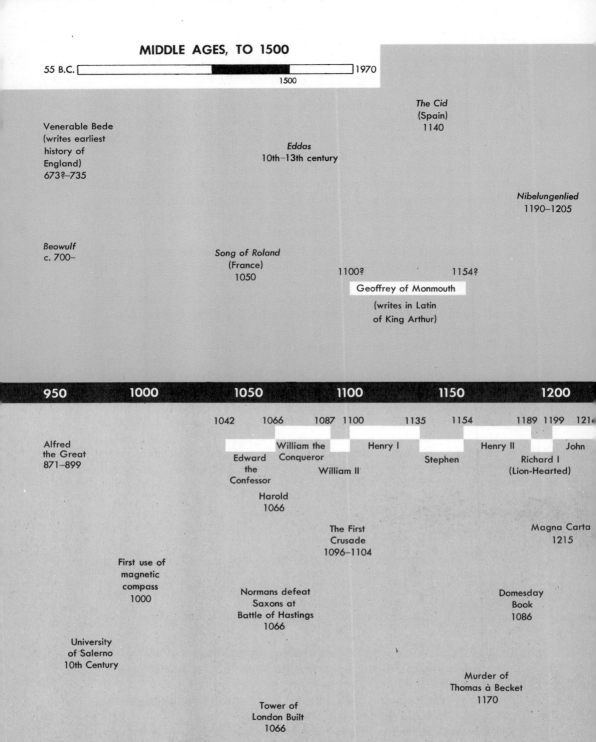

MIDDLE AGES, TO 1500

55 B.C. ━━━━━━━━━━━━━━━━━━━ 1970
                    1500

The Cid
(Spain)
1140

Venerable Bede
(writes earliest
history of
England)
673?–735

Eddas
10th–13th century

Nibelungenlied
1190–1205

Beowulf
c. 700–

Song of Roland
(France)
1050

1100?   1154?

Geoffrey of Monmouth

(writes in Latin
of King Arthur)

950	1000	1050	1100	1150	1200

1042   1066   1087 1100   1135   1154   1189 1199 121

Alfred
the Great
871–899

Edward
the
Confessor

William the
Conqueror

William II

Henry I

Stephen

Henry II

Richard I
(Lion-Hearted)

John

Harold
1066

The First
Crusade
1096–1104

Magna Carta
1215

First use of
magnetic
compass
1000

Normans defeat
Saxons at
Battle of Hastings
1066

Domesday
Book
1086

University
of Salerno
10th Century

Murder of
Thomas à Becket
1170

Tower of
London Built
1066

Boccaccio
(Italy)
1313–1375

First English
translation of Bible
1380's

Petrarch
(Italy)
1304–1374

Everyman
c. 1485

Langland writes
Piers Plowman
1362

Thomas Malory's
Morte Darthur
c. 1471

Guilds present
cycles of
miracle plays
1300–1450

*Sir Gawain
and the
Green Knight*
1370

William Caxton
sets up first
English
printing press
1476

1340?   1400
Geoffrey Chaucer

Dante (Italy);
Divine Comedy
1300–1319

1250	1300	1350	1400	1450	1500

1272   1307   1327   1377   1399 1413 1422   1461   1483 1485

Edward I   Edward III   Henry   Henry VI
Henry III   IV
          Edward II   Richard II   Henry   Edward   Richard
                                                            V   IV   III

                                                                              Edward V
                                                                              1483

Marco Polo
at the Court
of Kublai Khan
1275

First epidemic
of Black Death
1348–1350

Joan of Arc
1412?–1431

Parliaments
developed
in Eng., Fr., & Sp.
c. 1250

Peasants' Revolt
1381

War of the Roses
1455–1485

First Oxford
college
founded
1249

1338   Hundred Years' War   1453

First Cambridge
college founded
1284

Johann Gutenberg
(German printer;
invents movable type)
1398?–1468

Columbus
discovers
America
1492

Battle of
Agincourt
1415

117

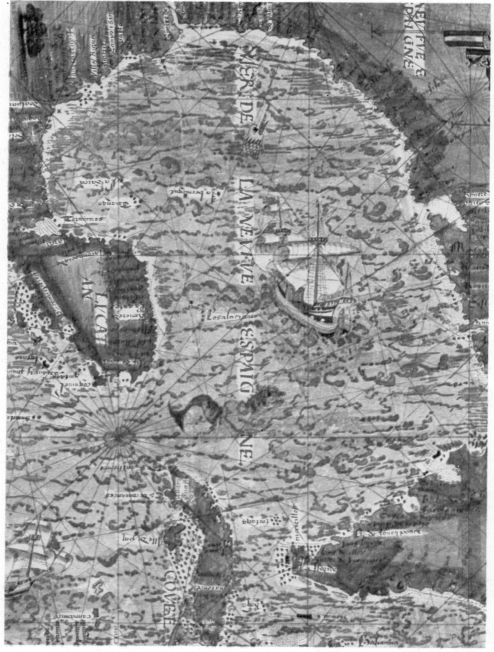

*A map of part of the New World—Florida, Cuba, Yucatan, and present-day Mexico—
by the French cartographer and navigator Guillaume Le Testu (1509–1572).*

1485-1660

The Renaissance

"*. . . imagination bodies forth*
The forms of things unknown. . . ."

WILLIAM SHAKESPEARE

THE WORD *Renaissance* did not come into general use until the 1840's, almost four hundred years after the beginning of the period to which it refers. Certainly so much happened between 1485 and 1660 in Britain and Europe that several centuries were required to understand it all. The word *Renaissance* means a rebirth, a reawakening; and historians have used it particularly to describe how the artists and scholars of Europe, starting in Italy in the 14th century, were reawakened to the literature and art of Greece and Rome. Yet the whole period of the Renaissance was more than a *re*birth. It was the period when new adventures began for all humankind—explorations by ship across uncharted seas and by telescope into remote heavens. And, most important for our concern, it was the period when there began new explorations by literature into the human mind and heart. "Imagination bodies forth/The forms of things unknown," wrote Shakespeare. Unknown lands and seas and heavens were opened up by the explorers and scientists. Yet greater unknowns were unlocked and given form by the imaginations of Renaissance writers.

Henry VIII's departure for the Field of Cloth of Gold to meet with Francis I of France in 1520—a conference marked by much pomp and splendor. The reign of Henry VIII saw the beginnings of the English navy.

The Writer's Language

The Language

WITH THE RENAISSANCE we come to a literature of books. Not that song, the drama, even the popular ballad—all the literature dependent upon the spoken word—ceased. Far from it. Rather, the Renaissance, at least in literature, is the time when readers and writers, poets and listeners, discover the power of the book. Writing, for some, becomes a full-time occupation, although many writers are still amateurs. And reading becomes an avenue to the most powerful ideas human beings are capable of. The book, too, begins to have its effect on literature and language by fixing in its print the spelling and the very shape of the words that writers use. Caxton, the first English printer and the printer of Malory, established his readers' expectations of how English should *look*. Caxton's spelling was, of course, to change, but it would change less than Chaucer's.

The conventions of printing, however, have concealed from us a long, slow process of change in the sound of the spoken language, a change in the sounds of vowels. In the Middle English word *name* the

Courtesy of the Honorable Simon Wingfield-Digby, M.P.

Queen Elizabeth in one of her many public appearances. She helped keep her great popularity by such progresses, or trips out among the people, as well as by the long periods of peace and plenty during her reign.

a was pronounced like the *a* of modern *father*, you recall; but by the early 17th century it was pronounced very much as we pronounce it now. (The final *-e* in Chaucer had become silent altogether.) The shift, from *ä* to *ā* in the example cited, occurred in a corresponding way for a number of the most important vowels and diphthongs (combinations of two vowels such as *ou* in *house*) of English and was virtually complete by about 1660.

At the same time the written language was subjected to another "invasion" from the continent, only this time an invasion of words, not of men. The Renaissance in Europe was first of all a renaissance, or rebirth, of learning. Scholars, especially Italian scholars, rediscovered the manuscripts of forgotten literatures: the plays and love poems of the Romans, the epic poetry of Homer, and the philosophical prose of Plato. And as these works made their way into Britain, along with scholarly commentaries upon them, the language of educated writers was greatly enriched by new terms, especially terms from the Latin. In everyday speech we may say *friendly* rather than *amicable*, or *happiness* rather than *felicity*. But for a writer on manners, say, the distinction between *friendly* and *amicable* behavior can be important. Or for a writer who is discussing philosophically the nature of the good life, *felicity* may connote a more dignified condition of mind than does *happiness*. The invasion of Latin words in the Renais-

The ruins of the church of Glastonbury Abbey, one of the monasteries dissolved by Henry VIII.

Lon McKee

sance thus tended to increase the distance between spoken and written English.

Latin, indeed, in the Renaissance replaced French as the great external modifying influence on English. It did much to standardize spelling: Chaucer, for example, writes *peynture*, from the French; but Shakespeare wrote *picture*, from the Latin. It gave us the adjectival forms of many English words: the adjective related to the English word *mind* is the Latin word *mental;* the adjective related to the English word *moon* is sometimes *moony,* but of course it is usually the Latin *lunar.*

Latin introduced some problems too, for it came to be regarded as a standard of grammatical correctness, even though, unlike English, it is a highly inflected language. There is, for example, the matter of ending a sentence with a preposition. This is a practice that makes many people who are proud of their correctness of speech wonder what the English language is coming to. Or perhaps they would rather wonder to what the English language is coming! The trouble is that the rule is based on the grammar of Latin, not of English. The Latin preposition is always close to its noun: in the phrase *magna cum celeritate* the preposition is the word *cum,* and the phrase means "with great speed." But if we followed the Latin exactly, we should have to say "great with speed." In Latin we must write *homo cui liberum dedi* ("the man to whom I gave the book"), because the "to whom" is contained in the single inflected word *cui.* It is simply impossible in Latin to say "the man I gave the book to," but there is nothing in the nature of English that makes it incorrect. For better or worse, such standards of correctness have come from the fact that

British Travel and Holidays Association

Compton Wynyates, a country home built in early Tudor times. During the long period of peace after the Wars of the Roses, wealthy men built many such impressive country seats, houses not designed for defense in time of war.

for hundreds of years generations of British schoolboys have been trained in the translating and the composing of Latin.

At the same time, however, the written English of the Renaissance continued to free itself of some awkward rules and practices. Chaucer writes "Whan that Aprill," and his *that* is a survival of the Old English conjunction *þæt*, which reinforces *Whan*. But Shakespeare begins one of his most famous sonnets with the simple *When:* "When, in disgrace with Fortune and men's eyes." And such a simplification, once more, can be traced to the emphatic stress of English. *Whan that* was pronounced as almost one word, with the stress on the first syllable—*Whánthat,* and by Shakespeare's time only the stressed *When* was left. The unstressed and unnecessary elements of words slowly disappeared. Chaucer's final *-e* marks the disappearance of the inflection of Old English grammar under the pressure of the native stress. And the disappearance of the final *-e* from Shakespeare's language shows us its continuing adaptability.

Despite the introduction of the new learning, then, the English language of the Renaissance was a supple, muscular, vigorous instrument. It was a language for writing sentences like the following one, which comes from a story in which a man has for many days and many miles been pursuing a bandit who has wronged him. The speaker, the hero, catches up with his foe in a town in Italy; he sees a crowd in the streets, asks who is at the center of it, and hears the name of the man he has been looking for. The very name of his enemy exhilarates him:

LANGUAGE

123

National Portrait Gallery, London

Sir Philip Sidney—poet, scholar, courtier, diplomat, and soldier—was thought by many to be the ideal Elizabethan gentleman.

The Louvre, Paris

Charles I, King from 1625 until his execution in 1649 at the end of the Civil War, which was the climax of the struggle between King and Parliament.

. . . answer was returned mee it was that notable Bandetto, Esdras of Granada. O so I was tickled in the spleene with that word, my heart hopt and daunst, my elbowes itcht, my fingers friskt, I wist[1] not what should become of my feete, nor knew what I did for joy.

This is a muscular language indeed!

The Writer

For the future of this energetic language the hopes of the Renaissance writer were high. Here is what one of them wrote on the subject of eloquence, the commanding power of words:

And who, in time, knows whither we may vent[1]
   The treasure of our tongue, to what strange shores
This gain of our best glory shall be sent
   To enrich unknowing nations with our stores?
What worlds in the yet unformed occident[2]
   May come[3] refined with accents that are ours?

1 wist: knew.   **1 vent:** send forth.   **2 occident:** the West.   **3 come:** become.

THE RENAISSANCE

Swans on the River Avon, at Stratford, where Shakespeare was born. Ben Jonson wrote of Shakespeare, "Sweet swan of Avon, what a sight it were / To see thee in our waters yet appear. . . ."

We, of course, know the answer that history gave to these questions, and we shall shortly see the answer to another question this poet went on to ask:

> Or who can tell for what great work in hand[4]
> The greatness of our style is now ordained?

The answer to this question is given in at least one great work, more than worthy of the greatness of Renaissance English, Shakespeare's *Macbeth*.

The high hopes and ambitions of those who used this language can perhaps best be seen in what they themselves said about writing, about books and poetry. Here are three famous Renaissance definitions of the power of the poet and his books:

> Nature never set forth the earth in so rich tapestry as divers poets have done—neither with so pleasant rivers, fruitful trees, sweet-smelling flowers, nor whatsoever else may make the too-much-loved earth more lovely. Her world is brazen; the poets only deliver a golden. SIR PHILIP SIDNEY

4 in hand: at home.

Poetry is a divine instinct and unnatural rage passing the reach
of common reason.

EDMUND SPENSER

For books are not absolutely dead things, but do contain a po-
tency of life in them to be as active as that soul was whose progeny they are; nay, they do preserve as in a vial the purest efficacy and extraction[1] of that living intellect that bred them.   I
know they are as lively and as vigorously productive as those
fabulous dragon's teeth, and being sown up and down may
chance to spring up armed men.[2]   And yet, on the other hand,
unless wariness be used, as good almost kill a man as kill a good
book: who kills a man kills a reasonable creature, God's image;
but he who destroys a good book kills reason itself, kills the image of God, as it were, in the eye.   Many a man lives a burden to
the earth; but a good book is the precious lifeblood of a master
spirit, embalmed and treasured up on purpose to a life beyond
life.

JOHN MILTON

The People and Their Times

THE GREATEST ACHIEVEMENTS of the Renaissance outdistanced the reach
of all but the most powerful imaginations.   The sailors and explorers
of England followed in the track of Columbus, and they made new
routes of their own to the New World.   And the "natural philosophers,"
or scientists, of Renaissance England followed the intellectual paths of
the new astronomers, Copernicus and Galileo, who charted new maps
of the heavens. One Englishman, a physician named William Harvey,
in 1616 made a new chart of the human body when he discovered the
circulation of the blood and showed that the heart is a pump that
keeps the circulation going.   The whole world, from the human heart
to the very stars, was seen anew.   But for some people this re-seeing
was not easy.   And for some it never happened at all.

The World of Knowledge

Old Science   For most people the world—what we call the universe had a shape and a structure that had been worked out long be-

---

1 **efficacy and extraction:** essential power.
2 **those fabulous . . . men:** a reference to a legend told of two Greek heroes. Each of
them sowed dragon's teeth in a field, and armed men sprang up who then turned on the
hero.

fore. Here is a picture of that world as outlined by a "Scholar" who is repeating a lesson to the teacher:

THE WORLD

SCHOLAR: This is the sum of all your doctrine[1] hitherto.

1. That the world is that entire body which containeth in it all the heavens and the elements, with all that in them is.

2. The parts of the world are two especial, the heavens which are eight in number, and the elements which are four in kind.

3. The order and situation of all these parts, as well elements as heavenly spheres, beginning at the highest, and proceeding to the lowest, is this: the Firmament, Saturn, Jupiter, Mars, the Sun, Venus, Mercury, and the Moon.

Fire, Air, Water, and Earth and ever the higher encloseth all that is under it.

4. The world and all his principal parts are round in form and shape, as a globe or ball.

5. The earth is in the middle of the world, as the center of it, and beareth no view of quantity in comparison to the world.[2]

6. The earth hath no motion of itself, no more than a stone, but resteth quietly; and so the other elements do, except they be forcibly moved.

7. The heavens do move continually from the east to the west, and that motion is called the daily motion, and is the measure of the common day.

8. The Moon hath a several[3] motion from the west toward the east, contrary to that moving of the daily course,[4] and that motion is the just measure of a month, and every quarter doth make a week.

9. The Sun also hath a peculiar motion from the west toward the east, which he accomplisheth in a year, and of that course the year taketh his measure and quantity.

This outline of the heavens, the planets, and the four elements comes from a popular textbook entitled *The Castle of Knowledge*. It was published in 1556, the first textbook on astronomy in English, and it summed up the world-picture of most people of the time. Yet in 1530 Copernicus had shown that the earth and the planets revolve around the sun, and that the earth itself turns on its own axis. In a few years Galileo was to demonstrate the proof of Copernicus's findings, by observations with his telescope and by calculations in his new mathematics. Mathematics, in fact, was soon to become the chief instrument in the recharting of our knowledge of the earth and humankind.

1 **doctrine:** teaching.
2 **beareth no . . . world:** is of an insignificant size (or "quantity") in comparison with the rest of the world.
3 **several:** separate.
4 **daily course:** i.e., the daily course of the heavens from east to west.

Old Science and New   The differences between the old science and the new appear in the following two descriptions of what happens when we move our bodies.   They were written just thirty years apart, in 1621 and 1651, but the differences between them would take many more years than that to reconcile.

I

Moving from place to place is a faculty . . . [by which] we locally move the body, or any part of it, and go from one place to another.   To the better performance of which, three things are requisite: that which moves; by what it moves; that which is moved.   That which moves is either the efficient cause, or end. The end is the object which is desired or eschewed, as in a dog to catch a hare, etc.   The efficient cause in man is reason, or his subordinate, fantasy, which apprehends good or bad objects. . . .   This faculty . . . by an admirable league of nature, and by mediation of the spirits,[1] commands the organ by which it moves; and that consists of nerves, muscles, cords, dispersed through the whole body, contracted and relaxed as the spirits will, which move the muscles or nerves in the midst of them, and draw the cord, and so . . . the joint, to the place intended. That which is moved is the body or some member apt to move. The motion of the body is divers, as going, running, leaping, dancing.

II

[The College of Physicians in London, a learned society of men, has] gone far toward the explication of the reasons and the manner of the motions of the muscles, by the principles of Mechanics:[2] an enterprise of great difficulty, and long desiderated, as leading us to understand the Geometry observed by the Creator in the fabric[3] [of man], and the verification of anatomical assertions by demonstrations mathematical.[4]   The same persons likewise have demonstrated, that we go, because we fall; that is, that each step we advance, is but a shifting the body to a fresh center of gravity; and our rest but a remaining or fixing of it upon the same: as also that in progression, the head of a man is moved through more of space, than his feet, by almost one part of four, in respect of[5] its greater distance from the center of the earth; which indeed was touched, and only touched upon, by that prodigy of the mathematical subtleties, Galileo.

---

1 the spirits: The "spirits" were thought to be an extremely fine and fluid substance in the body, intermediate between the finest "material" substance of the body—the blood, the nerves—and the "immaterial" part of the body that begins with the "fantasy" or imagination. The "spirits" are a kind of go-between connecting mind and body.
2 Mechanics: Our word would be *physics*. Here, the principles of physics are being applied to the study of anatomy ("anatomical assertions").
3 fabric: construction.
4 demonstrations mathematical: proofs as clear and as fixed as proofs of geometry.
5 in respect of: because of.

The first passage comes from one of the most fascinating books ever written, *The Anatomy of Melancholy,* by Robert Burton. It is a survey of human psychology—the organization of the mind and its faculties— as understood in the Renaissance; and it analyzes the disease of "melancholy" or extreme depression. The second passage comes from a book by a famous 17th-century physician, a man named Walter Charleton; and it is spoken to a group of French scientists by a visiting Englishman. "Our men are masters of the new science too," he says. And this science, with its emphasis on mathematics and physics, is far different from Robert Burton's talk of a "faculty" of motion. The old and the new here could not but live uneasily together.

Old Wonders and New Facts Again, the travelers and the explorers of Renaissance England visited remote parts of the globe. Sometimes they saw fresh wonders. But sometimes they saw, or thought they saw, wonders as old as literature: they saw what was already in their minds. Here are excerpts from the reports of two travelers. The first (named Fynes Moryson) visited the Holy Land and the Near East in the 1590's. The second, Sir Walter Raleigh, sent expeditions to North America in the 1580's to claim land in the name of Elizabeth, the Virgin Queen. (He claimed a good deal more than Virginia—the whole coast from Florida to Newfoundland!) And in the 1590's he sailed to the South American coast in search of gold. (He did not find gold there, but popularly associated with his name is the introduction to England of two American commodities more precious than gold to the Englishman—the potato and tobacco.) The second excerpt describes a river in what became British Guiana.

THE PHOENIX

Happy Arabia lies almost in the form of a chersonese or neck of land, between the two great gulfs of the sea, the Arabian Gulf and the Persian, and it yields cinnamon, frankincense, myrrh, the gum ladanum, and other precious odors,[1] and abounds with honey, wax, and all kinds of cattle, excepting swine only. It is said that grains of gold as big as acorns are found here among the clods of the earth. It hath the bird phoenix, of which kind there is never more than one only, which by striking of stones together, kindles a fire and burns herself in her nest of myrrh, and of the ashes comes a worm, which becomes a bird, and so the phoenix lives again. They fish pearls in the Arabian Gulf, and jewels are found upon the seashore.

THE LAGARTOS

On both sides of this river we passed the most beautiful country that ever mine eyes beheld; and whereas all that we had seen before was nothing but woods, prickles, bushes, and thorns, here we beheld plains of twenty miles in length, the grass short and

---

[1] **precious odors:** precious perfumes. The spices frankincense and myrrh were traditionally precious; they were brought by the three kings to Jesus's manger.

green, and in divers parts groves of trees by themselves, as if
they had been all the art and labor in the world so made of purpose; and still as we rowed, the deer came down feeding by the
water's side, as if they had been used to a keeper's call. Upon
this river there were great store[2] of fowl, and of many sorts; we
saw in it divers sorts of strange fishes, and of marvelous bigness;
but for lagartos it exceeded,[3] for there were thousands of those
ugly serpents; and the people call it, for the abundance of them,
the River of Lagartos, in their language. I had a Negro, a very
proper young fellow, who, leaping out of the galley[4] to swim in
the mouth of this river, was in all our sights taken and devoured
with one of those lagartos.

The phoenix of Arabia is the fabulous bird, first described by the
ancient Greeks, that has been a symbol in many poems of European
literature. Every five hundred years, the legend goes, the phoenix con-
sumes itself in a fire and then rises miraculously from its own ashes.
The phoenix is indeed a symbol of renaissance, or "rebirth." And in
Arabia, Moryson believed, the fabulous, the symbol, is a fact. But
what of the "lagartos" that Raleigh so carefully observed? Is not this
"ugly serpent" just as arresting as a fabulous legend of literature? Is
not an alligator a strange creature?

The World of Society

Ideal Leaders and Real People But what of the rulers of this expand-
ing new world? What should their training be? What should they
know? How should they conduct themselves? Here is one answer,
taken from *The Courtier*, published in 1561, and much read in the early
Renaissance. It is a translation by an English courtier, Sir Thomas
Hoby, from an earlier work by an Italian nobleman.

THE CHIEF CONDITIONS AND QUALITIES IN A COURTIER

To be well born and of a good stock.
To be of a mean stature, rather with the least than too high,[1]
and well made to his proportion. . . .
Not to praise himself unshamefully and out of reason. . . .
Not to carry about tales and trifling news. . . .
To be well spoken and fair languaged. . . .
To be seen[2] in tongues, and especially in Italian, French, and
Spanish. . . .

2 **store:** abundance.
3 **but . . . exceeded:** but it was excessively full of lagartos. The word comes from the
Spanish for "lizard," *al lagarto*. Do you hear the word it sounds like?
4 **galley:** rowboat.

1 **rather with the least:** rather too short than too tall.
2 **to be seen in:** to be expert in.

To fellowship himself for the most part with men of the best sort and of most estimation, and with his equals, so he be also beloved of his inferiors.

To play for his pastime at dice and cards, not wholly for money's sake, nor fume and chafe in his loss. . . .

To be handsome and cleanly in his apparel. . . .

To be brought to show his feats and qualities at the desire and request of others, and not rashly press to it of himself. . . .

To swim well.
To leap well.
To run well.
To vault well.
To wrestle well.
To cast the stone well.
To cast the bar well.

Seldom in open sight of the people but privily with himself alone, or among his friends and familiars.

* * *

To endeavor himself to love, please and obey his Prince in honesty. . . .

Not to love promotions so, that a man should think he could not live without them; nor unshamefastly[3] to beg any office.[4] . . .

His love toward women not to be sensual or fleshly, but honest and godly, and more ruled with reason than appetite; and to love better the beauty of the mind than of the body.

The Chief Conditions and Qualities in a Waiting Gentlewoman

To be well born and of a good house. . . .

To be witty and foreseeing, not heady and of a running wit.[5]

Not to be haughty, envious, ill-tongued, light, contentious, nor untowardly. . . .

To take heed that she give none occasion to be ill reported of. . . .

To have the understanding, being married, how to order her husband's substance,[6] her house and children, and to play the good housewife. . . .

Not willingly to give ear to such as report ill of other women. . . .

To come to dance, or to show her music, with suffering herself to be first prayed somewhat and drawn to it. . . .

To be learned.
To be seen in the most necessary languages.
To draw and paint.
To dance.
To devise sports and pastimes. . . .

To shape him that is oversaucy with her, or that hath small respect in his talk, such an answer that he may well understand she is offended with him. . . .

---

3 **shamefastly:** shamelessly.
4 **office:** An "office" is a position at court, such as the one Chaucer filled as Esquire of the Royal Household.
5 **not heady and of a running wit:** not impetuous and hasty.
6 **substance:** property.

To be heedful and remember that men may with less jeopardy show to be in love than women. . . .

To love one that she may marry withal,[7] being a maiden and minding to love. . . .

To make herself beloved for her deserts, amiableness, and good grace . . . with virtue and honest conditions.

The shaping of character and manners upon such models as these might well produce an admirable race of superior people. But not all Englishmen thought so. What does the courtier *do*? What is his trade? Can he really manage the affairs of a growing kingdom?

Here is one dissenting opinion, published in 1616, by Thomas Overbury, a man who had good reasons to dislike courtiers, for he died in prison as the result of the plotting of one.

A COURTIER

To all men's thinking [a courtier] is a man, and to most men the finest: all things else are defined by the understanding, but this by the senses,[1] but his surest mark is that he is to be found only about princes. He smells;[2] and putteth away much of his judgment[3] about the situation of his clothes. He knows no man that is not generally known. His wit, like the marigold, openeth with the sun, and therefore he riseth not before ten of the clock. He puts more confidence in his words than meaning, and more in his pronunciation than his words. Occasion is his Cupid,[4] and he hath but one receipt of[5] making love. He follows nothing but inconstancy, admires nothing but beauty, honors nothing but fortune, loves nothing. The sustenance of his discourse is news, and his censure like a shot depends upon the charging.[6] He is not,[7] if he be out of court, but fishlike breathes destruction, if out of his own element. Neither his motion or aspect are regular, but he moves by the upper spheres, and is the reflection of higher substances.[8]

If you find him not here, you shall in Paul's, with a pick-tooth in his hat, a cape-cloak, and a long stocking.[9]

7 **To love . . . to love:** to love a man whom it will be appropriate for her to marry, if love she must.

1 **but this by the senses:** All there is to a courtier is his appearance.
2 **He smells:** He uses perfume.
3 **putteth . . . judgment:** gives a lot of thought to.
4 **Occasion is his Cupid:** All he needs to fall in love is a chance, an occasion.
5 **receipt of:** recipe or rule for.
6 **his censure . . . charging:** The bullet ("shot") of a muzzle-loading gun must be "charged" with a ramrod: so the courtier's "censure" or bad report of someone depends on how well he has been rammed full of gossip.
7 **He is not:** He is nothing.
8 **Neither . . . substances:** "Motion" and "aspect" are words to describe the planets. The courtier is like a remote and unsubstantial star; he's almost "out of this world"—"in orbit."
9 **in Paul's . . . stocking:** He loiters near Saint Paul's Cathedral, where other idlers gather. His clothes are old-fashioned: men now wear trousers to the knee, not tights (long stockings).

THE RENAISSANCE

The New Ruler At the height of the Renaissance in England there was a ruler whose genius was beyond dispute. But this ruler was not a courtier nor was she simply a gentlewoman. She was Queen Elizabeth I, and in 1558 she came to the throne that she held until her death in 1603. There were troubles in her reign, as we shall see. But there were also glories, not just successes. Her navy made England the foremost sea-power by defeating the Spanish in 1588. Her domestic policies brought prosperity and stable prices to the middle class, together with generous provisions for the poor. And her playwrights brought English drama to a height it has never since attained.

Here is a portrait of Queen Elizabeth I written from direct observation by Sir John Hayward, a lawyer, historian, and knight, who shows us how she fulfilled her role in the early years of her reign.

THE QUEEN

Now, if ever any person had either the gift or the skill to win the hearts of people, it was this Queen; and if ever she did express the same, it was at that present,[1] in coupling mildness with majesty as she did, and in stately stooping to the meanest sort. All her faculties were in motion, and every motion seemed a well guided action. Her eye was set upon one, her ear listened to another, her judgment ran upon a third, to a fourth she addressed her speech. Her spirit seemed to be everywhere, and yet so entire in her self, as it seemed to be nowhere else. Some she commended, some she pitied, some she thanked, at others she pleasantly and wittily jested, condemning no person, neglecting no office; and generally casting forth such courteous countenances, gestures and speeches, that thereupon the people again redoubled the testimonies of their joy, and afterwards, raising every thing to the highest strain, filled the ears of all men with immoderate extolling their Prince.

She was a lady, upon whom nature had bestowed and well placed many of her fairest favors; of stature mean,[2] slender, straight, and amiably composed; of such state in her carriage, as every motion of her seemed to bear majesty: her hair was inclined to pale yellow, her forehead large and fair, a seemly seat for princely grace: her eyes lively and sweet, but shortsighted; her nose somewhat rising in the middest: the whole compass of her countenance somewhat long, but yet of admirable beauty, not so much in that which is termed the flower of youth, as in a most delightful composition of majesty and modesty in equal mixture. But without good qualities of mind, the gifts of nature are like painted flowers, without either virtue or sap; yea, sometimes they grow horrid and loathsome. Now her virtues were such as might suffice to make an ugly woman beau-

---

1 **at that present:** early in her reign, when she quickly won over all her people.
2 **mean:** moderate.

tiful, which the more a man can know and understand, the more he shall admire and love. In life she was most innocent, in desires moderate, in purpose just; of spirit above credit and almost capacity of her sex;[3] of divine wit,[4] as well for depth of judgment, as for quick conceit and speedy expedition;[5] of eloquence, as sweet in the utterance, so ready and easy to come to the utterance: of wonderful knowledge both in learning and affairs; skillful not only in Latin and Greek, but in divers other foreign languages: None knew better the hardest art of all others, that is, of commanding men. She was religious, magnanimous, merciful and just; respective of the honor of others, and exceeding tender in the touch of her own.[6] She was lovely and loving, the two principal bands of duty and obedience. She was very ripe and measured in counsel and experience, as well not to let go occasions, as not to take them when they were green.[7] She maintained justice at home, and arms abroad, with great wisdom and authority in either place. Her majesty seemed to all to shine through courtesy: but, as she was not easy to receive any to especial grace,[8] so was she most constant to those whom she received; and of great judgment to know to what point of greatness men were fit to be advanced. She was rather liberal than magnificent, making good choice of the receivers; and for this cause was thought weak by some against the desire of money.[9] But it is certain, that beside the want of treasure which she found,[10] her continual affairs in Scotland, France, the Low-countries,[11] and in Ireland, did occasion great provision of money, which could not be better supplied, than by cutting off either excessive or unnecessary expense at home.

To the traditional virtues of the leaders of England Queen Elizabeth added both the perceptiveness and the purposefulness that the new times required. If you will recall Malory's summary of the virtues of the medieval knight, as well as the list of the attainments of the Renaissance courtier, you will see the new skills, new power, and new bravery of this great ruler.

3 of spirit . . . sex: She had more courage than can be believed of a woman and almost more courage than a woman is capable of.
4 wit: general intellectual power.
5 quick conceit . . . expedition: for quick perception or imagination and for speedy decision.
6 tender . . . own: She was touchy about her own honor; i.e., she wanted others to respect her honor as she did theirs.
7 as well . . . green: She was wise enough not to let opportunities go by and wise enough not to seize them too soon.
8 easy . . . grace: She did not easily grant special favor or power.
9 weak . . . money: Because she gave away only liberal rather than magnificent sums, some people thought she was greedy—that she wanted the royal treasury for herself.
10 want . . . found: When she came to the throne, the treasury was low.
11 Low-countries: what are now the Netherlands, Belgium, and Luxembourg.

A large congregation listens to a sermon preached from Saint Paul's Cross outside Saint Paul's Cathedral in the early 17th century. The sermon was an important prose form in the 17th century.

The World of Religion

The Struggle in Society and in the Self The Renaissance in England was also a time of religious intensity. England was not immune to the violence and turmoil of the Reformation, the movement in which the Protestants of Europe, the followers of Martin Luther and John Calvin, separated themselves from the Roman Catholic Church. In the early 16th century, under Henry VIII (and for reasons that had less to do with religion than with that King's personal ambitions) an English Church had been established separate from Rome. The English Church, however, was subjected to two strong pressures: on the one hand, from Roman Catholics, who wanted to return to the Roman Church; and on the other, from Puritans, who wanted to "purify" the new Church of the practices and rituals that survived the break from Rome. English Puritans were, generally, followers of Calvin. One of Elizabeth's greatest achievements was her adjustment of the English Church to these pressures in such a way as to ensure religious peace during her reign.

In the English Renaissance, then, religious feelings were deep and intense. But the main effect on English literature of the divisions, the debates, the arguments, and the wars that marked the Reformation was the opening up of a new world of experience for the writer to explore. While nations and groups debated about the organization of religion, writers turned to examine the qualities of religious experience itself. And they found there a private struggle to understand, to feel, and to know the truth. Such a turning of the attention to what is inward is suggested by the following passage. It comes from a sermon preached in 1626 by John Donne, the Dean of Saint Paul's Cathedral (the foremost church in London).

THE STRUGGLE IN THE SELF

When we consider with a religious seriousness the manifold weaknesses of the strongest devotions in time of prayer, it is a sad consideration. I throw myself down in my chamber, and I call in, and invite God, and his angels thither, and when they are there, I neglect God and his angels, for the noise of a fly, for the rattling of a coach, for the whining of a door; I talk on, in the same posture of praying, eyes lifted up, knees bowed down, as though I prayed to God; and, if God or his angels should ask me when I thought last of God in that prayer, I cannot tell. Sometimes I find that I had forgot what I was about, but when I began to forget it, I cannot tell. A memory of yesterday's pleasures, a fear of tomorrow's dangers, a straw under my knee, a noise in mine ear, a light in mine eye, an anything, a nothing, a fancy, a chimera[1] in my brain, troubles me in my prayer. So certainly is there nothing, nothing in spiritual things, perfect in this world.

Prayer is not easy, says Donne. Nothing in spiritual things is perfect in this world. But his self-awareness, his description of the divided and wavering mind, heralds a new kind of self-analysis that enters literature decisively in the Renaissance.

Conflict

In a small way each of the preceding passages suggests the adventure of the Renaissance. New scientific discoveries conflicted with old assumptions. New sights turned out to be as astonishing as old marvels. The new state called for powers of persuasion and command that old educational ideals could not readily supply. The conflicts of religion gave people a new insight into the conflicts within the self. It is no wonder that the times required—and found—writers who believed that the powers of poetry could reveal to us a golden world beyond the conflicts of nature and human nature.

---

1 **chimera** (kĭ mĭr′ə): impossible fancy.

The Literature of

The Renaissance

The English Bible
The Book

No BOOK HAS more profoundly influenced our thinking and writing than
has the Bible. Its doctrines have been expounded in sermon upon sermon for hundreds of years. Its stories in the Middle Ages were told in
stained glass, in statues, and in plays. Its Psalms were part of the
earliest church services. It became extremely important in the 16th
century, for the Reformation that spread from Germany early in that
century was based on the belief that the Bible alone is the authority
for every person's faith and doctrine. It was therefore necessary that
the Bible be translated from the Latin of its official version into language that all people might read or learn to read. And so there began
in the 16th century the great work of providing an English Bible.

The first complete translation had been made in Chaucer's time, but
it had not been widely used, and indeed was no longer readable, so
fast was the language changing. The English Bible that has probably
had the greatest effect on literature in English is based upon the work
of William Tyndale, who in 1525 completed a translation of the
New Testament from Greek texts—texts older than the Vulgate, the
Latin Bible of the Church. And before his death (he was executed
as a heretic) ten years later, Tyndale had completed a translation
of some parts of the Old Testament. His version was revised when
the English Church under Henry VIII separated from Rome, and
during the 16th century other translations were made, including an
official Catholic text of the New Testament published in 1582 in France
at Reims by exiled English Catholics. (Their translation of the Old
Testament was published in Douai, France, in 1609-1610.) In 1604,
under James I, Elizabeth's successor, there began the project that gave
us the King James Version. Six committees of scholars were appointed
to consult the best texts available in the original languages, to compare
other English, Latin, and German translations, and to arrive at the best
readings their joint efforts could secure.

In 1611 their results appeared, the King James Version. None has
been more widely echoed throughout literature in English. Perhaps
most remarkable is the fact that the English language had reached a
stage of development at which fifty-four separate men could together
frame the many, many sentences that comprise a great monument of
English prose.

Psalm 8

The first selection is from the Book of Psalms. The word *psalm* comes from a Greek verb that signifies the plucking of a harp, and many of the Psalms are songs of praise for the Lord. They are perhaps the best-known and best-loved part of the Bible, for they have entered intimately into the speech and the memory of many generations.

Psalm 8

O Lord our Lord,
How excellent is thy name in all the earth!
Who hast set thy glory above the heavens.
Out of the mouth of babes and sucklings hast thou ordained strength
    because of thine enemies,
That thou mightest still the enemy and the avenger.   5
When I consider thy heavens, the work of thy fingers,
The moon and the stars, which thou hast ordained;
What is man, that thou art mindful of him?
And the son of man, that thou visitest him?
For thou hast made him a little lower than the angels,   10
And hast crowned him with glory and honor.
Thou madest him to have dominion over the works of thy hands;
Thou hast put all things under his feet:
All sheep and oxen,
Yea, and the beasts of the field;   15
The fowl of the air, and the fish of the sea,
And whatsoever passeth through the paths of the seas.
O Lord our Lord,
How excellent is thy name in all the earth!

The Book of Job

The story of Job, the man who suffers though he is innocent, has for centuries been a symbol of the mystery of pain and suffering. Clergy, philosophers, poets, and writers of tragedy have thought hard upon it. In the story of Job the distinction is made between an "I"—a suffering individual—and a "Thou" of infinite power, a power far beyond the comprehension, the knowledge, of faithful, sinless Job. The Book of Job has given many writers images of a power that no "I" can ever fully understand.

from **The Book of Job**

There was a man in the land of Uz,[1] whose name was Job; and that man was perfect and upright, and one that feared God, and eschewed evil. And there were born unto him seven sons and three daughters. His substance also was seven thousand sheep, and three thousand camels, and five hundred yoke of oxen, and five hundred she-asses, and a very great household; so that this man was the greatest of all the men of the east. And his sons went and feasted in their houses, every one his day; and sent and called for their three sisters to eat and to drink with them. And it was so, when the days of their feasting were gone about, that Job sent and sanctified them, and rose up early in the morning, and offered burnt offerings according to the number of them all: for Job said, "It may be that my sons have sinned, and cursed God in their hearts." Thus did Job continually.

Now there was a day when the sons of God[2] came to present themselves before the Lord, and Satan came also among them. And the Lord said unto Satan, "Whence comest thou?"

Then Satan answered the Lord, and said, "From going to and fro in the earth, and from walking up and down in it."

And the Lord said unto Satan, "Hast thou considered my servant Job, that there is none like him in the earth, a perfect and an upright man, one that feareth God, and escheweth evil?"

Then Satan answered the Lord, and said, "Doth Job fear God for nought? Hast not thou made an hedge about him, and about his house, and about all that he hath on every side? Thou hast blessed the work of his hands, and his substance is increased in the land. But put forth thine hand now, and touch all that he hath, and he will curse thee to thy face."

And the Lord said unto Satan, "Behold, all that he hath is in thy power; only upon himself put not forth thine hand." So Satan went forth from the presence of the Lord.

And there was a day when his sons and his daughters were eating and drinking wine in their eldest brother's house: and there came a messenger unto Job, and said, "The oxen were plowing, and the asses feeding beside them: and the Sabeans[3] fell upon them, and took them away; yea, they have slain the servants with the edge of the sword; and I only am escaped alone to tell thee."

While he was yet speaking, there came also another, and said, "The fire of God is fallen from heaven, and hath burned up the sheep, and the servants, and consumed them; and I only am escaped alone to tell thee."

While he was yet speaking, there came also another, and said, "The Chaldeans[4] made out three bands, and

---

1 **Uz** (ŭz): somewhere in northern Arabia.
2 **sons of God**: angels.

3 **Sabeans** (sə bē′ənz): an Arab tribe.
4 **Chaldeans** (kăl dē′ənz): Persians, from what is now southern Iraq.

fell upon the camels, and have carried them away, yea, and slain the servants with the edge of the sword; and I only am escaped alone to tell thee."

While he was yet speaking, there came also another, and said, "Thy sons and thy daughters were eating and drinking wine in their eldest brother's house: and, behold, there came a great wind from the wilderness, and smote the four corners of the house, and it fell upon the young men, and they are dead; and I only am escaped alone to tell thee."

Then Job arose, and rent his mantle, and shaved his head, and fell down upon the ground, and worshiped, and said, "Naked came I out of my mother's womb, and naked shall I return thither: the Lord gave, and the Lord hath taken away; blessed be the name of the Lord." In all this Job sinned not, nor charged God foolishly.

[*By afflicting him with boils, Satan then tempts Job to sin, to "charge God." And Job's friends, coming to commiserate with him, tempt him further to complain of his trouble. And so Job begins his lament.*]

After this opened Job his mouth, and
    cursed his day.
And Job spake, and said,
"Let the day perish wherein I was born,
And the night in which it was said,
    There is a man child conceived. 5
Let that day be darkness;
Let not God regard it from above,
Neither let the light shine upon it.
Let darkness and the shadow of death
    stain it;
Let a cloud dwell upon it;   10
Let the blackness of the day terrify it.
As for that night, let darkness seize
    upon it;

Let it not be joined unto the days of
    the year,
Let it not come into the number of the
    months.
Lo, let that night be solitary,   15
Let no joyful voice come therein.

* * *

My soul is weary of my life;
I will leave my complaint upon myself;
I will speak in the bitterness of my soul.
I will say unto God, 'Do not condemn
    me;   20
Shew me wherefore thou contendest
    with me.
Is it good unto thee that thou shouldest
    oppress,
That thou shouldest despise the work of
    thine hands,
And shine upon the counsel of the
    wicked?
Hast thou eyes of flesh?   25
Or seest thou as man seeth?
Are thy days as the days of man?
Are thy years as man's days,
That thou enquirest after mine iniquity,
And searchest after my sin?   30
Thou knowest that I am not wicked;
And there is none that can deliver out
    of thine hand.
Thine hands have made me and fash-
    ioned me
Together round about; yet thou dost
    destroy me.

* * *

Are not my days few? Cease then,   35
And let me alone, that I may take com-
    fort a little,
Before I go whence I shall not return,
Even to the land of darkness and the
    shadow of death;
A land of darkness, as darkness itself;
And of the shadow of death, without
    any order,   40
And where the light is as darkness.

* * *

Man that is born of a woman
Is of few days, and full of trouble.
He cometh forth like a flower, and is
   cut down:
He fleeth also as a shadow, and con-
   tinueth not.   45
And dost thou open thine eyes upon
   such an one,
And bringest me into judgment with
   thee,
Who can bring a clean thing out of an
   unclean? not one.
Seeing his days are determined,
The number of his months are with
   thee,   50
Thou hast appointed his bounds that he
   cannot pass:
Turn from him, that he may rest,
Till he shall accomplish, as an hireling,
   his day.
For there is hope of a tree,
If it be cut down, that it will sprout
   again,   55
And that the tender branch thereof will
   not cease.
Though the root thereof wax old in the
   earth,
And the stock thereof die in the ground;
Yet through the scent of water it will
   bud,
And bring forth boughs like a plant   60
But man dieth, and wasteth away:
Yea, man giveth up the ghost, and
   where is he?
As the waters fail from the sea,
And the flood decayeth and drieth up:
So man lieth down, and riseth not: 65
Till the heavens be no more, they shall
   not awake,
Nor be raised out of their sleep.
O that thou wouldest hide me in the
   grave,
That thou wouldest keep me secret, un-
   til thy wrath be past,
That thou wouldest appoint me a set
   time, and remember me!' "   70

[*Job's long lament to God finally ceases.
He is now quite alone; his wife and
friends have left him. Finally God
speaks to Job out of a whirlwind.*]

Then the Lord answered Job out of the
   whirlwind, and said,
"Who is this that darkeneth counsel
By words without knowledge?
Gird up now thy loins like a man;
For I will demand of thee, and answer
   thou me.   75
Where wast thou when I laid the foun-
   dations of the earth?
Declare, if thou hast understanding.
Who hath laid the measures thereof, if
   thou knowest?
Or who hath stretched the line upon it?
Whereupon are the foundations thereof
   fastened?   80
Or who laid the corner stone thereof;
When the morning stars sang together,
And all the sons of God shouted for
   joy?
Or who shut up the sea with doors,
When it brake forth, as if it had issued
   out of the womb?   85
When I made the cloud the garment
   thereof,
And thick darkness a swaddling band
   for it,
And brake up for it my decreed place,
And set bars and doors,
And said, Hitherto shalt thou come, but
   no further: 90
And here shall thy proud waves be
   stayed?
Hast thou commanded the morning
   since thy days;
And caused the dayspring⁵ to know his
   place? . . .
Hast thou entered into the springs of
   the sea?
Or has thou walked in the search of the
   depth?   95

5 **dayspring:** sun.

Fogg Museum of Art, Cambridge

*"Then the Lord answered Job out of the whirlwind. . . ." This engraving was done by
the poet William Blake to illustrate the Book of Job.*

Have the gates of death been opened
    unto thee?
Or hast thou seen the doors of the
    shadow of death?
Hast thou perceived the breadth of the
    earth?
Declare if thou knowest it all.
Where is the way where light
    dwelleth?   100
And as for darkness, where is the place
    thereof,
That thou shouldest take it to the bound
    thereof,
And that thou shouldest know the paths
    to the house thereof?
Knowest thou it, because thou wast
    then born?

Or because the number of thy days is
    great?   105
Hast thou entered into the treasures of
    the snow?
Or hast thou seen the treasures of the
    hail,
Which I have reserved against the time
    of trouble,
Against the day of battle and war?
By what way is the light parted,   110
Which scattereth the east wind upon
    the earth?
Who hath divided a watercourse for
    the overflowing of waters,
Or a way for the lightning of thunder;
To cause it to rain on the earth, where
    no man is;

On the wilderness, wherein there is no
   man;   115
To satisfy the desolate and waste
   ground;
And to cause the bud of the tender
   herb to spring forth? . . .
Wilt thou hunt the prey for the lion?
Or fill the appetite of the young lions,
When they couch in their dens,   120
And abide in the covert[6] to lie in wait?
Who provideth for the raven his food?
When his young ones cry unto God,
They wander for lack of meat.

＊ ＊ ＊

Doth the eagle mount up at thy com-
   mand,   125
And make her nest on high?
She dwelleth and abideth on the rock,
Upon the crag of the rock, and the
   strong place.
From thence she seeketh the prey,
And her eyes behold afar off.   130

Her young ones also suck up blood:
And where the slain are, there is she."

＊ ＊ ＊

Then Job answered the Lord, and said,
   "I know that thou canst do every
   thing,
And that no thought can be withholden
   from thee.   135
Who is he that hideth counsel without
   knowledge?
Therefore have I uttered that I under-
   stood not;
Things too wonderful for me, which I
   knew not.
Hear, I beseech thee, and I will speak:
I will demand of thee, and declare thou
   unto me.   140
I have heard of thee by the hearing of
   the ear:
But now mine eye seeth thee.
Wherefore I abhor myself,
And repent in dust and ashes."

6 in the covert: in hiding.

Comment

The Psalmist asks, "What is man, that thou art mindful of him?"
And his answer is a hymn of thanksgiving for his dominion over "all
things under his feet." Job asks the same question, but he believes that
God is mindful of him in quite a different way. And certainly he receives a different answer.

1. In his first lament, Job says "Let that day be darkness" in which he
was born. And the voice of God from the whirlwind, answering
him, asks, "Hast thou commanded the morning since thy days;/ And
caused the dayspring to know his place?" How does this question
answer Job's first lament? What does it tell us about Job? And
what does it tell us about God?
2. Find other passages from the Lord's answer to Job that balance
particular parts of Job's complaint. What does the voice of the Lord
chidingly ask Job again and again?
3. The Psalmist ends his praise of the Lord by exclaiming, "How excellent is thy name in all the earth!" Does Job finally answer the
Lord in any way like this?

OR SUMMARY

Songs and Sonnets:
The Nature of Love
and the Love of Nature

ONE OF THE commonest descriptive titles for a book of Renaissance poetry is "Songs and Sonnets." And it was indeed an age of song—of an easy outpouring of feeling in words. But it was also an age of the sonnet: of the carefully wrought poem, just fourteen lines long, its lines linked together with rhymes, and containing a "turn" or a kind of surprise ending. Whatever it does, the sonnet must end strongly.

The sonnet came to England from Italy (the word is Italian for "little song"), where it had been perfected by the great poet Petrarch. His name, indeed, describes one widely used sonnet form. The Petrarchan (or Italian) sonnet is typically divided into two parts: first, eight lines (the octave) with two rhymes, *abbaabba*, followed by a group of six lines (the sestet) that introduces a new set of rhymes, those commonly used being *cdcdcd, cdecde,* or *cdedce.* The other great sonnet form, perfected by Shakespeare, is divided differently. It is made up of three groups of four lines, called quatrains, and a final rhyming couplet that states a firm conclusion. The Shakespearean sonnet, also called Elizabethan or English, typically rhymes thus: *abab cdcd efef gg.* The conventions of rhyme were loosely observed. The first sonnet given here, for example, is Italian in general structure: it "turns" at line 9, when the octave is complete. But it does not have the usual Italian rhyme scheme.

What is important is the fact that there *were* rules and conventions: there was a craft to be learned, and it had rules and practices almost as definite as those governing the composition of music. For the sonnet, with its rhythms and its rhymes, adjusted the sound of a poem to its sense. A string of repeated rhymes will serve to evoke simple feelings: we all know what to feel when we hear ". . . June,/ . . . moon,/ . . . croon." But a sequence such as ". . . June,/ . . . fate,/ . . . moon,/ . . . mate" will suggest feelings that are perhaps not quite so simple.

The technical form of the sonnet performs a still more important function, for it regulates the speed, the pace, at which we move through the poem. The English followers of the Italian sonnet writers were learning how to match a flowing rush of words to the description of a moment of excitement. They were learning how to crowd and slow down the line that expresses sadness. They were learning how to suggest by sheer sound, simply by the repetition of a strong rhythm, connections between ideas or feelings that in cold prose could never seem to be related to each other. The song writers and sonneteers of the Renaissance were experimenters—and successful ones—in the subtle connection of sound and sense. In print they could fix the controls of the quiet voice that speaks to the inner ear.

And what were their songs about? What most songs have since been about: love, and springtime, and the great joyous parallel between people's feelings and their experience of nature. The songs and sonnets of the Renaissance poets set a fashion that has never quite been lost.

Sir Philip Sidney (1554-1586)

Sir Philip Sidney lived only thirty-two years, but in this time he distinguished himself in many ways: as poet, scholar, courtier, diplomat, and soldier. For many people in the early reign of Elizabeth I he was the foremost gentleman of his time. He died after being wounded in a minor skirmish in Holland, but not, so the story goes, before he had composed a song about his wound and had had it sung to him. On his death, it is said, every gentleman connected with Elizabeth's court went into mourning and wore somber clothes.

Like many of his contemporaries, Sidney wrote a long series of love poems, a sonnet sequence. They were addressed to a young girl named Penelope Devereux, daughter of one of the greatest noblemen of the kingdom; but, as in other sonnet sequences of the time, the lady's features are generalized, and she is given a name drawn from the literature of Greece and Rome. She is called Stella, meaning "star." You will shortly encounter a Celia and a Lucasta. Lesbia, Delia, Corinna, and Julia were other names for the disguised heroines of Renaissance love poems. The full title of Sidney's sonnet sequence is *Astrophel and Stella*, "The Star-lover and the Star." Here is the unforgettable sonnet that begins the sequence.

Sonnet

from *Astrophel and Stella*

Sir Philip Sidney

Loving in truth, and fain[1] in verse my love to show,
That she, dear she, might take some pleasure of my pain,[2]
Pleasure might cause her read, reading might make her know,
Knowledge might pity win, and pity grace obtain,
I sought fit words to paint the blackest face of woe,   5
Studying inventions fine,[3] her wits to entertain,
Oft turning others' leaves, to see if thence would flow
Some fresh and fruitful showers upon my sunburned brain.
But words came halting forth, wanting Invention's stay;[4]
Invention, Nature's child, fled step-dame Study's blows;[5]   10
And others' feet[6] still[7] seemed but strangers in my way.
Thus, great with child to speak, and helpless in my throes,
Biting my truant pen, beating myself for spite,
"Fool," said my Muse to me, "look in thy heart, and write."

1 **fain:** desirous.
2 **pleasure of my pain:** pleasure in my pain.
3 **inventions fine:** fine images, found in "others' leaves," other poets' works.
4 **stay:** steadying power.

5 **step-dame . . . blows:** Real imagination, which comes by nature, is frightened away by the urging ("blows") of Study, the cruel stepmother of Imagination.
6 **feet:** rhythms.
7 **still:** always.

Comment

The last line of this poem provides as fitting an introduction as there is to the poetry of the Renaissance. What does this poet find when he looks into his heart?

1. The poet speaks of his "pain" (l. 2); he "sought fit words to paint the blackest face of woe" (l. 5). What is his "pain" or "woe" as a lover? And what is his "pain" or "woe" as a writer?
2. Lines 3 and 4 move swiftly. Four short clauses in succession rush us on: "Pleasure . . . , reading . . . ,/ Knowledge . . . , and pity . . . ." What do these swift-moving lines describe? What "Knowledge" will win him pity from his lady?
3. In lines 12 and 13 there is a succession of phrases: "great with child . . . , helpless . . . ,/ Biting . . . , beating. . . ." How do these two lines echo the rhythm of lines 3 and 4? But what do lines 12 and 13 describe? Why does the poet bite his "truant pen"? Why is the rhythm appropriate in both instances?
4. What, then, does the poet find in his heart? What does it tell him about his pains and woes as a lover? What does it tell him about his pains and woes as a writer?

Henry Howard, Earl of Surrey (1517?-1547)

Henry Howard, Earl of Surrey, was one of the earliest English imitators and adaptors of Renaissance Italian sonnets. This poem is based on a sonnet by Petrarch. Surrey, a fiercely proud man, with his father, was suspected of plotting against Henry VIII. When Surrey would not come to terms with his accusers, he was beheaded for treason. Yet this bold man was a writer of gentle love songs. Such was the mixture of violence and the love of poetry among the early writers of the Renaissance.

Description of Spring

Wherein Each Thing Renews Save Only the Lover

Henry Howard, Earl of Surrey

The soote[1] season that bud and bloom forth brings
With green hath clad the hill and eke[2] the vale,
The nightingale with feathers new she sings,
The turtle to her make[3] hath told her tale.
Summer is come, for every spray now springs,   5
The hart hath hung his old head on the pale,[4]
The buck in brake[5] his winter coat he flings,
The fishes float with new repairèd scale,
The adder all her slough away she slings,
The swift swallow pursueth the flies smale,[6]   10
The busy bee her honey now she mings[7]—
Winter is worn, that was the flowers' bale:[8]
And thus I see, among these pleasant things
Each care decays—and yet my sorrow springs.

1 **soote:** sweet.
2 **eke:** also.
3 **turtle . . . make:** turtledove to her mate.
4 **The hart . . . pale:** The deer has rubbed off his old horns against the fence.
5 **brake:** thicket.
6 **smale:** small.
7 **mings:** mixes.
8 **bale:** disaster.

Comment

Love and spring have often been connected before and since the time of the Earl of Surrey. What does the connection mean in this poem?

1. The subtitle of the sonnet says that in spring "each thing renews." What are some images of "renewal" in the poem?
2. The subtitle says that in spring everything renews itself, "save only the lover"; the sonnet ends: "and yet my sorrow springs." How have the lover's feelings been affected by the changes he sees in nature? In what sense, then, has the lover been "renewed" by the spectacle of spring?

Thomas Nashe (1567-1601)

Thomas Nashe wrote the story from which you have read that muscular sentence ("my heart hopt and daunst"). The spring song that follows is from one of his plays. Nashe was one of a group of robust, irrepressible young writers known as University Wits, who flourished in the late 16th century.

Spring, the Sweet Spring

Thomas Nashe

Spring, the sweet spring, is the year's pleasant king;
Then blooms each thing, then maids dance in a ring,
Cold doth not sting, the pretty birds do sing:
    "Cuckoo, jug-jug,[1] pu-we, to-witta-woo!"

The palm[2] and may[3] make country houses gay,   5
Lambs frisk and play, the shepherds pipe all day,
And we hear aye[4] birds tune this merry lay:
    "Cuckoo, jug-jug, pu-we, to-witta-woo!"

The fields breathe sweet, the daisies kiss our feet,
Young lovers meet, old wives a-sunning sit,   10
In every street these tunes our ears do greet:
    "Cuckoo, jug-jug, pu-we, to-witta-woo!"
    Spring, the sweet spring!

1 **jug-jug:** sound of the nightingale.
2 **palm:** willow.
3 **may:** hawthorn.
4 **aye:** always.

Comment

Sometimes spring is celebrated for what Robert Frost once called "sheer morning gladness at the brim." How does this happy poem unite man and nature in gladness?

1. What images of people—of society—appear in the poem?
2. And what images of nature?
3. What unites these images of people and nature for the poet: What he sees? What he feels? What he hears?

Shakespeare was first a dramatist, but even his plays give us many examples of his lyric gift, his powers as a writer of songs. Here are two songs from plays written about ten years apart. The first is simpler than the second; the "chaliced flowers" and "winking Mary-buds" of the second perhaps reveal a ripening of his sensitivity for details.

Song *from Twelfth Night*

O mistress mine, where are you roaming?
O stay and hear! your true-love's coming,
   That can sing both high and low.
Trip no further, pretty sweeting;
Journeys end in lovers meeting,   5
   Every wise man's son doth know.

What is love? 'tis not hereafter;
Present mirth hath present laughter;
   What's to come is still unsure:
In delay there lies no plenty;   10
Then come kiss me, sweet and twenty!
   Youth's a stuff will not endure.

Song *from Cymbeline*

Hark, hark! the lark at heaven's gate sings,
   And Phoebus[1] 'gins arise,
His steeds to water[2] at those springs
   On chaliced[3] flowers that lies;
And winking Mary-buds[4] begin   5
   To ope their golden eyes.
With every thing that pretty is,
   My lady sweet, arise;
      Arise, arise!

1 Phoebus (fē′bəs): the sun.
2 His . . . water: The horses of the sun begin to drink the dew.
3 chaliced (chăl′ĭst): shaped like cups (holding the dew).
4 Mary-buds: marigolds.

Comment

Like a later poem you will shortly see ("To the Virgins, to Make Much of Time"), the song from *Twelfth Night* sings the old theme that comes from Latin poetry: *carpe diem*, "seize the day," for what is to come is unsure. How is this theme expressed in the last song?

Shakespeare's sonnets are perhaps his best-known work aside from some four or five of his plays. And yet we almost did not have them at all. They were apparently published in 1609 without his permission and in circumstances that have never been clarified. Their very arrangement remains a problem, for some are addressed to a woman, some to a man, and some to a friend who could be either. The four presented here are among the best-known love poems in English. They repeat—and they justify—the great hopes and claims made for poetry by the writers of the Renaissance.

Sonnets

William Shakespeare

18

Shall I compare thee to a summer's day?
Thou art more lovely and more temperate.
Rough winds do shake the darling buds of May,
And summer's lease hath all too short a date.[1]
Sometime too hot the eye of heaven shines,   5
And often is his gold complexion dimmed;
And every fair from fair sometime declines,[2]
By chance, or nature's changing course, untrimmed;[3]
But thy eternal summer shall not fade
Nor lose possession of that fair thou ow'st,[4]   10
Nor shall Death brag thou wand'rest in his shade
When in eternal lines to time thou grow'st.[5]
   So long as men can breathe or eyes can see,
   So long lives this, and this[6] gives life to thee.

1 **And . . . date:** Summer's lease (of the earth) expires in too short a time.
2 **from fair to fair . . . declines:** Every beautiful, fair thing from beauty, fairness, declines.
3 **nature's . . . untrimmed:** by nature's unregulated, changing course.
4 **fair . . . ow'st:** beauty you possess.
5 **to time thou grow'st:** become part of all time.
6 **this:** these lines.

29

When, in disgrace with Fortune and men's eyes,
I all alone beweep my outcast state,
And trouble deaf heaven with my bootless[1] cries,
And look upon myself and curse my fate,
Wishing me like to one more rich in hope,   5

4 lines per sentence
Then main theme

read

THE RENAISSANCE

Featured² like him, like him with friends possessed,
Desiring this man's art, and that man's scope,³
With what I most enjoy contented least;
Yet in these thoughts myself almost despising,
Haply⁴ I think on thee, and then my state,   10
Like to the lark at break of day arising
From sullen⁵ earth, sings hymns at heaven's gate;
   For thy sweet love rememb'red such wealth brings
   That then I scorn to change my state with kings.

1 bootless: profitless.
2 featured: formed.
3 scope: range of mind.

4 Haply: by chance.
5 sullen: gloomy.

55

Not marble nor the gilded monuments
Of princes shall outlive this powerful rhyme;
But you shall shine more bright in these contents¹
Than unswept stone, besmeared with sluttish² time.
When wasteful war shall statues overturn,   5
And broils³ root out the work of masonry,
Nor Mars his sword nor war's quick fire⁴ shall burn
The living record of your memory.
'Gainst death and all-oblivious enmity
Shall you pace forth; your praise shall still find room   10
Even in the eyes of all posterity
That wear this world out to the ending doom.⁵
   So, till the judgment that⁶ yourself arise,
   You live in this, and dwell in lovers' eyes.

1 contents: in what this poem contains.
2 sluttish: dirty; untidy.
3 broils: battles; struggles.
4 Nor Mars . . . quick fire: neither the sword of war nor war's quick fire.
5 ending doom: Judgment Day.
6 till the judgment that: until Judgment Day when.

116

Let me not to the marriage of true minds
Admit impediments.¹ Love is not love
Which alters when it alteration finds
Or bends with the remover² to remove.
O, no! it is an ever-fixèd mark   5
That looks on tempests and is never shaken;
It is the star to every wand'ring bark,³
Whose worth's unknown, although his height be taken.⁴
Love's not Time's fool,⁵ though rosy lips and cheeks
Within his bending sickle's compass come.⁶   10

Love alters not with his brief hours and weeks,
But bears it out[7] even to the edge of doom.
   If this be error, and upon me proved,
   I never writ, nor no man ever loved.

1 **admit impediments:** admit that there can be hindrances to the marriage of true minds.
2 **remover:** fickle person.
3 **bark:** ship.
4 **Whose . . . taken:** Although the height of a star can be calculated in navigation, the true worth, the real nature, of the star cannot be known.
5 **Time's fool:** True love is not a servant to time, not a jester employed to amuse time.
6 **Within . . . come:** although the beauty of youth ("rosy lips and cheeks") falls within the range of his swinging scythe (and thus can be destroyed by Time).
7 **bears it out:** endures.

Comment

Each of these sonnets explores the nature of true love. Each contrasts love with all that is impermanent in nature and in society, and two of them assert that what is permanent in true love can be captured and enshrined in verse. The poet knows what is permanent in love, and his lines contain this permanence.

1. The impermanent, the changing: how does it appear in these sonnets? In Sonnet 18 what are some images of change drawn from nature? In Sonnet 29 what changeableness does the poet find in himself?
2. The permanent, the unchanging: how does it appear? What main image of the unchanging quality of true love do you find in Sonnet 116? In Sonnet 29 what rescues the poet from the dissatisfaction and changeableness he finds in himself?
3. The permanence of poetry: how is this assurance expressed? In Sonnet 18 the poet says that the "eternal summer" of his mistress will not fade; she and her beauty will live on into all time in his "eternal lines." How does he say this in Sonnet 55? With what words does he refer to his poetry in this sonnet? With what kind of "monuments" is his poetry contrasted? Why are these monuments impermanent?
4. But all these sonnets are addressed to "thee," to "you." And this "you" is the object of his love. The poet is trying to assure her that he loves her deeply and truly. What, then, is his assurance to this "you" that he *does* love her truly?

John Donne (1572-1631)

With John Donne and the next three poets we enter the second stage of the Renaissance. As we have seen, Donne was a great churchman of the early 17th century. But in his youth he was well known to a circle of readers for his love poems, which circulated in manuscript and were not published until years later. Here, in a song of farewell to his wife, written when he went on a journey to the continent, Donne gives us a glimpse into a new sensibility, a new kind of love poem. It expresses a conception of love more complex, perhaps more subtle, but no less powerful than that which drove Sidney to bite his truant pen. Certainly Donne's love poetry is more intimate and more personal than that of his predecessors. We cannot be sure how near or how far from the poet is the "you" of Shakespeare's sonnets, but this poem, clearly, is addressed to an individual person.

Song

John Donne

Sweetest love, I do not go
    For weariness of thee,
Nor in hope the world can show
    A fitter love for me;
      But since that[1] I   5
Must die at last, 'tis best,
To use myself in jest
      Thus by feigned deaths to die.[2]

Yesternight the sun went hence,
    And yet is here today;   10
He hath no desire nor sense,
    Nor half so short a way.[3]
      Then fear not me,[4]
But believe that I shall make
Speedier journeys, since I take   15
    More wings and spurs than he.

O how feeble is man's power,
    That if good fortune fall,
Cannot add another hour,
    Nor a lost hour recall!   20
      But come bad chance,[5]
And we join to it our strength,
And we teach it art and length,
      Itself o'er us to advance.

---

1 **since that:** since.
2 **to use . . . to die:** to accustom myself to death in a joking way by pretended deaths.
3 **Nor . . . way:** nor so short a way to go as I have.
4 **fear not me:** fear not for me.
5 **bad chance:** bad luck.

When thou sigh'st, thou sigh'st not wind,　　　　　25
　　But sigh'st my soul away;
When thou weep'st unkindly kind,[6]
　　My life's blood doth decay.
　　　　It cannot be
That thou lov'st me as thou say'st,　　　　　30
If in thine my life thou waste;
　　Thou art the best of me.

Let not thy divining[7] heart
　　Forethink me any ill;
Destiny may take thy part,　　　　　35
　　And may thy fears fulfill;
　　　　But think that we
Are but turned aside to sleep;
They who one another keep
Alive, ne'er parted be.　　　　　40

6 unkindly kind: i.e., her kindness is hard on him.
7 divining: guessing.

Comment

The poet is reassuring his wife that, although he must go away on a journey, their love will keep them from being parted. How does he express the close relation he feels with her?

1. In lines 25-26 the poet says that the lady's sighs in sadness for his departure are not just exhalations of air, but exhalations of the substance of his soul. When she weeps, he says, his very lifeblood "decays" or is diminished. He compares his soul to the air she breathes; he compares her tears to his own blood. What do these comparisons tell us about their relationship?

2. Again, in the last stanza, he begs her not to "forethink" or imagine that any harm will come to him, lest Fate or Destiny make her fears and imaginings come true. He compares her "divining heart," thus, to a Destiny that can control him. What does this comparison tell us of their relationship?

3. What, therefore, is the foundation of the poet's assurance that he and his wife can never really be parted? How does he express it in the last two lines of the poem?

154

Ben Jonson (1572?-1637)

Ben Jonson, dramatist, poet, critic, was one of the leading men of letters of the early 17th century. He was praised by a later generation for his "smooth numbers"—for the easiness, the clarity, and the flow of his rhythms and his rhymes. This famous song certainly deserves the praise.

To Celia

Ben Jonson

Drink to me only with thine eyes,
   And I will pledge with mine;
Or leave a kiss but in the cup,
   And I'll not look for wine.
The thirst that from the soul doth rise   5
   Doth ask a drink divine;
But might I of Jove's nectar[1] sup,
   I would not change for thine.

I sent thee late a rosy wreath,
   Not so much honoring thee   10
As giving it a hope that there[2]
   It could not withered be.
But thou thereon didst only breathe,
   And sent'st it back to me;
Since when it grows, and smells, I swear,   15
   Not of itself but thee.

1 **Jove's nectar:** the drink of the gods.
2 **there:** with you.

Comment

This song was set to a melody by an 18th-century composer named Thomas Arne, and in this setting it has long been one of the best-known songs in English. Compare it with Shakespeare's song from *Twelfth Night*. What quality in Jonson's song emerges from the comparison?

Robert Herrick (1591-1674)

Robert Herrick lived at various times in his life in both the city of London and in the country—a village in Devonshire where he was a clergyman. And although he complained of the hardships of the country and spoke of his "banishment" from London, many of his poems are testimony to his real enjoyment of country scenes and life.

Although most of Herrick's poems were not published until almost the middle of the 17th century, they seem like poems of the early Renaissance. Many of his poems represent a sense of life—a freshness, a buoyancy—closer to Nashe than to Donne, closer to the 16th than to the 17th century. And yet in "To Daffodils" we can also hear the more pensive note that we find in Donne.

To the Virgins,
to Make Much of Time

Robert Herrick

Gather ye rosebuds while ye may:
    Old time is still a-flying;
And this same flower that smiles today
    Tomorrow will be dying.

The glorious lamp of heaven, the sun,   5
    The higher he's a-getting,
The sooner will his race be run,
    And nearer he's to setting.

That age is best which is the first,
    When youth and blood are warmer;   10
But being spent, the worse, and worst
    Times still succeed the former.

Then be not coy, but use your time,
    And, while ye may, go marry;
For, having lost but once your prime,   15
    You may forever tarry.

To Daffodils

Robert Herrick

Fair daffodils, we weep to see
　　You haste away so soon;
As yet the early-rising sun
　　Has not attained his noon.
　　　　Stay, stay,　　　　　　　　　　　　　5
　　Until the hasting day
　　　　Has run
　　But to the evensong;[1]
And, having prayed together, we
　　Will go with you along.　　　　　　　　　10

We have short time to stay, as you;
　　We have as short a spring;
As quick a growth to meet decay,[2]
　　As you, or anything.
　　　　We die,　　　　　　　　　　　　　15
　　As your hours do, and dry
　　　　Away
　　Like to the summer's rain;
Or as the pearls of morning's dew,
　　Ne'er to be found again.　　　　　　　　20

1 **evensong:** service of evening prayer.
2 **As . . . decay:** as short a season of growth to prepare for the season of decay.

Comment

Once more the theme is that of time passing. But each of these poems expresses the theme with a different emphasis and takes toward it a different attitude.

1. Consider the pace, the movement, of each poem. What rhythmic pattern do you find in "To the Virgins"? What pattern of rhyme? And what variety of rhythm do you find in "To Daffodils"? What pattern of rhyme? Which poem moves faster?
2. What difference of attitude toward the passing of time do you find between the two poems? For example, with what feeling must you say the line "Then be not coy, but use your time"? With what feeling must you say "Stay, stay"?
3. What relation do you see in each poem between its pace, its movement, and the attitude it expresses toward the passing of time?

Richard Lovelace (1618-1658)

Sidney and Surrey represent in the early Renaissance the nobleman-poet; that is, the soldier and courtier who studied poetry and wrote it. Richard Lovelace is their counterpart in the late Renaissance. He fought on the side of the king in the tragic civil war in which John Milton, as we shall see, fought with his pen on the opposing side. He was one of the handsomest and most talented of the "Cavalier Poets," who wrote and fought in a time of great public disorder and great private heroism. Whether there was a real lady behind his "Lucasta" we do not know.

To Lucasta,
Going to the Wars

Richard Lovelace

Tell me not, sweet, I am unkind,
 That from the nunnery
Of thy chaste breast and quiet mind
 To war and arms I fly.

True, a new mistress now I chase,   5
 The first foe in the field;
And with a stronger faith embrace
 A sword, a horse, a shield.

Yet this inconstancy is such
 As you too shall adore;   10
I could not love thee, dear, so much,
 Loved I not honor more.

Comment

The soldier leaves his lady for a new mistress, war; yet he contrives a compliment to them both.

1. In the first stanza the lover speaks of "nunnery" and "quiet mind." With what images does he characterize his "new mistress" in the second stanza?
2. What does "inconstancy" mean (l. 9)? Why should Lucasta adore this inconstancy?
3. The word *unkind* in line 1 means both "unfriendly" or "ungentle," and "unnatural." Why is the departure of the soldier not ungentle? Why is it not unnatural?

The World of Dreams

Edmund Spenser (1552?-1599)

THE 1590's WERE a period of great achievement in English literature. Shakespeare's happiest comedies and his most patriotic history plays were appearing. A poet and scholar named George Chapman began to publish his translation of Homer's *Iliad* (a translation that many years later would delight another English poet, John Keats). Richard Hakluyt proudly set his country's sailor-heroes before the world in his *Principal Navigations, Voyages, and Discoveries of the English Nation.* But no work of the period was more ambitious than *The Faerie Queene,* the first part of which was published in 1590. It was a work destined to be unfinished, like *The Canterbury Tales.* But it was thoroughly and elaborately planned, down to the very diction it employed.

The author was Edmund Spenser, a poet well known and admired by his contemporaries, though not altogether admired by some members of Queen Elizabeth's court. Spenser was never able to secure a government post at home; and from 1580 until his death he lived in Ireland, where he filled a number of different minor political offices. One of his early works, a political satire that attacked certain men powerful at court, seems to have left a sting that was not readily forgotten.

The Faerie Queene

In Ireland, at any rate, Spenser seems to have had time to write at least half of what, if it had been finished, would have been one of the longest poems ever written. *The Faerie Queene* combines two kinds of literature, the romance and the epic, and it combines them in a huge allegory in which the central figures are Arthur and Gloriana, or Queen Elizabeth. There were to have been twelve books or stories, each one describing, through the adventures of its hero, the characteristics of some moral virtue. One book, for example, tells of the adventures of Artegall, a knight who represents Justice. Another tells of Sir Guyon, or Temperance. Spenser based his stories on the legends of King Arthur (who, Spenser said, represents Magnificence, by which he probably meant Magnanimity, or "one of great soul"); and, through his retelling of the old tales, he comments on the moral virtues he believed the great age of Elizabeth required. As he said in a letter to Sir Walter Raleigh, "The general end therefore of all the book is to fashion a gentleman or noble person in virtuous and gentle discipline."

Spenser's knights, like those of Arthurian legend, protect ladies in distress, overcome wicked giants, and battle with traitors. One kind of adventure, though, is new in *The Faerie Queene.* This is the battle not against a giant, but against part of the mind itself. It is a battle in which the enemy is completely invisible to its foe.

Here are some portions of one such adventure. The Redcross Knight, who represents Holiness, is traveling with Una, or Truth.

They meet an old hermit, Archimago ("archmagician"), and go with him to his simple dwelling to rest. The Knight has just overcome a deadly dragon in the midst of the Forest of Error, and thus has protected the lady: Holiness protects Truth. But the adventure in the hermit's cottage is a different matter. There the magician contrives to separate Holiness from Truth, and it is long before they become reunited.

The Faerie Queene was deliberately written in archaic (old-fashioned) language. Spenser writes *ayre* rather than *air*, *deaw* rather than *dew*, or *steedes* rather than *steeds* because it is part of his purpose to remind his audience of their heritage: his old-fashioned language describes old-fashioned virtues. He invented also a new kind of stanza, one that bears his name (Spenserian) among the varieties of English verse. The rhymes (*ababbcbcc*) are closely woven, and the last line is two syllables (or one strong beat) longer than the other lines. (Final *-ed* is always pronounced as a separate syllable.) This long final line sets off each stanza as a unit. It slows the narrative down, to be sure, from Chaucer's brisk speed, but it makes each unit into something like a single detail of a huge and ancient tapestry.

from The Faerie Queene

Book I

Edmund Spenser

At lenth they chaunst to meet upon the way
An aged Sire, in long blacke weedes yclad,[1]
His feete all bare, his beard all hoarie gray,
And by his belt his booke[2] he hanging had.
Sober he seemde, and very sagely sad,[3]   5
And to the ground his eyes were lowly bent,
Simple in shew,[4] and voyde of malice bad;
And all the way he prayed as he went,
And often knockt his brest, as one that did repent.

---

1 **weedes yclad** (ĭ klăd′)**:** clad in black garments.
2 **booke:** prayer book.
3 **sad:** solemn.
4 **shew:** appearance.

He faire the knight saluted, louting⁵ low,
Who faire him quited, as that courteous was;⁶
And after asked him if he did know
Of straunge adventures, which abroad did pas.
"Ah, my deare Sonne," quoth he, "how should, alas,
Silly⁷ old man, that lives in hidden cell,
Bidding⁸ his beades all day for his trespas,
Tydings of warre and worldly trouble tell?
With holy father sits not with such things to mell.⁹

"But if of daunger which hereby doth dwell
And homebred¹⁰ evill ye desire to heare,
Of a straunge man I can you tidings tell,
That wasteth all this countrey farre and neare."
"Of such," said he, "I chiefly do inquere,
And shall you well reward to shew the place
In which that wicked wight¹¹ his dayes doth weare;
For to all knighthood it is foule disgrace,
That such a cursed creature lives so long a space."

"Far hence," quoth he, "in wastfull wildernesse¹²
His dwelling is, by which no living wight
May ever passe, but thorough¹³ great distresse."
"Now," sayd the Lady, "draweth toward night,¹⁴
And well I wote¹⁵ that of your later fight
Ye all forwearied¹⁶ be; for what so strong,
But, wanting rest, will also want of might?
The Sunne, that measures heaven all day long,
At night doth baite his steedes¹⁷ the Ocean waves emong.

"Then with the Sunne take, Sir, your timely rest,
And with new day new worke at once begin.
Untroubled night, they say, gives counsell best."
"Right well, Sir knight, ye have advised bin,"
Quoth then that aged man; "the way to win
Is wisely to advise.¹⁸ Now day is spent;
Therefore with me ye may take up your In¹⁹
For this same night." The knight was well content;
So with that godly father to his home they went.

---

5 **louting**: bowing.
6 **Who faire . . . was**: who repaid him courteously
with a bow in return.
7 **Silly**: simple.
8 **Bidding**: telling his beades, praying.
9 **With holy . . . mell**: It is not fitting for a holy
man to meddle with such things.
10 **homebred**: local, as opposed to wars and
worldly troubles.
11 **wight**: person

12 **wastfull wildernesse**: a wild wasteland.
13 **but thorough**: except with.
14 **draweth toward night**: night draws near.
15 **wote**: know.
16 **forwearied**: worn out.
17 **doth . . . steedes**: rests, or refreshes, the
horses that pull his chariot.
18 **the way . . . advise**: The way to prosper is to
be sensible.
19 **In**: inn, a shelter for the night.

EDMUND SPENSER   **161**

A little lowly Hermitage it was,
Downe in a dale, hard by a forest's side,
Far from resort of people that did pas
In travell to and froe.   A little wyde[20]
There was an holy Chappell edifyde,[21]   50
Wherein the Hermite dewly wont to say
His holy things each morne and eventyde.
Thereby a Christall streame did gently play,
Which from a sacred fountaine welled forth alway.

Arrived there, the little house they fill,   55
Ne looke for entertainement where none was.
Rest is their feast, and all things at their will;[22]
The noblest mind the best contentment has.
With faire discourse the evening so they pas,
For that old man of pleasing wordes had store. . . .   60

The drouping Night thus creepeth on them fast,
And the sad humour[23] loading their eye liddes,
As messenger of Morpheus[24] on them cast
Sweet slombring deaw, the which to sleepe them biddes.
Unto their lodgings then his guestes he riddes;[25]   65
Where when all drownd in deadly sleepe he findes,
He to his study goes, and there amiddes
His Magick bookes and artes of sundry kindes,
He seekes out mighty charmes, to trouble sleepy mindes.

Then choosing out few wordes most horrible   70
(Let none them read), thereof did verses frame,
With which and other spelles like terrible,[26]
He bad awake blacke Plutoe's griesly Dame,[27]
And cursed Heaven, and spake reprochfull shame
Of highest God, the Lord of life and light—   75
A bold bad man, that dar'd to call by name
Great Gorgon,[28] Prince of darknesse and dead night,
At which Cocytus quakes, and Styx is put to flight.[29]

And forth he cal'd out of deepe darknesse dred
Legions of Sprights, the which like little flyes   80
Flutt'ring about his ever damned hed,

20 **wyde:** off to one side.
21 **edifyde:** built; constructed.
22 **all things at their will:** Everything was as they
wanted it.
23 **sad humour:** heavy moisture.
24 **Morpheus:** god of sleep.
25 **riddes:** dismisses.
26 **like terrible:** similarly terrible.

27 **Plutoe's griesly Dame:** Proserpina, the fearful
(griesly) wife of Pluto, and thus queen of Hades,
or the classical underworld.
28 **Great Gorgon:** Demogorgon, a terrible demon
of the underworld.
29 **At which . . . flight:** i.e., the Demogorgon even
frightens the rivers of Hades.

162

A-waite whereto their service he applyes,
To aide his friends, or fray[30] his enimies.
Of those he chose out two, the falsest twoo,
And fittest for to forge true-seeming lyes: 85
The one of them he gave a message too;
The other by him selfe staide, other worke to doo.

He,[31] making speedy way through spersed ayre,
And through the world of waters wide and deepe,
To Morpheus' house doth hastily repaire.   90
Amid the bowels of the earth full steepe
And low, where dawning day doth never peepe,
His dwelling is; there Tethys[32] his wet bed
Doth ever wash, and Cynthia[33] still doth steepe
In silver deaw his ever-drouping hed,   95
Whiles sad Night over him her mantle black doth spred.

Whose double gates he findeth locked fast,
The one faire fram'd of burnisht Yvory,
The other all with silver overcast;
And wakefull dogges before them farre do lye,   100
Watching to banish Care, their enimy,
Who oft is wont to trouble gentle Sleepe.
By them the Sprite doth passe in quietly,
And unto Morpheus comes, whom drowned deepe
In drowsie fit he findes: of nothing he takes keepe.[34]   105

And more, to lulle him in his slumber soft,
A trickling streame from high rocke tumbling downe
And ever-drizling raine upon the loft,[35]
Mixt with a murmuring winde, much like the sowne
Of swarming Bees, did cast him in a swowne.   110
No other noyse, nor people's troublous cryes,
As still are wont t'annoy the walled towne,[36]
Might there be heard; but carelesse Quiet lyes,
Wrapt in eternall silence farre from enemyes.

The messenger approching to him spake,   115
But his wast wordes returned to him in vaine;
So sound he slept that nought mought[37] him awake.

EDMUND SPENSER

Then rudely he him thrust, and pusht with paine,
Whereat he gan to stretch; but he againe
Shooke him so hard that forced him to speake.   120
As one then in a dreame, whose dryer braine[38]
Is tost with troubled sights and fancies weake,
He mumbled soft, but would not all his silence breake.

The Sprite then gan more boldly him to wake,
And threatned unto him the dreaded name   125
Of Hecate;[39] whereat he gan to quake,
And, lifting up his lumpish head, with blame
Halfe angry asked him for what he came.
"Hither," quoth he, "me Archimago sent,
He that the stubborne Sprites can wisely tame;   130
He bids thee to him send for his intent[40]
A fit false dreame, that can delude the sleeper's sent."[41]

The God obayde and, calling forth straight way
A diverse[42] dreame out of his prison darke,
Delivered it to him, and downe did lay   135
His heavie head, devoide of carefull carke,[43]
Whose sences all were straight benumbd and starke.[44]
He, backe returning by the Yvorie dore,[45]
Remounted up as light as chearefull Larke;
And on his litle winges the dreame he bore   140
In hast unto his Lord, where he him left afore.

[*The sprite returns with the dream to Archimago, the archmagician,
who in the meantime has fashioned the other sprite into the shape of
an evil lady who is the twin or double of Una. He then confuses the
sleep of the knight with the false dream and the false Una: he makes
the knight believe that Una is unworthy of his protection, and so he
separates, for a time at least, Holiness from Truth.*]

38 dryer braine: Moisture produces a deep and
dreamless sleep. "Dry-brained" sleep would be
troubled by dreams.
39 Hecate (hĕk′ĭ tĭ) goddess of ghosts and magic.
40 intent: purpose.
41 sent: senses.

42 diverse: misleading.
43 carke: worry.
44 Whose . . . starke: He was dead to the world.
45 Yvorie dore: The gate for false dreams is of
ivory. The gate for the true is of horn.

Comment

The magician's sprite leaves the natural world, he enters the world
of sleep (the underworld), and he returns to the world above. But does
the god of sleep and dreams live in a world more mysterious than that
through which the knight and his lady are making their way? The
magic of a dream separates Holiness from Truth. But do dreams come
from an unnatural world?

1. What is the dominant imagery of Spenser's description of the house of Morpheus?
2. How does Morpheus behave as the sprite tries to awaken him?
3. Does Spenser's description of the underworld of sleep seem to you on the whole to make it a pleasant or an unpleasant place?
4. Yet the dream from the underworld helps to separate the Redcross Knight from Una, from Truth. What kind of enemy, then, besides monsters and dragons and giants, is Spenser's knight subjected to?
5. What does this adventure tell us about Spenser's conception of the moral struggle? Is evil always obvious? Can it always be seen and attacked directly?

OR SUMMARY

The World of Affairs

Francis Bacon (1561-1626)

NO OTHER MAN was more vigorously and widely active in the late 16th and early 17th centuries than was Sir Francis Bacon. His father was one of Queen Elizabeth's ministers, and he himself was at a very early age immersed in the rough politics of the court. He held a number of governmental positions and in 1618 was made Lord Chancellor, becoming head of the entire judicial system of the kingdom. The end of his public career was unfortunately darkened by scandal, for in 1621 a Parliamentary investigating committee found him guilty of accepting gifts and favors from persons whose suits were being tried in his court. (The accusation was in reality a veiled attack on King James, with whom Bacon had sided in his battles against Parliament.) In his own defense Bacon argued that his behavior differed in no way from that of any other judge of his time, but he was forced to retire.

Bacon turned then to the scientific interests that he had enthusiastically pursued all his life (in fact, he died of a cold he caught while gathering snow for an experiment), and he is remembered not as a lawyer but as the champion of new scientific procedures. His most famous work was called *The Advancement of Learning*, and the key word of the title is *Advancement*, or progress. Real progress would become possible, he argued, if science—"natural philosophy"—were to become more co-operative. Scientists must not work alone, each trying to discover a final truth, he said. They must work together in the progressive, gradual unfolding of truth. Above all they must test their truths or laws by practice, by experiment. These convictions may seem commonplace enough to us, but King James said of Bacon's *Advancement of Learning* that it was like the peace of God—"it passeth understanding"!

Bacon did not himself make scientific discoveries like those, say, of Galileo (though he did experiment enough to propose the theory that heat is a result of the violent activity of fine particles of matter, a theory which is indeed not unlike our present-day theory—that heat is a result of the motion of molecules). He did, however, have much to say about scientific method and what it might achieve.

The New Atlantis

In one of his last works Bacon sketched out his ideal scientific society in a book (written in Latin, but soon translated into English by an associate) entitled *The New Atlantis*. Atlantis is the name of a kingdom thought by the Greeks to have flourished so long ago that it had been covered over by the sea, and the name for centuries has been a symbol of a far-off perfect society in which men lived in purposeful harmony. Bacon retells the old legend. A group of Europeans, driven by a storm, sail to a strange island where they find a new and astonishing civilization. For some days they are kept in quarantine but are finally allowed to visit parts of the island and to learn something of its history and way of life. They are told particularly about Salomon's House, the institution central in the life of these far-off people. This selection comes from that portion of the story.

Salomon's House—the house of wisdom—provided the first detailed model of the scientific societies that grew up in the 17th century. Something like it came into being in England as The Royal Society of London for Improving Natural Knowledge. And something like it came into being in America when Benjamin Franklin founded The American Philosophical Society in Philadelphia in 1743.

From The New Atlantis

Francis Bacon

I WILL IMPART unto thee, for the love of God and men, a relation of the true state of Salomon's House. Son, to make you know the true state of Salomon's House, I will keep this order. First, I will set forth unto you the end of our foundation. Secondly, the preparations and instruments we have for our works. Thirdly, the several employments and functions whereto our fellows are assigned. And fourthly, the ordinances and rites which we observe.

The end of our foundation is the knowledge of causes and secret motions of things, and the enlarging of the bounds of human empire, to the effecting of all things possible.

The preparations and instruments are these. We have large and deep caves of several depths, the deepest are sunk six hundred fathom; and some of them are digged and made under great hills and mountains, so that if you reckon together the depth of the hill and the depth of the cave, they are (some of them) above three miles deep. For we find that the depth of a hill and the depth of a cave from the flat is the same thing, both remote alike from the sun and heaven's beams and from the open air. These caves we call the lower region. And we use them for all coagulations, indurations, refrigerations, and conservations of bodies.[1] We use them likewise for the imitation of natural mines and the producing also of new artificial metals by compositions and materials which we use, and lay there for many years. We use them also sometimes (which may seem strange) for curing of some diseases and for prolongation of life in some hermits that choose to live there, well accommodated of all things necessary; and indeed live very long, by whom also we learn many things. . . .

We have high towers, the highest about half a mile in height, and some of them likewise set upon high mountains, so that the vantage of the hill with the tower is in the highest of them three miles at least. And these places we call the upper region, accounting the air between the high places and the low as a middle region. We use these towers, according to their several heights and situations, for insolation, refrigeration, conservation, and for the view of divers meteors,[2] as winds, rain, snow, hail, and some of the fiery meteors[3] also. And upon them, in some places, are dwellings of hermits, whom we visit sometimes, and instruct what to observe. . . .

We have also great and spacious houses, where we imitate and demonstrate meteors, as snow, hail, rain, some artificial rains of bodies and not of water, thunders, lightnings; also generations of bodies in air, as frogs, flies, and divers others. . . .

---

1 **coagulations . . . of bodies:** names for activities of scientific research—the thickening, hardening, chilling, and preserving of matter.
2 **meteors:** various kinds of weather and climate.
3 **meteors:** This time the word means shooting star.

We have also means to make divers plants rise by mixtures of earths without seeds, and likewise to make divers new plants differing from the vulgar,[4] and to make one tree or plant turn into another.

We have also parks and enclosures of all sorts of beasts and birds, which we use not only for view or rareness but likewise for dissections and trials, that thereby we may take light what may be wrought upon the body of man. Wherein we find many strange effects: as continuing life in them, though divers parts, which you account vital, be perished and taken forth;[5] resuscitating of some that seem dead in appearance; and the like. We try also all poisons and other medicines upon them, as well of chirurgery as physic.[6] By art likewise we make them greater or taller than their kind is, and contrariwise dwarf them, and stay their growth; we make them more fruitful and bearing than their kind is, and contrariwise barren and not generative. . . .

We have also perspective-houses,[7] where we make demonstrations of all lights and radiations, and of all colors; and out of things uncolored and transparent we can represent unto you all several colors, not in rainbows, as it is in gems and prisms, but of themselves single. We represent also all multiplications of light,[8] which we carry to great distance, and make so sharp as to discern small points and lines; also all colorations of light, all delusions and deceits of the sight in figures, magnitudes, motions, colors, all demonstra-

tions of shadows. We find also divers means, yet unknown to you, of producing of light originally from divers bodies. We procure means of seeing objects afar off, as in the heaven and remote places, and represent things near as afar off and things afar off as near, making feigned distances. We have also helps for the sight, far above spectacles and glasses in use. We have also glasses and means to see small and minute bodies perfectly and distinctly, as the shapes and colors of small flies and worms, grains and flaws in gems, which cannot otherwise be seen. . . . We make artificial rainbows, halos, and circles about light. We represent also all manner of reflections, refractions, and multiplications of visual beams of objects. . . .

We have also sound-houses,[9] where we practice and demonstrate all sounds and their generation. We have harmonies, which you have not, of quarter-sounds and lesser slides of sounds.[10] Divers instruments of music likewise to you unknown, some sweeter than any you have, together with bells and rings that are dainty and sweet. We represent small sounds as great and deep, likewise great sounds extenuate[11] and sharp; we make divers tremblings and warblings of sounds, which in their original are entire. We represent and imitate all articulate sounds and letters, and the voices and notes of beasts and birds. We have certain helps which set to the ear do further the hearing greatly. . . .

We have also engine-houses,[12] where are prepared engines and instruments

<hr />

4 **the vulgar:** ordinary kinds.
5 **parts . . . taken forth:** though vital organs are removed.
6 **chirurgery** (kī rûr′jə rĭ) **as physic:** surgery and medicine.
7 **perspective houses:** laboratories for the study of optics or the nature of light.
8 **multiplications of light:** focusing beams of light.

9 **sound-houses:** laboratories for the study of acoustics. This is a subject in which Bacon himself as a student performed some fresh experiments.
10 **sounds:** subtle notes.
11 **extenuate:** very high-pitched.
12 **engine-houses:** An engine is any device for the production of force.

for all sorts of motions. There we imitate and practice to make swifter motions than any you have, either out of your muskets or any engine that you have; and to make them and multiply them more easily and with small force by wheels and other means, and to make them stronger and more violent than yours are, exceeding your greatest cannons and basilisks.[13] We represent also ordnance and instruments of war, and engines of all kinds, and likewise new mixtures and compositions of gunpowder, wildfires burning in water and unquenchable. Also fireworks of all variety both for pleasure and use. We imitate also flights of birds; we have some degrees of flying in the air; we have ships and boats for going under water, and brooking of seas; also swimming-girdles and supporters. We have divers curious clocks and other like motions of return and some perpetual motions. We imitate also motions of living creatures by images of men, beasts, birds, fishes, and serpents. We have also a great number of other various motions, strange for equality, fineness, and subtilty.

We have also a mathematical house, where are represented all instruments, as well of geometry as astronomy, exquisitely made. . . .

These are . . . the riches of Salomon's House.

For the several employments and offices of our fellows, we have twelve that sail into foreign countries, under the names of other nations (for our own we conceal),[14] who bring us the books and abstracts and patterns of experiments of all other parts. These we call Merchants of Light.

We have three that collect the experiments which are in all books. These we call Depredators.

We have three that collect the experiments of all mechanical arts, and also of liberal sciences, and also of practices which are not brought into arts. These we call Mystery-men.[15]

We have three that try new experiments, such as themselves think good. These we call Pioneers or Miners.

We have three that draw the experiments of the former four into titles and tables, to give the better light for the drawing of observations and axioms out of them. These we call Compilers.

We have three that bend themselves, looking into the experiments of their fellows, and cast about how to draw out of them things of use and practice for man's life, and knowledge as well for works as for plain demonstration of causes.[16] . . . These we call Dowry-men or Benefactors.

Then after divers meetings and consults of our whole number to consider of the former labors and collections, we have three that take care, out of them, to direct new experiments of a higher light,[17] more penetrating into nature than the former. These we call Lamps.

We have three others that do execute the experiments so directed, and report them. These we call Inoculators.

Lastly, we have three that raise the former discoveries by experiments into greater observations, axioms, and aphorisms. These we call Interpreters of Nature.

---

13 **basilisks:** long-barreled cannons.
14 **twelve . . . conceal:** The people of Bensalem, the far-off island, have visited Europe, but in disguise, to study its science; but no Europeans have visited Bensalem before.
15 **Mystery-men:** A "mystery" is a trade or craft that is not taught among the liberal sciences but is handed on to apprentices. Glass blowing would be an example.
16 **things of use . . . causes:** The Benefactors draw from experiments both practical applications and theoretical causes.
17 **higher light:** more general; more abstract.

The institution called Salomon's House is a giant research institute. It did not exist in all its branches anywhere in Bacon's time, but he hoped that it eventually would.

1. Make a list of all the modern scientific studies you can find represented in Salomon's House. Give them their modern names (for example, *meteorology*). What important modern subjects or studies do you find missing from your list? Consult an encyclopedia to find out when they came into being.
2. The last and most important officers of Salomon's House are called Interpreters of Nature. Why does Bacon grant to them the most important function? Where would you expect to find their equivalent today? What would their modern equivalent be called?

Bacon's Essays

Bacon wrote upon the conduct of life, as well as upon the conduct of science. His first *Essays, or Counsels Civil and Moral* appeared in 1597, and he kept adding to them throughout his life. As we read them we hear not only the tone of the man of affairs; we hear also the note of objectivity that grows from the scientist's pursuit of knowledge.

Of Boldness

Francis Bacon

IT IS A TRIVIAL grammar-school text, but yet worthy a wise man's consideration. Question was asked of Demosthenes[1] what was the chief part of an orator? He answered, "Action."[2] What next? "Action." What next again? "Action." He said it that knew it best, and had by nature himself no advantage in that he commended.[3] A strange thing that that part of an orator which is but superficial and rather the virtue of a player should be placed so high above those other noble parts of invention, elocu-

tion, and the rest; nay almost alone, as if it were all in all. But the reason is plain. There is in human nature generally more of the fool than of the wise; and therefore those faculties by which the foolish part of men's minds is taken are most potent. Wonderful like is the case of boldness in civil business; what first? Boldness; what second and third? Boldness. And yet boldness is a child of ignorance and baseness, far inferior to other parts. But nevertheless it doth fascinate and bind hand and foot those that are either shallow in judgment or weak in courage, which are the greatest part; yea and prevaileth with wise men at weak times. Therefore we see it hath done wonders in popular states,[4] but with senates and princes less; and more ever upon the first entrance of bold persons into action than soon after, for boldness is an ill keeper of promise.

1 **Demosthenes** (dĭ mŏs′thə nēz′): a great orator of ancient Greece.
2 **Action:** acting; i.e., being an actor.
3 **himself . . . commended:** Demosthenes was not naturally a good actor.

4 **popular states:** republics or democracies.

Greenwich Observatory was established in 1675 to promote the study of the movements of the moon and stars.

Surely as there are mountebanks[5] for the natural body, so are there mountebanks for the politic body, men that undertake great cures, and perhaps have been lucky in two or three experiments, but want[6] the grounds of science, and therefore cannot hold out. Nay you shall see a bold fellow many times do Mahomet's miracle. Mahomet made the people believe that he would call an hill to him, and from the top of it offer up his prayers for the observers of his law. The people assembled; Mahomet called the hill to come to him, again and again; and when the hill stood still, he was never a whit abashed, but said, "If the hill will not come to Mahomet, Mahomet will go to the hill." So these men, when they have promised great matters and failed most shamefully, yet (if they have the perfection of boldness) they will but slight it over, and make a turn, and no more ado. Certainly to men of great judgment, bold persons are a sport to behold; nay and to the vulgar also, boldness has somewhat of the ridiculous. For if absurdity be the subject of laughter, doubt you not but great boldness is seldom without some absurdity. Especially it is a sport to see, when a bold fellow is out of countenance,[7] for that puts his face into a most shrunken and wooden posture, as needs it must, for in bashfulness the spirits do a little go and come; but with bold men, upon like occasion, they stand at a stay, like a stale at chess,[8] where it is no mate, but yet the game cannot stir. But this last were fitter for a satire than for a serious observation. This is well to be weighed, that boldness is ever blind, for it seeth not dangers and inconveniences. Therefore it is ill in counsel, good in execution; so that the right use of bold persons is that they never command in chief, but be seconds and under the direction of others. For in counsel it is good to see dangers, and in execution not to see them, except they be very great.

7 **is . . . countenance:** is abashed.
8 **stale at chess:** stalemate but not checkmate. The game stops but neither side wins.

5 **mountebanks:** quacks.
6 **want:** lack.

FRANCIS BACON

Of Studies

Francis Bacon

STUDIES SERVE FOR delight, for ornament, and for ability. Their chief use for delight is in privateness and retiring; for ornament, is in discourse; and for ability, is in the judgment and disposition of business. For expert men can execute and perhaps judge of particulars, one by one, but the general counsels and the plots[1] and marshaling of affairs come best from those that are learned. To spend too much time in studies is sloth; to use them too much for ornament is affectation; to make judgment wholly by their rules is the humor of a scholar. They perfect nature, and are perfected by experience, for natural abilities are like natural plants, that need proyning[2] by study; and studies themselves do give forth directions too much at large, except they be bounded in by experience. Crafty men contemn studies, simple men admire them, and wise men use them, for they teach not their own use; but that is a wisdom without them and above them, won by observation. Read not to contradict and confute; nor to believe and take for granted; nor to find talk and discourse; but to weigh and consider. Some books are to be tasted, others to be swallowed, and some few to be chewed and digested; that is, some books are to be read only in parts; others to be read, but not curiously;[3] and some few to be read wholly and with diligence and attention. Some books also may be read by deputy,[4] and extracts made of them by others, but that would be only in the less important arguments and the meaner sort of books; else distilled books are like common distilled waters, flashy[5] things. Reading maketh a full man; conference a ready man; and writing an exact man. And therefore, if a man write little, he had need have a great memory; if he confer little, he had need have a present wit: and if he read little, he had need have much cunning, to seem to know that he doth not. Histories make men wise, poets witty, the mathematics subtile, natural philosophy deep, moral grave, logic and rhetoric able to contend. *Abeunt studia in mores.*[6] Nay there is no stond or impediment in the wit, but may be wrought out by fit studies,[7] like as diseases of the body may have appropriate exercises. Bowling is good for the stone and reins;[8] shooting for the lungs and breast; gentle walking for the stomach; riding for the head; and the like. So if a man's wit be wandering, let him study the mathematics, for in demonstrations, if his wit be called away never so little, he must begin again. If his wit be not apt to distinguish or find differences, let him study the schoolmen, for they are *cumini sectores.*[9] If he be not apt to beat over matters, and to call up one thing to prove and illustrate another, let him study the lawyers' cases. So every defect of the mind may have a special receipt.

1 **plots:** planning; organizing.
2 **proyning:** pruning.
3 **curiously:** too carefully.
4 **read by deputy:** read by another—by a research assistant.
5 **flashy:** showy.
6 **Abeunt . . . mores:** Studies affect behavior.
7 **stond . . . studies:** There is no intellectual obstacle that cannot be overcome by an appropriate study.
8 **reins:** kidneys. (Bowling is good for preventing kidney stones.)
9 **cumini sectores:** "hairsplitters."

The Ambassadors, painted by Hans Holbein (1497?-1543), is a portrait of Renaissance men of affairs, two French ambassadors. The objects in the painting represent their scientific and cultural interests.

Comment

Bacon's essays do not so much explore their subjects as give advice upon them. What sort of audience would value this advice? For whom is Bacon writing?

1. Some of Bacon's sentences are pithy and well-balanced; they lend themselves to the clear exposition of a particular point. "Studies serve for delight, for ornament, and for ability"—one, two, three. Locate other examples of such sentences.
2. Bacon's sentences give clear advice. Find examples of advice that seems to you clear and memorable.
3. Judging, then, by his style and by the character of his advice, what can you deduce about Bacon's audience? How would you describe his ideal reader? Would that person be a man or a woman? What would her/his tastes be? What would her/his interests be? How would he/she differ, in interests and training, from the Renaissance courtier you saw described at the beginning of this chapter?

The Dream of Power
and the Human World

William Shakespeare: Macbeth

IT WAS INEVITABLE that the greatest writer of the times should bring to
perfection a branch of literature in which conflict is central, namely,
tragedy. This you will see in *The Tragedy of Macbeth,* one of Shakespeare's greatest plays. Shakespeare's own description of the poet's
imagination applies to the central character, for Macbeth's imagination
indeed "bodies forth/The forms of things unknown." Or we may recall the definition of Edmund Spenser's: "Poetry is a divine instinct and
unnatural rage passing the reach of common reason." Macbeth is indeed possessed by an "unnatural rage," even to the point of its overwhelming his "divine instinct." But *Macbeth* is not the story of a
poet. It is the story of a man, a nobleman, in a world of other human
beings to whom his obligations are clear. And Macbeth, as we shall
see, is finally broken by the conflict between his dream of power and
the real world. It is a conflict that reveals to us a tragically divided
mind.

Shakespeare's Life Little is truly known of the circumstances by
which Shakespeare became a successful dramatist. The biographical
facts are few, though the conjectures about this great Elizabethan are
legion. He was born in April, 1564, in Stratford-on-Avon, to John
Shakespeare, an influential man in the town, and Mary Arden, a
gentlewoman. The grammar school at Stratford to which Shakespeare
is likely to have gone provided a good education for its students, with
emphasis upon Latin grammar, composition, and literature. Shakespeare was married in 1582 to Anne Hathaway, daughter of a Shottery
farmer; they had three children: Susanna and twins, Judith and Ham-
net. By 1588 he was known as a dramatist and was living in London,
and by 1592 he was well known as an actor. By 1598 Shakespeare had
written more than a dozen plays and had prospered so well that he
bought New Place, an imposing house in Stratford where his wife and
children lived. He continued writing sonnets and plays, a total of
thirty-five of the latter. In 1607 he retired from the theater, a wealthy
man, and lived in Stratford until his death, April 23, 1616. He was
buried in the chancel of the church at Stratford.

The Elizabethan Stage As you read *Macbeth,* keep in mind that
it was written not to be studied, but to be seen and heard as actors
performed the play on a stage. Although you may read the lines
silently, think of them as being spoken. From scene to scene ask yourself what are the expressions on the faces of the characters. Examine
the dialogue to determine what the key words in a passage are and
how they should be spoken: which exclaimed, which declared, which
questioned, which spoken softly or forcefully. At the same time, try to
be aware of the rhythm and sound of the poetry.

This portrait of Shakespeare by Martin Droeshout appeared in the first collected edition of Shakespeare's plays in 1623.

Folger Shakespeare Library, Washington

The Globe Theater, where many of Shakespeare's plays were performed, differed in several important ways from modern theaters. The stage of the Globe, as well as other Elizabethan playhouses, jutted into the yard (the main floor) and had the spectators on three sides. Since there were no curtains to conceal the main stage and only daylight to light it, contact between actors and spectators was close and intimate. Behind the main stage was the inner stage, a place where interior scenes were often enacted. When not in use, this area was concealed by curtains. Because of its position many spectators could not see the inner stage fully, and scenes begun here often moved down to the main stage quickly. Above the inner stage were second, third, and sometimes fourth levels. The second level often functioned as a bedroom or balcony. The third level was used occasionally for scenes but more often as a place where musicians performed. The fourth level was a place for sound effects—the ringing of a bell (alarum) or the rolling of cannon balls across the floor to simulate thunder. The main stage often used trap doors also: a large one center and well downstage, and two smaller ones right and left of the large one and upstage. There were doors connecting the inner stage with the upper levels and others leading to tiring (dressing) rooms, right and left of the main stage.

Since there were no curtains to conceal the main stage, plays had to flow smoothly from one scene to the next without interruption. Shakespeare used the platform (main stage), the inner stage, and the upper levels to indicate a change of scene. The inner stage could serve as Lady Macbeth's private chamber and then become the gathering place near Dunsinane for the armies. A change of scene was often indicated by the simple expedient of having a character exit by one door and reappear almost immediately at another.

Shakespeare also worked in a theater where there was little realistic scenery and where the actors usually wore costumes of their own time, not of the period in which the play was supposed to take place. Language had to tell the spectators where and when the story was taking place, to establish the nature of the characters and their conflict, and to reveal the feelings of the characters and the progress of the action.

One convention which the Elizabethan dramatist used to communicate directly what is in the mind of the central characters is the soliloquy. This is a speech delivered, as the term suggests, by a character alone on the stage. In *Macbeth* the hero speaks approximately 160 lines in several soliloquies. In almost every instance the soliloquy spoken by Macbeth is concerned with a dilemma—that is, he has two alternatives of action, neither of which is desirable, both of which will lead to misfortune. The presentation of opposing ideas in the soliloquy gives the spectator an opportunity to know what is on the mind of, and of deep concern to, the central character and to learn the possibilities of the character's future action. Developed metaphorically, the soliloquy not only reveals information to the spectators but also extracts emotional response from them.

Plot Source Shakespeare's genius worked too to shape a few bare historical facts into great tragedy. In Raphael Holinshed's *Chronicles*, a history of ancient England, Scotland, and Ireland, Shakespeare found the names of many of the characters of *Macbeth* and the basis for the plot of the play. He took liberties with the history he read in Holinshed's *Chronicles*, inventing, amplifying, and connecting the historically unconnected. From the borrowings, he developed not only the external, physical action of the drama but also the internal action, the conflict within the minds of characters. And although the physical stage on which the play is acted is limited, Shakespeare's poetic skill opens for us the whole vast interior stage of human thoughts and emotions. This interior action and the language to express it were not borrowed from Holinshed.

The Poetry Except for a few prose passages, *Macbeth* is written in blank verse. Unrhymed, but controlled by five iambic stresses, blank verse lends itself well to dramatic poetry because of its flexibility. It is easy in blank verse to approximate the naturalness of the spoken language, and spoken English falls naturally into the iambic pattern. The rhythmic character of blank verse never intrudes between the speaker and the sense of what is spoken.

The words Shakespeare used to tell Macbeth's story are not in themselves unusual; they are common words familiar to the audience of

Shakespeare's day, words which refer to everyday life. Yet they were able to evoke in that audience and in us now profound thought and feeling.

Perhaps the clue to the power of Shakespeare's language is in his use of imagery. The language brings to our minds things perceived through the senses, which in turn we connect with certain ideas and feelings.

Consider now an example of Shakespeare's use of language in *Macbeth* and see how it communicates the essential elements of the play. Remember that during the Renaissance kings were considered God's representatives on earth; they were sacred. For a subject to murder his king was almost unthinkable. When Macbeth murders Duncan, he commits a gross, unnatural act. The enormity of Macbeth's action becomes obvious through figurative language and through what have been called "image-clusters"—recurring imagery on one or two themes. In *Macbeth* there are many clusters of images which evoke darkness and violence. From this imagery, most of it metaphorical, comes a growing sense of evil caused by horrible, unnatural behavior. Notice the darkness and violence suggested by the images in the following passage.

> Ah, good father,
> Thou seest the heavens, as troubled with man's act,
> Threaten his bloody stage. By th' clock 'tis day,
> And yet dark night strangles the traveling lamp.
> Is't night's predominance, or the day's shame,
> That darkness does the face of earth entomb
> When living light should kiss it? (II, iv, 4-10)

In this passage such words as "bloody stage," "night strangles," "darkness does the face of earth entomb" communicate violence and evil.

Be aware as you read the play of other scenes where darkness and blood impress upon you the nightmarish quality of what happens in *Macbeth*. Notice, for example, that darkness dominates the three scenes in which the weird sisters appear. Darkness is coming as Duncan is approaching Inverness and his doom. In complete darkness Duncan is murdered. It is dark when the murderers strike down Banquo.

The Witches Before we discuss *Macbeth* as a tragic play, we should give attention to the witches, their origin, and their use in drama. Shakespeare adapted the term *Weird Sisters* from Holinshed. The Weird Sisters, as Holinshed described them, were goddesses of destiny, like the Norns of Scandinavian mythology, which corresponded to what the Anglo-Saxons called Wyrd, or Fate. Although there is this suggestion that the three are able to control man's destiny, they have in the play primarily the characteristics of the witch that the Elizabethan audience was familiar with. They are old women, ragged and poor, skinny and physically hideous, and full of hateful spite. In accordance

Macbeth and Banquo meet the weird sisters, or witches, as illustrated in Holinshed's Chronicles. *Shakespeare's conception of the witches differed somewhat from Holinshed's.*

with popular ideas of Elizabethan times, the witches have inherited from evil spirits certain supernatural powers: the ability to raise harmful storms, to become invisible and to pass from place to place unseen, to keep devils in the forms of toads and cats, to show things concealed and to foreshow things to come. The influence of the witches upon Macbeth is great. Because of his personal ambition he is susceptible to their influence. Innocent-minded Banquo is present when the witches first appear to Macbeth, yet he is unaffected by their prophecies. Although Shakespeare does have the witches exert some influence on Macbeth, the dramatist never goes so far as to make Macbeth their puppet—Macbeth never blames the Weird Sisters for his evil acts. He blames them only for deceiving him. The witches intensify the sense of fear, horror, mystery, and evil which characterize the atmosphere of the play. They also won the immediate attention of the Elizabethan spectator, who had no dimming lights or rising curtain in his theater to warn him when the play had begun.

Macbeth as Tragedy: Shakespeare wrote comedies, histories, and tragedies; *Macbeth* is a tragedy. If we examine the play as a whole, we may understand its tragic implications. Macbeth, the protagonist, is a person of high rank, a cousin of King Duncan, a royal thane, and a great general. When we first hear of him, we learn of his great bravery and courage in the battle to put down the rebellion against King Duncan; he stands as one of the three or four strongest men of the country. He is engaged in a noble action: to support his king and to save Scotland for its citizens. He fights energetically and courageously to put down the rebellion, to restore peace, and to reunite a people sundered by rebellion. He is a man noble, courageous, and righteous. Very early, however, we are made aware of another side of his nature. He is personally ambitious; he would destroy King Duncan in order to have the kingship for himself. The prophecies of the witches and the promptings of Lady Macbeth reinforce his own evil inclination. He murders his king. Although the prophetic suggestions of the witches and the strong influence of Lady Macbeth enter into his decision to kill Duncan and to seize the throne, they are of lesser importance than Macbeth's own evil ambition.

Having put down a rebellion and momentarily restored peace to Scotland, Macbeth immediately cancels these acts of a loyal subject when he murders Duncan. He becomes responsible for the terror which, as the play develops, begins to characterize Scotland. The King's sons flee their country. Banquo is murdered, his son Fleance barely escaping. Suspicion against Macbeth is aroused. Those who act with outright unfriendliness toward him suffer reprisals. Paid informers in the castles of the thanes breed a strong sense of insecurity among the noblemen. One nobleman is afraid to speak his honest mind to another for fear that the other may inform against him. Thus Macbeth has disrupted his kingdom, made its citizens fearful of each other, and struck terror to the heart of his country. Since the people of a country are united through their king, look to him as a moral example, and have security because a king is high-minded and generous, Macbeth's rule, so completely opposite to the ideal kingly role, has tragic consequences.

Another important element in the tragic struggle is within the character of Macbeth. Macbeth is a nobleman who is introspective and who possesses imagination and a conscience. Because of personal ambition, he commits a terrible act—the murder of his king. There is no extenuation for the murder itself, and the fact that King Duncan is benevolent and essentially good and trusting magnifies the horror of the action. Macbeth too has an inclination toward good; and, before he has gone far in his criminal career, his conscience speaks powerfully to him. Furthermore, he has unusual imaginative powers. Because of his powerful imagination and keen conscience, he has not a moment's peace, either physical or mental, from the time he conceives the act until he is himself slain at the end of the play. The physical act of the murder (which takes place off stage) and the other physical acts which occur throughout the rest of the play are not, *in themselves,* the action which engages the audience closely. It is the action taking place in the mind of Macbeth—the progress of his fear and the awful compunction of his conscience—which commands our close attention.

Although he makes a feeble effort at first to return to moral decency after each step in his moral decay, his fear of discovery and retribution

Chere begynneth a treatyse how þ hye
fader of heuen sendeth dethe to so-
mon euery creature to come and
gyue a counte of theyr lyues in
this worlde/and is in maner
of a morall playe.

A page from a 16th-century edition of Everyman, *the most famous of the English morality plays of the late Middle Ages and early Renaissance. Here Everyman is told by Death to prepare for a journey.*

leads him on. Just as he brings complete disorder to the Scottish nation, he brings complete disorder to his own life. He must die in order that Scotland may be restored to peace and decency and that he may rid his own soul of its horror. Macbeth's sense of righteousness is too weak to counteract his evil ambition. He must go down to defeat and death, the tragic consequences of his acts.

Although violence is done to King Duncan, to Banquo, to Macduff's family, and to the Scottish citizens at large, none of these events, each of which in itself one might call tragic, is central to the drama. Shakespeare wrote *The Tragedy of Macbeth.* Even though a whole nation has been disrupted, its citizens terrorized, its sense of decency and of the moral order lost, we find in the violence which Macbeth has done to *himself* the core of tragedy in the play. Witnessing Macbeth's tortured life and his tragic end, we feel both pity and terror. Yet with the death of Macbeth we feel that the ends of justice have ultimately been served.

The Tragedy of Macbeth

William Shakespeare

Dramatis Personae

DUNCAN, King of Scotland.

MALCOLM,
DONALBAIN, } his sons.

MACBETH,
BANQUO, } generals of the Scottish army.

MACDUFF,
LENNOX,
ROSS,
MENTEITH, } noblemen of Scotland.
ANGUS,
CAITHNESS,

FLEANCE, son to Banquo.

SIWARD, Earl of Northumberland, general of the English forces.

YOUNG SIWARD, his son.

SEYTON, an officer attending on Macbeth.

Boy, son to Macduff.

A Sergeant.

A Porter.

An Old Man.

An English Doctor.

A Scottish Doctor.

LADY MACBETH.

LADY MACDUFF.

A Gentlewoman, attending on Lady Macbeth.

The WEIRD SISTERS (WITCHES).

HECATE.

The Ghost of Banquo.

Apparitions.

Lords, Gentlemen, Officers, Soldiers, Murderers, Messengers, Attendants.

Scene—*Scotland; England.*

ACT I

Scene I. *Scotland. An open place.*

Thunder and lightning. Enter three WITCHES.

1 WITCH. When shall we three meet again
In thunder, lightning, or in rain?
  2 WITCH. When the hurlyburly's[1] done,
When the battle's lost and won.
5   **3 WITCH.** That will be ere the set of sun.
  1 WITCH. Where the place?
  2 WITCH.   Upon the heath.
  3 WITCH. There to meet with Macbeth.
  1 WITCH. I come, Graymalkin!
  2 WITCH. Paddock[2] calls.
  3 WITCH.   Anon![3]
10   **ALL.** Fair is foul, and foul is fair.
Hover through the fog and filthy air.   *(Exeunt.)*

1 hurlyburly : tumult; up-roar.

2 Graymalkin; Paddock : A cat, Graymalkin, and a frog, Paddock, are evil attendants on the Witches.
3 Anon : right away.

Scene II. *A camp near Forres.*

Alarum[1] within. Enter KING DUNCAN, MALCOLM, DONALBAIN, LENNOX, with Attendants, meeting a bleeding SERGEANT.

1 Alarum : a trumpet fanfare.

KING. What bloody man is that? He can report,
As seemeth by his plight, of the revolt
The newest state.
  MALCOLM.   This is the sergeant
Who like a good and hardy soldier fought
5 'Gainst my captivity.[2] Hail, brave friend!
Say to the King the knowledge of the broil[3]
As thou didst leave it.
  SERGEANT.   Doubtful it stood,
As two spent swimmers that do cling together
And choke their art.[4] The merciless Macdonwald
10 (Worthy to be a rebel, for to that[5]
The multiplying villanies of nature
Do swarm upon him) from the Western Isles
Of kerns and gallowglasses[6] is supplied;
And Fortune, on his damnèd quarrel smiling,
15 Showed like a rebel's whore.[7] But all's too weak;
For brave Macbeth (well he deserves that name),
Disdaining Fortune, with his brandished steel,
Which smoked with bloody execution
(Like valor's minion),[8] carved out his passage
20 Till he faced the slave;[9]
Which ne'er shook hands nor bade farewell to him
Till he unseamed him from the nave to th' chaps[10]

2 captivity : capture.
3 broil : battle.

4 choke their art : hamper each other.
5 to that : to that purpose.

6 kerns and gallowglasses : Irish foot soldiers.
7 And Fortune . . . whore : Fickle, changeable Fortune appeared to favor Macdonwald's evil cause for a time.
8 minion : favorite.
9 slave : villain.
10 Which . . . chaps : who [Macdonwald] was unable to avoid Macbeth until the latter cut him open from the navel to the jaws.

And fixed his head upon our battlements.

  KING. O valiant cousin! worthy gentleman!

25 SERGEANT. As whence the sun gins his reflection
Shipwracking storms and direful thunders break,
So from that spring whence comfort seemed to come
Discomfort swells.[11] Mark, King of Scotland, mark.
No sooner justice had, with valor armed,

30 Compelled these skipping[12] kerns to trust their heels
But the Norweyan lord, surveying vantage,[13]
With furbished arms and new supplies of men,
Began a fresh assault.

  KING.   Dismayed not this
Our captains, Macbeth and Banquo?

  SERGEANT.   Yes,

35 As sparrows eagles, or the hare the lion.
If I say sooth,[14] I must report they were
As cannons overcharged with double cracks, so they
Doubly redoubled strokes upon the foe.
Except[15] they meant to bathe in reeking wounds,

40 Or memorize another Golgotha,[16]
I cannot tell—
But I am faint; my gashes cry for help.

  KING. So well thy words become thee as thy wounds;
They smack of honor both. Go get him surgeons.

      (*Exit* SERGEANT, *attended.*)

     Enter Ross.

45 Who comes here?

  MALCOLM. The worthy Thane[17] of Ross.

  LENNOX. What a haste looks through his eyes! So should he
   look
That seems to speak things strange.

  ROSS.   God save the King!

  KING. Whence cam'st thou, worthy thane?

  ROSS.   From Fife, great King,
Where the Norweyan banners flout the sky

50 And fan our people cold.[18] Norway himself,
With terrible numbers,
Assisted by that most disloyal traitor
The Thane of Cawdor, began a dismal conflict,
Till that Bellona's bridegroom,[19] lapped in proof,[20]

55 Confronted him with self-comparisons,[21]
Point against point,[22] rebellious arm 'gainst arm,
Curbing his lavish[23] spirit; and to conclude,
The victory fell on us.

  KING.   Great happiness!

  ROSS.   That now

11 As . . . swells : As from the east, the sun first appears, bad weather also often comes; so from the source of content (victory over Macdonwald) comes disadvantage (King of Norway's attack).

12 skipping : of irregular tactics.

13 surveying vantage : noting an opportune moment for attack.

14 sooth : truth.

15 except : unless.

16 memorize . . . Golgotha (gŏl′gə thə): make the place memorable as a second Golgotha (field of the dead).

17 Thane : an early title of nobility in Scotland.

18 flout . . . cold : The Norwegian banner still flies but now serves only to cool off our soldiers.

19 Bellona's bridegroom : Macbeth is represented as the husband of Bellona, who was the Roman goddess of war.

20 lapped in proof : clad in well-tested (proved) armor.

21 confronted . . . comparisons : matched his movements with equal skill.

22 point against point : sword point to sword point.

23 lavish : reckless.

Sweno, the Norways' king, craves composition;[24]

60 Nor would we deign[25] him burial of his men
Till he disbursèd, at Saint Colme's Inch,[26]
Ten thousand dollars to our general use.
   KING. No more that Thane of Cawdor shall deceive
Our bosom interest.[27] Go pronounce his present death
65 And with his former title greet Macbeth.
   ROSS. I'll see it done.
   KING. What he hath lost noble Macbeth hath won.

(Exeunt.)

Scene III. *A blasted heath.*

Thunder. Enter the three WITCHES.

   1 WITCH. Where hast thou been, sister?
   2 WITCH. Killing swine.[1]
   3 WITCH. Sister, where thou?
   1 WITCH. A sailor's wife had chestnuts in her lap
5 And mounched and mounched and mounched. "Give me,"
      quoth I.
"Aroint thee,[2] witch!" the rump-fed ronyon[3] cries.
Her husband's to Aleppo gone, master o' th' Tiger;
But in a sieve[4] I'll thither sail
And, like[5] a rat without a tail,[6]
10 I'll do,[7] I'll do, and I'll do.
   2 WITCH. I'll give thee a wind.
   1 WITCH. Th' art kind.
   3 WITCH. And I another.
   1 WITCH. I myself have all the other,
15 And the very ports they blow,
All the quarters that they know
I' th' shipman's card.[8]
I will drain him dry as hay.
Sleep shall neither night nor day
20 Hang upon his penthouse lid.[9]
He shall live a man forbid.[10]
Weary sev'nights, nine times nine,
Shall he dwindle, peak, and pine.
Though his bark cannot be lost,
25 Yet it shall be tempest-tost.
Look what I have.
   2 WITCH. Show me! show me!
   1 WITCH. Here I have a pilot's thumb,[11]
Wracked as homeward he did come.

(Drum within.)

30 3 WITCH. A drum, a drum!
Macbeth doth come.

24 **craves composition :** asks terms of peace.
25 **deign :** grant.
26 **Saint Colme's Inch :** Incholm, an island in the Firth of Forth, near Edinburgh.
27 **deceive . . . interest :** deceive me in my most important and confidential affairs.

1 **swine :** Witches were believed to show malice by killing domestic animals such as swine.
2 **Aroint thee :** off with you.
3 **rump-fed ronyon :** fathipped, mangy person.
4 **sieve :** Witches supposedly could sail in sieves.
5 **like :** in the shape of.
6 **rat . . . tail :** The witch will board ship as a tailless rat because a devil's creature had to be imperfect.
7 **I'll do :** I'll cause trouble.

8 **card :** compass.

9 **penthouse lid :** The eyelid is compared to the slanting roof of a shed.
10 **forbid :** under a curse.

11 **thumb :** Parts of corpses were used in evil magic.

ALL. The Weird Sisters, hand in hand,
Posters[12] of the sea and land,
Thus do go about, about,
35 Thrice to thine, and thrice to mine,
And thrice again, to make up nine.
Peace! The charm's wound up.

Enter MACBETH *and* BANQUO.

MACBETH. So foul and fair a day I have not seen.[13]
BANQUO. How far is't called to Forres? What are these,
40 So withered, and so wild in their attire,
That look not like th' inhabitants o' th' earth,
And yet are on't? Live you? or are you aught
That man may question? You seem to understand me,
By each at once her choppy[14] finger laying
45 Upon her skinny lips. You should be women,
And yet your beards[15] forbid me to interpret
That you are so.
　　　MACBETH.　　Speak, if you can. What are you?
　　　1 WITCH. All hail, Macbeth! Hail to thee, Thane of Glamis!
　　　2 WITCH. All hail, Macbeth! Hail to thee, Thane of Cawdor!
50 　3 WITCH. All hail, Macbeth, that shalt be King hereafter!
　　　BANQUO. Good sir, why do you start and seem to fear
Things that do sound so fair? I' th' name of truth,
Are ye fantastical,[16] or that indeed
Which outwardly ye show? My noble partner
55 You greet with present grace and great prediction
Of noble having and of royal hope,
That he seems rapt withal.[17] To me you speak not.
If you can look into the seeds of time
And say which grain will grow and which will not,
60 Speak then to me, who neither beg nor fear
Your favors nor your hate.
　　　1 WITCH. Hail!
　　　2 WITCH. Hail!
　　　3 WITCH. Hail!
65 　1 WITCH. Lesser than Macbeth, and greater.
　　　2 WITCH. Not so happy, yet much happier.
　　　3 WITCH. Thou shalt get[18] kings, though thou be none.
So all hail, Macbeth and Banquo!
　　　1 WITCH. Banquo and Macbeth, all hail!
70　MACBETH. Stay, you imperfect speakers, tell me more!
By Sinel's[19] death I know I am Thane of Glamis;
But how of Cawdor? The Thane of Cawdor lives,
A prosperous gentleman; and to be King
Stands not within the prospect of belief,[20]
75 No more than to be Cawdor. Say from whence

12 Posters : rapid travelers.

13 So . . . seen : *foul* because of the weather; *fair* because of the victory. (Compare with I, i, 10.)

14 choppy : chapped.

15 beards : Witches were often pictured as bearded.

[handwritten note: positions in future & already this]

16 fantastical : imaginary.

17 That . . .withal : so that he seems in a trance.

[handwritten note: predictions for Banquo]

18 get : beget.

19 Sinel's (sī'nĕlz) : Macbeth's father's.

20 prospect of belief : farthest reach of belief.

WILLIAM SHAKESPEARE

You owe this strange intelligence,[21] or why
Upon this blasted heath you stop our way
With such prophetic greeting. Speak, I charge you.

(WITCHES *vanish*.)

BANQUO. The earth hath bubbles, as the water has,
80 And these are of them. Whither are they vanished?

MACBETH. Into the air, and what seemed corporal[22] melted
As breath into the wind. Would they had stayed!

BANQUO. Were such things here as we do speak about?
Or have we eaten on the insane root[23]
85 That takes the reason prisoner?

MACBETH. Your children shall be kings.

BANQUO.   You shall be King.

MACBETH. And Thane of Cawdor too. Went it not so?

BANQUO. To th' selfsame tune and words. Who's here?

Enter Ross *and* ANGUS.

Ross. The King hath happily received, Macbeth,
90 The news of thy success; and when he reads
Thy personal venture in the rebels' fight,
His wonders and his praises do contend
Which should be thine or his.[24] Silenced with that,[25]
In viewing o'er the rest o' th' selfsame day,
95 He finds thee in the stout Norweyan ranks,
Nothing afeard of what thyself didst make,
Strange images of death.[26] As thick as tale
Came post with post,[27] and every one did bear
Thy praises in his kingdom's great defense
And poured them down before him.

100 ANGUS.   We are sent
To give thee from our royal master thanks;
Only to herald thee into his sight,
Not pay thee.

Ross. And for an earnest[28] of a greater honor,
105 He bade me, from him, call thee Thane of Cawdor;
In which addition,[29] hail, most worthy Thane!
For it is thine.

BANQUO.   What, can the devil speak true?

MACBETH. The Thane of Cawdor lives. Why do you dress me
In borrowed robes?

ANGUS.   Who[30] was the Thane lives yet,
110 But under heavy judgment bears that life
Which he deserves to lose. Whether he was combined
With those of Norway, or did line the rebel[31]
With hidden help and vantage, or that with both
He labored in his country's wrack, I know not;
115 But treasons capital, confessed and proved,
Have overthrown him.

21 owe . . . intelligence :
got this strange news.

22 corporal (kôr′pə rəl) :
flesh and blood.

23 insane root : root, probably hemlock, causing in-
sanity.

24 His wonders . . . his :
The king's wonder struggles
with his desire to speak
your praises.
25 with that : by the struggle.
26 Nothing afeard . . . death :
not afraid of death, while
causing it.
27 As thick . . . post : As
quickly as could be counted
came messenger after mes-
senger.

28 earnest : token.

29 addition : title.

30 Who : he who.

31 line the rebel : support
Macdonwald.

MACBETH   (aside). Glamis, and Thane of Cawdor!
The greatest is behind.[32]—(To Ross and Angus.) Thanks for
    your pains.
(Aside to Banquo.) Do you not hope your children shall be
    kings,
When those that gave the Thane of Cawdor to me
Promised no less to them?
120   Banquo (aside to Macbeth). That, trusted home,[33]
Might yet enkindle you unto the crown,[34]
Besides the Thane of Cawdor. But 'tis strange!
And oftentimes, to win us[35] to our harm,
The instruments of darkness tell us truths,
125   Win us with honest trifles, to betray's
In deepest consequence.[36]—
Cousins, a word, I pray you.
    MACBETH   (aside). Two truths are told,
As happy prologues to the swelling act
Of the imperial theme.[37]—I thank you, gentlemen.—
130   (Aside.) This supernatural soliciting[38]
Cannot be ill; cannot be good. If ill,
Why hath it given me earnest of success,[39]
Commencing in a truth? I am Thane of Cawdor.
If good, why do I yield to that suggestion[40]
135   Whose horrid image doth unfix my hair
And make my seated[41] heart knock at my ribs
Against the use of nature?[42] Present fears
Are less than horrible imaginings.
My thought, whose murder yet is but fantastical,[43]
140   Shakes so my single state of man[44] that function[45]
Is smothered in surmise and nothing is
But what is not.
    BANQUO.   Look how our partner's rapt.[46]
    MACBETH (aside). If chance will have me King, why, chance
    may crown me,
Without my stir.[47]
    BANQUO.   New honors come upon him,
145   Like our strange garments, cleave not to their mold
But with the aid of use.[48]
    MACBETH   (aside). Come what come may,
Time and the hour runs through the roughest day.
    BANQUO. Worthy Macbeth, we stay upon your leisure.[49]
    MACBETH. Give me your favor.[50] My dull brain was wrought
150   With things forgotten.[51] Kind gentlemen, your pains
Are registered where every day I turn
The leaf to read them.[52] Let us toward the King.
    (Aside to Banquo.) Think upon what hath chanced; and, at
    more time,

32 behind : yet to come.

33 home : fully.
34 enkindle . . . crown : inspire you with hope.
35 win us : gain our confidence.

36 betray's . . . consequence : betray us with most serious results.
37 imperial theme : the idea of kingship.
38 soliciting : urging.

39 earnest of success : a pledge of what is to follow.
40 suggestion : temptation.
41 seated : firm.
42 Against . . . nature : unnaturally.

43 fantastical : imagined.
44 my single . . . man : my feeble human nature.
45 function : the power to act.
46 rapt : entranced.

47 stir : making an effort.

48 Like . . . use : like new garments, which are not comfortable until worn for a time.
49 stay . . . leisure : await your convenience.
50 favor : indulgence.
51 wrought . . . forgotten : agitated by things I had forgotten.
52 registered . . . them : recorded on the pages of memory.

The interim having weighed it, let us speak
Our free hearts each to other.
155   BANQUO   (*aside to* MACBETH). Very gladly.
      MACBETH (*aside to* BANQUO). Till then, enough.—Come,
      friends.   (*Exeunt.*)

Scene IV. *Forres. The palace.*

Flourish. Enter KING DUNCAN, LENNOX, MALCOLM,
DONALBAIN, *and Attendants.*

    KING. Is execution done on Cawdor? Are not
Those in commission[1] yet returned?
     MALCOLM.   My liege,
They are not yet come back. But I have spoke
With one that saw him die; who did report
5   That very frankly he confessed his treasons,
Implored your Highness' pardon, and set forth
A deep repentance. Nothing in his life
Became him like the leaving it. He died
  As one that had been studied in his death
10 To throw away the dearest thing he owed[2]
As 'twere a careless[3] trifle.
     DUNCAN.   There's no art
To find the mind's construction[4] in the face.
He was a gentleman on whom I built
An absolute trust.

     Enter MACBETH, BANQUO, *and* ANGUS.

              O worthiest cousin,
15 The sin of my ingratitude even now
Was heavy on me! Thou art so far before
That swiftest wing of recompense is slow
To overtake thee. Would thou hadst less deserved,
That the proportion[5] both of thanks and payment
20 Might have been mine! Only I have left to say,
More is thy due than more than all can pay.[6]
     MACBETH. The service and the loyalty I owe,
In doing it pays itself.[7] Your Highness' part
Is to receive our duties; and our duties
25 Are to your throne and state children and servants,
Which do but what they should by doing everything[8]
Safe toward your[9] love and honor.
     KING.   Welcome hither.
I have begun to plant thee and will labor
To make thee full of growing. Noble Banquo,
30 That hast no less deserved, nor must be known
No less to have done so, let me infold thee

1 commission : charge.

2 owed : owned.
3 careless : uncared for.

4 construction : meaning.

5 proportion : due amount.
6 More . . . pay : even more than I possess could pay.
7 pays itself : is its own payment.
8 our duties . . . everything : Our duties to you are like children's to parents or servants' to masters. We do no more than we ought no matter how much we do.
9 safe toward your : possibly "that will merit your" or "that shows toward you."

And hold thee to my heart.

    BANQUO.   There if I grow,
The harvest is your own.

    KING.   My plenteous joys,
Wanton[10] in fulness, seek to hide themselves
35 In drops of sorrow. Sons, kinsmen, thanes,
And you whose places are the nearest, know
We will establish our estate upon
Our eldest, Malcolm, whom we name hereafter
The Prince of Cumberland; which honor must
40 Not unaccompanied invest him only,[11]
But signs of nobleness, like stars, shall shine
On all deservers. From hence to Inverness,[12]
And bind us further to you.[13]

    MACBETH. The rest is labor, which is not used for you![14]
45 I'll be myself the harbinger,[15] and make joyful
The hearing of my wife with your approach;
So, humbly take my leave.

    KING.   My worthy Cawdor!

    MACBETH (aside). The Prince of Cumberland! That is a step
On which I must fall down, or else o'erleap,[16]
50 For in my way it lies. Stars, hide your fires!
Let not light see my black and deep desires.
The eye wink at the hand;[17] yet let that be,
Which the eye fears, when it is done, to see.
                                    (Exit.)

    KING. True, worthy Banquo: he is full so valiant,
55 And in his commendations I am fed;
It is a banquet to me. Let's after him,
Whose care is gone before to bid us welcome.
It is a peerless kinsman.   (Flourish. Exeunt.)

Scene V. Inverness. MACBETH's castle.

Enter LADY MACBETH, alone, with a letter.

    LADY MACBETH (reads). "They[1] met me in the day of success;
and I have learned by the perfect'st report they have more in
them than mortal knowledge. When I burned in desire to question them further, they made themselves air, into which they
5 vanished. Whiles I stood rapt in the wonder of it, came missives[2] from the King, who all-hailed me Thane of Cawdor, by
which title, before, these Weird Sisters saluted me, and referred
me to the coming of the time with 'Hail, King that shalt be!'
This have I thought good to deliver thee, my dearest partner of
10 greatness, that thou mightst not lose the dues of rejoicing by
being ignorant of what greatness is promised thee. Lay it to thy
heart, and farewell."

WILLIAM SHAKESPEARE

---

10 wanton : contrary.

11 which . . . only : Honor must not be given to Malcolm only.

12 Inverness (ĭn'vər nĕs') : site of Macbeth's castle.

13 bind . . . you : obligate me still further by accepting me as a guest.

14 The rest . . . you : Leisure is work unless I am serving you.

15 harbinger (här'bĭn jər) : messenger sent ahead to arrange for proper lodgings.

16 fall down . . . o'erleap : If Malcolm is Prince of Cumberland, I must abandon my hope to be king, or, by my own efforts become king in spite of him. (See I, iii, 143-144.)

17 The eye . . . hand : Let my eyes not see what my hands do.

1 They : the weird sisters.

2 missives : messengers.

Glamis thou art, and Cawdor, and shalt be—
What thou art promised. Yet do I fear thy nature.
15 It is too full o' th' milk of human kindness[3]
To catch the nearest way.[4] Thou wouldst be great;
Art not without ambition, but without
The illness[5] should attend it. What thou wouldst highly,
That wouldst thou holily; wouldst not play false,
20 And yet wouldst wrongly win. Thou'ldst[6] have, great Glamis,
That which cries "Thus thou must do," if thou have it;
And that which rather thou dost fear to do
Than wishest should be undone. Hie thee hither,
That I may pour my spirits[7] in thine ear
25 And chastise[8] with the valor of my tongue
All that impedes thee[9] from the golden round[10]
Which fate and metaphysical[11] aid doth seem
To have thee crowned withal.

Enter MESSENGER.

What is your tidings?
MESSENGER. The King comes here tonight.
LADY MACBETH.   Thou'rt mad to say it!
30 Is not thy master with him? who, were't so,
Would have informed for preparation.
MESSENGER. So please you, it is true. Our Thane is coming.
One of my fellows had the speed of him,[12]
Who, almost dead for breath, had scarcely more
Than would make up his message.
35 LADY MACBETH.   Give him tending;
He brings great news.   (*Exit* MESSENGER.)
                The raven himself is hoarse
That croaks the fatal entrance of Duncan
Under my battlements. Come, you spirits
That tend on mortal[13] thoughts, unsex me here,
40 And fill me, from the crown to the toe, top-full
Of direst cruelty! Make thick my blood;
Stop up th' access and passage to remorse,
That no compunctious visitings[14] of nature
Shake my fell[15] purpose nor keep peace between
45 Th' effect and it![16] Come to my woman's breasts
And take my milk for gall,[17] you murdering ministers,
Wherever in your sightless[18] substances
You wait on nature's mischief! Come, thick night,
And pall[19] thee in the dunnest smoke of hell,
50 That my keen knife see not the wound it makes,
Nor heaven peep through the blanket of the dark
To cry "Hold, hold!"

3 too . . . kindness : not hard or unnatural enough.
4 nearest way : i.e., killing Duncan.
5 illness : unscrupulousness.
6 Thou'ldst : thou wouldst.
7 spirits : my resolution and energy of will.
8 chastise : rebuke.
9 All . . . thee : any softness or scruples.
10 golden round : crown.
11 metaphysical : supernatural.

12 had . . . him : outstripped him.

13 mortal : deadly.

14 compunctious visitings : feelings of pity.
15 fell : cruel.
16 keep . . . it : come between my purpose and its carrying out.
17 And . . . gall : exchange any gentleness for bitter hate.
18 sightless : invisible.
19 pall : cover as with a shroud.

Enter MACBETH.

           Great Glamis! worthy Cawdor!
Greater than both, by the all-hail hereafter!
Thy letters have transported me beyond
55 This ignorant present, and I feel now
The future in the instant.
    MACBETH.   My dearest love,
Duncan comes here tonight.
    LADY MACBETH.   And when goes hence?
    MACBETH. Tomorrow, as he purposes.
    LADY MACBETH.   O, never
Shall sun that morrow see!
60 Your face, my Thane, is as a book where men
May read strange matters. To beguile the time,[20]
Look like the time; bear welcome in your eye,
Your hand, your tongue; look like the innocent flower,
But be the serpent under't. He that's coming
65 Must be provided for; and you shall put
This night's great business into my dispatch,
Which shall to all our nights and days to come
Give solely sovereign sway and masterdom.
    MACBETH. We will speak further.
    LADY MACBETH.   Only look up clear.
70 To alter favor ever is to fear.[21]
Leave all the rest to me.   (*Exeunt.*)

Scene VI. *Inverness. Before* MACBETH'S *castle. Hautboys*
   and torches. Enter KING DUNCAN, MALCOLM,
     DONALBAIN, BANQUO, LENNOX, MACDUFF,
       Ross, ANGUS, *and Attendants.*

    KING. This castle hath a pleasant seat.[1] The air
Nimbly and sweetly recommends itself
Unto our gentle senses.
    BANQUO.   This guest of summer,
The temple-haunting martlet,[2] does approve
5 By his loved mansionry[3] that the heaven's breath
Smells wooingly here. No jutty, frieze,
Buttress, nor coign of vantage,[4] but this bird
Hath made his pendent bed and procreant cradle.[5]
Where they most breed and haunt, I have observed
10 The air is delicate.

    Enter LADY MACBETH.

    KING.   See, see, our honored hostess!
The love that follows us sometime is our trouble,
Which still we thank as love.[6] Herein I teach you
How you shall bid God 'ield us for your pains

20 To beguile . . . time : to
delude men, look as one
normally would on such an
occasion.

21 To alter . . . fear : Your
changing expression is what
we have to fear (or, will
cause others to fear).

1 seat : location.
2 martlet : martin, which
often builds its nests about
churches.
3 does . . . mansionry :
does prove by building here.
4 coign of vantage : advantageous corner.
5 procreant (prō′krĭ ənt) cradle : nest where he breeds.

6 The love . . . love : Our
love for others can cause
them inconvenience, al-
though they do not mind
the trouble if its cause is
in our loving them.

WILLIAM SHAKESPEARE

And thank us for your trouble.[7]

LADY MACBETH.   All our service
15 In every point twice done, and then done double,
Were poor and single business to contend
Against those honors deep and broad wherewith
Your Majesty loads our house. For those of old,
And the late dignities[8] heaped up to them,
We rest your hermits.[9]
20   KING.   Where's the Thane of Cawdor?
We coursed[10] him at the heels and had a purpose
To be his purveyor;[11] but he rides well.
And his great love, sharp as his spur, hath holp[12] him
To his home before us. Fair and noble hostess,
We are your guest tonight.
25   LADY MACBETH.   Your servants ever
Have theirs, themselves, and what is theirs, in compt,
To make their audit at your Highness' pleasure,
Still to return your own.[13]
     DUNCAN.   Give me your hand;
Conduct me to mine host. We love him highly
30 And shall continue our graces towards him.
By your leave, hostess.   (*Exeunt.*)

Scene VII. *Inverness.* MACBETH's *castle.*

*Hautboys. Torches. Enter a Sewer,[1] and divers Servants with
dishes and service over the stage. Then enter* MACBETH.
     MACBETH. If it were done when 'tis done,[2] then 'twere well
It were done quickly. If th' assassination
Could trammel up the consequence, and catch,
With his surcease, success;[3] that but this blow
5 Might be the be-all and the end-all[4] here,
But here, upon this bank and shoal of time,[5]
We'd jump[6] the life to come. But in these cases
We still[7] have judgment here,[8] that[9] we but teach
Bloody instructions,[10] which, being taught, return
10 To plague th' inventor. This even-handed justice
Commends th' ingredience of our poisoned chalice
To our own lips. He's here in double trust:
First, as I am his kinsman and his subject—
Strong both against the deed; then, as his host,
15 Who should against his murtherer shut the door,
Not bear the knife myself. Besides, this Duncan
Hath borne his faculties[11] so meek, hath been
So clear[12] in his great office, that his virtues
Will plead like angels, trumpet-tongued, against
20 The deep damnation of his taking-off;[13]

7 Herein . . . trouble : The previous statement shows you that my visit, even though inconvenient, is a sign of my love and thus teaches you to bid God reward me for the trouble I cause.
8 late dignities : thaneships of Glamis and Cawdor.
9 We . . . hermits : We shall gratefully pray for you.
10 coursed : pursued.
11 purveyor : forerunner.
12 holp : helped.

13 Have . . . own : Everything we have is yours on account, to be rendered to you at your wish.

1 Sewer : steward.
2 If it were . . . 'tis done : if the whole business were to end with the murder itself.
3 trammel . . . success : ensnare, as in a net, any consequences
4 the be-all and the end-all : all there is to the matter.
5 But here . . . time : In this lifetime—man's life is as a sandbank (of time) surrounded by a sea (of eternity).
6 jump : risk.
7 still : always.
8 here : in this world.
9 that : so that.
10 Bloody instructions : i.e., murder.
11 borne his faculties : used his powers.
12 clear : free from reproach.
13 taking-off : death.

192

And pity, like a naked new-born babe,
Striding the blast, or heaven's cherubin, horsed
Upon the sightless couriers of the air,[14]
Shall blow the horrid deed in every eye,
25 That tears shall drown the wind.[15] I have no spur
To prick the sides of my intent, but only
Vaulting ambition, which o'erleaps itself
And falls on th' other side.

Enter LADY MACBETH.

How now? What news?

LADY MACBETH. He has almost supped. Why have you left
the chamber?

MACBETH. Hath he asked for me?

30 LADY MACBETH.   Know you not he has?

MACBETH. We will proceed no further in this business.
He hath honored me of late, and I have bought
Golden opinions from all sorts of people,
Which would be worn now in their newest gloss,
Not cast aside so soon.

35 LADY MACBETH.   Was the hope drunk
Wherein you dressed yourself? Hath it slept since?
And wakes it now to look so green and pale
At what it did so freely? From this time
Such[16] I account thy love. Art thou afeard
40 To be the same in thine own act and valor
As thou art in desire? Wouldst thou have that
Which thou esteem'st the ornament of life,[17]
And live a coward in thine own esteem,
Letting "I dare not" wait upon "I would,"
45 Like the poor cat i' th' adage?[18]

MACBETH.   Prithee peace!
I dare do all that may become a man.
Who dares do more is none.

LADY MACBETH.   What beast was't then
That made you break[19] this enterprise to me?
When you durst do it, then you were a man;
50 And to be more than what you were, you would
Be so much more the man. Nor time nor place
Did then adhere,[20] and yet you would make both.
They have made themselves,[21] and that their fitness now
Does unmake[22] you. I have given suck, and know
55 How tender 'tis to love the babe that milks me.
I would, while it was smiling in my face,
Have plucked my nipple from his boneless gums
And dashed the brains out, had I so sworn as you
Have done to this.

WILLIAM SHAKESPEARE

14 sightless . . . air : invisible winds.
15 That tears . . . wind : A heavy rain was supposed to drown the wind.

16 Such : just as changeable as your resolution has proved.
17 ornament of life : the crown.

18 the poor . . . adage : The proverb is: "The cat would eat fish, but she will not wet her feet."

19 break : disclose.

20 Nor time . . . adhere : Duncan was not then present.
21 They . . . themselves : Now Duncan is here and within your power.
22 unmake : unman.

MACBETH.   If we should fail?

LADY MACBETH.   We fail?

60 But screw your courage²³ to the sticking place,²⁴
And we'll not fail. When Duncan is asleep
(Whereto the rather shall his day's hard journey
Soundly invite him), his two chamberlains
Will I with wine and wassail so convince²⁵

65 That memory, the warder of the brain,
Shall be a fume, and the receipt of reason
A limebeck only.²⁶ When in swinish sleep
Their drenchèd natures lie as in a death,
What cannot you and I perform upon

70 Th' unguarded Duncan? what not put upon
His spongy²⁷ officers, who shall bear the guilt
Of our great quell?²⁸

MACBETH.   Bring forth men-children only;
For thy undaunted mettle should compose
Nothing but males. Will it not be received,

75 When we have marked with blood those sleepy two
Of his own chamber and used their very daggers,
That they have done't?

LADY MACBETH.   Who dares receive it other,²⁹
As we shall make our griefs and clamor roar
Upon his death?

MACBETH.   I am settled and bend up

80 Each corporal agent³⁰ to this terrible feat.
Away, and mock the time³¹ with fairest show;
False face must hide what the false heart doth know.

                                   (*Exeunt.*)

23 screw your courage : as in preparing a crossbow for firing.

24 sticking place : the notch of the crossbow in which the bowstring was caught and ready for firing.

25 convince : overpower.

26 memory . . . only : Memory, the watchman of the brain, shall be only a fume; and the mind (the receptacle of reason) only an alembic (the cap of a still, into which fumes rise during the process of distillation).

27 spongy : drunken (literally, absorbent).

28 quell : killing.

29 receive it other : take it otherwise.

30 bend . . . agent : stretch to its utmost each bodily power.

31 mock the time : mislead the world.

Questions for Study

ACT I

Scenes i, ii, iii

1. Aside from the physical appearance of the witches, what do the lines spoken by or about them indicate of their nature? Contrast the respective meanings of the witches and of Macbeth in their uses of the "foul and fair" phrase (i, 10 and iii, 38).
2. Two views of Macbeth emerge in scenes ii and iii. Explain what these two views reveal of Macbeth's character, citing the lines of the play which give these insights. What is the prevailing opinion of Macbeth held by the characters in scene ii?
3. What reaction does Macbeth have to the announcement that he is now Thane of Cawdor? See scene iii, lines 134-137. What does the tone of this passage suggest about Macbeth's thoughts? What do the lines imply respecting his conscience?

4. What does Banquo's reaction to the witches' prophecies say respecting his attitude toward them? respecting the state of his conscience?
5. With what lines does Macbeth dismiss his thought of the kingship? Explain in your own words what he means.

Scene iv

1. In what way are the lines of Duncan (ll. 11-14) concerning the former Thane of Cawdor prophetic as well as ironical?
2. In what lines does Macbeth state the duties of a thane to his king? What does he say about these duties? Discuss whether Macbeth here speaks sincerely or conventionally.
3. What qualities of Duncan are revealed in this scene?
4. What evidence is there in this scene that Macbeth did not dismiss his thoughts of the kingship of the preceding scene?

Scenes v, vi, and vii

1. From the two soliloquies spoken by Lady Macbeth in scene v, what do we learn of her nature? What is her judgment of her husband?
2. If you were directing this play, how would you have the parts of Macbeth and Lady Macbeth played in scene v, lines 52-71? Would you have the characters look at each other? How would you have Macbeth speak his lines? How, Lady Macbeth?
3. Describe the mood of the opening lines of scene vi. Why is this scene especially effective between scenes v and vii?
4. In what sense are Duncan's first lines in scene vi ironical?
5. In scene vi how is Lady Macbeth following the advice she gave to Macbeth in the preceding scene—to "look like the innocent flower,/ But be the serpent under 't" (v, 61-64)?
6. In scene vii what reasons does Macbeth give first for not murdering the King (ll. 1-12)? What next occurs to him (ll. 12-16)? And what is his final reason (ll. 16-25)?
7. In her first two long speeches in scene vii, what effect is the language Lady Macbeth uses likely to have on Macbeth?

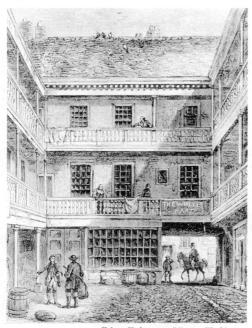

Three kinds of structures that gave the theater its form. The innyard (above left) was used by strolling companies of actors for their plays. Bullbaiting and bearbaiting, common entertainments in Elizabethan England, were watched (above right) in round, open buildings. Plays were given in the Great Hall of the Middle Temple (below), one of the Inns of Court (societies of lawyers) in London. The first production of Shakespeare's Twelfth Night *was here.*

Act II

Scene I. *Inverness. Court of* Macbeth's *castle*.

Enter Banquo, *and* Fleance *with a torch before him*.

Banquo. How goes the night, boy?
Fleance. The moon is down; I have not heard the clock.
Banquo. And she goes down at twelve.
Fleance.   I take't, 'tis later, sir.
Banquo. Hold, take my sword. There's husbandry[1] in heaven;
5 Their candles are all out. Take thee that too.
A heavy summons[2] lies like lead upon me,
And yet I would not sleep. Merciful powers,
Restrain in me the cursèd thoughts that nature
Gives way to in repose![3]

Enter Macbeth, *and a Servant with a torch*.

                         Give me my sword.
10 Who's there?
Macbeth. A friend.
Banquo. What, sir, not yet at rest? The King's abed.
He hath been in unusual pleasure and
Sent forth great largess[4] to your offices.
15 This diamond he greets your wife withal
By the name of most kind hostess, and shut up
In measureless content.[5]
Macbeth.   Being unprepared,
Our will became the servant to defect,
Which else should free have wrought.[6]
Banquo.   All's well.
20 I dreamt last night of the three Weird Sisters.
To you they have showed some truth.
Macbeth.   I think not of them.
Yet when we can entreat an hour to serve,[7]
We would spend it in some words upon that business,
If you would grant the time.
Banquo.   At your kind'st leisure.
25 Macbeth. If you shall cleave to my consent, when 'tis,[8]
It shall make honor for you.
Banquo.   So I lose none
In seeking to augment it but still keep
My bosom franchised[9] and allegiance clear,
I shall be counseled.
Macbeth.   Good repose the while!
30 Banquo. Thanks, sir. The like to you!

                    (*Exeunt* Banquo *and* Fleance.)

Macbeth. Go bid thy mistress, when my drink is ready,
She strike upon the bell. Get thee to bed.

---

1 husbandry : frugality.

2 summons : summons to sleep.

3 nature . . . repose : a prayer against a common idea of the time—that demons put evil thoughts in men's minds while they were helplessly asleep.

4 largess (lär′jĭs) : gifts.

5 shut up . . . content : ended by saying he was content beyond measure.
6 Our will . . . wrought : Our will to entertain the King lavishly was hampered by lack of preparation.

7 entreat . . . serve : find a free hour.

8 cleave . . . 'tis : support my interests when the time comes.

9 franchised : free of blame.

Is this a dagger which I see before me,
The handle toward my hand? Come, let me clutch thee!
35 I have thee not, and yet I see thee still.
Art thou not, fatal[10] vision, sensible[11]
To feeling as to sight? or art thou but
A dagger of the mind, a false creation,
Proceeding from the heat-oppressèd brain?
40 I see thee yet, in form as palpable
As this which now I draw.
Thou marshal'st me the way that I was going,
And such an instrument I was to use.
Mine eyes are made the fools o' th' other senses,
45 Or else worth all the rest.[12] I see thee still;
And on thy blade and dudgeon[13] gouts[14] of blood,
Which was not so before. There's no such thing.
It is the bloody business which informs[15]
Thus to mine eyes. Now o'er the one half-world
50 Nature seems dead, and wicked dreams abuse
The curtained sleep.[16] Now witchcraft celebrates
Pale Hecate's offerings; and withered murder,
Alarumed[17] by his sentinel, the wolf,
Whose howl's his watch,[18] thus with his stealthy pace,
55 With Tarquin's ravishing strides, towards his design
Moves like a ghost. Thou sure and firm-set earth,
Hear not my steps which way they walk, for fear
Thy very stones prate of my whereabout
And take the present horror[19] from the time,
60 Which now suits with it. Whiles I threat,[20] he lives;
Words to the heat of deeds too cold breath gives.

(*A bell rings.*)

I go, and it is done. The bell invites me.
Hear it not, Duncan, for it is a knell
That summons thee to heaven, or to hell.   (*Exit.*)

Scene II. *Inverness.* MACBETH's *castle.*

Enter LADY MACBETH.

LADY MACBETH. That which hath made them drunk hath
    made me bold;
What hath quenched them hath given me fire. Hark! Peace!
It was the owl that shrieked, the fatal bellman[1]
Which gives the stern'st good night. He is about it.
5 The doors are open, and the surfeited grooms
Do mock their charge[2] with snores. I have drugged their pos-
    sets,[3]

10 fatal : showing what is fated; also, deadly.
11 sensible : perceptible.

12 Mine eyes . . . rest : My eyes have become fools, if they are deluded by my imagination; or they are worth all my other senses combined, if the dagger represents reality.
13 dudgeon : hilt.
14 gouts : large drops.
15 informs : gives (false) information.
16 curtained sleep : sleeper in his curtained bed.
17 Alarumed : summoned to action.
18 watch : signal.
19 present horror : awful silence (which Macbeth fears to have broken lest his presence be revealed).
20 threat : make threats.

1 fatal bellman : It was customary in London for the town crier to visit condemned prisoners on the night before their execution.
2 mock their charge : make a mockery of their duty.
3 possets : a curdled drink.

That death and nature do contend about them
Whether they live or die.⁴

    MACBETH (*within*). Who's there? What, ho?

4 That death . . . die : so that they are drugged within an inch of their lives.

10   LADY MACBETH. Alack, I am afraid they have awaked,
And 'tis not done! Th' attempt, and not the deed,
Confounds⁵ us. Hark! I laid their daggers ready;
He could not miss 'em. Had he not resembled
My father as he slept, I had done't.

5 Confounds : ruins.

Enter MACBETH.

                My husband!

15   MACBETH. I have done the deed. Didst thou not hear a noise?

    LADY MACBETH. I heard the owl scream and the crickets cry.
Did you not speak?

    MACBETH.   When?

    LADY MACBETH.   Now.

    MACBETH.   As I descended?

    LADY MACBETH. Ay.

    MACBETH. Hark!
Who lies i' th' second chamber?

20   LADY MACBETH.   Donalbain.

    MACBETH. This is a sorry sight.   (*Looks on his hands.*)

    LADY MACBETH. A foolish thought, to say a sorry sight.

    MACBETH. There's one did laugh in's sleep, and one cried
        "Murder!"
That they did wake each other. I stood and heard them.

25 But they did say their prayers and addressed⁶ them
Again to sleep.

    LADY MACBETH. There are two lodged together.

6 addressed : prepared.

    MACBETH. One cried "God bless us!" and "Amen!" the other,
As they had seen me with these hangman's hands,
Listening their fear. I could not say "Amen!"
When they did say "God bless us!"

30   LADY MACBETH.   Consider it not so deeply.

    MACBETH. But wherefore could not I pronounce "Amen"?
I had most need of blessing, and "Amen"
Stuck in my throat.

    LADY MACBETH. These deeds must not be thought
After these ways. So,⁷ it will make us mad.

7 So : if we do so.

35   MACBETH. Methought I heard a voice cry "Sleep no more!
Macbeth does murder sleep"—the innocent sleep,
Sleep that knits up⁸ the raveled sleave⁹ of care,
The death of each day's life, sore labor's bath,
Balm of hurt minds, great nature's second course,¹⁰
Chief nourisher in life's feast.

40   LADY MACBETH.   What do you mean?

    MACBETH. Still it cried "Sleep no more!" to all the house;

8 knits up : untangles or ties up.
9 sleave : skein.
10 second course : The second course was the most substantial part of an Elizabethan dinner.

"Glamis hath murdered sleep, and therefore Cawdor
Shall sleep no more! Macbeth shall sleep no more!"
    LADY MACBETH. Who was it that thus cried? Why, worthy
        Thane,
45 You do unbend your noble strength to think
So brainsickly of things. Go get some water
And wash this filthy witness from your hand.
Why did you bring these daggers from the place?
They must lie there. Go carry them and smear
The sleepy grooms with blood.
50   MACBETH.   I'll go no more.
I am afraid to think what I have done;
Look on't again I dare not.
    LADY MACBETH.   Infirm of purpose!
Give me the daggers. The sleeping and the dead
Are but as pictures. 'Tis the eye of childhood
55 That fears a painted devil. If he do bleed,
I'll gild[11] the faces of the grooms withal,   11 gild : smear.
For it must seem their guilt.   (*Exit. Knocking within.*)
    MACBETH.   Whence is that knocking?
How is't with me when every noise appals me?
What hands are here? Ha! they pluck out mine eyes!
60 Will all great Neptune's ocean wash this blood
Clean from my hand? No. This my hand will rather
The multitudinous seas incarnadine,[12]   12 incarnadine : redden.
Making the green one red.

         Enter LADY MACBETH.

    LADY MACBETH. My hands are of your color, but I shame
65 To wear a heart so white. (*Knock.*) I hear a knocking
At the south entry. Retire we to our chamber.
A little water clears us of this deed.
How easy is it then! Your constancy
Hath left you unattended.[13] (*Knock.*) Hark! more knocking.   13 Your constancy . . . un-
70 Get on your nightgown, lest occasion call us   attended : Your firmness
And show us to be watchers. Be not lost   has deserted you.
So poorly in your thoughts.
    MACBETH. To know my deed, 'twere best not know myself.
                                 (*Knock.*)
Wake Duncan with thy knocking! I would thou couldst!
                               (*Exeunt.*)

      Scene III. *Inverness.* MACBETH'S *castle.*

      Enter a PORTER. *Knocking within.*

    PORTER. Here's a knocking indeed! If a man were porter of   1 should have old : would
hell gate, he should have old[1] turning the key. (*Knock.*) Knock,   have plenty of.

knock, knock! Who's there, i' th' name of Belzebub? Here's a
farmer that hanged himself on th' expectation of plenty. Come
5 in time!² Have napkins³ enow about you; here you'll sweat
for't. (*Knock.*) Knock, knock! Who's there, in th' other devil's
name? Faith, here's an equivocator,⁴ that could swear in both
the scales against either scale;⁵ who committed treason enough
for God's sake, yet could not equivocate to heaven. O, come in,
10 equivocator! (*Knock.*) Knock, knock, knock! Who's there? Faith,
here's an English tailor come hither for stealing out of a French
hose.⁶ Come in, tailor. Here you may roast your goose.⁷ (*Knock.*)
Knock, knock! Never at quiet! What are you? But this place is
too cold for hell. I'll devil-porter it no further. I had thought
15 to have let in some of all professions that go the primrose way
to th' everlasting bonfire.⁸ (*Knock.*) Anon, anon! (*Opens the
gate.*) I pray you remember the porter.⁹

Enter MACDUFF *and* LENNOX.

MACDUFF. Was it so late, friend, ere you went to bed,
That you do lie so late?
20 PORTER. Faith, sir, we were carousing till the second cock.¹⁰
MACDUFF. I believe drink gave thee the lie¹¹ last night.
PORTER. That it did, sir, i' the very throat on me; but I re-
quited him for his lie; and, I think, being too strong for him,
though he took up my legs sometime, yet I made a shift to
25 cast¹² him.
MACDUFF. Is thy master stirring?

Enter MACBETH.

Our knocking has awaked him; here he comes.
LENNOX. Good morrow, noble sir.
MACBETH.   Good morrow, both.
MACDUFF. Is the King stirring, worthy Thane?
MACBETH.   Not yet.
30 MACDUFF. He did command me to call timely¹³ on him;
I have almost slipped the hour.
MACBETH.   I'll bring you to him.
MACDUFF. I know this is a joyful trouble to you;
But yet 'tis one.
MACBETH. The labor we delight in physics pain.¹⁴
This is the door.
35 MACDUFF.   I'll make so bold to call,
For 'tis my limited¹⁵ service.   (*Exit.*)
LENNOX. Goes the King hence today?
MACBETH.   He does; he did appoint
so.
LENNOX. The night has been unruly. Where we lay,
Our chimneys were blown down; and, as they say,
40 Lamentings heard i' th' air, strange screams of death,

2 Come in time : Your ar-
rival is timely.
3 napkins : handkerchiefs.
4 equivocator : one who is
deceptively ambiguous.
5 swear . . . scale : swear
in a form of words with
two meanings so that,
whichever way the oath is
understood by the hearer,
the swearer can think to
himself that he meant the
other.
6 tailor . . . hose : Tailors
were said to steal cloth
when cutting out clothes
for their customers.
7 goose : pressing iron.
8 primrose . . . bonfire :
flowery path leading to hell-
fire.
9 remember the porter :
holding out his hand for a
tip.
10 second cock : 3:00 A.M.
11 gave thee the lie :
floored you and put you to
sleep (with a pun on *lie*).
12 cast : throw (as in wrestling); also, vomit.

13 timely : early.

14 the labor . . . pain : The
labor we enjoy relieves any
pain involved.
15 limited : appointed.

And prophesying, with accents terrible,
Of dire combustion[16] and confused events
New hatched to th' woeful time. The obscure bird[17]
Clamored the livelong night. Some say the earth
Was feverous and did shake.

45   MACBETH.   'Twas a rough night.

    LENNOX. My young remembrance cannot parallel
A fellow to it.

Enter MACDUFF.

    MACDUFF. O horror, horror, horror! Tongue nor heart
Cannot conceive nor name thee!

    MACBETH <i>and</i> LENNOX.   What's the matter?

50   MACDUFF. Confusion[18] now hath made his masterpiece!
Most sacrilegious murder hath broke ope
The Lord's anointed temple[19] and stole thence
The life o' th' building!

    MACBETH.   What is't you say? the life?

    LENNOX. Mean you his Majesty?

55   MACDUFF. Approach the chamber, and destroy your sight
With a new Gorgon. Do not bid me speak.
See, and then speak yourselves.

(Exeunt MACBETH and LENNOX.)

              Awake, awake!
Ring the alarum bell. Murder and treason!
Banquo and Donalbain! Malcolm! awake!

60 Shake off this downy sleep, death's counterfeit,
And look on death itself! Up, up, and see
The great doom's image![20] Malcolm! Banquo!
As from your graves rise up and walk like sprites[21]
To countenance[22] this horror! Ring the bell!

(Bell rings.)

Enter LADY MACBETH.

65   LADY MACBETH. What's the business,
That such a hideous trumpet calls to parley
The sleepers of the house? Speak, speak!

    MACDUFF.   O gentle lady,
'Tis not for you to hear what I can speak!
The repetition in a woman's ear
Would murder as it fell.

Enter BANQUO.

70   O Banquo, Banquo,
Our royal master's murdered!

    LADY MACBETH.   Woe, alas!
What, in our house?

    BANQUO.   Too cruel anywhere.

16 combustion : tumult.
17 obscure bird : owl.

18 Confusion : destruction.
19 Lord's anointed temple : sacred body of the King.

20 great doom's image : likeness of the Judgment Day.
21 sprites : spirits.
22 countenance : be in keeping with.

Dear Duff, I prithee contradict thyself
And say it is not so.

Enter MACBETH, LENNOX, *and* ROSS.

75 MACBETH. Had I but died an hour before this chance,
I had lived a blessed time; for from this instant
There's nothing serious in mortality;[23]
All is but toys;[24] renown and grace is dead;
The wine of life is drawn, and the mere lees
80 Is left this vault to brag of.

Enter MALCOLM *and* DONALBAIN.

DONALBAIN. What is amiss?
MACBETH.   You are, and do not know't.
The spring, the head, the fountain of your blood
Is stopped, the very source of it is stopped.
MACDUFF. Your royal father's murdered.
MALCOLM.   O, by whom?
85 LENNOX. Those of his chamber, as it seemed, had done't.
Their hands and faces were all badged[25] with blood;
So were their daggers, which unwiped we found
Upon their pillows.
They stared and were distracted. No man's life
90 Was to be trusted with them.
MACBETH. O, yet I do repent me of my fury
That I did kill them.
MACDUFF.   Wherefore did you so?
MACBETH. Who can be wise, amazed, temp'rate, and furious,
Loyal and neutral, in a moment? No man.
95 The expedition[26] of my violent love
Outrun the pauser, reason. Here lay Duncan,
His silver skin laced with his golden blood,
And his gashed stabs looked like a breach in nature
For ruin's wasteful entrance; there, the murderers,
100 Steeped in the colors of their trade, their daggers
Unmannerly breeched[27] with gore. Who could refrain
That had a heart to love and in that heart
Courage to make 's love known?
LADY MACBETH.   Help me hence, ho!
MACDUFF. Look to the lady.
105 MALCOLM (*aside to* DONALBAIN). Why do we hold our
          tongues,
That most may claim this argument for ours?[28]
DONALBAIN (*aside to* MALCOLM). What should be spoken
          here, where our fate,
Hid in an auger hole,[29] may rush and seize us?
Let's away.
Our tears are not yet brewed.

WILLIAM SHAKESPEARE

23 There's . . . mortality :
There is nothing worthwhile
in human life.
24 toys : trifles.

25 badged : marked.

26 expedition : haste.

27 breeched : covered, as
with breeches.

28 That . . . ours : who are
most concerned in this
matter?
29 hid . . . hole : lurking in
some unsuspected hiding
place.

110   MALCOLM   (*aside to* DONALBAIN). Nor our strong sorrow
    Upon the foot of motion.[30]

      BANQUO.   Look to the lady.

                  (LADY MACBETH *is carried out.*)

    And when we have our naked frailties[31] hid,
    That suffer in exposure, let us meet
    And question this most bloody piece of work,

115   To know it further. Fears and scruples[32] shake us.
    In the great hand of God I stand, and thence
    Against the undivulged pretense[33] I fight
    Of treasonous malice.

      MACDUFF.   And so do I.

      ALL.   So all.

      MACBETH. Let's briefly put on manly readiness
    And meet i' th' hall together.

120   ALL.   Well contented.

         (*Exeunt all but* MALCOLM *and* DONALBAIN.)

    MALCOLM. What will you do? Let's not consort with them.
    To show an unfelt sorrow is an office
    Which the false man does easy. I'll to England.

      DONALBAIN. To Ireland I. Our separated fortune

125   Shall keep us both the safer. Where we are,
    There's daggers in men's smiles; the near in blood,
    The nearer bloody.[34]

      MALCOLM.   This murderous shaft that's shot
    Hath not yet lighted, and our safest way
    Is to avoid the aim. Therefore to horse!

130   And let us not be dainty[35] of leave-taking
    But shift away. There's warrant in that theft
    Which steals itself when there's no mercy left.   (*Exeunt.*)

        Scene IV. *Inverness. Without* MACBETH's *castle.*

          Enter ROSS *with an* OLD MAN.

    OLD MAN. Threescore and ten I can remember well;
    Within the volume of which time I have seen
    Hours dreadful and things strange; but this sore night
    Hath trifled former knowings.[1]

      ROSS.   Ah, good father,

5   Thou seest the heavens, as troubled with man's act,
    Threaten his bloody stage.[2] By th' clock 'tis day,
    And yet dark night strangles the traveling lamp.[3]
    Is't night's predominance, or the day's shame,
    That darkness does the face of earth entomb
    When living light should kiss it?

10   OLD MAN.   'Tis unnatural,
    Even like the deed that's done. On Tuesday last

204

A falcon, towering in her pride of place,[4]
Was by a mousing owl hawked at and killed.
    Ross. And Duncan's horses (a thing most strange and certain),
15 Beauteous and swift, the minions[5] of their race,
Turned wild in nature, broke their stalls, flung out,
Contending 'gainst obedience, as they would make
War with mankind.
    Old Man.   'Tis said they eat each other.
    Ross. They did so, to th' amazement of mine eyes
That looked upon't.

Enter Macduff.

20   Here comes the good Macduff.
How goes the world, sir, now?
    Macduff.   Why, see you not?
    Ross. Is't known who did this more than bloody deed?
    Macduff. Those that Macbeth hath slain.
    Ross.   Alas, the day!
What good could they pretend?[6]
    Macduff.   They were suborned.[7]
25 Malcolm and Donalbain, the King's two sons,
Are stol'n away and fled, which puts upon them
Suspicion of the deed.
    Ross.   'Gainst nature still!
Thriftless ambition, that wilt raven up[8]
Thine own live's means! Then 'tis most like
30 The sovereignty will fall upon Macbeth.
    Macduff. He is already named, and gone to Scone
To be invested.[9]
    Ross.   Where is Duncan's body?
    Macduff. Carried to Colmekill,
The sacred storehouse of his predecessors
And guardian of their bones.
35   Ross.   Will you to Scone?
    Macduff. No, cousin, I'll to Fife.[10]
    Ross.   Well, I will thither.
    Macduff. Well, may you see things well done there. Adieu,
Lest our old robes sit easier than our new!
    Ross. Farewell, father.
40   Old Man. God's benison[11] go with you, and with those
That would make good of bad, and friends of foes!   (*Exeunt.*)

4 towering . . . place : soaring at the summit of her flight.

5 minions : favorites; hence, finest.

6 pretend : intend to gain.

7 suborned : bribed.

8 raven up : devour ravenously.

9 invested : crowned.

10 Fife : Macduff's own home.

11 benison : blessing.

Questions for Study

ACT II

Scenes i and ii

1. If you were the director, how would you instruct the person playing Macbeth to speak lines 25-26 in scene i? Consider matters of voice, tone, stress, volume, and the like. How would you have Banquo answer (ll. 26-29)?
2. How do you account for Macbeth's vision of the dagger? Notice how blood and darkness are associated with evil and violence in this soliloquy (i, 33-64).
3. What does Macbeth's hearing of the imaginary voice (ll. 35-36) tell us about his conscience in scene ii?
4. Contrast Macbeth and Lady Macbeth in their respective reactions to the blood on their hands. Which character shows the greater imagination? Prove your choice by reference to the poetry.
5. Discuss which you think preferable, giving reasons for your preference: Shakespeare's treatment of the murder of Duncan or a staging of it on the platform before the spectators.
6. What is the dramatic effect of the knocking in scene ii? What, possibly, does the knocking symbolize?

Scene iii

1. Although it may not appear so to you as you read it, the Porter scene was apparently a very funny one to Shakespeare's audiences. What is the dramatic purpose of comedy at this point in the play?
2. What does the imagery of Macduff's speech following his discovery of the murdered Duncan reveal concerning the regard in which he holds his king (ll. 50-53, 55-64)?
3. In this scene which character is in better control of himself, Macbeth or Lady Macbeth? Refer to their actions and statements to support your choice.

Scene iv

1. At the opening of this scene, how do Ross's and the Old Man's speeches concerning the night and its unnatural violence parallel, or reflect, what has happened within Macbeth's castle?
2. What do Macduff's answers to Ross's questions add to the plot? Do you think his answers to Ross's questions represent his own opinion or public opinion?

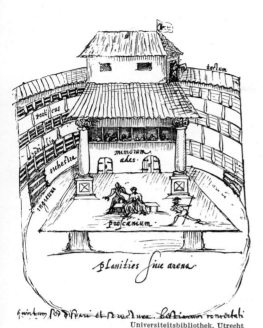

Public theaters in London. The sketch of the Swan Theater (left) was done from memory by a Dutch visitor in the 1590's. The Globe Theater (below) across the river from the city, was octagonal-shaped and open to the sky for lighting purposes.

The Fortune Theater (below left) was a private theater built between 1600 and 1620 for small, select audiences. Drolls, farcical fragments of plays, were popular during the time of the Civil War and Commonwealth. Notice the way the stage was lighted in the production of one such droll (right below).

ACT III

Scene I. *Forres. The palace.*

Enter BANQUO.

BANQUO. Thou hast it now—King, Cawdor, Glamis, all,
As the Weird Women promised; and I fear
Thou play'dst most foully for't. Yet it was said
It should not stand in thy posterity,
5   But that myself should be the root and father
Of many kings. If there come truth from them
(As upon thee, Macbeth, their speeches shine),
Why, by the verities on thee made good,
May they not be my oracles as well
10 And set me up in hope? But, hush, no more!

Sennet[1] sounded. Enter MACBETH *as King;* LADY MACBETH
    as Queen; LENNOX, ROSS, *Lords, and Attendants.*

MACBETH. Here's our chief guest.
LADY MACBETH.   If he had been forgotten,
It had been as a gap in our great feast,
And all-thing[2] unbecoming.
MACBETH. Tonight we hold a solemn[3] supper, sir,
And I'll request your presence.
15 BANQUO.   Let your Highness
Command upon me, to the which my duties
Are with a most indissoluble tie
Forever knit.
MACBETH. Ride you this afternoon?
20 BANQUO. Ay, my good lord.
MACBETH. We should have else desired your good advice
(Which still[4] hath been both grave and prosperous)[5]
In this day's council; but we'll take tomorrow.
Is't far you ride?
25 BANQUO. As far, my lord, as will fill up the time
'Twixt this and supper. Go not my horse the better,[6]
I must become a borrower of the night
For a dark hour or twain.
MACBETH.   Fail not our feast.
BANQUO. My lord, I will not.
30 MACBETH. We hear our bloody cousins are bestowed
In England and in Ireland, not confessing
Their cruel parricide, filling their hearers
With strange invention.[7] But of that tomorrow,
When therewithal we shall have cause of state
35 Craving us jointly.[8] Hie you to horse. Adieu,
Till you return at night. Goes Fleance with you?
BANQUO. Ay, my good lord. Our time does call upon's.

1 sennet : series of trumpet notes.

2 all-thing : altogether.
3 solemn : official; formal.

4 still : always.
5 grave and prosperous : weighty and good in its results.

6 go . . . better : unless my horse goes too fast to make that necessary.

7 strange invention : unlikely stories.
8 Craving us jointly : requiring both your and my attention.

208

MACBETH. I wish your horses swift and sure of foot,
And so I do commend you to their backs.
40 Farewell.   (*Exit* BANQUO.)
Let every man be master of his time
Till seven at night. To make society
The sweeter welcome, we will keep ourself
Till suppertime alone. While⁹ then, God be with you!   9 while : until.

(*Exeunt all but* MACBETH *and a* SERVANT.)

45 Sirrah, a word with you. Attend those men
Our pleasure?
    SERVANT. They are, my lord, without the palace gate.
    MACBETH. Bring them before us.   (*Exit* SERVANT.)
                              To be thus¹⁰ is nothing,   10 To be thus : to be king.
But to be safely thus.¹¹ Our fears in Banquo   11 But . . . thus : unless I
50 Stick deep, and in his royalty of nature   can be so safely.
Reigns that which would be feared. 'Tis much he dares,
And to¹² that dauntless temper of his mind   12 to : in addition to.
He hath a wisdom that doth guide his valor
To act in safety. There is none but he
55 Whose being I do fear; and under him
My Genius is rebuked,¹³ as it is said   13 Genius is rebuked :
Mark Antony's was by Caesar. He chid the Sisters   spirit is cowed.
When first they put the name of King upon me,
And bade them speak to him. Then, prophetlike,
60 They hailed him father to a line of kings.
Upon my head they placed a fruitless crown
And put a barren scepter in my gripe,
Thence to be wrenched with an unlineal hand,
No son of mine succeeding. If't be so,
65 For Banquo's issue have I filed¹⁴ my mind;   14 filed : defiled.
For them the gracious Duncan have I murdered;
Put rancors in the vessel of my peace
Only for them, and mine eternal jewel¹⁵   15 mine . . . jewel : my
Given to the common enemy of man¹⁶   soul.
                                                               16 common . . . man :
70 To make them kings, the seed of Banquo kings!   Satan.
Rather than so, come, Fate, into the list,¹⁷   17 list : lists.
And champion me to th' utterance!¹⁸ Who's there?   18 champion . . . utterance :
                                                               fight against me to the very
           Enter SERVANT *and two* MURDERERS.   death.
Now go to the door and stay there till we call.

                                              (*Exit* SERVANT.)

Was it not yesterday we spoke together?
    MURDERERS. It was, so please your Highness.
75   MACBETH.   Well then, now
Have you considered of my speeches? Know
That it was he,¹⁹ in the times past, which held you   19 he : Banquo.
So under fortune,²⁰ which you thought had been   20 held . . . fortune :
                                                               thwarted your careers.

WILLIAM SHAKESPEARE   **209**

Our innocent self. This I made good[21] to you
80　In our last conference, passed in probation with you[22]
How you were borne in hand,[23] how crossed; the instruments;[24]
Who wrought with them; and all things else that might
To half a soul[25] and to a notion[26] crazed
Say "Thus did Banquo."
　　　1 MURDERER.　　　　You made it known to us.
85　　MACBETH. I did so; and went further, which is now
Our point of second meeting. Do you find
Your patience so predominant in your nature
That you can let this go? Are you so gospeled[27]
To pray for this good man and for his issue,
90　Whose heavy hand hath bowed you to the grave
And beggared yours forever?
　　　1 MURDERER.　　　　We are men, my liege.
　　MACBETH. Ay, in the catalogue[28] ye go for men,
As hounds and greyhounds, mongrels, spaniels, curs,
Shoughs,[29] waterrugs,[30] and demiwolves[31] are clipt[32]
95　All by the name of dogs. The valued file[33]
Distinguishes the swift, the slow, the subtle,
The housekeeper,[34] the hunter, every one
According to the gift which bounteous nature
Hath in him closed;[35] whereby he does receive
100　Particular addition,[36] from the bill
That writes them all alike; and so of men.
Now, if you have a station in the file,
Not i' th' worst rank of manhood, say't;
And I will put that business in your bosoms
105　Whose execution takes your enemy off,
Grapples you to the heart and love of us,
Who wear our health but sickly in his life,
Which in his death were perfect.
　　　2 MURDERER.　　　　I am one, my liege,
Whom the vile blows and buffets of the world
110　Have so incensed that I am reckless what
I do to spite the world.
　　　1 MURDERER.　　And I another,
So weary with disasters, tugged[37] with fortune,
That I would set[38] my life on any chance,
To mend it or be rid on't.
　　MACBETH.　　　　Both of you.
115　Know Banquo was your enemy.
　　　MURDERERS.　　　　True, my lord.
　　MACBETH. So is he mine; and in such bloody distance[39]
That every minute of his being trusts
Against my near'st of life;[40] and though I could
With barefaced power sweep him from my sight

21 made good : proved.
22 passed . . . you : reviewed the facts of proof with you.
23 borne in hand : deluded.
24 instruments : agents (who worked against you).
25 half a soul : one who had only half a man's wits.
26 notion : judgment.

27 so gospeled : so filled with the spirit of the Gospel (forgiveness).

28 in the catalogue : in a general list.
29 Shoughs : shaggy Iceland lap dog.
30 waterrugs : rough water dogs.
31 demiwolves : animals half wolf, half dog.
32 clipt : called.
33 valued file : list which notes the valuable quality which distinguishes each breed.
34 housekeeper : watchdog.
35 in him closed : endowed him with.
36 Particular addition : a name or title which distinguishes him (from other dogs).

37 tugged : pulled about.
38 set : stake.

39 distance : discord; or (as a fencing term) the distance to be kept between two antagonists.
40 my near'st of life : my most vital spot.

120 And bid my will avouch it,[41] yet I must not,
    For certain friends that are both his and mine,
    Whose loves I may not drop, but wail[42] his fall
    Who I myself struck down. And thence it is
    That I to your assistance do make love,
125 Masking the business from the common eye
    For sundry weighty reasons.
        2 MURDERER.   We shall, my lord,
    Perform what you command us.
        1 MURDERER.   Though our lives—
        MACBETH. Your spirits[43] shine through you. Within this
            hour at most
    I will advise you where to plant yourselves,
130 Acquaint you with the perfect spy o' th' time,
    The moment on't; for't must be done tonight,
    And something from[44] the palace; always thought[45]
    That I require a clearness;[46] and with him,
    To leave no rubs[47] nor botches in the work,
135 Fleance his son, that keeps him company,
    Whose absence is no less material to me
    Than is his father's, must embrace the fate
    Of that dark hour. Resolve yourselves apart;[48]
    I'll come to you anon.
        MURDERERS.   We are resolved, my lord.
140   MACBETH. I'll call upon you straight.[49] Abide within.
                                    (*Exeunt* MURDERERS.)
    It is concluded. Banquo, thy soul's flight,
    If it find heaven, must find it out tonight.   (*Exit.*)

                Scene II. *Forres. The palace.*

            Enter LADY MACBETH *and a* SERVANT.

    LADY MACBETH. Is Banquo gone from court?
    SERVANT. Ay, madam, but returns again tonight.
    LADY MACBETH. Say to the King I would attend his leisure
    For a few words.
        SERVANT.   Madam, I will.   (*Exit.*)
        LADY MACBETH.   Naught's had, all's spent,
5   Where our desire is got without content.
    'Tis safer to be that which we destroy
    Than by destruction dwell in doubtful joy.

                    Enter MACBETH.

    How now, my lord? Why do you keep alone,
    Of sorriest[1] fancies your companions making,
10 Using[2] those thoughts which should indeed have died
    With them they think on? Things without all remedy
    Should be without regard. What's done is done.

WILLIAM SHAKESPEARE   **211**

---

41 avouch it : take responsibility for the deed.
42 but wail : But I must
wail.

43 spirits : courage and resolution.
44 something from : at
some distance from.
45 always thought : it being always understood.
46 clearness : freedom from
any suspicion.
47 rubs : flaws.

48 Resolve . . . apart :
Make up your minds pri-
vately (about this business).
49 straight : immediately.

1 sorriest : most despicable.
2 Using : associating with.

MACBETH. We have scotched[3] the snake, not killed it.
　　She'll close, and be herself, whilst our poor[4] malice

15　Remains in danger of her former tooth.
　　But let the frame of things disjoint, both the worlds suffer,[5]
　　Ere we will eat our meal in fear and sleep
　　In the affliction of these terrible dreams
　　That shake us nightly. Better be with the dead,

20　Whom we, to gain our peace, have sent to peace,
　　Than on the torture of the mind to lie[6]
　　In restless ecstasy.[7] Duncan is in his grave;
　　After life's fitful fever he sleeps well.
　　Treason has done his worst. Nor steel nor poison,

25　Malice domestic, foreign levy,[8] nothing,
　　Can touch him further.

　　LADY MACBETH.　　Come on.
　　Gentle my lord, sleek o'er your rugged looks;
　　Be bright and jovial among your guests tonight.

　　MACBETH. So shall I, love; and so, I pray, be you.

30　Let your remembrance apply to Banquo;
　　Present him eminence[9] both with eye and tongue—
　　Unsafe the while, that we
　　Must lave our honors in these flattering streams[10]
　　And make our faces vizards[11] to our hearts,
　　Disguising what they are.

35　**LADY MACBETH.**　　You must leave this.[12]

　　MACBETH. O, full of scorpions is my mind, dear wife!
　　Thou know'st that Banquo, and his Fleance, lives.

　　LADY MACBETH. But in them Nature's copy's not eterne.[13]

　　MACBETH. There's comfort yet! They are assailable.

40　Then be thou jocund. Ere the bat hath flown
　　His cloistered[14] flight,[15] ere to black Hecate's summons
　　The shard-borne beetle with his drowsy hums
　　Hath rung night's yawning peal,[16] there shall be done
　　A deed of dreadful note.[17]

　　LADY MACBETH.　　What's to be done?

45　**MACBETH.** Be innocent of the knowledge, dearest chuck,
　　Till thou applaud the deed. Come, seeling night,[18]
　　Scarf up[19] the tender eye of pitiful day,
　　And with thy bloody and invisible hand
　　Cancel and tear to pieces that great bond[20]

50　Which keeps me pale! Light thickens, and the crow
　　Makes wing to th' rooky wood.
　　Good things of day begin to droop and drowse,
　　Whiles night's black agents[21] to their preys do rouse.
　　Thou marvel'st at my words; but hold thee still:

55　Things bad begun make strong themselves by ill.
　　So prithee go with me.　　　　　　　(*Exeunt.*)

3 scotched : gashed.
4 poor : ineffective.
5 But let . . . suffer : Let the universe fall apart, and both this world and the next perish.
6 on . . . lie : metaphorical reference, perhaps to the torture of the rack.
7 ecstasy : mental suffering.
8 Malice . . . levy : in contrast to Macbeth, who fears both domestic malice from Banquo and Macduff and foreign levy from friends of Malcolm and Donalbain in England and Ireland.
9 Present . . . eminence : do him special honor.
10 Unsafe . . . streams : We are unsafe while we must wash our honors in streams of flattery to make them look clean.
11 vizards (vĭz′ərdz) : masks.
12 You . . . this : You must stop such remarks and the mood which causes them.
13 But . . . eterne : But nature has not granted them a perpetual lease on life.
14 cloistered : The bats inhabit belfries and cloisters.
15 Ere . . . flight : before dark.
16 ere . . . peal : ere the droning beetle, in obedience to Hecate's summons, has announced the coming of drowsy night.
17 of dreadful note : dreadful to be known.
18 seeling night : Night is like a falconer who sews up the eyelids of the falcon with silk thread to keep it in the dark while taming it.
19 Scarf up : blindfold.
20 bond : the prophecy by which Fate has bound itself to give the throne to Banquo's descendants.
21 black agents : all evil beings that act by night.

Scene III. *Forres. A park near the palace.*

Enter three MURDERERS.

1 MURDERER. But who did bid thee join with us?

3 MURDERER.   Macbeth.

2 MURDERER. He needs not our mistrust,[1] since he delivers[2]
Our offices,[3] and what we have to do,
To the direction just.[4]

1 MURDERER.   Then stand with us.

5 The west yet glimmers with some streaks of day.
Now spurs the lated[5] traveler apace
To gain the timely inn, and near approaches
The subject of our watch.

3 MURDERER.   Hark! I hear horses.

BANQUO (*within*). Give us a light there, ho!

2 MURDERER.   Then 'tis he! The rest

10 That are within the note of expectation[6]
Already are i' th' court.

1 MURDERER.   His horses go about.[7]

2 MURDERER. Almost a mile; but he does usually,
So all men do, from hence to th' palace gate
Make it their walk.

Enter BANQUO, *and* FLEANCE *with a torch.*

2 MURDERER.   A light, a light!

3 MURDERER.   'Tis he.

15   1 MURDERER. Stand to't.

BANQUO. It will be rain tonight.

1 MURDERER.   Let it come down!

                    (*They fall upon* BANQUO.)

BANQUO. O, treachery! Fly, good Fleance, fly, fly, fly!
Thou mayst revenge. O slave!

                    (*Dies.* FLEANCE *escapes.*)

3 MURDERER. Who did strike out the light?

1 MURDERER.   Was't not the way?

3 MURDERER. There's but one down; the son is fled.

20   2 MURDERER.   We have lost
Best half of our affair.

1 MURDERER. Well, let's away, and say how much is done.

                    (*Exeunt.*)

Scene IV. *Forres. Hall in the palace.*

Banquet prepared. Enter MACBETH, LADY MACBETH, ROSS,
LENNOX, LORDS, *and Attendants.*

MACBETH. You know your own degrees,[1] sit down. At first
And last the hearty welcome.

LORDS.   Thanks to your Majesty.

1 He . . . mistrust : We
need not mistrust him .
2 delivers : reports.
3 offices : duties.
4 To . . . just : exactly according to our instructions.
5 lated : belated.

6 within . . . expectation :
in the list of expected
guests.
7 go about : turn aside
(taken by servants, while
Banquo walks).

1 degrees : ranks, and
hence the seat which each
should take.

WILLIAM SHAKESPEARE   **213**

MACBETH. Ourself will mingle with society
And play the humble host.

5   Our hostess keeps her state,[2] but in best time[3]
We will require[4] her welcome.

LADY MACBETH. Pronounce it for me, sir, to all our friends,
For my heart speaks they are welcome.

Enter FIRST MURDERER *to the door.*

MACBETH. See, they encounter thee[5] with their hearts'
thanks.

10   Both sides are even.[6] Here I'll sit i' th' midst.
Be large in mirth; anon we'll drink a measure
The table round. (*Goes to the door.*) There's blood upon thy
face.

MURDERER. 'Tis Banquo's then.

MACBETH. 'Tis better thee without than he within.[7]

15   Is he dispatched?

MURDERER. My lord, his throat is cut. That I did for him.

MACBETH. Thou art the best o' th' cutthroats! Yet he's good
That did the like for Fleance. If thou didst it,
Thou art the nonpareil.[8]

MURDERER.   Most royal sir,

20   Fleance is scaped.

MACBETH (*aside*). Then comes my fit[9] again. I had else been
perfect;
Whole as the marble, founded as the rock,
As broad and general as the casing[10] air.
But now I am cabined, cribbed, confined, bound in

25   To saucy doubts and fears.—But Banquo's safe?

MURDERER. Ay, my good lord. Safe in a ditch he bides,
With twenty trenchèd[11] gashes on his head,
The least a death to nature.

MACBETH.   Thanks for that!
There the grown serpent lies; the worm that's fled

30   Hath nature that in time will venom breed,
No teeth for th' present. Get thee gone. Tomorrow
We'll hear ourselves again.   (*Exit* MURDERER.)

LADY MACBETH.   My royal lord,
You do not give the cheer.[12] The feast is sold
That is not often vouched, while 'tis a-making,

35   'Tis given with welcome.[13] To feed[14] were best at home.
From thence,[15] the sauce to meat is ceremony;
Meeting were bare without it.

Enter the Ghost of Banquo, and sits in MACBETH's *place.*

MACBETH.   Sweet remembrancer!
Now good digestion wait on appetite,
And health on both!

2 keeps her state : remains on her chair of state and thus separated from the guests' table.
3 in best time : when the proper moment comes.
4 require : request.

5 encounter thee : respond to you.
6 Both . . . even : All seats are full except for the one at the head reserved for Macbeth.

7 'Tis . . . within : It is better the blood should be outside you than inside Banquo.

8 nonpareil (nŏn'pə rĕl′) : one without equal.

9 my fit : my anxiety.

10 casing : enveloping.

11 trenched : deep-cut.

12 give the cheer : make your guests feel welcome.
13 the feast . . . welcome : Unless the host's words assure his guests they are welcome, he might as well be an innkeeper.
14 To feed : to eat merely to satisfy hunger.
15 From thence : away from home.

LENNOX.   May't please your Highness sit.

40   MACBETH. Here had we now our country's honor, roofed,[16]
Were the graced person of our Banquo present;
Who may I rather challenge for unkindness
Than pity for mischance![17]
      ROSS.   His absence, sir,
Lays blame upon his promise. Please't your Highness
45   To grace us with your royal company?
      MACBETH. The table's full.
      LENNOX.   Here is a place reserved, sir.
      MACBETH. Where?
      LENNOX. Here, my good lord. What is't that moves your
           Highness?
      MACBETH. Which of you have done this?
      LORDS.   What, my good lord?
50   MACBETH. Thou canst not say I did it. Never shake
Thy gory locks at me.
      ROSS. Gentlemen, rise. His Highness is not well.
      LADY MACBETH. Sit, worthy friends. My lord is often thus,
And hath been from his youth. Pray you keep seat.
55   The fit is momentary; upon a thought[18]
He will again be well. If much you note him,
You shall offend him and extend his passion.
Feed, and regard him not.—Are you a man?
      MACBETH. Ay, and a bold one, that dare look on that
Which might appal the devil.
60   LADY MACBETH.   O proper stuff![19]
This is the very painting of your fear.
This is the air-drawn dagger which you said
Led you to Duncan. O, these flaws and starts
(Impostors to[20] true fear) would well become
65   A woman's story at a winter's fire,
Authorized[21] by her grandam. Shame itself!
Why do you make such faces? When all's done,
You look but on a stool.
      MACBETH. Prithee see there! behold! look! lo! How say you?
70   Why, what care I? If thou canst nod, speak too.
If charnel houses[22] and our graves must send
Those that we bury back, our monuments
Shall be the maws of kites.[23]

                                              (*Exit Ghost.*)

      LADY MACBETH.   What, quite unmanned in folly?
      MACBETH. If I stand here, I saw him.
      LADY MACBETH.   Fie, for shame!
75   MACBETH. Blood hath been shed ere now, i' th' olden time,
Ere humane statute purged the gentle weal;[24]

16 had . . . roofed : We should now have all the noblest men of Scotland under one roof.

17 Who . . . mischance : whom I hope I may blame for staying away on purpose rather than pity for being prevented by an accident.

18 upon a thought : in a moment.

19 O proper stuff : A fine thing, this!

20 to : in comparison with.

21 Authorized : vouched for.

22 charnel houses : vaults or small buildings attached to churches for storage of bones coming to light as new graves were dug.

23 our monuments . . . kites : Our tombs will be the bellies of kites (who will devour the dead).

24 Ere . . . weal : before civilizing law purged the now gentle state of savagery.

Ay, and since too, murders have been performed
Too terrible for the ear. The time has been
That, when the brains were out, the man would die,
80 And there an end! But now they rise again,
With twenty mortal murders[25] on their crowns,
And push us from our stools. This is more strange
Than such a murder is.

    LADY MACBETH.   My worthy lord,
Your noble friends do lack you.[26]

    MACBETH.   I do forget.
85 Do not muse at me, my most worthy friends.
I have a strange infirmity, which is nothing
To those that know me. Come, love and health to all!
Then I'll sit down. Give me some wine, fill full.

Enter Ghost.

I drink to th' general joy o' th' whole table,
90 And to our dear friend Banquo, whom we miss.
Would he were here! To all, and him, we thirst,[27]
And all to all.[28]

    LORDS.   Our duties, and the pledge.[29]

    MACBETH. Avaunt, and quit my sight! Let the earth hide
    thee!
Thy bones are marrowless, thy blood is cold;
95 Thou hast no speculation[30] in those eyes
Which thou dost glare with!

    LADY MACBETH.   Think of this, good peers,
But as a thing of custom. 'Tis no other.
Only it spoils the pleasure of the time.

    MACBETH. What man dare, I dare.
100 Approach thou like the rugged Russian bear,
The armed[31] rhinoceros, or th' Hyrcan tiger;[32]
Take any shape but that, and my firm nerves
Shall never tremble. Or be alive again
And dare me to the desert[33] with thy sword.
105 If trembling I inhabit then,[34] protest me
The baby of a girl.[35] Hence, horrible shadow!
Unreal mock'ry,[36] hence!

                        (*Exit Ghost.*)

           Why, so! Being gone,
I am a man again. Pray you sit still.

    LADY MACBETH. You have displaced the mirth, broke the
    good meeting
With most admired[37] disorder.

110   MACBETH.   Can such things be,
And overcome us like a summer's cloud
Without our special wonder?[38] You make me strange

25 mortal murders : deadly wounds.

26 lack you : miss you.

27 thirst : drink.
28 And all to all : and let everybody drink to everybody.
29 Our duties . . . pledge : Homage to your Majesty, and a health to the whole table and Banquo.

30 speculation : power of sight.

31 armed : armored (by his thick hide).
32 Hyrcan (hûr′kən) tiger : alludes to a beast killed by Hercules.
33 to the desert : to a solitary place.
34 If trembling . . . then : If then, as now, I tremble.
35 baby . . . girl : i.e., weakling.
36 mock'ry : illusion.

37 admired : amazing.
38 overcome . . . wonder : pass over us as a cloud in summer, exciting no special surprise.

Even to the disposition that I owe,[39]
When now I think you can behold such sights
115 And keep the natural ruby of your cheeks
When mine is blanched with fear.

    Ross.   What sights, my lord?

    Lady Macbeth. I pray you speak not. He grows worse and
        worse;
Question enrages him. At once, good night.
Stand not upon the order of your going,[40]
But go at once.

120   **Lennox.**   Good night, and better health
Attend his Majesty!

    Lady Macbeth. A kind good night to all!

           (*Exeunt all but* **Macbeth** *and* **Lady Macbeth.**)

    Macbeth. It will have blood, they say; blood will have
    blood.
Stones have been known to move[41] and trees to speak;
Augures[42] and understood relations[43] have
125 By maggot-pies and choughs[44] and rooks brought **forth**
The secret'st man of blood.[45] What is the night?

    Lady Macbeth. Almost at odds[46] with morning, which is
    which.

    Macbeth. How say'st thou[47] that Macduff denies his per-
    son
At our great bidding?

    Lady Macbeth.   Did you send to him, sir?

130   **Macbeth.** I hear it by the way; but I will send.
There's not a one of them but in his house
I keep a servant feed.[48] I will tomorrow
(And betimes[49] I will) unto the Weird Sisters.
More shall they speak; for now I am bent to know
135 By the worst means the worst. For mine own good
All causes[50] shall give way. I am in blood
Stepped in so far that, should I wade no more,
Returning were as tedious as go o'er.
Strange things I have in head, that will to hand,[51]
140 Which must be acted ere they may be scanned.[52]

    Lady Macbeth. You lack the season of all natures, sleep.

    Macbeth. Come, we'll to sleep. My strange and self-abuse[53]
Is the initiate fear that wants hard use.[54]
We are yet but young in deed.   (*Exeunt.*)

           Scene V. *A heath.*

    Thunder. Enter the three **Witches,** *meeting* **Hecate.**

    1 Witch. Why, how now, Hecate? You look angerly.

---

39 You . . . owe : You make me feel that I do not know my own nature.

40 Stand . . . going : Do not take the time to leave in the order of your rank.

41 Stones . . . move : so as to reveal the body that murderers had hidden.
42 Augures : auguries—signs from the flight of birds.
43 understood relations : knowledge of the secret relation between things and events.
44 maggot-pies and choughs (chüfs) : magpies and crows.
45 Stones . . . blood : Macbeth recalls instances in which murders have been miraculously revealed.
46 at odds : disputing; therefore about midnight.
47 How . . . thou : What do you say to the fact?
48 feed : paid to spy.
49 betimes : early.

50 All causes : all considerations.
51 will to hand : are bound to be carried out.
52 scanned : studied.
53 My . . . self-abuse : my strange self-deception.
54 initiate . . . hard use : beginner's fear lacking in the use that hardens.

HECATE. Have I not reason, beldams[1] as you are,
Saucy and overbold? How did you dare
To trade and traffic with Macbeth
5   In riddles and affairs of death;
And I, the mistress of your charms,
The close[2] contriver of all harms,
Was never called to bear my part
Or show the glory of our art?
10   And, which is worse, all you have done
Hath been but for a wayward son,
Spiteful and wrathful, who, as others do,
Loves for his own ends, not for you.
But make amends now. Get you gone
15   And at the pit of Acheron[3]
Meet me i' th' morning. Thither he
Will come to know his destiny.
Your vessels and your spells provide,
Your charms and everything beside.
20   I am for th' air. This night I'll spend
Unto a dismal[4] and a fatal end.
Great business must be wrought ere noon.
Upon the corner of the moon
There hangs a vap'rous drop profound.[5]
25   I'll catch it ere it come to ground;
And that, distilled by magic sleights,[6]
Shall raise such artificial sprites
As by the strength of their illusion
Shall draw him on to his confusion.
30   He shall spurn fate, scorn death, and bear
His hopes 'bove wisdom, grace, and fear;
And you all know security
Is mortals' chiefest enemy.
        (*Music and a song within.* "Come away, come away," *etc.*)
Hark! I am called. My little spirit, see,
35   Sits in a foggy cloud and stays for me.   (*Exit.*)
    1 WITCH. Come, let's make haste. She'll soon be back again.
                                        (*Exeunt.*)

Scene VI. *Forres. The palace.*

Enter LENNOX *and another* LORD.

    LENNOX. My former speeches[1] have but hit[2] your thoughts,
Which can interpret farther.[3] Only I say
Things have been strangely borne.[4] The gracious Duncan
Was pitied of Macbeth. Marry,[5] he was dead!
5   And the right valiant Banquo walked too late;
Whom, you may say (if't please you) Fleance killed,

1 beldams : hags.

2 close : secret.

3 pit of Acheron (ăk'ə rŏn') : a Scottish cavern.

4 dismal : disastrous.

5 vap'rous drop profound : heavy drop of condensed vapor.
6 sleights : crafts.

1 My . . . speeches : Evidently Lennox has been expressing suspicions of Macbeth.
2 hit : agreed with.
3 interpret farther : draw their own further conclusions.
4 strangely borne : oddly managed.
5 Marry : indeed.

Goddess of ghosts

(Climax= escape of fleance)

For Fleance fled. Men must not walk too late.
Who cannot want the thought⁶ how monstrous
It was for Malcolm and for Donalbain
10 To kill their gracious father? Damnèd fact!⁷
How it did grieve Macbeth! Did he not straight,
In pious⁸ rage, the two delinquents tear,
That were the slaves of drink and thralls⁹ of sleep?
Was not that nobly done? Ay, and wisely too!
15 For 'twould have angered any heart alive
To hear the men deny't. So that I say
He has borne all things well; and I do think
That, had he Duncan's sons under his key
(As, an't please heaven, he shall not), they should find
20 What 'twere to kill a father. So should Fleance.
But peace! for from broad words,¹⁰ and 'cause he failed
His presence at the tyrant's feast, I hear
Macduff lives in disgrace. Sir, can you tell
Where he bestows himself?

    LORD.   The son of Duncan,
25 From whom this tyrant holds the due of birth,¹¹
Lives in the English court, and is received
Of the most pious Edward¹² with such grace
That the malevolence of fortune nothing
Takes from his high respect. Thither Macduff
30 Is gone to pray the holy King upon¹³ his aid
To wake¹⁴ Northumberland and warlike Siward;
That by the help of these (with Him above
To ratify the work) we may again
Give to our tables meat, sleep to our nights,
35 Free from our feasts and banquets bloody knives,
Do faithful homage and receive free honors—
All which we pine for now. And this report
Hath so exasperate the King that he
Prepares for some attempt of war.

    LENNOX.   Sent he to Macduff?
40   LORD. He did; and with an absolute "Sir, not I!"
The cloudy¹⁵ messenger turns me his back
And hums, as who should say, "You'll rue the time
That clogs me¹⁶ with this answer."

    LENNOX.   And that well might
Advise him to a caution t' hold what distance
45 His wisdom can provide. Some holy angel
Fly to the court of England and unfold
His message ere he come, that a swift blessing
May soon return to this our suffering country
Under a hand accursed!

    LORD.   I'll send my prayers with him. (*Exeunt.*)

WILLIAM SHAKESPEARE

6 Who . . . thought : Who can help thinking?

7 fact : evil deed.

8 pious : devoted; loyal.
9 thralls : slaves.

10 from broad words : because of too outspoken words.

11 holds . . . birth : withholds the throne.
12 Edward : King of England, 1042-1066.

13 upon : with
14 wake : call to arms

15 cloudy : frowning

16 clogs me : burdens.

Questions for Study

Act III

Scene i

1. If you were staging this scene, how would you have Macbeth and Lady Macbeth act toward Banquo? Why?
2. Now that Macbeth is King of Scotland, what does his soliloquy (ll. 48-72) tell us of the state of his mind? How does his language in this soliloquy reveal the value which he places on his soul?
3. How does Macbeth's talk with the murderers reveal his ability to manipulate men? What motive is there for this manipulation?

Scene ii

1. What speech by Lady Macbeth in this scene parallels a speech by Macbeth in the preceding scene? Contrast their points of view in these two scenes with their respective points of view in Act I, scene vii.
2. How has the relationship between Macbeth and Lady Macbeth changed from that of Act I and Act II?
3. In what respects are Macbeth's important speeches of this scene similar to Act II, scene i, lines 49-60? In this scene, what images of peace are contrasted with what images of evil? Find evidence here of the night-evil motif begun earlier in the play.

Scene iv

1. If you were staging this scene, which would you do and why: use an actor to pantomime the part of the ghost or depend upon the ability of the actor playing Macbeth to make the audience believe that he is seeing Banquo's ghost?
2. What similarities do you see between the ghost of this act and the illusionary dagger of Act I? What does each illusion tell us about Macbeth's conscience?
3. Notice Macbeth's two uses of blood imagery at the end of this scene. What is he expressing in each instance?
4. Lady Macbeth is one of Shakespeare's greatest creations. In scene iv several sides of her character are presented. Quote lines which reveal different facets of her personality, describing each of these facets.
5. The climax in a Shakespearean tragedy occurs at the point at which the hero's fortunes change. Up to the climax, things are going well; then an event occurs which begins the hero's downfall. Where does the climax occur in Act III? Defend your answer with evidence from the play.

Scene vi

1. What are the similarities between this scene and the final scene of Act II?

A form of drama much in demand in Shakespear's time was the masque, a spectacular dramatic entertainment presented at court, becoming very popular during the early 17th century. Inigo Jones, artist and architect, designed the scenery, costumes, lighting, and other effects for many of these productions. The evolution of Jones's talent is evident in the change from the relatively cautious design for Ben Jonson's Oberon, *1611 (top left), to the elaborate scene for William Davenant's* Temple of Love, *1635 (right). The costumes were very costly (top right). There was stage machinery for lifting whole choruses and chariots through the air (above). Figures called grotesques (above right) appeared in the humorous "antimasque" part of the play.*

Scene I. *A cavern. In the middle, a caldron boiling.*

Thunder. Enter the three WITCHES.

1 WITCH. Thrice the brinded[1] cat hath mewed.

2 WITCH. Thrice and once the hedgepig whined.

3 WITCH. Harpier[2] cries; 'tis time, 'tis time.

1 WITCH. Round about the caldron go;

5 In the poisoned entrails throw.

Toad, that under cold stone

Days and nights has thirty-one

Swelt'red venom sleeping got,

Boil thou first i' th' charmèd pot.

10 ALL. Double, double, toil and trouble;

Fire burn, and caldron bubble.

2 WITCH. Fillet of a fenny snake,

In the caldron boil and bake;

Eye of newt, and toe of frog,

15 Wool of bat, and tongue of dog,

Adder's fork, and blindworm's sting,

Lizard's leg, and howlet's[3] wing;

For a charm of pow'rful trouble

Like a hell-broth boil and bubble.

20 ALL. Double, double, toil and trouble;

Fire burn, and caldron bubble.

3 WITCH. Scale of dragon, tooth of wolf,

Witch's mummy,[4] maw and gulf[5]

Of the ravined[6] salt-sea shark,

25 Root of hemlock, digged i' th' dark;[7]

Liver of blaspheming Jew,

Gall of goat, and slips of yew[8]

Slivered in the moon's eclipse;

Nose of Turk and Tartar's lips;

30 Finger of birth-strangled babe

Ditch-delivered[9] by a drab:

Make the gruel thick and slab.[10]

Add thereto a tiger's chaudron[11]

For th' ingredience of our caldron.

35 ALL. Double, double, toil and trouble;

Fire burn, and caldron bubble.

2 WITCH. Cool it with a baboon's blood,

Then the charm is firm and good.

Enter HECATE *to the other three* WITCHES.

HECATE. O, well done! I commend your pains,

40 And every one shall share i' th' gains.

And now about the caldron sing

1 brinded (brĭn′dəd) : striped.

2 Harpier : name of an attendant spirit, derived from *harpy*.

3 howlet : owlet.

4 Witch's mummy : mumified fragment of a witch.

5 gulf : throat.

6 ravined (rāv′ənd) : ravenous.

7 i' th' dark : i.e., more potent.

8 yew : tree often grown in graveyards and regarded as poisonous.

9 Ditch-delivered : born in a ditch.

10 slab : slimy.

11 chaudron (shô′drôn) : entrails.

Like elves and fairies in a ring,
Enchanting all that you put in.

> (*Music and a song, "Black spirits," etc.*
>
> *Exit* HECATE.)

45 2 WITCH. By the pricking[12] of my thumbs,
Something wicked this way comes.

> Open locks,[13]
> Whoever knocks!
> *Enter* MACBETH.

MACBETH. How now, you secret, black, and midnight hags?
What is't you do?

ALL. A deed without a name.

50 MACBETH. I conjure you by that which you profess
(Howe'er you come to know it), answer me.
Though you untie the winds and let them fight
Against the churches; though the yesty[14] waves
Confound[15] and swallow navigation up;
55 Though bladed corn be lodged[16] and trees blown down;
Though castles topple on their warders' heads;
Though palaces and pyramids do slope
Their heads to their foundations; though the treasure
Of nature's germens[17] tumble all together,
60 Even till destruction sicken[18]—answer me
To what I ask you.

1 WITCH. Speak.

2 WITCH. Demand.

3 WITCH. We'll answer.

1 WITCH. Say, if th' hadst rather hear it from our mouths
Or from our masters.

MACBETH. Call 'em! Let me see 'em.

1 WITCH. Pour in sow's blood, that hath eaten
65 Her nine farrow; grease that's sweaten
From the murderer's gibbet[19] throw
Into the flame.

ALL. Come, high or low;[20]
Thyself and office deftly show!

> *Thunder. First* APPARITION, *an Armed Head.*[21]

MACBETH. Tell me, thou unknown power—

1 WITCH. He knows thy thought.
70 Hear his speech, but say thou naught.

1 APPARITION. Macbeth! Macbeth! Macbeth! Beware Macduff;
Beware the Thane of Fife. Dismiss me. Enough.

> (*He descends.*)

MACBETH. Whate'er thou art, for thy good caution thanks!
Thou hast harped[22] my fear aright. But one word more—

12 pricking : sign of the approach of a wicked person.
13 Open locks : a formula to release any spell forbidding the entrance of an intruder.

14 yesty : foaming.
15 Confound : destroy.
16 lodged : laid flat.

17 nature's germens : seeds, or sources, of all nature.
18 Though you untie . . . sicken : Though your evil spells bring utter ruin upon the earth.

19 gibbet (jĭb′ĭt) : gallows.
20 high or low : whether from earth or hell.

21 an armed Head : This may represent Macduff, a threat to Macbeth; it may represent Macbeth's own head (V, viii, 53).

22 harped : sounded.

75   1 Witch. He will not be commanded. Here's another,
More potent than the first.

               Thunder. Second Apparition, *a Bloody Child.*[23]

    2 Apparition. Macbeth! Macbeth! Macbeth!

    Macbeth. Had I three ears, I'd hear thee.

    2 Apparition. Be bloody, bold, and resolute; laugh to scorn
80   The pow'r of man, for none of woman born
Shall harm Macbeth.   *(Descends.)*

    Macbeth. Then live, Macduff. What need I fear of thee?
But yet I'll make assurance double sure
And take a bond of fate.[24] Thou shalt not live!
85   That I may tell pale-hearted fear it lies
And sleep in spite of thunder.

          Thunder. Third Apparition, *a Child Crowned,*[25] *with a*
                        tree in his hand.

                  What is this
That rises like the issue of a king
And wears upon his baby-brow the round
And top of sovereignty?[26]

    All.   Listen, but speak not to't.
90   3 Apparition. Be lion-mettled, proud, and take no care
Who chafes, who frets, or where conspirers are.
Macbeth shall never vanquished be until
Great Birnam Wood to high Dunsinane Hill
Shall come against him.   *(Descends.)*

    Macbeth.   That will never be.
95   Who can impress[27] the forest, bid the tree
Unfix his earth-bound root? Sweet bodements,[28] good!
Rebellion's head rise never till the Wood
Of Birnam rise, and our high-placed Macbeth
Shall live the lease of nature, pay his breath
100   To time and mortal custom.[29] Yet my heart
Throbs to know one thing. Tell me, if your art
Can tell so much—shall Banquo's issue ever
Reign in this kingdom?

    All.   Seek to know no more.

    Macbeth. I will be satisfied. Deny me this,
105   And an eternal curse fall on you! Let me know.
Why sinks that caldron? and what noise is this?

                        (Hautboys.)

    1 Witch. Show!

    2 Witch. Show!

    3 Witch. Show!
110   All. Show his eyes, and grieve his heart!
Come like shadows, so depart!

          (A show of eight Kings, the eighth with a glass in
                  his hand, and Banquo *last.)*

---

23 a Bloody Child : supposed to be Macduff (in a role yet unknown to Macbeth). *Caesarian section*

24 take . . . fate : bind fate to its promise.

25 a Child Crowned : Malcolm, heir of Duncan.

26 round . . . sovereignty : crown.

27 impress : enlist by force.

28 bodements (bōd'mənts) **:** prophecies.

29 live . . . custom : live the term of his natural life and die a natural death.

MACBETH. Thou art too like the spirit of Banquo. Down!
Thy crown does sear mine eyeballs. And thy hair,
Thou other gold-bound brow, is like the first.

115 A third is like the former. Filthy hags!
Why do you show me this? A fourth? Start,[30] eyes!
What, will the line stretch out to th' crack of doom?
Another yet? A seventh? I'll see no more.
And yet the eighth appears, who bears a glass[31]

120 Which shows me many more; and some I see
That twofold balls[32] and treble scepters carry.
Horrible sight! Now I see 'tis true;
For the blood-boltered[33] Banquo smiles upon me
And points at them for his. (**APPARITIONS** *vanish.*) What? Is
 this so?

125 1 **WITCH.** Ay, sir, all this is so. But why
Stands Macbeth thus amazedly?[34]
Come, sisters, cheer we up his sprites
And show the best of our delights.
I'll charm the air to give a sound

130 While you perform your antic[35] round,
That this great king may kindly say
Our duties did his welcome pay.
                (*Music. The* **WITCHES** *dance, and vanish.*)
   MACBETH. Where are they? Gone? Let this pernicious hour
Stand aye accursèd in the calendar!
Come in, without there!

                Enter **LENNOX.**

135 **LENNOX.**   What's your Grace's will?
   MACBETH. Saw you the Weird Sisters?
   LENNOX.   No, my lord.
   MACBETH. Came they not by you?
   LENNOX.   No, indeed, my lord.
   MACBETH. Infected be the air whereon they ride,
And damned all those that trust them! I did hear

140 The galloping of horse. Who was't came by?
   LENNOX. 'Tis two or three, my lord, that bring you word
Macduff is fled to England.
   MACBETH.   Fled to England?
   LENNOX. Ay, my good lord.
   MACBETH (*aside*). Time, thou anticipat'st[36] my dread ex-
    ploits.

145. The flighty[37] purpose never is o'ertook
Unless the deed go with it. From this moment
The very firstlings[38] of my heart shall be
The firstlings of my hand. And even now,
To crown my thoughts with acts, be it thought and done!

150 The castle of Macduff I will surprise,

WILLIAM SHAKESPEARE   **225**

30 Start : Start out of your sockets.

31 glass : mirror.

32 balls : symbols of sovereignty (*two-fold* suggesting Scotland and England; *treble* adding Ireland).
33 blood-boltered : having his hair matted with blood.

34 amazedly : as in a trance.

35 antic : fantastic.

36 anticipat'st : forestall.

37 flighty : fleeting.

38 firstlings : first-born; thus, the first purposes that he may form.

Seize upon Fife, give to the edge o' th' sword
His wife, his babes, and all unfortunate souls
That trace him in his line. No boasting like a fool!
This deed I'll do before this purpose cool.
155 But no more sights!—Where are these gentlemen?
Come, bring me where they are.   (*Exeunt.*)

Scene II. *Fife.* MACDUFF'S *castle.*

Enter LADY MACDUFF, *her* SON, *and* ROSS.

LADY MACDUFF. What had he done to make him fly the land?
Ross. You must have patience, madam.
LADY MACDUFF.   He had none.
His flight was madness. When our actions do not,
Our fears do make us traitors.
     Ross.   You know not
5 Whether it was his wisdom or his fear.
     LADY MACDUFF. Wisdom? To leave his wife, to leave his
          babes,
His mansion, and his titles, in a place
From whence himself does fly? He loves us not,
He wants the natural touch. For the poor wren,
10 (The most diminitive of birds) will fight,
Her young ones in her nest, against the owl.
All is the fear, and nothing is the love,
As little is the wisdom, where the flight
So runs against all reason.
     Ross.   My dearest coz,[1]
15 I pray you school yourself. But for your husband,
He is noble, wise, judicious, and best knows
The fits o' th' season.[2] I dare not speak much further;
But cruel are the times, when we are traitors
And do not know ourselves;[3] when we hold rumor
20 From[4] what we fear, yet know not what we fear,
But float upon a wild and violent sea
Each way and none. I take my leave of you.
Shall not be long but I'll be here again.
Things at the worst will cease, or else climb upward
25 To what they were before.—My pretty cousin,
Blessing upon you!
     LADY MACDUFF. Fathered he is, and yet he's fatherless.
     Ross. I am so much a fool, should I stay longer,
It would be my disgrace and your discomfort.[5]
30 I take my leave at once.   (*Exit.*)
     LADY MACDUFF.   Sirrah, your father's dead;
And what will you do now? How will you live?
     Son. As birds do, mother.

1 coz (kŭz) : an affectionate abbreviation of cousin.

2 fits . . . season : disorders of the present.
3 when . . . ourselves :
when we are traitors (to the
sovereign) but are unaware
of being such.
4 hold rumor / From : be-
lieve rumor because of.

5 It . . . discomfort : i.e., I
should shed tears (a dis-
grace to me as a man and
a distress to you).

THE RENAISSANCE

LADY MACDUFF. What, with worms and flies?

SON. With what I get, I mean; and so do they.

LADY MACDUFF. Poor bird! thou'dst never fear the net nor lime,[6]

35 The pitfall nor the gin.[7]

SON. Why should I, mother? Poor birds they are not set for.[8] My father is not dead, for all your saying.

LADY MACDUFF. Yes, he is dead. How wilt thou do for a father?

SON. Nay, how will you do for a husband?

40 LADY MACDUFF. Why, I can buy me twenty at any market.

SON. Then you'll buy 'em to sell again.

LADY MACDUFF. Thou speak'st with all thy wit; and yet, i' faith,

With wit enough for thee.[9]

SON. Was my father a traitor, mother?

45 LADY MACDUFF. Ay, that he was!

SON. What is a traitor?

LADY MACDUFF. Why, one that swears, and lies.

SON. And be all traitors that do so?

LADY MACDUFF. Every one that does so is a traitor and must

50 be hanged.

SON. And must they all be hanged that swear and lie?

LADY MACDUFF. Every one.

SON. Who must hang them?

LADY MACDUFF. Why, the honest men.

55 SON. Then the liars and swearers are fools; for there are liars and swearers enow[10] to beat the honest men and hang up them.

LADY MACDUFF. Now God help thee, poor monkey! But how wilt thou do for a father?

60 SON. If he were dead, you'd weep for him. If you would not, it were a good sign that I should quickly have a new father.

LADY MACDUFF. Poor prattler, how thou talk'st!

Enter a MESSENGER.

MESSENGER. Bless you, fair dame! I am not to you known,

65 Though in your state of honor I am perfect.[11]

I doubt[12] some danger does approach you nearly.

If you will take a homely man's advice,

Be not found here. Hence with your little ones!

To fright you thus methinks I am too savage;

70 To do worse to you were fell[13] cruelty,

Which is too nigh your person. Heaven preserve you!

I dare abide no longer. (*Exit.*)

LADY MACDUFF. Whither should I fly?

6 lime : birdlime—a sticky substance daubed on branches to catch birds.

7 gin : snare.

8 Poor . . . for : Traps are not set for such poor birds as I.

9 Thou . . . thee : What you say is a child's wisdom, and yet your wit is well enough.

10 enow : enough.

11 in your state . . . perfect : I know perfectly your honorable rank.

12 doubt : fear.

13 fell : deadly.

I have done no harm. But I remember now
I am in this earthly world, where to do harm
75 Is often laudable, to do good sometime
Accounted dangerous folly. Why then, alas,
Do I put up that womanly defense
To say I have done no harm?—What are these faces?

Enter MURDERERS.

80 MURDERER. Where is your husband?
LADY MACDUFF. I hope, in no place so unsanctified
Where such as thou mayst find him.
MURDERER.   He's a traitor.
SON. Thou liest, thou shag-eared[14] villain!
MURDERER.   What, you egg!

(Stabs him.)

Young fry of treachery!
SON.   He has killed me, mother.
85 Runaway, I pray you!   *(Dies.)*

(Exit LADY MACDUFF *crying "Murder" and pursued
by the* MURDERERS.)

14 shag-eared : shaggy-
haired.

Scene III. *England. Before King Edward's palace.*

Enter MALCOLM *and* MACDUFF.

MALCOLM. Let us seek out some desolate shade, and there
Weep our sad bosoms empty.
MACDUFF.   Let us rather
Hold fast the mortal sword and, like good men,
Bestride our downfallen birthdom.[1] Each new morn
5 New widows howl, new orphans cry, new sorrows
Strike heaven on the face, that it resounds
As if it felt with Scotland and yelled out
Like syllable of dolor.[2]
MALCOLM.   What I believe, I'll wail;
What know, believe; and what I can redress,
10 As I shall find the time to friend, I will.
What you have spoke, it may be so perchance.
This tyrant, whose sole[3] name blisters our tongues,
Was once thought honest; you have loved him well;
He hath not touched you yet. I am young; but something
15 You may deserve of him through me, and wisdom
To offer up a weak, poor, innocent lamb
T' appease an angry god.[4]
MACDUFF. I am not treacherous.
MALCOLM.   But Macbeth is.
A good and virtuous nature may recoil
20 In an imperial charge.[5] But I shall crave your pardon.
That which you are, my thoughts cannot transpose.

1 Bestride . . . birthdom :
defend our stricken land (as
a man in battle might stand
over a fallen friend to defend him).
2 Like . . . dolor : a similar
cry of pain.

3 sole : mere.

4 but . . . god : But you
may be trying to entrap me
in order to maintain yourself in Macbeth's favor.
5 may recoil . . . charge :
may give way under pres-
sure from a monarch.

THE RENAISSANCE

Angels are bright still, though the brightest[6] fell.
Though all things foul would wear the brows of grace,
Yet grace must still look so.

MACDUFF.   I have lost my hopes.

25   MALCOLM. Perchance even there where I did find my
              doubts.[7]
Why in that rawness[8] left you wife and child,
Those precious motives, those strong knots of love,
Without leave-taking? I pray you,
Let not my jealousies be your dishonors,
30   But mine own safeties. You may be rightly just,
Whatever I shall think.

MACDUFF.   Bleed, bleed, poor country!
Great tyranny, lay thou thy basis sure,
For goodness dare not check thee! Wear thou thy wrongs;[9]
The title is affeered![10] Fare thee well, lord.
35   I would not be the villain that thou think'st
For the whole space that's in the tyrant's grasp
And the rich East to boot.

MALCOLM.   Be not offended.
I speak not as in absolute fear of you.
I think our country sinks beneath the yoke,
40   It weeps, it bleeds, and each new day a gash
Is added to her wounds. I think withal
There would be hands uplifted in my right;
And here from gracious England have I offer
Of goodly thousands. But, for all this,
45   When I shall tread upon the tyrant's head
Or wear it on my sword, yet my poor country
Shall have more vices than it had before,
More suffer and more sundry ways than ever,
By him that shall succeed.

MACDUFF.   What should he be?[11]

50   MALCOLM. It is myself I mean; in whom I know
All the particulars[12] of vice so grafted[13]
That, when they shall be opened,[14] black Macbeth
Will seem as pure as snow, and the poor state
Esteem him as a lamb, being compared
With my confineless[15] harms.

55   MACDUFF.   Not in the legions
Of horrid hell can come a devil more damned
In evils to top Macbeth.

MALCOLM.   I grant him bloody,
Luxurious,[16] avaricious, false, deceitful,
Sudden,[17] malicious, smacking of every sin
60   That has a name. But there's no bottom, none,
In my voluptuousness. Your wives, your daughters,

6 the brightest : Lucifer.

7 Perchance . . . doubts :
Perhaps what has made you
lose your hopes is the very
circumstance that has made
me suspicious of you; i.e.,
your leaving your family in
Macbeth's power, as you
would hardly have done if
you were his enemy.
8 rawness : unprotected
condition.
9 Wear . . . wrongs : continue to hold your dishonest
gains.
10 affeered : confirmed
(since Malcolm refuses to
contest Macbeth's claim).

11 What . . . be : What or
who could be worse than
Macbeth?
12 particulars : particular
varieties.
13 grafted : implanted.
14 opened : brought to view.
15 confineless : boundless.

16 Luxurious : self-indul-
gent.
17 Sudden : violent.

Your matrons, and your maids could not fill up
The cistern of my lust; and my desire
All continent[18] impediments would o'erbear

65 That did oppose my will. Better Macbeth
Than such an one to reign.
    MACDUFF.   Boundless intemperance
In nature is a tyranny. It hath been
Th' untimely emptying of the happy throne
And fall of many kings. But fear not yet
70 To take upon you what is yours. You may
Convey[19] your pleasures in a spacious plenty,
And yet seem cold—the time you may so hoodwink.
We have willing dames enough. There cannot be
That vulture in you to devour so many
75 As will to greatness dedicate themselves,
Finding it so inclined.
    MALCOLM.   With this there grows
In my most ill-composed affection[20] such
A stanchless avarice that, were I King,
I should cut off the nobles for their lands,
80 Desire his jewels, and this other's house,
And my more-having would be as a sauce
To make me hunger more, that I should forge
Quarrels unjust against the good and loyal,
Destroying them for wealth.
    MACDUFF.   This avarice
85 Sticks deeper,[21] grows with more pernicious root
Than summer-seeming[22] lust; and it hath been
The sword of our slain[23] kings. Yet do not fear.
Scotland hath foisons[24] to fill up your will
Of your mere own.[25] All these are portable,
90 With other graces weighed.[26]
    MALCOLM. But I have none. The king-becoming graces,
As justice, verity, temperance, stableness,
Bounty, perseverance, mercy, lowliness,
Devotion, patience, courage, fortitude,
95 I have no relish of them, but abound
In the division of each several crime,[27]
Acting it many ways. Nay, had I power, I should
Pour the sweet milk of concord into hell,
Uproar the universal peace, confound
All unity on earth.
100   MACDUFF.   O Scotland, Scotland!
    MALCOLM. If such a one be fit to govern, speak.
I am as I have spoken.
    MACDUFF.   Fit to govern?
No, not to live. O nation miserable,

18 continent : restraining.

19 Convey : conduct secretly.

20 ill-composed affection : character made up of evil elements.

21 Sticks deeper : is less easily uprooted.
22 summer-seeming : summer-resembling (and thus temporary).
23 sword . . . kings : that which has caused their violent death.
24 foisons (foi′zənz) : abundance.
25 will . . . own : desires from what is yours alone.
26 all . . . weighed : All these vices are endurable weighed against your virtues.
27 abound . . . crime : am abundantly guilty of every possible form of each sin.

With an untitled tyrant bloody-scept'red,
105 When shalt thou see thy wholesome days again,
Since that the truest issue of thy throne
By his own interdiction[28] stands accursed
And does blaspheme his breed? Thy royal father
Was a most sainted king; the queen that bore thee,
110 Oftener upon her knees than on her feet,
Died every day she lived.[29] Fare thee well!
These evils thou repeat'st upon[30] thyself
Have banished me from Scotland. O my breast,
Thy hope ends here!
    MALCOLM.   Macduff, this noble passion,
115 Child of integrity, hath from my soul
Wiped the black scruples, reconciled my thoughts
To thy good truth and honor. Devilish Macbeth
By many of these trains[31] hath sought to win me
Into his power; and modest wisdom plucks me[32]
120 From overcredulous haste; but God above
Deal between thee and me! for even now
I put myself to thy direction and
Unspeak mine own detraction, here abjure
The taints and blames I laid upon myself
125 For strangers to my nature. I am yet
Unknown to woman, never was forsworn,
Scarcely have coveted what was mine own,
At no time broke my faith, would not betray
The devil to his fellow, and delight
130 No less in truth than life. My first false speaking
Was this upon myself. What I am truly,
Is thine and my poor country's to command;
Whither indeed, before thy here-approach,
Old Siward with ten thousand warlike men
135 Already at a point[33] was setting forth.
Now we'll together; and the chance of goodness
Be like our warranted quarrel![34] Why are you silent?
    MACDUFF. Such welcome and unwelcome things at once
'Tis hard to reconcile.

Enter a DOCTOR.

140   MALCOLM. Well, more anon. Comes the King forth, I pray
      you?
    DOCTOR. Ay, sir. There are a crew of wretched souls
That stay[35] his cure. Their malady convinces
The great assay of art;[36] but at his touch,
Such sanctity hath heaven given his hand,
They presently amend.
145   MALCOLM.   I thank you, doctor.   (*Exit* DOCTOR.)

28 interdiction : ban.

29 Died . . . lived : prepared herself daily for death through religious exercises; thus, was holy.
30 repeat'st upon : recitest against.

31 trains : subtle devices.
32 modest . . . me : Prudent wisdom restrains me.

33 at a point : fully prepared.

34 chance . . . quarrel : May our chance of success be as good as our cause is just!

35 stay : await.
36 convinces . . . art : baffles the utmost efforts of medical science.

WILLIAM SHAKESPEARE   **231**

MACDUFF. What's the disease he means?

MALCOLM.   'Tis called the evil:[37]

A most miraculous work in this good king,

Which often since my here-remain in England

I have seen him do. How he solicits heaven[38]

150 Himself best knows; but strangely visited people,

All swol'n and ulcerous, pitiful to the eye,

The mere despair of surgery, he cures,

Hanging a golden stamp[39] about their necks,

Put on with holy prayers; and 'tis spoken,

155 To the succeeding royalty he leaves

The healing benediction. With this strange virtue,

He hath a heavenly gift of prophecy,

And sundry blessings hang about his throne

That speak him full of grace.

Enter Ross.

MACDUFF.   See who comes here.

160 MALCOLM. My countryman; but yet I know[40] him not.

MACDUFF. My ever gentle cousin, welcome hither.

MALCOLM. I know him now. Good God betimes[41] remove

The means that makes us strangers!

Ross.   Sir, amen.

MACDUFF. Stands Scotland where it did?

Ross.   Alas, poor country,

165 Almost afraid to know itself! It cannot

Be called our mother, but our grave; where nothing,

But who knows nothing, is once seen to smile;

Where sighs and groans, and shrieks that rent the air,

Are made, not marked; where violent sorrow seems

170 A modern ecstasy.[42] The dead man's knell

Is there scarce asked for who; and good men's lives

Expire before the flowers in their caps,

Dying or ere they sicken.[43]

MACDUFF.   O, relation

Too nice,[44] and yet too true!

MALCOLM.   What's the newest grief?

175 Ross. That of an hour's age doth hiss the speaker;[45]

Each minute teems[46] a new one.

MACDUFF.   How does my wife?

Ross. Why, well.

MACDUFF.   And all my children?

Ross.   Well too.

MACDUFF. The tyrant has not battered at their peace?

Ross. No; they were well at peace when I did leave 'em.

180 MACDUFF. Be not a niggard of your speech. How goes't?

Ross. When I came hither to transport the tidings

Which I have heavily borne, there ran a rumor

37 evil : the disease scrofula.

38 solicits heaven : by prayer prevails upon heaven.

39 stamp : coin.

40 know : recognize.

41 betimes : speedily.

42 modern ecstasy : an ordinary disturbance of the mind.

43 Dying . . . sicken : i.e., die violently.

44 nice : particular.

45 That . . . speaker : If news is an hour old, the speaker is hissed for its staleness.

46 teems : brings forth.

Of many worthy fellows that were out;[47]

Which was to my belief witnessed the rather

185 For that I saw the tyrant's power afoot.

Now is the time of help. Your eye in Scotland

Would create soldiers, make our women fight

To doff their dire distresses.

    MALCOLM.   Be't their comfort

We are coming thither. Gracious England[48] hath

190 Lent us good Siward and ten thousand men.

An older and a better soldier none

That Christendom gives out.

    ROSS.   Would I could answer

This comfort with the like! But I have words

That would be howled out in the desert air,

Where hearing should not latch[49] them.

195   MACDUFF.   What concern they?

The general cause? or is it a fee-grief[50]

Due to some single breast?

    ROSS.   No mind that's honest

But in it shares some woe, though the main part

Pertains to you alone.

    MACDUFF.   If it be mine,

200 Keep it not from me, quickly let me have it.

    ROSS. Let not your ears despise my tongue forever,

Which shall possess them with the heaviest sound

That ever yet they heard.

    MACDUFF.   Humh! I guess at it.

    ROSS. Your castle is surprised; your wife and babes

205 Savagely slaughtered. To relate the manner,

Were, on the quarry[51] of these murdered deer,

To add the death of you.

    MALCOLM.   Merciful heaven!

What, man! Ne'er pull your hat upon your brows.

Give sorrow words. The grief that does not speak

210 Whispers the o'erfraught[52] heart and bids it break.

    MACDUFF. My children too?

    ROSS.   Wife, children, servants, all

That could be found.

    MACDUFF.   And I must be from thence?

My wife killed too?

    ROSS.   I have said.

    MALCOLM.   Be comforted.

Let's make us medicines of our great revenge

215 To cure this deadly grief.

    MACDUFF. He[53] has no children. All my pretty ones?

Did you say all? O hellkite! All?

What, all my pretty chickens and their dam[54]

WILLIAM SHAKESPEARE

---

47 out : in open revolt.

48 England : the King of England.

49 latch : catch.

50 fee-grief : personal sorrow.

51 quarry : slain heap.

52 o'erfraught : overburdened.

53 He : may refer to Malcolm or Macbeth.

54 dam : mother.

At one fell swoop?

MALCOLM. Dispute it like a man.

220 MACDUFF.   I shall do so;
But I must also feel it as a man.
I cannot but remember such things were
That were most precious to me. Did heaven look on
And would not take their part? Sinful Macduff,
225 They were all struck for thee! Naught[55] that I am,   55 Naught : wicked.
Not for their own demerits, but for mine,
Fell slaughter on their souls. Heaven rest them now!

MALCOLM. Be this the whetstone of your sword. Let grief
Convert to anger; blunt not the heart, enrage it.

230 MACDUFF. O, I could play the woman with mine eyes
And braggart with my tongue! But, gentle heavens,
Cut short all intermission. Front to front
Bring thou this fiend of Scotland and myself.
Within my sword's length set him. If he scape,
Heaven forgive him too!

235 MALCOLM.   This tune goes manly.
Come, go we to the King. Our power is ready;
Our lack is nothing but our leave.[56] Macbeth   56 Our lack . . . leave :
Is ripe for shaking, and the powers above   Nothing remains to do but
Put on their instruments.[57] Receive what cheer you may. to take our leave.
                                                        57 Put . . . instruments :
240 The night is long that never finds the day.   (*Exeunt.*) urge on us their agents.

Questions for Study

ACT IV

Scene i

1. How does Macbeth's second speech (ll. 50-61) reveal his desperation?
2. How do the three prophecies encourage Macbeth? During this scene, what disheartens him? How does his resolution at the end of this scene (ll. 144-155) reflect his increasing evil?

Scene ii

1. What does Ross's speech (ll. 17-22) reveal concerning the effects upon the Scottish people of Macbeth's rule?
2. By what means does Shakespeare involve us in sympathy for Lady Macduff and her son?
3. What does the slaying of Lady Macduff, her family, and her servants tell us of Macbeth's moral deterioration? of his chances for moral regeneration?

Mrs. Pritchard and the famous 18th-century actor David Garrick in a 1776 production of Macbeth.

Scene iii

1. What in this long and involved scene reveals the general demoralization of Scotland?
2. Because Malcolm suspects Macduff of being in the service of Macbeth, he gives himself a bad character to test Macduff's motives. But what are the virtues he really has which recommend him for the kingship?
3. The scene in which Macduff learns of the slaughter of his family is one of the most affecting in all Shakespeare. Reread carefully from line 159 to the end of the scene, and explain why this scene is so moving. What do you learn of Macduff's character in these lines?
4. Recall the darkness imagery used earlier in the play. What is the implication of the final line of the scene: "The night is long that never finds the day"?

WILLIAM SHAKESPEARE

Act V

Scene I. *Dunsinane.* Macbeth's *castle.*

Enter a Doctor *of Physic and a Waiting* Gentlewoman.

Doctor. I have two nights watched with you, but can perceive no truth in your report. When was it she last walked?

Gentlewoman. Since his Majesty went into the field[1] I have seen her rise from her bed, throw her nightgown upon her, unlock her closet, take forth paper, fold it, write upon't, read it, afterwards seal it, and again return to bed; yet all this while in a most fast sleep.

Doctor. A great perturbation in nature, to receive at once the benefit of sleep and do the effects of watching![2] In this slumbery agitation, besides her walking and other actual performances, what (at any time) have you heard her say?

Gentlewoman. That, sir, which I will not report after her.

Doctor. You may to me, and 'tis most meet you should.

Gentlewoman. Neither to you nor anyone, having no witness to confirm my speech.

Enter Lady Macbeth, *with a taper.*

Lo you, here she comes! This is her very guise, and, upon my life, fast asleep! Observe her; stand close.[3]

Doctor. How came she by that light?

Gentlewoman. Why, it stood by her. She has light by her continually. 'Tis her command.

Doctor. You see her eyes are open.

Gentlewoman. Ay; but their sense[4] is shut.

Doctor. What is it she does now? Look how she rubs her hands.

Gentlewoman. It is an accustomed action with her, to seem thus washing her hands. I have known her continue in this a quarter of an hour.

Lady Macbeth. Yet here's a spot.

Doctor. Hark, she speaks! I will set down what comes from her, to satisfy my remembrance the more strongly.

Lady Macbeth. Out, damnèd spot! out, I say! One; two.[5] Why then 'tis time to do't. Hell is murky. Fie, my lord, fie! a soldier, and afeard? What need we fear who knows it, when none can call our pow'r to accompt? Yet who would have thought the old man to have had so much blood in him?

Doctor. Do you mark that?

Lady Macbeth. The Thane of Fife had a wife. Where is she now? What, will these hands ne'er be clean? No more o' that, my lord, no more o' that! You mar all with this starting.

Doctor. Go to,[6] go to! You have known what you should not.

1 went . . . field : Macbeth has taken the field against his rebellious subjects.

2 effects of watching : the acts proper to a waking condition.

3 close : in concealment.

4 their sense : their faculty of sight.

5 One; two : referring to the hour at which Duncan was killed.

6 Go to : Go away; or, enough.

GENTLEWOMAN. She has spoke what she should not, I am sure of that. Heaven knows what she has known.

LADY MACBETH. Here's the smell of the blood still. All the perfumes of Arabia will not sweeten this little hand. Oh, oh, oh!

45   **DOCTOR.** What a sigh is there! The heart is sorely charged.[7]

GENTLEWOMAN. I would not have such a heart in my bosom for the dignity of the whole body.

DOCTOR. Well, well, well.

GENTLEWOMAN. Pray God it be, sir.

50   **DOCTOR.** This disease is beyond my practice. Yet I have known those which have walked in their sleep who have died holily in their beds.

LADY MACBETH. Wash your hands, put on your nightgown, look not so pale! I tell you yet again, Banquo's buried. He can-
55 not come out on's grave.

DOCTOR. Even so?

LADY MACBETH. To bed, to bed! There's knocking at the gate. Come, come, come, come, give me your hand! What's done cannot be undone. To bed, to bed, to bed!   (*Exit.*)

60   **DOCTOR.** Will she go now to bed?

GENTLEWOMAN. Directly.

DOCTOR. Foul whisp'rings[8] are abroad. Unnatural deeds
Do breed unnatural troubles. Infected[9] minds
To their deaf pillows will discharge their secrets.
65 More needs she the divine than the physician.
God, God forgive us all! Look after her;
Remove from her the means of all annoyance,[10]
And still keep eyes upon her. So good night.
My mind she has mated,[11] and amazed my sight.
I think, but dare not speak.

70   **GENTLEWOMAN.**   Good night, good doctor.

                                 (*Exeunt.*)

Scene II. *The country near Dunsinane.*

Drums and colors. Enter MENTIETH, CAITHNESS, ANGUS,
LENNOX, *Soldiers.*

MENTIETH. The English pow'r is near, led on by Malcolm,
His uncle Siward, and the good Macduff.
Revenges burn in them; for their dear causes
Would to the bleeding and the grim alarm
Excite the mortified man.[1]

5   **ANGUS.**   Near Birnam Wood
Shall we well[2] meet them; that way are they coming.

CAITHNESS. Who knows if Donalbain be with his brother?

LENNOX. For certain, sir, he is not. I have a file
Of all the gentry. There is Siward's son

---

7 charged : burdened.

8 Foul whisp'rings : evil rumors.
9 infected : diseased (because of guilt).

10 annoyance : injury.

11 mated : paralyzed.

1 Would . . . man : would rouse a paralytic to the bloody and grim onset.
2 well : probably.

10 And many unrough³ youths that even now
    Protest⁴ their first of manhood.

    MENTIETH.   What does the tyrant?

    CAITHNESS. Great Dunsinane he strongly fortifies.
    Some say he's mad; others, that lesser hate him,
    Do call it valiant fury; but for certain
15 He cannot buckle his distempered cause
    Within the belt of rule.⁵

    ANGUS.   Now does he feel
    His secret murders sticking on his hands.
    Now minutely⁶ revolts upbraid his faith-breach.
    Those he commands move only in command,
20 Nothing in love. Now does he feel his title
    Hang loose about him, like a giant's robe
    Upon a dwarfish thief.

    MENTIETH.   Who then shall blame
    His pestered senses to recoil and start,
    When all that is within him does condemn
    Itself for being there?⁷

25   CAITHNESS.   Well, march we on
    To give obedience where 'tis truly owed.
    Meet we the med'cine of the sickly weal;⁸
    And with him pour we in our country's purge
    Each drop of us.⁹

    LENNOX.   Or so much as it needs
30 To dew the sovereign flower and drown the weeds.¹⁰
    Make we our march towards Birnam.

                           (*Exeunt, marching.*)

Scene III. *Dunsinane. A room in the castle.*

Enter MACBETH, DOCTOR, *and Attendants.*

MACBETH. Bring me no more reports. Let them fly all!
Till Birnam Wood remove to Dunsinane,
I cannot taint¹ with fear. What's the boy Malcolm?
Was he not born of woman? The spirits that know
5 All mortal consequences² have pronounced me thus:
"Fear not, Macbeth. No man that's born of woman
Shall e'er have power upon thee." Then fly, false thanes,
And mingle with the English epicures.³
The mind I sway by⁴ and the heart I bear
10 Shall never sag with doubt nor shake with fear.

                Enter SERVANT.

The devil damn thee black, thou cream-faced loon!
Where got'st thou that goose look?

    SERVANT. There is ten thousand—

    MACBETH.   Geese, villain?

3 unrough : beardless.
4 Protest : assert.

5 He . . . rule : He cannot keep his diseased (evil) cause under control.
6 minutely : every minute.

7 When . . . there : when he is so full of guilt?
8 medicine . . . weal : remedy (or physician) for our sickly state, i.e., Malcolm.
9 pour . . . of us : shed our blood to cleanse (cure) our country.
10 To dew . . . weeds : to *water* the flower (Malcolm) of legitimate sovereignty and destroy the weeds (Macbeth).

1 taint : become tainted.

2 mortal consequences : future events in human life.

3 epicures (ĕp′ə kyōōrz′) : The Scots thought that the English lived in too great luxury.
4 sway by : guide myself by.

SERVANT.   Soldiers, sir.

MACBETH. Go prick thy face and over-red thy fear,
15 Thou lily-livered boy. What soldiers, patch?
Death of[5] thy soul! Those linen cheeks of thine
Are counselors to fear.[6] What soldiers, whey-face?
SERVANT. The English force, so please you.
MACBETH. Take thy face hence.

(Exit SERVANT.)

Seyton!—I am sick at heart,
20 When I behold—Seyton, I say!—This push[7]
Will cheer me ever, or disseat[8] me now.
I have lived long enough. My way of life
Is fallen into the sere,[9] the yellow leaf;
And that which should accompany old age,
25 As honor, love, obedience, troops of friends,
I must not look to have; but, in their stead,
Curses not loud but deep, mouth-honor,[10] breath,
Which the poor heart would fain deny, and dare not.
Seyton!

Enter SEYTON.

SEYTON. What's your gracious pleasure?
30 MACBETH.   What news more?
SEYTON. All is confirmed, my lord, which was reported.
MACBETH. I'll fight, till from my bones my flesh be hacked.
Give me my armor.
SEYTON.   'Tis not needed yet.
MACBETH. I'll put it on.
35 Send out moe[11] horses, skirr[12] the country round;
Hang those that talk of fear. Give me mine armor.
How does your patient, doctor?
DOCTOR.   Not so sick, my lord,
As she is troubled with thick-coming fancies
That keep her from her rest.
MACBETH.   Cure her of that!
40 Canst thou not minister to a mind diseased,
Pluck from the memory a rooted sorrow,
Raze out the written troubles of the brain,
And with some sweet oblivious[13] antidote
Cleanse the stuffed bosom[14] of that perilous stuff
Which weighs upon the heart?
45 DOCTOR.   Therein the patient
Must minister to himself.
MACBETH. Throw physic to the dogs, I'll none of it!—
Come, put mine armor on. Give me my staff.—
Seyton, send out.—Doctor, the thanes fly from me.—
50 Come, sir, dispatch.—If thou couldst, doctor, cast

Sidenotes:

5 of : upon.
6 Are . . . fear : prompt others to fear.

7 push : final effort.
8 disseat (dĭs sēt′) : unthrone.
9 sere : dry.

10 mouth-honor : homage from the mouth, not the heart.

11 moe : more.
12 skirr : scour.

13 oblivious : causing forgetfulness.
14 stuffed bosom : overburdened heart.

WILLIAM SHAKESPEARE

The water of my land,[15] find her disease,
And purge it to a sound and pristine[16] health,
I would applaud thee to the very echo,
That should applaud again.—Pull't off,[17] I say.—
55 What rhubarb, senna, or what purgative drug,
Would scour these English hence? Hear'st thou of them?
    DOCTOR. Ay, my good lord. Your royal preparation
Makes us hear something.
    MACBETH.   Bring it[18] after me!
I will not be afraid of death and bane
60 Till Birnam Forest come to Dunsinane.

                    (*Exeunt all but the* DOCTOR.)

    DOCTOR. Were I from Dunsinane away and clear,
Profit again should hardly draw me here.   (*Exit.*)

        Scene IV. *Country near Birnam Wood.*

Drums and Colors. Enter MALCOLM, SIWARD, MACDUFF, SIWARD'S
   SON, MENTIETH, CAITHNESS, ANGUS, LENNOX, ROSS,
       and SOLDIERS, *marching.*

    MALCOLM. Cousins, I hope the days are near at hand
That chambers will be safe.
    MENTIETH.   We doubt it nothing.
    SIWARD. What wood is this before us?
    MENTIETH.   The Wood of Birnam.
    MALCOLM. Let every soldier hew him down a bough
5 And bear't before him. Thereby shall we shadow
The numbers of our host and make discovery[1]
Err in report of us.
    SOLDIERS.   It shall be done.
    SIWARD. We learn no other but the confident tyrant
Keeps still in Dunsinane and will endure
Our setting down before't.[2]
10   MALCOLM.   'Tis his main hope;
For where there is advantage to be given,[3]
Both more and less[4] have given him the revolt;
And none serve with him but constrainèd things,
Whose hearts are absent too.
    MACDUFF.   Let our just censures
15 Attend the true event, and put we on
Industrious soldiership.[5]
    SIWARD.   The time approaches
That will with due decision make us know
What we shall say we have, and what we owe.
Thoughts speculative their unsure hopes relate,
20 But certain issue strokes must arbitrate;[6]
Towards which advance the war.   (*Exeunt, marching.*)

---

15 cast . . . land : make a diagnosis of Scotland's disease.

16 pristine (prĭs′tēn) : original.

17 Pull't off : i.e., some part of his armor.

18 it : the piece of armor he has just removed.

1 discovery : those who discover us.

2 setting down before't : laying siege to it.

3 advantage . . . given : an opportunity.

4 more and less : nobles and commoners.

5 Let . . . soldiership : Let our judgments await the actual outcome, and meantime let us devote ourselves to the campaign.

6 But . . . arbitrate : The actual result must be settled by fighting.

Scene V. *Dunsinane. Within the castle.*

Enter MACBETH, SEYTON, *and Soldiers, with drums and colors.*

MACBETH. Hang out our banners on the outward walls.
The cry is still, "They come!" Our castle's strength
Will laugh a siege to scorn. Here let them lie
Till famine and the ague eat them up.
5 Were they not forced[1] with those that should be ours,
We might have met them dareful, beard to beard,
And beat them backward home.

(A cry within of women.)

What is that noise?
SEYTON. It is the cry of women, my good lord.   *(Exit.)*
MACBETH. I have almost forgot the taste of fears.
10 The time has been, my senses would have cooled
To hear a night-shriek, and my fell of hair[2]
Would at a dismal treatise[3] rouse and stir
As life were in't. I have supped full with horrors.
Direness, familiar to my slaughterous thoughts,
Cannot once start me.

Enter SEYTON.

15   Wherefore was that cry?
SEYTON. The Queen, my lord, is dead.
MACBETH. She should[4] have died hereafter;
There would have been a time for such a word.
Tomorrow, and tomorrow, and tomorrow
20 Creeps in this petty pace from day to day
To the last syllable of recorded time;
And all our yesterdays have lighted fools
The way to dusty death. Out, out, brief candle!
Life's but a walking shadow, a poor player,
25 That struts and frets his hour upon the stage
And then is heard no more. It is a tale
Told by an idiot, full of sound and fury,
Signifying nothing.

Enter a MESSENGER.

Thou com'st to use thy tongue. Thy story quickly!
30 MESSENGER. Gracious my lord,
I should report that which I say I saw,
But know not how to do't.
MACBETH.   Well, say, sir!
MESSENGER. As I did stand my watch upon the hill,
I looked toward Birnam, and anon methought
The wood began to move.
35 MACBETH.   Liar and slave!
MESSENGER. Let me endure your wrath if't be not so.

1 forced : reinforced.

2 my fell of hair : the hair upon my skin.
3 treatise : story.

4 should : would (inevitably).

recite + memorize
write
15 pts

Within this three mile[5] may you see it coming;
I say, a moving grove.

    MACBETH.   If thou speak'st false,
Upon the next tree shalt thou hang alive,
40 Till famine cling[6] thee. If thy speech be sooth,
I care not if thou dost for me as much.
I pull in resolution, and begin
To doubt th' equivocation[7] of the fiend,
That lies like truth. "Fear not, till Birnam Wood
45 Do come to Dunsinane!" and now a wood
Comes toward Dunsinane. Arm, arm, and out!
If this which he avouches[8] does appear,
There is nor flying hence nor tarrying here.
I gin to be aweary of the sun,
50 And wish th' estate o' th' world were now undone.
Ring the alarum bell! Blow wind, come wrack,
At least we'll die with harness[9] on our back!

                              (*Exeunt.*)

5 mile : miles.

6 cling : shrivel.

7 equivocation (ĭ kwĭv′ə kā′ shən) : double-speaking.

8 avouches : affirms.

9 harness : armor.

Scene VI. *Dunsinane. Before the castle.*

Drums and colors. Enter MALCOLM, SIWARD, MACDUFF,
and their Army, with boughs.

    MALCOLM. Now near enough. Your leavy[1] screens throw
    down
And show like those you are. You, worthy uncle,[2]
Shall with my cousin, your right noble son,
Lead our first battle.[3] Worthy Macduff and we
5 Shall take upon's what else remains to do,
According to our order.[4]

    SIWARD.   Fare you well.
Do we but find the tyrant's power tonight,
Let us be beaten if we cannot fight.

    MACDUFF. Make all our trumpets speak, give them all breath,
10 Those clamorous harbingers of blood and death.

                (*Exeunt. Alarums continued.*)

1 leavy : leafy.

2 uncle : Siward.

3 battle : battalion; division.
4 order : plan.

Scene VII. *Another part of the field.*

Enter MACBETH.

    MACBETH. They have tied me to a stake.[1] I cannot fly,
But bearlike I must fight the course.[2] What's he
That was not born of woman? Such a one
Am I to fear, or none.

          Enter YOUNG SIWARD.

    YOUNG SIWARD. What is thy name?
5   MACBETH.   Thou'lt be afraid to hear it.

1 tied . . . stake : like the bear, in Elizabethan sport, who was tied to a stake and then attacked by dogs.
2 course : bout.

YOUNG SIWARD. No; though thou call'st thyself a hotter name
Than any is in hell.

    MACBETH.   My name's Macbeth.

    YOUNG SIWARD. The devil himself could not pronounce a title
More hateful to mine ear.

    MACBETH.   No, nor more fearful.

10   **YOUNG SIWARD.** Thou liest, abhorrèd tyrant! With my sword
I'll prove the lie thou speak'st.

                    (Fight, and YOUNG SIWARD *slain.)*

    MACBETH.   Thou wast born of woman.
But swords I smile at, weapons laugh to scorn,
Brandished by man that's of a woman born.   *(Exit.)*

            Alarums. Enter MACDUFF.

    MACDUFF. That way the noise is. Tyrant, show thy face!
15 If thou beest slain and with no stroke of mine,
My wife and children's ghosts will haunt me still.
I cannot strike at wretched kerns, whose arms
Are hired to bear their staves.[3] Either thou, Macbeth,
Or else my sword with an unbattered edge
20 I sheathe again undeeded.[4] There thou shouldst be.
By this great clatter one of greatest note
Seems bruited.[5] Let me find him, Fortune!
And more I beg not.   *(Exit. Alarums.)*

         Enter MALCOLM *and* SIWARD.

    SIWARD. This way, my lord. The castle's gently rendered:[6]
25 The tyrant's people on both sides do fight;
The noble thanes do bravely in the war;
The day almost itself professes yours,
And little is to do.

    MALCOLM.   We have met with foes
That strike beside us.[7]

    SIWARD.   Enter, sir, the castle.

                   (Exeunt. Alarum.)

    Scene VIII. *Another part of the field.*

             Enter MACBETH.

    MACBETH. Why should I play the Roman fool[1] and die
On mine own sword? Whiles I see lives,[2] the gashes
Do better upon them.

            Enter MACDUFF.

    MACDUFF.   Turn, hellhound, turn!

    MACBETH. Of all men else I have avoided thee.
5 But get thee back! My soul is too much charged
With blood of thine already.

    MACDUFF.   I have no words;
My voice is in my sword, thou bloodier villain

---

3 staves : spears.

4 undeeded : not honored
by any feat of arms.
5 bruited : proclaimed.

6 gently rendered : surrendered without active defense.

7 strike beside us : miss us
(intentionally).

1 Roman fool : Various Romans, such as Brutus, killed
themselves.
2 whiles . . . lives : while I
see living foes.

WILLIAM SHAKESPEARE

Than terms can give thee out![3]

3 Than . . . out : than words can declare you.

(Fight. Alarum.)

MACBETH.   Thou losest labor.
As easy mayst thou the intrenchant[4] air

4 intrenchant (ĭn trench′ənt) : uncuttable.

10 With thy keen sword impress as make me bleed.
Let fall thy blade on vulnerable crests.
I bear a charmèd life, which must not yield
To one of woman born.
        MACDUFF.   Despair thy charm!
And let the angel[5] whom thou still hast served

5 angel : demon.

15 Tell thee, Macduff was from his mother's womb
Untimely ripped.
        MACBETH. Accursèd be that tongue that tells me so,
For it hath cowed my better part of man![6]

6 my . . . man : courage.

And be these juggling fiends no more believed,
20 That palter[7] with us in a double sense,

7 palter : deal deceitfully.

That keep the word of promise to our ear
And break it to our hope![8] I'll not fight with thee!

8 keep . . . hope : fulfill their promise but not as expected.

        MACDUFF. Then yield thee, coward,
And live to be the show and gaze o' th' time!
25 We'll have thee, as our rarer monsters are,
Painted upon a pole,[9] and underwrit

9 Painted . . . pole : your picture painted on canvas and set up on a pole in front of a showman's booth.

"Here may you see the tyrant."
        MACBETH.   I will not yield,
To kiss the ground before young Malcolm's feet
And to be baited with the rabble's curse.
30 Though Birnam Wood be come to Dunsinane,
And thou opposed, being of no woman born,
Yet I will try the last.[10] Before my body

10 try the last : fight to the end.

I throw my warlike shield. Lay on, Macduff,
And damned be him that first cries "Hold, enough!"
(Exeunt fighting. Alarums.)
Retreat and flourish. Enter, with drum and colors, MALCOLM,
        SIWARD, ROSS, *Thanes and Soldiers.*
35   MALCOLM. I would the friends we miss were safe arrived.
        SIWARD. Some must go off;[11] and yet, by these I see,

11 go off : die.

So great a day as this is cheaply bought.
        MALCOLM. Macduff is missing, and your noble son.
        ROSS. Your son, my lord, has paid a soldier's debt.
40 He only lived but till he was a man,
The which[12] no sooner had his prowess confirmed

12 The which : the fact that he had become a man.

In the unshrinking station where he fought
But like a man he died.
        SIWARD.   Then he is dead?
        ROSS. Ay, and brought off the field. Your cause of sorrow
45 Must not be measured by his worth, for then
        It hath no end.

SIWARD.   Had he his hurts before?

Ross. Ay, on the front.

SIWARD.   Why then, God's soldier be he!
Had I as many sons as I have hairs,
I would not wish them to a fairer death.
And so his knell is knolled.[13]

50   MALCOLM.   He's worth more sorrow,
And that I'll spend for him.

SIWARD.   He's worth no more.
They say he parted well[14] and paid his score,
And so, God be with him! Here comes newer comfort.

              Enter MACDUFF, *with* MACBETH'S *head.*

MACDUFF. Hail, King! for so thou art. Behold where stands
55   Th' usurper's cursèd head. The time[15] is free.
I see thee compassed[16] with thy kingdom's pearl,
That speak my salutation in their minds;
Whose voices I desire aloud with mine—
Hail, King of Scotland!

ALL.   Hail, King of Scotland!   (*Flourish.*)

60   MALCOLM. We shall not spend a large expense of time
Before we reckon with your several loves[17]
And make us even with you. My thanes and kinsmen,
Henceforth be earls, the first that ever Scotland
In such an honor named. What's more to do[18]
65   Which would be planted newly with the time[19]—
As calling home our exiled friends abroad
That fled the snares of watchful tyranny,
Producing forth the cruel ministers
Of this dead butcher and his fiendlike queen,
70   Who (as 'tis thought) by self[20] and violent hands
Took off her life—this, and what needful else
That calls upon us, by the grace of Grace[21]
We will perform in measure,[22] time, and place.
So thanks to all at once and to each one,
75   Whom we invite to see us crowned at Scone.

              (*Flourish. Exeunt.*)

13 knolled : knelled; tolled.

14 parted well : departed (died) well.

15 time : world.
16 compassed : surrounded.

17 reckon . . . loves : reward the devotion of each of you.
18 What's . . . do : what remains to be done.
19 Which . . . time : any other reforms that these new times require.

20 self : her own.

21 of Grace : of God.
22 in measure : with propriety.

Questions for Study

ACT V

Scenes i, ii, iii, and iv

1. What lines much earlier in the play does "all the perfumes of Arabia will not sweeten this little hand" echo? Who spoke the earlier lines? What conclusion can you draw from your answers to these questions?

WILLIAM SHAKESPEARE

2. From the lines which she speaks while sleepwalking, tell what things have preyed upon Lady Macbeth's conscience and brought her to the state in which we see her now.
3. Which lines of scene ii reveal the state of Macbeth as the English soldiers approach Dunsinane? Explain why the imagery of these lines is effective in revealing his state.
4. In scene iii how does Macbeth reveal regret for the evil deeds of his life? How does he reveal here the courage characteristic of him in Act I, scene ii? How does his concern for his wife affect your feeling toward him?

Scenes v, vi, vii, and viii

1. Many of Shakespeare's lines have become so familiar and so much a part of our culture that we take for granted we know what they mean. Often we are mistaken. A case in point is Macbeth's speech which begins "Tomorrow and tomorrow and tomorrow" (v, 19-28). Reread these lines carefully. What *is* Macbeth saying about his life? about life in general? How would you have the actor playing Macbeth read the soliloquy in this scene?
2. What do the metaphors of this soliloquy tell us of the effect that the news of his wife's death has upon Macbeth? What words of the soliloquy suggest futility?
3. Why is Macbeth's death at the hand of Macduff appropriate?

The Play as a Whole

1. Recall the quotation from Shakespeare given at the beginning of this chapter on Renaissance literature: "imagination bodies forth/The forms of things unknown." Write an essay which relates this quotation to the character of Macbeth as you have seen it develop in the play.
2. In his *Chronicles*, Holinshed wrote that Macbeth was greatly encouraged by the words of the three Weird Sisters to usurp the kingdom by force. He has only the following to say of Lady Macbeth: "But speciallie his wife lay sore vpon him to attempt the thing, as she that was verie ambitious, burning in vnquenchable desire to beare the name of a queene." Working from this brief information, Shakespeare developed the character of Lady Macbeth as we find it in the play.

   By discussing the important elements of Lady Macbeth's character, write an essay respecting Shakespeare's ability to create character. Support your conclusions by reference to specific lines from the play.
3. Reread the selection from Malory's *Morte Darthur* in the preceding chapter (p. 72). Then write an essay comparing the attitude toward kings as it is shown in *Morte Darthur* and in *Macbeth*.

A view from behind the scenes of a stock company in an 18th-century presentation of Macbeth *in a makeshift theater.*

Consider what parallel characters and situations you find in the two selections. What contrasting ones. What do the similarities and the differences of attitude toward a king reveal concerning the periods represented? the authors represented?

4. At the opening of *Macbeth,* we find the line "Fair is foul, and foul is fair." Write an essay in which you prove that this line establishes a theme which appears several times throughout the drama. Give a number of examples from the play to illustrate how this paradoxical statement is interpreted and communicated.

5. "The proper subject of tragedy," it has been said, "is the downfall of one who is possessed of noble qualities and attainments, but who through weakness or defect in character gives way to great temptation, or through rashness or folly brings down ruin on his head."

Write an essay in which you discuss Macbeth as a "proper subject of tragedy." Use specific references to the play to support your statements.

WILLIAM SHAKESPEARE

The Religious Lyric: Meditation and Vision

THE 17TH-CENTURY poet still wrote about the earthly joys of spring, as did his older brother of the early Renaissance. But he often turned from the sight of the lark at break of day to an inward experience. He turned to the expression of religious meditation. The following poems are among the finest examples of the religious lyric.

John Donne

The first is by John Donne, who, as we have seen, also wrote love poetry. His "divine poems" (they were called so because their subject is divinity, or religion) were almost as well known as the sermons he preached from the pulpit of Saint Paul's Cathedral.

Death, Be Not Proud

John Donne

Death, be not proud, though some have called thee
Mighty and dreadful, for thou art not so;
For those whom thou think'st thou dost overthrow
Die not, poor Death, nor yet canst thou kill me.
From rest and sleep, which but thy pictures[1] be,   5
Much pleasure;[2] then from thee much more must flow,
And soonest our best men with thee do go,
Rest of their bones, and souls' delivery.[3]
Thou art slave to fate, chance, kings, and desperate men,
And dost with poison, war, and sickness dwell,   10
And poppy or charms[4] can make us sleep as well
And better than thy stroke; why swell'st[5] thou, then?
One short sleep past, we wake eternally,
And Death shall be no more; Death, thou shalt die.

1 **pictures:** imitations. (Rest and sleep look like death.)
2 **much pleasure:** We get much pleasure (from rest and sleep).
3 **soonest . . . delivery:** Those who have lived virtuous lives die easily and quickly (without painful lingering). They enjoy a rest of their bones and the freedom of their souls from their bodies.
4 **poppies or charms:** drugs or magic spells.
5 **why swell'st thou:** Why do you swell with pride?

Comment

No mystery is greater, no experience more universal, than that of death. Yet this poem expresses an attitude toward death that reduces its mystery and belittles its power.

1. The poet speaks directly to Death in this poem. Does he speak as to a superior, or to an equal, or to an inferior? What is his tone when he says (l. 4) "poor Death"? *Superior - Sarcastic -*
2. Why does he call Death (l. 9) the "slave" to fate, etc.? With what words at the beginning of the poem does "slave" contrast? *Mighty Dreadful* *Because He depends on fate befr* *he gets us*
3. In what tone of voice should the last words of the poem ("Death, thou shalt die") be spoken? What is the attitude of the poet toward death as he says this? *One of utter superiority complex / Forceful*
4. How has the poet reached the position he takes in this last line? What does he believe that supports him in this position?

Sleep looks like death
we enjoy sleep
we will enjoy our eternal
life after death. has to die.

George Herbert (1593-1633)

The next group of poems is by George Herbert, a country parson who lived in a quiet village near Salisbury Cathedral. Herbert came of a noble and important family, and he sought for a time to take his place in the affairs of the court. But after much self-questioning he gave his life to caring for a country parish.

Herbert's best-known work, published in 1633, is called *The Temple*. In it he collected a series of poems, each of which is a personal meditation on some part of the church building itself—its altar, its doors, or, as here, its windows—or on some one of the services held in the course of the year. The first poem below compares the preacher to the glass in the windows of his church: like the windows, his function is to let in light to his congregation, and he wants to make that light as beautiful and glowing as the light from a stained-glass window that tells a part of the Christian story.

The second poem, "Easter Wings," is an example of the emblem poem, a form very popular in the late Renaissance. If you turn the page on its side you will see that the shape of the lines of the page is like that of a pair of wings (actually, two pairs—one for each stanza). The adjustment of what the poem *says* about the occasion of Easter, to the very shape of the wings of the lark that rises on this day of Christ's rising, is more than ingenious.

The third poem from Herbert is his short, exquisite hymn to the virtuous soul—a soul that lives beyond the beauty of the spring or the flower.

The Church Windows

George Herbert

Lord, how can man preach Thy eternal word?
    He is a brittle, crazy glass;[1]
Yet in Thy temple Thou dost him afford
    This glorious and transcendent place,
    To be a window, through Thy grace.[2]   5

But when Thou dost anneal[3] in glass Thy story,
    Making Thy life to shine within
The holy preachers, then the light and glory
    More reverend grows, and more doth win,[4]
    Which else shows waterish, bleak, and thin.[5]   10

Doctrine and life, colors and light, in one
    When they combine and mingle, bring
A strong regard and awe; but speech alone
    Doth vanish like a flaring thing,[6]
    And in the ear, not conscience ring.   15

---

1 brittle, crazy glass: poorly made glass that distorts the light.
2 To . . . grace: The preacher is a "window" for his congregation. With God's help he lets them see the light of the "eternal word."
3 anneal: treat with intense heat, as in the manufacture of stained glass. The heat treatment fixes the colors.
4 more doth win: is more winning, or pleasing; and also wins or persuades more men to see the light of the preacher's message.
5 waterish . . . thin: Glass that has not been heat-treated makes the light look watery. So too the preacher who has not been heat-treated, i.e., has not suffered for his beliefs, and does not have the light of God's life shining within him, is a bleak, thin "window."
6 flaring thing: momentary flash.

Comment

The neatness of the comparison made in this poem shows us what writers in the 17th century meant by *wit*. For they were not, even in their serious poems, averse to what we might call punning; that is, the words that describe the window also describe the preacher.

1. What, briefly, is the question that Herbert asks in the first stanza?

2. How does the second stanza answer this question? What is the key word of the answer? How does this word apply to the window of a church? And how does it apply to a preacher?
3. This poem is built upon a single metaphor, or comparison. The first line of the last stanza reads: "Doctrine and life, colors and light, in one." How does this line sum up the two elements of the comparison?

Easter Wings

George Herbert

Lord, who createdst man in wealth and store,[1]
Though foolishly he lost the same,
Decaying more and more
Till he became
Most poor,   5
With Thee
O let me rise
As larks, harmoniously,
And sing this day Thy victories;
Then shall the fall further the flight in me.[2]   10

My tender age in sorrow did begin;
And still with sickness and shame
Thou didst so punish sin,
That I became
Most thin.   15
With Thee .
Let me combine,
And feel this day Thy victory;
For if I imp[3] my wing on Thine,
Affliction shall advance the flight in me.   20

1 **store:** abundance.
2 **Then shall . . . in me:** The fact that I have sunk so low means that I shall fly the higher.
3 **imp:** a term from falconry, meaning to graft fresh feathers to the injured wing of a falcon.

Comment

Easter for Christians is a day of rising, and the poet wishes to rise, too, as if on the wings of a lark. He rises not from the ground, but from a state of sin, of spiritual poverty.

1. Man, says the first stanza, has declined and decayed from the full glory in which he was first created. He is now "Most poor." But

what is still left to man? Why should "Most poor" and "With Thee" be the two shortest lines of the stanza? And why should the lines grow shorter before, then longer after, these two lines?

2. In the second stanza, why is the poet "Most thin"? And why should "With Thee" follow *this* line? How do the lengths of the lines in this stanza reinforce what the poet is saying about himself?

Virtue

George Herbert

Sweet day, so cool, so calm, so bright,
    The bridal¹ of the earth and sky,
The dew shall weep thy fall tonight,
    For thou must die.

Sweet rose, whose hue, angry and brave,²   5
    Bids the rash gazer wipe his eye,
Thy root is ever in its grave,
    And thou must die.

Sweet spring, full of sweet days and roses,
    A box where sweets compacted lie,   10
My music shows ye have your closes,³
    And all must die.

Only a sweet and virtuous soul,
    Like seasoned timber, never gives;
But though the whole world turn to coal,⁴   15
    Then chiefly lives.

1 **bridal:** joining, as in marriage.
2 **angry and brave:** bold and bright.
3 **closes:** the end of a musical phrase. (The poet's own music shows that the beauty of the day, the rose, and the spring must end.)
4 **though . . . coal:** Even if the beautiful world is destroyed by fire, the virtuous soul will live on.

Comment

The theme of this poem is simple, but it is expressed with the simplicity of great art. The day is sweet, the rose is sweet, the spring is sweet; but they must die. Only the soul can survive death. Herbert, of course, is not so crude as this paraphrase.

1. To whom is the speaker addressing himself in the first three stanzas? How does the tone of the poet change at the last stanza?

2. Each stanza ends with a refrain; the first three stanzas with almost identical refrains. Say these three refrains over to yourself. How do the stresses, the beats, fall in each one? Now say over to yourself the very last line: "Then chiefly lives." Obviously the last word has changed—it is the opposite of *die*. But what else has happened? What has happened to the rhythm that you have heard in the last line of the other stanzas?

Henry Vaughan (1622?-1695)

John Donne and George Herbert were churchmen, one a great city preacher, the other a village parson. Henry Vaughan, however, studied law and medicine, and he lived in a remote region where England and Wales border each other. He pursued a religious vision of his own, not necessarily at variance with the Church, but independent of it. In "The Retreat" he expresses a vision of innocence to which he wishes he could return.

The Retreat

Henry Vaughan

Happy those early days, when I
Shined in my angel infancy;
Before I understood this place
Appointed for my second race,[1]
Or taught my soul to fancy aught   5
But a white, celestial thought;
When yet I had not walked above
A mile or two from my first Love,
And looking back, at that short space,
Could see a glimpse of His bright face;   10
When on some gilded cloud or flower
My gazing soul would dwell an hour,
And in those weaker glories spy
Some shadows of eternity;
Before I taught my tongue to wound   15
My conscience with a sinful sound,
Or had the black art[2] to dispense
A several sin[3] to every sense,
But felt through all this fleshly dress[4]
Bright shoots of everlastingness.   20

1 second race: earthly life.
2 black art: harmful magic.
3 several . . . sense: separate sin for each of the five senses.
4 fleshly dress: my soul's garment of flesh.

Oh, how I long to travel back,
And tread again that ancient track!
That I might once more reach that plain
Where first I left my glorious train,[5]
From whence the enlightened spirit sees   25
That shady city[6] of palm trees.
But, ah! my soul with too much stay
Is drunk, and staggers in the way.
Some men a forward motion love,
But I by backward steps would move,   30
And when this dust falls to the urn,[7]
In that state I came, return.

5 train: the "bright shoots of everlastingness" left behind.
6 shady city: Paradise.
7 dust . . . urn: ashes of the funeral urn.

Comment

Vaughan contrasts his "angel infancy" with his later life, longing to return to the innocent state. How does he say this return may be possible?

1. In line 17 the poet speaks of a "black art" that transforms the senses into instruments of sin. With what images of his "angel infancy" does the "black art" contrast?
2. In line 31 he speaks of his death as a state when dust falls into a funeral urn. An urn is closed and limited. With what images of his early experience does it contrast?
3. Compare the conclusion of this poem with that of "Death, Be Not Proud."

Thomas Traherne (1637?-1674)

Thomas Traherne lived in the 17th century, but his important works were not published until early in the 20th century after they were found in a manuscript in a London bookstall. At first they were believed to be some forgotten writings of Henry Vaughan; but Traherne was a poet in his own right, close though his vision of life is to Vaughan's. One of his most interesting works is called *Centuries of Meditations,* a collection of loosely related meditative paragraphs arranged in groups of a hundred, or in "centuries." The following is one of the best known of these reflective passages. And, as you will see, it is no wonder that at first the finder of the manuscript believed he had found a prose work by Vaughan.

from

Centuries of
Meditations

Thomas Traherne

1

WILL YOU SEE the infancy of this sublime and celestial greatness? Those pure and virgin apprehensions I had from the womb and that divine light wherewith I was born are the best unto this day, wherein I can see the universe. By the gift of God they attended me into the world, and by His special favor I remember them till now. Verily they seem the greatest gifts His wisdom could bestow, for without them all other gifts had been dead and vain. They are unattainable by book, and therefore I will teach them by experience. Pray for them earnestly: for they will make you angelical, and wholly celestial. Certainly Adam in Paradise had not more sweet and curious apprehensions of the world than I when I was a child.

2

All appeared new, and strange at the first, inexpressibly rare and delightful and beautiful. I was a little stranger, which at my entrance into the world was saluted and surrounded with innumerable joys. My knowledge was divine. I knew by intuition those things which

since my apostasy[1] I collected again by the highest reason. My very ignorance was advantageous. I seemed as one brought into the estate of innocence. All things were spotless and pure and glorious: yea, and infinitely mine, and joyful and precious. I knew not that there were any sins, or complaints, or laws. I dreamed not of poverties, contentions, or vices. All tears and quarrels were hidden from mine eyes. Everything was at rest, free and immortal. I knew nothing of sickness or death or exaction.[2] In the absence of these I was entertained like an angel with the works of God in their splendor and glory; I saw all in the peace of Eden; heaven and earth did sing my Creator's praises and could not make more melody to Adam than to me. All time was eternity, and a perpetual Sabbath.[3] Is it not strange that an infant should be heir of the world and see those mysteries which the books of the learned never unfold?

3

The corn[4] was orient[5] and immortal wheat, which never should be reaped, nor was ever sown. I thought it had stood from everlasting to everlasting. The dust and stones of the street were as precious as gold: the gates were at first the end of the world. The green trees when I saw them first through one of the gates transported and ravished me; their sweetness and unusual beauty made my heart to leap, and almost mad with ecstasy, they were such strange and wonderful things. The men! O

---

1 **since my apostasy** (ə pŏs′tə sĭ): since abandoning the beliefs of my childhood.
2 **exaction:** money that must be paid for taxes.
3 **Sabbath:** day of rest.
4 **corn:** grain.
5 **orient:** shining.

what venerable and reverend creatures did the aged seem! Immortal cherubims! And young men glittering and sparkling angels and maids strange seraphic[6] pieces of life and beauty! Boys and girls tumbling in the street and playing were moving jewels. I knew not that they were born or should die. But all things abided eternally as they were in their proper places. Eternity was manifest in the light of the day, and something infinite behind everything appeared, which talked with my expectation and moved my desire. The city seemed to stand in Eden, or to be built in heaven. The streets were mine, the temple was mine, the people were mine, their clothes and gold and silver were mine, as much as their sparkling eyes, fair skins, and ruddy faces. The skies were mine, and so were the sun and moon and stars, and all the world was mine, and I the only spectator and enjoyer of it. I knew no churlish proprieties,[7] nor bounds, nor divisions: but all proprieties and divisions were mine: all treasures and the possessors of them. So that with much ado I was corrupted and made to learn the dirty devices of this world. Which now I unlearn and become, as it were, a little child again that I may enter into the Kingdom of God.

6 **seraphic** (sĭ răf′ĭk): angelic.

7 **churlish proprieties:** possessions that make us miserly.

Comment

Here, in prose, is a vision of innocence like that of "The Retreat." What are the elements of greatest similarity between them? What imagery do they both use to express the character of "angel infancy"? What attitude do they share toward the world of people, affairs, and property?

The Religious Lyric
Summing Up

The poetry gathered together in this section was written later than the "Songs and Sonnets" you read earlier. As you survey these two groups of poems, what general differences do you see?

1. Consider the image of the lark. It appears in Shakespeare's song from *Cymbeline* and in his 29th sonnet. And it appears too in Herbert's "Easter Wings." What does the image of the lark tell us in the two earlier poems? What does it tell us in Herbert's poem?

2. Consider the poems about spring in the earlier group. What does spring mean in such a poem as Nashe's "Spring, the Sweet Spring"? But Herbert too wrote of a "sweet spring." Does he see in spring the same values that Nashe did?

3. Again, both Vaughan and Traherne expressed a vision of innocence and delight that they knew in infancy but lost in growing up into a world of society. They have lost, they say, the fresh aware-

ness of nature—the "orient and immortal wheat"—of their youth. Leaving the earlier poems for the moment, and returning to Sir Francis Bacon, how does Bacon's "nature" differ from that to which Vaughan and Traherne want to return? How would you expect them to have responded to the scientific developments of the Renaissance that Bacon heralded?

4. Write a brief essay on "Nature in the Renaissance" as it is reflected in the literature you have read. What changes in attitude toward the world of nature can you trace through the literature of this period?

The Limits of Knowledge and the Scope of Wisdom

John Milton (1608-1674)

UNTIL FAIRLY recently the phrase "Miltonic conviction" carried a definite meaning to readers of English literature. It is a phrase meaning "I am destined to perform a great work," and it refers to a belief that John Milton held about himself from his earliest young manhood. It may sound like an egotistical belief, but it is not quite so simple a conviction. John Milton's belief in himself was also a belief that the English language and his fellow Englishmen were ready for a great work, and a belief that his training—his knowledge of literature, philosophy, and theology, together with his long apprenticeship in writing both Latin and English—was preparing him for the writing of a great book. The matter of his personal talent or genius was subordinated to his awareness of what the times demanded—and provided.

Milton's father was a prosperous scrivener, a man whose work included functions now distributed among lawyers, notaries, bankers, and stationers. Milton received the finest education available in the early 17th century; and, after he left Cambridge University in 1632, his father provided the resources for five years of study and writing at home. Then came a tour of Europe during which the young scholar and writer moved closer and closer to the Puritan position in the religious debates of the day. In 1639 John Milton returned to an England in which the difference between those who believed in the organization of the official Church and those who required freedom of worship was so intense that civil war was not far off. Milton entered the battle vigorously. He wrote—pamphlets, essays, debates—and became the leading literary spokesman of the

Pamphlet and ballad warfare was carried on before and during the Civil War in England by the Puritans and Cavaliers. This cartoon from a ballad sheet gives the Puritan's conception of the Cavaliers as luxury-loving and frivolous.

Puritan party, though he kept on, too, writing the poetry he had begun in his youth. His conviction that he would someday write a great book for a great English audience never left him.

In 1642 civil war erupted. The conflict was between the independents, or Puritans, and the official Church; and between Charles I and Parliament. It was, of course, not a simple war. The independents desired to be free of the religious rule of the bishops, and there were serious issues involving the rivalry between King and Parliament for power. Issues became confused and convictions distorted. Puritan fought against Bishop, Roundhead (from the close-cropped heads of the Puritan soliders) against Cavalier (those loyal to the court and to the official Church), and Parliament against King.

The most shocking result was the defeat of Charles I and his death under the executioner's ax in 1649. In an age in which many men believed that a king was God's substitute on earth, this act was appalling. It became the duty of John Milton to explain and defend the deeds of his fellow rebels to the governments of Europe. He had become Latin Secretary of State in the new government. (All diplomatic correspondence was conducted in Latin then.) And the great work he had promised himself was put off yet again.

The government that succeeded King Charles I was called the Commonwealth, or Protectorate. Its head was Oliver Cromwell, the leader of the forces that had overcome the King and his Cavaliers. Cromwell was a tough head of state with enough firmness to hold in a rough kind of balance the many divergent forces that had joined against the King. Upon his death in 1658 the difficulties and uncer-

This Cavalier cartoon from a ballad sheet depicts the Puritans as drab and hypocritical people. A tub was a contemptuous term for a pulpit—hence, the unusual structure from which the sermon is being delivered in the picture.

tainties of finding a successor to Cromwell prepared the way for the restoration of the monarchy in 1660. Charles II then came to the throne, and many of those who had fought against his father suffered severe penalties. Milton, however, was left alone, and he finally returned to the work that he was convinced was his. He was now blind. He had worked hard for the Commonwealth, and he had suffered bitter disappointment in the spectacle of the quarreling groups with which it had ended.

Milton had searched long for his subject, and he turned to it with full attention. He had at one stage planned to write an epic based on the King Arthur legend; it was to be a patriotic expression of the zeal and enthusiasm he felt when the Commonwealth was beginning. Moving further and further back from such an immediate subject to that which preceded all others, he finally wrote *Paradise Lost.* In this epic poem Milton presented in a long narrative the Biblical conception of the Creation and the Fall of Man. The poem's hero is perhaps not so clearly defined as, say, the heroes of Virgil (Aeneas) or of Homer (Hector or Ulysses)—models that he consciously set for himself. Milton's subject was not the founding of a nation (as in the *Aeneid*) or the trials of a warrior (as in the *Iliad* and the *Odyssey*). His subject is the war between God and the rebellious angel Satan—a war bequeathed to mankind. His subject is that which began human history: man's loss of innocence and the consequent necessity of his working in this world by the sweat of his brow. As we shall see, it is a very large subject indeed.

Milton wrote many different kinds of poems: a masque, or allegory, called *Comus;* a tragedy based on the Bible story of Samson, called *Samson Agonistes;* an elegy, entitled "Lycidas," on the death of a fellow student at Cambridge; and many others. And like all Renaissance poets, he often turned to the sonnet. The two presented here are from two different parts of his life: the first, from his public life as a member of the government established by Cromwell; the second, from his private life, as one whose most precious sense, his sight, has been lost.

To the Lord General Cromwell

On the Proposals of Certain Ministers at the Committee for Propagation of the Gospel

John Milton

Cromwell, our chief of men, who through a cloud
Not of war only, but detractions rude,[1]
Guided by faith and matchless fortitude,
To peace and truth thy glorious way hast plowed,
And on the neck of crownèd Fortune proud   5
Hast reared God's trophies[2] and his work pursued,
While Darwen stream with blood of Scots imbrued,
And Dunbar field resounds thy praises loud,
And Worcester's[3] laureate wreath; yet much remains
To conquer still; Peace hath her victories   10
No less renowned than War, new foes arise
Threatening to bind our souls with secular chains.
Help us to save free conscience from the paw
Of hireling wolves[4] whose Gospel is their maw.

1 detractions rude: Cromwell had many enemies among the men he led, especially among those who believed that he did not carry religious reform far enough.
2 God's trophies: Milton at this time believed that the soldiers of the Commonwealth had succeeded in bringing about religious reform.
3 Darwen, Dunbar, Worcester: Darwen (a river), Dunbar, and Worcester were three sites of battles won under Cromwell's generalship.
4 hireling wolves: certain Puritans who, Milton believed, wanted to take over for themselves the triumph of the Puritan forces under Cromwell and to set up yet another official state church. He compares them to wolves that want to get all into their own "maws" or stomachs.

Comment

This sonnet is altogether public, ending as an attack on "hireling wolves."

1. In what tone of voice should the last line of this sonnet be spoken?

2. What does the image of "maw" (stomach) tell you about Milton's attitude toward the "Gospel," or religious ideas, of these men whom he calls "hireling wolves"?

On His Blindness

John Milton

When I consider how my light is spent,
Ere half my days, in this dark world and wide,
And that one talent which is death to hide
Lodged with me useless, though my soul more bent
To serve therewith my Maker, and present   5
My true account, lest He returning chide;
"Doth God exact day-labor,[1] light denied,"
I fondly ask. But Patience to prevent
That murmur, soon replies, "God doth not need
Either man's works or his own gifts. Who best   10
Bear his mild yoke, they serve him best. His state
Is kingly: thousands at his bidding speed
And post o'er land and ocean without rest;
They also serve who only stand and wait."

1 **day-labor:** hard work; also work by daylight. But Milton, blind, cannot work so hard as once; he knows no daylight.

Comment

Milton was totally blind at the age of forty-four. For so prodigious a reader and writer as he, this would seem to be a catastrophe. But his faith rescued him from self-pity.

1. Read the parable of the talents in Matthew 25:14-30. What does *talent* mean in the Biblical parable? But what other meaning does the word have—in common speech and in this sonnet? Explain Milton's reference to the Biblical story of the talents (l. 3). How is Milton's situation like the parable? How is it unlike the parable?
2. What two attitudes toward blindness are expressed in this poem? At what point does Milton's attitude change?
3. Note the shift in point of view; for seven and a half lines Milton uses the word *I*. In the last six and a half lines he does not. How does this shift fit the meaning of the poem?

Paradise Lost

Milton's greatest work is his epic *Paradise Lost* (first published in 1667 though begun many years before). It fuses his enormous awareness of the literature of Greece and Rome with his commitment to the Old Testament story of the Creation and the Fall of Man. The Bible story of Adam and Eve—their temptation, fall, and expulsion from Paradise—provides the general framework of Milton's epic poem, which attempts to "justify the ways of God to men." In *Paradise Lost* Milton explores questions about man's life and his universe, about good and evil, about suffering, and about hopes and dreams.

Human limitation—the difference between our hopes or dreams and our powers—is a major theme in Milton's poem. Between what we imagine and what we are falls the limitation of human knowledge. The early poets of the Renaissance believed that the words of men made a golden world. As you read earlier in this chapter, Sir Philip Sidney wrote that nature's "world is brazen; the poets only deliver a golden." But though our dreams are unlimited, our powers are only human after all. Eating the fruit of the Tree of Knowledge did not make man divine, as the serpent told Eve it would; instead it gave him the knowledge of the long hard work needed to turn visions into realities in the world.

Yet at the end of *Paradise Lost* one has the sense of an adventure only just beginning, with Adam and Eve going forth out of Paradise, "the world all before them." Although we may indeed have to live in a brazen world, there is still, as Milton has the angel Michael say, "a Paradise within . . . happier far."

The many classical and Biblical allusions in the first lines of the poem may need some explanation for the modern reader. After describing the subject of his poem in the first five lines, Milton calls upon a Muse, or goddess of poetry, for aid, just as Homer and Virgil do at the opening of their epics. But Milton asks for the help of a Heavenly Muse who lives in a place higher than the "Aonian mount" (l. 15) where the classical Muses lived. His Muse is the spirit that in the Holy Land, "Oreb" and "Sinai" (l. 7) and "Siloa's brook" (l. 11), inspired the "shepherd" Moses (l. 8) to know and to tell how the world was created, for Moses was the author of the Book of Genesis. Milton relates this spirit to the spirit of God that lives in the conscience, or pure heart (l. 18), and then he identifies it (ll. 19-22) with the Holy Spirit that, according to Genesis, brooded over the darkness and gave it life. After the Holy Spirit "moved upon the face of the deep," Genesis tells us, "God said, 'Let there be light.' " And so Milton (ll. 22-23) asks for light or illumination like that which created the world. Milton's song is "adventurous" (l. 13); it soars on no "middle flight" (l. 14) because his subject is one "unattempted yet in prose or rhyme" (l. 16). No one ever before had written a poem about both the Creation and the Fall of Man. There were many separate treatments of each in the Renaissance, but this was the first that combined them.

[handwritten: Quiz 11-12-87 study Notes]

from Paradise Lost

John Milton

I

Of man's first disobedience,[1] and the fruit
Of that forbidden tree, whose mortal taste[2] *[handwritten: summary of poem]*
Brought death into the world, and all our woe,
With loss of Eden, till one greater Man[3]
Restore us, and regain the blissful seat,   5
Sing Heavenly Muse, that on the secret top
Of Oreb, or of Sinai, didst inspire
That shepherd, who first taught the chosen seed, *[handwritten: references of old testament passages that predict the future passages of the new testament]*
In the beginning how the Heavens and Earth
Rose out of Chaos; or if Sion hill   10
Delight thee more, and Siloa's brook that flowed
Fast by the oracle of God, I thence
Invoke thy aid to my adventurous song,
That with no middle flight intends to soar *[handwritten: I am about to do something that has never been done before]*
Above the Aonian mount; while it pursues   15
Things unattempted yet in prose or rhyme.
And chiefly thou O Spirit, that dost prefer
Before all temples the upright heart and pure,
Instruct me, for thou knowest; thou from the first
Wast present, and with mighty wings outspread   20
Dovelike sat'st brooding on the vast Abyss *[handwritten: asking the Gods to help]*
And madest it pregnant: what in me is dark
Illumine, what is low raise and support;
That to the height of this great argument
I may assert Eternal Providence,   25 *[handwritten: epic sentence (tells theme)]*
And justify[4] the ways of God to men.
     Say first, for Heaven hides nothing from thy view,
Nor the deep tract of Hell, say first what cause
Moved our grand parents[5] in that happy state,
Favored of Heaven so highly, to fall off   30 *[handwritten: do you know what caused our exile]*
From their Creator, and transgress his will
For one restraint, lords of the world besides?

---

1 first disobedience: both first in time and first in importance: it is the *original* sin that Milton will treat.
2 mortal taste: deadly taste.

3 greater Man: Jesus.
4 justify: explain the justice of; not "apologize for" but explain.
5 grand parents: Adam and Eve.

JOHN MILTON

en medias res – enter story in the middle

he does this

Who first seduced them to that foul revolt?
The infernal Serpent; he it was, whose guile,
Stirred up with envy and revenge, deceived   35
The Mother of Mankind;[6] what time his pride

This is the "Sin of Pride"

characteristics of SATAN
guile
deceptive
pride

Had cast him out from Heaven, with all his host
Of rebel angels, by whose aid aspiring
To set himself in glory above his peers,
He trusted to have equaled the Most High,   40
If he opposed;[7] and with ambitious aim
Against the throne and monarchy of God,
Raised impious war in Heaven and battle proud
With vain attempt. Him the Almighty Power
Hurled headlong flaming from the ethereal sky   45
With hideous ruin and combustion down
To bottomless perdition, there to dwell
In adamantine[8] chains and penal fire,
Who durst defy the Omnipotent to arms.
    Nine times the space that measures day and night   50
To mortal men, he with his horrid crew
Lay vanquished, rolling in the fiery gulf

SATAN:
Down there knows he's doomed
Does not give in

Confounded though immortal. But his doom
Reserved him to more wrath;[9] for now the thought
Both of lost happiness and lasting pain   55
Torments him; round he throws his baleful[10] eyes,
That witnessed huge affliction and dismay
Mixed with obdurate pride and steadfast hate.
At once as far as angels ken[11] he views
The dismal situation waste and wild: 60
A dungeon horrible, on all sides round

Conditions of HELL

As one great furnace flamed, yet from those flames
No light, but rather darkness visible[12] *oxymoron*
Served only to discover sights of woe,
Regions of sorrow, doleful shades, where peace   65
And rest can never dwell, hope never comes
That comes to all; but torture without end

Lucifer becomes SATAN in HELL

Still urges,[13] and a fiery deluge, fed
With ever-burning sulphur unconsumed:
Such place Eternal Justice had prepared   70
For those rebellious, here their prison ordained
In utter darkness,[14] and their portion set
As far removed from God and light of Heaven *as center of the earth to the poles*

6 what time: when (an example of Milton's frequent imitation of Latin phrasing).
7 He trusted . . . opposed: He believed he would be an equal match for God if he attacked Him.
8 adamantine (ăd'ə măn'tĭn): unbreakable.
9 his doom . . . wrath: Satan was fated to feel even more wrath from God.

10 baleful: full of woe.
11 ken: range of vision.
12 darkness visible: solid darkness.
13 urges: afflicts.
14 utter darkness: outer darkness. Hell is outside the region of light that fills the universe.

THE RENAISSANCE

As from the center thrice to the utmost pole.[15]   75
Oh how unlike the place from whence they fell!
There the companions of his fall, o'erwhelmed
With floods and whirlwinds of tempestuous fire,
He soon discerns, and weltering[16] by his side
One next himself in power, and next in crime,
Long after known in Palestine, and named   80
Beelzebub. To whom the Archenemy,[17]
And thence in Heaven called Satan; with bold words
Breaking the horrid silence thus began.
     "If thou beest he; but Oh how fallen! how changed
From him, who in the happy realms of light   85
Clothed with transcendent brightness didst outshine
Myriads,[18] though bright: if he whom mutual league,
United thoughts and counsels, equal hope
And hazard in the glorious enterprise,
Joined with me once, now misery hath joined   90
In equal ruin: into what pit thou seest
From what height fallen, so much the stronger proved
He with his thunder, and till then who knew
The force of those dire arms? Yet not for those,
Nor what the potent victor in his rage   95
Can else inflict, do I repent or change,
Though changed in outward luster, that fixed mind
And high disdain, from sense of injured merit,
That with the Mightiest raised me to contend,
And to the fierce contention brought along   100
Innumerable force of spirits armed
That durst dislike his reign, and, me preferring,[19]
His utmost power with adverse power opposed
In dubious battle on the plains of Heaven,
And shook his throne. What though the field be lost?   105
All is not lost; the unconquerable will,
And study of revenge, immortal hate,
And courage never to submit or yield:
And what is else not to be overcome?
That glory never shall his wrath or might   110
Extort from me. To bow and sue for grace
With suppliant knee, and deify his power
Who from the terror of this arm so late

[handwritten margin note: SATANS 2nd in Command]

[handwritten margin note: SATAN WILL NEVER GIVE UP DUE TO PRIDE]

JOHN MILTON   **265**

Doubted[20] his empire, that were low indeed,
That were an ignominy and shame beneath   115
This downfall; since by fate the strength of gods
And this empyreal substance[21] cannot fail,
Since through experience of this great event,
In arms not worse, in foresight much advanced,
We may with more successful hope resolve   120
To wage by force or guile eternal war,
Irreconcilable to our grand foe,
Who now triumphs, and in the excess of joy
Sole reigning holds the tyranny of Heaven."
    So spake the apostate Angel, though in pain,   125
Vaunting aloud, but racked with deep despair. . . .

This will go on Forever

in pain but God will NEVER get the best of him

[*Satan is answered by Beelzebub, who is less bold. He asks, "Suppose we are here in Hell not because we cannot be destroyed but because we are being eternally punished."*]

"What can it then avail, though yet we feel
Strength undiminished, or eternal being
To undergo eternal punishment?"
    Whereto with speedy words the Archfiend replied.   130
"Fallen Cherub, to be weak is miserable,
Doing or suffering: but of this be sure,
To do aught good never will be our task,
But ever to do ill our sole delight,
As being the contrary to his high will   135
Whom we resist. If then his providence
Out of our evil seek to bring forth good,
Our labor must be to pervert that end,
And out of good still to find means of evil;
Which ofttimes may succeed, so as perhaps   140
Shall grieve him, if I fail not,[22] and disturb
His inmost counsels from their destined aim.
But see the angry victor hath recalled
His ministers of vengeance and pursuit
Back to the gates of Heaven; the sulphurous hail   145
Shot after us in storm, o'erblown hath laid
The fiery surge, that from the precipice
Of Heaven received us falling, and the thunder,
Winged with red lightning and impetuous rage,
Perhaps hath spent his shafts, and ceases now   150
To bellow through the vast and boundless deep.
Let us not slip[23] the occasion, whether scorn,
Or satiate fury yield it from our foe.

Do you think he will leave us here forever

Devel

Be ready to suffer, BUT to do good will never be our goal - we like doing wrong so we can spite God - hasn't touched man at this point. SULKING

20 **doubted:** feared for. Satan insists that his attack did shake the power of God.
21 **empyreal** (ĕm pĭr'ĭ əl) **substance:** heavenly substance which cannot be destroyed; Satan, therefore, can go on waging war with hope of success.
22 **if I fail not:** unless I am mistaken.
23 **Let us not slip:** Let us not let slip.

THE RENAISSANCE

Seest thou yon dreary plain, forlorn and wild,
The seat of desolation, void of light,   155
Save what the glimmering of these livid flames
Casts pale and dreadful? Thither let us tend
From off the tossing of these fiery waves,
There rest, if any rest can harbor there,
And reassembling our afflicted powers,   160
Consult how we may henceforth most offend
Our enemy, our own loss how repair,
How overcome this dire calamity,
What reinforcement we may gain from hope,
If not what resolution from despair." . . .   165

probably no hope, but we can live on our determination to keep from submitting

Forthwith upright he rears from off the pool
His mighty stature; on each hand the flames
Driven backward slope their pointing spires, and rolled[24]
In billows, leave in the midst a horrid vale.
Then with expanded wings he steers his flight   170
Aloft, incumbent on the dusky air
That felt unusual weight till on dry land
He lights, if it were land that ever burned
With solid, as the lake with liquid fire. . . .

SATAN can move from HELL (effect us)

"Is this the region, this the soil, the clime,"   175
Said then the lost Archangel, "this the seat
That we must change for Heaven, this mournful gloom
For that celestial light? Be it so, since he
Who now is sovran can dispose and bid
What shall be right. Farthest from him is best,   180
Whom reason hath equaled, force hath made supreme[25]
Above his equals. Farewell happy fields
Where joy forever dwells: Hail horrors, hail
Infernal world, and thou profoundest Hell
Receive thy new possessor: one who brings   185
A mind not to be changed by place or time.
The mind is its own place, and in itself
Can make a Heaven of Hell, a Hell of Heaven.
What matter where, if I be still the same,
And what I should be, all but less than[26] he   190
Whom thunder hath made greater? Here at least
We shall be free; the Almighty hath not built
Here for his envy, will not drive us hence:
Here we may reign secure, and in my choice
To reign is worth ambition, though in Hell: 195
Better to reign in Hell than serve in Heaven.

SATAN is equal in reason + force & Better to reign in HELL than save in Heaven

---

24 **rolled:** being rolled (passive, like *driven*).
25 **Whom . . . supreme:** Satan again claims equality with God in reason though not in force. He
cannot imagine any superiority except that of
force; he can conceive of no god who is not a
"tyrant."
26 **all but less than:** almost equal to; i.e., "I am
equal to God in everything but power."

JOHN MILTON   267

(handwritten notes in margin: SATANS. PALACE IS IN HELL build by falling Angels and is called Pandemonium)

But wherefore let we then our faithful friends,
The associates and copartners of our loss,
Lie thus astonished on the oblivious pool,[27]
And call them not to share with us their part   200
In this unhappy mansion; or once more
With rallied arms to try what may be yet
Regained in Heaven, or what more lost in Hell?"

[*Satan then calls to the rest of the fallen angels: "Awake, arise, or be
forever fallen!" And they spring up like soldiers who have been
caught sleeping while on guard. Satan puts them to work to build a
huge palace, Pandemonium (from the Greek for "all" and "demon").
Then the fallen host assembles to discuss what they shall do.*]

(handwritten: 11-11-87)

(handwritten: 11-12-87)

II

[*The debate in Hell fills almost the next book of* Paradise Lost. *One
devil urges violent war against Heaven. Another says there is no point
in war—they know they will be defeated—and he urges "ignoble ease."
Still another urges that a kingdom rivaling that of Heaven be made in
Hell and thus arouse God's envy. Finally Beelzebub, speaking for
Satan, suggests a solution for the conflict of proposals: the fallen angels
can get back at God through Man.*]

"What if we find
Some easier enterprise? There is a place
(If ancient and prophetic fame[1] in Heaven
Err not), another world, the happy seat
Of some new race called Man, about this time   5
To be created like to us, though less
In power and excellence, but favored more
Of him who rules above; so was his will
Pronounced among the gods, and by an oath,
That shook Heaven's whole circumference, confirmed.   10
Thither let us bend all our thoughts, to learn
What creatures there inhabit, of what mold
Or substance, how endued, and what their power,
And where their weakness, how attempted best,
By force or subtlety. Though Heaven be shut,   15
And Heaven's high Arbitrator sit secure
In his own strength, this place may lie exposed,
The utmost border of his kingdom, left
To their defense who hold it; here perhaps
Some advantageous act may be achieved   20
By sudden onset, either with Hell fire

---

27 astonished . . . pool: stunned on the pool that
causes forgetfulness. In Greek mythology drinking
water from the river Lethe in Hades causes forgetfulness.   1 fame: rumor.

268

To waste his whole creation, or possess
All as our own, and drive as we were driven,
The puny habitants; or if not drive,
Seduce them to our party, that their God   25
May prove their foe, and with repenting hand
Abolish his own works. This would surpass
Common revenge, and interrupt his joy
In our confusion, and our joy upraise
In his disturbance; when his darling sons   30
Hurled headlong to partake with us, shall curse   *original*
Their frail original, and faded bliss,   *sin*
Faded so soon. Advise if this be worth
Attempting, or to sit in darkness here
Hatching vain empires." Thus Beelzebub   35
Pleaded his devilish counsel, first devised
By Satan. . . .

III

[*Satan then takes on himself the great mission. He flies out of Hell
across the vast chaotic darkness to the regions of light; he makes his
way to Earth and to the Garden of Eden. Although his presence is
known to God and the angels in Heaven, he proceeds to his plan of
corrupting mankind in order to injure God.*

*First he tempts Eve by entering her mind in a dream. Then he
tempts her in a disguise. He appears before her as a serpent; since the
time is before the Fall, all things are innocent and harmless to Eve, and
she is not afraid. She only wonders that a serpent has the power of
speech, and she speaks with him. He learns from her that all the fruits
of the Garden are for her use and Adam's except one, that of the
Tree of Knowledge. This tree stands near the Tree of Life, from
which they are permitted to eat. Without giving reason or explanation, God has forbidden them to eat of the Tree of Knowledge: "Ye
shall not eat/Thereof, nor shall ye touch it, lest ye die." Eve and
Satan, in his disguise, are before the forbidden tree. He delivers his
great speech of temptation. He has eaten of the Tree of Knowledge,
he falsely says, and since he, an animal, by eating of its fruit has become like a man (for he has the power of speech), so she, by eating of
it, shall become a god. It is a masterly speech—diabolically so. For
Satan knows that there are not "gods"; there is only one God. And
no magic, no knowledge, can circumvent His rule. To know why
God forbade the eating of the fruit is to know His reasons—is to be
His equal in intellect. And this cannot be.*

*But Eve does not know how perverse the serpent's reasoning is. She
cannot see that an animal that talks is a monster, a disorder of nature.
She is confounded, she is tempted, and she falls.*

It is in Book IX that the following scene is found. Satan speaks:]

"O sacred, wise, and wisdom-giving Plant,
Mother of science[1] now I feel thy power
Within me clear, not only to discern
Things in their causes, but to trace the ways
Of highest agents, deemed however wise.   5
Queen of this Universe, do not believe
Those rigid threats of death; ye shall not die:
How should ye? by the fruit? it gives you life
To knowledge; by the threatener? look on me,
Me who have touched and tasted, yet both live,   10
And life more perfect have attained than fate
Meant me, by venturing higher than my lot.
Shall that be shut to Man, which to the beast
Is open? or will God incense his ire
For such a petty trespass, and not praise   15
Rather your dauntless virtue, whom the pain
Of death denounced, whatever thing death be,
Deterred not from achieving what might lead
To happier life,[2] knowledge of good and evil;
Of good, how just? of evil, if what is evil   20
Be real, why not known, since easier shunned?[3]
God therefore cannot hurt ye, and be just;
Not just, not God; not feared then, nor obeyed:
Your fear itself of death removes the fear.
Why then was this forbid? Why but to awe,   25
Why but to keep ye low and ignorant,
His worshipers; he knows that in the day
Ye eat thereof, your eyes that seem so clear,
Yet are but dim, shall perfectly be then
Opened and cleared, and ye shall be as Gods,   30
Knowing both good and evil as they know.
That ye should be as Gods, since I as Man,
Internal Man, is but proportion meet,
I of brute human, ye of human Gods.[4]
So ye shall die perhaps, by putting off   35
Human, to put on Gods, death to be wished,
Though threatened, which no worse than this can bring.
And what are Gods, that Man may not become
As they, participating godlike food?[5]

---

1 **science:** knowledge.
2 **and not praise . . . life:** Shall not God rather praise your courage for trying to achieve a happier life even though you knew that death, whatever that is, was promised as penalty for this deed?
3 **Of good . . . shunned:** How can it be just to keep you from knowledge of good? Why is it not proper to know evil in order to avoid it?
4 **That ye . . . Gods:** Just as I am like a man, having risen from the condition of a brute animal, so, by a fitting proportion, you should rise from being human to being like gods.
5 **participating godlike food:** eating the food of gods.

The Gods are first, and that advantage use   40
On our belief, that all from them proceeds;
I question it, for this fair Earth I see,
Warmed by the sun, producing every kind,
Them nothing. If they all things, who enclosed
Knowledge of good and evil in this tree,   45
That whoso eats thereof, forthwith attains
Wisdom without their leave? and wherein lies
The offense, that Man should thus attain to know?
What can your knowledge hurt him, or this tree
Impart against his will, if all be his?   50
Or is it envy, and can envy dwell
In heavenly breasts? These, these and many more
Causes import your need of this fair fruit.
Goddess humane, reach then, and freely taste!"
He ended, and his words replete with guile   55
Into her heart too easy entrance won.

[Eve listens, then argues with herself. Finally she submits:]

. . . her rash hand in evil hour
Forth reaching to the fruit, she plucked, she eat.
Earth felt the wound; and Nature from her seat
Sighing through all her works gave signs of woe,   60
That all was lost. Back to the thicket slunk
The guilty Serpent, and well might, for Eve
Intent now only on her taste, nought else
Regarded; such delight till then, as seemed,
In fruit she never tasted, whether true   65
Or fancied so, through expectation high
Of knowledge, nor was Godhead from her thought.
Greedily she ingorged without restraint,
And knew not eating death.[6] Satiate at length,
And heightened as with wine, jocund and boon,   70
Thus to herself she pleasingly began.
"O sovran, virtuous, precious of all trees
In Paradise, of operation blest
To sapience,[7] hitherto obscured, infamed,
And thy fair fruit let hang, as to no end   75
Created; but henceforth my early care,
Not without song, each morning, and due praise,
Shall tend thee, and the fertile burden ease
Of thy full branches offered free to all;
Till dieted by thee I grow mature   80
In knowledge, as the Gods who all things know;

6 **knew not . . . death:** did not know she was eating death.

7 **of operation . . . sapience:** so blest as to have the power of giving wisdom.

Though others envy what they cannot give;
For had the gift been theirs, it had not here
Thus grown. Experience, next to thee I owe,
Best guide; not following thee, I had remained   85
In ignorance, thou open'st Wisdom's way,
And givest access, though secret she retire.
And I perhaps am secret; Heaven is high,
High and remote to see from thence distinct
Each thing on Earth; and other care perhaps   90
May have diverted from continual watch
Our great Forbidder, safe with all his spies
About him. But to Adam in what sort
Shall I appear? Shall I to him make known
As yet my change, and give him to partake   95
Full happiness with me, or rather not,
But keep the odds of knowledge in my power
Without copartner? so to add what wants
In female sex, the more to draw his love,
And render me more equal, and perhaps,   100
A thing not undesirable, sometime
Superior; for inferior who is free?
This may be well. But what if God have seen
And death ensue? then I shall be no more,
And Adam wedded to another Eve,   105
Shall live with her enjoying, I extinct;
A death to think."

IV

[After Eve has eaten the Forbidden Fruit, Adam returns. He is amazed at her disobedience, but he forgives her, and he eats of the fruit himself. With this act ends the harmony of Eden. Adam and Eve fall to accusing each other, as the enormity of their crime comes to be understood by them both, and they quarrel. Sin and death have been loosed upon the world, and there is rejoicing in Hell. Adam and Eve must leave the Garden to work in the world by the sweat of their brow. Before they leave, God sends the angel Michael to tell them all the events that will occur up to the time of the Flood. In the final Book XII Adam, having been instructed in what will befall his race, thanks the angel:]

"Greatly instructed I shall hence depart,
Greatly in peace of thought, and have my fill
Of knowledge, what this vessel can contain;
Beyond which was my folly to aspire.
Henceforth I learn, that to obey is best,   5
And love with fear the only God, to walk
As in his presence, ever to observe

His providence, and on him sole depend,
Merciful over all his works, with good
Still overcoming evil, and by small   10
Accomplishing great things, by things deemed weak
Subverting worldly strong, and worldly wise
By simply meek; that suffering for truth's sake
Is fortitude to highest victory,
And to the faithful death the gate of life;   15
Taught this by his example whom I now
Acknowledge my Redeemer ever blest."
      To whom thus also the Angel last replied.
"This having learned, thou hast attained the sum
Of wisdom; hope no higher, though all the stars   20
Thou knew'st by name, and all the ethereal powers,
All secrets of the deep, of Nature's works,
Or works of God in heaven, air, earth, or sea,
And all the riches of this world enjoy'dst,
And all the rule, one empire; only add   25
Deeds to thy knowledge answerable, add faith,
Add virtue, patience, temperance, add love,
By name to come called charity, the soul
Of all the rest: then wilt thou not be loth
To leave this Paradise, but shalt possess   30
A Paradise within thee, happier far."

[*And so Adam and Eve prepare to leave. They stand on a hill near the
eastern gate of Paradise and see the flames come to destroy the Garden
they have forfeited:*]

                   High in front advanced.
The brandished sword of God before them blazed
Fierce as a comet; which with torrid heat,
And vapor as the Libyan air adust,[1]   35
Began to parch that temperate clime; whereat
In either hand the hastening angel caught
Our lingering parents, and to the eastern gate
Led them direct, and down the cliff as fast
To the subjected[2] plain; then disappeared.   40
They looking back, all the eastern side beheld
Of Paradise, so late their happy seat,
Waved over by that flaming brand, the gate
With dreadful faces thronged and fiery arms.
Some natural tears they dropped, but wiped them soon,   45
The world was all before them, where to choose
Their place of rest, and Providence their guide.
They hand in hand with wandering steps and slow,
Through Eden took their solitary way.

---

1 **adust:** scorched by the sun.   2 **subjected:** lying below.

JOHN MILTON   273

Comment

Adam and Eve take their solitary way from Eden, the land of Paradise, into a world from which harmony and innocence have been lost. Milton has given us his version of the Biblical story of what took place before human history began. He has set forth the inevitable conditions under which that history must proceed. No larger subject has ever been treated in a poem. How does Milton make us feel the sheer *size* "Of Man's first disobedience"?

1. Consider the verse itself. Milton was aware that in writing in blank verse, rather than in pairs of rhyming lines (rhymed couplets), he was out of fashion. (Even plays in rhymed couplets would shortly be produced.) In a prefatory note he defended his use of blank verse. Here are some verses by a later poet (John Dryden) on a theme close to that of *Paradise Lost*. Dryden is speaking of religious truths that are beyond the rational understanding of man:

> Thus man by his own strength to Heaven would soar
> And would not be obliged to God for more.
> Vain, wretched creature, how art thou misled
> To think thy wit these godlike notions bred.

Compare these lines with the angel Michael's speech in Section IV. Dryden's couplets are neat and precise. But what qualities do you find in Milton's unrhymed lines that are not present here?

2. Milton frequently mingles (as in his opening lines) allusions to Greek and Roman mythology with allusions to the Bible. The practice raises difficulties for those who have not read, as Milton and the educated men of his times had, the literature of Greece and Rome. What kind of dimension does this mingling add to the poem? What does it suggest about the importance of Milton's subject? What does it suggest about the time in which his events occurred?

3. Many readers have felt that no character in the poem is so grand and so large as Satan. His defiance, in the speeches of Section I, is certainly untempered. From one of these opening speeches select what seems to you a particularly defiant assertion. What do you find in it that makes it a "big" speech?

4. Now consider the temptation scene (Section III). How does Satan's disguise here contrast with his bearing in the speech you have chosen from Section I? Consider again the speech he makes to Eve in Section III: What is he pretending to be, in relation to Eve? How does his role here compare with the stern commander who says to Beelzebub "to be weak is miserable"? And finally, what verb does Milton use to describe Satan's departure after Eve has eaten of the fruit? Where is the greatness of Satan in this whole scene?

5. After she has eaten of the fruit, Eve speaks. We know she has fallen because as she speaks she imitates Satan.

(*a*) Satan says, "O sacred, wise, and wisdom-giving Plant." And

Eve says, "O sovran, virtuous, precious of all trees." How does the rhythm of her speech imitate that of Satan?

(b) As she talks, Eve thinks for a moment that it will be well for her to deceive Adam. Why does she think of this? What will the deception do for her? How is this proposed deception another imitation of Satan? What deception of his does it resemble?

6. The archangel Michael in Section IV tells Adam that if he has learned the limitations of human knowledge and if he has added to this wisdom the virtue of charity, then Adam will have "A Paradise within thee, happier far." A Paradise *within*. What does this final teaching tell us about Milton's belief in what is "within"? How large does this belief make the human soul? How great does it make the adventure into which Adam and Eve now depart?

7. Milton has been called the last great humanist in English poetry: the last poet who *felt* a relation between the literature of the ancient Greeks and Romans on the one hand and the Christian religion on the other. He has also been called one of the first great modern minds: a mind that accepted boldly the ongoing adventure of man. Which judgment seems to you the more appropriate? Why?

The Renaissance
Summing Up

THE EPIGRAPH for this chapter is ". . . *imagination bodies forth/The forms of things unknown.* . . ." It comes from Shakespeare's comedy, *A Midsummer Night's Dream;* the full sentence reads:

> The poet's eye in a fine frenzy rolling,
> Doth glance from heaven to earth, from earth to heaven;
> And as imagination bodies forth
> The forms of things unknown, the poet's pen
> Turns them to shapes, and gives to airy nothings
> A local habitation and a name.

Poets look out on the world; and, as they do so, they imagine things that no one has ever seen or known before. These things poets turn into persons and places that everyone henceforth recognizes.

1. This quotation suggests that the *range* of the Renaissance writer was great—it stretched from earth to heaven. Consider the selections of this chapter; does such a claim seem justified? What selections seem occupied with "earth"? Which seem to express a view of "heaven"? Does any seem to be concerned with both?

2. The quotation suggests that the writer of the Renaissance brought mysteries ("airy nothings") within the knowledge of all people by giving them a place ("habitation") and a character ("name"). Which writers in this chapter seem to have done just this—given a permanent literary form to strange and wonderful things? Explain.

THE RENAISSANCE, 1500-1660

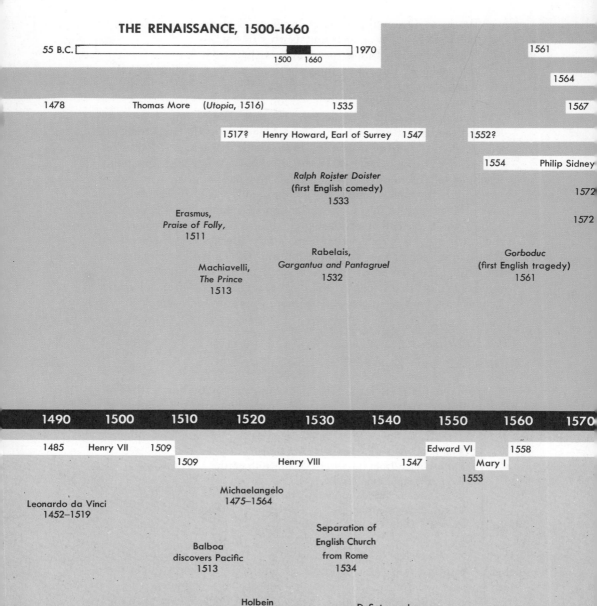

55 B.C. _____ 1970
1500 1660

1561

1564

1478   Thomas More   (*Utopia*, 1516)   1535   1567

1517?   Henry Howard, Earl of Surrey   1547   1552?

1554   Philip Sidney

Ralph Roister Doister
(first English comedy)
1533

1572

Erasmus,
Praise of Folly,
1511

1572

Rabelais,
Gargantua and Pantagruel
1532

Gorboduc
(first English tragedy)
1561

Machiavelli,
The Prince
1513

1490	1500	1510	1520	1530	1540	1550	1560	1570

1485   Henry VII   1509   Edward VI   1558

1509   Henry VIII   1547   Mary I

1553

Leonardo da Vinci
1452–1519

Michaelangelo
1475–1564

Separation of
English Church
from Rome
1534

Balboa
discovers Pacific
1513

Holbein
1497–1543

DeSoto explores
Southwest,
discovers Mississippi
1539–1542

Luther posts
his 95 theses
1517

Copernicus'
theory of the
Solar System
1543

Circumnavigation
of earth by
Magellan's fleet
1519–1522

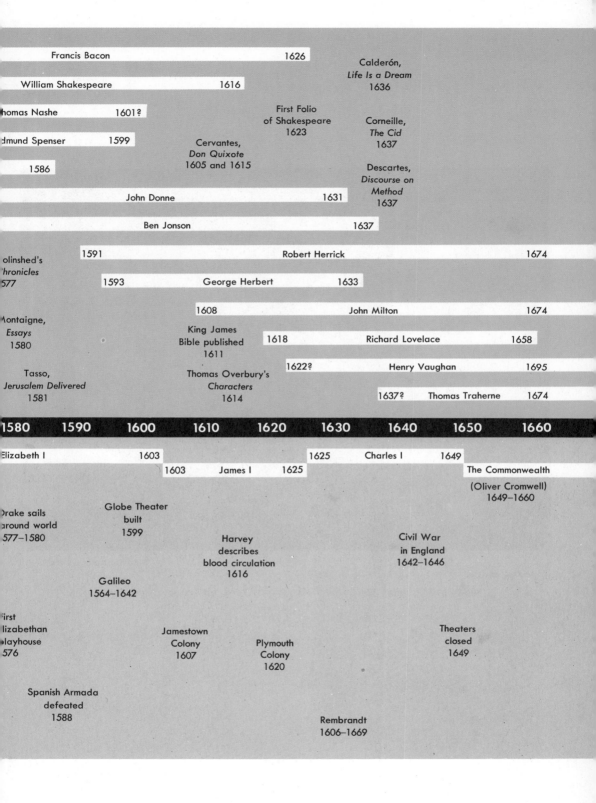

Francis Bacon 1626

Calderón,
Life Is a Dream
1636

William Shakespeare 1616

Thomas Nashe 1601?

First Folio
of Shakespeare
1623

Corneille,
The Cid
1637

Edmund Spenser 1599

Cervantes,
Don Quixote
1605 and 1615

1586

Descartes,
*Discourse on
Method*
1637

John Donne 1631

Ben Jonson 1637

1591 Robert Herrick 1674

Holinshed's
Chronicles
1577

1593 George Herbert 1633

1608 John Milton 1674

Montaigne,
Essays
1580

King James
Bible published
1611

1618 Richard Lovelace 1658

1622? Henry Vaughan 1695

Tasso,
Jerusalem Delivered
1581

Thomas Overbury's
Characters
1614

1637? Thomas Traherne 1674

1580   1590   1600   1610   1620   1630   1640   1650   1660

Elizabeth I 1603

1625 Charles I 1649

1603 James I 1625

The Commonwealth

(Oliver Cromwell)
1649–1660

Drake sails
around world
1577–1580

Globe Theater
built
1599

Harvey
describes
blood circulation
1616

Civil War
in England
1642–1646

Galileo
1564–1642

First
Elizabethan
playhouse
1576

Jamestown
Colony
1607

Plymouth
Colony
1620

Theaters
closed
1649

Spanish Armada
defeated
1588

Rembrandt
1606–1669

The Orrery, *a painting by Joseph Wright (1734–1797). An orrery is a model of the solar system, so named after the Earl of Orrery, for whom it was made.*

THE ENLIGHTENMENT

1660-1780

The Enlightenment

". . . repose on the stability of truth."

SAMUEL JOHNSON

> Hail! queen of manners, light of truth;
> Hail! charm of age, and guide of youth;
> Sweet refuge of distress:
> In business, thou! exact, polite;
> Thou giv'st retirement its delight,
> Prosperity its grace.

So runs one of the closing stanzas of a poem that appeared in 1739 in one of the most widely read periodicals of the day, *The Gentleman's Magazine.* What could its subject be? What is it that rules over manners and guides youth, that is present in business with exactness and politeness, that delights us when we are alone (in "retirement"), and that makes our prosperity graceful? The answer for the early 18th-century poet was clear: the title of his poem is "A Hymn to Science." It is quite literally a song of praise for the civilizing powers of learning and general knowledge (not of "science" in our more limited sense). The poet calls upon Science, or knowledge, as the "Sun of the soul!" And he begs of this sun, "Thy beams unveil," for the light of knowledge can illuminate all things:

> Of wealth, power, freedom, thou the cause;
> Foundress of order, cities, laws,
> Of arts inventress, thou!
> Without thee, what were humankind?
> How vast their wants, their thoughts how blind!
> Their joys how mean, how few!

Custom House Quay, *a painting by Samuel Scott (1702–1772), shows the waterfront activity along the Thames below London Bridge, then one of the busiest ports in the world. The great India merchant vessels fill the river as far as the eye can see.*

Knowledge, learning, is the great source of order: in the state, in the arts and skills of civilization, and in the private world of the person. Although we are likely to see in our periodicals today essays both on the glories of science and on its limitations, two and one-quarter centuries ago, at the height of the Enlightenment, the sentiments of this poem were fresh and interesting.

The poet's chief metaphor here is not in any sense original, for one of the oldest metaphors in all literature tells us that knowledge is light. An illuminating remark is one that helps us solve a problem. An enlightened people is free from ignorance and superstition. The next large period of English literature, then, is called the Enlightenment because it is a period during which authors and readers came to a new agreement about what people should know and how they should ex-

The Fruits of Early Industry and Economy, *a painting by George Morland (1763–1804). Increased foreign trade brought success to many thrifty tradesmen. The merchant's window here overlooks his docks and warehouses; his family is expensively dressed.*

press what they know. The writers of the late 17th and early 18th centuries did not believe that they knew everything, but they did believe that there were few problems of human life that could not be solved by reason and by learning.

The Writer's Language

ONE SUBJECT upon which writers and scholars became enlightened during the period from 1660 to 1780 was the English language itself. Some rediscovered the earliest English literature and studied the ancient manuscripts on which it was preserved. John Dryden, the foremost

Interior of the Rotunda, Ranelagh, London by Caneletto (1697–1768). Ranelagh was a fashionable resort for 18th-century Londoners who came here to promenade, drink tea, listen to music, and talk. In the winter it was heated by a huge central fireplace.

man of letters of the late 17th century, translated some of Chaucer's *Canterbury Tales* into a language that he believed his contemporaries could understand; and, in fact, the English of Chaucer's day was so different from his own that Dryden was uncertain how to pronounce it. (Chaucer's final *e*'s, for example, puzzled him.) Other scholars formulated the rules of English grammar, some by observing the usage of the best writers, but others, who eventually triumphed, by drawing up rules "according to the unalterable rules of right reason." By the late 18th century there had been established a system of English grammar that no well-informed person dared to ignore. The greatest achievement of students of language during the Enlightenment was the making of a full English dictionary. The rapid and constant changes of the language that had gone on since the time of Chaucer came almost to a halt, and the individual words of the English language stood still, as it were, to be counted and analyzed.

In the Middle Ages there had been special glossaries of "hard words" —lists of special terms in science or commerce—and in the Renaissance, as England became a nation along with other countries of Europe, there arose a need for special glossaries of foreign words needed by

THE ENLIGHTENMENT

Victoria and Albert Museum, London

An Elegant Establishment for Young Ladies by Edward Francis Burney (1760–1848), a satirical painting on women's education. The girl in the center is having her neck stretched while others learn how to faint and dance.

both the merchant and the student of literature. This publishing of special vocabularies continued into the 17th century; the first use of the words *English Dictionary* occurred in 1623, with, however, this subtitle, *An Interpreter of Hard Words*. But in 1721, one hundred years later, there appeared the first full dictionary of all the words in the written language; and in 1755 Samuel Johnson published his famous *Dictionary*. Johnson listed the words of "good English" only; he ignored slang words and the special terms of commerce and trade. Illustrating his definitions with quotations from the best writers of English, he set a standard of correctness in usage that held for a long time. It is said that a bill was thrown out of Parliament in the late 19th century because it used a word that was not in *the* dictionary, Johnson's *Dictionary*.

But neither Johnson's *Dictionary* nor any other could have been compiled if his material, the English language itself, had not reached maturity and stability. Some changes continued to occur, of course. The progressive verb form came to be widely used. People asked each other "What are you doing?" rather than "What doest thou?" *Thou* and *thee* and *ye* came to be reserved for poetry and for certain

A scene in the House of Commons with Pitt the Younger making a speech. Newspapers began in the 18th century to report Parliamentary debates, making Parliament publicly responsible for its actions.

religious groups, while *you* ceased to be used only for addressing one's inferiors or persons outside one's intimate circle. Certain impersonal constructions common in Shakespeare, such as "It likes me not," disappeared. The pronouns *who* and *which* began to supplant the universal *that*. And new words from French, German, and more remote languages continued to enrich the English vocabulary: *ballet, champagne, reservoir, envelope, cartoon, caramel, cigar, cosy, candy, smuggle.* Hundreds of words were adopted from places as far away as India. Yet none of these borrowings altered the structure of the language into which they came; English was firmly enough established to resist any "invasion" from other tongues.

The sound of the spoken language was less firmly fixed. A large number of words, far larger than in modern English, could be pronounced in more than one way. This seems to be indicated by such groups of rhyming words as *food, blood, wood,* and *heaven, seven, forgiven.* And rhymes like *obey, tea* and *name, stream* are evidence that one important group of words, frequently spelled with *ea* today, still had a vowel sound quite different from the modern one. Spelling, or orthography, was much more nearly standardized than pronunciation, a situation that still troubles many students and writers of English. Through most of the 18th century, as in Shakespeare's time, *fortune* was pronounced "fortin," *picture* was "pikter," *sermon* was "sarmon," and

THE ENLIGHTENMENT

Agricultural Laborers *by George Stubbs (1724–1806). In 18th-century England the poor agricultural laborer's lot was not improved by the many enclosure acts passed by Parliament, which "enclosed," or fenced off, the common land of the village formerly used by all.*

the final g of *ing* was dropped in the politest speech: a gentleman went "ridin'," not *riding*. And in spite of the "unalterable rules" of the grammarians, there was much "bad" grammar in the speech and correspondence of learned people: "It is me," "You was," "Who did you see?" appear frequently in the letters of the period.

Yet with all the uncertainties of pronunciation and its connection with spelling, and with all the inevitable difference between careless speaking and thoughtful writing, there was throughout the Enlightenment a great concern for regularity, stability, rules, and order in the spoken and written uses of English. The strongest concern, perhaps, was expressed by the growing and rising middle class. This vast number of tradespeople and merchants, whose power now began to equal that of the aristocracy, required for themselves and their families a "correctness" that would suit their new station in life. Their desire for an authority in usage was satisfied by Johnson's *Dictionary* and by the new grammar books.

New standards of correctness came from other sources. The "natural philosophers" of the period set strict requirements for those who wrote reports and accounts of experiments. In the mid-17th century there was founded an institution, patterned after the "Salomon's House" of Bacon's *New Atlantis,* called the Royal Society of London for Improving

Natural Knowledge. Its members included not only great scientists such as Robert Boyle or Sir Isaac Newton but also writers, doctors, churchmen, and many interested gentlemen and noblemen. Its "Transactions" (accounts of the activities it sponsored) contained reports on both theoretical and applied science. The members were interested, for example, in both the theory of air pressure and in devices for pumping water out of mines. Anyone who contributed to the proceedings of the Royal Society was required to be concise; he had to

> reject all the amplifications, digressions, and swellings of style: to return back to the primitive purity and shortness, when men delivered so many things almost in an equal number of words.

For the style of the natural philosopher must be modeled upon the plainness and clarity of mathematics:

> They have exacted from all their members a close, naked, natural way of speaking; positive expressions; clear senses; a native easiness; bringing all things as near the mathematical plainness as they can; and preferring the language of artisans, countrymen, and merchants, before that of wits or scholars.

The orderly knowledge of nature must be plainly expressed so that plain men could act upon it.

The "wits or scholars" of the Enlightenment also had a standard of "plainness" not very different from that of the scientists. Here, for example, is a passage from an essay by Jonathan Swift written to advise young men on how to speak and write well:

> Proper words in proper places, makes the true definition of a style. . . . When a man's thoughts are clear, the properest words will generally offer themselves first, and his own judgment will direct him in what order to place them, so as they may be best understood. . . . In short, that simplicity without which no human performance can arrive to any great perfection, is nowhere more eminently useful than in this [matter of style].

Swift's definition of style, "proper words in proper places," was reflected in much of the literary activity of the time. *Proper* means not only "correct" but also "one's own"; that is, what is proper to a thing pertains to what is essential in it. Upon what was proper to all kinds of literature most writers were in agreement. There was a style proper to the formal ode and one proper to informal satire. There were acknowledged rules and proprieties for tragedy, for the epic, for the elegy. There were even proper styles for various kinds of letter writing.

From this shared sense of the proper there developed during the Enlightenment a great body of literary criticism. Some of it was so severe in applying formal rules to earlier English literature that even Shakespeare was more than once called "barbarous" for the variety and profusion of his imagery or because his plots were not classically unified. The critical principles of the age, moreover, tended to separate poetry from prose and to encourage a special poetic diction. *Thou,* as we see in the stanzas from the "Hymn to Science," was proper for poetry. The prose writer might refer to *birds* and *flowers,* but the poet spoke of the *feathered choir* and the *vegetative tribe.* The moving air was regularly *gales,* and sheep were usually covered with *downy fleece.* If such diction seems affected to us now (as it certainly did to the writers of the next age), we must remember that it reflected a general desire for propriety and simplicity. It was one of the products of the constant refining and reforming of the English language that changed the language, as Samuel Johnson said, from brick to marble.

The literary ideal of the age was perhaps best summed up in a famous couplet by Alexander Pope:

> True wit is nature to advantage dressed,
> What oft was thought, but ne'er so well expressed.

The writer dresses up nature or thought ("Expression is the dress of thought," Pope goes on to say); but to do so he or she must know nature and people and what has been thought. Here is a passage from Samuel Johnson that describes the knowledge and the powers a poet must possess if he or she aspires to "true wit":

> The business of a poet . . . is to examine not the individual but the species; to remark general properties and large appearances. He does not number the streaks of the tulip, or describe the different shades in the verdure of the forest. He is to exhibit in his portraits of nature such prominent and striking features as recall the original to mind; and must neglect the minuter discriminations, which one may have remarked and another have neglected, for those characteristics which are alike obvious to vigilance and carelessness.
>
> But the knowledge of nature is only half the task of a poet; he must be acquainted likewise with all the modes of life. His character requires that he estimate the happiness and misery of every condition; observe the power of all the passions in all their combinations; and trace the changes of the human mind, as they are modified by various institutions and accidental influences of climate or custom, from the sprightliness of infancy to the despondence of decrepitude. He must divest himself of the prejudices of his age or country; he must consider right and wrong in their abstracted and invariable state; he must disregard present laws and opinions, and rise to general and transcendental truths, which will always be the same. He must therefore content himself with the slow progress of his name, condemn the applause of his own time, and commit his claims to the justice of pos-

terity. He must write as the interpreter of nature and the legislator of mankind, and consider himself as presiding over the thoughts and manners of future generations, as a being superior to time and place.

His labor is not yet at an end; he must know many languages and many sciences; and, that his style may be worthy of his thoughts, must by incessant practice familiarize to himself every delicacy of speech and grace of harmony.

The poet, says Johnson, must have a general knowledge of men and of nature. He must describe the large and obvious features of nature rather than the markings of a tulip or the different shades of greenness. He must know *all* the emotions ("passions") of men and all the changes of men's minds from infancy to old age; he must know enough to rise above the pressures of his own time and place. With so solemn and exacting a set of requirements we have moved far from that golden world made by the Renaissance poet by means of the power of an inspiration allied to madness. The poet now looks not only into his heart to write; he looks also into society and into history.

The wits of the Enlightenment were not, however, always solemn. They sometimes stood back and laughed even at their own interest in language and literature. Here is a scene from the play *The Rivals* by Richard Brinsley Sheridan, produced in 1775. Mrs. Malaprop and Sir Anthony Absolute are conspiring, without success, to arrange a match for Lydia Languish, the ward of Mrs. Malaprop. Sir Anthony blames Lydia's obstinacy upon her reading, and Lydia does talk a little like a storybook heroine. But the blunders committed by Mrs. Malaprop have made her name a noun in use to this day. All of us, perhaps, commit such malapropisms as confusing *orthodoxy* and *orthography*. Only a character in a play could commit so many thoroughly comic ones.

MRS. MALAPROP. There, Sir Anthony, there sits the deliberate Simpleton who wants to disgrace her family, and lavish herself on a fellow not worth a shilling!

LYDIA. Madam, I thought you once—

MRS. MALAPROP. You thought, miss! I don't know any business you have to think at all—thought does not become a young woman; the point we would request of you is, that you will promise to forget this fellow—to illiterate him, I say, quite from your memory.

LYDIA. Ah! madam! our memories are independent of our wills. It is not so easy to forget.

MRS. MALAPROP. But I say it is, miss; there is nothing on earth so easy as to *forget,* if a person chooses to set about it. I'm sure I have as much forgot your poor dear uncle as if he had never existed—and I thought it my duty so to do; and let me tell you, Lydia, these violent memories don't become a young woman.

SIR ANTHONY. Why sure she won't pretend to remember what she's ordered not! —Aye, this comes of her reading!

LYDIA. What crime, madam, have I committed, to be treated thus?

MRS. MALAPROP. Now don't attempt to extirpate yourself from the matter; you know I have proof controvertible of it. —But tell me, will you promise to do as you're bid? Will you take a husband of your friends' choosing?

LYDIA. Madam, I must tell you plainly, that had I no preference for any one else, the choice you have made would be my aversion.

MRS. MALAPROP. What business have you, miss, with *preference* and *aversion*? They don't become a young woman; and you ought to know, that as both always wear off, 'tis safest in matrimony to begin with a little *aversion*. I am sure I hated your poor dear uncle before marriage . . . —and yet, miss, you are sensible what a wife I made! —and when it pleased Heav'n to release me from him, 'tis unknown what tears I shed! —But suppose we were going to give you another choice, will you promise us to give up this Beverley?

LYDIA. Could I belie my thoughts so far, as to give that promise, my actions would certainly as far belie my words.

MRS. MALAPROP. Take yourself to your room. You are fit company for nothing but your own ill-humors.

LYDIA. Willingly, ma'am—I cannot change for the worse.

(*Exit* LYDIA)

MRS. MALAPROP. There's a little intricate hussy for you!

SIR ANTHONY. It is not to be wondered at, ma'am,—all this is the natural consequence of teaching girls to read. Had I a thousand daughters, by Heavens! I'd as soon have them taught the black art as their alphabet!

MRS. MALAPROP. Nay, nay, Sir Anthony, you are an absolute misanthropy.

SIR ANTHONY. In my way hither, Mrs. Malaprop, I observed your niece's maid coming forth from a circulating library! She had a book in each hand—they were half-bound volumes, with marbled covers! From that moment I guessed how full of duty I should see her mistress!

MRS. MALAPROP. Those are vile places, indeed!

SIR ANTHONY. Madam, a circulating library in a town is as an evergreen tree of diabolical knowledge! It blossoms through the year! And depend on it, Mrs. Malaprop, that they who are so fond of handling the leaves, will long for the fruit at last.

MRS. MALAPROP. Fie, fie, Sir Anthony, you surely speak laconically!

SIR ANTHONY. Why, Mrs. Malaprop, in moderation now, what would you have a woman know?

MRS. MALAPROP. Observe me, Sir Anthony. I would by no means wish a daughter of mine to be a progeny of learning; I don't think so much learning becomes a young woman; for instance—I would never let her meddle with Greek, or Hebrew, or Algebra, or Simony, or Fluxions, or Paradoxes, or such inflammatory branches of learning—neither would it be necessary for her to handle any of your mathematical, astronomical, diabolical instruments. But, Sir Anthony, I would send her, at nine years old, to a boarding school, in order to learn a little ingenuity and artifice. Then, sir, she should have a supercilious knowledge in accounts; and as she grew up, I would have her instructed in geometry, that she might know something of the contagious countries; but above all, Sir Anthony, she should be mistress of orthodoxy, that she might not misspell, and mispronounce words so shamefully as girls usually do; and likewise that she might reprehend the true meaning of what she is saying. —This, Sir Anthony, is what I would have a woman know; and I don't think there is a superstitious article in it.

SIR ANTHONY. Well, well, Mrs. Malaprop, I will dispute the point no further with you; though I must confess that you are a truly moderate and
polite arguer, for almost every third word you say is on my side of the
question. . . .

The People and Their Times

The refinement and correctness they attained in their language, the people of the Enlightenment desired also for society. They created and
perfected many institutions that brought a new orderliness into public
life. The new Post Office provided regular, dependable circulation of
social and business letters. The newspapers, although heavily taxed
at first, kept track of daily and weekly currents of opinion and information for a great middle-class audience. The Bank of England, founded
in 1694, organized the increasing foreign and domestic exchanges of
business. There were, of course, national crises and wars (during one
of which the American colonies were lost), and there was terrible poverty among the lowest laboring classes. The introduction of cheap
distilled spirits led to the depravity of many by drink. But the terrible
times of the Civil War had passed, and no revolution threatened at
home. The "Glorious Revolution" of 1688 without bloodshed brought
to the throne a new ruling family whose religious sympathies were
"correct"—neither Puritan nor Catholic—and the country sighed with
relief. Improvements in medicine and in hospitals lowered the death
rate, and the population increased rapidly: between 1700 and 1790
England and Wales grew from about five and one-half million to nine
million. And improvements in agriculture ensured an adequate supply
of food—both bread and meat—for the growing nation. (Because of
selective breeding the average weight of a sheep brought to market
more than doubled in the 18th century). Everywhere in England
people took a serious interest in society. The national ideal, as expressed by John Locke, the greatest philosopher of the period, was a
social man working with others to become "well-skilled in knowledge
of material causes of things in his power." In other words, people were
interested in what things were made of and how they worked rather
than in large matters beyond their power to understand or control. The
enlightened Englishman was constantly "directing his thought to the improvement of such arts and inventions, engines and utensils, as might
best contribute to his continuance with conveniency and delight."

The Intellectual Hero

"The Miracle of the Age"—this was the description by an early 18th-century writer of Sir Isaac Newton, the man who "unveiled" the very order of nature itself by formulating the laws of motion and the theory of gravitation. In his *Philosophiae Naturalis Principia Mathematica* ("The Mathematical Principles of Natural Philosophy, or Physics") Newton for the first time gave an account of the world of nature—the world of matter—entirely in the language of mathematics. He showed how nature could be understood as a mechanical system operating by principles and formulas as clear and as stable as the theorems of geometry. His work was one of the greatest achievements of the human mind; and, though not all people understood it, many praised and celebrated it. As Alexander Pope said in a couplet composed to the memory of Newton.

> Nature and Nature's laws lay hid in night;
> God said, "Let Newton be!" and all was light.

But what of the man himself? Here is a portrait of Newton written by the man who was his secretary and assistant during the years when he composed the *Principia*. It is the portrait of a scholar dedicated to the point of absent-mindedness, gentle, kindly, solitary, and strangely neglected and ignored by the other students and scholars of the university where he lived and worked. His thoughts were his library, the portrait tells us; they were also the house in which he lived and moved and had his real being.

Sir Isaac Newton

In the last year of King Charles II [1685], Sir Isaac was pleased, through the mediation of Mr. Walker (then schoolmaster at Grantham), to send for me up to Cambridge, of whom I had the opportunity, as well as honor, to wait [upon] for about five years. In such time he wrote his *Principia Mathematica*, which stupendous work, by his order, I copied out before it went to the press [in 1687]. After printing, Sir Isaac was pleased to send me with several of them in presents to some of the heads of Colleges, and others of his acquaintance, some of which (particularly Dr. Babington of Trinity) said that they might study seven years before they understood anything of it. His carriage then was very meek, sedate, and humble, never seemingly angry, of profound thought, his countenance mild, pleasant, and comely. I cannot say I ever saw him laugh but once. . . . He always kept close to his studies, very rarely went a-visiting, and had . . . few visitors. . . . I never knew him to take any recreation or pastime either in riding out to take the air, walking, bowling, or any other exercise whatever, thinking all hours lost that was not spent in his studies, to which he kept so close that he seldom left his chamber except at term time, when he read in the schools as being Lucasianus Professor,[1] where so few went to hear him, and fewer that understood him, that ofttimes he did in a manner, for want of hearers, read to the walls. Foreigners he received with a great deal of freedom, candor, and respect. When invited to a treat,[2] which was very seldom, he used to return it very handsomely, and with much satisfaction to himself. So intent, so serious upon his studies, that he ate very sparingly, nay, ofttimes he has forgot to eat at all, so that, going into his chamber, I have found his mess[3] untouched, of which, when I have reminded him, he would reply—"Have I?" and then making to the table, would eat a bit or two standing, for I cannot say I ever saw him sit at table by himself. . . . He very rarely went to bed till two or three of the clock, sometimes not until five or six, lying about four or five hours, especially at spring and fall of the leaf, at which times he used to employ about six weeks in his elaboratory,[4] the fire scarcely going out either night or day; he sitting up one night and I another, till he had finished his chemical experiments, in the performances of which he was the most accurate, strict, exact. What his aim might be I was not able to penetrate into, but his pains, his diligence at these set times made me think he aimed at something beyond the reach of human art and industry. I cannot say I ever saw him drink either wine, ale, or beer, excepting at meals, and then but very sparingly. He very rarely went to dine in the hall,[5] except on some public days, and then if he has not been minded, would go very carelessly, with shoes down at heels, stockings untied, surplice[6] on, and his head scarcely combed. . . .

Orderly Behavior

Business Efficiency If the greatest genius of the age was absent-minded, most people could not afford to be, particularly the buyers and sellers of goods. During the Enlightenment the market was transformed from a place where buyers and sellers might casually come together to exchange goods and information into an institution that regulated much of the society and most of the economy of England. Daniel Defoe, novelist and journalist, made a tour of Britain during which he surveyed the customs and institutions of his fellow countrymen; the first volume of his *Tour Through the Whole Island of Great Britain* appeared in 1727. Here is his description from that work of a market he saw in Leeds, in the Midlands, a market reserved exclusively for the selling of bolts of cloth. The "clothiers," or sellers, in this

---

1 Lucasianus Professor: Newton held a Cambridge professorship of mathematics that had been founded by a family named Lucas. His lectures were not well attended; the undergraduates scarcely knew him.
2 treat: dinner party.
3 mess: his food from the college kitchen.
4 elaboratory: laboratory.
5 dine in the hall: dine with other officials of the college at the "high table" in the college dining hall, a very formal occasion.
6 surplice (sûr′plĭs)**:** an outer garment not meant for wear in the dining hall; his academic gown would be proper there.

Bartholomew Fair, a view in 1721, was a place of business as well as of entertainment. Established in 1133, it became the principal market in England.

market paid local weavers for the products they wove at home on their looms, and some clothiers eventually became large manufacturers. They sold the fabrics, in turn, to the merchants, some of them representing other merchants from the colonies or other countries outside England. As you will see, what most impressed Defoe in this market was its silence, speed, and regularity. The cloth market almost becomes a symbol of a clocklike machine that runs the lives of those who participate in it.

THE MARKET

The market itself is worth describing, though no description can come up to the thing itself; however, take a sketch of it with its customs and usages as follows:

The street is a large, broad, fair and well-built street, beginning . . . at the bridge, and ascending gently to the north.

Early in the morning, there are tressels placed in two rows in the street, sometimes two rows on a side, but always one row at least; then there are boards laid cross those tressels, so that the boards lie like long counters on either side, from one end of the street to the other.

The clothiers come early in the morning with their cloth; and as few clothiers bring more than one piece, the market being so frequent, they go into the inns and public houses with it, and there set it down.

At seven o'clock in the morning, the clothiers being supposed to be all come by that time, even in the winter, but the hour is varied as the seasons advance (in the summer earlier, in the depth of winter a little later) I take it, at a medium, and as it was when I was there, at six or seven, I say, the market bell rings; it would surprise a stranger to see in how few minutes, without hurry or noise, and not the least disorder, the whole market is filled; all the boards upon the tressels are covered with cloth, close to one another as the pieces can lie long ways by one another, and behind every piece of cloth, the clothier standing to sell it. . . .

As soon as the bell has done ringing, the merchants and factors,[1] and buyers of all sorts, come down, and coming along the spaces between the rows of boards, they walk up the rows, and down as their occasions direct. Some of them have their foreign letters of orders, with patterns sealed on them, in rows,[2] in their hands; and with those they match colors, holding them to the cloths as they think they agree to; when they see any cloths to their colors, or that suit their occasions, they reach over to the clothier and whisper, and in the fewest words imaginable the price is stated; one asks, the other bids; and 'tis agree, or not agree, in a moment.

The merchants and buyers generally walk down and up twice on each side of the rows, and in little more than an hour all the business is done; in less than half an hour you will perceive the cloths begin to move off, the clothier taking it up upon his shoulder to carry it to the merchant's house, and by half an hour after eight o'clock the market bell rings again; immediately the buyers disappear, the cloth is all sold, or if here and there a piece happens not to be bought, 'tis carried back into the inn, and, in a quarter of an hour, there is not a piece of cloth to be seen in the market.

Thus, you see, ten or twenty thousand pounds value in cloth, and sometimes much more, bought and sold in little more than an hour, and the laws of the market the most strictly observed as ever I saw done in any market in England; for,

1. Before the market bell rings, no man shews a piece of cloth, nor can the clothiers sell any but in open market.

2. After the market bell rings again, nobody stays a moment in the market, but carries his cloth back if it be not sold.

3. And that which is most admirable is, 'tis all managed with the most profound silence, and you cannot hear a word spoken in the whole market, I mean, by the persons buying and selling; 'tis all done in whisper.

The reason of this silence, is chiefly because the clothiers stand so near to one another; and 'tis always reasonable that one should not know what another does, for that would be discovering their business, and exposing it to one another.

If a merchant has bidden a clothier a price, and he will not take it, he may go after him to his house, and tell him he has considered of it, and is willing to let him have it; but they are

---

1 **factors:** A factor is an agent for someone not present at a transaction.
2 **patterns . . . rows:** The agents for foreign merchants had swatches, or samples, fixed to their order sheets, which they then matched with the cloth for sale.

not to make any new agreement for it, so as to remove the market from the street to the merchant's house.

By nine o'clock the boards are taken down, the tressels are removed, and the street cleared, so that you see no market or goods any more than if there had been nothing to do; and this is done twice a week.

Minding Your Manners   The market required orderly behavior from all business persons. For the poor, and indeed for many of the middle class, one great regulator of behavior was the religious doctrine preached by such writers as John Bunyan, whose greatest work we shall sample later. The following passage comes from a book by Bunyan called *The Life and Death of Mr. Badman* (1680) that recounts the sufferings and deserved end of a man who cheated, swore, and drank, and who generally neglected the decencies of life that Bunyan wanted and expected all religious persons to observe. The story is frequently interrupted while one of the characters tells about a very hard case, like the following. Those who could be impressed by the story of Dorothy Mately, who swore herself right into the ground, were no doubt far removed from the library, laboratory, and study of Newton. And yet there is a strong insistence on the "facts" of this little story; the circumstances are detailed, the outcome is clear, and the moral is unmistakable. This was a story for simple, credulous persons; but it was also for those who were serious about the "godly behavior" they knew was proper. It is wrong to swear falsely, curse, lie, and steal—and here is the absolute, circumstantial proof!

The Devout Poor

Above all take that dreadful story of Dorothy Mately, an inhabitant of Ashover in the County of Darby.

This Dorothy Mately, saith the relator, was noted by the people of the town to be a great swearer, and curser, and liar, and thief (just like Mr. Badman). And the labor that she did usually follow was to wash the rubbish that came forth of the lead mines, and there to get sparks[1] of lead-ore; and her usual way of asserting of things was with these kind of imprecations: *"I would I might sink into the earth if it be not so, or I would God would make the earth open and swallow me up."* Now upon the 23. of March, 1660., this Dorothy was washing of ore upon the top of a steep hill, about a quarter of a mile from Ashover, and was there taxed[2] by a lad for taking of two single pence out of his pocket (for he had laid his breeches by, and was at work in his drawers), but she violently denied it, wishing *that the ground might swallow her up if she had them.* She also used the same wicked words on several other occasions that day.

1 **sparks:** nuggets or slivers of ore.
2 **taxed:** accused in a scolding way.

Now one George Hodgkinson of Ashover, a man of good report there, came accidently by where this Dorothy was, and stood still a while to talk with her, as she was washing her ore; there stood also a little child by her tub-side, and another a distance from her, calling aloud to her to come away; wherefore the said George took the girl by the hand to lead her away to her that called her. But behold, they had not gone above ten yards from Dorothy, but they heard her crying out for help; so looking back, he saw the woman, and her tub, and sieve, twirling round, and sinking into the ground. Then said the man, "Pray to God to pardon thy sin, for thou art never like to be seen alive any longer." So she and her tub twirled round, and round, till they sunk about three yards into the earth, and then for a while stayed. Then she called for help again, thinking, as she said, that she should stay there. Now the man though greatly amazed, did begin to think which way to help her, but immediately a great stone which appeared in the earth, fell upon her head, and brake her skull, and then the earth fell in upon her and covered her. She was afterwards digged up, and found about four yards within ground, with the boy's two single pence in her pocket, but her tub and sieve could not be found.

The consequences of swearing might be quite dreadful, but for some people they were as nothing compared to the terror of being excluded from polite society. There was even founded, in 1692, a Society for the Improvement of Manners. The following letter of advice, published in 1774 soon after its author's death, is one of many written in the 1740's by the Earl of Chesterfield to his son. Chesterfield himself was a most polished man who was a member of Parliament, a diplomat, and Secretary of State in the first half of the 18th century; and he did what he could for his son, in whom, however, he was to be disappointed.

Chesterfield's conception of manners is clear. Real merit, real honor, real virtue will make themselves felt; but the good manners that must accompany real character can be learned, and they too can make a person liked and respected. Certainly they are susceptible of minute description, as true honor is not, for Chesterfield wrote many, many letters like the following. It should be noted that his conception of manners extends even to the banning of proverbial speech. Yet Chesterfield's *Letters* provided much-needed advice to many who were rising to new positions of power and influence.

THE GENTRY

Dear Boy: I have often told you in my former letters (and it is most certainly true) that the strictest and most scrupulous honor and virtue can alone make you esteemed and valued by mankind; that parts and learning can alone make you admired and celebrated by them; but that the possession of lesser talents was most absolutely necessary toward making you liked, beloved, and sought after in private life. Of these lesser talents, good breeding is the principal and most necessary one, not only as it is very important in itself, but as it adds great luster to the more solid advantages both of the heart and the mind.

I have often touched upon good breeding to you before; so that this letter shall be upon the next necessary qualification to it, which is a genteel and easy manner and carriage, wholly free from those odd tricks, ill habits, and awkwardnesses, which even many very worthy and sensible people have in their behavior. However trifling a genteel manner may sound, it is of very great consequence toward pleasing in private life, especially the women, which, one time or other, you will think worth pleasing; and I have known many a man, from his awkwardness, give people such a dislike of him at first, that all his merit could not get the better of it afterward. Whereas a genteel manner prepossesses people in your favor, bends them toward you, and and makes them wish to be like you.

Awkwardness can proceed but from two causes: either from not having kept good company, or from not having attended to it. As for your keeping good company, I will take care of that; do you take care to observe their ways and manners, and to form your own upon them. Attention is absolutely necessary for this, as indeed it is for everything else; and a man without attention is not fit to live in the world. When an awkward fellow first comes into a room, it is highly probable that his sword gets between his legs, and throws him down, or makes him stumble, at least; when he has recovered this accident, he goes and places himself in the very place of the whole room where he should not; there he soon lets his hat fall down, and, in taking it up again, throws down his cane; in recovering his cane, his hat falls a second time, so that he is a quarter of an hour before he is in order again. If he drinks tea or coffee, he certainly scalds his mouth, and lets either the cup or the saucer fall, and spills either the tea or coffee in his breeches. At dinner, his awkwardness distinguishes itself particularly, as he has more to do; there he holds his knife, fork, and spoon differently from other people, eats with his knife, to the great danger of his mouth, picks his teeth with his fork, and puts his spoon, which has been in his throat twenty times, into the serving dishes again. If he is to carve, he can never hit the joint; but, in his vain efforts to cut through the bone, scatters the sauce in everybody's face. He generally daubs himself with soup and grease, though his napkin is commonly stuck through a buttonhole, and tickles his chin. When he drinks, he infallibly coughs in his glass, and besprinkles the company. Besides all this, he has strange tricks and gestures; such as snuffing up his nose, making faces, putting his finger in his nose, or blowing it and looking afterwards in his handkerchief, so as to make the company sick. His hands are troublesome to him when he has not something in them, and he does not know where to put them; but they are in perpetual motion between his bosom and his breeches; he does not wear his clothes, and, in short, does nothing like other people. All this, I own, is not in any degree criminal; but it is highly disagreeable and ridiculous in company, and ought most carefully to be avoided by whoever desires to please.

From this account of what you should not do, you may easily judge what you should do; and a due attention to the manners of people of fashion, and who have seen the world, will make it habitual and familiar to you.

There is, likewise, an awkwardness of expression and words, most carefully to be avoided; such as false English, bad pronunciation, old sayings, and common proverbs; which are so many proofs of having kept bad and low company. For example, if, instead of saying that tastes are different and that every man has his own peculiar one, you should let off a proverb and say, "What is one man's meat is another man's poison," or else, "Everyone as they like, as the good man said when he kissed his cow," everybody would be persuaded that you had never kept company with anybody above footmen and housemaids.

The Unexpected Grace

Unforeseen Tenderness Although "order" and "propriety" are keys to an understanding of the Enlightenment, in no other period were people more sensitive to feelings and insights that came upon them unexpectedly. A tender heart was as proper for an 18th-century gentleman as a set of rigorously formal manners, and occasions that spoke to his heart were welcome ones. The following passage comes from a journal kept by a great English novelist, Henry Fielding, during a voyage from England to Lisbon in 1754. Fielding tells us, with some amusement and detachment, about a tough sea captain who puts a ship out of its course to save a kitten. Fielding did not hail the captain as a fellow tenderhearted humanitarian, but the detail with which he records the incident tells us of his surprise and his pleasure in finding so susceptible a nature hidden under the captain's rough manner.

KITTEN OVERBOARD

Thursday, July 11. . . . A most tragical incident fell out this day at sea. While the ship was under sail, but making, as will appear, no great way, a kitten, one of four of the feline inhabitants of the cabin, fell from the window into the water: an alarm was immediately given to the captain, who was then upon deck, and received it with the utmost concern and many bitter oaths. He immediately gave orders to the steersman in favor of the poor thing, as he called it; the sails were instantly slackened, and all hands, as the phrase is, employed to recover the poor animal. I was, I own, extremely surprised at all this; less, indeed, at the captain's extreme tenderness, than at his conceiving any possibility of success; for, if puss had had nine thousand, instead of nine lives, I concluded they had been all lost. The boatswain, however, had more sanguine[1] hopes; for, having stripped himself of his jacket, breeches, and shirt, he leapt boldly into the water, and to my great astonishment, in a few minutes, returned to the ship, bearing the motionless animal in his mouth. Nor was this, I observed, a matter of such great difficulty as it appeared to my ignorance, and possibly may seem to that of my fresh-water reader: the kitten was now exposed to air and sun on the deck, where its life, of which it retained no symptoms, was despaired of by all.

The captain's humanity, if I may so call it, did not so totally destroy his philosophy, as to make him yield himself up to affliction on this melancholy occasion. Having felt his loss like a man, he resolved to shew he could bear it like one; and having declared, he had rather have lost a cask of rum or brandy, betook himself to threshing[2] at backgammon with the Portuguese friar, in which innocent amusement they had passed about two-thirds of their time.

But as I have, perhaps, a little too wantonly endeavored to raise the tender passions of my readers, in this narrative, I should think myself unpardonable if I concluded it, without giving them the satisfaction of hearing that the kitten at last recovered, to the great joy of the good captain; but to the great disappointment of some of the sailors, who asserted that the drowning a cat was the very surest way of raising a favorable wind: a supposition of which, though we have heard several plausible accounts, we will not presume to assign the true original reason.

---

1 **sanguine** (săng′gwĭn): optimistic.   2 **threshing:** playing the game with intensity.

The Literature of

The Enlightenment

Images of Order

John Bunyan *(1628-1688)* and The Pilgrim's Progress

EXCEPT FOR THE English Bible, no work in English has been so often reprinted or so widely translated as John Bunyan's *The Pilgrim's Progress*, first published in 1678. And no work in English is more dependent on the Bible for its phrasing, its imagery, and the very rhythm of its sentences. Bunyan knew the Bible intimately, for at every crisis or difficulty in his life—and he experienced many—he turned to it in an anxious search for assurance and comfort. If all the echoes, quotations, and paraphrases of the Bible were annotated in the following selection, the footnotes would begin to crowd the text off the page.

Bunyan was a "mechanick preacher": while he plied his trade of tinker, mending pots and pans as he traveled about the country, he preached to men and women in humble circumstances like himself. Just when Bunyan's preaching began to be famous, it became illegal. In 1660 the Restoration took place; that is, the Commonwealth of Oliver Cromwell ended, the House of Stuart was restored to the throne, and Charles II became King. In order to ensure religious conformity, the new government made it illegal for any person outside the Church of England to preach at public assemblies. Bunyan was a Baptist and therefore outside the official Church; but his strong convictions led him repeatedly and defiantly to break the new law, and he spent two long periods in jail for doing so. His confinement was not strict (nor was it so cruel as the Pilgrim's experience in the dungeon in the following selection); he frequently visited his home nearby, and during this period wrote many books and pamphlets, including *The Pilgrim's Progress*. Although he wrote it, as he says, "mine own self to gratify," more than 100,000 copies of *The Pilgrim's Progress* were sold in his lifetime; and there is no calculating the number that have appeared since. Somehow a simple, earnest, unlearned man wrote one of the world's great books.

Its full title should be noted: *The Pilgrim's Progress from This World to That Which Is to Come: Delivered under the Similitude of a Dream.* His story is told as if it were a dream. Bunyan's dream has been a dream of truth for many people. From a "den," a place of retirement from the world, he saw a vision of the nature of endeavor. Although the Pilgrim's "burden," the load of sin that he bears, is perhaps one that not all people now accept, his journey through difficulties is one that all understand.

300

from The Pilgrim's Progress

John Bunyan

As I WALKED through the wilderness of this world, I lighted on a certain place where was a Den, and I laid me down in that place to sleep: and as I slept I dreamed a dream. I dreamed, and behold, I saw a man clothed with rags, standing in a certain place, with his face from his own house, a book in his hand, and a great burden upon his back. I looked, and saw him open the book and read therein; and as he read, he wept and trembled; and not being able longer to contain, he brake[1] out with a lamentable cry, saying, "What shall I do?"

In this plight, therefore, he went home and refrained himself[2] as long as he could, that his wife and children should not perceive his distress; but he could not be silent long, because that his trouble increased. Wherefore at length he brake his mind to his wife and children; and thus he began to talk to them: "O my dear wife," said he, "and you the children of my bowels, I, your dear friend, am in myself undone by reason of a burden that lieth hard upon me; moreover, I am for certain informed that this our city will be burned with fire from heaven; in which fearful overthrow, both myself, with thee my wife, and you my sweet babes, shall miserably come to ruin; except (the which yet I see not) some way of escape can be found, whereby we may be delivered." At this his relations were sore amazed; not for that they believed that what he had said to them was true, but because they thought that some frenzy distemper[3] had got into his head; therefore, it drawing toward night, and they hoping that sleep might settle his brains, with all haste they got him to bed. But the night was as troublesome to him as the day; wherefore, instead of sleeping, he spent it in sighs and tears. So, when the morning was come, they would know how he did. He told them, "Worse and worse": he also set to talking to them again: but they began to be hardened. They also thought to drive away his distemper[4] by harsh and surly carriages to him; sometimes they would deride, sometimes they would chide, and sometimes they would quite neglect him. Wherefore he began to retire himself to his chamber, to pray for and pity them, and also to condole[5] his own misery; he would also walk solitarily in the fields, sometimes reading, and sometimes praying: and thus for some days he spent his time.

Now I saw, upon a time when he was walking in the fields, that he was, as he was wont,[6] reading in his book, and greatly distressed in his mind; and as he read, he burst out, as he had done be-

---

1 **brake:** broke.
2 **refrained himself:** restrained himself; refrained from speaking.

3 **frenzy distemper:** madness.
4 **distemper:** sickness.
5 **condole:** grieve over.
6 **as . . . wont:** as was his custom.

fore, crying, "What shall I do to be saved?"

I saw also that he looked this way and that way, as if he would run; yet he stood still, because, as I perceived, he could not tell which way to go. I looked then, and saw a man named Evangelist[7] coming to him, who asked, "Wherefore dost thou cry?"

He answered, "Sir, I perceive by the book in my hand that I am condemned to die, and after that to come to judgment, and I find that I am not willing to do the first, nor able to do the second."

Then said Evangelist, "Why not willing to die, since this life is attended with so many evils?" The man answered, "Because I fear that this burden that is upon my back will sink me lower than the grave, and I shall fall into Tophet.[8] And, sir, if I be not fit to go to prison, I am not fit to go to judgment, and from thence to execution; and the thoughts of these things make me cry."

Then said Evangelist, "If this be thy condition, why standest thou still?" He answered, "Because I know not whither to go." Then he gave him a parchment roll, and there was written within, "Fly from the wrath to come."

The man therefore read it, and looking upon Evangelist very carefully, said, "Whither must I fly?" Then said Evangelist, pointing with his finger over a very wide field, "Do you see yonder wicket-gate?"[9] The man said, "No." Then said the other, "Do you see yonder shining light?" He said, "I think I do." Then said Evangelist, "Keep that light in your eye, and go

up directly thereto: so shalt thou see the gate; at which, when thou knockest, it shall be told thee what thou shalt do." So I saw in my dream that the man began to run. Now, he had not run far from his own door, but his wife and children perceiving it, began to cry after him to return; but the man put his fingers in his ears, and ran on, crying, "Life! life! eternal life!" So he looked not behind him, but fled toward the middle of the plain.

The neighbors also came out to see him run; and as he ran, some mocked, others threatened, and some cried after him to return; and, among those that did so, there were two that resolved to fetch him back by force. The name of the one was Obstinate, and the name of the other Pliable. Now by this time the man was got a good distance from them; but, however, they were resolved to pursue him, which they did, and in a little time they overtook him. Then said the man, "Neighbors, wherefore are ye come?" They said, "To persuade you to go back with us." But he said, "That can by no means be; you dwell," said he, "in the City of Destruction, the place also where I was born: I see it to be so; and dying there, sooner or later, you will sink lower than the grave, into a place that burns with fire and brimstone:[10] be content, good neighbors, and go along with me."

OBST. "What!" said Obstinate, "and leave our friends and our comforts behind us?"

CHR. "Yes," said Christian (for that was his name), "because that ALL which you shall forsake is not worthy to be compared with a little of that which I am seeking to enjoy; and if you will go along with me, and hold it, you shall

---

7 **Evangelist:** literally, a messenger of good tidings; one who brings news of the gospel of salvation.

8 **Tophet** (tō'fĕt): Hell.

9 **wicket-gate:** gate set in a wall or a fence like a window.

10 **brimstone:** sulphur.

THE ENLIGHTENMENT

fare as I myself; for there where I go is enough and to spare. Come away, and prove my words."

Obst. "What are the things you seek, since you leave all the world to find them?"

Chr. "I seek an inheritance incorruptible, undefiled, and that fadeth not away, and it is laid up in heaven, and safe there, to be bestowed, at the time appointed, on them that diligently seek it. Read it so, if you will, in my book."

Obst. "Tush!" said Obstinate, "away with your book; will you go back with us or no?"

Chr. "No, not I," said the other, "because I have laid my hand to the plow."

Obst. "Come then, neighbor Pliable, let us turn again and go home without him; there is a company of these crazed-headed coxcombs,[11] that, when they take a fancy by the end, are wiser in their own eyes than seven men that can render a reason."[12]

Pli. Then said Pliable, "Don't revile; if what the good Christian says is true, the things he looks after are better than ours: my heart inclines to go with my neighbor."

Obst. "What! more fools still! Be ruled by me, and go back; who knows whither such a brainsick fellow will lead you? Go back, go back, and be wise."

Chr. "Nay, but do thou come with thy neighbor, Pliable; there are such things to be had which I spoke of, and many more glories besides. If you believe not me, read here in this book; and for the truth of what is expressed therein, behold all is confirmed by the blood of Him that made it."

Pli. "Well, neighbor Obstinate," said Pliable, "I begin to come to a point; I intend to go along with this good man, and to cast in my lot with him; but, my good companion, do you know the way to this desired place?"

Chr. "I am directed by a man whose name is Evangelist, to speed me to a little gate that is before us, where we shall receive instructions about the way."

Pli. "Come then, good neighbor, let us be going." Then they went both together.

Obst. "And I will go back to my place," said Obstinate; "I will be no companion of such misled, fantastical fellows."

Now I saw in my dream that, when Obstinate was gone back, Christian and Pliable went talking over the plain; and thus they began their discourse.

Chr. "Come, neighbor Pliable, how do you do? I am glad you are persuaded to go along with me. Had even Obstinate himself but felt what I have felt of the powers and terrors of what is yet unseen, he would not thus lightly have given us the back."

Pli. "Come, neighbor Christian, since there are none but us two here, tell me now further what the things are, and how to be enjoyed, whither we are going."

Chr. "I can better conceive of them with my mind, than speak of them with my tongue; but yet, since you are desirous to know, I will read of them in my book."

Pli. "And do you think that the words of your book are certainly true?"

Chr. "Yes, verily; for it was made by Him that cannot lie."

Pli. "Well said; what things are they?"

Chr. "There is an endless kingdom to be inhabited, and everlasting life to be given us, that we may inhabit that kingdom forever."

Pli. "Well said; and what else?"

11 **coxcombs** (kŏks′kōmz′): conceited men.
12 **render a reason:** have common sense.

CHR. "There are crowns of glory to be given us, and garments that will make us shine like the sun in the firmament of heaven."

PLI. "This is very pleasant; and what else?"

CHR. "There shall be no more crying nor sorrow; for He that is owner of the place will wipe all tears from our eyes."

PLI. "And what company shall we have there?"

CHR. "There we shall be with seraphims and cherubims,[13] creatures that will dazzle your eyes to look on them. There also you shall meet with thousands and ten thousands that have gone before us to that place; none of them are hurtful, but loving and holy; everyone walking in the sight of God, and standing in his presence with acceptance forever. In a word, there we shall see the elders with their golden crowns; there we shall see the holy virgins with their golden harps, there we shall see men that by the world were cut in pieces, burnt in flames, eaten of beasts, drowned in the seas, for the love that they bear to the Lord of the place, all well, and clothed with immortality as with a garment."

PLI. "The hearing of this is enough to ravish one's heart. But are these things to be enjoyed? How shall we get to be sharers thereof?"

CHR. "The Lord, the Governor of the country, hath recorded that in this book; the substance of which is, If we be truly willing to have it, he will bestow it upon us freely."

PLI. "Well, my good companion, glad am I to hear of these things; come on, let us mend our pace."

CHR. "I cannot go so fast as I would, by reason of this burden that is on my back."

Now I saw in my dream, that just as they had ended this talk they drew near to a very miry slough[14] that was in the midst of the plain; and they, being heedless, did both fall suddenly into the bog. The name of the slough was Despond.[15] Here, therefore, they wallowed for a time, being grievously bedaubed with the dirt; and Christian, because of the burden that was on his back, began to sink in the mire.

PLI. Then said Pliable, "Ah! neighbor Christian, where are you now?"

CHR. "Truly," said Christian, "I do not know."

PLI. At that Pliable began to be offended, and angrily said to his fellow, "Is this the happiness you have told me all this while of? If we have such ill speed at our first setting out, what may we expect betwixt this and our journey's end? May I get out again with my life, you shall possess the brave country alone for me." And with that he gave a desperate struggle or two, and got out of the mire on that side of the slough which was next to his own house: so away he went, and Christian saw him no more.

Wherefore Christian was left to tumble in the Slough of Despond alone: but still he endeavored to struggle to that side of the slough that was still further from his own house, and next to the wicket-gate; the which he did, but could not get out, because of the burden that was upon his back: but I beheld in my dream that a man came to him, whose name was Help, and asked him what he did there.

CHR. "Sir," said Christian, "I was bid go this way by a man called Evangelist, who directed me also to yonder gate, that I might escape the wrath to come;

---

13 **seraphims and cherubims:** two of the nine orders of angels.

14 **slough:** swamp.

15 **Despond** (dĭ spŏnd′): despondency; dejection.

and as I was going thither I fell in here."

HELP. "But why did not you look for the steps?"

CHR. "Fear followed me so hard that I fled the next way and fell in."

HELP. Then said he, "Give me thy hand": so he gave him his hand, and he drew him out, and set him upon sound ground, and bid him go on his way.

Then I stepped to him that plucked him out, and said, "Sir, wherefore, since over this place is the way from the City of Destruction to yonder gate, is it that this plat[16] is not mended, that poor travelers might go thither with more security?" And he said unto me, "This miry slough is such a place as cannot be mended; it is the descent whither the scum and filth that attends conviction for sin doth continually run, and therefore it is called the Slough of Despond; for still, as the sinner is awakened about his lost condition, there ariseth in his soul many fears, and doubts, and discouraging apprehensions, which all of them get together, and settle in this place. And this is the reason of the badness of this ground.

"It is not the pleasure of the King that this place should remain so bad. His laborers also have, by the direction of His Majesty's surveyors, been for above these sixteen hundred years employed about this patch of ground, if perhaps it might have been mended: yea, and to my knowledge," said he, "here have been swallowed up at least twenty thousand cartloads, yea, millions of wholesome instructions, that have at all seasons been brought from all places of the King's dominions, and they that can tell, say they are the best materials to make good ground of the place; if so be, it might have been mended, but it is the Slough of Despond still, and so will be when they have done what they can.

"True, there are, by the direction of the Lawgiver, certain good and substantial steps, placed even through the very midst of this slough; but at such time as this place doth much spew out its filth,[17] as it doth against change of weather, these steps are hardly seen; or if they be, men, through the dizziness of their heads, step beside, and then they are bemired to purpose, notwithstanding the steps be there; but the ground is good when they are once got in at the gate."

Now I saw in my dream that by this time Pliable was got home to his house again, so that his neighbors came to visit him; and some of them called him wise man for coming back, and some called him fool for hazarding himself with Christian: others again did mock at his cowardliness; saying, "Surely, since you began to venture, I would not have been so base to have given out for a few difficulties." So Pliable sat sneaking among them. But at last he got more confidence, and then they all turned their tales, and began to deride poor Christian behind his back. And thus much concerning Pliable.

Now as Christian was walking solitarily by himself, he espied one afar off come crossing over the field to meet him; and their hap was to meet just as they were crossing the way of each other. The gentleman's name that met him was Mr. Worldly Wiseman: he dwelt in the town of Carnal Policy,[18] a very great town, and also hard by from whence Christian came. This man, then, meeting with Christian, and hav-

16 plat: plot of ground.

17 spew . . . filth: overflow.
18 town of Carnal Policy: place ruled by the desire to be comfortable.

ing some inkling of him—for Christian's setting forth from the City of Destruction was much noised abroad, not only in the town where he dwelt, but also it began to be the town talk in some other places—Master Worldly Wiseman, therefore, having some guess of him, by beholding his laborious going, by observing his sighs and groans, and the like, began thus to enter into some talk with Christian.

WORLD. "How now, good fellow, whither away after this burdened manner?"

CHR. "A burdened manner indeed, as ever, I think, poor creature had! And whereas you ask me, 'Whither away?' I tell you, sir, I am going to yonder wicket-gate before me; for there, as I am informed, I shall be put into a way to be rid of my heavy burden."

WORLD. "Hast thou a wife and children?"

CHR. "Yes; but I am so laden with this burden that I cannot take that pleasure in them as formerly; methinks I am as if I had none."

WORLD. "Wilt thou hearken unto me if I give thee counsel?"

CHR. "If it be good, I will; for I stand in need of good counsel."

WORLD. "I would advise thee, then, that thou with all speed get thyself rid of thy burden; for thou wilt never be settled in thy mind till then; nor canst thou enjoy the benefits of the blessing which God hath bestowed upon thee till then."

CHR. "That is that which I seek for, even to be rid of this heavy burden; but get it off myself, I cannot; nor is there any man in our country that can take it off my shoulders; therefore am I going this way, as I told you, that I may be rid of my burden."

WORLD. "Who bid thee go this way to be rid of thy burden?"

CHR. "A man that appeared to me to be a very great and honorable person; his name, as I remember, is Evangelist."

WORLD. "I beshrew[19] him for his counsel; there is not a more dangerous and troublesome way in the world than is that unto which he hath directed thee; and that thou shalt find, if thou will be ruled by his counsel. Thou hast met with something, as I perceive, already; for I see the dirt of the Slough of Despond is upon thee; but that slough is the beginning of the sorrows that do attend those that go on in that way. Hear me, I am older than thou; thou art like to meet with, in the way which thou goest, wearisomeness, painfulness, hunger, perils, nakedness, sword, lions, dragons, darkness, and, in a word, death, and what not! These things are certainly true, having been confirmed by many testimonies. And why should a man so carelessly cast away himself, by giving heed to a stranger?"

CHR. "Why, sir, this burden upon my back is more terrible to me than are all these things which you have mentioned; nay, methinks I care not what I meet with in the way, if so be I can also meet with deliverance from my burden."

WORLD. "How camest thou by the burden at first?"

CHR. "By reading this book in my hand."

WORLD. "I thought so; and it is happened unto thee as to other weak men, who, meddling with things too high for them, do suddenly fall into thy distractions;[20] which distractions do not only unman men, as thine, I perceive, have done thee, but they run them upon desperate ventures to obtain they know not what."

19 **beshrew:** curse.
20 **distractions:** madness.

THE ENLIGHTENMENT

Illustrations from early editions of The Pilgrim's Progress. *Vanity Fair, a town where idleness and luxury are sold, is from an 18th-century edition. Dryden's play* All for Love *is offered as an allurement to the worldly and wicked. The Giant Despair outside Doubting Castle is from a 1683 edition.*

CHR. "I know what I would obtain; it is ease for my heavy burden."

[*Christian goes on, despite the advice of Mr. Worldly Wiseman. He fights and slays a dragon, an agent of the Devil, called Apollyon. He passes through the Valley of the Shadow. He and a companion named Faithful are mistreated in Vanity Fair, a town where idleness and worthlessness are sold. Their example converts one of the inhabitants of that town; and he, named Hopeful, accompanies Christian to the next adventure. After a night's rest they find themselves in the grounds of Doubting Castle.*]

Now there was, not far from the place where they lay, a castle called Doubting Castle, the owner whereof was Giant Despair; and it was in his ground they now were sleeping: wherefore he, getting up in the morning early, and walking up and down in his fields caught Christian and Hopeful asleep in his grounds. Then with a grim and surly voice he bid them awake, and asked them whence they were and what they did in his grounds. They told him they were pilgrims and that they had lost their way. Then said the giant, "You have this night trespassed on me by trampling in and lying on my grounds, and therefore you must go along with me." So they were forced to go, because he was stronger than they. They also had but little to say, for they knew themselves in a fault. The giant therefore drove them before him and put them into his castle, into a very dark dungeon, nasty and stinking to the spirits of these two men. Here then they lay from Wednesday morning till Saturday night, without one bit of bread, or drop of drink, or light, or any to ask how they did; they were therefore here in evil case, and were far from friends and acquaintance. Now in this place Christian had double sorrow, because 'twas through his unadvised haste that they were brought into this distress.

Now Giant Despair had a wife, and her name was Diffidence. So when he was gone to bed, he told his wife what he had done; to wit, that he had taken a couple of prisoners and cast them into his dungeon for trespassing on his grounds. Then he asked her also what he had best to do further to them. So she asked him what they were, whence they came, and whither they were bound; and he told her. Then she counseled him that when he arose in the morning he should beat them without any mercy. So when he arose, he getteth him a grievous crab-tree cudgel, and goes down into the dungeon to them, and there first falls to rating[21] of them as if they were dogs, although they never gave him a word of distaste. Then he falls upon them and beats them fearfully, in such sort that they were not able to help themselves, or to turn them upon the floor. This done, he withdraws and leaves them there to condole their misery and to mourn under their distress. So all that day they spent the time in nothing but sighs and bitter lamentations. The next night

21 **rating:** berating; scolding.

she, talking with her husband about them further, and understanding they were yet alive, did advise him to counsel them to make away themselves. So when morning was come, he goes to them in a surly manner as before, and perceiving them to be very sore with the stripes that he had given them the day before, he told them that since they were never like to come out of that place, their only way would be forthwith to make an end of themselves, either with knife, halter, or poison. "For why," said he, "should you choose life, seeing it is attended with so much bitterness?" But they desired him to let them go. With that he looked ugly upon them, and rushing to them, had doubtless made an end of them himself, but that he fell into one of his fits (for he sometimes in sunshiny weather fell into fits), and lost for a time the use of his hand; wherefore he withdrew, and left them as before to consider what to do. Then did the prisoners consult between themselves, whether 'twas best to take his counsel or no; and thus they began to discourse:

CHR. "Brother," said Christian. "what shall we do? The life that we now live is miserable. For my part I know not whether it is best to live thus, or to die out of hand. 'My soul chooseth strangling rather than life,' and the grave is more easy for me than this dungeon. Shall we be ruled by the giant?"

HOPE. "Indeed our present condition is dreadful, and death would be far more welcome to me than thus forever to abide; but yet let us consider, the Lord of the country to which we are going hath said, 'Thou shalt do no murder': no, not to another man's person; much more then are we forbidden to take his counsel to kill ourselves. Besides, he that kills another can but commit murder upon his body; but for one to kill himself is to kill body and soul at once. And moreover, my brother, thou talkest of ease in the grave; but hast thou forgotten the hell whither for certain the murderers go? For 'no murderer hath eternal life,' etc. And let us consider again that all the law is not in the hand of Giant Despair. Others, so far as I can understand, have been taken by him, as well as we; and yet have escaped out of his hand. Who knows but that God that made the world may cause that Giant Despair may die? or that at some time or other he may forget to lock us in? or but he may in short time have another of his fits before us, and may lose the use of his limbs? And if ever that should come to pass again, for my part, I am resolved to pluck up the heart of a man, and to try my utmost to get from under his hand. I was a fool that I did not try to do it before; but however, my brother, let's be patient, and endure a while. The time may come that may give us a happy release; but let us not be our own murderers." With these words Hopeful at present did moderate the mind of his brother; so they continued together (in the dark) that day, in their sad and doleful condition.

Well, toward evening the giant goes down into the dungeon again, to see if his prisoners had taken his counsel; but when he came there he found them alive; and truly, alive was all; for now, what for want of bread and water, and by reason of the wounds they received when he beat them, they could do little but breathe. But, I say, he found them alive; at which he fell into a grievous rage, and told them that, seeing they had disobeyed his counsel, it should be worse with them than if they had never been born.

At this they trembled greatly, and I think that Christian fell into a swoon; but coming a little to himself again, they renewed their discourse about the giant's counsel; and whether yet they had best to take it or no. Now Christian again seemed to be for doing it, but Hopeful made his second reply as followeth:

HOPE. "My brother," said he, "rememberest thou not how valiant thou hast been heretofore? Apollyon could not crush thee, nor could all that thou didst hear, or see, or feel, in the Valley of the Shadow of Death. What hardship, terror, and amazement hast thou already gone through, and art thou now nothing but fear? Thou seest that I am in the dungeon with thee, a far weaker man by nature than thou art; also this giant has wounded me as well as thee, and hath also cut off the bread and water from my mouth; and with thee I mourn without the light. But let us exercise a little more patience; remember how thou playedst the man at Vanity Fair, and wast neither afraid of the chain, nor cage, nor yet of bloody death. Wherefore let us (at least to avoid the shame that becomes not a Christian to be found in) bear up with patience as well as we can."

Now night being come again, and the giant and his wife being in bed, she asked him concerning the prisoners, and if they had taken his counsel. To which he replied, "They are sturdy rogues, they choose rather to bear all hardship, than to make away themselves." Then said she, "Take them into the castle-yard tomorrow, and show them the bones and skulls of those that thou hast already dispatched, and make them believe, ere a week comes to an end, thou also wilt tear them in pieces, as thou hast done their fellows before them."

So when the morning was come, the giant goes to them again, and takes them into the castle-yard, and shows them, as his wife had bidden him. "These," said he, "were pilgrims as you are once, and they trespassed in my grounds, as you have done; and when I thought fit, I tore them in pieces, and so within ten days I will do you. Go, get down to your den again"; and with that he beat them all the way thither. They lay therefore all day on Saturday in a lamentable case, as before. Now when night was come, and when Mrs. Diffidence and her husband the giant were got to bed, they began to renew their discourse of their prisoners; and withal the old giant wondered that he could neither by his blows nor his counsel bring them to an end. And with that his wife replied, "I fear," said she, "that they live in hope that some will come to relieve them, or that they have picklocks about them, by the means of which they hope to escape." "And sayest thou so, my dear?" said the giant; "I will therefore search them in the morning."

Well, on Saturday about midnight they began to pray, and continued in prayer till almost break of day.

Now a little before it was day, good Christian, as one half amazed, brake out in this passionate speech: "What a fool," quoth he, "am I, thus to lie in a stinking dungeon, when I may as well walk at liberty! I have a key in my bosom called Promise, that will, I am persuaded, open any lock in Doubting Castle." Then said Hopeful, "That is good news, good brother; pluck it out of thy bosom and try."

Then Christian pulled it out of his bosom, and began to try at the dungeon door, whose bolt (as he turned the key) gave back, and the door flew open with ease, and Christian and Hopeful both came out. Then he went to the outward door that leads into the castle-yard, and with his key opened that door also. After, he went to the iron gate, for that must be opened too; but that lock went damnable hard, yet the key did open it. Then they thrust open the gate to make their escape with speed, but that gate, as it opened, made such a creaking that it waked Giant Despair, who, hastily rising to pursue his prisoners, felt his limbs to fail, for his fits took him again, so that he could by no means go after them. Then they went on and came to the King's highway, and so were safe because they were out of his jurisdiction.

Comment

Besides the Bible, Bunyan's favorite book as a young man was *The Plain Man's Pathway to Heaven.* Bunyan's title—and his book—is more active. He describes a pathway or a road to the Celestial City, but he emphasizes the forward movement, the *progress,* of his pilgrim. And this progress is marked by the character of the pilgrim's difficulties and by the resources with which he overcomes them. What progress do you see in Bunyan's story as you move from the first of these two excerpts through the second?

1. The Slough of Despond: How is the character of Pliable revealed in this episode? And how is Pliable's character further revealed after he returns home? How is Christian saved from the Slough of

Despond? What does his rescue tell us about despondency and what most easily gets us out of it?

2. Doubting Castle: Giant Despair is cruel in word and deed, yet he suffers a "fit" that keeps him from killing the pilgrims. What do his violence and his "fit" tell us about the nature of despair?

   According to the dictionary, the word *diffidence* means "lacking confidence in oneself." What does the episode reveal about the nature of Diffidence? Why should she be the helpmeet of Despair? And why should both Diffidence and Despair be so hysterically cruel? How does Christian escape this difficulty, this adventure? What rescues him this time? Where does he find it?

3. As you compare these two episodes, then, which seems to you to be the worse, despondency or doubt? Which is the stronger obstacle to the Pilgrim's progress on his road? But which obstacle does he overcome by himself?

4. Write a paragraph on the kind of "progress" you now see Bunyan describing here. Is it a progress in which the way becomes easier or one in which the Pilgrim becomes stronger?

Poet-laureate - highest honor for poet [handwritten annotation]

John Dryden (1631-1700)

John Dryden, poet, dramatist, critic, translator, was the most eminent man of letters in the second half of the 17th century. Though there were better dramatists than he, his plays set the style for the drama of his time. His criticism set a standard of clarity and lightly carried learning that no other critic rivaled until Samuel Johnson's day. He was a member of the Royal Society, where he presided over a committee to refine and improve the English language (but which, perhaps fortunately, never took any real action), and he was for many years the leader of a group of "wits" who gathered at Will's, a London coffeehouse, to discuss literature and politics in a tone and a style that many eagerly imitated.

The quality called "wit" was for Dryden no mere capacity for making jokes; it was his name for the imagination, the faculty that no one could lack and still be a writer.

WIT — a great mental faculty of intelligence or inventiveness [handwritten annotation]

> The composition of all poems is or ought to be of wit; and wit in the poet . . . is no other than the faculty of imagination . . . which, like a nimble spaniel, beats over and ranges through the fields of memory, till it springs the quarry it hunteth after . . . . Wit written [i.e., the product of true wit] is that which is well defined, the happy result of thought, or product of imagination.

metaphysical — beyond the physical [handwritten annotation]

So wrote Dryden in 1666. Note that the imagination for him is a faculty that searches the memory, like a hunting dog searching for game. As Samuel Johnson implies in the passage we have seen (p. 287), the writer does not express him*self;* he rather defines and shapes the learning and experience stored in his memory. Dryden's critical pronouncements, such as this one, formed a conception of literature that was to endure for more than a hundred years.

Much of Dryden's poetry is satirical, attacking those from whom he differed in politics and literature. Its neat rhymed couplets, of the sort that we shall see in the poetry of Alexander Pope, set a verse style that endured almost as long as did his critical pronouncements. His translations of the Roman poet Virgil and of Chaucer (of whose works he said, " 'Tis sufficient to say, according to the proverb, 'Here is God's plenty' ") show the same clarity and ease that we find in his prose. And in that prose we find a modern voice.

"A Song for Saint Cecilia's Day"

The following selection is an ode written for a London musical society to celebrate the Feast of Saint Cecilia, a Christian martyr who became the patron saint of music. (The ode was later set to music by the composer Handel.) It is an example not only of Dryden's greatly varied skill but also of the conception of order that lies behind the concerns of the writer of the Enlightenment.

[handwritten: Teaches the communication of several instruments]

A Song for Saint Cecilia's Day

November 22, 1687

John Dryden

[handwritten: ODE - Long lyric poem - serious in subject elevated in style and elaborate in structure]

1

From harmony, from heavenly harmony,
    This universal frame began;
    When Nature underneath a heap
      Of jarring atoms lay,
    And could not heave her head,   5
The tuneful voice was heard from high,
    "Arise, ye more than dead."
Then cold and hot and moist and dry[1]
    In order to their stations leap,
      And Music's power obey.   10
From harmony, from heavenly harmony,
    This universal frame began:
    From harmony to harmony
Through all the compass of the notes it ran,
The diapason[2] closing full in Man.   15

2

What passion cannot Music raise and quell?
    When Jubal[3] struck the chorded shell,[4]
  His listening brethren stood around,
    And wondering, on their faces fell
    To worship that celestial sound: 20
Less than a god they thought there could not dwell
    Within the hollow of that shell
    That spoke so sweetly and so well.
What passion cannot Music raise and quell?

---

[1] **Then . . . dry:** the four elements that were believed to constitute all matter: earth ("cold"), fire ("hot"), water ("moist"), and air ("dry").
[2] **diapason** (dī′ə pā′zən): organ stop that sounds in octaves all the pitches of the notes the organist plays. This is the fullest sound the organ is capable of.
[3] **Jubal** (jōō′bəl): according to Genesis 4:21, the father of all who play the harp or organ.
[4] **chorded shell:** tortoise shell with strings stretched across it to form a lyre.

JOHN DRYDEN   313

3

The trumpet's loud clangor   25
    Excites us to arms
With shrill notes of anger
    And mortal alarms.
The double double double beat
    Of the thundering drum   30
    Cries, "Hark! the foes come;
Charge, charge, 'tis too late to retreat."

4

The soft complaining flute
    In dying notes discovers
    The woes of hopeless lovers,   35
Whose dirge[5] is whispered by the warbling lute.

5

    Sharp violins proclaim
Their jealous pangs and desperation,
Fury, frantic indignation,
Depth of pains and height of passion,   40
    For the fair, disdainful dame.

6

But oh! what art can teach,
What human voice can reach
    The sacred organ's praise?
Notes inspiring holy love,   45
Notes that wing their heavenly ways
    To mend the choirs above.

7

Orpheus[6] could lead the savage race,
And trees unrooted left their place,
    Sequacious of the lyre;   50
But bright Cecilia raised the wonder higher:
When to her organ vocal breath was given,
An angel heard, and straight appeared,
    Mistaking earth for heaven.

---

5 dirge: song of grief.
6 Orpheus (ôr′fi əs): in Greek mythology the musician who played so beautifully that even
beasts ("savage race") and trees followed (were "sequacious of") the sound of his lyre.

GRAND CHORUS

As from the power of sacred lays
   The spheres began to move,
And sung the great Creator's praise
   To all the blessed above; 55
So when the last and dreadful hour
This crumbling pageant[7] shall devour, 60
The trumpet shall be heard on high,
The dead shall live, the living die,
And Music shall untune the sky.[8]

---

7 **crumbling pageant:** human history.
8 **The trumpet . . . sky:** The Day of Judgment will be announced by the trumpet. At this last musical sound the world will end, and the music of the spheres will be "untuned."

Comment

Dryden's ode proceeds like a proportion: as heavenly harmony (the music of the spheres) brought order to the "jarring atoms" and four elements of the earth, so music (earthly harmony) brings order to the emotions ("passions") of mankind. As he describes these emotions, Dryden's own verse takes on musical qualities that are appropriate to each one. What changes of tone and rhythm do you hear as you move from stanza to stanza?

1. In stanzas 3, 4, 5, and 6 Dryden describes four "passions" that music can "raise and quell." Stanza 3, for example, refers to the "anger" of war. What emotions are 4, 5, and 6 concerned with?
2. What relation do you find between the emotions Dryden describes and the sound of the verses in which he describes them? For example, what is appropriate in the sound of line 29? in that of line 36? line 40? line 46?
3. "Wit written is that which is well defined," said Dryden. Once again, what is the subject of this poem? How has Dryden defined this subject well, making the poem, in Dryden's sense of the word, a "witty" poem?
4. Write a paragraph on the meaning of "harmony" as you find it expressed in this poem.

Alexander Pope (1688-1744)

It is difficult to imagine the learned reading public of the early 18th century praising the work of a mere youth. Yet at the age of twenty-three Alexander Pope was acknowledged by many as the foremost poet of the day, and a few years later with his *Essay on Criticism* (from which you have read the famous lines about "true wit") he achieved a general eminence that no 18th-century poet surpassed.

His success, moreover, came by his pen alone. Pope was deformed by a spinal infection suffered at the age of twelve. He never grew taller than four feet six, and for much of his life he was so helpless that he could not dress himself. Social life was difficult for him: he could not regularly visit the London coffeehouses where literary reputations were made (and broken); and he was by nature suspicious, quarrelsome, and ambitious. But at an early age he had stored his memory with years of attentive reading; he prepared himself well for the career of the writer who is fully aware of what goes on in the social world yet who lives somewhat apart from it.

Pope achieved his greatest skill in satire, as did Dryden. (Pope as a boy had met this famous poet.) We shall see a small sample of Pope's satire farther on. He wrote moral essays in verse (in the style of the Roman poet Horace, whom he admired); he wrote "epistles" or verse-letters to friends; and he made epigrams, all with a keen eye on the manners of his society. Like other men of letters of his time he was also a translator and an editor. He translated Homer's *Iliad* and *Odyssey* and made a fortune when "Mr. Pope's Homer" became, if not required reading, a required article of furniture in every gentleman's parlor. He edited Shakespeare, though not very well, and the adverse criticism this project received he repaid in full in his vast mock-heroic poem, *The Dunciad*, the most elaborate personal satire in English. It recounts the histories and fates of a number of "dunces," all of whom, not very strangely, are literary men from whom Pope had received real or imagined slights. And, as his enemies multiplied, he revised *The Dunciad* to include new victims. Yet bitter and personal as it is, this poem is organized around an important critical idea: that *dullness* in literature is not just a lack of power and liveliness, but a power itself, a power that encourages the growth of slovenliness and low standards. There is no dullness of the dunce in Pope. No writer polished and repolished his work to a higher brilliance than he did.

Essay on Man

Pope's early success came chiefly from his *Essay on Criticism* and from the vivacious *Rape of the Lock*, a witty satire on the polite society of the day. The *Essay on Man*, from which the following selection has been taken, is a much more ambitious enterprise. One of Pope's most intimate friends was the Tory political leader, Henry St. John, Viscount Bolingbroke, who, after the Whigs came into power—and after a number of other political adventures that included his temporary banishment as a traitor—turned to philosophy. He is "my St. John" (sĭn'jən) of the first line of the poem below, and from him Pope learned about the optimistic philosophy current among certain continental thinkers of the Enlightenment. Their belief that this is "the best of possible worlds" was distilled by Pope into the neat and pointed couplets of which he was the supreme master. Man, he argues, is limited; and he must restrain the pride that, like the ambition of Milton's Satan, tempts him to rise higher than his lot. Though man is limited, the world he lives in is not. It is, according to this philosophy, a vast "chain of being" that reaches from levels of creation lower than lifeless stones and earth, through the level of plant life, through animal life, through man, through angels, up to the very throne of God beyond the heavens. The great chain, however, remains unbroken only if each creature, each link, holds firm in its place. And in this theory man especially, since he alone of all earthly creatures is tempted to rise to the supernatural (to the condition of angels and spiritual beings), must know his place and stay in it. It is a comforting scheme of things for the conservative philosopher, for it makes any act of rebellion a crime against the whole order of the universe. But, as Pope describes it, it is also a conception of order both vast and subtle, both spacious and finely detailed.

from Essay on Man

Alexander Pope

I

Awake, my St. John! leave all meaner things
To low ambition and the pride of kings.
Let us (since life can little more supply
Than just to look about us, and to die)
Expatiate[1] free o'er all this scene of man;   5
A mighty maze! but not without a plan:
A wild, where weeds and flowers promiscuous[2] shoot;
Or garden, tempting with forbidden fruit.
Together let us beat[3] this ample field,
Try what the open, what the covert yield;   10
The latent tracts,[4] the giddy heights explore
Of all who blindly creep, or sightless soar;[5]
Eye Nature's walks, shoot folly as it flies,
And catch the manners living as they rise;
Laugh where we must, be candid[6] where we can;   15
But vindicate the ways of God to man.[7]

1 **expatiate** (ĭk spā′shĭ āt′): range; roam.
2 **promiscuous:** The weeds and flowers grow mixed together.
3 **beat:** walk.
4 **latent tracts:** hidden pathways.

5 **Of . . . soar:** of all who creep blindly (like moles) or fly beyond sight.
6 **candid:** kindly.
7 **But . . . man:** In *Paradise Lost* Milton writes, "I may assert Eternal Providence/And justify the ways of God to men."

Say first, of God above, or man below,
What can we reason, but from what we know?
Of man, what see we but his station here,
From which to reason, or to which refer? 20
Through worlds unnumbered, though the God be known,
'Tis ours to trace him only in our own.
He, who through vast immensity can pierce,[8]
See worlds on worlds compose one universe,
Observe how system into system runs, 25
What other planets circle other suns,
What varied being peoples every star,[9]
May tell why Heaven has made us as we are.
But of this frame the bearings and the ties,
The strong connections, nice dependencies,[10] 30
Gradations just,[11] has thy pervading soul
Looked through? or can a part contain the whole?
     Is the great chain, that draws all to agree,
And drawn supports, upheld by God or thee?

＊　＊　＊

     Heaven from all creatures hides the book of Fate, 35
All but the page prescribed, their present state:
From[12] brutes what men, from men what spirits know:
Or who could suffer being here below?
The lamb thy riot[13] dooms to bleed today,
Had he thy reason, would he skip and play? 40
Pleased to the last, he crops the flowery food,
And licks the hand just raised to shed his blood.
Oh blindness to the future! kindly given,
That each may fill the circle marked by Heaven:
Who sees with equal eye, as God of all, 45
A hero perish, or a sparrow fall,
Atoms or systems into ruin hurled,
And now a bubble burst, and now a world.
     Hope humbly then; with trembling pinions[14] soar;
Wait the great teacher, Death; and God adore. 50
What future bliss, He gives not thee to know,
But gives that hope to be thy blessing now.
Hope springs eternal in the human breast:
Man never Is, but always To be blest.
The soul, uneasy, and confined from home, 55
Rests and expatiates in a life to come.

---

8 **pierce:** rhymes with *verse*.
9 **What varied . . . star:** It was presumed in the
18th century that there might be certain kinds of
life ("being") on other planets.
10 **nice dependencies:** subtle relationships.

11 **gradations just:** exact degrees (of the scale of
creatures).
12 **From:** i.e., hides from.
13 **riot:** luxurious feasting.
14 **trembling pinions:** fearful wings.

THE ENLIGHTENMENT

Lo, the poor Indian! whose untutored mind
Sees God in clouds, or hears Him in the wind;
His soul, proud Science never taught to stray
Far as the solar walk,[15] or milky way;   60
Yet simple Nature to his hope has given,
Behind the cloud-topped hill, an   humbler Heaven,
Some safer world in depth of woods embraced,
Some happier island in the watery waste,
Where slaves once more their native land behold,   65
No fiends torment, no Christians thirst for gold.
To Be, contents his natural desire,
He asks no angel's wings, no seraph's fire;
But thinks, admitted to that equal sky,
His faithful dog shall bear him company.   70

                        ❖   ❖   ❖

What would this man?   Now upward will he soar,
And little less than angel, would be more;
Now looking downwards, just as grieved appears,
To want[16] the strength of bulls, the fur of bears.
Made for his use all creatures if he call,   75
Say what their use, had he the powers of all?[17]
Nature to these, without profusion, kind,
The proper organs, proper powers assigned;
Each seeming want compensated of course,[18]
Here with degrees of swiftness, there of force;   80
All in exact proportion to the state;
Nothing to add, and nothing to abate.[19]
Each beast, each insect, happy in its own:
Is Heaven unkind to man, and man alone?
Shall he alone, whom rational we call,   85
Be pleased with nothing, if not blest with all?
The bliss of man (could pride that blessing find)
Is not to act or think beyond mankind;
No powers of body or of soul to share,
But what his Nature and his state can bear.   90
Why has not man a microscopic eye?
For this plain reason, man is not a fly.
Say what the use, were finer optics given,
To inspect a mite, not comprehend the heaven?
Or touch, if trembling alive all o'er.   95
To smart and agonize at every pore?
Or quick effluvia darting through the brain,

---

15 **solar-walk:** sun's orbit.
16 **To want:** to lack.
17 **Made . . . of all:** Man asserts that all creatures
were made for his use, but what use would they
be if man had all their powers?

18 **Each . . . course:** Each apparent lack is duly
compensated for: timid creatures are swift; those
too large to hide are strong.
19 **abate:** subtract.

ALEXANDER POPE   319

Die of a rose in aromatic pain?[20]
If Nature thundered in his opening ears,
And stunned him with the music of the spheres,[21]   100
How would he wish that Heaven had left him still
The whisp'ring zephyr, and the purling rill?[22]
Who finds not Providence all good and wise,
Alike in what it gives and what it denies?

    Far as creation's ample range extends,
The scale of sensual, mental powers ascends:
Mark how it mounts to man's imperial race,
From the green myriads in the peopled grass:
What modes of sight betwixt each wide extreme,
The mole's dim curtain, and the lynx's beam:[23]   110
Of smell, the headlong lioness between,
And hound sagacious on the tainted green:[24]
Of hearing, from the life that fills the flood,[25]
To that which warbles through the vernal wood?
The spider's touch, how exquisitely fine!   115
Feels at each thread, and lives along the line:
In the nice[26] bee, what sense so subtly true
From poisonous herbs extract the healing dew?
How instinct varies in the grov'ling swine,
Compared, half-reasoning elephant, with thine!   120
'Twixt that, and reason, what a nice barrier.[27]
Forever separate, yet forever near!
Remembrance and reflection, how allied;
What thin partitions sense from thought divide;
And middle natures, how they long to join,   125
Yet never pass the insuperable line!
Without this just gradation could they be
Subjected, these to those,[28] or all to thee?
The powers of all subdued by thee alone,
Is not thy reason all these powers in one?   130

    See, through this air, this ocean, and this earth,
All matter quick, and bursting into birth.
Above, how high, progressive life may go!
Around, how wide! how deep extend below!
Vast chain of being! which from God began,   135

---

20 Say . . . pain: If man's senses of touch and smell were as keen as those of some insects, he would suffer; the odor of a rose would kill him.

21 stunned . . . spheres: The music of the spheres was inaudible to man; only celestial beings could hear it.

22 whisp'ring . . . rill: gentle winds and murmuring streams—the sounds man is "properly" pleased by.

23 lynx's beam: lynx's eyesight. (The lynx had keen eyes.)

24 Of smell . . . green: The dog is clever ("sagacious") enough to smell a trail that "taints" the grass, but the powerful lioness has a weaker sense of smell.

25 life . . . flood: fish.

26 nice: exact in discrimination.

27 nice barrier: fine distinction.

28 these to those: There are exact degrees of power in the animal world according to which some animals are superior to others.

THE ENLIGHTENMENT

Natures ethereal, human, angel, man,
Beast, bird, fish, insect, what no eye can see,
No glass can reach; from infinite to thee,
From thee to nothing. —On superior powers
Were we to press, inferior might on ours;[29]   140
Or in the full creation leave a void,
Where, one step broken, the great scale's destroyed:[30]
From Nature's chain whatever link you strike,
Tenth, or tenth thousandth, breaks the chain alike.

    And, if each system in gradation roll   145
Alike essential to the amazing whole,
The least confusion but in one, not all
That system only, but the whole must fall.
Let earth, unbalanced, from her orbit fly,
Planets and suns run lawless through the sky;   150
Let ruling angels from their spheres be hurled,
Being on being wrecked, and world on world;
Heaven's whole foundations to their center nod,[31]
And Nature trembles to the throne of God.
All this dread order break—for whom? for thee?   155
Vile worm!—oh madness! pride! impiety!

    What if the foot, ordained the dust to tread,
Or hand, to toil,[32] aspired to be the head?
What if the head, the eye, or ear repined[33]
To serve mere engines to the ruling mind?   160
Just as absurd for any part to claim
To be another, in this general frame;
Just as absurd, to mourn the tasks or pains
The great Directing Mind of all ordains.

    All are but parts of one stupendous whole,   165
Whose body Nature is, and God the soul;
That, changed through all, and yet in all the same;
Great in the earth, as in the ethereal frame;
Warms in the sun, refreshes in the breeze,
Glows in the stars, and blossoms in the trees;   170
Lives through all life, extends through all extent;
Spreads undivided, operates unspent!
Breathes in our soul, informs our mortal part,
As full, as perfect, in a hair as heart;
As full, as perfect in vile man that mourns,   175
As the rapt seraph that adores and burns:[34]
To him no high, no low, no great, no small;

---

29 On . . . ours: If we encroach upon powers
superior to man, powers lower than man will encroach upon us.
30 Or . . . destroyed: If any creature leaves a void
in the scale or chain of being, by rising above its
place, then the whole scale or chain collapses.

31 nod: collapse inwards.
32 to toil: i.e., ordained to toil.
33 repined: grumbled; complained.
34 rapt . . . burns: The angel burns with the light
of his adoration of God.

He fills, He bounds, connects, and equals all.
  Cease then, nor order imperfection name:
Our proper bliss depends on what we blame. 180
Know thy own point:[35] this kind, this due degree
Of blindness, weakness, Heaven bestows on thee.
Submit, in this, or any other sphere,
Secure to be as blest as thou canst bear:
Safe in the hand of one Disposing Power, 185
Or in the natal, or the mortal hour.[36]
All Nature is but art, unknown to thee
All chance, direction, which thou canst not see;
All discord, harmony not understood;
All partial evil, universal good: 190
And, spite of pride, in erring reason's spite,
One truth is clear, Whatever is, is right.

II

  Know then thyself, presume not God to scan,
The proper study of mankind is man.
Placed on this isthmus of a middle state,
A being darkly wise, and rudely great:
With too much knowledge for the skeptic side, 5
With too much weakness for the stoic's pride,[37]
He hangs between; in doubt to act, or rest;
In doubt to deem himself a god, or beast;
In doubt his mind or body to prefer;
Born but to die, and reasoning but to err; 10
Alike in ignorance, his reason such,
Whether he thinks too little, or too much:
Chaos of Thought and Passion, all confused;
Still by himself abused[38] or disabused;
Created half to rise, and half to fall; 15
Great lord of all things, yet a prey to all;
Sole judge of truth, in endless error hurled:
The glory, jest, and riddle of the world!

✸ ✸ ✸

---

35 **thy own point:** your exact and proper place.
36 **Or . . . hour:** either at birth or at death.

37 **With . . . pride:** knowing too much to doubt, but too little to be proud.
38 **abused:** deceived.

THE ENLIGHTENMENT

Comment

In his temptation speech to Eve, as you will recall, Satan (disguised as a serpent) argues that since he, a beast, has attained the power of speech, so Eve "by proportion meet" will become a goddess if she eats the forbidden fruit. The same "proportion meet" is the basis of Pope's conception of order:

> Pride still is aiming at the blest abodes,
> Men would be angels, angels would be gods.
> Aspiring to be gods, if angels fell,
> Aspiring to be angels, men rebel:
> And who but wishes to invert the laws
> Of Order, sins against th' Eternal Cause.

The order of the great scale, the great chain, must be preserved at every degree, in every link. Milton tried to justify the ways of God to humankind by emphasizing one's individual act of aspiring beyond one's lot. But Pope vindicates the ways of God to humankind by emphasizing the universe, the vast chain of being, which Pope believes is threatened by the act of so aspiring. What are some features of the order that Pope sees as threatened by human pride?

1. Vastness: Locate a passage in which Pope is concerned with the scope—the extent—of the universe. What imagery does he use to make you aware of its size?
2. Fine details: Locate a passage—a line or two—in which Pope is concerned with a single "link" of the great chain and its relation to other links. What imagery does he use to make you aware of the detail of the universe?
3. Balance: Notice the balance that so often appears in a single line:

   "A mighty maze!" balanced with "but not without a plan" (l. 6)
   "The latent tracts" balanced with "the giddy heights" (l. 11)
   "poisonous herbs" balanced with "healing dew" (l. 118).

   Locate some other examples of this balancing of opposites in single lines and couplets.
4. On the one hand, Pope's conception of order involves "one stupendous whole"; on the other hand, it involves many "gradations just." Both features, the large and the small, reinforce Pope's insistence that every person must "Know thy own point."

   What seems to you the chief power of Pope's verse; that is, does it more effectively describe "nice dependencies" or "creation's ample range"? Explain your answer, using illustrations from the poem.
5. Write a short essay on "Pride" as Pope conceives of it in this poem. Do not simply restate his idea of pride; comment also on the way he expresses this idea.

ALEXANDER POPE

323

Images of Order
Summing Up

Here then are three great images of order from the literature of the Enlightenment: the progress of man through hardships on the road of life; the harmony that "quells" the strident emotions; and the great chain of being.

As you think back to the literature of the Renaissance, and particularly to *Macbeth* and *Paradise Lost*, what great dimension of experience present in that earlier literature do you find missing from—or at least not emphasized in—these images of order? How does the writer of the Enlightenment look upon conflict in human experience? How did the Renaissance writer look upon it?

The Study of Humankind

"THE PROPER STUDY of mankind is man," said Pope. In essays, in poems, and, as we shall later see, in novels, the writers of the Enlightenment addressed themselves to the characteristics and customs—to the manners—of their fellows. Some looked upon humankind with the eyes of an innocent observer who saw a great deal but did not harshly judge the follies that were found mingled with virtue. Others, however, of whom the greatest representative is Jonathan Swift, beneath an appearance of innocence, judged with great severity not only the follies but even some of the virtues of the world.

The Innocent Observer

Joseph Addison (1672-1719) and Richard Steele (1672-1729)

The two most popular essayists of the early 18th century were Joseph Addison and Richard Steele. Together they edited and wrote the two most famous periodicals of their day: *The Tatler*, which appeared three times a week from 1709 to 1711, and *The Spectator*, which appeared daily from 1711 to the end of 1712. Each issue of *The Spectator* contained a single essay, and each essay was designed to instruct its readers in some branch of "polite learning," in some matter of good taste, or in some question of moral behavior. There were essays on Milton's *Paradise Lost*, on gardens, on the theater, on general religious faith, on the unhappy practice of dueling, even on such philosophical subjects as the nature of the imagination. Some sense of the learning of these two writers is given us when we reflect that each essay originally had for its motto an appropriate quotation from a classical author in Latin or Greek. Addison and Steele

The title page of the collected edition of The Spectator *shows the members of the club.*

considered themselves reformers of public taste and manners, but their methods were gentle. Through the voice of "Mr. Spectator" particularly, they exposed affectations of all kinds with an innocent air that made their readers smile at their own weaknesses—and eagerly await the next lesson.

Addison, the author of three of the following essays, wrote prose that Dr. Johnson called "the model of the middle style . . . always equable, and always easy, without glowing words or pointed sentences." He was the son of an important clergyman, the Dean of Lichfield Cathedral, and was educated at Charterhouse, a famous London school, and at Oxford. After graduation he lived the life of an Oxford scholar and then entered public life as a writer for the Whig party. He became a member of Parliament and an undersecretary of state; yet he also wrote for the stage and for many years contributed heavily to the periodicals he managed with Steele.

Richard Steele, the son of a Dublin lawyer, also attended Charterhouse and Oxford, but he left the latter and entered the army. Compared to Addison's, his life was sometimes wild and turbulent, and his style is less easy and equable. The idea for the periodical essay was his, and somewhat more earnestly than Addison he was committed to his misson of improving his fellow countrymen's manners and tastes.

The selections which follow are all taken from *The Spectator.*

Mr. Spectator

Joseph Addison

I HAVE OBSERVED that a reader seldom peruses a book with pleasure until he knows whether the writer of it be a black or a fair man, of a mild or choleric disposition, married or a bachelor, with other particulars of the like nature that conduce very much to the right understanding of an author. To gratify this curiosity, which is so natural to a reader, I design this paper and my next as prefatory discourses to my following writings, and shall give some account in them of the several persons that are engaged in this work. As the chief trouble of compiling, digesting, and correcting will fall to my share, I must do myself the justice to open the work with my own history.

I was born to a small hereditary estate, which, according to the tradition of the village where it lies, was bounded by the same hedges and ditches in William the Conqueror's time that it is at present, and has been delivered down from father to son whole and entire, without the loss or acquisition of a single field or meadow, during the space of six hundred years. There runs a story in the family that when my mother was gone with child

of me about three months she dreamt that she was brought to bed of a judge.[1] Whether this might proceed from a lawsuit which was then depending in the family, or my father's being a Justice of the Peace, I cannot determine; for I am not so vain as to think it presaged any dignity that I should arrive at in my future life, though that was the interpretation which the neighborhood put upon it. The gravity of my behavior at my very first appearance in the world, and all the time that I sucked, seemed to favor my mother's dream; for, as she has often told me, I threw away my rattle before I was two months old, and would not make use of my coral[2] until they had taken away the bells from it.

As for the rest of my infancy, there being nothing in it remarkable, I shall pass it over in silence. I find that during my nonage I had the reputation of a very sullen youth, but was always a favorite of my schoolmaster, who used to say that my parts[3] were solid, and would wear well. I had not been long at the University before I distinguished myself by a most profound silence; for during the space of eight years, excepting in the public exercises of the college, I scarce uttered the quantity of a hundred words; and, indeed, do not remember that I ever spoke three sentences together in my whole life. Whilst I was in this learned body I applied myself with so much diligence to my studies, that there are very few celebrated books, either in the learned or the modern tongues, which I am not acquainted with.

Upon the death of my father I was resolved to travel into foreign countries,

1 **mother . . . judge:** My mother dreamed that the child she was about to have (myself) would become a judge.
2 **coral:** teething ring.
3 **parts:** faculties; native capacities.

THE ENLIGHTENMENT

A coffeehouse where men met to talk, read newspapers, smoke, and drink coffee. Addison and Steele would often be found at the coffeehouse known as Will's.

and therefore left the University with the character[4] of an odd, unaccountable fellow that had a great deal of learning, if I would but show it. An insatiable thirst after knowledge carried me into all the countries of Europe in which there was anything new or strange to be seen; nay, to such a degree was my curiosity raised, that having read the controversies of some great men concerning the antiquities of Egypt, I made a voyage to Grand Cairo on purpose to take the measure of a pyramid; and as soon as I had set myself right in that particular, returned to my native country with great satisfaction.

I have passed my latter years in this city, where I am frequently seen in most public places, though there are not

above half a dozen of my select friends that know me; of whom my next paper shall give a more particular account. There is no place of general resort wherein I do not often make my appearance; sometimes I am seen thrusting my head into a round of politicians at Will's,[5] and listening with great attention to the narratives that are made in those little circular audiences. Sometimes I smoke a pipe at Child's,[6] and whilst I seem attentive to nothing but the *Postman*, overhear the conversation of every table in the room. I appear on Sunday nights at St. James's Coffee-

---

4 character of: reputation of being.

5 Will's: a coffeehouse that in Dryden's time had become a resort for poets and wits.
6 Child's: a coffeehouse patronized by physicians, clergymen, and others who were likely to be conservatives in politics. The newspaper, the *Postman*, that Mr. Spectator reads there, however, supported the Whigs!

ADDISON AND STEELE

House,[7] and sometimes join the little committee of politics in the inner room, as one who comes there to hear and improve. My face is likewise very well known at the Grecian,[8] the Cocoa-Tree,[9] and in the theaters, both of Drury Lane and the Haymarket. I have been taken for a merchant upon the Exchange for above these ten years. . . . In short, wherever I see a cluster of people I always mix with them, though I never open my lips but in my own club.

Thus I live in the world rather as a spectator of mankind than as one of the species, by which means I have made myself a speculative[10] statesman, soldier, merchant, and artisan, without ever meddling with any practical part in life. I am very well versed in the theory of a husband, or a father, and can discern the errors in the economy, business, and diversion of others, better than those who are engaged in them, as standers-by discover blots which are apt to escape those who are in the game. I never espoused any party with violence, and am resolved to observe an exact neutrality between the Whigs and Tories, unless I shall be forced to declare myself by the hostilities of either side. In short, I have acted in all the parts of my life as a looker-on, which is the character I intend to preserve in this paper.

I have given the reader just so much of my history and character as to let him see I am not altogether unqualified for the business I have undertaken. As for other particulars in my life and adventures, I shall insert them in following papers as I shall see occasion. In the meantime, when I consider how much I have seen, read, and heard, I begin to blame my own taciturnity; and since I have neither time nor inclination to communicate the fullness of my heart in speech, I am resolved to do it in writing, and to print myself out, if possible, before I die. I have been often told by my friends that it is pity so many useful discoveries which I have made should be in the possession of a silent man. For this reason, therefore, I shall publish a sheetful of thoughts every morning, for the benefit of my contemporaries; and if I can any way contribute to the diversion or improvement of the country in which I live, I shall leave it, when I am summoned out of it, with the secret satisfaction of thinking that I have not lived in vain.

There are three very material points which I have not spoken to in this paper, and which, for several important reasons, I must keep to myself, at least for some time: I mean an account of my name, my age, and my lodgings. I must confess I would gratify my reader in anything that is reasonable; but as for these three particulars, though I am sensible they might tend very much to the embellishment of my paper, I cannot yet come to a resolution of communicating them to the public. They would indeed draw me out of that obscurity which I have enjoyed for many years, and expose me in public places to several salutes and civilities, which have been always very disagreeable to me; for the greatest pain I can suffer is the being talked to and being stared at. It is for this reason likewise that I keep my complexion and dress as very great secrets, though it is not impossible but I may make discoveries of both in the progress of the work I have undertaken.

After having been thus particular upon myself, I shall in tomorrow's paper

---

7 **St. James's Coffee-House:** patronized by the Whigs (then out of office).
8 **Grecian:** coffeehouse favored by lawyers and scholars.
9 **Cocoa-Tree:** chocolate house favored by the Tories.
10 **speculative:** theorizing.

give an account of those gentlemen who are concerned with me in this work. For, as I have before intimated, a plan of it is laid and concerted (as all other matters of importance are) in a club. However, as my friends have engaged me to stand in the front, those who have a mind to correspond with me may direct their letters to the Spectator, at Mr. Buckley's in Little Britain.[11] For I must further acquaint the reader, that though our club meets only on Tuesdays and Thursdays, we have appointed a committee to sit every night, for the inspection of all such papers as may contribute to the advancement of the public weal.

11 **Britain:** a street of booksellers and printers.

The Spectator Club

Richard Steele

THE FIRST of our society is a gentleman of Worcestershire, of ancient descent, a baronet, his name Sir Roger de Coverley. His great-grandfather was inventor of that famous country-dance which is called after him. All who know that shire are very well acquainted with the parts and merits of Sir Roger. He is a gentleman that is very singular in his behavior, but his singularities proceed from his good sense, and are contradictions to the manners of the world only as he thinks the world is in the wrong. However, this humor creates him no enemies, for he does nothing with sourness or obstinacy, and his being unconfined to modes and forms makes him but the readier and more capable to please and oblige all who know him. When he is in town he lives in Soho Square:[1] it is said he keeps himself a bachelor by reason[2] he was crossed in love by a perverse beautiful widow of the next county to him. Before this disappointment, Sir Roger was what you call a fine gentleman, had often supped with my Lord Rochester and Sir George Etherege,[3] fought a duel upon his first coming to town, and kicked Bully Dawson[4] in a public coffeehouse for calling him "youngster." But being ill-used by the above-mentioned widow, he was very serious for a year and a half; and though, his temper being naturally jovial, he at last got over it, he grew careless of himself, and never dressed afterwards; he continues to wear a coat and doublet of the same cut that were in fashion at the time of his repulse, which, in his merry humors, he tells us has been in and out[5] twelve times since he first wore it. . . . He is now in his fifty-sixth year, cheerful, gay, and hearty; keeps a good house both in town and country; a great lover of mankind; but there is such a mirthful cast in his behavior that he is rather beloved

1 **Soho Square:** then a fashionable suburb west of central London.
2 **by reason:** because.
3 **Lord . . . Etherege:** courtiers and writers of the Restoration.
4 **Dawson:** a notorious man about town.
5 **in and out:** i.e., of fashion.

than esteemed. His tenants grow rich, his servants look satisfied, all the young women profess love to him, and the young men are glad of his company. When he comes into a house he calls the servants by their names, and talks all the way upstairs to a visit. I must not omit that Sir Roger is a Justice of the Quorum;[6] that he fills the chair at a Quarter Session[7] with great abilities, and three months ago gained universal applause by explaining a passage in the Game Act.[8]

The gentleman next in esteem and authority among us is another bachelor, who is a member of the Inner Temple;[9] a man of great probity, wit, and understanding; but he has chosen his place of residence rather to obey the direction of an old humorsome father than in pursuit of his own inclinations. He was placed there to study the laws of the land, and is the most learned of any of the House in those of the stage. Aristotle and Longinus are much better understood by him than Littleton or Coke.[10] The father sends up every post questions relating to marriage-articles,[11] leases, and tenures in the neighborhood; all which questions he agrees with an attorney to answer and take care of in the lump.[12] He is studying the passions themselves when he should be inquiring into the debates among men which arise from them. He knows the argument of each of the orations of Demosthenes and Tully,[13] but not one case in the reports of our own courts. No one ever took him for a fool, but none, except his intimate friends, know he has a great deal of wit. This turn makes him at once both disinterested and agreeable. As few of his thoughts are drawn from business, they are most of them fit for conversation. His taste of books is a little too just[14] for the age he lives in; he has read all, but approves of very few. His familiarity with the customs, manners, actions, and writings of the ancients makes him a very delicate observer of what occurs to him in the present world. He is an excellent critic, and the time of the play is his hour of business; exactly at five he passes through New Inn, crosses through Russell Court, and takes a turn at Will's until the play begins. He has his shoes rubbed and his periwig powdered at the barber's as you go into the Rose.[15] It is for the good of the audience when he is at a play, for the actors have an ambition to please him.

The person of next consideration is Sir Andrew Freeport, a merchant of great eminence in the city[16] of London: a person of indefatigable industry, strong reason, and great experience. His notions of trade are noble and generous, and, as every rich man has usually some sly way of jesting which would make no great figure were he not a rich man, he calls the sea the British Common.[17] He is acquainted with commerce in all its parts, and will tell you that it is a stupid and barbarous

6 **Quorum:** one of a select group of justices of the peace who had to be present before certain courts could proceed.
7 **Quarter Session:** a county court.
8 **Game Act:** a complicated law setting forth the rights of hunters and the penalties for poaching.
9 **member . . . Temple:** i.e., a lawyer.
10 **Aristotle** (ăr′ə stŏt′əl) . . . **Coke:** He understands literature better than law. (Coke and Littleton were early legal authorities.)
11 **marriage-articles:** property arrangements made before a marriage.
12 **all . . . lump:** He pays another to do the legal work he should do himself.

13 **Demosthenes** (dĭ mŏs′thə nēz′) **and Tully** (tŭl′ĭ): Demosthenes was the most famous Greek orator; Tully (Cicero), the most famous Roman.
14 **just:** scrupulous; exact.
15 **Rose:** a tavern near the theaters of 18th-century London.
16 **city:** central financial district.
17 **Common:** land to which all members of a town have certain rights, but which is under the control of the lord of the manor.

THE ENLIGHTENMENT

way to extend dominion by arms; for true power is to be got by arts and industry. He will often argue, that if this part of our trade were well cultivated we should gain from one nation; and if another, from another. I have heard him prove that diligence makes more lasting acquisitions than valor, and that sloth has ruined more nations than the sword. He abounds in several frugal maxims, among which the greatest favorite is "A penny saved is a penny got." A general trader of good sense is pleasanter company than a general scholar; and Sir Andrew having a natural unaffected eloquence, the perspicuity of his discourse gives the same pleasure that wit would in another man. He has made his fortunes himself, and says that England may be richer than other kingdoms by as plain methods as he himself is richer than other men; though at the same time I can say this of him, that there is not a point in the compass but blows home a ship in which he is an owner.

Next to Sir Andrew in the clubroom sits Captain Sentry, a gentleman of great courage, good understanding, but invincible modesty. He is one of those that deserve very well, but are very awkward at putting their talents within the observation of such as should take notice of them. He was some years a captain, and behaved himself with great gallantry in several engagements and at several sieges; but having a small estate of his own, and being next heir to Sir Roger, he has quitted a way of life in which no man can rise suitably to his merit who is not something of a courtier as well as a soldier. I have heard him often lament that, in a profession where merit is placed in so conspicuous a view, impudence should get the better of modesty. When he has talked to this purpose I never heard him make a

sour expression, but frankly confess that he left the world because he was not fit for it. A strict honesty, and an even, regular behavior are in themselves obstacles to him that must press through crowds who endeavor at the same end with himself, the favor of a commander. He will, however, in his way of talk excuse generals for not disposing according to men's desert, or inquiring into it; "For," says he, "that great man who has a mind to help me has as many to break through to come at me as I have to come at him." Therefore he will conclude that the man who would make a figure, especially in a military way, must get over all false modesty, and assist his patron against the importunity of other pretenders by a proper assurance in his own vindication. He says it is a civil cowardice to be backward in asserting what you ought to expect, as it is a military fear to be slow in attacking when it is your duty. With this candor does the gentleman speak of himself and others. The same frankness runs through all his conversation. The military part of his life has furnished him with many adventures, in the relation of which he is very agreeable to the company; for he is never overbearing, though accustomed to command men in the utmost degree below him; nor ever too obsequious, from a habit of obeying men highly above him.

But that our society may not appear a set of humorists[18] unacquainted with the gallantries and pleasures of the age, we have among us the gallant Will Honeycomb, a gentleman who according to his years should be in the decline of his life, but having ever been very careful of his person, and always had a very easy fortune, time has made

18 **humorists:** eccentric people.

but very little impression, either by wrinkles on his forehead or traces in his brain. His person is well turned, of a good height. He is very ready at that sort of discourse with which men usually entertain women. He has all his life dressed very well, and remembers habits as others do men. He can smile when one speaks to him, and laughs easily. He knows the history of every mode, and can inform you from which of the French king's wenches our wives and daughters had this manner of curling their hair, that way of placing their hoods; whose frailty was covered by such a sort of petticoat, and whose vanity to show her foot made that part of the dress so short in such a year. In a word, all his conversation and knowledge has been in the female world: as other men of his age will take notice to you what such a minister[19] said upon such and such an occasion, he will tell you when the Duke of Monmouth danced at court such a woman was then smitten, another was taken with him at the head of his troop in the Park. In all these important relations, he has ever about the same time received a kind glance or a blow of a fan from some celebrated beauty, mother of the present Lord such-a-one. If you speak of a young Commoner that said a lively thing in the House, he starts up, "He has good blood in his veins, Tom Mirabell begot him, the rogue cheated me in that affair; that young fellow's mother used me more like a dog than any woman I ever made

advances to." This way of talking of his very much enlivens the conversation among us of a more sedate turn; and I find there is not one of the company but myself, who rarely speak at all, but speaks of him as of that sort of man who is usually called a well-bred fine gentleman. To conclude his character, where women are not concerned he is an honest worthy man.

I cannot tell whether I am to account him whom I am next to speak of as one of our company, for he visits us but seldom, but when he does it adds to every man else a new enjoyment of himself. He is a clergyman, a very philosophic man, of general learning, great sanctity of life, and the most exact good breeding. He has the misfortune to be of a very weak constitution, and consequently cannot accept of such cares and business as preferments in his function[20] would oblige him to; he is therefore among divines[21] what a chamber-counselor[22] is among lawyers. The probity of his mind and the integrity of his life create him followers, as being eloquent or loud advances others. He seldom introduces the subject he speaks upon; but we are so far gone in years that he observes, when he is among us, an earnestness to have him fall on some divine topic, which he always treats with much authority, as one who has no interests in this world, as one who is hastening to the object of all his wishes, and conceives hope from his decays and infirmities. These are my ordinary companions.

---

19 minister: head of a government department.
20 preferments in his function: higher ecclesiastical office.

21 divines: theologians; clergymen.
22 chamber-counselor: lawyer who gives opinions in private, not in court.

Sir Roger in Church

Joseph Addison

I AM ALWAYS very well pleased with a country Sunday: and think, if keeping holy the seventh day were only a human institution, it would be the best method that could have been thought of for the polishing and civilizing of mankind. It is certain the country people would soon degenerate into a kind of savages and barbarians, were there not such frequent returns of a stated time, in which the whole village meet together with their best faces, and in their cleanliest habits, to converse with one another upon indifferent[1] subjects, hear their duties explained to them, and join together in adoration of the Supreme Being. Sunday clears away the rust of the whole week, not only as it refreshes in their minds the notions of religion, but as it puts both the sexes upon appearing in their most agreeable forms, and exerting all such qualities as are apt to give them a figure in the eye of the village. A country fellow distinguishes himself as much in the churchyard, as a citizen does upon the 'Change;[2] the whole parish politics being generally discussed in that place either after sermon or before the bell rings.

My friend Sir Roger being a good Churchman, has beautified the inside of his church with several texts of his own choosing: he has likewise given a handsome pulpit-cloth, and railed in the communion-table at his own expense. He has often told me, that at his coming to his estate he found his parishioners very irregular; and that in order to make them kneel and join in the responses, he gave every one of them a hassock[3] and a Common Prayer-Book; and at the same time employed an itinerant singing-master, who goes about the country for that purpose, to instruct them rightly in the tunes of the Psalms; upon which they now very much value themselves, and indeed outdo most of the country churches that I have ever heard.

As Sir Roger is landlord to the whole congregation, he keeps them in very good order, and will suffer nobody to sleep in it besides himself; for if by chance he has been surprised into a short nap at sermon, upon recovering out of it he stands up and looks about him, and if he sees anybody else nodding, either wakes them himself, or sends his servant to them. Several other of the old knight's particularities break out upon these occasions: sometimes he will be lengthening out a verse, in the singing Psalms, half a minute after the rest of the congregation have done with it; sometimes, when he is pleased with the matter of his devotion, he pronounces "Amen!" three or four times to the same prayer; and

1 indifferent: various.

2 'Change: Royal Exchange, a commercial center in London.
3 hassock: a small cushion to kneel on.

sometimes stands up when everybody else is upon their knees, to count the congregation, or see if any of his tenants are missing.

I was yesterday very much surprised to hear my old friend, in the midst of the service, calling out to one John Matthews to mind what he was about, and not disturb the congregation. This John Matthews, it seems, is remarkable for being an idle fellow, and at that time was kicking his heels for his diversion. This authority of the knight, though exerted in that odd manner which accompanies him in all circumstances of life, has a very good effect upon the parish, who are not polite enough to see anything ridiculous in his behavior; besides that, the general good sense and worthiness of his character, make his friends observe these little singularities as foils that rather set off than blemish his good qualities.

As soon as the sermon is finished, nobody presumes to stir till Sir Roger is gone out of the church. The knight walks down from his seat in the chancel[4] between a double row of his tenants, that stand bowing to him on each side; and every now and then inquires how such an one's wife, or mother, or son, or father do whom he does not see at church; which is understood as a secret reprimand to the person that is absent.

The chaplain has often told me, that upon a catechizing[5] day, when Sir Roger has been pleased with a boy that answers well, he has ordered a Bible to be given him next day for his encouragement; and sometimes accompanies it with a flitch[6] of bacon to his mother. Sir Roger has likewise added five pounds a year to the clerk's place;[7] and that he may encourage the young fellows to make themselves perfect in the Church service, has promised upon the death of the present incumbent, who is very old, to bestow it according to merit.

The fair understanding between Sir Roger and his chaplain, and their mutual concurrence in doing good, is the more remarkable, because the very next village is famous for the differences and contentions that rise between the parson and the squire, who live in a perpetual state of war. The parson is always preaching at the squire, and the squire, to be revenged on the parson, never comes to church. The squire has made all his tenants atheists and tithe-stealers: while the parson instructs them every Sunday in the dignity of his order, and insinuates to them in almost every sermon, that he is a better man than his patron. In short, matters are come to such an extremity, that the squire has not said his prayers either in public or private this half year; and that the parson threatens him, if he does not mend his manners, to pray for him in the face of the whole congregation.

Feuds of this nature, though too frequent in the country, are very fatal to the ordinary people; who are so used to be dazzled with riches, that they pay as much deference to the understanding of a man of an estate, as of a man of learning; and are very hardly brought to regard any truth, how important soever it may be, that is preached to them, when they know there are several men of five hundred a year who do not believe it.

---

4 **chancel** (chăn′səl): part of the church east of the nave, including the choir and the sanctuary. The knight sits "up front."
5 **catechizing day:** when children recite the parts of the church's teaching they are expected to have memorized.

6 **flitch:** side.
7 **place:** office; job.

A Young Lady of Fashion

Joseph Addison

THE JOURNAL[1] with which I presented my reader on Tuesday last has brought me in several letters with account of many private lives cast into that form. I have the "Rake's Journal," the "Sot's Journal," and among several others a very curious piece entitled "The Journal of a Mohock."[2] By these instances I find that the intention of my last Tuesday's paper has been mistaken by many of my readers. I did not design so much to expose vice as idleness, and aimed at those persons who pass away their time rather in trifle and impertinence than in crimes and immoralities. Offenses of this latter kind are not to be dallied with, or treated in so ludicrous a manner. In short, my journal only holds up folly to the light, and shows the disagreeableness of such actions as are indifferent in themselves, and blamable only as they proceed from creatures endowed with reason.

1 **The journal:** The "journal," or diary, was that of a "sober citizen" who was "of greater consequence in his own thoughts than in the eye of the world."
2 **Mohock:** hoodlums who made early 18th-century London dangerous at night.

My following correspondent, who calls herself Clarinda, is such a journalist as I require: she seems by her letter to be placed in a modish state of indifference between vice and virtue, and to be susceptible of either were there proper pains taken with her. Had her journal been filled with gallantries, or such occurrences as had shown her wholly divested of her natural innocence, notwithstanding it might have been more pleasing to the generality of readers, I should not have published it; but as it is only the picture of a life filled with a fashionable kind of gaiety and laziness, I shall set down five days of it as I have received it from the hand of my fair correspondent:—

"DEAR MR. SPECTATOR,

"You having set your readers an exercise in one of your last week's papers, I have performed mine according to your orders, and herewith send it you enclosed. You must know, Mr. Spectator, that I am a maiden lady of a good fortune, who have had several matches offered me for these ten years last past, and have at present warm applications made to me by a very pretty fellow. As I am at my own disposal, I come up to town every winter, and pass my time in it after the manner you will find in the following journal, which I began to write upon the very day after your *Spectator* upon that subject:—

TUESDAY *night.*—Could not go to sleep till one in the morning for thinking of my journal.

WEDNESDAY (*from eight till ten*).— Drank two dishes of chocolate in bed, and fell asleep after them.

From ten to eleven.—Ate a slice of bread and butter; drank a dish of bohea:[3] read the *Spectator*.

3 **dish of bohea:** cup of tea.

In the Grand Pump Room at Bath, a fashionable watering place of the 18th-century. Here the master of ceremonies introduces a partner to a wallflower.

From eleven to one.—At my toilet; tried a new head;[4] gave orders for Veny[5] to be combed and washed. *Mem.:*[6] I look best in blue.

From one till half-an-hour after two. —Drove to the 'Change. Cheapened[7] a couple of fans.

Till four.—At dinner. *Mem.:* Mr. Froth passed by in his new liveries.

From four to six.—Dressed; paid a visit to old Lady Blithe and her sister, having before heard they were gone out of town that day.

From six to eleven.—At basset.[8] *Mem.:* Never set again upon the ace of diamonds.

THURSDAY (*from eleven at night to eight in the morning*).—Dreamed that I punted to[9] Mr. Froth.

From eight to ten.—Chocolate. Read two acts in *Aurengzebe*[10] abed.

From ten to eleven.—Tea table. Sent to borrow Lady Faddle's Cupid for Veny. Read the playbills. Received a letter from Mr. Froth. *Mem.:* Locked it up in my strongbox.

Rest of the morning.—Fontange, the tirewoman,[11] her account of my Lady Blithe's wash. Broke a tooth in my little tortoise-shell comb. Sent Frank to know how my Lady Hectic rested after her monkey's leaping out at window. Looked pale. Fontange tells me

4 **head:** headdress.
5 **Veny:** her lap dog.
6 **Mem:** This frequently repeated word means "This is important; remember it."
7 **cheapened:** bargained with a shopkeeper for.
8 **basset:** a card game.

9 **punted to:** played cards with.
10 **Aurengzebe** (ôr′əng zēb′): a play by Dryden.
11 **Fontange, the tirewoman:** a famous French hair stylist.

my glass is not true. Dressed by three.

From three to four.—Dinner cold before I sat down.

From four to eleven.—Saw company. Mr. Froth's opinion of Milton. His account of the Mohocks. His fancy for a pincushion. Picture in the lid of his snuffbox. Old Lady Faddle promises me her woman to cut my hair. Lost five guineas at crimp.[12]

Twelve o'clock at night.—Went to bed.

FRIDAY, *eight in the morning.*—Abed. Read over all Mr. Froth's letters. Cupid and Veny.

Ten o'clock.—Stayed within all day; not at home.

From ten to twelve.—In conference with my mantua-maker.[13] Sorted a suit of ribbons. Broke my blue china cup.

From twelve to one.—Shut myself up in my chamber, practiced Lady Betty Modely's scuttle.[14]

One in the afternoon.—Called for my flowered handkerchief. Worked half a violet leaf in it. Eyes ached, and head out of order. Threw by my work, and read over the remaining part of *Aurengzebe.*

From three to four.—Dined.

From four to twelve.—Changed my mind, dressed, went abroad, and played at crimp until midnight. Found Mrs. Spitely at home. Conversation. Mrs. Brilliant's necklace false stones. Old Lady Loveday going to be married to a young fellow that is not worth a groat.[15] Miss Prue gone into the country. Tom Townly has red hair. *Mem.:* Mrs. Spitely whispered in my ear that she had something to tell me about Mr. Froth. I am sure it is not true.

Between twelve and one.—Dreamed that Mr. Froth lay at my feet, and called me Indamora.[16]

SATURDAY.—Rose at eight o'clock in the morning. Sat down to my toilet.

From eight to nine.—Shifted a patch[17] for half an hour before I could determine it. Fixed it above my left eyebrow.

From nine to twelve.—Drank my tea, and dressed.

From twelve to two.—At chapel. A great deal of good company. *Mem.:* The third air in the new opera. Lady Blithe dressed frightfully.

From three to four.—Dined. Miss Kitty called upon me to go to the opera before I was risen from the table.

From dinner to six.—Drank tea. Turned off[18] a footman for being rude to Veny.

Six o'clock.—Went to the opera. I did not see Mr. Froth till the beginning of the second act. Mr. Froth talked to a gentleman in a black wig. Bowed to a lady in the front box. Mr. Froth and his friend clapped Nicolini[19] in the third act. Mr. Froth cried out "Ancora!"[20] Mr. Froth led me to my chair. I think he squeezed my hand.

Eleven at night.—Went to bed. Melancholy dreams. Methought Nicolini said he was Mr. Froth.

SUNDAY.—Indisposed.

MONDAY, *eight o'clock.*—Waked by Miss Kitty. *Aurengzebe* lay upon the chair by me. Kitty repeated without book the eight best lines in the play. Went in our mobs[21] to the dumb man, according to appointment. Told me

---

16 **Indamora:** the heroine of Dryden's play.
17 **patch:** "beauty-patch" of black material often in the shape of a heart.
18 **Turned off:** got rid of; fired.
19 **Nicolini:** a famous Italian singer.
20 **Ancora:** Mr. Froth shows off his not very expert Italian in calling for "More."
21 **mobs:** caps with ribbons under the chin.

---

12 **crimp:** still another card game.
13 **mantua-maker:** dressmaker.
14 **scuttle:** mannered, rapid walk.
15 **not . . . groat:** "not worth a dime."

that my lover's name began with a *G*. *Mem.:* The conjurer was within a letter of Mr. Froth's name, etc.

"Upon looking back into this my journal, I find that I am at a loss to know whether I pass my time well or ill; and indeed never thought of considering how I did it, before I perused your speculation upon that subject. I scarce find a single action in these five days that I can thoroughly approve of, except the working upon the violet leaf, which I am resolved to finish the first day I am at leisure. As for Mr. Froth and Veny, I did not think they took up so much of my time and thoughts, as I find they do upon my journal. The latter of them I will turn off if you insist upon it; and if Mr. Froth does not bring matters to a conclusion very suddenly, I will not let my life run away in a dream.
    Your humble Servant,
            CLARINDA."

To resume one of the morals of my first paper, and to confirm Clarinda in her good inclinations, I would have her consider what a pretty figure she would make among posterity, were the history of her whole life published like these five days of it. I shall conclude my paper with an epitaph written by an uncertain author[22] on Sir Philip Sidney's sister, a lady who seems to have been of a temper very much different from that of Clarinda. The last thought of it is so very noble, that I dare say my reader will pardon me the quotation.

ON THE COUNTESS DOWAGER OF PEMBROKE

Underneath this marble hearse
Lies the subject of all verse,
Sidney's sister, Pembroke's mother;
Death, ere thou hast killed another,
Fair and learned, and good as she,
Time shall throw a dart at thee.

22 uncertain author: possibly the 17th-century poet Ben Jonson.

Comment

"There is no place of general resort wherein I do not often make my appearance," says the Spectator, but his appearance never can be identified. He is an anonymous guardian of manners who may be anywhere; his presence reminded those who knew of him that awkwardness and affectation might be almost as ridiculous as Lord Chesterfield would make them a little later in the century. But the presence of the Spectator encouraged a quality that Chesterfield knew little about: the 18th-century name for it is "good nature." The good-natured man is easy, tolerant, and not excessively formal. Addison and Steele were interested in manners, but they did not prescribe rules for them. By the art of the essay, rather, they tried to encourage the easiness and good nature that appears in the style of their paper.

1. Mr. Spectator. What sort of character is he? What sort of man would go to Egypt for the express purpose of measuring the pyramids? What is "odd" and "unaccountable" about him? But what is also very conventional about him? And why does he keep his "complexion and dress as very great secrets"? Why must he remain anonymous?

2. The Spectator Club. The members differ from each other, but what do they have in common? From what "station in life," or position in society, do they seem to you to come? Of which members of the Club does the Spectator most approve? Which does he criticize, however mildly? When you compare this little group with the band of Chaucer's pilgrims, what great difference (besides that of number) do you see?

3. Sir Roger in Church. What clumsiness does the Spectator see in the behavior of the knight here? But what gentleness does he also see? Consider the last sentence of this essay. What does it tell us about the values of the Spectator?

4. A Young Lady of Fashion. As you read the Spectator's last words in this essay, and the little poem with which he closes, what attitude do you take toward the frivolities you have seen in such detail? Do you scorn and despise the young lady? Or do you find yourself taking some other attitude?

5. What can you conclude about the audience for whom these essays were designed? What would their interest in them be, week after week? How would you expect them to differ from the audience of Bacon's *Essays?* Write a paragraph describing the audience that you infer Mr. Spectator was most interested in reaching and in pleasing.

Alexander Pope
The Rape of the Lock

You have already seen Pope occupied with human pride. His subject here is less grave. Sometime in the early 18th century, one Miss Arabella Fermor had a lock of hair snipped from her elegant headdress by an impetuous young baron. Partly because he was amused by the incident and partly to smooth the ruffled feelings of Miss Fermor's family, Pope wrote a mock epic, *The Rape of the Lock*. It was a mock epic, like Chaucer's tale of Chanticleer and Pertelote, because it treated a private, domestic matter with an elaborate, formal gravity that could be proper only for a large public occasion. The following short selection from *The Rape of the Lock* describes Belinda, the heroine, as she sits at her dressing table, attended by her maid, putting her hair and face in order for the day. The dressing table and all its mysterious charms and magic wands of beauty—her cosmetics—stand "unveiled." Like a true epic heroine, she is surrounded by a cloud of guardian spirits invisible to all save us. They do not warn her, and thus she does not know that her preparations are for a day of woe.

from The Rape of the Lock

The Dressing Table

Alexander Pope

Each silver vase in mystic order laid.
First, robed in white, the nymph intent adores,
With head uncovered, the cosmetic powers.
A heav'nly image in the glass appears,
To that she bends, to that her eye she rears;   5
Th' inferior priestess,[1] at her altar's side,
Trembling, begins the sacred rites of pride.
Unnumbered treasures ope at once, and here
The various offerings of the world appear;
From each she nicely culls with curious toil,   10
And decks the goddess with the glitt'ring spoil.
This casket India's glowing gems unlocks,
And all Arabia[2] breathes from yonder box.
The tortoise here and elephant unite,
Transformed to combs, the speckled and the white.   15
Here files of pins extend their shining rows,
Puffs, powders, patches, Bibles, billet-doux.[3]
Now awful beauty puts on all its arms;
The fair each moment rises in her charms,
Repairs her smiles, awakens every grace,   20
And calls forth all the wonders of her face:
Sees by degrees a purer blush arise,
And keener lightnings quicken in her eyes.
The busy sylphs[4] surround their darling care,
These set the head, and those divide the hair,   25
Some fold the sleeve, while others plait the gown;
And Betty's praised for labors not her own.

1 **priestess:** Betty, the maid.
2 **Arabia:** where the richest perfumes came from.
3 **billet-doux** (bill-ay-doo′): love letters.
4 **sylphs:** host of guardian spirits with which Pope surrounded his heroine.

Comment

The scene is one which might serve for Addison's young lady of fashion. But Pope is more general than Addison: he starts from a particular incident, but he turns it into a commentary on the general fashions of his day. What kind of comment is he making?

1. "Now awful beauty puts on all its arms," Pope writes (l. 18). What is the image here that describes the "nymph"—the young lady at her dressing table? Who is usually "awful" with "arms"? But is there a sense in which this image is appropriate in describing a young lady of fashion? (For example, what do we mean when we use the expression "dressed to kill"?)

2. Find another expression in the passage which at first seems to you to talk about dressing up, making up, in exaggerated language. How is it exaggerated? But how is it appropriate?

3. From this analysis what do you conclude Pope thought about the manners of his day—especially those of women? Has he a keener eye than Addison? Is he a more severe judge? Explain your answers by reference to the poem and the essays.

Oliver Goldsmith (1728-1774)

It is said that upon the news of the death of Oliver Goldsmith, the great orator Edmund Burke burst into tears, and Sir Joshua Reynolds, the great English painter, threw down his brush for the day. Goldsmith was the friend of Dr. Johnson and of the leading wits of his day, yet for much of his life he was a mere hack-writer, turning out anything the publishers thought would sell and carelessly squandering the results of the successes he achieved. He was born in Ireland and attended Trinity College, Dublin, as a "sizar" or scholarship student. Handicapped by his poverty, indecisive about his career, he apparently threw away his chances of joining the clergy by showing up in scarlet breeches when he was to be examined by a bishop. He studied medicine for a time in Edinburgh and then again at Leyden in Holland. But he evidently gave up all hope of a degree and set off on a tour of Europe, on foot, playing his flute for his dinners. He returned to England in 1756, and after a period of great poverty settled down to writing.

He wrote histories—of England, of Greece, of Rome. He wrote popular science, journalistic essays, and poetry. He revived the kind of polite essay that Addison and Steele had earlier made so popular. His one novel, *The Vicar of Wakefield*, has charmed readers since the day it was published. His best poem, *The Deserted Village*, laments the passing of the small village farmer.

She Stoops to Conquer

Goldsmith was also a dramatist. His first play, a comedy, *The Good Natur'd Man*, was an immediate success when it appeared in 1768. The theater into which it came was largely dominated by sentimental comedies—plays in which characters were either absurdly good or absurdly bad, and in which improbable plots were always arranged so that the good would triumph. In his essays Goldsmith had made fun of such plays; and in *She Stoops to Conquer*, his second comedy, produced in 1773, he virtually drove them off the stage.

The London theater had been through many changes of fashion since the great age of Shakespeare. In 1642, with the beginning of the Civil War, the theaters were closed. When they reopened at the Restoration, in 1660, the reigning fashion was the heroic play, an extravagant spectacle usually set in some remote land such as Mexico and with a warrior-hero whose deeds rivaled those of Homer's Achilles. Later in the Restoration period there began to appear plays about the manners of contemporary life, the comedy of manners. And it was to the comedy of manners that Goldsmith and others returned, in reaction against the sentimental fashion that had for some fifty years replaced it.

One of the settings for The Empress of Morocco, *1673, a highly spectacular Restoration play. The stage has become a three-sided room with an arch at the front called the proscenium arch; the illusion of depth is given by the use of a painted backdrop.*

She Stoops to Conquer is a comedy of manners written exclusively to amuse. Its characters are not vicious nor are they heroic. It concerns itself with a situation involving no very important people, as does *Macbeth,* but involving people from the "gentry" and from the lower classes. It makes comedy out of the manners of that very class of people whom Addison and Steele had set out to educate in their essays. No one is very wicked, no one is violently heroic; but everyone contributes to the humor that arises from the perpetration of blunder after blunder. Blunders are not crimes, but they are exposures of weakness and folly. No reader can miss the amusement that the opposing characters evoke—Tony as opposed to his mother, Mr. Hardcastle as opposed to Marlow, Kate Hardcastle herself as opposed to Kate Hardcastle in her role as barmaid. The substance of the play is the difference between the way people "really" act and the way they act when they put on false manners. It is a theme that has delighted audiences for almost two hundred years.

OLIVER GOLDSMITH

She Stoops to Conquer

or

The Mistakes of a Night

Oliver Goldsmith

DRAMATIS PERSONAE

MR. HARDCASTLE, *a country squire.*

MRS. HARDCASTLE, *his wife.*

MISS KATE HARDCASTLE, *their daughter.*

TONY LUMPKIN, *Mrs. Hardcastle's son by her first marriage.*

MISS CONSTANCE NEVILLE, *Mrs. Hardcastle's niece.*

DIGGORY, *a servant in the Hardcastle home.*

SIR CHARLES MARLOW, *an old friend of Mr. Hardcastle.*

Young CHARLES MARLOW, *his son.*

Young HASTINGS, *a friend of young Marlow.*

LANDLORD *at an inn, a* MAID, SERVANTS, *etc.*

ACT I

Scene I. *A chamber in an old-fashioned house.* ,

Enter MRS. HARDCASTLE *and* MR. HARDCASTLE.

MRS. HARDCASTLE. I vow, Mr. Hardcastle, you're very particular. Is there a creature in the whole country but ourselves that does not take a trip to town now and then, to rub off the rust a little? There's the two Miss Hoggs, and our neighbor Mrs. Grigsby, go to take a month's polishing every winter.

HARDCASTLE. Ay, and bring back vanity and affectation to last them the whole year. I wonder why London cannot keep its own fools at home! In my time, the follies of the town crept slowly among us, but now they travel faster than a stagecoach. Its fopperies come down not only as inside passengers, but in the very basket.[1]

MRS. HARDCASTLE. Ay, your times were fine times indeed; you have been telling us of them for many a long year. Here we live in an old rumbling mansion, that looks for all the world like an inn, but that we never see company. Our best visitors are old Mrs. Oddfish, the curate's wife, and little Cripplegate, the lame dancing master; and all our entertainment your old stories of Prince Eugene and the Duke of Marlborough.[2] I hate such old-fashioned trumpery.

1 the very basket: outside compartment of a stagecoach.
2 Prince Eugene . . . Duke of Marlborough: commanders of the Austrian and English armies who together defeated the French at the famous Battle of Blenheim (1704) in the War of the Spanish Succession.

HARDCASTLE. And I love it. I love everything that's old: old friends, old times, old manners, old books, old wine; and I believe, Dorothy (*taking her hand*), you'll own I have been pretty fond of an old wife.

MRS. HARDCASTLE. Lord, Mr. Hardcastle, you're forever at your Dorothys and your old wifes. You may be a Darby, but I'll be no Joan,[3] I promise you. I'm not so old as you'd make me, by more than one good year. Add twenty to twenty, and make money of that.

HARDCASTLE. Let me see; twenty added to twenty makes just fifty and seven.

MRS. HARDCASTLE. It's false, Mr. Hardcastle; I was but twenty when I was brought to bed of Tony, that I had by Mr. Lumpkin, my first husband; and he's not come to years of discretion yet.

HARDCASTLE. Nor ever will, I dare answer for him. Ay, you have taught him finely.

MRS. HARDCASTLE. No matter. Tony Lumpkin has a good fortune. My son is not to live by his learning. I don't think a boy wants much learning to spend fifteen hundred a year.

HARDCASTLE. Learning, quotha![4] a mere composition of tricks and mischief.

MRS. HARDCASTLE. Humor, my dear; nothing but humor. Come, Mr. Hardcastle, you must allow the boy a little humor.

HARDCASTLE. I'd sooner allow him a horsepond.[5] If burning the footmen's shoes, frighting the maids, and worrying the kittens be humor, he has it. It was but yesterday he fastened my wig to the back of my chair, and when I went to make a bow, I popped my bald head in Mrs. Frizzle's face.

MRS. HARDCASTLE. And am I to blame? The poor boy was always too sickly to do any good. A school would be his death. When he comes to be a little stronger, who knows what a year or two's Latin may do for him?

HARDCASTLE. Latin for him! A cat and fiddle. No, no; the alehouse and the stable are the only schools he'll ever go to.

MRS. HARDCASTLE. Well, we must not snub the poor boy now, for I believe we sha'n't have him long among us. Anybody that looks in his face may see he's consumptive.

HARDCASTLE. Ay, if growing too fat be one of the symptoms.

MRS. HARDCASTLE. He coughs sometimes.

HARDCASTLE. Yes, when his liquor goes the wrong way.

MRS. HARDCASTLE. I'm actually afraid of his lungs.

HARDCASTLE. And, truly, so am I; for he sometimes whoops like a speaking trumpet. (TONY *hallooing behind the scenes.*) Oh, there he goes—a very consumptive figure, truly.

Enter TONY, *crossing the stage.*

MRS. HARDCASTLE. Tony, where are you going, my charmer? Won't you give Papa and I a little of your company, lovee?

TONY. I'm in haste, Mother; I cannot stay.

MRS. HARDCASTLE. You sha'n't venture out this raw evening, my dear; you look most shockingly.

TONY. I can't stay, I tell you. The Three Pigeons expects me down every moment. There's some fun going forward.

HARDCASTLE. Ay; the alehouse, the old place; I thought so.

---

3 **Darby . . . Joan:** names traditionally used for an elderly husband and wife who are devoted to each other.
4 **quotha** (kwō′thə)**:** indeed!
5 **allow him a horsepond:** allow him to be ducked in a horsepond.

MRS. HARDCASTLE. A low, paltry set of fellows.

TONY. Not so low, neither. There's Dick Muggins, the exciseman; Jack Slang, the horse doctor; little Aminadab, that grinds the music box;[6] and Tom Twist, that spins the pewter platter.

MRS. HARDCASTLE. Pray, my dear, disappoint them for one night, at least.

TONY. As for disappointing them, I should not so much mind; but I can't abide to disappoint myself.

MRS. HARDCASTLE (*detaining him*). You sha'n't go.

TONY. I will, I tell you.

MRS. HARDCASTLE. I say you sha'n't.

TONY. We'll see which is strongest, you or I.

(*Exit, hauling her out.*)

HARDCASTLE (*alone*). Ay, there goes a pair that only spoil each other. But is not the whole age in a combination to drive sense and discretion out of doors? There's my pretty darling Kate; the fashions of the times have almost infected her, too. By living a year or two in town, she's as fond of gauze and French frippery as the best of them.

Enter KATE HARDCASTLE.

HARDCASTLE. Blessings on my pretty innocence! dressed out as usual, my Kate. Goodness! What a quantity of superfluous silk hast thou got about thee, girl! I could never teach the fools of this age that the indigent world could be clothed out of the trimmings of the vain.

KATE. You know our agreement, sir. You allow me the morning to receive and pay visits, and to dress in my own manner; and in the evening I put on my housewife's dress to please you.

HARDCASTLE. Well, remember, I insist on the terms of our agreement; and, by-the-bye, I believe I shall have occasion to try your obedience this very evening.

KATE. I protest, sir, I don't comprehend your meaning.

HARDCASTLE. Then, to be plain with you, Kate, I expect the young gentleman I have chosen to be your husband from town this very day. I have his father's letter, in which he informs me his son is set out, and that he intends to follow himself shortly after.

KATE. Indeed! I wish I had known something of this before. Bless me, how shall I behave? It's a thousand to one I sha'n't like him; our meeting will be so formal, and so like a thing of business, that I shall find no room for friendship or esteem.

HARDCASTLE. Depend upon it, child, I'll never control your choice: but Mr. Marlow, whom I have pitched upon,[7] is the son of my old friend Sir Charles Marlow, of whom you have heard me talk so often. The young gentleman has been bred a scholar, and is designed for an employment in the service of his country. I am told he's a man of an excellent understanding.

KATE. Is he?

HARDCASTLE. Very generous.

KATE. I believe I shall like him.

HARDCASTLE. Young and brave.

KATE. I'm sure I shall like him.

HARDCASTLE. And very handsome.

KATE. My dear Papa, say no more (*kissing his hand*); he's mine; I'll have him.

HARDCASTLE. And, to crown all, Kate, he's one of the most bashful and reserved young fellows in all the world.

KATE. Eh! you have frozen me to death again. That word *reserved* has undone all the rest of his accomplishments. A reserved lover, it is said, always makes a suspicious husband.

---

6 grinds . . . box: plays a barrel organ.

7 pitched upon: selected.

HARDCASTLE. On the contrary, modesty seldom resides in a breast that is not enriched with nobler virtues. It was the very feature in his character that first struck me.

KATE. He must have more striking features to catch me, I promise you. However, if he be so young, so handsome, and so everything as you mention, I believe he'll do still. I think I'll have him.

HARDCASTLE. Ay, Kate, but there is still an obstacle. It's more than an even wager he may not have you.

KATE. My dear Papa, why will you mortify one so? Well, if he refuses, instead of breaking my heart at his indifference, I'll only break my glass[8] for its flattery, set my cap to some newer fashion,[9] and look out for some less difficult admirer.

HARDCASTLE. Bravely resolved! In the meantime, I'll go prepare the servants for his reception: as we seldom see company, they want as much training as a company of recruits the first day's muster. (*Exit.*)

KATE (*alone*). Lud,[10] this news of Papa's puts me all in a flutter. Young, handsome: these he put last; but I put them foremost. Sensible, good-natured; I like all that. But then reserved and sheepish—that's much against him. Yet, can't he be cured of his timidity by being taught to be proud of his wife? Yes; and can't I— But, I vow, I'm disposing of the husband before I have secured the lover.

Enter CONSTANCE NEVILLE.

KATE. I'm glad you're come, Neville, my dear. Tell me, Constance, how do I look this evening? Is there anything whimsical[11] about me? Is it one of my well-looking days, child? Am I in face today?

CONSTANCE. Perfectly, my dear. Yet now I look again—bless me!—sure no accident has happened among the canary birds or the goldfishes! Has your brother or the cat been meddling? Or has the last novel been too moving?

KATE. No; nothing of all this. I have been threatened—I can scarce get it out —I have been threatened with a lover.

CONSTANCE. And his name—

KATE. Is Marlow.

CONSTANCE. Indeed!

KATE. The son of Sir Charles Marlow.

CONSTANCE. As I live, the most intimate friend of Mr. Hastings, my admirer. They are never asunder. I believe you must have seen him when we lived in town.

KATE. Never.

CONSTANCE. He's a very singular character, I assure you. Among women of reputation and virtue, he is the modestest man alive; but his acquaintance give him a very different character among creatures of another stamp: you understand me.

KATE. An odd character, indeed. I shall never be able to manage him. What shall I do? Pshaw! think no more of him, but trust to occurrences for success. But how goes on your own affair, my dear? has my mother been courting you for my brother Tony, as usual?

CONSTANCE. I have just come from one of our agreeable tête-à-têtes. She has been saying a hundred tender things, and setting off her pretty monster as the very pink of perfection.

KATE. And her partiality is such that she actually thinks him so. A fortune like yours is no small temptation. Be-

---

8 **glass:** mirror.
9 **set . . . fashion:** arrange my headdress according to some newer fashion.
10 **Lud:** Lord; an exclamation.

11 **whimsical:** odd.

sides, as she has the sole management of it, I'm not surprised to see her unwilling to let it go out of the family.

CONSTANCE. A fortune like mine, which chiefly consists in jewels, is no such mighty temptation. But, at any rate, if my dear Hastings be but constant, I make no doubt to be too hard for her at last. However, I let her suppose that I am in love with her son, and she never once dreams that my affections are fixed upon another.

KATE. My good brother holds out stoutly. I could almost love him for hating you so.

CONSTANCE. It is a good-natured creature at bottom, and I'm sure would wish to see me married to anybody but himself. But my aunt's bell rings for our afternoon's walk round the improvements. *Allons!*[12] Courage is necessary, as our affairs are critical.

KATE. "Would it were bedtime,[13] and all were well." (*Exeunt.*)

Scene II. *An alehouse room.*

Several shabby fellows with punch and tobacco. TONY *at the head of the table, a little higher than the rest, a mallet in his hand.*

ALL. Hurrea! hurrea! hurrea! bravo!

FIRST FELLOW. Now, gentlemen, silence for a song. The Squire is going to knock himself down[1] for a song.

ALL. Ay, a song, a song!

TONY. Then I'll sing you, gentlemen, a song I made upon this alehouse, the Three Pigeons.

SONG

Let schoolmasters puzzle their brain
   With grammar and nonsense and learning,
Good liquor, I stoutly maintain,
   Gives genus[2] a better discerning.
Let them brag of their heathenish gods,
   Their Lethes, their Styxes,[3] and Stygians,[4]
Their *Quis* and their *Quæs* and their *Quods*,[5]
   They're all but a parcel of Pigeons.[6]
      Toroddle, toroddle, toroll.

When Methodist preachers come down,
   A-preaching that drinking is sinful,
I'll wager the rascals a crown
   They always preach best with a skinful.
But when you come down with your pence
   For a slice of their scurvy religion,
I'll leave it to all men of sense,
   But you, my good friend, are the Pigeon.
      Toroddle, toroddle, toroll,

Then come, put the jorum[7] about,
   And let us be merry and clever;
Our hearts and our liquors are stout,
   Here's the Three Jolly Pigeons forever!
Let some cry up wookcock or hare,
   Your bustards, your ducks, and your widgeons.
But of all the *gay* birds in the air,
   Here's a health to the Three Jolly Pigeons.
      Toroddle, toroddle, toroll,

ALL. Bravo! bravo!

FIRST FELLOW. The Squire has got spunk in him.

---

12 **Allons** (ä lôN′): French for "Let's go."
13 **Would it were bedtime:** See *I Henry IV*, V, i, 125. Falstaff says, "I would twere bedtime, Hal, and all well."

1 **knock himself down:** pound the mallet as a signal for silence during his song.

2 **genus** (jē′nəs): Tony probably means *genius*.
3 **Lethes, Styxes:** The Lethe (lē′thĭ) and the Styx (stĭks) are two rivers of the Greek underworld.
4 **Stygians** (stĭj′ĭ ənz): formed from *Styx*.
5 **Quis, Quaes, Quods:** forms of a Latin pronoun.
6 **Pigeons:** dupes; fools.
7 **jorum** (jōr′əm): punch bowl.

THE ENLIGHTENMENT

SECOND FELLOW. I loves to hear him sing, bekeays he never gives us nothing that's low.

THIRD FELLOW. Oh, damn anything that's low! I cannot bear it.

FOURTH FELLOW. The genteel thing is the genteel thing any time: if so be that a gentleman bees in a concatenation[8] accordingly.

THIRD FELLOW. I like the maxum[9] of it, Master Muggins. What though I am obligated to dance a bear, a man may be a gentleman for all that. May this be my poison, if my bear ever dances but to the very genteelest of tunes—"Water Parted" or the minuet in "Ariadne."[10]

SECOND FELLOW. What a pity it is the Squire is not come to his own![11] It would be well for all the publicans within ten miles round of him.

TONY. Ecod,[12] and so it would, Master Slang. I'd then show what it was to keep choice of company.

SECOND FELLOW. Oh, he takes after his own father for that. To be sure, old Squire Lumpkin was the finest gentleman I ever set my eyes on. For winding the straight horn,[13] or beating a thicket for a hare or a wench, he never had his fellow. It was a saying in the place, that he kept the best horses, dogs, and girls in the whole county.

TONY. Ecod, and when I'm of age, I'll be no bastard, I promise you. I have been thinking of Bet Bouncer and the miller's gray mare to begin with. But, come, my boys, drink about and be merry, for you pay no reckoning. Well, Stingo, what's the matter?

Enter LANDLORD.

LANDLORD. There be two gentlemen in a post chaise[14] at the door. They have lost their way upo' the forest; and they are talking something about Mr. Hardcastle.

TONY. As sure as can be, one of them must be the gentleman that's coming down to court my sister. Do they seem to be Londoners?

LANDLORD. I believe they may. They look woundily[15] like Frenchmen.

TONY. Then desire them to step this way, and I'll set them right in a twinkling. (*Exit* LANDLORD.) Gentlemen, as they mayn't be good enough company for you, step down for a moment, and I'll be with you in the squeezing of a lemon. (*Exeunt mob.*)

TONY (*alone*). Father-in-law[16] has been calling me whelp and hound this half-year. Now, if I pleased, I could be so revenged upon the old grumbletonian. But then I'm afraid—afraid of what? I shall soon be worth fifteen hundred a year, and let him frighten me out of *that* if he can.

Enter LANDLORD, *conducting* MARLOW *and* HASTINGS.

MARLOW. What a tedious, uncomfortable day have we had of it! We were told it was but forty miles across the country, and we have come above threescore.

HASTINGS. And all, Marlow, from that unaccountable reserve of yours, that would not let us inquire more frequently on the way.

MARLOW. I own, Hastings, I am unwilling to lay myself under an obligation to everyone I meet, and often stand the chance of an unmannerly answer.

---

8 **concatenation:** a big word which this fellow does not know the meaning of but is proud to use.
9 **maxum:** maxim; moral.
10 **"Water Parted" or the minuet in "Ariadne":** songs from operas.
11 **come to his own:** received his inheritance.
12 **Ecod:** an oath.
13 **winding . . . horn:** blowing a hunting horn.

14 **post chaise:** hired carriage for conveying travelers from one post, or stage, to another.
15 **woundily:** exceedingly.
16 **Father-in-law:** stepfather.

HASTINGS. At present, however, we are not likely to receive any answer.

TONY. No offense, gentlemen. But I'm told you have been inquiring for one Mr. Hardcastle in these parts. Do you know what part of the country you are in?

HASTINGS. Not in the least, sir, but should thank you for information.

TONY. Nor the way you came?

HASTINGS. No, sir, but if you can inform us—

TONY. Why, gentlemen, if you know neither the road you are going, nor where you are, nor the road you came, the first thing I have to inform you is, that—you have lost your way.

MARLOW. We wanted no ghost to tell us that.[17]

TONY. Pray, gentlemen, may I be so bold as to ask the place from whence you came?

MARLOW. That's not necessary toward directing us where we are to go.

TONY. No offense; but question for question is all fair, you know. Pray, gentlemen, is not this same Hardcastle a cross-grained, old-fashioned, whimsical fellow, with an ugly face, a daughter, and a pretty son?

HASTINGS. We have not seen the gentleman; but he has the family you mention.

TONY. The daughter, a tall, traipsing, trolloping, talkative maypole; the son, a pretty, well-bred, agreeable youth, that everybody is fond of?

MARLOW. Our information differs in this. The daughter is said to be well-bred and beautiful; the son an awkward booby, reared up and spoiled at his mother's apron-string.

TONY. He-he-hem! Then, gentlemen, all I have to tell you is, that you won't reach Mr. Hardcastle's house this night, I believe.

HASTINGS. Unfortunate!

TONY. It's a damned long, dark, boggy, dirty, dangerous way. Stingo, tell the gentlemen the way to Mr. Hardcastle's! (*Winking upon the* LANDLORD.) Mr. Hardcastle's, of Quagmire Marsh, you understand me.

LANDLORD. Master Hardcastle's! Lock-a-daisy, my masters, you're come a deadly deal wrong! When you came to the bottom of the hill, you should have crossed down Squash Lane.

MARLOW. Cross down Squash Lane!

LANDLORD. Then you were to keep straight forward, till you came to four roads.

MARLOW. Come to where four roads meet?

TONY. Ay; but you must be sure to take only one of them.

MARLOW. O, sir, you're facetious.

TONY. Then keeping to the right, you are to go sideways, till you come upon Crackskull Common: there you must look sharp for the track of the wheel, and go forward till you come to farmer Murrain's barn. Coming to the farmer's barn, you are to turn to the right, and then to the left, and then to the right about again, till you find out the old mill—

MARLOW. Zounds, man! we could as soon find out the longitude!

HASTINGS. What's to be done, Marlow?

MARLOW. This house promises but a poor reception; though perhaps the landlord can accommodate us.

LANDLORD. Alack, master, we have but one spare bed in the whole house.

TONY. And to my knowledge, that's taken up by three lodgers already. (*After a pause, in which the rest seem disconcerted.*) I have hit it. Don't you think, Stingo, our landlady could ac-

17 We . . . that: See *Hamlet*, I, V, 125: "There needs no ghost, my lord, come from the grave,/To tell us this."

commodate the gentlemen by the fireside, with—three chairs and a bolster?

HASTINGS. I hate sleeping by the fireside.

MARLOW. And I detest your three chairs and a bolster.

TONY. You do, do you? Then, let me see; what if you go on a mile further, to the Buck's Head—the old Buck's Head on the hill, one of the best inns in the whole county?

HASTINGS. Oho! so we have escaped an adventure for this night, however.

LANDLORD (*apart to* TONY). Sure, you ben't sending them to your father's as an inn, be you?

TONY. Mum, you fool you. Let *them* find that out. (*To them.*) You have only to keep on straight forward till you come to a large old house by the roadside. You'll see a pair of large horns over the door. That's the sign. Drive up the yard, and call stoutly about you.

HASTINGS. Sir, we are obliged to you. The servants can't miss the way?

TONY. No, no; but I tell you, though, the landlord is rich, and going to leave off business; so he wants to be thought a gentleman, saving your presence[18]— he! he! he! He'll be for giving you his company; and, ecod, if you mind him, he'll persuade you that his mother was an alderman, and his aunt a justice of peace.

LANDLORD. A troublesome old blade, to be sure; but a keeps as good wines and beds as any in the whole country.

MARLOW. Well, if he supplies us with these, we shall want no further connection. We are to turn to the right, did you say?

TONY. No, no; straight forward. I'll just step myself, and show you a piece of the way. (*To the* LANDLORD.) Mum!

LANDLORD. Ah, bless your heart, for a sweet, pleasant—damned mischievous rogue! (*Exeunt.*)

18 **saving your presence:** a phrase used to apologize for an expression or remark which might offend.

Questions for Study

ACT I

Scene i

1. What is the situation as the play opens? Who are the people? Where are they? What does each expect to do?
2. How is each person characterized?

Scene ii

1. Judging by his song, what are Tony's interests?
2. What is Goldsmith satirizing in the opening part of this scene?
3. Why does Tony play his trick on the two travelers?
4. What makes Tony's misdirections humorous?
5. How does Tony's trick suggest a humorous complication that is likely to arise in the next act?

OLIVER GOLDSMITH

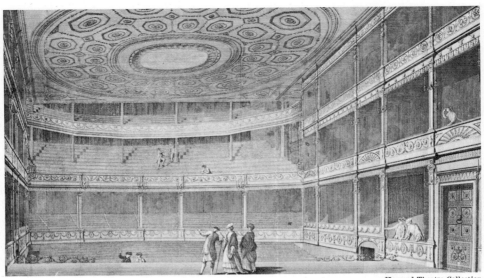

From the stage of the Theater Royal in Drury Lane, 1775. Note the boxes directly above the apron, the part of the stage projecting beyond the proscenium arch. One could see and hear well from every seat in the house.

Act II

An old-fashioned house.

Enter **Hardcastle,** *followed by three or four awkward* **Servants.**

Hardcastle. Well, I hope you are perfect in the table exercise I have been teaching you these three days. You all know your posts and your places, and can show that you have been used to good company, without ever stirring from home.

All. Ay, ay.

Hardcastle. When company comes you are not to pop out and stare, and then run in again, like frighted rabbits in a warren.

All. No, no.

Hardcastle. You, Diggory, whom I have taken from the barn, are to make a show at the side table; and you, Roger, whom I have advanced from the plow, are to place yourself behind my chair. But you're not to stand so, with your hands in your pockets. Take your hands from your pockets, Roger; and from your head, you blockhead you. See how Diggory carries his hands. They're a little too stiff, indeed, but that's no great matter.

Diggory. Ay, mind how I hold them. I learned to hold my hands this way when I was upon drill for the militia. And so being upon drill—

Hardcastle. You must not be so talkative, Diggory. You must be all attention to the guests. You must hear us talk, and not think of talking; you must see us drink, and not think of drinking; you must see us eat, and not think of eating.

Diggory. By the laws, your worship, that's perfectly unpossible. Whenever Diggory sees yeating going forward, ecod he's always wishing for a mouthful himself.

Hardcastle. Blockhead! Is not a bellyful in the kitchen as good as a

THE ENLIGHTENMENT

bellyful in the parlor? Stay your stomach with that reflection.

DIGGORY. Ecod, I thank your worship, I'll make a shift to stay my stomach with a slice of cold beef in the pantry.

HARDCASTLE. Diggory, you are too talkative.—Then, if I happen to say a good thing, or tell a good story at table, you must not all burst out a-laughing, as if you made part of the company.

DIGGORY. Then, ecod, your worship must not tell the story of Ould Grouse in the gun room: I can't help laughing at that—he! he! he!—for the soul of me. We have laughed at that these twenty years—ha! ha! ha!

HARDCASTLE. Ha! ha! ha! The story is a good one. Well, honest Diggory, you may laugh at that—but still remember to be attentive. Suppose one of the company should call for a glass of wine, how will you behave? A glass of wine, sir, if you please. (*To* DIGGORY.) Eh, why don't you move?

DIGGORY. Ecod, your worship, I never have courage till I see the eatables and drinkables brought upo' the table, and then I'm as bauld as a lion.

HARDCASTLE. What, will nobody move?

FIRST SERVANT. I'm not to leave this pleace.

SECOND SERVANT. I'm sure it's no pleace of mine.

THIRD SERVANT. Nor mine, for sartain.

DIGGORY. Wauns,[1] and I'm sure it canna be mine.

HARDCASTLE. You numskulls! and so while, like your betters, you are quarrelling for places, the guests must be starved. O you dunces! I find I must begin all over again— But don't I hear a coach drive into the yard? To your posts, you blockheads! I'll go, in the meantime, and give my old friend's son a hearty reception at the gate.

(*Exit* HARDCASTLE.)

DIGGORY. By the elevens,[2] my pleace is gone quite out of my head.

ROGER. I know that my pleace is to be everywhere.

FIRST SERVANT. Where the devil is mine?

SECOND SERVANT. My pleace is to be nowhere at all; and so I'ze go about my business.

(*Exeunt* SERVANTS, *running about, as if frighted, different ways.*)
Enter SERVANT *with candles, showing in* MARLOW *and* HASTINGS.

SERVANT. Welcome, gentlemen, very welcome! This way.

HASTINGS. After the disappointments of the day, welcome once more, Charles, to the comforts of a clean room and a good fire. Upon my word, a very well-looking house; antique but creditable.

MARLOW. The usual fate of a large mansion. Having first ruined the master by good housekeeping, it at last comes to levy contributions as an inn.

HASTINGS. As you say, we passengers are to be taxed to pay all these fineries. I have often seen a good sideboard or a marble chimney piece, though not actually put in the bill, inflame a reckoning[3] confoundedly.

MARLOW. Travelers, George, must pay in all places; the only difference is, that in good inns you pay dearly for luxuries, in bad inns you are fleeced and starved.

HASTINGS. You have lived very much among them. In truth, I have been often surprised that you who have seen so much of the world, with your natural good sense and your many opportunities, could never yet acquire a requisite share of assurance.

MARLOW. The Englishman's malady. But tell me, George, where could I have

---

1 **Wauns:** a mild oath.
2 **by the elevens:** an exclamation, probably original with Diggory.
3 **inflame a reckoning:** add to the bill.

learned that assurance you talk of? My life has been chiefly spent in a college or an inn, in seclusion from that lovely part of the creation that chiefly teach men confidence. I don't know that I was ever familiarly acquainted with a single modest woman, except my mother. But among females of another class, you know—

HASTINGS. Ay, among them you are impudent enough, of all conscience.

MARLOW. They are of *us*, you know.

HASTINGS. But in the company of women of reputation, I never saw such an idiot, such a trembler; you look for all the world as if you wanted an opportunity of stealing out of the room.

MARLOW. Why, man, that's because I *do* want to steal out of the room. Faith, I have often formed a resolution to break the ice, and rattle away at any rate. But I don't know how, a single glance from a pair of fine eyes has totally overset my resolution. An impudent fellow may counterfeit modesty, but I'll be hanged if a modest man can ever counterfeit impudence.

HASTINGS. If you could but say half the fine things to them that I have heard you lavish upon the barmaid of an inn, or even a college bedmaker—

MARLOW. Why, George, I can't say fine things to them; they freeze, they petrify me. They may talk of a comet or a burning mountain, or some such bagatelle; but to me, a modest woman, dressed out in all her finery, is the most tremendous object of the whole creation.

HASTINGS. Ha! ha! ha! At this rate, man, how can you ever expect to marry?

MARLOW. Never; unless, as among kings and princes, my bride were to be courted by proxy. If, indeed, like an Eastern bridegroom, one were to be introduced to a wife he never saw before, it might be endured. But to go

through all the terrors of a formal courtship, together with the episode of aunts, grandmothers, and cousins, and at last to blurt out the broad staring question of, "Madam, will you marry me?" No, no, that's a strain much above me, I assure you.

HASTINGS. I pity you. But how do you intend behaving to the lady you are come down to visit at the request of your father?

MARLOW. As I behave to all other ladies. Bow very low, answer "yes" or "no" to all her demands; but, for the rest, I don't think I shall venture to look in her face till I see my father's again.

HASTINGS. I'm surprised that one who is so warm a friend can be so cool a lover.

MARLOW. To be explicit, my dear Hastings, my chief inducement down was to be instrumental in forwarding your happiness, not my own. Miss Neville loves you, the family don't know you; as my friend you are sure of a reception, and let honor do the rest.

HASTINGS. My dear Marlow! but I'll suppress the emotion. Were I a wretch, meanly seeking to carry off a fortune, you should be the last man in the world I would apply to for assistance. But Miss Neville's person is all I ask, and that is mine, both from her deceased father's consent, and her own inclination.

MARLOW. Happy man! You have talents and art to captivate any woman. I'm doomed to adore the sex, and yet to converse with the only part of it I despise. This stammer in my address, and this awkward, prepossessing⁴ visage of mine, can never permit me to soar above the reach of a milliner's prentice, or one

4 **prepossessing:** producing an unfavorable impression; i.e., the opposite of its present meaning.

THE ENLIGHTENMENT

of the duchesses of Drury Lane.[5] Pshaw! this fellow here to interrupt us!

Enter HARDCASTLE.

HARDCASTLE. Gentlemen, once more you are heartily welcome. Which is Mr. Marlow? Sir, you are heartily welcome. It's not my way, you see, to receive my friends with my back to the fire. I like to give them a hearty reception in the old style at my gate. I like to see their horses and trunks taken care of.

MARLOW (*aside*). He has got our names from the servants already. (*To him.*) We approve your caution and hospitality, sir. (*To* HASTINGS.) I have been thinking, George, of changing our traveling dresses[6] in the morning. I am grown confoundedly ashamed of mine.

HARDCASTLE. I beg, Mr. Marlow, you'll use no ceremony in this house.

HASTINGS. I fancy, Charles, you're right: the first blow is half the battle. I intend opening the campaign with the white-and-gold.[7]

HARDCASTLE. Mr. Marlow—Mr. Hastings: gentlemen, pray be under no constraint in this house. This is Liberty Hall, gentlemen. You may do just as you please here.

MARLOW. Yet, George, if we open the campaign too fiercely at first, we may want ammunition before it is over. I think to reserve the embroidery to secure a retreat.

HARDCASTLE. Your talking of a retreat, Mr. Marlow, puts me in mind of the Duke of Marlborough when we went to besiege Denain.[8] He first summoned the garrison—

MARLOW. Don't you think the *ventre d'or*[9] waistcoat will do with the plain brown?

HARDCASTLE. He first summoned the garrison, which might consist of about five thousand men—

HASTINGS. I think not: brown and yellow mix but very poorly.

HARDCASTLE. I say, gentlemen, as I was telling you, he summoned the garrison, which might consist of about five thousand men—

MARLOW. The girls like finery.

HARDCASTLE. Which might consist of about five thousand men, well appointed with stores, ammunition, and other implements of war. Now, says the Duke of Marlborough to George Brooks, that stood next to him—you must have heard of George Brooks—I'll pawn my dukedom, says he, but I take that garrison without spilling a drop of blood. So—

MARLOW. What, my good friend, if you gave us a glass of punch in the meantime; it would help us to carry on the siege with vigor.

HARDCASTLE. Punch, sir! (*Aside.*) This is the most unaccountable kind of modesty I ever met with.

MARLOW. Yes, sir, punch. A glass of warm punch, after our journey, will be comfortable. This is Liberty Hall, you know.

HARDCASTLE. Here's a cup,[10] sir.

MARLOW (*aside*). So this fellow, in his Liberty Hall, will only let us have just what he pleases.

HARDCASTLE (*taking the cup*). I hope you'll find it to your mind. I have prepared it with my own hands, and I believe you'll own the ingredients are tolerable. Will you be so good as to

---

5 **duchesses . . . Lane:** low types of women.
6 **dresses:** clothing.
7 **white-and-gold:** suit of white with gold embroidery.
8 **Denain:** town in northeast France, scene of French victory over Prince Eugene's army. The Duke of Marlborough was *not* at this battle.

9 **ventre d'or** (väN′trə dôr′): with gold-embroidered front.
10 **cup:** sweetened, spiced wine.

pledge me, sir. Here, Mr. Marlow, here is to our better acquaintance. (*Drinks.*)

MARLOW (*aside*). A very impudent fellow this! but he's a character, and I'll humor him a little. Sir, my service to you. (*Drinks.*)

HASTINGS (*aside*). I see this fellow wants to give us his company, and forgets that he's an innkeeper before he has learned to be a gentleman.

MARLOW. From the excellence of your cup, my old friend, I suppose you have a good deal of business in this part of the country. Warm work, now and then, at elections, I suppose.

HARDCASTLE. No, sir, I have long given that work over. Since our betters have hit upon the expedient of electing each other, there is no business "for us that sell ale."

HASTINGS. So, then, you have no turn for politics, I find.

HARDCASTLE. Not in the least. There was a time, indeed, I fretted myself about the mistakes of government, like other people; but finding myself every day grow more angry, and the government growing no better, I left it to mend itself. Since that, I no more trouble my head about Hyder Ally, or Ally Cawn,[11] than about Ally Croker.[12] Sir, my service to you.

HASTINGS. So that with eating above stairs, and drinking below, with receiving your friends within, and amusing them without, you lead a good, pleasant, bustling life of it.

HARDCASTLE. I do stir about a great deal, that's certain. Half the differences of the parish are adjusted in this very parlor.

MARLOW (*after drinking*). And you have an argument in your cup, old gentleman, better than any in Westminster Hall.[13]

HARDCASTLE. Ay, young gentleman, that, and a little philosophy.

MARLOW (*aside*). Well, this is the first time I ever heard of an innkeeper's philosophy.

HASTINGS. So, then, like an experienced general, you attack them on every quarter. If you find their reason manageable, you attack it with your philosophy; if you find they have no reason, you attack them with this. Here's your health, my philosopher. (*Drinks.*)

HARDCASTLE. Good, very good, thank you—ha! ha! ha! Your generalship puts me in mind of Prince Eugene when he fought the Turks at the battle of Belgrade. You shall hear.

MARLOW. Instead of the battle of Belgrade, I believe it's almost time to talk about supper. What has your philosophy got in the house for supper?

HARDCASTLE. For supper, sir! (*Aside.*) Was ever such a request to a man in his own house?

MARLOW. Yes, sir, supper, sir; I begin to feel an appetite. I shall make devilish work tonight in the larder, I promise you.

HARDCASTLE (*aside*). Such a brazen dog sure never my eyes beheld. (*To him.*) Why, really, sir, as for supper, I can't well tell. My Dorothy and the cookmaid settle these things between them. I leave these kind of things entirely to them.

MARLOW. You do, do you?

HARDCASTLE. Entirely. By-the-bye, I believe they are in actual consultation upon what's for supper this moment in the kitchen.

MARLOW. Then I beg they'll admit me

11 **Hyder Ally, or Ally Cawn:** Heider Ali or Ali Khan, names of East Indians involved in the Indian troubles in which the English of 1773 were much interested.
12 **Ally Croker:** popular Irish song.

13 **Westminster Hall:** hall in London where the law courts were held.

THE ENLIGHTENMENT

as one of their privy council. It's a way I have got. When I travel, I always choose to regulate my own supper. Let the cook be called. No offense, I hope, sir?

HARDCASTLE. Oh no, sir, none in the least; yet I don't know how. Our Bridget, the cookmaid, is not very communicative upon these occasions. Should we send for her, she might scold us all out of the house.

HASTINGS. Let's see your list of the larder then. I ask it as a favor. I always match my appetite to my bill of fare.

MARLOW (to HARDCASTLE, *who looks at them with surprise*). Sir, he's very right, and it's my way too.

HARDCASTLE. Sir, you have a right to command here. Here, Roger, bring us the bill of fare for tonight's supper: I believe it's drawn out.—Your manner, Mr. Hastings, puts me in mind of my uncle, Colonel Wallop. It was a saying of his, that no man was sure of his supper till he had eaten it.

HASTINGS (*aside*). All upon the high ropes! His uncle a colonel! We shall soon hear of his mother being a justice of the peace. But let's hear the bill of fare.

MARLOW (*perusing*). What's here? For the first course; for the second course; for the dessert. The devil, sir, do you think we have brought down the whole Joiners' Company,[14] or the corporation of Bedford, to eat up such a supper? Two or three little things, clean and comfortable, will do.

HASTINGS. But let's hear it.

MARLOW (*reading*). For the first course at the top, a pig, and prune sauce.

HASTINGS. Damn your pig, I say.

MARLOW. And damn your prune sauce, say I.

HARDCASTLE. And yet, gentlemen, to men that are hungry, pig with prune sauce is very good eating.

MARLOW. At the bottom, a calf's tongue and brains.

HASTINGS. Let your brains be knocked out, my good sir; I don't like them.

MARLOW. Or you may clap them on a plate by themselves. I do.

HARDCASTLE (*aside*). Their impudence confounds me. (*To them.*) Gentlemen, you are my guests; make what alterations you please. Is there anything else you wish to retrench or alter, gentlemen?

MARLOW. Item. A pork pie, a boiled rabbit and sausages, a Florentine,[15] a shaking pudding,[16] and a dish of tiff—taff—taffety[17] cream.

HASTINGS. Confound your made dishes![18] I shall be as much at a loss in this house as at a green-and-yellow dinner at the French ambassador's table. I'm for plain eating.

HARDCASTLE. I'm sorry, gentlemen, that I have nothing you like; but if there be anything you have a particular fancy to—

MARLOW. Why, really, sir, your bill of fare is so exquisite that any one part of it is full as good as another. Send us what you please. So much for supper. And now to see that our beds are aired, and properly taken care of.

HARDCASTLE. I entreat you'll leave all that to me. You shall not stir a step.

MARLOW. Leave that to you! I protest, sir, you must excuse me, I always look to these things myself.

HARDCASTLE. I must insist, sir, you'll make yourself easy on that head.

---

14 **Joiners' Company:** one of the London trade guilds.

15 **Florentine:** a meat, vegetable, or fruit pie.
16 **shaking pudding:** a jelly.
17 **taffety cream:** a dish of thickened cream.
18 **made dishes:** elaborately prepared food.

MARLOW. You see I'm resolved on it. (*Aside.*) A very troublesome fellow this, as I ever met with.

HARDCASTLE. Well, sir, I'm resolved at least to attend you. (*Aside.*) This may be modern modesty, but I never saw anything look so like old-fashioned impudence.

(*Exeunt* MARLOW *and* HARDCASTLE.)

HASTINGS (*alone*). So I find this fellow's civilities begin to grow troublesome. But who can be angry at those assiduities which are meant to please him? —Ha! what do I see? Miss Neville, by all that's happy!

Enter CONSTANCE NEVILLE.

CONSTANCE. My dear Hastings! To what unexpected good fortune, to what accident, am I to ascribe this happy meeting?

HASTINGS. Rather let me ask the same question, as I could never have hoped to meet my dearest Constance at an inn.

CONSTANCE. An inn! sure you mistake; my aunt, my guardian, lives here. What could induce you to think this house an inn?

HASTINGS. My friend, Mr. Marlow, with whom I came down, and I, have been sent here as to an inn, I assure you. A young fellow, whom we accidentally met at a house hard by, directed us hither.

CONSTANCE. Certainly it must be one of my hopeful cousin's tricks, of whom you have heard me talk so often—ha! ha! ha!

HASTINGS. He whom your aunt intends for you? He of whom I have such just apprehensions?

CONSTANCE. You have nothing to fear from him, I assure you. You'd adore him if you knew how heartily he despises me. My aunt knows it too, and has undertaken to court me for him, and actually begins to think she has made a conquest.

HASTINGS. Thou dear dissembler! You must know, my Constance, I have just seized this happy opportunity of my friend's visit here to get admittance into the family. The horses that carried us down are now fatigued with their journey, but they'll soon be refreshed, and then, if my dearest girl will trust in her faithful Hastings, we shall soon be landed in France, where even among slaves the laws of marriage are respected.

CONSTANCE. I have often told you that, though ready to obey you, I yet should leave my little fortune behind with reluctance. The greatest part of it was left me by my uncle, the India director,[19] and chiefly consists in jewels. I have been for some time persuading my aunt to let me wear them. I fancy I'm very near succeeding. The instant they are put into my possession, you shall find me ready to make them and myself yours.

HASTINGS. Perish the baubles! Your person is all I desire. In the meantime, my friend Marlow must not be let into his mistake. I know the strange reserve of his temper is such that if abruptly informed of it, he would instantly quit the house before our plan was ripe for execution.

CONSTANCE. But how shall we keep him in the deception? Miss Hardcastle is just returned from walking; what if we still continue to deceive him? This, this way— (*They confer.*)

Enter MARLOW.

MARLOW. The assiduities of these good people tease me beyond bearing. My host seems to think it ill manners to leave me alone, and so he claps not only himself, but his old-fashioned wife on my back. They talk of coming to sup

19 **India director:** director in the East India Company.

with us, too; and then, I suppose, we are to run the gantlet through all the rest of the family.—What have we got here?

HASTINGS. My dear Charles! Let me congratulate you! The most fortunate accident! Who do you think is just alighted?

MARLOW. Cannot guess.

HASTINGS. Our mistresses, boy, Miss Hardcastle and Miss Neville. Give me leave to introduce Miss Constance Neville to your acquaintance. Happening to dine in the neighborhood, they called, on their return, to take fresh horses here. Miss Hardcastle has just stepped into the next room, and will be back in an instant. Wasn't it lucky, eh?

MARLOW (aside). I have been mortified enough of all conscience, and here comes something to complete my embarrassment.

HASTINGS. Well, but wasn't it the most fortunate thing in the world?

MARLOW. Oh yes. Very fortunate—a most joyful encounter. But our dresses, George, you know, are in disorder. What if we should postpone the happiness till tomorrow? Tomorrow at her own house. It will be every bit as convenient—and rather more respectful. Tomorrow let it be.   (Offering to go.)

CONSTANCE. By no means, sir. Your ceremony will displease her. The disorder of your dress will show the ardor of your impatience. Besides, she knows you are in the house, and will permit you to see her.

MARLOW. O the devil! how shall I support it? Hem! hem! Hastings, you must not go. You are to assist me, you know. I shall be confoundedly ridiculous. Yet, hang it! I'll take courage. Hem!

HASTINGS. Pshaw, man! it's but the first plunge, and all's over. She's but a woman, you know.

MARLOW. And of all women, she that I dread most to encounter.

Enter MISS HARDCASTLE, *as returning from walking, a bonnet, etc.*

HASTINGS (introducing them). Miss Hardcastle. Mr. Marlow. I'm proud of bringing two persons of such merit together, that only want to know, to esteem each other.

KATE (aside). Now for meeting my modest gentleman with a demure face, and quite in his own manner. (After a pause, in which he appears very uneasy and disconcerted.) I'm glad of your safe arrival, sir. I'm told you had some accidents by the way.

MARLOW. Only a few, madam. Yes, we had some. Yes, madam, a good many accidents, but should be sorry—madam—or rather glad of any accidents—that are so agreeably concluded. Hem!

HASTINGS (to him). You never spoke better in your whole life. Keep it up, and I'll insure you the victory.

KATE. I'm afraid you flatter, sir. You, that have seen so much of the finest company, can find little entertainment in an obscure corner of the country.

MARLOW (gathering courage). I have lived, indeed, in the world, madam; but I have kept very little company. I have been but an observer upon life, madam, while others were enjoying it.

CONSTANCE. But that, I am told, is the way to enjoy it at last.

HASTINGS (to him). Cicero[20] never spoke better. Once more, and you are confirmed in assurance forever.

MARLOW (to him). Hem! Stand by me, then; and when I'm down, throw in a word or two to set me up again.

KATE. An observer, like you, upon life were, I fear, disagreeably employed,

---

20 Cicero (sĭs′ə rō′): Marcus Tullius Cicero, Roman philosopher, orator, and statesman, 106-43 B.C.

since you must have had much more to censure than to approve.

MARLOW. Pardon me, madam. I was always willing to be amused. The folly of most people is rather an object of mirth than uneasiness.

HASTINGS (*to him*). Bravo, bravo. Never spoke so well in your whole life. Well, Miss Hardcastle, I see that you and Mr. Marlow are going to be very good company. I believe our being here will but embarrass the interview.

MARLOW. Not in the least, Mr. Hastings. We like your company of all things. (*To him.*) Zounds! George, sure you won't go? How can you leave us?

HASTINGS. Our presence will but spoil conversation, so we'll retire to the next room. (*To him.*) You don't consider, man, that we are to manage a little tête-à-tête of our own. (*Exeunt.*)

KATE (*after a pause*). But you have not been wholly an observer, I presume, sir; the ladies, I should hope, have employed some part of your addresses.

MARLOW (*relapsing into timidity*). Pardon me, madam, I—I—I—as yet have studied—only—to—deserve them.

KATE. And that, some say, is the very worst way to obtain them.

MARLOW. Perhaps so, madam. But I love to converse only with the more grave and sensible part of the sex. But I'm afraid I grow tiresome.

KATE. Not at all, sir; there is nothing I like so much as grave conversation myself; I could hear it forever. Indeed, I have often been surprised how a man of sentiment could ever admire those light airy pleasures where nothing reaches the heart.

MARLOW. It's—a disease—of the mind, madam. In the variety of tastes there must be some who, wanting a relish—for—um—a—um—

KATE. I understand you, sir. There must be some who, wanting a relish for refined pleasures, pretend to despise what they are incapable of tasting.

MARLOW. My meaning, madam, but infinitely better expressed. And I can't help observing—a—

KATE (*aside*). Who could ever suppose this fellow impudent upon some occasions? (*To him.*) You were going to observe, sir—

MARLOW. I was observing, madam—I protest, madam, I forget what I was going to observe.

KATE (*aside*). I vow and so do I. (*To him.*) You were observing, sir, that in this age of hypocrisy—something about hypocrisy, sir.

MARLOW. Yes, madam. In this age of hypocrisy there are few who, upon strict inquiry, do not—a—a—a—

KATE. I understand you perfectly, sir.

MARLOW (*aside*). Egad! and that's more than I do myself.

KATE. You mean that in this hypocritical age there are few that do not condemn in public what they practice in private, and think they pay every debt to virtue when they praise it.

MARLOW. True, madam; those who have most virtue in their mouths have least of it in their bosoms. But I'm sure I tire you, madam.

KATE. Not in the least, sir; there's something so agreeable and spirited in your manner, such life and force—pray, sir, go on.

MARLOW. Yes, madam. I was saying —that there are some occasions—when a total want of courage, madam, destroys all the—and puts us—upon a—a—a—

KATE. I agree with you entirely; a want of courage upon some occasions assumes the appearance of ignorance, and betrays us when we most want to excel. I beg you'll proceed.

MARLOW. Yes, madam. Morally

THE ENLIGHTENMENT

speaking, madam. But I see Miss Neville expecting us in the next room. I would not intrude for the world.

KATE. I protest, sir, I never was more agreeably entertained in all my life. Pray, go on.

MARLOW. Yes, madam, I was—. But she beckons us to join her. Madam, shall I do myself the honor to attend you?

KATE. Well, then, I'll follow.

MARLOW (aside). This pretty smooth dialogue has done for me. (Exit.)

KATE (alone). Ha! ha! ha! Was there ever such a sober, sentimental interview? I'm certain he scarce looked in my face the whole time. Yet the fellow, but for his unaccountable bashfulness, is pretty well too. He has good sense, but then so buried in his fears that it fatigues one more than ignorance. If I could teach him a little confidence, it would be doing somebody that I know of a piece of service. But who is that somebody? That, faith, is a question I can scarce answer. (Exit.)

Enter TONY *and* CONSTANCE, *followed*

TONY. What do you follow me for, Cousin Con? I wonder you're not ashamed to be so very engaging.[21]

CONSTANCE. I hope, cousin, one may speak to one's own relations, and not be to blame.

TONY. Ay, but I know what sort of a relation you want to make me, though; but it won't do. I tell you, Cousin Con, it won't do; so I beg you'll keep your distance. I want no nearer relationship.

(*She follows, coquetting him to the back scene.*)

MRS. HARDCASTLE. Well! I vow, Mr. Hastings, you are very entertaining. There is nothing in the world I love to talk of so much as London, and the fashions, though I was never there myself.

HASTINGS. Never there! You amaze me! From your air and manner, I concluded you had been bred all your life either at Ranelagh, St. James's, or Tower Wharf.[22]

MRS. HARDCASTLE. Oh, sir, you're only pleased to say so. We country persons can have no manner at all. I'm in love with the town, and that serves to raise me above some of our neighboring rustics; but who can have a manner that has never seen the Pantheon, the Grotto Gardens, the Borough,[23] and such places where the nobility chiefly resort? All I can do is to enjoy London at secondhand. I take care to know every tête-à-tête from the *Scandalous Magazine*, and have all the fashions, as they come out, in a letter from the two Miss Rickets of Crooked Lane. Pray how do you like this head,[24] Mr. Hastings?

HASTINGS. Extremely elegant and *dégagée*,[25] upon my word, madam. Your *friseur*[26] is a Frenchman, I suppose.

MRS. HARDCASTLE. I protest, I dressed it myself from a print in the *Ladies' Memorandum Book* for the last year.

HASTINGS. Indeed! Such a head in a side box at the playhouse would draw as many gazers as my Lady Mayoress at a city ball.

MRS. HARDCASTLE. I vow, since inoculation[27] began, there is no such thing to

---

21 **engaging:** seductive.

22 **Ranelagh** (răn′ə lä) . . . **Wharf:** The first two were fashionable spots; the last a disreputable resort. Hastings is mocking Mrs. Hardcastle's ignorance of London.

23 **Pantheon . . . Borough:** The Pantheon was a rival resort of Ranelagh; the Grotto Gardens and the Borough were in areas which were far from fashionable or aristocratic.

24 **this head:** coiffure.

25 **dégagée** (dĕ gà zhĕ′): free; natural.

26 **friseur** (frē zœr′): hairdresser.

27 **inoculation:** infecting with a light form of smallpox. This predecessor of vaccination was used to prevent the disease and its ugly marks.

be seen as a plain woman; so one must dress a little particular, or one may escape in the crowd.

HASTINGS. But that can never be your case, madam, in any dress. (*Bowing.*)

MRS. HARDCASTLE. Yet, what signifies my dressing when I have such a piece of antiquity by my side as Mr. Hardcastle; all I can say will never argue down a single button from his clothes. I have often wanted him to throw off his great flaxen wig, and where he was bald to plaster it over, like my Lord Pately, with powder.

HASTINGS. You are right, madam; for, as among the ladies there are none ugly, so among the men there are none old.

MRS. HARDCASTLE. But what do you think his answer was? Why, with his usual Gothic[28] vivacity, he said I only wanted him to throw off his wig to convert it into a *tête*[29] for my own wearing.

HASTINGS. Intolerable! At your age you may wear what you please, and it must become you.

MRS. HARDCASTLE. Pray, Mr. Hastings, what do you take to be the most fashionable age about town?

HASTINGS. Some time ago, forty was all the mode; but I'm told the ladies intend to bring up fifty for the ensuing winter.

MRS. HARDCASTLE. Seriously? Then I shall be too young for the fashion.

HASTINGS. No lady begins now to put on jewels till she's past forty. For instance, miss there, in a polite circle, would be considered as a child, as a mere maker of samplers.[30]

MRS. HARDCASTLE. And yet Mrs. Niece[31] thinks herself as much a woman, and is as fond of jewels, as the oldest of us all.

HASTINGS. Your niece, is she? And that young gentleman, a brother of yours, I should presume?

MRS. HARDCASTLE. My son, sir. They are contracted[32] to each other. Observe their little sports. They fall in and out ten times a day, as if they were man and wife already. (*To them.*) Well, Tony, child, what soft things are you saying to your cousin Constance this evening?

TONY. I have been saying no soft things; but that it's very hard to be followed about so. Ecod! I've not a place in the house now that's left to myself, but the stable.

MRS. HARDCASTLE. Never mind him, Con, my dear. He's in another story behind your back.

CONSTANCE. There's something generous in my cousin's manner. He falls out before faces to be forgiven in private.

TONY. That's a damned, confounded —crack.[33]

MRS. HARDCASTLE. Ah! he's a sly one. Don't you think they're like each other about the mouth, Mr. Hastings? The Blenkinsop mouth to a T. They're of a size, too. Back to back, my pretties, that Mr. Hastings may see you. Come, Tony.

TONY. You had as good not make me, I tell you. (*Measuring.*)

CONSTANCE. O lud! he has almost cracked my head.

MRS. HARDCASTLE. Oh, the monster! For shame, Tony! You a man, and behave so!

TONY. If I'm a man, let me have my fortin. Ecod! I'll not be made a fool of no longer.

MRS. HARDCASTLE. Is this, ungrateful boy, all that I'm to get for the pains I have taken in your education? I that

---

28 **Gothic:** uncivilized.
29 **tête** (tĕt): headdress.
30 **samplers:** pieces of needlework.
31 **Mrs. Niece:** Mistress niece.

32 **contracted:** betrothed.
33 **crack:** lie.

THE ENLIGHTENMENT

have rocked you in your cradle and fed that pretty mouth with a spoon! Did not I work[34] that waistcoat to make you genteel? Did not I prescribe for you every day, and weep while the receipt was operating?

TONY. Ecod! you had reason to weep, for you have been dosing me ever since I was born. I have gone through every receipt[35] in the *Complete Huswife* ten times over; and you have thoughts of coursing me through Quincy[36] next spring. But, ecod! I tell you, I'll not be made a fool of no longer.

MRS. HARDCASTLE. Wasn't it all for your good, viper? Wasn't it all for your good?

TONY. I wish you'd let me and my good alone, then. Snubbing this way when I'm in spirits! If I'm to have any good, let it come of itself; not to keep dinging it, dinging it into one so.

MRS. HARDCASTLE. That's false; I never see you when you're in spirits. No, Tony, you then go to the alehouse or kennel. I'm never to be delighted with your agreeable wild notes, unfeeling monster!

TONY. Ecod! Mamma, your own notes are the wildest of the two.

MRS. HARDCASTLE. Was ever the like? But I see he wants to break my heart; I see he does.

HASTINGS. Dear madam, permit me to lecture the young gentleman a little. I'm certain I can persuade him to his duty.

MRS. HARDCASTLE. Well, I must retire. Come, Constance, my love. You see, Mr. Hastings, the wretchedness of my situation: was ever poor woman so plagued with a dear, sweet, pretty, provoking, undutiful boy?

(*Exeunt* MRS. HARDCASTLE *and* CONSTANCE.)

34 **work:** embroider.
35 **receipt:** remedy.
36 **Quincy:** author of *The Complete English Dispensatory.*

TONY (*singing*). "There was a young man riding by, and fain would have his will. Rang do didlo dee."—Don't mind her. Let her cry. It's the comfort of her heart. I have seen her and sister cry over a book for an hour together; and they said they liked the book the better the more it made them cry.

HASTINGS. Then you're no friend to the ladies, I find, my pretty young gentleman?

TONY. That's as I find 'um.

HASTINGS. Not to her of your mother's choosing, I dare answer? And yet she appears to me a pretty, well-tempered girl.

TONY. That's because you don't know her as well as I. Ecod! I know every inch about her; and there's not a more bitter, cantankerous toad in all Christendom.

HASTINGS (*aside*). Pretty encouragement this for a lover!

TONY. I have seen her since the height of that. She has as many tricks as a hare in a thicket, or a colt the first day's breaking.

HASTINGS. To me she appears sensible and silent.

TONY. Ay, before company. But when she's with her playmate, she's as loud as a hog in a gate.

HASTINGS. But there is a meek modesty about her that charms me.

TONY. Yes, but curb her never so little, she kicks up, and you're flung in a ditch.

HASTINGS. Well, but you must allow her a little beauty. Yes, you must allow her some beauty.

TONY. Bandbox! She's all a made-up thing, mun. Ah! could you but see Bet Bouncer of these parts, you might then talk of beauty. Ecod, she has two eyes as black as sloes, and cheeks as broad and red as a pulpit cushion. She'd make two of she.

OLIVER GOLDSMITH

HASTINGS. Well, what say you to a friend that would take this bitter bargain off your hands?

TONY. Anon.[37]

HASTINGS. Would you thank him that would take Miss Neville, and leave you to happiness and your dear Betsy?

TONY. Ay; but where is there such a friend, for who would take *her*?

HASTINGS. I am he. If you but assist me, I'll engage to whip her off to France, and you shall never hear more of her.

TONY. Assist you! Ecod I will, to the last drop of my blood. I'll clap a pair of horses to your chaise that shall trundle you off in a twinkling, and may be get you a part of her fortin besides, in jewels, that you little dream of.

HASTINGS. My dear squire, this looks like a lad of spirit.

TONY. Come along, then, and you shall see more of my spirit before you have done with me. (*Singing.*)

We are the boys
That fears no noise
Where the thundering cannons roar.
(*Exeunt.*)

37 Anon: What? How's that?

Questions for Study

ACT II

1. How does the scene between Mr. Hardcastle and his servants fit the meaning of the play?
2. In the scene in which Hardcastle greets Marlow and Hastings, the last two speak often in *asides* (they and the audience hear, but Mr. Hardcastle does not). How would the scene be different if the *asides* were omitted?
3. When one considers that Marlow and Hastings think that they are at an inn, in what ways is their conduct toward Mr. Hardcastle reasonable?
4. Why does the author let Hastings in on the joke by having him meet Constance Neville at this time? How does the author keep Marlow away from the truth during this act?
5. How would you place Marlow and Kate Hardcastle on the stage during their conversation? In what manner would each of them speak?
6. In the scene in which Hastings and Mrs. Hardcastle discuss the social world and styles, what makes Mrs. Hardcastle ridiculous, a character at whom the audience is meant to laugh?
7. How does Tony add to our understanding of the weaknesses of Mrs. Hardcastle?
8. What causes Tony to change his attitude toward Hastings at the end of the scene? What does Tony's change of attitude suggest in respect to future plot development?

The house.

Enter HARDCASTLE, *alone.*

HARDCASTLE. What could my old friend Sir Charles mean by recommending his son as the modestest young man in town? To me he appears the most impudent piece of brass that ever spoke with a tongue. He has taken possession of the easy chair by the fireside already. He took off his boots in the parlor, and desired me to see them taken care of. I'm desirous to know how his impudence affects my daughter. She will certainly be shocked at it.

Enter KATE, *plainly dressed.*

HARDCASTLE. Well, my Kate, I see you have changed your dress, as I bid you; and yet, I believe, there was no great occasion.

KATE. I find such a pleasure, sir, in obeying your commands that I take care to observe them without ever debating their propriety.

HARDCASTLE. And yet, Kate, I sometimes give you some cause, particularly when I recommended my *modest* gentleman to you as a lover today.

KATE. You taught me to expect something extraordinary, and I find the original exceeds the description.

HARDCASTLE. I was never so surprised in my life! He has quite confounded all my faculties!

KATE. I never saw anything like it: and a man of the world too!

HARDCASTLE. Ay, he learned it all abroad. What a fool was I, to think a young man could learn modesty by traveling! He might as soon learn wit at a masquerade.

KATE. It seems all natural to him.

HARDCASTLE. A good deal assisted by bad company and a French dancing master.

KATE. Sure you mistake, Papa. A French dancing master could never have taught him that timid look—that awkward address—that bashful manner—

HARDCASTLE. Whose look? Whose manner, child?

KATE. Mr. Marlow's: his *mauvaise honte,*[1] his timidity, struck me at the first sight.

HARDCASTLE. Then your first sight deceived you; for I think him one of the most brazen first sights that ever astonished my senses.

KATE. Sure, sir, you rally! I never saw anyone so modest.

HARDCASTLE. And can you be serious? I never saw such a bouncing, swaggering puppy since I was born. Bully Dawson[2] was but a fool to him.

KATE. Surprising! He met me with a respectful bow, a stammering voice, and a look fixed on the ground.

HARDCASTLE. He met me with a loud voice, a lordly air, and a familiarity that made my blood freeze again.

KATE. He treated me with diffidence and respect; censured the manners of the age; admired the prudence of girls that never laughed; tired me with apologies for being tiresome; then left the room with a bow, and "Madam, I would not for the world detain you."

HARDCASTLE. He spoke to me as if he knew me all his life before; asked twenty questions, and never waited for an answer; interrupted my best remarks with some silly pun; and when I was in my best story of the Duke of Marlborough and Prince Eugene, he asked if I had not a good hand at making punch. Yes, Kate, he asked your father if he was a maker of punch!

1 mauvaise honte (mô′vĕz ōNt′): bashfulness.
2 Bully Dawson: a notorious London outlaw. Sir Roger de Coverley "kicked Bully Dawson in a coffeehouse for calling him 'youngster.'" (p 329)

KATE. One of us must certainly be mistaken.

HARDCASTLE. If he be what he has shown himself, I'm determined he shall never have my consent.

KATE. And if he be the sullen thing I take him, he shall never have mine.

HARDCASTLE. In one thing, then, we are agreed—to reject him.

KATE. Yes; but upon conditions. For if you should find him less impudent, and I more presuming; if you find him more respectful, and I more importunate, I don't know—the fellow is well enough for a man. Certainly, we don't meet many such at a horse race in the country.

HARDCASTLE. If we should find him so. But that's impossible. The first appearance has done my business. I'm seldom deceived in that.

KATE. And yet there may be many good qualities under that first appearance.

HARDCASTLE. Ay, when a girl finds a fellow's outside to her taste, she then sets about guessing the rest of his furniture. With her, a smooth face stands for good sense, and a genteel figure for every virtue.

KATE. I hope, sir, a conversation begun with a compliment to my good sense won't end with a sneer at my understanding?

HARDCASTLE. Pardon me, Kate. But if young Mr. Brazen can find the art of reconciling contradictions, he may please us both, perhaps.

KATE. And as one of us must be mistaken, what if we go to make further discoveries?

HARDCASTLE. Agreed. But depend on't I'm in the right.

KATE. And depend on't I'm not much in the wrong. (*Exeunt.*)

Enter TONY, *running in with a casket*

TONY. Ecod! I have got them. Here they are. My cousin Con's necklaces, bobs,[3] and all. My mother sha'n't cheat the poor souls out of their fortin neither. Oh, my genus, is that you?

Enter HASTINGS.

HASTINGS. My dear friend, how have you managed with your mother? I hope you have amused her with pretending love for your cousin, and that you are willing to be reconciled at last? Our horses will be refreshed in a short time, and we shall soon be ready to set off.

TONY. And here's something to bear your charges[4] by the way (*giving the casket*); your sweetheart's jewels. Keep them, and hang those, I say, that would rob you of one of them.

HASTINGS. But how have you procured them from your mother?

TONY. Ask me no questions, and I'll tell you no fibs. I procured them by the rule of thumb.[5] If I had not a key to every drawer in mother's bureau, how could I go to the alehouse so often as I do? An honest man may rob himself of his own at any time.

HASTINGS. Thousands do it every day. But to be plain with you, Miss Neville is endeavoring to procure them from her aunt this very instant. If she succeeds, it will be the most delicate way, at least, of obtaining them.

TONY. Well, keep them, till you know how it will be. But I know how it will be well enough; she'd as soon part with the only sound tooth in her head.

HASTINGS. But I dread the effects of her resentment, when she finds she has lost them.

TONY. Never you mind her resentment; leave *me* to manage that. I don't

3 bobs: earrings.
4 bear your charges: defray your expenses.
5 rule of thumb: practical experience.

value her resentment the bounce of a cracker.[6] Zounds! here they are. Morrice![7] Prance! (*Exit* HASTINGS.)

Enter MRS. HARDCASTLE *and* CONSTANCE.

MRS. HARDCASTLE. Indeed, Constance, you amaze me. Such a girl as you want jewels! It will be time enough for jewels, my dear, twenty years hence, when your beauty begins to want repairs.

CONSTANCE. But what will repair beauty at forty will certainly improve it at twenty, madam.

MRS. HARDCASTLE. Yours, my dear, can admit of none. That natural blush is beyond a thousand ornaments. Besides, child, jewels are quite out at present. Don't you see half the ladies of our acquaintance—my Lady Kill-daylight and Mrs. Crump and the rest of them—carry their jewels to town, and bring nothing but paste and marcasites[8] back?

CONSTANCE. But who knows, madam, but somebody that shall be nameless would like me best with all my little finery about me?

MRS. HARDCASTLE. Consult your glass, my dear, and then see if with such a pair of eyes you want any better sparklers. What do you think, Tony, my dear? Does your cousin Con want any jewels, in your eyes, to set off her beauty?

TONY. That's as thereafter may be.

CONSTANCE. My dear aunt, if you knew how it would oblige me.

MRS. HARDCASTLE. A parcel of old-fashioned rose and table-cut[9] things. They would make you look like the court of King Solomon at a puppet show. Besides, I believe, I can't readily

come at them. They may be missing, for aught I know to the contrary.

TONY (*apart to* MRS. HARDCASTLE). Then, why don't you tell her so at once, as she's so longing for them? Tell her they're lost. It's the only way to quiet her. Say they're lost, and call me to bear witness.

MRS. HARDCASTLE (*apart to* TONY). You know, my dear, I'm only keeping them for you. So if I say they're gone, you'll bear me witness, will you? He! he! he!

TONY. Never fear me. Ecod! I'll say I saw them taken out with my own eyes.

CONSTANCE. I desire them but for a day, madam. Just to be permitted to show them as relics, and then they may be locked up again.

MRS. HARDCASTLE. To be plain with you, my dear Constance, if I could find them you should have them. They're missing, I assure you. Lost, for aught I know; but we must have patience, wherever they are.

CONSTANCE. I'll not believe it! This is but a shallow pretense to deny me. I know they are too valuable to be so slightly kept; and as you are to answer for the loss—

MRS. HARDCASTLE. Don't be alarmed, Constance. If they be lost, I must restore an equivalent. But my son knows they are missing, and not to be found.

TONY. That I can bear witness to. They are missing, and not to be found; I'll take my oath on't.

MRS. HARDCASTLE. You must learn resignation, my dear; for though we lose our fortune, yet we should not lose our patience. See me, how calm I am.

CONSTANCE. Ay, people are generally calm at the misfortunes of others.

MRS. HARDCASTLE. Now I wonder a girl of your good sense should waste a thought upon such trumpery. We shall soon find them; and in the meantime

---

6 **bounce of a cracker:** burst of a firecracker.
7 **Morrice:** Get out!
8 **paste and marcasites:** imitation jewelry.
9 **rose . . . cut:** two ways of cutting gems.

you shall make use of my garnets till your jewels be found.

CONSTANCE. I detest garnets.

MRS. HARDCASTLE. The most becoming things in the world to set off a clear complexion. You have often seen how well they look upon me. You *shall* have them. (*Exit.*)

CONSTANCE. I dislike them of all things. You sha'n't stir. Was ever anything so provoking, to mislay my own jewels, and force me to wear her trumpery!

TONY. Don't be a fool. If she gives you the garnets, take what you can get. The jewels are your own already. I have stolen them out of her bureau, and she does not know it. Fly to your spark; he'll tell you more of the matter. Leave me to manage *her.*

CONSTANCE. My dear cousin!

TONY. Vanish. She's here, and has missed them already. (*Exit* CONSTANCE.) Zounds! how she fidgets and spits about like a Catherine wheel![10]

Enter MRS. HARDCASTLE.

MRS. HARDCASTLE. Confusion! thieves! robbers! We are cheated, plundered, broke open, undone!

TONY. What's the matter, what's the matter, Mamma? I hope nothing has happened to any of the good family!

MRS. HARDCASTLE. We are robbed. My bureau has been broken open, the jewels taken out, and I'm undone.

TONY. Oh! is that all? Ha! ha! ha! By the laws, I never saw it acted better in my life. Ecod, I thought you was ruined in earnest, ha! ha! ha!

MRS. HARDCASTLE. Why, boy, I *am* ruined in earnest. My bureau has been broke open, and all taken away.

TONY. Stick to that; ha! ha! ha! stick to that. I'll bear witness, you know; call me to bear witness.

MRS. HARDCASTLE. I tell you, Tony, by all that's precious, the jewels are gone, and I shall be ruined forever.

TONY. Sure, I know they are gone, and I am to say so.

MRS. HARDCASTLE. My dearest Tony, but hear me. They're gone, I say.

TONY. By the laws, Mamma, you make me for to laugh, ha! ha! I know who took them well enough, ha! ha! ha!

MRS. HARDCASTLE. Was there ever such a blockhead, that can't tell the difference between jest and earnest? I tell you I'm not in jest, booby.

TONY. That's right, that's right; you must be in a bitter passion, and then nobody will suspect either of us. I'll bear witness that they are gone.

MRS. HARDCASTLE. Was there ever such a cross-grained brute, that won't hear me? Can you bear witness that you are no better than a fool? Was ever poor woman so beset with fools on one hand, and thieves on the other?

TONY. I can bear witness to that.

MRS. HARDCASTLE. Bear witness again, you blockhead you, and I'll turn you out of the room directly. My poor niece, what will become of *her?* Do you laugh, you unfeeling brute, as if you enjoyed my distress?

TONY. I can bear witness to that.

MRS. HARDCASTLE. Do you insult me, monster? I'll teach you to vex your mother, I will.

TONY. I can bear witness to that.

(*He runs off; she follows him.*)

Enter KATE *and* MAID.

KATE. What an unaccountable creature is that brother of mine, to send them to the house as an inn, ha! ha! I don't wonder at his impudence.

MAID. But what is more, madam, the young gentleman, as you passed by in your present dress, asked me if you were the barmaid. He mistook you for the barmaid, madam.

10 Catherine wheel: pinwheel kind of fireworks.

KATE. Did he? Then, as I live, I'm resolved to keep up the delusion. Tell me, Pimple, how do you like my present dress? Don't you think I look something like Cherry in *The Beaux' Stratagem?*[11]

MAID. It's the dress, madam, that every lady wears in the country, but when she visits or receives company.

KATE. And are you sure he does not remember my face or person?

MAID. Certain of it.

KATE. I vow I thought so; for though we spoke for some time together, yet his fears were such that he never once looked up during the interview. Indeed, if he had, my bonnet would have kept him from seeing me.

MAID. But what do you hope from keeping him in his mistake?

KATE. In the first place, I shall be *seen,* and that is no small advantage to a girl who brings her face to market. Then I shall perhaps make an acquaintance, and that's no small victory gained over one who never addresses any but the wildest of her sex. But my chief aim is to take my gentleman off his guard, and, like an invisible champion of romance, examine the giant's force before I offer to combat.

MAID. But you are sure you can act your part, and disguise your voice so that he may mistake that, as he has already mistaken your person?

KATE. Never fear me. I think I have got the true bar cant—Did your honor call?—Attend the Lion there—Pipes and tobacco for the Angel—The Lamb[12] has been outrageous this half hour.

MAID. It will do, madam. But he's here. *(Exit* MAID.)

Enter MARLOW.

11 Cherry . . . *Strategem:* the landlord's daughter in a popular play of this name by George Farquhar.
12 Lion, Angel, Lamb: rooms of an inn.

MARLOW. What a bawling in every part of the house! I have scarce a moment's repose. If I go to the best room, there I find my host and his story; if I fly to the gallery, there we have my hostess with her courtesy down to the ground. I have at last got a moment to myself, and now for recollection.
(Walks and muses.)

KATE. Did you call, sir? Did your honor call?

MARLOW *(musing).* As for Miss Hardcastle, she's too grave and sentimental for me.

KATE. Did your honor call?
(She still places herself before him, he turning away.)

MARLOW. No, child. *(Musing.)* Besides, from the glimpse I had of her, I think she squints.

KATE. I'm sure, sir, I heard the bell ring.

MARLOW. No, no. *(Musing.)* I have pleased my father, however, by coming down, and I'll tomorrow please myself by returning.
(Taking out his tablets and perusing.)

KATE. Perhaps the other gentleman called, sir?

MARLOW. I tell you, no.

KATE. I should be glad to know, sir. We have such a parcel of servants!

MARLOW. No, no, I tell you. *(Looks full in her face.)* Yes, child, I think I did call. I wanted—I wanted— I vow, child, you are vastly handsome.

KATE. Oh la, sir, you'll make one ashamed.

MARLOW. Never saw a more sprightly, malicious eye. Yes, yes, my dear, I did call. Have you got any of your—a— what d'ye call it in the house?

KATE. No, sir; we have been out of that these ten days.

MARLOW. One may call in this house, I find, to very little purpose. Suppose I should call for a taste, just by way of trial, of the nectar of your lips; perhaps I might be disappointed in that too.

KATE. Nectar! nectar! That's a liquor there's no call for in these parts. French, I suppose. We keep no French wines here, sir.

MARLOW. Of true English growth, I assure you.

KATE. Then it's odd I should not know it. We brew all sorts of wines in this house, and I have lived here these eighteen years.

MARLOW. Eighteen years! Why, one would think, child, you kept the bar before you were born. How old are you?

KATE. Oh! sir, I must not tell my age. They say women and music should never be dated.

MARLOW. To guess at this distance, you can't be much above forty. (*Approaching.*) Yet nearer I don't think so much. (*Approaching.*) By coming close to some women, they look younger still; but when we come very close indeed—(*Attempting to kiss her.*)

KATE. Pray, sir, keep your distance. One would think you wanted to know one's age as they do horses, by mark of mouth.

MARLOW. I protest, child, you use me extremely ill. If you keep me at this distance, how is it possible you and I can be ever acquainted?

KATE. And who wants to be acquainted with you? I want no such acquaintance, not I. I'm sure you did not treat Miss Hardcastle, that was here a while ago, in this obstropalous[13] manner. I'll warrant me, before her you looked dashed, and kept bowing to the ground, and talked, for all the world, as if you was before a justice of peace.

MARLOW (*aside*). Egad, she has hit it, sure enough! (*To her.*) In awe of her,

child? Ha! ha! ha! A mere awkward squinting thing; no, no. I find you don't know me. I laughed and rallied her a little; but I was unwilling to be too severe. No, I could not be too severe, curse me!

KATE. Oh, then, sir, you are a favorite, I find, among the ladies?

MARLOW. Yes, my dear, a great favorite. And yet, hang me, I don't see what they find in me to follow. At the Ladies' Club in town I'm called their agreeable Rattle. Rattle, child, is not my real name, but one I'm known by. My name is Solomons; Mr. Solomons, my dear, at your service. (*Offering to salute her.*)

KATE. Hold, sir, you are introducing me to your club, not to yourself. And you're so great a favorite there, you say?

MARLOW. Yes, my dear. There's Mrs. Mantrap, Lady Betty Blackleg, the Countess of Sligo, Mrs. Langhorns, old Miss Biddy Buckskin,[14] and your humble servant keep up the spirit of the place.

KATE. Then, it is a very merry place, I suppose?

MARLOW. Yes, as merry as cards, supper, wine, and old women can make us.

KATE. And their agreeable Rattle, ha! ha! ha!

MARLOW (*aside*). Egad! I don't quite like this chit. She looks knowing, methinks. You laugh, child?

KATE. I can't but laugh, to think what time they all have for minding their work or their family.

MARLOW (*aside*). All's well; she don't laugh at me. (*To her.*) Do *you* ever work, child?

KATE. Ay, sure. There's not a screen or a quilt in the whole house but what can bear witness to that.

---

13 **obstropalous:** obstreperous.

14 Miss **Biddy Buckskin:** a real character, friend of Horace Walpole.

THE ENLIGHTENMENT

MARLOW. Odso! then you must show me your embroidery. I embroider and draw patterns myself a little. If you want a judge of your work, you must apply to me. (*Seizing her hand.*)

KATE. Ay, but the colors do not look well by candlelight. You shall see all in the morning. (*Struggling.*)

MARLOW. And why not now, my angel? Such beauty fires beyond the power of resistance. Pshaw! the father here! My old luck: I never nicked seven that I did not throw ambsace three times following.[15]

(*Exit MARLOW.*)

Enter HARDCASTLE, who stands in surprise.

HARDCASTLE. So, madam. So I find *this* is your *modest* lover. This is your humble admirer, that kept his eyes fixed on the ground, and only adored at humble distance. Kate, Kate, art thou not ashamed to deceive your father so?

KATE. Never trust me, dear Papa, but he's still the modest man I first took him for; you'll be convinced of it as well as I.

HARDCASTLE. By the hand of my body, I believe his impudence is infectious! Didn't I see him seize your

hand? Didn't I see him haul you about like a milkmaid? And now you talk of his respect and his modesty, forsooth!

KATE. But if I shortly convince you of his modesty, that he has only the faults that will pass off with time, and the virtues that will improve with age, I hope you'll forgive him.

HARDCASTLE. The girl would actually make one run mad! I tell you I'll not be convinced. I am convinced. He has scarcely been three hours in the house, and he has already encroached on all my prerogatives. You may like his impudence, and call it modesty; but my son-in-law, madam, must have very different qualifications.

KATE. Sir, I ask but this night to convince you.

HARDCASTLE. You shall not have half the time, for I have thoughts of turning him out this very hour.

KATE. Give me that hour, then, and I hope to satisfy you.

HARDCASTLE. Well, an hour let it be, then. But I'll have no trifling with your father. All fair and open. Do you mind me?

KATE. I hope, sir, you have ever found that I considered your commands as my pride; for your kindness is such that my duty as yet has been inclination.

(*Exeunt.*)

15 **I never . . . following:** in dice throwing, to have good luck followed by very bad.

Questions for Study

Act III

1. The opening conversation between Mr. Hardcastle and his daughter suggests that they agree in their estimate of Marlow. What is the true situation? What irony do you find in the conversation? What does the audience know beyond what they each know?
2. Contrast Mrs. Hardcastle before she misses the jewels with Mrs. Hardcastle after she discovers they are truly missing. What well-known truth do her actions and comments demonstrate? Although Tony seems to maintain the same attitude toward his mother's an-

The scene from one of the spectacular heroic plays of the early Restoration period (above) is in the Drury Lane Theater. Below is the tavern scene from She Stoops to Conquer.

nouncement that the jewels are missing, both before and after they are truly missing, why are his lines after the real loss of the jewels more humorous than the ones spoken before?

3. As Kate enters after the robbery scene, she now knows that Marlow thinks he is at an inn. How does she propose to take advantage of that knowledge?

4. How would you stage this scene between Marlow and Kate to make the situation of mistaken identity credible?

5. Near the end of this scene what is the dramatic significance of Kate's request: "Give me that hour, then"?

THE ENLIGHTENMENT

The house.

Enter Hastings *and* Constance.

Hastings. You surprise me; Sir Charles Marlow expected here this night! Where have you had your information?

Constance. You may depend upon it. I just saw his letter to Mr. Hardcastle, in which he tells him he intends setting out a few hours after his son.

Hastings. Then, my Constance, all must be completed before he arrives. He knows me; and should he find me here, would discover[1] my name, and perhaps my designs, to the rest of the family.

Constance. The jewels, I hope, are safe?

Hastings. Yes, yes. I have sent them to Marlow, who keeps the keys of our baggage. In the meantime I'll go to prepare matters for our elopement. I have had the squire's promise of a fresh pair of horses; and, if I should not see him again, will write him further directions. (*Exit.*)

Constance. Well, success attend you! In the meantime I'll go and amuse my aunt with the old pretense of a violent passion for my cousin. (*Exit.*)

Enter Marlow, *followed by a* Servant.

Marlow. I wonder what Hastings could mean by sending me so valuable a thing as a casket to keep for him, when he knows the only place I have is the seat of a post coach at an inn door. Have you deposited the casket with the landlady, as I ordered you? Have you put it into her own hands?

Servant. Yes, your honor.

Marlow. She said she'd keep it safe, did she?

Servant. Yes, she said she'd keep it safe enough; she asked me how I came

by it, and she said she had a great mind to make me give an account of myself. (*Exit* Servant.)

Marlow. Ha! ha! ha! They're safe, however. What an unaccountable set of beings have we got amongst! This little barmaid, though, runs in my head most strangely, and drives out the absurdities of all the rest of the family. She's mine, she must be mine, or I'm greatly mistaken.

Enter Hastings.

Hastings. Bless me! I quite forgot to tell her that I intended to prepare at the bottom of the garden. Marlow here, and in spirits too?

Marlow. Give me joy, George. Crown me, shadow me with laurels! Well, George, after all, we modest fellows don't want for success among the women.

Hastings. Some women, you mean. But what success has your honor's modesty been crowned with now, that it grows so insolent upon us?

Marlow. Didn't you see the tempting, brisk, lovely little thing that runs about the house with a bunch of keys to its girdle?

Hastings. Well, and what then?

Marlow. She's mine, you rogue you. Such fire, such motion, such eyes, such lips! but, egad! she would not let me kiss them though.

Hastings. But are you so sure, so very sure, of her?

Marlow. Why, man, she talked of showing me her work above stairs, and I am to improve the pattern.

Hastings. But how can *you*, Charles, go about to rob a woman of her honor?

Marlow. Pshaw! pshaw! We all know the honor of the barmaid of an inn. . . .

Hastings. I believe the girl has virtue.

Marlow. And if she has, I should be

1 discover: disclose.

the last man in the world that would attempt to corrupt it.

HASTINGS. You have taken care, I hope, of the casket I sent you to lock up? It's in safety?

MARLOW. Yes, yes. It's safe enough. I have taken care of it. But how could you think the seat of a post coach at an inn door a place of safety? Ah, numskull! I have taken better precautions for you than you did for yourself. I have—

HASTINGS. What?

MARLOW. I have sent it to the landlady to keep for you.

HASTINGS. To the landlady?

MARLOW. The landlady.

HASTINGS. You did?

MARLOW. I did. She's to be answerable for its forthcoming, you know.

HASTINGS. Yes, she'll bring it forth with a witness.

MARLOW. Wasn't I right? I believe you'll allow that I acted prudently upon this occasion.

HASTINGS (aside). He must not see my uneasiness.

MARLOW. You seem a little disconcerted though, methinks. Sure, nothing has happened?

HASTINGS. No, nothing. Never was in better spirits in all my life. And so you left it with the landlady, who, no doubt, very readily undertook the charge.

MARLOW. Rather too readily. For she not only kept the casket, but, through her great precaution, was going to keep the messenger too. Ha! ha! ha!

HASTINGS. He! he! he! They're safe, however.

MARLOW. As a guinea in a miser's purse.

HASTINGS (aside). So now all hopes of fortune are at an end, and we must set off without it. (To him.) Well, Charles, I'll leave you to your medita-

tions on the pretty barmaid, and—he! he! he!—may you be as successful for yourself as you have been for me!

(Exit.)

MARLOW. Thank ye, George; I ask no more. Ha! ha! ha!

Enter HARDCASTLE.

HARDCASTLE. I no longer know my own house. It's turned all topsy-turvy. His servants have got drunk already. I'll bear it no longer; and yet, from my respect for his father, I'll be calm. (To him.) Mr. Marlow, your servant. I'm your very humble servant. (Bowing low.)

MARLOW. Sir, your humble servant. (Aside.) What's to be the wonder now?

HARDCASTLE. I believe, sir, you must be sensible, sir, that no man alive ought to be more welcome than your father's son, sir. I hope you think so?

MARLOW. I do, from my soul, sir. I don't want much entreaty. I generally make my father's son welcome wherever he goes.

HARDCASTLE. I believe you do, from my soul, sir. But though I say nothing to your own conduct, that of your servants is insufferable. Their manner of drinking is setting a very bad example in this house, I assure you.

MARLOW. I protest, my very good sir, that is no fault of mine. If they don't drink as they ought, *they* are to blame. I ordered them not to spare the cellar. I did, I assure you. (To the side scene.) Here, let one of my servants come up. (To him.) My positive directions were, that as I did not drink myself, they should make up for my deficiencies below.

HARDCASTLE. Then they had your orders for what they do? I'm satisfied!

MARLOW. They had, I assure you. You shall hear from one of themselves.

Enter SERVANT, *drunk.*

THE ENLIGHTENMENT

MARLOW. You, Jeremy! Come forward, sirrah. What were my orders? Were you not told to drink freely, and call for what you thought fit, for the good of the house?

HARDCASTLE (*aside*). I begin to lose my patience.

JEREMY. Please your honor, liberty and Fleet Street[2] forever! Though I'm but a servant, I'm as good as another man. I'll drink for no man before supper, sir, damme! Good liquor will sit upon a good supper, but a good supper will not sit upon—hiccup—upon my conscience, sir.

MARLOW. You see, my old friend, the fellow is as drunk as he can possibly be. I don't know what you'd have more, unless you'd have the poor devil soused in a beer barrel.

HARDCASTLE. Zounds! he'll drive me distracted, if I contain myself any longer. Mr. Marlow—sir; I have submitted to your insolence for more than four hours, and I see no likelihood of its coming to an end. I'm now resolved to be master here, sir; and I desire that you and your drunken pack may leave my house directly.

MARLOW. Leave your house! Sure, you jest, my good friend! What? when I'm doing what I can to please you!

HARDCASTLE. I tell you, sir, you don't please me; so I desire you'll leave my house.

MARLOW. Sure you cannot be serious? At this time o' night, and such a night! You only mean to banter me.

HARDCASTLE. I tell you, sir, I'm serious! And, now that my passions are roused, I say this house is mine, sir; this house is mine, and I command you to leave it directly.

MARLOW. Ha! ha! ha! A puddle in a storm. I sha'n't stir a step, I assure you.

(*In a serious tone.*) This your house, fellow! It's my house. This is my house. Mine, while I choose to stay. What right have you to bid me leave this house, sir? I never met with such impudence, curse me; never in my whole life before!

HARDCASTLE. Nor I, confound me if ever I did! To come to my house, to call for what he likes, to turn me out of my own chair, to insult the family, to order his servants to get drunk, and then to tell me "This house is mine, sir!" By all that's impudent, it makes me laugh. Ha! ha! ha! Pray, sir (*bantering*), as you take the house, what think you of taking the rest of the furniture? There's a pair of silver candlesticks, and there's a fire screen, and here's a pair of brazen-nosed bellows; perhaps you may take a fancy to them.

MARLOW. Bring me your bill, sir; bring me your bill, and let's make no more words about it.

HARDCASTLE. There are a set of prints, too. What think you of the Rake's Progress,[3] for your own apartment?

MARLOW. Bring me your bill, I say; and I'll leave you and your infernal house directly.

HARDCASTLE. Then there's a mahogany table that you may see your own face in.

MARLOW. My bill, I say.

HARDCASTLE. I had forgot the great chair for your own particular slumbers, after a hearty meal.

MARLOW. Zounds! bring me my bill, I say, and let's hear no more on't.

HARDCASTLE. Young man, young man, from your father's letter to me, I was taught to expect a well-bred, modest man as a visitor here; but now I find him no better than a coxcomb and a

---

2 liberty and Fleet Street: a political slogan of the time.

3 Rake's Progress: a famous series of pictures by William Hogarth, showing the gradual ruin of a young man.

bully. But he will be down here presently, and shall hear more of it.

(*Exit.*)

MARLOW. How's this? Sure, I have not mistaken the house! Everything looks like an inn; the servants cry, "Coming"; the attendance is awkward; the barmaid, too, to attend us. But she's here, and will further inform me. Whither so fast, child? A word with you.

Enter KATE.

KATE. Let it be short, then. I'm in a hurry. (*Aside.*) I believe he begins to find out his mistake. But it's too soon quite to undeceive him.

MARLOW. Pray, child, answer me one question. What are you, and what may your business in this house be?

KATE. A relation of the family, sir.

MARLOW. What, a poor relation?

KATE. Yes, sir; a poor relation, appointed to keep the keys, and to see that the guests want nothing in my power to give them.

MARLOW. That is, you act as the barmaid of this inn.

KATE. Inn! O law! what brought that in your head? One of the best families in the country keep an inn! Ha! ha! ha! old Mr. Hardcastle's house an inn!

MARLOW. Mr. Hardcastle's house! Is this Mr. Hardcastle's house, child?

KATE. Ay, sure! Whose else should it be?

MARLOW. So, then, all's out, and I have been damnably imposed on. Oh, confound my stupid head, I shall be laughed at over the whole town! I shall be stuck up *in caricatura* in all the print shops. The *Dullissimo Macaroni.*[4] To mistake this house, of all others, for an inn, and my father's old friend for an innkeeper! What a swaggering puppy must he take me for! What a silly puppy do I find myself! There again, may I be hanged, my dear, but I mistook you for the barmaid!

KATE. Dear me! dear me! I'm sure there's nothing in my *behavior* to put me upon a level with one of that stamp.

MARLOW. Nothing, my dear, nothing. But I was in for a list of blunders, and could not help making you a subscriber. My stupidity saw everything the wrong way. I mistook your assiduity for assurance, and your simplicity for allurement. But it's over. This house I no more show *my* face in.

KATE. I hope, sir, I have done nothing to disoblige you. I'm sure I should be sorry to affront any gentleman who has been so polite, and said so many civil things to me. I'm sure I should be sorry (*pretending to cry*) if he left the family upon my account. I'm sure I should be sorry people said anything amiss, since I have no fortune but my character.

MARLOW (*aside*). By Heaven, she weeps! This is the first mark of tenderness I ever had from a modest woman, and it touches me. (*To her.*) Excuse me, my lovely girl; you are the only part of the family I leave with reluctance. But, to be plain with you, the difference of our birth, fortune, and education makes an honorable connection impossible; and I can never harbor a thought of seducing simplicity that trusted in my honor, of bringing ruin upon one whose only fault was being too lovely.

KATE (*aside*). Generous man! I now begin to admire him. (*To him.*) But I am sure my family is as good as Miss Hardcastle's; and though I'm poor, that's no great misfortune to a contented mind; and, until this moment, I never thought that it was bad to want fortune.

---

4 **Dullissimo Macaroni:** dullest of dandies.

MARLOW. And why now, my pretty simplicity?

KATE. Because it puts me at a distance from one that, if I had a thousand pound, I would give it all to.

MARLOW (*aside*). This simplicity bewitches me, so that if I stay, I'm undone. I must make one bold effort, and leave her. (*To her.*) Your partiality in my favor, my dear, touches me most sensibly; and were I to live for myself alone, I could easily fix my choice. But I owe too much to the opinion of the world, too much to the authority of a father; so that—I can scarcely speak it— it affects me. Farewell. (*Exit.*)

KATE. I never knew half his merit till now. He shall not go, if I have power or art to detain him. I'll still preserve the character in which *I stooped to conquer,* but will undeceive my papa, who perhaps may laugh him out of his resolution. (*Exit.*)

Enter TONY *and* CONSTANCE.

TONY. Ay, you may steal for yourselves the next time. I have done my duty. She has got the jewels again, that's a sure thing; but she believes it was all a mistake of the servants.

CONSTANCE. But, my dear cousin, sure you won't forsake us in this distress? If she in the least suspects that I am going off, I shall certainly be locked up, or sent to my Aunt Pedigree's, which is ten times worse.

TONY. To be sure, aunts of all kinds are damned bad things. But what can I do? I have got you a pair of horses that will fly like Whistle-jacket;[5] and I'm sure you can't say but I have courted you nicely before her face. Here she comes; we must court a bit or two more, for fear she should suspect us.

(*They retire, and seem to fondle.*)

Enter MRS. HARDCASTLE.

MRS. HARDCASTLE. Well, I was greatly fluttered, to be sure. But my son tells me it was all a mistake of the servants. I sha'n't be easy, however, till they are fairly married, and then let her keep her own fortune. But what do I see? Fondling together, as I'm alive! I never saw Tony so sprightly before. Ah! have I caught you, my pretty doves? What! billing, exchanging stolen glances and broken murmurs? Ah!

TONY. As for murmurs, Mother, we grumble a little now and then, to be sure. But there's no love lost between us.

MRS. HARDCASTLE. A mere sprinkling, Tony, upon the flame, only to make it burn brighter.

CONSTANCE. Cousin Tony promises to give us more of his company at home. Indeed, he sha'n't leave us any more. It won't leave us, Cousin Tony, will it?

TONY. Oh, it's a pretty creature! No, I'd sooner leave my horse in a pound than leave you when you smile upon one so. Your laugh makes you so becoming!

CONSTANCE. Agreeable cousin! Who can help admiring that natural humor, that pleasant, broad, red, thoughtless— (*patting his cheek*) ah! it's a bold face.

MRS. HARDCASTLE. Pretty innocence!

TONY. I'm sure, I always loved Cousin Con's hazel eyes, and her pretty long fingers, that she twists this way and that over the haspicholls,[6] like a parcel of bobbins.

MRS. HARDCASTLE. Ah, he would charm the bird from the tree. I was never so happy before. My boy takes after his father, poor Mr. Lumpkin, exactly. The jewels, my dear Con, shall be yours incontinently.[7] You shall have

---

5 Whistle-jacket: a famous race horse.

6 haspicholls: Tony's way of saying *harpsichord.*
7 incontinently: immediately.

them. Isn't he a sweet boy, my dear? You shall be married tomorrow, and we'll put off the rest of his education, like Dr. Drowsy's sermons, to a fitter opportunity.

Enter DIGGORY.

DIGGORY. Where's the squire? I have got a letter for your worship.

TONY. Give it to my mamma. She reads all my letters first.

DIGGORY. I had orders to deliver it into your own hands.

TONY. Who does it come from?

DIGGORY. Your worship mun[8] ask that o' the letter itself.

TONY. I could wish to know though. (*Turning the letter and gazing on it.*)

CONSTANCE (*aside*). Undone! undone! A letter to him from Hastings. I know the hand. If my aunt sees it, we are ruined forever. I'll keep her employed a little if I can. (*To* MRS. HARDCASTLE.) But I have not told you, madam, of my cousin's smart answer just now to Mr. Marlow. We so laughed. You must know, madam—. This way a little, for he must not hear us. (*They confer.*)

TONY (*still gazing*). A damned cramp piece of penmanship as ever I saw in my life! I can read your print hand very well. But here there are such handles, and shanks, and dashes, that one can scarce tell the head from the tail. "To Anthony Lumpkin, Esq." It's very odd, I can read the outside of my letters, where my own name is, well enough. But when I come to open it, it's all—buzz. That's hard, very hard; for the inside of the letter is always the cream of the correspondence.

MRS. HARDCASTLE. Ha! ha! ha! Very well, very well. And so my son was too hard for the philosopher?

CONSTANCE. Yes, madam; but you must hear the rest, madam. A little

more this way, or he may hear us. You'll hear how he puzzled him again.

MRS. HARDCASTLE. He seems strangely puzzled now himself, methinks.

TONY (*still gazing*). A damned up-and-down hand, as if it was disguised in liquor. (*Reading.*) "Dear Sir"—ay, that's that. Then there's an *M*, and a *T*, and an *S;* but whether the next be an izzard[9] or an *R*, confound me, I cannot tell.

MRS. HARDCASTLE. What's that, my dear? Can I give you any assistance?

CONSTANCE. Pray, aunt, let me read it. Nobody reads a cramp hand better than I. (*Twitching the letter from him.*) Do you know who it is from?

TONY. Can't tell, except from Dick Ginger, the feeder.[10]

CONSTANCE. Ay, so it is. (*Pretending to read.*) "Dear Squire,— Hoping that you're in health, as I am at this present. The gentlemen of the Shake-bag[11] Club has cut the gentlemen of Goose-green quite out of feather. The odds—um— odd battle—um—long fighting—um—" Here, here, it's all about cocks and fighting; it's of no consequence; here, put it up, put it up. (*Thrusting the crumpled letter upon him.*)

TONY. But I tell you, miss, it's of all the consequence in the world. I would not lose the rest of it for a guinea. Here, Mother, do you make it out. Of no consequence! (*Giving* MRS. HARDCASTLE *the letter.*)

MRS. HARDCASTLE. How's this! (*Reads.*) "Dear Squire,—I'm now waiting for Miss Neville, with a post chaise and pair, at the bottom of the garden, but I find my horses yet unable to perform the journey. I expect you'll assist us with a pair of fresh horses, as you promised. Dispatch is necessary, as the

---

8 mun: dialect word for *must.*

9 **izzard:** old name for the letter *z.*
10 **feeder:** trainer of gamecocks.
11 **Shake-bag:** large fighting cock.

THE ENLIGHTENMENT

hag [ay, the hag], your mother, will otherwise suspect us. Yours, Hastings." Grant me patience; I shall run distracted! My rage chokes me.

CONSTANCE. I hope, madam, you'll suspend your resentment for a few moments, and not impute to me any impertinence or sinister design that belongs to another.

MRS. HARDCASTLE (*courtesying very low*). Fine spoken, madam, you are most miraculously polite and engaging, and quite the very pink of courtesy and circumspection, madam. (*Changing her tone.*) And you, you great ill-fashioned oaf, with scarce sense enough to keep your mouth shut! were you, too, joined against me? But I'll defeat all your plots in a moment. As for you, madam, since you have got a pair of fresh horses ready, it would be cruel to disappoint them. So, if you please, instead of running away with your spark, prepare, this very moment, to run off with *me*. Your old Aunt Pedigree will keep you secure, I'll warrant me. You too, sir, may mount your horse, and guard us upon the way. Here, Thomas, Roger, Diggory! I'll show you that I wish you better than you do yourselves.

(*Exit.*)

CONSTANCE. So now I'm completely ruined.

TONY. Ay, that's a sure thing.

CONSTANCE. What better could be expected from being connected with such a stupid fool! And after all the nods and signs I made him!

TONY. By the laws, miss, it was your own cleverness, and not my stupidity, that did your business. You were so nice and so busy with your Shake-bags and Goose-greens that I thought you could never be making believe.

Enter HASTINGS.

HASTINGS. So, sir, I find, by my servant, that you have shown my letter and betrayed us. Was this well done, young gentleman?

TONY. Here's another. Ask miss, there, who betrayed you. Ecod, it was her doing, not mine.

Enter MARLOW.

MARLOW. So I have been finely used here among you. Rendered contemptible, driven into ill manners, despised, insulted, laughed at.

TONY. Here's another. We shall have old Bedlam[12] broke loose presently.

CONSTANCE. And there, sir, is the gentleman to whom we all owe every obligation.

MARLOW. What can I say to him? a mere boy, an idiot, whose ignorance and age are a protection.

HASTINGS. A poor contemptible booby, that would but disgrace correction.

CONSTANCE. Yet with cunning and malice enough to make himself merry with all our embarrassments.

HASTINGS. An insensible cub.

MARLOW. Replete with tricks and mischief.

TONY. Baw! damme, but I'll fight you both, one after the other—with baskets.[13]

MARLOW. As for him, he's below resentment. But your conduct, Mr. Hastings, requires an explanation. You knew of my mistakes, yet would not undeceive me.

HASTINGS. Tortured as I am with my own disappointments, is this a time for explanations? It is not friendly, Mr. Marlow.

MARLOW. But, sir—

CONSTANCE. Mr. Marlow, we never kept on your mistake till it was too late to undeceive you. Be pacified.

---

12 **Bedlam:** a lunatic asylum, Bethlehem Hospital in London.
13 **baskets:** fencing sticks with basketwork guards for the hands.

Enter SERVANT.

SERVANT. My mistress desires you'll get ready immediately, madam. The horses are putting to. Your hat and things are in the next room. We are to go thirty miles before morning.

(*Exit* SERVANT.)

CONSTANCE. Well, well; I'll come presently.

MARLOW (*to* HASTINGS). Was it well done, sir, to assist in rendering me ridiculous? To hang me out for the scorn of all my acquaintance? Depend upon it, sir, I shall expect an explanation.

HASTINGS. Was it well done, sir, if you're upon that subject, to deliver what I entrusted to yourself to the care of another, sir?

CONSTANCE. Mr. Hastings! Mr. Marlow! Why will you increase my distress by this groundless dispute? I implore, I entreat you—

Enter SERVANT.

SERVANT. Your cloak, madam. My mistress is impatient.

(*Exit* SERVANT.)

CONSTANCE. I come. Pray, be pacified. If I leave you thus, I shall die with apprehension.

Enter SERVANT.

SERVANT. Your fan, muff, and gloves, madam. The horses are waiting.

CONSTANCE. Oh, Mr. Marlow, if you knew what a scene of constraint and ill nature lies before me, I am sure it would convert your resentment into pity.

MARLOW. I'm so distracted with a variety of passions that I don't know what I do. Forgive me, madam. George, forgive me. You know my hasty temper, and should not exasperate it.

HASTINGS. The torture of my situation is my only excuse.

CONSTANCE. Well, my dear Hastings, if you have that esteem for me that I think—that I am sure you have, your constancy for three years will but increase the happiness of our future connection. If—

MRS. HARDCASTLE (*within*). Miss Neville! Constance, why, Constance, I say!

CONSTANCE. I'm coming. Well, constancy, remember, constancy is the word. (*Exit.*)

HASTINGS. My heart! how can I support this? To be so near happiness, and such happiness!

MARLOW (*to* TONY). You see now, young gentleman, the effects of your folly. What might be amusement to you is here disappointment, and even distress.

TONY (*from a reverie*). Ecod, I have hit it: it's here. Your hands. Yours and yours, my poor Sulky. My boots there, ho! Meet me two hours hence at the bottom of the garden; and if you don't find Tony Lumpkin a more good-natured fellow than you thought for, I'll give you leave to take my best horse, and Bet Bouncer into the bargain. Come along. My boots, ho! (*Exeunt.*)

Questions for Study

ACT IV

1. How are the complications of the several plot lines of the play intensified in this act?
2. How should this scene be played? Comment, as if you were a director, on entrances and exits, the speaking of the lines, the action.

Why is it dramatically appropriate in this scene to keep the dialogue between pairs or among groups short? How is continuity maintained?

3. How does Marlow's discovery of his mistake about the inn change his attitude toward Kate?

4. How does the reading of the letter hasten the solution of the plot?

Act V

Scene I. *The house.*

Enter Hastings *and* Servant.

HASTINGS. You saw the old lady and Miss Neville drive off, you say?

SERVANT. Yes, your honor. They went off in a post coach, and the young squire went on horseback. They're thirty miles off by this time.

HASTINGS. Then all my hopes are over.

SERVANT. Yes, sir. Old Sir Charles is arrived. He and the old gentleman of the house have been laughing at Mr. Marlow's mistake this half hour. They are coming this way.

HASTINGS. Then I must not be seen. So now to my fruitless appointment at the bottom of the garden. This is about the time. (*Exit.*)

Enter Sir Charles *and* Hardcastle.

HARDCASTLE. Ha! ha! ha! The peremptory tone in which he sent forth his sublime commands!

SIR CHARLES. And the reserve with which I suppose he treated all your advances.

HARDCASTLE. And yet he might have seen something in me above a common innkeeper, too.

SIR CHARLES. Yes, Dick, but he mistook you for an uncommon innkeeper; ha! ha! ha!

HARDCASTLE. Well, I'm in too good spirits to think of anything but joy. Yes, my dear friend, this union of our families will make our personal friendships hereditary; and though my daughter's fortune is but small—

SIR CHARLES. Why, Dick, will you talk of fortune to *me?* My son is possessed of more than a competence[1] already, and can want nothing but a good and virtuous girl to share his happiness, and increase it. If they like each other, as you say they do—

HARDCASTLE. *If*, man! I tell you they *do* like each other. My daughter as good as told me so.

SIR CHARLES. But girls are apt to flatter themselves, you know.

HARDCASTLE. I saw him grasp her hand in the warmest manner myself; and here he comes to put you out of your *ifs*, I warrant him.

Enter Marlow.

MARLOW. I come, sir, once more, to ask pardon for my strange conduct. I can scarce reflect on my insolence without confusion.

HARDCASTLE. Tut, boy; a trifle. You take it too gravely. An hour or two's laughing with my daughter will set all to rights again. She'll never like you the worse for it.

MARLOW. Sir, I shall be always proud of her approbation.

HARDCASTLE. Approbation is but a cold word, Mr. Marlow; if I am not deceived, you have something more than

1 competence: sufficient fortune.

OLIVER GOLDSMITH

approbation thereabouts. You take me?[2]

MARLOW. Really, sir, I have not that happiness.

HARDCASTLE. Come, boy, I'm an old fellow, and know what's what as well as you that are younger. I know what has passed between you; but mum.

MARLOW. Sure, sir, nothing has passed between us but the most profound respect on my side, and the most distant reserve on hers. You don't think, sir, that my impudence has been passed upon all the rest of the family?

HARDCASTLE. Impudence! No, I don't say that—not quite impudence; though girls like to be played with, and rumpled a little, too, sometimes. But she has told no tales, I assure you.

MARLOW. I never gave her the slightest cause.

HARDCASTLE. Well, well, I like modesty in its place well enough. But this is overacting, young gentleman. You may be open. Your father and I will like you the better for it.

MARLOW. May I die, sir, if I ever—

HARDCASTLE. I tell you, she don't dislike you; and as I'm sure you like her—

MARLOW. Dear sir, I protest, sir—

HARDCASTLE. I see no reason why you should not be joined as fast as the parson can tie you.

MARLOW. But hear me, sir—

HARDCASTLE. Your father approves the match, I admire it; every moment's delay will be doing mischief; so—

MARLOW. But why won't you hear me? By all that's just and true, I never gave Miss Hardcastle the slightest mark of my attachment, or even the most distant hint to suspect me of affection! We had but one interview, and that was formal, modest, and uninteresting.

HARDCASTLE (*aside*). This fellow's formal modest impudence is beyond bearing.

SIR CHARLES. And you never grasped her hand, or made any protestations?

MARLOW. As Heaven is my witness, I came down in obedience to your commands; I saw the lady without emotion, and parted without reluctance. I hope you'll exact no farther proofs of my duty, nor prevent me from leaving a house in which I suffer so many mortifications. (*Exit.*)

SIR CHARLES. I'm astonished at the air of sincerity with which he parted.

HARDCASTLE. And I'm astonished at the deliberate intrepidity of his assurance.

SIR CHARLES. I dare pledge my life and honor upon his truth.

HARDCASTLE. Here comes my daughter, and I would stake my happiness upon her veracity.

Enter KATE.

HARDCASTLE. Kate, come hither, child. Answer us sincerely and without reserve: has Mr. Marlow made you any professions of love and affection?

KATE. The question is very abrupt, sir! But since you require unreserved sincerity, I think he has.

HARDCASTLE (*to* SIR CHARLES). You see.

SIR CHARLES. And pray, madam, have you and my son had more than one interview?

KATE. Yes, sir, several.

HARDCASTLE (*to* SIR CHARLES). You see.

SIR CHARLES. But did he profess any attachment?

KATE. A lasting one.

SIR CHARLES. Did he talk of love?

KATE. Much, sir.

SIR CHARLES. Amazing! And all this formally?

KATE. Formally.

2 **You take me?:** You understand me?

HARDCASTLE. Now, my friend, I hope you are satisfied.

SIR CHARLES. And how did he behave, madam?

KATE. As most professed admirers do: said some civil things of my face; talked much of his want of merit, and the greatness of mine; mentioned his heart, gave a short tragedy speech, and ended with pretended rapture.

SIR CHARLES. Now I'm perfectly convinced indeed. I know his conversation among women to be modest and submissive; this forward, canting, ranting manner by no means describes him; and, I am confident, he never sat for the picture.

KATE. Then, what, sir, if I should convince you to your face of my sincerity? If you and my papa, in about half an hour, will place yourselves behind that screen, you shall hear him declare his passion to me in person.

SIR CHARLES. Agreed. And if I find him what you describe, all my happiness in him must have an end.

(*Exit.*)

KATE. And if you don't find him what I describe—I fear my happiness must never have a beginning. (*Exeunt.*)

Scene II. *The back of the garden.*

Enter **HASTINGS.**

HASTINGS. What an idiot am I, to wait here for a fellow who probably takes a delight in mortifying me! He never intended to be punctual, and I'll wait no longer. What do I see? It is he! and perhaps with news of my Constance.

Enter **TONY,** *booted and spattered.*

HASTINGS. My honest squire! I now find you a man of your word. This looks like friendship.

TONY. Ay, I'm your friend, and the best friend you have in the world, if you knew but all. This riding by night, by-the-bye, is cursedly tiresome. It has shook me worse than the basket of a stagecoach.

HASTINGS. But how? Where did you leave your fellow travelers? Are they in safety? Are they housed?

TONY. Five-and-twenty miles in two hours and a half is no such bad driving. The poor beasts have smoked for it. Rabbit me,[1] but I'd rather ride forty miles after a fox than ten with such varment.

HASTINGS. Well, but where have you left the ladies? I die with impatience.

TONY. Left them! Why, where should I leave them but where I found them?

HASTINGS. This is a riddle.

TONY. Riddle me this then. What's that goes round the house, and round the house, and never touches the house?

HASTINGS. I'm still astray.

TONY. Why, that's it, mon. I have led them astray. By jingo, there's not a pond or a slough within five miles of the place but they can tell the taste of.

HASTINGS. Ha! ha! ha! I understand: you took them in a round, while they supposed themselves going forward. And so you have at last brought them home again.

TONY. You shall hear. I first took them down Feather-bed Lane, where we stuck fast in the mud. I then rattled them crack over the stones of Up-and-down Hill. I then introduced them to the gibbet on Heavy-tree Heath; and from that, with a circumbendibus,[2] I fairly lodged them in the horse pond at the bottom of the garden.

HASTINGS. But no accident, I hope?

TONY. No, no, only Mother is confoundedly frightened. She thinks herself forty miles off. She's sick of the

1 **rabbit me:** confound me.
2 **circumbendibus:** circuitous way.

journey; and the cattle can scarce crawl. So if your own horses be ready, you may whip off with cousin, and I'll be bound that no soul here can budge a foot to follow you.

HASTINGS. My dear friend, how can I be grateful?

TONY. Ay, now it's dear friend, noble squire. Just now, it was all idiot, cub, and run me through the guts. Damn *your* way of fighting, I say. After we take a knock in this part of the country, we kiss and be friends. But if you had run me through the guts, then I should be dead, and you might go kiss the hangman.[3]

HASTINGS. The rebuke is just. But I must hasten to relieve Miss Neville; if you keep the old lady employed, I promise to take care of the young one.

(*Exit* HASTINGS.)

TONY. Never fear me. Here she comes. Vanish! She's got from the pond, and draggled up to the waist like a mermaid.

Enter MRS. HARDCASTLE.

MRS. HARDCASTLE. Oh, Tony, I'm killed! Shook! Battered to death! I shall never survive it. That last jolt, that laid us against the quickset hedge,[4] has done my business.

TONY. Alack, Mamma, it was all your own fault. You would be for running away by night, without knowing one inch of the way.

MRS. HARDCASTLE. I wish we were at home again. I never met so many accidents in so short a journey. Drenched in the mud, overturned in a ditch, stuck fast in a slough, jolted to a jelly, and at last to lose our way! Whereabouts do you think we are, Tony?

TONY. By my guess, we should come upon Crackskull Common, about forty miles from home.

MRS. HARDCASTLE. O lud! O lud! The most notorious spot in all the country. We only want a robbery to make a complete night on't.

TONY. Don't be afraid, Mamma, don't be afraid. Two of the five that kept here[5] are hanged, and the other three may not find us. Don't be afraid. Is that a man that's galloping behind us? No; it's only a tree. Don't be afraid.

MRS. HARDCASTLE. The fright will certainly kill me.

TONY. Do you see anything like a black hat moving behind the thicket?

MRS. HARDCASTLE. Oh, death!

TONY. No; it's only a cow. Don't be afraid, Mamma; don't be afraid.

MRS. HARDCASTLE. As I'm alive, Tony, I see a man coming towards us. Ah! I'm sure on't. If he perceives us, we are undone.

TONY (*aside*). Father-in-law, by all that's unlucky, come to take one of his night walks. (*To her.*) Ah! it's a highwayman with pistols as long as my arm; a damned ill-looking fellow.

MRS. HARDCASTLE. Good Heaven defend us! He approaches.

TONY. Do you hide yourself in that thicket, and leave me to manage him. If there be any danger, I'll cough, and cry hem. When I cough, be sure to keep close.[6]

(MRS. HARDCASTLE *hides behind a tree in the back scene.*)

Enter HARDCASTLE.

HARDCASTLE. I'm mistaken, or I heard voices of people in want of help. Oh, Tony! is that you? I did not expect you so soon back. Are your mother and her charge in safety?

TONY. Very safe, sir, at my Aunt Pedigree's. Hem!

MRS. HARDCASTLE (*from behind*). Ah, death! I find there's danger.

---

3 **kiss the hangman:** go to the gallows.
4 **quickset hedge:** hawthorn or box hedge.
5 **kept here:** frequented this place.
6 **keep close:** keep hidden.

THE ENLIGHTENMENT

HARDCASTLE. Forty miles in three hours; sure, that's too much, my youngster.

TONY. Stout horses and willing minds make short journeys, as they say. Hem!

MRS. HARDCASTLE (*from behind*). Sure he'll do the dear boy no harm.

HARDCASTLE. But I heard a voice here; I should be glad to know from whence it came.

TONY. It was I, sir, talking to myself, sir. I was saying that forty miles in four hours was very good going. Hem! As to be sure it was. Hem! I have got a sort of cold by being out in the air. We'll go in, if you please. Hem!

HARDCASTLE. But if you talked to yourself, you did not answer to yourself. I'm certain I heard two voices, and am resolved (*raising his voice*) to find the other out.

MRS. HARDCASTLE (*from behind*). Oh! he's coming to find me out. Oh!

TONY. What need you go, sir, if I tell you? Hem! I'll lay down my life for the truth—hem!—I'll tell you all, sir. (*Detaining him.*)

HARDCASTLE. I tell you I will not be detained. I insist on seeing. It's in vain to expect I'll believe you.

MRS. HARDCASTLE (*running forward from behind*). O lud! he'll murder my poor boy, my darling! Here, good gentleman, whet your rage upon me. Take my money, my life; but spare that young gentleman; spare my child, if you have any mercy.

HARDCASTLE. My wife, as I'm a Christian! From whence can she come? or what does she mean?

MRS. HARDCASTLE (*kneeling*). Take compassion on us, good Mr. Highwayman. Take our money, our watches, all we have; but spare our lives. We will never bring you to justice; indeed we won't, good Mr. Highwayman.

HARDCASTLE. I believe the woman's out of her senses. What, Dorothy! don't you know *me?*

MRS. HARDCASTLE. Mr. Hardcastle, as I'm alive! My fears blinded me. But who, my dear, could have expected to meet you here, in this frightful place, so far from home? What has brought you to follow us?

HARDCASTLE. Sure, Dorothy, you have not lost your wits? So far from home, when you are within forty yards of your own door! (*To him.*) This is one of your old tricks, you graceless rogue, you. (*To her.*) Don't you know the gate and the mulberry tree; and don't you remember the horse pond, my dear?

MRS. HARDCASTLE. Yes, I shall remember the horse pond as long as I live; I have caught my death in it. (*To Tony.*) And is it to you, you graceless varlet, I owe all this? I'll teach you to abuse your mother, I will.

TONY. Ecod, Mother, all the parish says you have spoiled me, and so you may take the fruits on't.

MRS. HARDCASTLE. I'll spoil you, I will. (*Follows him off the stage.*)

HARDCASTLE. There's morality,[7] however, in his reply. (*Exit.*)

Enter HASTINGS *and* CONSTANCE.

HASTINGS. My dear Constance, why will you deliberate thus? If we delay a moment, all is lost forever. Pluck up a little resolution, and we shall soon be out of the reach of her malignity.

CONSTANCE. I find it impossible. My spirits are so sunk with the agitations I have suffered that I am unable to face any new danger. Two or three years' patience will at last crown us with happiness.

HASTINGS. Such a tedious delay is worse than inconstancy. Let us fly, my charmer. Let us date our happiness from this very moment. Perish for-

7 **morality:** a lesson; truth.

OLIVER GOLDSMITH

tune! Love and content will increase what we possess beyond a monarch's revenue. Let me prevail!

CONSTANCE. No, Mr. Hastings, no. Prudence once more comes to my relief, and I will obey its dictates. In the moment of passion, fortune may be despised, but it ever produces a lasting repentance. I'm resolved to apply to Mr. Hardcastle's compassion and justice for redress.

HASTINGS. But though he had the will, he has not the power to relieve you.

CONSTANCE. But he has influence, and upon that I am resolved to rely.

HASTINGS. I have no hopes. But, since you persist, I must reluctantly obey you. *(Exeunt.)*

Scene III. *A room at*
MR. HARDCASTLE'S.

Enter SIR CHARLES *and* KATE.

SIR CHARLES. What a situation am I in! If what you say appears, I shall then find a guilty son. If what he says be true, I shall then lose one that, of all others, I most wished for a daughter.

KATE. I am proud of your approbation; and to show I merit it, if you place yourselves as I directed, you shall hear his explicit declaration. But he comes.

SIR CHARLES. I'll to your father, and keep him to the appointment.

(Exit SIR CHARLES.*)*
Enter MARLOW.

MARLOW. Though prepared for setting out, I come once more to take leave; nor did I, till this moment, know the pain I feel in the separation.

KATE (*in her own natural manner*). I believe these sufferings cannot be very great, sir, which you can so easily remove. A day or two longer, perhaps, might lessen your uneasiness by showing the little value of what you now think proper to regret.

MARLOW (*aside*). This girl every moment improves upon me.[1] (*To her.*) It must not be, madam. I have already trifled too long with my heart. My very pride begins to submit to my passion. The disparity of education and fortune, the anger of a parent, and the contempt of my equals begin to lose their weight; and nothing can restore me to myself but this painful effort of resolution.

KATE. Then go, sir; I'll urge nothing more to detain you. Though my family be as good as hers you came down to visit, and my education, I hope, not inferior, what are these advantages without equal affluence? I must remain contented with the slight approbation of imputed merit; I must have only the mockery of your addresses, while all your serious aims are fixed on fortune.

Enter HARDCASTLE *and* SIR CHARLES
from behind.

SIR CHARLES. Here, behind this screen.

HARDCASTLE. Ay, ay; make no noise. I'll engage my Kate covers him with confusion at last.

MARLOW. By heavens, madam! fortune was ever my smallest consideration. Your beauty at first caught my eye; for who could see that without emotion? But every moment that I converse with you steals in some new grace, heightens the picture, and gives it stronger expression. What at first seemed rustic plainness, now appears refined simplicity. What seemed forward assurance, now strikes me as the result of courageous innocence and conscious virtue.

SIR CHARLES. What can it mean? He amazes me!

HARDCASTLE. I told you how it would be. Hush!

1 improves upon me: rises in my estimation.

MARLOW. I am now determined to stay, madam, and I have too good an opinion of my father's discernment, when he sees you, to doubt his approbation.

KATE. No, Mr. Marlow, I will not, cannot, detain you. Do you think I could suffer a connection in which there is the smallest room for repentance? Do you think I would take the mean advantage of a transient passion, to load you with confusion? Do you think I could ever relish that happiness which was acquired by lessening yours?

MARLOW. By all that's good, I can have no happiness but what's in your power to grant me! Nor shall I ever feel repentance but in not having seen your merits before. I will stay, even contrary to your wishes; and, though you should persist to shun me, I will make my respectful assiduities atone for the levity of my past conduct.

KATE. Sir, I must entreat you'll desist. As our acquaintance began, so let it end, in indifference. I might have given an hour or two to levity; but, seriously, Mr. Marlow, do you think I could ever submit to a connection where I must appear mercenary and you imprudent? Do you think I could ever catch at the confident addresses of a secure admirer?

MARLOW (kneeling). Does this look like security? Does this look like confidence? No, madam; every moment that shows me your merit only serves to increase my diffidence and confusion. Here let me continue—

SIR CHARLES. I can hold it no longer. Charles, Charles, how hast thou deceived me! Is this your indifference, your uninteresting conversation?

HARDCASTLE. Your cold contempt, your formal interview? What have you to say now?

MARLOW. That I'm all amazement! What can it mean?

HARDCASTLE. It means that you can say and unsay things at pleasure; that you can address a lady in private, and deny it in public; that you have one story for us, and another for my daughter.

MARLOW. Daughter! This lady your daughter?

HARDCASTLE. Yes, sir, my only daughter; my Kate; whose else should she be?

MARLOW. Oh, the devil!

KATE. Yes, sir, that very identical tall, squinting lady you were pleased to take me for (courtesying); she that you addressed as the mild, modest, sentimental man of gravity, and the bold, forward, agreeable Rattle of the Ladies' Club. Ha! ha! ha!

MARLOW. Zounds! there's no bearing this; it's worse than death!

KATE. In which of your characters, sir, will you give us leave to address you? As the faltering gentleman, with looks on the ground, that speaks just to be heard, and hates hypocrisy; or the loud, confident creature that keeps it up[2] with Mrs. Mantrap and old Miss Biddy Buckskin till three in the morning? Ha! ha! ha!

MARLOW. Oh, curse on my noisy head! I never attempted to be impudent yet that I was not taken down! I must be gone.

HARDCASTLE. By the hand of my body, but you shall not! I see it was all a mistake, and I am rejoiced to find it. You shall not, sir, I tell you. I know she'll forgive you! Won't you forgive him, Kate? We'll all forgive you. Take courage, man.

(They retire, she tormenting him, to the back scene.)

Enter MRS. HARDCASTLE and TONY.

2 keeps it up: amuses himself.

MRS. HARDCASTLE. So, so, they're gone off. Let them go, I care not.

HARDCASTLE. Who gone?

MRS. HARDCASTLE. My dutiful niece and her gentleman, Mr. Hastings, from town. He who came down with our modest visitor here.

SIR CHARLES. Who, my honest George Hastings? As worthy a fellow as lives, and the girl could not have made a more prudent choice.

HARDCASTLE. Then, by the hand of my body, I'm proud of the connection!

MRS. HARDCASTLE. Well, if he has taken away the lady, he has not taken her fortune; that remains in this family to console us for her loss.

HARDCASTLE. Sure, Dorothy, you would not be so mercenary?

MRS. HARDCASTLE. Ay, that's my affair, not yours.

HARDCASTLE. But you know if your son, when of age, refuses to marry his cousin, her whole fortune is then at her own disposal.

MRS. HARDCASTLE. Ay, but he's not of age, and she has not thought proper to wait for his refusal.

Enter HASTINGS *and* CONSTANCE.

MRS. HARDCASTLE (*aside*). What, returned so soon! I begin not to like it.

HASTINGS (*to* HARDCASTLE). For my late attempt to fly off with your niece, let my present confusion be my punishment. We are now come back, to appeal from your justice to your humanity. By her father's consent I first paid her my addresses, and our passions were first founded in duty.

CONSTANCE. Since his death, I have been obliged to stoop to dissimulation to avoid oppression. In an hour of levity, I was ready to give up my fortune to secure my choice; but I am now recovered from the delusion, and hope from your tenderness what is denied me from a nearer connection.

MRS. HARDCASTLE. Pshaw, pshaw! this is all but the whining end of a modern novel.

HARDCASTLE. Be it what it will, I'm glad they're come back to reclaim their due. Come hither, Tony, boy. Do you refuse this lady's hand whom I now offer you?

TONY. What signifies my refusing? You know I can't refuse her till I'm of age, Father.

HARDCASTLE. While I thought concealing your age, boy, was likely to conduce to your improvement, I concurred with your mother's desire to keep it secret. But since I find she turns it to a wrong use, I must now declare you have been of age these three months.

TONY. Of age! Am I of age, father?

HARDCASTLE. Above three months.

TONY. Then you'll see the first use I'll make of my liberty. (*Taking* CONSTANCE'S *hand.*) Witness all men by these presents,[3] that I, Anthony Lumpkin, Esquire, of blank place, refuse you, Constantia Neville, spinster, of no place at all, for my true and lawful wife. So Constance Neville may marry whom she pleases, and Tony Lumpkin is his own man again.

SIR CHARLES. O brave squire!

HASTINGS. My worthy friend!

MRS. HARDCASTLE. My undutiful offspring!

MARLOW. Joy, my dear George, I give you joy sincerely. And could I prevail upon my little tyrant here to be less arbitrary, I should be the happiest man alive if you would return me the favor.

HASTINGS (*to* KATE). Come, madam, you are now driven to the very last scene of all your contrivances. I know you like him, I'm sure he loves you, and you must and shall have him.

---

3 **Witness . . . presents:** the form for beginning a legal declaration.

HARDCASTLE (*joining their hands*). And I say so too. And, Mr. Marlow, if she makes as good a wife as she has a daughter, I don't believe you'll ever repent your bargain. So, now to supper. Tomorrow we shall gather all the poor of the parish about us, and the mistakes of the night shall be crowned with a merry morning. So, boy, take her; and, as you have been mistaken in the mistress, my wish is that you may never be mistaken in the wife.

(*Exeunt* ALL.)

Questions for Study

ACT V

Scene i

1. What is the dramatic purpose for introducing Sir Charles at this point in the play?
2. Explain the meaning of the two following speeches and show how the problem which they signify remains to be settled before the end of the play:

> SIR CHARLES. Agreed. And if I find him what you describe, all my happiness in him must have an end.
> KATE. And if you don't find him what I describe—I fear my happiness must never have a beginning.

Scene ii

1. In what way should this scene be acted to make it credible to the audience?
2. What point does Mr. Hardcastle make when he says: "There's morality, however, in his reply"?
3. What causes Constance to reconsider her situation—elopement without her jewels or marriage with them? Why does she appeal her case to Mr. Hardcastle?

Scene iii

1. Which incident constitutes the climax of the play: Marlow's final realization of how he has been deceived throughout the play, Constance's getting both her jewels and permission to marry Hastings, Tony's final escape from his mother's attempt to dominate him, or another incident? Be prepared to support your choice with evidence from the play.
2. At the end of this scene, all the characters are on stage. How would you place them so as to present the best stage picture at the fall of the curtain? What determines which character should be downstage center, which to the right, which to the left, and which in the background?

OLIVER GOLDSMITH

389

A view of the interior of the Covent Garden Theater in the early 19th century. Theaters at this time were larger, and the audience became farther removed from the actors. Notice the full-size orchestra.

The Play as a Whole

Select one of the following topics upon which to write an essay:

1. The language used during the Enlightenment was both coarse and elegant—the coarse usually being spoken by the lower classes and the elegant by the upper. Keeping this statement in mind, examine the language used by two or more of the characters in *She Stoops to Conquer*. In what ways do Goldsmith's characters demonstrate the truth of this statement? In what ways does their language betray those of the lower class who aspire to the upper? In what instances is the language of the lower classes used as a form of disguise?

2. During the Enlightenment the emphasis upon reason and logic and upon symmetry and balance is evident in essays and poetry and in architecture and landscaping. Goldsmith in *She Stoops to Conquer* shows that he is a man of the Enlightenment. How does one action or statement start a logical chain of incidents, the second being the effect of the first, the third being the effect of the second, and so on?

3. The play is built largely on contrasts. Take any *one* of the following pairs of characters and show how they are different from each other: Tony and his mother; Marlow as he acts toward Kate when he knows who she is, and Marlow as he acts when she is pretending to be one of the servants; Mr. Hardcastle and Marlow.

THE ENLIGHTENMENT

The Study of Humankind
The Triumph of Satire

READ

SUMMARY

Jonathan Swift (1667-1745)

JONATHAN SWIFT was born and educated in Ireland; and to Ireland he returned in middle age, after tasting success and power in England. As a youth he first left Ireland to serve as private secretary to a distant relative, Sir William Temple, a scholar and diplomat; and, while in this service, he became a priest of the Church of England. After Temple's death Swift held a "living" (was the rector of a parish) in Ireland, but his ambitions looked toward London. Eventually, from 1710 to 1714, he enjoyed eminence and power as the writer whose political pamphlets did much to keep the Tories in office. He became the friend of Pope and other literary leaders, joined the most exclusive clubs, and was for a brief time one of the most influential men in England.

But the Whigs, the opposing party, came into office in 1714; and, upon leaving the government, the best reward Swift could secure was appointment as Dean of Saint Patrick's, the English Cathedral at Dublin. He went home to Ireland disappointed. He eventually roused himself to a vigorous pamphlet war on behalf of the Irish people, and for many years he fought against the incredible misgovernment exerted upon them by the absentee government in London. His later years were unhappy. From early manhood Swift suffered from a disorder of the inner ear which impaired his sense of balance. To this and other illness in old age was added the final injury of madness. Swift once said that, like a tree, he would die first at the top. By 1742 his prediction had come true.

Gulliver's Travels

Swift became the greatest prose satirist in English. As he once wrote to Pope, "The chief end I propose to myself in all my labors is to vex the world rather than divert it." He went on to explain his personal creed:

> I have ever hated all nations, professions, and communities, and all my love is toward individuals. . . . Principally I hate and detest that animal called man, although I heartily love John, Peter, Thomas, and so forth. . . . I have got materials toward a treatise, proving the falsity of that definition [of man as] *animal rationale* [rational animal], and to show it would be only *rationis capax* [capable of reason].

The treatise he speaks of was *Gulliver's Travels*, which vividly displays his aversion to man in the mass at the same time that it shows his love for the individual.

Swift had written a number of powerful satirical works before *Gulliver*. He savagely attacked groups who made sectarian wars on other groups in the name of Christianity. He attacked the absentee British landlords and governors of Ireland in a tract which argued that, since the government's policies seemed designed to swallow up Ireland's economy, they might as well do it the right way: he made the "Modest Proposal" that the Irish butcher and sell their infants and young children as special delicacies to please the voracious appetites of their landlords. The irony was harsh, but the plight of those he defended could be brought to public attention only by such harshness.

Gulliver's Travels was published in 1726. Its success was immediate and continuous. With some of its episodes left out, it has become a children's classic. With those episodes included, one can see the bitterness with which Swift regarded the practices of humankind in the mass.

The man invented by Jonathan Swift to tell the story of *Gulliver's Travels* was a good deal less refined than Addison's Spectator, though he was not uneducated. The original title page describes him as "Lemuel Gulliver, first a Surgeon (or ship's doctor), and then a Captain of several Ships." And as he describes his "Travels into Several Remote Nations of the World," Gulliver reveals human follies by comparing his own civilization with that of the strange lands he explores. The strangeness and absurdity he finds in the countries he visits, we soon see, are exaggerated features of his own people, and yet Gulliver is still the innocent observer. Indeed, as his name suggests, he is sometimes a gullible observer. But what he saw in his adventures, and the naïveté with which he saw it, together expose a depth of folly that Swift's contemporaries could only hint at.

Gulliver's first voyage begins with a shipwreck, and he is cast ashore alone on the island of Lilliput. It is a land in which he is a giant, for everything here—the people, their houses, their horses and cattle—is made on a scale in which a foot becomes an inch. Gulliver, exhausted by his long swim to shore, falls asleep and awakes to find himself bound down to the earth by threads running across his body and by tiny stakes driven through his long hair. His captors are perfectly formed little men, none more than six inches high: the Lilliputian army bound the giant invader as he slept. He is taken to the capital city and upon promises of good behavior is set free. He meets the Emperor and his court and learns the ways of Lilliputian society. He discovers, to his sorrow, that these exquisite, doll-like creatures are not so gentle as they seem.

from Gulliver's Travels

Jonathan Swift

A Voyage to Lilliput

My GENTLENESS and good behavior had gained so far on the Emperor and his court, and indeed upon the army and people in general, that I began to conceive hopes of getting my liberty in a short time. I took all possible methods to cultivate this favorable disposition. The natives came by degrees to be less apprehensive of any danger from me. I would sometimes lie down, and let five or six of them dance on my hand. And at last the boys and girls would venture to come and play at hide and seek in my hair. I had now made a good progress in understanding and speaking their language. The Emperor had a mind one day to entertain me with several of the country shows, wherein they exceed all nations I have known, both for dexterity and magnificence. I was diverted with none so much as that of the ropedancers, performed upon a slender white thread, extended about two foot, and twelve inches from the ground. Upon which I shall desire liberty, with the reader's patience, to enlarge a little.

This diversion is only practiced by those persons who are candidates for great employments and high favor at court. They were trained in this art from their youth, and are not always of noble birth, or liberal education. When a great office is vacant either by death or disgrace (which often happens) five or six of those candidates petition the Emperor to entertain his Majesty and the court with a dance on the rope; and whoever jumps the highest without falling, succeeds in the office. Very often the chief ministers themselves are commanded to show their skill, and to convince the Emperor that they have not lost their faculty. Flimnap, the Treasurer, is allowed[1] to cut a caper on the straight rope, at least an inch higher than any other lord in the whole empire. I have seen him do the summerset several times together upon a trencher[2] fixed on the rope, which is no thicker than a common packthread in England. My friend Reldresal, principal Secretary for Private Affairs, is, in my opinion, if I am not partial, the second after the Treasurer; the rest of the great officers are much upon a par.

These diversions are often attended with fatal accidents, whereof great numbers are on record. I myself have seen two or three candidates break a limb. But the danger is much greater when the ministers themselves are commanded to show their dexterity: for by contending to excel themselves and their fellows, they strain so far that there is hardly one of them who hath not received a fall, and some of them two or three. I was assured that a year or two before my arrival, Flimnap would have infallibly broke his neck, if one of the King's cushions, that accidentally lay on the ground, had not weakened the force of his fall.

There is likewise another diversion, which is only shown before the Em-

---

1 **allowed:** granted.
2 **trencher:** wooden plate.

peror and Empress, and first minister, upon particular occasions. The Emperor lays on a table three fine silken threads of six inches long. One is blue, the other red, and the third green.[3] These threads are proposed as prizes for those persons whom the Emperor hath a mind to distinguish by a peculiar mark of his favor. The ceremony is performed in his Majesty's great chamber of state, where the candidates are to undergo a trial of dexterity very different from the former, and such as I have not observed the least resemblance of in any other country of the old or the new world. The Emperor holds a stick in his hands, both ends parallel to the horizon, while the candidates, advancing one by one, sometimes leap over the stick, sometimes creep under it backwards and forwards several times, according as the stick is advanced or depressed. Sometimes the Emperor holds one end of the stick, and his first minister the other; sometimes the minister has it entirely to himself. Whoever performs his part with most agility, and holds out the longest in *leaping* and *creeping,* is rewarded with the blue-colored silk; the red is given to the next, and the green to the third, which they all wear girt twice round about the middle; and you see few great persons about this court who are not adorned with one of these girdles.

The horses of the army, and those of the royal stables, having been daily led before me, were no longer shy, but would come up to my very feet without starting. The riders would leap them over my hand as I held it on the ground, and one of the Emperor's huntsmen, upon a large courser, took my foot, shoe and all; which was indeed a prodigious leap. I had the good fortune to divert the Emperor one day, after a very extraordinary manner. I desired he would order several sticks of two foot high, and the thickness of an ordinary cane, to be brought me; whereupon his Majesty commanded the master of his woods to give directions accordingly; and the next morning six woodmen arrived with as many carriages, drawn by eight horses to each. I took nine of these sticks, and fixing them firmly in the ground in a quadrangular figure, two foot and a half square, I took four other sticks, and tied them parallel at each corner, about two foot from the ground; then I fastened my handkerchief to the nine sticks that stood erect, and extended it on all sides till it was as tight as the top of a drum; and the four parallel sticks rising about five inches higher than the handkerchief served as ledges on each side. When I had finished my work, I desired the Emperor to let a troop of his best horse, twenty-four in number, come and exercise upon this plain. His Majesty approved of the proposal, and I took them up one by one in my hands, ready mounted and armed, with the proper officers to exercise them. As soon as they got into order, they divided into two parties, performed mock skirmishes, discharged blunt arrows, drew their swords, fled and pursued, attacked and retired; and in short discovered[4] the best military discipline I ever beheld. The parallel sticks secured them and their horses from falling over the stage; and the Emperor was so much delighted that he ordered this entertainment to be repeated several days; and once was pleased to be lifted up and give the word of command; and, with

3 **green:** i.e., the ribbons of the highest honorary court offices in England.

4 **discovered:** exhibited.

great difficulty, persuaded even the Empress herself to let me hold her in her close chair, within two yards of the stage, from whence she was able to take a full view of the whole performance. It was my good fortune that no ill accident happened in these entertainments; only once a fiery horse that belonged to one of the captains, pawing with his hoof struck a hole in my handkerchief, and his foot slipping, he overthrew his rider and himself; but I immediately relieved them both; for covering the hole with one hand, I set down the troop with the other, in the same manner as I took them up. The horse that fell was strained in the left shoulder, but the rider got no hurt, and I repaired my handkerchief as well as I could: however, I would not trust to the strength of it any more in such dangerous enterprises.

About two or three days before I was set at liberty, as I was entertaining the court with these kinds of feats, there arrived an express to inform his Majesty that some of his subjects riding near the place where I was first taken up, had seen a great black substance lying on the ground, very oddly shaped, extending its edges round as wide as his Majesty's bedchamber, and rising up in the middle as high as a man: that it was no living creature, as they at first apprehended, for it lay on the grass without motion, and some of them had walked round it several times: that by mounting upon each other's shoulders, they had got to the top, which was flat and even; and stamping upon it they found it was hollow within: that they humbly conceived it might be something belonging to the Man-Mountain, and if his Majesty pleased, they would undertake to bring it with only five horses. I presently knew what they meant, and was glad at

heart to receive this intelligence. It seems, upon my first reaching the shore after our shipwreck, I was in such confusion that, before I came to the place where I went to sleep, my hat, which I had fastened with a string to my head while I was rowing, and had stuck on all the time I was swimming, fell off after I came to land; the string, as I conjecture, breaking by some accident which I never observed, but thought my hat had been lost at sea. I entreated his Imperial Majesty to give orders it might be brought to me as soon as possible, describing to him the use and the nature of it: and the next day the wagoners arrived with it, but not in a very good condition; they had bored two holes in the brim, within an inch and half of the edge, and fastened two hooks in the holes; these hooks were tied by a long cord to the harness, and thus my hat was dragged along for above half an English mile: but the ground in that country being extremely smooth and level, it received less damage than I expected. . . .

THE FIRST REQUEST I made after I had obtained my liberty was that I might have license to see Mildendo, the metropolis; which the Emperor easily granted me, but with a special charge to do no hurt either to the inhabitants or their houses. The people had notice by proclamation of my design to visit the town. The wall which encompassed it is two foot and an half high, and at least eleven inches broad, so that a coach and horses may be driven very safely round it; and it is flanked with strong towers at ten foot distance. I stept over the great Western Gate, and passed very gently, and sideling through the two principal streets, only in my short waistcoat, for fear of damaging the roofs and eaves of the house with the skirts of my coat. I walked with the utmost circumspection, to avoid treading on any stragglers, who might remain in the streets, although the orders were very strict, that all people should keep in their houses at their own peril. The garret windows and tops of houses were so crowded with spectators that I thought in all my travels I had not seen a more populous place. The city is an exact square, each side of the wall being five hundred foot long. The two great streets, which run cross and divide it into four quarters, are five foot wide. The lanes and alleys, which I could not enter, but only viewed them as I passed, are from twelve to eighteen inches. The town is capable of holding five hundred thousand souls. The houses are from three to five stories. The shops and markets well provided.

The Emperor's palace is in the center of the city, where the two great streets meet. It is enclosed by a wall of two foot high, and twenty foot distant from the buildings. I had his Majesty's permission to step over this wall; and the space being so wide between that and the palace, I could easily view it on every side. The outward court is a square of forty foot, and includes two other courts: in the inmost are the royal apartments, which I was very desirous to see, but found it extremely difficult; for the great gates, from one square into another, were but eighteen inches high and seven inches wide. Now the buildings of the outer court were at least five foot high, and it was impossible for me to stride over them without infinite damage to the pile, though the walls were strongly built of hewn stone, and four inches thick. At the same time the Emperor had a great desire that I should see the magnificence of his palace; but this I was not able to do till

three days after, which I spent in cutting down with my knife some of the largest trees in the royal park, about an hundred yards distant from the city. Of these trees I made two stools, each about three foot high, and strong enough to bear my weight. The people having received notice a second time, I went again through the city to the palace, with my two stools in my hands. When I came to the side of the outer court, I stood upon one stool, and took the other in my hand: this I lifted over the roof, and gently set it down on the space between the first and second court, which was eight foot wide. I then stept over the buildings very conveniently from one stool to the other, and drew up the first after me with a hooked stick. By this contrivance I got into the inmost court; and lying down upon my side, I applied my face to the windows of the middle stories, which were left open on purpose, and discovered the most splendid apartments that can be imagined. There I saw the Empress, and the young Princes, in their several lodgings, with their chief attendants about them. Her Imperial Majesty was pleased to smile very graciously upon me, and gave me out of the window her hand to kiss. . . .

ALTHOUGH I INTEND to leave the description of this empire to a particular treatise, yet in the meantime I am content to gratify the curious reader with some general ideas. As the common size of the natives is somewhat under six inches, so there is an exact proportion in all other animals, as well as plants and trees: for instance, the tallest horses and oxen are between four and five inches in height, the sheep an inch and a half, more or less: their geese about the bigness of a sparrow, and so the several gradations downwards till you come to the smallest, which, to my

A treadmill in debtors' prison from a pamphlet propagandizing the wrongs of the system in England. Swift: ". . . our laws were enforced only by penalties, without any mention of reward."

sight, were almost invisible; but nature hath adapted the eyes of the Lilliputians to all objects proper for their view: they see with great exactness, but at no great distance. And to show the sharpness of their sight towards objects that are near, I have been much pleased with observing a cook pulling[5] a lark, which was not so large as a common fly; and a young girl threading an invisible needle with invisible silk. Their tallest trees are about seven foot high; I mean some of those in the great royal park, the tops whereof I could but just reach with my fist clenched. The other vegetables are in the same proportion; but this I leave to the reader's imagination.

I shall say but little at present of their learning, which for many ages hath flourished in all its branches among them: but their manner of writing is very peculiar, being neither from the left to the right, like the Europeans; nor from the right to the left, like the Arabians; nor from up to down, like the Chinese; nor from down to up, like the Cascagians;[6] but aslant from one corner of the paper to the other, like ladies in England.

They bury their dead with their heads directly downwards; because they hold an opinion, that in eleven thousand moons they are all to rise again, in which period the earth (which they conceive to be flat) will turn upside down,

---

5 **pulling:** plucking the feathers from.

6 **Cascagians:** an invention of Swift's.

and by this means they shall, at their resurrection, be found ready standing on their feet. The learned among them confess the absurdity of this doctrine, but the practice still continues, in compliance to the vulgar.

There are some laws and customs in this empire very peculiar; and if they were not so directly contrary to those of my own dear country, I should be tempted to say a little in their justification. It is only to be wished that they were as well executed. The first I shall mention relates to informers. All crimes against the state are punished here with the utmost severity; but if the person accused maketh his innocence plainly to appear upon his trial, the accuser is immediately put to an ignominious death; and out of his goods or lands, the innocent person is quadruply recompensed for the loss of his time, for the danger he underwent, for the hardship of his imprisonment, and for all the charges he hath been at in making his defense. Or, if that fund be deficient, it is largely supplied by the Crown. The Emperor does also confer on him some public mark of his favor, and proclamation is made of his innocence through the whole city.

They look upon fraud as a greater crime than theft, and therefore seldom fail to punish it with death: for they allege, that care and vigilance, with a very common understanding, may preserve a man's goods from thieves, but honesty has no fence against superior cunning; and since it is necessary that there should be a perpetual intercourse of buying and selling, and dealing upon credit, where fraud is permitted and connived at, or hath no law to punish it, the honest dealer is always undone, and the knave gets the advantage. I remember when I was once interceding with the King for a criminal who had wronged his master of a great sum of money, which he had received by order, and ran away with; and happening to tell his Majesty, by way of extenuation, that it was only a breach of trust; the Emperor thought it monstrous in me to offer, as a defense, the greatest aggravation of the crime: and truly I had little to say in return, farther than the common answer, that different nations had different customs; for, I confess, I was heartily ashamed.

Although we usually call reward and punishment the two hinges upon which all government turns, yet I could never observe this maxim to be put in practice by any nation except that of Lilliput. Whoever can there bring sufficient proof that he hath strictly observed the laws of his country for seventy-three moons, hath a claim to certain privileges, according to his quality and condition of life, with a proportionable sum of money out of a fund appropriated for that use: he likewise acquires the title of *Snilpall*, or Legal, which is added to his name, but does not descend to his posterity. And these people thought it a prodigious defect of policy among us, when I told them that our laws were enforced only by penalties, without any mention of reward. It is upon this account that the image of Justice, in their courts of judicature, is formed with six eyes, two before, as many behind, and on each side one, to signify circumspection; with a bag of gold open in her right hand, and a sword sheathed in her left, to show she is more disposed to reward than to punish.

In choosing persons for all employments, they have more regard to good morals than to great abilities; for, since government is necessary to mankind, they believe that the common size of human understandings is fitted to some station or other; and that Providence never intended to make the management of public affairs a mystery, to be comprehended only by a few persons of sublime genius, of which there seldom are three born in an age: but they suppose truth, justice, temperance, and the like, to be in every man's power; the practice of which virtues, assisted by experience and a good intention, would qualify any man for the service of his country, except where a course of study is required. But they thought the want of moral virtues was so far from being supplied by superior endowments of the mind that employments could never be put into such dangerous hands as those of persons so qualified; and at least, that the mistakes committed by ignorance in a virtuous disposition would never be of such fatal consequence to the public weal, as the practices of a man whose inclinations led him to be corrupt, and had great abilities to manage, and multiply, and defend his corruptions.

In like manner, the disbelief of a Divine Providence renders a man uncapable of holding any public station: for, since kings avow themselves to be the deputies of Providence, the Lilliputians think nothing can be more absurd than for a prince to employ such men as disown the authority under which he acts.

In relating these and the following laws, I would only be understood to mean the original institutions, and not the most scandalous corruptions into which these people are fallen by the degenerate nature of man. For as to that infamous practice of acquiring great employments by dancing on the ropes, or badges of favor and distinction by leaping over sticks and creeping under them; the reader is to observe, that they were first introduced by the grandfather of the Emperor now reign-

ing, and grew to the present height by the gradual increase of party and faction. . . .

[After some further description of the customs of the Lilliputians, Gulliver tells how he was awarded the high honorary title of "Nardac" for saving them from their ancient enemies, the people of the island of Blefuscu. His new glory makes some Lilliputians jealous, and his enemies at court draw up "articles of impeachment" against him. They accuse him of a number of crimes, including that of high treason, and they ask that he be executed. The meeting at which his fate was debated by the Emperor and his Council is described to Gulliver by a friend who comes secretly at night to warn him. He tells Gulliver that the Emperor did not want him to be put to death—"his Majesty gave many marks of his great lenity, often urging the services you had done him, and endeavoring to extenuate your crimes." But the debate continued until]

"Reldresal, principal Secretary for Private Affairs, who always approved himself your true friend, was commanded by the Emperor to deliver his opinion, which he accordingly did; and therein justified the good thoughts you have of him. He allowed your crimes to be great, but that still there was room for mercy, the most commendable virtue in a prince, and for which his Majesty was so justly celebrated. He said, the friendship between you and him was so well known to the world, that perhaps the most honorable board might think him partial: however, in obedience to the command he had received, he would freely offer his sentiments. That if his Majesty, in consideration of your services, and pursuant to his own merciful disposition, would please to spare your life, and only give order to put out both your eyes, he humbly conceived that by this expedient justice might in some measure be satisfied, and all the world would applaud the lenity of the Emperor, as well as the fair and generous proceedings of those who have the honor to be his counselors. . . .

[*The Secretary's advice however, did not satisfy the rest of the council, and a compromise became necessary:*]

"His Imperial Majesty, fully determined against capital punishment, was graciously pleased to say, that since the Council thought the loss of your eyes too easy a censure, some other may be inflicted hereafter. And your friend the Secretary humbly desiring to be heard again, in answer to what the Treasurer had objected concerning the great charge[7] his Majesty was at in maintaining you, said that his Excellency, who had the sole disposal of the Emperor's revenue, might easily provide against that evil, by gradually lessening your establishment;[8] by which, for want of sufficient food, you would grow weak and faint, and lose your appetite, and consequently decay and consume in a few months; neither would the stench of your carcass be then so dangerous, when it should become more than half diminished; and immediately upon your death, five or six thousand of his Majesty's subjects might, in two or three days, cut your flesh from your bones, take it away by cartloads, and bury it in distant parts to prevent infection, leaving the skeleton as a monument of admiration to posterity.

"Thus by the great friendship of the Secretary, the whole affair was compro-

7 **charge:** expense.
8 **establishment:** provisions.

mised. It was strictly enjoined that the project of starving you by degrees should be kept a secret, but the sentence of putting out your eyes was entered on the books. . . ."

[*And so the debate, Gulliver is told, came to an end. The great "lenity" of the Emperor and the strong support of his friend the Secretary, had saved him from immediate execution; he was merely to be blinded and then slowly starved to death. Gulliver receives the information with "many doubts and perplexities of mind."*]

IT WAS A custom introduced by this prince and his ministry (very different, as I have been assured, from the practices of former times) that after the court had decreed any cruel execution, either to gratify the monarch's resentment, or the malice of a favorite, the Emperor always made a speech to his whole Council, expressing his *great lenity and tenderness, as qualities known and confessed by all the world.* This speech was immediately published through the kingdom; nor did anything terrify the people so much as those encomiums on his Majesty's mercy; because it was observed that the more these praises were enlarged and insisted on, the more *inhuman* was the punishment, and the *sufferer more innocent.* Yet, as to myself, I must confess, having never been designed for a courtier either by my birth or education, I was so ill a judge of things, that I could not discover the lenity and favor of this sentence, but conceived it (perhaps erroneously) rather to be rigorous than gentle. I sometimes thought of standing my trial, for although I could not deny the facts alleged in the several articles, yet I hoped they would admit of some extenuations. But having in my life perused many state trials, which I ever observed to terminate as the judges thought fit to direct, I durst not rely on so dangerous a decision, in so critical a juncture, and against such powerful enemies. Once I was strongly bent upon resistance: for while I had liberty, the whole strength of that empire could hardly subdue me, and I might easily with stones pelt the metropolis to pieces; but I soon rejected that project with horror, by remembering the oath I had made to the Emperor, the favors I received from him, and the high title of *Nardac* he conferred upon me. Neither had I so soon learned the gratitude of courtiers, to persuade myself that his Majesty's *present severities acquitted me of all past obligations. . . .*

[*After these rueful reflections on the nature of princes and ministers, Gulliver determines to escape. He goes to Blefuscu and there fits out a boat for himself. He puts out to sea and is picked up by a British ship whose captain, astonished by his tale, carries him home to England. And so ends the first voyage.*]

Comment

An 18th-century miniature is a tiny, jewel-like portrait of exquisite detail, and in his description of Lilliput Swift combines the art of the miniaturist with the perspective of one who looks at a nearby scene through the wrong end of a telescope. He shows us much that is fascinating and exquisite, but he shows us much too that seems quite out of normal perspective. Particularly when he comes to matters of government and politics, Swift's satire is most biting. Here, for example, the "diversions" of the court—such as the jumping and dancing on a tightrope—show us Swift's contempt for the endless scramble for power and the mean acts to which people are led by ambition. But Swift becomes most ironic when he tells us of Gulliver's response to the secret sentence against him.

1. Upon hearing that he is to be blinded and starved rather than killed at once, Gulliver says,

   I must confess, having never been designed for a courtier either by my birth or education, I was so ill a judge of things, that I could not discover the lenity and favor of this sentence, but conceived it (perhaps erroneously) rather to be rigorous than gentle.

   What is Gulliver's tone here? Note the parenthetical "perhaps erroneously." What sort of attitude toward his situation does it express? What is wrong with this attitude? What kind of reasoning makes blinding and starving more lenient than summary execution?

2. Gulliver says, however, that he would doubtless understand these things if he had been trained as a courtier. What does this tell us about Swift's conception of courtiers? Is Swift simply saying that political ambition makes people cruel, or does he suggest that there is a moral obliviousness—a deadness of heart—in people that is worse than cruelty? What folly, what absurdity, is Swift attacking here?

A VOYAGE TO BROBDINGNAG

[In Lilliput, humanity is reduced to a scale in which a foot becomes an inch. In the land of Gulliver's next voyage, Brobdingnag (brŏb' dĭng năg), *the scale is reversed: an inch becomes a foot. Here Swift shows us the world through the right end of a telescope; but because everything is so near to us our perspective is again disturbed, and the scene is magnified to grotesque proportions.*

The adventures of this voyage begin peacefully. Gulliver is ashore on an island somewhere in the Pacific Ocean with other crewmen looking for fresh water, when he wanders away from his shipmates. Soon, to his horror, he is picked up by a farmer, a giant who "appeared as tall as an ordinary spire-steeple, and took about ten yards with every stride." Gulliver is in a land where the inhabitants are to him as he was to the Lilliputians. When he is put to bed, the mattress is twenty yards wide and eight yards from the floor. The family cat is a huge, lionlike monster; Gulliver almost drowns in a huge tank—a bowl of cream. The farmer eventually transports his prize to the neighboring town. He carries him on his horse in a box, and the experience is shattering: "For the horse went about forty foot at every step, and trotted so high, that the agitation was equal to the rising and falling of a ship in a great storm, but much more frequent." Gulliver is taken into the household of the King and Queen, and once again he learns the ways of a strange and remote society.]

The King, who, as I before observed, was a prince of excellent understanding, would frequently order that I should be brought in my box, and set upon the table in his closet. He would then command me to bring one of my chairs out of the box, and sit down within three yards distance upon the top of the cabinet, which brought me almost to a level with his face. In this manner I had several conversations with him. I one day took the freedom to tell his Majesty that the contempt he discovered toward Europe, and the rest of the world did not seem answerable to those excellent qualities of mind that he was master of. That reason did not extend itself with the bulk of the body: on the contrary, we observed in our country that the tallest persons were usually least provided with it. That among other animals, bees and ants had the reputation of more industry, art, and sagacity than many of the larger kinds. And that, as inconsiderable as he took me to be, I hoped I might live to do his Majesty some signal service. The King heard me with attention, and began to conceive a much better opinion of me than he had ever before. He desired I would give him as exact an account of the government of England as I possibly could; because, as fond as princes commonly are of their own customs (for so he conjectured of other monarchs, by my former discourses), he should be glad to hear of anything that might deserve imitation.

Imagine with thyself, courteous reader, how often I then wished for the tongue of Demosthenes or Cicero,[1] that might have enabled me to celebrate the praise of my own dear native country in a style equal to its merits and felicity. I began my discourse by informing

---

1 Demosthenes (dĭ mŏs'thə nēz') **or Cicero** (sĭs' ə rō): the greatest orators of Greece and Rome.

THE ENLIGHTENMENT

The Poll, *one of a series of paintings by Hogarth (1697–1764) satirizing election practices. Note the cripple, the blind man, the dying man, and the idiot who are being brought in to cast their votes.*

his Majesty that our dominions consisted of two islands, which composed three mighty kingdoms under one sovereign, beside our plantations in America. I dwelt long upon the fertility of our soil, and the temperature of our climate. I then spoke at large upon the constitution of an English Parliament, partly made up of an illustrious body called the House of Peers, persons of the noblest blood, and of the most ancient and ample patrimonies. I described that extraordinary care always taken of their education in arts and arms, to qualify them for being counselors born to the king and kingdom; to have a share in the legislature, to be members of the highest Court of Judicature, from whence there could be no appeal; and to be champions always ready for the defense of their prince and country, by their valor, conduct, and fidelity. That these were the ornament and bulwark of the kingdom, worthy followers of their most renowned ancestors, whose honor had been the reward of their virtue; from which their posterity were never once known to degenerate. To these were joined several holy persons, as part of that assembly, under the title of Bishops, whose peculiar business it is to take care of religion, and of those who instruct the people therein. These were searched and sought out through the whole nation, by the prince and his wisest counselors, among such of the priesthood as were most deservedly distinguished by the sanctity of their lives, and the depth of their erudition; who were indeed the spiritual fathers of the clergy and the people.

JONATHAN SWIFT

That the other part of the Parliament consisted of an assembly called the House of Commons, who were all principal gentlemen, *freely* picked and culled out by the people themselves, for their great abilities and love of their country, to represent the wisdom of the whole nation. And these two bodies make up the most august assembly in Europe, to whom, in conjunction with the prince, the whole legislature is committed. . . .

This conversation was not ended under five audiences, each of several hours, and the King heard the whole with great attention, frequently taking notes of what I spoke, as well as memorandums of several questions he intended to ask me.

When I had put an end to these long discourses, his Majesty in a sixth audience consulting his notes, proposed many doubts, queries, and objections, upon every article. He asked what methods were used to cultivate the minds and bodies of our young nobility, and in what kind of business they commonly spent the first and teachable part of their lives. What course was taken to supply that assembly when any noble family became extinct. What qualifications were necessary in those who were to be created new lords. Whether the humor of the prince, a sum of money to a court lady, or a prime minister, or a design of strengthening a party opposite to the public interest, ever happened to be motives in those advancements. What share of knowledge these lords had in the laws of their country, and how they came by it, so as to enable them to decide the properties of their fellow subjects in the last resort. Whether they were always so free from avarice, partialities, or want, that a bribe, or some other sinister view, could have no place among them. Whether those holy lords I spoke of were constantly promoted to that rank upon account of their knowledge in religious matters, and the sanctity of their lives, had never been compliers with the times while they were common priests, or slavish prostitute chaplains to some nobleman, whose opinions they continued servilely to follow after they were admitted into that assembly.

He then desired to know what arts were practiced in electing those whom I called commoners. Whether a stranger with a strong purse might not influence the vulgar voters to choose him before their own landlord, or the most considerable gentleman in the neighborhood. How it came to pass that people were so violently bent upon getting into this assembly, which I allowed to be a great trouble and expense, often to the ruin of their families, without any salary or pension: because this appeared such an exalted strain of virtue and public spirit that his Majesty seemed to doubt it might possibly not be always sincere: and he desired to know whether such zealous gentlemen could have any views of refunding themselves for the charges and trouble they were at, by sacrificing the public good to the designs of a weak and vicious prince in conjunction with a corrupted ministry. He multiplied his questions, and sifted me thoroughly upon every part of this head, proposing numberless inquiries and objections, which I think it not prudent or convenient to repeat. . . .

He was perfectly astonished with the historical account I gave him of our affairs during the last century; protesting it was only an heap of conspiracies, rebellions, murders, massacres, revolutions, banishments, the very worst effects that avarice, faction, hypocrisy, perfidiousness, cruelty, rage, madness, hatred, envy, lust, malice, or ambition could produce.

His Majesty in another audience was at the pains to recapitulate the sum of all I had spoken; compared the questions he made with the answers I had given; then taking me into his hands, and stroking me gently, delivered himself in these words, which I shall never forget nor the manner he spoke them in. "My little friend Grildrig, you have made a most admirable panegyric upon your country. You have clearly proved that ignorance, idleness, and vice are the proper ingredients for qualifying a legislator. That laws are best explained, interpreted, and applied by those whose interests and abilities lie in perverting, confounding, and eluding them. I observe among you some lines of an institution which in its original might have been tolerable; but these half erased, and the rest wholly blurred and blotted by corruptions. It doth not appear from all you have said, how any one virtue is required toward the procurement of any one station among you; much less that men are ennobled on account of their virtue, that priests are advanced for their piety or learning, soldiers for their conduct or valor, judges for their integrity, senators for the love of their country, or counselors for their wisdom. As for yourself," continued the King, "who have spent the greatest part of your life in traveling, I am well disposed to hope you may hitherto have escaped many vices of your country. But by what I have gathered from your own relation, and the answers I have with much pains wringed and extorted from you, I cannot but conclude the bulk of your natives to be the most pernicious race of little odious vermin that nature ever suffered to crawl upon the surface of the earth."

NOTHING BUT AN extreme love of truth could have hindered me from concealing this part of my story. It was in vain to discover my resentments, which were always turned into ridicule: and I was forced to rest with patience while my noble and most beloved country was so injuriously treated. I am heartily sorry as any of my readers can possibly be, that such an occasion was given: but this prince happened to be so curious and inquisitive upon every particular that it could not consist either with gratitude or good manners to refuse giving him what satisfaction I was able. Yet thus much I may be allowed to say in my own vindication; that I artfully eluded many of his questions; and gave to every point a more favorable turn by many degrees than the strictness of truth would allow. For I have always borne that laudable partiality to my own country which Dionysius Halicarnassensis[2] with so much justice recommends to an historian. I would hide the frailties and deformities of my political mother, and place her virtues and beauties in the most advantageous light. This was my sincere endeavor in those many discourses I had with that mighty monarch, although it unfortunately failed of success.

But great allowances should be given to a King who lives wholly secluded from the rest of the world, and must therefore be altogether unacquainted with the manners and customs that most prevail in other nations: the want of which knowledge will ever produce many *prejudices*, and a certain *narrowness of thinking*; from which we and the politer countries of Europe are wholly exempted. And it would be hard indeed, if so remote a prince's notions of

2 **Dionysius** (dī′ə nĭsh′ĭ əs) **Halicarnassensis:** an ancient Greek writer.

virtue and vice were to be offered as a standard for all mankind.

To confirm what I have now said, and further, to show the miserable effects of a *confined education,* I shall here insert a passage which will hardly obtain belief. In hopes to ingratiate myself farther into his Majesty's favor, I told him of an invention discovered between three and four hundred years ago, to make a certain powder, into an heap of which the smallest spark of fire falling, would kindle the whole in a moment, although it were as big as a mountain, and make it all fly up in the air together, with a noise and agitation greater than thunder. That a proper quantity of this powder rammed into an hollow tube of brass or iron, according to its bigness, would drive a ball of iron or lead with such violence and speed, as nothing was able to sustain its force. That the largest balls thus discharged, would not only destroy whole ranks of an army at once; but batter the strongest walls to the ground; sink down ships with a thousand men in each, to the bottom of the sea; and, when linked together by a chain, would cut through masts and rigging; divide hundreds of bodies in the middle, and lay all waste before them. That we often put this powder into large hollow balls of iron, and discharged them by an engine into some city we were besieging; which would rip up the pavements, tear the houses to pieces, burst and throw splinters on every side, dashing out the brains of all who came near. That I knew the ingredients very well, which were cheap, and common; I understood the manner of compounding them, and could direct his workmen how to make those tubes of a size proportionable to all other things in his Majesty's kingdom, and the largest need not be above two hundred foot long;

twenty or thirty of which tubes, charged with the proper quantity of powder and balls, would batter down the walls of the strongest town in his dominions in a few hours; or destroy the whole metropolis, if ever it should pretend to dispute his absolute commands. This I humbly offered to his Majesty, as a small tribute of acknowledgment in return of so many marks that I had received of his royal favor and protection.

The King was struck with horror at the description I had given of those terrible engines, and the proposal I had made. He was amazed how so impotent and groveling an insect as I (these were his expressions) could entertain such inhuman ideas, and in so familiar a manner as to appear wholly unmoved at all the scenes of blood and desolation, which I had painted as the common effects of those destructive machines; whereof he said some evil genius, enemy to mankind, must have been the first contriver. As for himself, he protested that although few things delighted him so much as new discoveries in art or in nature; yet he would rather lose half his kingdom than be privy to such a secret; which he commanded me, as I valued my life, never to mention any more.

A strange effect of *narrow principles* and *short views!* that a prince possessed of every quality which procures veneration, love, and esteem; of strong parts, great wisdom, and profound learning; endued with admirable talents for government, and almost adored by his subjects; should from a *nice unnecessary scruple,* whereof in Europe we can have no conception, let slip an opportunity put into his hands, that would have made him absolute master of the lives, the liberties, and the fortunes of his people. Neither do I say this with the least intention to detract from the many

The horrors of war reach not only soldiers on the battlefield but civilians as well. Here the sacking and burning of a village during the Thirty Years' War (1618–1648) shows the vices and excesses of man in the mass.

virtues of that excellent King, whose character I am sensible will on this account be very much lessened in the opinion of an English reader: but I take this defect among them to have risen from their ignorance; they not having hitherto reduced politics into a science, as the more acute wits of Europe have done. For I remember very well, in a discourse one day with the King, when I happened to say there were several thousand books among us written upon the art of government; it gave him (directly contrary to my intention) a very mean opinion of our understandings. He professed both to abominate and despise all *mystery, refinement,* and *intrigue,* either in a prince or a minister. He could not tell what I meant by *secrets of state,* where an enemy or some rival nation were not in the case. He confined the knowledge of governing within very *narrow bounds;* to common sense and reason, to justice and lenity, to the speedy determination of civil and criminal causes; with some other obvious topics which are not worth considering. And he gave it for his opinion that whoever could make two ears of corn or two blades of grass to grow upon a spot of ground where only one grew before, would deserve better of mankind, and do more essential service to his country than the whole race of politicians put together.

The learning of this people is very defective; consisting only in morality, history, poetry, and mathematics; wherein they must be allowed to excel. But the last of these is wholly applied to what may be useful in life, to the improvement of agriculture, and all mechanical arts; so that among us it would be little esteemed. And as to ideas, entities, abstractions, and transcendentals, I could never drive the least conception into their heads.

Comment

Once again an affair of state provides Swift with an opportunity for his most powerful irony. The King, whose humanity and learning Gulliver admires, indignantly rejects the "proposal of much advantage" that Gulliver makes him. And in Gulliver's response, once again, we find the object of Swift's satire.

1. What is Gulliver's tone as he describes the powers of gunpowder to the King?
2. And what is his tone as he reflects upon the King's peremptory refusal to have anything to do with this invention?
3. In this episode Swift emphasizes such terms as "prejudices," "narrowness of thinking," "narrow principles," and "short views." To what sort of people are such terms usually applied? How do such people differ from those who believe in inventions and in progress?
4. What, then, is the real object of Swift's satire here? Does he simply praise that which is backward and provincial at the expense of that which is forward-looking? What is Gulliver being gullible about here? What folly and absurdity does his behavior reveal?

The Power of Common Sense

Samuel Johnson (1709-1784) and James Boswell (1740-1795)

Quotations from Samuel Johnson have appeared frequently in these pages, and probably no other writer has been quoted more often by the student of English literature. "The Great Cham" (khan, or lord), as he was later called, dominated the literary opinions of his day, and in no later age have his judgments been ignored. Johnson was a lexicographer, an essayist, a biographer, a poet, a playwright. In his early London days he even reported speeches in Parliament for the *Gentleman's Magazine*. (It was illegal to make public the procedures of Parliament, but Johnson reported them as proceedings of the senate of Lilliput!)

Johnson was born in Lichfield, in the Midlands, in 1709. His father was a bookseller, and at an early age the son had read most of his stock. He spent three years at Oxford, and, though he had to leave before taking his degree, the University in 1775 gave him the honorary degree that made him Doctor Johnson. As a young man he married a widow older than he and tried to earn a living as a schoolmaster. Few enrolled in his little institution, however (though he did have a famous pupil in David Garrick, who later became the greatest actor

Johnson and Boswell in a convivial mood on High Street in Edinburgh, an engraving by Rowlandson of the two well-known figures.

of his time); and he set out, as so many others had, to make his fortune in London. Success came slowly. His *Dictionary*, published in 1755, at first earned him no money though it brought him fame. Ten years later his edition of Shakespeare, a great work of scholarship, did not make him much richer. (The royal pension he was granted in 1762, he spent mostly on pensioners of his own—handicapped, destitute persons who filled his house and lived off his charity.) His reputation and literary influence, though, constantly grew. In 1764 he and Sir Joshua Reynolds, the great painter, formed "The Club," an association of men important in government and literature. Their sessions of conversation and "wit" were pervaded by Johnson's authority, just as his authority later pervaded all literary discussion.

Here are some of Johnson's critical pronouncements taken from various writings. Their weight and their tone could be duplicated many times over, in many of his other writings.

> If the language of theology were extracted from Hooker[1] and the translation of the Bible; the terms of natural knowledge from Bacon; the phrases of policy, war, and navigation from Raleigh; the dialect of poetry and fiction from Spenser and Sidney; and the diction of common life from Shakespeare, few ideas would be lost to mankind for want of English words in which they might be expressed.
>
> —Preface to the *English Dictionary* (1755)

1 **Hooker:** a great Elizabethan churchman who wrote on theology and government.

To judge rightly of an author, we must transport ourselves to his time, and examine what were the wants of his contemporaries, and what were his means of supplying them. That which is easy at one time was difficult at another.

—"Dryden," *Lives of the Poets* (1779-1781)

Words too familiar, or too remote, defeat the purpose of a poet. From those sounds which we hear on small or on coarse occasions, we do not easily receive strong impressions, or delightful images; and words to which we are nearly strangers, whenever they occur, draw that attention on themselves which they should transmit to things.

—"Dryden," *Lives of the Poets* (1779-1781)

Nothing can please many, and please long, but just representations of general nature. Particular manners can be known to few, and therefore few only can judge how nearly they are copied. The irregular combinations of fanciful invention may delight awhile, by that novelty of which the common satiety of life sends us all in quest; but the pleasures of sudden wonder are soon exhausted, and the mind can only repose on the stability of truth.

—Preface to *Shakespeare* (1765)

Boswell's Life of Samuel Johnson

An American scholar has said that there is no matter of fact about the life of an 18th-century man of letters that cannot be documented by research. It was an age in which correspondence was abundant and journals were widely and strictly kept; people formed regular habits of recording the social life around them. The supreme example of this interest in the record is James Boswell's *Life of Samuel Johnson*. Through the power of exact memory and hundreds of notes, Boswell gave us one of the fullest records ever made of a life. In its pages we not only hear Johnson's great talk; we also come to know one of the greatest personalities in literature.

James Boswell (1740-1795), the son of a distinguished Scottish judge, came from Ayrshire. He studied the law himself, but his real interest was in the literary and social life of London. In 1782 Boswell inherited his father's property and title: he became a "laird," the Master of Auchinleck, the family estate. He soon moved his family to London and there worked on his great biography. He was wild and unstable, yet apparently gifted with great charm. On his European journeys he presented himself to the leading writers and thinkers, and at home he determined to make the acquaintance of the most famous man of letters in the kingdom.

Here is an account of Boswell's first meeting with Johnson. The time is 1763; the place is a bookshop owned by a Mr. Davies. The account is from Boswell's *Life of Samuel Johnson*.

> Mr. Davies mentioned my name, and respectfully introduced me to him. I was much agitated; and recollecting his prejudice against the Scotch, of which I had heard much, I said to Davies, "Don't tell him where I come from." "From Scotland," cried Davies, roguishly. "Mr. Johnson," said I, "I do indeed come from Scotland, but I cannot help it." I am willing to flatter myself that I meant this as light pleasantry to soothe and conciliate him, and not as an humiliating abasement at the expense of my country. But however that might be, this speech was somewhat unlucky; for with that quickness of wit for which he was so remarkable, he seized the expression "come from Scotland," which I used in the sense of being of that country; and, as if I had said that I had come away from it, or left it, retorted, "That, sir, I find is what a very great many of your countrymen cannot help." This stroke stunned me a good deal; and when we had sat down, I felt myself not a little embarrassed, and apprehensive of what might come next. He then addressed himself to Davies: "What do you think of Garrick? He has refused me an order[1] for the play for Miss Williams,[2] because he knows the house will be full, and that an order will be worth three shillings." Eager to take any opening to get into conversation with him, I ventured to say, "O, sir, I cannot think Mr. Garrick would grudge such a trifle to you." "Sir," said he, with a stern look, "I have known David Garrick longer than you have done; and I know no right you have to talk to me on the subject." Perhaps I deserved this check; for it was rather presumptuous in me, an entire stranger, to express any doubt of the justice of his animadversion upon his old acquaintance and pupil. I now felt myself much mortified, and began to think that the hope which I had long indulged of obtaining his acquaintance was blasted. And, in truth, had not my ardor been uncommonly strong, and my resolution uncommonly persevering, so rough a reception might have deterred me forever from making any further attempts. Fortunately, however, I remained upon the field not wholly discomfited, and was soon rewarded by hearing some of his conversation. . . .

Boswell was encouraged when Davies whispered to him as he left, "Don't be uneasy. I can see he likes you very well." The acquaintance ripened into friendship, and "Bozzy" fulfilled his ambition by becoming an intimate of the great man.

Here, arranged under general topics, are more passages from Boswell's *Life*.

---

1 **order:** complimentary ticket.   2 **Miss Williams:** one of Johnson's pensioners.

from The Life
of
Samuel Johnson

James Boswell

The Dictionary

[*When he completed the plan for his dictionary, Johnson sought to persuade Lord Chesterfield to become its patron —one who would help finance its expenses and whose name would encourage others to subscribe to it before publication. Johnson was ignored by Chesterfield until the eve of publication, when, according to Boswell, he tried to* have the work dedicated to himself and let it be known that he had been its sponsor. Chesterfield wrote two letters to The World, a London newspaper, belatedly praising the project that was now completed, and they provoked from Johnson the following masterpiece. Boswell quotes it in full:]

February 7, 1755

To the Earl of Chesterfield

My Lord:

I have been lately informed, by the proprietor of *The World*, that two papers, in which my *Dictionary* is recommended to the public, were written by your lordship. To be so distinguished, is an honor, which, being very little accustomed to favors from the great, I know not well how to receive, or in what terms to acknowledge.

When, upon some slight encouragement, I first visited your lordship, I was overpowered, like the rest of mankind, by the enchantment of your address, and could not forbear to wish that I might boast myself *Le vainqueur du vainqueur de la terre*[1]—that I might obtain that regard for which I saw the world contending; but I found my attendance so little encouraged, that neither pride nor modesty would suffer me to continue it. When I had once addressed your lordship in public, I had exhausted all the art of pleasing which a retired and uncourtly scholar can possess. I had done all that I could; and no man is well pleased to have his all neglected, be it ever so little.

Seven years, my Lord, have now passed, since I waited in your outward rooms, or was repulsed from your door; during which time I have been pushing on my work through difficulties, of which it is useless to complain, and have brought it, at last, to the verge of publication, without one act of assistance, one word of encouragement, or one smile of favor. Such treatment I

---

1 **Le . . . terre:** the conqueror of the conqueror of the world. (Johnson quotes from an essay by the French writer Boileau.)

did not expect, for I never had a patron before.

The shepherd in Virgil grew at last acquainted with Love, and found him a native of the rocks.[2]

Is not a patron, my Lord, one who looks with unconcern on a man struggling for life in the water, and, when he has reached ground, encumbers him with help? The notice which you have been pleased to take of my labors, had it been early, had been kind; but it has been delayed till I am indifferent, and cannot enjoy it; till I am solitary,[3] and cannot impart it; till I am known, and do not want it. I hope it is no very cynical asperity not to confess obligations where no benefit has been received, or to be unwilling that the Public should consider me as owing that to a patron, which Providence has enabled me to do for myself.

Having carried on my work thus far with so little obligation to any favorer of learning, I shall not be disappointed though I should conclude it, if less be possible, with less; for I have been long wakened from that dream of hope, in which I once boasted myself with so much exultation, my Lord, your lordship's most humble, most obedient servant,

Sam. Johnson

* * *

The *Dictionary, with a Grammar and History of the English Language,* being now at length published, in two volumes folio,[4] the world contemplated with wonder so stupendous a work achieved by one man, while other countries had thought such undertakings fit only for whole academies. Vast as his powers were, I cannot but think that his imagination deceived him, when he supposed that by constant application he might have performed the task in three years. . . .

The extensive reading which was absolutely necessary for the accumulation of authorities, and which alone may account for Johnson's retentive mind being enriched with a very large and various store of knowledge and imagery, must have occupied several years. The Preface furnishes an eminent instance of a double talent, of which Johnson was fully conscious. Sir Joshua Reynolds heard him say, "There are two things which I am confident I can do very well: one is an introduction to any literary work, stating what it is to contain, and how it should be executed in the most perfect manner; the other is a conclusion, showing from various causes why the execution has not been equal to what the author promised to himself and to the public." . . .

A few of his definitions must be admitted to be erroneous. Thus *Windward* and *Leeward,* though directly of opposite meaning, are defined identically the same way; as to which inconsiderable specks it is enough to observe, that his Preface announces that he was aware there might be many such in so immense a work; nor was he at all disconcerted when an instance was pointed out to him. A lady once asked him how he came to define *Pastern* the *knee* of a horse: instead of making an elaborate defense, as she expected, he at once answered, "Ignorance, madam, pure ignorance." His definition of *Network*[5] has been often quoted with sportive malignity, as obscuring a thing in itself very plain. But

2 **shepherd . . . rocks:** an allusion to a poem by Virgil about rustic life.
3 **solitary:** Johnson's wife died in 1752.
4 **folio:** large page.

5 **Network:** "any thing reticulated or decussated at equal distances, with interstices between the intersections."

to these frivolous censures no other answer is necessary than that with which we are furnished by his own Preface. . . .

His introducing his own opinions, and even prejudices, under general definitions of words, while at the same time the original meaning of the words is not explained, as his *Tory, Whig, Pension, Oats, Excise,*[6] and a few more, cannot be fully defended, and must be placed to the account of capricious and humorous indulgence. . . .

Let it, however, be remembered, that this indulgence does not display itself only in sarcasm toward others, but sometimes in playful allusion to the notions commonly entertained of his own laborious task. Thus: *"Grubstreet,* the name of a street in London, much inhabited by writers of small histories, *dictionaries,* and temporary poems; whence any mean production is called *Grubstreet."—"Lexicographer,* a writer of dictionaries, a *harmless drudge."*

Proper Language

He observed, that a gentleman of eminence in literature had got into a bad style of poetry of late. "He puts," said he, "a very common thing in a strange dress, till he does not know it himself, and thinks other people do not know it." BOSWELL. "That is owing to his being so much versant in old English poetry." JOHNSON. "What

is that to the purpose, sir? If I say a man is drunk, and you tell me it is owing to his taking much drink, the matter is not mended. No, sir, ———[7] has taken to an odd mode. For example, he'd write thus:

Hermit hoar, in solemn cell,
　　Wearing out life's evening gray.

Gray evening is common enough; but *evening gray* he'd think fine.—Stay;— we'll make out the stanza:

Hermit hoar, in solemn cell,
　　Wearing out life's evening gray;
Smite thy bosom, sage, and tell,
　　What is bliss? and which the way?"

BOSWELL. "But why smite his bosom, sir?" JOHNSON. "Why, to show he was in earnest" (smiling). He at an after period added the following stanza:

Thus I spoke; and speaking sighed;
　—Scarce repressed the starting tears;—
When the smiling sage replied—
　—Come, my lad, and drink some beer.

* * *

Next day we got to Harwich,[8] to dinner; and my passage in the packet-boat to Helvoetsluys being secured, and my baggage put on board, we dined at our inn by ourselves. I happened to say it would be terrible if he should not find a speedy opportunity of returning to London, and be confined in so dull a place. JOHNSON. "Don't, sir, accustom yourself to use big words for little matters. It would *not* be *terrible,* though I *were* to be detained some time here."

* * *

BOSWELL. "I wish much to be in Parliament, sir." JOHNSON. "Why, sir, unless you come resolved to support

---

6 **Tory . . . Excise:** The definitions are: *Tory:* one who adheres to the ancient constitution of the state, and the apostolical hierarchy of the Church of England; opposed to a whig. *Whig:* the name of a faction. *Pension:* an allowance made to any one without an equivalent. In England it is generally understood to mean pay given to a state hireling for treason to his country. *Oats:* a grain which in England is generally given to horses, but in Scotland supports the people. *Excise:* a hateful tax levied upon commodities, and adjudged not by the common judges of property, but wretches hired by those to whom Excise is paid.

7 ———: Johnson is referring to a contemporary poet, Thomas Warton.
8 **Harwich:** Boswell was about to go to Europe by ship from Harwich to Holland.

any administration, you would be the worse for being in Parliament, because you would be obliged to live more expensively." BOSWELL. "Perhaps, sir, I should be the less happy for being in Parliament. I never would sell my vote, and I should be vexed if things went wrong." JOHNSON. "That's cant, sir. It would not vex you more in the House than in the gallery: public affairs vex no man." BOSWELL. "Have not they vexed yourself a little, sir? Have not you been vexed by all the turbulence of this reign, and by that absurd vote of the House of Commons, 'That the influence of the Crown has increased, is increasing, and ought to be diminished'?" JOHNSON. "Sir, I have never slept an hour less, nor ate an ounce less meat. I would have knocked the factious dogs on the head, to be sure; but I was not *vexed*." BOSWELL. "I declare, sir, upon my honor, I did imagine I was vexed, and took a pride in it; but it *was*, perhaps, cant; for I own I neither ate less nor slept less." JOHNSON. "My dear friend, clear your *mind* of cant. You may *talk* as other people do: you may say to a man, 'Sir, I am your most humble servant.' You are *not* his most humble servant. You may say, 'These are bad times; it is a melancholy thing to be reserved to such times.' You don't mind the times. You tell a man, 'I am sorry you had such bad weather the last day of your journey, and were so much wet.' You don't care sixpence whether he is wet or dry. You may *talk* in this manner; it is a mode of talking in society: but don't *think* foolishly."

Society

I described to him an impudent fellow from Scotland, who affected to be a savage, and railed at all established systems. JOHNSON. "There is nothing surprising in this, sir. He wants to make himself conspicuous. He would tumble in a hogsty, as long as you looked at him and called to him to come out. But let him alone, never mind him, and he'll soon give it over."

I added that the same person maintained that there was no distinction between virtue and vice. JOHNSON. "Why, sir, if the fellow does not think as he speaks, he is lying; and I see not what honor he can propose to himself from having the character of a liar. But if he does really think that there is no distinction between virtue and vice, why, sir, when he leaves our houses, let us count our spoons."

* * *

He again insisted on the duty of maintaining subordination of rank. "Sir, I would no more deprive a nobleman of his respect than of his money. I consider myself as acting a part in the great system of society, and I do to others as I would have them to do to me. I would behave to a nobleman as I should expect he would behave to me, were I a nobleman and he Sam. Johnson. Sir, there is one Mrs. Macaulay in this town, a great republican. One day when I was at her house, I put on a very grave countenance, and said to her, 'Madam, I am now become a convert to your way of thinking. I am convinced that all mankind are upon an equal footing; and to give you an unquestionable proof, madam, that I am in earnest, here is a very sensible, civil, well-behaved fellow citizen, your footman; I desire that he may be allowed to sit down and dine with us.' I thus, sir, showed her the absurdity of the leveling doctrine. She has never liked me since. Sir, your levelers wish to level *down* as far as themselves; but they cannot bear leveling *up* to themselves. They would all have some people under them; why not then have some people above them?" I mentioned a certain author who disgusted me by his forwardness, and by showing no deference to noblemen into whose company he was admitted. JOHNSON. "Suppose a shoemaker should claim an equality with him, as he does with a lord: how he would stare. 'Why, sir, do you stare?' says the shoemaker; 'I do great service to society. 'Tis true I am paid for doing it; but so are you, sir: and I am sorry to say it, better paid than I am, for doing something not so necessary. For mankind could do better without your books, than without my shoes.' Thus, sir, there would be a perpetual struggle for precedence were there no fixed invariable rules for the distinction of rank, which creates no jealousy, as it is allowed to be accidental."

✿ ✿ ✿

Feelings

He recommended to me to keep a journal of my life, full and unreserved. He said it would be a very good exercise, and would yield me great satisfaction when the particulars were faded from my remembrance. I was uncommonly fortunate in having had a previous coincidence of opinion with him upon this subject, for I had kept such a journal for some time; and it was no small pleasure to me to have this to tell him, and to receive his approbation. He counseled me to keep it private, and said I might surely have a friend who would burn it in case of my death. From this habit I have been enabled to give the world so many anecdotes, which would otherwise have been lost to posterity. I mentioned that I was afraid I put into my journal too many little incidents. JOHNSON. "There is nothing, sir, too little for so little a creature as man. It is by studying little things that we attain the great art of having as little misery and as much happiness as possible."

✿ ✿ ✿

On Wednesday, July 20, Dr. Johnson, Mr. Dempster, and my uncle Dr. Boswell, who happened to be now in London, supped with me at these chambers. JOHNSON. "Pity is not natural to man. Children are always cruel. Savages are always cruel. Pity is acquired and improved by the cultivation of reason. We may have uneasy sensations from seeing a creature in distress, without pity; for we have not pity unless we wish to relieve them. When I am on my way to dine with a friend, and finding it late, have bid the coachman make haste, if I happen to attend when he whips his horses, I may feel unpleasantly that the animals are put to pain, but I do not wish him to desist. No, sir, I wish him to drive on."

✿ ✿ ✿

Johnson's love of little children, which he discovered upon all occasions, calling them "pretty dears," and giving them sweetmeats, was an undoubted proof of the real humanity and gentleness of his disposition.

His uncommon kindness to his servants, and serious concern, not only for their comfort in this world, but their happiness in the next, was another unquestionable evidence of what all, who were intimately acquainted with him, knew to be true.

Nor would it be just, under this head, to omit the fondness which he showed for animals which he had taken under his protection. I never shall forget the indulgence with which he treated Hodge, his cat; for whom he himself used to go out and buy oysters, lest the servants, having that trouble, should take a dislike to the poor creature. I am, unluckily, one of those who have an antipathy to a cat, so that I am uneasy when in the room with one; and I own I frequently suffered a good deal from the presence of this same Hodge. I recollect him one day scrambling up Dr. Johnson's breast, apparently with much satisfaction, while my friend, smiling and half-whistling, rubbed down his back and pulled him by the tail; and when I observed he was a fine cat, saying, "Why, yes, sir, but I have had cats whom I liked better than this"; and then, as if perceiving Hodge to be out of countenance, adding, "but he is a very fine cat, a very fine cat indeed."

This reminds me of the ludicrous account which he gave Mr. Langton of the despicable state of a young gentleman of good family. "Sir, when I heard of him last, he was running about town shooting cats." And then, in a sort of kindly reverie, he bethought himself of his own favorite cat, and said, "But Hodge shan't be shot; no, no, Hodge shall not be shot."

* * *

We walked in the evening in Greenwich Park. He asked me, I suppose by way of trying my disposition, "Is not this very fine?" Having no exquisite relish of the beauties of nature, and being more delighted with "the busy hum of men,"[9] I answered, "Yes, sir; but not equal to Fleet Street." JOHNSON. "You are right, sir."

* * *

In our way, Johnson strongly expressed his love of driving fast in a post chaise. "If," said he, "I had no duties, and no reference to futurity, I would spend my life in driving briskly in a post chaise with a pretty woman; but she should be one who could understand me, and would add something to the conversation."

Comment

Johnson was a rich and various personality. His mind was clear, and he gave his opinions with emphasis because he knew his own mind. Sometimes the Latinity of his expression was excessive. Charles Dickens in the next century may have been making fun of such Latinity when he has Mr. Micawber say, speaking of yet another job that he has lost, "It is not an avocation of a remunerative description—in other words, it does *not* pay." Johnson's weightiness of expression led some to call him the "Great Bear," but Goldsmith said, "He has nothing of the bear but his skin." He was a huge, shaggy man, but he could be sensitive and gay.

Boswell once wrote a "character" of Johnson that appears in the preface to his book about a tour through Scotland that he and Johnson made together. The "character" is a short sketch that decribes the main traits of a personality by summing up many separate observations. From the record above—and including the passages of Johnson's literary criticism—write a "character" of Samuel Johnson.

9 the busy hum of men: a quotation from a poem by Milton, "L'Allegro."

Far from the Madding Crowd

DR. JOHNSON'S FIRST literary success was a poem entitled "London," and his love for the city emerges frequently in Boswell's *Life*. Some writers of the 18th century, however, especially toward its close, shunned the city and lived in country retirement. They were not quite the lovers of nature that the poets of the next age were to be; their attitudes were more melancholy. But their intimate knowledge of simple life and country ways was opposed to the sophistication of the "damned, dear, distracting town," as Pope called it.

Thomas Gray (1716-1771) and the "Elegy"

No other poem of the 18th century is a better example of "What oft was thought, but ne'er so well expressed" than Gray's "Elegy." As Dr. Johnson said, it "abounds with images which find a mirror in every mind, and with sentiments to which every bosom returns an echo."

Its author was born in London, and, supported by his mother, who kept a millinery shop, he attended Eton and Cambridge. After making the Grand Tour—the trip through Europe and the Alps that completed every gentleman's education—he returned to the university and lived there very much to himself for the rest of his life.

The "Elegy," published in 1751, was begun in 1742 after the death of Gray's close friend, Richard West, a friend whose experience Gray seems to remember in his closing lines.

Elegy Written in a Country Churchyard

Thomas Gray

The curfew tolls the knell of parting day,
The lowing herd wind slowly o'er the lea,
The plowman homeward plods his weary way,
And leaves the world to darkness and to me.

Now fades the glimmering landscape on the sight,   5
And all the air a solemn stillness holds,
Save where the beetle wheels his droning flight,
And drowsy tinklings lull the distant folds;[1]

Save that from yonder ivy-mantled tow'r,
The moping owl does to the moon complain   10
Of such as, wand'ring near her secret bow'r,
Molest her ancient solitary reign.

Beneath those rugged elms, that yew tree's shade,
Where heaves the turf in many a mold'ring heap,
Each in his narrow cell forever laid,   15
The rude forefathers of the hamlet sleep.

The breezy call of incense-breathing Morn,
The swallow twitt'ring from the straw-built shed,
The cock's shrill clarion, or the echoing horn,[2]
No more shall rouse them from their lowly bed.   20

For them no more the blazing hearth shall burn,
Or busy housewife ply her evening care;
No children run to lisp their sire's return,
Or climb his knees the envied kiss to share.

---

1 folds: pens for sheep.   **2 horn:** i.e., of the huntsman.

Oft did the harvest to their sickle yield;   25
Their furrow oft the stubborn glebe[3] has broke;
How jocund did they drive their team afield!
How bowed the woods beneath their sturdy stroke!

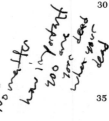

Let not Ambition mock their useful toil,
Their homely joys, and destiny obscure;   30
Nor Grandeur hear, with a disdainful smile,
The short and simple annals of the poor.

The boast of heraldry, the pomp of pow'r,
And all that beauty, all that wealth e'er gave
Awaits[4] alike th' inevitable hour.   35
The paths of glory lead but to the grave.

Nor you, ye proud, impute to these the fault,
If Mem'ry o'er their tomb no trophies raise,
Where through the long-drawn aisle and fretted vault[5]
The pealing anthem swells the note of praise.   40

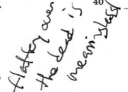

Can storied urn[6] or animated[7] bust
Back to its mansion call the fleeting breath?
Can Honor's voice provoke[8] the silent dust,
Or Flatt'ry soothe the dull cold ear of Death?

Perhaps in this neglected spot is laid   45
Some heart once pregnant with celestial fire;
Hands[9] that the rod of empire might have swayed,
Or waked to ecstasy the living lyre.

But Knowledge to their eyes her ample page,
Rich with the spoils of time, did ne'er unroll;   50
Chill Penury repressed their noble rage,[10]
And froze the genial[11] current of the soul.

Full many a gem of purest ray serene
The dark unfathomed caves of ocean bear;
Full many a flower is born to blush unseen,   55
And waste its sweetness on the desert air.

---

3 **glebe:** field.
4 **awaits:** The subject of this verb is *hour.*
5 **fretted vault:** arched, ornamented ceiling of a church.
6 **storied urn:** vase with painted figures on its sides.

7 **animated:** lifelike.
8 **provoke:** call forth to life.
9 **Hands:** subject of verb *might have swayed.*
10 **rage:** inspiration.
11 **genial:** creative.

Some village Hampden,[12] that with dauntless breast
The little tyrant of his fields withstood;
Some mute inglorious Milton here may rest,
Some Cromwell guiltless of his country's blood.   60

Th' applause of list'ning senates to command,
The threats of pain and ruin to despise,
To scatter plenty o'er a smiling land,
And read their hist'ry in a nation's eyes,

Their lot forbade;[13] nor circumscribed alone   65
Their growing virtues, but their crimes confined;
Forbade to wade through slaughter to a throne,
And shut the gates of mercy on mankind,

The struggling pangs of conscious truth to hide,
To quench the blushes of ingenuous shame,   70
Or heap the shrine of Luxury and Pride
With incense kindled at the Muse's flame.

Far from the madding[14] crowd's ignoble strife,
Their sober wishes never learned to stray;
Along the cool sequestered vale of life   75
They kept the noiseless tenor of their way.

Yet ev'n these bones from insult to protect,
Some frail memorial still erected nigh,
With uncouth rhymes and shapeless sculpture decked,
Implores the passing tribute of a sigh.   80

Their name, their years, spelt by th' unlettered Muse,
The place of fame and elegy supply;
And many a holy text around she strews,
That teach the rustic moralist to die.

For who, to dumb Forgetfulness a prey,   85
This pleasing anxious being e'er resigned,
Left the warm precincts of the cheerful day,
Nor cast one longing, ling'ring look behind?

On some fond breast the parting soul relies,
Some pious drops the closing eye requires;   90
Ev'n from the tomb the voice of Nature cries,
Ev'n in our ashes live their wonted fires.

---

12 Hampden: John Hampden, a member of Parliament, who led the opposition to Charles I.

13 forbade: The whole preceding stanza is the object of this verb.

14 madding: raving; wild (not *maddening*).

For[15] thee, who mindful of th' unhonored dead
Dost in these lines their artless tale relate,
If chance,[16] by lonely Contemplation led,   95
Some kindred spirit shall inquire thy fate,

Haply some hoary-headed swain may say,
"Oft have we seen him at the peep of dawn
Brushing with hasty steps the dews away
To meet the sun upon the upland lawn.   100

"There at the foot of yonder nodding beech,
That wreathes its old fantastic roots so high,
His listless length at noontide would he stretch,
And pore upon the brook that babbles by.

"Hard by yon wood, now smiling as in scorn,   105
Mutt'ring his wayward fancies he would rove,
Now drooping, woeful wan, like one forlorn,
Or crazed with care, or crossed in hopeless love.

"One morn I missed him on the customed hill,
Along the heath and near his fav'rite tree;   110
Another came; nor yet beside the rill,
Nor up the lawn, nor at the wood was he;

"The next with dirges due in sad array
Slow through the church-way path we saw him borne.
Approach and read (for thou canst read) the lay,   115
Graved on the stone beneath yon aged thorn."

The Epitaph

Here rests his head upon the lap of Earth
A youth to Fortune and to Fame unknown.
Fair Science[17] frowned not on his humble birth,
And Melancholy marked him for her own.   120

Large was his bounty, and his soul sincere,
Heav'n did a recompense as largely send:
He gave to Mis'ry all he had, a tear,
He gained from Heav'n ('twas all he wished) a friend.

No farther seek his merits to disclose,   125
Or draw his frailties from their dread abode,
(There they alike in trembling hope repose),
The bosom of his Father and his God.

15 For: i.e., as for.
16 if chance: if it should happen that.   **17 Science:** learning.

Comment

The "Elegy" progresses in several movements, each a group of four or five stanzas.

1. Lines 1-16. The first four stanzas describe the village at the end of the day. How are Gray's images here appropriate to his subject?
2. Lines 17-28. The next movement describes the life left behind by the "rude forefathers" who sleep in their graves. How do the images of daily life contrast here with the images describing the close of day in the first movement?
3. Lines 29-44. The next movement begins with a typical 18th-century personification: "Let not Ambition. . . ." What other moral qualities are personified in this movement? What comment do these four stanzas make on those who rest in the churchyard?
4. Lines 45-76. Here the poet comments more particularly on various persons who may be buried in "this neglected spot." Why are they all men? What sort of men does he imagine them to have been? With what metaphors and personifications does he describe them?
5. Lines 77-92. The poet refers to the "memorials" of the churchyard. What is their character? How are they appropriate to the lives they commemorate?
6. Lines 93-116. The poet turns from the scene and muses upon a "thee"—upon a poet like himself who remembers these "unhonored dead" with "artless lines." He wonders what might be said of such a poet if some "kindred spirit" should inquire about his fate. How does the reply of the "hoary-headed swain" relate the poet to those who are buried in the churchyard? How is the poet's imagined life like theirs?
7. The Epitaph. How do these final lines sum up the poem? What kind of a life do they commemorate?
8. As you reflect on the literature of the Renaissance that you have earlier read, what seems new to you in Gray's poem? Poets had expressed melancholy before. But what kind of melancholy does Gray express here? What kind of experience does he feel melancholy toward?

The Enlightenment
Summing Up

THE HEADNOTE TO this chapter of our survey is a quotation from Samuel Johnson: ". . . repose on the stability of truth." As you look back over the preceding selections from the literature of the Enlightenment, consider why this headnote, or motto, is an appropriate one. In the passage from which it comes (in the preface to his edition of Shakespeare), Johnson makes a contrast between "fanciful invention" and "the stability of truth":

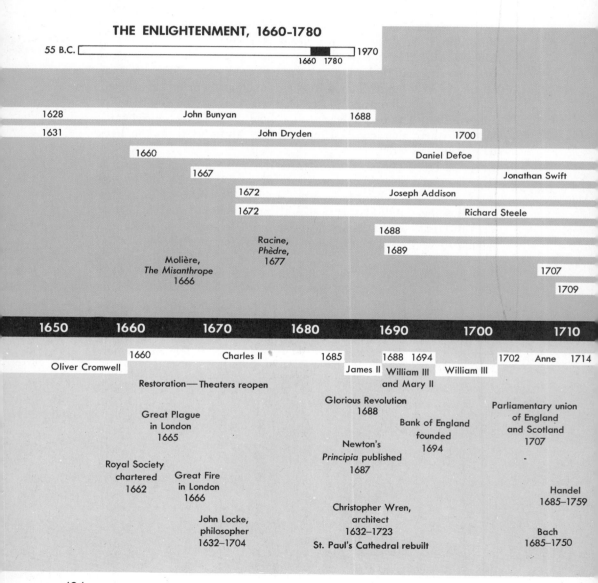

THE ENLIGHTENMENT, 1660-1780

55 B.C. ☐————————————■—☐ 1970
1660 1780

1628   John Bunyan   1688
1631   John Dryden   1700
1660   Daniel Defoe
1667   Jonathan Swift
1672   Joseph Addison
1672   Richard Steele
1688
1689
1707
1709

Racine,
Phèdre,
1677

Molière,
The Misanthrope
1666

| 1650 | 1660 | 1670 | 1680 | 1690 | 1700 | 1710 |

1660   Charles II   1685   1688 1694   1702   Anne   1714

Oliver Cromwell   James II   William III   William III
and Mary II

Restoration—Theaters reopen

Glorious Revolution   Parliamentary union
1688   of England
and Scotland
1707

Great Plague
in London   Bank of England
1665   founded
1694

Newton's
Royal Society   Principia published
chartered   Great Fire   1687
1662   in London
1666   Handel
1685–1759

Christopher Wren,
John Locke,   architect   Bach
philosopher   1632–1723   1685–1750
1632–1704   St. Paul's Cathedral rebuilt

The irregular combinations of fanciful invention may delight awhile, . . . but the pleasures of sudden wonder are soon exhausted, and the mind can only repose on the stability of truth.

Do the writers of the Enlightenment seem to you more interested in "the stability of truth" than in "irregular combinations of fanciful invention"? Do the major writers of the Enlightenment seem to you writers who knew and felt a real *stability* in the truths they tried to express? Explain the reasons for your conclusions.

Diderot, *Encyclopedia*, 1751–1772

1751 Richard Brinsley Sheridan	1816
1728 Oliver Goldsmith	1774
1721 Tobias Smollett	1771
716 Thomas Gray	1771
713 Laurence Sterne	1768
1731	
1745	

Voltaire, *Candide*, 1759

719

Jonathan Edwards, *A Personal Narrative*, 1739

Montesquieu, *The Spirit of Laws*, 1750

Rousseau, *Social Contract*, 1762

Thomas Paine, *Common Sense*, 1776

1729

Alexander Pope 1744

Samuel Richardson 1761

Henry Fielding 1754

Samuel Johnson 1784

1740 James Boswell 1795

1720   1730   1740   1750   1760   1770   1780

1727 George II 1760

George I 1727

1760 George III 1820

First full English dictionary 1721

Joshua Reynolds, painter 1723–1792

Spinning jenny invented 1764

Mozart 1756–1791

Robert Walpole Prime Minister 1721–1742

William Pitt the Elder, Prime Minister 1756–1761

Edmund Burke 1729–1797

American Declaration of Independence adopted 1776

1756 Seven Years' War 1763

William Hogarth 1697–1764

Benjamin Franklin 1706–1790

Haydn (Austria) 1732–1809

Steam engine patented by Watt 1769

A detail from The Lake from Petworth House–Sunset, *a painting by J. M. W. Turner* (1775–1851).

1780-1830

The Romantic Period

". . . magic casements opening . . ."

JOHN KEATS

IN 1802 Charles Lamb, a writer whom you will presently encounter, visited the Lake District, a region of peaks and fiord-like lakes in the northwest of England. He tramped through the countryside, he waded in streams, he climbed one of the highest mountains, and he wrote to a friend: "Such an impression I never received from objects of sight before. . . . I have satisfied myself that there is such a thing as that which tourists call *romantic.*" That word with which Lamb summed up his impressions was not new, and it is a word that his correspondent doubtless understood at once. But to give an exact definition of *romantic* would probably have been difficult for both of them. At the beginning of the 19th century, *romantic* to some people was a term of abuse, a word connoting irresponsibility. To others it meant a state of mind in which a faculty called imagination did something that that faculty had not done during the Enlightenment: it took over the power of another faculty called judgment. To still others, *romantic* was a synonym for such words as *wild,* or *extravagant,* or *visionary.*

Charles Lamb, of course, had been no more irresponsible during his walking tour of the Lake District than any other vacationer. His pleasures had certainly not been wild or extravagant, and he at least tried to exercise some judgment in telling his friend about all that he had enjoyed. The word *visionary* is perhaps the one synonym for *romantic* that Lamb might have accepted—though he would have qualified it. The other words leave out the serenity and the joy of his experience. They leave out, too, any reference to the most important condition of his vacation: that it occurred far from a bookkeeper's desk in London where Lamb spent his days keeping track of the affairs of a great business firm. His *romantic* experience occurred in a beautiful region in which, in solitude, he stored his mind with fresh images from nature. Lamb speaks of "an impression . . . received from objects of sight." It was what he *saw*, what exercised his powers of *vision*, that most moved him. Perhaps the only current meaning of *romantic* that he would have accepted is *visionary*.

The Writer's Language

THE GREATEST WRITERS of the Romantic period looked at mountains, forests, lakes, and streams with a new sensitivity and freshness. They did so partly because they were rebelling against the science that in the Enlightenment had described the natural world as a vast mechanism operating by mathematical laws. Samuel Taylor Coleridge, one of the greatest men of letters of the period, once summed up the achievements of that science in these words:

> In short, from the time of Kepler to that of Newton, and from Newton to [the present], not only all things in external nature, but the subtlest mysteries of life and organization, and even of the intellect and moral being, were conjured within the magic circle of mathematical formulae.

To combat this conjuring, this reducing of experience to "mathematical formulae," Coleridge and others proposed a new way of looking at the world. The poet Wordsworth, for example, as Coleridge tells us, set out to reveal "an inexhaustible treasure," the "loveliness and the wonders of the world before us." This wonder and loveliness, the Romantic poet believed, could be revealed to all people by a new kind of poetry. It was a kind of poetry that the Romantic writer explained by analogies from nature, from organic life. Expression for him was not the "dress," or outer clothing, of thought, as Pope wrote; it was the flesh, the body, of thought. Writing for him was a living process, and he regularly compared it to growing things: "If poetry comes not as naturally as the leaves to a tree it had better not come at all," said John Keats. "For all good poetry is the spontaneous overflow of powerful feelings," said Wordsworth; and *spontaneous* was for him a word that meant the opposite of *mechanical*.

How do writers achieve this naturalness? What enables them to see freshly into nature and to escape the "magic circle of mathematical formulae"? Writer after writer gave the same answer: the imagination. And for the Romantic poet the imagination was not a faculty standing in a certain relation to the judgment or anything else. It was a unique power. As the poet William Blake stated defiantly,

THE ROMANTIC PERIOD

The Cottage Door by Thomas Gainsborough (1727–1788). Both painters and writers of the Romantic Period saw virtue in the humble life of simple country people.

"One Power alone makes a Poet: Imagination, The Divine Vision."

By this power, the Romantics believed, people understand one another and become aware of their duties to one another:

> A man, to be greatly good, must imagine intensely and comprehensively; he must put himself in the place of another and of many others; the pains and pleasures of his species must become his own. The great instrument of moral good is the imagination. . . .

That is, poetry helps us to become good not by preaching abstract lessons but by showing us how to imagine the lives of others. And

This is the kind of landscape that Dorothy Wordsworth so carefully described in her notebooks and which led her brother to the awareness he sought.

the author of these sentences, the poet Shelley, went on to say: "Poets are the unacknowledged legislators of the world."

The Romantics believed that the power of imagination could bring people into a close relation with all living things. Human life, they believed, is not separate from the life of nature. As John Keats put it, with startling directness, "if a sparrow come before my window I take part in its existence and pick about the gravel." Indeed, for Keats, poets so constantly and so closely identify themselves with all that they grasp in their imaginations that they have almost no proper identity of their own. As Keats said in a letter to a friend, "A poet is the most unpoetical of anything in existence; because he has no identity—he is continually . . . filling some other body." Poets have no self because they are constantly losing it in the creatures of their imagination—the characters they imagine, the scenes they create.

But this loss of self in the world of the imagination is not a wild and irresponsible act. The Romantic poet believed that the imagination has its own discipline, its own method, which is very different from the discipline of science. Keats, again, described this discipline in another letter:

> . . . it struck me what quality went to form a Man of Achievement, especially in Literature, and which Shakespeare possessed

The Ironworks at Coalbrookdale. *The Industrial Revolution brought changes to the face of the English countryside.*

so enormously—I mean *Negative Capability*, that is, when a man is capable of being in uncertainties, mysteries, doubts, without any irritable reaching after fact and reason. . . .

To reach for "fact and reason" dispels uncertainty and mystery, but it does so by putting them into something like that "magic circle of mathematical formulae." When we reach for facts and reasons, we put our perceptions into a pattern different from that in which we immediately feel them. We cut off the imaginative projection through which the poet takes part in the life of the sparrow at his or her window. To be "negatively capable" means to be able to live with mysteries without explaining them away. The imagination, then, could bring to all people a new sense of the "loveliness and wonders of the world before us."

The poetry that would express this new kinship between people and the world must make new demands upon language. The Romantic writer is sometimes pictured as a shaggy dreamer who pours forth wild, incoherent words that no one can understand, but the greatest writers of the Romantic period worked hard at their craft. They had a new confidence in the power of words, and they tried to meet new standards of relevance and exactness. Coleridge once said that in poetry "the infallible test of a blameless style [is] its *untranslatableness*

The Battle of Yorktown, 1781, in the American Revolutionary War. The British were defeated in this action and three days later asked for a cease-fire.

in words of the same language without injury to the meaning." He was speaking of poetry in general, but what he says is especially true of the best poetry written in his own time. For it is easier to paraphrase or "translate" Pope's *Essay on Man* than Wordsworth's "Tintern Abbey," which you will shortly read. To paraphrase Pope, of course, immediately destroys the elegance, the balance, the pointedness of his couplets. To paraphrase Wordsworth destroys something quite different. For Wordsworth was not sketching the outlines of a philosophical system; he was not expressing the general truths that Samuel Johnson prescribed as the "business of the poet." Or rather, Wordsworth was not writing of such truths in their general form. He wrote of them in the form of the individual experience through which he discovered them for himself. Romantic poetry at its best is not "translatable" because one individual's experience is not another's. The moment in which we perceive some wonder or loveliness is not like any other moment, and the words in which we express it must be the right ones to reveal its unique character. The poets of the Romantic period were concerned with "the stability of truth," but they approached it through the "magic casements" of individual experience, individual perception, individual emotion.

The Romantic poet, therefore, unlike his predecessors of the Enlightenment, had no rules according to which the various kinds of literature should be written. Indeed, his favorite kind was the auto-

THE ROMANTIC PERIOD

A cartoon of 1793 contrasting English and French liberty. Many early supporters of the French Revolution became disillusioned during the Reign of Terror.

biographic, the literary genre that shows us a close connection between a man's ideas or truths and his living experience, and one that requires the individual to express himself in his own way. Wordsworth's longest poem, *The Prelude,* is an example; its subtitle is "The Growth of a Poet's Mind."

With the end of 18th-century rules, moreover, came an end to the special diction appropriate to each kind. Wordsworth quite consciously rebelled against the poetic diction of the 18th century. In his earliest poems he set out deliberately "to choose incidents and situations from common life," and to relate them in a "language really used by men." And he often chose "humble and rustic life," he tells us, "because in that condition, the essential passions of the heart . . . speak a plainer and more emphatic language." The scientists of the early Enlightenment recommended a language like that of "artisans and countrymen" because it had the plainness that science required. Yet 150 years later we find a poet recommending a similar language because it has the plainness that the heart requires! Wordsworth's practice, however, was often different from his preaching, for the language of his poetry is not simple and rustic. It follows no preconceived theory; much better, it follows the meditative, reflective calmness of Wordsworth's own mind. The language of Wordsworth, of Keats, of Shelley expresses the individual poet's sense of a new closeness to his subject, a subject revealed by the power of his imagination.

It will perhaps be wondered why no mention has been made here of the Romantic writer of prose, and why all the foregoing has been about the Romantic theory of poetry. There are two reasons. First, a discussion of the novel, the most important prose form of the Romantic period, is deferred until a later chapter. Second, all the Romantic writers had the highest hopes for the poet, the writer whose words echo the deepest rhythm of his emotions. All agreed that one great quality marked the highest uses of language—its rhythmic quality. Meter, an ordering of the rhythms of speech, was for them that which most distinguished poetry from prose, and only in metered—measured —language was the highest utterance possible. They would not have rhythm ordered as it is in the couplets of Dryden and Pope; they tried, rather, through meter to follow the movement of their own feelings.

Wordsworth asked, "What is a poet?" He answered with a simple affirmation of all his beliefs: "He is a man speaking to men." What does this man speaking to men do? Coleridge gave this answer: "The poet, described in *ideal* perfection, brings the whole soul of man into activity." This is a large requirement. But to attain the ideal was precisely why the Romantic poet wrote.

The People and Their Times

"A TYRANT IS the worst disease, and the cause of all others," said William Blake. Throughout the Romantic period writers and statesmen, leaders and followers, dreamed of a freedom that would cure this dread disease forever. The French Revolution with its rallying cry of "Liberty, Equality, Fraternity" seemed to many people in England the great hope for the future of man. The Declaration of the Rights of Man, which, it was hoped, would guarantee civil liberties, was the kind of political reform welcomed with enthusiasm by many Englishmen, including Blake, Burns, Wordsworth, and Coleridge.

Some cures, however, bring on worse sickness. It seemed that one form of tyranny was to replace another, and the coming of the Reign of Terror in France—the period of violence when thousands of "enemies of state" were killed—turned the enthusiasm to suspicion, fear, and disillusionment. And when Napoleon, having risen to leadership in the chaotic times, began his conquest of Europe, England went to war.

The greatest heroes of the time were an admiral, Lord Nelson, who defeated the French navy at Trafalgar in 1805; and a general, the Duke of Wellington, who led the armies that defeated Napoleon at Waterloo in 1815. Much of the country was prosperous during the war years. Country gentlemen refashioned their gardens to make them less formal than was the fashion earlier in the 18th century; tourists sought out "picturesque" views of the landscape. The moral energy of a churchman, Bishop Wilberforce, aroused the country to

From the original in the United Service Club, London, by permission of the Committee and Members

The Battle of Trafalgar. *Here in 1805 the British fleet under Lord Nelson's command annihilated its enemy, and here Nelson was wounded and died.*

put an end to the slave trade that supplied the plantations of the New World.

But there was much fear of revolutionary ideas in the early years of the 19th century. Government spies and informers denounced any men who spoke too loudly for freedom. Combination Acts—laws that made labor unions illegal—were in effect from 1799 to 1824. The growth of the factory system, while it made the country strong in the conduct of the war, introduced for many a new kind of tyranny, one that made them "wage slaves." From villages and farms, families flocked to the great new factories; and there, living in hideous crowding and dirt, they worked long hours at jobs which they left only when the demand for goods slackened at some far-off, mysterious market and the factory closed down. Great problems were piling up for the next age while poets and artists and soldiers won victories that had never before been imagined. The times called for new energies; they produced also new disciplines.

Energy and Discipline

Percy Bysshe Shelley was perhaps the most ethereal of the Romantic poets. Few writers used the word *soul* more often than he; no one was more convinced than he of the existence of an ideal world of the spirit into which the poetic imagination can penetrate. Yet as a student at Oxford Shelley was passionately interested in chemistry and mineralogy; the world of the spirit was real to him, but so too was the world of hard rocks. Here is a portrait of Shelley written by a fellow student who met him in 1810. It sets forth all the items that made Shelley's character as well as his appearance "a sum of many contradictions."

THE SCIENTIFIC POET

[His appearance] was a sum of many contradictions. His figure was slight and fragile, and yet his bones and joints were large and strong. He was tall, but he stooped so much that he seemed of a low stature. His clothes were expensive, and made according to the most approved mode of the day; but they were tumbled, rumpled, unbrushed. His gestures were abrupt and sometimes violent, occasionally even awkward, yet more frequently gentle and graceful. His complexion was delicate, and almost feminine, of the purest red and white; yet he was tanned and freckled by exposure to the sun, having passed the autumn, as he said, in shooting. His features, his whole face, and particularly his head, were, in fact, unusually small; yet the last *appeared* of a remarkable bulk, for his hair was long and bushy, and in fits of absence,[1] and in the agonies (if I may use the word) of anxious thought, he often rubbed it fiercely with his hands, or passed his fingers quickly through his locks unconsciously, so that it was singularly wild and rough. In times when it was the mode to imitate stage-coachmen as closely as possible in costume, and when the hair was invariably cropped, like that of our soldiers, this eccentricity was very striking. His features were not symmetrical (the mouth, perhaps, excepted), yet was the effect of the whole extremely powerful. They breathed an animation, a fire, an enthusiasm, a vivid and preternatural intelligence, that I never met within any other countenance. Nor was the moral expression less beautiful than the intellectual; for there was a softness, a delicacy, a gentleness, and especially (though this will surprise many) that air of profound religious veneration that characterizes the best works, and chiefly the frescoes[2] (and into those they infused their whole souls), of the great masters of Florence and of Rome. I recognized the very peculiar expression in those wonderful productions long afterwards, and with a satisfaction mingled with much sorrow, for it was after the decease of him in whose countenance I had first observed it. I admired the enthusiasm of my new acquaintance, his ardor in the cause of science, and his thirst for knowledge. I seemed to have found in him all those intellectual qualities which I had vainly expected to meet with in an university. But there was one physical

---

1 **absence:** absent-mindedness.
2 **air . . . frescoes:** Shelley's facial expression is compared to the religious wall paintings of the Italian Renaissance.

blemish that threatened to neutralize all his excellence. "This is a fine, clever fellow!" I said to myself, "but I can never bear his society; I shall never be able to endure his voice; it would kill me. What a pity it is!" I am very sensible of imperfections, and especially of painful sounds—and the voice of the stranger was excruciating: it was intolerably shrill, harsh, and discordant; of the most cruel intension[3]—it was perpetual, and without any remission—it excoriated[4] the ears. He continued to discourse of chemistry, sometimes sitting, sometimes standing before the fire, and sometimes pacing about the room; and when one of the innumerable clocks that speak in various notes during the day and the night at Oxford, proclaimed a quarter to seven, he said suddenly that he must go to a lecture on mineralogy, and declared enthusiastically that he expected to derive much pleasure and instruction from it. I am ashamed to own that the cruel voice made me hesitate for a moment; but it was impossible to omit so indispensable a civility—I invited him to return to tea; he gladly assented, promised that he would not be absent long, snatched his cap, hurried out of the room, and I heard his footsteps, as he ran through the silent quadrangle, and afterwards along High-street.

In 1813 Robert Southey, poet, friend of Wordsworth and Coleridge, lawyer, and civil servant, published his *Life of Nelson*. It is the most successful of the many books Southey wrote, for it celebrates one of the great heroes of British history; Nelson's monument to this day rises high above Trafalgar Square in central London. Lord Nelson, as the following passage reveals, was much loved by his officers and men. None of his men fought with more dash and abandon than he, yet no other officer more coolly prepared his battle plans or more thoroughly carried them out. Nelson's last words to his vice-commander, Blackwood, were prophetic, for he died of the wounds he received in the decisive battle off Cape Trafalgar, the greatest victory of his career.

THE PUBLIC HERO

He wore that day, as usual, his admiral's frock coat,[1] bearing on the left breast four stars, of the different orders with which he was invested.[2] Ornaments which rendered him so conspicuous a mark for the enemy were beheld with ominous apprehensions by his officers. It was known that there were riflemen on board the French ships; and it could not be doubted but that his life would be particularly aimed at. They communicated their fears to each other; and the surgeon, Mr. Beatty, spoke to the chaplain, Dr. Scott, and to Mr. Scott, the public secretary, desiring that some person would entreat him to change his dress, or cover the stars: but they knew that such a request would

3 intension: intensity.
4 excoriated: literally, "took the hide off"; irritated.

1 frock coat: coat with skirts to the knees.
2 orders . . . invested: badges of honorary office given him.

highly displease him. "In honor I gained them," he had said when such a thing had been hinted to him formerly, "and in honor I will die with them." Mr. Beatty, however, would not have been deterred by any fear of exciting his displeasure, from speaking to him himself upon a subject, in which the weal[3] of England as well as the life of Nelson was concerned, but he was ordered from the deck before he could find an opportunity. This was a point upon which Nelson's officers knew that it was hopeless to remonstrate or reason with him; but both Blackwood, and his own captain, Hardy, represented to him how advantageous to the fleet it would be for him to keep out of action as long as possible; and he consented at last to let the *Leviathan* and the *Téméraire*, which were sailing abreast of the *Victory*, be ordered to pass ahead. Yet even here the last infirmity of this noble mind[4] was indulged; for these ships could not pass ahead if the *Victory* continued to carry all her sail; and so far was Nelson from shortening sail, that it was evident he took pleasure in pressing on, and rendering it impossible for them to obey his own orders. A long swell was setting into the bay of Cadiz: our ships, crowding all sail, moved majestically before it, with light winds from the southwest. The sun shone on the sails of the enemy; and their well-formed line, with their numerous three-deckers, made an appearance which any other assailants would have thought formidable;—but the British sailors only admired the beauty and the splendor of the spectacle; and, in full confidence of winning what they saw, remarked to each other, what a fine sight yonder ships would make at Spithead![5]

The French admiral, from the *Bucentaure*, beheld the new manner in which his enemy was advancing, Nelson and Collingwood each leading his line; and, pointing them out to his officers, he is said to have exclaimed, that such conduct could not fail to be successful. Yet Villeneuve[6] had made his own dispositions with the utmost skill, and the fleets under his command waited for the attack with perfect coolness. Ten minutes before twelve they opened their fire. Eight or nine of the ships immediately ahead of the *Victory*, and across her bows, fired single guns at her, to ascertain whether she was yet within their range. As soon as Nelson perceived that their shot passed over him, he desired Blackwood, and Captain Prowse, of the *Sirius*, to repair to their respective frigates; and, on their way, to tell all the captains of the line of battle ships that he depended on their exertions; and that, if by the prescribed mode of attack they found it impracticable to get into action immediately, they might adopt whatever they thought best, provided it led them quickly and closely alongside an enemy. As they were standing on the front of the poop, Blackwood took him by the hand, saying, he

---

3 **weal:** well-being.
4 **last . . . mind:** Southey is quoting from a poem by Milton, "Lycidas," which speaks of the desire for fame as "that last infirmity of noble mind."
5 **Spithead:** the anchorage of the British fleet near Portsmouth.
6 **Villeneuve:** the French commander.

THE ROMANTIC PERIOD

hoped soon to return and find him in possession of twenty prizes. He replied: "God bless you, Blackwood: I shall never see you again."

Workdays and Schooldays

In 1807 Southey published a collection of essays which pretended to be letters from England written by a foreigner visiting the country for the first time. One spectacle, which he compared to a scene from one of the levels of hell in Dante's *Inferno*, moved him deeply: children working in a factory. Child-labor laws were far in the future when Southey visited this mill. "Hands" had to be supplied for the new mills to meet the demands of the huge new market, and not even the tenderest feelings for the young could be permitted to interfere in the free operation of that market. Southey's response to the sight of these children tending the bobbins and shuttles of a textile factory was shared by many.

WORKDAYS

Mr. —— remarked that nothing could be so beneficial to a country as manufactures. "You see these children, sir," said he. "In most parts of England poor children are a burden to their parents and to the parish; here the parish, which would else have to support them, is rid of all expense; they get their bread almost as soon as they can run about, and by the time they are seven or eight years old bring in money. There is no idleness among us: —they come at five in the morning; we allow them half an hour for breakfast, and an hour for dinner; they leave work at six, and another set relieves them for the night; the wheels never stand still." I was looking, while he spoke, at the unnatural dexterity with which the fingers of these little creatures were playing in the machinery, half giddy myself with the noise and the endless motion: and when he told me there was no rest in these walls, day nor night, I thought that if Dante had peopled one of his hells with children, here was a scene worthy to have supplied him with new images of torment.

Despite the cruelties of the factory system the lot of the child in the Romantic period was happier than it had ever been before. Educational reforms took place, and thoughtful men tried many experiments in an effort to provide schools that would produce a literate and informed population. One of these educational reformers was Joseph Lancaster, who introduced many "improvements and inventions," as he called them, into his school in Southwark, the suburb of London where Chaucer's pilgrims had gathered. Among Lancaster's reforms were new methods of discipline, and the following passage describes a few of them. It is clear that Lancaster was an ingenious man, but whether his methods of punishment were, for the pupils, an "improvement" over the traditional flogging is certainly arguable!

A traditional way of punishing young scholars shown here was perhaps less ingenious than Lancaster's methods—but probably no less effective.

SCHOOLDAYS

The Basket Occasionally boys are put in a sack, or in a basket, suspended to the roof of the school, in sight of all the pupils, who frequently smile at the birds in the cage. This punishment is one of the most terrible that can be inflicted on boys of sense and abilities. Above all, it is dreaded by the monitors;[1] the name of it is sufficient, and therefore it is but seldom resorted to on their account.

The Caravan Frequent or old offenders are yoked together, sometimes by a piece of wood that fastens round all their necks; and thus confined, they parade the school, walking backwards— being obliged to pay very great attention to their footsteps, for fear of running against any object that might cause the yoke to hurt their necks, or to keep from falling down. Four or six can be yoked together this way.

Proclamation of the Faults of an Offender before the School When a boy is disobedient to his parents, profane in his language, has committed any offense against morality, or is remarkable for slovenliness, it is usual for him to be dressed up with labels, describing his offense, and a tin or paper cap on his head. In that manner he walks round the school, two boys preceding

---

1 monitors: here, pupils chosen to teach other pupils. One of Lancaster's proposals was to increase the number of students by having the monitors repeat for the beginners the lesson taught by the teacher.

THE ROMANTIC PERIOD

him, and *proclaiming* his fault; varying the proclamation according to the different offenses.

Slovenliness   When a boy comes to school, with dirty face or hands, and it seems to be more the effect of habit than of accident, a girl is appointed to wash his face in the sight of the whole school.   This usually creates much diversion, especially when (as previously directed) she gives his cheeks a few *gentle taps of correction* with her hand.   *One punishment* of this kind has kept the boys' faces clean for two years.

Confinement after School Hours   Few punishments are so effectual as confinement after school hours.   It is, however, attended with one unpleasant circumstance.   In order to confine the bad boys in the schoolroom, after school hours, it is often needful that the master, or some proper substitute for him, should confine himself in school, to keep them in order.   This inconvenience may be avoided by tying them to the desks, or putting them in logs,[2] etc., in such a manner that they cannot loose themselves.   These variations in the *modes of unavoidable punishment* give it the continual force of novelty, whatever shape it may assume.   Any single kind of punishment, continued constantly in use, becomes familiar, and loses its effect.   Nothing but *variety* can continue the power of *novelty*.   Happily, in my institution, there are few occasions of punishment; and this conduces much to the pleasure it affords me.   The advantages of the various modes of correction are that they can be inflicted, so as to give much uneasiness to the delinquents, without disturbing the mind or temper of the master.

Nature and the Engine

The Romantic poet, as we have seen, looked upon nature with new eyes.   Samuel Johnson had said that the poet must not try to "number the streaks of the tulip," but the fine details of the scene before him were often what most moved the later poet, for it was his experience of such details that led him by a new route into the full awareness he sought.   Here are some passages from a diary kept by Dorothy Wordsworth, the poet's sister, in the early months of 1798.   She was living with her brother in the Lake District, and her observations often record details that can be traced in the poems Wordsworth was writing at this time.   But her own sensitivity was remarkable, as the following quiet passages testify.

NATURE

The green paths down the hillsides are channels for streams. The young wheat is streaked by silver lines of water running between the ridges, the sheep are gathered together on the slopes. After the wet dark days, the country seems more populous.   It

---

2 logs: a kind of portable stocks like that described in the second paragraph.

peoples itself in the sunbeams. The garden, mimic of spring, is gay with flowers. The purple-starred hepatica spreads itself in the sun, and the clustering snowdrops put forth their white heads, at first upright, ribbed with green, and like a rosebud when completely opened, hanging their heads downwards, but slowly lengthening their slender stems. The slanting woods of an unvarying brown, showing the light through the thin network of their upper boughs. Upon the highest ridge of that round hill covered with planted oaks, the shafts of the trees show in the light like the columns of a ruin.

Bright sunshine. I went out at three o'clock. The sea perfectly calm blue, streaked with deeper color by the clouds, and tongues or points of sand; on our return of a gloomy red. The sun gone down. The crescent moon, Jupiter, and Venus. The sound of the sea distinctly heard on the tops of the hills, which we could never hear in summer. We attribute this partly to the bareness of the trees, but chiefly to the absence of the singing of birds, the hum of insects, that noiseless noise which lives in the summer air. The villages marked out by beautiful beds of smoke. The turf fading into the mountain road. The scarlet flowers of the moss. . . .

Went to the hilltop. Sat a considerable time overlooking the country toward the sea. The air blew pleasantly round us. The landscape mildly interesting. The Welsh hills capped by a huge range of tumultuous white clouds. The sea, spotted with white, of a bluish-gray in general, and streaked with darker lines. The near shores clear; scattered farmhouses, half-concealed by green mossy orchards, fresh straw lying at the doors; haystacks in the fields. Brown fallows,[1] the springing wheat, like a shade of green over the brown earth, and the choice meadow plots, full of sheep and lambs, of a soft and vivid green; a few wreaths of blue smoke, spreading along the ground; the oaks and beeches in the hedges retaining their yellow leaves; the distant prospect on the land side, islanded with sunshine; the sea, like a basin full to the margin; the fresh-plowed fields dark; the turnips of a lively rough green. Returned through the wood.

While Dorothy Wordsworth watched the play of light and shade upon the fields and hills, others were looking at a new wonder of the age, the steam engine. The first one was made in 1765, but it was many years until it could be adapted to the machinery of the factories. James Watt, as the following passage tells us, was the man most responsible for making the steam engine generally useful in industry. This account of Watt and his invention was written in 1819 by a leading editor and journalist, Francis Jeffrey, and the admiration it expresses was almost universally shared.

---

1 Brown fallows: fields left fallow or uncultivated for a year to restore the soil.

We have said that Mr. Watt was the great *Improver* of the steam engine; but, in truth, as to all that is admirable in its structure, or vast in its utility, he should rather be described as its *Inventor*. It was by his inventions that its action was so regulated, as to make it capable of being applied to the finest and most delicate manufactures, and its power so increased, as to set weight and solidity at defiance. By his admirable contrivance, it has become a thing stupendous alike for its force and its flexibility—for the prodigious power which it can exert, and the ease, and precision, and ductility, with which that power can be varied, distributed, and applied. The trunk of an elephant, that can pick up a pin or rend an oak, is as nothing to it. It can engrave a seal,[1] and crush masses of obdurate metal before it—draw out, without breaking, a thread as fine as gossamer, and lift a ship of war like a bauble in the air. It can embroider muslin and forge anchors, cut steel into ribbands, and impel loaded vessels against the fury of the winds and waves.

It would be difficult to estimate the value of the benefits which these inventions have conferred upon this country. There is no branch of industry that has not been indebted to them; and, in all the most material, they have not only widened most magnificently the field of its exertions, but multiplied a thousandfold the amount of its productions. It was our improved steam engine, in short, that fought the battles of Europe, and exalted and sustained, through the late tremendous contest, the political greatness of our land. It is the same great power which now enables us to pay the interest of our debt, and to maintain the arduous struggle in which we are still engaged, with the skill and capital of countries less oppressed with taxation. But these are poor and narrow views of its importance. It has increased indefinitely the mass of human comforts and enjoyments; and rendered cheap and accessible, all over the world, the materials of wealth and prosperity. It has armed the feeble hand of man, in short, with a power to which no limits can be assigned; completed the dominion of mind over the most refractory qualities of matter; and laid a sure foundation for all those future miracles of mechanic power which are to aid and reward the labors of after generations. It is to the genius of one man, too, that all this is mainly owing! And certainly no man ever bestowed such a gift on his kind. The blessing is not only universal, but unbounded; and the fabled inventors of the plow and the loom, who were Deified by the erring gratitude of their rude contemporaries,[2] conferred less important benefits on mankind than the inventor of our present steam engine.

1 **engrave a seal:** stamp out a delicate design.
2 **fabled . . . contemporaries:** a reference to mythological stories of the invention of plowing and weaving.

A Quiet Life

James Woodforde was a quiet country parson known to few outside the village of his parish. But the great variety of the Romantic period, its contradictions, its combinations of new and old, emerge with a quaint clarity from the pages of his diary. Here are some extracts, from early March, 1791. Woodforde was kind and charitable to the poor, but he was never inattentive to the rich. He attended to his religious duties, but he also kept a sharp eye on the price of the butter that he sold in the village market. He was enthusiastic for the practice of inoculation for smallpox, but he treated a sty on his eye with a remedy as scientific as the one Huckleberry Finn used to cure warts. Quiet as it was, his was a life of the times.

A COUNTRY PARSON

Mar. 6, Sunday. . . . I read prayers, preached, and churched[1] a woman this afternoon at Weston Church. The woman being poor returned the fee to her—Mr. and Mrs. Custance at church, as was also my niece, it being a fine day and good walking. A young sow of mine had for her first litter—7 pigs.

Mar. 7, Monday. . . . Washing week at our house and a fine day. The smallpox spreads much in the parish. Abigail Roberts's husband was very bad in it in the natural way, who was supposed to have had it before and which he thought also. His children are inoculated[2] by Johnny Reeve, as are also Richmond's children near me. It is a pity that all the poor in the parish were not inoculated also. I am entirely for it.

Mar. 8, Tuesday. . . . Gave poor Roberts one of my old shirts to put on in the smallpox—his, poor fellow, being so extremely coarse and rough, that his having the smallpox so very full, his coarse shirt makes it very painful to him. I sent his family a basket of apples and some black currant robb.[3] There are many, many people in the parish yet [who] have never had the smallpox. Pray God all may do well that have it or shall have it. Went this afternoon and saw poor old John Peachman who is very lame, found him unable to walk and having no relief from the parish[4] gave him money. Called also at Tom Cary's shop and left some money for Roberts's family's use for such useful things as they might want and they have. Recd. for 4 Pints ½ Butter, at 9d. 0.3.4.[5] Lady Durrant at Weston House.

---

1 **churched:** offered prayers of thanks for the safe birth of her child.
2 **inoculated:** Inoculation with the live virus of smallpox in order to induce a light case and subsequent immunity was practiced among the nobility and the rich from about 1722. In 1798 Edward Jenner published his account of his discovery of vaccination, the inoculation of a patient with the virus of cowpox. Jenner's vaccination did not, like earlier inoculation, spread the disease; in fact, its general use has almost eliminated smallpox, which, during the 18th century, killed almost a third of the population.
3 **black currant robb:** syrup or conserve of black currants.
4 **relief from the parish:** The parish was both the local unit of the church and the unit of local government, the taxpayers of the parish contributing to the support of the poor.
5 **Recd. . . . 0.3.4:** Received for four and one-half pints of butter at ninepence per pint, no pounds, three shillings, and fourpence.

Mar. 9, Wednesday. . . . Henry Case of this parish who lately lost a cow came to my house this morning with a petition to give him something toward buying another, as he was a parishioner and a tenant of mine for some glebe land,[6] and having also a wife and many children and keeping an aged mother, I gave him towards the same 0.10.6. Had a note this evening from Mr. and Mrs. Custance requesting our company to dinner tomorrow at West House to meet Lady Durrant, etc. I sent a note back that we would wait on them. Mr. Custance's groom with three of Lady Durrant's servant men came with the above note.

Mar. 10, Thursday. . . . Mr. Jeanes called here this morning and stayed about an hour, but Nancy being dressing would not make her appearance. We dined and spent the afternoon at Weston House with Mr. and Mrs. Custance, Lady Durrant, old Mrs. Collyer and Mr. Press Custance. After coffee we all got to loo[7] limited to half a crown. I lost at it 0.6.0. Nancy won three shillings. We went and returned in Mr. Custance's coach. My right eyelid very much swelled and inflamed having a stiony[8] on it, very painful all day.

Mar. 11, Friday. . . . Mem. The stiony on my right eyelid still swelled and inflamed very much. As it is commonly said that the eyelid being rubbed by the tail of a black cat would do it much good if not entirely cure it, and having a black cat, a little before dinner I made a trial of it, and very soon after dinner I found my eyelid much abated of the swelling and almost free from pain. I cannot therefore but conclude it to be of the greatest service to a stiony on the eyelid. Any other cat's tail may have the above effect in all probability—but I did my eyelid with my own black tomcat's tail. Recd, for 2 Pints ½ of Butter at 9d. 0.1.10½. Lady Durrant and old Mrs. Collyer leave Weston today. The latter is breaking up very fast.

---

6 glebe land: agricultural land owned by the church and rented to tenants who paid in tithes, portions of their earnings, upon it.
7 loo: card game.
8 stiony: sty.

The Romantic Period

Uncommon Songs of Common People

IN THE EARLY 18th century, as you have seen, a number of writers raised themselves from poverty and obscurity to wealth and fame. The literary world in which they sought their fortunes was an ordered one: young writers could educate themselves for success in that world and could learn how to satisfy the expectations of the audience that bought and read their works. London was the literary capital, and writers who succeeded were known to each other in the theaters and clubs and coffee-houses where they discussed each other's work. In the late 18th century, however, the expectations of literature changed: the important centers of everyone's attention were France, where a political revolution ran its violent course, and America, where through another revolution a colony became a republic. It was a time of new impulses in thought and expression, impulses felt by people unknown to each other and often living far from the London literary world. Two poets who reveal the power of the new voices are Robert Burns and William Blake.

Robert Burns (1759-1796)

Robert Burns lived for only thirty-seven intense, passionate, work-filled years. He was born in Ayrshire, in southern Scotland, the oldest of seven children; his father, a small tenant farmer, wore himself out trying to raise and educate his large family. Robert, indeed, had to turn to the hard labor of the fields so young that it is believed he did permanent damage to his heart by his exertions to do an adult's work while still a child. Yet he was from his earliest years a buoyant, gay person; he once claimed that he wrote his first poem on the occasion when he first fell in love, at age fifteen.

Certainly he is best known as a writer of songs about love and friendship. Most of you know the first verse and chorus of his most famous song to friendship, "Auld Lang Syne," which is still sung all over the English-speaking world on New Year's Eve:

> Should auld acquaintance be forgot,
> And never brought to mind?
> Should auld acquaintance be forgot,
> And auld lang syne!
>
> For auld lang syne, my dear,
> For auld lang syne,
> We'll tak a cup o' kindness yet
> For auld lang syne!

Burns's patriotic poetry recalled to the Scots such battles as this one from a 13th-century manuscript showing a combat of the Scottish hero Wallace.

But not many know that "Long Ago" or "Old Times" (which is what "Auld Lang Syne" means in modern English) is Burns's version of a traditional Scottish drinking song. For although he wrote in the dialect of southern Scotland rather than in the literary English of Johnson or Gray, Burns was no simple, untutored singer. He studied the traditional songs and ballads of his native region, and he set out to fashion a poetry that would have the imaginative freshness of popular, oral literature. Some of his words and idioms have to be translated for the modern reader, yet the movement of his poetry is clearer than that of the old ballads that it so much resembles.

The fact that Burns wrote in his native dialect has somewhat obscured the range of his poetry. His songs were about patriotism and honor as well as about love. Many too were bitterly satirical, for Burns was a fiercely proud, self-educated man who was sensitive to the hypocrisies and injustices of society. His first book, published in 1786 in Kilmarnock, a town on the River Clyde, appealed to so many readers that almost overnight he became known as Caledonia's Bard, the poet of the Scottish people. He offended some by his democratic principles, and he offended others by his criticisms of the strict piety of the Scottish Church; but his generosity of spirit, his great good humor, and his fresh rendering of common experience in the language of his own people could not be denied. In 1788 Burns was appointed Excise Officer (a tax official), and, having married an early sweetheart, Jean Armour, the only one to whom he remained faithful, he settled down to writing and to collecting folk songs and ballads. His years of fame and relative security were short, though long enough to consolidate his position as a national poet whose achievements eventually brought him far more than national fame.

Almost as well known as the song to "old times" is Burns's song to the River Afton, a stream in his native Ayrshire. The musical setting of the song is hushed, and through it there flows the sentiment that the singer feels toward Mary.

Sweet Afton

Robert Burns

Flow gently, sweet Afton, among thy green braes![1]
Flow gently, I'll sing thee a song in thy praise!
My Mary's asleep by thy murmuring stream—
Flow gently, sweet Afton, disturb not her dream!

Thou stock dove[2] whose echo resounds thro' the glen,   5
Ye wild whistling blackbirds in yon thorny den,
Thou green-crested lapwing,[3] thy screaming forbear—
I charge you, disturb not my slumbering fair!

How lofty, sweet Afton, thy neighboring hills,
Far marked with the courses of clear, winding rills!   10
There daily I wander, as noon rises high,
My flocks and my Mary's sweet cot[4] in my eye.

How pleasant thy banks and green vallies below,
Where wild in the woodlands the primroses blow
There oft, as mild Ev'ning weeps over the lea,[5]   15
The sweet-scented birk[6] shades my Mary and me.

Thy crystal stream, Afton, how lovely it glides,
And winds by the cot where my Mary resides!
How wanton thy waters her snowy feet lave,
As, gathering sweet flowerets, she stems[7] thy clear wave!   20

Flow gently, sweet Afton, among thy green braes!
Flow gently, sweet river, the theme of my lays!
My Mary's asleep by thy murmuring stream—
Flow gently, sweet Afton, disturb not her dream!

---

1 **braes** (brāz): hillsides.
2 **stock dove:** wild pigeon.
3 **lapwing:** crested bird noted for its shrill cry.
4 **cot:** cottage.
5 **lea:** pasture; grassland.
6 **birk:** birch.
7 **stems:** checks (by standing in the shallow water).

Comment

The singer of this song is a shepherd who looks down from the hills where he pastures his sheep to see a valley and a cottage that contain all that he loves. Is it the place, or his Mary, that he most loves?

1. "Flow gently," the singer says to the stream. And how does the Afton flow? What are the images that describe its course, its banks? What (stanza 2) is the one possible source of disturbance in the scene?
2. If, then, with all the quietness of the scene before him, the poet repeats "Flow gently" in the last stanza, what must be the character of Mary and her dream? What does he tell us about her, and about his feeling for her, as he asks even this quietly beautiful scene to be gentle and disturb her not?

"For A' That"

"Is there anyone who, because he is honestly poor, hangs his head, and all that kind of thing? He's a coward and a slave; *we* pass him by." The "we" of this harsh but proud poem are those who shared with Burns in the 1790's the revolutionary conviction that rank and money are worthless to those who believe in the brotherhood of man. The very repetition of "a' that" is a conversational, almost intimate way of saying, "*We* know—we don't have to spell out the details of the differences between the rich and the poor." Yet other assertions are bold and defiant, not conversational at all—The man's the real gold; The honest man is king of men. Burns could be both conversational and defiant about his firm belief in Liberty, Equality, and Fraternity.

For A' That

Robert Burns

Is there for honest poverty
    That hings his head, an' a' that?
The coward slave, we pass him by—
    We dare be poor for a' that!
For a' that, an' a' that,   5
    Our toils obscure, an' a' that,
The rank is but the guinea's[1] stamp,
    The man's the gowd[2] for a' that.

---

1 **guinea:** an English gold coin, twenty-one shillings in value, no longer minted.
2 **gowd:** gold.

What though on hamely fare we dine,
    Wear hoddin gray,[3] an' a' that?   10
Gie fools their silks, and knaves their wine—
    A man's a man for a' that.
For a' that, an' a' that,
    Their tinsel show, an' a' that,
The honest man, tho' e'er sae poor,   15
    Is king o' men for a' that.

Ye see yon birkie[4] ca'd "a lord,"
    Wha struts, an' stares, an' a' that?
Tho' hundreds worship at his word,
    He's but a cuif[5] for a' that.   20
For a' that, an' a' that,
    His riband, star,[6] an' a' that,
The man o' independent mind,
    He looks an' laughs at a' that.
A prince can mak a belted knight,   25
    A marquis, duke, an' a' that!
But an honest man's aboon[7] his might—
    Guid faith, he mauna fa'[8] that!
For a' that, an' a' that,
    Their dignities, an' a' that,   30
The pith o' sense an' pride o' worth
    Are higher rank that a' that.

Then let us pray that come it may
    (As come it will for a' that)
That Sense and Worth o'er a' the earth   35
    Shall bear the gree[9] an' a' that!
For a' that, an' a' that,
    It's comin yet for a' that,
That man to man the world o'er
    Shall brithers be for a' that.   40

3 **hoddin gray:** coarse, undyed woolen cloth.
4 **birkie:** young "sport" or dandy.
5 **cuif:** lout; fool.
6 **riband, star:** badges of honors and titles.
7 **aboon:** above.
8 **mauna fa':** must not claim.
9 **bear the gree:** have the prize.

Comment

Certainly there is almost a monotony in the repetition of "a' that" in this poem; it may even be this monotony that made Burns once say to a friend that "For A' That" is not really a poem at all. Yet it makes some memorable assertions.

1. According to the poem, what are some of the superficial signs of a man's rank, whether high or low? How does the repetition of "a' that" make us feel that these signs *are* superficial?
2. But what qualities does the poem oppose to these superficial signs of rank? How does the repetition of "a' that" make us feel that these qualities are important?
3. In the last stanza the tone changes: from assertion to prophecy, from pointing out the way things are to praying for the way they will be. What does Burns prophesy will someday take place? Put in your own words the sense of "for a' that" as it occurs here.
4. How, then, does the repetition of the phrase "a' that" in this poem contribute to the certainty with which Burns communicates his message?

"To a Louse"

The difference between what we are and what we pretend to be was not always so serious a matter to Burns. Here, at any rate, it is a matter of sheer comedy—comedy with a moral, to be sure. Jenny enjoys the attention she is attracting because she thinks it is for her beauty and pretty clothes. Instead, it is a louse, usually associated with the unwashed poor, which is attracting the looks and pointing. Jenny, undoubtedly, would not be happy to see herself as others see her; however, having such a power would quickly free her from her foolish notion.

To a Louse

On Seeing One on a Lady's Bonnet at Church

Robert Burns

Ha! whare ye gaun,[1] ye crowlin ferlie?[2]
Your impudence protects you sairly,[3]
I canna say but ye strunt[4] rarely
    Owre[5] gauze and lace,
Tho' faith! I fear ye dine but sparely   5
    On sic[6] a place.

1 **gaun:** going.
2 **crowlin ferlie:** crawling wonder.
3 **sairly:** greatly.
4 **strunt:** strut.
5 **Owre:** over.
6 **sic:** such.

Ye ugly, creepin, blastit wonner,[7]
Detested, shunned by saunt an' sinner,
How daur ye set your fit[8] upon her—
        Sae fine a lady!   10
Gae somewhere else and seek your dinner
        On some poor body.

Swith![9] in some beggar's hauffet squattle:[10]
There ye may creep, and sprawl, and sprattle,[11]
Wi' ither kindred, jumping cattle,   15
        In shoals and nations;
Whare horn nor bane[12] ne'er daur unsettle
        Your thick plantations.

Now haud[13] you there! ye 're out o' sight,
Below the fatt'rils,[14] snug an' tight;   20
Na, faith ye yet! ye 'll no be right,
        Till ye 've got on it—
The vera tapmost, tow'ring height
        O' Miss's bonnet.

My sooth! right bauld[15] ye set your nose out,   25
As plump an' gray as onie grozet:[16]
O for some rank, mercurial rozet,[17]
        Or fell, red smeddum,[18]
I'd gie ye sic a hearty dose o 't.
        Wad dress your droddum.[19]   30

I wad na been surprised to spy
You on an auld wife's flainen toy;[20]
Or aiblins[21] some bit duddie[22] boy,
        On 's wyliecoat;[23]
But Miss's fine Lunardi![24] fye!   35
        How daur ye do 't?

7 **blastit wonner:** blasted wonder.
8 **fit:** foot.
9 **Swith:** be off.
10 **hauffet squattle:** temple settle.
11 **sprattle:** scramble.
12 **horn nor bane:** comb made of horn or bone.
13 **haud:** hold.
14 **fatt'rils:** ribbon ends.
15 **bauld:** bold.
16 **onie grozet:** any gooseberry.
17 **rozet:** rosin.
18 **fell, red smeddum:** deadly red powder.
19 **Wad dress your droddum:** would dress you down.
20 **flainen toy:** flannel cap.
21 **aiblins:** maybe.
22 **bit duddie:** small ragged.
23 **wyliecoat:** undervest.
24 **Lunardi:** balloon bonnet, named after Lunardi, a famed balloonist.

THE ROMANTIC PERIOD

O Jenny, dinna toss your head,
An' set your beauties a' abread![25]
Ye little ken what cursèd speed
   The blastie 's[26] makin!
Thae[27] winks an' finger-ends, I dread,
   Are notice takin'.

   40

O wad some Power the giftie[28] gie us
To see oursels as ithers see us!
It wad frae monie a blunder free us,
   An' foolish notion:
What airs in dress an' gait wad lea'e us,
   An' ev'n devotion!

   45

25 **abread:** abroad.
26 **blastie:** blasted creature.
27 **Thae:** those.
28 **giftie:** small gift.

Comment

In the first six stanzas of the poem, Burns addresses himself to the louse and lightly scolds it for presuming to take up residence on such a worthy lady. In the next to last stanza he speaks to Jenny, and in the last to all of us.

1. What kind of person is Jenny? How is she dressed?
2. Upon what sort of people does Burns say it is usual to see a louse?
3. How does Jenny react to the winks and finger-pointing? What does she think has attracted the others? As Burns turns to her and says "O Jenny," how does his tone change?
4. What happens to his tone in the last stanza, when he turns to us?
5. "What airs of dress and manner would leave us, and even devotion," says Burns at the very end. Jenny is in church, but what is her real devotion? Of what "devotion" would we rid ourselves if we could see ourselves as others see us?

"Scots, Wha Hae"

"Scots, Wha Hae," a war song, is one of the poems that endeared Burns to the Scottish nation. Often described as Scotland's anthem, it sings of the Battle of Bannockburn, at which King Robert Bruce, a great Scottish hero, in 1314 defeated the English under Edward II. Here Burns imagines Bruce addressing his troops before the battle.

Scots, Wha Hae

Robert Burns

Scots, wha hae[1] wi' Wallace[2] bled,
Scots, wham Bruce has aften led,
Welcome to your gory bed
   Or to victorie!

Now 's the day, and now 's the hour: 5
See the front o' battle lour,[3]
See approach proud Edward's power—
   Chains and slaverie!

Wha will be a traitor knave?
Wha can fill a coward's grave?   10
Wha sae base as be a slave?—
   Let him turn, and flee!

Wha for Scotland's King and Law
Freedom's sword will strongly draw,
Freeman stand or freeman fa',[4]   15
   Let him follow me!

By Oppression's woes and pains,
By your sons in servile chains,
We will drain our dearest veins
   But they shall be free!   20

Lay the proud usurpers low!
Tyrants fall in every foe!
Liberty 's in every blow!
   Let us do, or die!

1 **wha hae:** who have.
2 **Wallace:** a celebrated Scottish national hero (1272?-1305), a leader in the wars against the English.
3 **lour:** become threatening.
4 **fa':** fall.

Comment

In 1793, when this poem was written, Scotland was not under attack from any "proud power." As he witnessed from afar the French Revolution, Burns believed that the French people were throwing off tyranny, just as his own countrymen once had. He recalled a traditional tune that had been played as Scottish soldiers marched to battle, and to this ancient tune he fitted these new words to rouse his countrymen's sympathies for what he believed was the cause of the common people of France. Yet he roused his countrymen chiefly to a proud sense of their own history.

1. What does Burns attack in "For A' That"? Who is the coward and slave there? What, according to that poem, unites free men?
2. Who are the cowards and slaves of "Scots, Wha Hae"? What does "freedom" mean in this poem? And who are the "we" of this poem?
3. Considering the poems by Burns that you have read, write a short essay on Burns as a poet of the Scottish people. What are the ideals that he made his countrymen aware of?

William Blake (1757-1827)

In the 1790's William Blake, an obscure poet, painter, and engraver, began two poetical works that he never finished, *The French Revolution* and *America, A Prophecy,* in which he gave voice to his excitement in, and hopes for, the two great political events of the time. Blake went on to write even more ambitious works, long "prophetic" poems in which he tried to express his own system of political, religious, and philosophical ideas. "I must Create a System, or be enslaved by another Man's," he said. Blake's poetic efforts to make his "system" are complex and difficult; they are far different from the simple, direct songs that he first wrote and for which he is best known.

Indeed Blake's simplicity and directness are sometimes astonishing. When he was a child, he tells us, he saw God looking in at him through his window. At another time he saw a tree full of angels. He experienced religious visions, directly, completely, and in as matter-of-fact a manner as other men saw trees or rivers or hillsides. And such things happened to him, he believed, not because he was more religious, in the normal sense, than other men, or more holy. He saw visions because it

Blake himself designed, engraved, and colored the illustrations and text of these two pages from Songs of Innocence *and* Songs of Experience. *He personally manufactured all of his books except the first,* Poetical Sketches.

was in the power of his imagination to do so. It was this same power that made him a poet, for, according to him: "One Power alone makes a Poet: Imagination, The Divine Vision."

The man who so serenely and so confidently held these beliefs was the son of a London haberdasher. While still a boy he showed a talent for drawing, and his father sent him to art school and apprenticed him to an engraver. But William Blake could never become a conventional commercial artist. He read widely among religious poets and philosophers and from an early age was writing poetry in which he expressed his own imaginative vision of the world about him. At the age of twenty-four he married. His wife could neither read nor write, but her faith in the visions and the powers of her husband was as strong as his own; and she learned to help him as both poet and engraver.

Blake's first book of poems, *Poetical Sketches*, printed when he was twenty-six, was his only printed work. All his later works were unique creations of his own: he engraved each page on copper plate, surrounding the lines with decorations; and each page, after it had been

THE ROMANTIC PERIOD

impressed on paper, he colored with his own hand. Everything he published, after the first book, was therefore a unique work of art—and, of course, the small number of copies he could make by such a process means that his works are now among the rarest and most valuable works of literature in the world. Though they are so now, when in 1809 Blake arranged for an exhibition of his works, it was a failure. Not until very late in his life did other artists and writers begin to recognize his dedication and genius.

In 1794 Blake finished his first great work, *Songs of Innocence and Experience*. The title was exactly descriptive, for this engraved book consisted of two groups of poems: the first expressing a vision of the world as seen by the innocent eye of the child; the second, a vision of the world as seen by the eye of experience. And it was these two states, these two kinds of vision, that Blake later tried to unite in his efforts to make a "system." Blake had an enormous reverence for life. He knew that men must grow, that they cannot remain as children, that they must take their place in society. But the cruelties of society outraged him. Here, for example, are some couplets from a long, unfinished poem he left in manuscript:

> A Robin Redbreast in a Cage
> Puts all Heaven in a Rage. . . .
> A dog starved at his Master's Gate
> Predicts the ruin of the State.
> A Horse misused upon the Road
> Calls to Heaven for Human blood.

The unfinished work from which these couplets are taken was called "Auguries of Innocence"; that is, they are signs or omens seen by someone who knows what innocence really is. They are not mere appeals to be kind to animals; they are, rather, indications of man's inhumanity. The outrage Blake expresses is directed toward men who believe that they are worthy of heaven and that their society is secure, although they are oblivious to the cruelty they exert upon creatures lower than men. All life, all creation was precious to Blake; he wanted his readers

> To see a World in a Grain of Sand
> And a Heaven in a Wild Flower,
> Hold Infinity in the palm of your hand
> And Eternity in an hour.

And something like this vision, Blake believed, was possible for the child.

The following selection from *Songs of Innocence* is a song to a symbol of innocence as old as the Psalms of the Bible.

[handwritten marginal notes: monosyllabic — repetition — 4 beat — couplet]

The Lamb

William Blake

Little Lamb, who made thee?
Dost thou know who made thee?
Gave thee life, and bid thee feed
By the stream and o'er the mead;
Gave thee clothing of delight,   5
Softest clothing, woolly, bright;
Gave thee such a tender voice,
Making all the vales rejoice?
    Little Lamb, who made thee?
    Dost thou know who made thee?   10

    Little Lamb, I'll tell thee,
    Little Lamb, I'll tell thee:
He is callèd by thy name,
For he calls himself a Lamb.
He is meek, and he is mild;   15
He became a little child.
I a child, and thou a lamb,
We are callèd by his name.
    Little Lamb, God bless thee!
    Little Lamb, God bless thee!   20

Comment

The "I" of this delicate lyric, a child, is so innocent, so sure of the happiness of his world, that he can answer the question, "Dost thou know who made thee?" The answer is, "He is callèd by thy name," a Creator who "became a little child." Both the lamb and the child were created by someone as meek and mild as themselves.

Another song of innocence expresses the simple assurance that the father of all men will keep them from grief.

On Another's Sorrow

William Blake

Can I see another's woe,
And not be in sorrow too?
Can I see another's grief,
And not seek for kind relief?

Can I see a falling tear,   5
And not feel my sorrow's share?
Can a father see his child
Weep, nor be with sorrow filled?

Can a mother sit and hear
An infant groan an infant fear?   10
No, no! never can it be!
Never, never can it be!

And can he who smiles on all
Hear the wren with sorrows small,
Hear the small bird's grief and care,   15
Hear the woes that infants bear,

And not sit beside the nest,
Pouring pity in their breast;
And not sit the cradle near,
Weeping tear on infant's tear;   20

And not sit both night and day,
Wiping all our tears away?
O, no! never can it be!
Never, never can it be!

He doth give his joy to all;   25
He becomes an infant small;
He becomes a man of woe;
He doth feel the sorrow too.

Think not thou canst sigh a sigh
And thy maker is not by;
Think not thou canst weep a tear   30
And thy maker is not near.

O! he gives to us his joy
That our grief he may destroy;
Till our grief is fled and gone   35
He doth sit by us and moan.

"The Poison Tree"

The best comment on the preceding two songs of innocence, perhaps, is two selections from the *Songs of Experience*. The first, "A Poison Tree," tells of an awareness of another's pain that is quite different from the awareness of "On Another's Sorrow."

A Poison Tree

William Blake

I was angry with my friend:
I told my wrath, my wrath did end.
I was angry with my foe:
I told it not, my wrath did grow.

And I watered it in fears,   5
Night and morning with my tears;
And I sunnèd it with smiles,
And with soft deceitful wiles.

And it grew both day and night,
Till it bore an apple bright;   10
And my foe beheld it shine,
And he knew that it was mine,

And into my garden stole
When the night had veiled the pole:[1]
In the morning glad I see   15
My foe outstretched beneath the tree.

1 **pole:** polar star.

THE ROMANTIC PERIOD

Comment

Rhythmically "A Poison Tree" and "On Another's Sorrow" use the same songlike meter. Yet how different is the experience of "I" when he has left the world of innocence.

> Can I see another's woe
> And not be in sorrow too?

he asks in the song of innocence. But now, in the song of experience, he gloats:

> In the morning glad I see
> My foe outstretched beneath the tree.

What is the difference between innocence and experience here?

1. In "On Another's Sorrow" what is the relation between "I" and "another"? How is it like the relation between father and child, between mother and infant, and above all like the relation between "he who smiles on all" and the creatures he has made?
2. And what is the relation between "I" and "my foe" in "A Poison Tree"?
3. In the third and fourth stanzas of "A Poison Tree" the "I" tells us how his unspoken wrath became an apple tree in a garden. To what story is Blake alluding here?
4. In the morning, the "I" tells us, his foe is "outstretched"—dead. In what sense is he himself also poisoned by the tree of wrath? How has he made it grow? What sort of person is "glad" to see his foe "outstretched"?
5. Write a paragraph explaining the difference between innocence and experience as Blake conceives them in these two poems.

"The Tiger"

This second selection from *Songs of Experience* is perhaps Blake's most famous poem, "The Tiger." It is a poem that has puzzled many readers, even as it has fascinated them, and certainly it is not a poem that makes an explicit statement. Instead it asks, and asks again and again, a question. And this question can be answered only by grasping the qualities of the central symbol, the burning, dreadful, beautiful Tiger. Our understanding of this symbol can be greatly helped if we bear in mind that "The Tiger" is a song of experience. "Did he who made the Lamb make thee?" the poet asks. We read this poem, then, alongside the song of innocence, "The Lamb," and we come to see not only the meaning of each poem by itself but also the meaning of Blake's two worlds, innocence and experience.

The Tiger

William Blake

Tiger! Tiger! burning bright
In the forests of the night,
What immortal hand or eye
Could frame thy fearful symmetry?

In what distant deeps or skies   5
Burnt the fire of thine eyes?
On what wings dare he aspire?[1]
What the hand dare seize the fire?

And what shoulder, and what art,
Could twist the sinews of thy heart?   10
And when thy heart began to beat,
What dread hand? and what dread feet?

What the hammer? what the chain?
In what furnace was thy brain?
What the anvil? what dread grasp   15
Dare its deadly terrors clasp?

When the stars threw down their spears,
And watered heaven with their tears,[2]
Did he smile his work to see?
Did he who made the Lamb make thee?   20

Tiger! Tiger! burning bright
In the forests of the night,
What immortal hand or eye,
Dare frame thy fearful symmetry?

1 aspire: soar.
2 When . . . tears: The stars for Blake are a symbol of reason and order, as they are for many poets. Here, the stars—reason and order themselves—surrender before the awesome spectacle of the Tiger.

Comment

In the world of innocence the child knows that he who made the Lamb is one who "became a little child" like himself. In the world of experience there is no child, no person who asks and answers a question; there is only the large, unanswered question itself: "What immortal hand or eye, / Dare frame thy fearful symmetry?" Why must the question go unanswered in the world of experience?

1. The differences between the Lamb and the Tiger are startlingly direct. What are some of the images that characterize the Lamb? What are some of the images that characterize the Tiger?
2. In both "The Lamb" and "The Tiger" the speaker has a dramatic relation to the subject: the "I" is speaking to the Lamb; the poet addresses the Tiger. But are they equally close to their subjects? What is the tone of the "I" as he speaks to the Lamb? And what is the tone of the poet as he addresses the Tiger?
3. The speaker of "The Lamb," as we have seen, answers his own question: he knows who made the Lamb and himself. The speaker of "The Tiger" can only ask his question. But precisely because he can *not* answer his questions, does he not affirm something about the "immortal hand or eye" that frames the "fearful symmetry" of the Tiger? In the second stanza, for example, what remoteness is implied about the "distant deeps or skies" where the fire of the tiger's eye came from? In the fourth stanza, what qualities are implied about the forge, with its furnace and anvil, where the Tiger was made (just as the ancient god of war, Vulcan, was thought by the Romans to make weapons in his forge)?
4. The Tiger is beautiful, but also fearful: it is difficult to imagine the power that could make both the fearful Tiger and the little Lamb. What conclusion can you draw from the fact that it is in the world of experience that Blake confronts the Tiger?
5. Looking back to your observations on the poem "A Poison Tree," and reflecting on your reading of "The Tiger," write a short essay on "Experience" as Blake conceives it.

People Speaking to People

In 1798 THERE was published *Lyrical Ballads, with a Few Other Poems,* the joint work of two young poets, William Wordsworth and Samuel Taylor Coleridge. No book more clearly embodies the new impulse in literature. Wordsworth and Coleridge were not only writers *of* poetry; they were also writers *about* poetry. *Lyrical Ballads* was the result of many hours of discussion between them, and to the second edition of it Wordsworth added a Preface, planned with Coleridge, which set forth the principles of their poetry. *Lyrical Ballads* was a book that embodied their belief, as Wordsworth put it, that the poet is "a man speaking to men." He is not only an observer of society, not merely a scholar reviving ancient traditions of literature, not simply a preacher of moral truth, not just a singer of songs, but all these and something more, an individual who speaks directly and fully to other individuals.

British Information Services

A scene in the English Lake District. Wordsworth was born in this part of England, and here he and his sister settled in 1799.

William Wordsworth (1770-1850)

Wordsworth, the English Romantic who was most deeply admired here in America from the beginning of his career, spent most of his life in the Lake District, amid the natural scenes from which he drew the images that so distinctively mark his work. He was the second of five children; both his parents had died by the time he was thirteen, and his one sister, Dorothy, was for almost all his life his closest companion. Her journals, as you have seen, are full of observations of the light and shade, the fields and hills, of the countryside; and so close was her relation with her brother that one can often find the very phrases of her observations in his poems.

William went to Cambridge University in 1787, where he was an indifferent student who preferred doing his own reading and writing his own poetry to attending the required lectures and courses. In 1791 he went to France and became an enthusiastic witness to the French Revolution, then in its early stages. He was compelled to return to England when his money ran out, but a bequest left to him by a friend enabled him to establish a home for Dorothy and himself. Shortly afterwards he met Coleridge and entered into the intimate association that produced *Lyrical Ballads*.

By 1799 William and Dorothy had settled at Grasmere, in the Lake District, with Coleridge nearby; and in 1802 Wordsworth's small circle was completed with his marriage to Mary Hutchinson, whom he had known since childhood. Although his friendship with Coleridge did not last beyond 1810, Wordsworth lived quietly with his sister and his family in or near Grasmere until the end of his long life. Like Burns, he was made a tax official in his district, and, later, was given a government pension in recognition of his achievements. In 1843 he was made Poet Laureate, though by then his productive years were past. He traveled often, to London and to the continent; he knew many of the eminent persons of his time. But except for the exciting youthful period in France, Wordsworth's life was a quiet sojourn among the scenes he most loved. The very title of a long poem that he planned but never completed was *The Recluse*.

The Prelude

In 1798 Wordsworth began that long poem, *The Recluse*, by starting to write his autobiography in blank verse, and by the next year he had written much of the first two books, "Childhood" and "Schooltime." He had completed a draft of this autobiography by 1805 (his wife suggested the title that he gave it, *The Prelude*), and he kept revising it intermittently until his death, when it was published in its final version. The two following excerpts from *The Prelude*, then, are revisions of a long narrative poem that Wordsworth began in the same year in which he cooperated with Coleridge to produce *Lyrical Ballads*. It shows us clearly why Wordsworth is usually thought of as "the poet of nature," and it shows us too something of what he meant by "nature." He did not mean a picturesque landscape that the city-dweller looks at and sighs over. He did not mean the orderly scheme of things— mineral, vegetable, animal, and human—that the 18th-century poet celebrated. By nature Wordsworth meant all the living forms around people by which they become aware of the moral and religious feelings that shape their lives. For Wordsworth, to experience nature was never just to see a pretty picture. It was to feel the presence of spiritual powers greater than ours and his preoccupations with himself. He writes that when he was a boy he grew up "Fostered alike by beauty and by fear." Nature was to him a "ministry" that educated his emotions and his feelings toward others. The following selections from *The Prelude* tell how as a child Wordsworth experienced fear and beauty as he played in the wild country of the Lake District. The first begins as he describes how one night, led by "her"—by nature—he entered into a childish prank that ended by frightening him and by endowing him with large images of powers greater than his own.

WILLIAM WORDSWORTH

465

from The Prelude

William Wordsworth

One summer evening (led by her) I found
A little boat tied to a willow tree
Within a rocky cove, its usual home.
Straight I unloosed her chain, and stepping in
Pushed from the shore. It was an act of stealth   5
And troubled pleasure, nor without the voice
Of mountain echoes did my boat move on;
Leaving behind her still, on either side,
Small circles glittering idly in the moon,
Until they melted all into one track   10
Of sparkling light. But now, like one who rows,
Proud of his skill, to reach a chosen point
With an unswerving line, I fixed my view
Upon the summit of a craggy ridge,
The horizon's utmost boundary; far above   15
Was nothing but the stars and the gray sky.
She was an elfin pinnace;[1] lustily
I dipped my oars into the silent lake,
And, as I rose upon the stroke, my boat
Went heaving through the water like a swan;   20
When, from behind that craggy steep till then
The horizon's bound,[2] a huge peak, black and huge,
As if with voluntary power instinct,
Upreared its head. I struck and struck again,
And growing still in stature the grim shape   25
Towered up between me and the stars, and still,
For so it seemed, with purpose of its own
And measured motion like a living thing,
Strode after me. With trembling oars I turned,
And through the silent water stole my way   30
Back to the covert[3] of the willow tree;
There in her mooring place I left my bark,
And through the meadow homeward went, in grave
And serious mood; but after I had seen
That spectacle, for many days, my brain   35
Worked with a dim and undetermined sense

---

1 pinnace (pĭn′ĭs): light sailing vessel.
2 bound: boundary.
3 covert (kŭv′ərt): hidden place.

Of unknown modes of being; o'er my thoughts
There hung a darkness, call it solitude
Or blank desertion. No familiar shapes
Remained, no pleasant images of trees,   40
Of sea or sky, no colors of green fields;
But huge and mighty forms, that do not live
Like living men, moved slowly through the mind
By day, and were a trouble to my dreams.

[*The second selection from* The Prelude *turns to another season and to a more joyous experience, skating
in wintertime.*]

    And in the frosty season, when the sun   45
Was set, and visible for many a mile
The cottage windows blazed through twilight gloom,
I heeded not their summons; happy time
It was indeed for all of us—for me
It was a time of rapture! Clear and loud   50
The village clock tolled six—I wheeled about,
Proud and exulting like an untired horse
That cares not for his home. All shod with steel,
We hissed along the polished ice in games
Confederate, imitative of the chase   55
And woodland pleasures—the resounding horn,
The pack loud chiming, and the hunted hare.
So through the darkness and the cold we flew,
And not a voice was idle; with the din
Smitten, the precipices rang aloud;   60
The leafless trees and every icy crag
Tinkled like iron; while far distant hills
Into the tumult sent an alien sound
Of melancholy not unnoticed, while the stars
Eastward were sparkling clear, and in the west   65
The orange sky of evening died away.
Not seldom from the uproar I retired
Into a silent bay, or sportively
Glanced sideway, leaving the tumultuous throng,
To cut across the reflex of a star   70
That fled, and, flying still before me, gleamed
Upon the glassy plain; and oftentimes,
When we had given our bodies to the wind,
And all the shadowy banks on either side
Came sweeping through the darkness, spinning still   75
The rapid line of motion, then at once
Have I, reclining back upon my heels,

Stopped short; yet still the solitary cliffs
Wheeled by me—even as if the earth had rolled
With visible motion her diurnal⁴ round!   80
Behind me did they stretch in solemn train,
Feebler and feebler, and I stood and watched
Till all was tranquil as a dreamless sleep.

Ye Presences of Nature in the sky
And on the earth! Ye Visions of the hills!   85
And Souls of lonely places! can I think
A vulgar⁵ hope was yours when ye employed
Such ministry, when ye, through many a year
Haunting me thus among my boyish sports,
On caves and trees, upon the woods and hills,   90
Impressed, upon all forms, the characters
Of danger or desire; and thus did make
The surface of the universal earth,
With triumph and delight, with hope and fear,
Work like a sea?   95

4 **diurnal** (dī ûr′nəl)**:** daily.
5 **vulgar:** common.

Comment

Two boyhood experiences—slipping out to row a boat on a lake and
skating on a windy winter evening. Many men have been through
similar experiences; few, perhaps, have felt in them all that Wordsworth was aware of. And yet this *is* a man speaking to men about a
common awareness of a "ministry" that "Impressed, upon all forms, the
characters / Of danger or desire." From the "Presences of Nature"
Wordsworth learned some intensely personal meanings for the common
words *fear* and *hope*.

1. In the first selection Wordsworth finds "a little boat"; when he has
   slipped out on his forbidden journey, the boat becomes "an elfin pinnace." Which expression is the more natural, the less artificial?
   Why should the more artificial, the more unrealistic expression occur
   where it does in the little story?
2. As he rowed the boat, the young Wordsworth kept a straight course
   by fixing his eye on the top of a "craggy ridge." When he started,
   the ridge, which was nearby, hid the tall peak behind it. Soon, however, as he moved away from the shore, his line of sight suddenly included the peak behind the ridge. One can almost diagram the
   physical situation. But what of the moral situation? What happens
   to the boy as he sees the towering peak? Why does he turn back?
   And what is the "trouble" to his "dreams" as he thinks back upon the
   experience later?

3. The second selection begins: "happy time / It was indeed for all of us." What words describing the activity and the scene add to our idea of "happy"? What episodes of the experience explain still further what was "happy"?

4. In the first selection the peak seemed to stride after the boy as if in pursuit. Does anything similar seem to occur in the second selection?

5. The selection ends as Wordsworth says that the "Presences," "Visions," and "Souls" of the landscape around him "worked"—they moved like the surface of a sea of emotions with "triumph and delight," "hope and fear." He cannot believe that their "ministry" to him was a "vulgar hope"—just an ordinary concern for him. The world of his childhood, he implies, was alive to him, and alive not simply in the sense that it contained natural things. What kind of life did his early experience make him aware of? What awareness did these two occasions instill in him?

"Tintern Abbey"

The final poem of *Lyrical Ballads, with a Few Other Poems* was one of the "other" poems. It is a long, meditative contemplation of a landscape near a ruined medieval abbey, with a river and fields in the foreground. Wordsworth first saw this landscape in 1793 on his way to Wales (it is in Monmouthshire, in the Welsh border country), and five years later he revisited the scene with his sister Dorothy. The second visit reminded him of the pleasure and joy he had felt five years before, but with a difference: he was older, and he had experienced and suffered much. Had he lost, then, in the intervening years, all the awareness with which he had first looked on the scene? This is the question Wordsworth asks, and answers, in one of his greatest poems.

Lines

Composed a Few Miles above Tintern Abbey

William Wordsworth

Five years have passed; five summers, with the length
Of five long winters! and again I hear
These waters, rolling from their mountain springs
With a soft inland murmur.—Once again
Do I behold these steep and lofty cliffs,   5
That on a wild secluded scene impress
Thoughts of more deep seclusion; and connect

The landscape with the quiet of the sky.
The day is come when I again repose
Here, under this dark sycamore, and view   10
These plots of cottage ground, these orchard tufts,
Which at this season, with their unripe fruits,
Are clad in one green hue, and lose themselves
'Mid groves and copses. Once again I see
These hedgerows,[1] hardly hedgerows, little lines   15
Of sportive wood run wild: these pastoral farms,
Green to the very door; and wreaths of smoke
Sent up, in silence, from among the trees!
With some uncertain notice, as might seem
Of vagrant dwellers in the houseless woods,   20
Or of some Hermit's cave, where by his fire
The Hermit sits alone.

             These beauteous forms,
Through a long absence, have not been to me
As is a landscape to a blind man's eye:
But oft, in lonely rooms, and 'mid the din   25
Of towns and cities, I have owed to them
In hours of weariness, sensations sweet,
Felt in the blood, and felt along the heart;
And passing even into my purer mind,
With tranquil restoration:—feelings too   30
Of unremembered pleasure: such, perhaps,
As have no slight or trivial influence
On that best portion of a good man's life,
His little, nameless, unremembered, acts
Of kindness and of love. Nor less, I trust,   35
To them I may have owed another gift,
Of aspect more sublime; that blessed mood
In which the burthen of the mystery,
In which the heavy and the weary weight
Of all this unintelligible world,   40
Is lightened:—that serene and blessed mood,
In which the affections gently lead us on,—
Until, the breath of this corporeal[2] frame
And even the motion of our human blood
Almost suspended, we are laid asleep   45
In body, and become a living soul:
While with an eye made quiet by the power
Of harmony, and the deep power of joy,
We see into the life of things.

---

1 **hedgerows:** row of shrubs or trees, planted for enclosure or separation of fields.
2 **corporeal** (kôr pōr′ĭ əl): bodily.

THE ROMANTIC PERIOD

If this

Be but a vain belief, yet, oh! how oft— 50
In darkness and amid the many shapes
Of joyless daylight; when the fretful stir
Unprofitable, and the fever of the world,
Have hung upon the beatings of my heart—
How oft, in spirit, have I turned to thee, 55
O sylvan Wye![3] thou wanderer thro' the woods,
How often has my spirit turned to thee!

   And now, with gleams of half-extinguished thought,
With many recognitions dim and faint,
And somewhat of a sad perplexity, 60
The picture of the mind revives again:
While here I stand, not only with the sense
Of present pleasure, but with pleasing thoughts
That in this moment there is life and food
For future years. And so I dare to hope, 65
Though changed, no doubt, from what I was when first
I came among these hills; when like a roe
I bounded o'er the mountains, by the sides
Of the deep rivers, and the lonely streams,
Wherever nature led: more like a man 70
Flying from something that he dreads than one
Who sought the thing he loved. For nature then
(The coarser pleasures[4] of my boyish days,
And their glad animal movements all gone by)
To me was all in all.—I cannot paint 75
What then I was. The sounding cataract
Haunted me like a passion: the tall rock,
The mountain, and the deep and gloomy wood,
Their colors and their forms, were then to me
An appetite; a feeling and a love, 80
That had no need of a remoter charm,
By thought supplied, nor any interest
Unborrowed from the eye.—That time is past,
And all its aching joys are now no more,
And all its dizzy raptures. Not for this 85
Faint I, nor mourn nor murmur; other gifts
Have followed; for such loss, I would believe,
Abundant recompense. For I have learned
To look on nature, not as in the hour
Of thoughtless youth; but hearing oftentimes 90
The still, sad music of humanity,

---

3 **Wye:** a river of England and Wales, emptying into the Severn estuary.
4 **coarser pleasures:** outdoor sports; physical activities.

Nor harsh nor grating, though of ample power
To chasten and subdue. And I have felt
A presence that disturbs me with the joy
Of elevated thoughts; a sense sublime   95
Of something far more deeply interfused,
Whose dwelling is the light of setting suns,
And the round ocean and the living air,
And the blue sky, and in the mind of man:
A motion and a spirit, that impels   100
All thinking things, all objects of all thought,
And rolls through all things. Therefore am I still
A lover of the meadows and the woods,
And mountains; and of all that we behold
From this green earth; of all the mighty world   105
Of eye, and ear,—both what they half create,
And what perceive; well pleased to recognize
In nature and the language of the sense
The anchor of my purest thoughts, the nurse,
The guide, the guardian of my heart, and soul   110
Of all my moral being.
                            Nor perchance,
If I were not thus taught, should I the more
Suffer my genial spirits⁵ to decay:
For thou⁶ art with me here upon the banks
Of this fair river; thou my dearest Friend,   115
My dear, dear Friend; and in thy voice I catch
The language of my former heart, and read
My former pleasures in the shooting lights
Of thy wild eyes. Oh! yet a little while
May I behold in thee what I was once,   120
My dear, dear Sister! and this prayer I make,
Knowing that Nature never did betray
The heart that loved her; 'tis her privilege,
Through all the years of this our life, to lead
From joy to joy: for she can so inform⁷   125
The mind that is within us, so impress
With quietness and beauty, and so feed
With lofty thoughts, that neither evil tongues,
Rash judgments, nor the sneers of selfish men,
Nor greetings where no kindness is, nor all   130
The dreary intercourse of daily life,
Shall e'er prevail against us, or disturb
Our cheerful faith, that all which we behold
Is full of blessings. Therefore let the moon

5 genial spirits: native powers.
6 thou: Dorothy, the poet's sister.
7 inform: animate; inspire.

Shine on thee in thy solitary walk; 135
And let the misty mountain winds be free
To blow against thee: and, in after years,
When these wild ecstasies shall be matured
Into a sober pleasure; when thy mind
Shall be a mansion for all lovely forms, 140
Thy memory be as a dwelling place
For all sweet sounds and harmonies; oh! then,
If solitude, or fear, or pain, or grief,
Should be thy portion, with what healing thoughts
Of tender joy wilt thou remember me, 145
And these my exhortations! Nor, perchance—
If I should be where I no more can hear
Thy voice, nor catch from thy wild eyes these gleams
Of past existence[8]—wilt thou then forget
That on the banks of this delightful stream 150
We stood together; and that I, so long
A worshiper of Nature, hither came
Unwearied in that service: rather say
With warmer love—oh! with far deeper zeal
Of holier love. Nor wilt thou then forget, 155
That after many wanderings, many years
Of absence, these steep woods and lofty cliffs,
And this green pastoral landscape, were to me
More dear, both for themselves and for thy sake!

8 of past existence: the poet's own past.

Comment

As he stands looking down upon the landscape with its farms and woodlands (ll. 1-22), Wordsworth meditates on how the scene in the intervening five years has often been present in his mind and has indeed sometimes mingled itself with the "blessed mood" in which he has quietly, momentarily been aware of the harmony of life around him (ll. 22-49). And he voices the hope that this sense of harmony, in which the vision of the Wye valley has been mingled, is not a "vain belief," a delusion, for he has certainly often turned in memory to the "sylvan Wye" (ll. 49-57). Once again, as he stands there, his memories return, and with the present scene before him, he recalls how as a boy he felt the "dizzy raptures" of wandering in such a landscape (ll. 58-83). Now, he knows, that time is past, but that is no cause for grief (ll. 83-88); for as he has grown mature he has come to feel a deeper joy in nature, a "sense sublime" that there is a common living spirit shared by the sky, the ocean, the air—by all of nature—and by the mind of man (ll. 83-102). Therefore he is still a lover of all "this green earth," though he loves it now not for its "dizzy raptures" but for the fact that it has been the "nurse," "guide," and "guardian" (what in *The Prelude* he calls the "ministry") of his moral sense (ll. 102-111). Finally (ll. 112-end) he turns to his sister Dorothy, who stands beside him at the scene, and in her eyes, and in his awareness of her present and future experience, he sees the confirmation of his own experience: she too will remember this vision of the Wye valley, and in her future life it will be, as it has been for him, part of the "mansion for all lovely forms" in her mind, a source of pleasure, strength, and love in the unknown days ahead. The poem moves back and forth between a particular situation in the present and a general sense of the past; between a particular, present awareness and a general principle that is valid for past, present, and future. What is this general principle?

1. What is the character of the immediate scene as the poet looks upon it once again (ll. 1-22)? What is the character of the hedgerows as he sees them? And what is the character of the "pastoral farms" of the landscape?

2. Next, the poet gives us his first statement of what the memory of such scenes as this has meant to him in the past; he tells us that he has "owed" to them a "blessed mood." What is the character of that mood? In what sense is it like the image of the contemplating Hermit in the first twenty-two lines?

3. In lines 65-83 the poet tells us of his boyhood experience of nature. What are some of the images that characterize that experience? In what sense is it like the description of the hedgerows that opens the poem?

4. We come to the heart of the poem at lines 93-102, to the sense "Of something far more deeply interfused," and we notice the looseness —a string of *and's*—with which Wordsworth connects the "something" in the setting suns, the ocean, air, and sky, and the mind of man. What is his tone as he makes these connections? Is it the tone of a man who is defiant, unsteady, or unsure of himself? How has his opening contemplation of the scene before him prepared you for the connections he announces here between the something deeply interfused in nature and the mind of man?

5. And finally the poet turns to his sister. What does he see in her to corroborate and confirm his belief that even though we grow older, still nature can lead us "From joy to joy"? What evidence of present "joy" does he see in her? And what future joys does he foresee for her?

6. At line 48 Wordsworth speaks of the "deep power of joy" that enables him to "see into the life of things." You will have seen by now that "joy" is indeed a key principle in this poem. Write a brief essay on Wordsworth's meaning of "joy" in "Tintern Abbey"; how does "joy," as he conceives of it, connect our experience of youth and maturity, our awareness of "dizzy raptures" with our sense of "something far more deeply interfused"?

474

In 1800 Wordsworth brought out a second edition of *Lyrical Ballads* containing the Preface which set forth his conceptions of poetry and the poet. In 1807 he completed the greatest ten years of his life with the publication of *Poems in Two Volumes*. The latter contained many sonnets—the finest, it has been said, since Shakespeare's and Milton's. Wordsworth was the master of the long, meditative narrative poem in blank verse, yet he was equally at ease in the formal rhymes of the sonnet.

"Upon Westminster Bridge" The first of the sonnets below was written on the roof of a coach as Wordsworth left London on a journey in 1802.

Composed upon Westminster Bridge

William Wordsworth

Earth has not anything to show more fair:
Dull would he be of soul who could pass by
A sight so touching in its majesty:
This City now doth, like a garment, wear
The beauty of the morning; silent, bare,　　　　　5
Ships, towers, domes, theaters, and temples lie
Open unto the fields, and to the sky;
All bright and glittering in the smokeless air.
Never did sun more beautifully steep
In his first splendor, valley, rock, or hill;　　　　10
Ne'er saw I, never felt, a calm so deep!
The river glideth at his own sweet will:
Dear God! the very houses seem asleep;
And all that mighty heart is lying still!

Comment

Usually we think of Wordsworth as the poet of nature, but here his subject is a great city in the early morning light before the round of human activity begins. Is there anything in this vision of the city that reminds you of his vision of the River Wye near Tintern Abbey?

1. How does line 6 sound to you as you read it aloud? What characteristic of the city, of city life, is expressed in the very sound of

this line? How does the image of the city given us in this line contrast with that in line 11?

2. "Dear God!"—the poem ends with an exclamation. Is it an exclamation of dismay? of wonder? What has Wordsworth seen in this vision of the city that returns us to his vision of nature in "Tintern Abbey"?

"It Is a Beauteous Evening" The following sonnet was written on the beach near Calais, France, in the autumn of 1802. The child is Wordsworth's daughter.

It Is a Beauteous Evening

William Wordsworth

It is a beauteous evening, calm and free,
The holy time is quiet as a Nun
Breathless with adoration; the broad sun
Is sinking down in its tranquility;
The gentleness of heaven broods o'er the Sea: 5
Listen! the mighty Being is awake,
And doth with his eternal motion make
A sound like thunder—everlastingly.
Dear Child! dear Girl! that walkest with me here,
If thou appear untouched by solemn thought,   10
Thy nature is not therefore less divine:
Thou liest in Abraham's bosom[1] all the year;
And worship'st at the Temple's inner shrine,
God being with thee when we know it not.

1 **Abraham's bosom:** God's presence. See Luke 16:22.

Comment

Wordsworth begins with a description of the calmness of the evening. Then, as he listens, he hears a sound that has been present but unmentioned in the opening quatrain. He turns to his daughter to see whether she is aware of the meaning he finds in the contrast between the calmness of the evening and the steady beat of the sea.

1. "The holy time is quiet as a Nun / Breathless with adoration." Of what is a nun aware in her adoration? How is this simile continued in the metaphor that compares the sea to a "mighty Being"?

2. The poet turns to his child: is her appearance that of a nun? Is her awareness different from that of the poet, at the very beginning, be-

fore he hears the everlasting beat of the sea beneath the calmness of the evening?

3. In what sense does the last line of the poem describe both the poet and his daughter?

"London, 1802" In "London, 1802" Wordsworth speaks across the years to John Milton, the predecessor whom he most admired. As he expresses that admiration, Wordsworth speaks to his contemporaries somewhat as Burns spoke to his fellow Scotsmen in "Scots, Wha Hae." England in 1802 was hostile to the revolution in France, but in Milton's time it had been different. Then, the country lived through the revolutionary times of the Commonwealth, and Milton had set aside his poetry to become Latin Secretary of State.

London, 1802

William Wordsworth

Milton! thou shouldst be living at this hour:
England hath need of thee: she is a fen
Of stagnant waters: altar, sword, and pen,
Fireside, the heroic wealth of hall and bower,
Have forfeited their ancient English dower   5
Of inward happiness. We are selfish men;
Oh! raise us up, return to us again;
And give us manners, virtue, freedom, power.
Thy soul was like a Star, and dwelt apart;
Thou hadst a voice whose sound was like the sea: 10
Pure as the naked heavens, majestic, free,
So didst thou travel on life's common way,
In cheerful godliness; and yet thy heart
The lowliest duties on herself did lay.

Comment

The John Milton of the 1650's was, to Wordsworth, everything that the England of 1802 was not. Whether or not Milton was in fact quite so noble and lofty as Wordsworth makes him is less important than the virtues that Wordsworth believed would make his country great.

1. This sonnet, like most others, is in a basic meter of iambic pentameter: the normal line, the line we expect as we begin to read it, has five feet, each consisting of an unaccented syllable followed by an accented syllable. But here, at the very beginning, the first word,

"Milton!" disrupts our expectations. Compare the beginning of this line with the beginnings of the last three lines. What is the effect of this opening of the sonnet? What tone does it make us hear? How is this tone continued in the octave?

2. England, says Wordsworth, is "a fen / Of stagnant waters." With what contrasting images does he characterize Milton?

3. In the last three lines Wordsworth speaks of "life's common way," "cheerful godliness," and "lowliest duties." How do these phrases complete the heroic stature ascribed to Milton in the preceding three lines? How do they complete, too, our understanding of the "ancient English dower / Of inward happiness"?

"The World Is Too Much with Us" Wordsworth's sympathies with the revolution in France slowly died away, as did those of many of his fellow countrymen. By 1806, when he wrote the following sonnet, his subject was not England but the world, the daily "getting and spending" in which we lose the joyful communion with nature that for Wordsworth was the only real life.

The World
Is Too Much
with Us

William Wordsworth

The world is too much with us; late and soon,
Getting and spending, we lay waste our powers:
Little we see in Nature that is ours;
We have given our hearts away, a sordid boon![1]
This Sea that bares her bosom to the moon;   5
The winds that will be howling at all hours,
And are upgathered now like sleeping flowers;
For this, for everything, we are out of tune;
It moves us not.—Great God! I'd rather be
A Pagan suckled in a creed outworn;   10
So might I, standing on this pleasant lea,
Have glimpses that would make me less forlorn;
Have sight of Proteus rising from the sea;
Or hear old Triton[2] blow his wreathèd horn.

1 **sordid boon:** base or ignoble gift.
2 **Proteus** (prō′tūs) . . . **Triton** (trī′tən): sea-gods in classical, or "pagan," mythology. Proteus could transform himself into any shape, like the constantly shifting waves; Triton, by blowing on his conch-shell trumpet, which is "wreathed," or spiral, in shape, could make the waves stormy or calm.

Comment

Once more Wordsworth is meditating by the sea, but this time no sense of a "mighty Being" makes its way to him in the sound of the waves. Here he is "forlorn" because he is conscious only of waste and disharmony among men. He would rather be an ancient pagan whose mythology clothed the sea in human characteristics—he would rather see Proteus and Triton there—than see nothing "that is ours." And yet he does see something that is "ours."

1. At the end of the octave (ll. 5-8) how does Wordsworth see the sea and the winds? In what sense does his vision here deny his assertion, "Little we see in Nature that is ours."
2. What then is the nature of those "glimpses" that might make the poet "less forlorn"?
3. Wordsworth could not, of course, go back to the experience of the ancient "Pagans." But as you think of the selections from *The Prelude* and of "Tintern Abbey," what was the "creed" in which he did believe?

Samuel Taylor Coleridge (1772-1834)

In 1772 in a small Devonshire village there was born to the vicar and his wife their fourteenth child, a son destined to be one of the most puzzling and fascinating leaders of the English Romantic movement. His troubles began early. As a small boy of eight, after a bitter fight with one of his brothers, he ran away from home and spent the night hiding in the damp reeds on the bank of a nearby river. By morning he was suffering from a rheumatic inflammation so severe that he could not move his legs; throughout his life he was often to experience severe pain and illness. He was sent to school in London and then entered Cambridge, just after Wordsworth's time, and was a student even more indifferent than his friend. After two years, in fact, his situation was so hopeless that he ran away again: he joined a troop of cavalry as a common soldier (though he knew nothing about horses), enlisting under the unlikely name (though one with his own initials) of Silas Tomkyn Comberbacke. His older brothers soon managed to rescue him and return him to the university, but he never graduated. In the next year he was planning to emigrate to America with the poet Robert Southey and to found with him and some other young people an ideal community (Pantisocracy—"equal government for all"—was their name for it) on the Susquehanna River in Pennsylvania. When this scheme had to be abandoned, Coleridge, now married, turned to writing, to preaching as a Unitarian, and to the exploration of all kinds of literature and philosophy. In 1798 a young man, William Hazlitt, who was to become an important literary critic, met Coleridge and was

An illustration for "The Rime of the Ancient Mariner" from a drawing by Gustave Doré (1832–1883), a French illustrator and engraver who was very popular in England.

overwhelmed by his eloquence and knowledge. On a long walk with him, however, Hazlitt said

> I observed that he continually crossed me on the way by shift-ing from one side of the footpath to the other. This struck me as an odd movement; but I did not at that time connect it with any instability of purpose or involuntary change of principle, as I have done since. He seemed unable to keep on in a straight line.

The observation was prophetic, for Coleridge kept crossing from career to career throughout his life.

His association with Wordsworth was the most sustained episode of his life, though it was not always serene. Coleridge was frequently ill and in great bodily pain. He was forced to resort to a common remedy of the time, laudanum, a mixture of opiates and alcohol that relieved suffering but entailed also the risk of the horrors of addiction. From 1797 until 1810 Coleridge lived most of the time near the Words-worths (he lived with them from 1808 to 1810), his health precarious, his marriage unhappy, his struggles to earn a living by writing and lecturing often unavailing. He moved to London in 1810 and spent his last years cared for by still other friends. Yet with all his illness and pain he did a great deal of work. He wrote on philosophy and politics and religion; he lectured on Shakespeare and other writers to large and enthralled audiences. And he talked. He was one of the greatest conversationalists in the history of English letters, and few who met him could resist the spell of his learning and imagination.

Son of the vicar of a school – educated at Cambridge – met Southy at Cambridge – devoted themselves to pantisocracy – 1795 he got married – met Wordsworth – had deep friendship – wrote Kublakhan in 1797 (famous work) – 1806 retired to England and became heavily dependent on drugs (opium + alcohol) – lecture tour on English poets In 1825 introduced English thinkers to German Philospical works – literary critic! – The true end of poetry is to give pleasure. –

"The Rime of the Ancient Mariner"

Coleridge seems in fact to have exerted on many people the power felt by the wedding guest who listens to the tale of the strange old man in "The Rime of the Ancient Mariner." This, the opening poem of *Lyrical Ballads,* was begun in collaboration with Wordsworth, who contributed some lines (for example, stanza 4 of Part I; ll. 13-16) and proposed two of its most striking episodes, the shooting of the albatross and the sailing of the ship by the dead men. The finished poem belongs to Coleridge, however. In planning *Lyrical Ballads,* he tells us,

> it was agreed that my endeavors should be directed to persons and characters supernatural, or at least romantic; yet so as to transfer from our inward nature a human interest and a semblance of truth sufficient to procure for these shadows of imagination that willing suspension of disbelief for the moment, which constitutes poetic faith. Mr. Wordsworth, on the other hand, was to propose to himself as his object to give the charm of novelty to things of every day, and to excite a feeling analogous to the supernatural, by awakening the mind's attention to the lethargy of custom and directing it to the loveliness and the wonders of the world before us. . . .

Certainly some of the characters of Coleridge's poem are "supernatural"; whether they and the other "shadows of imagination" in the poem are so described as to cause you to suspend your disbelief in them, you can determine for yourself.

The Rime
of the
Ancient Mariner

IN SEVEN PARTS

Samuel Taylor Coleridge

Argument   How a Ship, having first sailed to the Equator, was driven by Storms to the cold Country toward the South Pole; how the Ancient Mariner cruelly and in contempt of the laws of hospitality killed a Sea bird and how he was followed by many and strange Judgments: and in what manner he came back to his own Country.

PART I

An ancient Mariner meeteth three Gallants bidden to a wedding feast, and detaineth one.

It is an ancient Mariner,
And he stoppeth one of three.
"By thy long gray beard and glittering eye,
Now wherefore stopp'st thou me?

"The Bridegroom's doors are opened wide,   5
And I am next of kin;
The guests are met, the feast is set:
May'st hear the merry din."

He holds him with his skinny hand,
"There was a ship," quoth he.   10
"Hold off! unhand me, graybeard loon!"
Eftsoons[1] his hand dropt he.

The Wedding Guest is spellbound by the eye of the old searfaring man, and constrained to hear his tale.

He holds him with his glittering eye—
The Wedding Guest stood still,
And listens like a three years' child: 15
The Mariner hath his will.

---

1 **Eftsoons:** soon after.

The Wedding Guest sat on a stone:
He cannot choose but hear;
And thus spake on that ancient man,
The bright-eyed Mariner.   20

"The ship was cheered, the harbor cleared,
Merrily did we drop
Below the kirk,² below the hill,
Below the lighthouse top.

The Mariner tells how the ship sailed southward with a good wind and fair weather, till it reached the Line.³
"The Sun came up upon the left,   25
Out of the sea came he!
And he shone bright, and on the right
Went down into the sea.

"Higher and higher every day,
Till over the mast at noon—"   30
The Wedding Guest here beat his breast,
For he heard the loud bassoon.

The Wedding Guest heareth the bridal music; but the Mariner continueth his tale.
The bride hath paced into the hall,
Red as a rose is she;
Nodding their heads before her goes   35
The merry minstrelsy.

The Wedding Guest he beat his breast,
Yet he cannot choose but hear;
And thus spake on that ancient man,
The bright-eyed Mariner.   40

The ship driven by a storm toward the South Pole.
"And now the STORM-BLAST came, and he
Was tyrannous and strong:
He struck with his o'ertaking wings,
And chased us south along.

"With sloping masts and dipping prow,   45
As who pursued with yell and blow
Still treads the shadow of his foe,
And forward bends his head,
The ship drove fast, loud roared the blast,
And southward aye we fled.   50

"And now there came both mist and snow,
And it grew wondrous cold:
And ice, mast-high, came floating by,
As green as emerald.

2 **kirk:** church.
3 **Line:** equator.

SAMUEL TAYLOR COLERIDGE   483

The land of ice, and of fearful sounds where no living thing was to be seen.

"And through the drifts the snowy clifts   55
Did send a dismal sheen:
Nor shapes of men nor beasts we ken—
The ice was all between.

"The ice was here, the ice was there,
The ice was all around: 60
It cracked and growled, and roared and howled,
Like noises in a swound!⁴

Till a great sea bird, called the Albatross, came through the snow-fog, and was received with great joy and hospitality

"At length did cross an Albatross,
Thorough the fog it came;
As if it had been a Christian soul,   65
We hailed it in God's name.

"It ate the food it ne'er had eat,
And round and round it flew.
The ice did split with a thunder-fit;
The helmsman steered us through!   70

And lo! the Albatross proveth a bird of good omen, and followeth the ship as it returned northward through fog and floating ice.

"And a good south wind sprung up behind;
The Albatross did follow,
And every day, for food or play,
Came to the mariner's hollo!

"In mist or cloud, on mast or shroud,⁵   75
It perched for vespers⁶ nine;
Whiles all the night, through fog-smoke white,
Glimmered the white Moonshine."

The ancient Mariner inhospitably killeth the pious bird of omen.

"God save thee, ancient Mariner!
From the fiends, that plague thee thus!—   80
Why look'st thou so?"—"With my crossbow
I shot the ALBATROSS.

PART II

"The Sun now rose upon the right:
Out of the sea came he,
Still hid in the mist, and on the left   85
Went down into the sea.⁷

4 swound: swoon.
5 shroud: rigging.
6 vespers: evenings.
7 The sun . . . into the sea: The ship has rounded Cape Horn into the Pacific.

"And the good south wind still blew behind,
But no sweet bird did follow,
Nor any day for food or play
Came to the mariners' hollo!   90

His shipmates cry out
against the ancient
Mariner, for killing
the bird of good luck.

"And I had done a hellish thing,
And it would work 'em woe:
For all averred, I had killed the bird
That made the breeze to blow.
Ah wretch! said they, the bird to slay,   95
That made the breeze to blow!

But when the fog cleared
off, they justify the same,
and thus make themselves
accomplices in the crime.

"Nor dim nor red, like God's own head,
The glorious Sun uprist:
Then all averred, I had killed the bird
That brought the fog and mist.   100
'Twas right, said they, such birds to slay,
That bring the fog and mist.

The fair breeze continues;
the ship enters the Pa-
cific Ocean, and sails
northward, even till it
reaches the Line.

"The fair breeze blew, the white foam flew,
The furrow followed free;
We were the first that ever burst   105
Into that silent sea.

"Down dropt the breeze, the sails dropt down,
'Twas sad as sad could be;
The ship hath been sud-
denly becalmed.
And we did speak only to break
The silence of the sea!   110

"All in a hot and copper sky,
The bloody Sun, at noon,
Right up above the mast did stand,
No bigger than the Moon.

"Day after day, day after day,   115
We stuck, nor breath nor motion;
As idle as a painted ship
Upon a painted ocean.

And the Albatross begins
to be avenged.
"Water, water, everywhere,
And all the boards did shrink;   120
Water, water, everywhere,
Nor any drop to drink.

"The very deep did rot: O Christ!
That ever this should be!
Yea, slimy things did crawl with legs   125
Upon the slimy sea.

"About, about, in reel and rout
The death-fires[8] danced at night;
The water, like a witch's oils,
Burnt green, and blue and white.   130

A Spirit had followed
them; one of the in-
visible inhabitants of
this planet, neither de-
parted souls nor angels;
concerning whom the
learned Jew, Josephus,[9]
and the Platonic Con-
stantinopolitan, Michael
Psellus,[10] may be con-
sulted. They are very
numerous, and there is
no climate or element
without one or more.

"And some in dreams assurèd were
Of the Spirit that plagued us so;
Nine fathom deep he had followed us
From the land of mist and snow.

"And every tongue, through utter drought, 135
Was withered at the root;
We could not speak, no more than if
We had been choked with soot.

The shipmates, in their
sore distress, would fain
throw the whole guilt
on the ancient Mariner:
in sign whereof they
hang the dead sea bird
round his neck.

"Ah! welladay! what evil looks
Had I from old and young!   140
Instead of the cross, the Albatross
About my neck was hung.

PART III

"There passed a weary time. Each throat
Was parched, and glazed each eye.
A weary time! a weary time!   145
How glazed each weary eye,
When looking westward, I beheld
A something in the sky.

The ancient Mariner be-
holdeth a sign in the element afar off.

"At first it seemed a little speck,
And then it seemed a mist;   150
It moved and moved, and took at last
A certain shape, I wist.[11]

"A speck, a mist, a shape, I wist!
And still it neared and neared:
As if it dodged a water sprite,[12]   155
It plunged and tacked and veered.

8 **death-fires:** phosphorescence.
9 **Josephus:** 1st-century historian and military commander.
10 **Psellus:** 11th-century writer, philosopher, and politcian.
11 **wist:** knew
12 **sprite:** spirit.

486

At its nearer approach, it
seemeth him to be a ship;
and at a dear ransom he
freeth his speech from the
bonds of thirst.

"With throats unslaked, with black lips baked,
We could nor laugh nor wail;
Through utter drought all dumb we stood!
I bit my arm, I sucked the blood,   160
And cried, A sail! a sail!

"With throats unslaked, with black lips baked,
Agape they heard me call:

A flash of joy;

Gramercy![13] they for joy did grin,
And all at once their breath drew in,   165
As[14] they were drinking all.

And horror follows. For
can it be a ship that
comes onward without
wind or tide?

"See! see! (I cried) she tacks no more!
Hither to work us weal;
Without a breeze, without a tide,
She steadies with upright keel!   170

"The western wave was all aflame.
The day was well nigh done!
Almost upon the western wave
Rested the broad bright Sun;
When that strange shape drove suddenly   175
Betwixt us and the Sun.

It seemeth him but the
skeleton of a ship.

"And straight the Sun was flecked with bars,
(Heaven's Mother send us grace!)
As if through a dungeon grate he peered
With broad and burning face.   180

"Alas! (thought I, and my heart beat loud)
How fast she nears and nears!
Are those *her* sails that glance in the Sun,
Like restless gossameres?[15]

And its ribs are seen
as bars on the face
of the setting Sun.
The Specter Woman
and her Deathmate,
and no other on board
the skeleton ship.

"Are those *her* ribs through which the Sun   185
Did peer, as through a grate?
And is that Woman all her crew?
Is that a DEATH?[16] and are there two?
Is DEATH that woman's mate?

"*Her* lips were red, *her* looks were free,   190
Her locks were yellow as gold:
Her skin was as white as leprosy,

13 **Gramercy:** May God give you great mercy!
14 **As:** as if.
15 **gossameres:** cobwebs.
16 **Death:** skeleton.

SAMUEL TAYLOR COLERIDGE   487

Like vessel, like crew!

The Nightmare LIFE-IN-DEATH was she,
Who thicks man's blood with cold.

Death and Life-in-Death have diced for the ship's crew, and she (the latter) winneth the ancient Mariner.

"The naked hulk alongside came,   195
And the twain were casting dice;
'The game is done! I've won! I've won!'
Quoth she, and whistles thrice.

No twilight within the courts of the Sun.

"The Sun's rim dips; the stars rush out:
At one stride comes the dark;   200
With far-heard whisper, o'er the sea,
Off shot the specter-bark.

At the rising of the Moon,

"We listened and looked sideways up!
Fear at my heart, as at a cup,
My lifeblood seemed to sip!
The stars were dim, and thick the night,
The steersman's face by his lamp gleamed white;
From the sails the dew did drip—
Till clomb above the eastern bar
The hornèd Moon, with one bright star   210
Within the nether tip.

One after another,

"One after one, by the star-dogged Moon,
Too quick for groan or sigh,
Each turned his face with a ghastly pang,
And cursed me with his eye.   215

His shipmates drop down dead.

"Four times fifty living men,
(And I heard nor sigh nor groan)
With heavy thump, a lifeless lump,
They dropped down one by one.

But Life-in-Death begins her work on the ancient Mariner.

"The souls did from their bodies fly—   220
They fled to bliss or woe!
And every soul, it passed me by,
Like the whizz of my crossbow!"

PART IV

The Wedding Guest feareth that a Spirit is talking to him;

"I fear thee, ancient Mariner!
I fear thy skinny hand!   225
And thou art long, and lank, and brown,
As is the ribbed sea sand.

"I fear thee and thy glittering eye,
And thy skinny hand, so brown."—

"Fear not, fear not, thou Wedding Guest!   230
This body dropt not down.

But the ancient Mariner
assureth him of his bodily
life, and proceedeth to relate his horrible penance.

"Alone, alone, all, all alone,
Alone on a wide wide sea!
And never a saint took pity on
My soul in agony.   235

He despiseth the crea-
tures of the calm,

"The many men, so beautiful!
And they all dead did lie:
And a thousand thousand slimy things
Lived on; and so did I.

And envieth that *they*
should live, and so
many lie dead.

"I looked upon the rotting sea,   240
And drew my eyes away;
I looked upon the rotting deck,
And there the dead men lay.

"I looked to heaven, and tried to pray;
But or[17] ever a prayer had gusht,   245
A wicked whisper came, and made
My heart as dry as dust.

"I closed my lids, and kept them close,
And the balls like pulses beat;
For the sky and the sea, and the sea and the sky   250
Lay like a load on my weary eye,
And the dead were at my feet.

But the curse liveth for
him in the eye of the
dead men.

"The cold sweat melted from their limbs,
Nor rot nor reek did they:
The look with which they looked on me   255
Had never passed away.

"An orphan's curse would drag to hell
A spirit from on high;
But oh! more horrible than that

In his loneliness and
fixedness he yearneth
toward the journey-
ing Moon, and the
stars that still sojourn,
yet still move onward;
and everywhere the
blue sky belongs to
them, and is their ap-
pointed rest, and their

Is the curse in a dead man's eye!   260
Seven days, seven nights, I saw that curse,
And yet I could not die.

"The moving Moon went up the sky,
And nowhere did abide:
Softly she was going up,   265
And a star or two beside—

17 or: before.

SAMUEL TAYLOR COLERIDGE   489

native country and their own natural homes, which they enter unannounced, as lords that are certainly expected and yet there is a silent joy at their arrival.

"Her beams bemocked the sultry main,
Like April hoarfrost spread;
But where the ship's huge shadow lay,
The charmèd water burnt alway
A still and awful red.

270

By the light of the Moon he beholdeth God's creatures of the great calm.

"Beyond the shadow of the ship,
I watched the water snakes:
They moved in tracks of shining white,
And when they reared, the elfish light
Fell off in hoary flakes.

275

"Within the shadow of the ship
I watched their rich attire:
Blue, glossy green, and velvet black,
They coiled and swam; and every track
Was a flash of golden fire.

280

Their beauty and their happiness.

"O happy living things! no tongue
Their beauty might declare:
A spring of love gushed from my heart,
And I blessed them unaware:
Sure my kind saint took pity on me,
And I blessed them unaware.

285

He blesseth them in his heart.

The spell begins to break.

"The selfsame moment I could pray;
And from my neck so free
The Albatross fell off, and sank
Like lead into the sea.

290

Part V

"Oh sleep! it is a gentle thing,
Beloved from pole to pole!
To Mary Queen the praise be given!
She sent the gentle sleep from Heaven,
That slid into my soul.

295

By grace of the holy Mother, the ancient Mariner is refreshed with rain.

"The silly[18] buckets on the deck,
That had so long remained,
I dreamt that they were filled with dew;
And when I awoke, it rained.

300

18 silly: simple.

THE ROMANTIC PERIOD

"My lips were wet, my throat was cold,
My garments all were dank;
Sure I had drunken in my dreams,
And still my body drank.

"I moved, and could not feel my limbs: 305
I was so light—almost
I thought that I had died in sleep,
And was a blessèd ghost.

He heareth sounds and
seeth strange sights and
commotions in the sky
and the element.
"And soon I heard a roaring wind:
It did not come anear;   310
But with its sound it shook the sails,
That were so thin and sere.[19]

"The upper air burst into life!
And a hundred fire flags sheen,[20]
To and fro they were hurried about!   315
And to and fro, and in and out,
The wan stars danced between.

"And the coming wind did roar more loud,
And the sails did sigh like sedge;[21]
And the rain poured down from one black cloud;   320
The Moon was at its edge.

"The thick black cloud was cleft, and still
The Moon was at its side:
Like water shot from some high crag,
The lightning fell with never a jag,   325
A river steep and wide.

The bodies of the ship's
crew are inspired, and
the ship moves on;
"The loud wind never reached the ship,
Yet now the ship moved on!
Beneath the lightning and the Moon
The dead men gave a groan.   330

"They groaned, they stirred, they all uprose,
Nor spake, nor moved their eyes;
It had been strange, even in a dream,
To have seen those dead men rise.

"The helmsman steered, the ship moved on;   335
Yet never a breeze upblew;

19 sere: dry; withered.
20 sheen: shone.
21 sedge: grassy plants.

SAMUEL TAYLOR COLERIDGE   491

The mariners all 'gan work the ropes,
Where they were wont to do;
They raised their limbs like lifeless tools—
We were a ghastly crew.   340

"The body of my brother's son
Stood by me, knee to knee:
The body and I pulled at one rope,
But he said nought to me.

"I fear thee, ancient Mariner!"   345
"Be calm, thou Wedding Guest!
'Twas not those souls that fled in pain,
Which to their corses²³ came again,
But a troop of spirits blest:

But not by the souls of the men, nor by daemons²² of earth or middle air, but by a blessed troop of angelic spirits, sent down by the invocation of the guardian saint.

"For when it dawned—they dropped their arms,   350
And clustered round the mast;
Sweet sounds rose slowly through their mouths,
And from their bodies passed.

"Around, around, flew each sweet sound,
Then darted to the Sun;   355
Slowly the sounds came back again,
Now mixed, now one by one.

"Sometimes a-dropping from the sky
I heard the skylark sing;
Sometimes all little birds that are,   360
How they seemed to fill the sea and air
With their sweet jargoning!

"And now 'twas like all instruments,
Now like a lonely flute;
And now it is an angel's song,   365
That makes the heavens be mute.

"It ceased; yet still the sails made on
A pleasant noise till noon,
A noise like of a hidden brook
In the leafy month of June,   370
That to the sleeping woods all night
Singeth a quiet tune.

---

22 **daemons:** spirits, not evil demons.
23 **corses:** corpses.

"Till noon we quietly sailed on,
Yet never a breeze did breathe:
Slowly and smoothly went the ship,   375
Moved onward from beneath.

"Under the keel nine fathom deep,
From the land of mist and snow,
The spirit slid: and it was he
That made the ship to go.   380
The sails at noon left off their tune,
And the ship stood still also.

"The Sun, right up above the mast,
Had fixed her to the ocean:
But in a minute she 'gan stir,   385
With a short uneasy motion—
Backwards and forwards half her length
With a short uneasy motion.

"Then like a pawing horse let go,
She made a sudden bound: 390
It flung the blood into my head,
And I fell down in a swound.

"How long in that same fit I lay,
I have not[24] to declare;
But ere my living life returned,   395
I heard and in my soul discerned
Two voices in the air.

" 'Is it he?' quoth one, 'Is this the man?
By him who died on cross,
With his cruel bow he laid full low   400
The harmless Albatross.

" 'The spirit who bideth by himself
In the land of mist and snow,
He loved the bird that loved the man
Who shot him with his bow.'   405

"The other was a softer voice,
As soft as honeydew:
Quoth he, 'The man hath penance done,
And penance more will do.'

---

24 **have not:** am unable.

Part VI

" 'But tell me, tell me! speak again,
Thy soft response renewing—
What makes that ship drive on so fast?
What is the ocean doing?'

410

SECOND VOICE

" 'Still as a slave before his lord,
The ocean hath no blast;
His great bright eye most silently
Up to the Moon is cast—

415

" 'If he may know which way to go;
For she guides him smooth or grim.
See, brother, see! how graciously
She looketh down on him.'

420

FIRST VOICE

The Mariner hath been cast into a trance; for the angelic power causeth the vessel to drive northward faster than human life could endure.

" 'But why drives on that ship so fast,
Without or wave or wind?'

SECOND VOICE

" 'The air is cut away before,
And closes from behind.

425

" 'Fly, brother, fly! more high, more high!
Or we shall be belated:
For slow and slow that ship will go,
When the Mariner's trance is abated.'

The supernatural motion is retarded; the Mariner awakes, and his penance begins anew.

"I woke, and we were sailing on
As in a gentle weather:
'Twas night, calm night, the moon was high;
The dead men stood together.

430

"All stood together on the deck,
For a charnel dungeon[25] fitter:
All fixed on me their stony eyes,
That in the Moon did glitter.

435

"The pang, the curse, with which they died,
Had never passed away:

---

25 **charnel dungeon:** vault for bones.

I could not draw my eyes from theirs,   440
Nor turn them up to pray.

The curse is finally
expiated. "And now this spell was snapt: once more
I viewed the ocean green,
And looked far forth, yet little saw
Of what had else been seen—   445

"Like one, that on a lonesome road
Doth walk in fear and dread,
And having once turned round walks on,
And turns no more his head;
Because he knows, a frightful fiend   450
Doth close behind him tread.

"But soon there breathed a wind on me,
Nor sound nor motion made:
Its path was not upon the sea,
In ripple or in shade.   455

"It raised my hair, it fanned my cheek
Like a meadow gale of spring—
It mingled strangely with my fears,
Yet it felt like a welcoming.

"Swiftly, swiftly flew the ship,   460
Yet she sailed softly too:
Sweetly, sweetly blew the breeze—
On me alone it blew.

And the ancient Mariner
beholdeth his native
country. "Oh! dream of joy! is this indeed
The lighthouse top I see?   465
Is this the hill? is this the kirk?
Is this mine own countree?

"We drifted o'er the harbor bar,
And I with sobs did pray—
O let me be awake, my God!   470
Or let me sleep alway.

"The harbor bay was clear as glass,
So smoothly it was strewn!
And on the bay the moonlight lay,
And the shadow of the Moon.   475

"The rock shone bright, the kirk no less,
That stands above the rock:
The moonlight steeped in silentness
The steady weathercock.

"And the bay was white with silent light,   480
Till rising from the same,
Full many shapes, that shadows were,
In crimson colors came.

The angelic spirits leave the dead bodies,

"A little distance from the prow
Those crimson shadows were: 485
I turned my eyes upon the desk—
Oh, Christ! what saw I there!

And appear in their own forms of light.

"Each corse lay flat, lifeless and flat,
And, by the holy rood![26]
A man all light, a seraph[27] man,   490
On every corse there stood.

"This seraph band, each waved his hand:
It was a heavenly sight!
They stood as signals to the land,
Each one a lovely light;   495

"The seraph band, each waved his hand,
No voice did they impart—
No voice; but oh! the silence sank
Like music on my heart.

"But soon I heard the dash of oars,   500
I heard the Pilot's[28] cheer;
My head was turned perforce away
And I saw a boat appear.

"The Pilot and the Pilot's boy,
I heard them coming fast: 505
Dear Lord in Heaven! it was a joy
The dead men could not blast.

"I saw a third—I heard his voice:
It is the Hermit good!
He singeth loud his godly hymns   510
That he makes in the wood.

26 **rood:** cross.
27 **seraph** (sĕr′əf): type of angel.
28 **Pilot:** harbor pilot.

He'll shrieve[29] my soul, he'll wash away
The Albatross's blood.

Part VII

The Hermit of the Wood, "This Hermit good lives in that wood
Which slopes down to the sea.   515
How loudly his sweet voice he rears!
He loves to talk with marineres[30]
That come from a far countree.

"He kneels at morn, and noon, and eve—
He hath a cushion plump: 520
It is the moss that wholly hides
The rotted old oak stump.

"The skiff boat neared: I heard them talk,
'Why, this is strange, I trow![31]
Where are those lights so many and fair,   525
That signal made but now?'

Approacheth the ship
with wonder. " 'Strange, by my faith!' the Hermit said—
'And they answered not our cheer!
The planks looked warped! and see those sails,
How thin they are and sere!   530
I never saw aught like to them,
Unless perchance it were

" 'Brown skeletons of leaves that lag
My forest brook along;
When the ivy tod[32] is heavy with snow,   535
And the owlet whoops to the wolf below,
That eats the she-wolf's young.'

" 'Dear Lord! it hath a fiendish look'—
(The Pilot made reply)
'I am a-feared'—'Push on, push on!'   540
Said the Hermit cheerily.

"The boat came closer to the ship,
But I nor spake nor stirred;
The boat came close beneath the ship,
And straight a sound was heard.   545

---

29 **shrieve:** shrive; absolve.
30 **marineres:** mariners.
31 **trow:** trust; think.
32 **tod:** bush.

SAMUEL TAYLOR COLERIDGE   **497**

The ship suddenly sinketh.

"Under the water it rumbled on,
Still louder and more dread:
It reached the ship, it split the bay;
The ship went down like lead.

The ancient Mariner is saved in the Pilot's boat.

"Stunned by that loud and dreadful sound,   550
Which sky and ocean smote,
Like one that hath been seven days drowned
My body lay afloat;
But swift as dreams, myself I found
Within the Pilot's boat.   555

"Upon the whirl, where sank the ship,
The boat spun round and round;
And all was still, save that the hill
Was telling of the sound.

"I moved my lips—the Pilot shrieked   560
And fell down in a fit;
The holy Hermit raised his eyes,
And prayed where he did sit.

"I took the oars: the Pilot's boy,
Who now doth crazy go,   565
Laughed loud and long, and all the while
His eyes went to and fro.
'Ha! ha!' quoth he, 'full plain I see,
The Devil knows how to row.'

"And now, all in my own countree,   570
I stood on the firm land!
The Hermit stepped forth from the boat,
And scarcely he could stand.

The Ancient Mariner earnestly entreateth the Hermit to shrieve him; and the penance of life falls on him.

" 'O shrieve me, shrieve me, holy man!'
The Hermit crossed his brow.   575
'Say quick,' quoth he, 'I bid thee say—
What manner of man art thou?'

"Forthwith this frame of mine was wrenched
With a woeful agony,
Which forced me to begin my tale;   580
And then it left me free.

And ever and anon throughout his future life an agony constraineth him to travel from land to land;

"Since then, at an uncertain hour,
That agony returns:
And till my ghastly tale is told,
This heart within me burns.   585

"I pass, like night, from land to land;
I have strange power of speech;
That moment that his face I see,
I know the man that must hear me:
To him my tale I teach.   590

"What loud uproar bursts from that door!
The wedding guests are there:
But in the garden bower the bride
And bridemaids singing are:
And hark the little vesper bell,   595
Which biddeth me to prayer!

"O Wedding Guest! this soul hath been
Alone on a wide wide sea:
So lonely 'twas, that God himself
Scarce seemèd there to be.   600

"O sweeter than the marriage feast,
'Tis sweeter far to me,
To walk together to the kirk
With a goodly company!—

"To walk together to the kirk,   605
And all together pray,
While each to his great Father bends,
Old men, and babes, and loving friends
And youths and maidens gay!

And to teach, by his own example, love and reverence to all things that God made and loveth.

"Farewell, farewell! but this I tell   610
To thee, thou Wedding Guest!
He prayeth well, who loveth well
Both man and bird and beast.

"He prayeth best, who loveth best
All things both great and small;   615
For the dear God who loveth us,
He made and loveth all."

The Mariner, whose eye is bright,
Whose beard with age is hoar,
Is gone: and now the Wedding Guest   620
Turned from the bridegroom's door.

He went like one that hath been stunned,
And is of sense forlorn:[33]
A sadder and a wiser man,
He rose the morrow morn.   625

Comment

"The Rime of the Ancient Mariner" is a literary ballad; that is, it was written by an author in imitation of the folk ballad and is even indebted for some of its details to traditional ballads of the supernatural. It is indebted still more, of course, for its archaic diction. The effect of this diction appears as soon as we give the chief character his name in modern English: it is the difference between saying "the ancient Mariner" and "the old sailor." Coleridge knew the old ballad language well, but apparently many of his readers did not, for to an edition of the poem published in 1817 he added the marginal prose commentary, or gloss, to ensure that his narrative would be clear.

The running gloss did more, however, than clarify the narrative; it called attention to certain symbols. For example, the gloss emphasizes the mysterious appearance of the ghost-ship bearing "Death" and "Life-in-Death." It emphasizes, too, the roles of the sun and the moon, of twilight and harsh sunlight, in the poem. It has been said, for example, that the Sun stands for reason and science—for the bright light of knowledge; while the Moon stands for the imagination—for that which veils the horrors of the world and makes them bearable. (By moonlight, for example, the mariner blesses the water snakes.) To elucidate every feature of the poem, however, is a long and difficult task. Its main dramatic movement is clear, and the moral significance of that movement is enough to keep us enthralled.

1. The tale is told to a man on his way to a joyous celebration. He says little, but his behavior in Part I and Part VII shows us the influence of the storyteller.
    (a) How do the Wedding Guest's responses and gestures characterize the Mariner in Part I?
    (b) The Wedding Guest does speak out at the end of Part I: How does his speech indicate the enormity of the Mariner's crime?
    (c) What other dramatic outbursts of the Wedding Guest characterize the Mariner and his adventure later in the poem?

33 forlorn: deprived.

2. At the end of Part II his shipmates hang the Albatross from the Mariner's neck as a sign of his guilt. At the end of Part IV the Albatross falls from his neck. Consider what has happened.
   (a) In Part IV (ll. 232-247) the Mariner looks at his dead companions. What is his response as he sees them lying there? Why does he try to pray?
   (b) Later in Part IV (ll. 272-287) the Mariner looks at the water snakes. What is his response to them? In line 245 no prayer "gusht" from him. What gushes from him now (l. 284)?
   (c) Why, then, does the Albatross fall from him when it does? How is its dropping away explained in the conclusion of the poem (ll. 610-617)?
3. The Mariner is saved from the fate of his shipmates: they are won by Death; he, by Life-in-Death (Part III). As the poem ends, in what sense is he still "Alone, alone, all, all alone"? How does his condition affect the Wedding Guest?
4. The Mariner's shooting of the Albatross is apparently simple, direct, unpremeditated. Yet it is cruel and evil. What does the conclusion of the poem imply about the effect of such inexplicable cruelty? Can it be thrown off and forgotten?
5. Write a paragraph explaining the relevance of the final description of the Wedding Guest. He is first stunned and shocked; next morning he rises sadder and wiser. What has happened to him? What has he learned?

Charles Lamb (1775-1834)

Although Charles Lamb worked for thirty-three years in the accounting department of the East India Company, one of the largest trading and commercial enterprises of the day, his main interests and chief friends were literary. He corresponded with Wordsworth; he befriended Coleridge; he knew William Hazlitt and many others. Not that his tastes were always the same as those of his literary friends: we have seen how he enjoyed his vacation in 1802 in the Lake District that so attracted the Romantic poets; but, like Samuel Johnson, he was a confirmed lover of city life. Although many of his friends were excited by the political ideas of the French Revolution, he himself was a conservative in both politics and religion. He greatly admired the poetry of Wordsworth and Coleridge, but not without reservations. In a letter to Wordsworth, for example, he said of Coleridge's "Rime of the Ancient Mariner" "I dislike all the miraculous part of it, but the feelings of the man dragged me along." "I was never so affected with any human tale," he said; but it was the human part of the poem that most gripped him.

Lamb was in many ways a spectator of, rather than a participant in, the life around him. He never married. His sister Mary, who suffered a periodically recurring mental illness, was the chief care of his life. Together they wrote *Tales from Shakespeare* (1807), an appreciative retelling for children of Shakespeare's plays. He himself edited a collection of plays by Shakespeare's less famous contemporaries, and he tried his own hand as a dramatist more than once. But he found a literary form which best suited him when, in 1820, he began to write informal essays for the *London Magazine* under the pen name of Elia (the name, originally, of an Italian clerk he had known early in his business career). The familiar essay, intimate in tone and informal in organization, became for Lamb the comfortable vehicle by which he spoke his mind, indulged his tastes, and expressed his most personal feelings.

"Dream Children"

"Dream Children" is one of the more personal of such essays. Lamb pretends to describe a scene in which he is telling his children—and of course he had no children—about a great-grandmother, Mary Field, who was in fact Lamb's own grandmother. He recalls his childhood visits to the great house where his grandmother was housekeeper and weaves into his recollections imaginary events taken from a contemporary ballad and from reminiscences of his own brother John (who had recently died) and his childhood sweetheart, Ann Simmons (who appears as "the fair Alice W—n").

Dream Children

A Reverie

Charles Lamb

CHILDREN LOVE to listen to stories about their elders, when *they* were children; to stretch their imagination to the conception of a traditionary great-uncle, or grandame, whom they never saw. It was in this spirit that my little ones crept about me the other evening to hear about their great-grandmother Field, who lived in a great house in Norfolk (a hundred times bigger than that in which they and Papa lived) which had been the scene—so at least it was generally believed in that part of the country—of the tragic incidents which they had lately become familiar with from the ballad of the Children in the Wood.[1] Certain it is that the whole story of the children and their cruel uncle was to be seen fairly carved out in wood upon the chimney piece of the great hall, the whole story down to the Robin Redbreasts, till a foolish rich person pulled it down to set up a marble one of modern invention in its stead,

with no story upon it. Here Alice put out one of her dear mother's looks, too tender to be called upbraiding. Then I went on to say, how religious and how good their great-grandmother Field was, how beloved and respected by everybody, though she was not indeed the mistress of this great house, but had only the charge of it (and yet in some respects she might be said to be the mistress of it too) committed to her by the owner, who preferred living in a newer and more fashionable mansion which he had purchased somewhere in the adjoining county; but still she lived in it in a manner as if it had been her own, and kept up the dignity of the great house in a sort while she lived, which afterward came to decay, and was nearly pulled down, and all its old ornaments stripped and carried away to the owner's other house, where they were set up, and looked as awkward as if someone were to carry away the old tombs they had seen lately at the Abbey, and stick them up in Lady C.'s tawdry gilt drawing room. Here John smiled, as much as to say, "that would be foolish indeed." And then I told how, when she came to die, her funeral was attended by a concourse of all the poor, and some of the gentry too, of the neighborhood for many miles round, to show their respect for her memory, because she had been such a good and religious woman; so good indeed that she knew all the Psaltery[2] by heart, ay, and a great part of the Testament besides. Here little Alice spread her hands. Then I told what a tall, upright, graceful person their great-grandmother Field once was; and how in her youth she was esteemed the best dancer—here Alice's little right foot played an involuntary

---

1 **ballad . . . Wood:** a story of the mysterious disappearance of two children.

2 **Psaltery** (sôl′tə rĭ): the Book of Psalms.

movement, till, upon my looking grave, it desisted—the best dancer, I was saying, in the county, till a cruel disease, called a cancer, came, and bowed her down with pain; but it could never bend her good spirits, or make them stoop, but they were still upright, because she was so good and religious. Then I told how she was used to sleep by herself in a lone chamber of the great lone house; and how she believed that an apparition of two infants was to be seen at midnight gliding up and down the great staircase near where she slept, but she said "those innocents would do her no harm"; and how frightened I used to be, though in those days I had my maid to sleep with me, because I was never half so good or religious as she—and yet I never saw the infants. Here John expanded all his eyebrows and tried to look courageous. Then I told how good she was to all her grandchildren, having us to the great house in the holydays, where I in particular used to spend many hours by myself, in gazing upon the old busts of the Twelve Caesars, that had been Emperors of Rome, till the old marble heads would seem to live again, or I to be turned into marble with them; how I never could be tired with roaming about that huge mansion, with its vast empty rooms, with their worn-out hangings, fluttering tapestry, and carved oaken panels, with the gilding almost rubbed out—sometimes in the spacious old-fashioned gardens, which I had almost to myself, unless when now and then a solitary gardening man would cross me —and how the nectarines and peaches hung upon the walls, without my ever offering to pluck them, because they were forbidden fruit, unless now and then—and because I had more pleasure in strolling about among the old melancholy-looking yew trees, or the firs, and picking up the red berries, and the fir apples, which were good for nothing but to look at—or in lying about upon the fresh grass, with all the fine garden smells around me—or basking in the orangery, till I could almost fancy myself ripening too along with the oranges and the limes in that grateful warmth— or in watching the dace that darted to and fro in the fishpond, at the bottom of the garden, with here and there a great sulky pike hanging midway down the water in silent state, as if it mocked at their impertinent friskings—I had more pleasure in these busy-idle diversions than in all the sweet flavors of peaches, nectarines, oranges, and such like common baits of children. Here John slyly deposited back upon the plate a bunch of grapes, which, not unobserved by Alice, he had meditated dividing with her, and both seemed willing to relinquish them for the present as irrelevant. Then in somewhat a more heightened tone, I told how, though their grandmother Field loved all her grandchildren, yet in an especial manner she might be said to love their uncle, John L———,[3] because he was so handsome and spirited a youth, and a king to the rest of us; and, instead of moping about in solitary corners, like some of us, he would mount the most mettlesome horse he could get, when but an imp no bigger than themselves, and make it carry him half over the county in a morning, and join the hunters when there were any out—and yet he loved the old great house and gardens too, but had too much spirit to be always pent up within their boundaries —and how their uncle grew up to man's estate as brave as he was handsome, to the admiration of everybody, but of their great-grandmother Field most es-

3 John L—: John Lamb; Charles's brother.

pecially; and how he used to carry me upon his back when I was a lame-footed boy[4]—for he was a good bit older than me—many a mile when I could not walk for pain; and how in afterlife he became lame-footed too, and I did not always (I fear) make allowances enough for him when he was impatient, and in pain, nor remember sufficiently how considerate he had been to me when I was lame-footed; and how when he died, though he had not been dead an hour, it seemed as if he had died a great while ago, such a distance there is betwixt life and death; and how I bore his death as I thought pretty well at first, but afterward it haunted and haunted me; and though I did not cry or take it to heart as some do, and as I think he would have done if I had died, yet I missed him all day long, and knew not till then how much I had loved him. I missed his kindness, and I missed his crossness, and wished him to be alive again, to be quarreling with him (for we quarreled sometimes), rather than not have him again, and was as uneasy without him as he their poor uncle must have been when the doctor took off his limb. Here the children fell a-crying, and asked if their little mourning which they had on was not for Uncle John, and they looked up, and prayed me not to go on about their uncle, but to tell them some stories about their pretty dead mother. Then I told how for seven long years, in hope sometimes, sometimes in despair, yet persisting ever, I courted the fair Alice W—n; and, as much as children could understand, I explained to them what coyness, and difficulty, and denial meant in maidens—when suddenly, turning to Alice, the soul of the first Alice looked out at her eyes with such a reality of representment, that I became in doubt which of them stood there before me, or whose that bright hair was; and while I stood gazing, both the children gradually grew fainter to my view, receding, and still receding till nothing at last but two mournful features were seen in the uttermost distance, which, without speech, strangely impressed upon me the effects of speech; "We are not of Alice, nor of thee, nor are we children at all. The children of Alice call Bartrum father. We are nothing; less than nothing, and dreams. We are only what might have been, and must wait upon the tedious shores of Lethe[5] millions of ages before we have existence, and a name"—and immediately awaking, I found myself quietly seated in my bachelor armchair, where I had fallen asleep, with the faithful Bridget[6] unchanged by my side—but John L. (or James Elia) was gone forever.

4 I . . . boy: There is no evidence that Lamb was permanently lame.

5 Lethe (lē'thĭ): in Greek mythology a river of Hades; drinking water from it caused forgetfulness of the past.
6 Bridget: Mary Lamb.

Comment

Although this essay is in many respects historically not true, it still expresses more fully than most autobiographies the personal feelings of its author. Its tone is easy and informal, its construction apparently casual. And yet its author's feelings are organized deftly and surely.

1. "Then I told": this clause, with some variations, is repeated a num-

ber of times. What do the repetitions do to the pace of the essay?

2. "Here Alice put out one of her dear mother's looks"—"Here John smiled": Lamb describes throughout the essay the dramatic responses of the dream children. How do their responses make the reader understand what is happening in Lamb's essay? And what do their responses tell us of Lamb's attitude toward children?

3. Consider the feelings that Lamb expresses as the essay comes to its close. He tells us, for example, that "both the children grew fainter and fainter to my view"; and at the very end he says, "but John L. (or James Elia) was gone forever." John Lamb had recently died. Dead, too, was the James Elia whose name Lamb had adopted as an author. Into what kind of world do the last words of the essay deliver us? What is the purpose of "dream children" in such a world? What attitude toward the real world, as opposed to the world of make believe, does the essay as a whole express?

Thomas De Quincey (1785-1859)

De Quincey was born wealthy, the son of a Manchester merchant; when he came into his inheritance he made a substantial and anonymous gift of money to Coleridge, whom he admired as he did Wordsworth, and whom in addition he resembled in several important respects. Like Coleridge he showed an early aptitude for learning; like him too he was a runaway: at the age of seventeen he hid himself away for one terrible winter in the slums of London. After returning to his family, he went to Oxford, but left suddenly in the midst of his final examinations. And, like Coleridge, he was driven by pain and illness to take laudanum. At the age of thirty-six he turned his sufferings into one of the most popular works of the day, *Confessions of an English Opium Eater.*

"On the Knocking at the Gate in Macbeth"

The essay which follows is one of the best-known pieces of Shakespearean criticism. De Quincey speaks out of his experience of *Macbeth.* He has *felt* something powerful in the knocking at the gate that follows the death of Duncan, but he cannot *understand* why he should have felt it. To resolve his perplexity he turns, not to literary theory, but to another experience, what he has heard about a recent crime of murder in London. Noblemen and a king were not involved in it. Late in 1811 (not 1812, as the essay states) a sailor, one John Williams, murdered two London families named Marr and Williamson. A servant of the Marrs', returning from an errand, knocked on the door of the house just after Williams had killed her employers. Starting from here, from a contemporary event as grisly as the one Shakespeare described, De Quincey proceeds to account for the power of the whole play of *Macbeth.*

from On the Knocking at the Gate in *Macbeth*

Thomas De Quincey

FROM my boyish days I had always felt a great perplexity on one point in *Macbeth*. It was this: The knocking at the gate which succeeds to the murder of Duncan produced to my feelings an effect for which I never could account. The effect was that it reflected back upon the murderer a peculiar awfulness and a depth of solemnity; yet, however obstinately I endeavored with my understanding to comprehend this, for many years I never could see *why* it should produce such an effect. . . .

In fact, my understanding said positively that it could *not* produce any effect. But I knew better; I felt that it did; and I waited and clung to the problem until further knowledge should enable me to solve it. At length, in 1812, Mr. Williams made his debut on the stage of Ratcliffe Highway,[1] and executed those unparalleled murders which have procured for him such a brilliant and undying reputation. On which

murders, by the way, I must observe that in one respect they have had an ill effect, by making the connoisseur in murder very fastidious in his taste, and dissatisfied by anything that has been since done in that line. All other murders look pale by the deep crimson of his; and, as an amateur[2] once said to me in a querulous tone, "There has been absolutely nothing *doing* since his time, or nothing that's worth speaking of." But this is wrong; for it is unreasonable to expect all men to be great artists, and born with the genius of Mr. Williams. Now, it will be remembered that in the first of these murders (that of the Marrs) the same incident (of a knocking at the door soon after the work of extermination was complete) did actually occur which the genius of Shakespeare has invented; and all good judges, and the most eminent dilettanti,[3] acknowledged the felicity of Shakespeare's suggestion as soon as it was actually realized. Here, then, was a fresh proof that I was right in relying on my own feeling, in opposition to my understanding; and I again set myself to study the problem. At length I solved it to my own satisfaction; and my solution is this: Murder, in ordinary cases, where the sympathy is wholly directed to the case of the murdered person, is an incident of coarse and vulgar horror; and for this reason—that it flings the interest exclusively upon the natural but ignoble instinct by which we cleave to life: an instinct which, as being indispensable to the primal law of self-preservation, is the same in kind (though different in degree) amongst all living creatures. This instinct, therefore, because it annihilates all distinctions, and degrades the greatest of men to the level of "the

---

1 **Ratcliffe Highway:** in the district of London where the Marr and Williamson murders occurred.

2 **amateur:** connoisseur; fan.
3 **dilettanti** (dĭl′ə tän′tĭ): persons interested in the fine arts.

poor beetle that we tread on,"[4] exhibits human nature in its most abject and humiliating attitude. Such an attitude would little suit the purposes of the poet. What then must he do? He must throw the interest on the murderer. Our sympathy must be with *him* (of course I mean a sympathy of comprehension, a sympathy by which we enter into his feelings, and are made to understand them—not a sympathy of pity or approbation). In the murdered person, all strife of thought, all flux and reflux[5] of passion and of purpose, are crushed by one overwhelming panic; the fear of instant death smites him "with its petrific mace."[6] But in the murderer, such a murderer as a poet will condescend to, there must be raging some great storm of passion—jealousy, ambition, vengeance, hatred—which will create a hell within him; and into this hell we are to look.

In *Macbeth,* for the sake of gratifying his own enormous and teeming faculty of creation, Shakespeare has introduced two murderers: and, as usual in his hands, they are remarkably discriminated: but—though in Macbeth the strife of mind is greater than in his wife, the tiger spirit not so awake, and his feelings caught chiefly by contagion from her—yet, as both were finally involved in the guilt of murder, the murderous mind of necessity is finally to be presumed in both. This was to be expressed; and, on its own account, as well as to make it a more proportionable antagonist to the unoffending nature of their victim, "the gracious Duncan,"[7] and adequately to expound "the deep damnation of his taking-off,"[8] this was to be expressed with peculiar energy. We were to be made to feel that the human nature—i.e., the divine nature of love and mercy, spread through the hearts of all creatures, and seldom utterly withdrawn from man—was gone, vanished, extinct, and that the fiendish nature had taken its place. And, as this effect is marvelously accomplished in the *dialogues* and *soliloquies* themselves, so it is finally consummated by the expedient under consideration;[9] and it is to this that I now solicit the reader's attention. If the reader has ever witnessed a wife, daughter, or sister in a fainting fit, he may chance to have observed that the most affecting moment in such a spectacle is *that* in which a sigh and a stirring announce the recommencement of suspended life. Or, if the reader has ever been present in a vast metropolis on the day when some great national idol was carried in funeral pomp to his grave, and, chancing to walk near the course through which it passed, has felt powerfully, in the silence and desertion of the streets, and in the stagnation of ordinary business, the deep interest which at that moment was possessing the heart of man—if all at once he should hear the deathlike stillness broken up by the sound of wheels rattling away from the scene, and making known that the transitory vision was dissolved, he will be aware that at no moment was his sense of the complete suspension and pause in ordinary human concerns so full and affecting as at that moment when the suspension ceases, and the goings-on of human life are suddenly resumed. All action in any direction is best expounded,

---

4 the poor . . . on: Shakespeare's *Measure for Measure,* III, i, 79.
5 flux and reflux: action and reaction.
6 with . . . mace: from *Paradise Lost; petrific* means "turning to stone."
7 the gracious Duncan: *Macbeth,* III, i, 66.

8 the deep . . . off: *Macbeth,* I, vii, 20.
9 expedient . . . consideration: i.e., the knocking at the gate.

THE ROMANTIC PERIOD

measured, and made apprehensible, by reaction. Now, apply this to the case in *Macbeth*. Here, as I have said, the retiring of the human heart and the entrance of the fiendish heart was to be expressed and made sensible. Another world has stepped in; and the murderers are taken out of the region of human things, human purposes, human desires. They are transfigured: Lady Macbeth is "unsexed";[10] Macbeth has forgot that he was born of woman; both are conformed to the image of devils; and the world of devils is suddenly revealed. But how shall this be conveyed and made palpable? In order that a new world may step in, this world must for a time disappear. The murderers and the murder must be insulated—cut off by an immeasurable gulf from the ordinary tide and succession of human affairs—locked up and sequestered in some deep recess; we must be made sensible that the world of ordinary life is suddenly arrested, laid asleep, tranced, racked into a dread armistice; time must be annihilated, relation to things without abolished; and all must pass self-withdrawn into a deep syncope[11] and suspension of earthly passion. Hence it is that, when the deed is done, when the work of darkness is perfect, then the world of darkness passes away like a pageantry in the clouds: the knocking at the gate is heard, and it makes known audibly that the reaction has commenced; the human has made its reflux upon the fiendish; the pulses of life are beginning to beat again; and the re-establishment of the goings-on of the world in which we live first makes us profoundly sensible of the awful parenthesis that had suspended them.

O mighty poet! Thy works are not as those of other men, simply and merely great work of art, but are also like the phenomena of nature, like the sun and the sea, the stars and the flowers, like frost and snow, rain and dew, hailstorm and thunder, which are to be studied with entire submission of our own faculties, and in the perfect faith that in them there can be no too much or too little, nothing useless or inert, but that, the farther we press in our discoveries, the more we shall see proofs of design and self-supporting arrangement where the careless eye had seen nothing but accident!

10 **unsexed:** *Macbeth,* I, v, 39.
11 **syncope** (sĭng′kə pĭ): fainting spell.

Comment

De Quincey's "understanding" could not account for the effects on him of the knocking at the gate. Worse, his understanding told him that this knocking *could not* affect him as it did. His essay, thus, tries to arrive at some other kind of understanding of the play. At what kind of understanding does it finally arrive?

1. In Macbeth, De Quincey tells us, "the strife of mind" is greater than in Lady Macbeth, but "the tiger spirit" is not so awake. Does this seem to you a valid distinction between the characterization of Macbeth and that of Lady Macbeth? Why?

THOMAS DE QUINCEY

2. "The knocking at the gate . . . makes known audibly that the reaction has commenced." What reaction? Does this seem to you a just account of the knocking at the gate? Why?
3. De Quincey's interpretation is clearly imaginative, and provocative. What experience of the play does it depend on: on simply reading it as one reads words on a page? on seeing and hearing it in a theater? How must you imagine *Macbeth* in order to follow this interpretation?

International Heroes

LIKE THE RENAISSANCE and the Enlightenment, Romanticism was an international movement. Democratic ideas from the French Revolution, you have seen, influenced Burns and the young Wordsworth. And the literary revolution developing simultaneously in England and Germany—its rise in France was temporarily checked by the political revolution—produced writers who were admired and imitated in all countries of the Western world. The two figures of English Romanticism whose fame quickly became international were not the most gifted writers of their day. But they perfected new departures in literature that won them admirers in many countries when William Blake, for example, or, later, John Keats were still unknown to most of their own countrymen. Both these international figures were aristocratic men, both were from time to time engaged in affairs other than literary, and both were among the most fluent and prolific writers in English literature. They were Sir Walter Scott and George Gordon, Lord Byron.

Sir Walter Scott (1771-1832)

Walter Scott did not become Sir Walter until 1820. He was the son of an Edinburgh attorney and became an attorney himself. His early childhood, after a severe illness, was spent at his grandfather's home in the Border Country, the scene in the past of many raids and battles between the English and the Scots and a region where many traditional stories and ballads of the warlike past were still current among the country people. At thirteen Scott discovered what was by then a famous book, a collection of folk ballads, *Reliques* [Remnants] *of Ancient English Poetry*, published in 1765 by Bishop Thomas Percy. Percy's *Reliques*, the foundation of all ballad collections, later inspired *Minstrelsy of the Scottish Border*, a collection Scott made among the people with whom he spent his childhood.

Scott had a prodigious memory. Not only could he recall great numbers of ballads he had heard sung among the Border peasants, he could also, simply by making a notch in his stick when he saw some view he liked during his explorations, fix in his mind all the details of a mountain landscape or a distant castle. He edited the works of other writers with exact knowledge and skill, he translated poems and plays by German writers, and, as Sheriff of Selkirkshire (he was appointed in 1799), he discharged many exacting legal and administrative duties.

He turned some of his intimate knowledge of the Border Country into narrative verse in *The Lay of the Last Minstrel*. This was the first of a series of romantic tales in verse published between 1805 and 1813 that made him the most popular poet in Britain. In 1814 he turned to prose with the publication of *Waverley*, the first in what was to be one of the greatest series of historical novels ever produced. They ranged in time and in setting from Scotland of the 17th and 18th centuries back to the days of the Crusades, and they gave to many generations of readers an exciting sense of a heroic past. The series was called the Waverley Novels because Scott kept his authorship a secret—the author's name on each succeeding novel was simply "By the Author of *Waverley*." Both Scott's romantic verse tales and his novels turned an unknown and neglected past into a tradition of heroic action.

Born in Edinbourgh -Son of Attourney Editor + Translator - Attourney - wrote a Series of Romantic Tales.— Interested in Mideavil Age

"Lochinvar"

Marmion is a verse tale of romantic intrigue set in the late Middle Ages. It contains an interlude—a song sung by a lady of the king's court—describing a young hero whose name, Lochinvar, has come to be a conventional title for the bold and dashing lover. The scene, of course, is the Border Country. There is a town called Netherby in northern Cumberland, with a lee, or lea, an open grassland, north of it near the town of Canobie. Lochinvar, however, is likely to be found in any country.

Equally at home with prose and poetry.

Lochinvar

Sir Walter Scott

Oh! young Lochinvar is come out of the west,
Through all the wide Border his steed was the best;
And save his good broadsword he weapons had none,
He rode all unarmed and he rode all alone.
So faithful in love and so dauntless in war, 5
There never was knight like the young Lochinvar.

He stayed not for brake[1] and he stopped not for stone,
He swam the Eske river where ford there was none;
But ere he alighted at Netherby gate
The bride had consented, the gallant came late: 10
For a laggard in love and a dastard in war
Was to wed the fair Ellen of brave Lochinvar.

L

1 brake: thicket.

So boldly he entered the Netherby Hall,
Among bridesmen, and kinsmen, and brothers, and all:
Then spoke the bride's father, his hand on his sword— 15
For the poor craven bridegroom said never a word—
"Oh! come ye in peace here, or come ye in war,
Or to dance at our bridal, young Lord Lochinvar?"

"I long wooed your daughter, my suit you denied;
Love swells like the Solway,[2] but ebbs like its tide— 20
And now am I come, with this lost love of mine,
To lead but one measure, drink one cup of wine.
There are maidens in Scotland more lovely by far,
That would gladly be bride to the young Lochinvar."

The bride kissed the goblet; the knight took it up, 25
He quaffed off the wine, and he threw down the cup.
She looked down to blush, and she looked up to sigh,
With a smile on her lips and a tear in her eye.
He took her soft hand ere her mother could bar—
"Now tread we a measure!" said young Lochinvar. 30

So stately his form, and so lovely her face,
That never a hall such a galliard[3] did grace;
While her mother did fret, and her father did fume,
And the bridegroom stood dangling his bonnet and plume;
And the bride-maidens whispered, " 'T were better by far 35
To have matched our fair cousin with young Lochinvar."

One touch to her hand and one word in her ear,
When they reached the hall door, and the charger stood near;
So light to the croupe[4] the fair lady he swung,
So light to the saddle before her he sprung! 40
"She is won! we are gone, over bank, bush, and scaur;[5]
They 'll have fleet steeds that follow," quoth young Lochinvar.

There was mounting 'mong Graemes of the Netherby clan;
Forsters, Fenwicks, and Musgraves, they rode and they ran:
There was racing and chasing on Cannobie Lee, 45
But the lost bride of Netherby ne'er did they see.
So daring in love and so dauntless in war,
Have ye e'er heard of gallant like young Lochinvar?

2 **Solway**: a long bay of the Irish Sea.
3 **galliard** (găl′yərd): lively dance.
4 **croupe** (kro͞op): croup; behind his saddle.
5 **scaur** (skär): rocky hill.

THE ROMANTIC PERIOD

Comment

One reason why the story of young Lochinvar is unforgettable is the rhythm of its lines. The meter, anapestic tetrameter, is not often used in English poetry: it consists of four feet (tetrameter), each foot consisting of two unaccented syllables followed by one accented syllable (anapest). The lines are therefore relatively long, yet the rhythm moves us through them with great speed.

1. Do you hear a strong caesura, or pause, in many lines? What effect does this medial pause have on the clarity of each line? What is its effect on the pace with which you read the poem?
2. In line 5 Lochinvar is "So faithful in love, and so dauntless in war." How is this line echoed in the description of Lochinvar's rival (1. 11)? Why in line 47 is "faithful" changed to "daring"?
3. "Have ye e'er heard of gallant like young Lochinvar?" How has Scott made us *hear* in an unforgettable way the story of this hero?

"Proud Maisie"

The following literary ballad comes from *The Heart of Midlothian*, a novel set in 18th-century Scotland. Scott wrote it as the deathbed song of Madge Wildfire, a mad peasant woman.

Proud Maisie

Sir Walter Scott

Proud Maisie is in the wood,
   Walking so early;
Sweet Robin sits on the bush,
   Singing so rarely.

"Tell me, thou bonny bird,
   When shall I marry me?"   5
"When six braw gentlemen
   Kirkward[1] shall carry ye."

"Who makes the bridal bed,
   Birdie, say truly?"   10
"The gray-headed sexton[2]
   That delves the grave duly.

"The glowworm o'er grave and stone
   Shall light thee steady.
The owl from the steeple sing,   15
   'Welcome, proud lady.'"

1 **Kirkward:** toward the church. The finely dressed ("braw") men are pallbearers.
2 **sexton:** church official in charge of church property; sometimes also the gravedigger.

SIR WALTER SCOTT   **513**

Comment

It has been said of this ballad that it is one of the most perfect imitations of the traditional ballad ever written. As you look back to the ballads from the late Middle Ages, does this seem to you a convincing imitation of them? In what respect is it most like "The Wife of Usher's Well" (p. 50), for example?

George Gordon, Lord Byron (1788-1824)

In 1814 there was published in London a long narrative poem entitled *The Corsair*, the tale of Conrad, a strange pirate of the Aegean Sea. It was an instantaneous best seller; on the day of publication ten thousand copies were sold. (Over the ensuing years a number of most unromantic little girls were to be called Medora, the name of its heroine.) The author was a young nobleman, George Gordon, Lord Byron, the most exciting literary personality of the day.

He had been raised in poverty by his Scottish mother, who had been deserted by his father. At the age of ten, however, young George Gordon's fortunes suddenly changed when he inherited the title of his great-uncle and became Lord Byron, the sixth Baron Byron. He proceeded to an old public school, Harrow, and then to Cambridge, where as an undergraduate he published his first book of poems. Its title, *Hours of Idleness*, described all too well the author's university career. Byron in 1809 began two years of travel abroad; he traveled farther and stayed longer than most of his contemporaries did on their Grand Tours of Europe, the postgraduate excursions customary then for wealthy young men. On his return these travels provided him with the materials with which he became a most successful author. They also provided England and all Europe with an unforgettable character, the Byronic hero.

Conrad the Corsair was a "man of loneliness and mystery." He was darkly handsome—"his forehead high and pale / The sable curls in rich profusion veil." Although he might not at first attract attention, on second glance

> His features' deepening lines and varying hue
> At times attracted, yet perplexed the view,
> As if within that murkiness of mind
> Worked feelings fearful, and yet undefined.

After many adventures, including the loss of Medora, who dies of grief upon a false report of his death, Conrad leaves his haunts of piracy and

514

A satirical print (left) with two Romantic heroes, one sitting lonely and brooding, the other expounding to the air. Byron's death is treated allegorically in the engraving at the right. A warrior crowns him with laurel, and Greece mourns for him.

returns, under the name of Lara, to his ancestral home. In this guise he is even more "Byronic." Here is Lara from the long narrative poem *Lara* published in 1814:

> There was in him a vital scorn of all:
> As if the worst had fallen which could befall,
> He stood a stranger in this breathing world,
> An erring Spirit from another hurled. . . .
> His presence haunted still; and from the breast
> He forced an all unwilling interest:
> Vain was the struggle in that mental net—
> His spirit seemed to dare you to forget!

Such are a few features of the brooding, lonely, haunting Byronic hero, the character who captured the imagination of readers and writers in every country of the Western world. He—or someone like him—has appeared in novel after novel (and in more recent times in movie after movie). He is the Romantic hero incarnate.

Of course Conrad-Lara was identified with his creator. But even though all Byron's major works are strongly autobiographical, he himself was not quite so simple as the romantic, brooding outsider that his public believed him to be. He was often scornful and aloof, but he was fond of company, generous to his friends, and high-spirited at congenial parties. He was extremely handsome, highly attractive to women, and full of physical daring and courage. Yet he suffered from a congenital lameness and made himself an accomplished rider, swordsman, and swimmer to conceal and to compensate for his handicap. (One of his most famous feats was to swim the Hellespont, now called the Dardanelles, a narrow body of water between Europe and Asia.) He was also inclined to be fat and was forced to starve himself periodically in order to avoid reaching grotesque proportions. As a member of the House of Lords he frequently spoke for liberalism in politics, yet his personal social attitudes were conservative and aristocratic. He died in Greece of a fever contracted when he selflessly and generously organized an expedition to aid the Greeks in their revolt for independence from the Turks. Yet he was doubtful that the cause could succeed and knew that his own motives for joining the fight were not completely idealistic, for he was profoundly bored with the life he left to become a soldier. He was capable of great tenderness and love, yet much of his life was scandalous. He loved England and the gentlemanly pleasures of country life, yet he lived in European exile from 1816 until his death. The only large fact about Byron that cannot be qualified is that he was the most fluent and prolific of the English Romantic poets and one of the best-known authors in the 19th-century world.

Childe Harold's Pilgrimage

In 1815 Byron married, most uncongenially and unhappily, as it soon became clear. His violent reactions to the unsuccessful marriage led, finally, to social ostracism, and in 1816 Byron left England never to return. From the Continent in that same year he sent back to his publishers the third canto of *Childe Harold's Pilgrimage*, a long narrative poem he had begun in 1809 after his travels abroad. Harold, the hero ("Childe" is a medieval word for a young noble awaiting knighthood), undergoes a number of adventures that parallel the events of Byron's turbulent life; and, when Canto III appeared in 1816, it was eagerly read for its reflection of Byron's exile. One section of it presents the Romantic hero in the situation in which many other writers would place him again and again: he is alone on an Alpine peak in Switzerland. His ambitions, like nature, lie spread out before him as he looks out upon a stormy mountain landscape. What does he want? He wants the power to make all men quaver at his words, as the scene before him bows before the lightning. The Romantic hero wants a power of imagination as irresistible as the powers of nature itself. (The following excerpt comes toward the end of Canto III.)

from Childe Harold's Pilgrimage

Lord Byron

All Heaven and Earth are still—though not in sleep,
But breathless, as we grow when feeling most;
And silent, as we stand in thoughts too deep—
All Heaven and Earth are still: From the high host
Of stars, to the lulled lake and mountain-coast,   5
All is concentered in a life intense,
Where not a beam, nor air, nor leaf is lost,
But hath a part of Being, and a sense
Of that which is of all Creator and Defense.

Then stirs the feeling infinite, so felt   10
In solitude, where we are *least* alone;
A truth, which through our being then doth melt,
And purifies from self: it is a tone,
The soul and source of Music, which makes known
Eternal harmony, and sheds a charm   15
Like to the fabled Cytherea's zone,[1]
Binding all things with beauty—'twould disarm
The specter Death, had he substantial power to harm.

Not vainly did the early Persian make
His altar the high places,[2] and the peak   20
Of earth-o'ergazing mountains, and thus take
A fit and unwalled temple, there to seek
The Spirit, in whose honor shrines are weak,
Upreared of human hands. Come, and compare
Columns and idol-dwellings—Goth or Greek—   25
With Nature's realms of worship, earth and air—
Nor fix on fond abodes to circumscribe thy prayer![3]

---

1 **Cytherea's** (sĭth'ə rē'əz) **zone:** belt, or sash, of Venus; worn by a mortal, it attracted love.
2 **Not vainly . . . places:** The early Persians, worshipers of nature, did not build temples, but sought mountain peaks and other high places of natural beauty that they deemed appropriate for the worship of nature.
3 **Come . . . prayer:** The poet implies that the structures erected by the Greeks and Goths were inferior as places of worship to naturally beautiful places.

The sky is changed! and such a change!   Oh Night,
And Storm, and Darkness, ye are wondrous strong,
Yet lovely in your strength, as is the light   30
Of a dark eye in Woman!   Far along,
From peak to peak, the rattling crags among
Leaps the live thunder!   Not from one lone cloud,
But every mountain now hath found a tongue,
And Jura⁴ answers, through her misty shroud,   35
Back to the joyous Alps, who call to her aloud!

And this⁵ is in the Night—Most glorious Night!
Thou wert not sent for slumber! let me be
A sharer in thy fierce and far delight,
A portion of the tempest and of thee!   40
How the lit lake shines, a phosphoric sea,
And the big rain comes dancing to the earth!
And now again 'tis black, and now, the glee
Of the loud hills shakes with its mountain-mirth,
As if they did rejoice o'er a young Earthquake's birth.   45

Now, where the swift Rhone⁶ cleaves his way between
Heights which appear as lovers who have parted
In hate, whose mining depths⁷ so intervene,
That they can meet no more, though brokenhearted:
Though in their souls, which thus each other thwarted,   50
Love was the very root of the fond rage
Which blighted their life's bloom, and then departed—
Itself expired, but leaving them an age
Of years all winter—war within themselves to wage:

Now, where the quick Rhone thus hath cleft his way,   55
The mightiest of the storms hath ta'en his stand:
For here, not one, but many,⁸ make their play
And fling their thunderbolts from hand to hand,
Flashing and cast around: of all the band,
The brightest through these parted hills hath forked   60
His lightnings, as if he did understand,
That in such gaps as Desolation worked,
There the hot shaft should blast whatever therein lurked.

---

4 **Jura:** a mountain range, mostly between France and Switzerland, its highest peaks over
five thousand feet.
5 **this:** the storm.
6 **Rhone:** a great river flowing from the Alps of Switzerland to the Gulf of Lions in France.
7 **mining depths:** The valleys between the peaks are deep as mines.
8 **many:** i.e., storms.

Sky—Mountains—River—Winds—Lake—Lightnings! ye!
With night, and clouds, and thunder—and a Soul   65
To make these felt and feeling, well may be
Things that have made me watchful; the far roll
Of your departing voices is the knoll[9]
Of what in me is sleepless—if I rest.
But where of ye, O Tempests! is the goal?   70
Are ye like those within the human breast?
Or do ye find, at length, like eagles, some high nest?

Could I embody and unbosom now
That which is most within me, could I wreak
My thoughts upon expression, and thus throw   75
Soul—heart—mind—passions—feelings—strong or weak—
All that I would have sought, and all I seek,
Bear, know, feel—and yet breathe—into *one* word,
And that one word were Lightning, I would speak;
But as it is, I live and die unheard,   80
With a most voiceless thought, sheathing it as a sword.

                    ✿   ✿   ✿

I have not loved the World, nor the World me;
I have not flattered its rank breath, nor bowed
To its idolatries a patient knee,
Nor coined my cheek to smiles, nor cried aloud   85
In worship of an echo: in the crowd
They could not deem me one of such—I stood
Among them, but not of them—in a shroud
Of thoughts which were not their thoughts, and still could,
Had I not filed[10] my mind, which thus itself subdued.   90

I have not loved the World, nor the World me,—
But let us part fair foes; I do believe,
Though I have found them not, that there may be
Words which are things—hopes which will not deceive,
And Virtues which are merciful, nor weave   95
Snares for the failing: I would also deem
O'er others' griefs that some sincerely grieve—
That two, or one, are almost what they seem—
That Goodness is no name—and Happiness no dream.

9 **knoll:** knell.
10 **filed:** defiled (see *Macbeth*, III, i, 65). He has defiled his mind by trying to have
thoughts like those of other men.

Comment

Byron's hero, momentarily at least, gives up "the World"—society—for nature. Alone and in exile he has set forth on a journey, or pilgrimage, in search of himself—a true self that he could not find in relations with other men.

1. In the first stanza, what is the condition of the natural world on which Harold is gazing? How does his own condition parallel that of the natural scene?
2. What happens to the natural scene beginning in lines 28-45? Why is it appropriate that the mountain peaks now (ll. 46-54) should be compared to lovers who have been separated by anger?
3. In lines 64-72 Harold calls out to a series of natural forces: "Sky—Mountains—River—Winds—Lake—Lightnings!" What forces in himself does he call upon in a similar series in lines 73-81?
4. What relation between himself and the natural world does Harold express in lines 64-81? How does it differ from his relation to "the World," as he expresses it in lines 82-90?

Don Juan

In 1818 Byron began a poem, *Don Juan,* with a different kind of hero. (It should be pronounced *dŏn jōō′ ən, not* as in Spanish.) Childe Harold was terribly serious about his ambitions. Don Juan, although Byron conducts him through many adventures more exciting and more violent than those of his predecessor, is never permitted to take himself quite so seriously. He is a figure through whom Byron could even make fun of the poetic ambitions of Childe Harold. In the following selection from Canto I, Juan is in a lonely situation somewhat like that of the previous passage, though he is not in solitary splendor on top of an alp. His situation is much more traditionally poetic: he is alone in a quiet woodland dreaming of love.

from **Don Juan**

Lord Byron

Silent and pensive, idle, restless, slow,
   His home deserted for the lonely wood,
Tormented with a wound he could not know,
   His, like all deep grief, plunged in solitude:
I'm fond myself of solitude or so,   5
   But then, I beg it may be understood,
By solitude I mean a Sultan's (not
A Hermit's), with a haram[1] for a grot.[2] . . .

Young Juan wandered by the glassy brooks,
   Thinking unutterable things; he threw   10
Himself at length within the leafy nooks
   Where the wild branch of the cork forest grew;
There poets find materials for their books,
   And every now and then we read them through,
So that their plan and prosody[3] are eligible,   15
Unless, like Wordsworth, they prove unintelligible.

He, Juan (and not Wordsworth), so pursued
   His self-communion with his own high soul,
Until his mighty heart, in its great mood,
   Had mitigated part, though not the whole   20
Of its disease; he did the best he could
   With things not very subject to control,
And turned, without perceiving his condition,
Like Coleridge, into a metaphysician.[4]

He thought about himself, and the whole earth,   25
   Of man the wonderful, and of the stars,
And how the deuce they ever could have birth;
   And then he thought of earthquakes, and of wars,
How many miles the moon might have in girth,
   Of air-balloons, and of the many bars   30
To perfect knowledge of the boundless skies—
And then he thought of Donna Julia's eyes.

1 **haram:** harem; women's quarters.
2 **grot:** cave.
3 **prosody** (prŏs′ə dĭ): system of versification.
4 **metaphysician:** one skilled in abstract reasoning.

In thoughts like these true Wisdom may discern
　　Longings sublime, and aspirations high,
Which some are born with, but the most part learn　　　35
　　To plague themselves withal, they know not why:
'Twas strange that one so young should thus concern
　　His brain about the action of the sky;
If *you* think 'twas Philosophy that this did,
I can't help thinking puberty assisted.　　　　　　　40

He pored upon the leaves, and on the flowers,
　　And heard a voice in all the winds; and then
He thought of wood-nymphs and immortal bowers,
　　And how the goddesses came down to men:
He missed the pathway, he forgot the hours,　　　　45
　　And when he looked upon his watch again,
He found how much old Time had been a winner—
He also found that he had lost[5] his dinner.

5 **lost**: missed.

Comment

It perhaps comes as a shock that Byron makes fun of Don Juan by
comparing him with Wordsworth and Coleridge, but Byron had no
sympathies with the poets of the Lake District. He respected only Shelley among his contemporaries, and in *Don Juan* he made many a satiric
joke at the expense of the solemnity and seriousness of Wordsworth,
Southey, and Coleridge. Through Don Juan, indeed, he made fun of
almost every contemporary manner and assumption.

1. How would you describe the tone of the first four lines of the first
   stanza? And what happens to this tone in the second half of the
   stanza? Do you find a repetition of this pattern in the next two
   stanzas?
2. The rhyme scheme of the stanzas of this passage is called ottava
   rima (it was used by Chaucer, among others), rhyming *abababcc*.
   How does Byron's use of the final couplet (*cc*) in each stanza emphasize his comic, satiric effect? Do you find any particularly outrageous final rhymes?
3. You have seen what his contemplation of nature does for Childe
   Harold. What does *his* do for Don Juan? Childe Harold, too, is
   presented to us as an "I"; *Don Juan* is in the third person. How
   does this difference in point of view assist Byron's satiric fun?

4. Childe Harold exclaims:

> I live and die unheard,
> With a most voiceless thought, sheathing it as a sword.

Speaking about Don Juan's condition, Byron says,

> Longings sublime, and aspirations high,
> Which some are born with, but the most part learn
> To plague themselves withal, they know not why. . . .

What difference do you see between these two assertions? What do they suggest to you about Byron's poetic development? How is he unlike other Romantic poets?

"She Walks in Beauty"

Byron was many-sided, and it would be unfair to leave him without a representative of his lovely lyrics. The following poem, written in 1814 while he was still in England, was occasioned by Byron's first sight of Mrs. Robert Wilmot, a second cousin, who came to a ball dressed in a black gown (for mourning) covered with spangles (the period of mourning was nearly over). The poem appeared in a book called *Hebrew Melodies*, a collection of lyrics made by a young friend of Byron's who adapted a number of contemporary poems to old Jewish airs. It expresses a kind of reverence for women that Byron's enemies thought he entirely lacked.

She Walks in Beauty

Lord Byron

She walks in beauty, like the night
 Of cloudless climes and starry skies;
And all that's best of dark and bright
 Meet in her aspect and her eyes:
Thus mellowed to that tender light   5
 Which Heaven to gaudy day denies.

One shade the more, one ray the less,
 Had half impaired the nameless grace
Which waves in every raven tress,
 Or softly lightens o'er her face;   10
Where thoughts serenely sweet express,
 How pure, how dear their dwelling place.

And on that cheek, and o'er that brow,
　　So soft, so calm, yet eloquent,
The smiles that win, the tints that glow,　　　　15
　　But tell of days in goodness spent,
A mind at peace with all below,
　　A heart whose love is innocent!

Comment

In the dress and appearance of his cousin, Byron finds an expression of her character. What is the full beauty she walks in?

1. The lady's dress, with silver spangles on a black background, is like the dark night with its bright stars. How is the combination of light and dark repeated farther on in stanza 1? And how (in stanza 2) is the light and dark motif repeated?
2. The combination of light and dark in dress, eyes, and face is a delicately balanced "nameless grace." The final stanza is exclamatory— it is not an assertion, it has no independent clause. How does the final stanza, in its grammar as well as in the characteristics it describes, make us aware of the lady's "nameless grace"?
3. As you consider the three selections from Byron presented here, what sort of figure does he seem to you to have been? Why is it impossible to label him simply and easily?

Unacknowledged Legislators

"POETS ARE THE unacknowledged legislators of the world," said Shelley, and he said "unacknowledged" without bitterness, for he did not mean that poets should necessarily be in Parliament. He did mean that poets are as necessary to society as are lawmakers or even as necessary to society as government itself. Legislators tell people their duties as members of a particular nation or state. Poets, however, tell people their duties as members of the human race—their duties as human beings. The imagination of the poet speaks to the imagination that is in every person and thereby reveals to all a tie, deeper than the bond of citizenship, that unites human beings whatever their nation, whatever their class. According to both Shelley and Keats, the poet speaks to the imaginative depths in all people, depths that would remain hidden from all until and unless their imaginations were spoken to by the poet.

Shelley and Keats were themselves two such "legislators." It is true that they were in their lifetime unknown and unacknowledged as compared with Scott and Byron; but their achievements, particularly those of Keats, have grown steadily in importance over the past century and a quarter.

Villa Magni, Shelley's home on the Gulf of Spezia. Shelley was sailing his boat, the Don Juan, *near here when it sank in a squall, and he was drowned.*

Percy Bysshe Shelley (1792-1822)

We have already seen a portrait of Shelley as a student at Oxford, an intense young man interested in chemistry and mineralogy. Six months later, having been expelled from the university for refusing to answer questions about an antireligious pamphlet he had written, he was living in London. From there he eloped with a young schoolmate of his sisters'; her family, he believed, were tyrants because they wanted to compel her to go to school. The young couple were married in Scotland, and after some wanderings in Ireland they returned to London, where Shelley came under the influence of William Godwin, a writer who argued for social justice and the perfectability of man. Shelley fell in love with Godwin's daughter Mary. (She is famous in literary history as the author of *Frankenstein*, a tale of terror about a young medical student who creates a monstrous artificial man that eventually destroys him.) And abandoning Harriet, his young wife, Shelley fled with Mary Godwin to France. Two years later Harriet drowned herself, and Shelley's conduct was regarded by many as so monstrous that he was refused the custody of their two children. He and Mary were married, and in 1818 moved to Italy for the last four years of his short, violent life. He was drowned in 1822.

Byron said of Shelley that he was "without exception the *best* and least selfish man I ever knew." It is a judgment that many believed only another irresponsible man could have made. And yet Shelley was in many respects generous and selfless. He inherited a fortune but gave it away to help his struggling young writer-friends. He tried to befriend Keats and wrote *Adonais,* a great elegy in his memory, when Keats died. Shelley's many acts of rebellion brought him no rewards: they were the acts of a visionary whose intense idealism was so uncompromising that it brought him much sorrow and unhappiness.

"To a Skylark"

The intensity of Shelley's convictions about the art of poetry appears in one of his best-known and most sustained lyrics, "To a Skylark." Mary Shelley described the origin of this poem: "It was on a beautiful summer evening while wandering [near Leghorn, Italy] among the lanes, whose myrtle hedges were the bowers of the fireflies, that we heard the caroling of the skylark, which inspired one of the most beautiful of his poems." Wordsworth, we have seen, believed in a "deep power of joy" that enabled him to "see into the life of things." For Shelley, the song of the unseen skylark rises in the evening air like something from the spiritual world—it is a "blithe spirit," an "unbodied joy." And it symbolizes to him the kind of poetry he most desires to utter.

To a Skylark

Percy Bysshe Shelley

Hail to thee, blithe spirit!
   Bird thou never wert,
That from heaven, or near it,
   Pourest thy full heart
In profuse strains of unpremeditated art.   5

Higher still and higher
   From the earth thou springest
Like a cloud of fire;
   The blue deep thou wingest,
And singing still dost soar, and soaring ever singest.   10

In the golden lightning
    Of the sunken sun,
O'er which clouds are bright'ning,
    Thou dost float and run;
Like an unbodied[1] joy whose race is just begun.   15

The pale purple even[2]
    Melts around thy flight;
Like a star of heaven,
    In the broad daylight
Thou art unseen, but yet I hear thy shrill delight,   20

Keen as are the arrows
    Of that silver sphere,[3]
Whose intense lamp narrows
    In the white dawn clear,
Until we hardly see, we feel that it is there.   25

All the earth and air
    With thy voice is loud,
As, when night is bare,
    From one lonely cloud
The moon rains out her beams, and heaven is overflowed.   30

What thou art we know not;
    What is most like thee?
From rainbow clouds there flow not
    Drops so bright to see,
As from thy presence showers a rain of melody.   35

Like a poet hidden
    In the light of thought,
Singing hymns unbidden,
    Till the world is wrought
To sympathy with hopes and fears it heeded not: 40

Like a high-born maiden
    In a palace tower,
Soothing her love-laden
    Soul in secret hour
With music sweet as love, which overflows her bower: 45

1 **unbodied:** disembodied.
2 **even:** evening.
3 **silver sphere:** the morning star.

PERCY BYSSHE SHELLEY   **527**

Like a glowworm golden
        In a dell of dew,
Scattering unbeholden
        Its aërial hue
Among the flowers and grass, which screen it from view: 50

Like a rose embowered
        In its own green leaves,
By warm winds deflowered,[4]
        Till the scent it gives
Makes faint with too much sweet these heavy-wingèd thieves:[5]   55

Sound of vernal showers
        On the twinkling grass,
Rain-awakened flowers,
        All that ever was
Joyous, and clear, and fresh, thy music doth surpass: 60

Teach us, sprite or bird,
        What sweet thoughts are thine:
I have never heard
        Praise of love or wine
That panted forth a flood of rapture so divine.   65

Chorus Hymeneal,[6]
        Or triumphal chant,
Matched with thine would be all
        But an empty vaunt,
A thing wherein we feel there is some hidden want.   70

What objects are the fountains[7]
        Of thy happy strain?
What fields, or waves, or mountains?
        What shapes of sky or plain?
What love of thine own kind? what ignorance of pain?   75

With thy clear keen joyance
        Languor cannot be:
Shadow of annoyance
        Never came near thee:
Thou lovest; but ne'er knew love's sad satiety.   80

---

4 **deflowered:** fully opened.
5 **thieves:** i.e., the winds.
6 **Chorus Hymeneal** (hī'mə nē'əl): wedding song.
7 **fountains:** sources.

Waking or asleep,
Thou of death must deem
Things more true and deep
Than we mortals dream,
Or how could thy notes flow in such a crystal stream?   85

We look before and after,
And pine for what is not:
Our sincerest laughter
With some pain is fraught;
Our sweetest songs are those that tell of saddest thought.   90

Yet if we could scorn
Hate, and pride, and fear;
If we were things born
Not to shed a tear,
I know not how thy joy we ever should come near.   95

Better than all measures
Of delightful sound,
Better than all treasures
That in books are found,
Thy skill to poet were, thou scorner of the ground!   100

Teach me half the gladness
That thy brain must know,
Such harmonious madness
From my lips would flow,
The world should listen then, as I am listening now.   105

Comment

From the invisible lark comes a song of joy that fills the evening air. No human song could be so joyous, Shelley says, for the "sweetest songs" of men "are those that tell of saddest thought." And yet any poet who knew but half the joy and gladness expressed in the song of the lark would make poems that the world could not resist hearing.

1. After the opening invocation—"Hail to thee"—Shelley describes the song of the lark by comparing it with phenomena of the sky (ll. 11-35). In lines 18-25, for example, he compares the song to the light of the morning star in the rising dawn. What other images of light appear in these opening stanzas? How does each emphasize both the lark's invisibility and the diffusion of its song?
2. Next, in lines 36-55, the song is compared to scenes and creatures of the earth, beginning with the poet who is "hidden" in the radi-

ance of his own thought. How is the "hidden" quality in this comparison repeated in the following similes? For example, the "high-born maiden" is soothing her soul in "*secret* hour."

3. The source of the song of the lark is then invisible, for the bird cannot be seen; and its source in another sense, the bird's gladness of heart and mind, is "hidden." The poet asks, "Teach us, sprite [spirit] or bird, / What sweet thoughts are thine." And although they are "hidden" from him, in what way does the poet believe these "thoughts" must differ from the thoughts and feelings he and other men share?

4. In his final address to the lark, the poet says that if the song could teach him "half the gladness" known to the bird, he would be able to utter a "harmonious madness" that all the world would listen to, as he listens to the lark. Why would the perfect song of the poet be a "harmonious madness"?

"Ode to the West Wind"

The song of a skylark inspired "To a Skylark." In the preceding year (1819) Shelley had experienced an inspiration even more intense; and about the "Ode to the West Wind," which he then wrote, he said, "This poem was conceived and chiefly written in a wood that skirts the Arno [River], near Florence, and on a day when that tempestuous wind, whose temperature is at once mild and animating, was collecting the vapors which pour down the autumnal rains." His observations of the autumnal Mediterranean wind recur throughout the poem in detail and with exactness. But they are more than observations of the weather and the cycle of the seasons. The west wind is the "breath of autumn's being," and a "Wild Spirit"; in Latin (and in other languages) the words for "breath," "spirit," "soul," and "wind" have a common root; in Latin, *spiritus* means both "breath" and "breath of life," or "spirit." Shelley's "Ode to the West Wind" is a poem of "inspiration"—of "breathing in"—in the deepest and oldest sense. It is a poem in which he asks to be inspired by the power of ongoing nature itself.

Ode
to the
West Wind

Percy Bysshe Shelley

[handwritten margin note: married a 16 yr old girl, Left her after 3 yrs started to wonder remarried but she drowned herself. Went to Italy + wrote many poems; Ode to the West Wind, and To a skylark. Wrote prose + several phuisophical essays]

1

O, wild West Wind, thou breath of Autumn's being,
Thou, from whose unseen presence the leaves dead
Are driven, like ghosts from an enchanter fleeing,

Yellow, and black, and pale, and hectic[1] red,   5
Pestilence-stricken multitudes: O, thou,
Who chariotest to their dark wintry bed   [handwritten: Earth]

The wingèd seeds, where they lie cold and low,
Each like a corpse within its grave, until
Thine azure sister of the Spring[2] shall blow

Her clarion[3] o'er the dreaming earth, and fill   10
(Driving sweet buds like flocks to feed in air)
With living hues and odors plain and hill:

Wild Spirit, which art moving everywhere;
Destroyer and preserver; hear, O, hear!

2   [handwritten: Air]

Thou on whose stream, 'mid the steep sky's commotion,   15
Loose clouds like earth's decaying leaves are shed,
Shook from the tangled boughs of Heaven and Ocean,

Angels of rain and lightning:[4] there are spread
On the blue surface of thine airy surge,
Like the bright hair uplifted from the head   20

1 **hectic:** feverish.
2 **Thine . . . Spring:** the reviving south wind of the springtime.
3 **clarion:** loud trumpet (see l. 69).
4 **Thou . . . lightning:** The streaming wind tears fragments of cloud ("leaves") from large clouds that are formed by the mixture of water and air ("tangled boughs of Heaven and Ocean"); the "Loose clouds" are messengers, indications ("angels") of the approaching autumnal storms.

Of some fierce Maenad,[5] even from the dim verge
Of the horizon to the zenith's height
The locks of the approaching storm.   Thou dirge

Of the dying year, to which this closing night
Will be the dome of a vast sepulcher,   25
Vaulted with all thy congregated might

Of vapors, from whose solid atmosphere
Black rain, and fire, and hail will burst: O, hear!

3

Thou who didst waken from his summer dreams
The blue Mediterranean, where he lay,   30
Lulled by the coil of his crystàlline streams,[6]

Beside a pumice[7] isle in Baiae's[8] bay,
And saw in sleep old palaces and towers
Quivering within the wave's intenser day,[9]

All overgrown with azure moss and flowers   35
So sweet, the sense faints picturing them!   Thou
For whose path the Atlantic's level powers

Cleave themselves into chasms, while far below
The sea-blooms and the oozy woods which wear
The sapless foliage of the ocean, know   40

Thy voice, and suddenly grow gray with fear,
And tremble and despoil themselves:[10] O, hear!

4

If I were a dead leaf thou mightest bear;
If I were a swift cloud to fly with thee;
A wave to pant beneath thy power, and share   45

The impulse of thy strength, only less free
Than thou, O, uncontrollable!   If even
I were as in my boyhood, and could be

---

5 **Maenad** (mē′năd): nymph; attendant of the Greek god of wine and vegetation.
6 **coil . . . streams:** currents of the sea, often multicolored.
7 **pumice** (pŭm′ĭs): porous volcanic stone.
8 **Baiae** (bā′yē): a village west of Naples.
9 **wave's intenser day:** Colors reflected in water, as Shelley once noted, are more vivid yet more harmonious than when seen directly.
10 **Thou . . . themselves:** In a note on these lines Shelley said that "The phenomenon . . . is well known to naturalists. The vegetation at the bottom of the sea . . . sympathizes with that of the land in the change of seasons. . . ."

The comrade of thy wanderings over heaven,
As then, when to outstrip thy skiey speed   50
Scarce seemed a vision; I would ne'er have striven

As thus with thee in prayer in my sore need.
Oh! lift me as a wave, a leaf, a cloud!
I fall upon the thorns of life!   I bleed!

A heavy weight of hours has chained and bowed   55
One too like thee: tameless, and swift, and proud.

5

Make me thy lyre,[11] even as the forest is:
What if my leaves are falling like its own!
The tumult of thy mighty harmonies

Will take from both[12] a deep, autumnal tone,   60
Sweet though in sadness.   Be thou, Spirit fierce,
My spirit!   Be thou me, impetuous one!

Drive my dead thoughts over the universe
Like withered leaves to quicken a new birth!
And, by the incantation of this verse,   65

Scatter, as from an unextinguished hearth
Ashes and sparks, my words among mankind!
Be through my lips to unawakened earth

The trumpet of a prophecy!   O, Wind,
If Winter comes, can Spring be far behind?   70

---

11 lyre (līr): a wind harp (aeolian lyre) that sounds a chord when the wind blows through it.
12 both: i.e., "the forest" and "me."

Comment

In *A Defense of Poetry* Shelley wrote,

> A man cannot say, "I will compose poetry." The greatest poet
> even cannot say it; for the mind in creation is as a fading coal,
> which some invisible influence, like an inconstant wind, awakens
> to transitory brightness. . . .

The true poet must be inspired, and in the west wind Shelley sees a
huge symbol of true inspiration. What can such inspiration accomplish?

1. "Ode to the West Wind" is most carefully wrought. Each stanza (or strophe, as it is sometimes called in an ode) is the length of a sonnet, with four tercets (or three-line units) rhyming *aba, bcb, cdc, ded,* and a final couplet *ee.* Read the final couplets of the five stanzas. How is the movement of the whole ode suggested by the sequence of the final couplets?
2. Each of the first three stanzas is concerned with the west wind's effects on a part of nature. How are these three stanzas summarized in the opening of the fourth stanza? But what has the poet now added to his observations of the effects of the autumnal wind? If he was observing before, what does he here begin to do?
3. What relation between the poet and the west wind is announced in the fourth stanza? How are they alike? But how are they different?
4. The fifth stanza begins "Make me thy lyre" and ends "Be through my lips . . . the trumpet. . . ." What difference do you find between these two images? What happens to the tone of the final stanza as we move from "lyre" to "trumpet"?
5. The "trumpet" will announce a "prophecy": How does the "prophecy" repeat the description of the west wind in the first stanza as "Destroyer and preserver" (l. 14)?
6. If the west wind symbolizes true inspiration for Shelley, what will the words of the inspired poet do to mankind? In what sense will his poetry, like the west wind, be both a "destroyer" and a "preserver"?

"Ozymandias"

In the preceding poems Shelley brings his observations of the lark and the wind to bear upon his desires and ambitions as a poet: the large word in each of them is "I." In the following poem, however, the "I" appears but once, to start the narrative told by a traveler from a distant place about a monument from a distant time.

Ozymandias

Percy Bysshe Shelley

I met a traveler from an antique land
Who said: Two vast and trunkless legs of stone
Stand in the desert. Near them, on the sand,
Half sunk, a shattered visage lies, whose frown,
And wrinkled lip, and sneer of cold command,   5
Tell that its sculptor well those passions read
Which yet survive, stamped on these lifeless things,
The hand that mocked them and the heart that fed:[1]
And on the pedestal these words appear:
"My name is Ozymandias, king of kings: 10
Look on my works, ye Mighty, and despair!"
Nothing beside[2] remains. Round the decay
Of that colossal wreck, boundless and bare
The lone and level sands stretch far away.

1 **Which . . . fed:** The passions expressed by the statue have survived the hand of the sculptor who imitated them and the heart of the king that fed them.
2 **beside:** besides; else.

Comment

Ozymandias was a legislator very much acknowledged. He was Ramses II of Egypt, and an ancient historian tells us that his statue, the largest in Egypt, had this inscription: "I am Ozymandias, king of kings; if any man wishes to know what I am and where I am buried, let him surpass me in some of my deeds." The sculptor, however, is nameless. What inference can we draw from this traveler's tale?

1. What comment is made by the contrast between the last three lines of the sonnet and the words of the inscription?
2. Whose "works," then, *do* survive, according to this story? Who has been the most permanent "legislator," the mighty king or the nameless sculptor?

John Keats (1795-1821)

Although John Keats died at twenty-five, an age at which most young men are but beginning their careers, he produced some poetic masterpieces—and in his letters expressed some insights—that few writers have equaled in full lifetimes. Most of his greatest achieve-

*In this building in Rome
next to the Spanish Steps
is the apartment where
Keats spent the last
months of his life and
where he died.*

ments, in fact, occurred in the months between January and September of 1819. It was as if he somehow knew how short his time would be.

Keats died of tuberculosis, the disease that killed his mother and one of his brothers. His father, a prosperous livery-stable owner, sent him to a good school. The guardian who managed the family affairs after the death of both parents apprenticed Keats to a doctor, and at the age of twenty he studied medicine at Guy's Hospital in London. A year later he abandoned medicine for poetry. In 1818 he fell deeply in love with Fanny Brawne, a girl without literary interests but with a great fund of good sense. They never married. In the autumn of 1820 Keats went to Italy seeking a warmer climate after his physician had told him that he could not survive another cold winter in England. On February 23, 1821, he died in Rome and was buried there in the Protestant cemetery.

Leigh Hunt, an editor, critic, and essayist who was close to Shelley and Godwin, wrote this description of Keats as he was near the end of his life:

> He was under the middle height; and his lower limbs were small in comparison with the upper, but neat and well turned. His shoulders were very broad for his size: he had a face in which energy and sensibility were remarkably mixed up; an

eager power, checked and made patient by ill health. Every feature was at once strongly cut, and delicately alive. If there was any faulty expression, it was in the mouth, which was not without something of a character of pugnacity. His face was rather long than otherwise; the upper lip projected a little over the under; the chin was bold, the cheeks sunken; the eyes mellow and glowing; large, dark, and sensitive. At the recital of a noble action, or a beautiful thought, they would suffuse with tears and his mouth trembled. In this, there was ill health as well as imagination, for he did not like these betrayals of emotion; and he had great personal as well as moral courage. He once chastised a butcher, who had been insolent, by a regular stand-up fight. His hair, of a brown color, was fine, and hung in natural ringlets. The head was a puzzle for the phrenologists, being remarkably small in the skull; a singularity which he had in common with Byron and Shelley, whose hats I could not get on. Keats was sensible of the disproportion above noticed, between his upper and lower extremities; and he would look at his hand, which was faded and swollen in the veins, and say it was the hand of a man of fifty.

Hunt speaks of Keats's dislike for "betrayals of emotion," and for all the richly sensuous qualities of his poetry, Keats rarely—at his best never—surrendered himself to his feelings as Shelley did. He dedicated himself to the achievement of an imaginative discipline, a discipline that would free him from both an "irritable reaching after fact and reason" and from what he called "the egotistical sublime"—the setting up of a huge "I." The poet must have no "self," he said, for he must lose himself in the scenes and experiences made by the imagination. Some of his contemporaries, Shelley among them, recognized his fresh and exciting powers. But the reviewers, especially of his early poems, did not; one of his poems, *Endymion*, received one of the most savagely hostile reviews of the early 19th century. Yet in the next generation—to the poet Tennyson, for example—Keats had become one of the glories of the Romantic movement.

"On First Looking into Chapman's Homer"

One night in the autumn of his twenty-first year Keats sat up until dawn reading an old book—new to him—with his former teacher, Charles Cowden Clarke. Clarke, who generously assisted Keats's literary education over many years, had introduced him to a vigorous translation of Homer's *Iliad* and *Odyssey* made by the Elizabethan poet George Chapman. In the ten o'clock mail, not many hours after they had separated, Clarke received this sonnet from his pupil and friend.

JOHN KEATS

537

On First
Looking into
Chapman's Homer

John Keats

Much have I traveled in the realms of gold,
    And many goodly states and kingdoms seen;
    Round many western islands have I been
Which bards in fealty[1] to Apollo[2] hold.
Oft of one wide expanse had I been told   5
    That deep-browed Homer ruled as his demesne;[3]
    Yet did I never breathe its pure serene[4]
Till I heard Chapman speak out loud and bold:
Then felt I like some watcher of the skies
    When a new planet swims into his ken;   10
Or like stout Cortez[5] when with eagle eyes
    He stared at the Pacific—and all his men
Looked at each other with a wild surmise—
    Silent, upon a peak in Darien.[6]

1 **fealty** (fē′əl tǐ): duty owed by a vassal to his feudal lord.
2 **Apollo:** Greek god of poetry and music.
3 **demesne** (dǐ mēn): estate ruled by a feudal lord.
4 **serene:** clear air.
5 **Cortez** (kôr tĕz′): It was Balboa, not Cortez, who discovered the Pacific.
6 **Darien** (dâr′ǐ ĕn′): Panama.

Comment

Keats's experience of Chapman's translation of Homer was an experience of discovery. It came upon him after he had read ("traveled in") much literature ("realms of gold") and had surveyed many works of modern European literature ("western islands"). What was this discovery like?

1. In the first six lines Keats uses a number of political metaphors; he speaks of works of literature as "realms," islands held in "fealty," and Homer's "demesne." What period of European history are these words drawn from?

2. In what period of European history did watchers of the skies begin to see new planets? In what period did Balboa stare at the Pacific? What happened to the worlds of astronomy and geography in that period?

3. The "wide expanse" of Homer's poetry was to Keats as vast as the Pacific. Yet Homer "ruled" this "wide expanse" as if it were his "demesne." What power does Keats attribute to Homer? Why is it a power that makes Keats "silent"?

Keats's first Shakespearean sonnet, and one of his most personal ones, is dated January, 1818. He was twenty-two, and he had many poetic ambitions to fulfill. It is a poem in which "I" does strongly appear, and the first line tells us why.

When I Have Fears

John Keats

When I have fears that I may cease to be
   Before my pen has gleaned my teeming brain,
Before high-pilèd books, in charact'ry,[1]
   Hold like rich garners the full-ripened grain;
When I behold, upon the night's starred face,   5
   Huge cloudy symbols of a high romance,
And think that I may never live to trace
   Their shadows, with the magic hand of chance;
And when I feel, fair creature of an hour!
   That I shall never look upon thee more,   10
Never have relish in the faery[2] power
   Of unreflecting love!—then on the shore
Of the wide world I stand alone, and think
Till love and fame to nothingness do sink.

1 **charact'ry:** characters; symbols used to express thought.
2 **faery:** magic; enchanting.

Comment

In the Italian sonnet, as you may remember, the "turn" comes after the first eight lines (the octave), and the last six (sestet) resolve the dramatic situation presented in the beginning. In the English or Shakespearean sonnet, as here, the resolution comes late—often not until the final couplet—after the dramatic situation has been presented in three divisions. What is most astonishing about this sonnet is the way its grammar rushes us on to its resolution.

1. "When I have fears . . . ," "When I behold . . . ," "And when I feel . . .": these are all subordinate clauses. Where do you find the conjunction that balances all the "when's"? And where do you find the independent verbs of the whole single sentence that makes up this sonnet?

2. In what metaphor does Keats describe his writing in the first four lines? And in what metaphor, in the second four lines? Which

metaphor seems to you to express more powerfully the promise and the fertility of the poetic imagination? Explain why it does so.

3. "I stand alone, and think," Keats says in the final couplet. Shelley, you recall, exclaimed, "I fall upon the thorns of life! I bleed!" What difference do you see between the "I" of this sonnet and the "I" of "Ode to the West Wind"?

"To Autumn"

It perhaps comes as a surprise that the Romantic poets, for all their desire to speak in the real language of men and to speak directly to the imagination that slumbers in all men, resorted frequently to the ode, the most formal and highly wrought of all lyric poems. The ode was originally a song sung by a Greek chorus; it was used by Roman poets; it was a favorite form of the English poets of the Enlightenment. Yet Wordsworth and Coleridge wrote odes, and we have seen Shelley's highly organized "Ode to the West Wind." In Keats's period of greatest productivity, in 1819, he turned again and again to this most formal of verse forms. No one, before or since, achieved the union of formality and natural imagery that we find in "To Autumn."

To Autumn

John Keats

Season of mists and mellow fruitfulness,
    Close bosom-friend of the maturing sun;
Conspiring with him how to load and bless
    With fruit the vines that round the thatch-eves run;
To bend with apples the mossed cottage trees,   5
    And fill all fruit with ripeness to the core;
        To swell the gourd, and plump the hazel shells
With a sweet kernel; to set budding more,
    And still more, later flowers for the bees,
Until they think warm days will never cease,   10
        For Summer has o'erbrimmed their clammy cells.

Who hath not seen thee oft amid thy store?
    Sometimes whoever seeks abroad may find
Thee sitting careless on a granary floor,
    Thy hair soft-lifted by the winnowing wind;   15
Or on a half-reaped furrow sound asleep,

Drowsed with the fume of poppies, while thy hook[1]
    Spares the next swath and all its twinèd flowers:
And sometimes like a gleaner thou dost keep
    Steady thy laden head across a brook;   20
    Or by a cider-press, with patient look,
      Thou watchest the last oozings hours by hours.

Where are the songs of Spring? Ay, where are they?
    Think not of them, thou hast thy music too—
While barrèd clouds bloom the soft-dying day,   25
    And touch the stubble plains with rosy hue;
Then in a wailful choir the small gnats mourn
    Among the river sallows,[2] borne aloft
      Or sinking as the light wind lives or dies;
And full-grown lambs loud bleat from hilly bourn;[3]   30
    Hedge crickets sing; and now with treble soft
The redbreast whistles from a garden croft;[4]
    And gathering swallows twitter in the skies.

1 **hook:** sickle or scythe.
2 **sallows:** willow trees.
3 **bourn:** region.
4 **croft:** plot.

Comment

Each stanza of this short ode is addressed to autumn: the first directly, the second as if autumn were both the lord of an estate and the laborers on it, and the last through the very being of the season, particularly its sounds. Each stanza, furthermore, has a pervading tone. Notice what the tone of each is and Keats's use of specific words and images to create each. Notice also the feeling of serenity characterizing the entire ode.

1. In stanza 1 what pervading characteristic does Keats give to autumn? Notice such words as *load, bend, fill, swell,* and *plump* and the part they play in creating this quality.
2. In stanza 2 what is the dominant tone? What images contribute to establishing this tone?
3. What gives the hint of melancholy, of things coming to an end, in the third stanza?
4. The poet here is an observer, but an observer without an obtrusive "I": he is neither the "innocent observer" of the Enlightenment nor the observer of the power of the autumnal west wind. How does this observer differ from those two? How would you characterize this observer?

JOHN KEATS   **541**

"Ode on a Grecian Urn"

The art of ancient Greece was to many writers in England, France, and Germany a source of inspiration in the late 18th and early 19th centuries. Keats saw with awe and delight works of art from ancient Greece that were exhibited in the British Museum. The urn, or vase, from ancient Greece that he contemplates in this ode is a generalized version of many of its kind. As one turns such an urn, he sees a series of groups in succession—young men pursuing young maidens in a dance, a piper playing under the trees, a pair of young lovers in the wood, and a religious procession led by a priest who is bringing a young ox to a sacrifice. Keats sees each of these designs in turn, and sees them as an example of the ancient art that moved naturally and inevitably from love between men and women to religion. His conclusion, that "Beauty is truth, truth beauty," is an expression that many people have quoted and interpreted, though not always in connection with its place in this poem. Its meaning, its conclusiveness, can be understood only through the poem.

Ode on
a Grecian Urn

John Keats

1

Thou still unravished bride of quietness,
    Thou foster child of silence and slow time,
Sylvan historian,[1] who canst thus express
    A flowery tale more sweetly than our rhyme:
What leaf-fringed[2] legend haunts about thy shape   5
    Of deities or mortals, or of both,
        In Tempe[3] or the dales of Arcady?[4]
What men or gods are these? What maidens loth?
    What mad pursuit? What struggle to escape?
        What pipes and timbrels?[5] What wild ecstasy?   10

---

1 **Sylvan historian:** The urn first presents a woodland (sylvan) scene.
2 **leaf-fringed:** Greek urns usually had a leaf-pattern "collar."
3 **Tempe** (tĕm′pĭ): a pleasant valley in Greece; in poetry a synonym for rural beauty.
4 **Arcady** (är′kə dĭ): Arcadia, in Greece; a carefree paradise.
5 **timbrels:** small hand drums.

Heard melodies are sweet, but those unheard
    Are sweeter; therefore, ye soft pipes, play on;
Not to the sensual ear, but, more endeared,
    Pipe to the spirit ditties of no tone:[6]
Fair youth, beneath the trees, thou canst not leave   15
    Thy song nor ever can those trees be bare;
        Bold Lover, never, never canst thou kiss,
Though winning near the goal—yet, do not grieve;
    She cannot fade, though thou hast not thy bliss,
        Forever wilt thou love, and she be fair!   20

3

Ah, happy, happy boughs! that cannot shed
    Your leaves, nor ever bid the Spring adieu;
And, happy melodist, unwearièd,
    Forever piping songs forever new;
More happy love! more happy, happy love!   25
    Forever warm and still to be enjoyed,
        Forever panting, and forever young;
All breathing human passion far above,
    That leaves a heart high-sorrowful and cloyed,
        A burning forehead, and a parching tongue.   30

4

Who are these coming to the sacrifice?
    To what green altar, O mysterious[7] priest,
Lead'st thou that heifer lowing at the skies,
    And all her silken flanks with garlands dressed?
What little town by river or sea shore,   35
    Or mountain-built with peaceful citadel,
        Is emptied of this folk, this pious morn?
And, little town, thy streets forevermore
    Will silent be; and not a soul to tell
        Why thou are desolate, can e'er return.   40

5

O Attic[8] shape! Fair attitude! with brede
    Of marble men and maidens overwrought,[9]
With forest branches and the trodden weed;

---

6 **ditties of no tone:** unheard songs, unheard by the ear of sense.
7 **mysterious:** concerned with religious mysteries.
8 **Attic:** Athenian; Greek.
9 **brede . . . overwrought:** ornamented with a connected pattern.

Thou, silent form, dost tease us out of thought
As doth eternity: Cold Pastoral![10]   45
When old age shall this generation waste,
Thou shalt remain, in midst of other woe
Than ours, a friend to man, to whom thou say'st,
"Beauty is truth, truth beauty"—that is all
Ye know on earth, and all ye need to know.   50

10 Pastoral: country scene or story.

Comment

The urn, clearly, is a thing of beauty to Keats. Just as clearly, it presents, unmoving and frozen in sculpture, scenes from a moving, vital way of life. That way of life has passed. Is its "truth," then, only to be found in the "beauty" of its representation—in the reliefs on the urn that commemorate it?

1. The groups or panels on the urn present ancient woodland scenes. They are thus a kind of "Sylvan historian"—they tell the history of a past way of life. Keats in the first stanza asks a series of questions about this way of life. Why should he be unsure whether the "legend"—the history—concerns "deities" or "mortals" or "both"?
2. In the second and third stanzas the poet begins to answer his questions. What sort of music is it that plays only to the spirit (l. 14)? And what sort of love is it (ll. 15-20) that can never cease pursuit and never fade? the love of gods or men or both?
3. What recapitulation of stanza 2 occurs in stanza 3?
4. In stanza 4 we come to the religious procession. The scene is clear, but why should the poet be puzzled—why should he ask about the "little town" from which the procession has come? The town, of course, is unrepresented on the urn. How is the poet's question about it related to his opening question about "deities or mortals"?
5. In the final stanza the poet exclaims, "Cold Pastoral!" The scenes themselves are "pastoral"—they are rural woodland scenes with men and maidens, the piper, the procession. And these scenes are "cold" in that they are now preserved in the cold material of the urn. In what other sense is the urn a "cold" pastoral? What is its effect on the poet (l. 44)?
6. The ode ends with the famous statement of the equivalence of beauty and truth. What is the beauty that he has seen in the urn? And what is the only truth he has found with which to answer his questions? Can the urn lead him back fully into the life of the ancient Greeks? Or can he know no more than the beauty of that life captured by one of its artists?

The nightingale's song has haunted English poets since the days of Chaucer (and with good reason: no other bird's song is like it). In the spring of 1819, while staying with a friend near London, Keats heard the song of a nightingale more than once, and from that experience came one of his greatest odes. Like Shelley listening to the song of the lark, he expresses a desire to lose himself in the "full-throated ease" of the nightingale. But unlike Shelley, he relinquishes his identification with the bird as its song dies away.

Ode to a Nightingale

John Keats

1

My heart aches, and a drowsy numbness pains
   My sense, as though of hemlock[1] I had drunk,
Or emptied some dull opiate to the drains
   One minute past, and Lethe-wards[2] had sunk:
'Tis not through envy of thy happy lot,   5
   But being too happy in thine happiness—
      That thou, light-wingèd Dryad[3] of the trees,
        In some melodious plot
Of beechen green, and shadows numberless,
      Singest of summer in full-throated ease.   10

2

O, for a draught of vintage! that hath been
   Cooled a long age in the deep-delvèd earth,
Tasting of Flora[4] and the country green,
   Dance, and Provençal song,[5] and sunburnt mirth!
O for a beaker full of the warm South,   15
   Full of the true, the blushful Hippocrene,[6]
      With beaded bubbles winking at the brim,
        And purple-stainèd mouth;
That I might drink, and leave the world unseen,
      And with thee fade away into the forest dim: 20

1 **hemlock:** a poisonous herb; not an evergreen.
2 **Lethe** (lē′thĭ)-**wards:** toward the river in Hades that causes forgetfulness.
3 **Dryad** (drī′əd): Greek tree nymph.
4 **Flora:** Roman goddess of flowers.
5 **Provençal** (prō′vən säl′) **song:** Provence in southern France was the home of the medieval troubadours.
6 **Hippocrene** (hĭp′ə krēn′): fountain of the Muses, Greek goddesses of the arts and sciences.

3

Fade far away, dissolve, and quite forget
   What thou among the leaves hast never known,
The weariness, the fever, and the fret
   Here, where men sit and hear each other groan;
Where palsy shakes a few, sad, last gray hairs,   25
   Where youth grows pale, and specter-thin, and dies;
   Where but to think is to be full of sorrow
      And leaden-eyed despairs,
Where Beauty cannot keep her lustrous eyes,
   Or new Love pine at them beyond tomorrow.   30

4

Away! away! for I will fly to thee,
   Not charioted by Bacchus and his pards,[7]
But on the viewless[8] wings of Poesy,[9]
   Though the dull brain perplexes and retards:
Already with thee! tender is the night,   35
   And haply[10] the Queen-Moon is on her throne,
     Clustered around by all her starry Fays;[11]
      But here there is no light,
Save what from heaven is with the breezes blown
   Through verdurous[12] glooms and winding mossy ways.   40

5

I cannot see what flowers are at my feet,
   Nor what soft incense hangs upon the boughs,
But, in embalmèd[13] darkness, guess each sweet
   Wherewith the seasonable month endows
The grass, the thicket, and the fruit tree wild;   45
   White hawthorn, and the pastoral eglantine;[14]
     Fast fading violets covered up in leaves;
      And mid-May's eldest child,
The coming musk rose, full of dewy wine,
   The murmurous haunt of flies on summer eves.   50

---

7 **Bacchus** (băk′əs) **and his pards:** The Roman god of wine had a chariot drawn by leopards.
8 **viewless:** invisible.
9 **Poesy:** poetry.
10 **haply:** perhaps.
11 **Fays:** fairies; attendants.
12 **verdurous:** thick and green.
13 **embalmed:** aromatic; perfumed.
14 **pastoral eglantine:** country honeysuckle.

                                  THE ROMANTIC PERIOD

6

Darkling[15] I listen; and, for many a time
    I have been half in love with easeful Death,
Called him soft names in many a musèd[16] rhyme,
    To take into the air my quiet breath;
Now more than ever seems it rich to die,   55
    To cease upon the midnight with no pain,
        While thou art pouring forth thy soul abroad
           In such an ecstasy!
    Still wouldst thou sing, and I have ears in vain—
    To thy high requiem become a sod.   60

7

Thou wast not born for death, immortal Bird!
    No hungry generations tread thee down;
The voice I hear this passing night was heard
    In ancient days by emperor and clown:
Perhaps the selfsame song that found a path   65
    Through the sad heart of Ruth,[17] when, sick for home,
        She stood in tears amid the alien corn;[18]
           The same that ofttimes hath
    Charmed magic casements, opening on the foam
    Of perilous seas, in faery[19] lands forlorn.   70

8

Forlorn! the very word is like a bell
    To toll me back from thee to my sole self!
Adieu! the fancy[20] cannot cheat so well
    As she is famed to do, deceiving elf
Adieu! adieu! thy plaintive anthem fades   75
    Past the near meadows, over the still stream,
        Up the hillside; and now 'tis buried deep
           In the next valley glades:
    Was it a vision, or a waking dream?
    Fled is that music—Do I wake or sleep?   80

15 Darkling: existing in the dark.
16 mused: meditated.
17 Ruth: heroine of the Old Testament Book of Ruth, who after her husband's death went to his mother's land and worked in the fields.
18 corn: wheat.
19 faery: magic; enchanted.
20 fancy: imagination.

Comment

Keats's meditation ends with a question, "Do I wake or sleep?" He asks whether his experience was "a vision, or a waking dream." But the questions do not mean simply "Where am I?" For he has been through an experience of listening, meditating, and thinking that has left him changed, even though he has had to return from it to the real world and to "my sole self." What has happened to him?

1. The duration of Keats's meditation on the nightingale's song is clearly marked, though often missed. What time of day is it, and where is he in relation to the bird at line 9? at line 35? What time at line 56? Where is he in relation to the bird at lines 75-78?

2. In stanza 1 Keats expresses a joy—"too happy in thine happiness"— in the song of the bird. But what is the character of this joy? Why is it like the condition of one who has drunk hemlock?

3. How in stanza 2 does Keats ask for an intensification of this joy? What does the verb "fade" (l. 20) tell us of his desire? What does it tell us about the song of the nightingale? And how does stanza 3, which picks up "fade," explain his desire?

4. In stanza 4 the poet reaches the nightingale, not by fading away but by the power of poetry. It is night; yet he knows where he is. What senses tell him where he is (stanzas 4 and 5)?

5. At stanza 6 his relation to the bird begins to change: he withdraws from the richness of the flowers and wood into himself. With what thoughts does he turn to himself? How are we prepared for these thoughts in stanza 3? And how does he turn away from them at the end of stanza 6, in lines 59-60?

6. In stanza 7 he addresses the nightingale again. What permanence does he now hear in the song? How has the song, for him, "charmed magic casements"? What "perilous seas," what "faery [magic] lands" has the song of the nightingale opened to him?

7. In the final stanza the poet returns to his "sole self." The "fancy," the "viewless wings of Poesy," cannot keep him permanently "with thee." His imagination cannot "cheat"—he must come back to the real world. Yet his concluding questions imply he has been changed by his experience. The nightingale and its song were, for a time, a part of his world. What did they show him? How did they change him?

The Romantic Period
Summing Up

1. The following passage comes from a long 14th-century romance, "The Flower and the Leaf." It was translated at the end of the 17th century by John Dryden, who thought it was by Chaucer. It describes another nightingale, one heard first by an unknown, late-medieval poet, and then reheard by one of the great poets of the Enlightenment.

> So sweet, so shrill, so variously she sung,
> That the grove echoed, and the valleys rung,
> And I so ravished with her heavenly note,

I stood entranced, and had no room for thought,
But all o'erpowered with ecstasy of bliss,   5
Was in a pleasing dream of Paradise:
At length I waked, and looking round the bower
Searched every tree, and pried on every flower,
If anywhere by chance I might espy
The rural poet of the melody;   10
For still methought she sung not far away:
At last I found her on a laurel spray.
Close by my side she sat, and fair in sight,
Full in a line, against her opposite,
Where stood with eglantine the laurel twined;   15
And both their native sweets were well conjoined.
    On the green bank I sat, and listened long;
(Sitting was more convenient for the song:)
Nor till her lay was ended could I move,
But wished to dwell forever in the grove.   20
Only methought the time too swiftly passed,
And every note I feared would be the last.
My sight and smell and hearing were employed,
And all three senses in full gust enjoyed.
And what alone did all the rest surpass,   25
The sweet possession of the fairy place;
Single, and conscious to my self alone
Of pleasures to the excluded world unknown;
Pleasures which nowhere else were to be found,
And all Elysium in a spot of ground.   30

Write an essay on the difference between "Nature" in this excerpt and "Nature" in the poetry of the Romantic period. How is the scene of this poem different from the landscape that Wordsworth looked at in "Tintern Abbey"? How does the effect of this nightingale's song differ from the effect on Shelley of the song of the soaring skylark? And, most important, how does this experience of a nightingale's song differ from that of Keats in his "Ode to a Nightingale"?

2. Shelley, Byron, and Keats all wrote plays that are called "closet dramas" because they do not lend themselves to the theater, but are poems to be read rather than performed. They also wrote poems of individual experience—often with an "I" at the center—that we cannot imagine as plays at all. Why can we not imagine "Tintern Abbey" or "Ode to the West Wind" or "Ode on a Grecian Urn" as plays? What experience did the poets of the Romantic period try to express that did not fall into dramatic form, as that of the Elizabethans did?

3. Write an essay comparing the essayists of the Enlightenment with the poets of the Romantic period as critics of their societies.

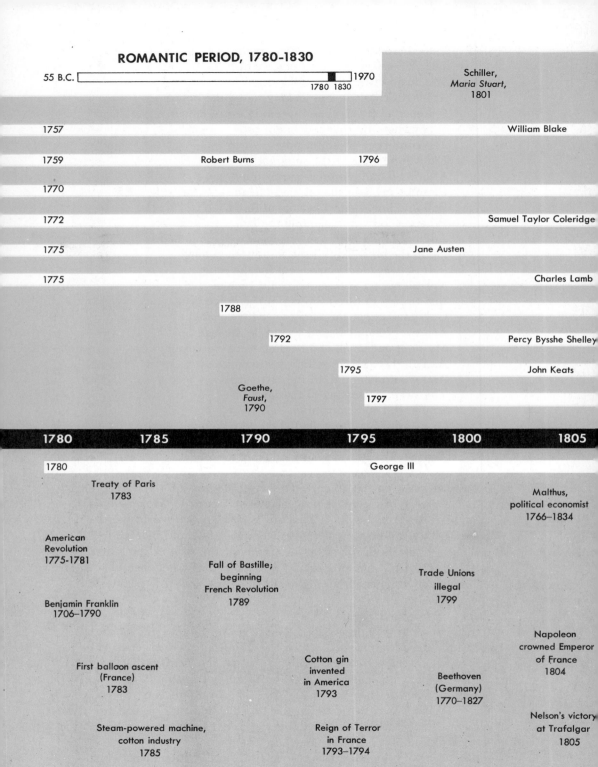

ROMANTIC PERIOD, 1780-1830

55 B.C. |▭▭▭▭▭▭▭▭▭▭▭▭▭▭▭▭■▭| 1970
1780 1830

Schiller,
Maria Stuart,
1801

1757 — William Blake

1759 — Robert Burns — 1796

1770

1772 — Samuel Taylor Coleridge

1775 — Jane Austen

1775 — Charles Lamb

1788

1792 — Percy Bysshe Shelley

1795 — John Keats

Goethe,
Faust,
1790 — 1797

| **1780** | **1785** | **1790** | **1795** | **1800** | **1805** |

1780 — George III

Treaty of Paris
1783

Malthus,
political economist
1766–1834

American
Revolution
1775-1781

Fall of Bastille;
beginning
French Revolution
1789

Trade Unions
illegal
1799

Benjamin Franklin
1706–1790

Napoleon
crowned Emperor
of France
1804

First balloon ascent
(France)
1783

Cotton gin
invented
in America
1793

Beethoven
(Germany)
1770–1827

Nelson's victory
at Trafalgar
1805

Steam-powered machine,
cotton industry
1785

Reign of Terror
in France
1793–1794

Washington Irving,
The Sketch Book,
1819–1820

1827

William Cullen Bryant,   Heine,
Thanatopsis,   *Book of Songs,*
1817   1827

William Wordsworth   1850

1834

1817   James Fenimore Cooper,
The Last of the Mohicans,
1826

1834

Lord Byron   1824

1822

1821

Mary Wollstonecraft Shelley (author of *Frankenstein*)   1851

| 1810 | 1815 | 1820 | 1825 | 1830 | 1835 |

1811 //////// Regency //////// 1820
1820   George IV   1830

Corn Laws
1815

Abolition of   Steam-powered   Monroe
slave trade   presses used on   Doctrine
by England   *The Times*   1823
1807   1814
                                               Trade Unions
                                               legalized
War of 1812   1824
1812–1815

                                               First photograph—Niepce
Napoleon's   Wellington   (France)
Russian   defeats Napoleon   1826
campaign   at Waterloo
1812   1815   Completion of
                                               first railroad
Congress of Vienna   in England
1814–1815   1825

551

A portrait of the young Queen Victoria in her coronation robes.

The Victorian Period

> WISDOM, *a name to shake*
> *All evil dreams of power.* . . .
>
> ALFRED, LORD TENNYSON

THOMAS CARLYLE, a great essayist and critic of the early Victorian period, characterized the times in which he lived with these words:

> Were we required to characterize this age of ours by any single epithet, we should be tempted to call it, not an Heroical, Devotional, Philosophical, or Moral Age, but, above all others, the Mechanical Age. It is the Age of Machinery, in every outward and inward sense of that word. . . .

Carlyle pointed to the new factories and mills that were driving "the living artisan" from his home workshop into the cities. He witnessed the application of coal power to the looms of the "clothiers" that Daniel Defoe had seen a hundred years earlier, and he saw the growth of mills even larger than the one Robert Southey had visited some twenty years earlier. By the middle of the 19th century the steam engine had made England the foremost industrial nation of the world. Machinery had turned the craft of the artisan into big business.

Carlyle granted that the progress of industry had changed many things for the better. He saw that the new factories made many people better fed, clothed, and housed than they had ever been before. But he warned his readers against the encroachments of machinery upon life:

> Not the external and physical alone is now managed by machinery, but the internal and spiritual also. . . . For the same habit regulates not our modes of action alone, but our modes of thought and feeling. Men are grown mechanical in head and in heart, as well as in hand.

The entrance to the railway in Liverpool in the early days of the pioneer Liverpool & Manchester Railway line, which opened in 1830. The locomotive revolutionized the transportation system of England.

And for Carlyle, as well as for many serious writers of his time, the task of the writer was to resist this mechanizing of the "head and heart." More and more people were reading books, and the invention of the steam-driven press produced a vast ocean of print—newspapers, magazines, pamphlets, and books in undreamed of numbers. Many were trash that revealed all too clearly Carlyle's contention that not only "the external and physical" world were being managed by machinery, but the spiritual world also. Some, however, and they are the works of writers in this chapter, tried to temper the new power of the machine with wisdom. The serious writers were critics of the life around them.

The Writer's Language

THE VICTORIAN writer lived in a society that had grown so large and continued to grow so fast that great talent was required of anyone who might try to disengage a single experience, a single individual character, from the buzzing life around him or her and make it into something representative of the whole. It was easier to report than to create —and sometimes more useful too. For the fast-growing society needed great quantities of information to keep in touch with itself, to connect all the rapidly diversifying functions of a modern industrial nation.

THE VICTORIAN PERIOD

The steamship Great Eastern *laying the Atlantic cable, which connected England and North America by telegraph. By the 1880's all but the most remote corners of the world were joined by deep-sea cables.*

Information was needed to run the new mills, to find new markets, to keep order in the crowded cities. The dependence of industries at home upon the affairs of nations abroad was clear, and news of the world was everyone's interest. Journalism came of age in the Victorian period.

Once again, machinery was behind it all. In 1814 *The Times* of London (still today a most influential newspaper) began printing with a steam-powered press; by the middle of the century its improved presses could print forty thousand copies of the paper in four hours. The tax on newspapers was ended in 1855, and in that year appeared the first penny paper, soon to be followed by many others. The new presses soon made newsprint as common as the paving stones of the street. Magazines and periodicals of all sorts flourished. For the leaders of society there were *The Times* and the quarterlies, solemn, lengthy, authoritative reviews of literature and politics. For the greater mass of the public there were the new Sunday papers with their supplements full of gossip about the rich and stories of sensational crimes. There were new magazines devoted to sporting news; there were old ones such as *The Newgate Calendar*, a weekly that since the late 18th century had been publishing stories of crime and reports of the final words of famous criminals sent to the scaffold. The presses ground out huge quantities of print, and the public eagerly bought and read.

The Crystal Palace was erected in Hyde Park for the Great Exhibition of 1851, which housed exhibits of England's industrial achievements for some six million visitors to see.

The relation of the reader to the page before him or her had changed enormously since the first printed books of the Renaissance. Not only had people learned to read silently, they now read as if to hypnotize themselves. Passengers in trams (streetcars), trains, and buses occupied their minds with reading that was quite literally a "pass-time." Reading became a way of insulating oneself from the noise and confusion of the crowded transport and the busy city. Journalists adapted their style to the new conditions; they produced quantities of simple, short articles that the mind could master almost at a glance. They dug up sensational stories and provided their readers with odd gossip. They were not interested in improving public tastes, but they gave people a great quantity of information in a style and a form that they could readily understand.

Journalistic practices even invaded the world of literature. Most of the novels of Charles Dickens were published in paperback monthly installments (or "numbers") that sold for a shilling; some appeared in installments in the two newspapers that Dickens himself managed. But while a mid-century bookseller or news distributor might sell 250 copies of a monthly number of one of Dickens's novels, he normally sold up to six thousand copies of the weekly numbers of "Ella the Out-

THE VICTORIAN PERIOD

London slums in the 1870's. This engraving by the French artist Gustave Doré shows the dirty, crowded workers' houses huddling beneath the shadow of the railway and its viaducts.

cast," or "Gentleman Jack," or "Gambler's Wife." The production of cheap fiction and "penny dreadfuls" became a lucrative industry. Early in the period certain publishers had produced encyclopedias in weekly numbers for a penny, and many men rose from the working class with the knowledge they made available. But public libraries came into being in 1850, and in 1870 there began the system of "board schools"—public education—that provided for the many what the few had earlier sought out for themselves. At mid-century, among the "lower orders" (as all those below the great middle class were called), about two-thirds to three-quarters of the population were literate, though many who could read did not know how to write. But in the last quarter of the century the almost universally literate population supported a great number of publishing enterprises that produced sensational stories and sober political analyses, humorous sketches and serious religious tracts, trashy novels and great summations of man's new social experience.

The new words that entered the English language during the Victorian period reflect the growth of society. Until the 1860's there was no word for unemployment; the economists spoke only of "overpopulation." "Altruism" was introduced near the middle of the century as

Ruins of the British Residency in Lucknow, India, after the mutiny of the Indian army in 1857 against the British. The British Empire expanded rapidly during the 19th century, particularly from 1870 on when England gained many colonies in Africa and Asia.

thinkers tried to clarify the role of charity in the new society. Jeremy Bentham, a philosopher and political scientist of the early Victorian period, first used the word *community* to refer to the country as a whole; he also coined the word *international*—and apologized for doing so! Words were proposed for new functions in society: *physicist, biologist, scientist* and other *ists* named the new specialists and their branches of knowledge.

Between the middle classes and the "lower orders" there were many differences that all were aware of—differences of income, of job (sometimes the "white-collar worker," as he came to be called, was paid less than the master machinist in overalls, but his job was more "respectable"); there were differences of dress, of interests in sport, of the hours for meals and the food eaten at them. But the most persistent differences were those of speech. The middle-class merchant who aspired to be "respectable," or more, to be a "gentleman," took care to imitate the educated speech that was based on the authority of Johnson's *Dictionary.* He did not drop his *h*'s: after a day at the office he went home, not "ome," and he looked after his health, not "is ealth." He tried, too, to remove all traces of the dialect of the region where he was born, if he did not come from London. He supported "good" literature

Chemistry   Landon Eason I

$$\frac{2.3 \text{ g Na}}{} \left| \frac{11 \text{ atoms}}{1 \text{ g}} \right. = 25.3 \text{ atoms}$$

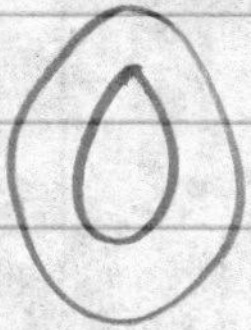

$$\frac{3.01 \times 10^{23} \text{M}}{} \left| \frac{211.4 \text{ g}}{1 \text{ M}} \right.$$

39.1
 3
‾‾‾‾
117.3

23
11
‾‾‾
23
230
‾‾‾
25.3

$39.1 \times 3 = 117.3$

$30.1 \times 1 = 30.1$

$16.0 \times 4 = \underline{64.0}$

211.4

16.0
 4
‾‾‾
64.0

3.01
211.40
12040
‾‾‾‾‾
30100

Many Happy Returns of the Day, *painted by William P. Frith in 1856, is a picture of comfortable, secure, middle-class Victorian family life.*

—at least his library table supported it—but he read the newspapers. He separated himself from those below him in society by many formidable barriers, though none was so formidable, so supple, and so subtle as the way in which he used his native language.

In a society such as this it is not surprising that the great hopes and achievements of the Romantic writer were ignored by most readers. We find traces of the Romantic vision in the early poetry of Tennyson, and we find it in the early poetry of Matthew Arnold, but we find it emerging most strongly only as we approach the close of the period. Arnold, a critic, a Professor of Poetry at Oxford, and an inspector of schools, as well as a leading poet, showed that the Romantic dream was not dead when he wrote in 1865:

> The grand power of poetry is its interpretative power; by which I mean, not a power of drawing out in black and white an explanation of the mystery of the universe, but the power of so dealing with things as to awaken in us a wonderfully full, new, and intimate sense of them, and of our relations with them. When this sense is awakened in us, as to objects without us, we feel ourselves to be in contact with the essential nature of those objects, to be no longer bewildered and oppressed by them, but

to have their secret, and to be in harmony with them; and this feeling calms and satisfies us as no other can.

With its emphasis on poetry as that which awakens in us a sense of the mystery of nature, this passage might have been written by Wordsworth or Keats.

But this was for Arnold only one of the powers of poetry. The other was "moral profundity." As he put it in what is perhaps the most famous statement about the nature of poetry in the 19th century:

It is important to hold fast to this: that poetry is at bottom a criticism of life; that the greatness of a poet lies in his powerful and beautiful application of ideas to life—to the question: How to live?

The fresh vision of the world was not quite enough; the poet must never forget that readers must learn "how to live."

With this power of poetry the prose writers, the novelists, were in full agreement. Both Charles Dickens and William Makepeace Thackeray, the two greatest novelists of the mid-century, never lost sight of the moral responsibilities of their calling. They thought of themselves as preachers, and indeed they sometimes interrupted their stories to preach a message based on the situations they described.

The problem of the writer was put a little differently by the essayist Thomas De Quincey, who not only knew Wordsworth and Coleridge but lived on into Carlyle's "Mechanical Age" until 1859. In a famous passage published in 1848 he described two kinds of literature:

In that great social organ, which collectively we call literature, there may be distinguished two separate offices that may blend and often *do* so, but capable severally of a severe insulation, and naturally fitted for reciprocal repulsion. There is, first, the literature of *knowledge*, and, secondly, the literature of *power*. The function of the first is—to *teach;* the function of the second is—to *move:* the first is a rudder, the second an oar or a sail. The first speaks to the *mere* discursive understanding; the second speaks ultimately, it may happen, to the higher understanding or reason, but always *through* affections [feelings] of pleasure and sympathy.

The difference between the literature of knowledge and the literature of power, as De Quincey saw it, was a deep one. They repel each other, and they are insulated from each other, although sometimes they may be blended. De Quincey went on, perhaps a little unfairly, to give as an example of the first, a cookbook, and as an example of the second, Milton's *Paradise Lost*. Certainly a cookbook can teach us something, and certainly Milton's great poem moves us. But most Victorian writers wanted to do both—they wanted the ship of literature to be complete, with both a rudder and oars or a sail. They tried to achieve a blend of knowledge and power.

To reach the great audience of the new society—to both teach them and move them—it was necessary to write naturally and simply. It was necessary to speak a language something like that which Wordsworth had called "the language really used by men." And sometimes it was not easy to satisfy that audience. Tennyson, the greatest poet of the age, once wrote:

> I have known an old fishwife, who had lost two sons at sea, clench her fist at the advancing tide on a stormy day, and cry out, "Ay! roar, do! how I hates to see thee show thy white teeth." Now if I had adopted her exclamation and put it into the mouth of some old woman in one of my poems, I dare say the critics would have thought it original enough, but would most likely have advised me to go to Nature for my old women and not to my imagination. . . .
>
> When I was about twenty-one I went on a tour to the Pyrenees. Lying among these mountains before a waterfall that comes down one thousand or twelve hundred feet I sketched it (according to my custom then) in these words:
> > Slow-dropping veils of thinnest lawn.
>
> When I printed this, a critic informed me that "lawn" was the material used in theaters to imitate a waterfall, and graciously added: "Mr. T. should not go to the boards [stage] of a theater but to Nature herself for his suggestions." And I *had* gone to Nature herself.

But whatever their difficulties, the poets and essayists and novelists of the Victorian Age were determined men and women, and their mission was clear to them. As Matthew Arnold put it,

> The future of poetry is immense, because in poetry, where it is worthy of its high destinies, our race, as time goes on, will find an ever surer and surer stay. There is not a creed which is not shaken, not an accredited dogma which is not shown to be questionable, not a received tradition which does not threaten to dissolve.

The poet, the writer, that is, in the fullest and most serious sense of the word, must provide the stay, the support, that people need as old customs and beliefs fall away. The people of his time, said Arnold, needed "ideas" with which to understand the bewildering variety of new facts that confronted them. Facts and machinery seemed to threaten the mental and moral lives of all. "But for poetry," said Arnold, "the idea is everything."

March of the Chartists in London, 1848. The Chartist movement, the first important effort of working-class self-help, was rooted in economic and social distress and demanded political and constitutional reform.

The People and Their Times

QUEEN VICTORIA succeeded to the throne in 1837, a young and inexperienced girl of eighteen. The entry she made in her diary on that occasion tells us much about the moral earnestness which she lived by and diffused among her subjects during her long reign (from 1837 to 1901):

> Since it has pleased Providence to place me in this station, I shall do my utmost to fullfil my duty toward my country; I am very young and perhaps in many, though not in all things, inexperienced, but I am sure, that few have more real good will and more real desire to do what is fit and right than I have.

"To do what is fit and right" and to do it by hard, earnest work is perhaps not the most exalted ideal in human history, but it is a practical one; it is an ideal that was within the grasp of the humblest citizen.

And certainly there was much to be done. There had lately (1832) been passed the Great Reform Bill that extended the power of the vote to members of the middle class whose new towns and industrial centers had for too long been unrepresented in Parliament. Much would have to be done to better the lot of the factory worker: children six and eight years old still worked ten to twelve hours a day in the mills and the mines. Women worked sixteen-hour days in garment factories for wages so small that we cannot believe them now. In one London

THE VICTORIAN PERIOD

block about four hundred yards square some 12,000 persons lived in some 1400 dwellings. Water and sanitary systems were so primitive that cholera broke out in London in the middle of the century. With the factory had come the *slums:* the origin of this word is uncertain, but it entered the language in the Victorian period, and what it referred to could no longer be ignored.

Changes came slowly: "self-help" was a favorite word of the century, and most men were wary of extending the powers of government to help improve conditions. In 1851 there occurred the Great Exhibition, a kind of World's Fair held in London in the spacious Crystal Palace, a huge structure of iron and glass built for the purpose; and in the official catalogue of the Exhibition is this representative sentence:

> The great constitutional freedom which this country enjoys, may be ascribed in some measure to the reluctance which the Government always shows to act on behalf of the people in any case where it is possible they can act for themselves.

And acting for themselves the British people accomplished much in the 19th century.

It is an old saying that an Englishman's home is his castle. The Victorian Englishman made for himself a domestic life as solid as a fortress. It was a world of heavy furniture, heavy meals, stern fathers, and strict mothers. There was much piety—in many households the servants and the family gathered each morning while the father read from the Bible. There were many good works—missions, hospitals, foundling homes, and charity wards multiplied in every city. But the ideal of "what is fit and right" was not shared by all, and the solid world of our Victorian ancestors came to an end with the beginning of yet another world that was ushered in by the first World War of 1914.

The Smugness of Success

Mr. Podsnap, the subject of the following sketch, was not a real person, for he was invented by Charles Dickens in one of his last novels, *Our Mutual Friend* (1865). Mr. Podsnap, as you will see, is something like the mechanical man that Carlyle warned against; he would indeed be a monster but for one thing: the humor with which Dickens has drawn his portrait. Mr. Podsnap represents the worst kind of Victorian smugness; but it is essential to remember that the man who imagined him was also a Victorian, and one who had a weapon more powerful against the machinery of smugness than any other: laughter. The most powerful critics of the Victorian scene were the Victorians themselves.

PODSNAPPERY

Mr. Podsnap was well to do, and stood very high in Mr. Podsnap's opinion. Beginning with a good inheritance, he had married a good inheritance, and had thriven exceedingly in the Marine Insurance way, and was quite satisfied. He never could make out why everybody was not quite satisfied, and he felt conscious that he set a brilliant social example in being particularly well satisfied with most things, and, above all other things, with himself.

Thus happily acquainted with his own merit and importance, Mr. Podsnap settled that whatever he put behind him he put out of existence. There was a dignified conclusiveness—not to add a grand convenience—in this way of getting rid of disagreeables which had done much toward establishing Mr. Podsnap in his lofty place in Mr. Podsnap's satisfaction. "I don't want to know about it; I don't choose to discuss it; I don't admit it!" Mr. Podsnap had even acquired a peculiar flourish of his right arm in often clearing the world of its most difficult problems, by sweeping them behind him (and consequently sheer away) with those words and a flushed face. For they affronted him.

Mr. Podsnap's world was not a very large world, morally; no, nor even geographically: seeing that although his business was sustained upon commerce with other countries, he considered other countries, with that important reservation, a mistake, and of their manners and customs would conclusively observe, "Not English!" when, Presto! with a flourish of the arm, and a flush of the face, they were swept away. Elsewise, the world got up at eight, shaved close at a quarter past, breakfasted at nine, went to the City[1] at ten, came home at half past five, and dined at seven. Mr. Podsnap's notions of the Arts in their integrity might have been stated thus. Literature: large print, respectfully descriptive of getting up at eight, shaving close at a quarter past, breakfasting at nine, going to the City at ten, coming home at half past five, and dining at seven. Painting and Sculpture: models and portraits representing Professors of getting up at eight, shaving close at a quarter past, breakfasting at nine, going to the City at ten, coming home at half past five, and dining at seven. Music: a respectable performance (without variations) on stringed and wind instruments, sedately expressive of getting up at eight, shaving close at a quarter past, breakfasting at nine, going to the City at ten, coming home at half past five, and dining at seven. Nothing else to be permitted to those same vagrants the Arts, on pain of excommunication. Nothing else To Be—anywhere!

As a so eminently respectable man, Mr. Podsnap was sensible of its being required of him to take Providence under his protection. Consequently he always knew exactly what Providence meant. Inferior and less respectable men might fall short of that mark, but Mr. Podsnap was always up to it. And it was very remarkable (and must have been very comfortable) that what Providence meant, was invariably what Mr. Podsnap meant.

---

1 the City: the financial district in central London.

THE VICTORIAN PERIOD

The Serenity of Success

As if in opposition to all that Mr. Podsnap stands for is the following sketch of the ideal gentleman. It was written by one of the greatest churchmen of the 19th century, Cardinal Newman, and is part of a famous series of lectures, later called *The Idea of a University*, that he delivered in 1852 at the newly founded Catholic University of Ireland in Dublin. The gentleman, as Cardinal Newman conceives him, conducts himself on a plane far above the fussiness and touchiness of Mr. Podsnap. The real gentleman is too wise and too serene to be smug.

THE GENTLEMAN

. . . It is almost a definition of a gentleman to say he is one who never inflicts pain. This description is both refined and, as far as it goes, accurate. He is mainly occupied in merely removing the obstacles which hinder the free and unembarrassed action of those about him; and he concurs with their movements rather than takes the initiative himself. His benefits may be considered as parallel to what are called comforts or conveniences in arrangements of a personal nature: like an easy chair or a good fire, which do their part in dispelling cold and fatigue, though nature provides both means of rest and animal heat without them. The true gentleman in like manner carefully avoids whatever may cause a jar or a jolt in the minds of those with whom he is cast—all clashing of opinion, or collision of feeling, all restraint, or suspicion, or gloom, or resentment—his great concern being to make every one at their ease and at home. He has his eyes on all his company; he is tender toward the bashful, gentle toward the distant, and merciful toward the absurd; he can recollect to whom he is speaking; he guards against unseasonable allusions, or topics which may irritate; he is seldom prominent in conversation, and never wearisome. He makes light of favors while he does them, and seems to be receiving when he is conferring. He never speaks of himself except when compelled, never defends himself by a mere retort; he has no ears for slander or gossip, is scrupulous in imputing motives to those who interfere with him, and interprets everything for the best. He is never mean or little in his disputes, never takes unfair advantage, never mistakes personalities or sharp sayings for arguments, or insinuates evil which he dare not say out. From a long-sighted prudence, he observes the maxim of the ancient sage, that we should ever conduct ourselves toward our enemy as if he were one day to be our friend. He has too much good sense to be affronted at insults; he is too well employed to remember injuries, and too indolent to bear malice. He is patient, forbearing, and resigned, on philosophical principles; he submits to pain, because it is inevitable, to bereavement, because it is irreparable, and to death, because it is his destiny. If he engages in controversy of any kind, his disciplined intellect preserves him from the blundering discourtesy of better, perhaps, but less edu-

*The Black Country. The machine ultimately made such scenes as this one,
the steel works in Sheffield, common in regions of England.*

cated minds; who, like blunt weapons, tear and hack instead of
cutting clean, who mistake the point in argument, waste their
strength on trifles, misconceive their adversary, and leave the
question more involved than they find it. He may be right or
wrong in his opinion, but he is too clearheaded to be unjust; he
is as simple as he is forcible, and as brief as he is decisive. Nowhere shall we find greater candor, consideration, indulgence:
he throws himself into the minds of his opponents; he accounts
for their mistakes. He knows the weakness of human reason as
well as its strength, its province and its limits.

Nature and Industry

Behind the prosperity of Mr. Podsnap was the power of the new factories, and to many 19th-century travelers factories meant "The Black
Country," a Midland region they entered soon after leaving the port of
Liverpool. Here is one account of that region by a man who actually
did something to bring about its character. He was James Nasmyth, an
engineer who invented the steam hammer. He shows us what happened
when the natural world so sensitively observed by Dorothy Wordsworth was mingled with the smoke and fumes of James Watt's steam
engine. Vulcan, the blacksmith god of industry, drove out Ceres, the
goddess of vegetation.

The Black Country is anything but picturesque. The earth seems to have been turned inside out. Its entrails are strewn about; nearly the entire surface of the ground is covered with cinder heaps and mounds of scoriae.[1] The coal, which has been drawn from below ground, is blazing on the surface. The district is crowded with iron furnaces, puddling furnaces,[2] and coal-pit engine furnaces. By day and by night the country is glowing with fire, and the smoke of the ironworks hovers over it. There is a rumbling and clanking of iron forges and rolling mills. Workmen covered with smut,[3] and with fierce white eyes, are seen moving about amongst the glowing iron and the dull thud of forge hammers.

Amidst these flaming, smoky, clanging works, I beheld the remains of what had once been happy farmhouses, now ruined and deserted. The ground underneath them had sunk by the working out of the coal, and they were falling to pieces. They had in former times been surrounded by clumps of trees; but only the skeletons of them remained, dilapidated, black, and life-less. The grass had been parched and killed by the vapors of sulphureous acid thrown out by the chimneys; and every herba-ceous[4] object was of a ghastly gray—the emblem of vegetable death in its saddest aspect. Vulcan had driven out Ceres. In some places I heard a sort of chirruping sound, as of some for-lorn bird haunting the ruins of the old farmsteads. But no! the chirrup was a vile delusion. It proceeded from the shrill creak-ing of the coal-winding chains,[5] which were placed in small tun-nels beneath the hedgeless road.

The Grandeur of the Tangled Bank

The fumes and slag heaps of the ironworks killed the green leaves of nature. But the idea of nature held by many Victorians, their whole conception of the world in which humankind and all creatures live, in 1859 received a shock as severe as the effects of machinery upon the landscape. In that year was published *On the Origin of Species by Means of Natural Selection* by Charles Darwin. Most biologists be-fore Darwin believed that each form of life was created fully and specifically as we now find it. But Darwin argued that "all the living forms of life are the lineal descendants of those which lived long before the Silurian epoch": all living things, including human beings, have evolved from a few simple forms of life that began millions of years ago in the Paleozoic period. Many were horrified by Darwin's argu-ment, not only because it did not coincide with the account of the

---

1 **scoriae** (skōr'ĭ ē'): slag heaps—the refuse from steelmaking.
2 **puddling furnaces:** furnaces for turning pig iron into steel.
3 **smut:** soot.
4 **herbaceous** (hûr bā'shəs): green-leafed.
5 **coal-winding chains:** continuous chain combined with small buckets which carried the coal through a shaft to the surface.

Creation in the Biblical Book of Genesis, but also because it introduced into their conception of the world a time-scale, an idea of geologic time, that reckoned by millions of years. The biological history of humankind completely dwarfed the history of civilization. One can imagine the response of Mr. Podsnap to a conception of history that made so little of his valuable lifetime.

Darwin believed, however, that there was a "grandeur" in the conception of human history that he proposed. Here is the final paragraph from his great work, *The Origin of Species*. It describes a grandeur different from the "spirit" which Wordsworth sensed in nature. Darwin's grandeur is that of a new complexity, a complexity of "endless forms" evolving from the simplest beginnings, and evolving by a long, slow process that only the fittest could survive.

A TANGLED BANK

It is interesting to contemplate a tangled bank, clothed with many plants of many kinds, with birds singing on the bushes, with various insects flitting about, and with worms crawling through the damp earth, and to reflect that these elaborately constructed forms, so different from each other, and dependent upon each other in so complex a manner, have all been produced by laws acting around us. These laws, taken in the largest sense, being Growth with Reproduction; Inheritance which is almost implied by reproduction; Variability from the indirect and direct action of the conditions of life, and from use and disuse: a Ratio of Increase so high as to lead to a Struggle for Life, and as a consequence to Natural Selection, entailing Divergence of Character and the Extinction of less-improved forms. Thus, from the war of nature, from famine and death, the most exalted object which we are capable of conceiving, namely, the production of the higher animals, directly follows. There is grandeur in this view of life, with its several powers, having been originally breathed by the Creator into a few forms or into one; and that, whilst this planet has gone cycling on according to the fixed law of gravity, from so simple a beginning endless forms most beautiful and most wonderful have been, and are being evolved.

The Literature of

The Victorian Period

Doubt and Faith

THE VICTORIAN WORLD, so full of change, so full of growth, with so much comfort for some, and so much harshness for others, was the scene of a drama that had been enacted before many times. Now, however, it became a drama that engaged many writers, poets, essayists, and novelists, as never before. It is the drama in which a person moves from doubt to despair—from depression, uncertainty, and frustration to happiness, serenity, and achievement.

In 1833 Thomas Carlyle published a book with the strange title *Sartor Resartus* (Latin for "The Tailor Reclothed"). It pretends to be the autobiography of a German sage (with the unlikely and almost unpronounceable name of Diogenes Teufelsdröchk), but it actually tells the story of a crisis through which Carlyle, the author, had himself earlier passed. At one stage of his life, he tells us, speaking through his wordy hero, he was sunk in apathy:

> To me the Universe was all void of Life, of Purpose, of Volition, even of Hostility: it was one huge, dead, immeasurable Steam engine, rolling on, in its dead indifference, to grind me limb from limb.

And he remained for a time sunk in this deadness of spirit, feeling that the world had become a vast, indifferent machine, until one day:

> . . . all at once, there rose a Thought in me, and I asked myself: "What *art* thou afraid of? Wherefore, like a coward, dost thou forever . . . whimper, and go cowering and trembling? . . . Let it [i.e., Death and all that the Devil and Man can do against thee] come, then; I will meet it and defy it!" And as I so thought, . . . I shook base Fear away from me forever. I was strong, of unknown strength. . . .

So Carlyle describes an experience that many Victorian writers and thinkers were to undergo after him. He had moved from a crippling doubt, a state that he called "the Everlasting No," to a brave faith in himself, a state that he called "the Everlasting Yea." As he summed it up, speaking first of the state of mind in which "To me the Universe was all void of life," he wrote: "Thus had the EVERLASTING No . . . pealed through all the recesses of my Being, of my ME. . . ." But he rebelled; he asserted himself:

> and then was it that my whole ME stood up, in native God-created majesty, and with emphasis recorded its Protest. . . . The Everlasting No had said: "Behold, thou art fatherless, outcast, and the Universe is mine . . ."; to which my whole ME now made answer: "I am not thine, but Free, and forever hate thee!"

Carlyle's vehement rejection of doubt, his defiant repudiation of "the Everlasting No," and his affirmation of "the Everlasting Yea"—this is the spiritual adventure that many people in modern times have undergone, and it is an adventure that many writers, artists, and political thinkers began 150 years ago.

Alfred, Lord Tennyson (1809-1892)

The poet who commanded the largest audience of Victorian times (and one of the largest audiences ever reached by a poet) was a huge, deep-voiced, shy man who from his earliest days lived much in seclusion. Alfred Tennyson was the fourth son of a not altogether happy family of twelve children. Their father, a deeply disappointed man (he was disinherited from the family estate in favor of a younger brother), was rector of the village church in Somersby, Lincolnshire, and he spent much of his time preparing his sons to become university students. Even in such isolated circumstances Alfred began to write. Before he entered Cambridge University he published a volume of poems with his brother Charles (*Poems of Two Brothers*, 1827), and at eighteen began the dedicated career as poet that ended only with his death sixty-five years later. Much of his life was spent in melancholy, uncertainty, and doubt—there is a story that even as a young child he wandered in the garden saying his name aloud over and over, "Alfred, Alfred," as if to make sure of who he was. But of his poetic gift he was never uncertain, and in its constant exercise he never wavered.

Tennyson arrived at Cambridge to find himself famous as the co-author of *Poems of Two Brothers*. He was shy and comparatively poor, but he was asked to join the "Apostles," a kind of informal fraternity of some of the most talented students at the university. Here he became the close friend of Arthur Henry Hallam (and Hallam later became his sister's fiancé), a promising young writer whose early and sudden death was a most painful blow to Alfred Tennyson. Tennyson's great elegy for Hallam, *In Memoriam*, was one of the most widely read poems of the 19th century. In 1831, however, Tennyson was forced by family circumstances to leave Cambridge without taking his degree. He went home and continued to study and write poetry, some of it in its melancholy reflecting the pressures of his father's uncertain temper and the family's limited circumstances. In 1833 he was plunged into sadness by the death of Hallam. Upon the death of his father, in 1836, he invested the family's meager resources in an invention, a wood-carving machine: the project failed, and Tennyson fell into a severe depression. Even so, he continued to write, and with constantly increasing range and skill. By 1850, with the publication of *In Memoriam*, he had become so famous that in the same year he succeeded Wordsworth as poet laureate. He was at last able to marry his fiancée, Emily Sellwood (they were first engaged in 1836), and his life thereafter was serene and comfortable. Tennyson's poetry, indeed, was eventually to make him a world-famous and wealthy man. He lived in seclusion in a large house on the Isle of Wight, off the south coast, though many visitors sought him out as the wisest sage of his time. In 1884 he became Lord Tennyson, and when he died in 1892 he was buried with national honors in Westminster Abbey.

No Victorian writer was finally more successful than Tennyson, though few were more acquainted with despair before success finally came. His tone is never brash, confident, and loud; nor on the other hand is it ever completely the tone of pessimism and gloom. His tone, rather, is that of the thinker and writer who longs for certainty, perhaps more certainty than he can have. Few poets, whatever their tone, have been more melodious: Tennyson's musical gifts, his skill in meter, rhythm, and sound, were unsurpassed by any other poets of his time.

"Ulysses"

Homer's Ulysses returns to his home in Ithaca after many adventures; he routs the suitors of his queen, Penelope, and rejoices in his reunion with his son, Telemachus. Their king has returned, and peace comes to the people of Ithaca. The Italian poet Dante, however, continued the story: In his *Inferno* he tells how Ulysses became restless and in old age set out with some of his followers on yet another voyage to the west. In 1833 Tennyson composed the following dramatic portrait of the restless Ulysses summoning his mariners to one last questing voyage. The portrait is a monologue—Ulysses alone speaks throughout.

Ulysses

Alfred, Lord Tennyson

It little profits that an idle king,
By this still hearth, among these barren crags,
Matched with an aged wife, I mete and dole
Unequal laws[1] unto a savage race,
That hoard, and sleep, and feed, and know not me.   5

I cannot rest from travel: I will drink
Life to the lees:[2] all times I have enjoyed
Greatly, have suffered greatly, both with those
That loved me, and alone; on shore, and when
Thro' scudding drifts[3] the rainy Hyades[4]   10
Vexed the dim sea: I am become a name;
For always roaming with a hungry heart
Much have I seen and known; cities of men
And manners, climates, councils, governments,
Myself not least, but honored of them all;   15
And drunk delight of battle with my peers,
Far on the ringing plains of windy Troy.
I am a part of all that I have met;
Yet all experience is an arch wherethro'
Gleams that untraveled world, whose margin fades   20
Forever and forever when I move.
How dull it is to pause, to make an end,
To rust unburnished, not to shine in use!
As tho' to breathe were life. Life piled on life

---

1 **mete . . . laws:** measure and give out rewards and punishments.
2 **lees:** dregs.
3 **scudding drifts:** driving showers.
4 **Hyades** (hī′ə dēz′): stars (in the constellation Taurus) thought to bring rain.

Were all too little, and of one to me   25
Little remains: but every hour is saved
From that eternal silence, something more,
A bringer of new things; and vile it were
For some three suns to store and hoard myself,
And this gray spirit yearning in desire   30
To follow knowledge like a sinking star,
Beyond the utmost bound of human thought.

    This is my son, mine own Telemachus,
To whom I leave the scepter and the isle[5]—
Well-loved of me, discerning[6] to fulfill   35
This labor, by slow prudence to make mild
A rugged people, and thro' soft degrees
Subdue them to the useful and the good.
Most blameless is he, centered in the sphere
Of common duties, decent not to fail   40
In offices[7] of tenderness, and pay
Meet adoration to my household gods,
When I am gone. He works his work, I mine.

    There lies the port; the vessel puffs her sail:
There gloom the dark broad seas. My mariners,   45
Souls that have toiled, and wrought, and thought with me—
That ever with a frolic welcome took
The thunder and the sunshine, and opposed
Free hearts, free foreheads—you and I are old;
Old age hath yet his honor and his toil;   50
Death closes all: but something ere the end,
Some work of noble note,[8] may yet be done,
Not unbecoming men that strove with Gods.
The lights begin to twinkle from the rocks:
The long day wanes: the slow moon climbs: the deep   55
Moans round with many voices. Come, my friends,
'Tis not too late to seek a newer world.
Push off, and sitting well in order smite
The sounding furrows;[9] for my purpose holds
To sail beyond the sunset, and the baths   60
Of all the western stars,[10] until I die.
It may be that the gulfs will wash us down:

---

5 **isle:** Ithaca, an island off the west coast of Greece, Ulysses's kingdom.
6 **discerning to:** knowing how to.
7 **offices:** duties.
8 **note:** fame.
9 **furrows:** i.e., of the waves.
10 **baths . . . stars:** ocean that the Greeks believed surrounded the flat, circular earth.

ALFRED, LORD TENNYSON

It may be we shall touch the Happy Isles,[11]
And see the great Achilles,[12] whom we knew.
Tho' much is taken, much abides; and tho'   65
We are not now that strength which in old days
Moved earth and heaven; that which we are, we are;
One equal temper of heroic hearts,
Made weak by time and fate, but strong in will
To strive, to seek, to find, and not to yield.   70

11 Happy Isles: place to which heroes went after their deaths.
12 Achilles (ə kĭl′ēz): the great hero of the Trojan war, in which Ulysses
had participated before his many adventures on the journey back to Ithaca.

Comment

Ulysses, the hero "with a hungry heart," speaks first about his past
as he reflects upon the sights he has seen, then about the present as he
looks upon his son, and then about the future as he looks upon his ship
and the sea. How does he characterize himself in these three movements of the poem?

1. "I will drink/Life to the lees," (ll. 6-7) says Ulysses in what is now
   almost a proverbial expression. What other expressions of desire
   do you find in the first thirty-two lines of the poem?
2. What contrast do you find in lines 33-43 between the virtues of "mine
   own Telemachus" and the character of Ulysses? What are some
   words Ulysses uses about his son that he cannot use about himself?
3. From line 44 to the end of the poem, Ulysses turns to his ship and
   his fellow mariners. How do we know that they too, like him, are
   men "with a hungry heart"?
4. " 'Tis not too late to seek a newer world," says Ulysses to his shipmates. For Tennyson, of course, Ulysses was more than a person;
   he was a symbol. What values does he symbolize in this poem?

In Memoriam

The death of his friend Hallam meant not only a severe personal grief to Tennyson. It meant also the larger, though still personal, question of the meaning of life. *In Memoriam* is not only an elegy, a poem of praise for one who has died; it is also a poem that asks whether the meaning of life is destroyed by death. It is a poem that asks whether the love which human beings bear one another provides a foundation for the faith that life is not in vain. And it answers affirmatively.

Tennyson's poem was written over a seventeen-year period, between 1833 and 1850. The early years of this period, as you have seen, were years of personal distress for the poet. They were also years during which many writers were troubled, and Tennyson among them, by the effects of certain scientific theories on traditional religious beliefs. Darwin and his theory of evolution were still a long way off. But there were scientists before Darwin, geologists especially, who raised questions similar to those raised by Darwin's *The Origin of Species.* They showed, for example, that the earth itself has a history, one that involves vast stretches of time. The very cliffs and hills of a landscape, they said, were not always there, but are the results of long geological processes of erosion, of far-off volcanic eruptions, or of vast, slow glacial processes that millions of years ago remade whole continents. The study of fossils, of coal deposits, and of other bygone forms of life held in the strata of the earth suggested that there had once lived whole tribes of plants and animals now vanished from the face of the earth.

Such considerations as these—and there were many before Darwin— could not but raise doubts among those who believed that the earth was made as we see it now, to delight and to serve us. Nature, indeed, to many people began to seem indifferent to humankind: the faith of Wordsworth, for example, that there is one spirit both in "the light of setting suns" and "in the mind of man," did not come easily to those who knew what the scientists of the early 19th century were saying about the structure and history of nature.

Tennyson's poem touches upon these and other disturbing doubts. It surmounts these doubts, however, by turning away from the world of nature, by leaving the proofs of the scientists and turning to the world of people, to the feelings by which we are bound to each other. The certainty of his love for his departed friend overcomes Tennyson's fear that the living may have no spiritual link with the dead.

In Memoriam is a long poem; it presents Tennyson's passage from doubt to faith in a sequence of 131 lyric poems, of which we can present only a few here. The first is the Prologue, a poem that was actually written last. It is addressed to "Thou," to the God of love in whom the poet trusts that his friend, the young man so tragically and so suddenly cut off, now lives.

from In Memoriam A. H. H.

Alfred, Lord Tennyson

Strong Son of God, immortal Love,
   Whom we, that have not seen thy face,
   By faith, and faith alone, embrace,
Believing where we cannot prove;[1]

Thine are these orbs[2] of light and shade;   5
   Thou madest Life in man and brute;
   Thou madest Death; and lo, thy foot
Is on the skull which thou hast made.

Thou wilt not leave us in the dust:
   Thou madest man, he knows not why,   10
   He thinks he was not made to die;
And thou has made him: thou art just.

Thou seemest human and divine,
   Thou highest, holiest manhood, thou:
   Our wills are ours, we know not how;   15
Our wills are ours, to make them thine.

Our little systems[3] have their day;
   They have their day and cease to be:
   They are but broken lights of thee,
And thou, O Lord, art more than they.   20

We have but faith: we cannot know;
   For knowledge is of things we see;
   And yet we trust it comes from thee,
A beam in darkness: let it grow.

Let knowledge grow from more to more,   25
   But more of reverence in us dwell:
   That mind and soul, according well,
May make one music as before,[4]

---

1 believing . . . prove: i.e., we believe in God without asking for proof.
2 orbs: planets.
3 systems: both solar systems and systems of philosophy and theology.
4 May . . . before: i.e., may become joined in harmony as in bygone days when men joined knowledge ("mind") and faith ("soul").

But vaster. We are fools and slight;
    We mock thee when we do not fear: 30
    But help thy foolish ones to bear;
Help thy vain worlds to bear thy light.

Forgive what seemed my sin in me;
    What seemed my worth since I began;
    For merit lives from man to man,   35
And not from man, O Lord, to thee.

Forgive my grief for one removed,
    Thy creature, whom I found so fair.
    I trust he lives in thee, and there
I find him worthier to be loved.   40

Forgive these wild and wandering cries,
    Confusions of a wasted[5] youth;
    Forgive them where they fail in truth,
And in thy wisdom make me wise.

[*Roughly the first half of* In Memoriam *expresses the poet's intense "grief for one removed." How can the death of one so young and so promising be accounted for—what faith can overcome my sorrow, he asks. His grief becomes despair as he looks at the apparent indifference of nature to forms of life other than human. He can find no consolation in nature, for nature seems only wasteful of life.*]

54

Oh yet we trust that somehow good
    Will be the final goal of ill,
    To pangs of nature, sins of will,
Defects of doubt, and taints of blood;[6]

That nothing walks with aimless feet;   5
    That not one life shall be destroyed,
    Or cast as rubbish to the void,
When God hath made the pile complete;

That not a worm is cloven in vain;
    That not a moth with vain desire   10
    Is shriveled in a fruitless fire,
Or but subserves another's gain.[7]

---

5 wasted: laid waste; made desolate.
6 To . . . blood: i.e., that good will succeed such evils as natural pains, deliberate sins, the blemish of doubt, and inherent wickedness.
7 Or . . . gain: or only serves the purpose of some more powerful creature in the struggle of nature.

Behold, we know not anything;
   I can but trust that good shall fall
   At last—far off—at last, to all,   15
And every winter change to spring.

So runs my dream: but what am I?
   An infant crying in the night:
   An infant crying for the light:
And with no language but a cry.   20

55

The wish, that of the living whole
   No life may fail beyond the grave,
   Derives it not from what we have
The likest God within the soul?

Are God and Nature then at strife,   5
   That Nature lends such evil dreams?
   So careful of the type[8] she seems,
So careless of the single life;

That I, considering everywhere
   Her secret meaning in her deeds,   10
   And finding that of fifty seeds
She often brings but one to bear,

I falter where I firmly trod,
   And falling with my weight of cares
   Upon the great world's altar stairs   15
That slope thro' darkness up to God,

I stretch lame hands of faith, and grope,
   And gather dust and chaff, and call
   To what I feel is Lord of all,
And faintly trust the larger hope.   20

56

"So careful of the type?" but no.
   From scarpèd[9] cliff and quarried stone
   She cries, "A thousand types are gone:
I care for nothing, all shall go.

---

8 **type:** species, or general kinds of life.
9 **scarped:** steep.

"Thou makest thine appeal to me: 5
    I bring to life, I bring to death:
    The spirit does but mean the breath:[10]
I know no more."   And he, shall he,

Man, her last work, who seemed so fair,
    Such splendid purpose in his eyes,   10
    Who rolled[11] the psalm to wintry skies,
Who built him fanes[12] of fruitless prayer,

Who trusted God was love indeed
    And love Creation's final law—
    Tho' Nature, red in tooth and claw   15
With ravine,[13] shrieked against his creed—

Who loved, who suffered countless ills,
    Who battled for the True, the Just,
    Be blown[14] about the desert dust,
Or sealed within the iron hills?   20

No more?   A monster then, a dream,
    A discord.   Dragons of the prime,
    That tare[15] each other in their slime,
Were mellow music matched with him.

O life as futile, then, as frail!   25
    O for thy voice[16] to soothe and bless!
    What hope of answer, or redress?
Behind the veil, behind the veil.

[*Even though he cannot hear his friend's voice, the poet cannot believe
that a man when he dies is no more than the dust of the desert or the
stone of the mountain.   And in the second half of the poem Tennyson
describes his slow ascent from the hopeless vision of nature's indifference—"I bring to life, I bring to death . . . / I know no more."   He
turns to his memories of his friend, to the life they shared, and to the
example that Hallam himself set.   For Hallam, he remembers, would
have understood his doubts.*]

---

10 **spirit . . . breath:** i.e., "spirit" means no more than the physical breath of life.
11 **rolled:** chanted.
12 **fanes:** temples.
13 **ravine** (răv′ən): plunder; something seized and devoured as prey.
14 **be blown:** The subject is "Man" (l. 9).
15 **tare:** tore.
16 **thy voice:** Hallam's voice.

ALFRED, LORD TENNYSON   579

. . . one indeed I knew
   In many a subtle question versed,
   Who touched a jarring lyre at first,
But ever strove to make it true:

Perplexed in faith, but pure in deeds,   5
   At last he beat his music out.
   There lives more faith in honest doubt,
Believe me, than in half the creeds.

He fought his doubts and gathered strength,
   He would not make his judgment blind,   10
   He faced the specters of the mind
And laid them: thus he came at length

To find a stronger faith his own;
   And Power was with him in the night,
   Which makes the darkness and the light,   15
And dwells not in the light alone,

But in the darkness and the cloud,
   As over Sinai's peaks of old,
   While Israel made their gods of gold,
Altho' the trumpet blew so loud.[17]   20

[The poet's faith is rekindled as he recalls the example of his friend. Once again, with the passing of time, a New Year comes, and as the bells ring out he gathers hope for the future.]

106

Ring out, wild bells, to the wild sky,
   The flying cloud, the frosty light:
   The year is dying in the night;
Ring out, wild bells, and let him die.

Ring out the old, ring in the new,   5
   Ring, happy bells, across the snow:
   The year is going, let him go;
Ring out the false, ring in the true.

Ring out the grief that saps the mind,
   For those that here we see no more;   10

17 But . . . loud: Just as God was hidden in a cloud of darkness over Mount Sinai before He spoke to the prophet Moses (Exodus 19:16-25), high above those who worshiped golden idols, so religious faith may emerge from the darkness of honest doubt.

Ring out the feud of rich and poor,
Ring in redress to all mankind.

Ring out a slowly dying cause,
   And ancient forms of party strife;
   Ring in the nobler modes of life,   15
With sweeter manners, purer laws.

Ring out the want, the care, the sin,
   The faithless coldness of the times;
   Ring out, ring out my mournful rhymes,
But ring the fuller minstrel in.   20

Ring out false pride in place and blood,
   The civic slander and the spite;
   Ring in the love of truth and right,
Ring in the common love of good.

Ring out old shapes of foul disease;   25
   Ring out the narrowing lust of gold;
   Ring out the thousand wars of old,
Ring in the thousand years of peace.

Ring in the valiant man and free,
   The larger heart, the kindlier hand;   30
   Ring out the darkness of the land,
Ring in the Christ that is to be.

[*And finally, emboldened by his hopes, heartened by the memory of his friend, who "faced the specters of the mind" and came "To find a stronger faith his own," Tennyson rejects his former despair.*]

120

I trust I have not wasted breath:[18]
   I think we are not wholly brain,
   Magnetic mockeries;[19] not in vain,
Like Paul[20] with beasts, I fought with Death;

Not only cunning casts in clay:[21]   5
   Let Science prove we are, and then
   What matters Science unto men,
At least to me? I would not stay.

18 **I . . . breath:** I trust that I possess something more than breath that wastes away.
19 **magnetic mockeries:** mere toys moved by magnetic force.
20 **Paul:** an apostle of Jesus; he was persecuted for his faith. (See I Corinthians 15:32.)
21 **Not . . . clay:** i.e., we are not only china figures.

ALFRED, LORD TENNYSON

Let him, the wiser[22] man who springs
   Hereafter, up from childhood shape   10
   His action like the greater ape,
But I was *born* to other things.

[*The geologists may be right, the very hills may "flow/ From form to form." But the poet will not believe that the history of man is merely a process of meaningless change. The assurance he feels is stronger than the evidence of science or the evidence of his senses.*]

123

There rolls the deep where grew the tree.[23]
   O earth, what changes hast thou seen!
   There where the long street roars, hath been
The stillness of the central sea.

The hills are shadows, and they flow   5
   From form to form, and nothing stands;
   They melt like mist, the solid lands,
Like clouds they shape themselves and go.

But in my spirit will I dwell,
   And dream my dream, and hold it true;   10
   For tho' my lips may breathe adieu,
I cannot think the thing farewell.[24]

124

That which we dare invoke to bless;
   Our dearest faith; our ghastliest doubt;
   He, They, One, All; within, without;[25]
The Power in darkness whom we guess;

I found Him not in world or sun,   5
   Or eagle's wing, or insect's eye;[26]
   Nor thro' the questions men may try,
The petty cobwebs we have spun:[27]

If e'er when faith had fall'n asleep,
   I heard a voice "believe no more"   10
   And heard an ever-breaking shore
That tumbled in the Godless deep;

22 wiser: i.e., more convinced of science—said ironically.
23 There . . . tree: By geologic change, forest-covered lands are at the bottom of oceans.
24 For . . . farewell: Even when I *say* I dismiss my dream, I cannot do so in my mind.
25 He . . . without: i.e., whatever name we may give to God, the subject of both our faith and our doubt.
26 I . . eye: I did not find God by looking at the design of the world and its creatures.
27 Nor . . . spun: Nor did I find God by abstruse argument.

A warmth within the breast would melt
   The freezing reason's colder part,
   And like a man in wrath the heart   15
Stood up and answered "I have felt."

No, like a child in doubt and fear:
   But that blind clamor made me wise;
   Then was I as a child that cries,
But, crying, knows his father near;   20

And what I am beheld again
   What is, and no man understands;
   And out of darkness came the hands
That reach thro' nature, molding men.

Comment

Such is the main movement of *In Memoriam*, the most ambitious and
certainly one of the most widely read poems of the Victorian period.
The movement is dramatic, for it presents us with the story of a profound alteration in a man's outlook. This story, however, is not told to
us in the direct narrative of a novel. It is rather a story that we infer,
that we work out for ourselves, as we move through the long succession
of individual lyric poems or sections of the whole work. Each stanza
of each individual poem, moreover, is an adaptation that Tennyson has
made of the traditional ballad stanza: each is a quatrain rhyming *abba*.
The individual poems, then, that comprise the whole, are not linked by
the supple blank verse that Milton, for example, used. Instead they are
linked by the interlocking of rhymes and by the recurrence of images
and figures and by changes of tone. Together, they give us the portrait
of a mind musing, communing with itself in grief, and rising from
doubt to faith.

1. Consider first the group of poems, 54-56, in which the poet's doubt is
   most intense.
   (*a*) With what image of himself does he conclude poem 54? Why
       does he say he has "no language but a cry"?
   (*b*) In poem 55 the poet finds a conflict between his "wish" that "No
       life may fail beyond the grave," on the one hand, and nature's
       "secret meaning in her deeds," on the other. What is this "secret
       meaning" of nature? How does it lead the poet to ask, "Are
       God and Nature then at strife"? How then does he describe
       himself in the last two stanzas of poem 55? What is his attitude
       toward the "strife" of God and nature? How does he express his
       attitude in the image of himself with which poem 55 concludes?
   (*c*) In poem 56, lines 8-20 ask one long question, beginning "And he,
       shall he . . . ?" What is the tone of this question? How does

the poet's own voice here contrast with the voice of nature that says, "I know no more" in the first two stanzas?

2. In poem 96 the poet turns to the example of his friend Hallam, who also had struggled with doubt, but who had won through to a strong faith.

(a) With what image does Tennyson describe Hallam's attainment of faith in lines 9-12? How does his image here of Hallam contrast with the earlier description of himself as one who possesses "no language but a cry"?

(b) And in lines 12-16 how does he describe Hallam? How does his imagery here contrast with the image of himself that Tennyson gives us in the last two stanzas of poem 55?

3. "Ring out, wild bells," Tennyson exclaims in poem 106. With what tone must the reader speak these lines? How does this tone contrast with the tone in which Tennyson asks the long question of poem 56?

4. In poems 120, 123, and 124, Tennyson returns to the doubts that he had expressed in poems 54-56. He asks many of the same questions, but with a difference, for now he does not need to answer them.

(a) What is his attitude toward the doubts raised by science in poem 120? In what way is his attitude here like that which he ascribes to Hallam in poem 96?

(b) In poems 123 and 124 Tennyson makes his protest and enters into his own state of "Everlasting Yea": he will "dream [his] dream, and hold it true." In the fourth stanza of poem 124, what is his act of defiance? In what respects is it like the example set by Hallam? In the fifth stanza of poem 124, however, Tennyson changes his image of himself—"No," he says, "I was not only like an angry man." What image of himself does he substitute for the "man of wrath"? How does this new image reiterate the image of himself that concludes poem 54? How does it reiterate the image that concludes poem 55? What has happened to his earlier "cry"?

5. Now return to the Prologue to *In Memoriam,* which, though it comes first, was written last. How does it sum up the story of himself that Tennyson implies in the main body of his poem?

Although it is not the last poem that he wrote, Tennyson asked that the following short lyric be placed at the end of all editions of his poetry.

Crossing the Bar[1]

Alfred, Lord Tennyson

Sunset and evening star,
    And one clear call for me!
And may there be no moaning of the bar,[2]
    When I put out to sea,

But such a tide as moving seems asleep,   5
    Too full for sound and foam,
When that which drew from out the boundless deep
    Turns again home.

Twilight and evening bell,
    And after that the dark!   10
And may there be no sadness of farewell,
    When I embark;

For tho' from out our bourne[3] of Time and Place
    The flood may bear me far,
I hope to see my Pilot face to face   15
    When I have crossed the bar.

1 bar: sand bar, lying across the harbor mouth; a peril to navigation except at high tide.
2 moaning of the bar: An old superstition is that when someone dies, the outgoing tide moans as it passes over the harbor bar.
3 bourne: domain; realm.

Comment

"Crossing the Bar" is an extended metaphor: What is the voyage that Tennyson is preparing to make? Is it a voyage like that which he describes in "Ulysses"?

1. "When I put out to sea": What does Tennyson symbolize in this voyage? What does he represent by the tide of line 5? by the bar at the harbor entrance? by the dark of line 10? and by "my Pilot" (l. 15)?

2. How do you characterize the tone of this lyric?
3. In "Ulysses," you have seen, Tennyson describes Homer's hero in old age about to set forth on one more voyage. What difference do you find between Ulysses and the "I" of "Crossing the Bar"? What does this difference tell you about Tennyson's experience of the Victorian struggle between doubt and faith?

John Stuart Mill (1806-1873)

One of the greatest essays of the 19th century, *On Liberty*, was published in 1859. Its author was John Stuart Mill, who (like Charles Lamb before him) was an employee of the East India Company, but who was known to his contemporaries as the author of many powerful essays on the philosophy of government. His father, James Mill, was likewise a political philosopher, and the writings of father and son together contributed much in the first half of the 19th century to the development of the ideas upon which our modern, populous, democratic society is based.

On Liberty is based, as Mill said, upon one simple principle, that "the sole end for which mankind are warranted, individually or collectively, in interfering with the liberty of action of any of their number, is self-protection." If society is to be healthy, all persons must be free to express themselves and develop themselves; the only restraint upon the right of individual self-development is that it must not take place at the expense of the development of another person. Mill's conception of a society of freely developing individual citizens has entered deeply into the political convictions of people all over the world. It is a conception that puts the individual first, and the state, or government, second.

John Stuart Mill came to his political ideas through a most unusual education. His father believed that most schools were wasteful and inefficient, and he therefore educated his son at home—starting him, indeed, on Greek at the age of three! The son was gifted with prodigious intellectual powers: by the age of twelve he had read nearly all the Latin and Greek, the history, and the mathematics that the most talented university graduates could have mastered. But what this education left out, you see below. Isolated from his contemporaries, undergoing the strict training imposed by his stern father, John Stuart Mill was intellectually complete long before any child of his time. The cost of this precocity, however, the price he paid for his early development, is revealed in the following passages from his *Autobiography*, published in 1873.

J. Keir Hardie, first leader of the Labor party, addresses a suffragette meeting in Trafalgar Square. The freedom of the individual, a concept that Mill championed in On Liberty, *has long been a part of England's tradition.*

Autobiography

Many Victorian thinkers, writers, and statesmen wrote autobiographies, and many novels of the period were based upon autobiography. The writer who told others the story of his or her life, who took stock of his or her failures and achievements, was eagerly read. The audience was the great number of readers who were seeking their way in a society very different from the settled world of the 18th century; for them the experience of another "I" in coping with the requirements of the job, relations with friends and family, problems of belief, provided an intimate and helpful guide. Mill's life was of course unique, for he had as a child been subjected to a discipline that few adults could have endured. Yet his account of his life reveals that he too experienced the drama that many others of his time went through, the experience of moving from doubt and despair to clarity and faith.

The selection begins with the fifth chapter of his *Autobiography,* which Mill entitled "A Crisis in My Mental History." He is just twenty-one years old as the selection begins. Despite his youth, he has been a regular contributor to a leading political journal and has been much occupied in discussing and analyzing the political theories of his father and his father's friends. But suddenly, and unaccountably, he comes to a virtual standstill.

JOHN STUART MILL

From

Autobiography

A CRISIS IN MY MENTAL HISTORY

John Stuart Mill

FROM THE WINTER of 1821, . . . I had what might truly be called an object in life; to be a reformer of the world. My conception of my own happiness was entirely identified with this object. The personal sympathies I wished for were those of fellow laborers in this enterprise. I endeavored to pick up as many flowers as I could by the way; but as a serious and permanent personal satisfaction to rest upon, my whole reliance was placed on this; and I was accustomed to felicitate myself on the certainty of a happy life which I enjoyed, through placing my happiness in something durable and distant, in which some progress might be always making, while it could never be exhausted by complete attainment. This did very well for several years, during which the general improvement going on in the world and the idea of myself as engaged with others in struggling to promote it, seemed enough to fill up an interesting and animated existence. But the time came when I awakened from this as from a dream. It was in the autumn of 1826. I was in a dull state of nerves, such as everybody is occasionally liable to; unsusceptible to enjoyment or pleasurable excitement; one of those moods

when what is pleasure at other times, becomes insipid or indifferent. . . . In this frame of mind it occurred to me to put the question directly to myself: "Suppose that all your objects in life were realized; that all the changes in institutions and opinions which you are looking forward to, could be completely effected at this very instant: would this be a great joy and happiness to you?" And an irrepressible self-consciousness distinctly answered, "No!" At this my heart sank within me: the whole foundation on which my life was constructed fell down. All my happiness was to have been found in the continual pursuit of this end. The end had ceased to charm, and how could there ever again be any interest in the means? I seemed to have nothing left to live for.

At first I hoped that the cloud would pass away of itself; but it did not. A night's sleep, the sovereign[1] remedy for the smaller vexations of life, had no effect on it. I awoke to a renewed consciousness of the woeful fact. I carried it with me into all companies, into all occupations. Hardly anything had power to cause me even a few minutes' oblivion of it. For some months the cloud seemed to grow thicker and thicker. The lines in Coleridge's "Dejection"[2]—I was not then acquainted with them—exactly describe my case:

A grief without a pang, void, dark
    and drear,
A drowsy, stifled, unimpassioned grief,
Which finds no natural outlet or relief
In word, or sigh, or tear.

In vain I sought relief from my favorite books; those memorials of past nobleness and greatness from which I had always hitherto drawn strength and

1 **sovereign:** effectual.
2 **"Dejection":** ode about an experience much like that of Mill's.

animation. I read them now without feeling, or with the accustomed feeling *minus* all its charm; and I became persuaded that my love of mankind and of excellence for its own sake had worn itself out. I sought no comfort by speaking to others of what I felt. If I had loved anyone sufficiently to make confiding my griefs a necessity, I should not have been in the condition I was. I felt, too, that mine was not an interesting, or in any way respectable distress. There was nothing in it to attract sympathy. Advice, if I had known where to seek it, would have been most precious. The words of Macbeth to the physician[3] often occurred to my thoughts. But there was no one on whom I could build the faintest hope of such assistance. My father, to whom it would have been natural to me to have recourse in any practical difficulties, was the last person to whom, in such a case as this, I looked for help. Everything convinced me that he had no knowledge of any such mental state as I was suffering from, and that even if he could be made to understand it, he was not the physician who could heal it. My education, which was wholly his work, had been conducted without any regard to the possibility of its ending in this result; and I saw no use in giving him the pain of thinking that his plans had failed, when the failure was probably irremediable, and, at all events, beyond the power of *his* remedies. Of other friends, I had at that time none to whom I had any hope of making my condition intelligible. It was however abundantly intelligible to myself; and the more I dwelt upon it, the more hopeless it appeared. . . .

For I now saw, or thought I saw, what I had always before received with incredulity—that the habit of analysis has a tendency to wear away the feelings: as indeed it has, when no other mental habit is cultivated, and the analyzing spirit remains without its natural complements and correctives. The very excellence of analysis (I argued) is that it tends to weaken and undermine whatever is the result of prejudice; that it enables us mentally to separate ideas which have only casually clung together: and no associations whatever could ultimately resist this dissolving force, were it not that we owe to analysis our clearest knowledge of the permanent sequences in nature; the real connections between Things, not dependent on our will and feelings; natural laws, by virtue of which, in many cases, one thing is inseparable from another in fact. . . . Analytic habits may thus even strengthen the associations between causes and effects, means and ends, but tend altogether to weaken those which are, to speak familiarly, a *mere* matter of feeling. They are therefore (I thought) favorable to prudence and clear-sightedness, but a perpetual worm at the root both of the passions and of the virtues; and, above all, fearfully undermine all desires, and all pleasures. . . . These were the laws of human nature, by which, as it seemed to me, I had been brought to my present state. All those to whom I looked up were of opinion that the pleasure of sympathy with human beings, and the feelings which made the good of others, and especially of mankind on a large scale, the object of existence, were the greatest and surest sources of happiness. Of the truth of this I was convinced, but to know that a feeling would make me happy if I had it, did not give me the feeling. My education, I thought, had failed to create these feelings in sufficient strength to resist the

---

3 **to the physician:** See *Macbeth*, V, iii, 40-45.

dissolving influence of analysis, while the whole course of my intellectual cultivation had made precocious and premature analysis the inveterate habit of my mind. I was thus, as I said to myself, left stranded at the commencement of my voyage, with a well-equipped ship and a rudder, but no sail; without any real desire for the ends which I had been so carefully fitted out to work for: no delight in virtue, or the general good, but also just as little in anything else. The fountains of vanity and ambition seemed to have dried up within me, as completely as those of benevolence. I had had (as I reflected) some gratification of vanity at too early an age: I had obtained some distinction, and felt myself of some importance, before the desire of distinction and of importance had grown into a passion: and little as it was which I had attained, yet having been attained too early, like all pleasures enjoyed too soon, it had made me blasé and indifferent to the pursuit. Thus neither selfish nor unselfish pleasures were pleasures to me. And there seemed no power in nature sufficient to begin the formation of my character anew, and create in a mind now irretrievably analytic, fresh associations of pleasure with any of the objects of human desire.

These were the thoughts which mingled with the dry heavy dejection of the melancholy winter of 1826-1827. During this time I was not incapable of my usual occupations. I went on with them mechanically, by the mere force of habit. I had been so drilled in a certain sort of mental exercise, that I could still carry it on when all the spirit had gone out of it. I even composed and spoke several speeches at the debating society, how, or with what degree of success, I know not. Of four years continual speaking at that society, this is

the only year of which I remember next to nothing. Two lines of Coleridge, in whom alone of all writers I have found a true description of what I felt, were often in my thoughts, not at this time (for I had never read them), but in a later period of the same mental malady:

> Work without hope draws nectar in a
> sieve,
> And hope without an object cannot
> live.

In all probability my case was by no means so peculiar as I fancied it, and I doubt not that many others have passed through a similar state; but the idiosyncrasies of my education had given to the general phenomenon a special character, which made it seem the natural effect of causes that it was hardly possible for time to remove. I frequently asked myself if I could, or if I was bound to go on living, when life must be passed in this manner. I generally answered to myself that I did not think I could possibly bear it beyond a year. When, however, not more than half that duration of time had elapsed, a small ray of light broke in upon my gloom. I was reading, accidentally, Marmontel's *Memoires*,[4] and came to the passage which relates his father's death, the distressed position of the family, and the sudden inspiration by which he, then a mere boy, felt and made them feel that he would be everything to them—would supply the place of all that they had lost. A vivid conception of the scene and its feelings came over me, and I was moved to tears. From this moment my burden grew lighter. The oppression of the thought that all feeling was dead within me, was gone. I was no longer hopeless: I was not a stock or a

4 **Marmontel's** *Memoires*: autobiographical work by Jean-François Marmontel, an 18th-century French novelist and dramatist.

stone. I had still, it seemed, some of the material out of which all worth of character, and all capacity for happiness, are made. Relieved from my ever present sense of irremediable wretchedness, I gradually found that the ordinary incidents of life could again give me some pleasure; that I could again find enjoyment, not intense, but sufficient for cheerfulness, in sunshine and sky, in books, in conversation, in public affairs; and that there was, once more, excitement, though of a moderate kind, in exerting myself for my opinions, and for the public good. Thus the cloud gradually drew off, and I again enjoyed life: and though I had several relapses, some of which lasted many months, I never again was as miserable as I had been.

The experiences of this period had two very marked effects on my opinions and character. In the first place, they led me to adopt a theory of life, very unlike that on which I had before acted. . . . I never, indeed, wavered in the conviction that happiness is the test of all rules of conduct, and the end of life. But I now thought that this end was only to be attained by not making it the direct end. Those only are happy (I thought) who have their minds fixed on some object other than their own happiness; on the happiness of others, on the improvement of mankind, even on some art or pursuit, followed not as a means, but as itself an ideal end. Aiming thus at something else, they find happiness by the way. The enjoyments of life (such was now my theory) are sufficient to make it a pleasant thing, when they are taken *en passant*,[5] without being made a principal object. Once make them so, and they are immediately felt to be insuffi-

cient. They will not bear a scrutinizing examination. Ask yourself whether you are happy, and you cease to be so. The only chance is to treat, not happiness, but some end external to it, as the purpose of life. Let your self-consciousness, your scrutiny, your self-interrogation, exhaust themselves on that; and if otherwise fortunately circumstanced you will inhale happiness with the air you breathe, without dwelling on it or thinking about it, without either forestalling it in imagination, or putting it to flight by fatal questioning. This theory now became the basis of my philosophy of life. And I still hold to it as the best theory for all those who have but a moderate degree of sensibility and of capacity for enjoyment, that is for the great majority of mankind.

The other important change which my opinions at this time underwent, was that I, for the first time, gave its proper place, among the prime necessities of human well-being, to the internal culture of the individual. I ceased to attach almost exclusive importance to the ordering of outward circumstances, and the training of the human being for speculation and for action.

I had now learnt by experience that the passive susceptibilities needed to be cultivated as well as the active capacities, and required to be nourished and enriched as well as guided. I did not, for an instant, lose sight of, or undervalue, that part of the truth which I had seen before; I never turned recreant to intellectual culture, or ceased to consider the power and practice of analysis as an essential condition both of individual and of social improvement. But I thought that it had consequences which required to be corrected, by joining other kinds of cultivation with it. The maintenance of a due balance

5 *en passant* (äN på säN'): French for "in passing."

among the faculties, now seemed to me of primary importance. The cultivation of the feelings became one of the cardinal points in my ethical and philosophical creed. And my thoughts and inclinations turned in an increasing degree towards whatever seemed capable of being instrumental to that object.

I now began to find meaning in the things which I had read or heard about the importance of poetry and art as instruments of human culture. But it was some time longer before I began to know this by personal experience. The only one of the imaginative arts in which I had from childhood taken great pleasure, was music; the best effect of which (and in this it surpasses perhaps every other art) consists in exciting enthusiasm; in winding up to a high pitch those feelings of an elevated kind which are already in the character, but to which this excitement gives a glow and a fervor, which, though transitory at its utmost height, is precious for sustaining them at other times. This effect of music I had often experienced; but like all my pleasurable susceptibilities it was suspended during the gloomy period. I had sought relief again and again from this quarter, but found none. After the tide had turned, and I was in process of recovery, I had been helped forward by music, but in a much less elevated manner. I at this time first became acquainted with Weber's *Oberon*,[6] and the extreme pleasure which I drew from its delicious melodies did me good, by showing me a source of pleasure to which I was as susceptible as ever. The good, however, was much impaired by the thought, that the pleasure of music (as is quite true of such pleasure as this

was, that of mere tune) fades with familiarity, and requires either to be revived by intermittence, or fed by continual novelty. And it is very characteristic both of my then state, and of the general tone of my mind at this period of my life, that I was seriously tormented by the thought of the exhaustibility of musical combinations. The octave consists only of five tones and two semitones, which can be put together in only a limited number of ways, of which but a small proportion are beautiful: most of these, it seemed to me, must have been already discovered, and there could not be room for a long succession of Mozarts and Webers, to strike out, as these had done, entirely new and surpassingly rich veins of musical beauty. This source of anxiety may, perhaps, be thought to resemble that of the philosophers of Laputa,[7] who feared lest the sun should be burnt out. It was, however, connected with the best feature in my character, and the only good point to be found in my very unromantic and in no way honorable distress. For though my dejection, honestly looked at, could not be called other than egotistical, produced by the ruin, as I thought, of my fabric of happiness, yet the destiny of mankind in general was ever in my thoughts, and could not be separated from my own. I felt that the flaw in my life, must be a flaw in life itself; that the question was, whether, if the reformers of society and government could succeed in their objects, and every person in the community were free and in a state of physical comfort, the pleasures of life, being no longer kept up by struggle and privation, would cease to be pleasures. And I felt that unless I could see my way to some better hope than this for human

6 *Oberon:* romantic opera by the German composer Karl Maria von Weber, who died in London in 1826 just after supervising its production there.

7 Laputa: strange country inhabited by even stranger scientists in Swift's *Gulliver's Travels.*

THE VICTORIAN PERIOD

happiness in general, my dejection must continue; but that if I could see such an outlet, I should then look on the world with pleasure; content as far as I was myself concerned, with any fair share of the general lot.

This state of my thoughts and feelings made the fact of my reading Wordsworth for the first time (in the autumn of 1828) an important event in my life. I took up the collection of his poems from curiosity, with no expectation of mental relief from it, though I had before resorted to poetry with that hope. In the worst period of my depression, I had read through the whole of Byron (then new to me), to try whether a poet, whose peculiar department was supposed to be that of the intenser feelings, could rouse any feeling in me. As might be expected, I got no good from this reading, but the reverse. The poet's state of mind was too like my own. His was the lament of a man who had worn out all pleasures, and who seemed to think that life, to all who possess the good things of it, must necessarily be the vapid, uninteresting thing which I found it. His Harold[8] and Manfred[9] had the same burden on them which I had. . . . But while Byron was exactly what did not suit my condition, Wordsworth was exactly what did. I had looked into the *Excursion*[10] two or three years before, and found little in it; and I should probably have found as little, had I read it at this time. But the miscellaneous poems, in the two-volume edition of 1815 (to which little of value was added in the latter part of the author's life), proved to be the precise thing for my mental wants at that particular juncture.

In the first place, these poems addressed themselves powerfully to one of the strongest of my pleasurable susceptibilities, the love of rural objects and natural scenery; to which I had been indebted not only for much of the pleasure of my life, but quite recently for relief from one of my longest relapses into depression. In this power of rural beauty over me, there was a foundation laid for taking pleasure in Wordsworth's poetry; the more so, as his scenery lies mostly among mountains, which, owing to my early Pyrenean[11] excursion, were my ideal of natural beauty. But Wordsworth would never have had any great effect on me, if he had merely placed before me beautiful pictures of natural scenery. Scott does this still better than Wordsworth, and a very second-rate landscape does it more effectually than any poet. What made Wordsworth's poems a medicine for my state of mind, was that they expressed, not mere outward beauty, but states of feeling, and of thought colored by feeling, under the excitement of beauty. They seemed to be the very culture of the feelings, which I was in quest of. In them I seemed to draw from a source of inward joy, of sympathetic and imaginative pleasure, which could be shared in by all human beings; which had no connection with struggle or imperfection, but would be made richer by every improvement in the physical or social condition of mankind. From them I seemed to learn what would be the perennial sources of happiness, when all the greater evils of life shall have been removed. And I felt myself at once better and happier as I came under their influence. There have certainly been, even in our own age, greater poets than Wordsworth; but poetry of deeper and

8 **Harold:** hero of *Childe Harold's Pilgrimage.*
9 **Manfred:** the hero of a play by Byron.
10 *Excursion:* long philosophic poem of 1814.

11 **Pyrenean** (pĭr ə nē'ən): adjective referring to the Pyrenees mountains in Spain.

JOHN STUART MILL

loftier feeling could not have done for me at that time what his did. I needed to be made to feel that there was real, permanent happiness in tranquil contemplation. Wordsworth taught me this, not only without turning away from, but with a greatly increased interest in the common feelings and common destiny of human beings. And the delight which these poems gave me, proved that with culture of this sort, there was nothing to dread from the most confirmed habit of analysis. . . . The result was that I gradually, but completely, emerged from my habitual depression, and was never again subject to it.

Comment

You now have seen for yourself more than one effect of Mill's severe education in this selection. His very style is that of one who has been rigorously trained in formal subjects: his vocabulary is heavily Latin. (Like Samuel Johnson, he uses such words as *felicitate, insipid, animation,* rather than their more informal equivalents with Anglo-Saxon roots.) And yet beneath the formality he tells a moving and human tale. It is the tale of one who moved from an "Everlasting No" to an "Everlasting Yea" when the power of his feelings, his buried emotional life, reasserted itself.

1. What do you learn about Mill's education and about the character of his father from his account of his depression?
2. As he was "accidentally" reading the passage in which the French writer Marmontel tells how he responded to the death of his father, something happened to Mill. "From this moment my burden grew lighter," he says. How do you account for the fact that Mill did not bring his habit of analysis to bear on this scene? What must it have shown him about his own father? What must it have shown him in himself? Why do you think his feelings here were, for him, unanalyzable?
3. Judging, then, by the values Mill came to discover in Wordsworth after this experience, what had been missing from his life? In what, alone, did he have faith before his "crisis"? And in what did he have faith after his "crisis" had passed?
4. As you have already read, Mill believed that all men must be free to express themselves and to develop themselves, each to his fullest capacity. What effect do you think Mill's "crisis" had on the formation of this, his deepest political belief?

Matthew Arnold (1822-1888)

Like many Victorian fathers, Thomas Arnold, the father of Matthew Arnold, was a most serious and dedicated man; he was, moreover, the Headmaster of Rugby School and one of the foremost educators of the 19th century. Young Matthew Arnold was raised and educated in his father's shadow at Rugby and proceeded to Oxford University. There, perhaps not surprisingly, he behaved for a time in a manner quite unlike that expected of the son of Thomas Arnold: he affected fancy waistcoats and the casual airs of an elegant dandy; he even came close to doing very badly as a student. In 1857 when he returned to Oxford to lecture as Professor of Poetry (a highly distinguished, part-time office), he asserted that "high seriousness" is the most important and most valuable characteristic of the man of letters. In the meantime, in 1847, he had become an inspector of schools in the government Education Office, a function that he performed with great conscientiousness for thirty-five years. His period of youthful casualness was short-lived.

To his contemporaries Arnold was better known as a critic and essayist than as a poet. John Stuart Mill, as you have seen, turned to Wordsworth's poetry for that "culture of the feelings" which he felt he needed after his crisis. In his most famous essay, *Culture and Anarchy*, Matthew Arnold argued that all human beings are in need of the cultivation of their emotional and spiritual lives, as Mill discovered. It was not enough, said Arnold, that his fellows were rich and practical, as many of them were. Those who were satisfied with wealth and machinery he called "Philistines," and to the narrow satisfactions of "Philistinism" Arnold opposed the discipline of what he called "sweetness and light."

Philistinism, according to Arnold, is the code of those who believe that culture is merely a matter of "doing as one likes." Arnold certainly believed, as did Mill, in individual self-development—as an educator, in fact, he devoted his life to it. But he also argued that if people did as they liked, and if the culture of the society had no goals beyond the assurance of wealth and the comforts of materialism, then society would lapse into a scramble that would be anarchy, or disorder. Arnold believed that the culture of his time required the civilizing influence of the "high seriousness" of great literature. For he believed that culture is "a study of perfection." But by "perfection" and "high seriousness" he did not mean some rigid and joyless standard that we must strive to live up to. He meant, rather, what he called "a harmonious expansion of *all* the powers which make the beauty and worth of human nature." And another name—it soon became a well-known phrase—that Arnold gave to this "harmonious expansion" was "sweetness and light." He meant nothing soft or shy by this famous phrase: he meant something like the human and humane values that John Stuart Mill discovered; he meant the human and humane values that England in the third quarter of the 19th century, a proud and wealthy nation, was in danger of forgetting. Arnold's phrases as a critic of his times were memorable. But though many remembered them, they did not, unfortunately, act upon them.

Most of Arnold's poetry was published in the 1850's. He wrote much less than Tennyson and his other famous contemporaries. Yet his best-known poems, melancholy and poignant as they sometimes are, present with great freshness both the wonder and the sadness of the 19th-century experience. It was an adventurous time, for it placed great value on the individual and the efforts made to achieve success. It was also a bewildering time, for new individual enterprises, in science, in industry, and in political life, came so fast and in such profusion that they swept away many traditional ways of feeling and believing. What could take their place? To this question Matthew Arnold's poems return again and again. The great question to be faced by the poet, by the writer, he said, is "How to live?" It is a question he never forgot in his own writing.

"Self-Dependence"

"Resolve to be thyself": this is one clear answer to the question of "How to live?" It is the answer given by one of Arnold's best-known poems, first published in 1852.

Self-Dependence

Matthew Arnold

Weary of myself, and sick of asking
What I am, and what I ought to be,
At this vessel's prow I stand, which bears me
Forwards, forwards, o'er the starlit sea.

And a look of passionate desire   5
O'er the sea and to the stars I send:
"Ye who from my childhood up have calmed me,
Calm me, ah, compose me to the end!

"Ah, once more," I cried, "ye stars, ye waters,
On my heart your mighty charm renew;   10
Still, still let me, as I gaze upon you,
Feel my soul becoming vast like you!"

From the intense, clear, star-sown vault of heaven,
Over the lit sea's unquiet way,
In the rustling night air came the answer: 15
"Wouldst thou *be* as these are? *Live* as they.

"Unaffrighted by the silence round them,
Undistracted by the sights they see,
These demand not that the things without them
Yield them love, amusement, sympathy.   20

"And with joy the stars perform their shining,
And the sea its long moon-silvered roll;
For self-poised they live, nor pine with noting
All the fever of some differing soul.[1]

"Bounded by themselves, and unregardful   25
In what state God's other works may be,
In their own tasks all their powers pouring,
These attain the mighty life you see."

O air-born voice! long since, severely clear,
A cry like thine in mine own heart I hear: 30
"Resolve to be thyself; and know that he,
Who finds himself, loses his misery!"

---

1 nor . . . soul: The sea and the stars do not jealously wish for the feverish activities of
natural elements different from themselves.

Comment

Once again a 19th-century poet imagines himself standing on a ship that bears him over the sea, and once again he asks what his proper destiny should be.

1. How does the poet describe himself as the poem begins? What similarity do you find between his condition and that of Tennyson in *In Memoriam* or Mill in his *Autobiography?*
2. What is the "mighty charm" of the sea and the stars that he asks to be renewed?
3. To the poet's cry there comes an answer, beginning at line 16. How does the answering voice describe the stars and the sea? According to the voice, what is the source of their power?
4. In the last two lines the poet speaks again: how do his words parallel those of the "air-born voice"?
5. The message of the answering voice is clear. But what of the source of the voice itself? It cannot be the stars and the sea speaking (it does not say "we" but "they"). What is it that speaks to the poet, ending his weariness and misery?

"Isolation"

In 1852, when this poem first appeared, it was entitled "To Marguerite, in Returning a Volume of the Letters of Ortis." (*The Letters of Ortis,* a novel by the Italian poet Ugo Foscolo, is a tragic tale of despair and suicide.) In the 1857 edition of his poems, Arnold gave it the title "Isolation," which is certainly more appropriate to its theme. The poem was originally one of a group in which there figures a mysterious Marguerite whom Arnold may have met during a visit to Switzerland in 1848. But whether there was such an actual person, and whether Arnold was in love with her and then parted from her, no one has been able to discover.

Isolation

Matthew Arnold

Yes! in the sea of life enisled,[1]
With echoing straits between us thrown,
Dotting the shoreless watery wild,[2]
We mortal millions live *alone*.
The islands feel the enclasping flow,   5
And then their endless bounds they know.

But when the moon their hollows lights,
And they are swept by balms of spring,
And in their glens, on starry nights,
The nightingales divinely sing;   10
And lovely notes, from shore to shore,
Across the sounds[3] and channels pour—

Oh! then a longing like despair
Is to their farthest caverns sent;
For surely once, they feel, we were   15
Parts of a single continent!
Now round us spreads the watery plain—
Oh might our marges[4] meet again!

Who ordered, that their longing's fire
Should be, as soon as kindled, cooled?   20
Who renders vain their deep desire?—
A God, a God their severance ruled![5]
And bade betwixt their shores to be
The unplumbed,[6] salt, estranging sea.

1 **enisled** (ĕn īld′): made an island of.
2 **wild:** wilderness.
3 **sounds:** straits.
4 **marges:** margins; shores.
5 **severance ruled:** decreed that they should be severed.
6 **unplumbed:** of unmeasured depth.

Comment

Individuals, according to "Self-Dependence," must be "Bounded by themselves," as are the stars and the sea. Here, in the poem "Isolation," Arnold stresses the loneliness of the human condition, the loneliness that is a consequence of such self-dependence as that of the stars or the sea.

1. "We mortal millions live alone," each an island in the sea of life: so the poem announces our isolation. What, then, is the tone of the

very first word, "Yes!"? Is this a "Yes" of affirmation? of despair? of resignation?

2. Stanzas 2 and 3 are one long sentence: in your own words, very briefly, what does this sentence say? What does Arnold seem to you to symbolize with the "lovely notes" of the "nightingales"? Why should the song of the nightingales make the islands feel they were once "Parts of a single continent"? What is the "longing" evoked by the nightingales' song?

3. In the final stanza the poet asks and answers a question. What does the question tell us about the desire that is stirred by the "lovely notes"? And what of the tone of the answer: what difference in tone do you find between stanza 3 (notice the two exclamations, "Oh") and the last three lines of the poem?

4. The "sea of life" (l. 1) of this poem becomes "The unplumbed, salt, estranging sea" (1.24). The longing of men once again to be "Parts of a single continent" is a longing that cannot be satisfied. How do you characterize Arnold's attitude toward human experience in this poem?

"Dover Beach"

As many American travelers know, and as thousands of Americans know who fought in World War II, Dover is the port on the English Channel nearest to France. It is so near that on a clear, moonlight night, standing on the white cliffs of Dover (they are cliffs of white, chalky limestone) one can catch glimpses of the French coast opposite. Below the cliffs, spreading out beside the busy harbor, are pebbly beaches upon which the tides and waves of the Channel ceaselessly move. Dover is the port that since the days of Chaucer has both joined and separated England from the Continent; its distance from Europe is short, yet it is a distance that has helped to preserve England's own long tradition of "self-dependence." "Dover Beach" is the title and the scene of Arnold's most famous poem.

600

Dover Beach

Matthew Arnold

The sea is calm tonight.
The tide is full, the moon lies fair
Upon the straits;—on the French coast the light
Gleams and is gone; the cliffs of England stand,
Glimmering and vast, out in the tranquil bay.   5
Come to the window, sweet is the night air!
Only, from the long line of spray
Where the sea meets the moon-blanched[1] land,
Listen! you hear the grating roar
Of pebbles which the waves draw back, and fling,   10
At their return, up the high strand,[2]
Begin, and cease, and then again begin,
With tremulous cadence slow, and bring
The eternal note of sadness in.

Sophocles long ago   15
Heard it on the Aegean, and it brought
Into his mind the turbid ebb and flow
Of human misery;[3] we
Find also in the sound a thought,
Hearing it by this distant northern sea.   ·   20

The Sea of Faith
Was once, too, at the full, and round earth's shore
Lay like the folds of a bright girdle furled.[4]
But now I only hear
Its melancholy, long, withdrawing roar,   25
Retreating, to the breath
Of the night wind, down the vast edges drear
And naked shingles[5] of the world.

---

1 moon-blanched: turned white by the moon.
2 strand: shore.
3 Sophocles (sŏf′ə klēz′) . . . **misery:** Arnold seems to be referring primarily to a passage from the Greek dramatist's tragedy *Antigone.* The passage to which he probably refers is one in which the whole human race is imagined as being buffeted by the waves of a hostile sea.
4 The Sea . . . furled: Arnold imagines a time in the past when the sea that surrounds men's lives did not ebb and flow, but was stationary at full tide: it surrounded the world of men like a sash ("girdle"), a piece of cloth that folded itself against the shore.
5 naked shingles: beaches with a hard surface covered with pebbles.

Ah, love, let us be true
To one another! for the world, which seems   30
To lie before us like a land of dreams,
So various, so beautiful, so new,
Hath really neither joy, nor love, nor light,
Nor certitude, nor peace, nor help for pain;
And we are here as on a darkling plain   35
Swept with confused alarms of struggle and flight,
Where ignorant armies clash by night.

Comment

The last stanza (it would be more correct, perhaps, to call it a verse-paragraph, for, although there is a system of rhymes in each "stanza," the lines are of unequal length)—the last stanza of "Dover Beach" was written some time previous to the rest of the poem. It contains, as you have seen, no reiteration of the imagery of the waves and tides of the sea. Yet it does propose a "faith" with which the poet will stand up against the ceaseless ebb and flow, the endless struggle of doubt and faith, that he sees in human history.

1. What is the situation presented in the first stanza? How do we know the speaker is not alone?
2. What does the speaker hear, in lines 9-14, that brings "The eternal note of sadness in"?
3. In the second stanza the speaker turns to an allusion to Sophocles, an ancient Greek dramatist. How does his reference to Sophocles support his line about the *eternal* "note of sadness"?
4. With what contrast of imagery in stanza 3 does the speaker describe his present situation?
5. The last stanza begins with a direct address: "Ah, love, let us be true/ To one another!"
   (*a*) When you come to the words "Ah, love. . . ." what change of tone must you make?
   (*b*) In lines 33-37 the world outside of "us" is contrasted with the world of the speaker and the person whom he addresses. What is the difference between the world of "us" and the world of the "darkling plain"?
6. "We mortal millions live *alone*," Arnold writes in "Isolation." How does "Dover Beach" modify this statement? Arnold's struggle between doubt and faith, it is clear, is less decisive than that of Tennyson or Mill. But does he come to a kind of faith in "Dover Beach"? And if so, how is his faith different from or similar to that of Tennyson and Mill?

Arthur Hugh Clough (1819-1861)

Matthew Arnold wrote a long poem, the elegy called "Thyrsis," to the memory of his close friend Arthur Hugh Clough. Like Arnold, Clough had been a student at Rugby and then at Oxford. Like Arnold too, he later went to work in the Education Office. And, like Arnold, he was a poet who addressed himself to the most troubling emotional and intellectual problems of his time.

Clough's short career, however, was less successful than that of his famous friend. He spent part of his childhood in Charleston, South Carolina, where his father had moved his family in order to look after his affairs as a cotton merchant. Later, after his university days, Clough returned to the United States and for a time planned to settle in Boston and establish a college preparatory school, but amid uncertainties he gave up the project and went back to England. His life was unsettled—in every sense; he was uncertain whether he belonged to the New World or the Old.

"Say Not the Struggle Nought Availeth"

Yet his doubts and his hopes gave rise to many striking poems. Most of them are long narrative poems that were not always understood by his contemporaries. One poem, however, spoke and still speaks from the center of the concern he shared with the greatest writers of his time.

Say Not
the Struggle
Nought Availeth

Arthur Hugh Clough

Say not the struggle nought availeth,
    The labor and the wounds are vain,
The enemy faints not, nor faileth,
    And as things have been they remain.

If hopes were dupes, fears may be liars;   5
    It may be, in yon smoke concealed,
Your comrades chase e'en now the fliers,
    And, but for you, possess the field.

For while the tired waves, vainly breaking,
    Seem here no painful inch to gain,   10
Far back, through creeks and inlets making,
    Comes silent, flooding in, the main,

And not by eastern windows only,
    When daylight comes, comes in the light,
In front, the sun climbs slow, how slowly,   15
    But westward, look, the land is bright.

Comment

Once more the familiar situation: the poet attempts to counter despair. He seems to speak only to himself, but he speaks for anyone who has heard a voice saying that the struggle is useless, that nothing is changed by fighting on.

1. The poem begins as if making a reply—"Say not": to what assertions is the poet replying "Say not" in stanza 1? What do you understand him to mean by "the enemy"? In stanza 2 the imagery of the battlefield is continued: what do you understand by the terms *smoke, comrades, fliers,* and *field?*
2. Stanza 3 presents the poet's situation in a new image. As he develops this image, how do lines 9 and 10 parallel what he has told us in stanza 1? But how is the situation seen differently in lines 11 and 12?
3. Stanza 4 presents the situation in yet another image. How does the development of this image reaffirm what we are told in lines 11 and 12?
4. Keeping in mind the theme of this poem and the three main images in which it is expressed, and remembering also the two words with which it begins, write an essay on "Say Not the Struggle Nought Availeth" as summing up the Victorian theme of doubt and faith.

The Nature of the Individual

"WHO FINDS HIMSELF, loses his misery," wrote Matthew Arnold. Today we still speak of people "finding themselves," and by this phrase we usually mean that someone has made a transition from doubt and uncertainty to faith and assurance. But we have also seen, in the preceding selections from Tennyson, Mill, and Arnold, that this finding of oneself, as Victorian authors imagined it, was not a simple task. For they saw that no "self" is simple, that every self, beginning with one's own, consists of both talents and blind spots, of both strengths and weaknesses, of qualities to be proud of mixed with others to be ashamed of. As you will see in the next chapter, the 19th-century interest in the individual was expressed mainly by the novel. But many writers other than novelists were interested in the character of the self, writers as different from each other as scientists and poets.

Reproduced by permission of The President and Council of The Royal College of Surgeons of England

Darwin's study at Down, his country house in Kent, where he did his writing each morning for many years. The house is now maintained as a museum.

Charles Robert Darwin (1809-1882)

It may at first sight seem surprising to include in a book of literature, selections from the autobiography of a great scientist—especially when that scientist says in his opening paragraph, "I have taken no pains about my style of writing." The following selections come from the *Autobiography* of Charles Darwin, which he wrote in the last years of his life. In his opening sentences, besides apologizing for his style, Darwin says that he wrote an account of his own life because "it would have interested me greatly to have read even so short and dull a sketch of the mind of my grandfather [Erasmus Darwin, a famous physician and poet], written by himself, and what he thought and did and how he worked." Darwin wrote his autobiographical sketch for his children and grandchildren because he suspected that they, like himself, would be interested in another person's self-analysis and self-appraisal.

As much of the following account will indicate, Charles Darwin was born into a prosperous family in Shrewsbury, an ancient town near the Welsh border, the site of a famous school which he attended. His father was a gifted and prosperous physician; he was related (as was his wife) to the Wedgwood family, descendants of the great 18th-century manufacturer of fine pottery and china. After university training at Edinburgh and Cambridge, Darwin spent five years as a naturalist on the voyage of a government ship, the *Beagle,* to South America to collect oceanographic and other scientific information. His own findings led him to publish important works on the formation of coral reefs and on volcanic islands; his narrative of the whole scientific adventure, *The Voyage of the "Beagle,"* based on his diaries, is one of the most fascinating scientific travel books of the 19th century. After his return to England and his marriage, Darwin lived a retired life at a remote country house, called Down, in Kent. His health was poor, and the number of hours that he could work in a day were few. He lived by a strict but quiet schedule: in his study in the morning, being read to and resting after lunch (he tells us how dependent he was on novels), a walk in his garden to inspect his growing plants, a quiet evening with his family—such was the day, for many years, of one of the great minds of the period. Others anticipated, in part, his formulation of the theory of evolution. But no one matched his full, carefully wrought, painstakingly argued account of that theory, the result of many years of persistent, imaginative, unceasing work.

From

Autobiography

Charles Darwin

I

I WAS BORN at Shrewsbury on February 12, 1809. I have heard my father say that he believed that persons with powerful minds generally had memories extending far back to a very early period of life. This is not my case for my earliest recollection goes back only to when I was a few months over four years old, when we went to near Abergele[1] for sea bathing, and I recollect

1 Abergele: on the northern coast of Wales.

some events and places there with some little distinctness.

My mother died in July, 1817, when I was a little over eight years old, and it is odd that I can remember hardly anything about her except her deathbed, her black velvet gown, and her curiously constructed worktable. I believe that my forgetfulness is partly due to my sisters, owing to their great grief, never being able to speak about her or mention her name; and partly to her previous invalid state. In the spring of this same year I was sent to a day school in Shrewsbury, where I stayed a year. Before going to school I was educated by my sister Caroline, but I doubt whether this plan answered. I have been told that I was much slower in learning than my younger sister Catherine, and I believe that I was in many ways a naughty boy. Caroline was extremely kind, clever and zealous; but she was too zealous in trying to improve me; for I clearly remember after this long interval of years, saying to myself when about to enter a room where she was—"What will she blame me for now?" and I made myself dogged so as not to care what she might say.

By the time I went to this day school my taste for natural history, and more especially for collecting, was well developed. I tried to make out the names of plants, and collected all sorts of things, shells, seals,[2] franks,[3] coins, and minerals. The passion for collecting, which leads a man to be a systematic naturalist, a virtuoso[4] or a miser, was very strong in me, and was clearly innate, as none of my sisters or brother ever had this taste.

One little event during this year has fixed itself very firmly in my mind, and I hope that it has done so from my conscience having been afterwards sorely troubled by it; it is curious as showing that apparently I was interested at this early age in the variability of plants! I told another little boy (I believe it was Leighton, who afterwards become a well-known lichenologist[5] and botanist) that I could produce variously colored polyanthuses[6] and primroses by watering them with certain colored fluids, which was of course a monstrous fable, and had never been tried by me. I may here also confess that as a little boy I was much given to inventing deliberate falsehoods, and this was always done for the sake of causing excitement. For instance, I once gathered much valuable fruit from my father's trees and hid them in the shrubbery, and then ran in breathless haste to spread the news that I had discovered a hoard of stolen fruit.

About this time, or as I hope at a somewhat earlier age, I sometimes stole fruit for the sake of eating it; and one of my schemes was ingenious. The kitchen garden was kept locked in the evening, and was surrounded by a high wall, but by the aid of neighboring trees I could easily get on the coping.[7] I then fixed a long stick into the hole at the bottom of a rather large flowerpot, and by dragging this upwards pulled off peaches and plums, which fell into the pot and the prizes were thus secured. When a very little boy I remember stealing apples from the orchard, for the sake of giving them away to some boys and young men who lived in a cottage not far off, but before I gave them the fruit I showed off how quickly I could run and it is wonderful that I did not perceive that the surprise and admiration which they expressed at my powers of running was given for the sake of the apples. But I well remember that I was delighted at them declaring that they had never seen a boy run so fast!

I remember clearly only one other incident during the years whilst at Mr. Case's daily school—namely, the burial of a dragoon[8] soldier; and it is surprising how clearly I can still see the horse with the man's empty boots and carbine suspended to the saddle, and the firing over the grave. This scene deeply stirred whatever poetic fancy there was in me.

In the summer of 1818 I went to Dr. Butler's great school in Shrewsbury, and remained there for seven years till midsummer 1825, when I was sixteen years old. I boarded at this school, so that I had the great advantage of living the life of a true schoolboy; but as the dis-

2 seals: engraved metal stamps.
3 franks: the signature (of a member of the House of Lords, for example) on letters sent free of postage.
4 virtuoso: ardent collector.
5 lichenologist (lī'kə nŏl'ə jĭst): botanist who studies lichens—mosses and fungi.
6 polyanthuses (pŏl'ĭ ăn'thəs əz): cultivated primroses, often colored.

7 coping: top, or covering, of a wall.
8 dragoon: cavalryman armed with a musket or carbine.

tance was hardly more than a mile to my home, I very often ran there in the longer intervals between the callings over[9] and before locking up at night. This I think was in many ways advantageous to me by keeping up home affections and interests. I remember in the early part of my school life that I often had to run very quickly to be in time, and from being a fleet runner was generally successful; but when in doubt I prayed earnestly to God to help me, and I well remember that I attributed my success to the prayers and not to my quick running, and marveled how generally I was aided.

I have heard my father and elder sisters say that I had, as a very young boy, a strong taste for long solitary walks; but what I thought about I know not. I often became quite absorbed, and once, whilst returning to school on the summit of the old fortifications round Shrewsbury, which had been converted into a public footpath with no parapet on one side, I walked off and fell to the ground, but the height was only seven or eight feet. Nevertheless the number of thoughts which passed through my mind during this very short, but sudden and wholly unexpected fall, was astonishing, and seem hardly compatible with what physiologists have, I believe, proved about each thought requiring quite an appreciable amount of time.

I must have been a very simple little fellow when I first went to the school. A boy of the name of Garnett took me into a cake shop one day, and bought some cakes for which he did not pay, as the shopman trusted him. When we came out I asked him why he did not pay for them, and he instantly answered, "Why, do you not know that my uncle left a great sum of money to the Town on condition that every tradesman should give whatever was wanted without payment to anyone who wore his old hat and moved it in a particular manner;" and he then showed me how it was moved. He then went into another shop where he was trusted, and asked for some small article, moving his hat in the proper manner, and of course obtained it without payment. When we came out he said, "Now if you like to go by yourself into that cake shop (how well I remember its exact position), I will lend you my hat, and you can get whatever you like if you move the hat on your head properly." I gladly accepted the generous offer, and went in and asked for some cakes, moved the old hat, and was walking out of the shop, when the shopman made a rush at me, so I dropped the cakes and ran away for dear life, and was astonished by being greeted with shouts of laughter by my false friend Garnett.

I can say in my own favor that I was as a boy humane, but I owed this entirely to the instruction and example of my sisters. I doubt indeed, whether humanity is a natural or innate quality. I was very fond of collecting eggs, but I never took more than a single egg out of a bird's nest, except on one single occasion, when I took all, not for their value, but from a sort of bravado.

I had a strong taste for angling, and would sit for any number of hours on the bank of a river or pond watching the float;[10] when at Maer[11] I was told that I could kill the worms with salt and water, and from that day I never spitted a living worm, though at the expense, probably, of some loss of success.

Once as a very little boy, whilst at the

9 callings over: roll calls.

10 float: attached to his fishing line.
11 Maer: the country estate of the Wedgwoods.

day school, or before that time, I acted cruelly, for I beat a puppy I believe, simply from enjoying the sense of power; but the beating could not have been severe, for the puppy did not howl, of which I feel sure as the spot was near to the house. This act lay heavily on my conscience, as is shown by my remembering the exact spot where the crime was committed. It probably lay all the heavier from my love of dogs being then, and for a long time afterwards, a passion. Dogs seemed to know this, for I was an adept in robbing their love from their masters.

Nothing could have been worse for the development of my mind than Dr. Butler's school, as it was strictly classical, nothing else[12] being taught except a little ancient geography and history. The school as a means of education to me was simply a blank. During my whole life I have been singularly incapable of mastering any language. Especial attention was paid to versemaking,[13] and this I could never do well. I had many friends, and got together a grand collection of old verses, which by patching together, sometimes aided by other boys, I could work into any subject. Much attention was paid to learning by heart the lessons of the previous day; this I could effect with great facility learning forty or fifty lines of Virgil or Homer, whilst I was in morning chapel; but this exercise was utterly useless, for every verse was forgotten in forty-eight hours. I was not idle, and with the exception of versification, generally worked conscientiously at my classics, not using cribs. The sole pleasure I ever received from such studies was from some of the odes of Horace, which I admired greatly. When I left the school I was for my age

neither high nor low in it; and I believe that I was considered by all my masters and by my father as a very ordinary boy, rather below the common standard in intellect. To my deep mortification my father once said to me, "You care for nothing but shooting, dogs, and rat-catching, and you will be a disgrace to yourself and all your family." But my father, who was the kindest man I ever knew, and whose memory I love with all my heart, must have been angry and somewhat unjust when he used such words.

* * *

Looking back as well as I can at my character during my school life, the only qualities which at this period promised well for the future were that I had strong and diversified tastes, much zeal for whatever interested me, and a keen pleasure in understanding any complex subject or thing. I was taught Euclid by a private tutor, and I distinctly remember the intense satisfaction which the clear geometrical proofs gave me. I remember with equal distinctness the delight which my uncle gave me (the father of Francis Galton[14]) by explaining the principle of the vernier[15] of a barometer. With respect to diversified tastes, independently of science, I was fond of reading various books, and I used to sit for hours reading the historical plays of Shakespeare, generally in an old window in the thick walls of the school. I read also other poetry, such as the recently published poems of Byron, Scott, and Thomson's *Seasons*. I mention this because later in life I wholly lost, to my great regret, all pleasure from poetry of any kind, including Shakespeare. In

---

12 **nothing else:** i.e., except Latin and Greek.
13 **versemaking:** composing Latin verses.

14 **Galton:** founder of the science of eugenics.
15 **vernier** (vûr′nĬ ər): a short, movable scale to indicate finer readings of the divisions of a graduated instrument. (Darwin refers to a mercury barometer.)

connection with pleasure from poetry I may add that in 1822 a vivid delight in scenery was first awakened in my mind, during a riding tour on the borders of Wales, and which has lasted longer than any other aesthetic pleasure.

[*The next passage comes from Darwin's account of his life as a student at Cambridge University, which he attended after two years of medical study at Edinburgh. At Cambridge he was interested in guns—he became an expert shot—and also in music. Music, indeed, gave him "intense pleasure, so that [his] backbone would sometimes shiver"; and yet he could not carry a tune! To the delight of his friends, he could not even recognize "God Save the King" if they played it very fast or very slow.*]

II

BUT NO PURSUIT at Cambridge was followed with nearly so much eagerness or gave me so much pleasure as collecting beetles. It was the mere passion for collecting, for I did not dissect them and rarely compared their external characters with published descriptions, but got them named anyhow. I will give a proof of my zeal: one day, on tearing off some old bark, I saw two rare beetles and seized one in each hand; then I saw a third and new kind, which I could not bear to lose, so that I popped the one which I held in my right hand into my mouth. Alas it ejected some intensely acrid fluid, which burnt my tongue so that I was forced to spit the beetle out, which was lost, as well as the third one.

I was very successful in collecting and invented two new methods; I employed a laborer to scrape during the winter, moss off old trees and place [it] in a large bag, and likewise to collect the rubbish at the bottom of the barges in which reeds are brought from the fens,[16] and thus I got some very rare species. No poet ever felt more delight at seeing his first poem published than I did at seeing in Stephen's *Illustrations of British Insects* the magic words, "captured by C. Darwin, Esq." I was introduced to entomology by my second cousin, W. Darwin Fox, a clever and most pleasant man, who was then at Christ's College, and with whom I became extremely intimate. Afterwards I became well acquainted with and went out collecting, with Albert Way of Trinity, who in after years became a well-known archaeologist; also with H. Thompson, of the same college, afterwards a leading agriculturist, chairman of a great railway, and Member of Parliament. It seems therefore that a taste for collecting beetles is some indication of future success in life!

I am surprised what an indelible impression many of the beetles which I caught at Cambridge have left on my mind. I can remember the exact appearance of certain posts, old trees and banks where I made a good capture. The pretty *Panagoeus crux-major* was a treasure in those days, and here at Down I saw a beetle running across a walk, and on picking it up instantly perceived that it differed slightly from *P. crux-major*, and it turned out to be *P. quadripunctatus*, which is only a variety or closely allied species, differing from it very slightly in outline. I had never seen in those old days Licinus alive, which to an uneducated eye hardly differs from many other black Carabidous beetles; but my sons found here a specimen and I instantly recognized that it was new to me; yet I had not looked at a British beetle for the last twenty years.

16 **fens:** marshes. (The reeds were used for thatching.)

[In the final pages of his autobiography, after commenting on each of his books, Darwin turns to an account of his powers of mind and how he used them as a scientist.]

III

I AM NOT conscious of any change in my mind during the last thirty years, excepting in one point presently to be mentioned; nor indeed could any change have been expected unless one of general deterioration. But my father lived to his eighty-third year with his mind as lively as ever it was, and all his faculties undimmed; and I hope that I may die before my mind fails to a sensible extent. I think that I have become a little more skillful in guessing right explanations and in devising experimental tests; but this may probably be the result of mere practice, and of a larger store of knowledge. I have as much difficulty as ever in expressing myself clearly and concisely; and this difficulty has caused me a very great loss of time; but it has had the compensating advantage of forcing me to think long and intently about every sentence, and thus I have been often led to see errors in reasoning and in my own observations or those of others.

There seems to be a sort of fatality in my mind leading me to put at first my statement and proposition in a wrong or awkward form. Formerly I used to think about my sentences before writing them down; but for several years I have found that it saves time to scribble in a vile hand whole pages as quickly as I possibly can, contracting half the words; and then correct deliberately. Sentences thus scribbled down are often better ones than I could have written deliberately.

Having said this much about my manner of writing, I will add that with my larger books I spend a good deal of time over the general arrangement of the matter. I first make the rudest outline in two or three pages, and then a larger one in several pages, a few words or one word standing for a whole discussion or series of facts. Each of these headings is again enlarged and often transformed before I begin to write in extenso.[17] As in several of my books facts observed by others have been very extensively used, and as I have always had several quite distinct subjects in hand at the same time, I may mention that I keep from thirty to forty large portfolios, in cabinets with labeled shelves, into which I can at once put a detached reference or memorandum. I have bought many books and at their ends I make an index of all the facts that concern my work; or, if the book is not my own, write out a separate abstract, and of such abstracts I have a large drawer full. Before beginning on any subject I look to all the short indexes and make a general and classified index, and by taking the one or more proper portfolios I have all the information collected during my life ready for use.

I have said that in one respect my mind has changed during the last twenty or thirty years. Up to the age of thirty, or beyond it, poetry of many kinds, such as the works of Milton, Gray, Byron, Wordsworth, Coleridge, and Shelley, gave me great pleasure, and even as a schoolboy I took intense delight in Shakespeare, especially in the historical plays. I have also said that formerly pictures gave me considerable, and music very great delight. But now for many years I cannot endure to read a line of poetry: I have tried lately to read Shakespeare, and found it so intolerably dull that it nauseated me. I

17 in extenso: in detailed length.

have also almost lost any taste for pictures or music.—Music generally sets me thinking too energetically on what I have been at work on, instead of giving me pleasure. I retain some taste for fine scenery, but it does not cause me the exquisite delight which it formerly did. On the other hand, novels which are works of the imagination, though not of a very high order, have been for years a wonderful relief and pleasure to me, and I often bless all novelists. A surprising number have been read aloud to me, and I like all if moderately good, and if they do not end unhappily—against which a law ought to be passed. A novel, according to my taste, does not come into the first class unless it contains some person whom one can thoroughly love, and if it be a pretty woman all the better.

This curious and lamentable loss of the higher aesthetic tastes is all the odder, as books on history, biographies and travels (independently of any scientific facts which they may contain), and essays on all sorts of subjects interest me as much as ever they did. My mind seems to have become a kind of machine for grinding general laws out of large collections of facts, but why this should have caused the atrophy of that part of the brain alone, on which the higher tastes depend, I cannot conceive. A man with a mind more highly organized or better constituted than mine, would not I suppose have thus suffered; and if I had to live my life again I would have made a rule to read some poetry and listen to some music at least once every week; for perhaps the parts of my brain now atrophied could thus have been kept active through use. The loss of these tastes is a loss of happiness, and may possibly be injurious to the intellect, and more probably to the moral character, by enfeebling the emotional part of our nature.

My books have sold largely in England, have been translated into many languages, and passed through several editions in foreign countries. I have heard it said that the success of a work abroad is the best test of its enduring value. I doubt whether this is at all trustworthy; but judged by this standard my name ought to last for a few years. Therefore it may be worthwhile for me to try to analyze the mental qualities and the conditions on which my success has depended; though I am aware that no man can do this correctly.

I have no great quickness of apprehension or wit which is so remarkable in some clever men, for instance Huxley.[18] I am therefore a poor critic: a paper or book, when first read, generally excites my admiration, and it is only after considerable reflection that I perceive the weak points. My power to follow a long and purely abstract train of thought is very limited; I should, moreover, never have succeeded with metaphysics or mathematics. My memory is extensive, yet hazy: it suffices to make me cautious by vaguely telling me that I have observed or read something opposed to the conclusion which I am drawing, or on the other hand in favor of it; and after a time I can generally recollect where to search for my authority. So poor in one sense is my memory, that I have never been able to remember for more than a few days a single date or a line of poetry.

Some of my critics have said, "Oh, he is a good observer, but has no power of reasoning." I do not think that this can be true, for the *Origin of Species* is one long argument from the beginning

---

18 **Huxley:** Thomas Henry Huxley (1825-1895), biologist and essayist, who did much to make Darwin's theories known.

to the end, and it has convinced not a few able men. No one could have written it without having some power of reasoning. I have a fair share of invention and of common sense or judgment, such as every fairly successful lawyer or doctor must have, but not I believe, in any higher degree.

On the favorable side of the balance, I think that I am superior to the common run of men in noticing things which easily escape attention, and in observing them carefully. My industry has been nearly as great as it could have been in the observation and collection of facts. What is far more important, my love of natural science has been steady and ardent. This pure love has, however, been much aided by the ambition to be esteemed by my fellow naturalists. From my early youth I have had the strongest desire to understand or explain whatever I observed—that is, to group all facts under some general laws. These causes combined have given me the patience to reflect or ponder for any number of years over any unexplained problem. As far as I can judge, I am not apt to follow blindly the lead of other men. I have steadily endeavored to keep my mind free, so as to give up any hypothesis, however much beloved (and I cannot resist forming one on every subject), as soon as facts are shown to be opposed to it. Indeed I have had no choice but to act in this manner, for with the exception of the Coral Reefs,[19] I cannot remember a single first-formed hypothesis which had not after a time to be given up or greatly modified. This has naturally led me to distrust greatly deductive reasoning in the mixed sciences. On the other hand, I am not very skeptical—a frame of mind which I believe to be injurious to the progress of science; a good deal of skepticism in a scientific man is advisable to avoid much loss of time; for I have met with not a few men, who I feel sure have often thus been deterred from experiment or observations, which would have proved directly or indirectly serviceable. . . .

My habits are methodical, and this has been of not a little use for my particular line of work. Lastly, I have had ample leisure from not having to earn my own bread. Even ill-health, though it has annihilated several years of my life, has saved me from the distractions of society and amusement.

Therefore, my success as a man of science, whatever this may have amounted to, has been determined, as far as I can judge, by complex and diversified mental qualities and conditions. Of these the most important have been—the love of science—unbounded patience in long reflecting over any subject—industry in observing and collecting facts—and a fair share of invention as well as of common sense. With such moderate abilities as I possess, it is truly surprising that thus I should have influenced to a considerable extent the beliefs of scientific men on some important points.

19 **Coral Reefs:** reference to his work on the structure and distribution of coral reefs, published after his voyage on the *Beagle*.

CHARLES ROBERT DARWIN

Comment

Personal stocktaking, especially in old age, is often a serious business. Most people, in fact, take themselves much too seriously when they analyze themselves. But Darwin is far from grim as he looks back over his past. There was of course much to be proud of in that past, but Darwin shows us that there were a few things to laugh at as well. His attitude toward himself is balanced, for he had a clear sense of what the *complete* individual should be, and it is with that sense that he measures himself.

1. What evidence do you find in Section I, "Schooldays," that Darwin was unusually observant as a boy? But what evidence, also, that he was unobservant? Do you find a similar combination of traits in his account of beetle-collecting at Cambridge, in Section II?
2. In Section III Darwin analyzes the qualities of his mind in maturity. What incompleteness does he find? Against what conception of the complete human being does he seem to you to measure himself?
3. "My mind seems to have become a kind of machine for grinding general laws out of large collections of facts," Darwin says. Does the mind that produced this autobiographical sketch seem to you "a kind of machine"? Judging by the account he gives of himself, how do you characterize Darwin's mind?

Robert Browning (1812-1889)

In 1881 a group of readers, critics, and amateur scholars met in London to form the first Browning Society. Their organization was something like a "fan club," except that its members collected papers and essays on their favorite poet (rather than pictures of him) and devoted their meetings to discussions of his work. Soon Browning Societies began to spring up here in the United States—indeed Robert Browning had a large and enthusiastic public here through much of his career; his poems were even reprinted as part of the timetable of the Chicago and Alton Railroad in the late 19th century.

Such fame had come slowly. Though he was but three years younger than Tennyson, Browning was recognized much later than the poet laureate. He was born in a suburb of London, the son of a banker, a learned man interested in history and the arts. His education came chiefly from his wide reading in his father's large library; for six months he was a student at the University of London, but he was always too restless to be satisfied with formal studies. His first poems (he was first published at twenty-one) were so close to their author's own preoccupations with himself that they were often less than clear to other readers (as was said by John Stuart Mill, one of his early reviewers). Browning then turned to the drama, and between 1837 and 1846, the year of his marriage, he completed eight plays, every one of them a failure or at least far from a smash hit. Yet from his experiments in the theater he learned where his greatest strength was to be.

The elopement and marriage of Robert Browning and Elizabeth Barrett in 1846 is perhaps the most famous literary romance of the 19th century. Miss Barrett was six years older than Robert Browning; she was a semi-invalid jealously watched over by her father (as everyone knows who has seen the play or the movie *The Barretts of Wimpole Street* by Rudolph Besier). Miss Barrett was a much more famous writer than the impetuous young man who dared to court her in her father's house; his fame was to come later.

The Brownings' happy married life was spent in Italy. There they watched with interest and enthusiasm the efforts of the Italians to achieve independence and unification. And there too in Florence and Rome Robert Browning lived among the pictures, statues, and buildings of the Italian Renaissance, the period in which he found many analogues with the world of Victorian England. His poetry deepened in power and excitement as he became more and more interested in bringing to life characters from the Italian past, imagined or real, in whom he could see aspects of the moral struggle of his own time. Browning perfected the dramatic monologue, the poem (Tennyson's "Ulysses" is an example) in which we hear but one character speaking. We hear this character, this "I," describing himself, and we come to understand him not only by what he directly says, but also by becoming aware of what he cannot say: in the dramatic monologue the speaker, without meaning to, exposes himself.

Browning's dramatic monologues were powerful analyses of the nature of the individual, his strengths and weaknesses, his self-knowledge and self-ignorance. Browning's most ambitious achievement in this genre, or literary method, was *The Ring and the Book*, a huge four-volume poem published in 1868-1869, in which a 17th-century Roman murder case is presented from successive points of view in twelve dramatic monologues. He had begun experimenting with the monologue much earlier, while he was trying to write for the theater, and in this literary form he found a way of studying character that differs from the way of the novelist or that of the dramatist, yet possesses many of the strengths of both.

"My Last Duchess"

One of Browning's finest dramatic monologues is among his earliest, first published in 1842. It is the portrait of an Italian duke of the Renaissance, apparently based on Duke Alfonso II of Ferrara, who lived in the second half of the 16th century. The Duke is a widower and is here entertaining the agent of another nobleman whose "fair daughter" he seeks to marry: the agent has come to discuss the financial arrangements involved in such a union of two noble houses. The Duke is the only speaker. As he proudly shows his visitor through his palace he pauses before the painting of his late wife, a painting that has caught her characteristic expression. The Duke, we see, is still puzzled by this expression, even as he was when it appeared in life, and he reveals himself as he tries to explain the meaning of the "earnest glance" that the artist has so perfectly caught.

My Last Duchess

FERRARA

Robert Browning

That's my last Duchess painted on the wall,
Looking as if she were alive. I call
That piece a wonder, now: Fra Pandolf's[1] hands
Worked busily a day, and there she stands.
Will 't please you sit and look at her? I said   5
"Fra Pandolf" by design, for never read
Strangers like you that pictured countenance,
The depth and passion of its earnest glance,
But to myself they turned (since none puts by
The curtain I have drawn for you, but I)   10
And seemed as they would ask me, if they durst,
How such a glance came there; so, not the first
Are you to turn and ask thus. Sir, 'twas not
Her husband's presence only, called that spot
Of joy into the Duchess' cheek: perhaps   15
Fra Pandolf chanced to say "Her mantle laps
Over my lady's wrist too much," or "Paint
Must never hope to reproduce the faint
Half-flush that dies along her throat": such stuff
Was courtesy, she thought, and cause enough   20
For calling up that spot of joy. She had
A heart—how shall I say?—too soon made glad,

---

1 **Fra Pandolf:** an imaginary artist, who is also a friar.

Too easily impressed; she liked whate'er
She looked on, and her looks went everywhere.
Sir, 'twas all one!   My favor at her breast,   25
The dropping of the daylight in the west,
The bough of cherries some officious fool
Broke in the orchard for her, the white mule
She rode with round the terrace—all and each
Would draw from her alike the approving speech,   30
Or blush, at least.   She thanked men—good! but thanked
Somehow—I know not how—as if she ranked
My gift of a nine-hundred-years-old name
With anybody's gift.   Who'd stoop to blame
This sort of trifling?   Even had you skill   35
In speech—(which I have not)—to make your will
Quite clear to such an one, and say, "Just this
Or that in you disgusts me; here you miss,
Or there exceed the mark"—and if she let
Herself be lessoned so, nor plainly set   40
Her wits to yours,[2] forsooth, and made excuse,
—E'en then would be some stooping; and I choose
Never to stoop.   Oh sir, she smiled, no doubt,
Whene'er I passed her; but who passed without
Much the same smile?   This grew; I gave commands;   45
Then all smiles stopped together.   There she stands
As if alive.   Will 't please you rise?   We'll meet
The company below, then.   I repeat,
The Count your master's known munificence
Is ample warrant that no just pretense   50
Of mine for dowry will be disallowed;
Though his fair daughter's self, as I avowed
At starting, is my object.   Nay, we'll go
Together down, sir.   Notice Neptune,[3] though,   '
Taming a sea horse, thought a rarity,   55
Which Claus of Innsbruck[4] cast in bronze for me!

2 **nor . . . yours:** nor was obstinate.
3 **Neptune:** Greek god of the sea.
4 **Claus of Innsbruck:** an imaginary sculptor.

Comment

The Duke portrays himself as he speaks: he is a proud man, proud of
his possessions and of his "nine-hundred-years-old name."   He is con-
descendingly polite—"Nay, we'll go / Together down, sir," he says, and
we can imagine how his visitor is standing back deferentially as they
are about to leave the room.   And yet with all his pride and superiority
the Duke seems to have been unable to understand his late wife.   In-

deed, she so exasperated him that he "gave commands," and we infer that she was either put to death or shut away in a prison. What is the nature of this proud man?

1. If this monologue were acted as part of a play, what would happen on the stage? What physical movements do the Duke and his visitor perform in the course of the poem? The visitor, the agent, of course says nothing, but what expressions would you have him register as he looks and listens?

2. According to the Duke, his Duchess had "A heart . . . too soon made glad"; she valued his ancient name no more highly than other, quite simple pleasures and possessions. What conclusions about the character of the Duchess does the reader draw from the Duke's complaints?

3. The Duke's memories of his *last* Duchess, we note, are stirred by the painting on the wall. Again, as he leaves he asks his visitor to notice a bronze statue of the god of the sea "Taming a sea horse." We see that he is a collector and connoisseur of art; we also see his attitude toward people. How does he speak of the daughter of the Count to whom, presumably, he will next be married? Note that after speaking of the large dowry he expects, he says that of course the lady's "fair . . . self" is his "object." When he speaks of a "self" as an "object," how is his attitude like that which we find in his description of his late wife?

4. Browning the poet, of course, does not speak in his own voice in this poem to deliver his judgment of the Duke. But what does he make us infer about the Duke's nature? How does he make us feel toward a man who can experience nature and people only if he can collect them as works of art?

"Home Thoughts"

Travel, we say, is broadening, but in a most important sense it can be narrowing too, for it makes the traveler aware of the scenes he has left behind and of the parts of his own character that have been shaped by his homeland. Browning twice traveled to Italy before he went to live there with his wife. The first of the following poems was written after his return from his first Italian journey; the next, during the sea voyage of his second.

Home Thoughts, from Abroad

Robert Browning

Oh, to be in England
Now that April's there,
And whoever wakes in England
Sees, some morning, unaware,
That the lowest boughs and brushwood sheaf   5
Round the elm tree bole are in tiny leaf,
While the chaffinch sings on the orchard bough
In England—now!

And after April, when May follows,
And the whitethroat builds, and all the swallows!   10
Hark, where my blossomed pear tree in the hedge
Leans to the field and scatters on the clover
Blossoms and dewdrops—at the bent spray's edge—
That's the wise thrush; he sings each song twice over,
Lest you should think he never could recapture   15
The first fine careless rapture!
And though the fields look rough with hoary dew
All will be gay when noontide wakes anew
The buttercups, the little children's dower
—Far brighter than this gaudy melon flower!   20

Home Thoughts, from the Sea

Robert Browning

Nobly, nobly Cape Saint Vincent[1] to the northwest died away;
Sunset ran, one glorious blood-red, reeking into Cadiz Bay;[2]
Bluish 'mid the burning water, full in face Trafalgar lay;
In the dimmest northeast distance dawned Gibraltar grand and
    gray;
"Here and here did England help me: how can I help England?"—
    say,   5
Whoso turns as I, this evening, turn to God to praise and pray,
While Jove's planet[3] rises yonder, silent over Africa.

1 **Cape Saint Vincent:** the southwest tip of Portugal, where Nelson defeated the Spanish
in a sea battle in 1797.
2 **Cadiz Bay:** on the southern coast of Spain; to the east is Cape Trafalgar, where Nelson
defeated the combined French and Spanish fleets in 1805.
3 **Jove's planet:** Jupiter.

Comment

Browning does not just vaguely see an English landscape: he sees fine details, such as the early leaves of the low boughs and saplings around the trunk, "bole," of the elm. Nor does he just see a vast sea-scape: he sees English history in the sites of two great naval battles. How do these two sets of "home thoughts" complement each other?

1. With what kind of imagery does the first poem characterize England? And how does Browning make us feel toward the images he selects? Why, for example, does he call the buttercups "the little children's dower [wealth]"?

2. But how does Browning characterize the scene before him in the second poem? What, for example, is the effect of "Nobly, nobly" at the beginning? What associations are evoked by the phrases he uses in line 2 to describe the sunset?

3. How would you characterize the rhythm and meter of the first poem? of the second? What appropriateness do you find in the meter and rhythm of each?

4. These two poems are usually printed together: write a paragraph in which you show how Browning's full meaning of "home" would be incomplete if we read either poem without the other.

"Prospice"

In 1861 Elizabeth Barrett Browning died. With their son, who had been born in 1849, Browning sadly left Italy, the scene of his happy marriage, and returned to England. He wrote a great deal, he lived close to the literary and social life of the time, and he became a famous personage. Yet the happiest days of his life were past. The following poem, which he wrote soon after his wife's death, was first published in the *Atlantic Monthly* in 1864. Its title is Latin for "look forward."

Prospice

Robert Browning

Fear death?—to feel the fog in my throat,
    The mist in my face,
When the snows begin, and the blasts denote
    I am nearing the place,
The power of the night, the press of the storm,   5
    The post of the foe;
Where he stands, the Arch Fear in a visible form,
    Yet the strong man must go:
For the journey is done and the summit attained,
    And the barriers fall,   10

Though a battle's to fight ere the guerdon[1] be gained,
  The reward of it all.
I was ever a fighter, so—one fight more,
  The best and the last!
I would hate that death bandaged my eyes, and forbore,[2]   15
  And bade me creep past.
No! let me taste the whole of it, fare like my peers
  The heroes of old,
Bear the brunt, in a minute pay glad life's arrears[3]
  Of pain, darkness and cold.   20
For sudden the worst turns the best to the brave,
  The black minute's at end,
And the elements' rage, the fiend-voices[4] that rave,
  Shall dwindle, shall blend,
Shall change, shall become first a peace out of pain,   25
  Then a light, then thy breast,
O thou soul of my soul![5] I shall clasp thee again,
  And with God be the rest!

1 guerdon (gûr'dən): reward.
2 forebore: i.e., only partially killed me.
3 arrears: what I owe.
4 fiend-voices: reference to a legend that fiends cry loudly and try to grasp the soul as it leaves the body.
5 soul of my soul: his wife.

Comment

For many of his readers "Prospice" was Browning's most eloquent expression of the optimism and courage they found throughout his works. "To the brave," he says (l. 21) the worst can suddenly become the best, even at the moment of death. The individual who has courage can defeat even the "everlasting no" of death.

1. Where, in one word, is the answer given to the question with which the poem opens? How does this answer comment on the one fate he does fear and hate (ll. 15-16)?
2. How does Browning characterize himself in the first twenty lines of the poem? In what situation, in what kind of action, does he imagine himself?
3. "For sudden the worst turns the best to the brave" (l. 21): how, in the remainder of the poem, does "the worst turn the best"? How will the "black minute" end for Browning?
4. "Prospice" is not only a poem about the fear of death: it is also a poem that expresses Browning's love for his wife. How do we understand that love as we reach the end of the poem?

A drawing by Cruikshank pointing up the evils of child labor. Elizabeth Barrett Browning's early poetry concerned itself with such causes.

Elizabeth Barrett Browning (1806-1861)

Robert Browning made his first visit to Elizabeth Barrett as an admirer of her poems, for despite her invalid condition (she had injured her spine as a child) she was one of the best-known writers of her generation. The man whom she was to marry was of course a serious poet, though, as you have seen, his concern for issues of life and death, good and evil, was expressed dramatically and obliquely. Elizabeth Barrett, however, wrote poetry of a different sort. As she once wrote, in one of her longer poems, the poet should "speak the truth in/Worthy song from earnest soul." Her own earnestness showed itself before her marriage in poetry that urged such humanitarian reforms as the abolition of slavery and of child labor.

Sonnets from the Portuguese

The sonnets she wrote after her marriage to Robert Browning, though they are less public in theme, are not less earnest and direct. They are among the most eloquent love poems of the 19th century. Their general title is *Sonnets from the Portuguese*, for it is thought that upon Robert Browning's suggestion, Mrs. Browning pretended that they were translations from a Portuguese poet.

Sonnet 26

Elizabeth Barrett Browning

I lived with visions for my company
Instead of men and women, years ago,
And found them gentle mates, nor thought to know
A sweeter music than they played to me.
But soon their trailing purple was not free   5
Of this world's dust—their lutes did silent grow,
And I myself grew faint and blind below
Their vanishing eyes. Then THOU didst come . . to *be,*
Beloved, what they *seemed.* Their shining fronts,
Their songs, their splendors . . (better, yet the same, . .   10
As river water hallowed into fonts[1] . .)
Met in thee, and from out thee overcame
My soul with satisfaction of all wants—
Because God's gifts put man's best dreams to shame.

1 better . . . fonts: i.e., just as river water, blessed by the priest, becomes the holy water of the church, so when you came my visions changed into life-giving reality.

Sonnet 14

Elizabeth Barrett Browning

If thou must love me, let it be for nought
Except for love's sake only. Do not say
"I love her for her smile . . her look . . her way
Of speaking gently, . . for a trick of thought
That falls in well with mine, and certes[1] brought   5
A sense of pleasant ease on such a day"—
For these things in themselves, Beloved, may
Be changed, or change for thee—and love so wrought,
May be unwrought so. Neither love me for
Thine own dear pity's wiping my cheeks dry,   10
Since one might well forget to weep who bore
Thy comfort long, and lose thy love thereby.
But love me for love's sake, that evermore
Thou may'st love on through love's eternity.

1 certes (sûr′tēz): assuredly; certainly.

Comment

Each of these poems makes a distinction between true love and some other state. The first distinguishes between dreams or visions and the love that replaces them; the second, between symptoms of love that may change and a reality that cannot change.

1. In the first poem, what is the character of the "visions" that have preceded the arrival of "THOU"? Why, for example, are the visions imagined as dressed in "trailing purple"? How does the comparison in lines 10-11 prepare for the last line, with its distinction between "God's gifts" and "man's best dreams"?
2. The second poem rejects a love based on "comfort": what are some ways in which this comfort or assurance is described? What does the speaker claim is more powerful than such "comfort"?
3. You have already read Browning's "Prospice," the poem in memory of his wife. These two sonnets, of course, were written earlier than "Prospice," but do they seem to you to conceive of love in the same way as that poem does? Explain.

Dante Gabriel Rossetti (1828-1882)

Poetry and painting are sometimes closely related—in speaking of the former we often use such words as "portrait" or "picture." Yet the two arts are seldom practiced by the same man. Dante Gabriel Rossetti, however, was both poet and painter. He was the son of a political exile who took refuge in England from the rule of Austria over Italy. Like his father, he was a devoted student of the great Italian poet Dante, for whom he was named, and from the era of Dante he drew his convictions about art. With William Holman Hunt, John Everett Millais, and others he formed the "Pre-Raphaelite Brotherhood," a group of painters critical of the conventional painting done by popular artists of their time and convinced that the artist should paint in the manner and spirit of the early Renaissance artists from Giotto to Leonardo da Vinci, with a naturalness and directness and sincerity that conventional painting had lost.

"Lost Days"

In his poetry Rossetti also asserted his artistic convictions. In the following poem, for example, rather than moralizing on the wasted days of the past, he expresses himself in strikingly pictorial images. It is one of a long series of sonnets that Rossetti called *The House of Life*.

Lost Days

Dante Gabriel Rossetti

The lost days of my life until today,
    What were they, could[1] I see them on the street
    Lie as they fell? Would they be ears of wheat
Sown once for food but trodden into clay?
Or golden coins squandered and still to pay?   5
    Or drops of blood dabbling the guilty feet?
    Or such spilt water as in dreams must cheat
The undying throats of Hell, athirst alway?

I do not see them here; but after death
    God knows I know the faces I shall see,   10
Each one a murdered self, with low last breath.
    "I am thyself,—what hast thou done to me?"
"And I—and I—thyself," (lo! each one saith,)
    "And thou thyself to all eternity!"

1 **could:** i.e., if I could.

Comment

Many moralists have written on "lost days," wasted time, opportunities let slip. But few have imagined such losses so violently as Rossetti has here. He does not say "Live every minute of your life"; rather, he says that the days you have not lived are as parts of yourself that you have killed.

1. In the octave of this Italian sonnet, how does the poet imagine the lost days of his life? Which of the four successive images seems to you the most startling? Why?
2. How does he imagine the lost days of his life in the sestet? How does the image of "each one a murdered self" continue and conclude the violent images of the octave?
3. What attitude toward life, toward experience, does the poem seem to you finally to express?

William Ernest Henley (1849-1903)

In 1888 there was published a book of poems entitled *In Hospital,* a startling and powerful collection of sketches, in free, unrhymed verse, of the experience of a patient in a large city hospital. The author, William Ernest Henley, was in fact a patient at the Edinburgh Infirmary) and he had fought for many years against the then terrible disease of tuberculosis.

> Lived on one's back,
> In the long hours of repose
> Life is a practical nightmare—
> Hideous, asleep or awake.

"Invictus"

One of Henley's most famous poems—it has been set to music and sung by many choruses—is the following, the Latin title of which means "Unconquered." It is a poem that has all but obscured Henley's other and considerable writings. Yet it is a crucial poem too, for it sums up what many have believed to be the essential faith of the 19th century. Whether its creed is thus representative you can decide.

Invictus

William Ernest Henley

Out of the night that covers me,
  Black as the pit[1] from pole to pole,
I thank whatever gods may be
  For my unconquerable soul.

In the fell[2] clutch of circumstance   5
  I have not winced nor cried aloud.
Under the bludgeonings of chance
  My head is bloody, but unbowed.

Beyond this place of wrath and tears
  Looms but the Horror of the shade,[3]   10
And yet the menace of the years
  Finds and shall find me unafraid.

It matters not how strait[4] the gate,
  How charged with punishments the scroll,[5]
I am the master of my fate: 15
  I am the captain of my soul.

---

1 **pit:** Hell.
2 **fell:** deadly; evil.
3 **shade:** netherworld, abode of disembodied ghosts.
4 **strait:** narrow.
5 **charged . . . scroll:** punishments listed on the individual's record.

Comment

"I am the master of my fate": Does this summarize Victorian person's dream of himself or herself? Courage and self-sufficiency—were these enough for the battle of life? Or is Henley's vision of the "I," the individual, too simple?

1. As you look back upon the selections of this section, explain whether Henley's "I" seems to you to sum up the individual as Darwin, Browning, and others see him. Does Henley's creed seem to you to leave out any important features of the full individual suggested or portrayed in the other selections? Explain.

Old Themes and New Voices

AS THE 19TH century drew to a close, the writers of England, and of most Western countries as well, were moving in many different directions. Some had turned to realism, to the reporter-like accounts of life in modern society, accounts that many readers found uncomfortably frank and unflattering. Others had turned toward a vision of life like that of the early 19th-century Romantic. And between these extremes were many paths both traditional and freshly original. This survey of Victorian writers closes with selections to illustrate both the persistence of old themes and the emergence of new voices with which the 19th century ended and our contemporary world began.

George Meredith (1828-1909)

Like Thomas Hardy, whom we shall encounter shortly, George Meredith is better known for his novels than for his poetry. Meredith's novels are concerned with the conflict between the codes of society and the desires and aspirations of the individual—a conflict sometimes tragic, as in *The Ordeal of Richard Feverel* (1859), but more often comic, as in *The Egoist* (1879). Like Hardy again, however, Meredith was seriously committed to the writing of poetry, and some of his most characteristic ideas and feelings emerge more clearly from his poems than from his novels.

"Lucifer in Starlight"

In the following sonnet Meredith presents his own version of a part of the story told by Milton in *Paradise Lost*. Lucifer, the leader of the fallen angels, and the embodiment of dark and evil power, flies from his "dominion," Hell, deep in the universe. This time he does not reach the earth, but sinks back, overcome by the spectacle of the stars in the heavens above the earth. It is a poem in which Meredith restates for us the epigraph of this Victorian chapter, for it is a poem in which something like "wisdom" does indeed "shake" an "evil dream of power."

Lucifer
in
Starlight

George Meredith

On a starred night Prince Lucifer uprose.
Tired of his dark dominion swung the fiend
Above the rolling ball in cloud part screened,
Where sinners hugged their specter[1] of repose.
Poor prey to his hot fit of pride were those.   5
And now upon his western wing he leaned,
Now his huge bulk o'er Afric's sands careened,
Now the black planet[2] shadowed Arctic snows.
Soaring through wider zones that pricked his scars[3]
With memory of the old revolt from Awe,[4]   10
He reached the middle height, and at the stars,
Which are the brain of heaven, he looked, and sank.
Around the ancient track marched, rank on rank,
The army of unalterable law.

1 **specter:** illusion.
2 **black planet:** the flying Lucifer.
3 **pricked his scars:** reminded him of his expulsion from heaven.
4 **Awe:** God.

Comment

"He looked, and sank": what is it that overwhelms the huge fallen angel as he pauses in his vast, soaring flight?

1. What are some of the verbs that describe the flight of Lucifer? And what is the verb that describes the movement of the stars?
2. A sonnet can sometimes consist of a single sentence; often, with run-on lines, it will consist of no more than two or three. In this sonnet, however, are six sentences, two of them but one line long. The effect of such short sentences is often one of choppiness, but what is their effect here? What tone do they reinforce?
3. The very last line of the sonnet is short, yet it is as metrically regular as, for example, line 6: into the one long word *unalterable* are crowded five syllables. What is the effect of this word as we read it in the last line? Why, for example, would the substitution of the word *unchanging* for *unalterable* weaken the line?
4. "He looked, and sank": what do these simple, unmodified verbs tell us of the order, the "law," that Lucifer sees? Meredith does not elaborate: what is the effect of the simple "looked, and sank" in this poem?

Charles Lutwidge Dodgson, "Lewis Carroll" (1832-1898)

Alice's Adventures in Wonderland (1865) and *Through the Looking-Glass* (1878), as almost everyone knows, were written by a man named Lewis Carroll. What is less well known is that "Lewis Carroll" was in fact a gifted lecturer in mathematics at Oxford whose real name was Dodgson and who most of his life busied himself with matters of university policy and with questions in logic and mathematics that only experts can understand. His two most famous books were written to amuse a young friend named Alice Liddell, daughter of Dean Liddell of Oxford, a great classical scholar. Lewis Carroll made her the heroine of a pair of books that have delighted both children and adults since they were first published. Both were originally illustrated by Sir John Tenniel with drawings that are as unforgettable as the texts.

The immense attraction of the "Alice" books is not that they are nonsense, but that they are in a strange way "logical nonsense." They are made up of elaborate games played with words. Sometimes the game consists in humorously dislocating and recombining elements of familiar words. In "Jabberwocky," the strange poem that Alice reads in *Through the Looking-Glass,* for example, we find "chortle," which seems to combine "chuckle" and "snort"; and "galumphing," a combination of "gallop" and "triumph." Sometimes the word-play is parody, as in the following selection when the Hatter makes fun of the well-known poem that begins, "Twinkle, twinkle, little star / How I wonder what you are!" Sometimes the game is a kind of outrageous punning, as when Alice says that she has to beat time when she learns music, and the Hatter says that Time, whom he knows well, "won't stand beating"! Carroll's endless play with language makes us dance between the literal and the fantastic meaning of words in a game as old as the nursery rhyme.

There were other writers of charming and high-spirited nonsense in the 19th century. The best known, perhaps, besides Carroll, was his older contemporary Edward Lear, who in addition to writing "The Owl and the Pussy Cat" and "The Jumblies" made the limerick the popular comic form that it remains to this day. Both Lewis Carroll and Edward Lear wrote their comic nonsense for children. But their works have been read—and quoted—with delight by generations of adults. Their "nonsense," indeed, was really an exploration of associations among words that many modern writers have pursued with great seriousness.

"A Mad Tea Party"

The following selection, one of the most famous episodes in Victorian literature, describes Alice's adventures at a strange tea party. Alice has come to a fantastic underground world: she followed a white rabbit into its burrow and has entered a world where animals talk—and even talk with a weird consistency that bewilders her but amuses us.

A Mad Tea Party

From ALICE IN WONDERLAND

Lewis Carroll

THERE WAS A TABLE set out under a tree in front of the house, and the March Hare[1] and the Hatter[2] were having tea at it: a Dormouse[3] was sitting between them, fast asleep, and the other two were using it as a cushion, resting their elbows on it, and talking over its head. "Very uncomfortable for the Dormouse," thought Alice; "only as it's asleep, I suppose it doesn't mind."

The table was a large one, but the three were all crowded together at one corner of it. "No room! No room!" they cried out when they saw Alice coming. "There's *plenty* of room!" said Alice indignantly, and she sat down in a large armchair at one end of the table.

"Have some wine," the March Hare said in an encouraging tone.

Alice looked all round the table, but there was nothing on it but tea. "I don't see any wine," she remarked.

"There isn't any," said the March Hare.

---

1 March Hare: "Mad as a March hare" is a proverbial expression dating back to the Renaissance.
2 Hatter: a dealer in (or maker of) hats; "mad as a hatter" is another proverbial expression.
3 Dormouse: a small rodent noted for its long hibernation period.

"Then it wasn't very civil of you to offer it," said Alice angrily.

"It wasn't very civil of you to sit down without being invited," said the March Hare.

"I didn't know it was *your* table," said Alice: "it's laid for a great many more than three."

"Your hair wants cutting," said the Hatter. He had been looking at Alice for some time with great curiosity, and this was his first speech.

"You should learn not to make personal remarks," Alice said with some severity: "it's very rude."

The Hatter opened his eyes very wide on hearing this; but all he *said* was "Why is a raven like a writing desk?"

"Come, we shall have some fun now!" thought Alice. I'm glad they've begun asking riddles—"I believe I can guess that," she added aloud.

"Do you mean that you think you can find out the answer to it?" said the March Hare.

"Exactly so," said Alice.

"Then you should say what you mean," the March Hare went on.

"I do," Alice hastily replied; "at least —at least I mean what I say—that's the same thing, you know."

"Not the same thing a bit!" said the Hatter. "Why, you might just as well say that 'I see what I eat' is the same thing as 'I eat what I see'!"

"You might just as well say," added the March Hare, "that 'I like what I get' is the same thing as 'I get what I like'!"

"You might just as well say," added the Dormouse, which seemed to be talking in its sleep, "that 'I breathe when I sleep' is the same thing as 'I sleep when I breathe'!"

"It *is* the same thing with you," said the Hatter, and here the conversation dropped, and the party sat silent for a minute, while Alice thought over all she could remember about ravens and writing desks, which wasn't much.

The Hatter was the first to break the silence. "What day of the month is it?" he said, turning to Alice: he had taken his watch out of his pocket, and was looking at it uneasily, shaking it every now and then, and holding it to his ear.

Alice considered a little, and then said, "The fourth."

"Two days wrong!"[4] sighed the Hatter. "I told you butter wouldn't suit the works!" he added, looking angrily at the March Hare.

"It was the *best* butter," the March Hare meekly replied.

"Yes, but some crumbs must have got in as well," the Hatter grumbled: "you shouldn't have put it in with the bread knife."

The March Hare took the watch and looked at it gloomily: then he dipped it into his cup of tea, and looked at it again: but he could think of nothing better to say than his first remark, "It was the *best* butter, you know."

Alice had been looking over his shoulder with some curiosity. "What a funny watch!" she remarked. "It tells the day of the month, and doesn't tell what o'clock it is!"

"Why should it?" muttered the Hatter. "Does *your* watch tell you what year it is?"

"Of course not," Alice replied very readily: "but that's because it stays the same year for such a long time together."

"Which is just the case with *mine*," said the Hatter.

Alice felt dreadfully puzzled. The Hatter's remark seemed to her to have no sort of meaning in it, and yet it was certainly English. "I don't quite understand you," she said, as politely as she could.

"The Dormouse is asleep again," said the Hatter, and he poured a little hot tea upon its nose.

The Dormouse shook its head impatiently, and said, without opening its eyes, "Of course, of course: just what I was going to remark myself."

"Have you guessed the riddle yet?" the Hatter said, turning to Alice again.

"No, I give it up," Alice replied. "What's the answer?"

"I haven't the slightest idea," said the Hatter.

"Nor I," said the March Hare.

Alice sighed wearily. "I think you might do something better with the time," she said, "than wasting it in asking riddles that have no answers."

"If you knew Time as well as I do,' said the Hatter, "you wouldn't talk about wasting *it*. It's *him*."

"I don't know what you mean," said Alice.

"Of course you don't!" the Hatter said, tossing his head contemptuously. "I dare say you never even spoke to Time!"

"Perhaps not," Alice cautiously replied; "but I know I have to beat time when I learn music."

"Ah! That accounts for it," said the Hatter. "He won't stand beating. Now, if you only kept on good terms with him, he'd do almost anything you liked with the clock. For instance, suppose it were nine o'clock in the morning, just time to begin lessons: you'd only have to whisper a hint to Time, and round goes the clock in a twinkling! Half past one, time for dinner!"

("I only wish it was," the March Hare said to itself in a whisper.)

"That would be grand, certainly,"

4 Two . . . wrong: The Hatter's watch keeps time by the month; i.e., it follows the phases of the moon, as befits a lunatic's watch.

The Mad Tea Party, an illustration from Alice in Wonderland *done by Tenniel, the original illustrator of the book.*

said Alice thoughtfully; "but then—I shouldn't be hungry for it, you know."

"Not at first perhaps," said the Hatter: "but you could keep it to half past one as long as you liked."

"Is that the way *you* manage?" Alice asked.

The Hatter shook his head mournfully. "Not I!" he replied. "We quarreled last March——just before *he* went mad, you know——" (pointing with his teaspoon at the March Hare) "——it was at the great concert given by the Queen of Hearts, and I had to sing

Twinkle, twinkle, little bat!
How I wonder what you're at!

You know the song, perhaps?"

"I've heard something like it," said Alice.

"It goes on, you know," the Hatter continued, "in this way:—

Up above the world you fly,
Like a tea tray in the sky.
　　Twinkle, twinkle—"

Here the Dormouse shook itself, and began singing in its sleep "Twinkle, twinkle, twinkle, twinkle——" and went on so long that they had to pinch it to make it stop.

"Well, I'd hardly finished the first verse," said the Hatter, "when the Queen bawled out 'He's murdering the time![5] Off with his head!'"

"How dreadfully savage!" exclaimed Alice.

"And ever since that," the Hatter

5 He's . . . time: i.e., he has not got the rhythm right.

632   THE VICTORIAN PERIOD

went on in a mournful tone, "he won't do a thing I ask! It's always six o'clock now."

A bright idea came into Alice's head. "Is that the reason so many tea things are put out here?" she asked.

"Yes, that's it," said the Hatter with a sigh: "it's always teatime, and we've no time to wash the things between whiles."

"Then you keep moving round, I suppose?" said Alice.

"Exactly so," said the Hatter: "as the things get used up."

"But what happens when you come to the beginning again?" Alice ventured to ask.

"Suppose we change the subject," the March Hare interrupted, yawning. "I'm getting tired of this. I vote the young lady tells us a story."

"I'm afraid I don't know one," said Alice, rather alarmed at the proposal.

"Then the Dormouse shall!" they both cried. "Wake up, Dormouse!" And they pinched it on both sides at once.

The Dormouse slowly opened its eyes. "I wasn't asleep," it said in a hoarse, feeble voice, "I heard every word you fellows were saying."

"Tell us a story!" said the March Hare.

"Yes, please do!" pleaded Alice.

"And be quick about it," added the Hatter, "or you'll be asleep again before it's done."

"Once upon a time there were three little sisters," the Dormouse began in a great hurry; "and their names were Elsie, Lacie, and Tillie; and they lived at the bottom of a well——"

"What did they live on?" said Alice, who always took a great interest in questions of eating and drinking.

"They lived on treacle,"[6] said the Dormouse, after thinking a minute or two.

"They couldn't have done that, you know," Alice gently remarked. "They'd have been ill."

"So they were," said the Dormouse; "*very* ill."

Alice tried a little to fancy to herself what such an extraordinary way of living would be like, but it puzzled her too much: so she went on: "But why did they live at the bottom of a well?"

"Take some more tea," the March Hare said to Alice, very earnestly.

"I've had nothing yet," Alice replied in an offended tone: "so I can't take more."

"You mean you can't take *less*," said the Hatter: "it's very easy to take *more* than nothing."

"Nobody asked *your* opinion," said Alice.

"Who's making personal remarks now?" the Hatter asked triumphantly.

Alice did not quite know what to say to this: so she helped herself to some tea and bread and butter, and then turned to the Dormouse, and repeated her question. "Why did they live at the bottom of a well?"

The Dormouse again took a minute or two to think about it, and then said, "It was a treacle well."

"There's no such thing!" Alice was beginning very angrily, but the Hatter and the March Hare went "Sh! Sh!" and the Dormouse sulkily remarked, "If you can't be civil, you'd better finish the story for yourself."

"No, please go on!" Alice said very humbly. "I won't interrupt you again. I dare say there may be *one*."

"One, indeed!" said the Dormouse indignantly. However, he consented to go on. "And so these three little sisters—they were learning to draw, you know——"

"What did they draw?" said Alice, quite forgetting her promise.

6 **treacle:** sweet molasses.

"Treacle," said the Dormouse, without considering at all, this time.

"I want a clean cup," interrupted the Hatter: "let's all move one place on."

He moved on as he spoke, and the Dormouse followed him: the March Hare moved into the Dormouse's place, and Alice rather unwillingly took the place of the March Hare. The Hatter was the only one who got any advantage from the change; and Alice was a good deal worse off than before, as the March Hare had just upset the milk jug into his plate.

Alice did not wish to offend the Dormouse again, so she began very cautiously: "But I don't understand. Where did they draw the treacle from?"

"You can draw water out of a water well," said the Hatter; "so I should think you could draw treacle out of a treacle well—eh, stupid?"

"But they were *in* the well," Alice said to the Dormouse, not choosing to notice this last remark.

"Of course they were," said the Dormouse: "well in."

This answer so confused poor Alice, that she let the Dormouse go on for some time without interrupting it.

"They were learning to draw," the Dormouse went on, yawning and rubbing its eyes, for it was getting very sleepy; "and they drew all manner of things—everything that begins with an M——"

"Why with an M?" said Alice.

"Why not?" said the March Hare.

Alice was silent.

The Dormouse had closed its eyes by this time, and was going off into a doze; but, on being pinched by the Hatter, it woke up again with a little shriek, and went on: "——that begins with an M, such as mousetraps, and the moon, and memory, and muchness—you know you say things are 'much of a muchness'[7]— did you ever see such a thing as a drawing of a muchness!"

"Really, now you ask me," said Alice, very much confused, "I don't think——"

"Then you shouldn't talk," said the Hatter.

This piece of rudeness was more than Alice could bear: she got up in great disgust, and walked off: the Dormouse fell asleep instantly, and neither of the others took the least notice of her going, though she looked back once or twice, half hoping that they would call after her: the last time she saw them, they were trying to put the Dormouse into the teapot.

"At any rate I'll never go *there* again!" said Alice, as she picked her way through the wood. "It's the stupidest tea party I ever was at in all my life!"

7 much of a muchness: Carroll, the logician, is making fun of a fashionable expression that meant "very much alike."

Comment

Poor Alice is puzzled, bewildered, and finally disgusted by the behavior of the other three members of the tea party, yet her responses make no impression on them. The Hatter, the Hare, and the Dormouse "live" by their own system, and we may be sure that as they judge, it is Alice who is unreasonable. The party is as mad as a joke, and almost as mad as a nightmare.

1. At the beginning of the tea party the Mad Hatter tells Alice that she should say what she means; at the end he tells her that if she doesn't

think she shouldn't talk. Good advice? What is its effect on Alice?

2. How, then, is Alice "right" during the tea party? And how is she "wrong"? How does she differ from the three strange figures to whose party she invites herself?

Gerard Manley Hopkins (1844-1889)

As a student at Oxford in the 1860's Gerard Manley Hopkins, a sensitive, imaginative young man, was exposed to the continuation of a religious controversy that had begun there thirty years earlier. In Hopkins's time the opposing groups were the "Broad" and the "High" churchmen. The latter stressed the authoritative and ritual elements of the Anglican Church and were followers of those who, with John Henry Newman, had earlier founded the Oxford Movement, an association of scholars, theologians, and priests who set out to reform the English Church by affirming the central dogmas of Christianity. The Broad Churchmen, who emphasized the private conscience and judgment in spiritual matters, were followers of those who had originally opposed the Oxford Movement. Though the controversy was less intense in Hopkins's time than in Newman's, the young scholar's sympathies were strongly with the High Churchmen, and like Newman, whom he consulted, Hopkins eventually left the Anglican Church to become a Roman Catholic. In 1868 he joined the Society of Jesus (the Jesuits) and for the rest of his short life was a dedicated priest working among the poor of the slums of Liverpool and teaching Latin and Greek in the new Catholic University in Dublin.

Hopkins wrote little after his entrance into the Jesuit Order, and much that he had written earlier he destroyed. None of his poetry was published in his lifetime: he left manuscripts in the care of a friend, Robert Bridges, and they were not published until 1918. Long though the delay in their publication was, Hopkins's poems have been widely and enthusiastically read since their appearance and have had a strong effect on modern poetry.

Hopkins is of course a religious poet; the writing of his poetry was indeed for him a kind of religious exercise. The rapturous intensity of his religious feelings could not be satisfied by the poetic techniques in vogue in his day, and he experimented constantly in his notebooks, trying to achieve the mode of expression his vision required. His most notable innovation is "sprung rhythm," a way of setting words in a line much as the notes are set in a bar of music: what matters is not the number of syllables (or notes) but the number of accents (or beats). The norm of English verse is iambic pentameter, that is, a line of ten syllables with five stresses. A line of Hopkins's poetry, which contains five stresses, may well have more or fewer syllables than a line of iambic pentameter verse, but it will have the rising (from unaccented to accented) sound of iambic meter. The effect is striking, for Hopkins achieves a style that is at once close to normal speech and intense enough to suggest his religious feeling. In many ways Gerard Manley Hopkins was unlike the other poets of his time. Yet he was sufficiently like them to bring his great gifts, and especially his great musical gift, to bear on the world of experience that he shared with his contemporaries.

"Spring"

The beauty of springtime, as you have seen again and again, is a constant theme of English poetry. Hopkins saw the spring not only in its natural richness and excitement of new growth; for him the spring was also an emblem, a symbol, of the very beginning of the world—"the earth's sweet being in the beginning / In Eden. . . ."

Spring

Gerard Manley Hopkins

Nothing is so beautiful as spring—
   When weeds, in wheels,[1] shoot long and lovely and lush;
   Thrush's eggs look little low heavens, and thrush
Through the echoing timber does so rinse and wring
The ear, it strikes like lightnings to hear him sing;   5
   The glassy peartree leaves and blooms, they brush
   The descending blue; that blue is all in a rush
With richness; the racing lambs too have fair their fling.

What is all this juice and all this joy?
   A strain of the earth's sweet being in the beginning   10
In Eden garden.—Have, get, before it cloy,
   Before it cloud,[2] Christ, lord, and sour with sinning,
Innocent mind and Mayday in girl and boy,
   Most, O maid's[3] child, thy choice and worthy the winning.

1 **wheels:** possibly whorls (an arrangement of leaves around the same point in a stem); or possibly arching stems.
2 **before . . . cloud:** The word "it" refers to the preceding line, to the similarity between the spring and the beginning of the world in Eden. The poet asks "Christ, lord" to take to himself the innocent minds of the young before they are spoiled and soured by the beauty of the spring—for it is, after all, only natural beauty.
3 **maid's:** the Virgin Mary's.

Comment

In the octave of this sonnet the poet rapturously fills out his opening statement, "Nothing is so beautiful as spring." And in the sestet he makes a religious application of the freshness he has seen. He calls on "Christ, lord" to keep "girl and boy"—human beings in their springtime—to himself. For beautiful as it is, the beauty of nature can only spoil ("cloy") and cloud and sour the innocence of human beings. Beautiful as it is, the natural world is less "worthy the winning" than are people.

A word must be said about Hopkins's extraordinary rhythms in this poem. The first line is regular enough: we hear five strong beats—"Nothing is so beautiful as spring"—and we begin to hear too the characteristic "rising accent" of the whole poem. It would be clearer, perhaps, if the line were more conventionally regular and began with an unaccented syllable—say, "And nóthing ís so beáutiful as spríng." But the rising accent is firmly established by the second line: "When weéds, in wheéls, shoŏt lóng and lóvely and lúsh." Our expectations are now attuned to the accentual pattern. But look at—or rather, listen to—what happens in the climactic line of the poem, at the point where the speaker turns away from his own musing and speaks out to his God: "In Eden garden.—Have, get, before it cloy." We must pronounce the imperatives, "Have, get," strongly, and we must therefore rush on to the final "cloy," because the strong, rising, five-beat pattern is now so firmly fixed. With Hopkins the rhythm of a single line is as supple as speech, as intense as his strongest feeling.

1. The beauty of the spring is alive for the speaker—it moves, it acts, it rushes. What are some of the words (verbs, adverbial phrases, adjectives) that express the motion, the activity that the speaker sees?
2. At the beginning of the sestet the poet asks and answers a question, and the key word of his answer is an odd word, *strain*. We hear it clearly, for the rhythm makes us hear it. But what does "strain" mean? Does it mean "strain" in the biological sense of descendant from a common ancestor, in the sense that a rancher tries to breed certain strains of horses? Does it mean "strain" in the musical sense? Does it mean "strain" in the sense of tension or great exertion, as when we speak of muscle-strain? Or does it mean all three? Is the beauty of the spring a descendant of the beautiful beginning of the earth? Is it a note or melody sustained since the beginning of time? And is it also a hopeless straining after that beautiful beginning? Explain.
3. How do you read the last sentence of this poem, beginning, "Have, get . . ."? Hopkins's tone changes, for he now speaks directly to Christ. To what "springtime" does he now turn? How does he elevate this springtime above the beauty he has praised in the octave?

"God's Grandeur"

Although for Hopkins the beauty of spring was less "worthy" than the beautiful innocence of the child, still, as it was to others of his time, nature was to him more beautiful than the works of human beings—of children whose innocence has been lost in worldliness. In this poem, though in a way opposite to that of "Spring," the difference between humankind and nature assures him of the presence of a spirit that is above both.

God's Grandeur

Gerard Manley Hopkins

The world is charged with the grandeur of God.
    It will flame out, like shining from shook foil;[1]
    It gathers to a greatness, like the ooze of oil
Crushed.[2] Why do men then now not reck his rod?[3]
Generations have trod, have trod, have trod;   5
    And all is seared with trade; bleared, smeared with toil;
    And wears man's smudge and shares man's smell: the soil
Is bare now, nor can foot feel, being shod.

And for all this, nature is never spent;
    There lives the dearest freshness deep down things;   10
And though the last lights off the black West went
    Oh, morning, at the brown brink eastward, springs—
Because the Holy Ghost over the bent
    World broods with warm breast and with ah! bright wings.

1 **shining . . . foil:** like the reflection from aluminum or tin foil when we shake it in sunlight; or, perhaps, like the gleaming foil of a fencer.
2 **ooze . . . crushed:** like oil crushed from olives.
3 **reck his rod:** attend to his law or authority.

Comment

For Hopkins, most people are not only blind to the beauty of the world; worse, they are blind to the power that causes that beauty to "flame out." The dawn, with its rising morning light, is not only the beautiful return of light to earth; it is also the manifestation of the "bright wings" of God.

1. This sonnet opens with a large declaration in the first line. How do lines 2 and 3 expand this statement?

2. Line 4 (except for the first word) asks the question with which the speaker moves on from his opening declaration of "grandeur": "Why do men then now . . ." a question crowded with monosyllables. How must we read "then"? Does it mean "therefore"? Does it mean "in time past" (to go along with time "now")? Or both? Explain.

3. The next line, line 5, is certainly one of the boldest lines written in the 19th century—two monosyllables, "have trod," repeated three times. How does this line contrast, in sound and sense, with line 2, which describes how the "grandeur" will "flame out"? What change of feeling in the speaker is expressed by the repetition of "have trod"? And how do the rest of the verbs of the octave, verbs describing man's ways, add to the effect of the repetition?

4. With the beginning of the sestet the tone changes once more. How does the imagery of the sestet contrast with that of the second half of the octave?

5. The final image of the poem is that of the "Holy Ghost" brooding over the world. At the beginning of the poem, God's grandeur "will flame out"; at the end God is imagined as brooding "with warm breast and with ah! bright wings." What then is God's grandeur in this poem? Is it a flaming, a gathering greatness, that will oppose "man's smudge"? Or is it a grandeur less fierce? What is the grandeur that Hopkins finally sees?

Robert Bridges (1844-1930)

When Robert Bridges was made poet laureate in 1913, many newspapers wondered at the appointment, for he was not well known. Nor did he, until after his eightieth year, become in any sense a popular poet. His first book was published in 1873, his last in 1929—he lived through many changes of fashion, yet he himself was never fashionable. Bridges had a scholar's interest in the art of verse, in languages, and in literature generally. He was the man to whom Gerard Manley Hopkins entrusted his manuscripts and the friend with whom Hopkins carried on a correspondence about the art of poetry. His last work, *The Testament of Beauty* (1929), a long, meditative, philosophical poem, was widely read, yet, ironically, his best lyrics were neglected.

"Nightingales"

In our own time, however, Bridges's poems have won the respect that too few accorded them in his lifetime. One of his finest is the following dramatic lyric. It is a poem that for many readers distills the Romantic vision that many lesser poets tried in vain to recapture late in the 19th century.

Nightingales

Robert Bridges

Beautiful must be the mountains whence ye come,
And bright in the fruitful valleys the streams, wherefrom
      Ye learn your song:
Where are those starry woods? O might I wander there,
  Among the flowers, which in that heavenly air   5
      Bloom the year long!

Nay, barren are those mountains and spent the streams:
Our song is the voice of desire, that haunts our dreams,
      A throe of the heart,
Whose pining visions dim, forbidden hopes profound,   10
  No dying cadence nor long sigh can sound,
      For all our art.

Alone, aloud in the raptured ear of men
We pour our dark nocturnal secret; and then,
      As night is withdrawn   15
From these sweet-springing meads and bursting boughs of May,
  Dream, while the innumerable choir of day
      Welcome the dawn.

Comment

The nightingale of Keats's ode, you will remember, does not answer to the questionings and the importunings of the poet. Here, the poet asks the nightingales, a symbol of art and imagination since the days of Chaucer, about the nature of their land and their life. And he is answered, but not with the answer he expects.

1. In the first stanza, how does the speaker imagine the mountains, streams, and woods where he believes the nightingales live? Why should he believe that their land is a beautiful one?
2. The nightingales reply in stanzas 2 and 3; their adjectives for their land are different from the poet's. What antonym for "barren" (1.7) and for "spent" (1.7) do you find in the first stanza?
3. What further contrast between the human world and the world of the nightingales is implied by the difference between "Alone" (1.13) and "innumerable" (1.17)?
4. Line 17, the next to the last line of the last stanza, begins with the monosyllable "Dream." How do lines 5 and 11, the corresponding lines of the other stanzas, begin? Why is it appropriate that "Dream" should be so heavily stressed?
5. The "I" of this poem is a poet, an artist. He asks the nightingales, who symbolize art, to tell him the source of their power. What does their answer tell us about his conception of art? What is the nature of the "land," what is the nature of the desire, that brings forth the nightingales' song?

Rudyard Kipling (1865-1936)

The year 1897 marked the sixtieth anniversary of Queen Victoria's reign and occasioned a national celebration, the "Diamond Jubilee." And toward the end of that celebration there was published a poem entitled "Recessional," which means the hymn that is sung at the end of a religious service. The author was Rudyard Kipling, who had begun his long career as a reporter in India and had gone on to write many poems and stories based on the experience of soldiers and governing officials in the land that was then the largest of the possessions in the British Empire. Kipling had been born in Bombay and returned to India after receiving his education in England, but he spent most of his later life in England (except for a brief residence in Vermont—his wife was an American). His experience and his talents made him a most successful interpreter of the conditions and the responsibilities of the far-flung British Empire, and it was the responsibilities that he emphasized in his poem for the Diamond Jubilee. Most of the speech-making on that occasion proudly praised the glory and might of the Empire. Kipling's "Recessional" reminded the people of England that imperial power even so great as theirs might not last forever.

Recessional

Rudyard Kipling

God of our fathers, known of old,
　　Lord of our far-flung battle - line,
Beneath whose awful Hand we hold
　　Dominion over palm and pine—
Lord God of Hosts, be with us yet,　　　　　　5
Lest we forget—lest we forget!

The tumult and the shouting dies;
　　The captains and the kings depart:
Still stands Thine ancient sacrifice,
　　An humble and a contrite heart.[1]　　　　10
Lord God of Hosts, be with us yet,
Lest we forget—lest we forget!

Far-called, our navies melt away;
　　On dune and headland sinks the fire:[2]
Lo, all our pomp of yesterday　　　　　　　15
　　Is one with Nineveh[3] and Tyre![4]
Judge of the Nations, spare us yet,
Lest we forget—lest we forget!

If, drunk with sight of power, we loose
　　Wild tongues that have not Thee in awe,　　20
Such boastings as the Gentiles[5] use,
　　Or lesser breeds without the Law—
Lord God of Hosts, be with us yet,
Lest we forget—lest we forget!

For heathen heart that puts her trust　　　25
　　In reeking tube[6] and iron shard,[7]
All valiant dust that builds on dust,
　　And guarding, calls not Thee to guard,
For frantic boast and foolish word—
Thy Mercy on Thy People, Lord!　　　　　　30

　　　　　　　　　　　Amen.

---

1 **An . . . heart:** See Psalm 51.
2 **On . . . fire:** Fires were lighted on signal encircling the island of Great Britain as a part of the opening ceremonies to celebrate Queen Victoria's Diamond Jubilee.
3 **Nineveh** (nĭn'ə və)**:** The fall of this ancient capital of Assyria (612 B.C.) ended the prestige of the Assyrian Empire after centuries of success.
4 **Tyre** (tīr)**:** This ancient Phoenician city, once a great port of the Mediterranean, is now but a small town in Lebanon.
5 **Gentiles:** used in the Biblical sense and meaning not belonging to the chosen people— i.e., not English.
6 **tube:** barrel of a gun.
7 **shard:** shrapnel; fragments of the bombshell.

Comment

By 1897 Britain had achieved great political power in the world, and was proudly conscious of the fact. How does Kipling ask his country to temper its pride of power?

1. The words of most hymns are not those of ordinary language, for they must reflect the solemnity of a religious occasion. Does Kipling's diction seem to you in any way special, formal, or elevated?
2. What is the effect of the repetition of "Lest we forget" at the end of the first four stanzas? How is Kipling's message to his fellow countrymen emphasized by the ending of the last stanza?
3. Write a paragraph on the appropriateness of Kipling's title, "Recessional." It was written, of course, to conclude a great national celebration or service. But in what other ways is it like a recessional *hymn*?

Alfred Edward Housman (1859-1936)

A. E. Housman was Professor of Latin at University College, London, and then at Oxford, and most of his life was spent in the meticulous scholarship required of an editor of classical texts. He was born near the Shropshire border, in Worcestershire; his brilliant career as an undergraduate at Oxford came to a shocking end when, apparently under the pressure of some psychological distress, he failed his final examinations. He went to London and found employment that left him sufficient free time to pursue an independent career of study and research. By intense application he re-established himself as a distinguished scholar, and his university appointments followed.

It is perhaps difficult to imagine the severe scholar who stands behind the following poems. Yet in their spareness, their simple elegance, we can sense a highly disciplined imagination. Housman is "modern" in his concentrated directness—his poems are never highly wrought, like Kipling's hymn, for example. But he is also traditional in theme and subject, and his poetry therefore stands by itself, without obligations to any "school" and with no pretensions to found one.

A Shropshire Lad

All the following selections come from Housman's first book, *A Shropshire Lad*, published in 1896. They evoke the simple incidents and scenes of a countryside removed from the turmoil of industrial England, and they contemplate with stoic calm the passage of life.

Loveliest of Trees

A. E. Housman

Loveliest of trees, the cherry now
Is hung with bloom along the bough,
And stands about the woodland ride[1]
Wearing white for Eastertide.

Now, of my threescore years and ten,[2]   5
Twenty will not come again,
And take from seventy springs a score,
It only leaves me fifty more.

And since to look at things in bloom
Fifty springs are little room,   10
About the woodlands I will go
To see the cherry hung with snow.

1 **ride:** track for riding.
2 **my . . . ten:** "The days of our years are threescore years and ten." (Psalm 90.)

Comment

The speaker looks upon the blossoming cherry trees; he is young, the trees are in their springtime bloom, and yet he is reminded of his mortality.

1. How old *is* the speaker? When he says, "It only leaves me fifty more," what does he tell us of his feeling for the "Loveliest of trees"? How do the first two lines of the last stanza enforce this feeling?
2. The poem ends, "To see the cherry hung with snow." How does the image "hung with snow" echo the last line of the first stanza? But "snow" also connotes winter, and connotes old age. How does this final image describe both the beauty of the cherry trees and the man's sense of his own life?

"To an Athlete Dying Young"

The next poem is a meditation on the death of a young man, an athlete cut off in his prime. The theme is an ancient one, and we may expect it to evoke pity. Housman, however, seems to treat the theme almost cynically—"You are better off," he seems to say. And yet, as we reach the end of the poem, we hear a tragic note in the speaker's voice that is much more powerful even than cynicism.

To an Athlete
Dying Young

A. E. Housman

The time you won your town the race
We chaired you through the market place;
Man and boy stood cheering by,
And home we brought you shoulder-high.

Today, the road all runners come,   5
Shoulder-high we bring you home,
And set you at your threshold down,
Townsman of a stiller town.

Smart lad, to slip betimes away
From fields where glory does not stay   10
And early though the laurel[1] grows
It withers quicker than the rose.

Eyes the shady night has shut
Cannot see the record cut,[2]
And silence sounds no worse than cheers   15
After earth has stopped the ears:

Now you will not swell the rout
Of lads that wore their honors out,
Runners whom renown outran
And the name died before the man.   20

So set, before its echoes fade,
The fleet foot on the sill of shade,[3]
And hold to the low lintel[4] up
The still-defended challenge cup.

And round that early-laureled head   25
Will flock to gaze the strengthless dead,
And find unwithered on its curls
The garland briefer than a girl's.

1 **laurel:** The laurel wreath was awarded by the Greeks to the victors in athletic games.
2 **record cut:** i.e., the record beaten.
3 **sill of shade:** the doorsill of death.
4 **lintel:** beam at the top of a doorway. (This beam is "low" because death has come early.)

"Smart lad, to slip betimes away," says the speaker, in a colloquial, familiar tone. The fallen athlete will not know the defeat of seeing his victory outdone. But the speaker's tone is not quite so knowing at the end of the poem: how does he finally see the dead youth?

1. In the first stanza the speaker remembers how his townsmen carried the victorious athlete ("chaired") on their shoulders in triumph. How is this image repeated in the second stanza? What is the meaning of "Townsman of a stiller town"?

2. In stanzas 3, 4, and 5, the speaker offers a kind of comfort to the dead athlete. What does he imply about life, about experience, as he does so?

3. In the sixth stanza the speaker urges a gesture upon the athlete: what would this gesture express?

4. In the final stanza the speaker promises a result, an effect, from the gesture he urges: the "strengthless dead" will gather to "gaze" on the athlete's "unwithered" crown or wreath of victory. What attitude does the speaker now take toward the athlete's early death?

"On Wenlock Edge"

Wenlock is a town in Shropshire near the region where Housman grew up. Wenlock Edge is a long ridge nearby; from its top one can see far into the ancient hills and valleys of the countryside. The speaker in the following poem is an English yeoman, a countryman with a small farm. He watches a storm sweeping over the countryside and reflects that winds of similar storms must have troubled those who preceded him, even back to the time when the Romans were settled in the district.

On Wenlock Edge

A. E. Housman

On Wenlock Edge the wood's in trouble;
    His forest fleece the Wrekin[1] heaves;
The gale, it plies[2] the saplings double,
    And thick on Severn[3] snow the leaves.

'Twould blow like this through holt[4] and hanger[5]   5
    When Uricon[6] the city stood:

1 **Wrekin:** an isolated extinct volcano.
2 **plies:** bends.
3 **Severn:** the Severn River, which flows through Shropshire.
4 **holt:** woods.
5 **hanger:** woods on the steep side of a hill.
6 **Uricon:** a Roman city that stood near the site of modern Shrewsbury.

'Tis the old wind in the old anger,
　　But then it threshed another wood.

Then, 'twas before my time, the Roman
　　At yonder heaving hill would stare:　　　　　　10
The blood that warms an English yeoman,
　　The thoughts that hurt him, they were there.

There, like the wind through woods in riot,
　　Through him the gale of life blew high;
The tree of man was never quiet:　　　　　　　　15
　　Then 'twas the Roman, now 'tis I.

The gale, it plies the saplings double,
　　It blows so hard, 'twill soon be gone:
Today the Roman and his trouble
　　Are ashes under Uricon.　　　　　　　　　　20

Comment

"Then 'twas the Roman, now 'tis I," says the speaker. Housman not only expresses human subjection to unheeding natural forces; he tells us also that this subjection is one of our bonds with past generations.

1. The storm is announced with the words, "the wood's in trouble," and in the next line a mountain is described as heaving its "fleece," its hairy hide. When does an animal raise or "heave" its fur?
2. What does the word *stare* imply about the way the Roman experienced the storm?
3. In the fourth stanza the storm now becomes "the gale of life," the forests become "The tree of man." How does the speaker of these words differ from the "staring" Roman? But how do these words show us his link with the ancient Roman?
4. How does the last stanza enlarge and enforce what the speaker says at line 16, "Then 'twas the Roman, now 'tis I"? What does the last stanza suggest about the speaker's "now"? What does his "now" include that the Roman's could not?
5. What attitude toward experience, toward the movement of life, do you find in this poem and the two preceding? Housman is clearly not a poet of hope. But is he the opposite, a poet of despair? Explain.

Thomas Hardy (1840-1928)

The world knows Thomas Hardy as a novelist (in our next chapter we shall discuss one of his most famous novels, *The Return of the Native*), but his writing life was also given to poetry, and in both his novels and his poems he expressed a stern and sometimes tragic vision of life that disturbed his contemporaries. After the publication of *Jude the Obscure* (1895), in fact, Hardy turned almost exclusively to the writing of poetry for the rest of his long life. Jude, a young stonemason, tries in vain to better his condition; his ambition is to enter an ancient university and become a learned scholar or preacher, but he fails, bitterly and sadly, the victim of his own natural impulse. *Jude the Obscure* angered many readers—Hardy was by this time so well known that he had a large public—and the author, rather than battle in vain with his public, simply gave up writing novels. Jude is a tragic hero, but his tragedy offended late-Victorian readers who demanded not only "happy endings" (as Charles Darwin had) but also a "message" of hopefulness and optimism. Hardy's poetry does not give its readers a comfortable sense that all is well, any more than did his novels. But his poems often bring back to us the stark, unadorned qualities of the medieval ballads, and his vision of the smallness of humankind beside the vast and indifferent forces of nature and history belongs with the balladlike manner of his poems.

Hardy was born and raised in Dorsetshire, the region of southwest England that he called "Wessex" in his novels. It is a region full of the most ancient lore and traditions of British history: there, King Alfred defeated the Danes; there, too, the Romans set up their earliest camps. Hardy knew the region well. His father was a carpenter and mason who formed with his sons a group of fiddlers who played at many a country dance. At fifteen Thomas Hardy was apprenticed to an architect in Dorchester who specialized in renovating and rebuilding old churches in the district. Hardy's work, as well as his fiddling, took him into many a remote village of the ancient Wessex world. He was largely self-educated, and read widely in the small leisure from work that he could find. His works echo the Bible and Shakespeare, though no writer of his time was more aware of contemporary intellectual movements. Yet Hardy is in no sense sophisticated or "literary"; his works came directly from his own deeply pondered experience in a region where the modern and the ancient lived side by side.

"The Darkling Thrush"

The following poem is dated December 31, 1900; the poet stands at the threshold of a new century. He stands in the desolate half-light of winter, the world around him and he himself, "fervourless"—lifeless. Can he escape from the dying year, the dying century, the dying world? He cannot know, he cannot tell, yet he hears a sound of hope.

The Darkling[1] Thrush

Thomas Hardy

I leant upon a coppice[2] gate
    When Frost was spectre-gray,
And Winter's dregs made desolate
    The weakening eye of day.[3]
The tangled bine-stems scored[4] the sky   5
    Like strings from broken lyres,
And all mankind that haunted[5] nigh
    Had sought their household fires.

The land's sharp features seemed to be
    The Century's corpse outleant,[6]   10
His crypt the cloudy canopy,
    The wind his death-lament.
The ancient pulse of germ and birth[7]
    Was shrunken hard and dry,
And every spirit upon earth   15
    Seemed fervourless as I.

At once a voice arose among
    The bleak twigs overhead
In a full-hearted evensong
    Of joy illimited;[8]   20
An aged thrush, frail, gaunt, and small,
    In blast-beruffled plume,
Had chosen thus to fling his soul
    Upon the growing gloom.

So little cause for carollings   25
    Of such ecstatic sound
Was written on terrestrial things
    Afar or nigh around,
That I could think there trembled through
    His happy good-night air   30
Some blessed Hope, whereof he knew
    And I was unaware.

1 **Darkling:** in the dark.
2 **coppice** (kŏp′ĭs) **gate:** gate into the woods.
3 **eye of day:** the sun.
4 **bine-stems scored:** stems of woodbine were like marks on.
5 **haunted:** lived.
6 **Century's . . . outleant:** The 19th century, like a dead body, is stretched out.
7 **ancient . . . birth:** endless cycle of reproduction and birth.
8 **illimited:** unlimited.

Comment

"The Darkling Thrush" is divided exactly in its center. In the first half, the poet, the "I," describes his situation, and in the second half he tells how he hears the "full-hearted song" of the "aged thrush." Do the two halves of the poem exactly balance each other? Or does one outweigh the other?

1. The first half of the poem ends, "And every spirit upon earth/ Seemed fervourless as I." What are some images of the first two stanzas that prepare us for the full meaning of "fervourless"?

2. In stanza 3 the situation begins to change. But how does the first line of stanza 3 announce the change—stridently? tentatively? Notice the succession of "a" sounds: "*At* once *a* voice *a*rose *a*mong"— what is their effect on the speaker's tone here?

3. The voice rises to a "full-hearted evensong [a song of praise]/Of joy illimited." But the source of the song is identified in a line that echoes the sounds of the first line of stanza 3: "An *a*ged thrush, fr*a*il, g*a*unt, and sm*a*ll." These "a" sounds are stronger than the "uh" sound of hesitation, but are they boldly confident and affirmative?

4. How do the last lines, "Some blessed Hope, whereof he knew/And I was unaware," in both sound and sense contrast the situation of the speaker with the song of the thrush? Note especially the very last word of the poem, describing the "I."

5. Does Hardy's thrush symbolize here the hope and deliverance symbolized by the water snakes in *The Rime of the Ancient Mariner?* Does it symbolize in this poem the creative power of the song of Shelley's skylark? Write a paragraph on Hardy's thrush as a symbol that is both like and unlike the symbols from bird or animal life in poems you have read.

"Channel Firing"

The similarity between Hardy's poetry and the medieval ballads is especially strong in the following poem, which even in its quatrains is close to the ballad stanza. It comes upon us suddenly, and yet as the most natural thing in the world, that the speakers, "we," are dead men speaking from a churchyard. And God speaks to them, not in omnipotent tones, but in tones as familiar as their own. This is a poem in which the supernatural is made as familiar as it is in "The Wife of Usher's Well." It is also a poem with which we may fittingly take leave of the Victorian era, for it gives us Hardy's reflections upon the sound of gunnery practice at sea, in the English Channel, in April, 1914. In August, 1914, four months later, the guns on land and sea were firing in earnest, for World War I had begun.

Channel Firing

Thomas Hardy

That night your great guns, unawares,
Shook all our coffins as we lay,
And broke the chancel window-squares,
We thought it was the Judgment-day

And sat upright. While drearisome   5
Arose the howl of wakened hounds:
The mouse let fall the altar-crumb,
The worms drew back into the mounds,[1]

The glebe cow[2] drooled. Till God called, "No;
It's gunnery practice out at sea   10
Just as before you went below;
The world is as it used to be:

"All nations striving strong to make
Red war yet redder. Mad as hatters[3]
They do no more for Christès[4] sake   15
Than you who are helpless in such matters.

"That this is not the judgment-hour
For some of them's a blessed thing,
For if it were they'd have to scour
Hell's floor for so much threatening. . . .   20

"Ha, ha. It will be warmer when
I blow the trumpet (if indeed
I ever do; for you are men,
And rest eternal sorely need)."

So down we lay again. "I wonder,   25
Will the world ever saner be,"
Said one, "than when He sent us under
In our indifferent century!"

---

1 **mounds:** of the graves.
2 **glebe cow:** the cow that grazed on the "glebe," or land belonging to the parish.
3 **Mad as hatters:** See *Alice in Wonderland*.
4 **Christès:** archaic spelling and pronunciation as in a medieval ballad.

And many a skeleton shook his head.
"Instead of preaching forty year,"
My neighbour Parson Thirdly said,
"I wish I had stuck to pipes and beer."

Again the guns disturbed the hour,
Roaring their readiness to avenge,
As far inland as Stourton Tower,
And Camelot, and starlit Stonehenge.[5]

30

35

---

5 **Stourton . . . Stonehenge:** Stourton Tower was erected in "Wessex" in the 18th century to commemorate the victory of Alfred over the Danes in the 9th century; Camelot is the legendary site of King Arthur's court; Stonehenge is a circle of huge stones, apparently an outdoor temple in which to worship the sun, erected by prehistoric inhabitants of Britain.

Comment

Although the sound of naval gunfire is enough to waken the dead, Judgment Day has not yet come. The world goes on as before, says God, and He laughs wryly—yet with compassion for the awakened dead. And muttering to themselves the dead go back to sleep, while the guns continue to shake the land. Hardy paints a grim picture, yet it is one not without humor. Is it also without pity or hope?

1. The dead awake in sudden fear; how do the images of the animals surrounding them in the church and churchyard add to their terror?
2. But God speaks—"No," it's not yet Judgment Day. How does the speech of God reassure the awakened dead? How does it also add to their sense of impending doom?
3. The dead become silent again. But again "the guns disturbed the hour," and their sound is heard inland at the most ancient sites in England. How does the last stanza modify God's statement in stanza 4, that men, preparing for war, are "Mad as hatters"? With what tone does the poem end?

The Victorian Period
Summing Up

1. Two of the most famous lines of Victorian poetry appear in a long poem by Browning called "Pippa Passes." (They are lines known to many who have no idea where they come from.) They are said by an innocent—and ignorant—girl whose life and whose attitudes are contrasted with the cynicism and wickedness of various people who live near her. Here are the lines:

> God's in his heaven—
> All's right with the world!

These lines have been quoted often as summarizing the main theme and message of Victorian poetry. Do they seem to you to do so? Explain why.

2. Nature—sometimes the sea, sometimes the mountains, sometimes the forest—furnishes many of the most memorable images and settings of Victorian literature. Nature is also a major philosophic and scientific concept among the Victorians. And so, too, is nature in the poetry and prose of Wordsworth, perhaps the greatest Romantic writer. What differences do you find between Wordsworth's nature and Tennyson's? Or what would Wordsworth have made of Meredith's conception of the stars as the "army of unalterable law"? Locate other comparisons for yourself and write an essay on nature in Wordsworth and in his Victorian successors.

3. The motto, or epigraph, chosen for this Victorian chapter, you will recall, is "WISDOM, a name to shake/ All evil dreams of power." The lines come from a poem by Tennyson (a poem about the powers of the poet). As you reflect on your reading in this chapter, does this epigraph seem to you relevant? Do the Victorian writers you have studied seem to you to have been concerned with opposing some kind of wisdom to dreams of power? If so, how have they imagined this "power"? And how have they imagined "wisdom"?

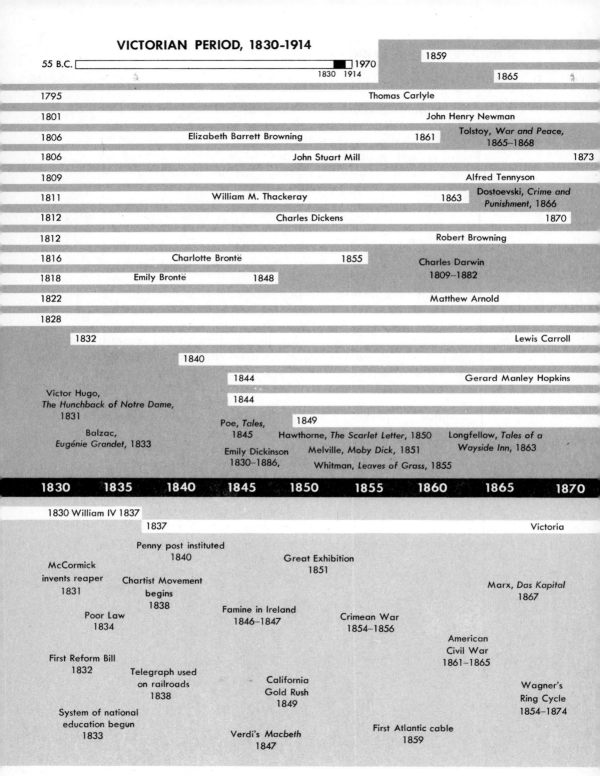

VICTORIAN PERIOD, 1830–1914

55 B.C. ☐☐☐☐☐☐☐☐☐☐☐☐☐■ ☐1970
1830 1914

1859

1865

1795   Thomas Carlyle

1801   John Henry Newman

1806   Elizabeth Barrett Browning   1861   Tolstoy, *War and Peace*, 1865–1868

1806   John Stuart Mill   1873

1809   Alfred Tennyson

1811   William M. Thackeray   1863   Dostoevski, *Crime and Punishment*, 1866

1812   Charles Dickens   1870

1812   Robert Browning

1816   Charlotte Brontë   1855   Charles Darwin 1809–1882

1818   Emily Brontë   1848

1822   Matthew Arnold

1828

1832   Lewis Carroll

1840

1844   Gerard Manley Hopkins

Victor Hugo, *The Hunchback of Notre Dame*, 1831

1844

Balzac, *Eugénie Grandet*, 1833

Poe, *Tales*, 1845

1849

Hawthorne, *The Scarlet Letter*, 1850

Longfellow, *Tales of a Wayside Inn*, 1863

Emily Dickinson 1830–1886,

Melville, *Moby Dick*, 1851

Whitman, *Leaves of Grass*, 1855

| 1830 | 1835 | 1840 | 1845 | 1850 | 1855 | 1860 | 1865 | 1870 |

1830 William IV 1837

1837   Victoria

Penny post instituted 1840

Great Exhibition 1851

McCormick invents reaper 1831

Chartist Movement begins 1838

Marx, *Das Kapital* 1867

Poor Law 1834

Famine in Ireland 1846–1847

Crimean War 1854–1856

First Reform Bill 1832

Telegraph used on railroads 1838

California Gold Rush 1849

American Civil War 1861–1865

Wagner's Ring Cycle 1854–1874

System of national education begun 1833

Verdi's *Macbeth* 1847

First Atlantic cable 1859

654

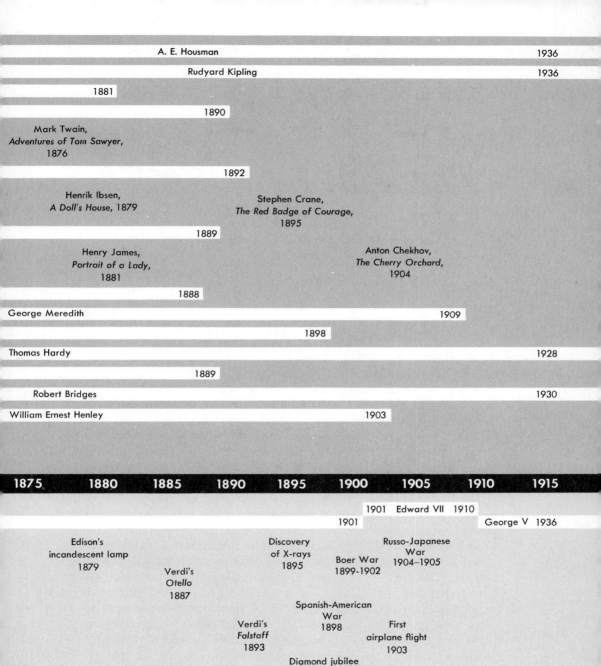

A. E. Housman   1936

Rudyard Kipling   1936

1881

1890

Mark Twain,
Adventures of Tom Sawyer,
1876

1892

Henrik Ibsen,
A Doll's House, 1879

Stephen Crane,
The Red Badge of Courage,
1895

1889

Henry James,
Portrait of a Lady,
1881

Anton Chekhov,
The Cherry Orchard,
1904

1888

George Meredith   1909

1898

Thomas Hardy   1928

1889

Robert Bridges   1930

William Ernest Henley   1903

1875	1880	1885	1890	1895	1900	1905	1910	1915

1901   Edward VII   1910

1901   George V   1936

Edison's
incandescent lamp
1879

Discovery
of X-rays
1895

Boer War
1899-1902

Russo-Japanese
War
1904–1905

Verdi's
Otello
1887

Spanish-American
War
1898

Verdi's
Falstaff
1893

First
airplane flight
1903

Diamond jubilee
of Queen Victoria
1897

Alexander
Graham Bell
invents telephone
1876

Boxer Rebellion
in China
1900

Einstein
publishes
theory
of relativity
1905

The English Novel

*". . . to strike the balance between the uncommon
and the ordinary so as on the one hand to give interest,
on the other to give reality."*

THOMAS HARDY

The Elements of the Novel

As YOU HAVE seen throughout the foregoing pages, English writers have
been telling stories since the days of the unknown author of *Beowulf*.
The magic words *Once upon a time* have worked their spell upon
countless generations of listeners and readers. What is the novel, then?
Everyone knows that a novel tells a story; true, it is usually a long
story, and it is told in prose, not verse. But what else is there to it? If
it is not just a story, what *is* a novel?

The best answer to this question is a historical answer, for it is no
easier to define the novel than it is to define poetry. We have already
seen how each period of English literature has proposed its own conception of the poet and his language. The Renaissance idea of poetry
differs from that of the Enlightenment; the Romantic idea differs from
both; and the Victorian (as well as that of the 20th Century, you will
later see) differs yet again. These very differences, in fact, give us an
important clue to the nature of the novel, for although there have always been storytellers, the character of the story has changed during
the course of English literary history just as the character of poetry has
changed.

The first use of the words *"the* novel" occurred in 1757. Toward the
middle of the 18th century something had appeared on the literary
scene that required—and received—a name of its own. The name was
not new. During the 17th century there had arisen a vogue for stories
of rogues, bandits, and travelers. These stories were called novels to
distinguish them from romances, the tales of knights, chivalry, and
magical events that were popular from the Middle Ages on. But

Omnibus Life in London *by William M. Egley gives a vivid glimpse of the crowded interior of a London bus in the 19th century.*

A miniature from a 15th-century romance. The romance, allegorical stories of chivalry and magic, was one of the early precursors of the novel. Here the allegorical figure of Love hands the author's heart to Desire. There is a kind of dreamy reality to this illustration which embodies the quality of the romance itself.

toward the end of the Enlightenment the novel came to be recognized as more than a high-spirited story of life on the road. The novelist had begun to bring together in a new form a number of different kinds of writing that had hitherto stood by themselves. And each of these ingredients, each of these newly combined elements, has already been before us in its original setting.

We have seen two of them in the selections from the Renaissance. The first of these is the "character," the short sketch that sums up, sometimes wittily, either a particular type of person or some historical personage. You will recall the witty, if uncomplimentary, "character" of the courtier as sketched by Sir Thomas Overbury. And you will recall, too, Sir John Hayward's portrait or "character" of Queen Elizabeth I. Both are examples of a new literary interest that appeared in the Renaissance. And while character-writing was practiced by historians and biographers in the late Renaissance, and while it was a discipline

A miniature from a 14th-century edition of Lancelot du Lac. *The Arthurian legends, early ancestors of the novel, were popular in France as well as in England. The drawing here has little regard for perspective, and the size of a figure symbolizes his importance in relation to others.*

useful to the dramatist too, it was destined to come to its full development when, combined with other ingredients, it would be used by the novelist.

A second element of the novel that comes from the Renaissance is at first sight not so obvious as the character. Perhaps you will remember the passage of prose in which the preacher and poet John Donne analyzed the distractions that overcame his attention as he knelt in prayer. The kind of self-analysis that Donne carried out in that little passage was performed by many men and women during the 17th century. Many of the Puritans in both America and Britain kept diaries in which they noted only in a secondary way the obvious events of each day: their primary purpose was to probe and analyze their thoughts and motives. They kept strict accounts of themselves to see whether their private thoughts conformed to the code of their religion as did their public lives. Many of them wrote not only diaries and meditations

The frontispiece to the 1680 edition of The Pilgrim's Progress, *showing Bunyan's dream and the pilgrim on the road. Not truly a novel, the book was a sustained allegory.*

but also autobiographies in which they considered in detail their most personal fears and joys, doubts and certainties, temptations and triumphs. John Bunyan's great story, *The Pilgrim's Progress*, coming at the end of the Renaissance, worked powerfully on an audience who had probed their own hearts to find there impulses like those represented by Pliable or Diffidence and who hoped to triumph as Christian did.

But *The Pilgrim's Progress* was not yet a novel. It still says much to us about the difficulties of the traveler on the road of life, but it does not describe these difficulties in what we think of as a "real" world. For by "real world" we usually mean a social world, a world in which people interact with each other in the vast system of public institutions and private relationships that we call society. And this is the world in which the writer of the Enlightenment was primarily interested. The difference between Samuel Johnson's ideal poet and Sir Philip Sidney's, you will remember, is that for Johnson the poet must know the social world both intimately and generally: he or she must know the history of the institutions by which people live, and he or she must observe the ways in which people at all ages of their lives respond to the life around them. For Sidney, the poet is first of all a "maker": he makes a "golden" world out of the "brazen" world of nature. The poet was still a maker in the 18th century; but the poet was also a student, and the great object of his or her study was society.

We say, quite properly, that the portraits of the pilgrims in the Prologue to *The Canterbury Tales* give us a picture of Chaucer's society. We find there a collection of individuals ranging from a Plowman to a Knight, from an elegant religious lady to a sociable widow. Yet Chau-

Oliver Twist in the workhouse asks for more gruel. The drawing is by George Cruikshank, from an early edition of Dickens's Oliver Twist. The cruelties and injustices of society were often exposed by Dickens and other Victorian novelists.

cer was not trying to describe his society; he simply described a complete band of religious pilgrims, and they *were* society. By the 18th century had come many changes. People were separated from each other not only by hereditary rank, as were the Plowman and the Knight; or by the fact that they normally stood on opposite sides of the market-stall, as did the Merchant and the Wife of Bath; or by the fact that some lived in the city, like the Lawyer, others in the country, like the Franklin. There were other differences now, such as that between the person who could understand Sir Isaac Newton's mathematical *Principia* and the person who listened with rapt attention to the story of Dorothy Mately and her terrible fate. Britain was growing; the population both at home and in the New World was rapidly increasing, and among the people at home and abroad new political ideas were beginning to emerge. London, the center of the kingdom, was spreading out into the green fields of the countryside. And beyond London, deeper in that countryside, amid old villages and noble estates there were also the beginnings of new industrial towns. No one pilgrimage could gather up the representatives of all these new people, places, and ideas. How then could they be related? What *is* the nature of society?

Writers of the 18th century answered the question in many ways, but the answer to which they returned again and again was—manners. We can understand the nature of society if we understand how people act; the character of any society is revealed by the behavior of its members. And not only can we understand society through its manners; we can also improve society by exposing its manners. To this exposure, as we have seen, conducted ruthlessly by Swift, more gently by Addison and Pope, the 18th-century writers turned their best efforts.

You will recall that the essays of Addison and Steele were written as if they came from the pen of an anonymous bystander, "The Spectator"; and you will recall that Mr. Spectator described himself as an observer of manners who would not identify himself fully and specifically. He exposed the society around him by moving through it as if clad in a cloak of invisibility. He was as likely to be found among the Whigs as among the Tories; he was as familiar with the country as with the city; he knew in intimate detail the ways of a sober, old-fashioned lawyer as well as the tedious hours in the day of a fashionable young lady. The Spectator was a mysterious, affable stranger whose presence reminded men and women that their manners related them to society.

But all the exposing and describing of society carried on by the poets and essayists of the Enlightenment does not by itself account for what we think of as the novel. Certainly the novel does give society a picture of itself. And yet novels—at their best—are not social documents only. At their best they do what Shelley, at the height of the Romantic movement, said must be done by the poet:

> A man, to be greatly good, must imagine intensely and comprehensively; he must put himself in the place of another and of many others.

It is just this putting oneself "in the place of another and of many others" that the novelist accomplishes as he looks into society. Shelley's requirement seems more appropriate for the novel than for poetry, and indeed it is this requirement that made the novel so important in the Romantic movement.

A skill in the drawing of character. A skill in the probing of private thoughts and motives. An invisible observer who can see into all the corners of contemporary society. An observer, moreover, who shows us how to put ourselves in the place of other people. These ingredients, by the late 18th century, had been formed by the teller of tales into something new, something, as we know, that was destined to grow into that branch of literature larger than any other, the novel. Its period of greatest growth was the 19th century; then, the introduction of cheaper, speedier printing put the greatest novelists of the day in touch with a vast new audience. Charles Dickens, William Makepeace Thackeray, George Eliot, and many others published some of their best works in monthly shilling numbers which were eagerly read aloud in thousands of family circles. And the 19th-century novelist, especially at mid-century, was fully aware of a new power and influence. At this time, as we have seen, Matthew Arnold said that poetry must be a criticism of life: the poet must never lose sight of the great question "How to live?" To this principle the Victorian novelists readily subscribed. It was a powerful conviction with which they combined the elements they inherited from the writers who preceded them. Indeed, the great novelists of the 19th century did their work so well that more than once in our own time there have been predictions that the novel is finished—that it has exhausted its potentialities and can grow no further. Whether such predictions are justified you will someday determine for yourselves.

The Range of the Novel

ALTHOUGH PUTTING oneself "in the place of another and of many others" was an important principle of poetry for Shelley, it had been practiced before him by many novelists. In 1712, for example, there was published in London an account of a voyage round the world, some of the most memorable passages of which described a castaway named Alexander Selkirk found by the author's crew on a small, far-off island. Selkirk, "a man clothed in goatskins, who looked wilder than the first owners of them," had been marooned for four years and four months. He had almost lost the use of his native language, but he had ingeniously kept himself alive and clothed even though he had "no other needle but a nail; and when his knife was wore to the back, he made others as well as he could of some iron hoops that were left ashore, which he beat thin and ground upon stones." From such hints as these Daniel Defoe wrote *The Life and Strange Surprising Adventures of Robinson Crusoe, of York, Mariner,* one of the earliest and still one of the most famous of all English novels. So thoroughly did Defoe imagine the life of his shipwrecked hero that many could not believe his book was fiction. It was treated as yet another history of the dangers of the sea, and Defoe himself was called a liar by critics who found certain of his details unprofessional.

In 1748 was published what is still the longest novel in English and one that reveals the power of imagining the "place" of a very different sort of person. Its title is *Clarissa, or The History of a Young Lady;* its author was a middle-aged printer, Samuel Richardson, who had become a novelist by accident. Some years before, he had set out to make a collection of letters to serve as models for the uneducated to follow in their correspondence, but instead of composing model letters Richardson found that he was imagining the concerns of fictitious letter writers, and he went on to write three long novels consisting entirely of letters sent to one another by the main characters. A Richardson novel is something like a very long play in which each character speaks at great length about actions that we never see directly before us on the stage. The correspondents analyze their feelings in detail, and the situations in which they are involved are developed for us as slowly and as inevitably as the movement of the minute hand of a watch.

Here, for example, is a passage from one of the hundreds of letters Clarissa Harlowe writes to her friend Miss Howe. It describes an occasion when she must be agreeable to Mr. Solmes, the rich old man whom her family want her to marry, and it tells in detail her efforts to forestall him as he "hems up"—clears his throat—to deliver the proposal speech he knows she expects and that her family have given their blessing to.

from Clarissa

I went down this morning when breakfast was ready with a very uneasy heart, from what Hannah had informed me of yesterday afternoon; wishing for an opportunity, however, to appeal to my mother, in hopes to engage her interest in my behalf, and purposing to try to find one when she retired to her own apartment after breakfast: but unluckily there was the odious Solmes sitting asquat between my mother and sister, with _so much_ assurance in his looks! But you know, my dear, that those we love not cannot do anything to please us.

Had the wretch kept his seat, it might have been well enough: but the bent and broad-shouldered creature must needs rise and stalk toward a chair, which was just by that which was set for me.

I removed it to a distance, as if to make way to my own: and down I sat, abruptly I believe; what I had heard all in my head.

But this was not enough to daunt him. The man is a very confident, he is a very bold, staring man! Indeed, my dear, the man is very confident!

He took the removed chair and drew it so near mine, squatting in it with his ugly weight, that he pressed upon my hoop. I was so offended (all I had heard, as I said, in my head) that I removed to another chair. I own I had too little command of myself. It gave my brother and sister too much advantage. I dare say they took it. But

I did it involuntarily, I think. I could not help it. I knew not what I did.

I saw that my father was excessively displeased. When angry, no man's countenance ever shows it so much as my father's. "Clarissa Harlowe!" said he with a big voice—and there he stopped. "Sir!" said I, trembling and curtsying (for I had not then sat down again): and put my chair nearer the wretch, and sat down—my face, as I could feel, all in a glow.

"Make tea, child," said my kind mamma; "sit by me, love, and make tea."

I removed with pleasure to the seat the man had quitted; and being thus indulgently put into employment, soon recovered myself; and in the course of the breakfasting officiously asked two or three questions of Mr. Solmes, which I would not have done, but to make up with my father. _"Proud spirits may be brought to!"_ whisperingly spoke my sister to me over her shoulder, with an air of triumph and scorn: but I did not mind her.

My mother was all kindness and condescension. I asked her once if she were pleased with the tea? She said softly (and again called me _dear_) she was pleased with all I did. I was very proud of this encouraging goodness: and all blew over, as I hoped, between my father and me; for he also spoke kindly to me two or three times.

Small incidents these, my dear, to trouble you with; only as they lead to greater, as you shall hear.

Before the usual breakfast time was over, my father withdrew with my mother, telling her he wanted to speak to her. Then my sister and next my aunt (who was with us) dropped away.

My brother gave himself some airs of insult, which I understood well enough; but which Mr. Solmes could make nothing of: and at last he arose from *his* seat. "Sister," said he, "I have a curiosity to show you. I will fetch it." And away he went shutting the door close after him.

I saw what all this was for. I arose; the man hemming up for a speech, rising and beginning to set his splay feet (indeed, my dear, the man in all his ways is hateful to me!) in an approaching posture. "I will save my brother the trouble of bringing to me his curiosity," said I. I curtsied—"Your servant, sir." The man cried, madam, madam, twice, and looked like a fool. But away I went—to find my brother, to save my word. But my brother, indifferent as the weather was, was gone to walk in the garden with my sister. A plain case that he had left his *curiosity* with me, and designed to show me no other.

Clarissa escapes "the odious Solmes" this time; but, so bent upon the marriage and the money it will bring are her family that, when she persists in refusing him, they make her a virtual prisoner. As will be readily suspected, Clarissa loves another, a dashing young man named Lovelace; but, alas, his intentions are not honorable. It is perhaps difficult to imagine that Clarissa's troubles should have been spun out to almost a million words. And yet, as we can see in this passage, Richardson's method, his close attention to the details even of the seating arrangements at the table, the rising and falling of Clarissa's apprehensions, the meanness of the sister—all these fine features of the situation have not lost their power of fascination.

Richardson's meticulous psychological probing, we must bear in mind, was quite startlingly new in the mid-18th century. And it did not go uncriticized, for Richardson's first novel provoked Henry Fielding (who told the story of the kitten that fell overboard) to parody, and so another great novelist accidentally came into being. Fielding's gifts were those of the comic writer at his best; and, though he began his novelist's career by making fun of Richardson, he quickly moved on to the expression of a large, generous humanity, particularly in his masterpiece, *Tom Jones*. Fielding found much to laugh at in the human scene, but he never laughed at a generous act.

To suggest briefly the range of the novel, however, we must move on to Charles Dickens, the greatest, though sometimes the most uneven, novelist of the 19th century. In Dickens we find both Fielding's generous humanity and Richardson's interest in minute psychological details. It was an unstable combination, especially in Dickens's later works, yet it enabled him to show his readers ranges of experience and kinds of people that had not appeared in the English novel before. Here, for example, is Dickens's portrait of someone at the lowest level of his society: a young boy who earns the few pennies a day that constitute his living by sweeping aside the mud at a street-crossing so that pedestrians may pass without soiling their shoes. Jo lives in a hideous slum with the quaint name of "Tom-all-Alone's," and Dickens tells us that the reason for the dilapidation of "Tom" is that it is one of many properties being fought over in an endless lawsuit, the case of "Jarndyce and Jarndyce." Dickens not only tries to imagine the thoughts and feelings of an almost nameless boy; he also relates the plight of this waif to the neglect and misery that enter a society which cares only for money and for lawsuits to get more of it.

from Bleak House

Jo sweeps his crossing all day long, unconscious of the link, if any link there be. He sums up his mental condition, when asked a question, by replying that he "don't know nothink." He knows that it's hard to keep the mud off the crossing in dirty weather, and harder still to live by doing it. Nobody taught him, even that much; he found it out.

Jo lives—that is to say, Jo has not yet died—in a ruinous place, known to the like of him by the name of Tom-all-Alone's. It is a black, dilapidated street, avoided by all decent people; where the crazy houses were seized upon, when their decay was far advanced, by some bold vagrants, who, after establishing their own possession, took to letting them out in lodgings. Now, these tumbling tenements contain, by night, a swarm of misery. As on the ruined human wretch, vermin parasites appear, so these ruined shelters have bred a crowd of foul existence that crawls in and out of gaps in walls and boards; and coils itself to sleep, in maggot numbers, where the rain drips in; and comes and goes, fetching and carrying fever, and sowing more evil in its every footprint than Lord Coodle, and Sir Thomas Doodle, and the Duke of Foodle, and all the fine gentlemen in office, down to Zoodle, shall set right in five hundred years—though born expressly to do it.

Twice, lately, there has been a crash and a cloud of dust, like the springing of a mine, in Tom-all-Alone's; and, each time, a house has fallen. These accidents have made a paragraph in the newspapers, and have filled a bed or two in the nearest hospital. The gaps remain, and there are not unpopular lodgings among the rubbish. As several more houses are nearly ready to go, the next crash in Tom-all-Alone's may be expected to be a good one.

This desirable property is in Chancery, of course. It would be an insult to the discernment of any man with half an eye, to tell him so. Whether "Tom" is the popular representative of the original plaintiff or defendant in Jarndyce and Jarndyce; or whether Tom lived here when the suit had laid the street waste, all alone, until other settlers came to join him; or whether the traditional title is a comprehensive name for a retreat cut off from honest company and put out of the pale of hope; perhaps nobody knows. Certainly, Jo don't know.

"For *I* don't," says Jo, "*I* don't know nothink."

It must be a strange state to be like Jo! To shuffle through the streets, unfamiliar with the shapes, and in utter darkness as to the meaning, of those mysterious symbols, so abundant over the shops, and at the corners of streets, and on the doors, and in the windows! To see people read, and to see people write, and to see the postmen deliver letters, and not to have the least idea of all that language—to be, to every scrap of it, stone blind and dumb! It must be very puzzling to see the good company going to the churches on Sundays, with their books in their hands, and to think (for perhaps Jo *does* think, at odd times) what does it all mean, and if it means anything to anybody, how comes it that it means nothing to me? To be hustled, and jostled, and moved on; and really to feel that it would appear to be perfectly true that I have no business, here, or there, or anywhere; and yet to be perplexed by the consideration that I *am* here somehow, too, and everybody overlooked me until I became the creature that I am! It must be a strange state, not merely to be told that I am scarcely human (as in the case of my offering myself for a witness), but to feel it of my own knowledge all my life! To see the horses, dogs, and cattle go by me, and to know that in ignorance I belong to them, and not to the superior beings in my shape, whose delicacy I offend! Jo's ideas of a Criminal Trial, or a Judge, or a Bishop, or a Government, or that in-

estimable jewel to him (if he only knew it) the Constitution, should be strange! His whole material and immaterial life is wonderfully strange; his death, the strangest thing of all.

Jo comes out of Tom-all-Alone's, meeting the tardy morning which is always late in getting down there, and munches his dirty bit of bread as he comes along. His way lying through many streets, and the houses not yet being open, he sits down to breakfast on the doorstep of the Society for the Propagation of the Gospel in Foreign Parts, and gives it a brush when he has finished, as an acknowledgment of the accommodation. He admires the size of the edifice, and wonders what it's all about. He has no idea, poor wretch, of the spiritual destitution of a coral reef in the Pacific, or what it costs to look up the precious souls among the coconuts and breadfruit.

He goes to his crossing, and begins to lay it out for the day. The town awakes; the great teetotum is set up for its daily spin and whirl; all that unaccountable reading and writing, which has been suspended for a few hours, recommences. Jo, and the other lower animals, get on in the unintelligible mess as they can.

Dickens, as you see, not only suggests what it must feel like to be poor and illiterate, though this by itself would have been startling enough; he also, at the end, says something about the society that surrounds Jo. Let charity begin at home, he seems to say. The very building from which missionaries are sent out to coral islands in the Pacific is unrecognizable to Jo.

There is bitterness in this passage from Dickens's *Bleak House,* but we can certainly see that it is the work of a warm, humane imagination; and, when we come to the references to Coodle, Doodle, Foodle, and Zoodle, we begin to suspect that it is the work of a thoroughly comic imagination as well. Dickens's immense talent for comedy constantly exposed the dishevelment, the disorderliness, and the hypocrisy he found in Victorian society, especially in his later works. Yet even there we sometimes find the sheer high spirits of the following passage. It comes from his first novel, *Pickwick Papers,* which recounts the adventures of the Pickwick Club—Mr. Pickwick, Tupman, Snodgrass, Winkle, and Mr. Pickwick's servant, a Cockney named Sam Weller. The members of the Club are enjoying the country hospitality of Mr. Wardle of Dingley Dell. Benjamin Allen and Bob Sawyer are two young medical students who have appeared to escort a young lady of the party, Arabella Allen, back to her home. Mr. Winkle, who has been mightily smitten by Miss Arabella, has just experienced a moment of torture in witnessing the greeting between her and Sawyer:

> Arabella gracefully held out her hand, in acknowledgment of Bob Sawyer's presence. A thrill of hatred struck to Mr. Winkle's heart, as Bob Sawyer inflicted on the proffered hand a perceptible squeeze.

Injury is added to insult, then, when poor Mr. Winkle is compelled against his better judgment to put on skates with the rest of the party. Afraid to look ridiculous before Arabella by refusing, he turns out to be even more ridiculous by accepting.

from The Pickwick Papers

Old Wardle led the way to a pretty large sheet of ice; and the fat boy and Mr. Weller, having shoveled and swept away the snow which had fallen on it during the night, Mr. Bob Sawyer adjusted his skates with a dexterity which to Mr. Winkle was perfectly marvelous, and described circles with his left leg, and cut figures of eight, and inscribed upon the ice, without once stopping for breath, a great many other pleasant and astonishing devices, to the excessive satisfaction of Mr. Pickwick, Mr. Tupman, and the ladies: which reached a pitch of positive enthusiasm, when old Wardle and Benjamin Allen, assisted by the aforesaid Bob Sawyer, performed some mystic evolutions, which they called a reel.

All this time Mr. Winkle, with his face and hands blue with the cold, had been forcing a gimlet into the soles of his feet, and putting his skates on, with the points behind, and getting the straps into a very complicated and entangled state, with the assistance of Mr. Snodgrass, who knew rather less about skates than a Hindoo. At length, however, with the assistance of Mr. Weller, the unfortunate skates were firmly screwed and buckled on, and Mr. Winkle was raised to his feet.

"Now, then, sir," said Sam, in an encouraging tone; "off with you, and show 'em how to do it."

"Stop, Sam, stop!" said Mr. Winkle, trembling violently, and clutching hold of Sam's arms with the grasp of a drowning man. "How slippery it is, Sam!"

"Not an uncommon thing upon ice, sir," replied Mr. Weller. "Hold up, sir!"

This last observation of Mr. Weller's bore reference to a demonstration Mr.

Winkle made at the instant, of a frantic desire to throw his feet in the air, and dash the back of his head on the ice.

"These—these—are very awkward skates, ain't they, Sam?" inquired Mr. Winkle, staggering.

"I'm afeerd there's a orkard gen'l'm'n in 'em, sir," replied Sam.

"Now, Winkle," cried Mr. Pickwick, quite unconscious that there was anything the matter. "Come; the ladies are all anxiety."

"Yes, yes," replied Mr. Winkle, with a ghastly smile, "I'm coming."

"Just a goin' to begin," said Sam, endeavoring to disengage himself. "Now, sir, start off!"

"Stop an instant, Sam," gasped Mr. Winkle, clinging most affectionately to Mr. Weller. "I find I've got a couple of coats at home that I don't want, Sam. You may have them, Sam."

"Thank'ee, sir," replied Mr. Weller.

"Never mind touching your hat, Sam," said Mr. Winkle, hastily. "You needn't take your hand away to do that. I meant to have given you five shillings this morning for a Christmas box, Sam. I'll give it you this afternoon, Sam."

"You're wery good, sir," replied Mr. Weller.

"Just hold me at first, Sam; will you?" said Mr. Winkle. "There—that's right. I shall soon get in the way of it, Sam. Not too fast, Sam; not too fast."

Mr. Winkle stooping forward, with his body half doubled up, was being assisted over the ice by Mr. Weller, in a very singular and unswanlike manner, when Mr. Pickwick most innocently shouted from the opposite bank:

"Sam!"

"Sir?"

"Here. I want you."

"Let go, sir," said Sam. "Don't you hear the governor a callin'? Let go, sir."

With a violent effort, Mr. Weller disengaged himself from the grasp of the agonized Pickwickian, and, in so doing, administered a considerable impetus to the unhappy Mr. Winkle. With an accuracy which no degree of dexterity or practice could have insured, that unfortunate gentleman bore swiftly down into the center of the reel, at the very moment when Mr. Bob Sawyer was performing a flourish of unparalleled beauty. Mr. Winkle struck wildly against him, and with a loud crash they both fell heavily down. Mr. Pickwick ran to the spot. Bob Sawyer had risen to his feet, but Mr. Winkle was far too wise to do anything of the kind, in skates. He was seated on the ice, making spasmodic efforts to smile; but anguish was depicted on every lineament of his countenance.

"Are you hurt?" inquired Mr. Benjaman Allen, with great anxiety.

"Not much," said Mr. Winkle, rubbing his back very hard.

"I wish you'd let me bleed you," said Mr. Benjamin, with great eagerness.

"No, thank you," replied Mr. Winkle hurriedly.

"I really think you had better," said Allen.

"Thank you," replied Mr. Winkle; "I'd rather not."

"What do you think, Mr. Pickwick?" inquired Bob Sawyer.

Mr. Pickwick was excited and indignant. He beckoned to Mr. Weller, and said in a stern voice, "Take his skates off."

"No; but really I had scarcely begun," remonstrated Mr. Winkle.

"Take his skates off," repeated Mr. Pickwick firmly.

The command was not to be resisted. Mr. Winkle allowed Sam to obey it in silence.

"Lift him up," said Mr. Pickwick.

Sam assisted him to rise.

Mr. Pickwick retired a few paces apart from the bystanders; and, beckoning his friend to approach, fixed a searching look upon him, and uttered in a low, but distinct and emphatic tone, these remarkable words:

"You're a humbug, sir."

"A what?" said Mr. Winkle, starting.

"A humbug, sir. I will speak plainer, if you wish it. An impostor, sir."

With those words, Mr. Pickwick turned slowly on his heel, and rejoined his friends.

While Mr. Pickwick was delivering himself of the sentiment just recorded, Mr. Weller and the fat boy, having by their joint endeavors cut out a slide, were exercising themselves thereupon, in a very masterly and brilliant manner. Sam Weller, in particular, was displaying that beautiful feat of fancy-sliding which is currently denominated "knocking at the cobbler's door," and which is achieved by skimming over the ice on one foot, and occasionally giving a postman's knock upon it with the other. It was a good long slide, and there was something in the motion which Mr. Pickwick, who was very cold with standing still, could not help envying.

"It looks a nice warm exercise that, doesn't it?" he inquired of Wardle, when that gentleman was thoroughly out of breath, by reason of the indefatigable manner in which he had converted his legs into a pair of compasses, and drawn complicated problems on the ice.

"Ah, it does indeed," replied Wardle. "Do you slide?"

"I used to do so, on the gutters when I was a boy," replied Mr. Pickwick.

"Try it now," said Wardle.

"Oh, do, please, Mr. Pickwick!" cried all the ladies.

"I should be very happy to afford you any amusement," replied Mr. Pickwick, "but I haven't done such a thing these thirty years."

"Pooh! pooh! Nonsense!" said Wardle, dragging off his skates with the impetuosity which characterized all his proceedings. "Here; I'll keep you company; come along!" And away went the good-tempered old fellow down the slide, with a rapidity which came very close upon Mr. Weller, and beat the fat boy all to nothing.

Mr. Pickwick paused, considered, pulled off his gloves and put them in his hat: took two or three short runs, balked himself as often and at last took another run, and went slowly and gravely down the slide, with his feet about a yard and a quarter apart, amidst the gratified shouts of all the spectators.

"Keep the pot a bilin', sir!" said Sam; and down went Wardle again, and then Mr. Pickwick, and then Sam, and then Mr. Winkle, and then Mr. Bob Sawyer, and then the fat boy, and then Mr. Snodgrass, following closely upon each other's heels, and running after each other with as much eagerness as if all their future prospects in life depended on their expedition.

It was the most intensely interesting thing, to observe the manner in which Mr. Pickwick performed his share in the ceremony; to watch the torture of anxiety with which he viewed the person behind, gaining upon him at the imminent hazard of tripping him up; to see him gradually expend the painful force he had put on at first, and turn slowly round on the slide, with his face toward the point from which he had started; to contemplate the playful smile which mantled on his face when he had accomplished the distance, and the eagerness with which he turned round when he had done so, and ran after his predecessor: his black gaiters trip-

The skating party, from an early edition of The Pickwick Papers. *The artist is Phiz, the pseudonym for H. K. Browne, who illustrated many of Dickens's novels.*

ping pleasantly through the snow, and his eyes beaming cheerfulness and gladness through his spectacles. And when he was knocked down (which happened upon the average every third round), it was the most invigorating sight that can possibly be imagined, to behold him gather up his hat, gloves, and handkerchief, with a glowing countenance, and resume his station in the rank, with an ardor and enthusiasm that nothing could abate.

The sport was at its height, the sliding was at the quickest, the laughter was at the loudest, when a sharp smart crack was heard. There was a quick rush toward the bank, a wild scream from the ladies, and a shout from Mr. Tupman. A large mass of ice disappeared; the water bubbled up over it; Mr. Pickwick's hat, gloves, and handkerchief were floating on the surface; and this was all of Mr. Pickwick that anybody could see.

Dismay and anguish were depicted on every countenance, the males turned pale, and the females fainted, Mr. Snodgrass and Mr. Winkle grasped each other by the hand, and gazed at the spot where their leader had gone down, with frenzied eagerness: while Mr. Tupman, by way of rendering the promptest assistance, and at the same time conveying to any persons who might be within hearing, the clearest possible notion of the catastrophe, ran off across the country at his utmost speed, screaming "Fire!" with all his might.

It was at this moment, when old Wardle and Sam Weller were approaching the hole with cautious steps, and Mr. Benjamin Allen was holding a hurried consultation with Mr. Bob Sawyer, on the advisability of bleeding the company generally, as an improving little bit of professional practice—it was at this very moment, that a face, head, and shoulders, emerged from beneath the water, and disclosed the features and spectacles of Mr. Pickwick.

"Keep yourself up for an instant—for only one instant!" bawled Mr. Snodgrass.

"Yes, do; let me implore you—for my sake!" roared Mr. Winkle, deeply affected. The adjuration was rather unnecessary; the probability being, that if Mr. Pickwick had declined to keep himself up for anybody else's sake, it would have occurred to him that he might as well do so, for his own.

"Do you feel the bottom there, old fellow?" said Wardle.

"Yes, certainly," replied Mr. Pickwick, wringing the water from his head and face, and gasping for breath. "I fell upon my back. I couldn't get on my feet at first."

The clay upon so much of Mr. Pickwick's coat as was yet visible, bore testimony to the accuracy of this statement; and as the fears of the spectators were still further relieved by the fat boy's suddenly recollecting that the water was nowhere more than five feet deep, prodigies of valor were performed to get him out. After a vast quantity of splashing, and cracking, and struggling, Mr. Pickwick was at length fairly extricated from his unpleasant position, and once more stood on dry land.

"Oh, he'll catch his death of cold," said Emily.

"Dear old thing!" said Arabella. "Let me wrap this shawl round you, Mr. Pickwick."

"Ah, that's the best thing you can do," said Wardle; "and when you've got it on, run home as fast as your legs can carry you, and jump into bed directly."

A dozen shawls were offered on the instant. Three or four of the thickest having been selected, Mr. Pickwick was wrapped up, and started off, under the guidance of Mr. Weller: presenting the singular phenomenon of an elderly gentleman, dripping wet, and without a hat, with his arms bound down to his sides, skimming over the ground, without any clearly defined purpose, at the rate of six good English miles an hour.

But Mr. Pickwick cared not for appearances in such an extreme case, and urged on by Sam Weller, he kept at the very top of his speed until he reached the door of Manor Farm, where Mr. Tupman had arrived some five minutes before, and had frightened the old lady into palpitations of the heart by impressing her with the unalterable conviction that the kitchen chimney was on fire—a calamity which always presented itself in glowing colors to the old lady's mind, when anybody about her evinced the smallest agitation.

Mr. Pickwick paused not an instant until he was snug in bed. Sam Weller lighted a blazing fire in the room, and took up his dinner: a bowl of punch was carried up afterward, and a grand carouse held in honor of his safety. Old Wardle would not hear of his rising, so they made the bed the chair, and Mr. Pickwick presided. A second and a third bowl were ordered in; and when Mr. Pickwick awoke next morning, there was not a symptom of rheumatism about him: which proves, as Mr. Bob Sawyer very justly observed, that there is nothing like hot punch in such cases: and that if ever hot punch did fail to act as a preventive, it was merely because the patient fell into the vulgar error of not taking enough of it.

That Mr. Winkle should crash into Bob Sawyer is comic justice enough, but that the medical students should offer to bleed him afterwards makes the comic confusion complete. And Mr. Pickwick, despite his stern treatment of Winkle, goes through an adventure of his own that is almost a parody of the misfortune of his fellow Pickwickian. Moreover, even before we begin, it is hard to imagine a more incongruous set of people—the medical students, the young ladies, the cheerful squire, the Cockney Sam Weller, the portly Mr. Pickwick himself. Perhaps only a sliding party—a pilgrimage to an ice pond—could bring together such an unlikely gathering of people. Dickens's range was as large as his capacity for humor.

Literary Expectation

IT IS PERHAPS difficult to imagine the next adventure that would befall Clarissa Harlowe or Jo the sweeper or Mr. Pickwick and his friends. These passages have been taken from their contexts; they should be read by the reader who is making his progress through the novels from which they come. For that reader, as we all know, comes upon each new episode with an attitude of expectancy. How will this turn out? What will happen next? To read a novel is to be constantly leaning forward; the reader adopts an attitude of expectation that he or she does not always drop, even with the end of the book, for the reader sometimes goes on imagining further adventures for the hero and heroine after he or she has reached the last page.

This interest in narrative, of course, is not simply engaged by a mere succession of events—if it were, we should read calendars and chronologies instead of novels. We are held by the narrative because it is *shaping* something: everything that happens in a novel modifies our knowledge of the characters and their relationships. Something is being developed for us as we move from chapter to chapter.

What is this "something" developed by a novel? Does not development occur in the drama as well? Don't we follow a play with the same sense of expectation? We do, of course. And indeed the great scenes of many a novel are dramatic in the way that any play is: their dialogue and action can often be transferred to the stage (or the movie screen) without the slightest change. But a novel is not exclusively dramatic, for the novelist is an observer who sees differently from the dramatist. The novelist sees the main characters not only standing face to face in the dramatic climax; he or she sees them also when they are alone—he or she annotates for us their most private thoughts and feelings and describes for us motives and feelings that cannot be represented directly on any stage. The novelist not only presents the characters directly in action and dialogue; he or she also gives us the history and background of their situations. He or she shows us a world that extends from the most private feelings to the most public institutions. He or she shows us not only poor Jo's starved, illiterate imagination; he or she shows us also a connection between Jo's condition and a complicated lawsuit in the High Court of Chancery.

The novelist, then, makes a social world for us, and we lean forward expectantly as its outlines gradually take shape. The story moves, the characters change, and, through their experience, we discover the kind of world they live in. It is as if the novelist were performing an experiment. In a laboratory the scientist may test a chemical element to determine its properties. The experiment is limited—often to the highly purified walls of a test tube. Yet limited as it is, the experiment is a model, the model of a process in nature. The novelist is studying society, not nature, and he or she does so by imagining relationships— sometimes between men and women, sometimes between parts of the mind of a single individual. These relationships are the novelist's models of the endless, constantly moving processes that make up society. An analogy between the writer and the scientist must not be carried too far, for the study of human character in action is more complex than even the study of the nucleus of the atom, and the discipline that makes a great novelist is more mysterious than that which makes a great scientist. But both require that those who study their works shall be responsible interpreters.

Scientists do not answer the question "What is matter?" by laying down a complete set of laws. They devise experiments within the power of their equipment and their ingenuity, and produce a model of one of the infinite number of processes in matter. What they produce is valid or invalid, useful or trivial, depending upon the interpretation of other scientists, sometimes hundreds of them, each with a model which he or she is measuring against the models of others. Novelists, for their part, do not tell us "how to live" by laying down a simple moral or a set of rules for conduct. They shape our expectations by requiring us to interpret what they put before us—sometimes even at the cost of having to reshape the model of society that we hold most dear because we have painfully constructed it for ourselves. Novelists' answers to the great question "How to live?" is: by interpretation, by a constant alertness to all the words and gestures that surround us all through our lives. Their vision may discover in these words and gestures a pattern as simple and crude as the experiment performed by the first-year student of physics; it may reveal a pattern as grand as that discovered by a winner of the Nobel Prize. Whatever their vision reveals, it must be interpreted with attention and with discipline.

In reading a novel our expectations are fullest and freshest as we begin it. And the way in which we read the opening chapter of a novel all too often determines the way in which we shall get on with it. Indeed, if our powers of interpretation are not then at their fullest, we may well look ahead to a kind of development that the novelist has no intention of giving us. Here are the opening chapters of five famous

English novels. They are arranged chronologically to indicate some of the stages of the history of the novel itself, but they have been chosen also to suggest once more the great range of experience the novel offers us. It is a range that requires a great variety of interpretation: we cannot read all novels as if they were the same; we must be alert for many different effects. The best measure of your interpretation of each of these opening chapters, of course, is to test it by reading the novels from which they come.

Pride and Prejudice

Jane Austen, the author of the first selection, was born the year before America's Declaration of Independence and lived through the turbulent period of the Napoleonic Wars and the Battle of Waterloo. (Two of her brothers were distinguished officers in the Royal Navy.) Yet her life was quiet, perhaps more quiet than that of any other major novelist. Most of it she spent looking after her widowed father, a clergyman, and caring for a succession of nephews and nieces. Her novels rarely depart from the quiet country scenes she knew so well, and they are concerned with characters from the comfortable, elegant upper-middle class into which she was born. And yet as we read them we are not conscious of the limitations of their scene. For Jane Austen was first of all a critic; her first stories were parodies that made fun of the novels of her time that tried to transport readers into a world of castles and dungeons and violence; more than that, they made fun of those readers who, nurtured upon cheap fiction, came to expect that life itself was an adventure of violent cruelty and violent emotions. She moved on to write novels in which, again and again, the principal characters cannot see what is before their eyes unless it conforms to some romantic model they are carrying in their own heads. They learn to know themselves and those around them by relinquishing the "pride" or the "prejudice" which has kept them from seeing the truth. *Pride and Prejudice*, in fact, is the title of her best-known novel, and here is the way it begins:

Pride and Prejudice

Jane Austen

CHAPTER I

IT IS A truth universally acknowledged, that a single man in possession of a good fortune must be in want of a wife.

However little known the feelings or views of such a man may be on his first entering a neighborhood, this truth is so well fixed in the minds of the surrounding families, that he is considered as the rightful property of some one or other of their daughters.

"My dear Mr. Bennet," said his lady to him one day, "have you heard that Netherfield Park is let[1] at last?"

Mr. Bennet replied that he had not.

"But it is," returned she; "for Mrs. Long has just been here, and she told me all about it."

Mr. Bennet made no answer.

"Do not you want to know who has taken it?" cried his wife impatiently.

"*You* want to tell me, and I have no objection to hearing it."

This was invitation enough.

"Why, my dear, you must know, Mrs. Long says that Netherfield is taken by a young man of large fortune from the north of England; that he came down on Monday in a chaise and four[2] to see the place, and was so much delighted with it, that he agreed with Mr. Morris immediately; that he is to take possession before Michaelmas,[3] and some of his servants are to be in the house by the end of next week."

"What is his name?"

"Bingley."

"Is he married or single?"

"Oh! single, my dear, to be sure! A single man of large fortune; four or five thousand[4] a year. What a fine thing for our girls!"

"How so? How can it affect them?"

"My dear Mr. Bennet," replied his wife, "how can you be so tiresome! You must know that I am thinking of his marrying one of them."

"Is that his design in settling here?"

"Design! nonsense, how can you talk so! But it is very likely that he *may* fall in love with one of them, and therefore you must visit him as soon as he comes."

"I see no occasion for that. You and the girls may go, or you may send them by themselves, which perhaps will be still better, for as you are as handsome as any of them, Mr. Bingley might like you the best of the party."

"My dear, you flatter me. I certainly *have* had my share of beauty, but I do not pretend to be anything extraordinary now. When a woman has five grown-up daughters, she ought to give over thinking of her own beauty."

"In such cases, a woman has not often much beauty to think of."

"But, my dear, you must indeed go and see Mr. Bingley when he comes into the neighborhood."

---

1 **let:** rented.

2 **chaise** (shāz) **and four:** light traveling carriage with four horses.

3 **Michaelmas** (mĭk′əl məs): the feast of Saint Michael, September 29.

4 **four or five thousand:** the equivalent of $20,000 or $25,000 a year—a very large income.

"It is more than I engage for, I assure you."

"But consider your daughters. Only think what an establishment it would be for one of them. Sir William and Lady Lucas are determined to go, merely on that account, for in general, you know, they visit no newcomers. Indeed you must go, for it will be impossible for *us* to visit him if you do not."

"You are overscrupulous, surely. I dare say Mr. Bingley will be very glad to see you; and I will send a few lines by you to assure him of my hearty consent to his marrying whichever he chooses of the girls: though I must throw in a good word for my little Lizzy."

"I desire you will do no such thing. Lizzy is not a bit better than the others; and I am sure she is not half so handsome as Jane, nor half so good-humored as Lydia. But you are always giving *her* the preference."

"They have none of them much to recommend them," replied he; "they are all silly and ignorant, like other girls: but Lizzy has something more of quickness than her sisters."

"Mr. Bennet, how can you abuse your own children in such a way! You take delight in vexing me. You have no compassion on my poor nerves."

"You mistake me, my dear. I have a high respect for your nerves. They are my old friends. I have heard you mention them with consideration these twenty years at least."

"Ah! you do not know what I suffer."

"But I hope you will get over it, and live to see many young men of four thousand a year come into the neighborhood."

"It will be no use to us, if twenty such should come, since you will not visit them."

"Depend upon it, my dear, that when there are twenty, I will visit them all."

Mr. Bennet was so odd a mixture of quick parts,[5] sarcastic humor, reserve, and caprice, that the experience of three-and-twenty years had been insufficient to make his wife understand his character. *Her* mind was less difficult to develop.[6] She was a woman of mean understanding, little information, and uncertain temper. When she was discontented, she fancied herself nervous. The business of her life was to get her daughters married; its solace was visiting and news.

5 **quick parts:** cleverness.
6 **develop:** disclose or reveal.

Comment

The very first sentence of this novel puts us on the alert. "It is a truth universally acknowledged, that a single man in possession of a good fortune must be in want of a wife." Any "truth universally acknowledged," especially in the late 18th and early 19th centuries, is a serious matter, sometimes as serious as the "truths self-evident" with which our own Declaration of Independence begins. But what solemn truth have we here? That a man who is rich wants to be married? True? Or perhaps the truth here concerns someone else: the people of a community, especially the mothers, who want to believe that their daughters will be married to rich men. The novel opens with playful irony, and the dialogue carries it on, for it is a dialogue between someone who does believe in this "universal truth" and someone who does not.

1. Consider the following little exchange between Mr. and Mrs. Bennet:

   "How so, how can it affect them?"

   ". . . You must know that I am thinking of his marrying one of them."

   "Is that his design in settling here?"

   With what tone do you hear Mr. Bennet pronounce the word *design?* What does this word in his reply tell you about the difference between Mr. Bennet and his wife?

2. In the last paragraph Jane Austen sums up the characters of Mr. and Mrs. Bennet. How do the qualities she attributes to each of them appear in the dialogue of this chapter. How, for example, does Mr. Bennet appear as a man of "quick parts"?

3. It is clear that this novel is going to have a good deal to do with the business of courtship and marriage. But how do you expect such a subject will be developed in the following chapters? Could a conventional, romantic love story, in which a dashing hero meets the girl of his dreams (or vice versa), follow from such a beginning? Why?

Jane Eyre

The following passage, from the opening of *Jane Eyre,* by Charlotte Brontë, is, as you will see, quite different from the opening of *Pride and Prejudice.* Here the narrator and the main character are one and the same: the story is told by an "I." In the opening of *Pride and Prejudice* the entrance of a rich young man into the neighborhood is an event that has one meaning for Mrs. Bennet and another for her husband. But here, the "I" who is telling the story is also the victim of its events, and there can be no two ways of seeing these events. It is the grim and passionate opening of a novel in which there is no room for playful irony. The author, Charlotte Brontë, was the eldest of three sisters and a brother in whose lives there was indeed little playfulness. They grew up in the wild, barren moorland north of the Midlands, and from their earliest days, literature—the composing of poems and stories as well as reading—was the intense and passionate interest with which the sisters and brother passed their isolated days. *Jane Eyre* itself recounts some of Charlotte Brontë's life—her experience at a miserable charity school, her eventual employment as a governess, her intense interest in books and literature. But *Jane Eyre* is not merely an autobiographical novel. It is also a dream of freedom that attempts to justify itself by making us feel that, no matter what happens, we must side with its heroine.

Jane Eyre

Charlotte Brontë

CHAPTER I

THERE WAS no possibility of taking a walk that day. We had been wandering, indeed, in the leafless shrubbery[1] an hour in the morning; but since dinner (Mrs. Reed, when there was no company, dined early) the cold winter wind had brought with it clouds so somber, and a rain so penetrating, that further outdoor exercise was now out of the question.

I was glad of it: I never liked long walks, especially on chilly afternoons: dreadful to me was the coming home in the raw twilight, with nipped fingers and toes, and a heart saddened by the chidings of Bessie, the nurse, and humbled by the consciousness of my physical inferiority to Eliza, John, and Georgiana Reed.

The said Eliza, John, and Georgiana were now clustered round their mama in the drawing room: she lay reclined on a sofa by the fireside, and with her darlings about her (for the time neither quarreling nor crying) looked perfectly happy. Me, she had dispensed from joining the group; saying, "She regretted to be under the necessity of keeping me at a distance; but that until she heard from Bessie, and could discover by her own observation that I was endeavoring in good earnest to acquire a more sociable and childlike disposition, a more attractive and sprightly manner —something lighter, franker, more natural as it were—she really must exclude me from privileges intended only for contented, happy little children."

"What does Bessie say I have done?" I asked.

"Jane, I don't like cavilers or questioners: besides, there is something truly forbidding in a child taking up her elders in that manner. Be seated somewhere; and until you can speak pleasantly, remain silent."

A small breakfast room adjoined the drawing room. I slipped in there. It contained a bookcase: I soon possessed myself of a volume, taking care that it should be one stored with pictures. I mounted into the window seat: gathering up my feet, I sat cross-legged, like a Turk; and, having drawn the red moreen[2] curtain nearly close, I was shrined in double retirement.

Folds of scarlet drapery shut in my view to the right hand; to the left were the clear panes of glass, protecting, but not separating me from the drear November day. At intervals, while turning over the leaves of my book, I studied the aspect of that winter afternoon. Afar, it offered a pale blank of mist and cloud; near, a scene of wet lawn and storm-beat shrub, with ceaseless rain sweeping away wildly before a long and lamentable blast.

I returned to my book—Bewick's *History of British Birds:* the letterpress[3] thereof I cared little for, generally speaking; and yet there were certain introductory pages that, child as I was,

---

1 **shrubbery:** plot of ground planted with woody plants lower than trees.

2 **moreen:** heavy woolen material.
3 **letterpress:** print.

Philip Boucas, Magnum

Charlotte Brontë was familiar with such scenes as this one, typical of the moors near the remote Yorkshire village in which she spent most of her life.

I could not pass quite as a blank. They were those which treat of the haunts of seafowl; of "the solitary rocks and promontories" by them only inhabited; of the coast of Norway, studded with isles from its southern extremity, the Lindeness, or Naze, to the North Cape—

"Where the Northern Ocean, in vast whirls,
Boils round the naked, melancholy isles
Of farthest Thule;[4] and the Atlantic surge
Pours in among the stormy Hebrides."[5]

Nor could I pass unnoticed the suggestion of the bleak shores of Lapland, Siberia, Spitzbergen,[6] Nova Zembla,[7]

4 **Thule** (thōōˊlē): a classical term for a northerly, remote land; also an Eskimo settlement in northwestern Greenland.
5 **Hebrides** (hĕbˊrə dēz): islands about five hundred miles west of Scotland.
6 **Spitzbergen:** cluster of islands, belonging to Norway, in the Arctic Ocean.
7 **Nova Zembla:** Russian islands in the Arctic Ocean.

Iceland, Greenland, with "the vast sweep of the Arctic Zone, and those forlorn regions of dreary space—that reservoir of frost and snow, where firm fields of ice, the accumulation of centuries of winters, glazed in Alpine heights above heights, surround the pole, and concenter the multiplied rigors of extreme cold." Of these death-white realms I formed an idea of my own: shadowy, like all the half-comprehended notions that float dim through children's brains, but strangely impressive. The words in these introductory pages connected themselves with the succeeding vignettes, and gave significance to the rock standing up alone in a sea of billow and spray; to the broken boat stranded on a desolate coast; to the cold and ghastly moon glancing through bars of cloud at a wreck just sinking.

I cannot tell what sentiment haunted the quiet solitary churchyard, with its inscribed headstone; its gate, its two trees, its low horizon, girdled by a broken wall, and its newly risen crescent, attesting the hour of eventide.

The two ships becalmed on a torpid sea, I believed to be marine phantoms.

The fiend pinning down the thief's pack behind him, I passed over quickly: it was an object of terror.

So was the black, horned thing seated aloof on a rock, surveying a distant crowd surrounding a gallows.

Each picture told a story; mysterious often to my undeveloped understanding and imperfect feelings, yet ever profoundly interesting: as interesting as the tales Bessie sometimes narrated on winter evenings, when she chanced to be in good humor; and when, having brought her ironing table to the nursery hearth, she allowed us to sit about it, and while she got up Mrs. Reed's lace frills, and crimped her nightcap borders, fed our eager attention with passages of love and adventure taken from old fairy tales and older ballads; or (as at a later period I discovered) from the pages of *Pamela*, and *Henry, Earl of Moreland*.

With Bewick on my knee, I was then happy: happy at least in my way. I feared nothing but interruption, and that came too soon. The breakfast room door opened.

"Boh! Madame Mope!" cried the voice of John Reed; then he paused: he found the room apparently empty.

"Where the dickens is she?" he continued. "Lizzy! Georgy! (calling to his sisters) Joan is not here: tell mama she is run out into the rain—bad animal!"

"It is well I drew the curtain," thought I; and I wished fervently he might not discover my hiding place: nor would John Reed have found it out himself; he was not quick either of vision or conception; but Eliza just put her head in at the door, and said at once:

"She is in the window seat, to be sure, Jack."

And I came out immediately, for I trembled at the idea of being dragged forth by the said Jack.

"What do you want?" I asked, with awkward diffidence.

"Say, 'what do you want, Master Reed,'" was the answer. "I want you to come here;" and seating himself in an armchair, he intimated by a gesture that I was to approach and stand before him.

John Reed was a schoolboy of fourteen years old; four years older than I, for I was but ten; large and stout for his age, with a dingy and unwholesome skin; thick lineaments in a spacious visage, heavy limbs and large extremities. He gorged himself habitually at table, which made him bilious, and gave him a dim and bleared eye and flabby cheeks. He ought now to have been at school; but his mama had taken him home for a month or two, "on account of his delicate health." Mr. Miles, the master, affirmed that he would do very well if he had fewer cakes and sweetmeats sent him from home; but the mother's heart turned from an opinion so harsh, and inclined rather to the more refined idea that John's sallowness was owing to over-application and, perhaps, to pining after home.

John had not much affection for his mother and sisters, and an antipathy to me. He bullied and punished me; not two or three times in the week, nor once or twice in the day, but continually: every nerve I had feared him, and every morsel of flesh on my bones shrank when he came near. There were moments when I was bewildered by the terror he inspired, because I had no appeal whatever against either his menaces or his inflictions; the servants did not like to offend their young master by taking my part against him, and Mrs. Reed was blind and deaf on the subject: she never saw him strike or heard him abuse me, though he did both now and then in her very presence; more frequently, however, behind her back.

Habitually obedient to John, I came up to his chair: he spent some three minutes in thrusting out his tongue at me as far as he could without damaging the roots: I knew he would soon strike, and while dreading the blow, I mused on the disgusting and ugly appearance of him who would presently deal it. I wonder if he read that notion in my face; for, all at once, without speaking, he struck suddenly and strongly. I tottered, and on regaining my equilibrium retired back a step or two from his chair.

"That is for your impudence in answering mama awhile since," said he, "and for your sneaking way of getting behind curtains, and for the look you had in your eyes two minutes since, you rat!"

Accustomed to John Reed's abuse, I never had an idea of replying to it; my care was how to endure the blow which would certainly follow the insult.

"What were you doing behind the curtain?" he asked.

"I was reading."

"Shew the book."

I returned to the window and fetched it thence.

"You have no business to take our books; you are a dependent, mama says; you have no money; your father left you none; you ought to beg, and not to live here with gentlemen's children like us, and eat the same meals we do,

and wear clothes at our mama's expense. Now, I'll teach you to rummage my bookshelves: for they *are* mine; all the house belongs to me, or will do in a few years. Go and stand by the door, out of the way of the mirror and the windows."

I did so, not at first aware what was his intention; but when I saw him lift and poise the book and stand in act to hurl it, I instinctively started aside with a cry of alarm: not soon enough, however; the volume was flung, it hit me, and I fell, striking my head against the door and cutting it. The cut bled, the pain was sharp; my terror had passed its climax; other feelings succeeded.

"Wicked and cruel boy!" I said. "You are like a murderer—you are like a slave driver—you are like the Roman emperors!"

I had read Goldsmith's *History of Rome,* and had formed my opinion of Nero, Caligula, etc. Also I had drawn parallels in silence, which I never thought thus to have declared aloud.

"What! what!" he cried. "Did you say that to me? Did you hear her, Eliza and Georgiana? Won't I tell mama? but first"—

He ran headlong at me: I felt him grasp my hair and my shoulder: he had closed with a desperate thing. I really saw in him a tyrant: a murderer. I felt a drop or two of blood from my head trickle down my neck, and was sensible of somewhat pungent sufferings: these sensations for the time predominated over fear, and I received him in frantic sort. I don't very well know what I did with my hands, but he called me "Rat! rat!" and bellowed out aloud. Aid was near him: Eliza and Georgiana had run for Mrs. Reed, who was gone upstairs; she now came upon the scene, followed by Bessie and her maid Abbot. We were parted: I heard the words:

"Dear! dear! What a fury to fly at Master John!"

"Did ever anybody see such a picture of passion!"

Then Mrs. Reed subjoined:

"Take her away to the red room,[8]

and lock her in there." Four hands were immediately laid upon me, and I was borne upstairs.

8 **red room:** room decorated in red; Mr. Reed had died there.

Comment

This novel's opening is decidedly in earnest when we compare it with that of our preceding sample. From the very outset we feel the constraint, if not the imprisonment, of the chief character: no possibility of a walk, no possibility of getting out. Her freedom can come, apparently, only through the thoughts and dreams that she escapes into with her book. The thoughts and dreams stimulated by reading are indeed her sole weapon against the cruelty of John Reed.

1. What attitude toward John Reed and his mother and sisters do you take by the end of this passage? Do you find them, and John especially, in any way comic? Why? What compels you to take the attitude you do?
2. What, then, are your expectations as you finish this opening chapter? What do you *want* to happen as the story develops?
3. Do you find that your expectations are clearer about the rest of this novel than they were about the rest of *Pride and Prejudice?* How do you account for the difference?

Vanity Fair

Next, let us look at the opening of one of the most famous novels of the mid-19th century, *Vanity Fair,* by William Makepeace Thackeray. Although it claims to begin "While the present century was in its teens," that is, more than thirty years before, it reflects Thackeray's concern with the question "How to live?" and how to live in Victorian England. He got his title from *The Pilgrim's Progress,* from an episode in which Bunyan describes a market town in which idleness and luxury are sold; and the word *Fair* was perhaps more important for Thackeray than *Vanity.* For he was writing about the way in which the fair, the market, buying and selling, had begun to dominate the lives of many of his contemporaries. Two of the most famous chapters of the novel are entitled "How to Live Well on Nothing a Year," in which he describes people borrowing far beyond their abilities to repay and extending their debts far beyond their limited assets. The "fair," or market, in which 19th-century "vanities" were sold was a large one, and Thackeray tried to urge his contemporaries to live without it. But the most memorable feature of this "Novel without a Hero," as Thackeray called it, is Becky Sharp, whom we first meet in this opening chapter.

Vanity Fair

William Makepeace Thackeray

CHAPTER I

Chiswick Mall

WHILE THE PRESENT century was in its teens, and on one sunshiny morning in June, there drove up to the great iron gate of Miss Pinkerton's academy for young ladies, on Chiswick Mall,[1] a large family coach, with two fat horses in blazing harness, driven by a fat coachman in a three-cornered hat and wig, at the rate of four miles an hour. A black servant, who reposed on the box beside the fat coachman, uncurled his bandy legs as soon as the equipage drew up opposite Miss Pinkerton's shining brass plate, and as he pulled the bell, at least a score of young heads were seen peering out of the narrow windows of the stately old brick house. Nay, the acute observer might have recognized the little red nose of good-natured Miss Jemima Pinkerton herself, rising over some geranium pots in the window of that lady's own drawing room.

"It is Mrs. Sedley's coach, sister," said Miss Jemima. "Sambo, the black servant, has just rung the bell; and the coachman has a new red waistcoat."

"Have you completed all the necessary preparations incident to Miss Sedley's departure, Miss Jemima?" asked Miss Pinkerton herself, that majestic lady: the Semiramis of Hammersmith,[2] the friend of Doctor Johnson, the correspondent of Mrs. Chapone[3] herself.

"The girls were up at four this morning, packing her trunks, sister," replied Miss Jemima; "we have made her a bow-pot."

"Say a bouquet, sister Jemima, 'tis more genteel."

"Well, a booky as big almost as a haystack; I have put up two bottles of the gillyflower[4]-water for Mrs. Sedley, and the receipt for making it, in Amelia's box."

"And I trust, Miss Jemima, you have made a copy of Miss Sedley's account. This is it, is it? Very good—ninety-three pounds, four shillings. Be kind enough to address it to John Sedley, Esquire, and to seal this billet[5] which I have written to his lady."

In Miss Jemima's eyes an autograph letter of her sister, Miss Pinkerton, was an object of as deep veneration, as would have been a letter from a sovereign. Only when her pupils quitted the establishment, or when they were about to be married, and once, when poor Miss Birch died of the scarlet fever, was Miss Pinkerton known to write personally to the parents of her pupils; and it was Jemima's opinion that if anything *could* console Mrs.

---

1 **Chiswick Mall:** A mall was originally an area for games, and then a sheltered walk, or promenade. Chiswick Mall is still in existence, a road in a district west of central London.

2 **Semiramis of Hammersmith:** Semiramis, Queen of Nineveh, was the legendary conqueror of Asia. Hammersmith in the early 19th century was a quiet suburb of London.

3 **Mrs. Chapone:** Hester Chapone, a learned lady of the 18th century. One of her books was entitled *Letters on the Improvement of the Mind.*

4 **gillyflower** (jĭl′ĭ flou′ər): clove-scented pink flower.

5 **billet:** short letter.

Birch for her daughter's loss, it would be that pious and eloquent composition in which Miss Pinkerton announced the event.

In the present instance Miss Pinkerton's "billet" was to the following effect:

> "The Mall, Chiswick
> June 15, 18—
>
> "Madam,
>
> "After her six years' residence at the Mall, I have the honor and happiness of presenting Miss Amelia Sedley to her parents, as a young lady not unworthy to occupy a fitting position in their polished and refined circle. Those virtues which characterize the young English gentlewoman, those accomplishments which become her birth and station, will not be found wanting in the amiable Miss Sedley, whose *industry* and *obedience* have endeared her to her instructors, and whose delightful sweetness of temper has charmed her *aged* and her *youthful* companions.
>
> "In music, in dancing, in orthography, in every variety of embroidery and needlework, she will be found to have realized her friends' *fondest wishes.* In geography there is still much to be desired; and a careful and undeviating use of the backboard,[6] for four hours daily during the next three years, is recommended as necessary to the acquirement of that dignified *deportment and carriage,* so requisite for every young lady of *fashion.*
>
> "In the principles of religion and morality, Miss Sedley will be found worthy of an establishment which has been honored by the presence of *The Great Lexicographer,* and the patronage of the admirable Mrs. Chapone. In leaving the Mall, Miss Amelia carries with her the hearts of her companions, and the affectionate regards of her mistress, who has the honor to subscribe herself,

> "Madam,
> "Your most obliged humble servant,
> "Barbara Pinkerton.
>
> "P.S. Miss Sharp accompanies Miss Sedley. It is particularly requested that Miss Sharp's stay in Russell Square may not exceed ten days. The family of distinction with whom she is engaged, desire to avail themselves of her services as soon as possible."

This letter completed, Miss Pinkerton proceeded to write her own name, and Miss Sedley's, in the flyleaf of a Johnson's Dictionary—the interesting work which she invariably presented to her scholars, on their departure from the Mall. On the cover was inserted a copy of "Lines addressed[7] to a young lady on quitting Miss Pinkerton's school, at the Mall; by the late revered Doctor Samuel Johnson." In fact, the Lexicographer's name was always on the lips of this majestic woman, and a visit he had paid to her was the cause of her reputation and her fortune.

Being commanded by her elder sister to get "the Dictionary" from the cupboard, Miss Jemima had extracted two copies of the book from the receptacle in question. When Miss Pinkerton had finished the inscription in the first, Jemima, with rather a dubious and timid air, handed her the second.

"For whom is this, Miss Jemima?" said Miss Pinkerton, with awful coldness.

"For Becky Sharp," answered Jemima, trembling very much, and blushing over her withered face and neck, as she turned her back on her sister. "For Becky Sharp: she's going too."

---

6 **backboard:** board strapped across the back to promote erect posture.

7 **Lines . . . Johnson:** a humorous fiction of Thackeray's.

"MISS JEMIMA!" exclaimed Miss Pinkerton, in the largest capitals. "Are you in your senses? Replace the Dixonary in the closet, and never venture to take such a liberty in future."

"Well, sister, it's only two-and-ninepence, and poor Becky will be miserable if she don't get one."

"Send Miss Sedley instantly to me," said Miss Pinkerton. And so venturing not to say another word, poor Jemima trotted off, exceedingly flurried and nervous.

Miss Sedley's papa was a merchant in London, and a man of some wealth; whereas Miss Sharp was an articled pupil,[8] for whom Miss Pinkerton had done, as she thought, quite enough, without conferring upon her at parting the high honor of the Dixonary.

Although schoolmistresses' letters are to be trusted no more nor less than churchyard epitaphs; yet, as it sometimes happens that a person departs this life, who is really deserving of all the praises the stonecutter carves over his bones; who *is* a good Christian, a good parent, child, wife or husband; who actually *does* leave a disconsolate family to mourn his loss; so in academies of the male and female sex it occurs every now and then, that the pupil is fully worthy of the praises bestowed by the disinterested instructor. Now, Miss Amelia Sedley was a young lady of this singular species; and deserved not only all that Miss Pinkerton said in her praise, but had many charming qualities which that pompous old Minerva[9] of a woman could not see, from the differences of rank and age between her pupil and herself.

For she could not only sing like a lark, or a Mrs. Billington,[10] and dance like Hillisberg or Parisot;[11] and embroider beautifully; and spell as well as the Dixonary itself; but she had such a kindly, smiling, tender, gentle, generous heart of her own, as won the love of everybody who came near her, from Minerva herself down to the poor girl in the scullery, and the one-eyed tartwoman's[12] daughter, who was permitted to vend her wares once a week to the young ladies in the Mall. She had twelve intimate and bosom friends out of the twenty-four young ladies. Even envious Miss Briggs never spoke ill of her; high and mighty Miss Saltire (Lord Dexter's granddaughter) allowed that her figure was genteel; and as for Miss Swartz, the rich woolly-haired mulatto from St. Kitt's, on the day Amelia went away, she was in such a passion of tears, that they were obliged to send for Dr. Floss, and half tipsify[13] her with sal volatile.[14] Miss Pinkerton's attachment was, as may be supposed, from the high position and eminent virtues of that lady, calm and dignified; but Miss Jemima had already blubbered several times at the idea of Amelia's departure; and, but for fear of her sister, would have gone off in downright hysterics, like the heiress (who paid double) of St. Kitt's. Such luxury of grief, however, is only allowed to parlor boarders.[15] Honest Jemima had all the bills, and the washing, and the mending, and the puddings, and the plate and crockery, and the servants to superintend. But why speak about her? It is probable that we shall not hear of her again from this moment to the end of time, and that when the

8 **articled pupil:** student apprenticed to learn to be a teacher.
9 **Minerva:** Roman goddess of wisdom.
10 **Mrs. Billington:** a famous English opera singer.
11 **Hillisberg or Parisot:** well-known ballet dancers.
12 **tartwoman:** one who sold small sweet pastries.
13 **tipsify:** make dizzy.
14 **sal volatile** (săl vō lăt'ə lē'): smelling salts.
15 **parlor boarders:** boarding-school pupils who live with the family of the principal.

great filligree iron gates are once closed on her, she and her sister will never issue therefrom into this little world of history.

But as we are to see a great deal of Amelia, there is no harm in saying at the outset of our acquaintance, that she was one of the best and dearest creatures that ever lived; and a great mercy it is, both in life and in novels, which (and the latter especially) abound in villains of the most somber sort, that we are to have for a constant companion, so guileless and good-natured a person. As she is not a heroine, there is no need to describe her person; indeed I am afraid that her nose was rather short than otherwise, and her cheeks a great deal too round and red for a heroine; but her face blushed with rosy health, and her lips with the freshest of smiles, and she had a pair of eyes, which sparkled with the brightest and honestest good humor, except indeed when they filled with tears, and that was a great deal too often; for the silly thing would cry over a dead canary-bird, or over a mouse, that the cat haply had seized upon, or over the end of a novel, were it ever so stupid; and as for saying an unkind word to her, were any one hard-hearted enough to do so—why, so much the worse for them. Even Miss Pinkerton, that austere and godlike woman, ceased scolding her after the first time, and though she no more comprehended sensibility than she did Algebra, gave all masters and teachers particular orders to treat Miss Sedley with the utmost gentleness, as harsh treatment was injurious to her.

So that when the day of departure came, between her two customs of laughing and crying, Miss Sedley was greatly puzzled how to act. She was glad to go home, and yet most woefully sad at leaving school. For three days before, little Laura Martin, the orphan, followed her about, like a little dog. She had to make and receive at least fourteen presents—to make fourteen solemn promises of writing every week: "Send my letters under cover to my grandpapa, the Earl of Dexter," said Miss Saltire (who, by the way, was rather shabby): "Never mind the postage, but write every day, you dear darling," said the impetuous and woolly-headed, but generous and affectionate Miss Swartz; and little Laura Martin (who was just in round hand) took her friend's hand and said, looking up in her face wistfully, "Amelia, when I write to you I shall call you Mamma." All which details, I have no doubt, Jones, who reads this book at his Club, will pronounce to be excessively foolish, trivial, twaddling, and ultra-sentimental. Yes; I can see Jones at this minute (rather flushed with his joint of mutton and half-pint of wine), taking out his pencil and scoring under the words *foolish, twaddling*, etc., and adding to them his own remark of *"quite true."* Well, he is a lofty man of genius, and admires the great and heroic in life and novels; and so had better take warning and go elsewhere.

Well, then. The flowers, and the presents, and the trunks, and bonnet-boxes of Miss Sedley having been arranged by Mr. Sambo in the carriage, together with a very small and weather-beaten old cowskin trunk with Miss Sharp's card neatly nailed upon it, which was delivered by Sambo with a grin, and packed by the coachman with a corresponding sneer—the hour for parting came; and the grief of that moment was considerably lessened by the admirable discourse which Miss Pinkerton addressed to her pupil. Not that the parting speech caused Amelia to philosophize, or that it armed her in any

In an illustration done for Vanity Fair *by Thackeray himself, Becky Sharp flings Johnson's*
Dictionary *back at Miss Pinkerton's school.*

way with a calmness, the result of argument; but it was intolerably dull, pompous, and tedious; and having the fear of her schoolmistress greatly before her eyes, Miss Sedley did not venture, in her presence, to give way to any ebullitions of private grief. A seedcake[16] and a bottle of wine were produced in the drawing room, as on the solemn occasions of the visit of parents, and these refreshments being partaken of, Miss Sedley was at liberty to depart.

16 seedcake: sweet cake flavored with caraway seeds.

"You'll go in and say good-by to Miss Pinkerton, Becky?" said Miss Jemima to a young lady of whom nobody took any notice, and who was coming downstairs with her own bandbox.

"I suppose I must," said Miss Sharp calmly, and much to the wonder of Miss Jemima; and the latter having knocked at the door, and receiving permission to come in, Miss Sharp advanced in a very unconcerned manner, and said in French, and with a perfect accent, *"Mademoiselle, je viens vous faire mes adieux."*

Miss Pinkerton did not understand French; she only directed those who did: but biting her lips and throwing up her venerable and Roman-nosed head (on the top of which figured a large and solemn turban), she said, "Miss Sharp, I wish you a good morning." As the Hammersmith Semiramis spoke, she waved one hand both by way of adieu, and to give Miss Sharp an opportunity of shaking one of the fingers of the hand which was left out for that purpose.

Miss Sharp only folded her own hands with a very frigid smile and bow, and quite declined to accept the proffered honor; on which Semiramis tossed up her turban more indignantly than ever. In fact, it was a little battle between the young lady and the old one, and the latter was worsted. "Heaven bless you, my child," said she, embracing Amelia, and scowling the while over the girl's shoulder at Miss Sharp. "Come away, Becky," said Miss Jemima, pulling the young woman away in great alarm, and the drawing room door closed upon them forever.

Then came the struggle and parting below. Words refuse to tell it. All the servants were there in the hall—all the dear friends—all the young ladies—the dancing master who had just arrived; and there was such a scuffling, and hugging, and kissing, and crying, with the hysterical *yoops* of Miss Swartz, the parlor boarder, from her room, as no pen can depict, and as the tender heart would fain pass over. The embracing was over; they parted—that is, Miss Sedley parted from her friends. Miss Sharp had demurely entered the carriage some minutes before. Nobody cried for leaving *her*.

Sambo of the bandy legs slammed the carriage door on his young weeping mistress. He sprang up behind the carriage. "Stop!" cried Miss Jemima, rushing to the gate with a parcel.

"It's some sandwiches, my dear," said she to Amelia. "You may be hungry, you know; and Becky, Becky Sharp, here's a book for you that my sister—that is, I—Johnson's Dixonary, you know; you mustn't leave us without that. Good-by. Drive on, coachman. God bless you!"

And the kind creature retreated into the garden, overcome with emotions.

But, lo! and just as the coach drove off, Miss Sharp put her pale face out of the window, and actually flung the book back into the garden.

This almost caused Jemima to faint with terror. "Well, I never—" said she—"what an audacious—" Emotion prevented her from completing either sentence. The carriage rolled away; the great gates were closed; the bell rang for the dancing lesson. The world is before the two young ladies; and so, farewell to Chiswick Mall.

Comment

Thackeray's opening words suggest that he is aiming at a sense of history: he speaks of the "present century"; he refers to such historical personages as Dr. Johnson and Hester Chapone. It is an informal kind of history, to be sure, for Thackeray writes with a keen eye for the comic detail, and his tone is easy, familiar, even confidential. (You and I, reader, know more about life than the impatient Mr. Jones in his club, he seems to say.) Thackeray wanted his readers to believe that the world before the two young ladies was a world that historically existed, and he leads us into it gaily but firmly. Before writing *Vanity Fair* Thackeray had been, chiefly, a journalist—he had even tried for a time to publish a newspaper in France for the many English visitors and residents. Most recently he had done a series of sketches, eventually called *The Book of Snobs*, in which he satirized the social climbers of his day. *Vanity Fair* was begun, in fact, as a kind of large-scale continuation of Thackeray's history of snobbery, and we find traces of his intention not only in his portrait of Miss Pinkerton but also in such details as the sneer the coachman directs toward Becky Sharp's inelegant luggage. Thackeray was also an illustrator and cartoonist, and his own illustrations to *Vanity Fair* helped in its success. But *Vanity Fair* turned Thackeray into something more than a journalistic critic of manners. It made him a novelist and brought him a large audience who found in his works a sense of history and an awareness of living society—a quality in which he was surpassed by no other writer of his time.

1. Thackeray makes much of the pretentiousness of Miss Pinkerton, calling her, for example, "Semiramis" and "Minerva." How is this introductory portrait dramatized in the farewell between Miss Pinkerton and Becky Sharp?
2. What difference do you find between the official description of Amelia in Miss Pinkerton's letter and the unofficial, confidential description of her given us by the author? If the official version of Amelia belongs to the 18th-century world of formality and propriety, what does Thackeray suggest happened to that world in the 19th century?
3. You have earlier heard much about Dr. Johnson and his *Dictionary*; and, as this opening chapter ends, you see Becky Sharp fling the great volume back into the garden at Chiswick Mall. Suppose we think of Becky's act as a symbol: What does such a symbol tell us about the "teens" of the 19th century?

The Return of the Native

The following passage is from Thomas Hardy's *The Return of the Native*, published in 1878. Hardy, as you have seen, was a poet as well as a novelist, and the world with which he surrounded the words and gestures of his characters had a history as ancient—as timeless—as the open, uncultivated heath-land described here. While Jane Austen, Dickens, and Thackeray could approach the novel with comic genius, Hardy is like Charlotte Brontë in his seriousness of style. And yet it would not have occurred to him to write a first-person novel such as *Jane Eyre*. The "I" for Hardy was too small to come first: what came first for him is suggested by this opening chapter, which bears the enigmatic title, "A Face on Which Time Makes But Little Impression."

The Return of the Native

Thomas Hardy

A Face on Which Time Makes But Little Impression

A SATURDAY afternoon in November was approaching the time of twilight, and the vast tract of unenclosed[1] wild known as Egdon Heath[2] embrowned itself moment by moment. Overhead the hollow stretch of whitish cloud shutting out the sky was as a tent which had the whole heath for its floor.

The heaven being spread with this pallid screen and the earth with the darkest vegetation, their meeting-line at the horizon was clearly marked. In such contrast the heath wore the appearance of an installment of night which had taken up its place before its astronomical hour was come: darkness had to a great extent arrived hereon, while day stood distinct in the sky. Looking upward, a furze-cutter[3] would have been inclined to continue work; looking down, he would have decided to finish his fagot[4] and go home. The distant rims of the world and of the firmament seemed to be a division in time no less than a division in matter. The face of the heath by its mere complexion added half an hour to evening; it could in like manner retard the dawn, sadden noon, anticipate the frowning of storms scarcely generated, and intensify the opacity of a moonless midnight to a cause of shaking and dread.

In fact, precisely at this transitional point of its nightly roll into darkness the great and particular glory of the Egdon waste[5] began, and nobody could be said to understand the heath who had not been there at such a time. It could best be felt when it could not clearly be seen, its complete effect and explanation lying in this and the succeeding hours before the next dawn: then, and only then, did it tell its true tale. The spot was, indeed, a near relation of night, and when night showed itself an apparent tendency to gravitate together could be perceived in its shades and the scene. The somber stretch of rounds and hollows seemed to rise and meet the evening gloom in pure sympathy, the heath exhaling darkness as rapidly as the heavens precipitated it. And so the obscurity in the air and the obscurity in the land closed together in a black fraternization toward which each advanced halfway.

The place became full of a watchful intentness now; for when other things sank brooding to sleep the heath appeared slowly to awake and listen. Every night its Titanic form seemed to await something; but it had waited thus, unmoved, during so many centuries, through the crisis of so many things, that it could only be imagined to await one last crisis—the final overthrow.

It was a spot which returned upon the memory of those who loved it with

1 **unenclosed:** unfenced.
2 **Heath:** open, uncultivated ground.
3 **furze:** gorse, a low evergreen shrub with yellow flowers, cut for fuel.
4 **fagot:** bundle of sticks or twigs.

5 **waste:** uncultivated land.

an aspect of peculiar and kindly congruity. Smiling champaigns[6] of flowers and fruit hardly do this, for they are permanently harmonious only with an existence of better reputation as to its issues than the present. Twilight combined with the scenery of Egdon Heath to evolve a thing majestic without severity, impressive without showiness, emphatic in its admonitions, grand in its simplicity. The qualifications which frequently invest the façade of a prison with far more dignity than is found in the façade of a palace double its size lent to this heath a sublimity in which spots renowned for beauty of the accepted kind are utterly wanting. Fair prospects wed happily with fair times; but alas, if times be not fair! Men have oftener suffered from the mockery of a place too smiling for their reason than from the oppression of surroundings oversadly tinged. Haggard Egdon appealed to a subtler and scarcer instinct, to a more recently learned emotion, than that which responds to the sort of beauty called charming and fair.

Indeed, it is a question if the exclusive reign of this orthodox beauty is not approaching its last quarter. The new Vale of Tempe[7] may be a gaunt waste in Thule:[8] human souls may find themselves in closer and closer harmony with external things wearing a somberness distasteful to our race when it was young. The time seems near, if it has not actually arrived, when the chastened sublimity of a moor, a sea, or a mountain will be all of nature that is absolutely in keeping with the moods of the more thinking among mankind. And

ultimately, to the commonest tourist, spots like Iceland may become what the vineyards and myrtle-gardens of South Europe are to him now; and Heidelberg[9] and Baden[10] be passed unheeded as he hastens from the Alps to the sand dunes of Scheveningen.[11]

The most thorough-going ascetic could feel that he had a natural right to wander on Egdon: he was keeping within the line of legitimate indulgence when he laid himself open to influences such as these. Colors and beauties so far subdued were, at least, the birthright of all. Only in summer days of highest feather did its mood touch the level of gaiety. Intensity was more usually reached by way of the solemn than by way of the brilliant, and such a sort of intensity was often arrived at during winter darkness, tempests, and mists. Then Egdon was aroused to reciprocity; for the storm was its lover, and the wind its friend. Then it became the home of strange phantoms; and it was found to be the hitherto unrecognized original of those wild regions of obscurity which are vaguely felt to be compassing us about in midnight dreams of flight and disaster, and are never thought of after the dream till revived by scenes like this.

It was at present a place perfectly accordant with man's nature—neither ghastly, hateful, nor ugly: neither commonplace, unmeaning, nor tame; but, like man, slighted and enduring; and withal singularly colossal and mysterious in its swarthy monotony. As with some persons who have long lived apart, solitude seemed to look out of its

---

6 champaigns: fields.
7 Vale of Tempe: valley in Thessaly, Greece, noted for its beauty; hence any place of charm and beauty.
8 Thule (thōō′lē): a classical term for a northerly remote land; also an Eskimo settlement in northwestern Greenland.

9 Heidelberg: picturesque university city in Germany.
10 Baden: resorts in both Austria and Switzerland; noted for their mineral waters used for curative baths, or *baden.*
11 Scheveningen (SKHā′vən ĭng′ən): seaside resort in the Netherlands.

THE ENGLISH NOVEL

countenance. It had a lonely face, suggesting tragical possibilities.

This obscure, obsolete, superseded country figures in Domesday.[12] Its condition is recorded therein as that of heathy, furzy, briary wilderness—"Bruaria." Then follows the length and breadth in leagues; and, though some uncertainty exists as to the exact extent of this ancient lineal measure, it appears from the figures that the area of Egdon down to the present day has but little diminished. "Turbaria Bruaria"— the right of cutting heath-turf—occurs in charters relating to the district. "Overgrown with heth and mosse," says Leland[13] of the same dark sweep of country.

Here at least were intelligible facts regarding landscape—far-reaching proofs productive of genuine satisfaction. The untamable, Ishmaelitish[14] thing that Egdon now was it always had been. Civilization was its enemy; and ever since the beginning of vegetation its soil had worn the same antique brown dress, the natural and invariable garment of the particular formation. In its venerable one coat lay a certain vein of satire on human vanity in clothes. A person on a heath in raiment of modern cut and colors has more or less an anomalous look. We seem to want the oldest and simplest human clothing where the clothing of the earth is so primitive.

To recline on a stump of thorn in the central valley of Egdon, between afternoon and night, as now, where the eye could reach nothing of the world outside the summits and shoulders of heathland which filled the whole circumference of its glance, and to know that everything around and underneath had been from prehistoric times as unaltered as the stars overhead, gave ballast to the mind adrift on change, and harassed by the irrepressible New. The great inviolate place had an ancient permanence which the sea cannot claim. Who can say of a particular sea that it is old? Distilled by the sun, kneaded by the moon, it is renewed in a year, in a day, or in an hour. The sea changed, the fields changed, the rivers, the villages, and the people changed, yet Egdon remained. Those surfaces were neither so steep as to be destructible by weather, nor so flat as to be the victims of floods and deposits. With the exception of an aged highway, and a still more aged barrow presently to be referred to—themselves almost crystallized to natural products by long continuance— even the trifling irregularities were not caused by pickax, plow, or spade, but remained as the very finger-touches of the last geological change.

The above-mentioned highway traversed the lower levels of the heath, from one horizon to another. In many portions of its course it overlaid an old vicinal way, which branched from the great Western road of the Romans, the Via Iceniana, or Ikenild Street, hard by. On the evening under consideration it would have been noticed that, though the gloom had increased sufficiently to confuse the minor features of the heath, the white surface of the road remained almost as clear as ever.

12 Domesday (dōōmz'dā'): The Domesday Book records a survey, made in the 11th century, of the lands of England.
13 Leland: John Leland, in the 16th century, made studies of ancient Britain.
14 Ishmaelitish: on unfriendly terms with society (from Ishmael, the outcast son of Abraham in the Bible.)

THOMAS HARDY

Comment

Egdon Heath is Hardy's name for a district of southwest England, though regions like it can be found in other parts of England as well. These opening paragraphs describe its topography in detail; there is no dialogue, and no character appears on the scene. Yet it is clear that we are not beginning a book about nature; the heath is more than a remote, uncultivated area of land.

1. Hardy calls the heath "a place perfectly accordant with man's nature." With what conception of the nature of man, then, does this novel begin?

2. With what expectations would you move into Hardy's story after this opening? What will happen here? What kind of action will be appropriate to such a scene?

To the Lighthouse

We must now make a long leap, from 1878 to 1927, for our final example. It is from the beginning of *To the Lighthouse*, by Virginia
Woolf, and it suggests, when put beside these four earlier examples,
what has happened to the novel in the 20th century. Virginia Woolf,
the daughter of a distinguished philosopher and historian, wife of a
distinguished publisher and writer on politics, lived from 1882 to 1941.
She wrote many essays on the novel and other literary subjects, she
wrote biographies, and she assisted in translating works of Tolstoy, the
great Russian novelist. But she was first of all a novelist, and always a
boldly experimental one. She—along with others of her generation—
was dissatisfied with the kind of novel that narrates its episodes in a
straight line, event following event so clearly that we can easily separate
the "plot" from "setting" and "character." Our consciousness of our own
experience, she believed, does not move forward in discrete steps, like
a clock. Rather, it flows like a stream: any one moment of experience
will contain an awareness of the past that surrounds it like a kind of
halo. Virginia Woolf tried many new techniques to produce the sense
of flow in experience.

The opening pages of *To the Lighthouse*, for example, contain a dialogue that runs like this:

> "Yes, of course, if it's fine tomorrow. But you'll have to be up
> with the lark."
> "But it won't be fine."
> "It's due west. There'll be no landing at the Lighthouse to-
> morrow. No going to the Lighthouse, James."
> "Perhaps you will wake and find the sun shining and the birds
> singing. Perhaps it will be fine tomorrow."

Several voices, at least two, perhaps three, seem to be discussing some
kind of trip or outing. Apparently there is some difference of opinion
about whether someone named James will be able to sail to a certain
"Lighthouse" tomorrow, for he seems to require good weather for the
voyage. Perhaps it is a family discussion; perhaps they are planning
an excursion during a vacation.

But now let us see all that Virginia Woolf has put around and between these speeches; the passage from which they have been taken is
many pages long.

To
the Lighthouse*

Virginia Woolf

I

"YES, OF COURSE, if it's fine tomorrow," said Mrs. Ramsay. "But you'll have to be up with the lark," she added.

To her son these words conveyed an extraordinary joy, as if it were settled, the expedition were bound to take place, and the wonder to which he had looked forward, for years and years it seemed, was, after a night's darkness and a day's sail, within touch. Since he belonged, even at the age of six, to that great clan which cannot keep this feeling separate from that, but must let future prospects, with their joys and sorrows, cloud what is actually at hand, since to such people even in earliest childhood any turn in the wheel of sensation has the power to crystallize and transfix the moment upon which its gloom or radiance rests, James Ramsay, sitting on the floor cutting out pictures from the illustrated catalogue of the Army and Navy Stores,[1] endowed the picture of a refrigerator, as his mother spoke, with heavenly bliss. It was fringed with joy. The wheelbar-

row, the lawn mower, the sound of poplar trees, leaves whitening before rain, rooks cawing, brooms knocking, dresses rustling—all these were so colored and distinguished in his mind that he had already his private code, his secret language, though he appeared the image of stark and uncompromising severity, with his high forehead and his fierce blue eyes, impeccably candid and pure, frowning slightly at the sight of human frailty, so that his mother, watching him guide his scissors neatly round the refrigerator, imagined him all red and ermine on the Bench[2] or directing a stern and momentous enterprise in some crisis of public affairs.

"But," said his father, stopping in front of the drawing-room window, "it won't be fine."

Had there been an ax handy, or a poker, any weapon that would have gashed a hole in his father's breast and killed him, there and then, James would have seized it. Such were the extremes of emotion that Mr. Ramsay excited in his children's breasts by his mere presence; standing, as now, lean as a knife, narrow as the blade of one, grinning sarcastically, not only with the pleasure of disillusioning his son and casting ridicule upon his wife, who was ten thousand times better in every way than he was (James thought), but also with some secret conceit at his own accuracy of judgment. What he said was true. It was always true. He was incapable of untruth; never tampered with a fact; never altered a disagreeable word to suit the pleasure or convenience of any mortal being, least of all of his own children, who, sprung from his loins, should be aware from childhood that life is difficult; facts uncompromising;

1 **Army and Navy Stores:** a large London department store.

2 **red . . . Bench:** i.e., she imagines him in the robes of a judge.

and the passage to that fabled land where our brightest hopes are extinguished, our frail barks founder in darkness (here Mr. Ramsay would straighten his back and narrow his little blue eyes upon the horizon), one that needs, above all, courage, truth, and the power to endure.

"But it may be fine—I expect it will be fine," said Mrs. Ramsay, making some little twist of the reddish-brown stocking she was knitting, impatiently. If she finished it tonight, if they did go to the Lighthouse after all, it was to be given to the Lighthouse keeper for his little boy, who was threatened with a tuberculous hip; together with a pile of old magazines, and some tobacco, indeed, whatever she could find lying about, not really wanted, but only littering the room, to give those poor fellows, who must be bored to death sitting all day with nothing to do but polish the lamp and trim the wick and rake about on their scrap of garden, something to amuse them. For how would you like to be shut up for a whole month at a time, and possibly more in stormy weather, upon a rock the size of a tennis lawn?[3] she would ask; and to have no letters or newspapers, and to see nobody; if you were married, not to see your wife, not to know how your children were,—if they were ill, if they had fallen down and broken their legs or arms; to see the same dreary waves breaking week after week, and then a dreadful storm coming, and the windows covered with spray, and birds dashed against the lamp, and the whole place rocking, and not be able to put your nose out of doors for fear of being swept into the sea? How would you like that? she asked, addressing herself particularly to her daughters. So

3 tennis lawn: tennis court.

she added, rather differently, one must take them what comforts one can.

"It's due west," said the atheist Tansley, holding his bony fingers spread so that the wind blew through them, for he was sharing Mr. Ramsay's evening walk up and down, up and down the terrace. That is to say, the wind blew from the worst possible direction for landing at the Lighthouse. Yes, he did say disagreeable things, Mrs. Ramsay admitted; it was odious of him to rub this in, and make James still more disappointed; but at the same time, she would not let them laugh at him. "The atheist," they called him; "the little atheist." Rose mocked him; Prue mocked him; Andrew, Jasper, Roger mocked him; even old Badger without a tooth in his head had bit him, for being (as Nancy put it) the hundred and tenth young man to chase them all the way up to the Hebrides when it was ever so much nicer to be alone.

"Nonsense," said Mrs. Ramsay, with great severity. Apart from the habit of exaggeration which they had from her, and from the implication (which was true) that she asked too many people to stay, and had to lodge some in the town, she could not bear incivility to her guests, to young men in particular, who were poor as church mice, "exceptionally able," her husband said, his great admirers, and come there for a holiday. Indeed, she had the whole of the other sex under her protection; for reasons she could not explain, for their chivalry and valor, for the fact that they negotiated treaties, ruled India, controlled finance; finally for an attitude towards herself which no woman could fail to feel or to find agreeable, something trustful, childlike, reverential; which an old woman could take from a young man without loss of dignity, and woe betide the girl—pray Heaven it was none of her daughters!—who did not feel the worth of it, and all that it implied, to the marrow of her bones!

She turned with severity upon Nancy. He had not chased them, she said. He had been asked.

They must find a way out of it all. There might be some simpler way, some less laborious way, she sighed. When she looked in the glass and saw her hair gray, her cheek sunk, at fifty, she thought, possibly she might have managed things better—her husband; money; his books. But for her own part she would never for a single second regret her decision, evade difficulties, or slur over duties. She was now formidable to behold, and it was only in silence, looking up from their plates, after she had spoken so severely about Charles Tansley, that her daughters, Prue, Nancy, Rose—could sport with infidel ideas which they had brewed for themselves of a life different from hers; in Paris, perhaps; a wilder life; not always taking care of some man or other; for there was in all their minds a mute questioning of deference and chivalry, of the Bank of England and the Indian Empire, of ringed fingers and lace, though to them all there was something in this of the essence of beauty, which called out the manliness in their girlish hearts, and made them, as they sat at table beneath their mother's eyes, honor her strange severity, her extreme courtesy, like a queen's raising from the mud to wash a beggar's dirty foot, when she thus admonished them so very severely about that wretched atheist who had chased them—or, speaking accurately, been invited to stay with them—in the Isles of Skye.

"There'll be no landing at the Lighthouse tomorrow," said Charles Tansley, clapping his hands together as he stood at the window with her husband.

Surely, he had said enough. She wished they would both leave her and James alone and go on talking. She looked at him. He was such a miserable specimen, the child said, all humps and hollows. He couldn't play cricket; he poked; he shuffled. He was a sarcastic brute, Andrew said. They knew what he liked best—to be forever walking up and down, up and down, with Mr. Ramsay, and saying who had won this, who had won that, who was a "first-rate man" at Latin verses, who was "brilliant but I think fundamentally unsound," who was undoubtedly the "ablest fellow in Balliol," who had buried his light temporarily at Bristol or Bedford[4] but was bound to be heard of later when his Prolegomena,[5] of which Mr. Tansley had the first pages in proof with him if Mr. Ramsay would like to see them, to some branch of mathematics or philosophy saw the light of day. That was what they talked about.

She could not help laughing herself sometimes. She said, the other day, something about "waves mountains high." Yes, said Charles Tansley, it was a little rough. "Aren't you drenched to the skin?" she had said. "Damp, not wet through," said Mr. Tansley, pinching his sleeve, feeling his socks.

But it was not that they minded, the children said. It was not his face; it was not his manners. It was him—his point of view. When they talked about something interesting, people, music, history, anything, even said it was a fine evening so why not sit out of doors, then what they complained of about Charles

---

4 **Balliol** (bāl'yəl) . . . **Bristol** . . . **Bedford:** colleges in England. Balliol, one of the colleges that constitute Oxford University, was assumed to be superior to "red-brick," or provincial, centers of learning such as Bedford in London or Bristol in the west—an assumption that is now not quite so firm.

5 **Prolegomena** (prō'lə gŏm'ə nə): an academic word meaning "introductory treatise."

Tansley was that until he had turned the whole thing round and made it somehow reflect himself and disparage them—he was not satisfied. And he would go to picture galleries they said and he would ask one, did one like his tie? God knows, said Rose, one did not.

Disappearing as stealthily as stags from the dinner table directly the meal was over, the eight sons and daughters of Mr. and Mrs. Ramsay sought their bedrooms, their fastnesses in a house where there was no other privacy to debate anything, everything; Tansley's tie; the passing of the Reform Bill; sea birds and butterflies; people; while the sun poured into those attics, which a plank alone separated from each other so that every footstep could be plainly heard and the Swiss girl sobbing for her father who was dying of cancer in a valley of the Grisons, and lit up bats, flannels, straw hats, inkpots, paintpots, beetles, and the skulls of small birds, while it drew from the long frilled strips of seaweed pinned to the wall a smell of salt and weeds, which was in the towels too, gritty with sand from bathing.

Strife, divisions, difference of opinion, prejudices twisted into the very fiber of being, oh, that they should begin so early, Mrs. Ramsay deplored. They were so critical, her children. They talked such nonsense. She went from the dining room, holding James by the hand, since he would not go with the others. It seemed to her such nonsense—inventing differences, when people, heaven knows, were different enough without that. The real differences, she thought, standing by the drawing-room window, are enough, quite enough. She had in mind at the moment, rich and poor, high and low; the great in birth receiving from her, some half grudgingly, half respect, for had she not in her veins the blood of that very noble, if slightly mythical, Italian house, whose daughters, scattered about English drawing rooms in the 19th century, had lisped so charmingly, had stormed so wildly, and all her wit and her bearing and her temper came from them, and not from the sluggish English, or the cold Scotch; but more profoundly, she ruminated the other problem, of rich and poor, and the things she saw with her own eyes, weekly, daily, here or in London, when she visited this widow, or that struggling wife in person with a bag on her arm, and a notebook and pencil with which she wrote down in columns carefully ruled for the purpose wages and spendings, employment and unemployment, in the hope that thus she would cease to be a private woman whose charity was half a sop to her own indignation, half a relief to her own curiosity, and become what with her untrained mind she greatly admired, an investigator, elucidating the social problem.

Insoluble questions they were, it seemed to her, standing there, holding James by the hand. He had followed her into the drawing room, that young man they laughed at; he was standing by the table, fidgeting with something, awkwardly, feeling himself out of things, as she knew without looking round. They had all gone—the children; Minta Doyle and Paul Rayley; Augustus Carmichael; her husband—they had all gone. So she turned with a sigh and said, "Would it bore you to come with me, Mr. Tansley?"

She had a dull errand in the town; she had a letter or two to write; she would be ten minutes perhaps; she would put on her hat. And, with her basket and her parasol, there she was again, ten minutes later, giving out a sense of being ready, of being equipped for a jaunt, which, however, she must interrupt for a moment, as they passed the tennis lawn, to ask Mr. Carmichael, who was basking with his yellow cat's eyes ajar, so that like a cat's they seemed to reflect the branches moving or the clouds passing, but to give no inkling of any inner thoughts or emotion whatsoever, if he wanted anything.

For they were making the great expedition, she said, laughing. They were going to the town. "Stamps, writing paper, tobacco?" she suggested, stopping by his side. But no, he wanted nothing. His hands clasped themselves over his capacious paunch, his eyes blinked, as if he would have liked to reply kindly to these blandishments (she was seductive but a little nervous) but could not, sunk as he was in a gray-green somnolence which embraced them all, without need of words, in a vast and benevolent lethargy of well-wishing; all the house; all the world; all the people in it, for he had slipped into his glass at lunch a few drops of something, which accounted, the children thought, for the vivid streak of canary-yellow in mustache and beard that were otherwise milk-white. No, nothing, he murmured.

He should have been a great philosopher, said Mrs. Ramsay, as they went down the road to the fishing village, but he had made an unfortunate marriage. Holding her black parasol very erect, and moving with an indescribable air of expectation, as if she were going to meet someone round the corner, she told the story; an affair at Oxford with some girl; an early marriage; poverty; going to India; translating a little poetry "very beautifully, I believe," being willing to teach the boys Persian or Hindustanee, but what really was the use of

that?—and then lying, as they saw him, on the lawn.

It flattered him; snubbed as he had been, it soothed him that Mrs. Ramsay should tell him this. Charles Tansley revived. Insinuating, too, as she did the greatness of man's intellect, even in its decay, the subjection of all wives—not that she blamed the girl, and the marriage had been happy enough, she believed—to their husband's labors, she made him feel better pleased with himself than he had done yet, and he would have liked, had they taken a cab, for example, to have paid for it. As for her little bag, might he not carry that? No, no, she said, she always carried *that* herself. She did too. Yes, he felt that in her. He felt many things, something in particular that excited him and disturbed him for reasons which he could not give. He would like her to see him, gowned and hooded, walking in a procession. A fellowship, a professorship, he felt capable of anything and saw himself—but what was she looking at? At a man pasting a bill. The vast flapping sheet flattened itself out, and each shove of the brush revealed fresh legs, hoops, horses, glistening reds and blues, beautifully smooth, until half the wall was covered with the advertisement of a circus; a hundred horsemen, twenty performing seals, lions, tigers . . . Craning forwards, for she was short-sighted, she read it out . . . "will visit this town," she read. It was terribly dangerous work for a one-armed man, she exclaimed, to stand on top of a ladder like that—his left arm had been cut off in a reaping machine two years ago.

"Let us all go!" she cried, moving on, as if all those riders and horses had filled her with childlike exultation and made her forget her pity.

"Let's go," he said, repeating her words, clicking them out, however, with a self-consciousness that made her wince. "Let us go to the circus." No. He could not say it right. He could not feel it right. But why not? she wondered. What was wrong with him then? She liked him warmly, at the moment. Had they not been taken, she asked, to circuses when they were children? Never, he answered, as if she asked the very thing he wanted; had been longing all these days to say, how they did not go to circuses. It was a large family, nine brothers and sisters, and his father was a working man. "My father is a chemist,[6] Mrs. Ramsay. He keeps a shop." He himself had paid his own way since he was thirteen. Often he went without a greatcoat in winter. He could never "return hospitality" (those were his parched stiff words) at college. He had to make things last twice the time other people did; he smoked the cheapest tobacco; shag; the same the old men did in the quays. He worked hard—seven hours a day; his subject was now the influence of something upon somebody—they were walking on and Mrs. Ramsay did not quite catch the meaning, only the words, here and there . . . dissertation . . . fellowship . . . readership . . . lectureship. She could not follow the ugly academic jargon, that rattled itself off so glibly, but said to herself that she saw now why going to the circus had knocked him off his perch, poor little man, and why he came out, instantly, with all that about his father and mother and brothers and sisters, and she would see to it that they didn't laugh at him any more; she would tell Prue about it. What he would have liked, she supposed, would have been to say how he had gone not to the circus but to Ibsen with the Ramsays. He was an awful prig—oh yes, an insuffer-

6 chemist: manager of a drugstore.

able bore. For, though they had reached the town now and were in the main street, with carts grinding past on the cobbles, still he went on talking, about settlements, and teaching, and workingmen, and helping our own class, and lectures, till she gathered that he had got back entire self-confidence, had recovered from the circus, and was about (and now again she liked him warmly) to tell her—but here, the houses falling away on both sides, they came out on the quay, and the whole bay spread before them and Mrs. Ramsay could not help exclaiming, "Oh, how beautiful!" For the great plateful of blue water was before her; the hoary Lighthouse, distant, austere, in the midst; and on the right, as far as the eye could see, fading and falling, in soft low pleats, the green sand dunes with the wild flowing grasses on them, which always seemed to be running away into some moon country, uninhabited of men.

That was the view, she said, stopping, growing grayer-eyed, that her husband loved.

She paused a moment. But now, she said, artists had come here. There indeed, only a few paces off, stood one of them, in Panama hat and yellow boots, seriously, softly, absorbedly, for all that he was watched by ten little boys, with an air of profound contentment on his round red face gazing, and then, when he had gazed, dipping; imbuing the tip of his brush in some soft mound of green or pink. Since Mr. Paunceforte had been there, three years before, all the pictures were like that, she said, green and gray, with lemon-colored sailing boats, and pink women on the beach.

But her grandmother's friends, she said, glancing discreetly as they passed, took the greatest pains; first they mixed their own colors, and then they ground them, and then they put damp cloths to keep them moist.

So Mr. Tansley supposed she meant him to see that the man's picture was skimpy, was that what one said? The colors weren't solid? Was that what one said? Under the influence of that extraordinary emotion which had been growing all the walk, had begun in the garden when he had wanted to take her bag, had increased in the town when he had wanted to tell her everything about himself, he was coming to see himself, and everything he had ever known gone crooked a little. It was awfully strange.

There he stood in the parlor of the poky little house where she had taken him, waiting for her, while she went upstairs a moment to see a woman. He heard her quick step above; heard her voice cheerful, then low; looked at the mats, tea caddies,[7] glass shades; waited quite impatiently; looked forward eagerly to the walk home; determined to carry her bag; then heard her come out; shut a door; say they must keep the windows open and the doors shut, ask at the house for anything they wanted (she must be talking to a child) when, suddenly, in she came, stood for a moment silent (as if she had been pretending up there, and for a moment let herself be now), stood quite motionless for a moment against a picture of Queen Victoria wearing the blue ribbon of the Garter; when all at once he realized that it was this: it was this:—she was the most beautiful person he had ever seen.

With stars in her eyes and veils in her hair, with cyclamen[8] and wild violets— what nonsense was he thinking? She was fifty at least; she had eight children. Stepping through fields of flowers and taking to her breast buds that had

broken and lambs that had fallen; with the stars in her eyes and the wind in her hair— He took her bag.

"Good-by, Elsie," she said, and they walked up the street, she holding her parasol erect and walking as if she expected to meet someone round the corner, while for the first time in his life Charles Tansley felt an extraordinary pride; a man digging in a drain stopped digging and looked at her, let his arm fall down and looked at her; for the first time in his life Charles Tansley felt an extraordinary pride; felt the wind and the cyclamen and the violets for he was walking with a beautiful woman. He had hold of her bag.

II

"No going to the Lighthouse, James," he said, as he stood by the window, speaking awkwardly, but trying in deference to Mrs. Ramsay to soften his voice into some semblance of geniality at least.

Odious little man, thought Mrs. Ramsay, why go on saying that?

III

"Perhaps you will wake up and find the sun shining and the birds singing," she said compassionately, smoothing the little boy's hair, for her husband, with his caustic saying that it would not be fine, had dashed his spirits she could see. This going to the Lighthouse was a passion of his, she saw, and then, as if her husband had not said enough, with his caustic saying that it would not be fine tomorrow, this odious little man went and rubbed it in all over again.

"Perhaps it will be fine tomorrow," she said, smoothing his hair.

7 **tea caddies:** small boxes to hold tea.
8 **cyclamen** (sĭk/lə mən): the primula, an early-blooming flower.

All she could do now was to admire the refrigerator, and turn the pages of the Stores list in the hope that she might come upon something like a rake, or a mowing machine, which, with its prongs and its handles, would need the greatest skill and care in cutting out. All these young men parodied her husband, she reflected; he said it would rain; they said it would be a positive tornado.

But here, as she turned the page, suddenly her search for the picture of a rake or a mowing machine was interrupted. The gruff murmur, irregularly broken by the taking out of pipes and the putting in of pipes which had kept on assuring her, though she could not hear what was said (as she sat in the window which opened on the terrace), that the men were happily talking; this sound, which had lasted now half an hour and had taken its place soothingly in the scale of sounds pressing on top of her, such as the tap of balls upon bats, the sharp, sudden bark now and then, "How's that? How's that?" of the children playing cricket, had ceased; so that the monotonous fall of the waves on the beach, which for the most part beat a measured and soothing tattoo to her thoughts and seemed consolingly to repeat over and over again as she sat with the children the words of some old cradle song, murmured by nature, "I am guarding you—I am your support," but at other times suddenly and unexpectedly, especially when her mind raised itself slightly from the task actually in hand, had no such kindly meaning, but like a ghostly roll of drums remorselessly beat the measure of life, made one think of the destruction of the island and its engulfment in the sea, and warned her whose day had slipped past in one quick doing after another that it was all ephemeral as a rainbow—this sound which had been obscured and concealed under the other sounds suddenly thundered hollow in her ears and made her look up with an impulse of terror.

They had ceased to talk; that was the explanation. Falling in one second from the tension which had gripped her to the other extreme which, as if to recoup her for her unnecessary expense of emotion, was cool, amused, and even faintly malicious, she concluded that poor Charles Tansley had been shed. That was of little account to her. If her husband required sacrifices (and indeed he did) she cheerfully offered up to him Charles Tansley, who had snubbed her little boy.

One moment more, with her head raised, she listened, as if she waited for some habitual sound, some regular mechanical sound; and then, hearing something rhythmical, half said, half chanted, beginning in the garden, as her husband beat up and down the terrace, something between a croak and a song, she was soothed once more, assured again that all was well, and looking down at the book on her knee found the picture of a pocket knife with six blades which could only be cut out if James was very careful.

Comment

If we go back now to the dialogue by itself ("Yes, of course, if it's fine . . ."; "But it won't be . . ."; "No going to the Lighthouse, James"; "Perhaps it will be fine . . ."), we find that each of the direct speeches reverberates with individual meanings. This is no casual discussion of plans for a summer day; from behind the words of Mrs. Ramsay, Mr. Ramsay, and Tansley, we feel the weight of an individual personality; we are aware not only of three different characters but also of three different ways of accepting (and rejecting) life. Through Mrs. Ramsay's memory of earlier events of the day on which occurs the little debate about going to the Lighthouse, we become aware of all that is involved in her hope that James shall not be disappointed in his excursion. The whole passage, we may assume, covers but a minute or two of "actual" time. But the time of awareness, the time of consciousness, is but remotely connected with the clock.

The Ramsays are spending the summer holidays at their cottage in Skye, an island off the west coast of Scotland. They are a highly cultivated family: Mr. Ramsay is a university professor whom younger scholars often seek out, and one is there now, a philosophy student named Tansley. Mrs. Ramsay, some of whose ancestors were a noble Italian family, is interested in various charities and in bringing up her large family to be respectful of others. There are various guests besides Tansley; there are the eight sons and daughters, some of whom are impatient with their father's earnest students; and there is a Swiss servant girl. The youngest of the household is James Ramsay, who has been promised a trip in the sailboat to a nearby lighthouse. Mrs. Ramsay hopes very much that he will not be disappointed.

Such would be a conventional outline of these opening pages from *To the Lighthouse,* and of course such an outline reads like a heavy-handed joke. For this passage cannot be reduced to such capsule form; it is not about family plans and circumstances and backgrounds, though of course these things appear. Rather, it is about the feelings, chiefly, that radiate from Mrs. Ramsay like the ceaseless sound of the waves that suddenly and overwhelmingly emerges at the end of the passage. The words exchanged about the trip to the Lighthouse provide the dramatic situation. But the real action, the real drama, is below the level of speech; it is the unspoken awareness of James, of Tansley, and, especially, of Mrs. Ramsay, that fills a moment or two at the end of an uncertain summer day. The passage contains all the ingredients we expect in a novel: it comes to us as if from the pen of an invisible observer who is most perceptive about manners, who is skilled in the sketching of character, who can probe into individual feelings, who certainly knows much about the "place" of others, and who cares deeply about "how to live." But these ingredients are put together differently here; the novel, as Virginia Woolf and others in the 20th century have shaped it, has found new patterns among the words and gestures of society.

Summing Up

1. The opening chapter of *Pride and Prejudice* gives us two versions of the importance of Mr. Bingley's entrance into the neighborhood, and the two versions serve to characterize those who express them. The subject discussed in the opening of *To the Lighthouse* is the weather, a notoriously changeable subject; but how do their opinions of tomorrow's weather characterize Mrs. Ramsay and Tansley?
2. *Jane Eyre* begins with unforgettable violence. Do you find anything like it in the passage from *To the Lighthouse?* Where does the violence occur in this passage?
3. What features of the opening of *To the Lighthouse* can you find to correspond to Thackeray's references to real history, real personages, real society?
4. And what, in the opening of *To the Lighthouse,* fulfills a role like that of the heath in the passage from *The Return of the Native,* even though it is less extensively described than the heath?
5. You can, then, find certain elements of the traditional novel represented in this passage by Virginia Woolf. But what has been changed? What do you find here that the other opening passages do not contain? What expectations, based on this opening, do you form for the rest of the novel? What do you want to happen?

The Cathedral Church of Saint Michael in Coventry. The 15th-century cathedral was destroyed by the Germans in 1940, leaving only two spires and a shell. In 1962 the new cathedral was consecrated. The design of the new is integrated with that of the old.

1914–

The Twentieth Century

"Only connect!"

E. M. FORSTER

"HISTORY IS A NIGHTMARE from which I am trying to awake": so speaks
the hero of a novel published in 1922. He is speaking not only of the
past but also of the present; history here is the whole ongoing life of
the modern world. Certainly the 20th century has sometimes seemed
a nightmare, and sometimes it has seemed a golden vision of plenty
and peace. But whether nightmare or utopia, the 20th century has
produced great numbers of articulate persons who have tried to wake
up from the history of their own times—to stand off from and describe
these times. The duty that they have imposed on themselves is a
difficult one, for it is not easy to look into all that is happening around
us and to point to some event in politics, in literature, or in science, and
say *this* is the beginning of something important, *this* will never be
forgotten. How can we describe our own times? What are the permanent trends and characteristics of an age in which we daily, hourly,
participate? How can we awake from our own history fully enough
and long enough to describe it? We know much about the past. But
what of the present? Where are we? And where are we going?

Every thoughtful person makes his or her own answer, of course,
and every thoughtful person makes different answers at different times
of his or her life. But perhaps the answers most frequently given can
be grouped under two large generalizations: We live in an Age of
Science. We live in an Age of Violence.

The achievements of 20th-century science have been no less visible
in Great Britain than here in America. The first radio broadcast in
England occurred in 1920; the first television broadcast, in 1936. The

*At the Henley Regatta in the summer of 1914. The peace of that summer
was abruptly ended in August, when England declared war on Germany.*

first jet airplane engine was tested there in 1930; the first generating
plant run by atomic energy was put into operation there in 1956;
penicillin, the first of the antibiotics of modern medicine, was discovered by an English scientist in 1928. The science that has so
changed our lives in the 20th century is indeed international.

It is international not only in its achievements but also in the training
and the discipline required of those who contribute to its achievements. Modern science is built upon theories developed by the insight and genius of great minds, often solitary great minds, of the
present and the past; it rests upon the work of the Newtons and the
Einsteins of history. It is built also upon the practice of cooperation
among all scientists, whatever their contributions. The biologist, the
chemist, the physicist—every scientist today is immersed in a discipline
that he or she shares with hundreds of others. The scientist may arrive at his or her ideas in solitude, but they can be no more than day-
dreams until he or she has communicated them to others and has
submitted them to the tests that, with the rest of the profession, he or
she agrees will determine their validity. It is of no use to throw a
tantrum in a laboratory; only the patient exercise of reason and observation, the disciplining of imagination by facts, will reveal the truth.

THE TWENTIETH CENTURY

Dunkirk Beaches, May 1940 by Richard Eurich. Here a third of a million British troops who had been forced to retreat to the sea were rescued from the exposed beaches and taken across the Channel to England by the British navy, private yachts, and some two hundred small motorboats manned by civilian amateurs.

The violence of the 20th century is international also. English men and women who began their lives with the century were infants during the Boer War (1899-1903), in which only Great Britain and one of her colonies were involved. When Britons born in 1900 were fourteen, they saw the start of World War I, an enormous conflict involving nations from every continent, and many of them saw service in it before the end in 1918. When those born in 1900 were twenty-nine and raising their own young families, they began to suffer the effects of a world-wide depression; and ten years later, as they were about to turn forty, they felt the bombings that began World War II. In World War I the loss of life on the battlefields and at sea was greater than had ever occurred before: some eight and a half million men in uniform were killed. But by the end of World War II, it has been estimated, more than twenty-two million *civilians* had lost their lives. The total casualties, civilian and military, can never be counted. Men and women now in their sixties were seventeen years old when the terrors of the Russian Revolution began; they were in their middle thirties during the Spanish Civil War, the bloody testing-ground for World War II; and since early middle age they have lived in a world of mass killings, concentration camps, gas chambers, and threats of violence even greater.

People on holiday at the seashore in Cornwall. Vacations with pay and increased leisure time have made it possible for many Britons in the 20th century to enjoy the great seaside resorts.

On the one hand, then, an Age of Science, with all its progress in the arts of transportation, communication, and healing—with all its clarity of organization, its discipline of the imagination, its constant balance of what we wish against what is the fact. And on the other hand, an Age of Violence, the mass violence of civilian bombing, forced labor, and the displacing of millions from their jobs and homes by war and revolution. Each description is true, yet neither· is more than half the truth.

What then of 20th-century writers? What is the character of the age as they see it? Like other citizens, they hope that the uses of science will never be completely at the service of the forces of violence—they hope that peace, freedom, and plenty will triumph over nightmare. Sometimes, like other citizens, they are hopeful, but sometimes too they can only be skeptical and full of forebodings. It is no wonder that a famous modern poet, W. H. Auden, who was born in 1907 in England and who lived in the United States, should have hit upon yet another title for the 20th century: the Age of Anxiety.

Of course no writer tries to understand an age merely through descriptive titles. Rather the writer of every age tries to see through such generalizations into the experience behind them. The 20th-century writer has seen violence and science together; his/her vision has included both the achievements and the failures of the 20th century; he/she has expressed our clarities and our confusions as they are, side by side. The modern writer sees both the humanitarianism of the great hospital, and the cruel suffering of one patient. He/she sees both the incredible knowledge of those who turn atomic energy into the current that runs a washing machine, and the dark ignorance of the person who can read only the cheapest comic book. The modern writer sees both the violence of the criminal and the self-discipline of the artist, both the arrogance of the dictator and the dedication of the judge. He/she has tried to connect the fragments and contradictions of the modern world in a vision of his/her own.

One possible motto, then, for the literature of the 20th century—for the writers who make it and for the readers who explore it—is "Only connect!" It comes from a novel by E. M. Forster (whom you will shortly meet) published early in the century, in 1910, and is the message that the heroine hopes to get across to the man she is about to marry. She is imaginative, sensitive, and happy in solitude; he is practical, efficient, always in the company of others, yet curiously unaware of the feelings of others. She hopes that a bridge can be built between them, a bridge of "quiet indications."

> Only connect! That was the whole of her sermon.
> Only connect the prose with the passion, and both
> will be exalted, and human love will be seen at its
> height. Live in fragments no longer.

The 20th-century writer has not always succeeded in connecting the prose of science with the violence of passion; he/she has not always connected the prose of everyday life with the passion of great moments of insight. But since the beginning of the century the writer has tried to show readers how to "live in fragments no longer."

The Writer's Language

The Language

WHATEVER CONNECTIONS writers may make, they must express them in language, and in the 20th century language has been studied more extensively and intensively than ever before.

In 1928 there was published in England the final installment of *A New English Dictionary on Historical Principles*, the culmination of more than fifty years of work by many scholars. The *Oxford English Dictionary*, as it is usually called (for it was published by the Oxford University Press), runs to ten large volumes. Its pages, each with three columns of close-packed information, are about the size of the pages in popular picture-magazines, and there are more than fifteen thousand pages in the ten volumes. These pages contain the definitions of more

Piccadilly Circus, one of the busiest traffic circles in London. Here are the colors and shapes of advertising displays, one of the methods of communication other than language that have become important in the 20th century.

than half a million words. Each definition, moreover—and this is why it is a dictionary "on historical principles"—is illustrated by quotations showing how the word has been used in written sources, and there are almost two million such quotations. The first recorded use of a word, sometimes taken from manuscripts dating back to 1250, and then all the major changes, extensions, or sometimes contractions of its meaning through all the centuries it has been in use—all these are illustrated by carefully selected quotations from poems, plays, essays, scientific papers, and every other kind of source in which the English language has been responsibly used. Never before had so complete an inventory of a language been taken, and never before had so complete an analysis of each word in a language been made.

Just one year later, in 1929, a project of quite a different kind was copyrighted. It was a list of 850 carefully selected English words, all of them fairly simple and all within the vocabulary of anyone who can pass a literacy test. It consisted of 600 common nouns; 150 adjectives; 100 "operators"—assorted pronouns, prepositions, conjunctions, adverbs, and 18 verbs. The list was called "Basic English," and it has been used both to teach those whose native language is not English and to pro-

THE TWENTIETH CENTURY

vide a tool for those who study the ways in which language works. Almost any passage of prose or poetry will contain many words that are not among the 850 selected to form Basic English; to translate a sonnet of Shakespeare into Basic, for example, might well produce a clumsy and graceless paraphrase of the original. The person who does the translating, however, as he or she chooses words from the list and combines them to do justice to Shakespeare's rich meanings, will learn a great deal about the power and uniqueness of Shakespeare's art. The construction of Basic English was one of many important steps taken in modern times to find out how language functions, language as used by great writers and by everyone who reads, writes, listens, and speaks.

In the 20th century, in fact, the study of the English language and of every language, alive or dead, written or spoken, has become the business of many scholars. There have been many investigations into the history of language, as typified by the *Oxford English Dictionary*. There have been many investigations into the ways in which the words of a language communicate meanings, as typified by the research that constructed Basic English. And there have been, particularly since World War II, a great many investigations into the structure of language, investigations in the field called "linguistics." In its most general sense linguistics is the scientific, systematic study of language. The linguist examines and isolates the characteristic sounds of a language, both as those sounds have historically changed (as the sounds of English have changed from Chaucer's day to our own) and as they function in the living speech by which we communicate (as in the difference of sound between "It is here" and "It is here?"). The linguist examines the characteristic internal forms of the words of a language, tracing their histories and describing their functions (and thus explaining, to take a very small example, why we say "mouse" and "mice" but "house" and "houses"). Linguists also analyze the characteristic syntax of a language and make comparative studies of the ways in which words "go together" in the grammars of different languages. And linguists are of course concerned with semantics, with the constant problem of the relation between what we say—the sounds of our speeches to each other—and the meanings that we share (and sometimes mistake!) through these sounds. The basic material of linguistics is the spoken language—the unending sounds of human voices that surround us most of our waking hours. Many devices from radio and electronic engineering have been produced to assist the linguist, the most generally useful and important of which is the tape recorder, the device that records living speech and presents it for analysis.

All these interests—in the structure of the spoken language, in the history of the written language, and in the ways in which both the written and the spoken language function in a society, whether by the jokes of a radio comedian, by the articles in the newspaper, or in the most imaginative lines of a poet—all these interests have suggested that yet another title for the 20th century is the Age of Analysis. The very word *analysis,* of course, suggests something scientific, objective, and probing. Not that all 20th-century investigations into the ways in which we talk in everyday life, or the ways in which our greatest writers express their sense of life, have been altogether cool, objective, and detached. Yet there has never been a time when so many scholars have been busily analyzing and interpreting the literature of the past. The analysis of meaning, the discussion of myth, metaphor, and symbol —indeed the kind of analysis that you have been engaged in throughout this book—has not been confined to students of literature. It has been pursued by psychologists, by anthropologists, and by social scientists of many kinds. Historians have searched through documents of the past to discover the dominant "images" of certain periods. Public opinion experts have learned much about how propaganda works and how group opinions are swayed. There has lately risen another specialist, the scholar who analyzes popular culture—movies, comic strips, even comic postcards, not to mention television programs—to learn what can be discovered there about society as a whole.

All this communications research, analysis of opinion, and literary criticism would seem to suggest that the English language and all the gestures and expressions that accompany it have finally stood still to be looked at and analyzed as we analyze a specimen under the microscope. But of course the only language that really stands still is the dead language, and we know that our English language is very much alive. We know, for example, that new words are being added to it every year; not a year goes by that does not present another new chemical element or industrial process to be named. No dictionary can ever be completely up to date. Nor can we predict the more subtle deepenings and modifications of the meanings of words in our language that will occur as a result of the works yet to come from the unknown writers and thinkers of the future: *spring,* we remember, is not quite so simple a word for us here and now as it was so many years ago for Chaucer. And yet we know that the language that will contain all the new words from science and industry, that will contain the deepened meanings of such old words as *spring,* has in its forms and its sounds probably changed less in the last two hundred years than in any previous two centuries.

English is spoken and written over more of the globe than at any time in the past. The radio and television, no less in Britain than here, have done much since the 1930's to standardize the way English is spoken. There are still differences of accent and pronunciation that vary according to economic and social position, though such variations are fewer than they were fifty years ago, and it is no longer so easy to tell the rich from the poor just by the way they talk. There are still regional differences too; the Scot speaks differently from the Cornishman, although, again, the standard or "educated" speech set by the British Broadcasting Corporation is widely diffused. It is true, of course, that many of these standardizing influences have had an unhappy effect on the English language, at least on our respect for the spoken word. For when a radio is going all day, we can only half-listen to what is said, and the inattention, not to mention the bad manners, sometimes evident in large assemblies of people springs at least in part from our habit of ignoring the clamor of the loud-speaker. The stabilizing and standardizing of English has also made it possible, on the other hand, to attain the goal of universal literacy and to create an educational system in which millions are taught to read efficiently and intelligently.

There are methods of communication other than the English language that have assumed great importance in modern civilization. The blips of the radar screen, the symbols of the calculus, the images of the movie screen, the colors and shapes of public displays and advertising —all these are methods of communication that work very differently from words. There are some indications that we no longer call only upon the language the Oxford scholars charted so thoroughly when they made their dictionary early in this century and that modern society, and especially the modern city, relies on signals and symbols other than words for the conduct of daily affairs. Although the English language is not growing and changing so rapidly as it did three hundred years ago, it is certainly here to stay, and it will outlive us. Our children and our children's children will go on speaking to each other in the words we know so well: *love, friend, family, home, city, country, freedom.* Such words will not quickly become obsolete. And they cannot decay if we use them well.

The Writer

The 20th-century writer has given much thought to this matter of using the language well; indeed the major poets and novelists have all written a good deal of literary criticism, much of it directed against shoddiness and imprecision in the use of words. Joseph Conrad, the great novelist, in one of his prefaces speaks of the "unremitting . . . care" that the writer must exercise if he or she would bring once again "the light of magic suggestiveness" to "the old, old words, worn thin, defaced by ages of careless usage." The task of the novelist, Conrad believed, is "by the power of the written word to make you hear, to make you feel—it is, before all, to make you *see*." And this seeing, this direct vision, the novelist can capture only when he or she captures "the shape and ring of sentences" that are his or her own.

Many serious writers, ranging from poets to journalists, have argued that the main source of the "careless usage" that has impoverished "the old, old words" is pretentiousness. They have urged a plainness and naturalness of style that makes readers see the subject rather than the elaborate vocabulary of the author. Sir Arthur Quiller-Couch, a novelist, critic, and professor at Cambridge University, in an essay on the art of writing once attacked something he called "jargon." Jargon, according to "Q" (as he was called), is the excessive use of abstract nouns and passive verbs, and it can result in a ridiculous windiness and vagueness. He illustrates by rewriting Hamlet's famous soliloquy, "To be, or not to be," as a jargoneer would write it:

> To be, or the contrary? Whether the former or the latter be preferable would seem to admit of some difference of opinion; the answer in the present case being of an affirmative or of an negative character according as to whether one elects on the one hand to mentally suffer the disfavor of fortune, albeit in an extreme degree, or on the other to boldly envisage adverse conditions in the prospect of eventually bringing them to a conclusion. The condition of sleep is similar to, if not indistinguishable from, that of death; and with the addition of finality the former might be considered identical with the latter: so that in this connection it might be argued with regard to sleep that, could the addition be effected, a termination would be put to the endurance of a multiplicity of inconveniences, not to mention a number of downright evils incidental to our fallen humanity, and thus a consummation achieved of a most gratifying nature.

A glance at the original will quickly show you how far jargon is from poetry: reading it by itself certainly shows how near jargon is to pretentious nonsense.

But sometimes, it has been argued, bad, muddy writing results from slavishly following the "rules" of "good form": this kind of writing is vague not because it is pretentious but because it is frightened—frightened of sounding like a person talking. Here is a passage from the farewell broadcast of John Hilton, one of the most famous radio commentators of the B.B.C. before World War II. He is explaining how he wrote the radio scripts that so many of his audience admired.

> I don't know anything about others, as I say, but my way is to speak my sentences aloud as I write them. In fact here's my rule, all pat: "To write as you would talk you must talk while you write." If you were outside my room while I'm writing a talk you'd hear muttering and mumbling and outright declaration from beginning to end. You'd say, "There's somebody in there with a slate loose; he never stops talking to himself." No, I wouldn't be talking to *myself* but to you. . . .
>
> You can scrap, in writing a talk, most of what you've been told all your life was literary good form. You have to; if you want your talk to ring the bell and walk in and sit down by the hearth. You've been told, for instance, that it's bad form to end a sentence with a preposition. It may be, in print. But not in talk. Not in talk. I'm coming to the view that what I call the "prepositional verb" (I'm no grammarian—I invent my own names for those things)—that what I call the prepositional verb is one of the glories of the English language. You start with a simple verb like "to stand"; and with the help of a pocketful

A 1923 English radio broadcast of Shakespeare.

of prepositions you get all those lovely changes: to stand up, to stand down, to stand off, to stand in, to stand by, to stand over—and twenty others. We score over the French there. The Germans have it; but they stick their prepositions in front of the verbs. I think our way has much more punch to it. And what bull's-eyes you can score with the prepositional verb if only you'll search for it and, having found it, let the preposition come at the end of the sentence.

You know how odd moments stick in the memory. One stays in mine. I was dealing with retirement pensions. I was tired. Tired to the point of writing that awful jargon that passes for English. I'd written something like "I don't want what I've said to discourage you from pursuing this question further; rather I would wish that my arguments should prove an added stimulus. . . ." At that point I said to myself, "Now, come on, John, pull yourself together. That won't do: what is it you're trying to say?" And I pulled myself together (tired as I was)—I pulled myself together and searched and found it. "I don't want to put you off. I want rather to set you on." That was all. (What torment we have to go through to find what it is we're trying to say and how to say it in simple words.) That was all. Two simple sentences: put you *off*—set you *on*. Each ending with a preposition.

It is one thing to write naturally in order to reach a mass audience, but quite another to do so in order to express a vision of one's own. William Butler Yeats, the Irish poet who won the Nobel Prize for literature in 1923 and whose influence has been felt by every poet and playwright of our period, has told us in his *Autobiographies* that early in his career he resolved to "escape from rhetoric and abstraction" and to achieve "personal utterance." This "personal utterance," however, could not be won simply by giving up the "rhetoric and abstraction" of the jargoneer or by refusing the fussiness of one who slavishly follows rules. Yeats demanded something more intimate and personal. "We should write out our own thoughts in as nearly as possible the language we thought them in, as though in a letter to an intimate friend," he said. Yeats resolved, he said, "to write out of my emotions exactly as they came to me in life, not changing them to make them more beautiful." To achieve "personal utterance" a writer must keep faith with the experience that is most personally his own.

Yeats says that he would not change his emotions by making them more beautiful; he might well have said that he would not change them by making them more public. For in an age of mass literacy, when every member of a nation is continuously subjected to the public language of the newspapers, of radio, and television, it is not only language that becomes standardized; the feelings and experience behind language become so too. No one can fully participate in the life of any modern nation unless he can read and write, and the spread of literacy, the great extension and development of public education, is perhaps the greatest achievement of all English-speaking countries in the 20th century. The 20th-century writer, perhaps more than anyone, is aware of the vast systems of communication that organize millions of people for the progress of industry, for the great enterprises of government, for the very maintenance of a national way of life. He is also aware that the difference between mass communication and personal utterance has never been so acute: we cannot have a society without the first, but none of us can have a self without the second. The relation between personal utterance and public language is not an easy one, but it is a relation that our best writers are determined to make.

The modern writer who struggles to achieve personal utterance, the style of the one, does not turn his or her back on mass communication, the style of the many. It has been said that a novelist is someone who takes himself or herself off from people and starts talking to himself or herself. He or she soon discovers that he or she is saying what many others are saying to themselves silently. Through its writers a society utters its secrets, its silent thoughts. With all those who are conscious of the difference between public language and private, between the way we know ourselves and the way we know the world, the modern writer shares his or her deepest concern.

Modern writers, then, and especially modern poets, have been very much aware that their situation is a new one in the history of literature, and they have often written of their works in terms very different from great writers who have preceded them. The poet Louis Mac-Neice, for example, whom we shall shortly meet, once had this to say:

> I consider that the poet is a blend of the entertainer and the critic or informer; he is not a legislator, however unacknowledged, nor yet, essentially, a prophet. As informer, he is not a photographic or scientific informer, but more like the "informer" in the derogatory sense.

This description does indeed make the poet a retailer of secrets. Again, T. S. Eliot, like Yeats a Nobel prize winner and a writer of wide and profound influence, has said this:

> [Poetry] is a concentration, and a new thing resulting from the concentration, of a very great number of experiences which to the practical and active person would not seem to be experiences at all. . . . Poetry is not a turning loose of emotion, but an escape from emotion; it is not the expression of personality, but an escape from personality. But, of course, only those who have personality and emotions know what it means to want to escape from these things.*

The "concentration" of which Eliot speaks has sometimes led the modern poet far indeed from the "emotion" and "personality" which figure so largely in the mass-circulation magazine stories, or the quickly forgotten, run-of-the-mill movies and television serials that pass the time for many. It is a concentration that sometimes achieves an unforgettable effect, an effect like that which William Butler Yeats discusses in the following passage:

> There are no lines with more melancholy beauty than these by Burns:—
>
> > The White moon is setting behind the white wave,
> > And Time is setting with me, O!
>
> and these lines are perfectly symbolical. Take from them the whiteness of the moon and of the wave, whose relation to the setting of Time is too subtle for the intellect, and you take from them their beauty. But, when all are together, moon and wave and whiteness and setting Time and the last melancholy cry, they evoke an emotion which cannot be evoked by any other arrangement of colors and sounds and forms. We may call this metaphorical writing, but it is better to call it symbolical writing, because metaphors are not profound enough to be moving, when they are not symbols, and when they are symbols they are most perfect of all, because the most subtle, outside of pure sound, and through them one can best find out what symbols are.

The concentration of modern writers, their efforts to restore to "the old, old words" some of the "light of magic suggestiveness," has led

* From "Tradition and the Individual Talent" in *Selected Essays,* New Edition, by T. S. Eliot, copyright 1932, 1936, 1950 by Harcourt Brace Jovanovich, Inc.; renewed 1960, 1964, by T. S. Eliot. Reprinted by permission of the publishers. Also reprinted by permission of Faber and Faber Ltd from *Selected Essays* by T. S. Eliot.

them to discover, or rather to rediscover, the kind of symbol that Yeats describes here. Modern literature, especially when we compare it with the literature of the last century, is often difficult. It does not beautify emotions that are ugly. It does not offer us large abstractions that are as easy to "get" as the message on a billboard. It has much to say about the public world and it is often harshly critical of that world. But it does not do so in the easy language of the public world. Modern writers, sometimes by the use of symbolism, often by the use of irony, and always by a persistent concentration of their language, try to bring together parts of their own world in a design through which we can see ourselves.

The People and Their Times

EVEN THOUGH more than three-fourths of it have gone by, the century in which we ourselves are living is so full of surprises—and terrors— that it is not easy to characterize. Many possibilities, some of them frightening, some heartening, all of them challenging, lie in the present and future of all who speak and write English. No one can say with finality, "This is where we have been, and this is where we are going." The 20th century, so far, has been as unpredictable and as exciting as an adventure.

An Adventurous Leader

Perhaps the most relevant introduction, then, to the way in which the British people have lived in the first half of the 20th century is the following passage. It describes the escape of a young British officer from his captors during the Boer War in 1899. The officer, as you will see, has been hidden away in a freight car ("goods truck") in a small space among bales of wool. Thirty years later, at the time of writing, he can still remember the names of the towns through which he moved on his slow, two-day journey from the interior to the seacoast. There may be names of persons and places in this passage that will mean little to you, but it can quickly be read as an adventure story—as indeed it is.

JOURNEY TO FREEDOM

There was plenty of light now in the recess in which I was confined. There were many crevices in the boards composing the sides and floor of the truck, and through these the light found its way between the wool bales. Working along the tunnel to the end of the truck, I found a chink which must have been nearly an eighth of an inch in width, and through which it was possible to gain a partial view of the outer world. To check the progress of the journey I had learnt by heart beforehand the names of all the stations on the route. I can remember many of them today: Witbank, Middleburg, Bergendal, Belfast, Dalmanutha, Machadodorp, Waterval Boven, Waterval Onder, Elands, Nooidgedacht, and so on to Komati Poort. We had by now reached the first of these. At this point the branch line from the mine joined the railway. Here, after two or three hours' delay and shunting, we were evidently coupled up to a regular train, and soon started off at a superior and very satisfactory pace. . . .

Late in the afternoon we reached the dreaded Komati Poort. Peeping through my chink, I could see this was a considerable place, with numerous tracks of rails and several trains standing on them. Numbers of people were moving about. There were many voices and much shouting and whistling. After a preliminary inspection of the scene I retreated, as the train pulled up, into the very center of my fastness, and covering myself up with a piece of sacking lay flat on the floor of the truck and awaited developments with a beating heart.

Three or four hours passed, and I did not know whether we had been searched or not. Several times people had passed up and down the train talking in Dutch. But the tarpaulins had not been removed, and no special examination seemed to have been made of the truck. Meanwhile darkness had come on, and I had to resign myself to an indefinite continuance of my uncertainties. It was tantalizing to be held so long in jeopardy after all these hundreds of miles had been accomplished, and I was now within a few hundred yards of the frontier. . . .

We were still stationary when I awoke. Perhaps they were searching the train so thoroughly that there was consequently a great delay! Alternatively, perhaps we were forgotten on the siding and would be left there for days or weeks. I was greatly tempted to peer out, but I resisted. At last, at eleven o'clock, we were coupled up, and almost immediately started. If I had been right in thinking that the station in which we had passed the night was Komati Poort, I was already in Portuguese territory. But perhaps I had made a mistake . . . all these doubts were dispelled when the train arrived at the next station. I peered through my chink and saw the uniform caps of the Portuguese officials on the platform and the name Resana Garcia painted on a board. I restrained all expression of my joy until we moved on again. Then, as we rumbled and banged along, I pushed my head out of the tarpaulin and sang and shouted and crowed at the top of my voice. Indeed, I was so carried away by thankfulness and delight that I fired my revolver two or three times in the air as a *feu de joie*.[1] None of these follies led to any evil results.

It was late in the afternoon when we reached Lourenço Marques. My train ran into a goods yard, and a crowd of Kaffirs advanced to unload it. I thought the moment had now come for me to quit my hiding place, in which I had passed nearly three anxious and uncomfortable days. . . . I now slipped out at the end of the truck between the couplings, and mingling unnoticed with the Kaffirs and loafers in the yard— which my slovenly and unkempt appearance well fitted me to

1 *feu de joie*: firing of guns as a sign of joy.

do—I strolled my way toward the gates and found myself in the streets of Lourenço Marques.

Burgener was waiting outside the gates. We exchanged glances. He turned and walked off into the town, and I followed twenty yards behind. We walked through several streets and turned a number of corners. Presently he stopped and stood for a moment gazing up at the roof of the opposite house. I looked in the same direction, and there—blest vision!—I saw floating the gay colors of the Union Jack. It was the British Consulate.

The secretary of the British Consul evidently did not expect my arrival.

"Be off," he said. "The Consul cannot see you today. Come to his office at nine tomorrow, if you want anything."

At this I became so angry, and repeated so loudly that I insisted on seeing the Consul personally at once, that that gentleman himself looked out of the window and finally came down to the door and asked me my name. From that moment every resource of hospitality and welcome was at my disposal. A hot bath, clean clothing, an excellent dinner, means of telegraphing —all I could want.

The author of this passage is not a writer of adventure stories, though he has in fact lived through the greatest adventures anyone could know in the 20th century. Nor is he a writer by profession, though he has written many books about history and politics. The author is Sir Winston Churchill, and the "I" of the story is himself as a young man. This adventure story is history, it is autobiography, and it was written by the man who became the greatest political leader in Britain in the first half of the 20th century.

What can it tell us about those years? First, it plainly suggests a good deal about bravery—not only about courage, but about the gallantry and high spirits that mean bravery too. It suggests also something about self-confidence: this young man was not going to be pushed around by any official of the consular office, any more than he hesitated in his determination to get through. And it tells us also a good deal about taking hardships for granted: at the best they can be made light of; at worst they can be defied; generally they can be endured.

Two World Wars with the ravages of a world-wide depression between them: these are the hardest facts of the first half of the 20th century in Britain. They have of course been the hardest facts in the life of every 20th-century nation, but their consequences have been graver for the British than for us. Britain is no longer the center of an Empire. Since World War II many of her former colonies, with the best training and the highest hopes she could offer them, have become independent nations—India, Ghana, and others. The British Commonwealth of Nations (the most important of which are Australia, New Zealand, India, Pakistan, Ceylon, and Canada) has supplanted the proud Empire of the last two centuries; although members of the Com-

European Picture Service

Winston Churchill as a prisoner of war in 1899 during the Boer War.

monwealth exchange certain preferential trade advantages, they are bound to each other and to Great Britain more by ties of heritage and language than by the stricter political and economic ties of Empire. At home, Britain's reserves of coal, the great resource behind her industrial leadership in the 19th century, have been seriously depleted, and her industrial plant has had to be modernized to meet new competition. Great Britain is a trading nation that must export more than she imports to stay ahead, and in this century the battle to stay ahead has not been easy.

Such developments of his country's history and his involvement in them were of course unknown to the young man who so exuberantly shot off his revolver when he reached free territory that night near the beginning of the century. No one, however, was to play a larger role than his in the making of that history for the next fifty years. In 1900 Winston Churchill was elected to Parliament for the first of many terms. In 1906 he became a member of the administrative branch of the government, as the Secretary for Colonies, the first of many administrative offices that he would hold. In 1910, as Home Secretary (a Secretary of State for internal affairs) he helped to reduce the power of the House of Lords (the legislative body whose members hold office by hereditary right rather than by election) by depriving them of the power of veto over acts passed by Parliament. In 1911, as First Lord of the Admiralty he saw signs of the coming of World War

I that some other high officials could not or did not see, and built up the Navy so that when war came in 1914 it was the strongest of the armed services. In 1915 Winston Churchill fought in France, in the Army, and returned in the next year to become first the Minister for Munitions and then Secretary for War and Air. After World War I, he wrote books, on history, on the world crisis that led to the War, and from 1933 as a member of Parliament was almost alone in warning against the growing military threat of Nazi Germany. When World War II came, in September, 1939, he became, once more, First Lord of the Admiralty and, in 1940, Prime Minister and the leader of Britain in the darkest moments of her history. In 1954, having refused the honor once before, he became *Sir* Winston Churchill.

Such was the man who would say to his countrymen in 1940, in the dark beginnings of World War II, "I have nothing to offer but blood, toil, tears, and sweat." A month later, in June, 1940, when the British Army had been driven out of Europe at Dunkirk, and when the outlook was as bleak as it had ever been in Britain's history, he said this:

> . . . We shall not flag or fail. We shall go on to the end, we shall fight in France, we shall fight on the seas and oceans, we shall fight with growing confidence and growing strength in the air, we shall defend our Island, whatever the cost may be, we shall fight on the beaches, we shall fight on the landing grounds, we shall fight in the fields and in the streets, we shall fight in the hills; we shall never surrender.

With his powers of leadership and his ringing phrases Churchill rallied his countrymen in World War II and afterward. In 1963 he was made an honorary citizen of the United States—just seventeen years after he had distinguished the free world from the world on the other side of "The Iron Curtain," in a speech in 1946 at Westminster College in Missouri.

Everyman in War and Peace

Such was the character of the leader. But what of those whom he led? What of their character and their experience? Here are some portraits of citizens in war and peace. The first, written by a well-known journalist, Sir Philip Gibbs, describes a scene that was paralleled many times during the depression years of the 1930's. Men were "on the dole"—they were receiving unemployment assistance—and their inaction was for many the worst hardship of the depression.

ON THE DOLE

I went up to the distressed areas in Yorkshire, Northumberland, and Durham. It was all very tragic up there, especially in the mining villages with their rows of little houses reaching out to the slag heaps. In some of them there was complete unemployment. The mines had closed down, having become "uneconomical" to work. The men lounged about, just able to keep body and soul together on the dole. Rent took a lion's share of their dole—as much as 17s. 6d. in some districts.

Men still working on a few shifts a week were haunted by the menace of being paid off and joining the big battalions of workless men. Their women lived in the constant dread that their men would come home one evening with the news that another pit had been closed forever.

"There's not much doing," I was told by one of the Durham miners, standing under the shadow of a slag heap in one of these villages. "Men who are working are not much better off than those on the dole. One goes down there and sweats, and takes a risk of one's life, for wages which don't give a man much of a time, especially if he's married with a family. . . . All the same it's best working. It keeps a man from fretting."

He stared away beyond the slag heap.

"These young fellows round here," he said, "haven't a chance of a day's shift. They're closing down many of the pits. And it's worse for the older men who are put off first, and won't get another week's wage as long as they live. It's a black shame when men have no kind of hope. That's what's happening in this country, but perhaps it's nobody's fault."

How tolerant was this man looking into the face of misery! . . .

War came, and the miners went back to their pits or into uniform. It was a war in which the civilian population suffered as never before: when the German bombers did not strike, the threat of bombing made every night an uneasy one. Here is one writer's description of the morning in London after a night of air raids in 1940. The author is Elizabeth Bowen, one of the finest novelists of the mid-century. Like Conrad's ideal novelist, by the shape and ring of her sentences she makes you see not only the city itself but also the character of its stunned inhabitants.

After the Raid

Early September morning in Oxford Street. The smell of charred dust hangs on what should be crystal pure air. Sun, just up, floods the once more innocent sky, strikes silver balloons and the intact building tops. The whole length of Oxford Street, west to east, is empty, looks polished like a ballroom, glitters with smashed glass. Down the distances, natural mists of morning are brown with the last of smoke. Fumes still come from the shell of a shop. At this corner where the burst gas main flaming floors high made a scene like hell in the night, you still feel heat. The silence is now the enormous thing—it appears to amaze the street. Sections and blocks have been roped off; there is no traffic; the men in the helmets say not a person may pass (but some sneak through). Besides the high explosives that did the work, this quarter has been seeded with time bombs—so we are herded, waiting for those to go off. This is the top of Oxford

Ludgate Hill in London, May 1944, after an incendiary air attack.

Street, near where it joins the corner of Hyde Park at Marble Arch.

We people have come up out of the ground, or out from the bottom floors of the damaged houses: we now see what we heard happen throughout the night. Roped away from the rest of London we seem to be on an island—when shall we be taken off? Standing, as might the risen dead in the doors of tombs, in the mouths of shelters, we have nothing to do but yawn at each other or down the void of streets, meanwhile rubbing the smoke-smart deeper into our eyes with our dirty fists. . . . It has been a dirty night. The side has been ripped off one near block—the open gash is nothing but dusty, colorless. (As bodies shed blood, buildings shed mousy dust.) Up there the sun strikes a mirror over a mantelpiece; shreds of a carpet sag out over the void. An A.R.P.[1] man, like a chamois, already runs up the debris; we stare. The charred taint thickens everyone's lips and tongues—what we want is bacon and eggs, coffee. We attempt little sorties—"Keep BACK, please! Keep OFF the street!" The hungry try to slake down with smoking. "PLEASE —that cigarette *out!* Main gone—gas all over the place—d'*you* want to blow up London?" Cigarette trodden guiltily into the trodden glass. We loaf on and on in our cave-mouths; the sun goes on and on up. Some of us are dressed, some of us are not: pajama-legs show below overcoats. There are some Poles, who having lost everything all over again sit down whenever and

1 A.R.P.: Air Raid Precautions.

wherever they can. They are our seniors in this experience: we cannot but watch them. There are two or three unmistakable pairs of disturbed lovers—making one think "Oh yes, how odd—love." There are squads of ageless "residents" from aquarium-like private hotels just round the corner. There are the nomads of two or three nights ago who, having been bombed out of where they were, pitched on this part, to be bombed out again. There is the very old gentleman wrapped up in the blanket, who had been heard to say, humbly, between the blasts in the night, "The truth is, I have outlived my generation. . . ." We are none of us—except perhaps the Poles?—the very very poor: our predicament is not a great predicament. The lady in the fur coat has hair in two stiff little bedroomy gray plaits. She appeals for hairpins: most of us have short hair—pins for her are extracted from one of the Poles' heads. Girls stepping further into the light look into pocket mirrors. "Gosh," they say remotely. Two or three people have, somehow, begun walking when one time bomb goes off at Marble Arch. The street puffs itself empty; more glass splinters. Everyone laughs.

It is a fine morning and we are still alive.

Finally, let us hear of the holiday of a London family of modest circumstances after the war had ended. The time is before the end of the wartime rationing of food and during the period in which the economy was slowly turning back to the production of the goods and services of peace. It was necessary still to be resourceful, but it was possible, too, to be happy and gay. The passage comes from an interview recorded by the B.B.C.

Holiday at the Seaside

It all happened one Monday morning. I was busy dishing dinner up for all my gang, and I just happened to say how fed up I was. It was washday and I'd rather be at the seaside than washing over the dolly tub.[1] And Father said to me "What's wrong with you taking a day off and going down to the coast with your youngest boy?" That properly put the cat among the pigeons because everybody wanted to come as well. So we argued it this way and we argued it that way and we dived in among the money boxes, and in the end we all went down for the day. We chose the nearest seaside place because of the fares and we chose a Saturday actually because Father having the day off, it made it easier for him to come too. And having arrived down on the beach, it was a lovely day and the boys immediately set off down to the water's edge, they couldn't wait two minutes—they didn't hardly wait to get into their bathing costumes. And Father and I were just sitting there stretched out, and I kicked off my shoes—my feet were just killing me, and I said "Oh, isn't this just grand?" and Father said, "Yes it was" and we just was there, just enjoying it and I said to Dad, "Isn't it lovely down here—would you like to have a holiday down here?" So he said "What's the good of us

---

1 **dolly tub:** a washtub; a dolly is an agitator used to stir the clothes.

wanting a holiday down here—you know perfectly well, Lil, that we just can't manage it this year." So, I says "Oh well—we'll see if we can get a bungalow—do you think we really could?" He said "Now forget it." He says "You know we can't." So I just sat down, just sat there thinking it all out, and I thought, well, I don't know, maybe we would be able to manage it. So I said "Well supposing I went and had a look round?" I said "I did happen to see some sandals up in the High Street that I rather fancied. I'll go and have a look at them, and if, in the meantime, a bungalow happens to hit me head-on—I'll take it." So he said "You've got a hope anyway." Well I collected one of the twins—one that wasn't so fond of the water (he couldn't swim so well as the others), and took him with me. So I said to Terry: "Guess what, Terry?" He says "What Mum?" I says "Well, I'm going to try and get a bungalow." He says "You're not!" I says "Yes I am. Would you like to have a holiday down here?" He says "Oh I'd love it!" So we went up the High Street and I didn't really know who to ask or where to go to get this bungalow, so I saw a bus pull up and I went down and asked the bus conductress if she knew where to go. So she said "You haven't got a chance, mate, but try over there, there's no harm in trying." So I went over to the Estate Agents,[2] and staring me in the face was a huge notice "No bungalows." So I said to Terry "Can you read Terry?" He said "Yes." So I says "Well I can't. Come on love, let's go in and see what's doing." And the attendant was busy at the moment and then my turn came. I says, "Is that notice right?" She said "Yes I'm afraid it is." I said, "Hasn't anybody given you one back —well, *you* know, rejected one?" So she said "No I'm afraid not, but," she says, "but look, would you take a part bungalow?" I said "Do you mean with another family?" She said "No—the people live in there." So I said "Well I'll try it anyway." So she said "Well go along to the address," and I went along to the address, and it was a very nice bungalow, and at once I said to Terry "Oh Terry, it's too nice. It will be awfully expensive here. Don't let's go in." He said "Come on Mum, come on—try." So just then, round the corner, came a very very nice old lady. And one look at her—I thought "Oh, *she* seems all right." So she asked us what we wanted. I told her we was looking for accommodation. She said "How many of them are you?" so I said "There's five lads," I said, "myself and my husband." I said "They are lads that'll pay you." So she said "Well come in and have a look round." So she took me in, and everywhere was all white counterpanes and shining—it was just lovely, and there was plenty of accommodation, and it was so nice that my heart just went down in my boots, because I knew perfectly well it couldn't be cheap. But anyway, I asked her how much it was and she told me it was four pounds fifteen.[3] So I was most astonished—I really was. I just couldn't

THE TWENTIETH CENTURY

A queue of women in London in 1949 wait to buy food, a familiar scene during the years of austerity following World War II.

believe it. I expected at least five guineas, and not to be nice at that. So I paid a deposit and Terry and I literally danced out of the bungalow and down to the beach, and I said "Oh Terry, when we get down to the beach, don't say a thing to your father. Just say nothing—pull a long face and make out we haven't got it." So we sits alongside Dad, and Dad looks at me and "Well," says he—looks at Terry—"no go?" I say "no go." He says "I told you so. You might just as well have sat down and rested your feet," he says, "you must go gallivanting about," he says, "you can't sit down for five minutes. You moan you never sit down, and when you get the chance you don't sit down." So he said "Did you get your sandals?" So Terry said "No Dad, she spent the money on the deposit." He said "The deposit? For what?" He said "the bungalow!" He said "You haven't—." I said "Yes—I've got a bungalow." He says "Well—how are you going to manage it now? Now come on mate, let's work it out," he said, "there's the fares down, that's going to cost us at least thirty shillings." He said, "There's the four pound fifteen to be found for the lodgings." He said, "The boys will want little odds and ends and little extras, you know that." I said,—and gradually, we went over each item—I said "I've covered them all," I said. I said the family allowance would cover the clothing problem and I had him stymied at every problem he brought up. I said I'd put points away to save for the food and I said the fares would come out of his week's allowance that he'd get from his holiday money—you see, he'd get a week's holiday money in advance—and the ordinary housekeeping money they gave me would pay for all our food. We wouldn't eat any more food. Now he's getting holidays with pay, that week would help us to tide over, you see. That would pay the necessaries, and the eldest boy but one, he does a grocery round and I'm sure he'd pool his pocket money to help the other boys out, and one by one, we went over everything. That was O.K. We relaxed and sat there running it over in our minds and we were there according to ourselves, and all of a sudden Father dropped a bombshell and he said, "I thought there was something said about me getting a new pair of flannels." So "Uh! uh!" I thought, "How do you do!" Anyway, we talked *that* over, and I decided that if I could get a bit of material I could make him a pair. It was my first attempt at flannels. I'd made pajamas, but nothing so good as flannels, but we thought we'd give it a try, and indeed, I got the stuff. The stuff cost just over one pound. And they turned out quite O.K. Anyway, they suited Father and that's saying something. . . . The week following I didn't touch my fat ration[4] so that we could have a—we could put butter on the bread without scraping it on, and we could have it just how we wanted it, and also I—every little thing I could save up, I did. Everybody had a box and everybody saved, even to the baby—he saved too. He has his little box. . . . So the grand day came for the holiday. Well, the weather was lovely and we traveled down on the Saturday. The train journey was quite easy because we chose a time, it was the end of August—we chose a time when everybody else had had their holiday, and the day we got down there we just had a quick eggs and bacon—well Daddy and I had a quick eggs and bacon dinner, and all the boys, with the exception of the wee one—he stayed with us—all the boys flocked to the beach, collecting themselves a fish and chip dinner on the way, and they thought that was fun having it out of the newspaper.[5] That was grand. And on the Sunday, the boys all got ready—on the Sunday they all got ready and had a quick breakfast and went down to the beach. And of course, I was clearing the dishes up and the landlady and I got together. And I cooked a whole batch of pastry in her kitchen. She was very sweet about it. She even got me the apples out of her orchard and peeled them for me—helped me, so that lets you see what she was like—she made you feel right at home. They put themselves out to make us feel at home. And a most unheard of thing, that Sunday morning I had three hours relaxation in a deckchair and we had our dinners bang-on[6] at one o'clock. And the boys went on ahead, down to the beach, and Daddy and I followed afterwards. And there were

4 **fat ration:** amount of butter and other fats allowed per person per week.
5 **newspaper:** Fish and chips ("french fries") are sold in cones made of newspaper.
6 **bang-on:** exactly.

just one or two people on the beach. We found a nice spot to ourselves—the boys weren't in sight and I never bothered about that for the simple reason my boys always find me when their tummy calls. We never bother. I was sitting there very peaceful, young David at our feet playing, and I said to Daddy, "This must be like how people feel who's only got one child—just the one at your feet all peaceful and quiet." He said "Yes it must be, mate,"[7] and all of a sudden, there was a terrific "hallo" across the beach "Mam, Mam, Mam" . . . and I said "Don't look mate, don't look for goodness sake," and there were three figures coming across the beach, plastered from head to toe in thick black mud—thick black mud! I said "Oh my goodness!" and as they got up to us, they did a merry war dance round us chanting "Down on the beach there's lots of mud,—smack it on and slap it on it will do you plenty good," so—after Father had chased them down and got them clean we tried to get a snap[8] of them. We got them all lined up beautifully, and I said "Right Dad—get them now." And then all of a sudden Terry said "Look Dad, our Ted's pulling a face like a monkey—like this," and so the snap turned out with them both looking like monkeys. Anyway, we're keeping it—it's awfully good. . . .

It may seem a dull holiday to some people but the great thing about it was it was so unexpected—everything went right— not a thing went wrong, the weather was lovely, no tempers were lost and everybody was kind, even the landlady. So that the really unexpected thing about it all was it came up to all our expectations and we'd been without a holiday for nearly ten years at that.

And it was all done for under fourteen pounds, the whole lot of us bang-on. What do you think of that?

7 **mate:** a common form of address; perhaps "pal" is the nearest American equivalent.
8 **snap:** snapshot.

At war or in peace, at work or play, the English are a reserved and puzzling nation. They rarely complain or grumble, but they will not submit to dictation; they are given to understating their experience, but their awareness and perceptions are acute; they believe in privacy, but they love companionship. Perhaps the following passage, by the novelist E. M. Forster, who has supplied us with the motto for this chapter, sums up the mystery of the British character as neatly and as wittily as it can be done.

THE LAST WORD *

The trouble is that the English nature is not at all easy to understand. It has a great air of simplicity, it advertises itself as simple, but the more we consider it, the greater the problems we shall encounter. People talk of the mysterious East, but the

* From *Abinger Harvest,* copyright, 1936, 1964, by E. M. Forster. Reprinted by permission of Harcourt Brace Jovanovich, Inc., and Edward Arnold (Publishers) Ltd.

West also is mysterious. It has depths that do not reveal themselves at the first gaze. We know what the sea looks like from a distance: it is of one color, and level, and obviously cannot contain such creatures as fish. But if we look into the sea over the edge of a boat, we see a dozen colors, and depth below depth, and fish swimming in them. That sea is the English character—apparently imperturbable and even. The depths and the colors are the English romanticism and the English sensitiveness—we do not expect to find such things, but they exist. And—to continue my metaphor—the fish are the English emotions, which are always trying to get up to the surface, but don't quite know how. For the most part we see them moving far below, distorted and obscure. Now and then they succeed and we exclaim, "Why, the Englishman has emotions! He actually can feel!" And occasionally we see that beautiful creature the flying fish, which rises out of the water altogether into the air and the sunlight. English literature is a flying fish. It is a sample of the life that goes on day after day beneath the surface; it is a proof that beauty and emotion exist in the salt, inhospitable sea.

The Literature of

The Twentieth Century

The Need for Renewal

ALTHOUGH LITERARY periods are often assigned dates that come from political history (and although they often coincide with periods of political history), we nevertheless distinguish any period of literature from that which precedes it by observing a change of interest, of concern, and of expectation in the works of a cluster of writers. We begin to hear new voices.

In the first quarter of the 20th century, and particularly in the years during and following the first World War, a number of such new voices began to be heard. Some were tragically cut off by that war. Others—two of whom you will shortly be reading—went on to influence and shape a revolution in English literature as decisive as that made by the Romantic poets. It was a literary revolution that met the need for renewal.

Many Victorian writers, as you have seen, described the spiritual adventure of passing from an "everlasting no" to an "everlasting yes." Like Tennyson in *In Memoriam*, or Mill in his *Autobiography*, they described personal crises, crises of feeling in themselves, in which they moved from doubt, uncertainty, and spiritual deadness to hope, confidence, and a zest for productive life.

Something like this adventure has been recorded by many 20th-century writers. For them, however, the "no," the state of despair from which they tried to free themselves, has been pressing and immediate. From the beginning of this century the major writers have felt an oppression, a deadness, a sense of drift, in the very society surrounding them. They have had to move, not just from personal crises, but from crises of feeling and of direction that they felt they shared with others. Their passage to new certainty, new freedom—to a new "yes"—has accordingly been more painful and difficult.

In presenting their new conception of an old adventure, modern writers have been compelled to use new techniques, sometimes drastically new methods of composition. While these new methods often mean difficulties for the reader, as some of the following selections will reveal, they also show us how thoroughly the modern writer has concentrated on his or her task.

E. M. Forster (1879-1970)

The following story was written about fifty years ago by Edward Morgan Forster (usually known as E. M. Forster), a writer who returned to live in the Cambridge where he was at college more than sixty years ago. Forster wrote all but one of his five novels before World War I; his best-known, *A Passage to India*, was published in 1924. It describes not only the conflicts between the English and the then colonial Indians but also the subtle conflicts among the Indians themselves. Since this last novel he has published a well-known critical book, *Aspects of the Novel*, and a number of essays on moral and political matters. Through all his works there runs a conviction that he phrased in an essay published in 1939. "Where do I start?" he asked. And he answered decisively: "With personal relationships." Forster's writings return again and again to this subject, and you will readily see how it appears in the following story. He here places in opposition the humanity of personal relationships and the inhumanity of a planned society in which even parents and children rarely confront each other, and in which "direct experience" is the one thing to be feared before all else. The time of this story is to be imagined as far in the future: remember that it was written before 1914, and that its mixture of prophecy and fantasy was a good deal stranger then than it might appear now.

The Machine Stops[*]

E. M. Forster

Part I

THE AIRSHIP

IMAGINE, if you can, a small room, hexagonal in shape, like the cell of a bee. It is lighted neither by window nor by lamp, yet it is filled with a soft radiance. There are no apertures for ventilation, yet the air is fresh. There are no musical instruments, and yet, at the moment that my meditation opens, this room is throbbing with melodious sounds. An armchair is in the center, by its side a reading desk—that is all the furniture. And in the armchair there sits a swaddled lump of flesh—a woman, about five feet high, with a face as white as a fungus. It is to her that the little room belongs.

An electric bell rang.

The woman touched a switch and the music was silent.

"I suppose I must see who it is," she thought, and set her chair in motion. The chair, like the music, was worked by machinery, and it rolled her to the other side of the room, where the bell still rang importunately.

"Who is it?" she called. Her voice was irritable, for she had been interrupted often since the **music** began.

* From *The Eternal Moment and Other Stories* by E. M. Forster, copyright, 1928, by Harcourt Brace Jovanovich, Inc.; renewed, 1956, by E. M. Forster. Reprinted by permission of the publishers.

She knew several thousand people; in certain directions human intercourse had advanced enormously.

But when she listened into the receiver, her white face wrinkled into smiles, and she said:

"Very well. Let us talk, I will isolate myself. I do not expect anything important will happen for the next five minutes—for I can give you fully five minutes, Kuno. Then I must deliver my lecture on 'Music during the Australian Period.'"

She touched the isolation knob, so that no one else could speak to her. Then she touched the lighting apparatus, and the little room was plunged into darkness.

"Be quick!" she called, her irritation returning. "Be quick, Kuno; here I am in the dark wasting my time."

But it was fully fifteen seconds before the round plate that she held in her hands began to glow. A faint blue light shot across it, darkening to purple, and presently she could see the image of her son, who lived on the other side of the earth, and he could see her.

"Kuno, how slow you are."

He smiled gravely.

"I really believe you enjoy dawdling."

"I have called you before, Mother, but you were always busy or isolated. I have something particular to say."

"What is it, dearest boy? Be quick. Why could you not send it by pneumatic post?"[1]

"Because I prefer saying such a thing. I want——"

"Well?"

"I want you to come and see me."

Vashti watched his face in the blue plate.

"But I can see you!" she exclaimed.

1 pneumatic post: a system of transmitting mail in capsules shot through tubes by air pressure.

"What more do you want?"

"I want to see you not through the Machine," said Kuno. "I want to speak to you not through the wearisome Machine."

"Oh, hush!" said his mother, vaguely shocked. "You mustn't say anything against the Machine."

"Why not?"

"One mustn't."

"You talk as if a god had made the Machine," cried the other. "I believe that you pray to it when you are unhappy. Men made it, do not forget that. Great men, but men. The Machine is much, but it is not everything. I see something like you in this plate, but I do not see you. I hear something like you through this telephone, but I do not hear you. That is why I want you to come. Come and stop with me. Pay me a visit, so that we can meet face to face, and talk about the hopes that are in my mind."

She replied that she could scarcely spare the time for a visit.

"The airship barely takes two days to fly between me and you."

"I dislike airships."

"Why?"

"I dislike seeing the horrible brown earth, and the sea, and the stars when it is dark. I get no ideas in an airship."

"I do not get them anywhere else."

"What kind of ideas can the air give you?"

He paused for an instant.

"Do you not know four big stars that form an oblong, and three stars close together in the middle of the oblong, and hanging from these stars, three other stars?"

"No, I do not. I dislike the stars. But did they give you an idea? How interesting; tell me."

"I had an idea that they were like a man."

"I do not understand."

"The four big stars are the man's shoulders and his knees. The three stars in the middle are like the belts that men wore once, and the three stars hanging are like a sword."

"A sword?"

"Men carried swords about with them, to kill animals and other men."

"It does not strike me as a very good idea, but it is certainly original. When did it come to you first?"

"In the airship——" He broke off, and she fancied that he looked sad. She could not be sure, for the Machine did not transmit nuances of expression. It only gave a general idea of people— an idea that was good enough for all practical purposes, Vashti thought. The imponderable bloom, declared by a discredited philosophy to be the actual essence of intercourse, was rightly ignored by the Machine, just as the imponderable bloom of the grape was ignored by the manufacturers of artificial fruit. Something "good enough" had long since been accepted by our race.

"The truth is," he continued, "that I want to see these stars again. They are curious stars. I want to see them not from the airship, but from the surface of the earth, as our ancestors did, thousands of years ago. I want to visit the surface of the earth."

She was shocked again.

"Mother, you must come, if only to explain to me what is the harm of visiting the surface of the earth."

"No harm," she replied, controlling herself. "But no advantage. The surface of the earth is only dust and mud, no life remains on it, and you would need a respirator, or the cold of the outer air would kill you. One dies immediately in the outer air."

"I know; of course I shall take all precautions."

"And besides——"

"Well?"

She considered, and chose her words with care. Her son had a queer temper, and she wished to dissuade him from the expedition.

"It is contrary to the spirit of the age," she asserted.

"Do you mean by that, contrary to the Machine?"

"In a sense, but——"

His image in the blue plate faded.

"Kuno!"

He had isolated himself.

For a moment Vashti felt lonely.

Then she generated the light, and the sight of her room, flooded with radiance and studded with electric buttons, revived her. There were buttons and switches everywhere—buttons to call for food, for music, for clothing. There was the hot-bath button, by pressure of which a basin of (imitation) marble rose out of the floor, filled to the brim with a warm deodorized liquid. There was the cold-bath button. There was the button that produced literature. And there were of course the buttons by which she communicated with her friends. The room, though it contained nothing, was in touch with all that she cared for in the world.

Vashti's next move was to turn off the isolation switch, and all the accumulations of the last three minutes burst upon her. The room was filled with the noise of bells, and speaking tubes. What was the new food like? Could she recommend it? Had she had any ideas lately? Might one tell her one's own ideas? Would she make an engagement to visit the public nurseries at an early date?—say this day month.[2]

To most of these questions she replied with irritation—a growing quality

in that accelerated age. She said that the new food was horrible. That she could not visit the public nurseries through press of engagements. That she had no ideas of her own but had just been told one—that four stars and three in the middle were like a man: she doubted there was much in it. Then she switched off her correspondents, for it was time to deliver her lecture on Australian music.

The clumsy system of public gatherings had been long since abandoned; neither Vashti nor her audience stirred from their rooms. Seated in her armchair she spoke, while they in their armchairs heard her, fairly well, and saw her, fairly well. She opened with a humorous account of music in the pre-Mongolian epoch,[3] and went on to describe the great outburst of song that followed the Chinese conquest. Remote and primeval as were the methods of I-San-So and the Brisbane school, she yet felt (she said) that study of them might repay the musician of today: they had freshness; they had, above all, ideas.

Her lecture, which lasted ten minutes, was well received, and at its conclusion she and many of her audience listened to a lecture on the sea; there were ideas to be got from the sea; the speaker had donned a respirator and visited it lately. Then she fed, talked to many friends, had a bath, talked again, and summoned her bed.

The bed was not to her liking. It was too large, and she had a feeling for a small bed. Complaint was useless, for beds were of the same dimension all over the world, and to have had an alternative size would have in-

---

[3] **pre-Mongolian epoch:** the first of several pretended historical terms. Vashti and Kuno live in a time so far in the future that our epoch is presumably to them about as far in the past as the Dark Ages are to us.

[2] **this day month:** a month from today.

volved vast alterations in the Machine. Vashti isolated herself—it was necessary, for neither day nor night existed under the ground—and reviewed all that had happened since she had summoned the bed last. Ideas? Scarcely any. Events—was Kuno's invitation an event?

By her side, on the little reading desk, was a survival from the ages of litter—one book. This was the Book of the Machine. In it were instructions against every possible contingency. If she was hot or cold or dyspeptic or at loss for a word, she went to the book, and it told her which button to press. The Central Committee published it. In accordance with a growing habit, it was richly bound.

Sitting up in the bed, she took it reverently in her hands. She glanced round the glowing room as if someone might be watching her. Then, half ashamed, half joyful, she murmured "O Machine! O Machine!" and raised the volume to her lips. Thrice she kissed it, thrice inclined her head, thrice she felt the delirium of acquiescence. Her ritual performed, she turned to page 1367, which gave the times of the departure of the airships from the island in the southern hemisphere, under whose soil she lived, to the island in the northern hemisphere, whereunder lived her son.

She thought, "I have not the time."

She made the room dark and slept; she awoke and made the room light; she ate and exchanged ideas with her friends, and listened to music and attended lectures; she made the room dark and slept. Above her, beneath her, and around her, the Machine hummed eternally; she did not notice the noise, for she had been born with it in her ears. The earth, carrying her, hummed as it sped through silence, turning her now to the invisible sun, now to the invisible stars. She awoke and made the room light.

"Kuno!"

"I will not talk to you," he answered, "until you come."

"Have you been on the surface of the earth since we spoke last?"

His image faded.

Again she consulted the book. She became very nervous and lay back in her chair palpitating. Think of her as without teeth or hair. Presently she directed the chair to the wall, and pressed an unfamiliar button. The wall swung apart slowly. Through the opening she saw a tunnel that curved slightly, so that its goal was not visible. Should she go to see her son, here was the beginning of the journey.

Of course she knew all about the communication system. There was nothing mysterious in it. She would summon a car and it would fly with her down the tunnel until it reached the lift that communicated with the airship station: the system had been in use for many, many years, long before the universal establishment of the Machine. And of course she had studied the civilization that had immediately preceded her own—the civilization that had mistaken the functions of the system, and had used it for bringing people to things, instead of for bringing things to people. Those funny old days, when men went for change of air instead of changing the air in their rooms! And yet—she was frightened of the tunnel: she had not seen it since her last child was born. It curved—but not quite as she remembered; it was brilliant—but not quite as brilliant as a lecturer had suggested. Vashti was seized with the terrors of direct experience. She shrank back into the room, and the wall closed up again.

Writers have often described fantastic worlds, as Forster does in "The Machine Stops." Sir Thomas More's Utopia *(meaning, literally, "no place") of the 16th century describes the mythical kingdom of Utopia, comparing England unfavorably with it.* The Plan of Utopia *(left) is from a 1518 edition. The utopia in Francis Godwin's* Man in the Moone *(1638) is out of this world—on the moon. The hero is carried there by wild swans who fly in harness.*

"Kuno," she said, "I cannot come to see you. I am not well."

Immediately an enormous apparatus fell on to her out of the ceiling, a thermometer was automatically inserted between her lips, a stethoscope was automatically laid upon her heart. She lay powerless. Cool pads soothed her forehead. Kuno had telegraphed to her doctor.

So the human passions still blundered up and down in the Machine. Vashti drank the medicine that the doctor projected into her mouth, and the machinery retired into the ceiling. The voice of Kuno was heard asking how she felt.

"Better." Then with irritation: "But why do you not come to me instead?"

"Because I cannot leave this place."

"Why?"

"Because, any moment, something tremendous may happen."

"Have you been on the surface of the earth yet?"

"Not yet."

"Then what is it?"

"I will not tell you through the Machine."

She resumed her life.

But she thought of Kuno as a baby, his birth, his removal to the public nurseries, her one visit to him there, his visits to her—visits which stopped when the Machine had assigned him a room on the other side of the earth. "Parents, duties of," said the book of the Machine, "cease at the moment of birth. P. 42232-7483." True, but there was something special about Kuno—indeed there had been something special about all her children—and, after all, she must brave the journey if he desired it. And "something tremendous might happen." What did that mean? The nonsense of a youthful man, no doubt, but she must go. Again she pressed the unfamiliar button, again the wall swung back, and she saw the tunnel that curved out of sight. Clasping the Book, she rose, tottered on to the platform, and summoned the car. Her room closed behind her: the journey to the northern hemisphere had begun.

Of course it was perfectly easy. The car approached and in it she found armchairs exactly like her own. When she signaled, it stopped, and she tottered into the lift.[4] One other passenger was in the lift, the first fellow creature she had seen face to face for months. Few traveled in these days, for, thanks to the advance of science, the earth was exactly alike all over. Rapid intercourse, from which the previous civilization had hoped so much, had ended by defeating itself. What was the good of going to Pekin when it was just like Shrewsbury? Why return to Shrewsbury when it would be just like Pekin? Men seldom moved their bodies; all unrest was concentrated in the soul.

The airship service was a relic from the former age. It was kept up, because it was easier to keep it up than to stop it or to diminish it, but it now far exceeded the wants of the population. Vessel after vessel would rise from the vomitories[5] of Rye or of Christchurch

(I use the antique names), would sail into the crowded sky, and would draw up at the wharves of the south—empty. So nicely adjusted was the system, so independent of meteorology, that the sky, whether calm or cloudy, resembled a vast kaleidoscope whereon the same patterns periodically recurred. The ship on which Vashti sailed started now at sunset, now at dawn. But always, as it passed above Rheims, it would neighbor the ship that served between Helsingfors and the Brazils, and, every third time it surmounted the Alps, the fleet of Palermo would cross its track behind. Night and day, wind and storm, tide and earthquake, impeded man no longer. He had harnessed Leviathan.[6] All the old literature, with its praise of Nature, and its fear of Nature, rang false as the prattle of a child.

Yet as Vashti saw the vast flank of the ship, stained with exposure to the outer air, her horror of direct experience returned. It was not quite like the airship in the cinematophote.[7] For one thing it smelt—not strongly or unpleasantly, but it did smell, and with her eyes shut she should have known that a new thing was close to her. Then she had to walk to it from the lift, had to submit to glances from the other passengers. The man in front dropped his Book—no great matter, but it disquieted them all. In the rooms, if the Book was dropped, the floor raised it mechanically, but the gangway to the airship was not so prepared, and the sacred volume lay motionless. They stopped—the thing was unforeseen—and

underground cities of each hemisphere with the surface of the earth. Rye is in southern England; Christchurch is in New Zealand. To ascend through a "vomitory" to an airship one needs an "Egression-permit"—a permit to go out.
6 Leviathan (lĭ vī′ə thən): in the Bible, a sea monster; here a symbol of the great energies of nature.
7 cinematophote: another elaborate, invented word; presumably a kind of television screen.

4 lift: elevator.
5 vomitories: a pedantic or high-sounding word for the deep elevator shafts that connect the

THE TWENTIETH CENTURY

the man, instead of picking up his property, felt the muscles of his arm to see how they had failed him. Then someone actually said with direct utterance: "We shall be late"—and they trooped on board, Vashti treading on the pages as she did so.

Inside, her anxiety increased. The arrangements were old-fashioned and rough. There was even a female attendant, to whom she would have to announce her wants during the voyage. Of course a revolving platform ran the length of the boat, but she was expected to walk from it to her cabin. Some cabins were better than others, and she did not get the best. She thought the attendant had been unfair, and spasms of rage shook her. The glass valves had closed, she could not go back. She saw, at the end of the vestibule, the lift in which she had ascended going quietly up and down, empty. Beneath those corridors of shining tiles were rooms, tier below tier, reaching far into the earth, and in each room there sat a human being, eating, or sleeping, or producing ideas. And buried deep in the hive was her own room. Vashti was afraid.

"O Machine! O Machine!" she murmured, and caressed her Book, and was comforted.

Then the sides of the vestibule seemed to melt together, as do the passages that we see in dreams, the lift vanished, the Book that had been dropped slid to the left and vanished, polished tiles rushed by like a stream of water, there was a slight jar, and the airship, issuing from its tunnel, soared above the waters of a tropical ocean.

It was night. For a moment she saw the coast of Sumatra edged by the phosphorescence of waves, and crowned by lighthouses, still sending forth their disregarded beams. These also vanished, and only the stars distracted her. They were not motionless, but swayed to and fro above her head, thronging out of one skylight into another, as if the universe and not the airship was careening. And, as often happens on clear nights, they seemed now to be in perspective, now on a plane; now piled tier beyond tier into the infinite heavens, now concealing infinity, a roof limiting forever the visions of men. In either case they seemed intolerable. "Are we to travel in the dark?" called the passengers angrily, and the attendant, who had been careless, generated the light, and pulled down the blinds of pliable metal. When the airships had been built, the desire to look direct at things still lingered in the world. Hence the extraordinary number of skylights and windows, and the proportionate discomfort to those who were civilized and refined. Even in Vashti's cabin one star peeped through a flaw in the blind, and after a few hours' uneasy slumber, she was disturbed by an unfamiliar glow, which was the dawn.

Quick as the ship had sped westwards, the earth had rolled eastwards quicker still, and had dragged back Vashti and her companions toward the sun. Science could prolong the night, but only for a little, and those high hopes of neutralizing the earth's diurnal revolution had passed, together with hopes that were possibly higher. To "keep pace with the sun," or even to outstrip it, had been the aim of the civilization preceding this. Racing aeroplanes had been built for the purpose, capable of enormous speed, and steered by the greatest intellects of the epoch. Round the globe they went, round and round, westward, westward, round and round, amidst humanity's applause. In vain. The globe went eastward quicker still, horrible accidents occurred, and the Committee of the Machine, at the time rising into prominence, declared the pursuit illegal, unmechanical, and punishable by Homelessness.

Of Homelessness more will be said later.

Doubtless the Committee was right. Yet the attempt to "defeat the sun" aroused the last common interest that our race experienced about the heavenly bodies, or indeed about anything. It was the last time that men were compacted by thinking of a power outside the world. The sun had conquered, yet it was the end of his spiritual dominion. Dawn, midday, twilight, the zodiacal path, touched neither men's lives nor their hearts, and science retreated into the ground, to concentrate herself upon problems that she was certain of solving.

So when Vashti found her cabin invaded by a rosy finger of light, she was annoyed, and tried to adjust the blind. But the blind flew up altogether, and she saw through the skylight small pink clouds, swaying against a background of blue, and as the sun crept higher, its radiance entered direct, brimming down the wall, like a golden sea. It rose and fell with the airship's motion, just as waves rise and fall, but it advanced steadily, as a tide advances. Unless she was careful, it would strike her face. A spasm of horror shook her and she rang for the attendant. The attendant too was horrified, but she could do nothing; it was not her place to mend the blind. She could only suggest that the lady should change her cabin, which she accordingly prepared to do.

People were almost exactly alike all over the world, but the attendant of the airship, perhaps owing to her exceptional duties, had grown a little out of the common. She had often to address passengers with direct speech, and this had given her a certain roughness and

originality of manner. When Vashti swerved away from the sunbeams with a cry, she behaved barbarically—she put out her hand to steady her.

"How dare you!" exclaimed the passenger. "You forget yourself!"

The woman was confused, and apologized for not having let her fall. People never touched one another. The custom had become obsolete, owing to the Machine.

"Where are we now?" asked Vashti haughtily.

"We are over Asia," said the attendant, anxious to be polite.

"Asia?"

"You must excuse my common way of speaking. I have got into the habit of calling places over which I pass by their unmechanical names."

"Oh, I remember Asia. The Mongols came from it."

"Beneath us, in the open air, stood a city that was once called Simla."

"Have you ever heard of the Mongols and of the Brisbane school?"

"No."

"Brisbane also stood in the open air."

"Those mountains to the right—let me show you them." She pushed back a metal blind. The main chain of the Himalayas was revealed. "They were once called the Roof of the World, those mountains."

"What a foolish name!"

"You must remember that, before the dawn of civilization, they seemed to be an impenetrable wall that touched the stars. It was supposed that no one but the gods could exist above their summits. How we have advanced, thanks to the Machine!"

"How we have advanced, thanks to the Machine!" said Vashti.

"How we have advanced, thanks to the Machine!" echoed the passenger who had dropped his Book the night before, and who was standing in the passage.

"And that white stuff in the cracks?—what is it?"

"I have forgotten its name."

"Cover the window, please. These mountains give me no ideas."

The northern aspect of the Himalayas was in deep shadow: on the Indian slope the sun had just prevailed. The forests had been destroyed during the literature epoch for the purpose of making newspaper-pulp, but the snows were awakening to their morning glory, and clouds still hung on the breasts of Kinchinjunga. In the plain were seen the ruins of cities, with diminished rivers creeping by their walls, and by the sides of these were sometimes the signs of vomitories, marking the cities of to-day. Over the whole prospect airships rushed, crossing and intercrossing with incredible aplomb, and rising nonchalantly when they desired to escape the perturbations of the lower atmosphere and to traverse the Roof of the World.

"We have indeed advanced, thanks to the Machine," repeated the attendant, and hid the Himalayas behind a metal blind.

The day dragged wearily forward. The passengers sat each in his cabin, avoiding one another with an almost physical repulsion and longing to be once more under the surface of the earth. There were eight or ten of them, mostly young males, sent out from the public nurseries to inhabit the rooms of those who had died in various parts of the earth. The man who had dropped his Book was on the homeward journey. He had been sent to Sumatra for the purpose of propagating the race. Vashti alone was traveling by her private will.

At midday she took a second glance at the earth. The airship was crossing another range of mountains, but she could see little, owing to clouds. Masses of black rock hovered below her, and merged indistinctly into gray. Their shapes were fantastic; one of them resembled a prostrate man.

"No ideas here," murmured Vashti, and hid the Caucasus behind a metal blind.

In the evening she looked again. They were crossing a golden sea, in which lay many small islands and one peninsula.

She repeated, "No ideas here," and hid Greece behind a metal blind.

Part II

THE MENDING APPARATUS

By a vestibule, by a lift, by a tubular railway, by a platform, by a sliding door—by reversing all the steps of her departure did Vashti arrive at her son's room, which exactly resembled her own. She might well declare that the visit was superfluous. The buttons, the knobs, the reading desk with the Book, the temperature, the atmosphere, the illumination—all were exactly the same. And if Kuno himself, flesh of her flesh, stood close beside her at last, what profit was there in that? She was too well-bred to shake him by the hand.

Averting her eyes, she spoke as follows:

"Here I am. I have had the most terrible journey and greatly retarded the development of my soul. It is not worth it, Kuno, it is not worth it. My time is too precious. The sunlight almost touched me, and I have met with the rudest people. I can only stop a few minutes. Say what you want to say, and then I must return."

"I have been threatened with Homelessness," said Kuno.

She looked at him now.

"I have been threatened with Homelessness, and I could not tell you such a thing through the Machine."

Homelessness means death. The victim is exposed to the air, which kills him.

"I have been outside since I spoke to you last. The tremendous thing has happened, and they have discovered me."

"But why shouldn't you go outside!" she exclaimed. "It is perfectly legal, perfectly mechanical, to visit the surface of the earth. I have lately been to a lecture on the sea; there is no objection to that; one simply summons a respirator and gets an Egression-permit. It is not the kind of thing that spiritually minded people do, and I begged you not to do it, but there is no legal objection to it."

"I did not get an Egression-permit."

"Then how did you get out?"

"I found out a way of my own."

The phrase conveyed no meaning to her, and he had to repeat it.

"A way of your own?" she whispered. "But that would be wrong."

"Why?"

The question shocked her beyond measure.

"You are beginning to worship the Machine," he said coldly. "You think it irreligious of me to have found out a way of my own. It was just what the Committee thought, when they threatened me with Homelessness."

At this she grew angry. "I worship nothing!" she cried. "I am most advanced. I don't think you irreligious, for there is no such thing as religion left. All the fear and the superstition that existed once have been destroyed by the Machine. I only meant that to find out a way of your own was—— Besides, there is no new way out."

"So it is always supposed."

"Except through the vomitories, for which one must have an Egression-permit, it is impossible to get out. The Book says so."

"Well, the Book's wrong, for I have been out on my feet."

For Kuno was possessed of a certain physical strength.

By these days it was a demerit to be muscular. Each infant was examined at birth, and all who promised undue strength were destroyed. Humanitarians may protest, but it would have been no true kindness to let an athlete live; he would never have been happy in that state of life to which the Machine had called him; he would have yearned for trees to climb, rivers to bathe in, meadows and hills against which he might measure his body. Man must be adapted to his surroundings, must he not? In the dawn of the world our weakly must be exposed on Mount Taygetus,[8] in its twilight our strong will suffer euthanasia, that the Machine may progress, that the Machine may progress, that the Machine may progress eternally.

"You know that we have lost the sense of space. We say 'space is annihilated,' but we have annihilated not space, but the sense thereof. We have lost a part of ourselves. I determined to recover it, and I began by walking up and down the platform of the railway outside my room. Up and down, until I was tired, and so did recapture the meaning of 'Near' and 'Far.' 'Near' is a place to which I can get quickly *on my feet*, not a place to which the train or the airship will take me quickly. 'Far' is a place to which I cannot get quickly on my feet; the vomitory is 'far,' though

8 **Mount Taygetus** (tā ĭ′jə təs): a wild and rugged mountain in the ancient Greek land of the Spartans. Sparta was a military kingdom governed by harsh laws and customs, among them the custom of putting weak or deformed infants out into the hills to die of exposure.

I could be there in thirty-eight seconds by summoning the train. Man is the measure. That was my first lesson. Man's feet are the measure for distance, his hands are the measure for ownership, his body is the measure for all that is lovable and desirable and strong. Then I went further: it was then that I called to you for the first time, and you would not come.

"This city, as you know, is built deep beneath the surface of the earth, with only the vomitories protruding. Having paced the platform outside my own room, I took the lift to the next platform and paced that also, and so with each in turn, until I came to the topmost, above which begins the earth. All the platforms were exactly alike, and all that I gained by visiting them was to develop my sense of space and my muscles. I think I should have been content with this—it is not a little thing—but as I walked and brooded, it occurred to me that our cities had been built in the days when men still breathed the outer air, and that there had been ventilation shafts for the workmen. I could think of nothing but these ventilation shafts. Had they been destroyed by all the food-tubes and medicine-tubes and music-tubes that the Machine has evolved lately? Or did traces of them remain? One thing was certain. If I came upon them anywhere, it would be in the railway tunnels of the topmost story. Everywhere else, all space was accounted for.

"I am telling my story quickly, but don't think that I was not a coward or that your answers never depressed me. It is not the proper thing, it is not mechanical, it is not decent to walk along a railway tunnel. I did not fear that I might tread upon a live rail and be killed. I feared something far more intangible—doing what was not contemplated by the Machine. Then I said to myself, 'Man is the measure,' and I went, and after many visits I found an opening.

"The tunnels, of course, were lighted. Everything is light, artificial light; darkness is the exception. So when I saw a black gap in the tiles, I knew that it was an exception, and rejoiced. I put in my arm—I could put in no more at first—and waved it round and round in ecstasy. I loosened another tile, and put in my head, and shouted into the darkness: 'I am coming, I shall do it yet,' and my voice reverberated down endless passages. I seemed to hear the spirits of those dead workmen who had returned each evening to the starlight and to their wives, and all the generations who had lived in the open air called back to me, 'You will do it yet, you are coming.'"

He paused, and, absurd as he was, his last words moved her. For Kuno had lately asked to be a father, and his request had been refused by the Committee. His was not a type that the Machine desired to hand on.

"Then a train passed. It brushed by me, but I thrust my head and arms into the hole. I had done enough for one day, so I crawled back to the platform, went down in the lift, and summoned my bed. Ah, what dreams! And again I called you, and again you refused."

She shook her head and said:

"Don't. Don't talk of these terrible things. You make me miserable. You are throwing civilization away."

"But I had got back the sense of space and a man cannot rest then. I determined to get in at the hole and climb the shaft. And so I exercised my arms. Day after day I went through ridiculous movements, until my flesh ached, and I could hang by my hands and hold the pillow of my bed out-

The tradition of utopian literature was carried on in the 19th century. William Morris's News from Nowhere *looks forward to a social paradise. The frontispiece to the book (left) symbolizes the fulfillment of the dreams of 19th-century socialism. But in Jules Verne's reverse utopia in* The Begum's Fortune *(1879), humanity is mastered by the machine. "Stahlstadt" (right) is a huge munitions factory run like a concentration camp.*

stretched for many minutes. Then I summoned a respirator, and started.

"It was easy at first. The mortar had somehow rotted, and I soon pushed some more tiles in, and clambered after them into the darkness, and the spirits of the dead comforted me. I don't know what I mean by that. I just say what I felt. I felt, for the first time, that a protest had been lodged against corruption, and that even as the dead were comforting me, so I was comforting the unborn. I felt that humanity existed, and that it existed without clothes. How can I possibly explain this? It was naked, humanity seemed naked, and all these tubes and buttons and machineries neither came into the world with us, nor will they follow us

out, nor do they matter supremely while we are here. Had I been strong, I would have torn off every garment I had, and gone out into the outer air unswaddled. But this is not for me, nor perhaps for my generation. I climbed with my respirator and my hygienic clothes and my dietetic tabloids![9] Better thus than not at all.

"There was a ladder, made of some primeval metal.[10] The light from the railway fell upon its lowest rungs, and I saw that it led straight upwards out of the rubble at the bottom of the shaft. Perhaps our ancestors ran up and down it a dozen times daily, in their building.

9 dietetic tabloids: food pills.
10 primeval (prī mē′vəl) **metal:** Presumably the men of the future will have developed new alloys and metals; steel would then be "primeval."

As I climbed, the rough edges cut through my gloves so that my hands bled. The light helped me for a little, and then came darkness and, worse still, silence which pierced my ears like a sword. The Machine hums! Did you know that? Its hum penetrates our blood, and may even guide our thoughts. Who knows! I was getting beyond its power. Then I thought: 'This silence means that I am doing wrong.' But I heard voices in the silence, and again they strengthened me." He laughed. "I had need of them. The next moment I cracked my head against something."

She sighed.

"I had reached one of those pneumatic stoppers[11] that defend us from the outer air. You may have noticed them on the airship. Pitch dark, my feet on the rungs of an invisible ladder, my hands cut; I cannot explain how I lived through this part, but the voices still comforted me, and I felt for fastenings. The stopper, I suppose, was about eight feet across. I passed my hand over it as far as I could reach. It was perfectly smooth. I felt it almost to the center. Not quite to the center, for my arm was too short. Then the voice said: 'Jump. It is worth it. There may be a handle in the center, and you may catch hold of it and so come to us your own way. And if there is no handle, so that you may fall and are dashed to pieces—it is still worth it: you will still come to us your own way.' So I jumped. There was a handle, and——"

He paused. Tears gathered in his mother's eyes. She knew that he was fated. If he did not die today he would die tomorrow. There was not room for such a person in the world. And with her pity disgust mingled. She was ashamed at having borne such a son, she who had always been so respectable and so full of ideas. Was he really the little boy to whom she had taught the use of his stops and buttons, and to whom she had given his first lessons in the Book? The very hair that disfigured his lip showed that he was reverting to some savage type. On atavism the Machine can have no mercy.

"There was a handle, and I did catch it. I hung tranced[12] over the darkness and heard the hum of these workings as the last whisper in a dying dream. All the things I had cared about and all the people I had spoken to through tubes appeared infinitely little. Meanwhile the handle revolved. My weight had set something in motion and I span slowly, and then——

"I cannot describe it. I was lying with my face to the sunshine. Blood poured from my nose and ears and I heard a tremendous roaring. The stopper, with me clinging to it, had simply been blown out of the earth, and the air that we make down here was escaping through the vent into the air above. It burst up like a fountain. I crawled back to it—for the upper air hurts—and, as it were, I took great sips from the edge. My respirator had flown goodness knows where, my clothes were torn. I just lay with my lips close to the hole, and I sipped until the bleeding stopped. You can imagine nothing so curious. This hollow in the grass—I will speak of it in a minute,—the sun shining into it, not brilliantly but through marbled clouds—the peace, the nonchalance, the sense of space, and, brushing my cheek, the roaring fountain of our artificial air! Soon I spied my respira-

11 **pneumatic stoppers:** The mine shafts made when the underground city was built, unlike the "vomitories," are sealed with a cap to hold in the rarefied air breathed by the worshipers of the Machine.

12 **tranced:** in a daze.

tor, bobbing up and down in the current high above my head, and higher still were many airships. But no one ever looks out of airships, and in my case they could not have picked me up. There I was, stranded. The sun shone a little way down the shaft, and revealed the topmost rung of the ladder, but it was hopeless trying to reach it. I should either have been tossed up again by the escape,[13] or else have fallen in, and died. I could only lie on the grass, sipping and sipping, and from time to time glancing around me.

"I knew that I was in Wessex,[14] for I had taken care to go to a lecture on the subject before starting. Wessex lies above the room in which we are talking now. It was once an important state. Its kings held all the southern coast from the Andredswald to Cornwall, while the Wansdyke protected them on the north, running over the high ground. The lecturer was only concerned with the rise of Wessex, so I do not know how long it remained an international power, nor would the knowledge have assisted me. To tell the truth I could do nothing but laugh, during this part. There was I, with a pneumatic stopper by my side and a respirator bobbing over my head, imprisoned, all three of us, in a grass-grown hollow that was edged with fern."

Then he grew grave again.

"Lucky for me that it was a hollow. For the air began to fall back into it and fill it as water fills a bowl. I could crawl about. Presently I stood. I breathed a mixture, in which the air that hurts predominated whenever I tried to climb the sides. This was not so bad. I had not lost my tabloids and remained ridiculously cheerful, and as for the Machine, I forgot about it altogether. My one aim now was to get to the top, where the ferns were, and to view whatever objects lay beyond.

"I rushed the slope. The new air was still too bitter for me and I came rolling back, after a momentary vision of something gray. The sun grew very feeble, and I remembered that he was in Scorpio[15]—I had been to a lecture on that too. If the sun is in Scorpio and you are in Wessex, it means that you must be as quick as you can, or it will get too dark. (This is the first bit of useful information I have ever got from a lecture, and I expect it will be the last.) It made me try frantically to breathe the new air, and to advance as far as I dared out of my pond.[16] The hollow filled so slowly. At times I thought that the fountain played with less vigor. My respirator seemed to dance nearer the earth; the roar was decreasing."

He broke off.

"I don't think this is interesting you. The rest will interest you even less. There are no ideas in it, and I wish that I had not troubled you to come. We are too different, Mother."

She told him to continue.

"It was evening before I climbed the bank. The sun had very nearly slipped out of the sky by this time, and I could not get a good view. You, who have just crossed the Roof of the World, will not want to hear an account of the little hills that I saw—low colorless hills. But to me they were living and the turf that covered them was a skin, under which their muscles rippled, and I felt that those hills had called with incalculable

13 tossed . . . by the escape: i.e., by the refined air pouring like a fountain from the shaft.
14 Wessex: the region southwest of London where the West Saxons under King Alfred ("Aelfrid," p. 749, col. 1) defeated the invading Danes in 987.

15 Scorpio: the eighth sign of the zodiac; the sun is "in" Scorpio beginning October 24.
16 out of my pond: i.e., the "pond" of air from underground that filled the bottom of the dell.

force to men in the past, and that men had loved them. Now they sleep—perhaps forever. They commune with humanity in dreams. Happy the man, happy the woman, who awakes the hills of Wessex. For though they sleep, they will never die."

His voice rose passionately.

"Cannot you see, cannot all your lecturers see, that it is we who are dying, and that down here the only thing that really lives is the Machine? We created the Machine, to do our will, but we cannot make it do our will now. It has robbed us of the sense of space and of the sense of touch, it has blurred every human relation and narrowed down love to a carnal act, it has paralyzed our bodies and our wills, and now it compels us to worship it. The Machine develops—but not on our lines. The Machine proceeds—but not to our goal. We only exist as the blood corpuscles that course through its arteries, and if it could work without us, it would let us die. Oh, I have no remedy —or, at least, only one—to tell men again and again that I have seen the hills of Wessex as Aelfrid saw them when he overthrew the Danes.

"So the sun set. I forgot to mention that a belt of mist lay between my hill and other hills, and that it was the color of pearl."

He broke off for the second time.

"Go on," said his mother wearily.

He shook his head.

"Go on. Nothing that you say can distress me now. I am hardened."

"I had meant to tell you the rest, but I cannot: I know that I cannot: good-by."

Vashti stood irresolute. All her nerves were tingling with his blasphemies. But she was also inquisitive.

"This is unfair," she complained. "You have called me across the world to hear your story, and hear it I will. Tell me—as briefly as possible, for this is a disastrous waste of time—tell me how you returned to civilization."

"Oh—that!" he said, starting. "You would like to hear about civilization. Certainly. Had I got to where my respirator fell down?"

"No—but I understand everything now. You put on your respirator, and managed to walk along the surface of the earth to a vomitory, and there your conduct was reported to the Central Committee."

"By no means."

He passed his hand over his forehead, as if dispelling some strong impression. Then, resuming his narrative, he warmed to it again.

"My respirator fell about sunset. I had mentioned that the fountain seemed feebler, had I not?"

"Yes."

"About sunset, it let the respirator fall. As I said, I had entirely forgotten about the Machine, and I paid no great attention at the time, being occupied with other things. I had my pool of air, into which I could dip when the outer keenness became intolerable, and which would possibly remain for days, provided that no wind sprang up to disperse it. Not until it was too late, did I realize what the stoppage of the escape implied. You see—the gap in the tunnel had been mended; the Mending Apparatus; the Mending Apparatus, was after me.

"One other warning I had, but I neglected it. The sky at night was clearer than it had been in the day, and the moon, which was about half the sky behind the sun, shone into the dell at moments quite brightly. I was in my usual place—on the boundary between the two atmospheres—when I thought I saw something dark move across the bottom of the dell, and vanish into the shaft. In my folly, I ran down. I bent over and listened, and I thought I heard a faint scraping noise in the depths.

"At this—but it was too late—I took alarm. I determined to put on my respirator and to walk right out of the dell. But my respirator had gone. I knew exactly where it had fallen—between the stopper and the aperture—and I could even feel the mark that it had made in the turf. It had gone, and I realized that something evil was at work, and I had better escape to the other air, and, if I must die, die running toward the cloud that had been the color of a pearl. I never started. Out of the shaft—it is too horrible. A worm, a long white worm, had crawled out of the shaft and was gliding over the moonlit grass.

"I screamed. I did everything that I should not have done, I stamped upon the creature instead of flying from it, and it at once curled round the ankle. Then we fought. The worm let me run all over the dell, but edged up my leg as I ran. 'Help!' I cried. (That part is too awful. It belongs to the part that you will never know.) 'Help!' I cried. (Why cannot we suffer in silence?) 'Help!' I cried. Then my feet were wound together, I fell, I was dragged away from the dear ferns and the living hills, and past the great metal stopper (I can tell you this part), and I thought it might save me again if I caught hold of the handle. It also was enwrapped, it also. Oh, the whole dell was full of things. They were searching it in all directions, they were denuding it, and the white snouts of others peeped out of the hole, ready if needed. Everything that could be moved they brought—brushwood, bundles of fern, everything, and down we all went intertwined into hell. The last things that I saw, ere the stopper closed after us, were certain stars, and I felt that a man of my sort lived in the sky. For I did fight, I fought till the very end, and it was only my head hitting against the ladder that quieted me. I woke up in this room. The worms had vanished. I was surrounded by artificial air, artificial light, artificial peace, and my friends were calling to me down speaking tubes to know whether I had come across any new ideas lately."

Here his story ended. Discussion of it was impossible, and Vashti turned to go.

"It will end in Homelessness," she said quietly.

"I wish it would," retorted Kuno.

"The Machine has been most merciful."

"I prefer the mercy of God."

"By that superstitious phrase, do you mean that you could live in the outer air?"

"Yes."

"Have you ever seen, round the vomitories, the bones of those who were extruded after the Great Rebellion?"

"Yes."

"They were left where they perished for our edification. A few crawled away, but they perished, too—who can doubt it? And so with the Homeless of our own day. The surface of the earth supports life no longer."

"Indeed."

"Ferns and a little grass may survive, but all higher forms have perished. Has any airship detected them?"

"No."

"Has any lecturer dealt with them?"

"No."

"Then why this obstinacy?"

"Because I have seen them," he exploded.

"Seen *what?*"

"Because I have seen her in the twilight—because she came to my help when I called—because she, too, was entangled by the worms, and, luckier than I, was killed by one of them piercing her throat."

He was mad. Vashti departed, nor, in the troubles that followed, did she ever see his face again.

Part III

THE HOMELESS

During the years that followed Kuno's escapade, two important developments took place in the Machine. On the surface they were revolutionary, but in either case men's minds had been prepared beforehand, and they did but express tendencies that were latent already.

The first of these was the abolition of respirators.

Advanced thinkers, like Vashti, had always held it foolish to visit the surface of the earth. Airships might be necessary, but what was the good of going out for mere curiosity and crawling along for a mile or two in a terrestrial motor? The habit was vulgar and perhaps faintly improper: it was unproductive of ideas, and had no connection with the habits that really mattered. So respirators were abolished, and with them, of course, the terrestrial motors, and except for a few lecturers, who complained that they were debarred access to their subject matter, the development was accepted quietly. Those who still wanted to know what the earth was like had after all only to listen to some gramophone, or to look into some cinematophote. And even the lecturers acquiesced when they found that a lecture on the sea was none the less stimulating when compiled out of other lectures that had

already been delivered on the same subject. "Beware of firsthand ideas!" exclaimed one of the most advanced of them. "Firsthand ideas do not really exist. They are but the physical impressions produced by love and fear, and on this gross foundation who could erect a philosophy? Let your ideas be secondhand, and if possible tenthhand, for then they will be far removed from that disturbing element—direct observation. Do not learn anything about this subject of mine—the French Revolution. Learn instead what I think that Enicharmon thought Urizen thought Gutch thought Ho-Yung thought Chi-Bo-Sing thought Lafcadio Hearn thought Carlyle thought Mirabeau said about the French Revolution. Through the medium of these eight great minds, the blood that was shed at Paris and the windows that were broken at Versailles will be clarified to an idea which you may employ most profitably in your daily lives. But be sure that the intermediates are many and varied, for in history one authority exists to counteract another. Urizen must counteract the skepticism of Ho-Yung and Enicharmon, I must myself counteract the impetuosity of Gutch. You who listen to me are in a better position to judge about the French Revolution than I am. Your descendants will be even in a better position than you, for they will learn what you think I think, and yet another intermediate will be added to the chain. And in time"—his voice rose—"there will come a generation that has got beyond facts, beyond impressions, a generation absolutely colorless, a generation

'seraphically free
From taint of personality,'

which will see the French Revolution not as it happened, nor as they would like it to have happened, but as it

In modern times utopian literature is generally negative. H. G. Wells's When the Sleeper Wakes *tells of a man who wakes up in a world where there is security but no freedom and all culture is canned, as is the climate—under domes.*

would have happened, had it taken place in the days of the Machine."

Tremendous applause greeted this lecture, which did but voice a feeling already latent in the minds of men—a feeling that terrestrial facts must be ignored, and that the abolition of respirators was a positive gain. It was even suggested the airships should be abolished too. This was not done, because airships had somehow worked themselves into the Machine's system. But year by year they were used less, and mentioned less by thoughtful men.

The second great development was the re-establishment of religion.

This, too, had been voiced in the celebrated lecture. No one could mistake the reverent tone in which the peroration had concluded, and it awakened a responsive echo in the heart of each. Those who had long worshiped

silently, now began to talk. They described the strange feeling of peace that came over them when they handled the Book of the Machine, the pleasure that it was to repeat certain numerals out of it, however little meaning those numerals conveyed to the outward ear, the ecstasy of touching a button, however unimportant, or of ringing an electric bell, however superfluously.

"The Machine," they exclaimed, "feeds us and clothes us and houses us; through it we speak to one another, through it we see one another, in it we have our being. The Machine is the friend of ideas and the enemy of superstition: the Machine is omnipotent, eternal; blessed is the Machine." And before long this allocution was printed on the first page of the Book, and in subsequent editions the ritual swelled into a complicated system of praise and prayer. The word *religion* was sedulously avoided, and in theory the Machine was still the creation and the implement of man. But in practice all, save a few retrogrades, worshiped it as divine. Nor was it worshiped in unity. One believer would be chiefly impressed by the blue optic plates, through which he saw other believers; another by the mending apparatus, which sinful Kuno had compared to worms; another by the lifts, another by the Book. And each would pray to this or to that, and ask it to intercede for him with the Machine as a whole. Persecution—that also was present. It did not break out, for reasons that will be set forward shortly. But it was latent, and all who did not accept the minimum known as "undenominational Mechanism" lived in danger of Homelessness, which means death, as we know.

To attribute these two great developments to the Central Committee, is to take a very narrow view of civilization. The Central Committee announced the developments, it is true, but they were no more the cause of them than were the kings of the imperialistic period the cause of war. Rather did they yield to some invincible pressure, which came no one knew whither, and which, when gratified, was succeeded by some new pressure equally invincible. To such a state of affairs it is convenient to give the name of progress. No one confessed the Machine was out of hand. Year by year it was served with increased efficiency and decreased intelligence. The better a man knew his own duties upon it, the less he understood the duties of his neighbor, and in all the world there was not one who understood the monster as a whole. Those master brains had perished. They had left full directions, it is true, and their successors had each of them mastered a portion of those directions. But Humanity, in its desire for comfort, had overreached itself. It had exploited the riches of nature too far. Quietly and complacently, it was sinking into decadence, and progress had come to mean the progress of the Machine.

As for Vashti, her life went peacefully forward until the final disaster. She made her room dark and slept; she awoke and made the room light. She lectured and attended lectures. She exchanged ideas with her innumerable friends and believed she was growing more spiritual. At times a friend was granted Euthanasia, and left his or her room for the homelessness that is beyond all human conception. Vashti did not much mind. After an unsuccessful lecture, she would sometimes ask for Euthanasia herself. But the death rate was not permitted to exceed the birth rate, and the Machine had hitherto refused it to her.

The troubles began quietly, long before she was conscious of them.

One day she was astonished at receiving a message from her son. They never communicated, having nothing in common, and she had only heard indirectly that he was still alive, and had been transferred from the northern hemisphere, where he had behaved so mischievously, to the southern—indeed, to a room not far from her own.

"Does he want me to visit him?" she thought. "Never again, never. And I have not the time."

No, it was madness of another kind.

He refused to visualize his face upon the blue plate, and speaking out of the darkness with solemnity said:

"The Machine stops."

"What do you say?"

"The Machine is stopping, I know it, I know the signs."

She burst into a peal of laughter. He

heard her and was angry, and they spoke no more.

"Can you imagine anything more absurd?" she cried to a friend. "A man who was my son believes that the Machine is stopping. It would be impious if it was not mad."

"The Machine is stopping?" her friend replied. "What does that mean? The phrase conveys nothing to me."

"Nor to me."

"He does not refer, I suppose, to the trouble there has been lately with the music?"

"Oh no, of course not. Let us talk about music."

"Have you complained to the authorities?"

"Yes, and they say it wants mending, and referred me to the Committee of the Mending Apparatus. I complained of those curious gasping sighs that disfigure the symphonies of the Brisbane school. They sound like someone in pain. The Committee of the Mending Apparatus say that it shall be remedied shortly."

Obscurely worried, she resumed her life. For one thing, the defect in the music irritated her. For another thing, she could not forget Kuno's speech. If he had known that the music was out of repair—he could not know it, for he detested music—if he had known that it was wrong, "the Machine stops" was exactly the venomous sort of remark he would have made. Of course he had made it at a venture, but the coincidence annoyed her, and she spoke with some petulance to the Committee of the Mending Apparatus.

They replied, as before, that the defect would be set right shortly.

"Shortly! At once!" she retorted. "Why should I be worried by imperfect music? Things are always put right at once. If you do not mend it at once, I shall complain to the Central Committee."

"No personal complaints are received by the Central Committee," the Committee of the Mending Apparatus replied.

"Through whom am I to make my complaint, then?"

"Through us."

"I complain then."

"Your complaint shall be forwarded in its turn."

"Have others complained?"

This question was unmechanical, and the Committee of the Mending Apparatus refused to answer it.

"It is too bad!" she exclaimed to another of her friends. "There never was such an unfortunate woman as myself. I can never be sure of my music now. It gets worse and worse each time I summon it."

"I too have my troubles," the friend replied. "Sometimes my ideas are interrupted by a slight jarring noise."

"What is it?"

"I do not know whether it is inside my head, or inside the wall."

"Complain, in either case."

"I have complained, and my complaint will be forwarded in its turn to the Central Committee."

Time passed, and they resented the defects no longer. The defects had not been remedied, but the human tissues in that latter day had become so subservient, that they readily adapted themselves to every caprice of the Machine. The sigh at the crisis of the Brisbane symphony no longer irritated Vashti; she accepted it as part of the melody. The jarring noise, whether in the head or in the wall, was no longer resented by her friend. And so with the moldy artificial fruit, so with the bath water that began to stink, so with the defective rhymes that the poetry machine had taken to emit. All were bitterly complained of at first, and then acquiesced in and forgotten. Things went from bad to worse unchallenged.

It was otherwise with the failure of the sleeping apparatus. That was a more serious stoppage. There came a day when over the whole world—in Sumatra, in Wessex, in the innumerable cities of Courland[17] and Brazil—the beds, when summoned by their tired owners, failed to appear. It may seem a ludicrous matter, but from it we may date the collapse of humanity. The Committee responsible for the failure was assailed by complainants, whom it referred, as usual, to the Committee of the Mending Apparatus, who in its turn assured them that their complaints would be forwarded to the Central Committee. But the discontent grew, for mankind was not yet sufficiently adaptable to do without sleeping.

"Someone is meddling with the Machine——" they began.

"Someone is trying to make himself king, to reintroduce the personal element."

"Punish that man with Homelessness."

"To the rescue! Avenge the Machine! Avenge the Machine!"

"War! Kill the man!"

But the Committee of the Mending Apparatus now came forward, and allayed the panic with well-chosen words. It confessed that the Mending Apparatus was itself in need of repair.

The effect of this frank confession was admirable.

"Of course," said a famous lecturer —he of the French Revolution, who gilded each new decay with splendor— "of course we shall not press our complaints now. The Mending Apparatus has treated us so well in the past that we all sympathize with it, and will wait patiently for its recovery. In its own good time it will resume its duties. Meanwhile let us do without our beds, our tabloids, our other little wants. Such, I feel sure, would be the wish of the Machine."

Thousands of miles away his audience applauded. The Machine still linked them. Under the seas, beneath the roots of the mountains, ran the wires through which they saw and heard, the enormous eyes and ears that were their heritage, and the hum of many workings clothed their thoughts in one garment of subserviency. Only the old and the sick remained ungrateful, for it was rumored that Euthanasia, too, was out of order, and that pain had reappeared among men.

It became difficult to read. A blight entered the atmosphere and dulled its luminosity. At times Vashti could scarcely see across her room. The air, too, was foul. Loud were the complaints, impotent the remedies, heroic the tone of the lecturer as he cried: "Courage, courage! What matter so long as the Machine goes on? To it the darkness and the light are one." And though things improved again after a time, the old brilliancy was never recaptured, and humanity never recovered from its entrance into twilight. There was an hysterical talk of "measures," of "provisional dictatorship," and the inhabitants of Sumatra were asked to familiarize themselves with the workings of the central power station, the said power station being situated in France. But for the most part panic reigned, and men spent their strength praying to their Books, tangible proofs of the Machine's omnipotence. There were gradations of terror—at times came rumors of hope—the Mending Ap-

17 Courland: Kurland, a part of Latvia.

paratus was almost mended—the enemies of the Machine had been got under—new "nerve-centers" were evolving which would do the work even more magnificently than before. But there came a day when, without the slightest warning, without any previous hint of feebleness, the entire communication system broke down, all over the world, and the world, as they understood it, ended.

Vashti was lecturing at the time and her earlier remarks had been punctuated with applause. As she proceeded the audience became silent, and at the conclusion there was no sound. Somewhat displeased, she called to a friend who was a specialist in sympathy. No sound: doubtless the friend was sleeping. And so with the next friend whom she tried to summon, and so with the next, until she remembered Kuno's cryptic remark, "The Machine stops."

The phrase still conveyed nothing. If Eternity was stopping it would of course be set going shortly.

For example, there was still a little light and air—the atmosphere had improved a few hours previously. There was still the Book, and while there was the Book there was security.

Then she broke down, for with the cessation of activity came an unexpected terror—silence.

She had never known silence, and the coming of it nearly killed her—it did kill many thousands of people outright. Ever since her birth she had been surrounded by the steady hum. It was to the ear what artificial air was to the lungs, and agonizing pains shot across her head. And scarcely knowing what she did, she stumbled forward and pressed the unfamiliar button, the one that opened the door of her cell.

Now the door of the cell worked on a simple hinge of its own. It was not connected with the central power station, dying far away in France. It opened, rousing immoderate hopes in Vashti, for she thought that the Machine had been mended. It opened, and she saw the dim tunnel that curved far away toward freedom. One look, and then she shrank back. For the tunnel was full of people—she was almost the last in the city to have taken alarm.

People at any time repelled her, and these were nightmares from her worst dreams. People were crawling about, people were screaming, whimpering, gasping for breath, touching each other, vanishing in the dark, and ever and anon being pushed off the platform on to the live rail. Some were fighting round the electric bells, trying to summon trains which could not be summoned. Others were yelling for Euthanasia or for respirators, or blaspheming the Machine. Others stood at the doors of their cells fearing, like herself, either to stop in them or to leave them. And behind all the uproar was silence—the silence which is the voice of the earth and of the generations who have gone.

No—it was worse than solitude. She closed the door again and sat down to wait for the end. The disintegration went on, accompanied by horrible cracks and rumbling. The valves that restrained the Medical Apparatus must have been weakened, for it ruptured and hung hideously from the ceiling. The floor heaved and fell and flung her from her chair. A tube oozed toward her serpent fashion. And at last the final horror approached—light began to ebb, and she knew that civilization's long day was closing.

She whirled round, praying to be saved from this, at any rate, kissing the Book, pressing button after button.

The uproar outside was increasing, and even penetrated the wall. Slowly the brilliancy of her cell was dimmed, the reflections faded from her metal switches. Now she could not see the reading stand, now not the Book, though she held it in her hand. Light followed the flight of sound, air was following light, and the original void returned to the cavern from which it had been so long excluded. Vashti continued to whirl, like the devotees of an earlier religion,[18] screaming, praying, striking at the buttons with bleeding hands.

It was thus that she opened her prison and escaped—escaped in the spirit: at least so it seems to me, ere my meditation closes. That she escapes in the body—I cannot perceive that. She struck, by chance, the switch that released the door, and the rush of foul air on her skin, the loud throbbing whispers in her ears, told her that she was facing the tunnel again, and that tremendous platform on which she had seen men fighting. They were not fighting now. Only the whispers remained, and the little whimpering groans. They were dying by hundreds out in the dark.

She burst into tears.

Tears answered her.

They wept for humanity, those two, not for themselves. They could not bear that this should be the end. Ere silence was completed their hearts were opened, and they knew what had been important on the earth. Man, the flower of all flesh, the noblest of all creatures visible, man who had once made god in his image, and had mirrored his strength on the constella-

tions, beautiful naked man was dying, strangled in the garments that he had woven. Century after century had he toiled, and here was his reward. Truly the garment had seemed heavenly at first, shot with the colors of culture, sewn with the threads of self-denial. And heavenly it had been so long as it was a garment and no more, so long as man could shed it at will and live by the essence that is his soul, and the essence, equally divine, that is his body. The sin against the body—it was for that they wept in chief; the centuries of wrong against the muscles and the nerves, and those five portals by which we can alone apprehend—glozing it over with talk of evolution, until the body was white pap, the home of ideas as colorless, last sloshy stirrings of a spirit that had grasped the stars.

"Where are you?" she sobbed.

His voice in the darkness said, "Here."

"Is there any hope, Kuno?"

"None for us."

"Where are you?"

She crawled toward him over the bodies of the dead. His blood spurted over her hands.

"Quicker," he gasped, "I am dying—but we touch, we talk, not through the Machine."

He kissed her.

"We have come back to our own. We die, but we have recaptured life, as it was in Wessex, when Aelfrid overthrew the Danes. We know what they know outside, they who dwelt in the cloud that is the color of a pearl."

"But, Kuno, is it true? Are there still men on the surface of the earth? Is this—this tunnel, this poisoned darkness—really not the end?"

He replied:

"I have seen them, spoken to them, loved them. They are hiding in the mist and the ferns until our civilization

18 **whirl . . . earlier religion:** Among the Moslems the members of some religious orders, called dervishes, engage in trancelike ritual dances during which they whirl violently.

stops. Today they are the Homeless—tomorrow——"

"Oh, tomorrow—some fool will start the Machine again, tomorrow."

"Never," said Kuno, "never. Humanity has learnt its lesson."

As he spoke, the whole city was broken like a honeycomb. An airship had sailed in through the vomitory into a ruined wharf. It crashed downwards, exploding as it went, rending gallery after gallery with its wings of steel. For a moment they saw the nations of the dead, and, before they joined them, scraps of the untainted sky.

Comment

The world of this story seems quite literally a terrible one. It is a world in which people are so isolated from nature that they die in the "outer air"; it is a world in which they are so isolated from each other that they may know "several thousand people" but never or rarely meet another face to face. Each person lives in his or her little cell, breathing machine-made air, listening to abstract "ideas," and following the requirements of the Book, a huge set of instructions that tell how to live by the Machine. This world, in short, seems one in which human beings have lost their humanity.

Yet at the same time that he describes this dreadful world, Forster shows us many values that oppose it. Indeed, the fantasy, the exaggeration, of the story is itself an affirmation of these values. How does Forster suggest these opposing values, and what are some of them?

1. What is meant in the story by: "the Machine," "Homelessness," "civilization," "firsthand ideas"?

2. At the very beginning of the story (p. 735, col. 2) Vashti tells her son, "I can give you fully five minutes." Later (p. 743, col. 2) when she finally sees him she is "too well-bred to shake him by the hand." What do such details as these tell us about her attitude toward people? What other such details tell us of her attitude toward direct experience?

3. According to Vashti (p. 744, col. 1) the Machine has destroyed all "fear and superstition." But how would you describe her attitude toward the Book? How do you account for her distress when Kuno speaks against the Machine?

4. Kuno looks up at the stars and sees a constellation shaped like a man with a sword. How do the stars appear to Vashti from the airship? And what does she say to Kuno's "idea" about the constellation? What seems to you missing from the "ideas" that Vashti finds "interesting"?

5. At the end of the story, as Vashti and Kuno perish, "they knew what had been important on earth. Man, the flower of all flesh, the

noblest of all creatures visible . . . was dying, strangled in the garments that he had woven."

(*a*) What seem to you the real "garments" that are strangling man in this story? Are they the Machine, the Book, the Committee? Or are they something for which the Machine, for example, is a symbol?

(*b*) Write a short essay in which you describe the idea of man that this story communicates to you. According to this story, what *should* man believe in?

T. S. Eliot (1888-1965)

In the introduction to this book we compared the opening of Chaucer's *Canterbury Tales* with the opening of *The Waste Land,* a poem published in 1922 by Thomas Stearns Eliot. The comparison is a just one not only because both poets, as you will recall, wrote of the coming of April, but also because each poet has had many, many imitators and followers. Greatness in poetry, as in anything else, consists at least partly in weight and extent of influence, and T. S. Eliot has been a major influence in the 20th century not only on English literature but on the literatures of other languages.

He was born in St. Louis, Missouri, educated at Harvard, at the Sorbonne (in Paris), and at Oxford, and could easily have become a university professor of ancient literature or of philosophy. In 1917, however, after a brief period of schoolteaching, he went to work for a bank in London, and later became a director of an English publishing firm. He was first of all a writer, however, and besides composing his own startling and revolutionary poetry, he edited and contributed to a number of influential literary magazines. Although he often revisited the United States, he moved to England in 1914, and in 1927 became a British citizen.

In the years after World War II Eliot had three much-discussed plays produced in London and on Broadway, the most notable of them, perhaps, *The Cocktail Party* of 1950. But before that to many serious readers and students of literature everywhere he was the best-known figure in modern letters. His books of criticism, his poems, his earlier dramas (especially *Murder in the Cathedral,* 1935, a play in verse about the death of Thomas à Becket, the "holy, blissful martyr" of Chaucer's Canterbury)—all these works, and his more general essays on culture and history besides, were widely read and discussed.

In his own life Eliot met the disorders of the modern world with a philosophy of conservatism and orthodoxy both more serious and more flexible than that which we have seen in other writers. The *traditional,* in literature as well as in politics, he argued, must guide the developments of the present. (See the last essay in this book.) But the present, he also argued, has so far forgotten the traditions of history, and has so far succumbed to something like Forster's "Machine," that the traditional forms and concerns of literature often look strange and obscure in the present. If the modern poet is difficult, his argument implies, it is because modern readers have lost touch with the buried life of the past. To remind them of that buried life, to show them their roots, was much of Eliot's endeavor.

"Preludes"

The two following poems will suggest the direction and the movement of Eliot's poetry. The first is an early poem, published in 1915, at the beginning of his English residence. It shows a startling new use of imagery, a use that has been compared to the projection of a series of images on a picture-screen. The links between the images, links that we should normally expect, have been dropped out: one image after another is flashed before us, and we supply the feelings that link them.

Preludes *

T. S. Eliot

I

The winter evening settles down
With smell of steaks in passageways.
Six o'clock.
The burnt-out ends of smoky days.
And now a gusty shower wraps   5
The grimy scraps
Of withered leaves about your feet
And newspapers from vacant lots;
The showers beat
On broken blinds[1] and chimney-pots,   10
And at the corner of the street
A lonely cab-horse steams and stamps.
And then the lighting of the lamps.

II

The morning comes to consciousness
Of faint stale smells of beer   15
From the sawdust[2]-trampled street
With all its muddy feet that press
To early coffee-stands.
With the other masquerades
That time resumes,   20
One thinks of all the hands
That are raising dingy shades
In a thousand furnished rooms.

1 **blinds:** window shutters.   2 **sawdust:** from the floors of barrooms.

III

You tossed a blanket from the bed,
You lay upon your back, and waited;   25
You dozed, and watched the night revealing
The thousand sordid images
Of which your soul was constituted;
They flickered against the ceiling.
And when all the world came back   30
And the light crept up between the shutters
And you heard the sparrows in the gutters,
You had such a vision of the street
As the street hardly understands;
Sitting along the bed's edge, where   35
You curled the papers from your hair,
Or clasped the yellow soles of feet
In the palms of both soiled hands.

IV

His soul stretched tight across the skies
That fade behind a city block,   40
Or trampled by insistent feet
At four and five and six o'clock;
And short square fingers stuffing pipes,
And evening newspapers, and eyes
Assured of certain certainties,   45
The conscience of a blackened street
Impatient to assume[3] the world.

I am moved by fancies that are curled
Around these images, and cling:
The notion of some infinitely gentle   50
Infinitely suffering thing.

Wipe your hand across your mouth, and laugh;
The worlds revolve like ancient women
Gathering fuel in vacant lots.

3 **assume:** take over; lay claim to.

Comment

A prelude is the opening, the beginning of something, and each of these "Preludes" is the introduction to a part of the daily round of life in the 20th-century city. The first gives us the winter evening, the burnt-out end of another smoky day. The next gives us the morning, any morning after a night of forgetfulness, though we come closer to a particular individual's experience with "One thinks . . ." (l. 21). And we come still closer to individual experience in the next, where "you" are awake, and there comes to "you" "such a vision of the street/As the street hardly understands." What is this vision? Its character is suggested in the final "Prelude," not only by the "stretched" soul of someone who has now become "he," someone who hears the trampling of feet, sees the workmen preparing their tobacco pipes, and sees the arrogant eyes of each isolated passer-by. This vision that the street "hardly understands" is also suggested by the last two paragraphs of the poem. What do they say? More important, *how* must each one be said?

1. At line 48, for the first time, an "I" appears: the poet himself speaks. What are the "fancies" that "cling" for him around "these images"? What attitude toward these images of city life is suggested by "The notion of some infinitely gentle/Infinitely suffering thing"?
2. But what happens to this "notion" in the last three lines of the poem? Is the poet here being "moved by fancies"? What is his mood? What change in his tone is expressed by the difference between the "notion of some infinitely gentle . . . thing" and the simile with which the poem ends?
3. A prelude is an opening, a beginning. But of what, finally, are these "Preludes" the beginning? What attitude toward the city, its streets, and people, does the poet finally take?

(Quiz 1)

"Journey of the Magi"

The next poem was published in 1927, twelve years after the "Preludes." In the meantime Eliot had published *The Waste Land*, his most ambitious single poem, which in images drawn from contemporary life and figures of ancient myth and literature pictures the modern world as a sterile, rocky place where nothing will grow. This was followed in 1925 by "The Hollow Men," in which the religious themes and images of almost all the later poems begin to be asserted more strongly. Yet the last lines of "The Hollow Men" also echo the feelings of the last lines of "Preludes":

> This is the way the world ends
> Not with a bang but a whimper.

The following poem, however, may fairly be taken as representing the movement Eliot followed from *The Waste Land* to the *Four Quartets*, four long religious meditations published together in 1943, though the writing of some dates from much earlier.

In "The Journey of the Magi" the Magus, one of the Three Wise Men, tells, many years later, of the journey he and his companions made to bring gifts to Jesus. They went to see a miraculous birth, and they experienced great hardships to get there. Moreover, the birth they saw, the birth of a new religion, meant death to the old ways, to the religious codes that had been in force. And even in their sight of the spectacle itself, there were signs of the death that Jesus would eventually suffer. The Magus is not exultant; he uses no more than understatement: "it was (you may say) satisfactory." The birth of a new religion, of a new way of life, does not come about easily.

Journey
of the Magi *

T. S. Eliot

> "A cold coming we had of it,
> Just the worst time of the year
> For a journey, and such a long journey:
> The ways deep and the weather sharp,
> The very dead of winter."[1]   5
> And the camels galled, sore-footed, refractory,
> Lying down in the melting snow.
> There were times we regretted
> The summer palaces on slopes, the terraces,
> And the silken girls bringing sherbet.   10
> Then the camel men cursing and grumbling
> And running away, and wanting their liquor and women,

---

1 **A cold coming . . . winter:** This quotation comes from a sermon by Bishop Lancelot Andrewes, one of the members of the committee that made the King James Bible. Andrewes, a great churchman in Elizabethan times, was studied and admired by Eliot.

And the night-fires going out, and the lack of shelters,
And the cities hostile and the towns unfriendly
And the villages dirty and charging high prices: 15
A hard time we had of it.
At the end we preferred to travel all night,
Sleeping in snatches,
With the voices singing in our ears, saying
That this was all folly.   20

   Then at dawn we came down to a temperate valley,
Wet, below the snow line, smelling of vegetation;
With a running stream and a water-mill beating the darkness,
And three trees on the low sky,[2]
And an old white horse[3] galloped away in the meadow.   25
Then we came to a tavern with vine-leaves over the lintel,
Six hands at an open door dicing for pieces of silver,[4]
And feet kicking the empty wine-skins.
But there was no information, and so we continued
And arrived at evening, not a moment too soon   30
Finding the place; it was (you may say) satisfactory.

   All this was a long time ago, I remember,
And I would do it again, but set down
This set down
This: were we led all that way for   35
Birth or Death? There was a Birth, certainly,
We had evidence and no doubt. I had seen birth and death,
But had thought they were different; this Birth was
Hard and bitter agony for us, like Death, our death.
We returned to our places, these Kingdoms,   40
But no longer at ease here, in the old dispensation,[5]
With an alien people clutching their gods.
I should be glad of another death.

Comment

   The poem is presented in three stages, in each of which details are
accumulated both in short, clipped lines and in long, loose ones. The
whole movement of the poem is suggested by the last line of each of
the three divisions: "That this was all folly"; "it was (you may say) sat-

---

2 three trees on the low sky: an image that foreshadows the three crosses of the
Crucifixion.
3 old white horse: In the Bible a white horse carries a rider with a bow and crown, who
"went forth conquering and to conquer" (Revelation 6:2); later in the chapter a reference
is made to "a white horse; and he that sat upon him was called Faithful and True (Revelation 19:11). But there is also (Revelation 6:8) "a pale horse: and his name that sat
upon him was Death."
4 Six hands . . . silver: This line fuses the image of the Roman soldiers gambling with
each other for Jesus's garments, and the image of Judas, who betrayed Jesus for thirty
pieces of silver.
5 old dispensation: codes of religion in force before the coming of Jesus.

isfactory"; and "I should be glad of another death." But the movement as a whole does not take us to an exultant climax; it takes us instead to a troubling question: "were we led all that way for/Birth or Death?" and the enigmatic statement of the last line of the poem.

1. What are some of the images of the first movement that justify the "voices" that say "this was all folly"?
2. The first three lines of the second movement present natural images of fertility and respite from the cold journey. But how do the images of the next five lines qualify the prospect of the "temperate valley," making the "place," when the Magi have arrived, no more than "satisfactory"?
3. How do the images of the last part of the second movement prepare you for the question the Magus so earnestly asks, "were we led . . . for Birth or Death"? Notice the shortness of line 34: "This set down"; is the "This" of line 34 the object of the imperative "set down" that comes in line 33? Or is it the object of the "set down" in line 34? What does the ambiguity of the grammar tell you here about the state of mind of the speaker?
4. How do you read the very last line of the poem? What does "another death" mean here?
5. Write an essay on the conclusions of these two poems of T. S. Eliot. Does the Magus seem to you to be sure of the "notion of some infinitely gentle/Infinitely suffering thing"? Does he bitterly dismiss it all by saying, "Wipe your hand across your mouth, and laugh . . ."?

William Butler Yeats (1865-1939)

"A sixty-year-old smiling public man"—so Yeats described himself in a poem he wrote in 1926. He was indeed a public man, for he had been made a senator in the newly founded Irish Free State in 1922, and in 1923 he had won the Nobel Prize for literature. Yeats had been for a time associated with the Irish revolutionary movement that had preceded the Free State, he had helped to found the Abbey Theater in Dublin, where the first great plays in modern Irish literary history were produced, and from 1900 to about 1925 he had been one of the leaders of the greatest literary movement in Irish history.

But Yeats was a restless man of profound imaginative energy for whom no public life would have been enough. He was the son of a painter and studied art himself as a young man in London and Dublin. Most of his youth was spent in County Sligo and the hills of western Ireland, where he learned about Celtic heroes and legends from a people for whom they were still alive. For a time during his young manhood in London he was interested in occult religions and philosophies, and at a much later period of his life he turned again to the study of such mysteries as communication with spirits, automatic writing, and other manifestations of the occult. In 1925 he published *A Vision,* an elaborate treatise on symbolism, the cycles of history, and the nature of man. But he was always a poet, first and last. Some of his strange interests got into his poetry, but most of them did not—and indeed many persons who have known only his poetry have been unaware of those interests.

"The Lake Isle of Innisfree"

Yeats lived through several different styles as poet, but it is possible to trace only two of them here. The first is a style that he shared with many poets writing in England at the end of the 19th century (only they did not write it so well as he!), and it is perhaps most beautifully represented in the following poem, which appeared first in 1890. Lough Gill (lŏKH gĭl′), in Sligo, is the beautiful lake in which stands the island of Innisfree. In his autobiography Yeats says that he wanted to live in a cottage on Innisfree just as Thoreau lived in his cabin at Walden Pond. Innisfree, however, is not just a place; it is a symbol of what many men have longed for while standing "on the roadway, or on the pavements grey."

The Lake Isle of Innisfree

William Butler Yeats

I will arise and go now, and go to Innisfree,
And a small cabin build there, of clay and wattles[1] made:
Nine bean-rows[2] will I have there, a hive for the honey bee,
And live alone in the bee loud glade.

And I shall have some peace there, for peace comes dropping
    slow,   5
Dropping from the veils of the morning to where the cricket
    sings;
There midnight's all a glimmer, and noon a purple glow,
And evening full of the linnet's wings.

I will arise and go now, for always night and day
I hear lake water lapping with low sounds by the shore;   10
While I stand on the roadway, or on the pavements[3] grey,
I hear it in the deep heart's core.

---

1 **wattles:** woven twigs and small branches.
2 **bean-rows:** Yeats had indeed been reading *Walden;* Thoreau, as he hoed his crop, said, "I was determined to *know beans.*"
3 **pavements:** sidewalks.

Comment

Many poems have been written about a land of the heart's desire far from the streets of the city, but none was ever written with such beautifully quiet modulation as this.

1. In the second stanza, what metaphor describes the "peace" of the lake isle? How does this metaphor emphasize the bond between nature and humanity in the lake isle?
2. In the last stanza Yeats repeats, "I will arise and go now": Where is he "now"? In what sense is he himself an island where he now is?

"Sailing to Byzantium"

The next poem comes from the period when Yeats was perhaps at the very height of his powers. "Sailing to Byzantium" is one of the most quoted and most influential poems of the 20th century, and though it is not without its difficulties, its movement and theme are clear when we read it beside "Innisfree." Written in 1926, it marks the culmination of a deliberate change of style that Yeats had set out to achieve many years before. In 1914, for example, he had written a poem describing an ideal reader, the sort of reader to whom he wanted to address himself, and it ended:

> Before I am old
> I shall have written him one
> Poem maybe as cold
> And passionate as the dawn.

And "Sailing to Byzantium" is a poem both cold—as cold as abstract art —and passionate—as passionate as the desire to be free from one's dying body; but its coldness and passion no longer find their model in anything so much a part of nature as the dawn. Yeats is both expressing a wish and describing a journey; the object of both is not a peaceful land where human beings are one with nature, but a "holy city" where they will be one with great art. "Byzantium," of course, was the capital of the Eastern Roman Empire, and a "holy city" because it was the chief center of Greek Orthodox Christianity. But it is no more a "place" here than "Innisfree" was in the earlier poem. It is an ideal city where the soul may live in the contemplation of ideas and art. The poem begins with the rejection of another land: "That is no country for old men." And "That country" is here, of course, Ireland and Innisfree, but it is also the country that is idealized by "Innisfree," a country of *natural* rather than intellectual beauty.

Sailing to Byzantium

William Butler Yeats

1

That is no country for old men.   The young
In one another's arms, birds in the trees
—Those dying generations—at their song,
The salmon-falls, the mackerel-crowded seas,
Fish, flesh, or fowl, commend all summer long   5
Whatever is begotten, born, and dies.
Caught in that sensual music all neglect
Monuments of unageing intellect.

2

An aged man is but a paltry thing,
A tattered coat upon a stick, unless   10
Soul clap its hands and sing, and louder sing
For every tatter in its mortal dress,
Nor is there singing school but studying
Monuments of its own magnificence;
And therefore I have sailed the seas and come   15
To the holy city of Byzantium.

3

O sages standing in God's holy fire
As in the gold mosaic of a wall,[1]
Come from the holy fire, perne in a gyre,[2]
And be the singing-masters of my soul.   20
Consume my heart away; sick with desire
And fastened to a dying animal
It knows not what it is; and gather me
Into the artifice of eternity.

---

[1] **sages . . . wall:** One of the greatest achievements of Byzantine art is the Church of
Hagia Sophia, the Church of "Holy Wisdom," and on its walls are figures in mosaic.
The figures are not lifelike, but are stylized and abstract, and each is surrounded by a
nimbus, or halo, that resembles a golden fire.
[2] **come . . . gyre** (jīr): Yeats begs the sages to come down to him, to descend in a
whirling, spiral motion: *gyre* means spiral form; *perne* is Yeats's own word for "spin" or
"whirl" (it comes from a west-of-Ireland word for "spool").

4

Once out of nature I shall never take   25
My bodily form from any natural thing,
But such a form as Grecian goldsmiths[3] make
Of hammered gold and gold enameling
To keep a drowsy Emperor awake;
Or set upon a golden bough to sing   30
To lords and ladies of Byzantium
Of what is past, or passing, or to come.

[3] **Grecian goldsmiths:** In a note on this line, Yeats has said: "I have read somewhere that in the Emperor's palace at Byzantium was a tree made of gold and silver, and artificial birds that sang."

Comment

This poem, like both of the poems of T. S. Eliot that we have read, is indeed an example of concentration. Once again, it is the story of a journey, but many of the links, certain details of the journey, that we should expect in earlier narrative poetry have been suppressed. And yet the stages of Yeats's journey to Byzantium are clear. First comes the rejection of the land where animal and natural life go on and on, but where no one can hear the monumental music of intellects that do not grow old and die as natural creatures do. For (2) unless an old man has a soul that can sing for joy at every sign of decay of his body ("every tatter in its mortal dress"), he is a "paltry thing." And no school can teach him this song; he can learn it only by studying the monuments made by the soul itself, apart from the body. That is why Yeats, now old himself, has sailed away from a world of natural birth, life, and death, to the symbolic city where the greatest creations are ageless. And now that he has arrived—or dreams that he has arrived (3)—he begs the "sages" to come to him, to teach him to sing—to sing something different from the "sensual music" (1) of nature. He begs to be gathered into an "artifice of eternity"—that is, into an eternity, or an "agelessness," that is created as art is created. For (4) he would himself become a work of art, he would be "out of nature," if his prayer could be answered. Yet he would not lose the real world after all, for although he would not take his "bodily form from any natural thing," yet he would be a bird formed by art to sing a song of all history, a song "Of what is past, or passing, or to come." He would, if his wish were granted, if his journey could be made, live in a world outside of nature, outside of history, and still be able to sing—to write poetry—about the world he has left behind. The difference between the "young," the birds, the rivers and seas of the first stanza and the bird "Of hammered gold" of the last stanza, is the difference between those who are overwhelmed by life and those who can stand off from life and shape it into art.

With these observations on the poem in mind, read it again—and yet again. Then write a brief comparison between "The Lake Isle of Innisfree" and "Sailing to Byzantium." Each one expresses a wish to go "out of this world." But what is "this world" that the poet would go out of in the first poem? And what is "this world" that he would leave in the second? Which poem is the more concentrated—that is, which leaves out more of the links and connections that we normally expect in a poem? Why do you think it does so?

The Need For Renewal
Summing Up

You have read three different examples of the concern of the 20th-century writer with the need for renewal. The short story by E. M. Forster sets forth this theme in a parable made out of science fiction. The two poets describe this need for renewal both in individual poems and in the differences we can see when we move from one of their early poems to one of their later ones. What do these three writers tell you about the most representative adventure in modern literature? What is the character of the journey, as they see it, from skepticism to renewal, from domination by "the Machine" to freedom of the mind? What is so difficult in this journey, as these writers make it out? And how do they make you feel this difficulty?

Human Beings and Inhuman Society

IT IS A WELL-FOUNDED common belief that 20th-century literature was most concerned with society—with social criticism and social protest—during the 1930's. But the pressures of society upon the individual have also been the theme—and have often supplied the humor—of stories, poems, and plays since the 20th century began. The following works will suggest how variously this theme has been treated. It has been treated sometimes with bitterness, sometimes with gentle humor, though always with irony. The irony reflects the astonishing fact that around the individual there has grown a society so large and often so overwhelming that it seems sometimes to be an enemy rather than a home.

D. H. Lawrence (1885-1930)

The first twenty-five years of this century were a period of great innovation and experiment in English literature, and some of the boldest new writers of this period, even though their public was small, were greeted with bewilderment and hostility. Some of the words of David Herbert Lawrence (1885-1930) still arouse violent hostility, yet others of them are today widely read and admired (the following story has even been made into a movie), and many of the convictions he tried to express in his short life seem neither strange nor dangerous after all. Lawrence, the son of a coal miner from the Midlands of England, was an intense, troubled, outspoken rebel. He believed that the conditions of life in an industrial, mechanized society keep men and women and families from being fully and warmly human.

"The Rocking-Horse Winner"

You will see, for example, that the story presented here begins by describing a mother who "knew that at the center of her heart was a hard little place that could not feel love," and you will see that it goes on to suggest that it is her anxiety about money that has made her bitter and hard. Many writers have said, all too easily, that love is more important than money. Lawrence said it with a passionate belief that grew out of his experience. He traveled far, in the old world and the new, looking for a natural way of life, a simple society in which human instincts could be expressed freely and naturally, undistorted by the desire for status, things, and machines. He lived for a time in Taos, New Mexico, amid the strong colors and wild scenery that he loved. Indeed, his love for lands of sunlight was a necessity, for he was often unwell and eventually died of tuberculosis. Lawrence not only believed that all we mean by "love" is more important than all we mean by "money." He also believed that many people in the modern world are sick at heart, sick in spirit, because they do not see how the values of love and money may be opposed to each other.

The Rocking-Horse Winner

D. H. Lawrence

THERE was a woman who was beautiful, who started with all the advantages, yet she had no luck. She married for love, and the love turned to dust. She had bonny[1] children, yet she felt they had been thrust upon her, and she could not love them. They looked at her coldly, as if they were finding fault with her. And hurriedly she felt she must cover up some fault in herself. Yet what it was that she must cover up she never knew. Nevertheless, when her children were present, she always felt the center of her heart go hard. This troubled her, and in her manner she was all the more gentle and anxious for her children, as if she loved them very much. Only she herself knew that at the center of her heart was a hard little place that could not feel love, no, not for anybody. Everybody else said of her: "She is such a good mother. She adores her children." Only she herself, and her children themselves, knew it was not so. They read it in each other's eyes.

There were a boy and two little girls. They lived in a pleasant house, with a garden, and they had discreet servants,

1 **bonny:** Scottish and north-English for "pretty," or "pleasant to look at."

and felt themselves superior to anyone in the neighborhood.

Although they lived in style, they felt always an anxiety in the house. There was never enough money. The mother had a small income, and the father had a small income, but not nearly enough for the social position which they had to keep up. The father went in to town to some office. But though he had good prospects, these prospects never materialized. There was always the grinding sense of the shortage of money, though the style was always kept up.

At last the mother said, "I will see if *I* can't make something." But she did not know where to begin. She racked her brains, and tried this thing and the other, but could not find anything successful. The failure made deep lines come into her face. Her children were growing up, they would have to go to school. There must be more money, there must be more money. The father, who was always very handsome and expensive in his tastes, seemed as if he never *would* be able to do anything worth doing. And the mother, who had a great belief in herself, did not succeed any better, and her tastes were just as expensive.

And so the house came to be haunted by the unspoken phrase: *There must be more money! There must be more money!* The children could hear it all the time, though nobody said it aloud. They heard it at Christmas, when the expensive and splendid toys filled the nursery. Behind the shining modern rocking horse, behind the smart doll's-house, a voice would start whispering: "There *must* be more money! There *must* be more money!" And the children would stop playing, to listen for a moment. They would look into each other's eyes, to see if they had all heard. And each one saw in the eyes of the other two that they too had heard. "There *must* be more money! There *must* be more money!"

It came whispering from the springs of the still-swaying rocking horse, and even the horse, bending his wooden, champing head, heard it. The big doll, sitting so pink and smirking in her new pram, could hear it quite plainly, and seemed to be smirking all the more self-consciously because of it. The foolish puppy, too, that took the place of the teddy bear, he was looking so extraordinarily foolish for no other reason but that he heard the secret whisper all over the house: "There *must* be more money!"

Yet nobody ever said it aloud. The whisper was everywhere, and therefore no one spoke it. Just as no one ever says: "We are breathing!" in spite of the fact that breath is coming and going all the time.

"Mother," said the boy Paul one day, "why don't we keep a car of our own? Why do we always use Uncle's, or else a taxi?"

"Because we're the poor members of the family," said the mother.

"But why *are* we, Mother?"

"Well—I suppose," she said slowly and bitterly, "it's because your father has no luck."

The boy was silent for some time.

"Is luck money, Mother?" he asked, rather timidly.

"No, Paul. Not quite. It's what causes you to have money."

"Oh!" said Paul vaguely. "I thought when Uncle Oscar said *filthy lucker*,[2] it meant money."

"*Filthy lucre* does mean money," said

the mother. "But it's lucre, not luck."

"Oh!" said the boy. "Then what *is* luck, Mother?"

"It's what causes you to have money. If you're lucky you have money. That's why it's better to be born lucky than rich. If you're rich, you may lose your money. But if you're lucky, you will always get more money."

"Oh! Will you? And is Father not lucky?"

"Very unlucky, I should say," she said bitterly. The boy watched her with unsure eyes.

"Why?" he asked.

"I don't know. Nobody ever knows why one person is lucky and another unlucky."

"Don't they? Nobody at all? Does *nobody* know?"

"Perhaps God. But He never tells."

"He ought to, then. And aren't you lucky either, Mother?"

"I can't be, if I married an unlucky husband."

"But by yourself, aren't you?"

"I used to think I was, before I married. Now I think I am very unlucky indeed."

"Why?"

"Well—never mind! Perhaps I'm not really," she said.

The child looked at her, to see if she meant it. But he saw, by the lines of her mouth, that she was only trying to hide something from him.

"Well, anyhow," he said stoutly, "I'm a lucky person."

"Why?" said his mother, with a sudden laugh.

He stared at her. He didn't even know why he had said it.

"God told me," he asserted, brazening it out.

"I hope He did, dear!" she said, again with a laugh, but rather bitter.

"He did, Mother!"

---

2 **filthy lucker:** a mispronunciation of the slang phrase "filthy lucre" (lōō′kər) which means money that has been much handled. The word *lucre* is French. What English word does Paul confuse it with?

"Excellent!" said the mother, using one of her husband's exclamations.

The boy saw she did not believe him; or rather, that she paid no attention to his assertion. This angered him somewhere, and made him want to compel her attention.

He went off by himself, vaguely, in a childish way, seeking for the clue to "luck." Absorbed, taking no heed of other people, he went about with a sort of stealth, seeking inwardly for luck. He wanted luck, he wanted it, he wanted it. When the two girls were playing dolls in the nursery, he would sit on his big rocking horse, charging madly into space, with a frenzy that made the little girls peer at him uneasily. Wildly the horse careered, the waving dark hair of the boy tossed, his eyes had a strange glare in them. The little girls dared not speak to him.

When he had ridden to the end of his mad little journey, he climbed down and stood in front of his rocking horse, staring fixedly into its lowered face. Its red mouth was slightly open, its big eye was wide and glassy-bright.

"Now!" he would silently command the snorting steed. "Now, take me to where there is luck! Now take me!"

And he would slash the horse on the neck with the little whip he had asked Uncle Oscar for. He *knew* the horse could take him to where there was luck, if only he forced it. So he would mount again, and start on his furious ride, hoping at last to get there. He knew he could get there.

"You'll break your horse, Paul!" said the nurse.

"He's always riding like that! I wish he'd leave off!" said his elder sister Joan.

But he only glared down on them in silence. Nurse gave him up. She could make nothing of him. Anyhow he was growing beyond her.

One day his mother and his uncle Oscar came in when he was on one of his furious rides. He did not speak to them.

"Hallo, you young jockey! Riding a winner?" said his uncle.

"Aren't you growing too big for a rocking horse? You're not a very little boy any longer, you know," said his mother.

But Paul only gave a blue glare from his big, rather close-set eyes. He would speak to nobody when he was in full tilt. His mother watched him with an anxious expression on her face.

At last he suddenly stopped forcing his horse into the mechanical gallop, and slid down.

"Well, I got there!" he announced fiercely, his blue eyes still flaring, and his sturdy long legs straddling apart.

"Where did you get to?" asked his mother.

"Where I wanted to go," he flared back at her.

"That's right, son!" said Uncle Oscar. "Don't you stop till you get there. What's the horse's name?"

"He doesn't have a name," said the boy.

"Gets on without all right?" asked the uncle.

"Well, he has different names. He was called Sansovino[3] last week."

"Sansovino, eh? Won the Ascot.[4] How did you know his name?"

"He always talks about horse races with Bassett," said Joan.

The uncle was delighted to find that his small nephew was posted with all the racing news. Bassett, the young gardener, who had been wounded in

3 **Sansovino:** the (invented) name of a race horse, like Daffodil, Malabar, and others that appear later.
4 **Ascot:** a famous race, like the Kentucky Derby; the Leger and the Derby are others that appear later.

the left foot in the war and had got his present job through Oscar Cresswell, whose batman[5] he had been, was a perfect blade of the "turf."[6] He lived in the racing events, and the small boy lived with him.

Oscar Cresswell got it all from Bassett.

"Master Paul comes and asks me, so I can't do more than tell him, sir," said Bassett, his face terribly serious, as if he were speaking of religious matters.

"And does he ever put anything on a horse he fancies?"

"Well—I don't want to give him away —he's a young sport, a fine sport, sir. Would you mind asking him himself? He sort of takes a pleasure in it, and perhaps he'd feel I was giving him away, sir, if you don't mind."

Bassett was serious as a church.

The uncle went back to his nephew, and took him off for a ride in the car.

"Say, Paul, old man, do you ever put anything on a horse?" the uncle asked.

The boy watched the handsome man closely.

"Why, do you think I oughtn't to?" he parried.

"Not a bit of it! I thought perhaps you might give me a tip for the Lincoln."

The car sped on into the country, going down to Uncle Oscar's place in Hampshire.

"Honor bright?" said the nephew.

"Honor bright, son!" said the uncle.

"Well, then, Daffodil."

"Daffodil! I doubt it, sonny. What about Mirza?"

"I only know the winner," said the boy. "That's Daffodil."

"Daffodil, eh?"

There was a pause. Daffodil was an obscure horse comparatively.

"Uncle!"

"Yes, son?"

"You won't let it go any further, will you? I promised Bassett."

"Bassett be damned, old man! What's he got to do with it?"

"We're partners. We've been partners from the first. Uncle, he lent me my first five shillings, which I lost. I promised him, honor bright, it was only between me and him; only you gave me that ten-shilling note I started winning with, so I thought you were lucky. You won't let it go any further, will you?"

The boy gazed at his uncle from those big, hot, blue eyes, set rather close together. The uncle stirred and laughed uneasily.

"Right you are, son! I'll keep your tip private. Daffodil, eh? How much are you putting on him?"

"All except twenty pounds," said the boy. "I keep that in reserve."

The uncle thought it a good joke.

"You keep twenty pounds in reserve, do you, you young romancer? What are you betting, then?"

"I'm betting three hundred," said the boy gravely. "But it's between you and me, Uncle Oscar! Honor bright?"

The uncle burst into a roar of laughter.

"It's between you and me all right, you young Nat Gould,"[7] he said, laughing. "But where's your three hundred?"

"Bassett keeps it for me. We're partners."

"You are, are you! And what is Bassett putting on Daffodil?"

"He won't go quite as high as I do, I expect. Perhaps he'll go a hundred and fifty."

---

5 **batman:** enlisted man attached as a private servant to a British army officer.
6 **blade of the turf:** explained in the next sentence. "Turf" is the race track.

7 **Nat Gould:** journalist and author who was a well-known racing authority.

"What, pennies?" laughed the uncle.

"Pounds," said the child, with a surprised look at his uncle. "Bassett keeps a bigger reserve than I do."

Between wonder and amusement Uncle Oscar was silent. He pursued the matter no further, but he determined to take his nephew with him to the Lincoln races.

"Now, son," he said, "I'm putting twenty on Mirza, and I'll put five for you on any horse you fancy. What's your pick?"

"Daffodil, Uncle."

"No, not the fiver on Daffodil!"

"I should if it was my own fiver," said the child.

"Good! Good! Right you are! A fiver for me and a fiver for you on Daffodil."

The child had never been to a race-meeting before, and his eyes were blue fire. He pursed his mouth tight, and watched. A Frenchman just in front had put his money on Lancelot. Wild with excitement, he flayed his arms up and down, yelling *"Lancelot! Lancelot!"* in his French accent.

Daffodil came in first, Lancelot second, Mirza third. The child, flushed and with eyes blazing, was curiously serene. His uncle brought him four five-pound notes, four to one.

"What am I to do with these?" he cried, waving them before the boy's eyes.

"I suppose we'll talk to Bassett," said the boy. "I expect I have fifteen hundred now; and twenty in reserve; and this twenty."

His uncle studied him for some moments.

"Look here, son!" he said. "You're not serious about Bassett and that fifteen hundred, are you?"

"Yes, I am. But it's between you and me, Uncle. Honor bright!"

"Honor bright all right, son! But I must talk to Bassett."

"If you'd like to be a partner, Uncle, with Bassett and me, we could all be partners. Only, you'd have to promise, honor bright, Uncle, not to let it go beyond us three. Bassett and I are lucky, and you must be lucky, because it was your ten shillings I started winning with. . . ."

Uncle Oscar took both Bassett and Paul into Richmond Park for an afternoon, and there they talked.

"It's like this, you see, sir," Bassett said. "Master Paul would get me talking about racing events, spinning yarns, you know, sir. And he was always keen on knowing if I'd made or if I'd lost. It's about a year since, now, that I put five shillings on Blush of Dawn for him: and we lost. Then the luck turned, with that ten shillings he had from you: that we put on Singhalese. And since that time, it's been pretty steady, all things considering. What do you say, Master Paul?"

"We're all right when we're sure," said Paul. "It's when we're not quite sure that we go down."

"Oh, but we're careful then," said Bassett.

"But when are you *sure?*" smiled Uncle Oscar.

"It's Master Paul, sir," said Bassett, in a secret, religious voice. "It's as if he had it from heaven. Like Daffodil, now, for the Lincoln. That was as sure as eggs."

"Did you put anything on Daffodil?" asked Oscar Cresswell.

"Yes, sir. I made my bit."

"And my nephew?"

Bassett was obstinately silent, looking at Paul.

"I made twelve hundred, didn't I, Bassett? I told Uncle I was putting three hundred on Daffodil."

"That's right," said Bassett, nodding.

"But where's the money?" asked the uncle.

"I keep it safe locked up, sir. Master Paul he can have it any minute he likes to ask for it."

"What, fifteen hundred pounds?"

"And twenty! And *forty*, that is, with the twenty he made on the course."

"It's amazing!" said the uncle.

"If Master Paul offers you to be partners, sir, I would, if I were you: if you'll excuse me," said Bassett.

Oscar Cresswell thought about it.

"I'll see the money," he said.

They drove home again, and, sure enough, Bassett came round to the garden-house with fifteen hundred pounds in notes. The twenty pounds reserve was left with Joe Glee, in the Turf Commission deposit.[8]

"You see, it's all right, Uncle, when I'm *sure!* Then we go strong, for all we're worth. Don't we, Bassett?"

"We do that, Master Paul."

"And when are you sure?" said the uncle, laughing.

"Oh, well, sometimes I'm *absolutely* sure, like about Daffodil," said the boy; "and sometimes I have an idea; and sometimes I haven't even an idea, have I, Bassett? Then we're careful, because we mostly go down."

"You do, do you! And when you're sure, like about Daffodil, what makes you sure, sonny?"

"Oh, well, I don't know," said the boy uneasily. "I'm sure, you know, Uncle; that's all."

"It's as if he had it from heaven, sir," Bassett reiterated.

"I should say so!" said the uncle.

But he became a partner. And when the Leger was coming on, Paul was "sure" about Lively Spark, which was a quite inconsiderable horse. The boy insisted on putting a thousand on the horse, Bassett went for five hundred, and Oscar Cresswell two hundred. Lively Spark came in first, and the betting had been ten to one against him. Paul had made ten thousand.

"You see," he said, "I was absolutely sure of him."

Even Oscar Cresswell had cleared two thousand.

"Look here, son," he said, "this sort of thing makes me nervous."

"It needn't, Uncle! Perhaps I shan't be sure again for a long time."

"But what are you going to do with your money?" asked the uncle.

"Of course," said the boy, "I started it for Mother. She said she had no luck, because Father is unlucky, so I thought if *I* was lucky, it might stop whispering."

"What might stop whispering?"

"Our house. I *hate* our house for whispering."

"What does it whisper?"

"Why—why"—the boy fidgeted—"why, I don't know. But it's always short of money, you know, Uncle."

"I know it, son, I know it."

"You know people send Mother writs,[9] don't you, Uncle?"

"I'm afraid I do," said the uncle.

"And then the house whispers, like people laughing at you behind your back. It's awful, that is! I thought if I was lucky—"

"You might stop it," added the uncle.

The boy watched him with big blue eyes, that had an uncanny cold fire in them, and he said never a word.

"Well, then!" said the uncle. "What are we doing?"

"I shouldn't like Mother to know I was lucky," said the boy.

---

8 Turf Commission deposit: a kind of bank in which a better can deposit money to bet with.

9 writs: a legal document; here, signifying that legal action is about to be taken to recover an unpaid bill.

THE TWENTIETH CENTURY

"Why not, son?"

"She'd stop me."

"I don't think she would."

"Oh!"—and the boy writhed in an odd way—"I *don't* want her to know, Uncle."

"All right, son! We'll manage it without her knowing."

They managed it very easily. Paul, at the other's suggestion, handed over five thousand pounds to his uncle, who deposited it with the family lawyer, who was then to inform Paul's mother that a relative had put five thousand pounds into his hands, which sum was to be paid out a thousand pounds at a time, on the mother's birthday, for the next five years.

"So she'll have a birthday present of a thousand pounds for five successive years," said Uncle Oscar. "I hope it won't make it all the harder for her later."

Paul's mother had her birthday in November. The house had been "whispering" worse than ever lately, and, even in spite of his luck, Paul could not bear up against it. He was very anxious to see the effect of the birthday letter, telling his mother about the thousand pounds.

When there were no visitors, Paul now took his meals with his parents, as he was beyond the nursery control. His mother went into town nearly every day. She had discovered that she had an odd knack of sketching furs and dress materials, so she worked secretly in the studio of a friend who was the chief "artist" for the leading drapers. She drew the figures of ladies in furs and ladies in silk and sequins for the newspaper advertisements. This young woman artist earned several thousand pounds a year, but Paul's mother only made several hundreds, and she was again dissatisfied. She so wanted to be first in something, and she did not suc-ceed, even in making sketches for drapery advertisements.[10]

She was down to breakfast on the morning of her birthday. Paul watched her face as she read her letters. He knew the lawyer's letter. As his mother read it, her face hardened and became more expressionless. Then a cold, determined look came on her mouth. She hid the letter under the pile of others, and said not a word about it.

"Didn't you have anything nice in the post for your birthday, Mother?" said Paul.

"Quite moderately nice," she said, her voice cold and absent.

She went away to town without saying more.

But in the afternoon Uncle Oscar appeared. He said Paul's mother had had a long interview with the lawyer, asking if the whole five thousand could not be advanced at once, as she was in debt.

"What do you think, Uncle?" said the boy.

"I leave it to you, son."

"Oh, let her have it, then! We can get some more with the other," said the boy.

"A bird in the hand is worth two in the bush, laddie!" said Uncle Oscar.

"But I'm sure to *know* for the Grand National; or the Lincolnshire; or else the Derby. I'm sure to know for *one* of them," said Paul.

So Uncle Oscar signed the agreement, and Paul's mother touched the whole five thousand. Then something very curious happened. The voices in the house suddenly went mad, like a chorus of frogs on a spring evening. There were certain new furnishings, and Paul had a tutor. He was *really* going to Eton, his father's school, in the following autumn. There were flowers

10 **drapery advertisements:** advertisements for clothing and dress goods.

D. H. LAWRENCE

in the winter, and a blossoming of the luxury Paul's mother had been used to. And yet the voices in the house, behind the sprays of mimosa and almond blossom, and from under the piles of iridescent cushions, simply trilled and screamed in a sort of ecstasy: "There *must* be more money! Oh-h-h; there *must* be more money. Oh, now, now-w! Now-w-w—there *must* be more money! —more than ever! More than ever!"

It frightened Paul terribly. He studied away at his Latin and Greek with his tutors. But his intense hours were spent with Bassett. The Grand National had gone by: he had not "known," and had lost a hundred pounds. Summer was at hand. He was in agony for the Lincoln. But even for the Lincoln he didn't "know," and he lost fifty pounds. He became wild-eyed and strange, as if something were going to explode in him.

"Let it alone, son! Don't you bother about it!" urged Uncle Oscar. But it was if the boy couldn't really hear what his uncle was saying.

"I've got to know for the Derby! I've got to know for the Derby!" the child reiterated, his big blue eyes blazing with a sort of madness.

His mother noticed how overwrought he was.

"You'd better go to the seaside. Wouldn't you like to go now to the seaside, instead of waiting? I think you'd better," she said, looking down at him anxiously, her heart curiously heavy because of him.

But the child lifted his uncanny blue eyes.

"I couldn't possibly go before the Derby, Mother!" he said. "I couldn't possibly!"

"Why not?" she said, her voice becoming heavy when she was opposed. "Why not? You can still go from the seaside to see the Derby with your uncle Oscar, if that's what you wish. No need for you to wait here. Besides, I think you care too much about these races. It's a bad sign. My family has been a gambling family, and you won't know till you grow up how much damage it has done. But it has done damage. I shall have to send Bassett away, and ask Uncle Oscar not to talk racing to you, unless you promise to be reasonable about it: go away to the seaside and forget it. You're all nerves!"

"I'll do what you like, Mother, so long as you don't send me away till after the Derby," the boy said.

"Send you away from where? Just from this house?"

"Yes," he said, gazing at her.

"Why, you curious child, what makes you care about this house so much, suddenly? I never knew you loved it."

He gazed at her without speaking. He had a secret within a secret, something he had not divulged, even to Bassett or to his uncle Oscar.

But his mother, after standing undecided and a little bit sullen for some moments, said:

"Very well, then! Don't go to the seaside till after the Derby, if you don't wish it. But promise me you won't let your nerves go to pieces. Promise you won't think so much about horse racing and *events,* as you call them!"

"Oh, no," said the boy casually. "I won't think much about them, Mother. You needn't worry. I wouldn't worry, Mother, if I were you."

"If you were me and I were you," said his mother, "I wonder what we *should* do!"

"But you know you needn't worry, Mother, don't you?" the boy repeated.

"I should be awfully glad to know it," she said wearily.

"Oh, well, you *can,* you know. I

mean, you *ought* to know you needn't worry," he insisted.

"Ought I? Then I'll see about it," she said.

Paul's secret of secrets was his wooden horse, that which had no name. Since he was emancipated from a nurse and a nursery-governess, he had had his rocking horse removed to his own bedroom at the top of the house.

"Surely, you're too big for a rocking horse!" his mother had remonstrated.

"Well, you see, Mother, till I can have a *real* horse, I like to have *some* sort of animal about," had been his quaint answer.

"Do you feel he keeps you company?" she laughed.

"Oh, yes! He's very good, he always keeps me company, when I'm there," said Paul.

So the horse, rather shabby, stood in an arrested prance in the boy's bedroom.

The Derby was drawing near, and the boy grew more and more tense. He hardly heard what was spoken to him, he was very frail, and his eyes were really uncanny. His mother had sudden strange seizures of uneasiness about him. Sometimes, for half-an-hour, she would feel a sudden anxiety about him that was almost anguish. She wanted to rush to him at once, and know he was safe.

Two nights before the Derby, she was at a big party in town, when one of her rushes of anxiety about her boy, her first-born, gripped her heart till she could hardly speak. She fought with the feeling, might and main, for she believed in common sense. But it was too strong. She had to leave the dance and go downstairs to telephone to the country. The children's nursery-governess was terribly surprised and startled at being rung up in the night.

"Are the children all right, Miss Wilmot?"

"Oh, yes, they are quite all right."

"Master Paul? Is he all right?"

"He went to bed as right as a trivet. Shall I run up and look at him?"

"No," said Paul's mother reluctantly. "No! Don't trouble. It's all right. Don't sit up. We shall be home fairly soon." She did not want her son's privacy intruded upon.

"Very good," said the governess.

It was about one o'clock when Paul's mother and father drove up to their house. All was still. Paul's mother went to her room and slipped off her white fur cloak. She had told her maid not to wait up for her. She heard her husband downstairs, mixing a whisky and soda.

And then, because of the strange anxiety at her heart, she stole upstairs to her son's room. Noiselessly she went along the upper corridor. Was there a faint noise? What was it?

She stood, with arrested muscles, outside his door, listening. There was a strange, heavy, and yet not loud noise. Her heart stood still. It was a soundless noise, yet rushing and powerful. Something huge, in violent, hushed motion. What was it? What in God's name was it? She ought to know. She felt that she knew the noise. She knew what it was.

Yet she could not place it. She couldn't say what it was. And on and on it went, like a madness.

Softly, frozen with anxiety and fear, she turned the door handle.

The room was dark. Yet in the space near the window, she heard and saw something plunging to and fro. She gazed in fear and amazement.

Then suddenly she switched on the light, and saw her son, in his green pajamas, madly surging on the rocking horse. The blaze of light suddenly lit him up, as he urged the wooden horse, and lit her up, as she stood, blonde, in her dress of pale green and crystal, in the doorway.

"Paul!" she cried. "Whatever are you doing?"

"It's Malabar!" he screamed, in a powerful, strange voice. "It's Malabar!"

His eyes blazed at her for one strange and senseless second, as he ceased urging his wooden horse. Then he fell with a crash to the ground, and she, all her tormented motherhood flooding upon her, rushed to gather him up.

But he was unconscious, and unconscious he remained, with some brain fever. He talked and tossed, and his mother sat stonily by his side.

"Malabar! It's Malabar! Bassett, Bassett, I *know*! It's Malabar!"

So the child cried, trying to get up and urge the rocking horse that gave him his inspiration.

"What does he mean by Malabar?" asked the heart-frozen mother.

"I don't know," said the father stonily.

"What does he mean by Malabar?" she asked her brother Oscar.

"It's one of the horses running for the Derby," was the answer.

And, in spite of himself, Oscar Cresswell spoke to Bassett, and himself put a thousand on Malabar: at fourteen to one.

The third day of the illness was critical: they were waiting for a change. The boy, with his rather long, curly hair, was tossing ceaselessly on the pillow. He neither slept nor regained consciousness, and his eyes were like blue stones. His mother sat, feeling her heart had gone, turned actually into a stone.

In the evening, Oscar Cresswell did not come, but Bassett sent a message, saying could he come up for one moment, just one moment? Paul's mother was very angry at the intrusion, but on second thoughts she agreed. The boy was the same. Perhaps Bassett might bring him to consciousness.

The gardener, a shortish fellow with a little brown mustache, and sharp little brown eyes, tiptoed into the room, touched his imaginary cap to Paul's mother, and stole to the bedside, staring with glittering, smallish eyes at the tossing, dying child.

"Master Paul!" he whispered. "Master Paul! Malabar came in first all right, a clean win. I did as you told me. You've made over seventy thousand pounds, you have; you've got over eighty thousand. Malabar came in all right, Master Paul."

"Malabar! Malabar! Did I say Malabar, Mother? Did I say Malabar? Do you think I'm lucky, Mother? I knew Malabar, didn't I? Over eighty thousand pounds! I call that lucky, don't you, Mother? Over eighty thousand pounds! I knew, didn't I know I knew? Malabar came in all right. If I ride my horse till I'm sure, then I tell you, Bassett, you can go as high as you like. Did you go for all you were worth, Bassett?"

"I went a thousand on it, Master Paul."

"I never told you, Mother, that if I can ride my horse, and *get there*, then I'm absolutely sure—oh, absolutely! Mother, did I ever tell you? I *am* lucky!"

"No, you never did," said the mother.

But the boy died in the night.

And even as he lay dead, his mother heard her brother's voice saying to her: "My God, Hester, you're eighty-odd thousand to the good, and a poor devil of a son to the bad. But, poor devil, poor devil, he's best gone out of a life where he rides his rocking horse to find a winner."

Comment

We usually think of "luck" as a mysterious something that is kind to us, that makes our dreams come true. We often say, too, that life is a game or a gamble—you have to take chances, and if you are lucky, they "pan out." "Pan out" is an American slang phrase that comes down to us from the days when gold was discovered in the West, and the man who made a lucky claim (or lucky strike) was one who found gold in the bottom of his miner's pan as he swirled out the water and the gravel. In England, however, and in many parts of our country too, the example of having "luck" that everyone recognizes is the winning bet on a race horse. "Lady luck" is kind to those who win. In this story, however, the luck that wins is not kind; it is inhumanly cruel. Paul has a power over luck, and he uses it to give his mother what she wants, what he thinks will make her happy—perhaps, what will even melt the hard place in her heart. Yet it is a power that exhausts Paul as he exercises it. He tries to silence the "whisperings" in the house; he tries to make his family content; but the burden and the effort are too much.

Here, we say, people try to "keep up with the Joneses"; in England, they say "keep up appearances." However we express it, anxiety about money, position, appearances does distress many people. Lawrence suggests that this anxiety is not merely distressing: it is inhuman, for it makes us cold to people around us, even to members of our own family. Lawrence suggests this, of course, by fantasy, by an improbable occurrence. Paul's secret power of riding his rocking horse until he "arrives" at the name of a winning horse may well seem fantastic and absurd. Yet Lawrence's account of it is not silly or childish, for it expresses his convictions about those who put money before love and humanity.

1. In the first description of the whispering in Paul's house (p. 773, col. 2), we are told that it is heard by the children and their toys, but apparently not by the adults. What does this description, fantastic as it seems, tell you about the moral atmosphere of the house? What does it tell you about the relation between the children and their parents?

2. In the last description of the whispering (p. 779, col. 2), we are told that after Paul's mother has received his five thousand pounds, and after she has bought new furnishings and filled the house with expensive flowers and cushions, the voices are louder than ever. Why is the whispering louder now? Why not quieter? What is Lawrence saying about money here?

3. The fact that the whispering grew louder "frightened Paul terribly" (p. 780, col. 1). Is Paul afraid of ghosts—afraid as any child might be in a haunted house? Or is he frightened by the effort he knows he must make to silence these voices? What is Lawrence telling you about Paul here?

4. The night he rides to his last winner, Paul's mother, coming to his room in her anxiety, hears a "strange, heavy, and yet not loud noise," the sound of his rocking horse. But is this sound in any way like the whispering that Paul has heard?

5. And in this final scene, when Paul falls from his rocking horse, his mother, "all her tormented motherhood flooding upon her, rushed to gather him up." She cannot know, as we do, what he has done for her, yet she responds as if she did know. What has happened at this moment to Paul's mother? Why does she *say* nothing?

6. The last word in this story is Uncle Oscar's: "he's best gone out of a life where he rides his rocking horse to find a winner." Uncle Oscar knows more than anyone else except Bassett about what Paul has gone through, yet he has made use of Paul's gift for picking winners. How deep, therefore, is the pity and understanding with which he says this last word?

7. But Lawrence, the author, is also speaking to us through this last sentence, and he certainly knows all that has happened. What does he make Paul out to be? What sort of "life" does he believe Paul has "gone out of"?

8. Write a short essay explaining how this last sentence, as Lawrence means it, is ironic. Show how it expresses both Uncle Oscar's attitude toward Paul and the discovery of her son that Paul's mother experiences.

Katherine Mansfield (1888-1923)

Most short-story writers are novelists too; indeed, most writers have looked upon the short story as a kind of training or apprenticeship for the larger and more serious business of writing novels. But a few have brought all their imagination and skill to bear exclusively upon the short story, and of these no one has set a higher standard than Katherine Mansfield. No writer in modern times, certainly, has been more dedicated than she to perfecting this literary form. She was born in Wellington, New Zealand, in 1888 (the story below reflects her childhood there), but went to London in 1903 to continue her education, particularly in music. Except for one two-year period, from 1906 to 1908, when she returned to New Zealand, she spent the rest of her short life in England and Europe, her very last years in various European centers for the treatment of tuberculosis. She died near Paris in 1923, leaving behind her husband, John Middleton Murry, himself a distinguished English writer. Murry has edited her notebooks and letters as well as her stories, and has provided readers of literature with one of the fullest records available of an important modern writer. "The Apple Tree," although it is not one of the best-known of Katherine Mansfield's stories, has been reprinted here because it so clearly represents both the seriousness and the playfulness that her best works deftly combine.

The Apple Tree

Katherine Mansfield

THERE WERE TWO orchards belonging to the old house. One, that we called the "wild" orchard, lay beyond the vegetable garden; it was planted with bitter cherries and damsons[1] and transparent yellow plums. For some reason it lay under a cloud; we never played there, we did not even trouble to pick up the fallen fruit; and there, every Monday morning, to the round open space in the middle, the servant girl and the washerwoman carried the wet linen—Grandmother's nightdresses, Father's striped shirts, the hired man's cotton trousers and the servant girl's "dreadfully vulgar" salmon-pink flannelette drawers jigged and slapped in horrid familiarity.

But the other orchard, far away and hidden from the house, lay at the foot of a little hill and stretched right over to the edge of the paddocks[2]—to the clumps of wattles[3] bobbing yellow in the bright sun and the blue gums with their streaming sickle-shaped leaves. There, under the fruit trees, the grass grew so thick and coarse that it tangled and knotted in your shoes as you walked, and even on the hottest day it was damp

1 **damsons:** small purple plums.
2 **paddocks:** enclosed fields.
3 **wattles:** acacia trees—small flowering trees.

to touch when you stopped and parted it this way and that, looking for windfalls—the apples marked with a bird's beak, the big bruised pears, the quinces, so good to eat with a pinch of salt, but so delicious to smell that you could not bite for sniffing. . . .

One year the orchard had its Forbidden Tree. It was an apple tree discovered by Father and a friend during an after-dinner prowl one Sunday afternoon.

"Great Scott!" said the friend, lighting upon it with every appearance of admiring astonishment: "Isn't that a ——?" And a rich, splendid name settled like an unknown bird on the tree.

"Yes, I believe it is," said Father lightly. He knew nothing whatever about the names of fruit trees.

"Great Scott!" said the friend again: "They're wonderful apples. Nothing like 'em—and you're going to have a tiptop crop. Marvelous apples! You can't beat 'em!"

"No, they're very fine—very fine," said Father carelessly, but looking upon the tree with new and lively interest.

"They're rare—they're very rare. Hardly ever see 'em in England nowadays," said the visitor and set a seal on Father's delight. For Father was a self-made man and the price he had to pay for everything was so huge and so painful that nothing rang so sweet to him as to hear his purchase praised. He was young and sensitive still. He still wondered whether in the deepest sense he got his money's worth. He still had hours when he walked up and down in the moonlight half deciding to "chuck this confounded rushing to the office every day—and clear out—clear out once and for all." And now to discover that he'd a valuable apple tree thrown in with the orchard—an apple tree that this Johnny from England positively envied!

"Don't touch that tree! Do you hear me, children!" said he, bland and firm; and when the guest had gone, with quite another voice and manner:

"If I catch either of you touching those apples you shall not only go to bed—you shall each have a good sound whipping." Which merely added to its magnificence.

Every Sunday morning after church Father, with Bogey and me tailing after, walked through the flower garden, down the violet path, past the lace-bark tree, past the white rose and syringa bushes, and down the hill to the orchard. The apple tree—like the Virgin Mary—seemed to have been miraculously warned of its high honor, standing apart from its fellows, bending a little under its rich clusters, fluttering its polished leaves, important and exquisite before Father's awful eye. His heart swelled to the sight—we knew his heart swelled. He put his hands behind his back and screwed up his eyes in the way he had. There it stood—the accidental thing—the thing that no one had been aware of when the hard bargain was driven. It hadn't been counted in, hadn't in a way been paid for. If the house had been burned to the ground at that time it would have meant less to him than the destruction of his tree. And how we played up to him, Bogey and I—Bogey with his scratched knees pressed together, his hands behind his back, too, and a round cap on his head with "*H.M.S. Thunderbolt*"[4] printed across it.

The apples turned from pale green to yellow; then they had deep pink stripes painted on them, and then the pink melted all over the yellow, reddened, and spread into a fine clear crimson.

At last the day came when Father took out of his waistcoat pocket a little pearl penknife. He reached up. Very slowly and very carefully he picked two apples growing on a bough.

"By Jove! They're warm," cried Father in amazement. "They're wonderful apples! Tiptop! Marvelous!" he echoed. He rolled them over in his hands.

"Look at that!" he said. "Not a spot—not a blemish!" And he walked through the orchard with Bogey and me stumbling after, to a tree stump under the wattles. We sat, one on either side of Father. He laid one apple down, opened the pearl penknife and neatly and beautifully cut the other in half.

"By Jove! Look at that!" he exclaimed.

"Father!" we cried, dutiful but really enthusiastic, too. For the lovely red color had bitten right through the white flesh of the apple; it was pink to the shiny black pips lying so justly in their scaly pods. It looked as though the apple had been dipped in wine.

"Never seen *that* before," said Father. "You won't find an apple like that in a hurry!" He put it to his nose and pronounced an unfamiliar word. "Bouquet![5] What a bouquet!" And then he handed to Bogey one half, to me the other.

"Don't *bolt* it!" said he. It was agony to give even so much away. I knew it, while I took mine humbly and humbly Bogey took his.

Then he divided the second with the same neat beautiful little cut of the pearl knife.

I kept my eyes on Bogey. Together we took a bite. Our mouths were full of

---

4 *H.M.S. Thunderbolt:* Bogey is wearing a sailor hat with the name of a battleship printed on the band.

5 **Bouquet:** aroma, or fragrance, usually used by experts in speaking of fine wines.

THE TWENTIETH CENTURY

a floury stuff, a hard, faintly bitter skin—a horrible taste of something dry. . . .

"Well?" asked Father, very jovial. He had cut his two halves into quarters and was taking out the little pods. "Well?"

Bogey and I stared at each other, chewing desperately. In that second of chewing and swallowing a long silent conversation passed between us—and a strange meaning smile. We swallowed. We edged near Father, just touching him.

"Perfect!" we lied. "Perfect—Father! Simply lovely!"

But it was no use. Father spat his out and never went near the apple tree again.

Comment

"Father was a self-made man. . . ." This little story gently exposes the anxieties of a man who constantly worries about success. The exposure is gentler and more comical than many writers would make it, but it is nevertheless deft and sure. And it is surest in its details.

1. After the visitor from England has praised his tree, the father warns his children not to touch it. While the guest is there, he is *"bland and firm,"* but later he speaks differently. What does *bland* mean here? What does the change in the father's manner tell you about him?
2. "For some reason," the children never played in the orchard nearer the house. A few sentences later the appearance of this nearer orchard on washday is described. Where is the humor in this description? Does the way this orchard looks every Monday suggest a reason, perhaps even *the* reason, why the children and their father never go there?
3. The apple tree with the "rich, splendid name" is called "a Forbidden Tree." Why is this phrase capitalized? How does this phrase emphasize the seriousness of the father about his possessions? But how does it also gently tease his attitude toward his possessions? Do you see a similar irony in the comparison of the tree to the Virgin Mary?
4. The children take their sections of apple "humbly" and they try to conceal the taste from their father. What does their behavior tell you about their attitude toward him? Do they fear him? Or do they sympathize with him? Write a paragraph in which you sketch the father's character as you understand it at the end of the story.

In 1948 the poet Wystan Hugh Auden said,

> "Why do you want to write poetry?" If the young man answers: "I have important things to say," then he is not a poet. If he answers: "I like hanging around words listening to what they say," then maybe he is going to be a poet.

This has not, however, always been Auden's position, or his practice. Certainly his own poetry shows that he himself as a young man liked hanging around all sorts of words—words drawn from his widely ranging studies in science and psychology as well as literature. He was born in York in 1907, educated at Oxford, and after participating as an ambulance driver in the Spanish Civil War, came to America in 1939, where he has mainly resided ever since, though in 1956 he became Professor of Poetry at Oxford. When all his work is considered—his poems, essays, lectures, and librettos for operas—he seems to believe that in the modern world no one who does care about words can ever be at a loss for something important to say with them. In the following poem, indeed, he shows how even an "unknown citizen," the person who is only a file number in public records and opinion surveys, is a subject on which a poet can say a good deal, and imply even more.

The Unknown Citizen

W. H. Auden

(To JS/07/M/378[1]
This Marble Monument
Is Erected by the State)

He was found by the Bureau of Statistics to be
One against whom there was no official complaint,
And all the reports on his conduct agree
That, in the modern sense of an old-fashioned word, he was a
    saint,
For in everything he did he served the Greater Community.   5
Except for the War till the day he retired
He worked in a factory and never got fired,
But satisfied his employers, Fudge Motors Inc.
Yet he wasn't a scab[2] or odd in his views,
For his Union reports that he paid his dues,   10
(Our report on his Union shows it was sound)
And our Social Psychology workers found
That he was popular with his mates and liked a drink.

---

1 **JS/07/M/378**: the unknown citizen's file number. It has been suggested that "JS" might mean "John Smith"; what might the rest mean? Note the rhyme in the full title.
2 **scab**: strikebreaker.

The Press are convinced that he bought a paper every day
And that his reactions to advertisements were normal in every
    way.   15
Policies taken out in his name prove that he was fully insured,
And his Health-card shows he was once in hospital but left it
    cured.
Both Producers Research and High-Grade Living declare
He was fully sensible to the advantages of the Instalment Plan
And had everything necessary to the Modern Man,   20
A phonograph, a radio, a car and a frigidaire.
Our researchers into Public Opinion are content
That he held the proper opinions for the time of year;
When there was peace, he was for peace; when there was war,
    he went.
He was married and added five children to the population,   25
Which our Eugenist says was the right number for a parent of
    his generation,
And our teachers report that he never interfered with their
    education.
Was he free? Was he happy? The question is absurd:
Had anything been wrong, we should certainly have heard.

Comment

In this poem Auden makes us face the difference between public language and what Yeats called "personal utterance."

1. This poem may seem to be in free verse. But what formal device of poetry does it contain? Does the presence of this device make the poem more serious or more comic?
2. Why is no direct sense experience presented in this poem? Why should each sentence be a flat statement?
3. But do you find anything like a pun in line 27? Does "their" education mean the one they were giving, or the one they were acquiring? How could anyone interfere in either process?
4. Questions about the Citizen's happiness or freedom are "absurd," we are told. "Had anything been wrong, we should certainly have heard." What is the only kind of "wrong" that the "we" of this poem can hear or know?

"Elegy for J.F.K."

This is an elegy for a man who was, at his tragic death, the best-known citizen of the United States—whose Presidents are regarded with particular interest by the English people. Many poems were written on the occasion of President Kennedy's death, but few were more perfect examples of the elegy—a poem of lamentation and praise —than this.

Elegy for J.F.K.

(November 22nd, 1963)

W. H. Auden

Why *then*, why *there*,
Why *thus*, we cry, did he die?
The heavens are silent.

What he was, he was:
What he is fated to become   5
Depends on us.

Remembering his death,
How we choose to live
Will decide its meaning.

When a just man dies,   10
Lamentation and praise,
Sorrow and joy, are one.

Comment

There is no answer to our cries of lamentation; the meaning of his death will be decided by "How we choose to live."

Reflect upon the final stanza: what does it tell us of the nature of the "just man"? And what hope does it offer for the future of the society in which the "just man" dies?

Human Beings and Inhuman Society
Summing Up

None of the selections of this group directly tells us of a conflict between personal and social values, yet each in its way is concerned with just such a conflict. What do these selections tell you, then, about the way in which 20th-century writers express the personal, individual values in which they believe? How has their way of expressing these values changed from the way of Wordsworth or Shelley or Keats?

Trench warfare on the Western Front, 1916. Lancashire Fusileers fix their bayonets before an assault on the German lines.

War and Peace

THE TWO World Wars of the 20th century caused everyone whom they touched to ask of himself and his world some searching questions. For Homer, for Shakespeare, and for other great writers of the past, war was a heroic action; but the heroic endeavors of modern war seem overshadowed by its huge destruction of resources, of talent, and of all kinds of life. The experience of modern war is not limited to those who fight, nor is the expression of that experience limited to the time of war. The two World Wars, together with the many violent engagements and revolutions that came before and after each of them, have engaged the minds of the most imaginative writers, not because these events are isolated, but because they engaged all men everywhere in the questions and sufferings, the hopes and defiances, that are always present to the dedicated writer. Wars do not make writers; they do enlarge the audience that can understand the questions raised by war, the questions that have always concerned serious writers.

W. H. AUDEN

Rupert Brooke (1887-1915)

"Joyous, fearless, versatile, deeply instructed, with a classic symmetry of mind and body"—this description of Rupert Brooke was written in the London *Times* by Winston Churchill in April, 1915. A few days earlier, the young poet, an officer on his way to Egypt in a troopship early in World War I, had died of blood poisoning and had been buried on the Greek Island of Scyros, the island from which Achilles had set out for the Trojan War. Rupert Brooke was raised and educated at Rugby, the famous school, where his father was a master, and at Cambridge. He was a gifted scholar—he was made a Fellow of his Cambridge college; he was an adventurous traveler—he journeyed through the United States and Canada and out to the South Seas; and he was a promising poet—his first volume had been published in 1911, when he was but twenty-four. He was strikingly handsome, and his great charm as well as his great gifts made him one of the most admired men of his generation. The following poem, perhaps the most famous of all poems associated with World War I, was written by a young man whose untimely death symbolized for many the terrible cost of war in human talent.

The Soldier

Rupert Brooke

If I should die, think only this of me:
   That there's some corner of a foreign field
That is forever England. There shall be
   In that rich earth a richer dust concealed;
A dust whom England bore, shaped, made aware,   5
   Gave, once, her flowers to love, her ways to roam,
A body of England's, breathing English air,
   Washed by the rivers, blest by suns of home.

And think, this heart, all evil shed away,
   A pulse in the eternal mind, no less   10
      Gives somewhere back the thoughts by England given;
Her sights and sounds; dreams happy as her day;
   And laughter, learnt of friends; and gentleness,
      In hearts at peace, under an English heaven.

Comment

The soldier who speaks these lines is not yet in battle, but he is far away from the country for which he is about to fight. What is the nature of his bond to that country?

1. In the English *Book of Common Prayer,* these words are a part of the service for the burial of the dead: "We therefore commit his body to the ground; earth to earth, ashes to ashes, dust to dust." How are these words echoed in the first division of the poem? What part of himself does the soldier say is bound to England in this division of the poem?
2. Into what has the "dust" of the first division of the poem been transformed in the second division? And what part of himself does the poet say is bound to England in this division?
3. But are these two parts of himself, and their bonds with England, so separate? How does the verb "think" in the first line of each division join the two divisions?
4. "The Soldier," then, is not a poem of two separate parts. It is a sonnet: the octave is completed by the sestet. What is the full nature of the bond between the soldier and his country that this sonnet celebrates?

Wilfred Owen (1893-1918)

> My subject is War, and the pity of War.
> The Poetry is in the pity.

These sentences were found among the papers of a young officer killed on the Western Front just one week before the Armistice of November 11, 1918. His name was Wilfred Owen, and he was killed by machine-gun fire as he helped his men to bridge a canal near the Belgian border. He came from an ancient town on the border between England and Wales, and had been educated in Birmingham and at London University. Owen was in almost every way less favored by fortune than was Rupert Brooke; but his achievements, most of them unpublished when he died, have made him for later poets and students of literature the greatest poetic talent that was cut off by the first World War. He had been invalided home in 1917, after an exhausting experience of trench warfare, and had returned to the battlefield only in August of 1918. Yet wherever he was, he kept writing and thinking, and the manuscripts he left behind him will not soon be forgotten.

The following poem of Wilfred Owen has had a large influence on 20th-century poetry both for its technique and its vision. The speaker dreams that he has escaped from battle down into a Hell like the ancient Hades of the Greeks. There he meets the enemy he slew and hears that enemy voice regret for both of them. The strangeness of this "Strange Meeting" is enhanced by Owen's use of consonance: if you look at the rhyming words of the first four lines, for example (*escaped-scooped, groined-groaned*), you will see that their consonants are similar but that their vowels are not. The near-rhyme haunts the ear as the images do the eye.

Strange Meeting

Wilfred Owen

It seemed that out of battle I escaped
Down some profound dull tunnel, long since scooped
Through granites which titanic wars had groined.[1]
Yet also there encumbered sleepers groaned,
Too fast in thought or death to be bestirred.   5
Then, as I probed them, one sprang up, and stared
With piteous recognition in fixed eyes,
Lifting distressful hands as if to bless.
And by his smile, I knew that sullen hall,
By his dead smile I knew we stood in Hell.   10
With a thousand pains that vision's face was grained;
Yet no blood reached there from the upper ground,
And no guns thumped, or down the flues made moan.
"Strange friend," I said, "here is no cause to mourn."
"None," said the other, "save the undone years,   15
The hopelessness. Whatever hope is yours,
Was my life also; I went hunting wild
After the wildest beauty in the world,
Which lies not calm in eyes, or braided hair,
But mocks the steady running of the hour,[2]   20
And if it grieves, grieves richlier than here.
For by my glee[3] might many men have laughed,
And of my weeping something had been left,
Which must die now. I mean the truth untold,
The pity of war, the pity war distilled.   25

1 **groined:** A groin is the edge made by the intersection of two vaults or tunnels; the verb here means "carved out."
2 **mocks . . . hour:** is too firm to pass away with time.
3 **glee:** joyful melody.

Now men will go content with what we spoiled.
Or, discontent, boil bloody, and be spilled.
They will be swift with swiftness of the tigress,
None will break ranks, though nations trek[4] from progress.
Courage was mine, and I had mystery,   30
Wisdom was mine, and I had mastery;
To miss the march of this retreating world
Into vain citadels that are not walled.[5]
Then, when much blood had clogged their chariot-wheels
I would go up and wash them from sweet wells,   35
Even with truths that lie too deep for taint.
I would have poured my spirit without stint
But not through wounds; not on the cess[6] of war.
Foreheads of men have bled where no wounds were.[7]
I am the enemy you killed, my friend.   40
I knew you in this dark; for so you frowned
Yesterday through me as you jabbed and killed.
I parried; but my hands were loath and cold.
Let us sleep now. . . ."

4 **trek:** migrate; move away from.
5 **To . . . walled:** I was strong enough to resist the world as it marched,
foolishly, into the unsafe, useless fortress of war.
6 **cess:** assessment; obligation; also, here, the sense of *cess* as in *cesspool*.
7 **Foreheads . . . were:** In an early draft of this poem Owen wrote: "Even
as One [Christ] who bled where no wounds were."

Comment

The dialogue between these two speakers is indeed a strange meeting in a strange place, for although they are enemies, there is a deep
kinship between them that can be uttered only here.

1. How does the first speaker know that "we stood in Hell"? What
   does he see that convinces him?
2. What kind of man is "the other"? What was he searching for?
   What were his hopes?
3. How does the second speaker, "the other," recognize the first one?
   What does he see that is the opposite of what the first speaker saw?
4. Suppose both speakers are the same man—suppose they are two aspects, one frowning and one smiling, of one person: What then is
   "strange" about this "meeting"? What "piteous recognition" (l. 7)
   does this one man experience? What has the war done to the one
   man of whom these two speakers are two tragically separate parts?

Henry Reed (1914-   )

Here is yet one more "strange meeting" of different areas of experience in wartime: this one in a poem about a young soldier undergoing his training in the early days of World War II. The author, Henry Reed, a graduate of Birmingham University, served in both the Army and the Foreign Office, and since the war has written for radio and newspapers. "Naming of Parts" is one of a group of three poems called "Lessons of the War"; each poem, like this one, is an ironic lesson in the strange distance—and nearness—between peace and war.

Naming of Parts

Henry Reed

To-day we have naming of parts. Yesterday,
We had daily cleaning. And to-morrow morning,
We shall have what to do after firing. But to-day,
To-day we have naming of parts. Japonica[1]
Glistens like coral in all of the neighbouring gardens,   5
    And to-day we have naming of parts.

This is the lower sling swivel.[2] And this
Is the upper sling swivel, whose use you will see,
When you are given your slings. And this is the piling swivel,[3]
Which in your case you have not got. The branches   10
Hold in the gardens their silent, eloquent gestures,
    Which in our case we have not got.

This is the safety-catch, which is always released
With an easy flick of the thumb. And please do not let me
See anyone using his finger. You can do it quite easy   15
If you have any strength in your thumb. The blossoms
Are fragile and motionless, never letting anyone see
    Any of them using their finger.

And this you can see is the bolt. The purpose of this
Is to open the breech, as you see. We can slide it   20
Rapidly backwards and forwards: we call this

---

1 Japonica (jə pŏn′ə kə): the flowering quince.
2 sling swivel: One on the stock and one near the muzzle of the rifle, they are fastenings through which the leather sling of the rifle is passed so that it may be carried over the shoulder with the arms free.
3 piling swivel: the fastening used in piling or stacking guns together.

Easing the spring. And rapidly backwards and forwards
The early bees are assaulting and fumbling the flowers:
   They call it easing the Spring.

They call it easing the Spring: it is perfectly easy   25
If you have any strength in your thumb: like the bolt,
And the breech, and the cocking-piece, and the point of balance,
Which in our case we have not got; and the almond-blossom
Silent in all of the gardens and the bees going backwards and
     forwards,   30
   For to-day we have naming of parts.

Comment

There are two voices in this poem, the first that of the new soldier,
the other that of the drill instructor. The training session occurs early
in the war, and some parts of the soldiers' equipment are not yet available ("Which in your case you have not got"). What is the difference
between the voice of the trainee and that of the instructor?

1. How, in each stanza, does the last sentence express a change in point
   of view? And how, in each final sentence, does this change in point
   of view affect the words repeated from the first part of the stanza?
2. "For today we have naming of parts," says the last line. Why can
   there be only naming of *parts?* Why can the young soldier not
   name the *whole?*

C. Day Lewis (1904-1972)

Looking back on almost twenty-five years of writing, C. (Cecil) Day
Lewis wrote in 1951: "Poetry is a vocation, a habit, and a search for
truth. . . . We write in order to understand, not in order to be understood." The second sentence is an exaggeration, but of the sort that
sometimes tells more of the truth than the most precise remark. It fits
well, at any rate, with the large element of autobiography in Lewis's
poems; for he has written to understand himself, and yet he is one of
the most widely understood poets of his generation.

He was born in Ireland and studied at Oxford. Upon graduation he
became a schoolmaster, writing poetry and interesting himself in political affairs when he could take time from his classroom. After a period
of residence in the south of England near the scene of the following
poem, he worked during the war in the Ministry of Information. Later
he worked in broadcasting, at lecturing on literature, and at the understanding that comes to him in writing poetry.

"Watching Post"

The scene of the following poem, written when Lewis was in the
Home Guard at the start of the war, is the historic Axe valley in Dorset,

in the region Hardy called Wessex in his novels. The watching post looks out over a village where Marlborough, the general who defeated the French at Blenheim in 1704, was born; it looks upon the church containing the family vault of Sir Francis Drake, the first Englishman to sail around the world; and it stands above the valley from which the Duke of Monmouth began his unsuccessful rebellion against the king in the late 17th century. These are some of "the old ramparts" of the night in which the poet and the farmer keep watch.

Watching Post

C. Day Lewis

A hill flank overlooking the Axe valley.
Among the stubble a farmer and I keep watch
For whatever may come to injure our countryside—
Light-signals, parachutes, bombs, or sea-invaders,
The moon looks over the hill's shoulder, and hope   5
Mans the old ramparts of an English night.

In a house down there was Marlborough born. One night
Monmouth marched to his ruin out of that valley.
Beneath our castled hill, where Britons[1] kept watch,
Is a church where the Drakes, old lords of this countryside,   10
Sleep under their painted effigies.[2] No invaders
Can dispute their legacy of toughness and hope.

Two counties away, over Bristol,[3] the searchlights hope
To find what danger is in the air tonight.
Presently gunfire from Portland[4] reaches our valley   15
Tapping like an ill-hung door in a draught. My watch
Says nearly twelve. All over the countryside
Moon-dazzled men are peering out for invaders.

---

1 Britons: the native population who watched for raids from the Danes.
2 effigies: statues on the tombs in the church.
3 Bristol: some sixty miles to the north; an important center for the manufacture of airplanes.
4 Portland: a limestone peninsula that Hardy called "The Gibraltar of Wessex."

The farmer and I talk for a while of invaders:
But soon we turn to crops—the annual hope,   20
Making of cider, prizes for ewes.   Tonight
How many hearts along this war-mazed valley
Dream of a day when at peace they may work and watch
The small sufficient wonders of the countryside.

Image or fact, we both in the countryside   25
Have found our natural law, and until invaders
Come will answer its need: for both of us, hope
Means a harvest from small beginnings, who this night
While the moon sorts out into shadow and shape our valley,
A farmer and a poet, are keeping watch.   30

Comment

A farmer and a poet keep watch over their country in time of war; together they watch and hope.

1. In the first stanza, "hope/Mans the old ramparts of an English night."   What are some of the "ramparts" in the scene before the poet and the farmer?
2. In the last stanza, "hope/Means a harvest from small beginnings." What are some of the "small beginnings" in which the poet and farmer share?   What is the "harvest" they both hope for?
3. "Hope/Mans. . . ."; "hope/Means. . . .": How does the similarity of sound in these two metaphorical statements help to bind together the first and the last parts of the poem?

Laurence Binyon (1869-1943)

The following poem was written during the days when Britain was under fire from the air.   Laurence Binyon, its author, died before World War II ended, but in his long life he had seen one other great war end. In both war and peace he had witnessed many changes that might have led him to say, as he does here: "The world that was ours is a world that is ours no more."   But he does not say this with bitterness or sadness.

Binyon was an authority on oriental art.   He wrote the first book in English on Far Eastern painting, and some of the characteristics of this art, especially its finely drawn images of flowers, appear in his poetry. He wrote, too, on the religious drawings and engravings of William Blake, the visionary poet of the Romantic period.   One of the strongest influences on Binyon's poetry was Dante Alighieri, the great Italian poet of the Middle Ages. Binyon translated Dante's *Divine Comedy*, one of the world's greatest religious poems, and a work whose main images have become symbols of moral and religious values for many subsequent writers. One such symbol is that of fire or flame, and its central importance to "The Burning of the Leaves" is implied by the very title.

The Burning of the Leaves

Laurence Binyon

Now is the time for the burning of the leaves.
They go to the fire; the nostril pricks with smoke
Wandering slowly into the weeping mist.
Brittle and blotched, ragged and rotten sheaves!
A flame seizes the smoldering ruin, and bites   5
On stubborn stalks that crackle as they resist.

The last hollyhock's fallen tower is dust:
All the spices of June are a bitter reek,
All the extravagant riches spent and mean.
All burns! the reddest rose is a ghost.   10
Sparks whirl up, to expire in the mist: the wild
Fingers of fire are making corruption clean.

Now is the time for stripping the spirit bare,
Time for the burning of days ended and done,
Idle solace of things that have gone before.   15
Rootless hope and fruitless desire are there:
Let them go to the fire with never a look behind.
The world that was ours is a world that is ours no more.

They will come again, the leaf and the flower, to arise
From squalor of rottenness into the old splendor,   20
And magical scents to a wondering memory bring;
The same glory, to shine upon different eyes.
Earth cares for her own ruins, naught for ours.
Nothing is certain, only the certain spring.

Comment

The situation of this poem is familiar: it is autumn, the time when we burn the leaves and debris of the garden. But it is an autumn too in which another kind of burning occurs, the burning caused by fire bombs dropped in air raids.

1. Consider what the poet sees in the first two stanzas of this poem. He says that "the reddest rose is a ghost," obviously because the time when roses bloom is over. But "ghosts" are pale: what in the scene before him does the poet find so red that a rose is a "ghost" in comparison? How do "Fingers of fire" make "corruption clean"?
2. "Now is the time for stripping the spirit bare": How does this opening line of stanza 3 echo the first line of the poem? What change, what new subject, in the poet's meditation does it announce? What are some words in stanza 3 that explain "spirit"?
3. The last line of the poem refers to spring, not autumn: "Nothing is certain, only the certain spring." With this spring, he tells us, will come "the leaf and the flower" (l. 19). But what else will come? What other renewal of life does the poet see in the autumn burning of the leaves?

William Sansom (1912-   )

The experiences of William Sansom as a London fireman during World War II, he has said, made him a serious writer. He was born in London and has lived there all his life. He has worked in a bank, in an advertising agency, and has traveled and studied in Western Europe; but since 1944, when *Fireman Flower*, his first collection of short stories, was published, he has been a dedicated and prolific writer. The following story, written at the end of the war, brings before us a ghastly failure of communication, a mistake as terrible in its absurdity as the wreckage of war that litters the country where it occurs. Claeys, a Belgian, is a civilian relief worker. The war has ended and he is trying to help in the return of displaced people and prisoners to their homes in Eastern Europe. The tragic death of Claeys is itself an example of the great question he is thinking about when he is cut down, the question whether order, growth, and peace or disorder, death and war are supreme.

LAURENCE BINYON   **801**

How Claeys Died

William Sansom

In Germany, two months after the capitulation,[1] tall green grass and corn had grown up round every remnant of battle, so that the war seemed to have happened many years ago. A tank, nosing up from the corn like pale gray toad, would already be rusted, ancient: the underside of an overturned carrier exposed intricacies red-brown and clogged like an agricultural machine abandoned for years. Such objects were no longer the contemporary traffic, they were exceptional carcasses;[2] one expected their armor to melt like the armor of crushed beetles, to enter the earth and help fertilize further the green growth in which they were already drowned.

Claeys and his party—two officers and a driver—drove past many of these histories, through miles of such fertile green growth stretching flatly to either side of the straight and endlessly gray avenues. Presently they entered the out-

skirts of a town. This was a cathedral town, not large, not known much—until by virtue of a battle its name now resounded in black letters the size of the capital letters on the maps of whole countries. This name would now ring huge for generations, it would take its part in the hymn of a national glory; such a name had already become sacred, stony, a symbol of valor. Claeys looked about him with interest—he had never seen the town before, only heard of the battle and suffered with the soldiers who had taken it and held it for four hopeful days with the hope dying each hour until nearly all were dead, hope and soldiers. Now as they entered the main street, where already the white tram-trains were hooting, where the pale walls were chipped and bullet-chopped, where nevertheless there had never been the broad damage of heavy bombs and where therefore the pavements and shop-fronts were already washed and civil—as they entered these streets decked with summer dresses and flecked with leaf patterns, Claeys looked in vain for the town of big letters, and smelled only perfume; a wall of perfume; they seemed to have entered a scent-burg, a sissy-burg, a town of female essences, Grasse[3]—but it was only that this town happened to be planted with lime trees, lime trees everywhere, and these limes were all in flower, their shaded greenery alive with the golden powdery flower, whose essence drifted down to the streets and filled them. The blood was gone, the effort of blood had evaporated. Only scent, flowers, sunlight, trams, white dresses.

"A nice memorial," Claeys thought.

"Keep it in the geography book." Then the car stopped outside a barracks. The officers got out. Claeys said he would wait in the car. He was not in uniform, he was on a civil mission, attached temporarily to the army. It does not matter what mission. It was never fulfilled. All that need be said is that Claeys was a teacher, engaged then on relief measures, a volunteer for this work of rehabilitation of the enemy, perhaps a sort of half-brother-of-mercy as during the occupation he had been a sort of half-killer. Now he wanted to construct quickly the world of which he had dreamed during the shadow years; now he was often as impatient of inaction as he had learned to be patient before. Patience bends before promise: perhaps this curiosity for spheres of action quickened his interest as now a lorryload of soldiers drew up and jumped down at the barrack gate. One of the soldiers said: "They're using mortars."[4] Another was saying: "And do you blame 'em?"

There had been trouble, they told Claeys, up at the camp for expatriates—the camp where forced laborers imported from all over Europe waited for shipment home. A group of these had heard that a released German prisoner-of-war was returning to work his farm in the vicinity of the camp. They had decided to raid the farm at nightfall, grab as much food as possible, teach the German a trick or two. But the German had somehow got hold of a grenade—from the fields, or perhaps hidden in the farmhouse. At any rate, he had thrown it and killed two of the expatriates. The others had retreated, the story had spat round, before long the expatriates were coming back on the farm in full strength. They had rifles

and even mortars. The news got back to the occupational military and a picket[5] had been sent over. The mortars were opening fire as it arrived, but they were stopped: the expatriates respected the British. Yet to maintain this respect they had to keep a picket out there for the night. Not all the polskis or czechskis[6] or whoever they were had gone home. A few had hung about, grumbling. The air was by no means clear.

When the officers returned, Claeys told them that he had altered his plans, he wanted to go up and take a look at this expatriates' camp. He gave no reason, and it is doubtful whether he had then a special reason; he felt only that he ought to see these expatriates and talk to them. He had no idea of what to say, but something of the circumstances might suggest a line later.

So they drove out into the country again, into the green. Rich lucent corn stretched endlessly to either side of the straight and endless road. Regularly, in perfect order, precisely intervaled beeches flashed by: a rich, easy, discreet roof of leaves shaded their passage as the foliage met high above. Occasionally a notice at the roadside reminded them of mines uncleared beyond the verges,[7] occasionally a tree bore an orderly white notice addressed to civil traffic. And occasionally a unit of civil traffic passed—a family wheeling a handcart, a cyclist and his passenger, and once a slow-trudging German soldier making his gray way back along the long road to his farm. But there was nothing about this figure in gray-green to suggest more than a farmer dressed as a soldier; he walked slowly,

---

4 mortars: short, portable cannons that fire shells in a high arc.

5 picket: squad of soldiers who serve as guards.
6 polskis or czechskis: men from Poland or Czechoslovakia.
7 verges: edges or shoulders of the road.

WILLIAM SANSOM

he seemed to be thinking slowly, secure in his destination and free of time as any countryman walking slowly home on an empty road.

All was order. Birds, of course, sang. A green land, unbelievably quiet and rich, sunned its moisture. Each square yard lay unconcerned with the next, just as each measure of the road lay back as they passed, unconcerned with their passing, contented, remaining where it had always been under its own beech, a piece of land. And when at last the beech-rows stopped, the whole of that flat country seemed to spread itself suddenly open. The sky appeared, blue and sailing small white clouds to give it air. Those who deny the flatlands forget the sky—over flat country the sky approaches closer than anywhere else, it takes shape, it becomes the blue-domed lid on a flat plate of earth. Here is a greater intimacy between the elements; and for once, for a little, the world appears finite.

The carload of four traveled like a speck over this flat space. And Claeys was thinking: "Such a summer, such still air—something like a mother presiding heavily and quietly, while down in her young the little vigors boil and breed . . . air almost solid, a sort of unseen fruit fiber . . . a husk guarding the orderly chaos of the breeding ground. . . ."

Such a strict order seemed indeed to preside within the intricate anarchy—success and failure, vigorous saplings from the seeds of good fortune, a pennyworth of gas[8] from the seeds that fall on stony ground: yet a sum total of what might appear to be complete achievement, and what on the human level appears to be peace. And on that level, the only real level, there appeared—

over by the poplar plumes? Or by the windmill? Or at some flat point among the converged hedges?—there appeared one scar, a scar of purely human disorder: over somewhere lay this camp of ten thousand displaced souls, newly freed but imprisoned still by their strange environment and by their great expectations born and then as instantly barred. On the face of it, these seemed to represent disorder, or at most a residue of disorder. But was this really so? Would such disorder not have appeared elsewhere, in similar quantity and under conditions of apparent order? Were they, perhaps, not anything more than stony-grounders—the disfavored residue of an anarchic nature never governed directly, only impalpably guided by more general and less concerned governments? Was it right to rationalize, to impose order upon such seed, was it right—or at least, was it sensible? It was right, obviously—for a brain made to reason is itself a part of nature and it would be wrong to divert it from its necessitous reasoning. But right though reason may be, there was no more reason to put one's faith in the impeccable work of the reasoning brain than to imagine that any other impressive yet deluded machine—like, for instance, the parachute seed—should by its apparent ingenuity succeed. Look at the parachute seed—this amazing seed actually flies off the insensate plant-mother! It sails on to the wind! The seed itself hangs beneath such an intricate parasol, it is carried from the roots of its mother to land on fertile ground far away and set up there an emissary generation![9] And more—when it lands, this engine is so constructed that draughts inch-close to the soil drag, drag, drag at the little

8 **pennyworth of gas:** The seed that falls on stony ground does not grow; its life dries up and passes into the air like gas.

9 **emissary generation:** An emissary is an agent, sometimes a secret agent, of a country; the parachute seeds fly to strange regions and start a new, hidden generation or crop.

parachute, so that the seed beneath actually erodes the earth, digs for itself a little trench of shelter, buries itself! Amazing! And what if the clever little seed is borne on the wrong wind to a basin of basalt?[10]

Claeys was thinking: "The rule of natural anarchy—a few succeed, many waste and die. No material waste: only a huge waste of effort. The only sure survival is the survival of the greater framework that includes the seed and all other things on the earth—the furious landcrab, the bright young Eskimo, the Antiguan cornbroker[11]—every thing and body . . . and these thrive and decay and compensate . . . just as we, on the threshold of some golden age of reason, just as we are the ones to harness some little nuclear genius, pack it into neat canisters, store it ready to blow up all those sunny new clinics when the time comes, the time for compensation. . . ."

Just then the car drove into a small town on the bank of a broad river. Instantly, in a matter of yards, the green withered and the party found themselves abruptly in what seemed to be some sort of a quarry, dry, dug-about, dust-pale, slagged up on either side with excavated stones.

It was indeed an excavation; it was of course the street of a town. This town was dead. It had been bombed by a thousand aircraft, shelled by an entire corps of artillery, and then fought through by land soldiers. No houses were left, no streets. The whole had been churned up, smashed and jig-

sawed down again, with some of the jigsaw pieces left upended—those gaunt walls remaining—and the rest of the pieces desiccated into mounds and hollows and flats. No grass grew. The air hung sharp with vaporized dust. A few new alleys had been bulldozed through; these seemed pointless, for now there was no traffic, the armies had passed through, the town was deserted. Somewhere in the center Claeys stopped the car. He held up his hand for silence. The four men listened. Throughout that wasted city there was no sound. No distant muttering, no murmur. No lost hammering, no drowned cry. No word, no footstep. No wheels. No wind shifting a branch—for there were no trees. No flapping of torn cloth, this avalanche had covered all the cloth. No birds—but one, a small bird that flew straight over, without singing; above such a desert it moved like a small vulture, a shadow, a bird without destination. Brick, concrete, gravel-dust—with only two shaped objects as far all round as they could see: one, an intestinal engine[12] of fat iron pipes, black and big as an upended lorry,[13] something thrown out of a factory; and leaning on its side a pale copper-green byzantine cupola like a gigantic sweet-kiosk[14] blown over by the wind, the tower fallen from what had been the town church. This—in a town that had been the size of Reading.[15]

Almost reverently, as on sacred ground, they started the car and drove

---

10 **basin of basalt** (bə sôlt′): valley of hard, dark rock in which no plants can live.
11 **landcrab . . . cornbroker:** The landcrab lives both on land and in water. Eskimos, of course, live in the Arctic; Antigua is an island southwest of Puerto Rico, and a cornbroker there would be in the business of importing wheat. The three suggest the vast extent of the life of man and animals on earth.

12 **intestinal engine:** The boiler pipes of a discarded and wrecked steam engine look like coils of intestines.
13 **lorry:** truck.
14 **byzantine** (bĭz′ən tēn) **cupola . . . sweet-kiosk** (kĭ ŏsk′): The dome of the wrecked church tower, covered with copper, looks like the kind of newsstand found on the streets of European cities where candy (sweets) and other small items are sold.
15 **Reading:** a city in southern England with a population of 113,000.

off again. Through the pinkish-white mounds the sound of the motor seemed now to intrude garishly. Claeys wanted only to be out of the place. Again, this destruction seemed to have occurred years before; but now because of the very absence of green, of any life at all, of any reason to believe that people had ever lived there. Not even a torn curtain. They wormed through and soon, as abruptly as before, the country began and as from a seasonless pause the summer embraced them once more.

Claeys stood up off his seat to look over the passing hedges. The camp was somewhere near now. The driver said, two kilometers.[16] Surely, Claeys thought, surely with that dead town so near the men in this camp could realize the extent of the upheaval, the need for a pause before their journey could be organized? Surely they must see the disruption, this town, the one-way bridges over every stream far around, the roads pitted and impassable? Yet . . . what real meaning had these evidences? Really, they were too negative to be understood, too much again of something long finished. It was not as if something positive, like an army passing, held up one's own purpose; not even a stream of aircraft, showing that at least somewhere there was an effort and direction. No, over these fields there was nothing, not even the sense of a pause, when something might be restarted; instead a vacuity stretched abroad, a vacuum of human endeavor, with the appalling contrast of this vegetable growth continuing evenly and unconcerned. That was really the comprehensible evidence, this sense of the land and of the essence of life continuing, so that one must wish to be up and walk-

ing away, to be off to take part not in a regrowth but in a simple continuation of what had always been. For every immediate moment there was food to be sought, the pleasures of taste to be enjoyed: what was more simple than to walk out and put one's hands on a capful of eggs, a pig, a few fat hens? And if a gray uniform intervened, then it was above all a gray uniform,[17] something instinctively obstructive, in no real sense connected with the dead town. The only real sympathy that ever came sometimes to soften the grayness of this gray was a discovery, felt occasionally with senses of wonder and unease, that this uniform went walking and working through its own mined cornfields and sometimes blew itself up—that therefore there must be a man inside it, a farmer more than a soldier. But the gray was mostly an obstruction to the ordinary daily desire for food, for fun, for something to be tasted. The day for these men was definitely a day. It was no twenty-four hours building up to a day in the future when something would happen. No future day had been promised. There was, therefore, no succession of days, no days for ticking off, for passing through and storing in preparation. There were in fact the days themselves, each one a matter for living, each a separate dawning and tasting and setting.

Suddenly Claeys heard singing, a chorus of men's voices. A second later the driver down behind the windshield heard it. He nodded, as though they had arrived. The singing grew louder, intimate—as though it came from round a corner that twisted the road immediately ahead. But it came from a lane just before, it flourished suddenly into

---

16 **kilometers** (kĭl′ə mē′tərz): A kilometer is about five-eighths of a mile.

17 **gray uniform:** worn by the demobilized German soldier who has returned to his farm.

a full-throated Slavic anthem[18]—and there was the lane crowded with men, some sitting, others marching four abreast out into the road. The car whirred down to a dead halt. The singing wavered and stopped. Claeys saw that the driver had only his left hand on the wheel—his other hand was down gripping the black butt of a revolver at his knee. (He had never done this driving through German crowds earlier.)

"It's not the camp," the driver said. "These are some of them, though. The camp's a kilometer up the road." He kept his eyes scanning slowly up and down the line of men crowding in the lane's entry, he never looked up at Claeys. Then the men came a few paces forward, though they looked scarcely interested. Probably they were pushed forward by the crowd behind, many of whom could not have seen the car, many of whom were still singing.

Claeys stood upright and said: "I'd like to talk to these . . . you drive on, get round the corner and wait. I don't want that military feeling."

The men looked on with mild interest, as though they might have had many better things to do. They looked scarcely "displaced"; they had a self-contained air, an independence. There was no censure in their stare; equally no greeting; nor any love. Their clothes were simple, shirts and grayish trousers and boots: though these were weather-stained, they were not ragged.

Claeys jumped down. An interest seemed to quicken in some of the watching men as they saw how Claeys was dressed—beret, plus fours, leather jacket. It was because of these clothes that the military in the car gave Claeys no salute as they drove off; also because they disapproved of this kind of non-sense, and this may have been why they neither smiled nor waved, but rather nodded impersonally and whirred off round the corner. They might, for instance, have been dropping Claeys after giving him some sort of a lift.

So that Claeys was left quite alone on the road, standing and smiling at the crowd of expatriates grouped at the entrance to the lane. The car had disappeared. It had driven off the road and round the corner. There, as often happens when a vehicle disappears from view, its noise had seemed to vanish too. Presumably it had stopped. But equally it might have been presumed far away on its journey to the next town.

The men took a pace or two forward, now beginning to form a crescent shape round Claeys, while Claeys began to speak in English: "Good afternoon, mates. Excuse me, I'm Pieter Claeys—native of Belge." None of the men smiled. They only stared hard at him. They were too absorbed now even to mutter a word between themselves. They were searching for an explanation, a sign that would clarify this stranger. They were unsure, and certainly it seemed unimpressed. "Good afternoon, comrades," Claeys shouted. "Gentlemen, hello!"

Without waiting, for the silence was beginning to weigh, he turned into French. *"Suis Claeys de Belge. Je veux vous aider. Vous permettez—on peut causer un peu?"*

He repeated: *"Peut-être?"*[19] And in the pause while no one answered he looked up and above the heads of these

---

18 **Slavic anthem:** The song sounds like the national hymn not just of one country but of all Slavic-speaking people.

19 *Suis . . . Peut-être?:* "I'm Claeys from Belgium. I want to help you. Will you let me—can we talk a little . . . How about it?"

men, feeling that his smile might be losing its first flavor, that somehow an embarrassment might be dissolved if he looked away.

The country again stretched wide and green. Claeys was startled then to see sudden huge shapes of paint-box color erecting themselves in the distance. But then immediately he saw what they were—the wings and fuselages of broken gliders. They rose like the fins of huge fish, tilted at queer angles, grounded and breathlessly still. Difficult at first to understand, for their shapes were strange and sudden, and of an artifice dangerously like something natural: brightly colored, they might have been shapes torn from an abstract canvas and stuck willfully on this green background: or the bright broken toys left by some giant child.

Claeys tried again: "*Gijmijneheeren zijt blijkbaar in moeilijkheden. Ik zou die gaarne vernemen. . . .*"[20]

The Dutch words came ruggedly out with a revival of his first vigor, for Claeys was more used to Dutch and its familiarity brought some ease again to his smile. It brought also a first muttering from the men.

They began to mutter to each other in a Slav-sounding dialect—Polish, Ukrainian, Czech, Russian?—and as this muttering grew it seemed to become an argument. Claeys wanted instantly to make himself clearer, he seemed to have made some headway at last and so now again he repeated the Dutch. This time he nodded, raised his arm in a gesture, even took a pace forward in his enthusiasm. But now one of the men behind began to shout angrily, and would have pushed himself forward shaking his fist—had the others not held him.

It was not clear to Claeys—he felt that the Dutch had been understood, and yet what he had said was friendly . . . he began to repeat the words again. Then, halfway through, he thought of a clearer way. He broke into German. There was every chance that someone might understand German; they might have been working here for three years or more; or anyway it was the obvious second language. ". . . *so bin ich hier um Ihnen zu hilfen gekommen. Bitte Kameraden, hören Sie mal. . . .*"[21]

The muttering rose, they were plainly talking—and now not to each other but to him. The crescent had converged into a half-circle, these many men with livening faces were half round him. Clays stood still. Overhead the summer sky made its huge dome, under which this small group seemed to make the pin-point center. The green quiet stretched endlessly away to either side, the painted gliders stuck up brightly. No traffic.

". . . *bitte ein moment . . . ich bin Freund, Freund, FREUND . . .*"[22] And as he repeated this word *friend* he realized what his tongue had been quicker to understand—that none of his listeners knew the meaning of these German words. They knew only that he was speaking German, they knew the intonation well.

He stopped. For a moment, as the men nudged each other nearer, as the Slav words grew into accusation and imprecation, Claeys's mind fogged up appalled by this muddle, helplessly overwhelmed by such absurdity, such disorder and misunderstanding.

Then, making an effort to clear himself, he shook his head and looked

---

20 *Gijmijneheeren . . . vernemen:* a repetition of the preceding, in Dutch.

21 *so bin . . . mal:* "So I've come to help you. Please, friends, listen . . ."
22 *bitte . . . FREUND:* "Just a moment, please, I'm a friend, friend, FRIEND . . ."

London Eaon

Did you read it? 6
Quiz

1. It tells how we are constantly sroving is all kinds of
ways as we live.

2. Cletus

3. ~~00000000~~ The narrators parents

4. the narrator

5. Because it is something he doesn't want to remind them of.

closely from one man to the other. But the composure had gone: they were all mouths, eyes, anger and desire—they were no longer independent. And this was accumulating, breeding itself beyond the men as men. They had become a crowd.

Knowing that words were of no further use, Claeys did the natural thing—wearily, slowly he raised his arm in a last despairing bid for silence.

An unfortunate gesture. The shouting compounded into one confused roar. One of the men on the edge of the crowd jumped out and swung something in the air—a scythe. It cut Claeys down, and then all the pack of them were on him, kicking, striking, grunting and shouting less.

Claeys must have screamed as the scythe hit him—two shots thundered like two full stops into that muddle, there was an abrupt silence and two men fell forward; and then another shot and the men scattered crying into the lane.

Those three soldiers came running up to Claeys's body. They shot again into the men crowding the lane; but then the men bottled up in the narrow lane, suddenly turned and raised their arms above their heads. The soldiers held their fire, their particular discipline actuated more strongly than their emotions. Two of them kept their guns alert, gestured the men forward. They came, hands raised, shambling awkwardly. The other officer bent down to Claeys.

He was almost finished, messed with blood and blue-white where the flesh showed. He was breathing, trying to speak; and the officer knelt down on both his knees and raised Claeys's head up. But Claeys never opened his eyes—they were bruised shut. And no words came from his lips, though the officer lowered his head and listened very carefully.

Through the pain, through his battered head, one thought muddled out enormously. "Mistake . . . mistake . . ." And this split into two other confused, unanswered questions, weakening dulling questions. Broadly, if they could have been straightened out, these questions would have been: "Order or Disorder? Those fellows were the victims of an attempt to rule men into an impeccable order; my killing was the result of the worst, that is, the most stupid disorder. . . ."

But he couldn't get the words out, or any like them. Only—weakly, slowly he raised his right hand. He groped for the officer's hand, and the officer knew what he wanted and met the hand with his own in a handshake. Claeys just managed to point at the place where the men had been, where they still were. Then his head sank deep on to his neck. Again the officer knew what he wanted. He rose, his hand still outstretched from Claeys's grasp, like a hand held out by a splint. Then he started over toward the men.

Instinctively, for this hand of his was wet with blood, he wiped it on his tunic as he walked forward. Without knowing this, he raised his hand again into its gesture of greeting. There was a distasteful expression on his face, for he hardly liked such a duty.

So that when he shook hands with the first of the men, proffering to them, in fact, Claeys's handshake, none of these expatriates knew whether the officer was giving them Claeys's hand or whether he had wiped Claeys's gesture away in distaste and was now offering them his congratulation for killing such a common enemy as Claeys.

Comment

The main action of this story takes place after Claeys jumps down from the military vehicle and begins to speak to the crowd of prisoners. They cannot understand his language, whether French, Dutch, or German, but they think they understand his gestures and, when he speaks German, his intonation. They mistake him for their enemy, for one of the Germans who sent them here, far from the homes they are impatient to return to. The action is brief, tragic, and violent. Yet we cannot fully appreciate its tragic violence unless we understand all that we are told in the first part of the story. For, as we learn, if Claeys's dying thoughts could have been spoken, they would have been uttered as the question that has occupied him—and us—all through the journey to this place. The question is, "Order or Disorder?" And we see that it is not even to be answered by Claeys's horrible death. For as the officer goes to shake hands with the prisoners, in accordance with Claeys's dying wish, his gesture is not clear to them. They do not know whether he is thanking them or forgiving them. The first half of this story, then, where Claeys's question is first put to us, is of great importance to our understanding of the last half.

1. The story opens with a simile: The rusted machines of war are compared to abandoned agricultural machines—the instruments of war surrounded by green grass seem like instruments of peace. The tanks and carriers are then compared to another agricultural instrument, fertilizer, for they look like crushed beetles that enrich the soil as they rot away. How do these opening similes prepare you for the great question that Claeys is trying to answer as he dies?

2. In a town made famous by a battle, Claeys is surprised to find rows of lime trees blooming and giving off a scent like the atmosphere of the region of France where perfume is made. He finds not a ruined town smelling of battle, but a pleasant, perfumed, busy city. As the journey of Claeys and the officers continues into the flat, green farming country, he sees a land that because of its flatness seems close to the sky, a land that seems "finite" and orderly. But somewhere in the green farmland is the camp for displaced persons, "a scar of purely human disorder," a stony area where nothing will grow. Claeys thinks of the amazing parachute seed and recalls that at the end of its drifting fall it drags on the soil for a little way and makes a trench for itself. Parachute troops had dropped down on the land here during the war, and of them, too, some lived and some did not. How do the sweet-smelling town, the green fields surrounding the camp, and the description of the parachute seed prepare still further for Claeys's dying question?

3. The journey of Claeys and the officers is now almost over. They have come to the bombed-out town near the "scar" of the camp. Here, we are told, "the green withered." Claeys has asked himself, "And what if the clever little seed is borne on the wrong wind to a

basin of basalt?" How is Claeys something like a seed that has been blown by the wrong wind to stony ground rather than fertile, green land?

4. As he confronts the displaced persons, the men he wants to help, whom he wants to reassure about the delay of their return to their homes, Claeys cannot make them understand. He suddenly realizes that they do not understand his words but recognize only the German sounds in his speech. He then does "the natural thing": he raises his arm to signal for silence. But this "natural thing" is also "an unfortunate gesture." Why? Is Claeys's behavior orderly and peaceful? Or is it the opposite? Explain.

5. Claeys asks for silence, but the men roar all together. And then, "One of the men on the edge of the crowd jumped out and swung something in the air—a scythe." Write an essay in which you show how this sentence is the climax of this story: the climax of the action that occurs, but the climax too of the theme of order and disorder, war and peace, fertile soil and stony ground, that the author has woven into the action.

War and Peace
Summing Up

Claeys is killed by a scythe, an instrument of peace, in the midst of the confusion that war has brought about. The weapons of war and the instruments of peace are mingled together throughout Claeys's experience in this final story. As you look back at the poems in this section, do you find that their authors are similarly aware of the mingling of war and peace in their wartime experiences? What poems seem to you to ask the same question—order or disorder—that Claeys is asking? Do they answer this question as William Sansom seems to you to anwer it in this story?

The Adventure of Growth

IN A WORLD struggling toward new affirmations, in a society that sometimes presses hard on the individual, and in a time when the wonder
of a far-ranging science and the pity of war stand side by side, no
adventure is more challenging than the adventure of growth. And
this is the theme to which the 20th-century writer has turned again and
again. What does it feel like to grow up in the modern world? How
is the experience of young people today different from that of their
grandparents? What does the 20th century look like to those who will
live through it into the 21st? "The child is father of the man," said
Wordsworth, and modern psychology says it too. The subject treated
more often than any other by the 20th-century writer is the experience
of growth and development.

Setting Forth

The moment of setting forth and the first awareness that there is a
large and strange world ahead have been the theme of many works
of English literature. The following story and poems address this
theme in ways characteristic of their authors and of the modern period.

Mary Lavin (1912-   )

Although Mary Lavin (Mrs. William Walsh) was born in Massachu-
setts, she lives in County Meath, Ireland, near Dublin. There, when
not keeping house for her lawyer husband and their three daughters,
she has for more than twenty years been writing short stories and
novels. She was educated in Ireland and received the M.A. degree in
1937 from the National University in Dublin. Her master's thesis was
a study of Jane Austen, whose neatness of style and sense of comedy
are reflected in her own works. Mary Lavin's first story was published
in 1938, and her first collection of stories, published in 1942, won an
award somewhat like our Pulitzer prize. She has gone on to publish
three novels and many short stories, all of them about Irish people and
places. As the following story reveals, she has a keen but gentle interest in the terrors and the joys of growing up. The adventure of the
little boy who tells the story shows us how he changes from being
"nothing but an old babby," as his friend Mickser calls him, to becoming a person even more mature than his forceful friend.

The Living

Mary Lavin

"How MANY dead people do you know?" said Mickser suddenly.

Immediately, painfully, I felt my answer would show me once more inferior to him. He was eight and I was a year younger. "Do you mean ghosts?" I said slowly, to gain time.

We were sitting one on each post of the big gate at the schoolhouse that was down on the main road.

"No," said Mickser, "I mean corpses."

"But don't they get buried?" I cried.

"They're not buried for three days," said Mickser scathingly. "They have to be scrubbed and laid out and waked.[1] You're not allowed to keep them any longer than that, though, because their eyes go like this," and he put his hands up to his eyes and drew down the lower lids to show the inner lids swimming with watery blood. "They rot," he explained.

"Mind would you fall!"[2] said I hastily, thinking he might let go his eyelids if he had to steady himself on the gatepost.

We were sitting there watching the cars coming home from the Carlow and Kerry football finals. But it wasn't much fun. Cars were going past in plentiful numbers, all right, but spaced out fairly on the road, and moving nearly as slow as a funeral. As Mickser said, it was only the family man that came home straight after a match. The real followers didn't come home till night—or near morning, maybe.

"The sport is when the drunks are coming home," Mickser said. "Passing each other out on the roads—on the corners, mind! But your mammy wouldn't let a little fellow like you stay out long enough for that."

It was only too true. It was a wonder she'd let me down to the road at all. She had a terrible dread of danger, my mammy. "You can go down to the schoolhouse and look at the cars coming home if you're careful. And mind yourself!" she said to me. "Keep well in from the road! And wait a minute. Don't sit up on that high wall, the way I saw you doing once."

That was why we were up on the gateposts, although they were much higher than the wall. "Gateposts isn't walls," Mickser had said definitively.

That was Mickser all over. You could count on him to get you out of anything. But he could get you into anything, too. You never knew where a word would lead you with him. Still, this talk about dead people seemed safe enough.

"How many do you know, Mickser?" I asked, fearful but fascinated.

"Oh, I couldn't count them," said Mickser loftily. "I bet you don't know any at all."

"My grandfather's dead."

"How long is he dead?"

"He died the year I was born," I said. "On the very day after," I added importantly, having heard it told by my mother to many people.

---

1 **waked:** A wake is the watching, sometimes all night, of relatives and friends beside the body of a dead person.
2 **Mind would you fall:** Watch out or you'll fall.

"Bah!" said Mickser. "You can't count him. If you could, then you could count your great-grandfather, and your great-great-grandfather, and your great-great-great-grandfather, and—" He stopped enumerating them. "Sure, isn't the ground full of dead people that nobody knew?" He pointed down below us to where, through the nettles, the clay under the wall showed black and sour. "If you took up a spade this minute," he said, "and began digging down there, or anywhere, you'd be no time digging till you'd come on bones; somebody's bones! Oh, no!" He shook his head. "You can't count people you didn't *see* dead, like my Uncle Bat that was sitting up eating a boiled egg one minute and lying back dead the next minute. He's the best one on my list, though," he added magnanimously. "I saw him alive *and* dead. But most of them I only saw dead—like my two aunts that died within a week of each other. Everyone said it was a pity, if they had to go, it couldn't have been closer together, so they could have made the one wake of it. How many is that?" he asked. "How many have I now?"

"Only three," I said, and my heart rose. He mightn't be able to think of any more.

He looked at me severely. He was a bit of a mind reader, as well as everything else. "I wanted to pick out the good ones for first," he said.

That overwhelmed me altogether. "Ah, sure, Mickser," I said. "You needn't strain yourself thinking of good ones for one, because I never saw one at all. One of my aunts died a year ago, all right, and they had to take me to the funeral because they had no one to leave me with, but they wouldn't let me into the house till the funeral was ready to move off. They took it in turns to sit out in the car with me."

"And what was that for?" said Mickser, looking blankly at me.

"I don't know," I said in a grieved voice, but after a bit, in fairness to my mother and father, I felt obliged to hazard a reason for their behavior. "Maybe they thought I'd dream about it."

This seemed to give Mickser cause for profound reflection. We sat saying nothing for a long time. I was thinking back over it myself. "Not that it did much good keeping me outside," I said. "Because I dreamt about it all the same. I kept them up till morning, nightmaring about coffins and hearses!"

"Coffins and hearses?" Mickser repeated. "What was there about them to have you nightmaring? It's corpses that give people the creeps." He looked at me with genuine interest. "I wonder what way you'd take on if you saw a corpse," he said. And then he snapped his fingers. "I have it!" he said. "There's a wake in a cottage the other side of the town."

"Mind would you fall!" I cried—urgently this time, because of the way he was hopping about on his pants with excitement.

"Do you know the cottage I mean? It's at the level crossing. Do you know the woman in it—the one that opens and shuts the railway gates? Well, her man is dead."

"A big fellow with red hair, is it?"

"That's the one!" he cried. "She used to have him sitting outside the cottage most days, on a chair in the sun. He was a class of delicate[3] ever since he was hit by the train." Deftly Mickser tapped his own pate. "Up here," he said. "He died this morning. Isn't it a bit of luck I was put in mind of it? But we'd want to get there quick," he

---

3 class of delicate: extremely weak.

said, taking one jump down off the gate-post, into the nettles and all, without minding them any more than if he was a dog. "Before the crowds," he said. "They'll be glad to see us no matter who we are if we're the first to come. They're always glad to see the first signs of people arriving after the cleaning and work they've been doing. And they love to see children above all—at first, that is to say. 'Look who we have here,' they say," he mimicked in a voice that nearly made myself fall off the post. "'Bless their little hearts,'" he went on. "'Come in, child,' they say, and they lead you inside, telling each other that there's no prayers like the prayers of a child. Up they bring you straight to the bed, and down they put you kneeling beside it where you can get a good gawk at everything. Oh, but it's a different story altogether, I can tell you, if you leave it till late in the evening. You haven't a chance of getting inside the door. 'Out of this with you, you little brats!' That's all you'd hear then. 'This is no place for children—out of it, now!' They'd take the yard brush to you if you didn't get yourself out of sight double quick. So we'd better get up there immediately," he said. "What are you waiting for?"

I was hanging back for more reasons than one. "I was told to stay here," I said.

"You were told not to be climbing, too," said Mickser, as quick as a lawyer. "So you can't say you were doing what you were told anyway—not but that it's doing all you're told that has you the way you are this day, knowing nothing about anything. To think they wouldn't let you see your own aunt laid out! I know it wouldn't be me that would be done out of a thing like that. And what's more, you oughtn't to put up with it, either. You ought to tell them

there'd be no nightmaring or carrying on about corpses if you were let get used to them like me. Are you coming, or are you not?"

It was a sweet, mild afternoon as we set out for the edge of the town to where the level crossing was, and the small slate-roofed house to one side of it. It was very familiar to me when I was a bit smaller and my mother used to take me for a walk out of town into the country air. We often had to wait for the gates to be opened for us, although the train would have thundered past.

"What is the delay?" my mother would ask impatiently.

"I have to wait for the signals, ma'am," the woman in charge of the gates would say. "You can pass through the wicket gate if you like, ma'am, but that's none of my responsibility."

"Oh, we're not in a hurry," my mother would say hastily, doubtless to give me a good example of caution.

But there was no need. I had heard Mickser say he put a halfpenny on the line one day and the train made a penny out of it.[4] I had no fancy for being flattened out to the size of a man. And anyway, I used to be very curious about the big white-faced man that would always be sitting in the little bit of garden on a chair—a chair brought out of the house, not one you'd leave outside, like we had in the garden at home.

"Do they take it in at night?" I asked once.

"Of course she does," said my mother in a shocked voice, but she must have thought I meant the man. "Please don't stare," she'd say to me. "Why do I have to keep telling you!"

4 he put . . . out of it: The diameter of a British halfpenny is roughly that of our quarter; that of the penny is roughly that of our half dollar.

Only when the gates were opened, and we were starting to cross over the rails, would she let on to see him for her part. It was always the same. "How is he today?" she'd ask the woman.

And the woman's answer was always the same, too. "Poorly." That's what she'd say. At times, though rarely, she'd add, "It's a great cross to me, but I suppose God knows what He's doing."

"We must hope so anyway," my mother would say to that, and she'd step over the rails more quickly, till we were on the other side. "How is it," she said testily to me when we were out of earshot, "those gates are always shut no matter what time of the day we want to pass?"

And now here, today, for the first time in my life, the railway gates were wide open.

"Do you think they might have forgot to close them, on account of the wake?" I said, hanging back nervously.

Mickser stood in the middle of the tracks and looked back at me. "God knows it's high time someone took you in hand," he said. "You're nothing but an old babby. What harm would it be if they did forget? Haven't you eyes? Haven't you ears? And if it comes to that, haven't you legs? Come on out of that!" But he slowed down himself, and looked up and down the line.

"We're the first here," he said when we got to the cottage. He sized up the look of the little house expertly. "They're not finished yet," he said.

To me the house looked as if it had been washed down from top to bottom, the way I was washed down myself every Sunday night, and the bit of garden outside it was the same, neatened and tidied, and the big stones that I used to remark around the flower beds, keeping back the clay from the grass, were whitewashed, every one of them. It was a treat—the stones bright white, and the clay bright black, with not one weed to be seen out of all the weeds there used to be everywhere. But the chair wasn't out.

"We're too early," Mickser said, and he stepped suddenly over to the window that was to one side of the door, me at his heels. Being behind him, I couldn't see near so well, but I saw enough to open my mouth. Between white counterpanes[5] and white tablecloths and white mantle cloths and white doilies, the place was got up like the chapel at Lady Day. And in the middle of it all, like the high altar, was a big bed with a counterpane as white and glossy as marble, and—

But Mickser didn't let me see any more. He pulled me away. "I don't think they're ready yet," he said. He seemed to be losing courage just as I was getting mine. He put his hands in his pockets and sauntered toward the door. "There now, what did I tell you!" he cried as we only missed getting drenched to the skin by a big basin of slops that was sloshed out the door at that minute.

"Did you ever walk the railroad tracks?" he asked suddenly. And I knew he'd let up altogether on going to the wake.

"I'm not allowed walk on the tracks," I said. Anyway, I was bent on seeing the bed better, and what was on it. "Let me get a look in the window, at least," I said, and I skipped back over the flowers and pasted my face to the glass.

What did I expect to see? I don't know. Not the great gray man that was carved out on the bed, hard as stone, all but his red hair; that was real-

5 **counterpanes:** bedspreads.

looking, like the hair on a doll. "Eh, Mickser. Could you give me a leg-up on the window sill?" I cried, getting more and more curious and excited.

"Are you pots?"[6] said Mickser. "If they came out and caught you up on that window sill, you'd be clouted out of here with one of those stones."

"A true word if ever there was one!" said a voice at that moment, and a thin bit of a woman in black came round the gable end with her sleeves rolled up and no smile on her, I can tell you. "Out of here with you!" she shouted. "This is no place for you!" Just the very thing Mickser said wouldn't be said to us.

But before we had time to get out of the flower bed, another woman came running out of the front door—the woman herself that used to have charge of the crossing gates. "It's not right to send anyone from the door of a dead-house,"[7] she said dully.

"Hush now, they're only gossoons,"[8] said the other one.

"He was only a gossoon, too, in the latter end," said our woman. "Only a child—that was what the priest said to me many a time. Not that I had much chance of knowing what a real child is like! Sure, we were no length married when he was struck by the train. I never thought on our wedding day that he'd be all the babby I'd ever have!"

"There now! There now!" said the other one. "Isn't it better God took him before yourself, anyway."

"I used to pray He would," said the woman. "But now I'm not so sure. Wasn't it the unnatural thing to have to pray for, anyway? Doesn't every woman pray for the opposite—to die before them and not be left a lonesome widda-

6 **pots:** crazy.
7 **deadhouse:** house in which a dead person awaits burial.
8 **gossoons:** boys (from the French *garçon*).

woman. Ah, wasn't it a hard thing to be one year praying God to send you a man, and the next praying to have him taken. Oh, it's little you know about it."

She was getting a bit wild-looking, and the other woman began dragging at her to get her back into the house. "Hush now, you'll feel different when time goes on."

"Will I?" said the woman, looking wonderingly at the other one. "I'll feel different, maybe, sometimes when I look at the clock and have to pull off my apron and run out to throw back the gates. I'll feel different, maybe, when some woman stops to have a word with me, or when I have to take the jug and go down the road for a cup of milk. But in the middle of the night, or first thing when the jackdaws start screaming in the chimney and wake me out of my sleep, will I feel different then? And what if I do forget?" she cried, suddenly pulling her arm free. "I'll have nothing at all then! It will be like as if I never had him at all." She put her hand up to her head at that and began brushing her hair back from her forehead.

Stepping behind her back, the woman that wanted to be rid of us signaled at us to make off with ourselves, but it was too late. The dead man's wife started forward and caught us by the hands. "We must make the most of every minute we have him!" she cried. "Come inside and see him." She pushed us in the doorway.

"Kneel down and say a prayer for him," she commanded, pushing us down on our knees, but her voice was wonderfully gentle now where it had been wild. "It's many a day since he was able to pray for himself," she said softly. "I used to long for him to be able to say one little prayer, and I was always trying to bring them to his mind, but he couldn't recall a word of them. When he'd be sitting out in the sun on his chair, I used to show him the flowers and remind him God made them. And do you know all he'd say?" She gave a little laugh before she told us. "'Who's that fellow?' he'd say. And he'd look round to see if He was behind him! But the priest said God wouldn't heed him; he said He'd make allowances for him."

I was half listening. When she had us kneel down, I put my hands up to my face and I started to say my prayers, but after a minute or two I opened my fingers and took a look out through them at the man on the bed. Why was she saying he was like a child? He was a man if ever I saw one! Just then the woman swooped down on me. She saw me looking at him. I thought she might be mad with me, but it was the opposite.

"If only he could see you here now beside him," she said. She leaned across me and began to stroke his hands. "Here's two nice little boys come to see you!" she said, and then her eyes got very bright and wild again. "He never had a soul come into the house to see him in twenty years. He never had another human being but one as much as put out a hand and touch him—isn't that a lonely thing to think? Him that was so friendly before his accident that he knew every man on the whole line, even to the engine drivers and stokers. He knew them all by their names. And as for the passengers! Do you know what? Look out at that garden. Every twig in it was grown from a shoot or a cutting thrown out to him in a paper parcel by somebody that got to know him shuttling back and forth past the gates! Oh, there never was such a man for making friends! And to think it's

twenty years since anyone shook him by the hand. Oh, isn't it a queer world?"

It was indeed, I thought. I wonder would it be any use me shaking hands with him now, I thought, and it might be she saw the thought in my eyes.

"Would it be asking too much of you to stroke his hand?" she said, and then, as if she had settled it in her own mind that it wouldn't be asking much at all, she got very excited. "Stand up, like good boys," she said, "and stroke his hands. No, wait a minute!" she cried, and she got another idea, and she delved her hand into her pocket. "How would you like to comb his hair?" she cried.

I was nearer to the head of the bed than Mickser, but Mickser was nearer to her than me, and I couldn't be sure which of us she meant. I wanted above all to be polite, and I stood up, so as to be ready in case it was me she meant. She was taking a few big red hairs off the comb. Mickser stood up, too, but it was only to give me a shove out of his way.

"Let me out of here!" he shouted, and, putting the woman and me to either side of him, he bolted for the door. The next minute he was flying across the tracks.

And me after him. I told you I wanted to be polite to the people, the dead one included, but after all it was Mickser brought me, and it wouldn't be very polite to him to stay on after him. Not that he showed any appreciation.

I was full of talk. "Well! I have one for my list anyway now," I said cheerfully.

"I suppose you have," he said—kind of grudgingly, I thought—and then he nearly spoiled it all on me. "That one oughtn't to count, by rights," he said. "He wasn't all in it[9] when he was alive;
9 all in it: "all there."

he was sort of dead all along." He tapped his pate again, as he did the first time. "Up here!" he added.

I thought about that for a minute. "He looked all in it there on the bed!" I said.

But Mickser didn't seem to take well to talking about him at all. "Come on back to the main road," he said. "The cars are coming along now. Can't you hear them? Some of those boyos have a few jars in them, I'd say, in spite of the wives. Come on!"

"Ah, you can go and watch them yourself," I said. "I'm going home."

The truth was I was too excited to sit on any wall for long. I wanted to go home because there were a few things I'd like to find out from Mother, if I could bring the talk around to the topic of corpses without letting on where I got the information I had already.

As I ran off from Mickser across the fields for home, I felt that I was a new man, and I felt sure they would all notice a change in me when I went into the house. The next time there was a funeral, there would be no need to leave me sitting out in a car.

"Wipe your feet, son!" my mother cried out to me through the open door of the kitchen the minute I came in sight. "Not that you'd be the only one to put tracks all over the place," she said, and I could see what she meant, because there in the middle of the floor was my brother's old bike, upended, with the wheels in the air, and he busy mending a puncture. Or was it my father she meant? Because he was sitting the other side of the fire, with his feet in a basin of water.

It must have been my father she meant, because she lit on him just then. "This is no place for washing your feet," she said. "There's a fire inside in the parlor. Why don't you go in there

and wash them? I haven't got room to turn around with you all."

"The parlor is no place for washing feet," said my father quietly, and he pointed to the bike in the middle of the floor. "When that fellow's done with that bike, you'll be glad to have a bit of water on the floor to swish out the mess he'll have made. Why don't you make him take it out in the yard?"

My mother sighed. She was always sighing, but they weren't the kind of sighs you'd heed. They were caused by something we'd done on her, but they were sighs of patience, if you know what I mean, and not complaint.

"It's a bit cold outside," she said. "Here, you, son," she said, turning to me. She picked up my satchel and shoved it under my arm. "Let you set a good example and go into the parlor and do your homework there by the nice fire."

But I wasn't going into the empty parlor.

"Dear *knows!* I don't know why I waste my time lighting that fire every day and none of you ever set foot in there until it's nearly night. I only wish I could go in and sit by it. Then I'd leave you the kitchen and welcome."

But I think she knew well that if she was to go in there that minute, it wouldn't be many minutes more till we'd all be in there along with her, myself and my satchel, and my father with his feet in the basin, and the old bike as well, if it could be squeezed in at all between the piano and the chiffonier and all the other big, useless pieces of furniture that were kept in there out of the way.

"Ah, sure aren't we all right here!" said my father. "Where we can be looking at you?"

"You must have very little worth looking at if you want to be looking at me," said my mother, in a sort of voice I knew well; it sounded cross but couldn't be, because she always stretched up when she spoke like that, so she'd see into the little mirror on the mantelshelf, and she always smiled at what she saw in the glass. And well she might. She was a pretty woman, my mother, and never more so than when we were all around her in the kitchen, annoying her and making her cheeks red with the fuss of keeping us in order.

"Mind would you catch your finger in the spokes of that wheel!" she cried just then to my brother.

"Mind would you catch your hair in it, my girl," said Father, because as the kettle boiled and the little kitchen got full of steam, her hair used to loosen and lop around her face like a girl's. And he caught ahold of her as if to pull her back from the bike.

"Let go of me!" she cried. "Will you never get sense?"

"I hope not," said my father. "And what is more, I don't want you to get too much of it, either," he said.

"Oh, go on with you and your old talk, before the boys and all!" she cried, and she tried to drag herself free.

"She's not as strong as her tongue would have us believe, boys," said my father, tightening his hold. And then he laughed. "You'll never be the man I am!" he said, and this time it was my mother herself that giggled.

That very minute, in the middle of tricking and laughing, my father's face changed, and it was as if he wasn't holding her for fun at all but the way he'd hold us if he had something against us.

"You're feeling all right these days, aren't you?" he cried. "You'd tell me if you weren't, wouldn't you?" And then he let her go and put his hands up to his head. "Oh, my God, what would I do if anything happened to you!" he said.

"Such talk!" said my mother again, but her voice sounded different, too. And although she was free, she didn't ask to move away but stood there beside him, with such a sad look on her face I wanted to cry.

And I knew I couldn't pester her with questions about the poor fellow at the level crossing. But I thought about him. And I thought of the words of the prayers we said every night, ". . . the living and the dead. . . ."[10] Over and over we'd said them, night after night, and I never had paid any heed. But I suddenly felt that they were terrible, terrible words, and if we were to be kneeling down at that moment saying them, I couldn't bear it; I'd start nightmaring there and then, in the middle of them all, with the lamps lit, and it not dark.

The kettle began to spit on the range, and my mother ran over and lifted it back from the blaze. "How about us taking our tea in the parlor?" she cried. "All of us. The kitchen is no fitter than the back yard with you!"

And in the excitement I forgot all about the living and the dead. For a long time.

10 the living . . . dead: The evening prayer is based upon the Apostles' Creed, and the boy remembers the lines: "From thence He shall come to judge the living and the dead."

Comment

If "The Living" were a play, it would have three acts—short acts, to be sure, but three well-defined parts of a single large action. In the first act the young narrator and his friend Mickser are alone by the road curiously watching the adult world of cars and men returning from a football match. In the next, they are at the house where the former crossing watchman has died, a home in which there is now no family at all. And finally the narrator is with his own family at home. What happens to him as he moves through these three acts of his adventure?

1. In the first part of the story, Mickser speaks "scathingly," "definitively," "magnanimously." What do these words mean? (Refer to the glossary for those which you are unsure of.) What difference between Mickser and the young narrator do these words emphasize? What is the relation between the two boys in this first part of the story?

2. After Mickser has "bolted" from the house of the dead man and his widow, it is the narrator who is "full of talk" and Mickser who does not "take well to talking about him at all." How has their relation changed? Is the little boy who tells the story really braver than Mickser now?

3. At almost the end of the story, as he thinks about the words of the prayer, "the living and the dead," the little boy says, "But I suddenly felt that they were terrible, terrible words, and if we were to be kneeling down at that moment saying them, I couldn't bear it." The boy feels it "suddenly," but does the reader feel it so? What contrast, especially between what happens at the watchman's house and what happens at home, prepares you for what the boy here feels *suddenly?*

4. Yet, terrible as the words sound to him now, the little boy does not start "nightmaring there and then"; instead, in the "excitement" of tea all together in the parlor, he says, "I forgot all about the living and the dead. For a long time." Has he just "forgotten," or has he changed in some other way? During most of the story he and Mickser are curious and spying: they watch the men coming home from the game; they look in the windows of the watchman's house. But why is *curious* not the word to describe the boy at the end of the story?

5. In a paragraph, and by referring to the details of the story that seem to you most important, characterize the adventure of this little boy. Is it a painful one? a joyous one? Or is it somehow both?

Dylan Thomas (1914-1953)

Early in the 1950's a large number of American audiences, most of them in colleges, were electrified by readings given by an English poet with the voice and manner of a bard. Dylan Thomas's readings, from his own works and from those of older poets whom he admired, persuaded many who had not known it before that poetry is first of all meant to be heard, and that indeed if we can but *hear* modern poetry many of the difficulties it seems to present to the silent reader will vanish.

Certainly Thomas's own poetry is often full of the most rhapsodic sound. He was born and raised in the seaside town of Swansea in Wales, and from his earliest days was accustomed to hearing both modern "correct" English and the ancient Celtic sounds of Welsh. (His name, Dylan, is the Welsh for "tide" or "water," and it is also the name for an ancient Welsh god of the sea.) Upon leaving school he became a newspaper reporter, but the most important event of his youth was the publication, in 1934 when he was twenty, of his first book of poems. Thomas was destined to earn his living by the uses of language, but the use most natural to him was from the beginning the writing of poetry in which modern English is combined with the cadences and rhythms of an ancient, primitive tongue.

During the war Thomas worked for the B.B.C. (British Broadcasting Corporation) as a writer and broadcaster and began also to write for films. And his books of poetry kept coming—along with his short stories—with so steady a growth of power that many critics believed him the greatest poet of the age. He died, tragically and suddenly, in New York while on a lecture tour in 1953.

"Fern Hill"

The following poem, first published in 1945, is characteristic of Thomas's verse, though he did not always write with such buoyancy and so keen a sense of delight as here, for he was often almost too aware of sadness and tragedy. But like all Thomas's poems, it is not just *about* a subject, it is the *celebration* of a subject: he does not merely remember the joys of childhood on the farm; he commemorates that childhood. His language is formal—it is not that of everyday conversation but is instead a language that gives us highly wrought images of gladness in youth. Some of the ways in which Thomas forged and wrought his lines we will look at in detail. But first, read them, preferably aloud, boldly and without self-consciousness.

Fern Hill

Dylan Thomas

Now as I was young and easy under the apple boughs
About the lilting house and happy as the grass was green,
   The night above the dingle[1] starry,
    Time let me hail and climb
   Golden in the heydays of his eyes,   5
And honored among wagons I was prince of the apple towns
And once below a time I lordly had the trees and leaves
    Trail with daisies and barley
   Down the rivers of the windfall light.

And as I was green and carefree, famous among the barns   10
About the happy yard and singing as the farm was home,
   In the sun that is young once only,
    Time let me play and be
   Golden in the mercy of his means,
And green and golden I was huntsman and herdsman, the
     calves   15
Sang to my horn, the foxes on the hills barked clear and cold,
    And the sabbath rang slowly
   In the pebbles of the holy streams.

All the sun long it was running, it was lovely, the hay
Fields high as the house, the tunes from the chimneys, it was air   20
   And playing, lovely and watery
    And fire green as grass.
   And nightly under the simple stars
As I rode to sleep the owls were bearing the farm away,
All the moon long I heard, blessed among stables, the nightjars[2]   25
   Flying with the ricks,[3] and the horses
    Flashing into the dark.

And then to awake, and the farm, like a wanderer white
With the dew, come back, the cock on his shoulder: it was all
   Shining, it was Adam and maiden,   30
    The sky gathered again
   And the sun grew round that very day.

1 **dingle:** small, narrow, wooded valley.
2 **nightjars:** small birds, also called goatsuckers.
3 **ricks:** stacks or piles, as of grain, straw, or hay, in the open air.

So it must have been after the birth of the simple light
In the first, spinning place,[4] the spellbound horses walking
    warm
  Out of the whinnying green stable   35
    On to the fields of praise.

And honored among foxes and pheasants by the gay house
Under the new made clouds and happy as the heart was long,
  In the sun born over and over
    I ran my heedless ways,   40
    My wishes raced through the househigh hay
And nothing I cared, at my sky blue trades, that time allows
In all his tuneful turning so few and such morning songs
  Before the children green and golden
    Follow him out of grace,   45

Nothing I cared, in the lamb white days, that time would take
    me
Up to the swallow thronged loft by the shadow of my hand,
  In the moon that is always rising,
    Nor that riding to sleep
  I should hear him fly with the high fields   50
And wake to the farm forever fled from the childless land.
Oh as I was young and easy in the mercy of his means,
    Time held me green and dying
    Though I sang in my chains like the sea.

4 So . . . place: So it must have been at the Creation of the earth, when light was first made.

Comment

Whatever puzzlement some of the details of this poem may have left with you, as a whole it must certainly have left a strong sense of the breathless wonder and joy of childhood, the relish of all that lives in farmyard, field, and woods. But this wonder is not sheer outpouring; Thomas, in fact, uses some techniques as complex as the ancient alliterative devices of Anglo-Saxon poetry.

Some of these techniques appear at the very beginning of the poem. In the first stanza, for example, instead of the familiar "once upon a time" we have the strange "once below a time." Yet its meaning soon comes clear: The poet is looking back to the days when he was not yet conscious of the passing of time; he was "below" time rather than "upon" it because he had not yet begun to exist in time fully, as we all must when we have passed childhood. Or there is "prince of the apple towns": This phrase, we soon see, is a compounding or a compressing of the kind of simile that is usually written out much more fully—"the apple trees were so full of fruit that they seemed to me like towns full of people, and if they were towns full of people, naturally I should be their ruler." Or there is the clause, "Time let me hail and climb/Golden in the heyday of his eyes." The word *heyday* means "prosperity" or "vigor," but it is also a salutation, something like "hurrah" or even "wow." In the days of his childhood, the poet is saying, he climbed trees so happily and freely that it seemed as if the time that surrounded him was like a sun that poured cheers and blessings on him. Or there is the strange phrase at the end of the stanza, "rivers of windfall light." The word *windfall*, of course, means apples or fruit that fall to the ground without being picked, and they are usually fair game for any-one who wanders in the orchard. In his joyous childhood on the farm, then, everything around him—the daisies, the crops, the trees and their leaves, even the light from the sun itself—seemed to pour down for him, like a windfall, for his easy delight.

Such hints as these will encourage you to be bold for yourself about later examples of Thomas's compressed images. But what of the sound of this poem? Again, looking at the first stanza, we see no rhyme. And yet we have a sense of something like rhyme, something like ordered sound. And we should, for it is indeed there. But it is not an ordering of sound that can make its way to us if we read merely with the eye. Take the first line, for example: How do you say "as I" and "easy"? Do you hear a similarity of sound that binds the line together? Again, the first line ends with the word *boughs*, and if this were conventionally rhyming poetry we would expect a rhyming word at the end of the next line, or of some line soon, while the sound of *boughs* is still in our ears. But *green,* at the end of line 2, will not do, nor will any of the other words that end the lines of this stanza. But a rhyming word, in fact, is very close—so close that we hear it without noticing it: it is the word *house* in the middle of the next line. And what does this rhyme, or near-rhyme—this similarity of sound between *boughs* and *house*— do for us? It prepares us for the compressed image of line 6, the im-age of the trees as "apple towns": each bough of a tree is a house in a town. Of course Thomas does not *say* this, as one says "childhood is full of wonders." He is a poet; by all the resources of words, both their sense *and* their sound, he makes us feel the wondrous—perhaps, by adult standards, even slightly crazy—connections that the child makes among parts of his world.

But enough has been said. Read the poem to yourself again, and yet again. It is not necessary to spell out every phrase and line to your satisfaction as a maker of paraphrase, for the satisfaction of this poem is an effect on our inner ear that occurs faster and more surely than we can confidently say. But there is one large question to consider.

1. In the last stanza the poet says that he did not care that he would someday enter into time and history so far that the farm and its joys

would have receded into the past—"the farm forever fled from the childless land." Why does he conclude by saying "Time held me green and dying/Though I sang in my chains like the sea"? In what sense was he chained? And what was he chained to? What does he mean when he says that he sang in these childhood chains?

The Adventure of Growth

Awkwardness and Rapture

ONCE THE exhilaration of setting forth is over, the experience of growing up is sometimes awkward and painful, but it has its moments of rapturous happiness too. The awkwardness of the young, at least in the last hundred years or so, has provided some of the most comic passages in literature—Dickens, for one, was a master of it. And the raptures of youth have figured in works of all kinds since the period and the example of Wordsworth. But the pain of youthful experience has been treated more sympathetically and compassionately in the 20th century than ever before. The 20th-century writer has seen in the young people whom he has written about, a range of experience and emotion that few earlier writers have been aware of.

Stephen Spender (1909-   )

Stephen Spender is the youngest of the three poets—W. H. Auden and C. Day Lewis are the other two—who were in the 1930's the center of what was less a particular school of poetry than a new hope for poetry, a hope that it might provide the world with new social ideals. The ties among these three poets, however, and with others who shared their hopes, were so loose that each has moved in his own direction in the last quarter-century, and now it is difficult to see any more kinship among them than they bear to other serious writers of their time.

Stephen Spender, at any rate, from the beginning has shown more kinship with the Romantic poets, especially with Shelley, than with his contemporaries. Like the Romantics, he has a gift for the arresting image:

> Eye, gazelle, delicate wanderer,
> Drinker of horizon's fluid line.

Or speaking of great men of the past, "those who in their lives fought for life," he writes:

> Born of the sun, they travelled a short while towards the sun,
> And left the vivid air signed with their honour.

This, certainly, is a 20th-century image.

Like W. H. Auden, Spender was a student at Oxford and there contributed to the remarkable series of poetry collections published by Oxford students in the late 1920's and early 1930's. But even before going to the university he had printed a small volume of his own poems on his own printing press. In 1933 the publication in both the United States and in England of a volume called, simply, *Poems* won him a success and an importance that his later works have never diminished. He has brought his learning and taste to bear on the works of other modern writers in many critical essays, and he has written on politics and painting as well.

"What I expected"

The first of the two poems below has no title, but its theme is announced in the first three words: "What I expected." For it is a poem about the difference between what the speaker has expected and what he has in fact found.

> What I expected, was
> Thunder, fighting,
> Long struggles with men
> And climbing.
> After continual straining   5
> I should grow strong;
> Then the rocks would shake,
> And I rest long.
>
> What I had not foreseen
> Was the gradual day   10
> Weakening the will
> Leaking the brightness away,
> The lack of good to touch,
> The fading of body and soul
> —Smoke before wind,   15
> Corrupt, unsubstantial.
>
> The wearing of Time,
> And the watching of cripples pass
> With limbs shaped like questions
> In their odd twist,   20
> The pulverous grief
> Melting the bones with pity,
> The sick falling from earth—
> These, I could not foresee.

STEPHEN SPENDER

Expecting always   25
Some brightness to hold in trust,
Some final innocence
Exempt from dust,
That, hanging solid,
Would dangle through all,   30
Like the created poem,
Or faceted crystal.

Comment

One of the distinctive features of this poem is its use of verbal nouns and adjectives—"fighting," "weakening," "melting," "faceted." How do these verbal nouns and adjectives reveal the movement of the poem?

1. In the first stanza, what are the main verbal nouns? What main images in this stanza do they reinforce? How do these images tell us about "What I expected"?
2. The next two stanzas tell us "What I had not foreseen": What are the main verbal nouns or adjectives of these stanzas? And how do they support the main images of these two stanzas? How do these images tell us about "What I had not foreseen"?
3. What are the main images of the last stanza? How do they differ from those of the two preceding stanzas?
4. As you finish this poem, does it seem to you a poem of despair? Do you find anything like a renewed affirmation in the last stanza? What is the state of the "I" as it is revealed to us at the end?

"The Express"

In the catalogue of the "dear names" of things he has loved, Rupert Brooke's "The Great Lover" includes "the keen / Unpassioned beauty of a great machine." Here, in Stephen Spender's "The Express," is a detailed picture of one such beautiful machine.

The Express

Stephen Spender

After the first powerful, plain manifesto
The black statement of pistons, without more fuss
But gliding like a queen, she leaves the station.
Without bowing and with restrained unconcern
She passes the houses which humbly crowd outside,   5
The gasworks, and at last the heavy page
Of death, printed by gravestones in the cemetery.
Beyond the town, there lies the open country
Where, gathering speed, she acquires mystery,

The luminous self-possession of ships on ocean.   10
It is now she begins to sing—at first quite low
Then loud, and at last with a jazzy madness—
The song of her whistle screaming at curves,
Of deafening tunnels, brakes, innumerable bolts.
And always light, aerial, underneath,   15
Retreats the elate metre of her wheels.
Steaming through metal landscape on her lines,
She plunges new eras of white happiness,
Where speed throws up strange shapes, broad curves
And parallels clean like trajectories from guns.   20
At last, further than Edinburgh or Rome,
Beyond the crest of the world, she reaches night
Where only a low stream-line brightness
Of phosphorus on the tossing hills is light.
Ah, like a comet through flame, she moves entranced,   25
Wrapt in her music no bird song, no, nor bough
Breaking with honey buds, shall ever equal.

Comment

"The Express" is of course a steam-driven engine, and it is one of the
ironies of recent history that many people now in their teens have never
actually seen a steam locomotive. But it was for Stephen Spender a
marvel both to see and to hear; it was above all a marvel of history.

1. A manifesto is a public statement. The metaphor of language is
   continued in the description of the cemetery at the edge of town,
   which is called "the heavy page/Of death." Why should the express, with its "powerful, plain manifesto," *pass* this "heavy page"?
2. Once in the open country the express takes on "The luminous self-
   possession of ships on ocean." What is literally true about the "self-
   possession" of a train far out in the open country? And what is
   there about it that can literally be called "luminous"? How is the
   image of the train as a ship on the ocean repeated in lines 23 and
   24? (Have you ever seen the wake of a ship at night?)
3. At line 16 the poet refers to the "elate metre" of the wheels. In an
   early draft of this poem he had written "tapping metre": is the
   change from "tapping" to "elate" an improvement? Why?
4. The last two lines of the poem compare the beauty of the express
   with two much more traditional symbols of beauty:

   > Wrapt in her music no bird song, no, nor bough
   > Breaking with honey buds, shall ever equal.

   How is the express superior to these traditional symbols of beauty?
   If the song and the bough are symbols from the past, what is the
   greatest beauty that the poet sees in the express? What is, quite
   literally, so wonderful about the steam locomotive?

STEPHEN SPENDER

John Betjeman (1906-   )

To John Betjeman belongs the unusual distinction of being the only 20th-century poet who has written his autobiography in verse, *Summoned by Bells* (1960), which was received with considerable success, both here and in Britain. Like so many of the leading poets of the second quarter of the century, Betjeman went to Oxford. He has always earned his living as a writer. He has written guidebooks for travelers interested in the antiquities and buildings of England, and he has commented often, in both verse and prose, on the ugliness and the charm of many 19th-century buildings and monuments. The materials of his poetry, in fact, seem at first sight not poetic at all, for they are the materials that most writers of sketches and short stories usually make fun of. With an almost casual lightness of touch, Betjeman finds, sometimes, real pathos in the ordinary scenes of suburban life.

"Norfolk"

In both the following poems the poet is remembering his youth. In the first, he is revisiting Norfolk, a county northeast of London that contains a fenny, marshy district known as the Norfolk Broads—a succession of shallow lagoons linked together by three rivers, of which the largest is the River Bure. It is a district famous for fishing and boating, and the poet here recalls happy excursions in the family boat with his father.

Norfolk

John Betjeman

How did the Devil come? When first attack?
   These Norfolk lanes recall lost innocence,
The years fall off and find me walking back
   Dragging a stick along the wooden fence
Down this same path, where, forty years ago,   5
My father strolled behind me, calm and slow.

I used to fill my hand with sorrel seeds
   And shower him with them from the tops of stiles,
I used to butt my head into his tweeds
   To make him hurry down those languorous miles   10
Of ash and alder-shaded lanes, till here
Our moorings and the masthead would appear.

There after supper lit by lantern light
   Warm in the cabin I could lie secure
And hear against the polished sides at night   15
   The lap lap lapping of the weedy Bure,

A whispering and watery Norfolk sound
Telling of all the moonlit reeds around.

How did the Devil come? When first attack?
 The church is just the same, though now I know   20
Fowler of Louth restored it. Time, bring back
 The rapturous ignorance of long ago,
The peace, before the dreadful daylight starts,
Of unkept promises and broken hearts.

Comment

The theme of "lost innocence" is sometimes a large and serious one—
you remember *Paradise Lost*. What is the character of the youthful
paradise remembered here?

1. What relations between father and son does the poet recall?
2. How is the character of these relations summed up in the third
   stanza?
3. Why, in the next to the last line, does the poet speak of "*dreadful
   daylight*"? What does "daylight" fully mean here?
4. What is the meaning of the question, "How did the Devil come?"
   which opens the first and the last stanza?

"Original Sin on the Sussex Coast"

In the next poem we find something like an answer to the question
that has just been asked. Once again the poet is revisiting a childhood
scene, this time on the south coast of England, a suburban district of
upper-middle-class homes, with the Sussex Downs, a treeless, hilly
upland rising behind them.

Original Sin
On the
Sussex Coast

John Betjeman

Now on this out of season afternoon
Day schools which cater for the sort of boy
Whose parents go by Pullman[1] once a month
To do a show in town, pour out their young
Into the sharply red October light.   5
Here where The Drive[2] and Buckhurst Road converge
I watch the rival gangs and am myself

---

1 **Pullman:** first-class.
2 **The Drive:** the first of many fancy street-names of the sort to be found
in a new and prosperous suburb.

A schoolboy once again in shivering shorts.
I see the dust of sherbet on the chin
Of Andrew Knox well-dressed, well-born, well-fed,   10
Even at nine a perfect gentleman,
Willie Buchanan waiting at his side
Another Scot, eruptions on his skin.
I hear Jack Drayton whistling from the fence
Which hides the copper domes of "Cooch Behar."[3]   15
That was the signal.   So there's no escape.
A race for Willow Way and jump the hedge
Behind the Granville Bowling Club?   Too late.
They'll catch me coming out in Seapink Lane.
Across the Garden of Remembrance?[4]   No,   20
That would be blasphemy and bring bad luck.
Well then, I'm *for* it.   Andrew's at me first,
He pinions me in that especial grip
His brother learned in Kobë from a Jap
(No chance for me against the Japanese).   25
Willie arrives and winds me with a punch
Plum in the tummy, grips the other arm.
"You're to be booted.   Hold him steady chaps!"
A wait for taking aim.   Oh trees and sky!
Then crack against the column of my spine,   30
Blackness and breathlessness and sick with pain
I stumble on the asphalt.   Off they go
Away, away, thank God, and out of sight
So that I lie quite still and climb to sense
Too out of breath and strength to make a sound.   35
      Now over Polegate[5] vastly sets the sun;
Dark rise the Downs from darker looking elms,
And out of Southern railway trains to tea
Run happy boys down various Station Roads,
Satchels of homework jogging on their backs,   40
So trivial and so healthy in the shade
Of these enormous Downs.   And when they're home,
When the Post-Toasties mixed with Golden Shred
Make for the kiddies such a scrumptious feast,
Does Mum, the Persil[6]-user, still believe   45
That there's no Devil and that youth is bliss?
As certain as the sun behind the Downs
And quite as plain to see, the Devil walks.

---

3 **Cooch Behar:** a house named after a region in West Bengal, India, presumably owned by someone retired from government service in India.
4 **Garden of Remembrance:** the War Memorial.
5 **Polegate:** a town just below the eastern end of the Downs.
6 **Persil:** scented soap.

"How did the Devil come? When first attack?" the poet asks in "Norfolk." Whether this poem tells of the Devil's first attack is not clear, but it does tell us that the poet is sure that "the Devil walks" even among the respectable and well-to-do children of this suburban community.

1. What are some of the characterizing details of the town that the poet is revisiting? What sort of place, with what sorts of streets and houses, does it seem to you to be?
2. What contrast do you see between the town and the Downs?
3. The attack on the speaker by Andrew and Willie and Jack was apparently casual: we do not know what provoked it, nor do we know what followed it. What contrast do you see between the attack and the teatime comfort of the children home from school?
4. Is the contrast you found in question 3 anything like the contrast between the suburban town and the "enormous Downs"?
5. The speaker, the poet returning to his youth, is certain that "the Devil walks." Why is he so certain? Is he bitter or angry in his certainty?

The Adventure of Growth

The Journey Alone

GROWTH IS A continual setting forth, a constant setting out on new journeys; and perhaps the journey most difficult is the one that takes the traveler through a region, a world, a fate, that is indifferent to his or her passage. The traps set by enemies, the difficulties of adjusting one's hopes to the way things are, the encounter of cruelty—these are hardships enough. But the encounter of indifference, the discovery that the way ahead is simply dark, that it contains nothing and no one either for or against the traveler—this is a prospect even worse. In the 20th century many writers have written of a world that is neither hostile nor friendly to human endeavor but only indifferent to it. The solitude of the individual, strangely, has become a major theme of literature at a time when the world contains more people, and more human-made things, than it ever has before.

"Departure in the Dark"

The following poem by C. Day Lewis, whose "Watching Post" we have seen earlier, might well have been placed among the poems of "War and Peace," for it was first published in Lewis's wartime collection of poems. But the sudden, strange departure in the dark for an undisclosed destination occurs not only in wartime.

Departure in the Dark

C. Day Lewis

Nothing so sharply reminds a man he is mortal
As leaving a place
In a winter morning's dark, the air on his face
Unkind as the touch of sweating metal:
Simple good-bys to children or friends become   5
A felon's numb
Farewell, and love that was a warm, a meeting place—
Love is the suicide's grave under the nettles.[1]

Gloomed and clemmed[2] as if by an imminent ice-age
Lies the dear world   10
Of your street-strolling, field-faring.[3]   The senses, curled
At the dead end of a shrinking passage,
Care not if close the inveterate hunters creep,
And memories sleep
Like mammoths in lost caves.   Drear, extinct is the world,   15
And has no voice for consolation or presage.

There is always something at such times of the passover,[4]
When the dazed heart
Beats for it knows not what, whether you part
From home or prison, acquaintance or lover—   20
Something wrong with the timetable, something unreal
In the scrambled meal
And the bag ready packed by the door, as though the heart
Has gone ahead, or is staying here forever.

No doubt for the Israelites that early morning   25
It was hard to be sure
If home were prison or prison home: the desire
Going forth meets the desire returning.
This land,[5] that had cut their pride down to the bone
Was now their own   30
By ancient deeds of sorrow.   Beyond, there was nothing sure
But a desert of freedom to quench their fugitive yearnings.

---

1 **suicide . . . nettles:** The suicide cannot be buried in the churchyard; his grave is the unkept field by the road.
2 **field-faring:** frowning and pinched with cold.
3 **field-faring:** strolling in the country.
4 **passover:** yearly feast of the Jews to commemorate both the sparing of the children of Israel in Egypt when God smote the first-born in each Egyptian household and also the subsequent flight of the Israelites from their enslavement in Egypt.   (See the Bible, Exodus 12.)
5 **This land:** Egypt, where they were persecuted by the Pharoahs.

At this blind hour the heart is informed of nature's
Ruling that man
Should be nowhere a more tenacious settler than   35
Among wry thorns and ruins, yet nurture
A seed of discontent in his ripest ease.
There's a kind of release
And a kind of torment in every good-by for every man
And will be, even to the last of his dark departures.   40

Comment

A departure, a separation from what one knows, must be painful;
but a departure in the dark, a journey through a world in which we
cannot see, is doubly so. It is the commonest of experiences—leaving
home early in the morning, perhaps for an adventure—and yet one of
the most strangely disturbing.

1. "Nothing so sharply reminds a man he is mortal": how is this first
   line echoed in the last line of the poem?
2. What are some images in the first two stanzas that suggest the
   strangeness of departing in the dark?
3. In stanzas 3 and 4 the departure is compared with the Exodus of
   the Israelites in the ancient time of Moses. Consider these expressions:

   > as though the heart
   > Has gone ahead, or is staying here forever.   (11.23-24)

   > It was hard to be sure
   > If home were prison or prison home.   (11.26-27)

   How do these lines explain the experience of those who lived
   through the first Passover and Exodus?
4. In the last stanza the poet sums up the experience of departure as
   "a kind of release / And a kind of torment." What is the difference
   between "release" and "torment"? How do these two words together sum up what the poet means by "Departure in the Dark"?
   What is the nature of the experience that he is here evoking?

"Musée des Beaux Arts"

The ancient story of Daedalus and Icarus has been told many times.
In order to escape from King Minos of Crete, Daedalus the craftsman
made for himself and his son Icarus wings of feathers held in place
by wax. He warned Icarus not to fly too near the sun lest the wax
melt and his wings collapse, but the young man did not heed him. He
flew higher and higher, lost his wings, and fell into the sea. The old
myth is the subject of a famous painting by the Renaissance Flemish
painter Pieter Brueghel (it hangs in the Royal Museum in Brussels),
and in Brueghel's interpretation of the story, the fall of Icarus is a

matter of indifference to the world of nature and people—no one notices, and thus no one can care.

The following poem by W. H. Auden is a meditation on this picture and on others like it: how did early painters treat the subject of individual suffering?

Musée des Beaux Arts[1]

W. H. Auden

About suffering they were never wrong,
The Old Masters:[2] how well they understood
Its human position; how it takes place
While someone else is eating or opening a window or just
    walking dully along;
How, when the aged are reverently, passionately waiting   5
For the miraculous birth, there always must be
Children who did not specially want it to happen, skating
On a pond at the edge of the wood:
They never forgot
That even the dreadful martyrdom must run its course   10
Anyhow in a corner, some untidy spot
Where the dogs go on with their doggy life and the torturer's
    horse
Scratches its innocent behind on a tree.

In Brueghel's *Icarus,* for instance: how everything turns away
Quite leisurely from the disaster; the plowman may   15
Have heard the splash, the forsaken cry,
But for him it was not an important failure; the sun shone
As it had to on the white legs[3] disappearing into the green
Water; and the expensive delicate ship that must have seen
Something amazing, a boy falling out of the sky,   20
Had somewhere to get to and sailed calmly on.

1 *Musée des Beaux Arts:* French for "Museum of Fine Arts."
2 **Old Masters:** a term for any great European painter who lived before the 18th century.
3 **white legs:** i.e., those of Icarus in Brueghel's painting.

THE TWENTIETH CENTURY

Comment

In a great museum a man has been looking at many pictures that describe human suffering, and as he muses it comes to him that they treat this subject with a strange, and yet quite human, indifference.

1. How did the "Old Masters" understand the "human position" of suffering—that is, its relation to those who are themselves not undergoing the suffering?
2. How does the poet's account of Brueghel's *Icarus*, in the second stanza of the poem, support his account of the "Old Masters" in the first stanza?
3. What do you make of the language and rhythm of this poem? Is it formal and highly ordered, as, for example, Dylan Thomas's "Fern Hill"? How would you characterize its rhythms, the movement of its lines? In what tone of voice must you read these lines, especially the longer ones? What relation do you see between this tone of voice and the theme of the poem?

John Millington Synge (1871-1909)

"*Riders to the Sea* is in every sense a play written on the edge of the world." This was said of the play which concludes this section called "The Journey Alone." The author of the play, John Millington Synge, was born near Dublin and after studying to be a painter became a poet and dramatist. This, his second play to be produced, was first acted in Dublin in 1904, and though it was at first not widely appreciated it has come to be called the most perfect one-act play of the modern theater. *Riders to the Sea* was written *on* the edge of the world because Synge worked on it while visiting the Aran Islands, a group of rocky outposts off the west coast of Ireland, the edge of the Old World. The play is also written *about* the edge of the world because it presents us with two characters, a young man and his old mother, who are as near to the edge of life—as close to death—as any characters in modern literature.

A Revival of Drama When *Riders to the Sea* was first performed, the drama was beginning to flourish once again after a long period of decline and disuse. During the 19th century the novel, not the drama, was the major literary form. The few attempts at playwriting made by Shelley, Byron, and other Romantic poets, did not deal with the large conflicts that we find in the Elizabethan theater, or with the amusements of social manners that we find in Goldsmith and other writers of drama in the Enlightenment. Although there were many theaters and great actors and actresses in 19th-century Britain there were few contemporary plays except blood-and-thunder melodramas; the greatest

A scene from a television production of Macbeth. *Radio, movies, and television have made available to a large audience a wide variety of types of drama, some plays being written specifically for these new media and others adapted for them.*

productions, indeed, were of the major tragedies of Shakespeare. At the turn of the century, however, partly under the influence of the great Norwegian dramatist, Henrik Ibsen, the drama began to be once again the powerful literary force it had been in Shakespeare's day. Ibsen saw in dramatic terms the problems of middle-class people that had hitherto been treated chiefly by the novelist—indeed, he saw some problems that had not been treated before at all. Ibsen's main influence, however, comes from his development of the drama of conversation—the play in which the characters reveal themselves and their predicaments in excited, passionate talk with each other, rather than in more obvious direct action. Ibsen was followed in England by George Bernard Shaw (1856-1950), the master of the conversation drama who in more than fifty plays brought wit, wisdom, satire, and a living sense of society back into the English theater.

The Abbey Theater and Poetic Drama Another force in modern drama first appeared decisively in the Abbey Theater in Dublin, where *Riders to the Sea* was first performed. The Abbey Players (more formally, The Irish National Theater), in whose organization the poet Yeats played a large part, awakened poetic drama from its long sleep

THE TWENTIETH CENTURY

A scene from Shakespeare's Much Ado About Nothing *in the open-air theater, Regent's Park, London. Plays given in outdoor theaters have become popular in recent years in many cities and at colleges and universities.*

since Shakespeare and the Elizabethans. Their purpose at first was to introduce into the theater the ancient Irish heritage of folkways and folk traditions. (This purpose is evident in *Riders to the Sea*.) Yeats himself wrote a number of verse plays with such ancient themes— though Synge and others wrote their plays in prose. The possibility of the verse drama was revived, and has been exploited most successfully by T. S. Eliot. His *Murder in the Cathedral* (1935), a dramatization of the martyrdom of Thomas à Becket, Chaucer's "holy blissful martyr," has shown many audiences that blank verse can produce a powerful effect in the theater; *The Cocktail Party*—a play also about martyrdom—was a success in both London and New York in 1950.

New Media and Techniques The enormous popularity of the movies and of the radio and television play has changed the outlook for the drama since those days early in this century when Shaw and Synge, each in a different way, led many to rediscover the theater. Yet even these new media are still dependent on the two strong forces that began to work on the drama more than half a century ago: the realistic impulse to deal with contemporary moral and social problems, sometimes satirically, sometimes wittily; and the poetic impulse to bring

JOHN MILLINGTON SYNGE   **839** audiences to an awareness of ancient ways of feeling and thinking, sometimes tragically, always compassionately. The techniques of 20th-century drama have multiplied; its central concerns have remained astonishingly unchanged.

The Aran Islands The author of *Riders to the Sea* went to the Aran Islands on the advice of the poet Yeats. Yeats urged Synge to visit this primitive community in order to learn for himself the ancient, down-to-earth—and also down-to-sea—traditions of the Irish peasant. Around the year 1900 Synge made several visits, staying in the cottages of fishermen. Once he was present in a small community when a family received from Donegal, on the northern coast, the clothes of a drowned man. Only the dead fisherman's clothing, by its special stitching, could identify him. All of the action and characters of this play are similarly rooted in Synge's intimate and compassionate observations of a people with whom the civilization of the mainland was only intermittently and uncertainly connected. Some of their ways have since disappeared, for example, the "keening," or moaning in groups upon the death of the member of a family. Many other ways of life observed by Synge have remained, most notably the idiom in which his characters speak. The daughters of Maurya, the old mother, refer to her not as "Mother" but as "herself," a usage that can still be heard. The use of "after"—"I'm after doing it," meaning "I've just done it,"—continues, as does the use of the phrase "at all," in the sense of "anyhow."

But *Riders to the Sea* is not just a quaint play. It is a play both realistic—for this is what Synge witnessed—and poetic—for it shows us in an unforgettable way the tragic meaning of the journey alone.

Riders
to the Sea

John Millington Synge

PERSONS

MAURYA, *an old woman.*
BARTLEY, *her son.*
CATHLEEN, *her daughter.*
NORA, *a younger daughter.*
MEN *and* WOMEN.

SCENE—*An island off the west of Ireland.*

(*Cottage kitchen, with nets, oilskins, spinning wheel, some new boards standing by the wall, etc.* CATHLEEN, *a girl of about twenty, finishes kneading cake, and puts it down in the pot oven by the fire; then wipes her hands, and begins to spin at the wheel.* NORA, *a young girl, puts her head in at the door.*)

NORA (*in a low voice*). Where is she?

CATHLEEN. She's lying down, God help her, and may be sleeping, if she's able.

(NORA *comes in softly, and takes a bundle from under her shawl.*)

CATHLEEN (*spinning the wheel rapidly*). What is it you have?

NORA. The young priest is after bringing them. It's a shirt and a plain stocking were got off a drowned man in Donegal.[1]

(CATHLEEN *stops her wheel with a sudden movement, and leans out to listen.*)

NORA. We're to find out if it's Michael's they are; sometime herself will be down looking by the sea.

CATHLEEN. How would they be Michael's, Nora? How would he go the length of that way to the far north?

NORA. The young priest says he's known the like of it. "If it's Michael's they are," says he, "you can tell herself he's got a clean burial by the grace of God, and if they're not his, let no one say a word about them, for she'll be getting her death," says he, "with crying and lamenting."

(*The door which* NORA *half closed is blown open by a gust of wind.*)

CATHLEEN (*looking out anxiously*). Did you ask him would he stop Bartley going this day with the horses to the Galway fair?[2]

NORA. "I won't stop him," says he, "but let you not be afraid. Herself does be saying prayers half through the night, and the Almighty God won't leave her destitute," says he, "with no son living."

CATHLEEN. Is the sea bad by the white rocks, Nora?

NORA. Middling bad, God help us. There's a great roaring in the west, and it's worse it'll be getting when the tide's turned to the wind. (*She goes over to the table with the bundle.*) Shall I open it now?

CATHLEEN. Maybe she'd wake up on us, and come in before we'd done. (*Coming to the table.*) It's a long time

---

1 **Donegal:** a northwest county of the mainland.
2 **Galway fair:** the market in Galway, the seaport off which stand the Aran Islands.

we'll be, and the two of us crying.

NORA (*goes to the inner door and listens*). She's moving about on the bed. She'll be coming in a minute.

CATHLEEN. Give me the ladder, and I'll put them up in the turf loft,[3] the way she won't know of them at all, and maybe when the tide turns she'll be going down to see would he be floating from the east.

> (*They put the ladder against the gable of the chimney;* CATHLEEN *goes up a few steps and hides the bundle in the turf loft.* MAURYA *comes from the inner room.*)

MAURYA (*looking up at* CATHLEEN *and speaking querulously*). Isn't it turf enough you have for this day and evening?

CATHLEEN. There's a cake baking at the fire for a short space (*throwing down the turf*) and Bartley will want it when the tide turns if he goes to Connemara.[4]

> (NORA *picks up the turf and puts it round the pot oven.*)

MAURYA (*sitting down on a stool at the fire*). He won't go this day with the wind rising from the south and west. He won't go this day, for the young priest will stop him surely.

NORA. He'll not stop him, Mother, and I heard Eamon Simon and Stephen Pheety and Colum Shawn saying he would go.

MAURYA. Where is he itself?

NORA. He went down to see would there be another boat sailing in the week, and I'm thinking it won't be long till he's here now, for the tide's turning at the green head,[5] and the hooker's[6] tacking from the east.

CATHLEEN. I hear someone passing the big stones.

NORA (*looking out*). He's coming now, and he in a hurry.

BARTLEY (*comes in and looks round the room; speaking sadly and quietly*). Where is the bit of new rope, Cathleen, was bought in Connemara?

CATHLEEN (*coming down*). Give it to him, Nora; it's on a nail by the white boards. I hung it up this morning, for the pig with the black feet was eating it.

NORA (*giving him a rope*). Is that it, Bartley?

MAURYA. You'd do right to leave that rope, Bartley, hanging by the boards. (BARTLEY *takes the rope.*) It will be wanting in this place, I'm telling you, if Michael is washed up tomorrow morning, or the next morning, or any morning in the week, for it's a deep grave we'll make him by the grace of God.[7]

BARTLEY (*beginning to work with the rope*). I've no halter the way[8] I can ride down on the mare, and I must go now quickly. This is the one boat going for two weeks or beyond it, and the fair will be a good fair for horses I heard them saying below.

MAURYA. It's a hard thing they'll be saying below if the body is washed up and there's no man in it to make the coffin, and I after giving a big price for the finest white boards you'd find in Connemara. (*She looks round at the boards.*)

BARTLEY. How would it be washed up, and we after looking each day for nine days, and a strong wind blowing a while back from the west and south?

MAURYA. If it wasn't found itself, that wind is raising the sea, and there was

---

3 **turf loft:** attic for the storage of peat, or "turf."
4 **Connemara:** the region around Galway.
5 **green head:** grass-covered headland of the harbor.

6 **hooker:** one-masted fishing boat.
7 **It will . . . God:** The rope would be needed to lower the coffin into the grave.
8 **the way:** so that.

THE TWENTIETH CENTURY

a star up against the moon, and it rising in the night. If it was a hundred horses, or a thousand horses you had itself, what is the price of a thousand horses against a son where there is one son only?

BARTLEY (*working at the halter, to* CATHLEEN). Let you go down each day, and see the sheep aren't jumping in on the rye, and if the jobber[9] comes you can sell the pig with the black feet if there is a good price going.

MAURYA. How would the like of her get a good price for a pig?

BARTLEY (*to* CATHLEEN). If the west wind holds with the last bit of the moon let you and Nora get up weed enough for another cock for the kelp.[10] It's hard set we'll be from this day with no one in it but one man to work.

MAURYA. It's hard set we'll be surely the day you're drownd'd with the rest. What way will I live and the girls with me, and I an old woman looking for the grave?

(BARTLEY *lays down the halter, takes off his old coat, and puts on a newer one of the same flannel.*)

BARTLEY (*to* NORA). Is she coming to the pier?

NORA (*looking out*). She's passing the green head and letting fall her sails.

BARTLEY (*getting his purse and tobacco*). I'll have half an hour to go down, and you'll see me coming again in two days, or in three days, or maybe in four days if the wind is bad.

MAURYA (*turning round to the fire, and putting her shawl over her head*). Isn't it a hard and cruel man won't hear a word from an old woman, and she holding him from the sea?

CATHLEEN. It's the life of a young man to be going on the sea, and who would listen to an old woman with one thing and she saying it over?

BARTLEY (*taking the halter*). I must go now quickly. I'll ride down on the red mare, and the gray pony'll run behind me. . . . The blessing of God on you.

(*He goes out.*)

MAURYA (*crying out as he is in the door*). He's gone now, God spare us, and we'll not see him again. He's gone now, and when the black night is falling I'll have no son left me in the world.

CATHLEEN. Why wouldn't you give him your blessing and he looking round in the door? Isn't it sorrow enough is on everyone in this house without your sending him out with an unlucky word behind him, and a hard word in his ear?

(MAURYA *takes up the tongs and begins raking the fire aimlessly without looking round.*)

NORA (*turning toward her*). You're taking away the turf from the cake.

CATHLEEN (*crying out*). The Son of God forgive us, Nora, we're after forgetting his bit of bread. (*She comes over to the fire.*)

NORA. And it's destroyed he'll be going till dark night, and he after eating nothing since the sun went up.

CATHLEEN (*turning the cake out of the oven*). It's destroyed he'll be, surely. There's no sense left on any person in a house where an old woman will be talking forever.

(MAURYA *sways herself on her stool.*)

CATHLEEN (*cutting off some of the bread and rolling it in a cloth; to* MAURYA). Let you go down now to the spring well and give him this and he passing. You'll see him then and the

---

9 **jobber**: buyer of farm products.
10 **cock** . . . **kelp**: pile of seaweed, sold for chemical purposes.

dark word will be broken, and you can say "God speed you," the way he'll be easy in his mind.

MAURYA (*taking the bread*). Will I be in it as soon as himself?

CATHLEEN. If you go now quickly.

MAURYA (*standing up unsteadily*). It's hard set I am to walk.

CATHLEEN (*looking at her anxiously*). Give her the stick, Nora, or maybe she'll slip on the big stones.

NORA. What stick?

CATHLEEN. The stick Michael brought from Connemara.

MAURYA (*taking a stick* NORA *gives her*). In the big world the old people do be leaving things after them for their sons and children, but in this place it is the young men do be leaving things behind for them that do be old.

(*She goes out slowly.* NORA *goes over to the ladder.*)

CATHLEEN. Wait, Nora, maybe she'd turn back quickly. She's that sorry, God help her, you wouldn't know the thing she'd do.

NORA. Is she gone round by the bush?

CATHLEEN (*looking out*). She's gone now. Throw it down quickly, for the Lord knows when she'll be out of it[11] again.

NORA (*getting the bundle from the loft*). The young priest said he'd be passing tomorrow, and we might go down and speak to him below if it's Michael's they are surely.

CATHLEEN (*taking the bundle*). Did he say what way they were found?

NORA (*coming down*). "There were two men," says he, "and they rowing round with poteen[12] before the cocks crowed, and the oar of one of them caught the body, and they passing the black cliffs of the north."

CATHLEEN (*trying to open the bun-*

dle). Give me a knife, Nora, the string's perished[13] with the salt water, and there's a black knot on it you wouldn't loosen in a week.

NORA (*giving her a knife*). I've heard tell it was a long way to Donegal.

CATHLEEN (*cutting the string*). It is surely. There was a man in here a while ago—the man sold us that knife—and he said if you set off walking from the rocks beyond, it would be seven days you'd be in Donegal.

NORA. And what time would a man take, and he floating?

(CATHLEEN *opens the bundle and takes out a bit of a stocking. They look at them eagerly.*)

CATHLEEN (*in a low voice*). The Lord spare us, Nora! isn't it a queer hard thing to say if it's his they are surely?

NORA. I'll get his shirt off the hook the way we can put the one flannel on the other. (*She looks through some clothes hanging in the corner.*) It's not with them, Cathleen, and where will it be?

CATHLEEN. I'm thinking Bartley put it on him in the morning, for his own shirt was heavy with the salt in it. (*Pointing to the corner.*) There's a bit of a sleeve was of the same stuff. Give me that and it will do.

(NORA *brings it to her and they compare the flannel.*)

CATHLEEN. It's the same stuff, Nora; but if it is itself aren't there great rolls of it in the shops of Galway, and isn't it many another man may have a shirt of it as well as Michael himself?

NORA (*who has taken up the stocking and counted the stitches, crying out*). It's Michael, Cathleen, it's Michael; God spare his soul, and what will herself say when she hears this story, and Bartley on the sea?

---

11 **out of it:** out of the house.
12 **poteen:** whisky illegally distilled; "moonshine."

13 **perished:** hardened.

CATHLEEN (*taking the stocking*). It's a plain stocking.

NORA. It's the second one of the third pair I knitted, and I put up three score stitches, and I dropped four of them.

CATHLEEN (*counts the stitches*). It's that number is in it. (*Crying out.*) Ah, Nora, isn't it a bitter thing to think of him floating that way to the far north, and no one to keen[14] him but the black hags[15] that do be flying on the sea?

NORA (*swinging herself round, and throwing out her arms on the clothes*). And isn't it a pitiful thing when there is nothing left of a man who was a great rower and fisher, but a bit of an old shirt and a plain stocking?

CATHLEEN (*after an instant*). Tell me is herself coming, Nora? I hear a little sound on the path.

NORA (*looking out*). She is, Cathleen. She's coming up to the door.

CATHLEEN. Put these things away before she'll come in. Maybe it's easier she'll be after giving her blessing to Bartley, and we won't let on we've heard anything the time he's on the sea.

NORA (*helping* CATHLEEN *close the bundle*). We'll put them here in the corner.

(*They put them into a hole in the chimney corner.* CATHLEEN *goes back to the spinning wheel.*)

NORA. Will she see it was crying I was?

CATHLEEN. Keep your back to the door the way the light'll not be on you.

(NORA *sits down at the chimney corner, with her back to the door.* MAURYA *comes in very slowly, without looking at the girls, and goes over to her stool*

at the other side of the fire. The cloth with the bread is still in her hand. The girls look at each other, and NORA points to the bundle of bread.*)

CATHLEEN (*after spinning for a moment*). You didn't give him his bit of bread?

(MAURYA *begins to keen softly, without turning round.*)

CATHLEEN. Did you see him riding down?

(MAURYA *goes on keening.*)

CATHLEEN (*a little impatiently*). God forgive you; isn't it a better thing to raise your voice and tell what you seen, than to be making lamentation for a thing that's done? Did you see Bartley, I'm saying to you.

MAURYA (*with a weak voice*). My heart's broken from this day.

CATHLEEN (*as before*). Did you see Bartley?

MAURYA. I seen the fearfulest thing.

CATHLEEN (*leaves her wheel and looks out*). God forgive you; he's riding the mare now over the green head, and the gray pony behind him.

MAURYA (*starts, so that her shawl falls back from her head and shows her white tossed hair; with a frightened voice*). The gray pony behind him.

CATHLEEN (*coming to the fire*). What is it ails you, at all?

MAURYA (*speaking very slowly*). I've seen the fearfulest thing any person has seen, since the day Bride Dara seen the dead man with the child in his arms.

CATHLEEN AND NORA. Uah.

(*They crouch down in front of the old woman at the fire.*)

NORA. Tell us what it is you seen.

MAURYA. I went down to the spring well, and I stood there saying a prayer to myself. Then Bartley came along,

14 keen: wail in lamentation for the dead.
15 black hags: primitive witches.

and he riding on the red mare with the gray pony behind him. (*She puts up her hands, as if to hide something from her eyes.*) The Son of God spare us, Nora!

CATHLEEN. What is it you seen?

MAURYA. I seen Michael himself.

CATHLEEN (*speaking softly*). You did not, Mother; it wasn't Michael you seen, for his body is after being found in the far north, and he's got a clean burial by the grace of God.

MAURYA (*a little defiantly*). I'm after seeing him this day, and he riding and galloping. Bartley came first on the red mare; and I tried to say "God speed you," but something choked the words in my throat. He went by quickly; and "the blessing of God on you," says he, and I could say nothing. I looked up then, and I crying, at the gray pony, and there was Michael upon it—with fine clothes on him, and new shoes on his feet.

CATHLEEN (*begins to keen*). It's destroyed we are from this day. It's destroyed, surely.

NORA. Didn't the young priest say the Almighty God wouldn't leave her destitute with no son living?

MAURYA (*in a low voice, but clearly*). It's little the like of him knows of the sea. . . . Bartley will be lost now, and let you call in Eamon and make me a good coffin out of the white boards, for I won't live after them. I've had a husband, and a husband's father, and six sons in this house—six fine men, though it was a hard birth I had with every one of them and they coming to the world—and some of them were found and some of them were not found, but they're gone now the lot of them. . . . There were Stephen, and Shawn, were lost in the great wind, and found after in the Bay of Gregory of the Golden Mouth, and carried up the two of them on the one plank, and in by that door.

> (*She pauses for a moment; the girls start as if they heard something through the door that is half open behind them.*)

NORA (*in a whisper*). Did you hear that, Cathleen? Did you hear a noise in the northeast?

CATHLEEN (*in a whisper*). There's someone after crying out by the seashore.

MAURYA (*continues without hearing anything*). There was Sheamus and his father, and his own father again, were lost in a dark night, and not a stick or sign was seen of them when the sun went up. There was Patch after was drowned out of a curagh[16] that turned over. I was sitting here with Bartley, and he a baby, lying on my two knees, and I seen two women, and three women, and four women coming in, and they crossing themselves, and not saying a word. I looked out then, and there were men coming after them, and they holding a thing in the half of a red sail, and water dripping out of it—it was a dry day, Nora—and leaving a track to the door.

> (*She pauses again with her hand stretched out toward the door. It opens softly and old women begin to come in, crossing themselves on the threshold, and kneeling down in front of the stage with red petticoats over their heads.*)

MAURYA (*half in a dream, to* **CATHLEEN**). Is it Patch, or Michael, or what is it at all?

CATHLEEN. Michael is after being found in the far north, and when he is found there how could he be here in this place?

16 curagh (kŭr′əKH): small boat.

MAURYA. There does be a power of young men floating round in the sea, and what way would they know if it was Michael they had, or another man like him, for when a man is nine days in the sea, and the wind blowing, it's hard set his own mother would be to say what man was it.

CATHLEEN. It's Michael, God spare him, for they're after sending us a bit of his clothes from the far north.

(*She reaches out and hands* MAURYA *the clothes that belonged to* Michael. MAURYA *stands up slowly, and takes them in her hands.* NORA *looks out.*)

NORA. They're carrying a thing among them and there's water dripping out of it and leaving a track by the big stones.

CATHLEEN (*in a whisper to the women who have come in*). Is it Bartley it is?

ONE OF THE WOMEN. It is surely, God rest his soul.

(*Two younger women come in and pull out the table. Then men carry in the body of* BARTLEY, *laid on a plank, with a bit of a sail over it, and lay it on the table.*)

CATHLEEN (*to the women, as they are doing so*). What way was he drowned?

ONE OF THE WOMEN. The gray pony knocked him into the sea, and he was washed out where there is a great surf on the white rocks.

(MAURYA *has gone over and knelt down at the head of the table. The women are keening softly and swaying themselves with a slow movement.* CATHLEEN *and* NORA *kneel at the other end of the table. The men kneel near the door.*)

MAURYA (*raising her head and speaking as if she did not see the people around her*). They're all gone now, and there isn't anything more the sea can do to me. . . . I'll have no call now to be up crying and praying when the wind breaks from the south, and you can hear the surf is in the east, and the surf is in the west, making a great stir with the two noises, and they hitting one on the other. I'll have no call now to be going down and getting holy water in the dark nights after Samhain,[17] and I won't care what way the sea is when the other women will be keening. (*To* NORA). Give me the holy water, Nora; there's a small cup still on the dresser.

(NORA *gives it to her.*)

MAURYA (*drops Michael's clothes across* BARTLEY'S *feet, and sprinkles the holy water over him*). It isn't that I haven't prayed for you, Bartley, to the Almighty God. It isn't that I haven't said prayers in the dark night till you wouldn't know what I'd be saying; but it's a great rest I'll have now, and it's time surely. It's a great rest I'll have now, and great sleeping in the long nights after Samhain, if it's only a bit of wet flour we do have to eat, and maybe a fish that would be stinking.

(*She kneels down again, crossing herself, and saying prayers under her breath.*)

CATHLEEN (*to an old man*). Maybe yourself and Eamon would make a coffin when the sun rises. We have fine white boards herself bought, God help her, thinking Michael would be found, and I have a new cake you can eat while you'll be working.

THE OLD MAN (*looking at the boards*). Are there nails with them?

CATHLEEN. There are not, Colum; we didn't think of the nails.

ANOTHER MAN. It's a great wonder she wouldn't think of the nails, and all the coffins she's seen made already.

17 **Samhain:** an ancient Celtic feast.

CATHLEEN. It's getting old she is, and broken.

(MAURYA *stands up again very slowly and spreads out the pieces of Michael's clothes beside the body, sprinkling them with the last of the holy water.*)

NORA (*in a whisper to* CATHLEEN). She's quiet now and easy; but the day Michael was drowned you could hear her crying out from this to the spring well. It's fonder she was of Michael, and would anyone have thought that?

CATHLEEN (*slowly and clearly*). An old woman will be soon tired with anything she will do, and isn't it nine days herself is after crying and keening, and making great sorrow in the house?

MAURYA (*puts the empty cup mouth downwards on the table, and lays her hands together on* BARTLEY'S *feet*). They're all together this time, and the end is come. May the Almighty God have mercy on Bartley's soul, and on Michael's soul, and on the souls of Sheamus and Patch, and Stephen and Shawn (*bending her head*); and may He have mercy on my soul, Nora, and on the soul of everyone is left living in the world.

(*She pauses, and the keen rises a little more loudly from the women, then sinks away.*)

MAURYA (*continuing*). Michael has a clean burial in the far north, by the grace of the Almighty God. Bartley will have a fine coffin out of the white boards, and a deep grave surely. What more can we want than that? No man at all can be living forever, and we must be satisfied.

(*She kneels down again and the curtain falls slowly.*)

Comment

Knowledge, in the modern world, is power: what we know, we can control. By our knowledge of nature, through science, we can control huge sources of power in the 20th century. Yet Maurya, the old peasant mother, for all her frightening foreknowledge of her last son's death, cannot stop it. Yeats gave Synge good advice when he urged him to go to the Aran Islands, for Synge found there an awareness of nature, of life, and of death. He described people who know more than they can control.

1. A number of references are made to the new rope, the clean white boards, and, at the end, to the necessity of nails for the coffin. What do these details—and any others like them that you observe—tell us of the conditions in which Maurya and her family live? What do they tell us of the hard facts of their life?
2. Do such details tell us anything more? For example, Bartley asks for the rope in order to make a halter for the horse he wants to sell on the mainland. But for what purpose does his mother want to keep the rope? We know that when she goes out to take Bartley his bit of bread she sees a vision that convinces her that he will die. Do you see any relation between the use she wants to make of the rope and her foreknowledge of Bartley's death?

3. Bartley appears but briefly. What is his chief concern when he talks to his mother and sisters before he leaves? What are his instructions to them? What is his attention fixed on?

4. In contrast to her son, where is the mother's attention centered? What is her concern as he leaves his last instructions? Why does she not think to bless him when he leaves?

5. Maurya's lament (p. 847) seems to be ignored by the man who comes to help with the burial and is annoyed to find no nails for the coffin boards. How does his attitude show the same awareness of the inevitability of death from the sea that Maurya is expressing in her keening?

6. Do you find any similarity between this play and Auden's "Musée des Beaux Arts"? The latter presents a sophisticated museum-goer meditating on a picture he has seen. *Riders to the Sea* presents us with the sudden death of a young man whose mother knows, before he dies, that he is doomed. What similarity do you see between this short modern poem and this one-act modern play?

The Adventure of Growth

Toward the Future

ALTHOUGH SOMETIMES it may be painful, sometimes exhilarating, and often lonely, the adventure of growth as modern writers have imagined it must lead to self-knowledge. The following poems and essay suggest the kind of self-knowledge that is both required by a person's setting forth and also granted to him or her after many hardships.

Louis MacNeice (1907-1963)

We have already encountered Louis MacNeice as the author of the statement that the modern poet must be an "informer"—a kind of spy who reports on the secret thoughts and feelings of all of us. Mac-Neice was born in Belfast. He studied at Oxford, took a first-class degree in classics, and then taught at Birmingham and London universities. He has translated the Greek dramatist Aeschylus and the German poet Goethe; he has written radio plays and critical essays; and, between 1929, when his first book of poems appeared, and 1961 he published seven books of poetry.

MacNeice's poetry is in many ways more traditional than that of Spender or Auden, and yet its attitudes and its diction, as you will see, place it as fully in a contemporary idiom as theirs.

This poem comes from a MacNeice collection called *Solstices* (1961), and it tells of what happened to a "box of truisms"—a collection of obvious and generally accepted truths—given to a young man by his father.

The Truisms

Louis MacNeice

His father gave him a box of truisms
Shaped like a coffin, then his father died;
The truisms remained on the mantelpiece
As wooden as the playbox they had been packed in
Or that other[1] his father skulked inside.   5

Then he left home, left the truisms behind him
Still on the mantelpiece, met love, met war,
Sordor,[2] disappointment, defeat, betrayal,
Till through disbeliefs he arrived at a house
He could not remember seeing before.   10

And he walked straight in; it was where he had come from
And something told him the way to behave.
He raised his hand and blessed his home;
The truisms flew and perched on his shoulders
And a tall tree sprouted from his father's grave.   15

1 **that other:** his father's coffin.
2 **Sordor:** sordidness.

Comment

This poem tells the story of a setting out and a return home. Where does the traveler go? And what does he find when he returns?

1. Describe the journey of the young man as you understand it: What does he leave behind him? What kind of adventures does he journey through? Why does he not "remember seeing" the "house" to which he finally comes?
2. Why do the "truisms" fly and perch on his shoulders? What has he done to make them come alive? And why does the tree sprout from his father's grave? What has come alive between him and his now dead father?
3. What then does this poem make "truisms" out to be?

Laurie Lee (1914-   )

Laurie Lee was born in the Cotswolds, a range of hills in Glouces-
tershire containing some of the loveliest villages in England.   He
traveled in Spain before the outbreak of the Spanish Civil War in 1936
and came to admire the work of the modern Spanish poet García Lorca.
Like Dylan Thomas, Lee has written for the radio; one of his scripts,
a verse drama entitled *The Voyage of Magellan*, has been published.
His autobiography, *Cider with Rosie*, was a success both in Britain
and the United States.   "April Rise" is one of twelve poems published
together as "verses from a poet's year."   April, here, is not "the cruellest month"; it is "blessed."

April Rise

Laurie Lee

If ever I saw blessing in the air
   I see it now in this still early day
Where lemon-green the vaporous morning drips
   Wet sunlight on the powder of my eye.

Blown bubble-film of blue, the sky wraps round   5
   Weeds of warm light whose every root and rod
Splutters with soapy green, and all the world
   Sweats with the bead of summer in its bud.

If ever I heard blessing it is there
   Where birds in trees that shoals and shadows are   10
Splash with their hidden wings and drops of sound
   Break on my ears their crests of throbbing air.

Pure in the haze the emerald sun dilates,
   The lips of sparrows milk the mossy stones,
While white as water by the lake a girl   15
   Swims her green hand among the gathered swans.

Now, as the almond burns its smoking wick,
   Dropping small flames to light the candled grass;
Now, as my low blood scales its second chance,
   If ever world were blessed, now it is.   20

Comment

It is a springtime morning so rich and fresh that the warm sun and moist dew combine in one rain of light upon the earth. The day, the world, and the poet "rise" together.

1. Why should the sky be likened to a "Blown bubble-film of blue" (l. 5)? How is this image continued in line 7, where the root and stem ("rod") of every plant "Splutters with soapy green"?

2. How is the water-sunlight imagery continued in the third stanza? Why are the trees likened to "shoals"? In what element do the birds' wings "splash"? How do "drops" of sound come to have "crests"—how does the poet use the scientific notion of sound-waves here?

3. When we reach the last two stanzas, the mixture of light and moisture—the "Wet sunlight" of stanza 1—has become so intense that the sun is emerald-green, the rocks are mossy, and the sharp beaks of sparrows have become soft lips. The hand of the girl by the swans is green in the water, and the dusty-pink blossoms of the flowering almond (they are less red than the color of clear flame) fall from the upright stem ("wick") of the bush and lie upon the grass like small, lighted, green candles. The light of the sun and the moisture of the dew has permeated the world. But what of the poet himself? How is April a "rise" for him too?

   (a) At the end of line 4, how do you understand the phrase "powder of my eye"? Powder must be kept dry: what happens when moisture drops on and saturates it?

   (b) And in line 19 the poet says, "my low blood scales its second chance." In the country people sometimes speak of their blood as "low" in the spring—it has been thinned out by the rigors of winter. The word "scale" means "climb" but it also means "weigh" or "measure"; and it also means "remove"—the scaling off of a winter coat. Which of these meanings seems to you the right one here? What does the whole clause, "my low blood scales its second chance," mean?

   (c) How then does the poet here experience an "April Rise"? What "adventure of growth" does he experience?

Epilogue

THE ESSAY which completes this survey of English literature comes from the early 20th century. It was written in 1919, just after World War I, by T. S. Eliot, then a young man who was soon to become one of the greatest men of letters of modern times. It begins, as you will see, by defending the word, and the concept, *tradition*, for this was not a fashionable approach to literature when Eliot wrote. That *tradition* is now a term that normally appears in literary discussions of all kinds is largely the result of this essay—and of course of Eliot's great influence through his other works.

"Tradition and the Individual Talent" was originally conceived as a kind of letter of advice to young poets and writers who began their work as our century began its life. Eliot warns them that if they ignore the past their work will be eccentric and short-lived rather than genuinely fresh and original. But he speaks not only to poets; his advice applies to readers and students of literature as well. For his real subject is the awareness of both present and past literature, a sense of how "the whole of literature . . . has a simultaneous existence and composes a simultaneous order." Such an awareness, Eliot argues, is of great importance to the writer. This book of English literature has been an argument that it is of great importance to the student of literature. For this awareness in fact is the student's goal.

from

Tradition and the Individual Talent*

T. S. Eliot

IN ENGLISH WRITING we seldom speak of tradition, though we occasionally apply its name in deploring its absence. We cannot refer to "the tradition" or to "a tradition"; at most, we employ the adjective in saying that the poetry of So-and-so is "traditional" or even "too traditional." Seldom, perhaps, does the word appear except in a phrase of censure. If otherwise, it is vaguely approbative, with the implication, as to the work approved, of some pleasing archaeological reconstruction. You can hardly make the word agreeable to English ears without this comfortable reference to the reassuring science of archaeology.

Certainly the word is not likely to appear in our appreciations of living or dead writers. Every nation, every race, has not only its own creative, but its own critical turn of mind; and is even more oblivious of the shortcomings and limitations of its critical habits than of those of its creative genius. We know, or think we know, from the enormous mass of critical writing that has appeared in the French language the critical method or habit of the French; we

only conclude (we are such unconscious people) that the French are "more critical" than we, and sometimes even plume ourselves a little with the fact, as if the French were the less spontaneous. Perhaps they are; but we might remind ourselves that criticism is as inevitable as breathing, and that we should be none the worse for articulating what passes in our minds when we read a book and feel an emotion about it, for criticizing our own minds in their work of criticism. One of the facts that might come to light in this process is our tendency to insist, when we praise a poet, upon those aspects of his work in which he least resembles any one else. In these aspects or parts of his work we pretend to find what is individual, what is the peculiar essence of the man. We dwell with satisfaction upon the poet's difference from his predecessors, especially his immediate predecessors; we endeavour to find something that can be isolated in order to be enjoyed. Whereas if we approach a poet without this prejudice we shall often find that not only the best, but the most individual parts of his work may be those in which the dead poets, his ancestors, assert their immortality most vigorously. And I do not mean the impressionable period of adolescence, but the period of full maturity.[1]

Yet if the only form of tradition, of handing down, consisted in following the ways of the immediate generation before us in a blind or timid adherence to its successes, "tradition" should positively be discouraged. We have seen many such simple currents soon lost in the sand; and novelty is better than repetition. Tradition is a matter of

1 And . . . maturity: i.e., when he is young, a writer usually reveals most clearly the predecessors that have influenced him; but when he is mature, a writer's very strength will relate him to his predecessors.

854

much wider significance. It cannot be inherited, and if you want it you must obtain it by great labour. It involves, in the first place, the historical sense, which we may call nearly indispensable to any one who would continue to be a poet beyond his twenty-fifth year; and the historical sense involves a perception, not only of the pastness of the past, but of its presence; the historical sense compels a man to write not merely with his own generation in his bones, but with a feeling that the whole of the literature of Europe from Homer and within it the whole of the literature of his own country has a simultaneous existence and composes a simultaneous order. This historical sense, which is a sense of the timeless as well as of the temporal and of the timeless and of the temporal together, is what makes a writer traditional. And it is at the same time what makes a writer most acutely conscious of his place in time, of his own contemporaneity.

No poet, no artist of any art, has his complete meaning alone. His significance, his appreciation is the appreciation of his relation to the dead poets and artists. You cannot value him alone; you must set him, for contrast and comparison, among the dead. I mean this as a principle of aesthetic, not merely historical, criticism. The necessity that he shall conform, that he shall cohere, is not onesided; what happens when a new work of art is created is something that happens simultaneously to all the works of art which preceded it. The existing monuments form an ideal order among themselves, which is modified by the introduction of the new (the really new) work of art among them. The existing order is complete before the new work arrives; for order to persist after the supervention of novelty, the *whole* existing order must be, if ever so

slightly, altered; and so the relations, proportions, values of each work of art toward the whole are readjusted; and this is conformity between the old and the new. Whoever has approved this idea of order, of the form of European, of English literature will not find it preposterous that the past should be altered by the present as much as the present is directed by the past. And the poet who is aware of this will be aware of great difficulties and responsibilities.

In a peculiar sense he will be aware also that he must inevitably be judged by the standards of the past. I say judged, not amputated, by them; not judged to be as good as, or worse or better than, the dead; and certainly not judged by the canons of dead critics. It is a judgment, a comparison, in which two things are measured by each other. To conform merely would be for the new work not really to conform at all; it would not be new, and would therefore not be a work of art. And we do not quite say that the new is more valuable because it fits in; but its fitting in is a test of its value—a test, it is true, which can only be slowly and cautiously applied, for we are none of us infallible judges of conformity. We say: it appears to conform, and is perhaps individual, or it appears individual, and may conform; but we are hardly likely to find that it is one and not the other.

To proceed to a more intelligible exposition of the relation of the poet to the past: he can neither take the past as a lump, an indiscriminate bolus,[2] nor can he form himself wholly on one or two private admirations, nor can he form himself wholly upon one preferred period. The first course is inadmissible, the second is an important ex-

2 **indiscriminate bolus:** large pill.

perience of youth, and the third is a pleasant and highly desirable supplement. The poet must be very conscious of the main current, which does not at all flow invariably through the most distinguished reputations. He must be quite aware of the obvious fact that art never improves, but that the material of art is never quite the same. He must be aware that the mind of Europe—the mind of his own country—a mind which he learns in time to be much more important than his own private mind—is a mind which changes, and that this change is a development which abandons nothing *en route*, which does not superannuate either Shakespeare, or Homer, or the rock drawing of the Magdalenian[3] draughtsmen. That this development, refinement perhaps, complication certainly, is not, from the point of view of the artist, any improvement. Perhaps not even an improvement from the point of view of the psychologist or not to the extent which we imagine; perhaps only in the end based upon a complication in economics and machinery. But the difference between the present and the past is that the conscious present is an awareness of the past in a way and to an extent which the past's awareness of itself cannot show.

Some one said: "The dead writers are remote from us because we *know* so much more than they did." Precisely, and they are that which we know.

* * *

It is not in his personal emotions, the emotions provoked by particular events in his life, that the poet is in any way remarkable or interesting. His particular emotions may be simple, or crude, or flat. The emotion in his poetry will be a very complex thing, but not with the complexity of the emotions of people who have very complex or unusual emotions in life. One error, in fact, of eccentricity in poetry is to seek for new human emotions to express; and in this search for novelty in the wrong place it discovers the perverse. The business of the poet is not to find new emotions, but to use the ordinary ones and, in working them up into poetry, to express feelings which are not in actual emotions at all. And emotions which he has never experienced will serve his turn as well as those familiar to him. Consequently, we must believe that "emotion recollected in tranquillity"[4] is an inexact formula. For it is neither emotion, nor recollection, nor, without distortion of meaning, tranquillity. It is a concentration, and a new thing resulting from the concentration, of a very great number of experiences which to the practical and active person would not seem to be experiences at all; it is a concentration which does not happen consciously or of deliberation. These experiences are not "recollected," and they finally unite in an atmosphere which is "tranquil" only in that it is a passive attending upon the event. Of course this is not quite the whole story. There is a great deal, in the writing of poetry, which must be conscious and deliberate. In fact, the bad poet is usually unconscious where he ought to be conscious, and conscious where he ought to be unconscious. Both errors tend to make him "personal." Poetry is not a turning loose of emotion, but an escape from emotion; it is not the expression of personality, but an escape from personality. But, of course, only those who have personality and emo-

---

3 **Magdalenian:** caves at La Madeleine, France, where prehistoric drawings have been found.

4 **emotion . . . tranquillity:** Poetry, said Wordsworth in the Preface to *Lyrical Ballads*, "takes its origin from emotion recollected in tranquillity."

THE TWENTIETH CENTURY

tions know what it means to want to escape from these things. . . .

The emotion of art is impersonal. And the poet cannot reach this impersonality without surrendering himself wholly to the work to be done. And he is not likely to know what is to be done unless he lives in what is not merely the present, but the present moment of the past, unless he is conscious, not of what is dead, but of what is already living.

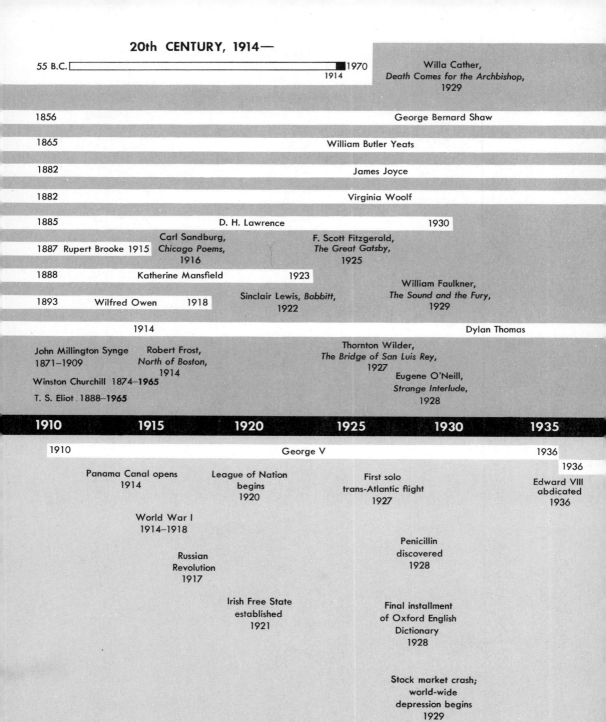

20th CENTURY, 1914—

55 B.C. ☐───────────────■ 1970
                        1914

Willa Cather,
Death Comes for the Archbishop,
1929

1856   George Bernard Shaw

1865   William Butler Yeats

1882   James Joyce

1882   Virginia Woolf

1885   D. H. Lawrence   1930

        Carl Sandburg,   F. Scott Fitzgerald,
1887 Rupert Brooke 1915 *Chicago Poems,* *The Great Gatsby,*
                            1916   1925

1888   Katherine Mansfield   1923

                              Sinclair Lewis, *Babbitt,*   William Faulkner,
                                      1922   *The Sound and the Fury,*
1893   Wilfred Owen   1918   1929

        1914   Dylan Thomas

John Millington Synge   Robert Frost,   Thornton Wilder,
1871–1909   *North of Boston,*   *The Bridge of San Luis Rey,*
                            1914   1927
Winston Churchill 1874–**1965**   Eugene O'Neill,
                                              Strange Interlude,
T. S. Eliot 1888–**1965**   1928

| **1910** | **1915** | **1920** | **1925** | **1930** | **1935** |

1910   George V   1936
                                                            1936
Panama Canal opens   League of Nation   First solo   Edward VIII
       1914   begins   trans-Atlantic flight abdicated
                          1920   1927   1936

        World War I
        1914–1918

             Russian   Penicillin
             Revolution   discovered
               1917   1928

        Irish Free State
          established   Final installment
             1921   of Oxford English
                                    Dictionary
                                       1928

                                Stock market crash;
                                    world-wide
                                 depression begins
                                       1929

Stephen Spender 1909–
Mary Lavin 1912–
William Sansom 1912–
Henry Reed 1914–

Ernest Hemingway,
The Old Man and the Sea,
1952

1950

1939

1941

1941

Arthur Miller,
Death of a Salesman,
1949

Marianne Moore,
Collected Poems,
1951

E. M. Forster 1879–**1970**

C. Day Lewis 1904–**1972**

John Betjeman 1906–

W. H. Auden 1907–**1973**

Louis MacNeice 1907–1963

J. D. Salinger,
Nine Stories,
1953

1953

Tennessee Williams,
The Glass Menagerie,
1945

| 1940 | 1945 | 1950 | 1955 | 1960 | 1965 |

1952

Elizabeth II

George VI

1952

Suez crisis
1956

Spanish
Civil War
1936–1939

U.S.S.R. launches
Sputnik
1957

U.S.S.R. and U.S.
men in space
1961

Korean War
1950–1953

India gains
independence
1947

World War II
1939–1945

Telstar
1962

Munich
Conference
1938

First use of
atomic bomb
1945

Vatican Council II
1962–63

Establishment of
United Nations
1945

Glossary

The glossary is a convenient means for looking up unfamiliar words in this book. Footnoted words are not in the glossary.

The following abbreviations are used:

adj.	adjective	esp.	especially	pl.	plural
adv.	adverb	Fr.	French	pron.	pronoun
Brit.	British	Ger.	German	sing.	singular
cap.	capital	n.	noun	U. S.	United States
Colloq.	colloquial	Obs.	obsolete	v.	verb

Pronunciation Key*

ă	act	ī	ice	ou	out	y	yes
ā	able	j	just	p	page	z	zeal
â	air	k	kept	r	read	zh	vision
ä	art	l	low	s	see	ə	a in *alone*
b	back	m	my	sh	shoe		e in *system*
ch	chief	n	now	t	ten		i in *easily*
d	do	ng	sing	th	thin		o in *gallop*
ĕ	ebb	ŏ	box	th	that		u in *circus*
ē	equal	ō	over	ŭ	up	à	as in Fr. *ami*
f	fit	ô	order	ū	use	KH	as in Ger. *ach*
g	give	oi	oil	û	urge	N	as in Fr. *bon*
h	hit	o͝o	book	v	voice	œ	as in Ger. *schon*
ĭ	if	o͞o	ooze	w	west	Y	as in Ger. *uber*

*The pronunciation system of *The American College Dictionary*, © Copyright 1947, 1963, Random House, Inc., New York. Used by permission.

Glossary

a·bate (ə bāt′), v. to lessen.

ab·ject (ăb′jěkt, ăb jěkt′), adj. utterly humiliating. 2. downcast.

ab·stract (ăb′străkt, ăb străkt′), adj. thought of apart from particular instances or objects; theoretical. —n. (ăb′străkt), a summary.

ac·cord·ant (ə kôr′dənt), adj. agreeing.

ac·qui·esce (ăk′wĭ ĕs′), v. to accept quietly, without protesting and without enthusiasm.

ac·rid (ăk′rĭd), adj. sharp, bitter, or irritating to the taste.

ac·tu·ate (ăk′chŏŏ āt′), v. to put into action.

a·cute (ə kūt′), adj. 1. sharp-pointed. 2. keen. 3. intense; crucial.

ad·jure (ə jŏŏr′), v. to command or entreat earnestly. —ad·ju·ra·tion (ăj′ŏŏ rā′shən), n.

aes·thet·ic (ĕs thĕt′ĭk), adj. pertaining to the beautiful.

af·fa·ble (ăf′ə bəl), adj. easy to talk to.

af·flu·ence (ăf′lŏŏ əns), n. abundance of material possessions; wealth.

af·front (ə frŭnt′), v. to offend openly.

ag·gra·va·tion (ăg′rə vā′shən), n. 1. *In earlier times,* provocation. 2. the act of making worse.

ag·gre·gate (ăg′rə gĭt), n. a group of things gathered together.

a·ghast (ə găst′), adj. filled with sudden fright.

a·gil·i·ty (ə jĭl′ə tĭ), n. ease and quickness of movement.

al·lege (ə lĕj′), v. to declare.

al·lit·er·a·tive (ə lĭt′ə rā′tĭv), adj. having several words of a group beginning with the same letter or sound.

al·lo·cu·tion (ăl′ə kū′shən), n. a formal address.

al·lude (ə lŏŏd′), v. to refer to indirectly.

al·ter·ca·tion (ôl′tər kā′shən), n. angry dispute.

a·nach·ro·nism (ə năk′ rə nĭz′əm), n. the introduction into past times of things or events that occurred only in a later time.

a·nal·o·gous (ə năl′ə gəs), adj. similar or comparable in certain respects.

a·nal·o·gy (ə năl′ə jĭ), n. a partial similarity on which a comparison may be based.

an·ar·chy (ăn′ər kĭ), n. absence of government or governmental control; lawlessness; disorder. —**an·ar′chic,** adj.

an·i·mad·ver·sion (ăn′ə măd vûr′zhən), n. an unfavorable remark.

an·no·tate (ăn′ō tāt′), v. to remark upon in notes.

a·nom·a·lous (ə nŏm′ə ləs), adj. abnormal.

an·thro·pol·o·gy (ăn′thrə pŏl′ə jĭ), n. the study of the races of mankind—their characteristics, distribution, customs, etc.

an·tip·a·thy (ăn tĭp′ə thĭ), n. a natural or settled dislike.

ap·a·thy (ăp′ə thĭ), n. lack of feeling.

ap·er·ture (ăp′ər chər), n. an opening.

aph·o·rism (ăf′ə rĭz′əm), n. a concise statement of a general truth.

a·plomb (ə plŏm′), n. assurance of manner.

a·pos·ta·sy (ə pŏs′tə sĭ), n. an abandonment of one's faith or cause.

a·pos·tate (ə pŏs′tāt), n. one who forsakes his faith or cause. —adj. guilty of apostasy.

ap·pre·hend (ăp′rĭ hĕnd′), v. 1. to take into custody. 2. to grasp the meaning of; understand. —**ap′pre·hen′si·ble,** adj.

ap·pre·hen·sion (ăp′rĭ hĕn′shən), n. 1. arrest. 2. understanding. 3. foreboding; fear.

ap·pro·ba·tion (ăp′rə bā′shən), n. approval.

ap·pro·ba·tive (ăp′rə bā′tĭv), adj. approving.

ar·bi·trar·y (är′bə trĕr′ĭ), adj. unreasonable.

ar·chae·ol·o·gy (är′kĭ ŏl′ə jĭ), n. the scientific study of ancient peoples by the excavation of ancient cities, relics, etc.

ar·dor (är′dər), n. eagerness.

ar·du·ous (är′jŏŏ əs), adj. difficult to do.

ar·tic·u·late (adj. är tĭk′yə lĭt; v. är tĭk′yə lāt′) —adj. 1. spoken clearly. 2. capable of speaking clearly. —v. to speak clearly.

ăct, āble, dâre, ärt; ĕbb, ēqual; ĭf, īce; hŏt, ōver, ôrder, oil, bŏŏk, ōōze, out; ŭp, ūse, ûrge; ə = a in *alone;* ch, chief; g, give; j, judge; ng, ring; sh, shoe; th, thin; th, that; zh, vision. See the full key at the beginning of this glossary.

ar·ti·fice (är′tə fĭs), *n.* **1.** skill. **2.** skill in deceiving. **3.** an artful device.

ar·ti·san (är′tə zən), *n.* a skilled craftsman.

as·cet·ic (ə sĕt′ĭk), *n.* one who leads a life of rigorous self-denial.

as·cribe (ə skrīb′), *v.* to assign; attribute.

as·per·i·ty (ăs pĕr′ə tĭ), *n.* harshness.

as·si·du·i·ty (ăs′ə dū′ə tĭ), *n.* **1.** diligence. **2.** *in the plural,* solicitous attentions.

at·a·vism (ăt′ə vĭz′əm), *n.* reversion to an earlier type.

a·the·ist (ā′thĭ ĭst), *n.* one who denies the existence of God.

a·tone (ə tōn′), *v.* to make amends (for wrongdoing).

au·da·cious (ô dā′shəs), *adj.* daring; bold.

au·gust (ô gŭst′), *adj.* inspiring reverence and awe; imposing.

aus·tere (ô stĭr′), *adj.* **1.** stern. **2.** morally strict. **3.** severely simple; without ornament.

av·a·rice (ăv′ə rĭs), *n.* greed for riches.

a·verse (ə vûrs′), *adj.* opposed (to).

a·ver·sion (ə vûr′zhən), *n.* intense dislike.

av·o·ca·tion (ăv′ə kā′shən), *n.* a subordinate occupation.

ax·i·om (ăk′sĭ əm), *n.* an established principle.

az·ure (ăzh′ər), *adj.* of a sky-blue color. —*n.* a blue pigment.

bag·a·telle (băg′ə tĕl′), *n.* a trifle.

band·box (bănd′bŏks′), *n.* a light box for holding collar bands, hats, etc.

bard (bärd), *n.* a poet.

base (bās), *adj.* morally low; vile.

bau·ble (bô′bəl), *n.* a cheap ornament.

ben·e·fice (bĕn′ə fĭs), *n.* an endowed church office that provides a living for a vicar or other churchmen.

be·nign (bĭ nīn′), *adj.* kindly.

be·shrew (bĭ shrōō′), *v.* to curse.

bland (blănd), *adj.* **1.** smooth; agreeable.

blan·dish·ment (blăn′dĭsh mənt), *n.* flattering speech or action.

blas·pheme (blăs fēm′), *v.* to speak irreverently of God or sacred things.

blas·phe·my (blăs′fə mĭ), *n.* mocking abuse of God or anything regarded as sacred.

blight (blīt), *v.* to cause to wither.

blip (blĭp), *n.* a spot of light on a radar screen indicating the position of a plane, ship, or other object.

blithe (blīth), *adj.* joyous.

bob·bin (bŏb′ĭn), *n.* a spool or reel on which thread or yarn is wound for spinning, machine sewing, and weaving.

Boer (bōr), *n.* a South African descended from the Dutch colonists.

boon (bōōn), *n.* **1.** a welcome benefit. **2.** a favor. *adj.* **1.** *Archaic.* kind; pleasant. **2.** merry (now only in *boon* companion).

brash (brăsh), *adj.* insolent.

bra·zen (brā′zən), *adj.* made of brass; like brass, as in sound, color, etc.; shameless. —*v.* (followed by *out*), to face shamelessly.

breach (brēch), *n.* **1.** an opening made by breaking something. **2.** a break in relations, as a *breach* of trust.

brim·stone (brĭm′stōn′), *n.* sulphur.

brooch (brōch), *n.* an ornament for the dress.

brunt (brŭnt), *n.* the main force of an attack.

Brython (brĭth′ən), *n.* a Celt in Britain using the Brythonic form of the Celtic language, and confined chiefly to southwest Britain.

bu·bon·ic (bū bŏn′ĭk) **plague,** *n.* a contagious disease carried by fleas from infected rats.

buf·foon (bə fōōn′), *n.* one who tries to amuse others by tricks and jokes.

bu·reau·crat (byōōr′ə krăt′), *n.* an official in a bureaucracy; one who works by inflexible routine without exercising judgment.

Byz·an·tine (bĭz′ən tēn′), *adj.* of or pertaining to Byzantium or the Byzantine Empire.

ca·dence (kā′dəns), *n.* rhythmic flow.

can·did (kăn′dĭd), *adj.* frank; open.

can·dor (kăn′dər), *n.* frankness; sincerity.

can·on (kăn′ən), *n.* a law or body of laws.

cant (kănt), *n.* **1.** whining, singsong speech, esp. as used by beggars. **2.** the special words used by a particular occupation.

can·tan·ker·ous (kăn tăng′kər əs), *adj.* ill-natured.

ca·pa·cious (kə pā′shəs), *adj.* able to hold much.

ca·price (kə prēs′), *n.* a sudden turn of mind without apparent or adequate reason.

ca·pri·cious (kə prĭsh′əs), *adj.* subject to caprices; flighty; unpredictable.

car·nal (kär′nəl), *adj.* of the flesh; worldly.

car·riage (kăr′ĭj), *n.* **1.** manner of carrying oneself or behaving. **2.** a wheeled vehicle.

caulk (kôk), *v.* to stop up cracks with filler, as the seams of a boat.

caus·tic (kôs′tĭk), *adj.* **1.** capable of burning or destroying living tissue by chemical action. **2.** biting; sarcastic.

cav·il (kăv′əl), *v.* to raise trivial objections; to find fault unnecessarily. —**cav′il·er,** *n.*

Celt (sĕlt; *esp. Brit.* kĕlt), *n.* a member of an Indo-European people, now chiefly the Irish, Welsh, Gaels, and Bretons.

cen·sure (sĕn′shər), *n.* reprimand.

ce·su·ra (sə zhŏŏr′ə), *n.* a break or pause in a line of verse, in English verse usually about the middle of the line. Also spelled **caesura.**

chaff (chăf), *n.* husks of wheat and other grain separated from the seed.

chaf·finch (chăf′ĭnch), *n.* a common European finch with a short, sweet song.

chaise (shāz), *n.* a lightweight carriage with a collapsible top, esp. a two-wheeled carriage for two persons.

cham·ois (shăm′ĭ), *n.* a goatlike animal from the mountains of Europe.

cha·ot·ic (kā ŏt′ĭk), *adj.* in utter confusion.

chas·ten (chā′sən), *v.* 1. to punish in order to correct. 2. to restrain; subdue.

cher·ub (chĕr′əb), *n., pl.* **cherubs** for 2; **cherubim** (chĕr′ə bĭm) for 1. 1. a kind of celestial being often represented as a beautiful winged child. 2. a beautiful or innocent person, esp. a child.

chide (chīd), *v.* to reprove.

chol·er (kŏl′ər), *n.* 1. *Obs.* bile, in medieval times considered the source of anger and irascibility. 2. anger; irascibility.

chol·er·ic (kŏl′ər ĭk), *adj.* irascible.

churl (chûrl), *n.* 1. a peasant. 2. an ill-bred person. 3. a miser. —**churl′ish,** *adj.*

cir·cum·spect (sûr′kəm spĕkt), *adj.* watchful on all sides; prudent. —**cir′cum·spec′tion** *n.*

cir·cum·vent (sûr′kəm vĕnt′), *v.* to go around by trickery.

ci·vil·i·ty (sĭ vĭl′ə tĭ), *n.* courtesy.

clar·i·on (klăr′ĭ ən), *n.* a kind of trumpet that produces clear, shrill sounds.

clime (klīm), *n. Poetic.* climate.

cloy (kloi), *v.* to weary by too much of anything, esp. anything sweet.

come·ly (kŭm′lĭ), *adj.* pleasing in appearance.

com·mit·ment (kə mĭt′mənt), *n.* a promise.

com·pla·cent (kəm plā′sənt), *adj.* pleased with oneself.

com·pre·hen·sive (kŏm′prĭ hĕn′sĭv), *adj.* inclusive.

com·punc·tion (kəm pŭngk′shən), *n.* a feeling of uneasiness caused by a sense of guilt.

con·cen·ter (kŏn sĕn′tər), *v.* to bring to a common center; to concentrate.

con·cept (kŏn′sĕpt), *n.* an idea of a class of objects; a general idea.

con·course (kŏn′kōrs), *n.* 1. a throng. 2. a place where crowds gather.

con·de·scend (kŏn′dĭ sĕnd′), *v.* 1. to descend voluntarily to the level of an inferior that one is dealing with. 2. to behave as if one were stooping from a superior position or rank; to patronize. —**con′de·scen′sion,** *n.*

con·dole (kən dōl′), *v.* to mourn in sympathy.

con·fed·er·ate (kən fĕd′ər ĭt), *adj.* united in a league or alliance.

con·found (kŏn found′), *v.* to throw into confusion.

con·front (kən frŭnt′), *v.* to meet face to face.

con·fute (kən fūt′), *v.* to prove to be false.

con·gen·i·tal (kən jĕn′ə təl), *adj.* existing from one's birth.

con·jur·er (kŭn′jər ər), *n.* 1. a magician or sorcerer. 2. one who entreats solemnly.

con·jure (kŭn′jər), *v.* 1. to summon a devil or spirit by magic. 2. to appeal earnestly.

con·nive (kə nīv′), *v.* to pretend not to look (at some wrongdoing), thus giving it aid. —**con·niv′ance,** *n.*

con·nois·seur (kŏn′ə sûr′), *n.* one who has expert knowledge and fine discrimination in some field, especially the fine arts.

con·strain (kən strān′), *v.* to force.

con·sum·mate (kŏn′sə māt′), *v.* to bring to completion or perfection.

con·ten·tion (kən tĕn′shən), *n.* dispute.

con·tin·gen·cy (kən tĭn′jən sĭ), *n.* a chance event.

cop·y·right (kŏp′ĭ rīt′), *n.* the exclusive right to publish, produce, or sell a literary, musical, or artistic work, granted by law for a specified number of years.

coun·ter (koun′tər), *v.* to oppose.

cov·ert (kŭv′ərt), *adj.* covered; concealed. —*n.* a hiding place; a thicket giving shelter to game.

cox·comb (kŏks′kōm′), *n.* a conceited dandy.

cra·ven (krā′vən), *adj.* cowardly.

cred·u·lous (krĕj′ə ləs), *adj.* tending to believe too readily.

croft (krôft), *n.* a small piece of enclosed ground for tillage.

cu·bit (kū′bĭt), *n.* an ancient unit of length, based on the length of the arm from the end of the middle finger to the elbow, usually from 17 to 21 inches.

cull (kŭl), *v.* to select.

cyn·ic (sĭn′ĭk), *n.* one who doubts or denies the goodness of people. —**cyn′i·cal,** *adj.*

ăct, āble, dâre, ärt; ĕbb, ēqual; ĭf, īce; hŏt, ōver, ôrder, oil, bŏŏk, ōōze, out; ŭp, ūse, ûrge; ə = a in *alone;* ch, chief; g, give; j, judge; ng, ring; sh, shoe; th, thin; th, that; zh, vision. See the full key at the beginning of this glossary.

dale (dāl), *n.* a valley.

dap·pled (dăp'əld), *adj.* having spots of different colors or shades.

dap·ple-gray (dăp'əl grā'), *adj.* gray spotted with darker gray.

das·tard (dăs'tərd), *n.* a mean coward.

daunt·less (dônt'lĭs), *adj.* fearless.

deb·o·nair (dĕb'ə nâr'), *adj.* 1. of pleasant manners. 2. gay; sprightly.

de·but, dé·but (dĭ bū', dā'bū), *n.* a first public appearance.

de·ca·dence (dĭ kā'dəns, dĕk'ə dəns), *n.* the process of falling into decay.

de·clen·sion (dĭ klĕn'shən), *n.* in grammar, a class of nouns, pronouns, or adjectives having a similar system of inflections.

de·crep·i·tude (dĭ krĕp'ə tūd'), *n.* feebleness, esp. of old age.

deem (dēm), *v.* to think.

de·fer (dĭ fûr'), *v.* to put off.

def·er·ence (dĕf'ər əns), *n.* respectful regard.

def·er·en·tial (dĕf'ə rĕn'shəl), *adj.* very respectful.

de·fin·i·tive (dĭ fĭn'ə tĭv), *adj.* conclusive.

deft (dĕft), *adj.* skillful; dexterous.

deign (dān), *v.* to think fitting to one's dignity (to do something).

de·mure (dĭ myo͞or'), *adj.* modest.

de·nude (dĭ nūd'), *v.* to make bare.

de·plete (dĭ plēt'), *v.* to reduce the amount of.

de·plore (dĭ plôr'), *v.* to express regret about.

de·praved (dĭ prāvd'), *adj.* corrupt; wicked.

de·prav·i·ty (dĭ prăv'ə tĭ), *n.* corruption.

de·ride (dĭ rīd'), *v.* to laugh at in ridicule.

de·rog·a·to·ry (dĭ rŏg'ə tôr'ĭ), *adj.* belittling; disparaging.

des·ic·cat·ed (dĕs'ə kā'tĕd), *adj.* dried up; powdered.

de·sist (dĭ zĭst', dĭ sĭst'), *v.* to cease.

des·pi·ca·ble (dĕs'pĭ kə bəl), *adj.* that is or should be despised; contemptible.

des·ti·tu·tion (dĕs'tə tū'shən), *n.* utter poverty.

de·vi·ate (dē'vĭ āt'), *v.* to turn aside (from a course, a standard, etc.)

de·vise (dĭ vīz'), *v.* to think out; plan.

dex·ter·i·ty (dĕks tĕr'ə tĭ), *n.* 1. skill in using the hands or body. 2. mental skill.

dic·tion (dĭk'shən), *n.* style of speaking or writing.

dif·fi·dence (dĭf'ə dəns), *n.* lack of confidence in oneself; shyness.

dif·fuse (dĭ fūz'), *v.* to pour out and spread, as a liquid.

di·gres·sion (dĭ grĕsh'ən), *n.* a turning aside from the main topic in talking or writing.

dil·i·gence (dĭl'ə jəns), *n.* constant and careful effort.

diph·thong (dĭf'thŏng), *n.* a speech sound made by gliding continuously from one vowel sound to another so that it gives the impression of one sound, as *ou* in *house.*

dire (dīr), *adj.* dreadful.

dirge (dûrj), *n.* a funeral hymn.

dis·cern·ment (dĭ zûrn'mənt), *n.* keenness of perception or judgment.

dis·com·fit (dĭs kŭm'fĭt), *v.* 1. to defeat utterly. 2. to disconcert.

dis·creet (dĭs krēt'), *adj.* wise in avoiding mistakes or faults; prudent.

dis·cur·sive (dĭs kûr'sĭv), *adj.* passing rapidly from one subject to another.

dis·in·ter·est·ed (dĭs ĭn'tə rĕs'tĭd), *adj.* not influenced by personal interest.

dis·par·age (dĭs păr'ĭj), *v.* to belittle.

dis·par·i·ty (dĭs păr'ə tĭ), *n.* inequality.

dis·sem·ble (dĭ sĕm'bəl), *v.* to conceal the true facts under a false appearance. —**dis·sem'bler,** *n.*

dis·sim·u·late (dĭ sĭm'yə lāt'), *v.* to hide (one's feelings) under a false appearance. —**dis·sim'u·la'tion,** *n.*

dis·si·pate (dĭs'ə pāt'), *v.* to scatter.

dis·taff (dĭs'tăf), *n.* a staff on which wool, etc., is wound for use in spinning.

dis·til (dĭs tĭl'), *v.* to heat a mixture so as to separate the more volatile from the less volatile parts, and thus to produce a purer substance.

dis·tort (dĭs tôrt'), *v.* to twist out of shape. —**dis·tort'ed,** *adj.* —**dis·tor'tion,** *n.*

dit·ty (dĭt'ĭ), *n.* a short, simple song.

di·ur·nal (dĭ ûr'nəl), *adj.* daily.

di·ver·gent (dĭ vûr'jənt), *adj.* going in different directions.

di·vers (dī'vərz), *adj.* various.

di·ver·sion (dĭ vûr'zhən), *n.* 1. a turning aside. 2. an amusement.

di·vert (dĭ vûrt'), *v.* 1. to turn aside. 2. to amuse.

di·vest (dĭ vĕst'), *v.* to strip (of clothing, etc.); to dispossess.

di·vulge (dĭ vŭlj'), *v.* to disclose something private or not known before.

dog·ged (dôg'ĭd), *adj.* stubborn.

dog·ma (dôg'mə), *n.* a body of doctrines laid down authoritatively.

dole (dōl), *n.* food or money given out as charity.

dole·ful (dōl'fəl), *adj.* sorrowful; gloomy.

dra·goon (drə go͞on'), *n.* a heavily armed cavalryman. —*v.* to persecute by dragoons; to force.

dra·per (drā'pər), *n.* in England, a dealer in dry goods, etc.

draught (drăft), *n.* the amount taken in one drink.

du·bi·ous (dū′bĭ əs), *adj.* **1.** causing doubt. **2.** feeling doubt. **3.** of uncertain outcome.

duc·tile (dŭk′təl), *adj.* **1.** capable of being molded or shaped. **2.** easily shaped or managed. —**duc·til′i·ty,** *n.*

dupe (dūp), *n.* a person easily deceived.

eb·ul·li·tion (ĕb′ə lĭsh′ən), *n.* a boiling up, as of passion or feeling.

ec·cen·tric (ĭk sĕn′trĭk), *adj.* *literally* off-center; peculiar.

ef·fi·ca·cy (ĕf′ə kə sĭ), *n.* effectiveness.

ef·flu·vi·um (ĭ flōō′vĭ əm), *n. pl.* —**via** (—vĭ ə). a slight or invisible outflow in the form of vapor or a stream of invisible particles.

e·ject (ĭ jĕkt′), *v.* to force out.

e·late (ĭ lāt′), *adj.* in high spirits; jubilant.

el·e·gy (ĕl′ə jĭ), *n.* a poem or song lamenting the dead.

E·ly·si·um (ĭ lĭzh′ĭ əm), *n.* **1.** *in Greek mythology,* the abode of the blessed after death. **2.** any place or state of perfect happiness.

e·man·ci·pate (ĭ măn′sə pāt′), *v.* to free.

em·i·nent (ĕm′ə nənt), *adj.* conspicuous; distinguished.

em·u·late (ĕm′yə lāt′), *v.* imitate with effort to equal or excel.

en·co·mi·um (ĕn kō′mĭ əm), *n.* a formal expression of high praise.

en·croach (ĕn krōch′), *v.* to trespass (upon the rights or properties of another). —**en·croach′ment,** *n.*

en·cum·ber (ĕn kŭm′bər), *v.* to burden; weigh down.

en·gen·der (ĕn jĕn′dər), *v.* to produce or cause.

e·nig·ma (ĭ nĭg′mə), *n.* a statement containing a hidden meaning; something puzzling. —**en′ig·mat′ic,** *adj.*

e·nor·mi·ty (ĭ nôr′mə tĭ), *n.* great wickedness.

en·sue (ĕn sōō′), *v.* **1.** to follow immediately. **2.** to follow as a consequence.

en·thrall (ĕn thrôl′), *v.* to captivate; enchant.

en·tice (ĕn tīs′), *v.* to attract by exciting hope of reward or pleasure; tempt.

en·to·mol·o·gy (ĕn′tə mŏl′ə jĭ), *n.* a branch of zoology that deals with insects.

e·phem·er·al (ĭ fĕm′ər əl), *adj.* lasting only one day; short-lived.

ep·i·gram (ĕp′ə grăm′), *n.* a compact, witty statement.

ep·i·thet (ĕp′ə thĕt′), *n.* an adjective or phrase thought to express some characteristic of a person.

eq·ui·page (ĕk′wə pĭj), *n.* a carriage, esp. one with horses and liveried servants.

er·u·di·tion (ĕr′ōō dĭsh′ən), *n.* learning acquired by reading and study; scholarship.

es·chew (ĕs chōō′), *v.* to shun.

es·pouse (ĕs pouz′), *v.* to adopt (a cause or idea).

e·the·re·al (ĭ thĭr′ĭ əl), *adj.* **1.** of the ether, or upper regions of space. **2.** airy; delicate. **3.** heavenly.

eu·tha·na·sia (ū′thə nā′zhə), *n.* the act of putting a person to death painlessly, especially one suffering from an incurable and painful disease.

e·vince (ĭ vĭns′), *v.* to show clearly.

e·voke (ĭ vōk′), *v.* to call up.

ex·co·ri·ate (ĭk skōr′ĭ āt′), *v.* to strip off the skin.

ex·cru·ci·at·ing (ĭk skrōō′shĭ ā′tĭng), *adj.* extremely painful.

ex·pa·ti·ate (ĭk spā′shĭ āt′), *v.* **1.** *Now Rare.* to wander at large (in). **2.** to enlarge (upon) in talking or writing.

ex·pa·tri·ate (ĕks pā′trĭ ĭt′), *n.* an exile.

ex·pe·di·ent (ĭk spē′dĭ ənt), *adj.* **1.** useful for bringing about a desired result. **2.** serving personal interest rather than what is right or just. —*n.* a means to an end, often implying shiftiness of means.

ex·pi·ate (ĕks′pĭ āt′), *v.* to make amends for.

ex·ploit (ĕks′ploit), *n.* bold act. *v.* (ĭk sploit′) to utilize for profit, esp. selfishly.

ex·pound (ĭk spound′), *v.* to explain in detail; interpret.

ex·ten·u·ate (ĭk stĕn′yōō āt′), *v.* to lessen the seriousness of an offense by giving excuses. —**ex·ten′u·a′tion,** *n.*

ex·tir·pate (ĕk′stər pāt′), *v.* to pull up by the roots. —**ex′tir·pa′tion,** *n.*

ex·tort (ĭk stôrt′), *v.* to force something from a person by violence, threat, or the like.

ex·tri·cate (ĕks′trə kāt′), *v.* to disentangle; to set free.

fa·çade (fə säd′), *n.* the front of a building, often used figuratively of a deceptive outward appearance.

ăct, āble, dâre, ärt; ĕbb, ēqual; ĭf, īce; hŏt, ōver, ôrder, oil, bŏŏk, ōōze, out; ŭp, ūse, ûrge; ə = a in *alone;* ch, chief; g, give; j, judge; ng, ring; sh, shoe; th, thin; t̶h̶, that; zh, vision. See the full key at the beginning of this glossary.

fa·ce·tious (fə sē'shəs), *adj.* trying to be amusing.

fac·tion (făk'shən), *n.* a group of people within a larger group and, usually, at odds with the main group.

fac·tious (făk'shəs), *adj.* addicted to cause arguments and quarrels within the group or party.

fal·low (făl'ō), *n.* land which has been plowed but left unseeded for a year or more to enrich the soil.

fas·tid·i·ous (făs tĭd'ĭ əs), *adj.* 1. not easy to please. 2. delicately refined.

feigned (fānd), *adj.* pretended.

fe·lic·i·tate (fĭ lĭs'ə tāt'), *v.* to congratulate.

fe·lic·i·ty (fĭ lĭs'ə tĭ), *n.* 1. extreme happiness; bliss. 2. the quality of pleasing expression in writing or speech.

fel·on (fĕl'ən), *n.* one who has committed a grave offense such as murder or burglary.

fen (fĕn), *n.* *Brit.* low land covered wholly or partially with water.

fil·i·gree (fĭl'ə grē'), *n.* ornamental work of fine wires. —*adj.* resembling filigree.

flur·ry (flûr'ĭ), *v.* to make nervous; to agitate.

for·mi·da·ble (fôr'mĭ də bəl), *adj.* causing fear or awe.

found·ling (found'lĭng), *n.* an infant found abandoned.

frat·er·nize (frăt'ər nīz'), *v.* to associate in a brotherly manner. —**frat'er·ni·za'tion,** *n.*

fraud·u·lent (frô'jə lənt), *adj.* dishonest.

fraught (frôt), *adj.* laden (with).

fres·co (frĕs'kō), *n.* a wall painting made with water colors on wet plaster.

fret (frĕt), *n.* an interlaced design of straight lines joining one another at right angles within a border. —*v.* to provide with frets.

frig·ate (frĭg'ĭt), *n.* a sailing war vessel of the 18th and early 19th centuries.

fru·gal (froo'gəl), *adj.* thrifty; economical.

frus·trate (frŭs'trāt), *v.* to cause (someone's plans) to have no effect. —**frus·tra'tion,** *n.*

fur·row (fûr'ō), *n.* a narrow groove made in the ground, esp. by a plow.

fus·tian (fŭs'chən), *n.* a coarse cloth.

gai·ter (gā'tər), *n.* a cloth or leather covering for the instep and ankle, and sometimes leg.

gant·let (gănt'lĭt), *n.* a former military punishment in which the offender ran between two rows of men who struck as he passed: *to run the gantlet.*

gar·ish (gâr'ĭsh), *adj.* showy.

gar·nish (gär'nĭsh), *v.* to decorate or trim.

gen·re (zhän'r), *n.* kind; type.

gen·teel (jĕn tēl'), *adj.* well-bred; stylish.

ghoul (gool), *n.* an evil spirit that robs graves and feeds on the dead.

gim·let (gĭm'lĭt), *n.* a tool for boring holes.

gird (gûrd), *v.* 1. to encircle with a girdle or belt. 2. to surround.

glee·man (glē'mən), *n.* a wandering minstrel.

glib (glĭb), *adj.* speaking or spoken in a smooth, offhand manner. —**glib'ly,** *adv.*

gloze (glōz), *v.* to explain away; to gloss over.

gob·bet (gŏb'ĭt), *n.* a fragment or chunk.

gos·sa·mer (gŏs'ə mər), *n.* a fine cobweb floating in the air.

gris·ly (grĭz'lĭ), *adj.* causing a shuddering horror.

gross (grōs), *adj.* 1. total, with no deductions, as one's *gross income.* 2. coarse; not delicate. 3. big, as *gross error.*

gro·tesque (grō tĕsk'), *adj.* fantastically odd or unnatural in appearance.

grov·el (grŭv'əl), *v.* 1. to lie or move face downward, esp. in abject humility or fear. 2. to humble oneself abjectly.

guile (gīl), *n.* sly, deceitful conduct.

guin·ea (gĭn'ĭ), *n.* a British gold coin issued from 1663 to 1813, with a value of 21 shillings; hence, now, the amount of 21 shillings, though there is no coin.

guise (gīz), *n.* 1. manner of dress. 2. assumed appearance.

gul·li·ble (gŭl'ə bəl), *adj.* easily deceived.

hab·er·dash·er (hăb'ər dăsh'ər), *n.* 1. one who sells men's furnishings. 2. *Chiefly Brit.* a dealer in small wares, such as buttons and needles, and, in Chaucer's time, hats.

hack (hăk), *n.* 1. a horse for hire. 2. a person who hires himself out for routine writing. 3. a carriage for hire.

half·pen·ny (hā'pə nĭ), *n.* a British bronze coin equal to half a penny.

hank (hăngk), *n.* a skein; a standard length of coiled thread or yarn.

har·ass (hăr'əs), *v.* to trouble by repeated attacks.

hart (härt), *n.* a male deer.

hav·oc (hăv'ək), *n.* great destruction.

heath (hēth), *n.* a tract of open, uncultivated land, in Britain often covered with heather.

her·e·tic (hĕr'ə tĭk), *n.* one who professes a religious belief contrary to those accepted by his church, or who rejects the official doctrines of his church.

hey·day (hā'dā'), *n.* a period of highest vigor.

hind (hīnd), *n.* a female deer.

hire·ling (hīr′lĭng), *n.* one who follows someone else's orders for pay. —*adj.* serving for hire (now usually contemptuous).

hoar·y (hōr′ĭ), *adj.* gray or white with age.

hos·tel·ry (hŏs′təl rĭ), *n.* a lodging place; inn.

hy·poc·ri·sy (hĭ pŏk′rə sĭ), *n.* pretense of being what one is not.

hy·poth·e·sis (hĭ pŏth′ə sĭs), *n.* an unproved theory accepted tentatively to explain certain facts or as a basis for further investigation.

id·i·o·syn·cra·sy (ĭd′ĭ ə sĭng′krə sĭ), *n.* peculiarity.

ig·no·min·i·ous (ĭg′nə mĭn′ĭ əs), *adj.* disgraceful.

im·bue (ĭm bū′), *v.* to fill with moisture or with color.

im·mi·nent (ĭm′ə nənt), *adj.* likely to happen at any moment.

im·pal·pa·ble (ĭm păl′pə bəl), *adj.* 1. not perceptible to the touch. 2. too slight or subtle to be grasped by the mind.

im·pec·ca·ble (ĭm pĕk′ə bəl), *adj.* faultless. —**im·pec′ca·bly,** *adv.*

im·per·turb·a·ble (ĭm′pər tûr′bə bəl), *adj.* not easily agitated; calm.

im·pe·tus (ĭm′pə təs), *n.* moving force; incentive.

im·pi·ous (ĭm′pĭ əs), *adj.* lacking reverence for God.

im·pli·ca·tion (ĭm′plə kā′ shən), *n.* something suggested without being said openly.

im·pon·der·a·ble (ĭm pŏn′dər ə bəl), *adj.* incapable of being weighed.

im·port (*v.* ĭm pōrt′, *n.* ĭm′pōrt), *v.* 1. to bring in from the outside. 2. to convey a meaning; to signify.

im·por·tu·nate (ĭm pôr′chə nĭt), *adj.* annoyingly urgent.

im·pose (ĭm pōz′), *v.* to lay on.

im·po·tent (ĭm′pə tənt), *adj.* lacking in physical strength; helpless.

im·pre·ca·tion (ĭm′prə kā′shən), *n.* a curse.

im·pute (ĭm pūt′), *v.* to attribute (something, especially something discreditable) to another person.

in·car·nate (ĭn kär′nĭt), *adj.* embodied in flesh; personified.

in·ces·sant (ĭn sĕs′ənt), *adj.* unceasing.

in·ci·dent (ĭn′sə dənt), *adj.* naturally connected with.

in·con·gru·ous (ĭn kŏng′grŏŏ əs), *adj.* inharmonious in character.

in·cre·ment (ĭn′krə mənt), *n.* an addition.

in·cum·bent (ĭn kŭm′bənt), *adj.* lying or leaning on something. —*n.* the holder of an office; in Britain, one who holds an ecclesiastical benefice.

in·de·fat·i·ga·ble (ĭn′dĭ făt′ə gə bəl), *adj.* incapable of fatigue; tireless.

in·di·gent (ĭn′də jənt), *adj.* needy.

in·do·lent (ĭn′də lənt), *adj.* disliking or avoiding work; idle.

in·ert (ĭn ûrt′), *adj.* of an inactive nature.

in·es·ti·ma·ble (ĭn ĕs′tə mə bəl), *adj.* of value too great to be estimated.

in·fal·li·ble (ĭn făl′ə bəl), *adj.* 1. incapable of error. 2. not liable to fail. —**in·fal′li·bly,** *adv.*

in·flect (ĭn flĕkt′), *v.* 1. to vary the tone or pitch (of the voice). 2. to change the form of a word to indicate certain grammatical relationships, as case, number, etc.

in·gen·ious (ĭn jēn′yəs), *adj.* having cleverness at inventing or constructing. —**in·gen′ious·ly,** *adv.*

in·gen·u·ous (ĭn jĕn′yŏŏ əs), *adj.* simple; artless.

in·gra·ti·ate (ĭn grā′shĭ āt′), *v.* to bring (oneself) into the favor of another.

in·iq·ui·ty (ĭ nĭk′wə tĭ), *n.* sin.

ink·ling (ĭngk′lĭng), *n.* hint.

in·nate (ĭ nāt′), *adj.* inborn.

in·no·va·tion (ĭn′ə vā′shən), *n.* something new.

in·sen·sate (ĭn sĕn′sāt), *adj.* lacking sensation.

in·sin·u·ate (ĭn sĭn′yŏŏ āt′), *v.* to suggest slyly.

in·ter·cede (ĭn′tər sēd′), *v.* to go between two parties for the purpose of producing agreement; to plead in behalf of someone.

in·trep·id (ĭn trĕp′ĭd), *adj.* fearless. —**in′tre·pid′i·ty,** *n.*

in·vet·er·ate (ĭn vĕt′ər ĭt), *adj.* firmly established in a habit or practice.

in·voke (ĭn vōk′), *v.* to call on.

i·ras·ci·ble (ĭ răs′ə bəl), *adj.* easily made angry.

i·ro·ny (ī′rə nĭ), *n.* an expression in which the intended meaning of the words is the opposite of the usual meaning.

ir·rep·a·ra·ble (ĭ rĕp′ə rə bəl), *adj.* that cannot be repaired or remedied.

i·tin·er·ant (ī tĭn′ər ənt), *adj.* traveling from place to place.

ăct, āble, dâre, ärt; ĕbb, ēqual; ĭf, īce; hŏt, ōver, ôrder, oil, bŏŏk, ōōze, out; ŭp, ūse, ûrge; ə = a in *alone*; ch, chief; g, give; j, judge; ng, ring; sh, shoe; th, thin; t̶h̶, that; zh, vision. See the full key at the beginning of this glossary.

jar·gon (jär′gən), *n.* meaningless talk.

jeop·ard·y (jĕp′ər dĭ), *n.* danger.

joc·und (jŏk′ənd), *adj.* merry.

ju·ris·dic·tion (jŏŏr′ĭs dĭk′shən), *n.* **1.** the power to administer justice. **2.** the territory over which authority is exercised.

ka·lei·do·scope (kə lī′də skōp′), *n.* an instrument made up of a small tube containing loose bits of colored glass that are reflected in a set of mirrors and form changing symmetrical patterns when the tube is rotated.

keen (kēn), *v. Irish.* to wail in lamentation for the dead.

kine (kīn), *n. pl. Archaic.* pl. of cow.

knave (nāv), *n.* a dishonest fellow.

knell (nĕl), *n.* the sound of a bell rung slowly, as for a funeral.

la·con·ic (lə kŏn′ĭk), *adj.* sparing of words, as were the Laconians (Spartans) of ancient Greece. —**la·con′i·cal·ly,** *adv.*

lan·guor (lăng′gər), *n.* lack of energy. — **lan′guor·ous,** *adj.*

la·tent (lā′tənt), *adj.* hidden.

lay (lā), *adj.* of the laity, or ordinary people, as distinguished from the clergy. *n.* a short poem, especially a narrative poem to be sung.

lea (lē), *n. Chiefly Poetic.* a meadow.

len·i·ty (lĕn′ə tĭ), *n.* gentleness; mercifulness.

le·thal (lē′thəl), *adj.* deadly.

leth·ar·gy (lĕth′ər jĭ), *n.* an abnormal drowsiness; sluggish inactivity.

lev·i·ty (lĕv′ə tĭ), *n.* lightness of mind; lack of seriousness.

lex·i·cog·ra·pher (lĕk′sə kŏg′rə fər), *n.* a person who writes or compiles a dictionary.

lilt (lĭlt), *v.* to sing, speak, or play in a light, tripping manner.

lin·e·al (lĭn′ĭ əl), *adj.* in the direct line of descent.

lin·e·a·ment (lĭn′ĭ ə mənt), *n.* any of the features of the face, esp. in regard to its outline.

lin·net (lĭn′ĭt), *n.* a small European songbird.

lin·tel (lĭn′təl), *n.* the supporting crosspiece over a door or window.

liv·id (lĭv′ĭd), *adj.* discolored as by a bruise; gray-blue.

loath (lōth), *adj.* reluctant.

loth (lōth), *adj.* loath.

lu·cent (lōō′sənt), *adj.* shining.

lu·cra·tive (lōō′krə tĭv), *adj.* profitable.

lu·di·crous (lōō′də krəs), *adj.* ridiculous.

lush (lŭsh), *adj.* tender and juicy, as plants.

lyre (līr), *n.* a stringed instrument of ancient Greece used to accompany the voice.

mag·got (măg′ət), *n.* the legless larva of a fly living in decaying matter.

mag·nan·i·mous (măg năn′ə məs), *adj.* generous in overlooking injuries and insults; free from pettiness.

ma·lig·ni·ty (mə lĭg′nə tĭ), *n.* desire to do harm.

man·i·fes·to (măn′ə fĕs′tō), *n.* a public declaration of intentions made by a government or important person.

ma·raud (mə rôd′), *v.* to rove in search of plunder; to raid for plunder. —**ma·raud′-ing,** *adj.*

mar·mo·set (mär′mə zĕt′), *n.* a small, squirrel-like monkey.

ma·roon (mə rōōn′), *v.* to put (a person) ashore in some desolate place and leave him there as punishment.

max·im (măk′sĭm), *n.* a concise rule of conduct; a proverbial saying.

mel·o·dra·ma (mĕl′ə drä′mə), *n.* a sensational play that exaggerates passion and sentiment and usually has a happy ending.

me·ter (mē′tər), *n.* a regular rhythmic pattern.

me·tic·u·lous (mə tĭk′yə ləs), *adj.* careful about minute details.

met·tle·some (mĕt′əl səm), *adj.* spirited.

mi·mo·sa (mĭ mō′sə), *n.* a tropical flowering tree or shrub.

mis·an·thro·py (mĭs ăn′ thrə pĭ), *n.* the hatred or distrust of all people.

mit·i·gate (mĭt′ə gāt′), *v.* to make less severe; moderate.

mode (mōd), *n.* **1.** a way of acting or doing. **2.** customary usage or style.

mod·u·late (mŏj′ə lāt′), *v.* **1.** to soften; tone down. **2.** to vary in tone.

mor·ti·fy (môr′tə fī′), *v.* to humiliate. —**mor′-ti·fi·ca′tion,** *n.*

mu·ta·tion (mū tā′shən), *n.* change.

myr·i·ad (mĭr′ĭ əd), *n.* **1.** ten thousand. **2.** an indefinitely great number.

na·ive (nä ēv′), *adj.* artless; unsophisticated. —**na·ive·té** (nä ēv′tā′), *n.*

na·tal (nā′təl), *adj.* pertaining to one's birth.

nec·tar·ine (nĕk′tə rēn′), *n.* a kind of peach with a smooth skin.

nice (nīs), *adj.* **1.** calling for accuracy. **2.** precisely accurate or discriminating. **3.** agreeable.

nig·gard (nĭg′ərd), *n.* a very stingy person.

no·mad (nō′măd), *n.* a member of a tribe with no permanent home that wanders constantly in search of pasture.

non·cha·lant (nŏn'shə lənt, nŏn'chə länt'), *adj.* coolly unconcerned. **—non'cha·lance,** *n.*

nu·ance (nū äns'), *n.* a slight variation of color, expression, or meaning.

nu·cle·us (nū'klĭ əs), *n.* **1.** a central part or thing about which other parts or things are grouped. **2.** *Physics.* the central part of an atom.

nur·ture (nûr'chər), *v.* to feed or nourish.

nymph (nĭmf), *n.* **1.** any of the minor nature goddesses conceived of as living in trees, rivers, etc. **2.** a beautiful young woman.

oaf (ōf), *n.* a stupid, clumsy fellow.

ob·du·rate (ŏb'dyə rĭt), *adj.* hardened and unrepenting; stubborn.

ob·liv·i·ous (ə blĭv'ĭ əs), *adj.* **1.** forgetful; unmindful (*of* or *to*). **2.** inducing forgetfulness. **—ob·liv'i·ous·ness,** *n.*

oc·cult (ə kŭlt'), *adj.* beyond the bounds of ordinary knowledge; mysterious.

o·di·ous (ō' dĭ əs), *adj.* hateful.

of·fi·cious (ə fĭsh'əs), *adj.* forward in offering unwanted advice or services.

om·i·nous (ŏm'ə nəs), *adj.* serving as an evil omen; threatening.

om·nip·o·tent (ŏm nĭp'ə tənt), *adj.* all-powerful. **—om·nip'o·tence,** *n.*

o·pac·i·ty (ō păs'ə tĭ), *n.* the state of being opaque.

o·paque (ō pāk'), *adj.* not able to transmit light.

ord·nance (ôrd'nəns), *n.* artillery.

or·gan·ic (ôr găn'ĭk), *adj.* pertaining to living organisms.

or·tho·dox (ôr'thə dŏks'), *adj.* conforming to usual beliefs and practices. **—or'tho·dox'y,** *n.*

or·thog·ra·phy (ôr thŏg'rə fĭ), *n.* correct spelling.

pa·gan (pā'gən), *n.* **1.** formerly a person not a Christian, and especially applied to the ancient Greeks and Romans. **2.** an irreligious person.

Pa·le·o·zo·ic (pā'lĭ ə zō'ĭk), *adj.* of the oldest geological period to have fossils.

pal·lid (păl'ĭd), *adj.* pale.

pal·pa·ble (păl'pə bəl), *adj.* **1.** that can be touched, felt, etc. **2.** easily perceived.

pal·pi·tate (păl'pə tāt'), *v.* to beat rapidly, as the heart. **—pal'pi·ta'tion,** *n.*

pal·try (pôl'trĭ), *adj.* trifling; worthless.

pan·e·gyr·ic (păn'ə jĭr'ĭk), *n.* formal and elaborate praise of a person or thing.

par·a·phrase (păr'ə frāz'), *v.* to restate the sense of a passage in other words.

par·a·site (păr'ə sīt'), *n.* **1.** a plant or animal that lives on or in another, from which it obtains its food. **2.** a person who lives at others' expense.

par·ish (păr'ĭsh), *n.* **1.** an ecclesiastic district having its own church and clergyman. **2.** *Chiefly Brit.* a civil district.

par·o·dy (păr'ə dĭ), *v.* to imitate in such a way as to ridicule.

par·ry (păr'ĭ), *v.* to turn aside an attack.

pa·tron (pā'trən), *n.* a rich or influential person who sponsors and supports some person or activity.

peer (pĭr), *n.* **1.** an equal before the law. **2.** a nobleman. *v.* **1.** to look closely, in an effort to see clearly. **2.** to peep out.

pe·nal (pē'nəl), *adj.* of or for punishment.

pence (pĕns), *n. Brit.* pl. of **penny** when value is indicated; used also in compounds, as *he gave two pennies for twopence worth.*

pen·ny (pĕn'ĭ), *n., pl.* **pennies,** (*esp. collectively*) **pence. 1.** a British bronze coin equal to 1/12 shilling (now about 1 U.S. cent but once of greater value). **2.** a U.S. or Canadian cent.

pen·sive (pĕn'sĭv), *adj.* deeply thoughtful.

per·di·tion (pər dĭsh'ən), *n.* **1.** utter ruin. **2.** in theology, loss of the soul; damnation.

per·emp·to·ry (pə rĕmp'tə rĭ), *adj.* intolerantly decisive.

per·fid·i·ous (pər fĭd'ĭ əs), *adj.* treacherous.

per·fi·dy (pûr'fə dĭ), *n.* betrayal of trust.

per·force (pər fōrs'), *adv.* of necessity.

per·i·wig (pĕr'ə wĭg'), *n.* a wig, now usually a white or powdered wig worn by men in the late 17th and 18th centuries.

per·o·ra·tion (pĕr'ə rā' shən), *n.* the concluding part of a speech.

per·spi·cu·i·ty (pûr'spə kū'ə tĭ), *n.* clearness of statement.

per·turb (pər tûrb'), *v.* to disturb greatly; agitate. **—per'tur·ba'tion** (pûr'tər bā'shən), *n.*

pe·ruse (pə rōōz'), *v.* to read thoroughly.

per·vade (pər vād'), *v.* **1.** to spread throughout. **2.** to influence throughout.

per·verse (pər vûrs'), *adj.* stubbornly contrary.

ăct, āble, dâre, ärt; ĕbb, ēqual; ĭf, īce; hŏt, ōver, ôrder, oil, bŏŏk, ōōze, out; ŭp, ūse, ûrge; ə = a in *alone;* **ch,** chief; **g,** give; **j,** judge; **ng,** ring; **sh,** shoe; **th,** thin; **th,** that; **zh,** vision. See the full key at the beginning of this glossary.

per·vert (pər vûrt′), *v.* to turn aside from the right course.

pet·u·lant (pĕch′ə lənt), *adj.* irritable, esp. over some trifling annoyance. —**pet′u·lance**, *n.*

phi·lol·o·gy (fĭ lŏl′ə jĭ), *n.* the study of written texts in order to determine their authenticity, meaning, etc.

phre·nol·o·gy (frĕ nŏl′ə jĭ), *n.* the theory that one's mental faculties can be determined by studying the shape of the skull. —**phre·nol′o·gist**, *n.*

pin·ion (pĭn′yən), *n.* a wing.

pink (pĭngk), *n.* 1. any of various plants with pale-red flowers. 2. the color of the flower. 3. the highest type of excellence.

pith·y (pĭth′ĭ), *adj.* full of meaning.

plain·tiff (plān′tĭf), *n.* one who brings suit into a court of law.

pli·a·ble (plī′ə bəl), *adj.* easily bent; easily influenced.

plume (plōōm), *v.* to display pride in oneself.

pneu·mat·ic (nū măt′ĭk), *adj.* operated by air.

poign·ant (poin′ənt), *adj.* sharply painful to the feelings.

pok·y (pō′kĭ), *adj.* (of a place) small and cramped.

pol·troon (pŏl trōōn′), *n.* a complete coward.

post chaise (pōst shāz), *n.* a carriage for hire for traveling rapidly, esp. a closed, four-wheeled carriage for two or four persons.

post coach (pōst kōch), *n.* a coach that runs regularly over a fixed route carrying passengers and mail; a stagecoach.

po·tent (pō′tənt), *adj.* powerful.

po·ten·ti·al·i·ty (pə tĕn′ shĭ ăl′ə tĭ), *n.* possibility of being or becoming.

pound (pound), *n., pl.* **pounds,** (*collectively*) **pound.** 1. a unit of weight. 2. in Great Britain, a unit of money equal to 20 shillings (now about $2.80 but once of greater value): symbol £. 3. an enclosure maintained by the city or town for confining stray animals until claimed.

pre·car·i·ous (prĭ kâr′ĭ əs), *adj.* 1. uncertain. 2. dangerous.

pre·co·cious (prĭ kō′shəs), *adj.* forward in mental development. —**pre·coc·i·ty** (prĭ kŏs′ə tĭ), *n.*

preg·nant (prĕg′nənt), *adj.* 1. being with child. 2. filled (*with*) or rich (*in*): *pregnant with meaning; pregnant in ideas.*

pre·oc·cu·pied (prĭ ŏk′yə pīd′), *adj.* completely engrossed. —**pre·oc·cu·pa·tion** (prĭ ŏk′yə-pā′shən), *n.*

pre·rog·a·tive (prĭ rŏg′ə tĭv), *n.* an exclusive privilege, especially one due to rank or office.

pres·age (prĭ sāj′), *v.* to predict, esp. as a warning. —*n.* (prĕs′ĭj), a foreboding.

pre·sume (prĭ zōōm′), *v.* 1. to take for granted. 2. to venture to do something without permission or authority.

pre·sump·tu·ous (prĭ zŭmp′chōō əs), *adj.* impertinently bold; forward.

pre·ten·tious (prĭ tĕn′shəs), *adj.* making claims to some dignity or importance. —**pre·ten′tious·ness**, *n.*

pre·ter·nat·u·ral (prē′tər năch′ə rəl), *adj.* differing from what is natural; out of the ordinary.

pre·var·i·cate (prĭ văr′ə kāt′), *v.* to turn aside from the truth. —**pre·var′i·ca′tion**, *n.*

pri·me·val (prī mē′vəl), *adj.* of the first age or ages of the world.

priv·y (prĭv′ĭ), *adj.* 1. having knowledge of something private or confidential (followed by *to*): *he was privy to the plot.* 2. private.

pro·bi·ty (prō′bə tĭ), *n.* integrity; honesty.

pro·di·gious (prə dĭj′əs), *adj.* extraordinary in size, amount, etc.

prod·i·gy (prŏd′ə jĭ), *n.* 1. a person endowed with unusual gifts or powers. 2. something marvelous.

prof·fer (prŏf′ər), *v.* to offer something by putting it before the person.

pro·fuse (prə fūs′), *adj.* poured forth freely and abundantly.

pro·fu·sion (prə fū′zhən), *n.* a pouring forth with great liberality or wastefulness.

pro·lif·ic (prō lĭf′ĭk), *adj.* producing abundantly.

prop·a·gan·da (prŏp′ə găn′də), *n.* 1. any organization or movement for the propagation of particular ideas or doctrines. 2. the ideas spread in this way.

prop·a·gate (prŏp′ə gāt′), *v.* 1. to cause (a plant or animal) to reproduce itself. 2. to spread (ideas, etc.). —**prop′a·ga′tion**, *n.*

pro·pri·e·ty (prə prī′ə tĭ), *n.* 1. conformity to accepted standards of behavior. 2. *Obs.* privately owned property or possessions.

pros·ti·tute (prŏs′tə tūt′), *v.* to sell (oneself, one's integrity, etc.) for unworthy purposes. *adj.* base; corrupt.

pros·trate (prŏs′trāt), *adj.* lying flat with face to the ground.

pro·tag·o·nist (prō tăg′ə nĭst), *n.* the main character in a play.

pro·voc·a·tive (prə vŏk′ə tĭv), *adj.* tending to provoke to action or thought; stimulating.

psal·ter·y (sôl′ tə rĭ), *n.* an ancient musical instrument consisting of a flat sounding box with strings that were plucked.

pug·na·cious (pŭg nā′shəs), *adj.* given to fighting; combative. —**pug·nac·i·ty** (pŭg-năs′ə tĭ), *n.*

pul·ver·ize (pŭl′və rīz′), *v.* to crush or grind into powder. —**pul′ver·ous,** *adj.*

pun·gent (pŭn′jənt), *adj.* 1. producing a sharp sensation of taste or smell. 2. sharply penetrating.

quaff (kwăf), *v.* to drink in large drafts with enjoyment.

quay (kē), *n.* a wharf with facilities for loading and unloading ships.

quell (kwĕl), *v.* to suppress; subdue.

quer·u·lous (kwĕr′ə ləs), *adj.* peevishly complaining.

rack (răk), *v.* to torture, as on a rack.

rail (rāl), *v.* to utter vehement reproaches.

rav·en·ing (răv′ən ĭng), *adj.* eagerly searching for prey.

rav·ish (răv′ĭsh), *v.* to fill with great joy.

re·ca·pit·u·late (rē′kə pĭch′ə lāt′), *v.* to summarize. —**re′ca·pit′u·la′tion,** *n.*

re·cip·ro·cal (rĭ sĭp′rə kəl), *adj.* mutual.

rec·i·proc·i·ty (rĕs′ə prŏs′ə tĭ), *n.* mutual exchange.

re·coup (rĭ kōōp′), *v.* to make up for.

rec·re·ant (rĕk′rĭ ənt), *adj.* disloyal. —*n.* a traitor.

re·frac·to·ry (rĭ frăk′tə rĭ), *adj.* difficult to manage.

re·mon·strate (rĭ mŏn′strāt), *v.* to plead in protest.

re·morse (rĭ môrs′), *n.* 1. a deep and painful sense of guilt for one's actions. 2. pity: now only in the negative, as *without remorse; remorseless.*

re·plete (rĭ plēt′), *adj.* well-filled; abundantly supplied. —**re·ple′tion,** *n.*

re·pris·al (rĭ prī′zəl), *n.* injury done in return for injury received.

re·pu·di·ate (rĭ pū′dĭ āt′), *v.* 1. to disown. 2. to refuse to accept. —**re·pu′di·a′tion,** *n.*

re·qui·em (rē′kwĭ əm, rĕk′wĭ əm), *n.* a hymn or Mass for the repose of the dead.

req·ui·site (rĕk′wə zĭt), *adj.* necessary.

res·pite (rĕs′pĭt), *n.* temporary relief.

re·trench (rĭ trĕnch′), *v.* to cut down; reduce.

ret·ri·bu·tion (rĕt′ rə bū′shən), *n.* punishment for evil done.

ret·ro·grade (rĕt′rə grād′), *adj.* moving backward.

rhap·so·dy (răp′sə dĭ), *adj.* an ecstatic expression of feeling in speech or writing.

rue·ful (rōō′fəl), *adj.* mournful.

ru·mi·nate (rōō′mə nāt′), *v.* to ponder; meditate on.

sa·gac·i·ty (sə găs′ə tĭ), *n.* wisdom.

san·guine (săng′gwĭn), *adj.* 1. (in early physiology) having blood as the predominating humor; hence, ruddy-faced; cheerful. 2. disposed to be cheerful and hopeful.

sa·ti·ate (*v.* sā′shĭ āt′; *adj.* sā′shĭ ĭt), *v.* to supply with more than enough so as to weary or disgust. —*adj.* satiated.

sa·ti·e·ty (sə tī′ə tĭ), *n.* the state of having had enough or more than enough.

sat·ire (săt īr′), *n.* a literary work in which vices and follies are held up for abuse or contempt. —**sa·tir′i·cal,** *adj.*

scath·ing (skā′thĭng), *adj.* severely critical.

scope (skōp), *n.* extent, of view or activity.

scribe (skrīb), *n.* a person who copied manuscripts before the invention of printing.

scriv·e·ner (skrĭv′nər), *n. Archaic.* 1. a public clerk. 2. a notary.

scru·ple (skrōō′pəl), *n.* 1. a very small amount. 2. hesitation or doubt caused by uncertainty as to what is right.

scru·pu·lous (skrōō′pyə ləs), *adj.* having a strict regard for what is right. —**scru·pu·los·i·ty** (skrōō′pyə lŏs′ə tĭ), *n.*

scul·ler·y (skŭl′ə rĭ), *n.* a small room where the rough, dirty work of the kitchen is done.

scur·vy (skûr′vĭ), *adj.* mean; contemptible.

sear (sīr), *v.* to dry up; scorch.

sect (sĕkt), *n.* a religious group, especially one that has broken away from an established church.

sec·tar·i·an (sĕk târ′ĭ ən), *adj.* confined to a particular sect.

sec·u·lar (sĕk′yə lər), *adj.* not pertaining to sacred or religious things but to the world.

se·duce (sĭ dūs′), *v.* to lead astray; entice away from duty or one's principles.

se·duc·tive (sĭ dŭk′tĭv), *adj.* enticing.

sed·u·lous (sĕj′ə ləs), *adj.* careful and steady; diligent.

seem·ly (sēm′lĭ), *adj.* fitting; in good taste.

ăct, āble, dâre, ärt; ĕbb, ēqual; ĭf, īce; hŏt, ōver, ôrder, oil, bŏŏk, ōōze, out; ŭp, ūse, ûrge; ə = a in alone; ch, chief; g, give; j, judge; ng, ring; sh, shoe; th, thin; th, that; zh, vision. See the full key at the beginning of this glossary.

se·man·tics (sǐ măn′tǐks), *n.* the study of the development and changes of the meaning of words.

sem·blance (sĕm′bləns), *n.* resemblance; likeness.

se·qua·cious (sǐ kwā′shəs), *adj. Rare.* following another person unreasoningly.

se·ques·tered (sǐ kwĕs′tərd), *adj.* out-of-the-way; secluded.

ser·aph (sĕr′əf), *n. pl.* **-aphs, -aphim** (-ə fĭm). a member of the highest order of celestial beings, the fiery and purifying beings closest to God.

serf (sûrf), *n.* a person bound to his master's land and transferred with it.

sheer (shĭr), *adj.* not mixed with anything else; pure.

shil·ling (shǐl′ĭng), *n.* a British silver coin worth 12 pence and now equivalent to about 14 U.S. cents.

shod·dy (shŏd′ĭ), *n.* an inferior woolen yarn or cloth made from used materials. *adj.* made of inferior materials. **—shod′di·ness,** *n.*

shroud (shroud), *n.* **1.** a cloth used to wrap a corpse for burial. **2.** something which covers like a garment.

shunt (shŭnt), *v.* to shove out of the way.

shut·tle (shŭt′əl), *n.* an instrument used in weaving for passing the weft thread back and forth between the warp threads.

Si·lu·ri·an (sǐ lōōr′ǐ ən), *adj.* of an early geological period of the Paleozoic Era.

sin·ew (sǐn′ū), *n.* **1.** any of the tough connective cords by which the muscles are attached to the bones. **2.** that which supplies strength.

skep·tic (skĕp′tǐk), *n.* one who habitually doubts or questions matters generally accepted. **skep′ti·cal,** *adj.*

slag (slăg), *n.* the fused refuse separated from a metal in smelting.

sloe (slō), *n.* a small, blackish, plumlike fruit.

sloth (slŏth), *n.* laziness.

slough (slou), *n.* a place of soft, deep mud.

slough (slŭf), *n.* the skin of a snake.

slur (slûr), *v.* to pass over quickly.

sol·ace (sŏl′ĭs), *n.* comfort.

som·no·lent (sŏm′nə lənt), *adj.* sleepy; drowsy. **—som′no·lence,** *n.*

span (spăn), *n.* a measure of length equal to 9 inches, based on the distance from the tip of the thumb to the tip of the little finger when the hand is extended.

spent (spĕnt), *adj.* used up; worn out.

spew (spū), *v.* to throw up; vomit.

splay (splā), *adj.* turned outward.

stark (stärk), *adj.* **1.** utter; downright. **2.** stiff; rigid.

sta·tus (stā′təs, stă′təs), *n.* a position or standing, socially, professionally, or otherwise.

stoat (stōt), *n.* the ermine, a weasel of northern regions, especially when in its brown summer coat.

sto·ic (stō′ĭk), *n.* **1.** one of the schools of philosophy founded by the Greek Zeno in the 4th century B.C. and teaching that men should be free from all passion, whether of joy or grief, and submit unmoved to whatever happens. **2.** one who maintains the attitude of this philosophy.

stri·dent (strī′dənt), *adj.* harsh-sounding.

sub·tle (sŭt′əl), *adj.* **1.** fine or delicate. **2.** intricate. **—sub·tly** (sŭt′lǐ), *adv.*

sub·vert (səb vûrt′), *v.* to overthrow or destroy (something established).

sun·der (sŭn dər), *v.* to break apart.

sun·dry (sŭn′drǐ), *adj.* various, miscellaneous.

su·per·sede (sōō′pər sēd′), *v.* to take the place of.

su·per·vene (sōō′pər vēn′), *v.* to come as something additional. **—su·per·ven·tion** (sōō′pər vĕn′shən), *n.*

sup·ple (sŭp′əl), *adj.* flexible.

sus·cep·ti·ble (sə sĕp′tə bəl), *adj.* sensitive. **—susceptible of,** allowing. **—n. sus·cep·ti·bil′i·ty,** sensitivity.

swad·dle (swŏd′əl), *v.* to wrap (a baby) round with long, narrow strips of cloth.

swarth·y (swôr′thǐ), *adj.* dark-colored.

swath (swŏth), *n.* the space covered by one stroke of a scythe.

swoon (swōōn), *v.* to faint. *n.* a fainting fit.

syc·a·more (sǐk′ə mōr′), *n.* **1.** a maple shade tree found in Europe and Asia. **2.** any of various American plane trees.

syn·tax (sǐn′tăks), *n.* sentence structure.

tac·i·turn (tăs′ə tûrn), *adj.* inclined not to talk. **—tac·i·tur·ni·ty** (tăs′ə tûr′nə tǐ), *n.*

tal·ent (tăl′ənt), *n.* **1.** a varying unit of weight or money used in ancient Greece, Rome, and the Middle East. **2.** any special natural ability.

tan·gi·ble (tăn′jə bəl), *adj.* **1.** capable of being touched. **2.** definite; not vague.

tan·ta·lize (tăn′tə līz′), *v.* to show or promise something to someone and then take it away.

taw·dry (tô′drǐ), *adj.* showy and cheap.

teem (tēm), *v.* to abound; be fertile.

tee·to·tum (tē tō′təm), *n.* a kind of top spun with the fingers.

tem·per (tĕm′pər), *v.* to moderate.

tem·per·ate (tĕm′pər ĭt), *adj.* moderate.

te·na·cious (tĭ nā′shəs), *adj.* holding fast; persistent.

ten·or (tĕn′ər), *n.* general course.

tes·ty (tĕs′tĭ), *adj.* touchy.

thane (thān), *n.* 1. in early England, a freeman who held land from the king or a lord in exchange for military service. 2. in early Scotland, a person of rank who held land from the king.

ti·tan·ic (tī tăn′ĭk), *adj.* characteristic of the Titans, hence huge in size and strength.

toll (tōl), *v.* to sound (a large bell) with slow, regular strokes.

to·pog·ra·phy (tə pŏg′rə fĭ), *n.* the description of the surface features of a region.

tract (trăkt), *n.* a pamphlet, esp. one on a religious subject.

traipse (trāps), *v.* to wander about idly.

tran·scend·ent (trăn sĕn′dənt), *adj.* going beyond the ordinary limits; surpassing.

tran·scen·den·tal (trăn′sĕn dĕn′təl), *adj.* rising above ordinary experience or thought. *—n.* (*pl.*) categories that have universal application, as good, true.

tran·sient (trăn′shənt), *adj.* lasting for only a short time.

tran·si·to·ry (trăn′sə tōr′ĭ), *adj.* not lasting.

tran·spire (trăn spīr′), *v.* to occur.

triv·et (trĭv′ĭt), *n.* a three-legged stand for holding kettles over or near the fire.

trump·er·y (trŭm′pə rĭ), *n.* showy but worthless finery.

tur·bid (tûr′bĭd), *adj.* not clear, because of sediment that has been stirred up; muddy.

two·pence (tŭp′əns), *n.* two pence; two British pennies.

un·a·vail·ing (ŭn′ə vā′lĭng), *adj.* ineffectual; useless.

un·can·ny (ŭn kăn′ĭ), *adj.* strange in a weird way.

un·couth (ŭn kōōth′), *adj.* uncultured; crude.

un·due (ŭn dū′), *adj.* not necessary; too great.

un·kempt (ŭn kĕmpt′), *adj.* 1. not combed. 2. untidy.

un·re·mit·ting (ŭn′rĭ mĭt′ĭng), *adj.* unceasing.

vap·id (văp′ĭd), *adj.* tasteless; dull.

var·let (vär′lĭt), *n.* 1. *Archaic.* an attendant. 2. a low fellow or rascal.

vault (vôlt), *n.* an arched ceiling or roof.

vaunt (vônt), *v.* to boast.

vend (vĕnd), *v.* to offer for sale.

ven·er·a·ble (vĕn′ər ə bəl), *adj.* commanding respect because of age and dignity of appearance.

ven·er·a·tion (vĕn′ə rā′shən), *n.* reverence.

ven·om·ous (vĕn′əm əs), *adj.* poisonous.

ve·rac·i·ty (və răs′ə tĭ), *n.* truthfulness.

ver·dure (vûr′jər), *n.* greenness of vegetation.

verge (vûrj), *n.* the edge.

ver·nal (vûr′nəl), *adj.* occurring in the spring.

ver·sa·tile (vûr′sə tĭl), *adj.* able to turn with ease from one subject or occupation to another.

vi·gnette (vĭn yĕt′), *n.* 1. a picture shading off gradually at the edges. 2. a word picture.

vin·di·cate (vĭn′də kāt′), *v.* to clear of a charge or suspicion; justify.

vint·ner (vĭnt′nər), *n.* a wine merchant.

vis·age (vĭz′ĭj), *n.* face.

vo·ra·cious (vō rā′shəs), *adj.* greedy in eating.

vul·gar (vŭl′gər), *adj.* 1. of the great mass of people in general. 2. characterized by lack of taste or good breeding.

waif (wāf), *n.* a person without home or friends, esp. a child.

war·y (wâr′ĭ), *adj.* cautious. **—war′i·ness,** *n.*

weal (wēl), *n.* well-being.

whelp (hwĕlp), *n.* the young of a dog or other flesh-eating animal.

wick·et (wĭk′ĭt), *n.* a small door or gate, especially one set in or near a larger one. **—wicket-gate,** *n.*

wim·ple (wĭm′pəl), *n.* a woman's headcloth so arranged that only the face is exposed: still worn by certain orders of nuns.

wran·gle (răng′gəl), *v.* to argue in a noisy or angry manner. **—wran′gler,** *n.*

wrought (wrôt), *adj.* 1. worked. 2. shaped by beating with a hammer.

wry (rī), *adj.* turned to one side; twisted; distorted.

yeo·man (yō′mən), *n.* an independent farmer.

yew (ū), *n.* a cone-bearing evergreen tree that has dark-green leaves.

zeal·ous (zĕl′əs), *adj.* full of zeal; warmly devoted to a cause.

zeph·yr (zĕf′ər), *n.* a gentle breeze.

ăct, āble, dâre, ärt; ĕbb, ēqual; ĭf, īce; hŏt, ōver, ôrder, oil, bŏŏk, ōōze, out; ŭp, ūse, ûrge; ə = a in *alone*; **ch**, chief; **g**, give; **j**, judge; **ng**, ring; **sh**, shoe; **th**, thin; **th**, that; **zh**, vision. See the full key at the beginning of this glossary.

Index

Boldface type indicates those selections and authors that have with them introductions, questions, or other extensive editorial material.

Index of Illustrations

D E F G H 9 8 7 6 5 4
PRINTED IN THE UNITED STATES OF AMERICA